6-06-02

Routing and Switching

Routing and Switching

TIME OF CONVERGENCE?

Rita Pužmanová

Addison-Wesley

An imprint of PEARSON EDUCATION
Boston · San Francisco · New York · Toronto · Montreal · London · Munich ·
Paris · Madrid · Cape Town · Sydney · Tokyo · Singapore · Mexico City

PEARSON EDUCATION LIMITED

Head Office:
Edinburgh Gate, Harlow, Essex CM20 2JE
Tel: +44 (0)1279 623623 Fax: +44 (0)1279 431059

London Office:
128 Long Acre, London WC2E 9AN
Tel: +44 (0)20 7447 2000 Fax: +44 (0)20 7240 5771

Website: www.aw.com/cseng

First published in Great Britain 2002
© Pearson Education Limited 2002

The right of Rita Pužmanová to be identified as author of this work has been asserted by her in accordance with the Copyright, Designs and Patents Act 1988.

ISBN 0-201-39861-3

British Library Cataloguing in Publication Data
A catalogue record for this book is available from the British Library.

Library of Congress Cataloging in Publication Data applied for.

The programs in this book have been included for their instructional value. The publisher does not offer any warranties or representations in respect of their fitness for a particular purpose, nor does the publisher accept any liability for any loss or damage (other than for personal injury or death) arising from their use.

Many of the designations used by manufacturers and sellers to distinguish their products are claimed as trademarks. Pearson Education Limited has made every attempt to supply trademark information about manufacturers and their products mentioned in this book.

10 9 8 7 6 5 4 3 2 1

Typeset by Pantek Arts Ltd, Maidstone, Kent.
Printed and bound by Biddles Ltd, Guildford and King's Lynn

The publishers' policy is to use paper manufactured from sustainable forests.

To my father, in memoriam,
whom I owe more than I thanked for

About the author

Rita Pužmanová, PhD, MBA, is an independent internetworking expert, course developer and trainer. She holds an MSc in systems engineering while her PhD is in telecommunications. As a Cisco Systems' affiliated consultant and instructor, she keeps abreast of the developments in networking technologies. She completed her MBA with the University of Calgary, a qualification which has helped her to run successfully her own specialized independent internetworking consultancy business.

Rita has been developing and teaching (inter)networking live courses for a worldwide business and technical audience for almost ten years. Recently she has become involved in on-line web education in the networking field and is currently running a TCP/IP course offered via the University of California, Los Angeles. She participates in the IEEE and IETF standardization work in the area of LANs and TCP/IP, and since 1993 has also been active in ETSI (the European Telecommunications Standards Institute) in the French Silicon Valley. In addition, she is also a founding member of the national Telecommunication Users Association supporting users' needs and collaborating worldwide on EU and other transnational telecommunications issues.

Rita has already published several books in the field of communication networks, TCP/IP, routing and switching, ITU-T standardization, and technical terminology (including the *Communications Technology Terms and Abbreviations Dictionary*). She has also written numerous articles for national and international technical magazines, such as *Data Communications, Computer Communications, ComputerWorld*, and *PCWorld*, and has presented papers at international conferences and seminars.

Having studied and worked in several countries, Rita is multilingual. She is also interested in non-technical issues such as creative thinking and holds an Edward de Bono certificate on General Thinking Skills.

Rita can be reached at rita@ieee.org.

Contents

Icons

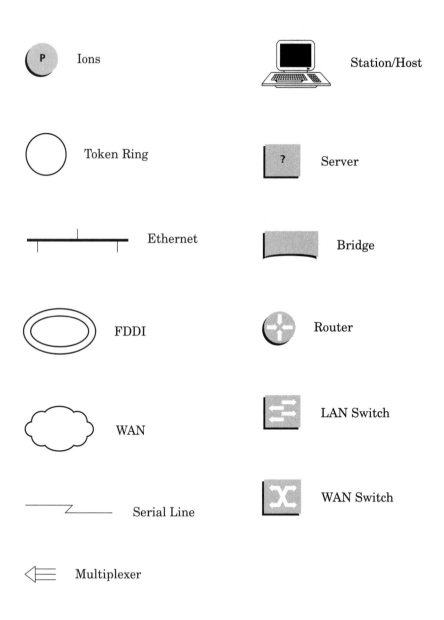

Ions	Station/Host
Token Ring	Server
Ethernet	Bridge
FDDI	Router
WAN	LAN Switch
Serial Line	WAN Switch
Multiplexer	

Preface

Why this book came into existence

What follows is a personal note on the reasons that brought me to develop the idea for a book and how it came to be.

I have been acquainted with networking for more than a decade, a decade in which major breakthroughs in internetworking development and deployment have been made. I first got involved in network management during my PhD studies, having had a wonderful opportunity to complete my degree in Spain at the University of Vallodolid and the Politecnica de Madrid. It was here I met knowledgeable teams dedicated to IP networking and network management and it was then that, for the first time, I could appreciate the fascinating resource that was the Internet. But it was also a time when OSI was being intensively promoted and also a time when the IETF made a number of moves towards eventual convergence with OSI. (CMOT was not to become a historic protocol for a number of years.)

As I delved deeper into network management I had to make sure I understood the operation of all the various layers. Moving from the top down, I began to be fascinated by the relaying (routing) concept in building internets, and the introduction of LAN switches to the market added to my interest. However, what fascinates me most about network interconnections is the routing technology, the algorithms and the diverse routing protocols which handle the ever-changing topology and determine the proper path through the wild network jungle. (We may not actually see them as they are transparent to us but we are all familiar with the tangible black, or white, or blue boxes which perform the routing functions.)

As time went by I kept a close eye on developments in internetworking and made my first contribution to the topic in 1996 (although it was then too early to draw any, even interim, conclusions or recommendations about the merging of routing and switching). However, the move towards integration has now reached a point where it is necessary to make some clear distinctions between the options available and their viability. As an unbiased, lifelong, independent networking specialist I try to keep an objective viewpoint about both open and proprietary proposals.

I hope the reader who has not as yet been gripped by internetworking technology will share my enthusiasm after getting through this book. Although we will be discussing the technology running through the programs based on man-made algorithms there are still a number of 'mysteries' in the background (which we sometimes call 'bugs'). Trying to get to the bottom of these mysteries, the hidden issues, the 'black holes,' requires a deal of hard work, intuition, and luck, but the result is very satisfying. Although this book is not essentially about troubleshooting *per se*, it will be prerequisite reading for any sensible person intending to troubleshoot on an internet. The same may be said about internet design – while this book is not about designing internets, it does cover design issues related to individual technologies and protocols.

The need for bandwidth, speed, and performance are the major drivers of developments in the internetworking arena. New features and new proposed technologies – both in hardware and software – seem to appear almost every day. Not all will succeed in today's highly competitive networking market, but all contribute to a solid global understanding of what is happening at network interconnect points now, and what needs to be happening there tomorrow. It is still a vendor-driven field today, but it is much less so than it was ten years ago, and everyone can benefit from the current multivendor proposals which have resulted from the Internet community itself.

Note for readers

This book has been written in precise and technical language with the intention of eliminating marketing hype and other inappropriate descriptions. (Indeed the book is no light read as the topics covered are taken most seriously by myself.) The terminology used is derived from standard use (i.e. internationally approved through the standardization process), and new terms are defined to avoid any confusion. However, occasionally, even among the creators of the technology, the terminology is not consistent so I have chosen those terms which seem most appropriate for consistency throughout the text. Although I personally do not always feel comfortable with the terms that have been endorsed, I do believe that the developers always try to advance the most appropriate terminology and so should not be castigated unduly afterwards.

Routing and Switching: Time of Convergence? provides a global and complex overview of the issues surrounding internetworking, together with sufficient detail to satisfy the internet professional as well as provide a proper understanding of the underlying principles. The primary aim of the text is to show what is behind the evolution in network interconnection, and give some clue as to where industry developments and standardization efforts are heading: to gain performance by avoiding unnecessary processing in the internetworking device, whether router or switch.

To make the book easier to use I have broken the text into sections of reasonable length and included a wealth of illustrations and tables to complement the individual topics. More importantly, I have included highlighted *Snapshots* and *Hints* to summarize the important concepts in a nutshell to aid comprehension, while the *Quick Tips* will help the reader to get to the bottom of ideas that may not be quite so obvious. Also included throughout are highlighted references to the appropriate standards and RFCs – *Standards and RFC Watches* – with additional details of the organizations from which they originate. The chapters or major sections also conclude with a complete list of all standards and RFCs mentioned throughout the text.

A word of caution should be added here. Due to the speed of developments in the areas on which this book concentrates it has not been possible to avoid mentioning enhancements which are 'only' at the proposal stage (usually in the form of Internet Drafts). New drafts appear every day and a great many of them will –

directly or partially – relate to the topics of interest here. I have tried to concentrate on those proposals which have already gathered significant attention and seem viable for future development. However, readers should consider sections where 'work in progress' is mentioned with care and check how far any proposals have been taken by the time the book is read. For similar reasons I have not included the links to or names of such drafts as they may well be renamed, their current versions become obsolete, or their status may have changed by the time the section is read.

Let me conclude with a motto to bear in mind before you start to read the text which follows:

Read not to contradict and confute, nor to believe and take for granted, nor to find talk or discourse, but to weigh and consider.

(FRANCIS BACON)

Rita Pužnanová
Independent Networking Specialist

Acknowledgments

I feel obliged and at the same time delighted to take this opportunity to express my gratitude to all the networking specialists I have met and learned from throughout my career, either in person or via Internet discussion groups. Without all these knowledgeable colleagues and partners I would not even have had the idea for this book. I am also proud that several of the specialists who have given me invaluable help in the preparation of this book actually participated in my networking courses in the past and have reached a level of specialization such that they were able to offer professional advice on the text itself.

In terms of direct involvement in finalizing and rounding off the rough edges of the book, a major acknowledgement belongs to my reviewer, Farid Hajji, who was not afraid to question the finest of details or suggest the slightest of improvements while at the same time not losing sight of the high-level practicalities of day-to-day networking. I would also like to express my thanks to friends and colleagues who generously dedicated their precious time to reading and commenting on sections closest to their expertise: Miloš Bárta (Cisco TAC Team, Brussels), Robert Hanžl (MPLS Cisco Development Team, Brussels), and Jarry Pilař (Cisco Office, Prague).

No book could ever be written without the support of close family, who share not only the glory of the writer's ups but also the burden of the writer's downs, in the field of technical writing as much as in that of *belles lettres*. Hence my biggest thanks go to my mother who was most helpful, especially during the final stages of producing the manuscript, although she knew the book was not her genre.

Introduction

Some books are to be tasted, others to be swallowed, and some few to be chewed and digested: that is, some books are to be read only in parts, others to be read, but not curiously, and some few to be read wholly, and with diligence and attention.

(FRANCIS BACON)

It has become a challenge to design a scalable high-performance network that would meet current, ever evolving and continuously more demanding business requirements. There are many options in terms of networking technologies and even broader choice when we come to interconnecting networks. The two leading, yet complementing ways of interconnecting networks – routing and switching – seem to come closer to each other: they exist side by side in the current networks and in many cases may not even exist one without the other (e.g. interconnected Virtual LANs). However, does it mean that routing and switching merged or even converged? Is it at all possible? Are the hot issues mentioned frequently in the press, such as 'multilayer switching' or 'routing switch' or 'Layer 4 switching,' simply marketing terms so that the vendors try to get more attention for their products? To answer this question it is necessary to fully understand what the **switching** (mostly, but not exclusively, we will deal with LAN switching in this book – network interconnecting at Layer 2) and **routing** (network interconnecting at Layer 3) technologies are all about. Only then we may rationalize about the possible options available, feasible and deployable in current complex internets, using high-speed optical infrastructures and carrying (among others) the traffic sensitive to delays and losses.

Networking at the dawn of the 21st century

The networking technologies have penetrated into almost everybody's life, as a supportive part of daily work in various business sectors or as a home-tool to access the information contents and to use other benefits of the Internet (for family use or home workers, a.k.a. teleworkers). The underlying technologies have emerged in types and variety, hence there is no longer a simple corporate network or internet (based on single technology and single vendor product). Commonly even a single company uses in its distant branches (different) local networks interconnected together through switches and routers, and all branches are interconnected through various WAN links (over Frame Relay, ATM, PSTN, ISDN, etc.) again requiring routers for WAN connection and WAN switches (transparent) in the wide-area transport network. Particularly, the way how the network segments are interconnected has become a crucial decision for network planners not only to fulfill the current business requirements but also to allow for future extension and development.

There are various techniques and equipment types to interconnect networks; however; several years ago two of them were combating for the leading place 'on the market': **routing** and **switching**. The networking experience shows that both technologies are, by their principles, not competitive but rather complementary and have their specific place in current internets. Although some manufacturers still try to push through only their single vision, there have evolved different approaches to integrate the two techniques. Therefore it is very interesting to overview the principles of both and see the current development in their 'convergence phase.'

This book, ***Routing and Switching: Time of Convergence?***, aims to help users, network designers and technicians, and IT decision makers, in their proper understanding of the interconnecting possibilities of today and potential for tomorrow (which may come more quickly than we might have thought yesterday). The book you have just opened provides a detailed explanation of all related principles, starting from an overview of communication networks, through the operation of Layer 2 internetworking devices – **bridges** and **switches**, the latter both in LANs and WANs – to the operation of Layer 3 devices – **routers**. This book devotes more time to more complex routing technologies and their application in **IP** and non-IP environments, such as (still present) **Novell IPX/SPX**, **AppleTalk**, (very slowly penetrating) **OSI**, (almost forgotten but not completely) **DecNet**, **Banyan VINES**, and (where it all started) **XNS**.

None of the important details regarding the building blocks of routing protocols or their implementation issues will be omitted – with a clear preference for IP internet deployment. The book looks not only at routing protocol issues but also at **router architectures** and internal **operation**. The book goes beyond common and well-known issues. You as a reader will gain knowledge of the network interconnections gradually, from the lowest layers up, finally reaching an advanced stage and a discussion of the most pressing issues of today's networks – quality of service deployment through **IntServ**, **DiffServ**, **RSVP**, and **MPLS** (what the interconnect devices need to know and do to support all that), and speed of packet transmission (how to improve the internal interconnect device processing), particularly with the advent of **optical switching**. We can then have a closer look at what is possible in terms of routing and switching 'integration' with the aim of speeding up user traffic across the interconnected network.

Special points

In comparison to somewhat similar books currently available on the market and dealing with network interconnect issues, this book differs (positively) in addressing the following concerns:

■ up-to-date overview of interconnect technologies covering all aspects related to proper understanding, choice, and deployment;

■ guidelines for network designers from the point of view of individual technologies;

- putting routing and switching in the right perspective with an exploration of how far integration of both can possibly go;
- detailed technical background of all routing, switching (LAN and WAN), and bridging aspects;
- relation not only to TCP/IP, but to other architectures (namely Novell NetWare, OSI, DECnet);
- covering the advanced – sometimes still under development – aspects of QoS support (DiffServ, IntServ) and operations of label switching (MPLS), and recent developments in optical switching.

There are several other books on the market which are excellent sources of information on more individual pieces of the interconnect puzzle and these are appropriately listed in the **Recommended Reading** section (Appendix F). They should help readers who need further details on a particular protocol, but as the last (or first – depending on how you to look at it) resort the reader should look at a relevant standard or specification. All approved standards, recommendations, RFCs, or industry fora specifications are clearly identified throughout the book. (In rare cases reference is also made to the draft spec, mainly in the case of Internet drafts; however, it is highly likely that these will be RFCs by the time the book is published.) In any case, the reader is recommended to check the most up-to-date standard or RFC status to be sure that the latest version is being used. (All the information included in the book is current as of time of writing, i.e. April 2001.)

For whom the book is written

The topics discussed in this book are at the top of the list for network specialists and internetwork designers. Switching and routing is not only of interest to ISPs or large enterprises with corporate networks of wide span, but is equally important for small and medium-sized businesses with branch networks interconnected over a wide area. The position of both switching and routing has stabilized over the past two years and it should be understood by now that both will be present in future networks. The development of Layer 3 switching, the combination of routing and switch functionality into a single box, and other industry proposals like tag switching and IP switching have paved the way to introduce QoS and MPLS into the networks. While not all issues have been widely endorsed by standardization bodies or the Internet community and are still described as work in progress, the cornerstones are already laid down.

Specifically this book is aimed at:

- *network designers and planners* (in large private enterprises, public administrations, and SMEs) who could use the book as a technology and design guide;
- *network administrators and technicians* (systems integrator companies, VADs/VARs of leading networking manufacturers) who could use the book as a description of background principles with the outlook for the future;
- *developers* in relative fields who could use the book as a base reference;

■ *technical university students and teachers* who could use the book as a detailed technical textbook and reference.

The book will be helpful to students, technicians, and professionals in need of reference material on the wide range of topics that are covered, while offering additional help by directing them to topics under development and further information. The book will prove invaluable as a reference for students on numerous computer science, networking and TCP/IP related courses, while helping those specialized in networking overcome difficulies in real life.

This is not a book on research or for research purposes; it is instead a guide to all matters related to routing and switching – from background information to advanced issues (both in terms of complexity and time evolution). The text, as a result, provides a mix of broad coverage and yet sufficiently detailed description.

The book has been written to be easy to follow, the basic ideas being built up one at a time. The reader is helped throughout with reminders (*Snapshots*, *Quick Tips*), links to base specs and useful appendices:

■ **abbreviations**
■ **network standardization overview**
■ **quick guide to internetworking troubleshooting**
■ **overview of transmission speeds**
■ **useful numbers**.

What is *not* covered

While the reader may easily grasp in detail – by looking at the table of contents – what this book is about, it may be worth noting what is *not* in this book for good reasons of objectivity and conciseness, and the provision of a high-level technological view:

■ references to specific vendor technology solutions (except some occasional cases of milestones of historical development such as Ipsilon's IP switching or Cisco's Tag switching);
■ references to existing products on the market and their prices;
■ configuration guidelines and examples for a particular routing and switching software;
■ complex internetworking network design examples.

Note: This is not a Cisco book. Although my experience in internetworking is mostly derived from working on Cisco equipment and teaching how to use it effectively, and although I acknowledge the power of the company in pushing forward high-tech solutions, I have been as objective as possible in this book. Moreover, there are many excellent Cisco-oriented books dedicated to individual topics or to individual networking certification needs.

PART I

Communications networks

In this introductory part, the basic networking issues relevant to internetworking will be covered. However, there is no space or need to go into every detail in specific network types and topologies. The main concern here is to provide a concise, overview of a hierarchical network architecture and various types of standardized and widely used networks in the local, metropolitan, and wide area environment.

The **local and wide area networking technologies** discussed later are as follows:

- **local area network** (LAN) technologies – Ethernet, Fast and Gigabit Ethernet, Token Ring, Wireless LANs (IEEE 802.x), FDDI, and Fiber Channel;
- **metropolitan area network** (MAN) – 802.6 DQDB;
- **data link protocols** – HDLC, LAPB, PPP;
- **wide area network** (WAN) technologies – ISDN, X.25, Frame Relay, SMDS, and ATM.

For our internetworking purposes the main topics discussed here are:

- **addressing** scheme used;
- **layered architecture** used in individual network cases;
- main **network characteristics** relevant for further switching and routing considerations;
- network **topologies**, **media**, and **network management**;
- differences between **connectionless and connection-oriented service** types;
- use of **Quality of Service** (QoS) classes in networks (for more detailed discussion on QoS enforcement with relation to the routers and switches see Part V).

We will refer to the basic terms, operation, and protocols mentioned in this part throughout the book.

This book will use extensively the term **internetworking** for **interconnecting networks** for communication into **internets**. Please note the difference between an **internet** (a general set of interconnected physical network segments) and the **Internet** (a specific and the largest TCP/IP internet, spanning the globe).

CHAPTER 1

Architecture of communications systems

Communications systems, which are the cornerstones of every network, have to perform numerous tasks defined altogether as **communication control**. Such a set of tasks, **functions**, and **services** which have to be provided for successful communication between systems is better controlled and more manageable when divided into smaller groupings, called **layers**. At the beginning of the (remarkably) short history of networking the layering principle of communication control was agreed as the best approach. However, the **network architectures**, a synonym for the structure of communication control, were developed by (then) various leading networking vendors as their proprietary solutions. This did not allow for interoperability between **multivendor** systems which is a common requirement today.

Therefore, under the auspices of the **International Organization for Standardization** (ISO), this requirement was looked at more closely, with the aim of producing a model hierarchical, layered network architecture to support the overall open interconnection between communications systems. Such **systems** would be **open**, i.e. not tied to a vendor solution, but open for **interoperable** network implementation. The standardization effort in the area of **Open Systems Interconnection** (OSI) bore the first fruit in 1984 when the **OSI Reference Model** (RM/OSI) was approved (IS 7498).

STANDARDS WATCH	Open Systems Interconnection

ISO/IEC 7498-1:1994 Information Technology – Open Systems Interconnection – Basic Reference Model: The Basic Model

ISO/IEC 7498-3:1997 Information Technology – Open Systems Interconnection – Basic Reference Model: Naming and Addressing

X.200 (07/94) Information Technology – Open Systems Interconnection – Basic Reference Model: The Basic Model

1.1 The OSI reference model of hierarchical communication

The hierarchical model divides the whole communications control task into **seven layers** (this number and definition of the individual layers have been frequently questioned but today we can only agree it was a lucky choice) – see Figure 1.1. Each of the seven smaller problems created through layering was chosen because each was reasonably self-contained and therefore more easily solved without excessive reliance on external information.

Each **layer** is defined by:

- the set of **functions** it has to perform;
- the **services** which it has to provide to its upper immediate neighbor layer.

FIGURE 1-1   The hierarchical OSI reference model

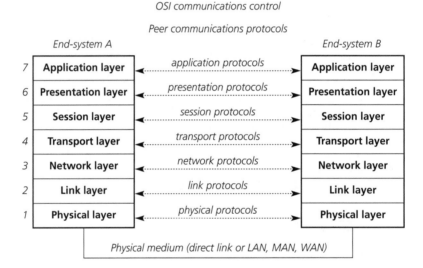

The division of the task into layers was done in a way that results in logical **function** grouping and minimum **interfacing** between the layers (see Figure 1.2): in fact through only a single (for instance communications) interface, the **Service Access Point** (SAP). The functions, for efficiency reasons, should not be duplicated in other layers. (Error control implemented in several layers has a different meaning and importance for the overall communication.)

The **services** between adjacent layers are expressed in terms of **primitive**s specifying the functions to be performed, and control **parameters**. Each layer (except the lowest one) may use services provided only by the underlying adjacent layer (and through the layering process thus uses services by all underlying layers, though this is not known), hence each layer recognizes only its adjacent layers to which it interfaces.

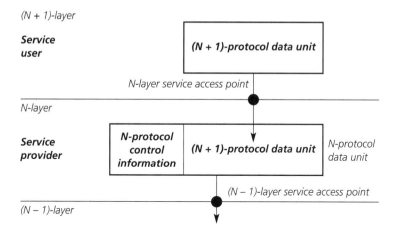

| FIGURE 1-2 | The relationship between adjacent layers in a communications system |

And, to allow for full interconnection between systems, the change in the implementation of one layer should not have an impact on the other system's layers which is also supported by having more than a single SAP for an individual layer.

The network operation appears as a direct **peer-to-peer communication** to the user. The user message appears to travel from a user to the local system's application (highest) layer and directly to the receiving (remote) system's application layer as if the devices were directly attached. In actuality, the user message is first passed from the local application layer down through all the other layers of the system, through their adjacent interfaces. Each layer performs its tasks and, among others, adds to the message the control information according to the network operating system's protocol for each layer. The message itself should not be modified at any layer except for special cases such as encryption or compression.

Communication protocol is what makes us believe that every layer directly communicates with its peer layer in other system: it is a set of rules and formats allowing the peer layers to understand each other completely (and at the same time not understand any other layer's information). Thus the communication between peer layers is fully governed by the communication protocol (of a particular layer) but it is in fact a virtual communication as the only physical communication is provided over the physical medium (inter)connecting the communicating devices.

| SNAPSHOT | protocol |

Protocol (communication protocol) = set of rules and formats for communication with peer layer.

Each layer of the sending system, upon receipt of the data unit (no longer the original user data as we move down the ladder) from the upper adjacent layer, performs its functions (including **segmentation** of data into smaller units, if necessary) and adds **Protocol Control Information** (PCI) to that data (see Figure 1.3). PCI may take the form of a **header** and/or **trailer**. By adding PCI each layer in fact **encapsulates** the received data into the **protocol data unit** (PDU).

FIGURE 1-3 Encapsulation of protocol data units

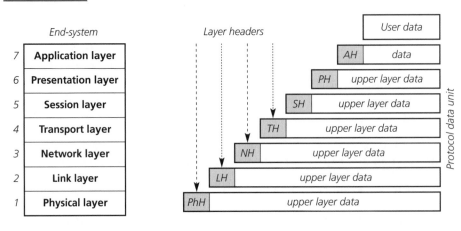

From the physical channel, separating sending and receiving systems, the encapsulated message passes upward through the same layers at the destination device. As the message progresses from layer to layer, each layer **decapsulates** the data unit, i.e. strips off protocol control information that was added by its counterpart in the transmitting station, and performs all its appropriate tasks (including **reassembly**, when segmentation was performed along the path). The result is the same message as was originally sent, arriving through the destination application layer to the user.

Each layer performs a specific function with respect to the complete communications process. Each of the seven problem areas is solved using a cooperation of instances within the N-layer of the model utilizing the **N-layer protocol**. Two peer instances of N-layer (one at each end of the virtual communication path) cooperate to solve the N-layer problem. For example, TCP performs a retransmission of missing packets. If more than two instances are communicating, more than two instances of N-layer can participate in solving the N-problem. Each layer is characterized by at least one protocol, and in many cases a choice from a variety of N-layer protocols is available (a typical example is the highest layer providing numerous application protocols), each providing a different service to the upper layer (if such exists). Choosing a different N-layer protocol often means a different set of SAPs and primitives between N and N + 1 to be used.

The OSI reference model is not a network implementation. Instead, it defines the functions of each layer and serves for the concrete protocol standardization.

Although for full compliance with the OSI reference model all seven layers should be implemented, actual network implementations may skip one or more layers. As we will see later on, while the full protocol set is obligatory for the end communications systems, simpler layered configuration is efficient for **intermediate systems** providing network relaying functions.

The lower two layers are implemented with hardware and software; the upper five layers are generally implemented in software.

1.2 The seven layers of the OSI reference model

The seven layers of the OSI reference model could be further divided into two sets:

- local procedures (Layers 1, 2, and 3) – **lower layers** – govern the communications across any communications line in a network and include the physical interface (physical layer), error detection and correction (link layer), and routing (network layer);
- end-to-end procedures (Layers 4 through 7) – **upper layers** – provide the means of linking communicating applications to networks and reside namely in end user systems.

Common functions performed with different aims at various layers, such as addressing or flow control, will be discussed later, relating, with anticipation, to comparison of different network types.

For our brief discussion of the functions of the seven OSI layers we will start at the top of the layered model.

1.2.1 Application layer – Layer 7

The application layer is the layer closest to the user and provides him or her with access to the communications system. It differs from the other layers in that it does not provide services to any other layer, but rather to application processes outside the scope of the OSI reference model, such as file transfer, remote terminal access and electronic mail. All underlying layers exist to support the requirements of this layer. The application layer identifies and establishes the availability of intended communication partners and determines whether sufficient resources for the intended communication exist. The application layer encapsulates into the **application data unit** the original user data (not comprehensible and not relevant to the layer's operation) together with its **application control information**.

1.2.2 Presentation layer – Layer 6

The presentation layer ensures that information sent by the application layer of one system will be comprehensible by the application layer of another system. If necessary, the presentation layer translates between multiple data representation formats by using a common data representation format. The presentation layer concerns itself not only with the **format** and **representation** of actual user data, but also with **data structures** used by programs. Therefore, in addition to actual **data format transformation** (if necessary), the presentation layer negotiates the **data transfer syntax** for the application layer. The presentation layer encapsulates into its data unit the whole application data unit, not just the original user data.

1.2.3 Session layer – Layer 5

The session layer **establishes**, **manages**, and **terminates sessions** between applications. Sessions consist of dialogue between two or more presentation layer entities. The session layer **synchronizes dialogue** between presentation layer entities and manages their data exchange. In addition to basic regulation of conversations (sessions), the session layer offers provisions for data expedition, class of service, and exception reporting of session-layer, presentation-layer, and application-layer problems.

1.2.4 Transport layer – Layer 4

The transport layer forms the boundary between application-layer protocols and lower-layer protocols. Whereas the application, presentation, and session layers are concerned with application issues, the lower four layers are concerned with data transport issues. The transport layer ensures the data transfer from source to destination by optionally managing the network data flow and implementing the **Quality of Service** requested by the session layer.

The transport layer provides a transport, **end-to-end**, service to the upper layers, in the form of reliable or unreliable transport. A **connection-oriented transport service** over an internet is accomplished through mechanisms for the establishment, maintenance, and orderly termination of connection, including sequence numbering and positive or negative acknowledgment of received data units, and data loss recovery through retransmissions. A **connectionless transport service** is concerned only with actual data transport without establishing a specific connection for it and without the possibility of detecting lost or duplicate data units. The connection-oriented service therefore provides reliable data transport as opposed to the connectionless service. Among other functions performed at the transport layer are transport **fault detection** and recovery, and **end-to-end flow control** (to prevent one system from overrunning another with data).

1.2.5 Network layer – Layer 3

The network layer provides **connectivity and path selection** between two end systems that may be located on geographically diverse networks (or subnets). Because a substantial geographic distance and many network segments can separate two end systems wishing to communicate, the network layer is the domain of **routing**. There would not be any routing without proper network addressing, hence the other major function of the network layer is network, **logical addressing** (see Part IV). Routing protocols, residing in the network layer, select optimal paths through the series of interconnected networks based on the destination network address. Individual network-layer protocols then move network data units, called commonly **packets** (or **datagrams** in Internet parlance), along these paths.

Similarly to transport layer, network layer provides two types of service (see also Section 1.6):

■ **Connectionless network service** – each packet is sent without regard for its context with respect to other elements. Consecutive packets, forming the single original message, sent this way may be delivered out of order because they may take different routes through a network; some may not be delivered at all, others may be delivered in duplicate. As this type of service is successfully used in the Internet, it is often referred to as **datagram service**.

■ **Connection-oriented network service** – a specific route is established for packets (cells) flowing between parties and that route is always taken within the communications. Packets are always delivered in order and any loss is detected.

The main difference between the connectionless and connection-oriented network services with respect to routers is that they do not need to keep state in the connectionless communication case, whereas they do in the connection-oriented case. Keeping state is costly in terms of memory and CPU cycles in the routing infrastructure and is therefore not very widespread. Keeping state is often considered redundant at Layer 3, because similar functions can be performed at Layer 4 at the end nodes.

Throughout the book we will often refer to services and protocol at the network layer as pertaining to **Layer 3**.

1.2.6 Link layer – Layer 2

The link layer was formerly referred to as the data link layer but it is no longer providing a link only for data but also for voice and video (for once I will deliberately divert from the standard term). It provides reliable transit of data units, called **frames**, across a physical link. The link layer is concerned with **physical** (as opposed to network, or logical) **addressing**, network topology, line discipline (how end systems will use the network link), link error checking, ordered delivery of frames, and link flow control to ensure the frame (Layer 2 data unit) is reliably transmitted down the wire to the neighbor. Link layer protocols always run only among the physically connected neighbors (or adjacent nodes in wireless environments), while upper layer protocols may involve intermediate nodes.

Throughout the book we will often refer to services and protocols at the link layer as pertaining to **Layer 2**.

1.2.7 Physical layer – Layer 1

The physical layer defines the electrical, mechanical, procedural, and functional specifications for activating, maintaining, and deactivating the physical link between end systems, and deals with such characteristics as coding the binary 'data,' voltage levels, timing of voltage changes, physical data rates, maximum transmission distances, and physical connectors.

1.2.8 Sublayering

OSI provides for subdivision of the individual layer(s), where necessary, into **sublayers**. This method was very efficiently used at the link layer (Layer 2) in the case of local network standardization (see further) where two sublayers, medium access control, and logical link control are commonly used.

1.3 Actual network architectures

We can easily find more or less resemblance to the above described layers (or rather their functions) in different **network architectures**, *de facto* standard (TCP/IP) and proprietary (namely Novell NetWare, XNS, Banyan VINES, AppleTalk, DECnet). In terms of their individual layering protocols the lower layers are built mostly around standardized physical connectors and standard link protocols (LANs, WANs) (see further) while from the network layer up the solutions are purely proprietary (we will consider aspects of these architectures relevant to their internetworking in Part IV). The only architecture complying fully with the layering rules above is, obviously, OSI itself as the *de jure* standard (only one but rarely fully implemented). Among the vendors which started before the OSI reference model was approved, only Digital decided to follow that path and recently created their DECnet PhaseV/OSI network architecture (sometimes seen).

1.4 Addressing

Locating and identifying computer systems on an internetwork is an essential component of any network system. Two basic types of address are closely related to the two layers where the addressing is performed:

- **Link-layer addresse**s (physical, hardware or MAC addresses, Layer 2) – unique to each network connection, for most local area networks these are burnt in (hence BIA) the interface circuitry and are assigned by the adapter manufacturer. Most end systems have one physical network connection, therefore they have only a **single** physical address. Devices interconnecting network segments have **multiple** link-layer addresses.
- **Network-layer addresses** (logical or virtual addresses, Layer 3) – unlike link-layer addresses, which usually exist within a flat address space, network-layer addresses are usually hierarchical. Hierarchical addresses make address sorting and recall easier by eliminating large blocks of logically similar addresses through a series of comparison operations. Routers use network-layer addresses as the basis for routing. Network-layer addresses differ depending on the protocol family being used, but they typically use similar logical divisions to find computer systems on an internet, usually in **network** and **host** parts.

It is necessary that for proper encapsulation and decapsulation of data units the network and link layers, the **mapping** between these two types of addresses must be resolved. In Part IV we will see how this function is performed by routers.

SNAPSHOT **addressing**

Logical addressing = network-layer (Layer 3) addressing (topology based) – **used in routing decisions**.

Physical addressing = link-layer (Layer 2) addressing (flat) – **used in bridging/switching decisions**.

1.5 Flow control

The primary reason for flow control is to **reduce the flow of excess traffic**. To reduce the flow one can use feedback mechanisms. To redirect the flow one can use routing techniques, and to clean the buffers from excess traffic one can drop the entire packet (i.e. early packet discards). The principal aspects of **congestion control** are to reduce the flow of traffic entering the network in order to relieve congestion at a point within the network and to redirect the flow away from those congested nodes that are experiencing unwanted traffic.

What really governs control is its basic rule, which is often formulated in the design algorithms and dictates how to control the flow. Control mechanisms were designed by researchers at several points and layers in the network, such as between neighboring switches, between edge network devices, or between end user systems. For example, **source-to-destination flow control** is known as **end-to-end flow control** and is often governed by transport protocol window flow control. **Node-to-node** or **switch-to-switch flow control** is known as **hop-by-hop flow control** and is a Layer 2 responsibility. Entry-to-exit flow control is Layer 3 flow control; it polices certain edges of the network from incoming traffic.

The layers of control are interchangeable: the end-to-end flow control at Layer 2 or below of the Asynchronous Transfer Mode (ATM see 3.8) can assume the end-to-end flow control responsibilities of Layer 4. The implementation could take place in hardware rather than software so that the switch can catch up with the speed of the incoming and outgoing cells.

Each layer controls different fragments in size. There is a difference between controlling a few large segments and many small fragments. It is like comparing a big truck on a fast lane with a small and efficient car on a highway. Sequencing and keeping track of all the small fragments are often more difficult. Small fragments, like many cells, tend to be switched faster than large packets; thus, their interarrival time at the destination, the time between arrivals, is shorter. Moreover, small fragments are also retransmitted more quickly (in case of errors) and reduce the overall traffic load. On the other hand, the overhead of small fragment's headers is higher than with big fragments.

1.5.1 Congestion control

Congestion occurs when resources are scarce and highly in demand, and processing and transmission speeds lag behind the speed of incoming traffic. Traditionally, congestion problems in low-speed networks are addressed with techniques that depend on the design of the network layer. For example, congestion is usually controlled in datagram networks by use of choke packets to concentrate on reducing the rate of input to the network. In virtual circuit networks congestion is frequently solved by use of **back pressure** which concentrates on distributing the storage of excess traffic.

There are two principal methods of congestion control: passive and active. **Passive mechanisms** are preventive actions and are implemented at the time of design. One example of such control is oversizing of resources, though this is something often avoided for fear of increasing the cost of the network; however, excess capacity can take care of some of the bursty behavior of traffic when it peaks and persists. Another example is limiting the number of available input and output buffers in a switch. This action will force the network to favor the traffic already in the network over that trying to enter. Similarly, fixed path routing limits the help that routing can provide. Call Admission Control (CAC) is another example of preventive action.

In **active mechanisms** the control reacts when congestion is experienced (also called reactive mechanisms). Active flow control asks for the estimation of network states, propagation of information, and source traffic reduction. For example, in active control an ATM switch is able to detect and measure the congestion levels by average trunk utilization, average buffer utilization, and/or average queue length on the output trunks local to the switch.

1.5.2 Flow control mechanisms

Credit-based window flow control

Credit-based window flow control is a sliding-window flow control which assumes a pair of entities that control data flow between them. For each direction, there is a sending entity and a receiving entity, and the sending entity transmits packets with a sequence number and receives acknowledgments (ACKs) from the receiving entity. The receiving entity may stop the sending entity from transmitting by not acknowledging receipt of packets, though this will not stop the sending entity immediately if the number of outstanding packets is smaller than the window size. This technique is used in low-speed packet-switched networks.

Backpressure

The concept of backpressure is similar to that of fluids flowing down a pipe. When one closes a pipe, the fluid tends to back up the pipe to the point of origin, where no more flow is allowed. The backpressure method implements per-VC (virtual circuit) flow control on every link; when a node detects congestion, it ceases to acknowledge packets on VCs that contribute to the congestion. This technique is used in low-speed packet-switched networks. Normally the window or credit on the link flow control will be significantly smaller than that of an end-to-end flow control window. When an upstream node (closer to the VC source) sees the link VC window becoming exhausted, it ceases to acknowledge incoming packets on those VCs, and the process continues up the path until the source is throttled. The significant features are that every VC on every link must be individually flow-controlled, and that during congestion each node stores for each congested VC a number of packets or cells equal to the link VC window flow control. This concept applies whether a packet- or cell-switched network is under consideration. The only difference is that the acknowledgment cells do not exist in cell-switched networks.

Choke packet

A choke packet is a control packet that has been generated at a congested node; it travels against the flow. The significant feature of the design is the use of end-to-end flow control to support congestion control in which flow control is not implemented. Years after it first appeared, this concept was also adapted to flow control in cell-switched technology. In the ATM world, the concept of a choke packet was adapted in VC connections and was named after resource management cells. The source generates a number of resource management cells for so many cells to send; resource management cells travel through the uncongested and congested nodes and convey the congested states back to the source. Some of the resource management cells also travel to the destinations as well, depending on the technique being implemented. The choke packet method concentrates on reducing input to the network; it reduces the input immediately, but tends to store the excess traffic in the congested node.

1.5.3 Credit-based and rate-based flow control

Credit-based control consists of per-link, per-VC (virtual circuit) window flow control. Each link consists of a sender node (either a source end system or a switch) and a receiver node (either a switch or a destination end system). Each node maintains a separate queue for each VC. The **receiver** monitors the queue lengths of each VC and determines the number of cells the sender can transmit on that VC. This number is called a **credit**. The sender transmits only as many cells as are allowed by the credit. If there is only one active VC, the credit must be large enough to allow the whole bandwidth to be utilized at all times and also match the smallest link on the path. The link cell rate can be computed by dividing the link bandwidth by the cell size.

In the later version, the credit-based approach was enhanced to give adaptive credit where each VC only gets a fraction of the round-trip delay's buffer allocation. The fraction depends on the rate at which the VC uses the credit. For highly active VCs, the fraction is larger; for less active VCs, the fraction is smaller. Inactive VCs receive a small fixed credit. If a VC does not use its credit and its observed usage rate over a period is low, it gets a smaller buffer allocation in the next cycle. If a VC becomes active, it may take some time to go through cycles before it can use the full capacity of the link even if there are no other users. The credit-based approach has some implementation complexity at the switches; it requires per-VC queuing.

The proposal for a **rate-based flow control approach** consists of end-to-end control using a single-bit feedback from the network. In this approach the switches monitor their queue lengths and, if congested, set the **explicit forward congestion indication** (EFCI) bit in the cell header. The destinations monitor EFCI bits; if set, the destinations generate a resource management cell back to the source. The sources use an additive increase and multiplicative decrease algorithm to adjust the incoming rates. The **resource management** cells are sent only to decrease the rate, but no resource management cells are required to increase the rate. The problem is that resource management cells may be lost due to heavy congestion in the reverse path, and the sources will keep increasing their load on the forward path.

The rate-based approach has been enhanced to include positive feedback as well (i.e. sending resource management cells on increase but not on decrease). When resource management cells are sent for both increase and decrease, the algorithm is considered bipolar. The current rate-based algorithm not only supports the EFCI control mechanism, it also provides options for **explicit rate control** (ERC) as well as segmentation of the flow in the control loop using virtual source and destination. The ERC limits the source's **allowed current rate** (ACR) to a specific value fluctuating between the minimum and maximum cell rates agreed during connection setup. This algorithm is sensitive to feedback round-trip delay.

Rate-based and credit-based approaches work quite differently. The rate-based method concentrates on reducing input traffic to the network, while the credit-based method concentrates on distributing the storage of the excess traffic. Differences are seen in both the processing overhead and the storage required by the algorithm.

The processing overhead in credit-based per-VC link flow control is considerable and present at all times. The rate-based method requires moderate processing. It escalates when congestion is detected and cleared. In the credit-based approach, a per-VC flow control scheme must be implemented at all nodes. To implement per-VC flow control additional bits and pieces are needed; that is, acknowledgments have to be present for every n cell.

The credit-based method stores more cells within the network during congestion than does the rate-based, but distributes them over more switches. The rate-based method stores fewer cells, but the storage tends to be concentrated at the congested switch. The congested switch is the best place for the stored cells in order to maintain a smooth flow, but this approach may require more buffer space.

If congestion is short-term and frequent, the rate-based method will generate appreciable overhead; if congestion is infrequent but long-term, the rate-based method will generate little overhead. The same considerations apply to storage: under relatively long-term congestion the credit-based method will tend to load up the network buffers with stored cells and the user may not be aware of the congestion until after a delay has been experienced. In general, the rate-based method seems best suited to a network in which congestion is relatively infrequent and long term. This situation could arise in an ATM network if a network busy hour were intense but infrequent, for example largely due to file and image transfer. Different methods are best suited for different services. If cost and implementation permits, the two methods could coexist at all times.

1.6 Connectionless and connection-oriented network services

With the growth of the Internet, a major portion of endpoint-generated traffic is expected to be carried in IP packets. Using **connection-oriented** networks to transport this traffic is beneficial to both users and service providers. Connection-oriented networks are those in which connection setup is performed prior to information transfer. In contrast, in **connectionless** networks, no explicit connection setup actions are executed prior to transmitting data; instead, data packets are routed to their destinations based on information in their headers.

QUICK TIP	connection-oriented protocols and reliability

Connection-oriented protocols are not necessarily reliable or error-recovering protocols although often implemented by a single protocol. Connection-oriented protocols do not have to provide error recovery (Frame Relay and ATM are examples), and error-recovering protocols do not have to be connection-oriented. Error recovery means that the protocol reacts to the lost or corrupted data and causes the data to be retransmitted.

Connectionless networks do not suffer the delay and processing overhead associated with connection setup. However, information about the connections in connection-oriented networks helps in providing service guarantees and, furthermore, makes it possible to most efficiently use network resources (e.g. bandwidth) by lending them to appropriate connections as they are set up.

It is with this goal of providing users with service guarantees and service providers with improved bandwidth utilization that there is an interest in carrying IP traffic over various connection-oriented networks. Examples of connection-oriented networks include Asynchronous Transfer Mode (ATM), Multiprotocol Label Switching (MPLS), Synchronous Optical Network/Synchronous Digital Hierarchy (SONET/SDH), and Wavelength Division Multiplexed (WDM) networks.

Connection-oriented networks can be packet- or circuit-switched. The **switching mode** of a network indicates whether the network nodes are circuit switches or packet switches. **Circuit switches** are position-based, in that bits arriving in a certain position are switched to a different position, with the position determined by a combination of one or more of three dimensions: space (interface number), time, and wavelength. **Packet switches** are label-based, in that they use information in packet headers (labels) to decide how to switch a packet.

A common definition of circuit switching is that a circuit-switched network is one in which a circuit is set up prior to user data exchange. While this property is a characteristic of circuit-switched networks, it is not the defining property, because with the invention of packet-switched connection-oriented networking (e.g. ATM), even in packet-switched networks a connection can be set up prior to data exchange. Whether a connection is set up prior to data exchange or not is a property of whether the network is connection-oriented or connectionless, not whether the network is packet- or circuit-switched. Connection-oriented networks can be operated in two modes: provisioned or switched. In the **provisioned mode**, connections can be set up a priori based on expected traffic. In the **switched mode**, connections are set up on demand and released after the data exchange is completed.

A networking technique is defined by its **switching and networking modes**. Connectionless networking implies the use of packet switches, but a network of packet switches can be operated in connectionless or connection-oriented mode. Also, a network of circuit switches implies the use of connection-oriented networking, but a connection-oriented network can consist of packet switches or circuit switches.

1.7 Connections and network topology

There are several different **network connection** arrangements for networks which then determine network topologies as discussed later:

- **point-to-point** – data flows between point A and point B;
- **multipoint** – data flows from point A to point B, from point A to point C, and so on. It also flows from points B, C, and D, to point A;
- **multilink** – data travels from point A to B, then to C, then to D, and so on. If one mode on the link fails, all subsequent modes are also affected;
- **multidrop** – one mode is a master, or primary station; the rest are secondary stations, or slaves. A failure on one secondary station will not prevent data from being transmitted to other secondary stations. Each location has its own address, and no two terminals on a multidrop line transmit data at the same time, although they are able to receive simultaneously.

In most data communications networks, a host computer serves more than one terminal, and it is possible to have a 'party line,' in which a single circuit connects many terminals to the host. In multidrop circuits, the terminals share the transmission facility, providing cost savings to the user.

STANDARDS WATCH	Summarized Standards watch

The following standards have been brought to your attention in this chapter:

ISO/IEC 7498-1:1994 *Information Technology – Open Systems Interconnection – Basic Reference Model: The Basic Model*

ISO/IEC 7498-3:1997 *Information Technology – Open Systems Interconnection – Basic Reference Model: Naming and Addressing*

ITU-T X.200 (07/94) *Information Technology – Open Systems Interconnection – Basic Reference Model: The Basic Model*

C H A P T E R   2

Local and metropolitan
area networking

This section is dedicated to **Local Area Networks** (LANs) and **Metropolitan Area Networks** (MANs). We will concentrate on their technical aspects with relevance to their potential for interconnection. We will first look at the LAN general layered architecture and then will overview the issues which distinguish individual types of LANs:

- **topology** (logical and physical);
- **shared transmission media**;
- **access method** to the common media.

A **Local Area Network** (LAN) is a communications network which is usually owned and operated by the business customer. A LAN operates over a limited geographical area (although some types of LANs, and interconnected LANs, may span quite broadly) and enables many independent peripheral devices, such as terminals, to be linked to a network through which they can share central processing units, memory banks, and a variety of other resources. LAN used to be only data oriented but with the advent of new applications LANs also started to support in an integrated way voice and video information.

To overcome certain limits of individual LANs and allow for their easy interconnection over a larger area, **Metropolitan Area Networks** (MAN) were defined. MANs may be private and serve a single organization for its branch interconnect, or may be public and serve the needs of various organizations for their information transfer within the 'city limits.'

Below are summarized the **major characteristics of local networks** which make them differ in some respects from their wide area counterparts:

- they work in **connectionless** mode;
- they provide for media access shared by multiple stations – **multiaccess networks**;
- they transmit frames using **broadcast** on the transmission media (each station has to assess the signal on the LAN media);
- they support **frames of variable length** (with limit dictated by each LAN spec).

Other LAN aspects which once were typical are now much the same as for WANs:

- **rates** – from an initial 1–16 Mbps LANs now ordinarily support up to 1 Gbps while 10 Gbps is currently being specified (ATM has taken away the speed advantages off LANs supporting 2.5 Gbps);
- **administration** – LANs are still typically owned and administered privately (corporate or home) while WANs may be either private or public (with VPNs using public infrastructure).

We need to understand the LAN architecture and various types because, as we will see later on, switch and router operation must obviously conform to that of the connected medium.

2.1 LAN architecture

Local area networks allow nodes to share a common medium and thus create a **broadcast multiaccess network**. With reference to the overview of the seven layers of the OSI hierarchy, it is clear that in the case of LAN architecture not all layers are necessary for purely local transport. Although the end nodes will have implemented a full protocol stack of some kind (standard, *de facto* standard, or proprietary), for actual LAN access only a few lower layers will be of importance. Routing or end flow control is not necessary on single shared media, as with functions of the upper layers. The core lies with the physical and link layers (see Figure 2.1).

FIGURE 2-1 LAN architecture

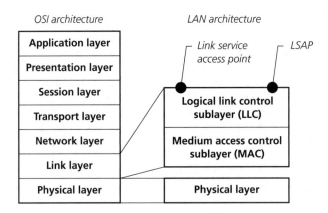

The **physical layer** is very specific to each individual LAN type as we will see later on.

The **link layer** is divided into two sublayers:

- the **Media Access Control sublayer** (MAC);
- the **Logical Link Control sublayer** (LLC).

> **SNAPSHOT**   **Local Area Network (LAN)**
>
> **LANs** incorporate the lower two layers of the hierarchical architecture, the **physical and link layers**, while the link layer is further effectively divided into **MAC and LLC sublayers**.

2.1.1 Media access control sublayer

Media Access Control (MAC) is responsible for several areas of operation. On the transmit side the MAC sublayer is responsible for receiving data from the Logical Link Control sublayer and encapsulating it into a MAC frame ready for transmission. The MAC sublayer is also responsible for determining if the communications channel is available and ready for transmission through the particular access method. If the channel is available, the MAC layer transmits the data onto the cable through the physical layer and monitors the physical layer status for e.g. an indication of a collision (more than one station transmitting at the same time). In case of contention network when there is a collision, the MAC layer also handles the backoff and retransmission function. On the receiving side, the MAC layer follows the reverse of the above steps. It checks the frame for errors, strips control information then passes the remainder of the packet to the upper layers by way of logical link control.

MAC addressing

As has already been mentioned, the link layer is responsible for the **physical addressing** of a device's interface to the network. From the LAN point of view, it is the MAC sublayer address which is used for unambiguous identification of each network interface. MAC addresses have two possible lengths (see Figure 2.2): **16 bits** (only locally meaningful) or **48 bits** (most common as it should be globally unique).

FIGURE 2-2   MAC address formats

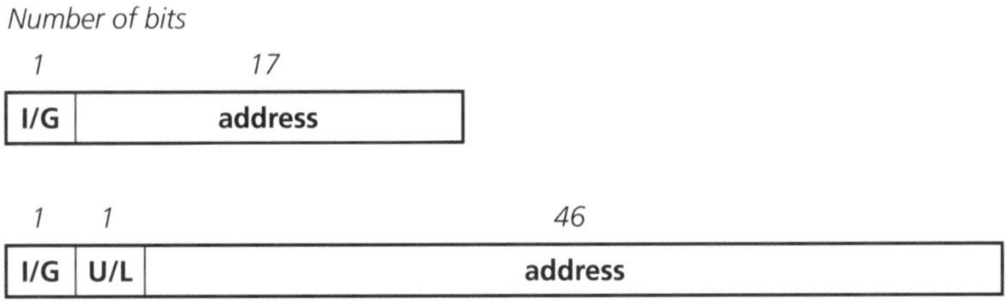

Notes:
Field values I/G (Individual/Group) and U/L (Universal/Local):
I/G = 0: individual address MAC   U/L = 0: universally allocated address
I/G = 1: group address MAC   U/L = 1: locally allocated address

They are typically expressed in hexadecimal format and have two parts:

■ an ***organization unique identifier*** (OUI, vendor code) – first three octets of MAC address assigned to manufacturer by IEEE;

■ an ***interface identifier*** – next three octets, assigned uniquely by manufacturer.

Besides **individual** addresses identifying every single interface in the world it is also possible to address a **group** of interfaces. Group MAC addresses serve for multicasting at Layer 2. There are numerous reserved globally assigned multicast MAC addresses which will be mentioned at appropriate places throughout the book. The I/G part of the MAC address indicates whether it is an individual or group address. An example of a group MAC address is shown in Figure 2.4. The address *FF-FF-FF-FF-FF-FF* means **broadcast** MAC address, i.e. a frame with such a destination address is for all stations.

FIGURE 2-3	Example of MAC address – hexadecimal and binary representation

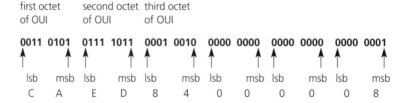

SNAPSHOT	MAC addressing

MAC addressing represents the **physical flat addressing** performed at the link layer.

The binary representation of an address is formed by taking each octet in order and expressing it as a sequence of eight bits, least significant bit (lsb) to most significant bit (msb), left to right. For example, the address *AC-DE-48-00-00-80* has the binary representation shown in Figure 2.3.

The first (leftmost) bit in the binary representation is the I/G address bit. If set to 0 as above, it indicates an individual address. It may be set to 1 in an address allocated by the assignee to indicate that that address is a group address.

The proper **bit order** in which the address is represented and transmitted may lead to serious troubles. The IEEE 802.1 committee has defined a canonical format for writing addresses where each octet is represented by two hexadecimal digits. **Canonical format** assumes the least significant bit goes first (see Figure 2.5).

FIGURE 2-4 Example of MAC group address

AD-DE-48-00-00-80

1011 0101   0111 1011   0001 0010   0000 0000   0000 0000   0000 0001
↑

I/G Address Bit
(D   A   E   D   8   4   0   0   0   0   0   8)

FIGURE 2-5 Transmission order of bits in MAC address as per canonical format

1011 0101   0111 1011   0001 0010   0000 0000   0000 0000   0000 0001
↑↑   ↑

| next bit transmitted
first bit transmitted   last bit transmitted

This may cause the main discrepancy between the 802.3 and 802.5 way of understanding addresses:

■ in 802.3 – least significant bit transmitted first (in conformance with the above rule on MAC addresses);

■ in 802.5 – most significant bit transmitted first (not in conformance with the above rule on MAC addresses).

While in general transmission the bit order is looked after properly by relevant adapters (as per specification), the addressing may cause some troubles. This is due to the fact that the *Individual/Group* bit in the address is defined as the first bit on the wire. Therefore, due to the different transmission bit order, the group address for 802.3 would not necessarily mean group address when transmitted on 802.5 because a different bit would be transmitted first. Hence, the addresses for transmission must be stored in a different format as they will transmit the most significant bit first.

2.1.2 Logical link control sublayer

The **Logical Link Control** (LLC), the upper part of the link layer, is responsible for shielding the upper layers from any particular access method or media. The upper layers need not worry about whether they are connected to a Token Ring or Ethernet network because the logical link control handles the interface (IEEE 802.2). All widely used LANs (except proprietary Ethernet version 2) follow the rule that common LLC is implemented over the specific LAN physical layer and MAC sublayer.

STANDARDS WATCH | **Logical Link Control (LLC)**

LLC: IEEE 802.2 – ISO/IEC 8802-2 (1997)

IEEE 802.2 offers three types of service:

- **Type 1** (LLC 1) provides **unacknowledged connectionless service** (the most commonly used as upper-layer protocols may provide for reliable data transfer);
- **Type 2** (LLC 2) provides **connection-oriented service** (establishes logical connections between sender and acknowledges data upon receipt);
- **Type 3** (LLC 3) provides **acknowledged connectionless service** (compromise between the two services above – without establishing connections acknowledges data receipt).

End stations can support multiple LLC service types. A Class I device supports only Type 1 service. A Class II device supports both Type 1 and Type 2 service. Class III devices support both Type 1 and Type 3 service, while Class IV devices support all three types of service.

LLC frame format

LLC headers include the following fields:

- *destination and source SAPs* – in the seven relevant bits of source or destination SAP, the identifier of the upper (network) layer protocol (source or destination) is encoded (for the meaning of the left bit in each SAP see Figure 2.6). The protocols addressed are standard, not proprietary;
- *control* – format similar to HDLC protocol with sequence numbers (see link protocols).

FIGURE 2-6 LLC frame format

Number of octets:

1	1	1 or 2	N (N ≥ 0)
DSAP destination SAP first bit = I/G	**SSAP** source SAP first bit = C/R	control	data

Notes:

I/G = Individual/Group:
I/G = 0: individual DSAP
I/G = 1: group DSAP

C/R = Command/Response:
C/R = 0: command
C/R = 1: response

2.1.3 SubNetwork access protocol

The **SubNetwork Access Protocol** (SNAP) is an alternative to the LLC protocol allowing for extension of the **network protocol address** field. SNAP was first defined by the IETF (standard protocol, RFC 1042) for the IP protocol over IEEE 802.x LANs but then extended for use by other network protocols. SNAP is therefore used for the majority of proprietary network protocols which are not addressed through the standard network SAP. SNAP uses two octets instead of one to identify an upper layer protocol through so called **Ethertype** hexadecimal code. The SNAP frame format, which conserves all LLC fields (with assigned constant values) and adds two new ones, is shown on Figure 2.7.

RFC WATCH	SubNetwork Access Protocol (SNAP)

RFC 1042 **Standard for the transmission of IP datagrams over IEEE 802 networks,** 1988 (Standard)

FIGURE 2-7   SNAP frame format

Number of octets:

1	1	1	3	2	N (N ≥ 0)
DSAP = AA	SSAP = AA	control = 03	OUI	protocol	data

2.2 LAN standardization

The majority of LAN standards, i.e. LLC and MAC sublayers and physical layer, were developed by IEEE Committee 802 and issued under the numbers of specific subcommittees, **IEEE 802.x** (see Table 2.1). All have also been adopted (or are undertaking the adoption process) by the ISO, where their numbering is similar to that of the IEEE, **ISO 8802-x.**

The Fiber Distributed Data Interface (FDDI), another common LAN, has not been standardized by the IEEE but by **ANSI** (as X3T9.5) and adopted by ISO (as ISO 9314). For the relationship between the most common LAN standards see Figure 2.8. The figure shows all standardized IEEE/ANSI local networks with their major characteristics. In the following discussion, however, we will concentrate only on the most popular local networks which are subject to interconnection:

- **Ethernet/IEEE 802.3 (differences from Token Ring are discussed in Section 6.6.1);**
- **Token Ring/IEEE 802.5;**
- **FDDI;**
- **Wireless LANs;**
- **Fibre Channel and SANs.**

| TABLE 2-1 | IEEE 802 subcommittees dedicated to LAN and MAN standardization |

IEEE Subcommittee/ Standard number	Subcommittee title
802.1	Higher Layer LAN Protocols
802.2	Logical Link Control
802.3	Ethernet (CSMA/CD) type networks
802.4	Token Bus networks (inactive working group (WG))
802.5	Token Ring Networks
802.6	Metropolitan Area Networks (MANs; inactive WG)
802.7	Technical advisory group (TAG) for broadband networks (inactive WG)
802.8	Technical advisory group for fiber optic networks
802.9	Isochronous LANs
802.10	LAN security
802.11	Wireless local networks (WLANs)
802.12	Demand Priority (VG-AnyLAN) networks
802.13	*Never used*
802.14	Cable Modems
802.15	Wireless Personal Area Networks (WPANs)
802.16	Broadband Wireless Access
802.17	Resilient Packet Ring

New IEEE standards group **802.17** has been recently approved to create a new MAC layer standard for **Resilient Packet Rings** (RPR). This activity is embraced by equipment vendors, silicon providers, carriers, ISPs, and user communities. The IEEE 802.17 Resilient Packet Ring Working Group (RPR WG) will define a Resilient Packet Ring Access Protocol for use in Local, Metropolitan and Wide Area Networks for transfer of data packets at rates scalable to many gigabits per second.

FIGURE 2-8 Relationship between LAN standards and their main characteristics

LINK	Logical link control (LLC) IEEE 802.2					
LAYER	Medium access control (MAC)					
	Ethernet *Carrier sense multiple access (CSMA/CD)* IEEE	Token bus *Token passing* IEEE	Token ring *Token passing* IEEE	IsoEthernet IEEE	100VG-AnyLAN *Demand priority* IEEE	Fiber distributed data interface *(FDDI)* ANSI
PHYSICAL LAYER	802.3 coax, UTP, optics 1; 10; 100; 1000 Mbps	802.4 coax, optics 1; 5; 10; 20 Mbps	802.5 STP, UTP 4; 16 Mbps	802.9 16.144 Mbps	802.12 STP, UTP, optics 100 Mbps	X3T9.5 optics 100 Mbps

STANDARDS WATCH **LAN standards available from (see also Appendix B):**

IEEE **(Institute of Electrical and Electronics Engineers): http://standards.ieee.org**

ANSI **(American National Standards Institute): http://www.ansi.org**

ISO **(International Organization for Standardization): http://www.iso.ch**

2.2.1 Local network topologies

We introduced the concept of network topology earlier in this Part. We will now have a look at how LAN topologies vary across the LAN types spectrum (see Figure 2.9). However, we should carefully distinguish between the logical and physical topology, as the logical topology is dictated by the access method but the physical topology may not correspond.

■ **Bus** (e.g. Ethernet). This comprises a single data path to which all workstations directly attach and on which all transmissions are available to every workstation. The aim is that only the workstation to which the transmission is addressed can actually read it, however. Every workstation can be put in so-called promiscuous mode and can therefore see the traffic that is not directly addressed to it. Programs like *etherdump, snoop, tcpdump* use this feature for debugging purposes and for hacking/cracking. Buggy networking software can cause big problems on shared media like bus. A bus cable must be

FIGURE 2-9 LAN topologies

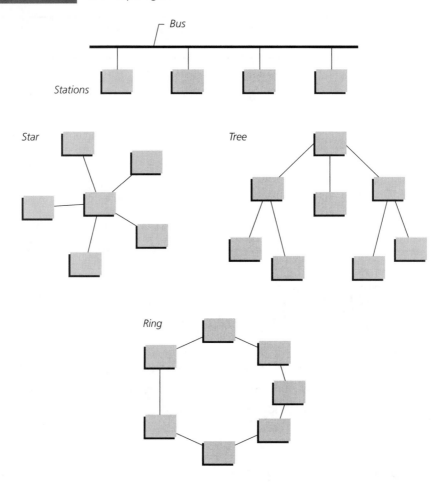

terminated at both ends to present a specified impedance to the network workstations, so any break in the bus cable takes the entire network down. Example of 'discrepancy' between logical and physical topology is IEEE 802.3 10BASE-T (see further) which is physically a star but logically a bus (as are all the other Ethernet types).

■ **Ring** (e.g. Token Ring, FDDI). Each workstation is connected to another adjacent workstation in a closed loop. Such a ring, however, shares with the bus-based Ethernet the disadvantage of a single-point failure. For this reason, most ring networks in use today are actually implemented as physical stars. To avoid single-point failures, some ring topologies (such as FDDI) use double rings that automatically revert to a single ring (of double length) if a single trunk between adjacent stations happens to be cut.

■ **Star/tree** (e.g. 100VG-AnyLAN). The star topology requires a center device, concentrator, or hub to allow single attached stations to communicate via it.

The point of failure is not the individual stations nor their connections, but only the central node. Once we start connecting stars together we can create more complex tree topologies.

2.2.2 Media

The transmission media used in LANs can either be tangible or not as no longer are LAN devices interconnected by hard wire (**wireline**), but also through the air in the case of **wireless** communication.

In terms of wires used nowadays, the following are the possibilities, but the actual choice is dictated by the concrete LAN standard:

- **Coaxial cable**. While coaxial cable carries higher bandwidth and spans medium distances, its limitations are expense, bulkiness, and inflexibility. Physically it consists of two conductors, a copper mesh tube and a wire that runs down the cable's central axis. A 'dielectric' separates the two conductors and provides insulation so that they cannot contact one another. A cable that consists of two central conductors in the same mesh tube is called twinaxial cable or twinax.

- **Twisted-pair wire**. Physically this comprises two conductors twisted around each other, which is a technique that minimizes the amount of interference the pair causes in adjacent pairs. The twisted-pair wire required for reliable data transmission is of a heavier gauge than telephone wire – 24 to 26 American Wire Gauge (AWG). There are two varieties of twisted pair in wide use:
  - **Unshielded Twisted Pair** (UTP) cabling is produced in a number of overall quality levels defined by the EIA/TIA, called Categories (Cats 3, 4, and 5 are used in LANs with the higher number the better the tolerance to interference);
  - **Shielded Twisted Pair** (STP) cabling, also known as IBM Type 1 cabling, allows longer cable runs and is less susceptible to interference of any kind. Shielded twisted pair is also more expensive and more difficult to pull into walls than unshielded twisted pair.

- **Fiber cable** (optical or plastic). This type of cable is immune to electrical interference and theoretically capable of supporting virtually unlimited transmission speed. With new technologies it is easy to install and with the price dropping it is more and more deployed even outside backbones. Two types of fiber media are in common use in LANs:
  - **multimode fiber** allows the use of light-emitting diodes (LEDs) as the light source and is capable of high transmission speeds within shorter distances;
  - **single-mode fiber** requires a laser as the light source and is generally used for longer distances.

Among other criteria for proper network technology choice is delay. Delay, when applied to network cabling, typically refers to the **propagation delay** of the segment or network. As signals in both electrically conductive cables and fiber optic cables travel through the transmission media at a fraction of the speed of light, there is an appreciable delay between the transmission of a signal on one end of a cable and the reception of the same signal on the other end. Network delay is typically measured in microseconds. Latency introduced by opto/electrical converters and repeaters (signal regenerators) limit the transmission speed as well. Optical media (fiber) have varying transmission characteristics at different frequencies.

2.2.3 Access methods

There have been developed two different approaches to how to allocate station access to the common shared medium when there is a need for transmission:

■ **random access** – any station can initiate a transmission at any time unless another station is already transmitting and the medium is busy, hence there is no explicit supervision allowing individual stations to transmit;

■ **deterministic access** – each station must wait for its turn to transmit as its access to the medium is not 'deliberate' but allowed explicitly, through token or poll.

2.3 Ethernet/IEEE 802.3

The most popular LAN so far with lots of potential for the future is Ethernet/IEEE 802.3. Ethernet is a natural fit into corporate and industrial networks because of its speed, robust performance, low cost of deployment, and constantly updated technology. Ethernet was originally developed by the Xerox Corporation's Palo Alto Research Center (PARC) in the 1970s. The specification was the technological basis for the IEEE 802.3 standard, which was initially released in 1980. Shortly thereafter, Digital, Intel Corporation, and Xerox Corporation jointly developed and released yet another **Ethernet specification Version 2.0** (called DIX). The standard IEEE 802.3 and Ethernet version 2 are very similar in the way they operate; however, due to incompatibility in frame structure, they cannot cooperate. Therefore it is necessary to distinguish properly between the two. While the Ethernet version 2 spec describes physical and link layers, IEEE 802.3 defines only the physical layer and MAC sublayer because IEEE 802.2 LLC is used.

STANDARDS WATCH	IEEE 802.3

10 Mbps Ethernet: IEEE 802.3 – ISO/IEC 8802-3, including:

10BASE2: 802.3a-1992

10BROAD36: 802.3b-1985

Repeater Unit for 10 Mbps Baseband Networks: 802.3c-1985

Fiber Optic Inter Repeater Link: 802.3d-1987

1BASE5 STARLAN: 802.3e-1987

10BASE-F: 802.3j-1993

Layer Management for 10 Mbps Baseband Repeaters: 802.3k-1992

In the following section, the basic Ethernet characteristics are described. Information closely related to hubs and repeaters in Ethernet/IEEE 802.3 networks is to be found in Section 5.1 and switching issues are summarized in Part III.

2.3.1 CSMA/CD access method

Carrier Sense Multiple Access with Collision Detection (CSMA/CD) allows stations to access the network at any time but before sending data, the station listens to the network to see if it is already in use by detecting a busy signal. If the network is busy, the station wishing to transmit waits. If the network is not in use, the station transmits. Because of propagation delays in the network, it is possible for two stations to simultaneously find the bus available, in which case both stations will begin transmitting frames. When these signals meet on the cable, a **collision** occurs. Upon detecting a collision all stations are informed by a special signal (jam) about collision occurrence. The stations which caused the collision must retransmit at some later time. Backoff algorithms determine when the colliding stations retransmit to ensure the best randomization to avoid subsequent collisions.

Both Ethernet and IEEE 802.3 LANs are broadcast networks. In other words, all stations see all frames, regardless of whether they represent an intended destination. Each station must examine received frames to determine if it is a specified destination address. If so, the frame is passed to a higher protocol layer for appropriate processing.

2.3.2 Ethernet and IEEE 802.3 frame

Ethernet and IEEE 802.3 frame formats are similar with the important exception of length/type field which makes them incompatible. Individual fields have the following meanings (see Figure 2.10):

FIGURE 2-10   Incompatibility of Ethernet and IEEE 802.3 frame formats

(a) Ethernet version 2

Number of octets:

8	6	6	2	46-1500	4
preamble	destination address	source address	protocol type	data	FCS

(b) IEEE 802.3

Number of octets:

8	6 (2)	6 (2)	2		4
preamble	destination address	source address	length	data LLC/SNAP	FCS

- **Preamble** – indicates the beginning of frame transmission and allows for frame timing at the receiving station. The signal pattern is a repeating sequence of alternating ones and zeros for a total of 56 bits (seven octet); it is not taken into account for the maximum frame length or the error checking procedure.

- **Start of Frame Delimiter** (SFD) – signal pattern is *10101011* for a total of 8 bits (1 octet). It follows the preamble and indicates the start of information by the last two bits, *11*; it is not taken into account for the maximum frame length or the error checking procedure.

- **Destination address** – address of destination station (MAC unicast), group of stations (multicast) or all stations (broadcast).

- **Source address** – indicates the address of the station initiating the transmission. The source address is always a unicast address of 48 bits (six octets) in length.

- **Length field** (IEEE 802.3) – indicates the length of the data field. The length field is 16 bits long.

- **Type field** (Ethernet version 2.0) – indicates the network protocol (e.g. *hex0800* for IP).

- **Data** – data of 46 octets minimum to a maximum of 1500 octets in length (in case of smaller data units padding is necessary to the minimum limit). For Ethernet data means network data unit. For IEEE 802.3 actual encapsulation may be either LLC or SNAP.

- **Frame Check Sequence** (FCS) – Cyclic Redundancy Check (CRC) across all fields but preamble, SFD and FCS performed by source and destination station for error check (in interconnected network by bridge, or switch working in store-and-forward mode, or router).

Total frame length is between 64 and 1518 octets (while the frame header takes 18 octets not taking into account the preamble and start of frame bits) and the obligatory Interframe Gap (IFG) is 96 bits, i.e. 9.6 microseconds which the stations must wait between any two consequently sent frames. (For a global comparison of framing and rate features see Table 2.2.)

TABLE 2-2 Framing and data rate constraints across typical LANs and WANs

	Interframe gap	Minimum frame length	Maximum frame length	Bandwidth
Ethernet	96 bits	64 octets	1518 octets	10 Mbps
Fast Ethernet	96 bits	64 octets	1518 octets	100 Mbps
Token Ring	4 bits	32 octets	16 K octets	16 Mbps
FDDI	0	34 octets	4500 octets	100 Mbps
BRI ISDN	0	24 octets (PPP)	1500 octets (PPP)	128 Kbps

TABLE 2-2	Continued			
	Interframe gap	*Minimum frame length*	*Maximum frame length*	*Bandwidth*
PRI ISDN	0	24 octets (PPP)	1500 octets (PPP)	1.472 Mbps
T1	0	14 octets (HDLC)	Non-existent (theoretically) 4500 octets (in reality)	1.5 Mbps
ATM	0	30 octets (AAL5)	16 K octets (AAL5)	155 Mbps

2.3.3 Ethernet/IEEE 802.3 physical layer

IEEE 802.3 specifies several different physical layers, whereas Ethernet defines only one. Each IEEE 802.3 physical layer protocol has a name that summarizes its characteristics. The IEEE 802.3 physical layer types are shown in Table 2.3.

TABLE 2-3	IEEE 802.3 physical layer					
Types	*10Base-5*	*10Base-2*	*1Base-5*	*10Base-T*	*10Broad-36*	*10Base-F*
Nickname	*Thick Ethernet*	*Thin Ethernet (Cheapernet)*	*Starlan*			
Media	Coaxial cable (50 ohm)	Coaxial cable (50 ohm)	UTP	UTP	Coaxial cable (75 ohm)	Optical cable (single or multimode)
Bandwidth	10 Mbps	10 Mbps	1 Mbps	10 Mbps	10 Mbps	10 Mbps
Max. segment length	500 m	185 m	500 m 250 m	100 m	1800 m	2000 m (multimode) 5000 m (singlemode)
Network span	2.5 km	0.925 km	2.5 km	0.5 km	3.6 km	2 km (active hub), 500 m (passive hub)
Max. stations on segment	100	30				

▶

TABLE 2-3	Continued					
Types	*10Base-5*	*10Base-2*	*1Base-5*	*10Base-T*	*10Broad-36*	*10Base-F*
Signaling, coding	Baseband Manchester II	Baseband Manchester II	Baseband Manchester II	Baseband Manchester II	Broadband DPSK	
Minimal distance between stations	2.5 m	0.5 m			2.5 m	
Cable diameter	10 mm	5 mm	0.4–0.6 mm	0.4–0.6 mm	10 mm	0.125 mm
Max. number of transceivers	100	30	2	2	6	2

Thick Ethernet workstations use a device called a transceiver to attach to the coaxial media. An installer first pierces the insulation of the coax to expose the central conductor. The transceiver is then clamped onto the cable so that a small spike is in contact with the exposed central conductor. This kind of connection is often termed a **vampire tap**; vampire taps are susceptible to corrosion. The transceiver is connected to the workstation by a nine-conductor, non-coaxial cable that can be up to 50 meters long. At the workstation, the Ethernet network interface card is equipped with a 15-pin 'D' connector called an attachment unit interface (AUI) to which the transceiver cable is connected.

Thin Ethernet network interface cards are equipped with an onboard transceiver unit, and the coaxial bus cable attaches directly to the card by means of a BNC 'T' connector. This T-shaped connector attaches to a male BNC connector that juts out of the back of the interface card. Two coaxial cable ends are then attached to the arms of the 'T.' Workstations at either end of the bus require a 50 ohm terminating resistor 'endcap' on one arm of the 'T' connector.

Logical IEEE 802.3 **topology** is always a bus, but physically it is sometimes implemented as a star with center in the hub (10BaseT). The principles of interconnecting several segments using **repeaters** is specified in the standard (due to overall propagation delay still allowing collision detection). The rule known as **5-4-3** limits the overall number of five segments interconnected by four repeaters while only three segments are inhabited by stations and the others are inter-repeater links.

2.3.4 Fast Ethernet IEEE 802.3u, y

Fast Ethernet with data rate of 100 Mbps is derived in the main from 10 Mbps IEEE 802.3. It uses the CSMA/CD access method, the same MAC frame and a similar physical layer. Due to a tenfold increase in the data rate the span of the network is more limited (to 205 m only). Currently there are four options for the physical layer (for comparison with 10BaseT and 100VG-AnyLAN only two are displayed in Table 2.4):

- **100BASE-TX** – UTP category 5 or STP with two pairs;
- **100BASE-T4** – UTP category 3, 4, 5 with four pairs;
- **100BASE-T2** – UTP category 3 (*voice-grade*), or 4, 5 with two pairs;
- **100BASE-FX** – two optical cables.

STANDARDS WATCH	Fast Ethernet

Fast Ethernet: IEEE 802.3 u, y

100BASE-T: 802.3u-1995

100BASE-T2: 802.3y-1997

The standard also defines the support for **autonegotiation** of the individual attached adaptor's speeds to choose the optimum (10 Mbps or 100 Mbps), and **autosensing** to agree on the manner of operation (half or full-duplex). 100Base-T station upon start-up automatically advertises its capabilities by sending a burst of link integrity test pulses (fast link pulse, FLP). If the receiving station is capable of 10Base-T operation only, it will ignore the FLP and the communication will use 10 Mbps operation as a fallback. Otherwise the adaptor will detect the FLP and will determine the highest possible segment speed to use.

TABLE 2-4 Comparison of Ethernet, Fast Ethernet, and 100VG-AnyLAN technologies

	10Base-T	100Base-TX	100Base-T4	100VG-AnyLAN
Cabling	UTP Cat 3, 5 (2 or 4 pairs)	UTP Cat 5 (2 pairs)	UTP Cat 3, 4, 5 (4 pairs)	UTP Cat 3, 4, 5 (4 pairs)
Network diameter	2500 m	205 m	205 m	205 m
Max. distance between hub and station	100 m	100 m	100 m	100 m
Support for full duplex (FDX)	Yes	Yes	No	No
Max. throughput	10 Mbps (20 Mbps FDX)	100 Mbps (200 Mbps FDX)	100 Mbps	100 Mbps

While the initial Ethernet specification allowed only half-duplex operation, full-duplex support (see Figure 2.11) was added and in the latest IEEE 802.3 standard forms an integral part. The simultaneous transmitting and receiving of frames requires a non-collision environment, therefore CSMA/CD must be disabled. This is useful in switched environments for connecting server to switch or two switches together.

FIGURE 2-11   Full duplex operation

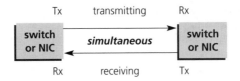

Two classes of **repeater** are defined for Fast Ethernet:

- **Class I** interconnects different media by converting signals between sequence 4B/5B code in 100Base-X and parallel code 8B/6T in 100Base-T4. Due to the delay incurred during this conversion only one repeater of class I is allowed in a single collision domain.
- **Class II** does not provide for interconnection of various media so there could be up to two class II repeaters in a collision domain.

The resulting Fast Ethernet topology comprises direct connection between nodes without repeaters, star connection with one repeater class I or star connection with one or two repeaters class II within 10 m of each other. More complex topology is allowed only through the use of switches and, of course, routers (see Parts III and IV).

2.3.5 Gigabit Ethernet IEEE 802.3z, ab

Gigabit Ethernet uses as many of the popular characteristics of the initial 10 Mbps IEEE 802.3 as possible:

- **CSMA/CD** access method;
- **frame** structure including its minimum and maximum sizes. This last compatibility requirement was solved through so-called **carrier extension** of

STANDARDS WATCH	Gigabit Ethernet

Gigabit Ethernet: IEEE 802.3z-1998
1000BASE-T: 802.3ab-1999

small frames to 512 octets (by adding a special signal after the frame is transmitted) which allows reasonable segment/network length.

The **physical layer** offers four choices (for distance limits see Figure 2.12):

- **1000BASE-SX** – optical fiber for short wavelengths (using Fibre Channel technology) for up to 260 meters distance over 62.5 micron multimode fiber, or up to 550 meters over 50 micron multimode fiber in a full duplex, switch-to-switch connection;
- **1000BASE-LX** – optical fiber for long wavelengths (using Fibre Channel technology) for up to 440 meters over 62.5 micron multimode fiber, and up to 550 meters over 50 micron multimode fiber, or up to 10 kilometers over 10 micron single mode fiber in a full duplex, switch-to-switch connection;
- **1000BASE-CX** – coaxial cable (twinax, balanced copper) for up to 25 m distance;
- **1000BASE-T** – four pairs of UTP Cat 5 for up to 100 m distance.

FIGURE 2-12   Distances in Gigabit Ethernet

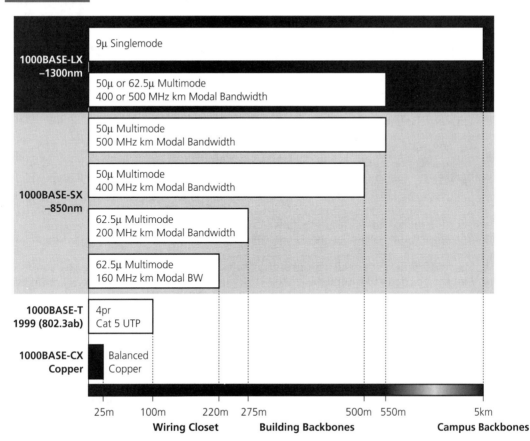

Half-duplex **repeaters** only allow two segments to be interconnected in a Gigabit Ethernet network. A new type of full-duplex hubs, **buffered distributors**, were standardized for use in the gigabit LAN. They implement flow control as defined in IEEE 802.3x (for more details see Part III on LAN switching) to provide for 100% network throughput due to simultaneous acceptance of incoming frames, while buffering them when necessary. Distributors position themselves between simple repeaters and LAN switches with their facilities.

STANDARDS WATCH	industry forum

10GEA (10Gigabit Ethernet Alliance): **http://www.10gea.org**

2.3.6 IEEE 802.1p and 802.1Q

While faster Ethernet technologies such as 100 Mbps Ethernet continue to reduce the probability of the collisions which cause the delays in transmitting data, they still leave a concern that collisions can occur and thus prevent data packets from getting to their destination in a predetermined time. The **IEEE 802.1p** standard addresses the need to deliver time-critical messages in a deterministic fashion. Designed for multimedia applications, this standard directly impacts on Ethernet as a control network by allowing system designers to prioritize messages, guaranteeing the bandwidth for time-critical data so that it is sent ahead of other less sensitive traffic. The companion standards **IEEE 802.1p/Q** are discussed in detail in Part III; here we only introduce their aims:

- **802.1Q** deals with the standardization of Virtual LANs and of the GVRP, a protocol to control the propagation of multicast/broadcast traffic on VLANs;
- **802.1p** deals with the definition of traffic classes on (V)LANs, and of GARP, a protocol to record attributes at the VLAN level. It is a generic protocol whose applications are useful to the network manager: these applications are GMRP (to manage the multicast groups on the LAN) and GVRP (to manage the propagation of the multicast/broadcast traffic).

Gigabit Ethernet's wider bandwidths help improve QoS regulating the timing of latency periods to minimize jittery video and audio delays. In the past, ATM was the only reliable way to achieve any kind of QoS. Gigabit Ethernet is achieving almost similar results (together with IEEE 802.1p and Q) with considerably more cost-effectiveness, backward compatibility and interoperability with other technologies. Therefore, after several years of attempts, it seems that ATM will remain at the WAN level of interconnectivity. ATM deployment at the workgroup or desktop requires a complete change of network interface hardware, software and management protocols. Instead, the opposite direction is expected nowadays: Gigabit Ethernet moving more into wide area networking, namely through its newly developed 10 Gbps version.

2.3.7 10 Gbps Ethernet

The latest specification for the very high-speed Ethernet is currently being developed in IEEE to become a standard denominated as **IEEE 802.3az**. The first draft was ready in September 2000 with standard completion expected in 2002. Two physical layers will be supported (10 Gbps LAN and OC-192 WAN) to allow for both local and wide area backbone interconnections. In the traditional LAN space the goal is to support transmission of data on dark fiber and dark wavelength while maintaining the traditional simplicity of Ethernet. In the WAN environment support for the transmission of Ethernet on an installed base of the SONET/SDH transport infrastructure will be added (operating at a data rate compatible with the OC-192c and SDH VC-4-64c payload rate, see Appendix D). The frame limits should be kept the same while the mode of operation will be full-duplex only.

The new proposed Ethernet will extend the 802.3 protocol to an operating speed of 10 Gbps and to expand the Ethernet application space to include wide area network links in order to provide a significant increase in bandwidth while maintaining maximum compatibility with the installed base of 802.3 interfaces, previous investment in research and development, and principles of network operation and management.

STANDARDS WATCH   industry forum

10-Gigabit Ethernet Alliance: http://www.10gea.org

STANDARDS WATCH   10 Gigabit Ethernet

10 Gbps Ethernet: IEEE 802.3ae

The **physical layer** will offer the following choices (based on current work in progress):

- **10GBASE-SX** – multimode optical fiber for network span up to 300 m;
- **10GBASE-LX** – multimode or singlemode optical fiber up to max. 5–15 km;
- **10GBASE-EX** – singlemode optical fiber up to tens of kilometers.

2.3.8 Shared vs. switched Ethernet

Shared Ethernet based on its media access method is always subject to collisions as it represents a contentious access method. Only one station may use the medium, in the half-duplex mode either for frame transmission (Tx mode) or reception (Rx mode). Hence the **switched Ethernet** became a useful option allowing for dedicated access to media for a smaller group of stations or a single station (usually a server). As switches divide the network into as many collision domains as they have physical segments connected (see Part III), the stations attached may feel a certain relief over the continuous battle over media access. When a dedicated, private LAN connects a single node to the switch, the operation mode may change from half to full duplex (using the autosensing procedure). This eliminates the CSMA/CD operation, thus no collisions are possible, and allows for potentially simultaneous transmitting and receiving of data. Although the data rate does not mysteriously double due to the change of operation (as some vendors still like to imply), full duplex in effect allows the user to transmit and receive at full media speed with nicely aggregated performance.

Switched Ethernet attempts to eliminate the cause of network congestion, but it does not offer the ultimate cure. Switched Ethernet may dedicate each LAN segment to a single user. A switch acts as the hub connecting the individual segments, but, unlike a hub, the switch may be capable of forwarding packets between segments at wire-speed, and it can support multiple conversations simultaneously. The potential for contention and congestion due to shared media access is removed. Switched Ethernet moves the contention problem from the user's network adapter to the switch. Contention is handled within the switch by buffering frames from multiple users who are trying to access the same destination simultaneously.

Switched Ethernet is subject to the same limitations as network hubs with respect to scalability: the advantage of the technology is limited by the number of ports on a switch, although users physically connected to the same switch receive a high-quality service. When communication takes place between switches across the backbone, the potential for congestion recurs.

The advantages and disadvantages of high-speed Ethernet networks are summarized in Table 2.5.

TABLE 2-5   Advantages and disadvantages of high-speed Ethernet networks

Advantages	Disadvantages
Very efficient with low network load (up to 30%)	With growing load networks become inefficient (attempting to retransmit after collisions, resulting in low user traffic throughput)
Simple protocol to implement and operate	Non-deterministic medium access method
Easy upgrading from previous slower Ethernet versions and possibility for combinations	Network span limited (max. segment size plus max. number of repeaters)
Cost-effective performance improvement	
Segmentation in collision domains with switches	

2.4 Token Ring/IEEE 802.5

The Token Ring network was originally developed by IBM in the 1970s. It is still IBM's primary local area network (LAN) technology, and is second only to Ethernet/IEEE 802.3: the in general LAN popularity. The IEEE 802.5 specification is almost identical to, and completely compatible with, IBM's Token Ring network.

2.4.1 Token passing access method

Token Ring and IEEE 802.5 apply a totally different access method to the Ethernet/IEEE 802.3: the **deterministic** method (all the differences between Ethernet and Token Ring are discussed in Section 6.6.1). It is possible to calculate the maximum time that will elapse before any end station is allocated access to the shared transmission medium. The right of access is granted to the station based on the receipt of a **token**, a special type of frame (see Figure 2.13 overleaf). If a node receiving the token has no information to send, it simply passes the token to the next end station. Each station can hold the token for a maximum period of time. If a station possessing the token does have information to transmit, it seizes the token, alters one bit of the token (which turns the token into a start-of-frame sequence), appends the information it wishes to transmit, and finally sends this information to the next station on the ring. While the information frame is circling the ring, there is no token on the network (unless the ring supports early token release), so other stations wishing to transmit must wait. Therefore, collisions cannot occur in Token Ring networks. If early token release is supported, a new token can be released when frame transmission is completed.

STANDARDS WATCH   **Token Ring**

Token Ring: IEEE 802.5-1997

The **information frame** circulates around the ring until it reaches the destination station, which copies the information for further processing. The information frame continues to circle the ring and is finally removed when it reaches the sending station. The sending station checks the returning frame to see whether the frame was seen and subsequently copied by the destination.

Token Ring networks use a sophisticated **priority** system that permits stations to use the network with priority access for critical data. Token Ring frames use bits that control priority: the **priority** and the **reservation** bits. Only stations with a priority equal to or higher than the priority value contained in a token can seize that token. Once the token is seized and changed to an information frame, only stations with a priority value higher than that of the transmitting station can reserve the token for the next pass around the network. When the next token is generated, it includes the higher priority of the reserving station. Stations that raise a token's priority level must reinstate the previous priority after their transmission is complete.

2.4.2 Fault management mechanisms

Token Ring networks use a robust protocol to handle various problems which may occur on the network through several fault management mechanisms. One station in the Token Ring network is selected to be the **active monitor**. This station, which can potentially be any station on the network, acts as a centralized source of timing information for other ring stations and performs a variety of ring maintenance functions. One of these functions is the removal of continuously circulating frames from the ring. When a sending device fails, its frame may continue to circle the ring. The active monitor can detect such frames (through a monitor bit in the access control field), remove them from the ring, and generate a new token.

Another Token Ring algorithm called **beaconing** detects and tries to repair certain network faults. Whenever a station detects a serious problem with the network (such as a cable break), it sends a beacon frame. The beacon frame defines a failure domain, which includes the station reporting the failure, its **nearest active upstream neighbor** (NAUN), and everything in between. Beaconing initiates a process called **autoreconfiguration**, where nodes within the failure domain automatically perform diagnostics in an attempt to reconfigure the network around the failed area. A station suspicious of a problem disconnects from the network and performs diagnostics 'off-line.' Unless the result of such diagnosis is positive (i.e. no problems) it cannot rejoin the ring.

2.4.3 Token Ring/IEEE 802.5 frames

There are three types of frames in use on the network (see Figure 2.13):

■ data (information) frame;
■ command frame;
■ token.

FIGURE 2-13 Token Ring/IEEE 802.5 frame format

(a) Data frame

Number of octets:

1	1	1	2 or 6	2 or 6		4	1	1
starting delimiter JK0JK000	**access control** PPPTMRRR	**frame control** FFxxZZZZ	**destination address**	**source address**	**data** LLC/ SNAP	**FCS**	**ending delimiter** JK1JK1IE	**frame status** ACxxACxx

Notes: J,K = empty data symbols; P = station priority; T = token bit; M = monitor bit; Z = control bit; R = reservation bit; FF = 00 (MAC Frame)/01 (LLC Frame); A = destination address recognized; C = frame copied

(b) Token frame

Number of octets:

1	1	1
starting delimiter	**access control**	**frame status**

Data/command frames vary in size, depending on the size of the information field. Data frames carry information for upper-layer protocols; command frames contain control information and have no data for upper-layer protocols. Token frames use only three fields.

Token Ring frame fields are as follows:

- ***Starting (frame) delimiter*** – has a similar function to the preamble in the Ethernet/IEEE 802.3 frame.

- ***Access control*** – all eight bits have some importance for several tasks: station priority and transmission reservation, token/other frame indication, and for frame circulating control (monitor bit).

- ***Frame control*** – indicates whether the frame contains data or control information. In control frames, this octet specifies the type of control information.

- ***Destination*** and ***source address*** – where the first bit of the source address is crucial for source route bridging in a token ring internet (see Part II) as it indicates the presence of a routing information field (RIF) in the data frame (if present it follows immediately after the source address).

- ***Data*** – the length of encapsulated (LLC or SNAP) data is limited by the ring token holding time, which defines the maximum time a station may hold the token.

- ***Frame Check Sequence*** (FCS) – filled by the source station with a calculated value depending on the frame contents. The destination station recalculates the value to determine whether the frame may have been damaged in transit. If so, the frame is discarded.

- ***End delimiter*** – completes the data/command frame.

- ***Frame status*** – indicates the success of frame delivery (i.e. frame successfully received by hardware, although congestion in the node could still force the frame to be dropped), as it is modified only by the receiving station (alternatively the source route bridge – see Part II) and after full circulation is checked by the source station.

The Token Ring does not have minimum limit for length of data field and as a **maximum** may support frames of 4500 octets (for 4 Mbps data rate) and 16 Koctets (for 16 Mbps data rate). (For global comparison of framing and rate features see Table 2.2 on p. 30.)

2.4.4 Token Ring addressing

The Token Ring provides several types of addressing mechanisms: individual (unicast) and group addresses (multicast). A special subtype of group addresses is called a **functional address** and is indicated by a **Functional Address Indicator** bit in the destination MAC address. They were designed for widely used functions such as ring monitoring, NETBIOS, Bridge, and LAN Manager frames. There are a limited number of functional addresses, 31 in all, and therefore several unrelated functions must share the same functional address.

The destination MAC address consists of six octets. In Figure 2.14 a MAC address shows the order of transmission of the octets from top to bottom (octet 0 to octet 5), and the order of transmission of the bits within each octet from right to left (bit 0 to bit 7). This is the canonical bit order for MAC addresses. Addresses supplied to or received from token ring interfaces are usually laid out in memory with the bits of each octet in the opposite order from that illustrated, i.e. with bit 0 in the high-order (leftmost) position within the octet.

FIGURE 2-14 Canonical format of Token Ring address

bits	7	6	5	4	3	2	1	0
octet 0							U/L	I/G
octet 1								
octet 2								FAI
octet 3								
octet 4								
octet 5								

The low order bit of the high order octet is called the I/G bit. It signifies whether the address is an individual address (0) or a group address (1). This is comparable to the multicast bit in the DIX Ethernet addressing format. Bit position 1 of the high order octet, called the U/L bit, specifies whether the address is universally administered (0) or locally administered (1). Universally administered addresses are those specified by a standards organization such as the IEEE. If the I/G bit is set to 1 and the U/L bit is 0, the address must be a universally administered group address. If the I/G bit is 1 and the U/L bit is a 1, the address may be either a local administered group address or a functional address. This distinction is determined by the **Functional Address Indicator** (FAI) bit located in bit position 0 of octet 2. If the FAI bit is 0, the address is considered a functional address. And if the FAI bit is 1, this indicates a locally administered group address.

Different functional addresses are made by setting one of the remaining 31 bits in the address field. These bits include the seven remaining bits in octet 2 as well as the eight bits in octets 3, 4, and 5. It is not possible to create more functional addresses by setting more than one of these bits at a time.

Three methods exist for mapping between an IP multicast address and a hardware address in the Token Ring environment:

■ the all rings broadcast address;
■ the assigned functional address;
■ the existing IEEE assigned IP Multicast group addresses.

In order to ensure interoperability, all systems supporting IP multicasting on each physical ring must agree on the hardware address to be used. Because there is a shortage of Token Ring functional addresses, all IP multicast addresses (see Part IV) have been mapped to a single Token Ring functional address (RFC 1469). In canonical form, this address is *03-00-00-20-00-00*. In non-canonical form, it is

C0-00-00-04-00-00. It should be noted that since there are only 31 possible functional addresses, there may be other protocols that are assigned this functional address as well.

2.4.5 Token Ring/IEEE 802.5 physical layer

Token Ring, while having a logical ring topology, is implemented on a physical star (see Figure 2.15). At the center of the star is a device similar to a hub called a **multistation access unit** (MAU or, less unambiguously, MSAU). Each station is attached to it so that the MSAU provides for a logical flow through its ports, called 'ring in' and 'ring out,' in the form of ring. MSAUs can be interconnected, again to form a ring.

FIGURE 2-15   Token Ring physical topology

Token Ring 4/16 Mbps

logical topology = RING

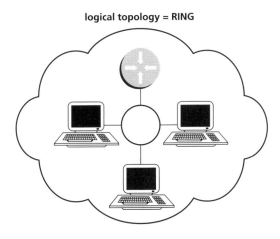

physical topology = STAR

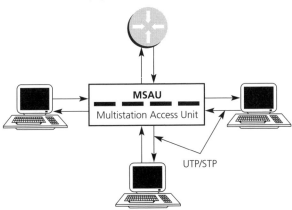

The specification allows for up to 255 stations to be attached to a Token Ring segment but the actual maximum limit depends on the physical media which varies from **STP**, **UTP** (Categories 3, 4, and 5) to **optical cable**. The **maximum distance** of a station from the MSAU varies similarly (100–200 m) and with the interconnection of several MSAUs the Token Ring network may easily span several kilometers.

Token Ring so far allows for only two data rates of **4 and 16 Mbps** but there are similar intentions to developments in the Ethernet: to achieve 100 Mbps and a Gigabit Token Ring in the near future.

2.4.6 High-speed Token Ring

The Token Ring has also been subject to increased bandwidth requirements, hence the specification for a *High-Speed Token Ring (HSTR)* has been under development. As the work is quite slow (not having enough support from users and vendors) the idea is to standardize both 100 Mbps and 1 Gbps versions at the same time. Vendors are participating in a *High-Speed Token Ring Alliance (HSTRA)* the aim of which is to spread the word about the revitalized Token Ring network once development is complete.

STANDARDS WATCH   **high-speed Token Ring**

100 Mbps Dedicated Token Ring: IEEE 802.5t-2000
Gigabit Token Ring: IEEE 802.5v

The obvious advantage will be the maximum frame length of 18 000 B which will lower the overall overhead proportional to the payload data (compared to Ethernet MTU supported of 1518 B). For an easy upgrade from 4/16 Mbps to 100/1000 Mbps Token Ring all network characteristics will be kept with the extension for full-duplex operation on the point-to-point links (IEEE 802.5r).

As presently defined, each token ring station shares the ring's total available bandwidth. The dedicated attachment extension to the original specification will provide a significant increase in the available bandwidth to each station. Additionally, it will decouple the operating speed of the concentrator from its attaching stations.

STANDARDS WATCH   **Token Ring advanced features**

Dedicated Token Ring Operation: 802.5r-1997
Aggregation of Multiple Link Segments: IEEE 802.5z

STANDARDS WATCH   industry forum

HSTRA (High-Speed Token Ring Alliance): **http://www.hstra.com**

The advantages and disadvantages of the Token Ring are summarized in Table 2.6.

TABLE 2-6   Advantages and disadvantages of the Token Ring

Advantages	Disadvantages
Deterministic access method	Complex and complicated protocol
Network management as part of the LAN protocol	Much less deployed than Ethernet
Efficient fault-tolerant network	High cost (especially switched network)

2.5 Fiber distributed data interface

The **Fiber Distributed Data Interface** (FDDI) standard was produced by the ANSI X3T9.5 standards committee in the mid-1980s and later adopted as ISO 9314. Its merit lies especially in high-speed LAN backbones with high fault tolerance and self-management.

STANDARDS WATCH   FDDI

FDDI: ANSI X3T9.5 = ISO 9314
ANSI (American National Standards Institute): **http://www.ansi.org**

2.5.1 FDDI architecture

FDDI specifies a 100 Mbps, token-passing, dual ring topology using a fiber transmission medium. It defines the physical layer and media-access portion of the link layer, while using IEEE 802.2 as LLC sublayer. FDDI share many features with Token Ring, including topology (ring), media-access technique (token passing), and broad management features.

The architecture structure differs from the IEEE approach and comprises the following sublayers:

- **Media Access Control** (MAC) sublayer – defines the access method, frame format, token handling, addressing, algorithm for calculating a cyclic redundancy check value, and error recovery mechanisms;

- **Physical Layer Protocol** (PHY) sublayer – defines data encoding/decoding procedures (4B/5B), clocking requirements, framing, and other functions;

- **Physical Medium Dependent** (PMD) sublayer – defines the characteristics of the transmission medium, including the fiber-optic link, power levels, bit error rates, optical components, and connectors;

- **Station Management** (SMT) – defines the FDDI station configuration, ring configuration, and ring control features, including station insertion and removal, initialization, fault isolation and recovery, scheduling, and collection of statistics.

2.5.2 FDDI topology

FDDI specifies the use of **dual rings**, primary and secondary. The primary ring is used for data transmission, while the secondary ring is generally used as a backup. Traffic on these rings is designed to travel in opposite directions. Physically, the rings consist of two or more point-to-point connections between adjacent stations.

There are two main **types of FDDI nodes**:

- **Class A** nodes reside on the ring backbone.
- **Class B** nodes are non-ring nodes; they may be standalone devices or elements within tree or star subnetworks.

As nodes may generally be stations or concentrators, the following categories of devices may become a part of the FDDI:

- **Dual Attached Concentrator** (DAC) – attached to both rings, providing connections for multiple SASs and SACs;
- **Single Attached Concentrator** (SAC) – attached to DAC;
- **Single Attached Station** (SAS) – with single attachment to the concentrators;
- **Dual Attached Station** (DAS) – with dual attachment to two concentrators (dual homed) or both rings direct.

FDDI provides a number of **fault-tolerant features**. The primary fault-tolerant feature is the dual ring. If a station on the dual ring fails or is powered down or if the cable is damaged, the dual ring is automatically 'wrapped' (doubled back onto itself) into a single ring using the (so far) secondary ring. This single failure does not disrupt FDDI operation. When two ring failures occur, the ring will be wrapped in both cases, effectively segmenting the ring into two separate rings that cannot communicate with each other (which may have an important impact on the routing to the FDDI network – see Part IV). Subsequent failures cause additional **ring segmentation**.

Dual homing provides additional redundancy and helps guarantee operation. In dual-homing situations, the critical device is attached to two concentrators. One pair of concentrator links is declared the active link; the other pair is declared passive. The passive link stays in backup mode until the primary link (or the concentrator to which it is attached) is determined to have failed. When this occurs, the passive link is automatically activated.

2.5.3 FDDI frame format

FDDI frame format is similar to that of Token Ring (see Figure 2.16).

FIGURE 2-16   FDDI frame formats

(a) General FDDI frame

Number of bits (number of symbols):

≥ 64 (18)	8 (2)	16 (4)/48 (12)	16 (4)/48 (12)		32 (8)	4 (1)	≥ 12 (3)
preamble and starting delimiter	frame control	destination address	source address	data LLC/ SNAP	FCS	ending delimiter	frame status

(b) FDDI token frame

≥ 64 (18)	8 (2)	8 (2)	8 (2)
preamble	starting delimiter	frame control	ending delimiter

The fields of an FDDI frame are as follows:

- *Preamble* – prepares each station for the upcoming frame.
- *Start delimiter* – as last octet of preamble indicates the beginning of the frame. It consists of signaling patterns that differentiate it from the rest of the frame.
- *Frame control* – indicates the size of the address fields, whether the frame contains asynchronous or synchronous data, and other control information.
- *Destination address* – a unicast, multicast, or broadcast MAC address.
- *Source address* – identifies the single station that sent the frame.
- *Data* – contains either information destined for an upper-layer protocol (LLC or SNAP encapsulated) or control information.
- *Frame Check Sequence* (FCS) – CRC for error checking.
- *End delimiter* – contains non-data symbols that indicate the end of the frame.
- *Frame status* – allows the source station to determine if the frame was recognized and copied by a receiving station.

FDDI does not have minimum limit for data field length and as a **maximum** may support frames of 4500 octets. (For global comparison of framing and rate features see Table 2.2 on p. 30.)

2.5.4 FDDI physical layer

FDDI defines use of two types of fiber: single-mode (sometimes called monomode) and multimode. **Single-mode fiber** allows only one mode of light to propagate through the fiber, while **multimode fiber** allows multiple modes of light to propagate through. Because multiple modes of light propagating through the fiber may travel different distances (depending on the entry angles), causing them to arrive at the destination at different times (a phenomenon called modal dispersion), single-mode fiber is capable of higher bandwidth and greater cable run distances than multimode fiber. Multimode fiber uses light-emitting diodes (LEDs) as the light-generating devices, while single-mode fiber generally uses lasers.

When no data is being sent, FDDI transmits an **idle pattern** that consists of a string of binary ones. FDDI is originally based on the single- and multi-mode fiber use which, with the distance between stations in the order of kilometers, allow for a very large span in the network. The network can support a total cable distance of 100 km per ring, tolerate up to 2 km of fiber between stations, and serve up to 500 attached devices or 1000 physical connections (two per device). Later developments have allowed the technology to be implemented over less expensive **copper media**, UTP Category 5 and STP Type 1, while limiting maximum distances between stations to 100 m.

FDDI can also support **synchronous** and **asynchronous** data transmission, as well as **isochronous** channels for real-time digitized voice and compressed video (through FDDI-II spec).

The advantages and disadvantages of FDDI are summarized in Table 2.7.

TABLE 2-7   Advantages and disadvantages of FDDI

Advantages	Disadvantages
Deterministic access method	High cost
Fault-tolerant protocol	Complex protocol
Back-up by secondary ring	Requirements to installation
Useful for backbone networks	

2.6 Wireless local networks

Currently more nomadic ways of performing business (on the road, in the presence of clients, from cars and other means of transport) and teleworking arrangements call for different solutions for the mobile workforce. While a lot can be accomplished with the use of a mobile phone and notebook or PDA, in the local area environment there is yet another appealing way of solving the problem indoors: **wireless LANs** (WLANs). These networks eliminate the need for cabling, i.e. the cost of procurement, installation, and maintenance, although the last of these may turn out to be quite costly with stations moving around and users frequently attaching to or leaving the network, and with connection problems requiring cable troubleshooting.

STANDARDS WATCH wireless LANs (WLANs)

IEEE 802.11a-1999 **High Speed Physical Layer in the 5 GHz band**

IEEE 802.11b-1999 **Higher Speed Physical Layer (PHY) extension in the 2.4 GHz band**

WLANs use an **air interface** for signal transmission which provides more flexible medium for users to move within and among networks. The standard covers not only the relevant interfaces and access method, but also effective methods of power supply from batteries in each attached portable device. Wireless LANs are useful in *ad hoc* working arrangements, in manufacturing or warehousing areas, or in difficult or even dangerous places where cables cannot be installed. However, the complete replacement of cable LANs with WLANs is not foreseen and is unlikely to happen in the future, mainly because of the lower transmission rates, higher cost of equipment, and possible communication quality problems.

The wireless technologies have their drawbacks too. Transmission over airwaves is subject to interference from all the other devices working on those particular frequencies (which may even be microwaves). Also, the overlapping of WLANs may cause unwanted possible intrusions or at least non-secure transmissions. Security of communication in the wireless environment is one of the major issues to be solved. The quality of communication is dependent of many factors, including the distances between the communicating devices.

2.6.1 WLAN configuration

A WLAN station equipped with the relevant adapter may operate in two configuration modes:

- **Independent configuration** – stations communicate directly without any supporting infrastructure; this arrangement is used for *ad hoc* LANs but is not suitable for a wider network span.
- **Configuration with distribution system** – requires an access point functioning as a communication bridge equipped with a transceiver. The number of access points depends on the network size, and each connected station chooses its access point with which it keeps contact. The standard defines the way of moving the station from the reach of one access point to the

scope of another. The distribution system may be viewed as a backbone network which may be realized in different ways (even by a traditional cable-based LAN). The standard specifies only the interface between stations and access points, not the distribution system itself.

2.6.2 WLAN physical characteristics

The physical layer at WLANs may be implemented in one of three specified ways, all so far supporting rates at only 1 Mbps, optionally 2 Mbps. Two use radio waves for communication in the band 2.4–2.4835 GHz; the third uses infrared. Radio WLANs have the usual intra-building span up to 100 m while infrared WLANs are limited to operation within a single space as waves cannot pass through solid objects like walls. Infrared solutions are also significantly more costly than the radio-based options.

2.6.3 WLAN MAC protocol

IEEE 802.11 is based on the non-deterministic access method, **Carrier Sense Multiple Access/Collision Avoidance** (CSMA/CA). Radio systems cannot detect collisions while transmitting therefore the Ethernet method CSMA/CD may not be applied here. The detection of a busy channel is performed by measuring the signal at the antenna. WLAN MAC has embedded frame prioritization.

New developments in wireless LAN standardization allow for transmission speeds of 5.5 or 11 Mbps, and 6 to 54 Mbps, respectively. In the latter case orthogonal frequency-division multiplexing (OFDM) will be used for the first time in packet communication.

An alternative solution to IEEE 802.11 has been developed in ETSI. Its **HiPerLan** (*High Performance Radio LAN*) is based on wireless ATM.

2.6.4 Wireless personal area networks

IEEE subcommittee 802.15 has also started work on **Wireless Personal Area Networks** (WPAN) to define PHY and MAC specifications for wireless connectivity with fixed, portable, and moving devices within or entering a **Personal Operating Space** (POS). The standard will provide for low complexity, low power consumption, wireless connectivity to support interoperability among devices within or entering the POS. This includes devices that are carried, worn, or located near the body. The proposed standard will address Quality of Service to support a variety of traffic classes.

STANDARDS WATCH   **WPAN**

Wireless Personal Area Networks (WPAN): 802.15.1-2001

2.6.5 Enhancements – work in progress

Wireless local area networking has become a hot area recently:

- **IEEE 802.11g** extends 802.11b to 22 Mbps. It is intended to be compatible with the 11 Mbps WLANs. First products are expected in 2002.
- **IEEE 802.11a** uses the more powerful 5 Hz band, with more channels and a higher aggregate bandwidth than 802.11b WLANs.
- **High data rates** are intended, from 6 Mbps to 54 Mbps. However, at the higher rates, the range of the radio is shorter compared to 802.11b. First products are expected late 2001 or early 2002.
- **HiperLAN/2** is a mainly European standard that also uses the 5 GHz band, and will reach similar speeds as 802.11a using a completely different, broadband modulation technique called orthogonal frequency division multiplexing. Work is being done to try to make the two interoperable.

With the advent of these higher speeds, users will have to install many more wireless access points than today's wireless LANs need and prepare for the fact that interface cards from one vendor might not work with the access point from another.

The advantages and disadvantages of WLANs are summarized in Table 2.8.

STANDARDS WATCH wireless industry fora (see Appendix B):

WLANA (Wireless LANs Association): **http://www.wlana.com**
IRDA (Infrared Data Association): **http://www.irda.org/**
WECA (Wireless Ethernet Compatibility Alliance):
   http://www.wirelessethernet.org
Hiperlan2: **http://www.hiperlan2.com**

STANDARDS WATCH standards on wireless LANs available from:

IEEE (Institute of Electrical and Electronics Engineers): **http://standards.ieee.org**
ETSI (European Telecommunications Standards Institute): **http://www.etsi.org**

TABLE 2-8	Advantages and disadvantages of WLANs

Advantages	Disadvantages
Minimal requirements for cabling provision and maintenance	Low transmission speed
Useful both for manufacturing and warehousing, meeting rooms and lecture halls	Limited network span
Applicable for small portable end devices powered from batteries	Unreliable quality (interference)

2.7 Fibre Channel and SANs

Fibre Channel (FC) is a new intelligent high-performance connection system that supports not only its own protocol, but also those of FDDI, SCSI, IP, and several others. Originally meant for WANs, FC can easily be converted to LAN standards by using a switch on the network. FC supports both channel and networking interfaces over one computer port, lessening the network burden on the station. It also supports both electrical and optical media on the network, with speeds ranging from 133 Mbps to 1062 Mbps. A key piece of FC is the **fabric**, an abstract entity that represents the interim network device, be it a loop, active hub, or circuit switch. FC has found its place as the core of recently developed **Storage Area Networks** (SANs).

SANs bring benefits such as high availability and centralized management to large amounts of data, addressing many of the issues critical to today's information needs. They take advantage of the benefits of advanced networking technologies and merge the worlds of storage and networking. Many companies are moving firmly down the SAN path, implementing successful SANs and beginning to migrate their high-availability production data to the SAN.

Initial SAN technology included Fibre Channel Arbitrated Loop and evolved into more advanced switched fabric. As SANs continue to evolve, there will be convergence of these early devices, allowing a single device to provide both loop and switch capability. Since the focus of the SAN is to make information available to the corporate network, and since without access to the information the network is irrelevant, the availability requirements and visibility of SANs today are extremely high.

STANDARDS WATCH	Fibre Channel and SANs related fora (see Appendix B):

FCIA (Fibre Channel Industry Association): **http://www.fibrechannel.com**

SNIA (Storage Networking Industry Association): **http://www.snia.org**

The storage-over-IP market is growing rapidly, and a lot of companies are currently developing IP storage products. Although many large companies have adopted Fibre Channel SANs, a number of smaller companies want to transport data over Gigabit Ethernet networks using the SCSI protocol. The router in storage area network typically sits on a Fibre Channel and links to a WAN or Metropolitan Area Network (MAN) connection to transport data across the IP-based network.

SAN routers will have to provide access for multiple transport methods such as Fibre Channel over IP, Gigabit Ethernet, SCSI over IP, and Fibre Channel backbone, all in a single box to satisfy the varying demands for SAN internal technology deployment. In addition, the successful devices will let business customers use existing Gigabit Ethernet networks to move data over IP natively, using the SCSI protocol. Next generation SAN optical switches will tie SANs to WANs through multiple Fibre Channel ports and offer support for ATM, Enterprise Systems Connection, OC-3, OC-12, OC-48, and SONET. More on optical networking and switching will be found in Part V.

The advantages and disadvantages of Fibre Channel are summarized in Table 2.9.

TABLE 2-9 Advantages and disadvantages of Fibre Channel

Advantages	Disadvantages
High-speed technology useful for small networks	Interoperability issues
High reliability	Lack of experience
Low delay	
Embedded network management	
Deployment in SANs	

STANDARDS WATCH **Summarized Standards watch**

The following standards have been brought to your attention in this chapter:

IEEE 802.2 – ISO/IEC 8802-2 (1997) LLC

IEEE 802.3 – ISO/IEC 8802-3 10 Mbps Ethernet: including:

- **IEEE 802.3a-**1992 10BASE2
- **IEEE 802.3b-**1985 10BROAD36

IEEE 802.3c-1985 Repeater Unit for 10 Mbps Baseband Networks

IEEE 802.3d-1987 Fiber Optic Inter Repeater Link

IEEE 802.3e-1987 1BASE5 STARLAN

▶

IEEE 802.3j-1993 10BASE-F

IEEE 802.3k-1992 Layer Management for 10 Mbps Baseband Repeaters

IEEE 802.3u-1995 Fast Ethernet 100BASE-T

IEEE 802.3y-1997 Fast Ethernet 100BASE-T2

IEEE 802.3z-1998 Gigabit Ethernet

IEEE 802.3ab-1999 1000BASE-T

IEEE 802.3ae 10 Gbps Ethernet

IEEE 802.5-1997 Token Ring

IEEE 802.5r-1997 Dedicated Token Ring Operation

IEEE 802.5t-2000 100 Mbps Dedicated Token Ring

IEEE 802.5v Gigabit Token Ring

IEEE 802.5z Aggregation of Multiple Link Segments

ANSI X3T9.5 = ISO 9314 FDDI

IEEE 802.11a-1999 High Speed Physical Layer in the 5 GHz band (WLAN)

IEEE 802.11b-1999 Higher Speed Physical Layer (PHY) Extension in the 2.4 GHz band (WLAN)

IEEE 802.15.1-2001 Wireless Personal Area Networks (WPAN)

CHAPTER 3

██████████████████████

Wide area networking

Leaving the environment of local and metropolitan networks we move to the long-distance transmission possibilities provided by private or public **Wide Area Networks** (WANs). We will first look at the distinction between switched and non-switched facilities in general, as we will discuss WAN switching in detail later (see Part III).

An overview of WAN link protocols will then be given, followed by important details on widely used WANs:

- **Integrated Services Data Network** (ISDN);
- **X.25**;
- **Frame Relay**;
- **Switched Multimegabit Data Service/Connectionless Broadband Data Service** (SMDS/CBDS);
- **Asynchronous Transmission Mode (ATM)**;
- **Synchronous Optical Network (SONET)**.

Similar to the approach used in the overview of LAN and MAN in the previous chapter, the emphasis will be given to:

- **network architecture**;
- **addressing**;
- **other issues** important to network interconnection.

For an overall comparison of the basic features of these WANs refer to Table 3.1.

TABLE 3-1   Comparison of wide area networks and services

Feature	X.25	Frame Relay	SMDS/CBDS	ATM
Standard	CCITT/ISO 1976–1988	CCITT/ANSI/ industry	Bellcore/ETSI	ITU-T/ATM Forum
Speeds	9.6–64 kbps	56 kbps–45 Mbps	1–45 Mbps	45 Mbps–2.5 Gbps
Information size	Max. 4096 B	Max. 4096 B	Max. 9188 B	Fixed 53 B

▶

TABLE 3-1	Continued

Feature	X.25	Frame Relay	SMDS/CBDS	ATM
Address	X.121 (up to 15 digits) 4-digit DNIC + 10–11 spec.	Fixed length DLCI 10 bit (0-1023)	E.164 10–15 digits	Fixed length VPI/VCI 24-bit NSAP
Multicast support	No	Yes (DLCI 1019-1022)	Yes	Yes
CL/CO	Connection-oriented	Connection-oriented	Connectionless	Connection-oriented
PVC/SVC	PVC/SVC	PVC/ SVC (from 1996)	N/a	PVC/SVC
Explicit per VC flow control	Yes	No	N/a	No
Data link layer error correction	Yes	No	No	No

3.1 Switched and non-switched facilities

A **non-switched** facility used to be referred as an analog or digital line that does not go through a central switch and can, therefore, be rented or leased exclusively to one customer for voice and/or data communications. It is less prone to errors and ideal for data transfer. Currently, non-switched facilities are mostly implemented as Virtual Circuits (VCs) on top of an SDH-fragment (Synchronous Digital Hierarchy), or using a fixed channel in Frequency Division Multiplexing (FDM) or Time Division Multiplexing (TDM) transparent sharing. VCs are also used for high-speed constant communications, e.g. setting ATM VCs on SDH channels for high-speed backbones.

The **switched network** comprises analog and digital lines that go through a central switch. It handles many parties at once and users pay only for their time on the line. The switched network, frequently composed of analog lines, is mainly used for low-speed, sporadic transmissions. The two basic forms of a switched network are circuit-switched and packet-switched (the form of message switching seems to be no longer in real use).

- **Circuit switching** – networks establish a circuit between the calling and called parties for the duration of the call. During this time, the full traffic capacity of the circuit is available only to the connected parties (e.g. ISDN). Usually they use a separate network system for signaling, typically standard ITU-T Signaling System #7 (SS7).

■ **Packet switching** – a networking technology used in private networks or public data networks (PDNs). Packet-switched networks can support a variety of special or customized services and functions, which, when combined, form value-added networks (VANs). On a packet-switched network, data travels in packets with control information in the headers. Packets are dynamically routed through a network; that is, if a line fails or is overloaded, the system automatically reroutes packets over the most efficient path. This allows multiple packets of one message to be sent via different routes. Therefore packets require sequence numbering so that they can be reassembled at their destination in the correct order.

The packet service can either be connection-oriented (e.g. X.25, Frame Relay, or ATM) or connectionless (SMDS). In **a connectionless packet service**, each transfer of data between source and destination is considered an independent, autonomous transaction. Therefore the addressing information must be included in every packet and resolved at each switching device. Switching tables then associate destination addresses with the next switching device along the path.

In a **connection-oriented packet service**, end station pairs are associated with a connection identifier. Each switching device constructs a table mapping connection identifiers to outbound ports according to the path established prior to sending the first packet into the network. More detailed discussion on connectionless and connection-mode network services is to be found in Chapter 1.

3.2 DTE vs. DCE

When we get beyond the local environment and start talking about using the transmission capability of some chosen type of WAN we are primarily interested in how to connect devices or LANs to the network. Here we have to distinguish between two categories of device (Figure 3.1), from the point of view of the actual network:

FIGURE 3-1 Position of DCE and DTE in WANs

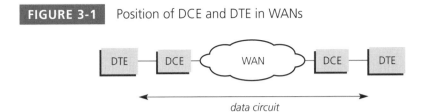

data circuit

■ **Data Circuit-terminating Equipment** (sometimes referred to as Data Communications Equipment, DCE) – device at the edge of the particular network, but still part of it (under the supervision of the WAN provider) and providing access to the network. In other words, it is the network side of the user-network interface. DCE is also responsible for clocking; typical DCEs are modem, CSU/DSU (see Frame Relay or SMDS) or TA/NT1 (see ISDN).

■ **Data Terminal Equipment** (DTE) – the terminal equipment which connects to the DCE and is not under the control of the public WAN provider. In other words it is the user side of the user-network interface. Despite the 'terminal' in the title, it may well be any interconnecting device which is not terminal at all.

The interface between the DTE and DCE is of major interest with all WAN networks and services, as it is the basic part of the definition and standardization.

3.3 Link protocols

There are currently several standard and *de facto* standard link protocols commonly used for direct interconnection over serial lines between devices and which support popular WANs.

Two types of links we may wish to support are:

■ **point-to-point** – between the pair of devices;

■ **point-to-multipoint** – one node may communicate to several nodes.

Nowadays all link protocols are based on IBM's **Synchronous Data Link Control** (SDLC), still the primary SNA link-layer protocol for WAN links. The first standard link protocol based on IBM's SDLC protocol was High-level Data Link Control (HDLC) adopted by the ISO. The CCITT then modified HDLC to create the Link Access Procedure (LAP) and then the Link Access Procedure, Balanced (LAPB).

3.3.1 High-level data link control

High-level Data Link Control (HDLC) was standardized as ISO 3309 (1979). HDLC shares the frame format of SDLC, supports synchronous, **full-duplex** operation, and point-to-point and point-to-multipoint configurations.

The HDLC frame format is shown in Figure 3.2.

FIGURE 3-2   HDLC frame format

Number of octets:

1	1(2)	1(2)	variable	2(4)	1
flag *01111110*	address	control	data	FCS	flag *01111110*

■ *Flag* – unique pattern serving for synchronization over serial line.

■ *Address* – identity of the destination station (where necessary, i.e. in the case of a point-to-multipoint line).

- *Control* – uses three different formats, depending on the type of HDLC frame used:

  - *Information (I)* frames – used to carry network-layer information and some control information. They contain send and receive sequence numbers and the poll/final *(P/F)* bit which performs flow and error control. The send and receive sequence number refers to the number of the frame to be sent next or to be received next, respectively. Both the sender and the receiver maintain send and receive sequence numbers. The primary station uses the *P/F* bit to tell the secondary whether it requires an immediate response. The secondary station uses this bit to tell the primary station whether the current frame is the last in its current response.

  - *Supervisory (S)* frames – provide control information: request and suspend transmission, report on status, and acknowledge the receipt of *I* frames. There is no information field.

  - *Unnumbered (U)* frames – used for control purposes and not sequenced. Depending on the function of the unnumbered frame, its control field is one or two octets. Some unnumbered frames have an information field.

- *Frame Check Sequence* (FCS) – Cyclic Redundancy Check (CRC) calculation remainder. The CRC calculation is redone in the receiver. If the result differs from the value in the sender's frame, an error is assumed.

HDLC supports three **transfer modes**:

- **Normal Response Mode** (NRM);
- **Asynchronous Response Mode** (ARM);
- **Asynchronous Balanced Mode** (ABM).

3.3.2 Link access procedure balanced

The LAPB is best known for its presence in the X.25 protocol stack. LAPB shares the same frame format, frame types, and field functions as HDLC. It is, however, restricted to the ABM transfer mode, and so is appropriate only for combined (primary/secondary) stations. Also, LAPB circuits can be established by either the DTE or the DCE. The station initiating the call is determined to be the primary, while the responding station is the secondary.

The LAPB uses three **frame types**:

- *Information (I)* frame – carries upper-layer information and some control information (necessary for full-duplex operation). Send and receive sequence numbers and the poll/final *(P/F)* bit perform flow control and error recovery. The send sequence number refers to the number of the current frame. The receive sequence number records the number of the frame to be received next. In full-duplex conversation, both the sender and the receiver keep send and receive sequence numbers. The poll bit is used to force a final bit message in response; this is used for error detection and recovery.

- *Supervisory (S)* frame – provides control information. Such frames request and suspend transmission, report on status, and acknowledge the receipt of *I* frames. They do not have an information field.

■ *Unnumbered* (U) frame – used for control purposes and not sequenced. For example, such frames can initiate a connection using standard or extended windowing (modulo 8 versus 128), disconnect the link, report a protocol error, or carry out similar functions.

LAPB frame format

The LAPB frame format is shown in Figure 3.3:

FIGURE 3-3 LAPB frame format

Number of octets:

1	1	1	variable	2	1
flag *01111110*	address	control	data	FCS	flag *01111110*

■ *Flag* – delimits the LAPB frame (bit stuffing must be used to ensure that the flag pattern does not occur within the body of the frame).
■ *Address* – indicates whether the frame carries a **command** or a **response**.
■ *Control* – provides further qualifications to the command and response frames, and also indicates the frame type (*U, I,* or *S*), frame function (for example, receiver ready or disconnect), and the send/receive sequence number.
■ *Data* – carries upper-layer data. Its size and format vary depending on the Layer 3 packet type. The maximum length of this field is set by agreement between a packet switched network administrator and the subscriber at subscription time.
■ *Frame Check Sequence* (FCS) – ensures the integrity of the transmitted data.

3.3.3 Point-to-point protocol

Traditionally, interoperability across serial links was restricted to equipment supplied by the same manufacturer. To overcome this, the **point-to-point protocol** (PPP) was defined as the *de facto* standard to allow **multivendor interoperability**. PPP was first proposed as a *de facto* standard in 1990 by the IETF to replace its predecessor **Serial Line Internet Protocol** (SLIP) that requires links to be established and torn down manually. However, unlike SLIP which only supports IP, PPP is not limited in network protocol support. PPP can also simultaneously transmit **multiple protocols** across a single serial link, eliminating the need to set up a separate link for each protocol. PPP is also ideal for interconnecting dissimilar devices such as hosts, bridges, and routers over serial links.

RFC WATCH **Point-to-Point Protocol (PPP)**

RFC 1570 **PPP LCP Extensions**, 1994 (Proposed Standard)

RFC 1661 **Point-to-Point Protocol (PPP)**, 1994 (Standard)

RFC 1662 **PPP in HDLC-like Framing**, 1994 (Standard)

RFC 1663 **PPP Reliable Transmission**, 1994 (Proposed Standard)

RFC 1962 **PPP Compression Control Protocol (CCP)**, 1996 (Proposed Standard)

RFC 1968 **The PPP Encryption Control Protocol (ECP)**, 1996 (Proposed Standard)

RFC 1990 **The PPP Multilink Protocol (MP)**, 1996 (Draft Standard)

RFC 1994 **PPP Challenge Handshake Authentication Protocol (CHAP)**, 1996 (Draft Standard)

RFC 2125 **The PPP Bandwidth Allocation Protocol (BAP) / The PPP Bandwidth Allocation Control Protocol (BACP)**, 1997 (Proposed Standard)

RFC 2153 **PPP Vendor Extensions**, 1997 (Informational)

RFC 2284 **PPP Extensible Authentication Protocol**, 1998 (Proposed Standard)

RFC 2484 **PPP LCP Internationalization Configuration Option**, 1999 (Proposed Standard)

RFC 2637 **Point-to-Point Tunneling Protocol (PPTP)**, 1999 (Informational)

RFC 2661 **Layer Two Tunneling Protocol (L2TP)**, 1999 (Proposed Standard)

RFC 2686 **The Multi-Class Extension to Multi-Link PPP**, 1999 (Proposed Standard)

RFC 2878 **PPP Bridging Control Protocol (BCP)**, 2000 (Proposed Standard)

RFC 3070 **Layer Two Tunneling Protocol (L2TP) over Frame Relay**, 2001 (Proposed Standard)

PPP is a **full-duplex**, bit-oriented protocol that can run over **synchronous** or **asynchronous** links which may be dedicated or circuit-switched. PPP can work over copper, fiber optic, microwave, or satellite leased lines. PPP provides data error detection while higher layer protocols are responsible for error recovery. Currently PPP is defined in RFC 1661 with vendor extensions in RFC 2153.

PPP provides a method for transmitting datagrams over serial point-to-point links. It is not a single uniform protocol, but instead has following main components:

■ The **Link Control Protocol** (LCP) serves to establish, configure, and test the data link connection to determine link quality. In a four-phase process, it establishes the link between two PPP peers and negotiates configuration options. Only phases one (link establishment and negotiation) and four (link ready) are necessary to establish communications. Phases two (authentication using additional protocols like PAP or CHAP, RFC 1994) and three (link quality determination) are optional and completely dependent on the PPP implementations at both ends of the link, e.g. PPP extensions, data compression.

■ The **Network Control Protocols** (NCP) are used for establishing and configuring different network layer protocols. NCPs are a series of independently defined protocols that encapsulate network layer protocols of network architectures like TCP/IP, DECnet, AppleTalk, IPX, XNS, and OSI. Each NCP has individual requirements for addressing and advertising connectivity for its network layer protocol. Each NCP is defined in a separate RFC.

In order to establish communications over a point-to-point link, the originating PPP first sends LCP frames to configure and (optionally) test the data link. After the link has been established and optional facilities have been negotiated as needed by the LCP, the originating PPP sends NCP frames to choose and configure one or more network layer protocols. When each of the chosen network layer protocols has been configured, packets from each network layer protocol can be sent over the link. The link will remain configured for communications until explicit LCP or NCP frames close the link, or until some external event occurs (for example, an inactivity timer expires or a user intervenes).

PPP frame format

PPP uses a similar frame format to the HDLC protocol (see Figure 3.4):

FIGURE 3-4   PPP frame format

Number of octets:

1	*1*	*1*	*2*	*variable*	*2(4)*
flag *01111110*	address	control	protocol	data	FCS

■ *Flag* – indicates the beginning or end of a frame. The flag field consists of the binary sequence *01111110*.

■ *Address* – as PPP does not need to assign individual destination station addresses (operates only on point-to-point links) it uses the standard broadcast address *(11111111)*.

■ *Control* – contains the binary sequence *00000011*, which calls for the transmission of user data in an unsequenced frame. A connectionless link service similar to that of Logical Link Control (LLC) Type 1 is provided.

■ *Protocol* – this field is different to the other link protocols as it identifies the protocol encapsulated in the information field of the frame. The most up-to-date values of the protocol field are specified in the most recent Assigned Numbers Request for Comments (RFC 1700).

- *Data* – zero or more octets that contain the network unit for the protocol specified in the protocol field. The default maximum length of the information field is 1500 octets. By prior agreement, consenting PPP implementations can use other values for the maximum information field length.
- *Frame Check Sequence* (FCS) – usually 16 bits. By prior agreement, consenting PPP implementations can use a 32-bit FCS for improved error detection.

The LCP can negotiate modifications to the standard PPP frame structure. However, modified frames will always be clearly distinguishable from standard frames.

PPP extensions

PPP, as the preferred link protocol in a multivendor environment, has several extensions. Among the most popular are:

The **Multilink Point-to-Point Protocol (MLPPP)**, an extension to the PPP protocol, allows several serial lines to be combined to be used for single communication (RFC 1990). It is successfully used not only to carry data but also video and is an interesting choice for dial-on-demand lines where it can provide load balancing over multiple lines (synchronous, asynchronous, ISDN, or even a mix). Its task is to split and reassemble upper-layer PDUs between participating devices, sequence them, and transmit over multiple lines. The receiving device with multilink PPP enabled again reassembles the received PDUs. Multilink PPP supports true bandwidth on demand through inverse multiplexing, as circuits may be activated and added automatically to the logical pipe when more bandwidth is needed or some links in the used pipe fail. It also supports LAN protocol spoofing to keep unnecessary network traffic from traversing WAN links.

The **Point-to-Point Tunneling Protocol** (PPTP) is another extension to the standard Point-to-Point Protocol (PPP) that is used to create multiprotocol Virtual Private Networks (VPNs) via the Internet. VPNs connect both branch offices and telecommuters into an enterprise-wide corporate network, and can eliminate all long-distance charges, along with the management and security responsibilities of maintaining private networks. PPTP handles only point-to-point links. PPTP is specified in RFC 2637.

The **Layer Two Tunneling Protocol** (L2TP, RFC 2661 and 3070) describes a mechanism to tunnel Point-to-Point Protocol (PPP) sessions. The protocol has been designed to be independent of the media it runs over. The base specification describes how it should be implemented to run over the User Datagram Protocol (UDP) and the Internet Protocol (IP). Additionally, RFC 3070 describes how L2TP is implemented over Frame Relay Permanent Virtual Circuits (PVCs) and Switched Virtual Circuits (SVCs). L2TP defines a general purpose mechanism for tunneling PPP over various media. By design, it insulates L2TP operation from the details of the media over which it operates. The base protocol specification illustrates how L2TP may be used in IP environments.

The **Bandwidth Allocation Control Protocol** (BACP, RFC 2125) is aimed at providing standards-based interoperability for managing dynamic bandwidth on demand. It works in conjunction with multilink PPP, providing a standard set of rules by which to change the multilink PPP bandwidth bundle, channel by channel, on demand. BACP manages bandwidth by allowing two peers (both of which support BACP) to negotiate the addition or deletion of a link in a multilink bundle. These links could be voice or data channels in an ISDN line. While not limited to ISDN, BACP is especially useful in ISDN environments because ISDN is a medium that uses multiple channels. With BACP, large hunt groups over multiple channels are easy to manage. The benefits BACP offers are network flexibility, multivendor product interoperability, the ability to manipulate bandwidth to maximize network resources, and the ability for either end of a connection to manage the link, reducing operating costs.

3.4 Integrated services digital network

The **Integrated Services Digital Network** (ISDN) is defined and described in ITU-T recommendations. It aims to support a wide range of **voice** and **non-voice** applications in the same network. Built on top of standard **unshielded twisted pair telephone wire**, ISDN is an end-to-end digital network that integrates enhanced voice and image features with high-speed data and text transfer. ISDN provides two rates of service, basic and primary, over B and D channels. The **B channel** provides transparent digital channels for voice or high-speed data transmission at 64 kbps. The **D channel** provides a non-transparent channel for signaling, telemetry, and low-speed packet switching at 16 kbps or 64 kbps.

- The **basic rate interface** (BRI) provides two 64 kbps B channels and one 16 kbps D channel (i.e., 2B + D), defined in ITU-T recommendation I.430.
- The **primary rate interface** (PRI) provides 30 B channels and one 64 kbps D channel (30B + D) in Europe, and 23 B channels and one 64 kbps D channel (23B + D) in North America, defined in ITU-T recommendation I.431.

3.4.1 ISDN addressing

The addressing of individual devices attached to an ISDN network is defined in ITU-T I.331. The international ISDN number (the first three parts in the format) uniquely identifies every subscriber. It is a variable length number of up to 17 digits. The country code is based on the international telephony numbering plan defined in ITU-T E.164. Interworking between ISDN numbering and other network addresses is defined in the ITU I.330 series of standards. This includes interworking between ISDN and the North American Numbering Plan (NANP) for telephones, X.121 for public packet networks (X.25) and OSI network layer addresses.

Sub-addresses provide an additional addressing capability outside of the ISDN numbering plan. They can be used, for example, to provide additional addressing within a private network that is accessed via ISDN.

3.4.2 ISDN network cornerstones

ISDN introduces numerous new terms for its network parts and interfaces (Figure 3.5):

FIGURE 3-5 ISDN components and reference points

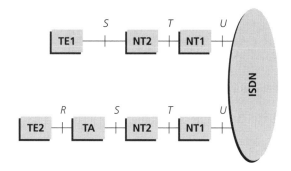

ISDN reference points:
- **R** – reference point between non-ISDN equipment and a TA;
- **S** – reference point between user terminals and the NT2;
- **T** – reference point between NT1 and NT2 devices;
- **U** – reference point between NT1 devices and line termination equipment in the carrier network. (The reference point is relevant only in North America, where the NT1 function is not provided by the carrier network.)

- **TE1 – terminal equipment** type 1 with direct connection to the ISDN network, e.g. ISDN telephone, G4 fax machine.

- **TE2 – terminal equipment** type 2 without capacity to directly connect to the ISDN line and with a need of TA, e.g. analog telephone, G3 fax machine, modem.

- **TA – terminal adapter** allowing non-ISDN devices to connect to the ISDN network. The ISDN TA can either be a standalone device or a board inside the TE2. If the TE2 is implemented as a standalone device, it connects to the TA via a standard physical-layer interface (like EIA/TIA-232-C, V.24, and V.35).

- **NT1** and **NT2 – network termination** type 1 and type 2. These are network-termination devices that connect the four-wire subscriber wiring to the conventional two-wire local loop. In North America, the NT1 is a customer premises equipment (CPE) device. In most other parts of the world, the NT1 is part of the network provided by the carrier. The NT2 is a more complicated device, typically found in digital private branch exchanges (PBXs) that performs Layer 2 and 3 protocol functions and concentration services. In an installation with more than one TE the NT is split into two parts, NT1 which terminates the subscriber line and NT2 to which ISDN-compatible TEs are connected. An NT1/2 device also exists as a single device that combines the functions of an NT1 and an NT2.

- **LT** – line termination, physical connection to the phone company.
- **ET** – exchange termination, local phone company's logical connection to the telephone network.

3.4.3 Services

Bearer services are the basic services used for information transfer. They are supported on the B channels. ISDN services are further subdivided into **circuit-switched mode services**, which provide dedicated end-to-end connections, and **packet-switched mode services**, which provide for packetized information (data, audio, and some video) transfer.

Besides bearer services additional **supplementary services** are provided by the network (call forwarding, speed calling, incoming calling line identification). The 1984 CCITT Red Book defines in Q.931 (I.451) messages and procedures for basic call set-up and disconnect, and includes a framework for supplementary voice services.

3.4.4 Basic operating characteristics

The basic structure for ISDN operating characteristics is **digitally encoded data** using a standard of 64 kbps at the basic rate, and using 1536 kbps at the primary rate. This is a derived channel using pulse code modulation techniques.

The **out-of-band signaling** infrastructure for the premises network is provided by the D channel in the BRI and PRI. It can also be provided by the public **common channel signaling** (CCS) network that transports the user-to-user signaling transparently from one premises switch to another. This extends the benefit of today's CCS network to premises network users, and facilitates the interconnection of geographically scattered premises switches. In the public network, the **ISDN user part** (ISUP) and the **signaling connection control part** (SCCP) of the CCITT **signaling system 7** (SS7) supports end-to-end ISDN features, while the **transaction capability** (TCAP) supports communications between the network switches and network application nodes.

3.4.5 Layer 2 signaling protocol LAPD

Link access protocol on D channel (LAPD) supports multiple logical links on a single physical link. The minimum functionality packet-switched service uses a portion of LAPD consisting of multiplexing, error detection, and frame delimiting. LAPD protocol, similar to HDLC and LAPB, runs over D channel. The format is shown on the Figure 3.6. The LAPD **flag** and **control fields** are identical to those of HDLC. The LAPD address field can be either one or two octets long. If the extended address bit of the first octet is set, the address is one octet; if it is not set, the address is two octets. The first address field octet contains the **service access point identifier** (SAPI), which identifies the portal at which LAPD services are provided to Layer 3. The **C/R** bit indicates whether the frame contains a command or a response. The **terminal end-point identifier** (TEI) field identifies either a single terminal or multiple terminals. A TEI of all ones indicates a broadcast.

FIGURE 3-6 LAPD frame format

Number of octets:

1	1	1	variable	1	1
flag 01111110	**address**	**control**	**data**	**FCS**	**flag** 01111110

3.4.6 Layer 3 signaling

Two Layer 3 specifications are used for ISDN signaling: ITU-T I.450 (also known as ITU-T Q.930) and ITU-T I.451 (also known as ITU-T Q.931). Together, these protocols support user-to-user, circuit-switched, and packet-switched connections. A variety of call establishment, call termination, information, and miscellaneous messages are specified, including *SETUP, CONNECT, RELEASE, USER INFOR-MATION, CANCEL, STATUS,* and *DISCONNECT.* These messages are functionally similar to those provided by the X.25 protocol.

For comparison of framing and data rate constraints across typical LANs and WANs see Table 2.2 on p. 30.

3.4.7 Narrowband and broadband ISDN (B-ISDN)

The traditional ISDN, described above, is narrowband while broadband ISDN should provide for broadband services, such as the transmission of video, which require variable bandwidth. For this reason, ITU has chosen Asynchronous Transfer Mode (ATM) as the target transfer mode for B-ISDN (see Section 3.8).

3.5 X.25

X.25 is the oldest **packet-switched network** (PSN) implemented, namely the public data network (PDN) by telcos. It provides a **connection-oriented network (packet) service** with numerous facilities to ensure reliability over unreliable and slow physical lines (for comparison with other WANs see Table 3.1 on p. 55, and supports point-to-point interaction between DCE and DTE. It has been standardized by CCITT ITU-T (X series of recommendations) and later adopted by the ISO as international standards. X.25 defines the interface between the DTE and DCE while intra-network communication may not necessarily use X.25.

X.25 is discussed from a WAN switching perspective in Part II.

3.5.1 X.25 architecture

The X.25 specification maps to Layers 1 through 3 of the OSI reference model although it was developed earlier, and the terminology uses **levels** instead of layers. **Level 3** (ISO 8208) describes packet formats and packet exchange procedures between peer Level 3 entities (incorrectly sometimes under X.25 notation whole network architecture is meant). **Level 2** of an X.25 network is

> **SNAPSHOT**   **X.25 features**
>
> ■ Implements physical, link and network layers for network access.
> ■ Standardized in CCITT/ITU-T.
> ■ Connection-oriented communication using PVCs and SVCs.
> ■ Multiprotocol support.
> ■ Typical speed up to 64 kbps.
> ■ Network address according to X.121, no multicast or broadcast support.

implemented by **Link Access Procedure, Balanced** (LAPB, ISO 7776) – for details see 3.3.2. LAPB defines packet framing for the DTE/DCE link, and is responsible for connection setup, information transfer, and final disconnect. Level 1 of X.25 defines the electrical and mechanical procedures for activating and deactivating the physical medium connecting the DTE and the DCE.

The **Level 3 packet header** consists of a **general format identifier** (GFI), a **logical channel identifier** (LCI), and a **packet type identifier** (PTI). The GFI is a four-bit field that indicates the general format of the packet header. The LCI is a 12-bit field that identifies the virtual circuit. The LCI is locally significant at the DTE/DCE interface. In other words, the PDN connects two logical channels, each with an independent LCI, on two DTE/DCE interfaces to establish a virtual circuit. The PTI field identifies one of the X.25's 17 packet types.

Network addressing fields in call setup packets provide source and destination DTE addresses. These are used to establish the virtual circuits that constitute X.25 communication. ITU-T recommendation X.121 specifies the source and destination address formats. **X.121 addresses** (also referred to as International Data Numbers, or IDNs) vary in length and can be up to 14 decimal digits long. Octet four in the call setup packet specifies the source DTE and destination DTE address lengths. The first four digits of an IDN are called the **data network identification code** (DNIC). The DNIC is divided into two parts, the first (three digits) specifying the country and the last specifying the network itself. The remaining digits are called the **national terminal number** (NTN), and are used to identify the specific DTE on the packet-switched network.

Level 1 uses the **X.21bis** physical-layer protocol and supports point-to-point connections, speeds of up to 19.2 kbps, and synchronous, full-duplex transmission over four-wire media. The maximum distance between DTE and DCE is 15 meters.

3.5.2 X.25 components

X.25 DTE can be a terminal that does not implement the complete X.25 functionality. A DTE is then connected to a DCE through a translation device called a **packet assembler/disassembler** (PAD). A **PAD** (defined in triple ITU-T X-series recommendations X.3, X.28, and X.29) converts information from a non-X.25 device or host computer into the X.25 data packet format. It can also perform line concentration and protocol conversion for multiple devices. User devices can access a PAD through a direct (local) connection, a public switched (dial-up) line, or a leased line. In normal operations, use of the PAD and X.25 network is transparent to both the sending and the receiving devices, except for added delay. For devices using the X.25 protocol, direct network connections without PADs are possible; a leased channel and the associated modems are the only equipment needed. With the X.25 connection, one synchronous interface eliminates the need for numerous asynchronous ports.

X.25 packet switch

An **X.25 packet switch** (DTE) receives data packets from PADs or other packet switches, performs error checking, and forwards the data packet to PADs or other packet switches. It also collects and maintains realtime information about the status of every network component, using that information to route data packets quickly and efficiently to their final destinations. The information is also forwarded to a network management system, enabling a system administrator to fine-tune the network and quickly correct operational problems from a workstation or dumb terminal.

Virtual circuits

Typically, a packet-switched network is implemented over leased channels and other conventional facilities. DTE-DCE interface can statistically multiplex a number of virtual circuits over a single physical transmission line. Data is transferred through either **switched virtual circuit** (SVC) or **permanent virtual circuit** (PVC) connections. A **PVC** is a connection for which a single dedicated path is predetermined therefore there is no setup phase. An **SVC** is one in which no single physical circuit is established between the sending and receiving stations. Instead, the network dynamically establishes the route of least delay for each packet of data. A logical circuit, which is an electronic circuit used to complete a logical function, is maintained only for the length of the virtual call. As each packet is physically transmitted, a temporary physical link is established through the network to the receiving station. SVC requires call setup, maintenance during packet transmissions, and closing phases. The DCE looks at the **virtual circuit number** to determine how to route the packet through the X.25 network. The Layer 3 X.25 protocol multiplexes between all the DTEs served by the DCE on the destination side of the network and the packet is delivered to the destination DTE.

The advantages and disadvantages of the X.25 network systems are summarized in Table 3.2.

TABLE 3-2   Advantages and disadvantages of X.25

Advantages	Disadvantages
Oldest packet-switched network	Low speed, high delays
Available (geographically and economically)	Does not match data, voice, and video integration
Charged per calls connected	Potential for network congestion with growing number of users
High reliability	Potential discrepancies between networks due to specification versions

3.6 Frame Relay

Frame Relay was first introduced in 1991 in the US as a high-speed connection-oriented data transport network. The term **relay** implies that the Layer 2 data frame is not terminated and/or processed at the end points of each network link, but is relayed to the destination, such as a LAN. In contrast with ITU-T's X.25-based packet switching, in a frame relaying service the physical line between nodes contains multiple data links, identified by the address in the data link frame.

Frame relay statistically multiplexes data to provide connectivity among user equipment (routers and nodal processors in particular), and between user equipment and carriers' frame relay network equipment (i.e. switches). The frame relay protocol supports data transmission only over a connection-oriented path and enables the transmission of variable-length data frames over an assigned virtual connection. Frame Relay supports access speeds of 56 kbps, N × 64 kbps, and 1.544 Mbps (2.048 Mbps in Europe). The data rate is achieved by eliminating unnecessary overheads of the protocols.

SNAPSHOT	**Frame Relay features**

- Speeds from 64 kbps to 2.048 Mbps (possibly 45 Mbps).
- Frames of variable length up to 8189 octets.
- Support for both PVCs and SVCs.
- Multiprotocol, transparent transmission.
- Only error detection performed by network (corrections done by end stations).

Frame Relay is based on more reliable physical infrastructure than was X.25 (the error rate on digital lines dropped to 10^{-7}), therefore it does not provide for heavy error checking. Error correction and per connection flow control are handled at network end points. Frame Relay accelerates the process of routing packets through a series of switches to a remote location by eliminating the need for each switch to check each packet it receives for errors before relaying it to the next switch. Instead, in most implementations, that function can be relegated in its entirety to the end users' Customer Premises Equipment (CPE). This error treatment increases performance and reduces bandwidth requirements, which can, in turn (in principle), reduce communications costs and decrease the number of packet-handling devices needed in a network.

Frame Relay is used to carry all types of protocols, network, bridged, or even other WANs (X.25), and for varying types of applications, from transaction processing and data transfer, to voice transmissions recently. As a multiprotocol transport service it is often used to build inter-site WANs.

Frame Relay technology is being applied successfully to LAN interconnection environments. **Frame Relay access device (assembly/disassembly**, FRAD) capability is now a standard feature on most routers. Since Frame Relay provides multiple logical connections (virtual circuits, similar to X.25) within a single physical connection, access costs are also reduced. Frame Relay requires fewer physical links to a carrier network so equipment costs are reduced. Fewer physical circuits are needed to reach the network so remote access devices have lower access line charges. This also allows full connectivity to be reached across the network with only a partial meshed network.

Frame Relay initially supported only **permanent virtual circuits**. However, recently support for **switched virtual circuits** has also been added although not extensively used so far. Each virtual circuit is associated with a minimum guaranteed bit rate, called the **committed information rate** (CIR). Frame Relay is implemented in both **public and private networks**. The support of Frame Relay interfaces to user devices, defined in standards mentioned later, does not necessarily dictate that the Frame Relay protocol is used between the network devices. No standards for interconnecting equipment inside a Frame Relay network currently exist. Thus, traditional circuit-switching, packet-switching, or a hybrid approach combining these technologies can be used.

Frame Relay has been standardized in ITU-T and ANSI, and a major support role in specifications development has been played by Frame Relay Forum. A basic comparison of Frame Relay with other described WANs is shown in Table 3.1 on p. 55.

Frame Relay switching is discussed in more detail in Part II.

3.6.1 Frame Relay frame format

The **link protocol** needed to support frame relay is based on the LAPD protocol (see section 3.4 on ISDN) and is called **LAP-F** (ITU-T, Q.922, Annex A; ANSI, T1.618). The Frame Relay data transfer protocol is intended to support multiple simultaneous end user protocols within a single physical channel. This protocol provides transparent transfer of user data and does not restrict information contents, format, or coding, or interpret the structure.

The Frame Relay frame format is shown in Figure 3.7.

FIGURE 3-7   LAPF frame format

Number of octets:

1	2	variable	2	1
flag *01111110*	address	data	FCS	flag *01111110*

- *Flags* – delimit the beginning and end of the frame.
- *Address* – ten bits of the two octets specify the actual circuit ID, the **data link connection** identifier (DLCI); the bit marked 'C/R' following the most significant DLCI octet is currently not used. Finally, three bits in the two-octet DLCI provide **congestion control**.
  - The **Forward Explicit Congestion Notification** (FECN) bit is set by the Frame Relay network in a frame to tell the DTE receiving that frame that congestion was experienced in the path from source to destination.

 – The **Backward Explicit Congestion Notification** (BECN) bit is set by the Frame Relay network in frames traveling in the opposite direction from frames encountering a congested path. The notion behind both of these bits is that the FECN or BECN indication can be promoted to a higher-level protocol that can take flow control action as appropriate (FECN bits are useful to higher-layer protocols that use receiver-controlled flow control, while BECN bits are significant to those that depend on 'emitter-controlled' flow control.)

 – The **Discard Eligibility** (DE) bit is set by the DTE to tell the Frame Relay network that a frame has lower importance than other frames and should be discarded before other frames if the network becomes short of resources. Thus, it represents a very simple priority mechanism. This bit is usually set only when the network is congested.

■ *Data* – may be up to maximum field size of 8189 octets.

■ *Frame Check Sequence* (FCS) – uses CRC-16 to detect bit errors in the address in the frame relay header. An error in the DLCI in the header results in a bad CRC, and the entire frame is discarded if the CRC does not match. This prevents the delivery of frames in which the DLCI has changed to the wrong location. Other errors, like error in the data, will also cause the frame to be deleted, but in this case, the upper-layer protocol will request the retransmission anyway. Further issues on error checking in Frame Relay are touched upon again in conjunction with ATM later in this chapter.

Frame Relay, through agreed multiprotocol encapsulation, allows the implementation to carry various protocols like IP, SNA, and IPX.

Frame Relay addressing – DLCI

The ten-bit DLCI value is the heart of the Frame Relay header. It identifies the logical connection that is multiplexed into the physical channel. In the basic (that is, not extended by the LMI, see further on) mode of addressing, DLCIs have local significance, i.e. the end devices at two different ends of a connection may use a different DLCI to refer to that same connection. At the end of each DLCI octet is an **extended address** (EA) bit. If this bit is one, the current octet is the last DLCI octet. All implementations currently use a two-octet DLCI, but the presence of the EA bits means that longer DLCIs may be agreed upon and used in the future. The DLCI has a number of reserved values; among the most important is DLCI 1023 reserved for LMI and four values 1019 to 1022 specifying multicast DLCI (optional LMI feature). Frames sent by a device using one of these multicast DLCIs are replicated by the network and sent to all exit points in the designated set. The multicasting extension also defines LMI messages that notify user devices of the addition, deletion, and presence of multicast groups.

As with other WANs there must exist a way to determine network addresses associated with each DLCI. In Frame Relay it can be done either statically (similar to X.25), through a configured mapping table at the DTE (router), or dynamically using an Inverse ARP protocol (RFC 2390).

3.6.2 Local management interface, UNI and NNI

The core of standardization activity for Frame Relay forms the **Local Management Interface** (LMI), **User-to-Network Interface** (UNI), and the **Network-to-Network Interface** (NNI) specifications developed by the **ITU-T** (according to the framework recommendation I.122) and later extended by ANSI. **ANSI** standards, published in final form in 1991, extend the I.122 principles into a set of specifications that can be used to deploy robust networks (private or public). Three key standards are Frame Relay service (ITU-T I.370, T1.606), access signaling and PVC management functions (Q.933, T.617, and T1.618).

In 1990 a number of vendors backed an interim frame relay specification in an effort to ensure some degree of interoperability among new products then being developed. Cisco Systems, Digital Equipment, Northern Telecom, and StrataCom jointly developed the Frame Relay **industry specification** which is currently the third LMI option and in fact is an enhancement to the standards (e.g. global addressing, multicast support).

The **LMI** transfers network messages notifying the user of the presence of an active DLCI, of the removal or failure of a DLCI, and providing realtime status monitoring of the physical and logical link between the network and each user device. In other words, the LMI solves the issue of a 'keepalive signal' between the network and the user's equipment. It also provides capabilities for downloading logical link addresses from the network to the user's equipment. A multicast facility for ease of address resolution by bridges and routers is included.

The LMI uses a connectionless data link protocol based on Q.921/LAP-D, making the procedure easy to implement; at Layer 3, Q.931 messages are used, similarly to ISDN. In LMI messages, the basic protocol header is the same as in normal data frames. The actual LMI message begins with four mandatory octets, followed by a variable number of **information elements** (IEs). The format and encoding of LMI messages is based on the ANSI T1S1 standard. The first of the mandatory octets (unnumbered information indicator) has the same format as the LAPB unnumbered information *(UI)* frame indicator with the poll/final bit set to zero (see 3.3.2). The next octet is referred to as the protocol discriminator, which is set to a value that indicates 'LMI.' The third mandatory octet (call reference) is always filled with zeros. The final mandatory octet is the message type field.

Two message types have been defined. *Status-enquiry messages* allow the user device to enquire about network status. *Status messages* respond to status-enquiry messages. *Keepalives* (messages sent through a connection to ensure that both sides will continue to regard the connection as active) and PVC status messages are examples of these messages and are the common LMI features that are expected to be a part of every implementation that conforms to the consortium specification. Together, status and status-enquiry messages help verify the integrity of logical and physical links. This information is critical in a routing environment because routing algorithms make decisions based on link integrity. Following the message type field is some number of IEs. Each IE consists of a single-octet IE identifier, an IE length field, and one or more octets containing actual data.

The **User-to-Network Interface** (UNI) defines communications procedures between data terminal equipment (DTE) and a frame relay switch (between access and egress networks). The **Network-to-Network Interface** (NNI) defines how two frame relay switches belonging to different public or private networks communicate. NNI plays a role in Frame Relay similar to that of the X.75 standard in packet switching. Definition of the relationship of Committed Information Rate (CIR), Committed Burst Size (Bc), and Excess Burst Size (Be) values, important for users attached to a public Frame Relay network, is provided by the NNI.

3.6.3 Frame Relay parameters

Frame Relay performance parameters are as follows:

- throughput;
- delay;
- CIR *(committed information rate)* – provider of Frame Relay service commits to guarantee this rate agreed with customer (and paid for);
- Bc *(committed burst)* – data volume related to CIR;
- EIR *(excess information rate)* – throughput above CIR;
- Be *(excess burst)* – data volume (above Bc), which may be transmitted if the network has currently excess capacities, such data is labeled with low priority and the DE bit set (in case of network congestion this data is thrown away first).

3.6.4 SLAs at Frame Relay networks

Frame Relay **Service Level Agreements** (SLA) currently encompass a number of key network system parameters, above and beyond what typical SNMP-managed systems are able to monitor. These parameters may cover the network as a whole, as individual sites, or even as a single PVC. To what level your SLA is defined depends on the criticality of the network to your business. SLAs covering individual components allow less downtime than those covering entire networks.

Frame Relay **service level components** include:

- *Network Availability* – measured over a month as a calculation of the following:

    [(Hours in a Day × Days in a Month × Number of Sites) – Network Outage Time]
    /[(Hours in a Day × Days in Month × Number of Sites)] = **Network Availability**

- *PVC Availability* – measured over a month as a calculation of the following:

    [(Hours in a Day × Days in a Month × Number of PVCs) – PVC Outage Time] /
    [(Hours in a Day × Days in Month × Number of PVCs)] = **PVC Availability**

■ *Roundtrip Network Delay* – measured over a month as a calculation of the following:

> [Cumulative Samples of End-to-End, Roundtrip Delay for All PVCs] [Number of Samples] = **Average Network Delay**

■ *Roundtrip PVC Delay* – measured over a month as a calculation of the following:

> [Cumulative Samples of End-to-End, Roundtrip Delay for the PVC] [Number of Samples] = **Average PVC Delay**

■ *Effective PVC Throughput* *(Frame Delivery Ratio)* – measured over a month as a calculation of the following:

> [Egress Frame Count] [Ingress Frame Count – (Frames Above Committed Burst Size + Excess Burst Size)] = **PVC Throughput**

■ *Mean Time to Respond* – measured as a monthly average of the time from inception of trouble ticket until repair personnel are on site as follows:

> [Total Time (in Hours) to Respond] [Total Number of Trouble Tickets] = **Mean Time to Respond**

■ *Mean Time to Repair or Restore* – measured as a monthly average of the time from inception of trouble ticket until outage is repaired to customer satisfaction as follows:

> [Total Outage Time (in Hours)] [Total Number of Trouble Tickets] = **Mean Time to Restore**

These SLA components, although calculated in a fairly standard manner among carriers, are implemented inconsistently. When working with a carrier to determine service levels, it is important to understand in detail the meaning of each of those measurements.

Until recently, vendors implemented their own, proprietary technology for **operations, administration**, and **maintenance** for Frame Relay networks. But that is changing with the new Frame Relay Forum implementation agreement: FRF.19 defines interoperable mechanisms for verifying that network performance meets the performance specified in service-level agreements. When implemented, these capabilities should soon mean higher service levels for customers. FRF.19 is designed for implementation within any frame relay network component. Primarily, though, it would be deployed in customer premises equipment, in frame relay network-to-network interfaces, and at the carrier end of the user-network interface. Because FRF.19 requires access at Layer 2, it will likely first appear in devices that reside at the Layer 1/Layer 2 border – in intelligent DSU/CSUs, Frame Relay access devices, and routers. Today, these classes of equipment support proprietary implementations for some, but not all, of the features of FRF.19.

The advantages and disadvantages of Frame Relay are summarized in Table 3.3.

TABLE 3-3	Advantages and disadvantages of Frame Relay

Advantages	Disadvantages
High performance (low transmission overhead), high-speed data burst transport	Frames of variable length – do not support implicitly delay-sensitive traffic
Ability to adjust bandwidth (BoD) and performance on demand (CIR), up to access speed (even asymmetric)	
Charges per CIR rather than distance	
Flexible topology (network scalability, management)	

3.7 Switched Megabit Data Service

The **Switched Megabit Data Service** (SMDS) is a Bellcore-defined (1989), public wide-area high-speed (1.544 Mbps = DS1 to 45 Mbps = DS3, see Appendix D), **connectionless** packet-switched service providing LAN-like features and performance. Since SMDS is a connectionless service (not technology), customers only need to have access to a network supporting SMDS to communicate with each other. As such, a customer does not have to establish point-to-point links or virtual connections to communicate using SMDS.

SNAPSHOT	SMDS features

- Connectionless network service.
- Packet size up to 9188 octets.
- Speed up to 45 Mbps.
- Addressing according to E.164 (64 bits), also supporting multicast addressing.
- Packets are fragmented into data units with constant size of 53 octets.

SMDS provides for the exchange of variable-length data units up to a maximum of 9188 octets. SMDS's **Subscriber-Network Interface** (SNI) complies with the IEEE 802.6 defining a DQDB MAN technology. It is important to note that SMDS is a service, not a technology by itself.

In Europe SMDS was adopted with slight modification as the **Connectionless Broadband Data Service** (CBDS) by ETSI. A basic comparison of SMDS with other described WANs is shown in Table 3.1 on p. 55.

3.7.1 SMDS components

SMDS is defined as, a three-tiered architecture:

- **switching infrastructure** comprising SMDS-compatible switches that may or may not be cell-based;

- **delivery system** made up of DS1 and DS3 circuits called **Subscriber – Network Interfaces** (SNIs); at the point of demarcation between the customer premises equipment (CPE) and the service provider's network at the SNI, the CSU/DSU connects to the network via a dedicated DS0, DS1, or DS3 link,

- **access control** system for users to connect to the switching infrastructure without becoming a part of it.

SMDS interface protocol

The **SMDS Interface Protocol** (SIP) operates on the SNI and defines how a customer connects to an SMDS network. The SIP is a three-level protocol. SIP Level 3 handles addressing and error detection, SIP Level 2 handles framing and error detection, and SIP Level 1 handles the physical transport. The functions of these three levels essentially perform OSI physical layer (Level 1) and link layer (Levels 2 and 3) operations.

The router takes the incoming packet and creates an SMDS packet, called a **Level 3 Protocol Data Unit** (L3PDU). The L3PDU consists of a 36-octet header with source and destination addresses and a four-octet trailer packaged between up to 9188 octets of user data. SMDS uses the E.164 **addressing** with variable number of digits (up to 15) divided into two parts, a country code and a nationally significant number. When an SMDS user addresses a data unit to a group address, the SMDS network delivers copies of the data unit to each destination address identified by that group address. SMDS users can also designate up to 16 addresses to a single SNI. Additionally, source addresses are validated by the network to ensure that the address in question is legitimately assigned to the SNI from which it originated. Thus, users are protected against address spoofing (a sender pretending to be someone else). Source and destination address screening is also possible. Source address screening acts on addresses as data units are leaving the network, while destination address screening acts on addresses as data units are entering the network. If the address is disallowed, the data unit is not delivered.

The payload portion of the L3PDU is called the **Service Data Unit** (SDU). The L3PDU is then segmented into multiple SIP Level 2 PDUs (L2PDUs) or cells of 44-octet payload packages with a seven-octet header and a two-octet trailer. As a result, the SMDS cell consists of a total of 53 octets like an ATM cell, although an ATM cell is comprised of 48 octets of payload data and a five-octet header (this similarity has meant appealingly easy migration to ATM through SMDS/CBDS).

The **Physical Layer Convergence Procedure** (PLCP) inserts an additional four octets between every SMDS cell including network-specific framing information and a parity-checking function.

SMDS technology platforms

There are three major technology platforms used for SMDS:

- **Cell-based platform based on DQDB** (Distributed Queue Dual Bus) – the first platform developed for SMDS. This platform is based on the **IEEE 802.6** standard. The DQDB-based platform has at its core a multilayer interface, the subscriber-network interface (SNI).

- **Frame-based platform based on SMDS DXI** (Digital eXchange Interface) – developed to support digital signal level 0 (DS0, see Appendix D) SMDS access at 56 and 64 kbps using the data exchange interface (DXI)/subscriber-network interface (SNI). The SMDS DXI, specified in the SMDS Interest Group (SIG) document SIG-TS-001/1991, was originally intended to provide an open interface between a router/host and an SMDS channel service unit (CSU)/data service unit (DSU). The router/host submits an SMDS packet that is encapsulated in an SMDS DXI frame. The format of the SMDS packet is based on the **IEEE 802.6** standard while the SMDS DXI data link protocol is based on the **high-level data link control** (HDLC) protocol.

- **Cell-based platform based on ATM** – instead of an SNI, the customer uses an ATM UNI to access SMDS. With this interface, the customer can access SMDS at rates ranging from 34 Mbps up to rates approaching 155 Mbps. Unlike the previous two technology platforms, the ATM-based platform is connection-oriented. To access SMDS using a UNI, the customer needs to establish at least one **virtual channel connection** (VCC) to the network. AAL 3/4 was chosen to transport SMDS traffic across an ATM network because of its commonality with the DQDB platform. In most cases, the AAL protocol field encodings and their associated procedures are identical, thus making the **interworking function** (IWF) implementation straightforward. The router/host submits a SIP connectionless service PDU (*SIP_CLS_PDU*) that is encapsulated in an AAL 3/4 common part convergence sublayer PDU (*AAL3/4_CPCS_PDU*).

There are strong commonalities between the frame-based, DQDB-based, and ATM-based platforms supporting SMDS. First, all three share a common PDU: the *SIP L3_PDU* or *AAL3/4_CPCS_PDU*. This is important because SMDS feature processing is driven by this PDU. With a common PDU, suppliers can develop SMDS feature processing functions independent of the lower levels of the technology platforms. While the AAL 5 encapsulation is different than the other platforms, the interworking functions are not all that complicated.

With these commonalities between platforms, the **Interworking Functions** (IWFs) required are significantly simplified. As such, suppliers should find the development of the IWFs for frame/DQDB, DQDB/ATM, and frame/ATM platforms straightforward. The major part of the IWFs for DQDB/ATM and frame/ATM platforms is the mapping between the VPI/VCI values (see 3.8) and SMDS addresses associated with SMDS VCCs. This aspect of the IWFs highlights the major difference between the ATM-based platform and the remaining two platforms: the ATM-based platform is connection-oriented while the frame-based and DQDB-based platforms are connectionless.

Currently, frame/DQDB interworking for SMDS is the most widely deployed of the interworking options. DQDB/ATM interworking for SMDS is already present in some switching system suppliers' products where ATM is used as the internal switching fabric. In addition, several ATM switching system suppliers are currently expanding their products to support SMDS. Finally, as with DQDB/ATM interworking, frame/ATM interworking for SMDS is already present in some switching system suppliers' products where ATM is used as the internal switching fabric.

The advantages and disadvantages of SMDS are summarized in Table 3.4.

TABLE 3-4   Advantages and disadvantages of SMDS

Advantages	Disadvantages
Connectionless service – useful for LAN interconnection	Not widely spread
Common features with ATM (constant data unit size)	
High speed	
Multiprotocol support	
Addressing according to E.164, including multicast address	

3.8 Asynchronous transfer mode

Asynchronous Transfer Mode (ATM) is the cell-switching and multiplexing technique (combining the benefits of circuit switching with those of packet switching) selected by the ITU – for the broadband access for ISDN. ATM transports information in **fixed-size** units of 53 octets that are commonly called **cells** where 48 octets make up the user information field and five octets make up the header. The cell header identifies the 'virtual path' to be used in routing a cell through the network. The virtual path defines the connections through which the cell is routed to reach its destination. ATM provides for cell switching in the network.

ATM is a **transfer mode** and as such is, in principle, independent of transmission technology as it does not refer to an asynchronous transmission technique. Transfer mode refers to the switching and multiplexing process and the term 'asynchronous' refers to the fact that cells allocated to the same connection may exhibit an irregular recurrence pattern as cells are filled according to the actual demand. ATM is a form of TDM and differs from synchronous multiplexing in that channel separation is not dependent on reference to a clock.

In contrast to ordinary LANs, ATM provides the **Quality of Service** guarantees required for realtime telephony, video streaming, videoconferencing, and other delay and delay-variation sensitive applications. However, even ATM does not guarantee data delivery; instead, it relies on the end nodes to provide this function.

- Connection-oriented service supporting high-speeds (1.5 Mbps – 2.5 Gbps) in full-duplex mode (10 Gbps ATM is in limited use and 70 Gbps in trials).
- Both PVC and SVC support.
- QoS guaranteed per data types.
- Constant data usits (cells) of 53 bits.
- Virtual addressing (VPI/VCI).
- No error detection or flow control within virtual circuit.

For standardization of ATM technology the ITU-T is responsible, and for the development of specifications and for implementations it is the ATM Forum which was founded in 1991. A basic comparison of ATM with other described WANs is shown in Table 3.1 on p. 55.

ATM is discussed in more detail with relation to its switching capabilities in Part II.

3.8.1 ATM components and operation

An ATM network is made up of an ATM switch and ATM end points. An **ATM switch** is responsible for cell transit through an ATM network. The ATM switch accepts the incoming cell from an ATM endpoint or another ATM switch. It then reads and updates the cell-header information and quickly switches the cell to an output interface toward its destination. An **ATM endpoint** (or end system) contains an ATM network interface adapter. Examples of ATM endpoints are workstations, routers, digital service units (DSUs), LAN switches, and video coder-decoders (CODECs).

An **ATM network** consists of a set of ATM switches interconnected by point-to-point ATM links or interfaces. ATM switches support two primary types of interface:

- **User-to-Network Interface** (UNI) – connects ATM end systems (such as hosts and routers) to an ATM switch;
- **Network-to-Network Interface** (NNI) – connects two ATM switches.

Depending on whether the switch is owned and located at the customer's premises or publicly owned and operated by the telephone company, UNI and NNI can be further subdivided into **public** and **private** UNIs and NNIs. A private UNI connects an ATM endpoint and a private ATM switch. Its public counterpart connects an ATM endpoint or private switch to a public switch. A private NNI connects two ATM switches within the same private organization. A public NNI connects two ATM switches within the same public organization.

When an ATM device wants to establish a connection with another ATM device, it sends a signaling-request packet to its directly connected ATM switch. This request contains the ATM address of the desired ATM endpoint, as well as any QoS parameters required for the connection. ATM signaling protocols vary by the type of ATM link, which can be either UNI signals or NNI signals. UNI is used between an ATM end system and ATM switch across ATM UNI, and NNI is used across NNI links.

ATM **signaling** uses the one-pass method of connection setup that is used in all modern telecommunication networks, such as the telephone network. An ATM connection setup proceeds in the following manner. First, the source end system sends a connection-signaling request. The connection request is propagated through the network. As a result, connections are set up through the network. The connection request reaches the final destination, which either accepts or rejects the connection request.

3.8.2 ATM architecture

The ATM model is based on a different approach than the OSI reference model as it adopts a three-dimensional model including **management**, **control**, and **user planes**. The actual layers, somewhat comparable to the OSI lower two layers, are as follows:

- **Physical layer** – physically transmitting data. Unlike conventional LANs, ATM has no inherent speed limit, therefore any increase in supported speed does not require any change in any the mode of operation nor does it imply any limit; currently speeds average 2.5 Gbps in operation; 10 Gbps in limited use and sparingly up to 70 Gbps in trials.

- **ATM layer** – responsible for providing appropriate routing information for cells (VPI/VCI) and for cell ordering.

- **ATM Adaptation Layer** (AAL) – basis for a variety of upper-layer protocols for different classes of service.

The following **ATM Adaptation Layers** (AAL) have been defined:

- **AAL1** – supports connection-oriented services (used for circuit emulation) that require constant bit rates and have specific timing and delay requirements. Examples are constant bit rate services like DS1 or DS3 transport. The *sequence number* (SN) and *sequence number protection* (SNP) fields provide the information that the receiving AAL1 needs to verify that it has received the cells in the correct order. The remainder of the payload field is filled with enough single octets to equal 48 octets. AAL1 is appropriate for transporting telephone traffic and uncompressed video traffic. It requires timing synchronization between the source and destination and, for that reason, depends on a media that supports clocking, such as SONET.

- **AAL2** – method for carrying voice over ATM, and compressed/non-compressed video.

- **AAL3/4** – intended for both connectionless and connection-oriented variable bit rate services. Originally two distinct adaptation layers AAL3 and 4, they have been merged into a single AAL named AAL3/4 for historical reasons. AAL3/4 was designed for network service providers and is closely aligned with Switched Multimegabit Data Service (SMDS). AAL3/4 will be used to transmit SMDS packets over an ATM network. The **Convergence Sublayer** (CS) creates a protocol data unit (PDU) by prepending a Beginning/End Tag header to the frame. The **Segmentation and Reassembly** (SAR) sublayer fragments the PDU and prepends to each PDU fragment a header consisting of the following fields:

- **type** – identifies whether the cell is the beginning of a message, continuation of a message, or end of a message;
- **sequence number** – identifies the order in which cells should be reassembled;
- **multiplexing identifier** – identifies cells from different traffic sources interleaved on the same Virtual Circuit Connection (VCC) so that the correct cells are reassembled at the destination.

The SAR sublayer also appends a CRC-10 trailer to each PDU fragment. The completed SAR PDU becomes the payload field of an ATM cell to which the ATM layer prepends the standard ATM header.

- **AAL5** – supports connection-oriented variable bit rate data services. It is a substantially lean AAL compared with AAL3/4 at the expense of error recovery and built-in retransmission. This tradeoff provides a smaller bandwidth overhead, simpler processing requirements, and reduced implementation complexity. The convergence sublayer of AAL5 appends a variable-length pad and an eight-octet trailer to a frame. The pad is long enough to ensure that the resulting PDU falls on the 48-octet boundary of the ATM cell. The trailer includes the length of the frame and a 32-bit CRC computed across the entire PDU, which allows AAL5 at the destination to detect bit errors and lost cells or cells that are out of sequence. Next, the segmentation and reassembly segments the CS PDU into 48-octet blocks. Then the ATM layer places each block into the payload field of an ATM cell. For all cells except the last cell, a bit in the payload type (PT) field is set to zero to indicate that the cell is not the last cell in a series that represents a single frame. For the last cell, the bit in the PT field is set to one. When the cell arrives at its destination, the ATM layer extracts the payload field from the cell, the SAR sublayer reassembles the CS PDU, and the CS uses the CRC and the length field to verify that the frame has been transmitted and reassembled correctly. AAL5 is the adaptation layer used to transfer most non-SMDS data, such as classical IP over ATM and local area network emulation.

Addressing

The ATM Forum has adopted the subnetwork model of **addressing**, in which the ATM layer is responsible for mapping network layer addresses to ATM addresses. Several ATM address formats have been developed, one for public networks and three for private networks.

Typically, **public ATM networks** will use E.164 numbers, which are also used by Narrow band Integrated Services Digital Network (N-ISDN) networks.

Figure 3.8 shows the format of **private network ATM addresses**. The three formats are Data Country Code (DCC), International Code Designator (ICD), and Network Service Access Point (NSAP) encapsulated E.164 addresses.

FIGURE 3-8 ATM address formats

(a) DCC address format

Number of octets:

1	2	1	3	2	2	2	6	1
AFI	DCC	DFI	AA	reserved	RD	area	ESI	selector

(b) ICD address format

Number of octets:

1	2	1	3	2	2	2	6	1
AFI	ICD	DFI	AA	reserved	RD	area	ESI	selector

(c) E.164 address format

Number of octets:

1	8	2	2	6	1
AFI	E.164	RD	area	ESI	selector

The fields of an **ATM address** are as follows:

- *AFI* – one octet of authority and format identifier. The AFI field identifies the type of address. The defined values are 45, 47, and 39 for E.164, ICD, and DCC addresses, respectively.
- *DCC* – two octets of data country code.
- *DFI* – one octet of domain-specific part (DSP) format identifier.
- *AA* – three octets of administrative authority.
- *RD* – two octets of routing domain.
- *Area* – two octets of area identifier.
- *ESI* – six octets of end system identifier, which is an IEEE 802 Media Access Control (MAC) address.
- *Sel* – one octet of NSAP selector (identifier of upper-layer protocol).
- *ICD* – two octets of international code designator.
- *E.164* – eight octets of Integrated Services Digital Network (ISDN) telephone number.

The ATM address formats are modeled on ISO NSAP addresses, but they identify SubNetwork Point of Attachment (SNPA) addresses. Incorporating the MAC address into the ATM address makes it easy to map ATM addresses into existing LANs.

3.8.3 Virtual connections and circuits

Two types of ATM connection exist:

- **virtual channels (VC)** – identified by the combination of a **Virtual Path Identifier** (VPI) and a **Virtual Channel Identifier** (VCI);
- **virtual path (VP)** – a bundle of virtual channels (see Figure 3.9), all of which are switched transparently across the ATM network on the basis of the common VPI. All VCIs and VPIs, however, have only local significance across a particular link and are remapped, as appropriate, at each switch. A transmission path is a bundle of VPs.

FIGURE 3-9 Transmission path consists of VCs and VPs

The basic operation of an **ATM switch** is very simple: to receive a cell across a link on a known VCI or VPI value; to look up the connection value in a local translation table to determine the outgoing port (or ports) of the connection and the new VPI/VCI value of the connection on that link; and then to retransmit the cell on that outgoing link with the appropriate connection identifiers. The switch operation is so simple because external mechanisms set up the local translation tables prior to the transmission of any data. The manner in which these tables are set up determine the two fundamental types of ATM connection, PVC and SVC (similar to X.25 or Frame Relay).

PVC in the usual meaning is a VC that is not signaled by the end points. Both of the endpoint (user) VC values are manually provisioned. The link-by-link route through the network is also manually provisioned. If any equipment fails, the PVC is down, unless the underlying physical network can reroute below ATM. So a PVC is a VC which is statically mapped at every point in the ATM network. A failure of any link that a PVC crosses results in the failure of the PVC.

A **Soft PVC** also has manually provisioned endpoint (user) VC values (which as defined above do not change), but the route through the network can be automatically revised if there is a failure. Historically this feature required a single-vendor network. A vendor may employ signaling (invisibly to the endpoints) within the network, or may just have a workstation somewhere sending proprietary configuration commands when it detects a failure. However, the P-NNI spec defines a standard way of doing this which does not require a vendor proprietary solution. So a Soft PVC is a VC that is programmed to be present at all times (like a PVC). It uses static routes to determine its path through the ATM network. The routes change through use of external management. The routes can be termed semi static but not dynamic, because there is nothing in the protocol of the switches that would provide for automatic rerouting. Soft PVC will be semi-automatically rerouted if a switch or link in the path fails, as opposed to simple PVC.

An **SVC** is established by UNI signaling methods. So an SVC is a demand connection initiated by the user. If a switch in the path fails, the SVC is broken and would have to be reconnected.

The ATM network is not a broadcast medium such as an LAN, therefore additional support is needed for broadcast traffic. As with X.25 where no multicasting or broadcasting is available, the packets/cells for broadcast must be replicated onto designated circuits/channels. To support broadcasting, a DTE (router) should be allowed to specify some virtual circuits as broadcast. When a protocol passes a packet with a broadcast address to the drivers, the packet is duplicated and sent to each circuit marked as broadcast in a point-to-multipoint mode.

3.8.4 Types of ATM connections

There are two fundamental types of ATM connection:

- **point-to-point connections**, which connect two ATM end systems and can be unidirectional or bidirectional;
- **point-to-multipoint connections**, which connect a single source end system (known as the root node) to multiple destination end systems (known as leaves). Cell replication is done within the network by the ATM switches at which the connection splits into two or more branches. Such connections are unidirectional, permitting the root to transmit to the leaves, but not the leaves to the root or to each other, on the same connection. The reason why such connections are only unidirectional are described below.

What is missing from these types of ATM connections is an analog to the multicasting or broadcasting capability common in many shared medium LAN technologies.

3.8.5 ATM cells

In ATM, information is packed into **fixed-size cells of 53 octets** (the cell format for the user-network interface is specified in ITU-T recommendation I.361). Cells are identified and switched throughout the network by means of a label in the header. The ATM header contains the label, which comprises a **virtual path identifier** (VPI), a **virtual channel identifier** (VCI), and an error detection field (see Figure 3.10(a)). Error detection on the ATM level is confined to the header. The network-node interface (NNI) cell is identical to the UNI format (see Figure 3.10(b)) except that the VPI occupies the entire first octet rather than just bits 1 through 4.

FIGURE 3-10 ATM cell format

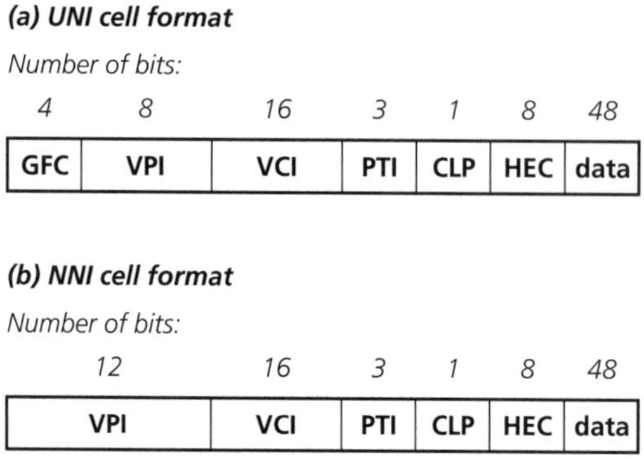

(a) UNI cell format

Number of bits:

4	8	16	3	1	8	48
GFC	VPI	VCI	PTI	CLP	HEC	data

(b) NNI cell format

Number of bits:

12	16	3	1	8	48
VPI	VCI	PTI	CLP	HEC	data

Cell fields have following functions:

- **Generic Flow Control** (GFC) – four-bit field allows encoding of 16 states for flow control.
- **Routing field** (VPI/VCI) – 24 bits available for routing: eight bits for the VPI and 16 bits for the VCI. Except for two reserved codes for signaling virtual channel identification and for general broadcast signaling virtual channel identification, the encoding methodology is still being studied by ITU-T. VPI/VCI is locally significant to the user interface but may undergo translation as it is being transported to another interface. The VPI/VCI constitutes a label used to allocate transmission resources; the label, rather than the position of a frame, determines the allocation. Usable capacity can be dynamically assigned; the network can take advantage of statistical fluctuations while maintaining an established grade of service. Multiple rate-dependent overlay networks are obviated, facilitating integration.
- **Payload Type** (PT) – three bits are available for payload type identification. They indicate whether the cell payload contains user information or network information. In user-information cells, the payload consists of user information and service-adaptation function information. In network information cells, the payload does not form part of the user's information transfer.
- **Cell Loss Priority** (CLP) – if the CLP is set (CLP value is 1), the cell may be subject to discard, depending on network conditions. If the CLP is not set (CLP value is 0), the cell has higher priority.
- **Header Error Control** (HEC) – consists of eight bits and is used for managing header errors. The NNI's HEC mechanism is identical to that at the UNI.

For comparison of framing and data rate constraints with typical LANs and other WANs see Table 2.2 on p. 30.

Error checking – ATM vs. Frame Relay

ATM uses a different approach to error checking in comparison to Frame Relay. The cyclic redundancy check-16 (CRC-16) error check at the end of a Frame Relay frame is used to detect an error in the frame, which could indicate an error in the address. It also determines that the maximum frame size for frame relay is about 4000 bytes. The CRC-16 has a very high probability of catching transmission errors when applied to frames of up to 4000 bytes. If the frames are longer, then the error checking is much less robust.

The ATM cell header consists of five bytes, and the last byte is an eight-bit error check on the first four bytes, out of which 24 (UNI) or 28 (NNI) comprise the address. The first contrast to Frame Relay checking is that in the case of ATM, the CRC covers only the address. Unlike Frame Relay, the ATM check does not include the payload and is more efficient. On the other hand, the ATM format required new chipsets to support this format, while Frame Relay could use existing hardware. Note that an eight-bit error check is sufficient to catch bit errors in ATM addresses, because the span of the information checked is only four bytes, as opposed to up to 4000 bytes.

3.8.6 ATM transport functions

The basic operation of an ATM switch is straightforward. The cell is received across a link on a known VCI or VPI value. The switch looks up the connection value in a local translation table to determine the outgoing port (or ports) of the connection and the new VPI/VCI value of the connection on that link. The switch then retransmits the cell on that outgoing link with the appropriate connection identifiers. Because all VCIs and VPIs have only local significance across a particular link, these values are remapped, as necessary, at each switch.

The transport functions of the ATM layer are subdivided into two levels: the virtual-channel level and the virtual-path level. The transport functions of the ATM layer are independent of the physical-layer implementation. Each ATM cell label explicitly identifies the virtual channel (VC) to which the cell belongs. A specific value of VCI is assigned each time a VC is switched in the network. With this in mind, a VC can be defined as a unidirectional capability for transporting ATM cells between two consecutive ATM entities, where the VCI value is translated. A VC link is originated or terminated by assigning or removing the VCI value.

ATM functions include the following:

- **Cell multiplexing and demultiplexing** – in the transmit direction, the cell-multiplexing function combines cells from individual virtual paths (VPs) and VCs into a non-continuous composite cell flow. In the receive direction, the cell-demultiplexing function directs individual cells from a non-continuous composite cell flow to the appropriate VP or VC.

- **Virtual-path identifier and virtual-channel identifier translation** – occurs at ATM switching points and/or cross-connect nodes. The value of the VPI and/or VCI fields of each incoming ATM cell is mapped into a new VPI and/or VCI value.

- **Cell header generation/extraction** – applies at points where the ATM layer is terminated. In the transmit direction, the cell-header generation function receives a cell information field from a higher layer and generates an appropriate ATM cell header except for the HEC sequence. This function could also include the translation from a service access point identifier to a VP and VC identifier. In the receive direction, the cell header extraction function removes the ATM cell's header and passes the cell information field to a higher layer. This function could also include a translation of VP and VC identifier into a service access point identifier.

■ **Flow control** – when applied at the ATM layer, the flow control information is carried in assigned and unassigned cells.

Additional functionality on top of the ATM layer is provided to accommodate various services. The boundary between the ATM layer and the AAL corresponds to the boundary between functions supported by the contents of the cell header and functions supported by AAL-specific information. The AAL-specific information is contained (nested) in the information field of the ATM cell. The AAL performs the function of adapting a given service to the ATM structure. The AAL can be used for an end-to-end service or terminated within the network. Several types of AALs have been identified; the key types are packet-switching service adaptation and circuit-switching service adaptation. In packet switching, a large packet may be presented to the ATM layer. Here, the AAL must segment the packet into many cells and then route them to the appropriate destination. At the far-end switch, a reassembly must take place. The AAL mechanism thus allows identification of the first segment, the second segment, and so on, to the last segment of the original packet. In serving a circuit-switched channel, the AAL buffers the arriving information, then places it into a cell and switches it to the destination. At the far-end switch, the cells are converted back to a continuous stream.

3.8.7 Service classes

Broadband integrated service digital networks (B-ISDNs) utilizing asynchronous transfer mode (ATM) technology are expected to support a wide variety of services. As defined by the ATM Forum, the different types of service supported by ATM are categorized into four service classes (see Table 3.5):

■ **Constant bit rate** (CBR) – offers strict bandwidth guarantees and minimal delay and delay variation. It is suitable for realtime applications such as telephony and video. It is intended to be the equivalent of a digital leased line service. This class of service cannot tolerate delay or loss.

■ **Variable bit rate** (VBR) – suited to LAN interconnection and similar applications that do not make stringent demands on bandwidth, delay or delay variation. Within the category, the ATM forum has defined **realtime** (RT) and **non-realtime** (NRT) traffic. VBR-RT is close to CBR in terms of its specifications and is intended for time-sensitive applications that can tolerate some minimal variation in delay or cell loss. The VBR-NRT is used for applications such as online transaction processing and static video.

■ **Available bit rate** (ABR) – makes use of the bandwidth that is available from moment to moment for applications such as file transfer that can tolerate low priority handling, but which still need minimal cell loss. These applications are not as time-sensitive and therefore can be superseded by more time sensitive applications.

■ **Unspecified bit rate** (UBR) – an economical class of service, which is similar to ABR in that it uses available bandwidth on a moment-to-moment basis, but without service level guarantees.

TABLE 3-5	Service classes and their features			
	Class A	*Class B*	*Class C*	*Class D*
Synchronization between source and destination stations	Necessary		Not necessary	
Transmission speed (throughput)	Constant	Variable		
Transport service	Connection-oriented		Connectionless	
Type AAL	**AAL1**	**AAL2**	**AAL3/4,5**	**AAL3/4**

CBR and VBR provide guaranteed service on demand, while ABR and UBR provide best-effort service (without guarantees of cell delivery).

3.8.8 Quality of service

According to the ATM Forum, CBR and realtime VBR connections have stringent delay and **Cell Loss Ratio** (CLR) requirements. Moreover, the CBR service class is designed for circuit-switching emulation, which requires a constant bandwidth capacity for each call. The traffic rate for a VBR connection may fluctuate around its average rate but not exceed its **Peak Cell Rate** (PCR).

The traffic rate for an ABR connection can be adjusted in real time, and its **minimum cell rate** (MCR) is specified. A UBR source may send as fast as it desires (up to its PCR), but the network does not guarantee any QoS for it. Traffic parameters for a call are specified in its ATM traffic descriptor. An ATM traffic descriptor is defined as a generic list of traffic parameters that can be used to capture the traffic characteristics of an ATM connection.

These QoS classes are implemented on the Virtual Channels (VCs) that are established as the traffic path through the network between end points. The ATM Forum standard requires that policers be used at the User-Network Interface (UNI) to ensure all traffic entering the network conforms to the parameters specified in the traffic descriptor. The **Generic Cell Rate Algorithm** (GCRA) has been standardized as a general policing scheme.

ATM supports QoS guarantees composed of traffic contract, traffic shaping, and traffic policing. A **traffic contract** specifies an envelope that describes the intended data flow. This envelope specifies values for peak bandwidth, average sustained bandwidth, and burst size, among others. When an ATM end system connects to an ATM network, it enters a contract with the network, based on QoS parameters.

Traffic shaping is the use of queues to constrain data bursts, limit peak data rate, and smooth jitters so that traffic will fit within the promised envelope. ATM devices are responsible for adhering to the contract by means of traffic shaping.

ATM switches can use **traffic policing.** This is carried out at each UNI by a function known as **Usage Parameter Control** (UPC) with a common method is known as leaky bucket policing, and maps directly into the algorithms used to specify the traffic descriptors. When a switch determines, using UPC, that the traffic sent across a UNI does not conform to the agreed traffic contract, it can do one of two things. First, it can simply drop the cell or, if adequate resources are available (as determined, for instance, by buffer thresholds), the switch can still pass the cell – but mark it non-conformant and subject to preferential dropping further along the path by setting a Cell Loss Priority bit (CLP). Switches along the path should give priority to cells without the CLP bit set and drop cells with the bit set first, if and when switch buffers start to fill. The traffic contract is not enforced, as long as there is enough bandwidth and buffer space in the switches to satisfy all allocated contracts.

There are numerous **performance parameters** defined for ATM. At the CPE interface **local parameters** are measured (see Table 3.6):

- **Peak Cell Rate** (PCR) – maximum cell transfer rate allowed at the interface;
- **Sustainable Cell Rate** (SCR) – average cell transfer rate allowed at the interface;
- **Cell Delay Variation Tolerance** (CDVT) – 'jitter,' or mean variation in the inter-cell timing;
- **Minimum Cell Rate** (MCR) – the lowest cell transfer rate allowed at the interface;
- **Burst Size** (BS) – maximum number of cells that can be transmitted at the peak cell rate.

TABLE 3-6   Service types and parameters

Parameters	CBR	RT-VBR	NRT-VBR	ABR	UBR	Parameter type
CLR	Specified	Specified	Specified	Specified	Not specified	QoS
CTD and CDV	CDV and maximum CTD	CDV and maximum CTD	Mean CTD	Not specified	Not specified	QoS
PCR and CDVT	Specified	Specified	Specified	Specified	Specified	Operational
SCR and BT	–	Specified	Specified	–	–	Operational
MCR	–	–	–	Specified	-	Operational
Congestion control	–	No	No	Yes	No	

Among **network parameters** measured between two points in the network the most important are:

- **cell delay** – maximum allowable end-to-end cell delay;
- **cell delay variation** – maximum allowable variation in cell delay;
- **cell loss** – maximum allowable percentage of traffic that can be lost or discarded.

3.8.9 ATM routing protocols

Since ATM is connection oriented, a connection request needs to be routed from the requesting node through the ATM network and to the destination node, much as packets are routed within a packet-switched network. The NNI protocols are hence to ATM networks what routing protocols (such as OSPF or IGRP) are to current IP networks. However, even before routing in ATM and routing in IP, it is necessary to remember that routing in IP occurs at a higher layer than ATM routing. In case of IP-over-ATM, both routing algorithms exist at the same time.

The P-NNI protocol consists of two components. The first is a P-NNI signaling protocol used to relay ATM connection requests within the networks, between the source and destination UNI. The UNI signaling request is mapped into NNI signaling at the source (ingress) switch. The NNI signaling is remapped back into UNI signaling at the destination (egress) switch.

The P-NNI protocols operate between ATM switching systems (which can represent either physical switches or entire networks operating as a single P-NNI entity), which are connected by P-NNI links. P-NNI links can be physical links or virtual, 'multi-hop' links. A typical example of a virtual link is a virtual path that connects two nodes together.

Since all virtual channels, including the connection carrying the P-NNI signaling, would be carried transparently through any intermediate switches between these two nodes on this virtual path, the two nodes are logically adjacent in relation to the P-NNI protocols. The **Interim Local Management Interface** (ILMI) protocol, first defined for use across UNI links, will also be used across both physical and virtual NNI links; enhancements to the ILMI MIBs allow for automatic recognition of NNI versus UNI links, and of private versus public UNI.

The current P-NNI signaling protocol developed by the ATM Forum is an extension of UNI signaling and incorporates additional Information Elements (IE) for such NNI-related parameters as Designated Transit Lists (DTL). P-NNI signaling is carried across NNI links on the same virtual channel, VCI = 5, which is used for signaling across the UNI. The VPI value depends on whether the NNI link is physical or virtual.

The second component of the P-NNI protocol is a virtual circuit routing protocol. This is used to route the signaling request through the ATM network. This is also the route on which the ATM connection is set up, and along which the data will flow. The operation of routing a signaling request through an ATM network, somewhat paradoxically, given ATM's connection oriented nature, is superficially similar to that of routing connectionless packets within existing network layer protocols (such as IP). This is due to the fact that prior to connection set up, there is, of course, no connection for the signaling request to follow.

As such, a VC routing protocol can use some of the concepts underlying many of the connectionless routing protocols that have been developed over the last few years. However, the P-NNI protocol is much more complex than any existing routing protocol. This complexity arises from two goals of the protocol: to allow for much greater scalability than is possible with any existing protocol, and to support true QoS-based routing.

Connection request routing and negotiation

Routing of the connection request is governed by an ATM routing protocol (which routes connections based on destination and source addresses), traffic, and the QoS parameters requested by the source end system. Negotiating a connection request that is rejected by the destination is limited because call routing is based on parameters of initial connection; changing parameters might, in turn, affect the connection routing.

A number of connection management message types, including setup, call proceeding, connect, and release, are used to establish and tear down an ATM connection. The source end system sends a setup message (including the destination end system address and any traffic QoS parameters) when it wants to set up a connection. The ingress switch sends a call proceeding message back to the source in response to the setup message. The destination end system next sends a connect message if the connection is accepted. The destination end system sends a release message back to the source end system if the connection is rejected, thereby clearing the connection.

Connection management messages are used to establish an ATM connection in the following manner. First, a source end system sends a setup message, which is forwarded to the first ATM switch (ingress switch) in the network. This switch sends a call proceeding message and invokes an ATM routing protocol. The signaling request is propagated across the network. The exit switch (called the egress switch) that is attached to the destination end system receives the setup message.

The **egress switch** forwards the setup message to the end system across its UNI, and the ATM end system sends a connect message if the connection is accepted. The connect message traverses back through the network along the same path to the source end system, which sends a connect acknowledge message back to the destination to acknowledge the connection. Data transfer can then begin.

The advantages and disadvantages of ATM are summarized in Table 3.7.

TABLE 3-7   Advantages and disadvantages of ATM

Advantages	Disadvantages
Guaranteed bandwidth on demand	Complexity
Integrated support for data, voice, and video	High cost
Flexibility, scalability	

3.8.10 ATM and Frame Relay interworking note – FUNI

The **Frame User-Network Interface** (FUNI) was a modification of the standard ATM service provided by the ATM User-Network Interface (UNI). The idea behind FUNI was to provide a frame-oriented version of ATM optimized for data traffic. Essentially, Frame Relay has long been regarded as a transport optimized for variable-length data traffic, while ATM, with its well-defined, specific classes of service, best supports an integrated mix of data, voice, and video on the network. FUNI held the promise of offering the best of both worlds, allowing frames and cells to be integrated seamlessly.

FUNI, in theory, enables CPE to submit variable-length frames to an ATM switch in a carrier's network. The ATM switch translates the FUNI frames to standard ATM cells and sends them on through the ATM network. FUNI had some significant advantages compared with traditional cell-based ATM:

- The overhead for transmitting variable-length frames generally fell below 1%, compared with 10% overhead in a cell-based ATM transmission. FUNI, then, could have been an efficient form of ATM for low-speed access links where giving up five out of every 53 cells to overhead takes a big bite out of bandwidth.
- CPE supporting FUNI was typically less expensive than ATM interfaces. This is because FUNI frames could be constructed in software, so hardware upgrades were not necessary.
- FUNI supports ATM network operations and network management, which is more extensive and standard than frame relay network management.
- Frame relay and ATM use different, yet equivalent, formats for multiprotocol encapsulation. Because of this, ATM–Frame Relay service interworking requires the translation of multiprotocol encapsulation formats when multiprotocol encapsulation is used. With FUNI, the functions of Frame Relay would be provided with the same multiprotocol encapsulation method used by ATM.

Admittedly, there were a couple of caveats with FUNI, such as not providing any benefits for voice and video compared with frame-based technologies. FUNI also lacked support for ATM's thousands of virtual circuits over a single interface. But these limitations were not the reason for the lack of FUNI acceptance. FUNI fell victim to the marketing and political forces in a community that failed to see the need for a smooth migration path for frame relay customers wishing to upgrade their service levels and network management but not yet ready for the expense and complexity of upgrading their hardware to cell-based ATM.

Guaranteeing accurate packet transmission

Frame Relay and ATM are considered connection-oriented because the frame header identifies the owner of the data, using a virtual circuit number. There is a call-establishment procedure that takes place using permanent virtual circuits or switched virtual circuits. This means that networked switches send the data to the eventual destination by looking up connections and doing a label swap on the virtual circuit number as data pass from one physical interface to another.

By contrast, IP is a connectionless technology in that the protocol has sufficient information about the destination address in the header of each packet for the packet to be delivered anywhere in the network without a predefined connection.

Frame Relay, IP, and ATM are, however, all quite similar, in that they depend on a higher-layer protocol to ensure accurate transmission of the information when guaranteed transmission is desired. Some types of information do not need retransmission: it is usually better to delete an erred voice packet than to retransmit it. Voice algorithms are better equipped to deal with lost packets than with the delays incurred with requesting a retransmission.

If guaranteed transmission is needed, the connection-oriented vs. connection-less question has no real bearing. In general, IP depends on TCP to guarantee delivery. Guaranteed delivery over Frame Relay or ATM depends on a TCP/IP stack, SNA, X.25, or some other upper-layer protocol to provide this function.

Sequencing in connection-oriented networks

Sequencing refers to whether the various packets in a single data flow arrive at a destination in the exact order they were transmitted. In a connection-oriented network, if upper-layer packets Nos. 3, 4, and 6 are received, there is really no need for the protocol layer to check the sequencing to wait to see if packet No. 5 arrives. It is safe to assume that packet No. 5 has been lost and that a retransmission should (in most cases) be requested.

No sequence numbering is used in the connection-oriented networks such as Frame Relay or ATM. Sequencing information is contained in the upper-layer protocol where the error detection and retransmission requests are happening. As an exception, in AAL-1 there is a four-bit sequence number in the header. However, AAL-1 is intended for constant bit-rate traffic, where the timing is very important. Thus, this sequence number is used only to detect lost cells so the timing may be adjusted for lost packets. There is no request for retransmission; only a detection of lost packets.

Because Frame Relay and ATM are connection-oriented, implicitly all packets will follow the same route through the network until some type of network event happens to initiate alternate routing. After the network path is rerouted, the packets will again arrive in sequence. Any packets that are received out of sequence indicate that the intermediate missing packets are lost.

3.8.11 LANE

LAN Emulation (LANE) was developed to provide smooth LAN interconnect across ATM networks by simulating the LAN broadcast nature (and sacrificing some ATM and LAN features). LANE is a Layer 2 framework that makes a connection-oriented ATM network seem like a shared connectionless Ethernet or Token Ring LAN segment. As a Layer 2 service, LANE can handle both routable protocols such as TCP/IP, IPX, and DECnet as well as non-routable protocols such as NetBIOS and SNA. LANE clearly integrates the advantages of ATM with existing LAN technologies such as Ethernet, TCP/IP, and IPX/SPX, enabling high performance communication within the workgroup.

LANE uses a client/server model, with emulated LANs made up of multiple LANE Clients (LECs) and a LANE Server (LES). The LES provides a MAC to ATM address resolution and broadcast service to the LANE Clients. Clients are implemented on ATM/LAN edge devices and ATM attached hosts, while the LANE Server can be implemented in a router, LAN or ATM switch, or in a standalone ATM equipped device.

While LANE is an ATM Forum specification, the IETF has worked on a way to support classical IP over ATM as well as various protocols using multiprotocol over ATM specifications.

FIGURE 3-11   LANE vs. OSI model

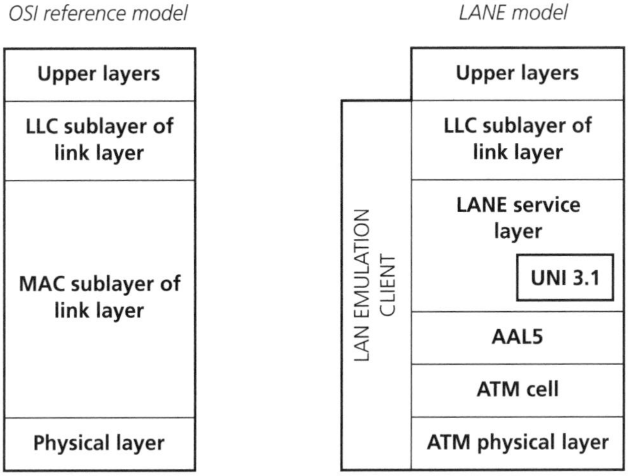

OSI reference model   *LANE model*

The components of LANE relate to the way LANs operate which includes broadcast search, address registration, and address caching. (The LAN emulation model is compared with the OSI model in Figure 3.11.) In addition, the client and server model approach that is common in a LAN environment is used by LANE components. As there is a large installed base of Ethernet LANs using bridges and routers, LANE needs to support this installed base in an effective manner. The following LANE components together provide the support for this key requirement:

■ **LAN Emulation Client** (LEC) – component residing in an ATM end system that participates in ATM LAN emulation network operations. ATM end systems include ATM hosts with native ATM interfaces such as using ATM Network Interface Cards (NICs), or ATM capable systems that support non-LANE systems to gain access to ATM. A non-LANE system typically is a legacy LAN host such as an Ethernet system, or can be another ATM host without LANE functionality. The ATM capable systems that support this LEC service can be ATM LAN bridges, switches, or LAN Network Operating System (NOS) clients. The LEC has to perform several functions (address resolution function, data transfer function, address caching function) and provides interfaces to other LANE components such as LECS, LES, and BUS servers as well as driver support for upper layer applications and services.

■ **LAN Emulation Server** (LES) – component and part of LAN emulation service typically residing in an ATM system such as a switch or a router that is part of an ATM network. This ATM network can be as small as one ATM switch or can be a large enterprise network with multiple ATM switches interconnected to each other. The LES is the central piece of LANE and provides the LECs with the necessary information and data to establish ATM connections to other LECs for LAN operations. The LES provides several functions, such as support to LECs, address registration support function and address resolution support function.

■ **Broadcast and Unknown Server** (BUS) – component and part of LANE service typically residing in an ATM system such as a switch or a router. The key function for BUS is to provide broadcasting support that is common to LAN through one point-to-multipoint VCC to all LECs (there is one BUS per Emulated LAN).

■ **LAN Emulation Configuration Server** (LECS) – component and part of LANE service typically residing in an ATM system such as a switch or a router. LECS provides support to LECs in the initialization phase, and supplies configuration information needed for LANE operations. These include registration of its address for Interim Local Management Interface (ILMI) support, and configuration support for LES addresses and their corresponding emulated LAN identifiers. The key function for LECS is to provide the respective LES addresses to the requested LECs. The LECS with interfaces to LEC and LES provides a registration function and configuration support function.

The LANE operations have two phases, initialization and operations. During the **initialization phase** the client (LEC):

■ connects to the configuration service (LECS);
■ gets the LES ATM address;
■ connects and joins to the LES;
■ connects to the BUS for multicast service;
■ sends address registrations to the LES.

And during **operation phase** then:

■ sends *LE_ARP* request to the LES to find out the partner ATM address;
■ receives *LE_ARP* reply from other LECs or from the LES;
■ sets up point-to-point connection with partner;
■ sends and receives multicast messages.

3.8.12 MULTIPROTOCOL OVER ATM

MULTIPROTOCOL OVER ATM (MPOA) uses **three complementary techniques** to form its fundamental capability. These are ATM Forum's **LAN Emulation** (LANE), the IETF's **Next Hop Resolution Protocol** (NHRP) and the concept of the **virtual router**. LANE supports native LAN environments over ATM in a transparent manner, while NHRP provides a mechanism to establish a shortcut over the ATM backbone based on network layer addressing.

Virtual Routers provide the ability to separate functions among various elements of the network, which reduces cost and improves efficiency.

MPOA provides unprecedented scalability and flexibility by introducing a concept known as a 'virtual router.' The 'virtual router' emulates the functionality of traditional routed networks, but eliminates the performance limitations of hop-by-hop routing. Shortcut connections are set up over the ATM fabric from any MPOA-capable host or edge device to any other, regardless of their subnet membership. In essence, MPOA identifies data 'flows' and maps them directly to ATM virtual channels. This technique of establishing shortcuts directly across the ATM network is sometimes referred to as 'cut-through' or 'zero-hop' routing.

The establishment of a shortcut connection over the ATM fabric provides a significant improvement in performance over pure router based inter-subnet solutions. Packets transported over the shortcut connection are no longer subjected to the hop-by-hop router processing in traditional networks. Besides improvement in performance the end-to-end delay between end LANE-MPOA overcomes some of the performance and scalability limitations of LANE-based networks. However, LANE Version 2 is an integral component of MPOA. LANE is used for intra-subnet communications, while the MPOA virtual router provides communications between subnets.

An MPOA network adds no more configuration requirements than a LAN Emulation-only network. This is because the default operation for an MPOA device will be standard LAN Emulation connectivity, over which all the MPOA-capable devices will autodiscover each other. Thus the configuration and startup operation is greatly simplified and conventional connectivity is available at all times. Building upon LAN Emulation also helps keep the MPOA edge device design simpler and less complicated or costly.

The ATM Forum has worked in cooperation with the IETF to develop MPOA – a powerful network layer routing solution that integrates and leverages existing protocols and standards to provide routing functionality over switched ATM networks.

MPOA architecture

In the MPOA architecture, conventional routers retain all of their traditional functions as they must run common routing protocols to discover how to reach other (sub)networks. They must also continue providing inter-VLAN multicast forwarding, as well as all the classical inter-VLAN forwarding for LAN emulation-only clients, and may also forward short-lived 'flows' on behalf of **MPOA Clients** (MPC). Essentially, routers continue to be the default forwarders for a network. MPOA defines logical components that can be implemented in various hardware configurations. The separation of function allows vendors to package their unique solutions to meet the particular needs of their customers.

■ **Edge devices** – inexpensive devices which forward packets between legacy LAN segments and ATM interfaces based on the destination network layer address and MAC layer address. Sometimes referred to as multilayer switches, these products allow for efficient transmission of legacy LAN traffic over ATM infrastructures; each can contain an MPC in addition to their one or more LAN Emulation Clients (LEC).

■ **MPOA Server** (MPS) a.k.a. **route server** – collection of functions that allow the mapping of Network Layer subnets to ATM. The route server can be implemented as a standalone product, or can be built into existing routers or switches. It maintains network layer, MAC-layer, and ATM address information to satisfy queries from edge devices and ATM-attached hosts. The information is used to establish direct virtual circuits between any two end-points that need to communicate with one another. The route server runs routing protocols (e.g. RIP and OSPF) to communicate routing information with traditional routers, allowing interoperability with existing routed LAN internetworks. Route servers may also be involved in forwarding broadcast and unknown frames in the MPOA network. In essence, the route server functions are a superset of the LES/BUS function in the ATM Forum's LAN emulation specification. The route server has additional extensions to accommodate Network Layer functions and to allow deployment of a virtual router; the MPS supplies all the cut-through forwarding information used by the MPCs. The MPS responds with this information upon receiving a query from an MPC. For this query and response function, MPOA is adopting and extending the Next Hop Resolution Protocol (NHRP).

■ **ATM-attached hosts** – ATM NIC cards that implement the MPOA protocol as part of their driver. They allow for efficient communication of ATM-attached hosts to each other, or to legacy LANs connected by an edge device.

■ **Virtual subnets** – MPOA uses network layer constructs in defining 'virtual' subnetworks. They denote both a Layer 3 protocol and an address range. In the case of IP, they can be thought of as 'virtual subnets.' The MPOA model supports all existing LAN internetwork data flows, including both intra-subnet and inter-subnet.

■ **MPOA router** – a collection of functions that allow the mapping of network layer subnets to ATM. The MPOA router can be implemented as a standalone product, or can be built into existing routers or switches. It maintains a local network layer, MAC-layer, and ATM address information in addition to routing tables. MPOA routers communicate via NHRP to resolve destination addresses so that MPCs can establish shortcuts. The routing engine runs routing protocols (e.g. RIP and OSPF) to communicate routing information with 'traditional routers,' allowing interoperability with existing routed LAN and WAN internetworks.

The MPOA model distributes routing among edge devices and ATM attached hosts with MPOA clients (ITPCs), which forward packets, and MPOA servers (MPSs), which supply routing information. MPCs examine the destination address of packets received on legacy LAN segments in order to make the correct forwarding decision. If the packet is to be routed, it will contain the destination MAC address of the MPOA router interface. If so, the MPC will look at the destination network layer address of the packet, and resolve this to the correct ATM address based on information received from the MPOA server, or use information in its cache. The MPC will then establish a direct virtual channel connection to the appropriate destination.

If the packet is destined to a host in the same subnet so that it can be bridged, the MPC will use LANE to resolve the ATM address and establish a virtual channel connection to the destination. If the local MPOA server does not know the appropriate ATM address, it can propagate the query to other MPOA servers or routers using NHRP functionality. The destination ATM address from the MPOA server can be the address of the host MPOA router.

Since it is commonplace for users in a routed internetwork to have repetitive and habitual external addresses to which they need to be connected, e.g. particular file servers or remote corporate destinations, the edge device can save ('cache') this virtual channel information to be reused without having to issue address resolution requests for every flow. This is a valuable aspect of the MPOA concept. A design goal of MPOA is to minimize the number of times the edge device must visit the route server to retrieve this information. To that end, the MPC maintains its own address cache. Much of the MPOA effort is devoted to devising performance. In the case of steady-stream transmissions such as video, this is highly efficient and superior to simple router-to-router operation.

Network layer mapping

MPOA works at network Layer 3 to recognize the beginning of a data transfer and respond with a network route destination address. The shortcut SVC is then used to forward traffic using standard Layer 2 switching. With both Layer 3 and Layer 2 capabilities, the MPOA model encompasses routing and switching:

- being able to route and switch network layer traffic;
- also being able to bridge non-routable traffic.

The network layer mapping enables the QoS properties of ATM to be used by network applications. For example, the IETF's RSVP protocol operates at the network layer, and provides mechanisms for applications to reserve a particular quality of service (see Part V). The MPOA framework allows the Layer 3 reservations to be mapped onto the underlying ATM fabric.

Next hop resolution protocol

The IETF has defined the **Next Hop Resolution Protocol** (NHRP) which, among other capabilities, allows the packet-forwarding function of intermediate routers on the data path to be bypassed. The NHRP was developed as a means of facilitating inter-LIS VCs in order to utilize the potential benefits of ATM which are lost with the classical models. NHRP is an **inter-LIS address resolution mechanism** that maps a destination's IP address to the destination's ATM address in cases where the destination resides within the same ATM cloud as the source.

The NHRP provides an extended address resolution protocol that permits **Next Hop Clients** (NHCs) to send queries between different **logical IP subnets** (LISs) sometimes referred to as Local Address Groups (LAGs). Queries are propagated using **Next Hop Servers** (NHSs) along paths discovered by standard routing protocols such as RIP and OSPF. This enables the establishment of ATM SVCs across subnet boundaries, allowing inter-subnet communications without using intermediate routers for qualified data flows. The MPOA servers run the full routing stack which results in a consolidated configuration for the entire network. The switches are standards-based ATM switches which results in a highly scalable, low cost, high performance network infrastructure. Edge devices are optimized for forwarding network layer and Layer 2 traffic resulting in network-wide virtual networks and zero-hop routing across the ATM network.

In cases where the destination resides outside the ATM cloud containing the source, the NHRP returns the ATM address of the source ATM cloud's egress router closest to the destination. Once the source receives the NHRP response, it can then open a direct cut-through VC to the destination using standard ATM signaling/routing protocols. However, opting to use the NHRP and end-to-end VC setup for every single data flow in an NHRP-capable network is unlikely to yield optimal results, especially in large ATM clouds within the Internet. This is because in such an environment the number of IP flows traversing the cloud may be quite large, in which case setting up a separate VC for each flow may result in an unmanageable number of VCs at switches within the cloud. Furthermore, setting up a cut-through VC may be unnecessary and even undesirable for certain short-lived flows where it would be hard to justify the associated overhead of the end-to-end connection and its setup, especially for flows that make no assumptions about QoS anyway.

The majority of flows would not be suitable for VC cut-through and so would continue to be forwarded in a connectionless hop-by-hop manner over the default VCs. However, the minority of flows that did receive cut-through would represent the majority of packets since these flows would be of much longer duration.

Although the NHRP unquestionably overcomes some of the weaknesses of the classical IP over ATM models, it is not without its own limitations. One of those is the NHRP's inability to directly support multicast. Also, an NHRP solution necessitates routing/signaling functionality in both the ATM and IP layers which adds to the overall complexity.

An NHRP example is shown in Figure 3.12.

FIGURE 3-12 NHRP example

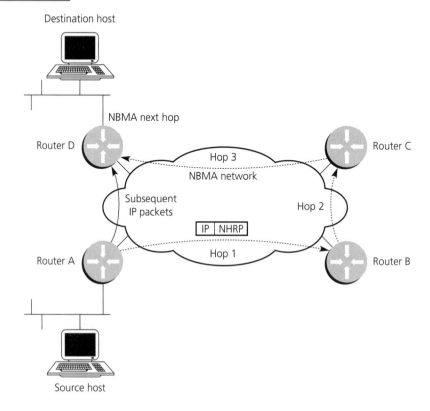

RFC WATCH **NHRP**

RFC 2332 **NBMA Next Hop Resolution Protocol** (NHRP), 1998 (Proposed Standard)

The next hop routing protocol is a way of finding an optimal shortcut through large public (non-broadcast multi-access) networks like X.25, SMDS, and ATM. It bypasses the normal IP routing paradigm by being able to establish direct connections to systems on a different IP-subnetwork. In this way it is possible to support interworking of thousands of systems belonging to different organizations on a common infrastructure in an efficient way.

A **virtual router** is a set of devices operating over a network which collectively provide the functionality of multiprotocol routed networks. In the case of MPOA the edge devices are analogous to router interface cards; the ATM switching fabric can be seen as the 'backplane' of the router, and the MPOA server is analogous to the control processor. The MPOA framework defines the protocols between the MPOA server and the edge devices that enable the 'virtual router' behavior.

LANE and MPOA comparison

While MPOA specifications are implemented to overcome some of the performance and scalability limitations of LANE specifications, LANE Version 2 is an integral component of MPOA. The default operation for an MPOA device is the standard LANE connectivity.

Both LANE and MPOA include methods for **establishing edge-to-edge connections** through the ATM network. Since this is the case, the performance through the ATM network is identical regardless of the protocol (once a cutthrough path is established). Thus, one can implement the edge strategy that best suits the desired network behavior whether that is router-based or VLAN-based.

MPOA integrates LANE and NHRP to preserve the benefits of LAN emulation, while allowing inter-subnet network layer protocol communication over ATM SVCs without requiring conventional routers in the data path. MPOA allows the physical separation of network layer route calculation and forwarding, a technique known as virtual routing. This separation provides a number of key benefits:

- high performance and efficient inter-subnet communication;
- increased manageability by decreasing the number of devices that must be configured to perform network layer route calculation;
- increased scalability by reducing the number of devices participating in the network layer route calculation;
- reduced complexity of the edge devices by eliminating the need to perform network layer route calculation;

■ resiliency in the campus network since multiple routers containing the MPS will likely be in use. Hence, there is no network-wide single point of failure in the MPOA architecture. Conventional routers in MPOA networks, each acting as the MPS for their respective (sub)networks, work together through the exchange of common routing protocols, such as Open Shortest Path First (OSPF), just as they did prior to the introduction of MPOA. Each subset of MPCs, which are using one MPS at any one time, can have a backup MPS by utilizing the same method used to provide inter-VLAN router redundancy, a feature already available from vendors today.

SNAPSHOT	MPOA benefits

■ Inter-VLAN cut-through connections.
■ Layer 3-to-ATM QoS exploitation.
■ Ability to utilize the existing infrastructure without requiring extra configuration.

MPOA vs. label switching

MPOA was adopted to facilitate integration of ATM and multiple protocols by the ATM Forum. Label switching has been introduced as a technology facilitating the ATM and IP integration. Although we will discuss label switching approaches in the final Part V, it may be interesting to preview the differences in the two.

MPOA and label switching each solve a somewhat different set of problems but that the sets partially overlap. For example, MPOA solves problems of communication among bridges on a single ATM subnet, which is not something that label switching addresses. Similarly, MPOA does not solve the problem of multicast communication among routers connected to a single ATM network in different subnets, which label switching does address. The area where the problem spaces most closely overlap is in establishing unicast communication among routers connected to an ATM network.

In setting up inter-subnet shortcuts, MPOA uses the Next Hop Resolution Protocol (NHRP). One of the most significant drawbacks with the NHRP is that, when run between routers, it can introduce persistent forwarding loops. The environments in which the NHRP can be applied must be constrained to prevent this from happening. The NHRP also requires a number of servers to enable the originator of the shortcut to determine the ATM address of the egress router, which it can then use to signal for a VC. Thus, there is a reasonable degree of complexity to set up the shortcut compared to establishing a label switched path. And the fact that NHRP is limited to unicast traffic further circumscribes its applicability.

Most of the other problems solved by MPOA are problems that label switching does not address. We have already mentioned bridging across a single ATM subnet. This seems worthwhile – to support non-IP or non-routable protocols, for example. However, this functionality can also be provided simply by using LAN emulation (LANE).

In summary, MPOA and label switching mostly address different problems. Where there is overlap, label switching seems the simpler and more generally applicable solution, as we will see in Part V.

3.8.13 Classical IP over ATM

Classical IP over ATM (CLIP, RFC 2225) is an approach that uses the power of ATM to forward IP traffic. It is used to connect subnets or workgroups that use only IP as the transport protocol. As in edge routing over ATM, QoS capabilities of ATM are ignored. It is possible to have multiple subnets on the same network, but at present each subnet must operate independently of the others and routers are required to provide communications between subnets.

RFC WATCH	**RFC watch**
	RFC 2225 **Classical IP and ARP over ATM** (Proposed Standard)

The classical IP over ATM approach follows the traditional IP subnet model. In this model, hosts in each **logical IP subnet** (LIS) communicate directly with each other and use routers to communicate to other hosts in a different LIS. Logical IP subnets are identical, in all 'protocol' aspects, to conventional LAN media subnets. The key aspects that matter in this context are that ATM-attached systems in the same LIS have the same network numbers and subnet masks, just as on an Ethernet or other conventional media. The LIS concept is shown in Figure 3.13.

FIGURE 3-13   Example of LIS use

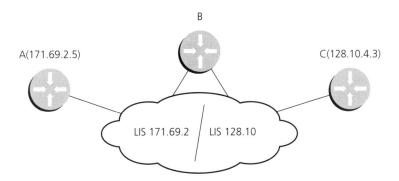

Hosts using the **Address Resolution Protocol** (ARP) can get the destination physical addresses of other hosts in the same LIS based on the IP addresses. The features for the classical IP over the ATM are as follows: IP datagrams are transmitted over ATM network using the ATM AAL-5, while the logical IP subnet model is maintained. That is routers do the forwarding from one IP subnet to another IP subnet. The ARP service is used to resolve IP addresses to ATM addresses for SVC network. The Inverse ARP is used for PVC network. ATM ARP and Inverse ARP are described in the following sections. Hosts within one subnet set up direct connections to communicate with each other. Although the classical IP over ATM approach works relatively well for small-sized networks, it does not scale well for big networks.

MARS

The IPv6 (see 10.8) address auto-configuration and neighbor discovery for LANs rely on the native-broadcast nature of the LAN. By using the native broadcast support, IPv6 protocols rely heavily on multicastings such as the all-routers multicast and all-nodes multicast addresses. As ATM does not have native broadcast capability, IPv6 hosts and routers connected to an ATM network will need to use some form of server that can provide this broadcast capability. One common way of supporting multicast in an ATM network is to use the **Multicast Address Resolution Server** (MARS) approach. MARS is a server that maintains mapping between Layer 3 multicast addresses and the corresponding groups of ATM addresses. Each Layer 3 multicast address will map to one or more ATM addresses.

Each node, a host or a router join their respective multicast Layer 3 address groups by registering their ATM addresses with MARS. When there is a need to send multicast packets by a node, it sends an address resolution request to MARS for the corresponding ATM addresses that belong to this multicast group. The node can then set up point-to-multipoint connections to the ATM addresses in the multicast group. In some ATM networks, the actual function of multicasting is supported using a MultiCast Server (MCS). The MCS acts as a proxy for doing the actual multicasting function. Nodes send the multicast data only to the MCS, and the MCS sets up the point-to-multipoint connections to the destinations in the group as needed and forwards the data.

3.9 SONET

The **Synchronous Optical Network** (SONET) was developed in 1984 as an optical network standard to support multiplexing on links capable of data rates of hundreds of megabits or more. Its main goal is to provide a single set of multiplexing standards for high-speed links. The standard provides various rates called Synchronous Transport Signal (STS) or Optical Carrier (OC) levels (see Appendix D for complete overview of levels and their related speeds). The basic **transmission rate** of SONET (51.840 Mbps), referred to as Synchronous Transport Signal level 1 (STS-1), is obtained by sampling the 810-byte frames at 8000 frames per second. Developed by Bellcore (now Telecordia), SONET features an octet-synchronous multiplexing scheme with transmission rates in multiples of 51.840 Mbps. Even though several other rates were originally specified, only the transmission rates in Table 3.8 have emerged as practical and only these have been implemented in real networks. Also shown in Table 3.8 are corresponding transmission rates and terminology for SDH. SDH is the SONET-equivalent specification proposed by the ITU-SDH supports only a subset of SONET data rates, starting from 155.520 Mbps, and it seems to be the most popular in Europe.

TABLE 3-8   SONET/SDH data rates

SONET	SDH	Data rates
STS-1		51.840 Mbps
STS-3	STM-1	155.520 Mbps
STS-12	STM-4	622.080 Mbps
STS-48	STM-16	2488.320 Mbps
STS-192	STM-48	9953.280 Mbps

SONET has the capacity to combine separate voice, data, and video networks into one broadband, multimedia network, by encapsulating fixed-length, variable position cells transported by super high-speed synchronized frames over the SONET network.

SONET is an end-to-end service designed to satisfy the following communication needs:

- automated maintenance and testing – embedded control channels enable carriers to track end-to-end performance of every transmission, and allow carriers to guarantee transmission performance, and users can readily verify compliance through on-premise management terminals;
- bandwidth administration;
- realtime rerouting – allows customers to bypass congested nodes or points of failure by reconfiguring the routes of affected circuits; reroutes are predetermined and stored in Automatic-Call-Routing (ACR) programs to provide immediate network recovery;
- digital cross-connecting;
- standard optical interface;
- synchronous multiplexing;
- worldwide connectivity.

SONET **synchronous transmission** offers the ability to directly access individual DS-0 and DS-1 channels. This provides a simple and effective means to achieve automated control over individual voice channels. Moreover, this control can take place in real time, providing true bandwidth-on-demand type capability. Synchronous multiplexing allows the high-speed transmission element within the multiplexer to observe and extract the lower-speed digital signals. This mode of operation enables add/drop time slot interchange multiplexing without bringing all the signals down to the digital signal 1 (DS-1) level.

3.9.1 SONET/SDH ring architecture

There are two categories of **SONET ring**:

- **Unidirectional Path-Switched Rings** (UPSR) – deployed in WANs; provides neighbor-to-neighbor traffic, shared protection (1:1).
- **Bidirectional Line-Switched Rings** (BLSR) – deployed in MANs; all traffic homing to central node, dedicated protection (1+1):
  - two-fiber Bidirectional-Line Switched Rings (BLSR2s);
  - four-fiber Bidirectional-Line Switched Rings (BLSR4s).

The ability to rapidly restore communications in the event of a node failure or fiber cut is achieved by designating half of the capacity of the ring as working capacity and the other half as protect capacity. When a failure occurs, affected traffic can still be switched to the protect capacity. It is possible to use the protect capacity of the ring to carry 'extra' traffic while the ring is in a normal (non-failure) operating mode. But the fact that this traffic will be completely pre-empted should a failure occur greatly limits the usefulness of this ability.

The SONET/SDH Bidirectional Line-Switched Ring (BLSR) delivers a scalable, highly reliable ring architecture with dual counter rotating rings with two unique paths per pair of interconnected nodes. As there are always two available paths, one is working (active), and the protect (secondary) is in standby mode.

SONET and Packet over SONET are further discussed with regard to optical switching in Part V.

3.10 Service level agreements

The network-wide **Service Level Agreements** (SLAs) that service providers strike with customers are becoming a key competitive differentiator among service offerings. SLAs can cover a certain level of service metrics for all customers as part of a base network service. They can also constitute customized contracts that guarantee more stringent metrics for which a customer is willing to pay a premium.

Delivering on SLAs becomes a technical challenge if the service provider is dealing with traffic that runs over disparate transports in its journey from point A to point B. For example, traffic might be prioritized in an IP network on the customer's premises using industry-standard Layer 3 IP precedence and then traverse an ATM with ATM's standard Layer 2 **Classes of Service** (CoS) in the carrier's WAN backbone.

For applications to perform well, network equipment must first be able to distinguish among packets generated by applications and users that require differentiated service. The equipment does this by looking at the IP precedence (for more details on IP see Part IV), a three-bit value in the **Type of Service** (ToS) byte in the IP version 4 (IPv4) packet header that can be used as a transmission preference indicator. When IP is running over a traditional WAN such as a leased line, IP Precedence is available for providing certain traffic with preferential treatment. A mapping function in IP-ATM CoS assigns an incoming IP packet with a given precedence value to an outgoing ATM permanent virtual circuit (PVC) so that priorities seamlessly traverse both IP and ATM infrastructures.

The IP-ATM CoS also supports per-PVC queuing. This means that instead of traffic forming a single queue to enter a PVC during a period of congestion, packets of different classes can line up in separate queues to enter the same PVC. Having separate queues allows traffic to be prioritized or to receive dedicated bandwidth within same PVC. The other option provided by this feature is to define separate PVCs for each traffic class. Each PVC, for example, could be designated to carry voice (highest priority), premium (mission-critical data), or best-effort traffic (lowest priority, such as Web traffic). Such service classes are often generically referred to as Gold, Silver, and Bronze, respectively.

SLAs are most attractive to customers if they constitute end-to-end guarantees. IP-ATM CoS functionality is imperative if Service Providers are to stick to their commitments to provide differentiated service classes for traffic that might traverse multiple transports with multiple prioritization schemes.

STANDARDS WATCH   **Summarized Standards watch**

The following standards and RFCs have been brought to your attention in this chapter:

ISO/IEC 3309:1993 *Information technology – Telecommunications and Information Exchange between Systems – High-level Data Link Control (HDLC) Procedures – Frame Structure*

ISO/IEC 7776:1995 *Information technology – Telecommunications and Information Exchange between Systems – High-level Data Link Control Procedures – Description of the X.25 LAPB-compatible DTE Data Link Procedures*

ITU-T Recommendation E.164/I.331 (05/97) *– The International Public Telecommunication Numbering Plan*

Recommendation I.330 (11/88) *– ISDN Numbering and Addressing Principles*

Recommendation I.370 (10/91) *– Congestion Management for the ISDN Frame Relaying Bearer Service*

Recommendation Q.930 (03/93) *– Digital Subscriber Signalling System No. 1 (DSS 1) – ISDN User-Network Interface Layer 3 – General Aspects*

Recommendation Q.931 (05/98) *– ISDN User-Network Interface Layer 3 Specification for Basic Call Control*

Recommendation X.3 (03/00) *– Packet Assembly/Disassembly Facility (PAD) in a Public Data Network*

Recommendation X.21 (09/92) *– Interface between Data Terminal Equipment and Data Circuit-terminating Equipment for Synchronous Operation on Public Data Networks*

Recommendation X.21 bis (11/88) *– Use on Public Data Networks of Data Terminal Equipment (DTE) which Is Designed for Interfacing to Synchronous V-Series Modems*

▶

Circuit-terminating *Equipment (DCE) for Terminals Operating in the Packet Mode and Connected to public Data Networks by Dedicated Circuit*

Recommendation X.25 (10/96) – *Interface between Data Terminal Equipment (DTE) and Data*

Recommendation X.28 (12/97) – *DTE/DCE Interface for a Start-Stop Mode Data Terminal Equipment Accessing the Packet Assembly/Disassembly Facility (PAD) in a Public Data Network Situated in the Same Country*

Recommendation X.29 (12/97) – *Procedures for the Exchange of Control Information and User Data between a Packet Assembly/Disassembly (PAD) Facility and a Packet Mode DTE or Another PAD*

Recommendation X.75 (10/96) – *Packet-Switched Signaling System between Public Networks Providing Data Transmission Services*

Recommendation Q.922 (02/92) – *ISDN Data Link Layer Specification for Frame Mode Bearer Services*

Recommendation Q.933 (10/95) – *Integrated Services Digital Network (ISDN) Digital Subscriber Signalling System No. 1 (DSS 1) – Signalling Specifications for Frame Mode Switched and Permanent Virtual Connection Control and Status Monitoring*

ANSI T1.606-1990 (R1996): *Telecommunications – Integrated Services Digital Network (ISDN) – Architectural Framework and Service Description for Frame-Relaying Bearer Service*

ANSI T1.617-1991 (R1997): *Telecommunications – Integrated Services Digital Network (ISDN) – Signaling Specification for Frame Relay Bearer Service for Digital Subscriber Signaling System Number 1 (DSS1)*

ANSI T1.618-1991 (R1997): *Telecommunications – Integrated Services Digital Network (ISDN) – Core Aspects of Frame Protocol for Use with Frame Relay Bearer Service*

ATM Forum LAN Emulation over ATM Version 2 – LNNI Specification, 1999

ATM Forum multiprotocol Over ATM Specification, Version 1.1, 1999

ATM Forum UNI Signaling 4.0, 1996

ATM Forum P-NNI V1.0, 1996

RFC 1570 PPP LCP Extensions, 1994 (Proposed Standard)

RFC 1661 Point-to-Point Protocol (PPP), 1994 (Standard)

RFC 1662 PPP in HDLC-like Framing, 1994 (Standard)

RFC 1663 PPP Reliable Transmission, 1994 (Proposed Standard)

RFC 1962 PPP Compression Control Protocol (CCP), 1996 (Proposed Standard)

RFC 1968 The PPP Encryption Control Protocol (ECP), 1996 (Proposed Standard)

RFC 1990 The PPP Multilink Protocol (MP), 1996 (Draft Standard)

RFC 1994 PPP Challenge Handshake Authentication Protocol (CHAP), 1996 (Draft Standard)

RFC 2125 The PPP Bandwidth Allocation Protocol (BAP) / The PPP Bandwidth Allocation Control Protocol (BACP), 1997 (Proposed Standard)

RFC 2153 PPP Vendor Extensions, 1997 (Informational)

RFC 2225 Classical IP and ARP over ATM (Proposed Standard)

RFC 2284 PPP Extensible Authentication Protocol, 1998 (Proposed Standard)

RFC 2332 NBMA Next Hop Resolution Protocol (NHRP), 1998 (Proposed Standard)

RFC 2484 PPP LCP Internationalization Configuration Option, 1999 (Proposed Standard)

RFC 2637 Point-to-Point Tunneling Protocol (PPTP), 1999 (Informational)

RFC 2661 Layer Two Tunneling Protocol (L2TP), 1999 (Proposed Standard)

RFC 2686 The Multi-Class Extension to Multi-Link PPP, 1999 (Proposed Standard)

RFC 2878 PPP Bridging Control Protocol (BCP), 2000 (Proposed Standard)

RFC 3070 Layer Two Tunneling Protocol (L2TP) over Frame Relay, 2001 (Proposed Standard)

C H A P T E R   4

![decorative bar]

Network management

The networking overview would be incomplete without at least briefly mentioning the position and importance of network management, especially in the more and more complex multivendor networking environment. However, there is no space to go into detail therefore we will just remind ourselves of the basic network management model, and the **two approaches to network management**:

- *de jure* standard – **Common Management Information Protocol**;
- *de facto* standard – **Simple Network Management Protocol**.

We started this Part with a definition of overall communication control performed at different layers of the network architecture. Here we get beyond controlling or managing just communications and concentrate more on complex network systems management.

It should be noted that today the interconnecting devices, switches and routers, would not be complete without sophisticated support to be managed, remotely and usually centrally, using various proprietary and common methods and management platforms. SNMP became a must, together with a support of **remote monitoring** (RMON) databases.

4.1 Distribution of management tasks

The management model recognizes two types of devices in the network: managers in the management stations and agents in the managed network hardware. Both managers and agents are implemented as pieces of software to support mutual communications for fulfilling various network management tasks. Generally **managers**, while looking after the agents, systematically poll them to find out their status. **Agents**, upon being asked, have to consult the repository of management information, the **Management Information Base** (MIB), where all the relevant managed objects in the form of records with values are contained (see Figure 4.1). MIB records and objects may be retrieved (*read*) or modified (*set*) by an authorized manager. Once the relevant response is found, the agent passes this information back to the manager, relying on it to perform further actions as necessary. Only in special cases will the agent initialize the management action by telling the manager that something important (usually wrong) is happening, and the event triggers an alarm. The way managers and agents communicate is governed by the **management protocol**.

FIGURE 4-1 Manager and agent collaboration on network management

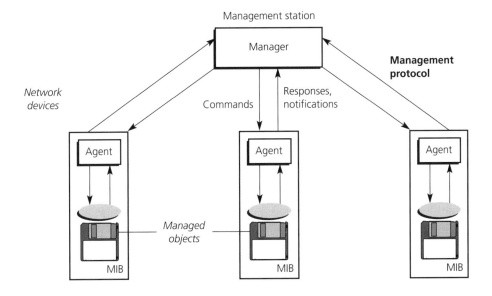

4.2 ISO network management model

The OSI network management model developed as an international *de jure* standard by the ISO divides the complex task of management into five conceptual **areas**:

■ **Fault management** – to detect, log, notify users of, and (to the extent possible) automatically isolate and, if possible, fix network problems in order to keep the network running effectively. Because faults can cause downtime or unacceptable network degradation, fault management is perhaps the most widely implemented of the ISO network management elements.

■ **Configuration management** – to monitor network and system configuration information so that the effects on network operation of various versions of hardware and software elements can be tracked and managed. Because all hardware and software elements have operational quirks, flaws, or both that might affect network operation, such information is important to maintaining a smooth-running network.

■ **Accounting management** – to measure network utilization parameters so that individual or group uses of the network can be regulated appropriately. Such regulation minimizes network problems (because network resources can be apportioned out based on resource capacities) and maximizes the fairness of network access across all users.

■ **Performance management** – to measure and make available various aspects of network performance so that internetwork performance can be maintained at an acceptable level. Examples of performance variables that might be provided include network throughput, user response times, and line utilization.

■ **Security management** – to control access to network resources according to local guidelines so that the network cannot be sabotaged (intentionally or unintentionally) and sensitive information cannot be accessed by those without appropriate authorization. For example, a security management subsystem can monitor users logging on to a network resource, refusing access to those who enter inappropriate access codes, optionally triggering an alarm at the management station. Besides port locking (as an example), security breaches are generally monitored at different levels at the management station. Highly sensitive networks, such as banking and in the military, require immediate action of management staff upon detected breaches.

STANDARDS WATCH	OSI network management

ISO/IEC 7498-4:1989 **Information Processing Systems – Open Systems Interconnection – Basic Reference Model – Part 4: Management Framework**

ISO/IEC 9596-x:1991 **Information Technology – Open Systems Interconnection – Common Management Information Protocol**

ISO/IEC 10040:1992 **Information Technology – Open Systems Interconnection – Systems Management Overview**

ISO/IEC 10165-x:1992-6 **Information Technology – Open Systems Interconnection – Management Information Services – Structure of Management Information**

ITU-T **X.700** series of recommendations

The OSI defines the **Common Management Information Protocol** (CMIP), an application layer protocol, as a way of communication between manager and agent, and **Common Management Information Services** (CMIS) to support the above mentioned management areas. It completes the definition of the management system by defining the **Structure of Management Information** (SMI) and various network management **functions**. All pieces of OSI network management are standardized in ISO and ITU-T (X.700 series recommendations).

SNAPSHOT   **Five management problem areas:**

FCAPS = fault, configuration, accounting, performance, security.

Despite its nowadays complete standardization, CMIP has not been widely accepted and deployed, and is superseded by the *de facto* standard of the Internet community, SNMP, which is simpler yet effectively operational.

4.3 TCP/IP network management

The Internet community responded to management needs by using the same basic management model while deploying a far simpler management protocol, **Simple Network Management Protocol** (SNMP). Particularly due to its simplicity it has became the preferred choice of network management implementations today. Although the initial *de facto* standards for SNMP (RFC 1157 from 1990) as well as related SMI (RFC 1155) and MIB (RFC 1213) have undergone serious revisions, namely SNMP v2, the initial version is still a valid standard for TCP/IP networks. Probably only the next version of the protocol, SNMP v3, will stand a chance of replacing the 'traditional' SNMP.

RFC WATCH   **SNMP**

RFC 1157 **Simple Network Management Protocol (SNMP)**, 1990 (Standard)

RFC 1213 **Management Information Base for Network Management of TCP/IP-based internets: MIB-II**, 1991 (updated by RFC 2011, RFC 2012, RFC 2013) (Standard)

RFC 1906 **Transport Mappings for Version 2 of the Simple Network Management Protocol (SNMPv2)**, 1996 (Draft Standard)

RFC 2011 **SNMPv2 Management Information Base for the Internet Protocol using SMIv2**, 1996 (Proposed Standard)

RFC 2012 **SNMPv2 Management Information Base for the Transmission Control Protocol using SMIv2**, 1996 (Proposed Standard)

RFC 2013 **SNMPv2 Management Information Base for the User Datagram Protocol using SMIv2**, 1996 (Proposed Standard)

RFC 2571 **An Architecture for Describing SNMP Management Frameworks**, 1999 (Draft Standard)

▶

RFC 2572 **Message Processing and Dispatching for the Simple Network Management Protocol (SNMP)**, 1999 (Draft Standard)

RFC 2573 **SNMP Applications**, 1999 (Draft Standard)

RFC 2574 **User-based Security Model (USM) for version 3 of the Simple Network Management Protocol (SNMPv3)**, 1999 (Draft Standard)

RFC 2576 **Coexistence between Version 1, Version 2, and Version 3 of the Internet-standard Network Management Framework**, 2000 (Proposed Standard).

SNMP, as opposed to CMIP, puts the emphasis on the managers' part allowing for agents to be implemented virtually on every device in the internet (due to memory and processing requirements). It does not support the number of various functions defined in the OSI framework, only several simple operations and messages: *get, get-next, set, trap*. For managed object description it uses an **abstract syntax** which is a subset of Abstract Syntax Notation One (ASN.1) and for **coding** a subset of Basic Encoding Rules (BER), both defined as part of OSI. **Managed objects** can be scalar (meaning that there is always exactly one instance) or tabular (meaning that there may be zero, one, or more instances). A MIB is depicted as a **tree**, with individual data items as leaves. Object identifiers uniquely identify MIB objects in the tree.

The major problem with SNMP is not the limited number of operations supported but the lack of **authentication** facilities to allow only an authorized entity to manage the network devices. This will be its core improvement in any future approved *de facto* standard.

4.4 Remote monitoring – RMON

Remote monitoring (RMON), specified in RFC 2819 (standard, RMON version 1) and RFC 2021 (proposed standard, RMON version 2), supports data collection on the current status of the local network. It uses a model similar to the one we saw above but simplified to probes designed for collecting the data. RMON2 probes will send a stream of information on the application activity to the management console which may help monitor the network but also will increase the traffic. RMON still supports Ethernet and Token Ring networks through 9 and 10 MIB groups, respectively.

Remote network monitoring devices, often called monitors or probes, are instruments that exist for the purpose of managing a network. Often these remote probes are standalone devices and devote significant internal resources for the sole purpose of managing a network. An organization may employ many of these devices, one per network segment, to manage its internet. In addition, these devices may be used for a network management service provider to access a client network, often geographically remote.

RFC WATCH — remote monitoring

RFC 2021 **Remote Network Monitoring Management Information Base Version 2 using SMIv2**, 1997 (Proposed Standard)

RFC 2819 **Remote Network Monitoring Management Information Base**, 2000 (Standard)

RFC 2895 **Remote Network Monitoring MIB Protocol Identifier Reference**, 2000 (Proposed Standard)

RFC 2896 **Remote Network Monitoring MIB Protocol Identifier Macros**, 2000 (Informational)

The **goals of remote network management** are manifold (RFC 2613):

- **Offline operation** – there are sometimes conditions when a management station will not be in constant contact with its remote monitoring devices. This is sometimes by design in an attempt to lower communications costs (especially when communicating over a WAN or dialup link), or by accident as network failures affect the communications between the management station and the probe. For this reason, this MIB allows a probe to be configured to perform diagnostics and to collect statistics continuously, even when communication with the management station may not be possible or efficient. The probe may then attempt to notify the management station when an exceptional condition occurs. Thus, even in circumstances where communication between management station and probe is not continuous, fault, performance, and configuration information may be continuously accumulated and communicated to the management station conveniently and efficiently.

- **Proactive monitoring** – given the resources available on the monitor, it is potentially helpful for it to continuously run diagnostics and to log network performance. The monitor is always available at the onset of any failure. It can notify the management station of the failure and can store historical statistical information about the failure. This historical information can be played back by the management station in an attempt to perform further diagnosis into the cause of the problem.

- **Problem detection and reporting** – the monitor can be configured to recognize conditions, most notably error conditions, and to continuously check for them. When one of these conditions occurs, the event may be logged and management stations may be notified in a number of ways.

- **Value-added data** – because a remote monitoring device represents a network resource dedicated exclusively to network management functions, and because it is located directly on the monitored portion of the network, the remote network monitoring device has the opportunity to add significant value to the data it collects. For instance, by highlighting those hosts on the network that generate the most traffic or errors, the probe can give the management station precisely the information it needs to solve a class of problems.

■ **Multiple managers** – an organization may have multiple management stations for different units of the organization, for different functions (e.g. engineering and operations), and in an attempt to provide disaster recovery. Because environments with multiple management stations are common, the remote network monitoring device has to deal with more than one management station, potentially using its resources concurrently.

4.5 Switch monitoring – SMON

Remote monitoring for **switched networks** requires an extension to the standard RMON, because switches differ from standard shared media protocols:

■ Data is not, in general, broadcast. This may be caused by the switch architecture or by the connection-oriented nature of the data. This means, therefore, that monitoring non-broadcast traffic needs to be considered.

■ Monitoring the multiple entry and exit points from a switching device requires a vast amount of resources – memory and CPU, and aggregation of the data in logical packets of information, determined by the application needs.

■ Switching incorporates logical segmentation such as Virtual LANs (VLANs).

■ Switching incorporates packet prioritization.

■ Data across the switch fabric can be in the form of cells. Like RMON, SMON is only concerned with the monitoring of packets.

> QUICK TIP **switch monitoring**
>
> For switched networks an RMON extension – **SMON** – is used for **port mirroring** and **VLAN statistics** collection.

LAN switches use RMON probes for collecting statistics on switch ports and generating alerts concerning the ports. The most complex monitoring involves passing the probe from one port to another, so-called port mirroring, for better single port monitoring. **Switch Monitoring** (SMON), proposed standard, RFC 2613 unifies the way port (or port group) **mirroring** is achieved and also provides for **steering** traffic to remote monitor. Besides, SMON helps identify VLAN frames according to the IEEE 802.1p and Q, and collect statistics data based on their priorities. The SMON MIB uses 64-bit counters for statistics collection as opposed to RMON with 32-bit counters.

RFC WATCH | switch monitoring

RFC 2613 **Remote Network Monitoring MIB Extensions for Switched Networks Version 1.0**, 1999 (Proposed Standard)

4.6 Web-based management

The current trend in network management is influenced by the increased use of WWW facilities and its browsers. **Web-based configuration and management** of individual devices seems to have become even more (Internet) user-friendly. It is aimed at managers of small networks who may not have their own network management system. These users want to configure and monitor the devices in their networks as easily as possible, and perhaps even gain some remote device management capabilities. What these users need is out-of-the-box device configuration tools using a Web browser. This is accomplished by providing the equipment to be configured with an agent that includes a native HTML interface. The manager then enters basic configuration parameters for each device by completing a simple online electronic form. Remote monitoring of simple device statistics can also be possible via the browser, using tabular and later graphical displays of basic device information and performance. Through a common Web browser running on any PC or laptop in the organization, the user can access the necessary application and continue the troubleshooting process, regardless of their location, while reducing the time and effort required to do the job.

Web-based management agents can be activated on some routers and switches, but are only suited to small networks that are managed *ad hoc*. Security breaches are possible and should be tightly controlled. Larger networks are managed through a mix of network-node-manager, template-driven generation of configurations from database data, etc. Manual intervention is not the normal mode of operations here (except for emergency fixes). Web-based tools are used to present the user with statistics, e.g. graphical or textual.

STANDARDS WATCH | Summarized Standards watch

The following standards and RFCs have been brought to your attention in this chapter:

ISO/IEC 7498-4:1989 *Information Processing Systems – Open Systems Interconnection – Basic Reference Model – Part 4: Management Framework*

ISO/IEC 9596-x:1991 *Information Technology – Open Systems Interconnection – Management Information Protocol*

ISO/IEC 10040:1992 *Information Technology – Open Systems Interconnection – Systems Management Overview*

ISO/IEC 10165-x:1992-6 *Information Technology – Open Systems Interconnection – Management Information Services – Structure of Management Information*

ITU-T X.700 series of recommendations

RFC 1157 *Simple Network Management Protocol (SNMP)*, 1990 (Standard)

RFC 1213 *Management Information Base for Network Management of TCP/IP-based Internets: MIB-II*, 1991 (updated by RFC2011, RFC2012, RFC2013) (Standard)

RFC 1906 *Transport Mappings for Version 2 of the Simple Network Management Protocol (SNMPv2)*, 1996 (Draft Standard)

RFC 2011 *SNMPv2 Management Information Base for the Internet Protocol using SMIv2*, 1996 (Proposed Standard)

RFC 2012 SNMPv2 *Management Information Base for the Transmission Control Protocol using SMIv2*, 1996 (Proposed Standard)

RFC 2013 SNMPv2 *Management Information Base for the User Datagram Protocol using SMIv2*, 1996 (Proposed Standard)

RFC 2021 *Remote Network Monitoring Management Information Base Version 2 using SMIv2*, 1997 (Proposed Standard)

RFC 2571 *An Architecture for Describing SNMP Management Frameworks*, 1999 (Draft Standard)

RFC 2572 *Message Processing and Dispatching for the Simple Network Management Protocol (SNMP)*, 1999 (Draft Standard)

RFC 2573 *SNMP Applications*, 1999 (Draft Standard)

RFC 2574 *User-based Security Model (USM) for Version 3 of the Simple Network Management Protocol (SNMPv3)*, 1999 (Draft Standard)

RFC 2576 *Coexistence between Version 1, Version 2, and Version 3 of the Internet-standard Network Management Framework*, 2000 (Proposed Standard)

RFC 2613 *Remote Network Monitoring MIB Extensions for Switched Networks Version 1.0*, 1999 (Proposed Standard)

RFC 2819 *Remote Network Monitoring Management Information Base*, 2000 (Standard)

RFC 2895 *Remote Network Monitoring MIB Protocol Identifier Reference*, 2000 (Proposed Standard)

RFC 2896 *Remote Network Monitoring MIB Protocol Identifier Macros*, 2000 (Informational)

CHAPTER 5

Principles of network interconnection

In the previous chapters we have discussed and reviewed individual network technologies without emphasizing their mutual relationships and possibilities to interconnect them. As this book is dedicated to two leading internetworking technologies and their combinations and convergence, we have to move forward and spend some time with the internetworking basics.

Internetworking devices offer communication between local area network segments, and between LANs and WANs. **Interworking functions** (IWF) between networks are performed by a separate device, the **interworking unit** (IWU), or may be integrated in network nodes. The standalone devices can be differentiated generally by the OSI layer at which they establish the connection between network segments. The OSI calls all types of interconnection devices simply **(N-layer) relays,** but we will distinguish between them in what follows according to the common denotations.

There are four primary types of internetworking devices, which will be described later:

- **repeaters**;
- **bridges** and **switches**;
- **routers**;
- **gateways**.

As we will concentrate on bridging, switching, and routing later in Parts II, III, and IV, respectively, in this chapter more space will be given to the other interconnecting devices, repeaters, and gateways.

5.1 Physical layer interconnection devices

On the lowest, physical layer operate several devices which are used to interconnect individual stations of a single LAN or two segments with a number of nodes attached to them. It should be noted that while some other interconnection devices may interface with WAN links, repeaters serve exclusively LAN environment.

All the devices described in the following have several characteristics in common which result from the layer they operate at (see Figure 5.1):

FIGURE 5-1 Physical layer relay architecture

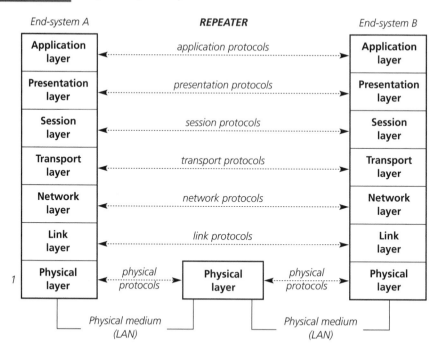

- **regenerate the signal** from one cable segment to the next;
- **do not make any decisions** based on the received signal or perform any error-checking;

- do not understand anything above the physical layer (namely any type of addressing);
- have **limited intelligence**.

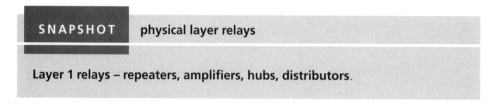

SNAPSHOT physical layer relays

Layer 1 relays – repeaters, amplifiers, hubs, distributors.

Repeaters enable the network to be extended by increasing the overall distance between communicating stations and thus allowing more network nodes. The latter reason was the main concern before the advent of MAC bridging: a limitation on the number of workstations that can be physically attached to a single network. While a maximum of hundreds of stations per segment is generally not a severe limiting factor, a maximum, for example, of 1024 stations in the entire network in Ethernet may cause problems, particularly in large enterprise networks.

Repeaters introduce minor **delays** in transmission that, coupled with propagation delays on the cable itself, can adversely affect access. **Design constraints** are imposed on LANs relating to the number of repeaters and the number of cable segments (see Chapter 2).

Using repeaters provides a great deal of **flexibility in wiring** even within the largest buildings, but one must remember that repeaters connect segments and links of the same network. All signals are **broadcast** on all segments and links through all repeaters.

5.1.1 Repeater types

The common physical-layer devices differ mostly only by the names used in relation to a specific LAN environment.

Repeaters or **amplifiers** simply extend the distance a signal can be driven within a single network. Once common in the traditional IEEE 10Base5 'thick' and 10Base2 'thin' Ethernet environments, standalone repeaters are rarely seen today. 10Base-T twisted-pair Ethernets are constructed on a hierarchical **hub** principle in which each hub is an active multiport repeater or **concentrator**. The hub thus replicates a traditional cable-based (e.g. Ethernet coax cable) shared LAN by replacing the common cable with a single shared media backplane. All data transmitted by any user attached to the hub are then broadcast across that backplane. In the token-passing ring, instead, each station in the ring provides a repeater function rebroadcasting signals to the next station.

QUICK TIP   **Ethernet rule for repeaters**

10 Mbps Ethernet – '5-4-3' rule limits the overall number of five segments interconnected by four repeaters while only three segments are inhabited by stations and the others are inter-repeater links.

Repeaters have evolved from standalone, single-segment devices designed simply to connect a fixed number of users to the same LAN. They are now sophisticated, scalable devices that are stackable, segmentable, or both:

- **stackable** repeater – allow more users to be added to the workgroup. When placed one atop the other and joined to the same inter-repeater bus, these scalable devices count as a single logical repeater. All stations connected to the stack share the same bandwidth. A set of stackable hubs effectively act as a single backplane, i.e. as if that set were a single repeater. However, there are physical constraints about the number of stackable repeater hubs.
- **segmentable** repeater – capable of subdividing the workgroup into smaller collision domains. These separate LAN segments share data when they are interconnected via switches or routers.

No buffering is supported with traditional repeaters, nor is full-duplex communication supported (as only two stations could be connected to a segment).

5.1.2 Collisions and auto partition in Ethernet/IEEE 802.3 LANs

For CSMA/CD, since the repeater physically separates the two coaxial segments, a collision on one segment could not be seen by devices on the other segment connected to the repeater. Therefore, the repeater is responsible for ensuring that the collision signal is propagated to all segments attached to it. To force a collision, the repeater sends out a jam signal to all segments attached to it to notify all stations on the network that a collision has occurred.

When the repeater detects 32 consecutive collisions on one port it will logically turn off or segment the port that it detected the problem on, thus allowing the rest of the network to function properly. When the repeater detects a collision on the segmented port, the collision will not be forwarded to the other segments of the network, leaving the port in segmented condition. When the repeater receives data on a good port, it attempts to transmit it to the segmented port. If the data transmits successfully, the repeater will turn the segmented port back on, bringing it out of segmentation.

5.1.3 Repeater development

With continuous development of IEEE 802.3, namely 100 Mbps and 1 Gbps versions, new repeater categories appeared.

Repeaters in **Fast Ethernet** are divided into two classes by the 100Base-TX standard. The difference between these Class I and Class II repeaters is the method each uses to handle received signals for transmission. The different techniques result in different rules of configuration for a Fast Ethernet network.

QUICK TIP   **repeaters in Fast Ethernet**

Fast Ethernet – one **Class I repeater** or two **Class II repeaters** allowed in a collision domain.

Class I repeaters receive the 100Base-TX electrical signal on one interface and translate that signal from its electrical form into a digital series, much the same way that a Fast Ethernet station receives a transmission. The Class I repeater then generates a new signal on each of its interfaces using the translated digital series for other Fast Ethernet physical types. The Class I repeater does not make any decisions based on the received signal, nor does it perform any error checking. The translation of the received signal is intended to improve the strength and validity of the repeated Fast Ethernet frame and allows different media to be interconnected which may be used for Fast Ethernet.

The **Class II repeater** receives and immediately repeats each received transmission without performing any translation. The repeating process is a simple electrical duplication and strengthening of the signal and can be used for interconnecting similar Fast Ethernet media.

Gigabit Ethernet in respect of the high speed it supports uses not only common half-duplex repeaters but introduces a brand new device which is half way between hubs and switches. The Full-Duplex Repeater (FDR) **buffered distributor** achieves switch-like performance while maintaining the cost and ease-of-use advantages of a shared hub. Like a switch, the FDR provides maximum throughput with full-duplex ports, frame forwarding in a non-collision environment, and congestion control, while allowing simultaneous acceptance of frames which can be buffered before further transmission. It ensures fair allocation of bandwidth among all ports with a fair round-robin forwarding mechanism. As opposed to a switch it does not perform address filtering.

QUICK TIP	repeaters in Gigabit Ethernet

Gigabit Ethernet – buffered distributor as full-duplex repeater.

The FDR aimed at workgroup environments, especially many-to-one networks. It can be used to supercharge high-end desktops, computer clusters, server farms, and transaction servers. The FDR can also be used as a gigabit port-expander to add more gigabit ports to the switch. FDR delivers switch performance at hub prices while having more sophisticated facilities to offer:

■ MAC frames are checked before forwarding.

■ Frames may be buffered which allows for error checking.

■ Each of the ports can provide traffic at a rate equal to the maximum rate of the shared bus.

■ Flow control is deployed which ensures that no frame is dropped (compliant with IEEE 802.3x see 7.4.3).

■ A fair allocation of bandwidth is provided for every station to have equal access to network, based on latency control, especially with delay-sensitive traffic in mind. The frame forwarder implements a simple and effective round-robin algorithm to determine which port may transmit onto the bus. The frame forwarder starts at the distributor's Port 1 and checks to see if a frame is in the buffer. If a frame is available, the port becomes active, one frame is transmitted, and the forwarder then moves on to the next port. If a frame is not available at the next port, the forwarder does not activate that port, and immediately moves on to the next port. The frame forwarder takes only one frame from a port at a time in order to ensure data from each port is treated fairly. This feature enables the FDR to shape traffic, therefore avoiding 'packet clumping,' which results in a jittered data stream. This feature, which is not even found on many switches today, is important for delay-sensitive traffic such as video.

Installation and maintenance of repeaters is easy compared with the more intelligent devices we will concentrate upon in the following section.

5.2 Link layer relays

Devices operating at the link layer, the second lowest layer of the OSI reference model (see Figure 5.2), offer features over repeaters which are derived from the information the link layer is dealing with. They commonly:

FIGURE 5-2 Link layer relay architecture

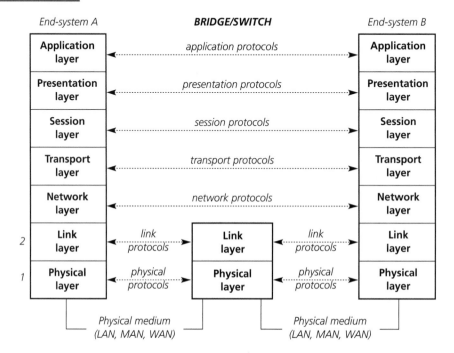

- forward or filter **frames**;
- base their decisions on **physical** (MAC) **addresses** of incoming frames and their address table(s);
- provide **error handling** and specific **flow control**;
- perform tasks related to **media access methods**;
- support **multiprotocol environment** (are network protocol transparent).

Initially only a single type of device was used to interconnect LANs, a **bridge**. Later another unit, the **switch**, was added to LAN operation to avoid problems with shared media by allowing dedicated bandwidth to network segments or even individual stations.

5.2.1 Bridging

Bridges became commercially available in the early 1980s. At the time of their introduction, bridges connected and enabled frame forwarding only between homogeneous local networks. More recently, bridging between different networks has also been defined and standardized, including the possibility to connect WAN links to bridges as transmission media (bridging is described in detail in Part II).

Some years ago bridges became less preferable than repeaters in comparison with newer routers and currently are not widely used for their pure basic functionality, but are rather enhanced by sophisticated filtering, pseudo-intelligent path selection, and high throughput rates.

Bridges are not complicated devices. They analyze incoming frames, make forwarding decisions based on information contained in the frames, and forward the frames toward the destination. In some cases (for example, source-route bridging), the entire path to the destination is contained in each frame. In other cases (for example, transparent bridging), frames are forwarded one hop at a time toward the destination. Bridges support the single frame processing mode, **store-and-forward**.

Network layer protocol transparency is a primary advantage of bridging. Because bridges operate at the link layer, they are not required to examine upper-layer information. This means that they can rapidly forward traffic representing any network-layer protocol. It is not uncommon for a bridge to support AppleTalk, DECnet, TCP/IP, XNS, and other traffic at the same time.

Bridges support two methods of **traffic filtering**:

- **inherent** – based on their address tables (in case of transparent bridging) which allows for keeping traffic local when source and destination stations are beyond the same bridge interface. This segments the bridged network and eliminates unnecessary traffic reaching other (uninterested) segments;

- **explicit** – dictated by configured filtering rules based on MAC addresses and protocol types in incoming frames (mostly for security reasons).

Bridges have a further important impact on the network because they act as a **firewall** for some potentially damaging network errors by error checking which is not carried out at the regular physical layer relays. Each frame, before it is forwarded, is always error checked.

Bridges **extend the size** of the network in terms of the physical span of a LAN and the number of nodes attached to a single network, as they segment the network into collision domains while creating one large broadcast domain.

Bridges and WAN connections

Besides **local bridges** which provide a direct connection between multiple LAN segments in the same area, remote bridges connect multiple LAN segments in different areas, usually over WAN links. **Remote bridging** presents several unique internetworking challenges. One of these is the difference between LAN and WAN speeds. Although several fast WAN technologies are now establishing a presence in geographically dispersed internets, LANs are often an order of magnitude faster than WAN speeds. Vastly different LAN and WAN speeds sometimes prevent users from running delay-sensitive LAN applications over the WAN.

Remote bridges cannot improve WAN speeds, but can compensate for speed discrepancies through sufficient buffering capability. If a LAN device capable of a Mbps transmission rate wishes to communicate with a device on a remote LAN, the local bridge must regulate the Mbps data stream so that it does not overwhelm the kbps serial link. This is done by storing the incoming data in onboard buffers and sending it over the serial link at a rate the serial link can accommodate. This can be achieved only for short bursts of data that do not overwhelm the bridge's buffering capability.

MAC and LLC bridges

Bridging between similar LAN media can be performed at the MAC sublayer. MAC bridges are the simplest bridges deployed and are of two types:

- **transparent bridges** (learning bridges) – used to interconnect Ethernet LANs, these are fully responsible for deciding how to handle a frame (create and maintain address table), and are transparent to end stations;
- **source-route bridges** – used to interconnect Token Ring LANs, such bridges only support forwarding based on the information contained in the frame (they do not keep any address table), while source station is responsible for finding the path to the destination and for inserting path information into its frame.

QUICK TIP   **easy bridging**

Bridges work efficiently when interconnecting **homogeneous networks** at Layer 2:

- Transparent bridges between Ethernet segments.
- Source-route bridges between Token Ring segments.

Should **heterogeneous** networks be interconnected by using a bridge, a MAC sublayer would not be enough as it differs and a **translation** between the environments needs to be provided. Therefore the LLC sublayer also gets involved. (We identify this as translational bridging which performs translation between the formats and transit principles of different media types.) How to bridge in mixed Ethernet and Token Ring environments and the issues to be taken into account are described in detail in Part II. It should be noted that a bridge's translation between networks of different types is never perfect because it is likely that one network will support certain frame fields and protocol functions not supported by the other network.

QUICK TIP   **complex bridging**

Interconnecting **heterogeneous networks** at Layer 2 requires **translational bridges**.

Broadcast domains

In a transparently bridged network, when a frame arrives in a bridge with an unknown destination address, the bridge will broadcast the same frame on all of its ports (except the one through which it was received). This is a very clever action as the bridge believes that the destination station exists somewhere in the bridged network, only it does not know (so far) where exactly. This event is unavoidable especially while bridges start dynamic learning of the addresses of active attached stations. Although their operations initially increases the bridged traffic, it is the only way to start and keep the network running. As the bridge learns, this situation should (almost) disappear.

We saw above that bridges segment the network to keep unnecessary traffic local. However, they still support only a **single broadcast domain**. Once a broadcast frame (with a destination broadcast MAC address) arrives on its port, the bridge will copy the frame on all the other ports. Thus the broadcast frame will shortly get into every corner in the network. Although true broadcast storms should be avoided by eliminating loops in the bridged network topology, broadcast frames permeating the whole network have an impact on the performance. The bridge typically deals with multicast frames in a similar way – it copies them onto all output ports.

To avoid loops in a bridged domain creating the potential for uncontrollable broadcast storms, the **spanning tree protocol** (STP, IEEE 802.1D) is used. It is covered extensively in Part II dedicated to bridging.

QUICK TIP   **segmenting with bridges**

Bridges segment networks into **collision domains**, but work within a single **broadcast domain**.

5.2.2 *LAN switches*

LAN switching is a form of Layer 2 bridging that delivers full LAN bandwidth to each port where the LAN segment (segment switches) or single station is attached (desktop switches or private switches). Like all link-layer schemes, LAN switching by itself cannot establish broadcast and security firewalls. This limitation makes it primarily a tool for local workgroups. In fact, LAN switching has not been developed primarily to interconnect local networks but rather to overcome the performance bottlenecks of shared LANs.

LAN switching improves **performance** by offering scalable bandwidth without the need for major network changes, modifying end stations, or scrapping existing investment in equipment. Switches eliminate backbone congestion because they provide high-speed pipes to clustered server farms and access to other campus locations. The main reasons for implementing LAN switching are the dedicated bandwidth for each connection, higher aggregate bandwidth, more refined management of connection procedures, faster access, and greater flexibility.

A LAN switch is actually a **multiport bridge** that simply forwards frames from a LAN segment on one port to another one on a different port. The forwarding decision is based on the destination MAC address at the header of the MAC frame. A switch will ignore a frame that is destined for a node located on the same port as the source node. Switches make their forwarding decisions based on link layer information.

SNAPSHOT	LAN switch

LAN switch – multiport **bridge**.

LAN switches share the following characteristics with (namely transparent) bridges, besides those relevant to all link-layer interconnecting devices:

- they **learn** the MAC addresses and accordingly modify their **address** (decision) **table**;
- they **interconnect similar media**;
- they **do not modify received frames** during processing;
- they create a **single broadcast domain**.

LAN switches differ from bridges in the following ways:

- they offer various **frame processing modes** (at a minimum, cut-through, and store-and-forward);
- they provide for LAN **segmentation**;
- they allow for **virtual LAN** creation;
- they **do not connect to WANs**.

LAN switching is described in detail in Part III.

5.3 Network layer relays

Routing is the main function of the network layer, so devices operating at the network layer and comprising the lowest three layers of the protocol architecture (see Figure 5.3), are now commonly called **routers**. In the Internet community they were formerly referred to as gateways but this ambiguous title has disappeared. (Routing is discussed in detail in Part IV.)

FIGURE 5-3   Network layer relay architecture

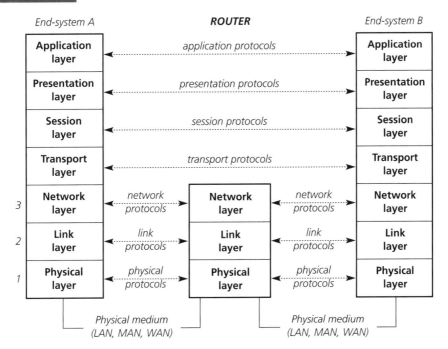

SNAPSHOT   **network layer relays**

Layer 3 internetworking device – router (formerly called a gateway in the Internet community).

In OSI parlance the N-relay is titled the **intermediate system** (which is also used in the OSI routing protocols). In accordance with ISO/IEC 8648 (1987) and 10028 (1993), the internal structure for the functions of an N-relay entity is shown in Figure 5.4.

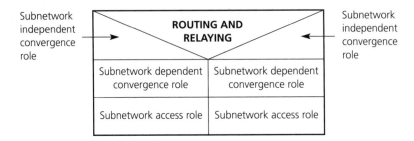

FIGURE 5-4   Internal structure for the functions of an N-relay entity

Routers share the following main characteristics:

- they create a true **internet** by the interconnection of network segments (networks or subnets);
- they process **packets** (datagrams);
- they base forwarding decisions on the destination **network** (logical) **address** of an incoming packet, comparing it with the routing table;
- they provide **link and network layer functions** including error handling, flow control, etc.;
- they are **transparent to physical media** attached (while performing the tasks of link-layer encapsulation and decapsulation), and interconnect LANs, MANs, and WANs;
- they are **dependent on network protocol**;
- they provide a **connectionless** (datagram) **service** between networks;
- they act as **broadcast firewalls** limiting the broadcast packet propagation through the Internet and eliminating broadcast storms, i.e. they segment the network into broadcast domains;
- they support **network security** through packet and routing information filtering (to the extreme of hiding private networks from the Internet);
- they interconnect LANs (similar or dissimilar), and LANs to WANs.

The topic of routing has been covered in computer science for over two decades, while the first analytical model for routing problems in data communications networks was proposed as early as 1962 by Kleinrock. However, routing only achieved commercial popularity in the mid-1980s. The primary reason for this time lag was the nature of networks in the 1970s. During this time, networks were fairly simple, homogeneous environments. Only recently has large-scale internetworking become popular.

5.3.1 Routing operation

Routing involves two basic activities (see Figure 5.5):

FIGURE 5-5 Path determination and packet forwarding

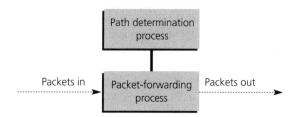

- **determination of optimal routing path**(s);
- **forwarding packets** through an internet (internal forwarding from ingoing interface to outgoing one(s) is called **switching**).

Switching is relatively straightforward. Path determination, on the other hand, can be very complex unless eliminated by manually configured static routes.

Path determination

To choose between existing paths to the destination network (if more than one exists) certain criteria are used. The criterion or criteria are called **metrics**, or standards of measurement, and are used by routing algorithms to determine the optimal path to a destination. Routers compare metrics to determine the optimal routes. Metrics differ depending on the design of the routing algorithm being used.

To aid the process of path determination, routing algorithms initialize and maintain **routing tables** which contain route information. Route information varies depending on the routing algorithm used. **Routing algorithms** fill routing tables with a variety of information. Destination/next hop associations tell a router that a particular destination can be gained optimally by sending the packet to a particular router representing the 'next hop' on the way to the final destination. When a router receives an incoming packet, it checks the destination address and attempts to associate this address with the next hop.

Routers need to communicate with one another to be able to create and maintain their routing tables. This communication is allowed by a variety of **routing protocols** supporting different network protocols. Routing protocol communication consists of a variety of messages, namely routing update messages or link-state advertisements. **Routing updates** generally consist of all or a portion of a routing table. By analyzing routing updates from all routers, a router can build a detailed picture of the network topology. **Link-state advertisements** inform other routers of the state of the sender's links. Link information can also be used to build a complete picture of network topology. Once the network topology is understood, routers can determine optimal routes to network destinations.

Forwarding packets

When a router receives a packet on its incoming interface, it actually receives the raw stream of bits in the physical layer. It then passes these for processing to the link layer which decapsulates the frame, i.e. takes away the link layer control information to perform an error check. Only after the link layer passes the decapsulated 'data' to the adjacent network layer as a packet may the process of path determination start, based on the destination station network address.

In the case where no general broadcast is involved, or the destination station does not sit in the network behind the incoming router's port, the path is found through the routing table look-up. After the outgoing port of the router is determined, the packet (without any change to network address fields) is passed down to the link layer responsible for operations relevant to the particular connection. Besides performing the functions pertinent to the media access control (LANs) or signaling (WANs), the packet has to be properly encapsulated here in the relevant frame.

It also means that the router must deploy some mechanism to resolve the mapping between the network and link layer addresses (logical and physical). When involving only LAN interconnections, the source physical address is the router's port address (MAC) while the destination physical address of a frame is either the destination station physical address itself (if the station is on the segment directly connected to the router), or the physical address of the next hop (the neighbor router's incoming port). We will see in Part III how to link or map physical and logical addresses differs from one network architecture to another.

When we mix together LANs and WANs, the 'border' router (interfacing WAN) has an even more difficult task. In this case, when a path across the WAN is found to the next hop behind the WAN, it has to map the network address of the neighbor to the address which is comprehensible to the WAN (X.121 address with X.25, E.164 number with ISDN, DLCI with Frame Relay, or VPI/VCI with ATM), and is either globally significant or understandable only to the local switch.

> **QUICK TIP**   **forwarding packets**
>
> **Forwarding packets** also involves **encapsulation/decapsulation** of frames and physical to logical **address mapping**.

Forwarding or switching algorithms are relatively simple, and are basically the same for many routing protocols. In most cases, they operate as follows. A host (often called an end system in routing literature) determines that it must send a packet to another host. Having acquired a router's address by some means, the source host sends a packet addressed specifically to a router's physical (MAC-layer) address, but with the protocol (network-layer) address of the destination host.

Upon examining the packet's destination protocol address, the router determines that it either knows or does not know how to forward the packet to the 'next hop.' In the latter case (where the router does not know how to forward the packet), the packet is typically dropped. In the former case, the router sends the packet to the next hop by changing the destination physical address to that of the next hop and transmitting the packet.

The next hop may or may not be the ultimate destination host. If not, the next hop is usually another router, which executes the same switching decision process. As the packet moves through the internetwork, its physical address changes, but its protocol address remains constant.

5.3.2 Router vs. switch – what is the difference?

What is the difference between a switch and a router? This is a good question because today we have switches that route and routers that bridge or switch. The best way to determine the difference is to look at the basic architecture of the box.

A switch architecture provides increased forwarding capacity as ports are added. This may be limited by the design of the bus or memory architecture, but when ports are added, each port module has additional hardware that is used to forward packets. A router typically has a single forwarding engine and additional ports share the capacity of this forwarding engine. This is somewhat similar to the difference between shared and switched media. For shared media, the capacity is shared by the users. For switched media the capacity is dedicated to the users.

We will deal in detail with the specifics of switches and routers (Parts III and IV), and will also look at the routing switches and alike 'hybrids' (Part V).

5.4 Application layer relays

To allow the interconnection of different network architectures (different network protocols) protocol translation gateways must be used. As it provides global translation between two protocol architectures, it comprises all layers of the two protocol stacks (see the gateway model operation in Figure 5.6). Earlier usage of the term **gateway** applied to any network interconnection device. Today the term is used exclusively for devices that actually map application functions as well as all of the supporting lower-layer implementations.

Routers, bridges, and repeaters are the most commonly implemented solutions in the LAN world. Protocol translation gateways at the application layer are rarely used to interconnect LANs, but are important in the context of providing interoperable solutions between organizations. A gateway consists of protocol conversion software that usually resides in a server, minicomputer or mainframe, or front-end device. Gateways allow LAN workstations to access a wide-area network or host environment as though each workstation had a dedicated terminal emulation facility or PC-to-WAN interface. By obviating the need to provide dedicated connection facilities for each LAN workstation, a gateway offers a cost-effective way to connect a large community of occasional users at a much lower cost per user.

Gateways go beyond the capabilities of bridges and routers in that they not only connect disparate networks, but ensure that the data transported from one network is compatible with that of other network at the application level. However, the gateway's translation capabilities impose a substantial processing burden on the gateway, resulting in a relatively slow throughput rate (i.e. hundreds of packets per second for a gateway versus up to tens of thousands of frames per second for a bridge). Consequently, the gateway may constitute a

FIGURE 5-6   Application layer relay architecture

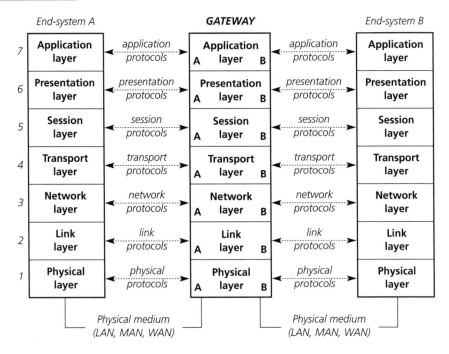

potential bottleneck when utilized frequently, unless the network is optimized for that possibility.

In addition to its translation capabilities, a gateway can check on the various protocols being used, ensuring that there is enough protocol processing power available for any given application. It also can ensure that the network links maintain a level of reliability for handling applications in conformance to user-defined error rate thresholds.

Gateways have a variety of applications. In addition to facilitating LAN work-station connections to various host environments, such as IBM SNA 3270 systems and IBM midrange systems, they facilitate connections to X.25 packet-switching networks. Other applications of gateways include the interconnection of various electronic mail systems, enabling mail to be exchanged between normally incompatible formats.

A gateway provides **protocol translation**. It does more than simply read a packet's address; it actually restructures the packet to be accommodated by the destination host. If a DECnet packet must be passed to an SNA network as an SNA packet, it must pass through a gateway. Because the gateway must read and then re-create the packet headers in a new form, it always affects performance to some extent.

The complete protocol translation and full gateway implementation between different network environments may be avoided by deploying **tunneling**. This method is used efficiently, especially for LAN interconnections which require traversing another, non-native environment. Tunneling is based on bypassing proper encapsulation/decapsulation where a data unit has to travel via all relevant layers down and up (as we saw in Chapter 1) by taking the packet belonging to a specific network protocol (passenger protocol) and putting it into the packet envelope of another network protocol (transport protocol). This is not usually done directly but by using additional mechanisms, mostly proprietary. The tunneling method is employed by most **router** vendors in their products. For IP, the GRE tunneling is common (RFC 1701) for setting up VPNs and MBone tunnels (discussed in Parts IV and V). Tunneling is also used at the link layer by **bridges** in cases of remote bridging (see Part II).

5.5 How to decide what to use

It would be too early to provide a definitive guide to how to decide among the basic choices currently available for LAN interconnection, as we still have lots of details ahead! However, it may be wise to keep repeating several basic rules and criteria which, if carefully considered, can eliminate many of the network administrators' headaches and business managers' disappointments.

In evaluating each of the alternatives, it is imperative to consider several important issues and features:

- **standards availability** – status of standards for various internetworking facilities and resulting capability for devices based on them to provide a level of interoperability in multivendor implementations;

- **connectivity** – physical interconnection options and topological considerations;

- **transparency** – extent to which protocol overhead is imposed in mapping dissimilar features and functions of the connected networks;

- **imposition of delay** – effect of throughput degradation on different types of traffic scenarios;

- **ease of implementation** – impact of initial installment and further maintenance;

- **scalability** – reserve for future improvements and enhancements, both dictated by business needs and allowed by technology development;

- **cost** – (last but, still, not least) not only at procuring hardware and software but related to its life cycle, such as cost for hiring, training, and keeping staff.

Further details and important issues will be considered under each of the 'headers' in this book.

5.6 Monitoring at internetworking devices

All of the above mentioned LAN interconnection devices provide for some monitoring and management functions (see also Chapter 4).

5.6.1 *Hubs as monitoring centers*

The intelligent wiring hub is a key element from a monitoring perspective. Hubs provide the 'first point of contact' for an end-system attached to a network, and serve as an observation point at which data flowing to and from the end-user can be examined. Virtually all hubs can allow monitoring and analysis of both the functioning of the hub itself and the traffic flowing through the hub. In a TCP/IP environment, the SNMP and RMON protocols are used for this purpose.

The current state and port configuration of a hub provides much information concerning topology and physical configuration schemes, an indication of the health of the network, and, more importantly, it allows the capture of traffic arriving from an end user's node.

Bridges and switches that operate at Layer 2 are also important network elements. It is this layer that most network monitors would examine to determine the quality of operation of a network.

5.6.2 *Routers as monitoring points*

Monitoring and analysis of the operation of routers and the routing process provides considerable information about the network. By detecting trends and events as seen by the routers, it is possible to take preventive actions, to isolate problem components, and to generally minimize the impact of faults.

5.6.3 *Monitoring elsewhere*

Monitoring the operation of applications and platforms is also highly desirable. **Gateways** provide for the interconnection of applications that are not directly compatible and for the conversion between different protocol suites. Middleware and platform applications provide services for distribution, for security, and for identification.

In any of these components there will be a trade-off between the processing load of the monitoring functions, the memory required for buffering the observations, and the amount of data collected. Spot checking, continuous monitoring, and targeted analysis change the amount of data collected and therefore the cost of performing the monitoring. The higher the speeds involved the more data that will need handling and the more important it is to operate at least at the wireline speeds.

5.7 Packet switching and cell relay

So far we have concentrated on the situations required for LAN interconnections or LAN attachment to WANs. Inside WANs we encounter a different situation which is usually either completely covered by the particular WAN standard or specification to ensure proper information unit handling throughout the network, or, on the contrary, is completely left to the manufacturers and providers. We will discuss the issues related to WAN switching in detail in Part III.

We saw in Chapter 3 that common WAN networks provide either packet switching or cell or frame relay functions, again depending on the highest layer at which they operate. The more the functions and thus overheads of the protocols are suppressed, the better results in terms of the higher transmission rates and lower delays that are achieved.

Older **packet switching** (namely in X.25) is similar to routing as we described it above while supporting a connection-oriented network service. It was emphasized throughout the overview of WAN services that today, in 'modern' WANs, the network layer is not implemented due to more reliable transmission media and the high processing capabilities of end nodes which can become finally responsible for error checking and end-flow control. Therefore lower layers are sufficient for providing the long-haul transport media using frame or cell relay.

Frame relay is in the middle way between packet switching and cell relaying. It eliminates the overhead of Layer 3 and operates only at Layer 2 leaving error checking and flow control fully on end node capabilities. Using virtual circuits it provides a connection-oriented service for transporting frames of variable lengths, each identified by the relatively short header. Based on the DLCI information the internal network switches make their decisions. Frame relay provides only an interface specification and providers can utilize proprietary internal protocols. This is similar to ITU-T X.25, where packet switches support a standardized interface but use internal transport, routing, and flow-control protocols.

Cell relay is a high-bandwidth, low-delay switching and multiplexing-packet technology. Cell relay in general can be either a connection-oriented service using virtual circuits (ATM) or a connectionless service if each cell is independently made to carry a protocol data unit. Cell-relay techniques implement procedures for allocating bandwidth at the user interface and allocating the bandwidth to various user services.

We can summarize the key basic differences between cell relay and packet switching as follows:

■ **Simplified protocol architecture** in cell relay – no error control for the information field (only the header field) and no flow control on the links, as the responsibility is moved to the edge of the network, and no windowing or processor-intensive protocol tasks are employed;

■ **Cells** – with fixed and very short length (53 bytes in ATM) which allows high-speed switching nodes, since the logical decisions are straightforward based on the header which identifies cells belonging to the same virtual circuit. Cells are switched by means of the label in the header. For comparison, classical packet switching uses large packets (128 or 256 octets) and, unlike cell relay, requires that every packet be brought entirely into each node and queued for output. As a result, classical packet switching suffers response time and throughput problems.

■ **Cell header** – with limited data-link layer functionality the transmission facility typically provides Layer 1 functionality. Cell relaying does not incorporate higher layer functionality as the responsibility is relegated to the edge of the network. As a result, information is transferred rapidly compared to other protocols. Cell-relay protocols can be implemented in hardware, expediting processing.

A number of functions of the data-link layer protocol are moved to the edge of the network, while core capabilities are supported directly by the cell switches, in addition to Layer 1 functions such as clocking, bit encoding, and physical-medium connection. The cell header is used for channel identification, in place of the positioned methodology for assigning octets inherent in traditional TDM DS1/DS3 systems. Cell sequence integrity is thus preserved within a virtual connection.

Cells associated with a given connection typically arrive in an irregular pattern, since cells are filled according to the actual bursty demand rather than following an inefficient preallocation scheme. Overall, however, cells arriving at a switch can show a statistically stable profile. Cell relay allows **bandwidth allocation** on demand to each user.

The **advantages of cell transport**, the currently best achieved technology, include the following:

- highly flexible network access due to the cell transport concept and specific cell transfer principles;
- dynamic bandwidth allocation on demand with a degree of granularity;
- flexible-bearer capability allocation and easy provisioning of (semi)permanent connections due to the virtual path concept;
- physical facility independence at the physical layer;
- functions implemented mostly in hardware.

5.8 Note on retransmission

Retransmission is not inherently part of routing or bridging. For most modern environments, retransmission is done between end hosts. This applies to networks that follow the end to end assumption of the Internet, and do not contain boxes such as NATs, firewalls, proxies, or tunneling devices. When retransmission is defined at the data link layer, it is done between whatever devices are at the two ends of the link – host to another host, host to router, router to router, etc.

STANDARDS WATCH   Summarized Standards watch

The following standards have been brought to your attention in this chapter:

ISO 8648:1988 *Information Processing Systems – Open Systems Interconnection – Internal Organization of the Network Layer*

ISO/IEC 10028:1993 *Information Technology – Telecommunications and Information Exchange between Systems – Definition of the Relaying Functions of a Network Layer Intermediate System*

PART I CONCLUDING REMARKS

Part I serves as a basis for the discussion that follows in subsequent Parts. It presents the overview of the layering principles in building and operating network architectures and illustrates the OSI seven-layer model we will refer to later on. It presents the basic characteristics and technical details of the currently widespread and new technologies in local area networks (all versions of IEEE 802.3, Token Ring, FDDI, and Fibre Channel) and wide area networking (link protocols, X.25, Frame Relay, ATM, and SONET). Briefly it describes approaches to network management, and also the remote monitoring of internetwork devices, such as switches. Finally, it builds the fundamentals in terms of internetworking at different network layers.

PART II

Bridging

Bridges first appeared in the 1980s and due to their ability to provide for basic **segmentation** of the large, flat network, provided a means of relieving congestion to network administrators. Bridges can connect LANs to one another and to WANs. Having the advantage of one more layer over repeaters or hubs, the **link layer**, bridges have the intelligence to keep the traffic which belongs to one segment local to that segment and to forward only the traffic which has to be passed through the bridged network.

Although pure bridges were several years later replaced almost entirely by more intelligent devices, routers, the bridging functionality has not disappeared at all and forms an integral part of today's routers. Initially the combined devices capable of both routing and bridging were called **brouters**, but this term is now obsolete as almost every router provides a bridging capability. However, in some cases standalone bridges may still appeal to the network administrators due to their transparency to network protocols, speed, simple configuration, and low price. Most importantly, there remain situations when only bridging can be deployed in the network, i.e. with **non-routable protocols** (LAT, MOP, NetBEUI, NetBIOS, etc.).

Although they no longer occupy the top of the networking equipment list, bridges remain important devices that **connect LANs, scrutinize the traffic**, and selectively **forward traffic**, depending on the source, destination, and protocol information contained in the data link frame.

In this Part, the following information is discussed:

- **bridging basics** – functionality, bridge types and requirements, bridge operation;
- **transparent bridging** – with details on bridge tasks and the spanning tree protocol;
- **source route bridging** – emphasizing how a source finds a route to the destination and how the route is advertised in a Token Ring frame;
- **remote bridging** – a method used to extend bridged networks;
- **source route transparent** and **translational bridging** – allowing a combination of two main bridging types;
- **bridge application and design** – recommendations.

SNAPSHOT why bridging

To summarize the **reasons for introducing bridges**, the following LAN limitations were to be overcome:

- limits in number of attached stations;
- limits in segment length;
- shared bandwidth.

CHAPTER 6

Bridging

6.1 Bridging basics

6.1.1 Bridging functionality

As was mentioned in the previous chapter, bridges represent the devices operating on the **link layer** (see Figure 6.1). This defines their functionality and limits their capabilities:

- Bridges work with **frames** – they check the MAC address fields, provide basic error checking and handling, conform to flow control mechanisms defined for particular MAC.
- Bridges depend fully on the **media access control mechanisms** deployed in the LAN segments they interconnect.
- Bridges may **filter** only on the basis of LAN frame fields, such as addresses and network protocol types – they cannot perform filtering based on higher layer (network and above) parameters.
- Bridges do not offer additional mechanisms for LAN interconnecting, such as traffic prioritization, queuing, or QoS support.

FIGURE 6-1   Internal organization of a MAC bridge

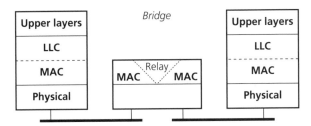

The bridge **mode of operation** is exclusively a store and forward one.

On the other hand, the limitations of the data link layer may in some cases prove to be advantageous: the **upper-layer protocols**, namely network protocols, are fully **transparent** to bridges. It simply does not matter to bridges whether the traffic they handle has been generated and belongs to, for example, TCP/IP (IP), NetWare (IPX), or AppleTalk (DDP).

QUICK TIP   independence on network protocols

Bridges may support any network protocol as upper-layer protocols are transparent to them.

One of the major issues which has to be taken into account is that bridges working on the link layer understand only the **physical addressing**, but not at all the logical addressing of the network layer. This means that a bridge does not provide any means for logical segmentation of the network and as a result a bridged network will always be a **flat network** with all stations, segments, and bridge ports belonging to the same logical network number (or, in an IP network, the same IP subnet). A bridge does not have any network address assigned; however, it has its unique identifier, usually derived from regular MAC addressing.

QUICK TIP   no segmentation into broadcast domains

Bridges create **flat networks** without logical segmentation into broadcast domains, only into collision domains in an Ethernet environment.

Bridges overcome the **physical limitations** of the particular local network (maximum length of segment, maximum number of stations on single segment) while at the same time they limit the unnecessary traffic traversing through the whole network and also prevent the propagation of error frames beyond the originating LAN segment. However, bridges do not inherently limit broadcast or multicast traffic. Additional mechanisms must be deployed to prevent **broadcast storms** from congesting the network.

While these constraints may seem in most cases significant and may lead to skipping the deployment of bridges altogether in favor of routers, there are still situations when bridges provide the only solution. The most noteworthy example of the necessity for bridging is when **non-routable protocols** like LAT, MOP, or NetBIOS (NetBIOS stations are addressed simply by an alphanumeric name which has no inherent hierarchical significance) are deployed and the LAN must be segmented to manage congestion and traffic load.

QUICK TIP   bridges support non-routable protocols

A bridge is the only internetworking device to support **non-routable protocols**.

6.1.2 Types of bridging

The types of bridging one can employ in the physical network are quite rigorous and do not allow much room for choice. The reason lies within the layer at which bridges operate, which makes them fully **dependent on the type of media** they interconnect and/or the media across which the bridged frames traverse. An overview of all the different bridging methods is shown in Table 6.1.

TABLE 6-1   Overview of bridging methods

Network environment	Media interconnected	Bridging type
Homogeneous environment (direct)	Ethernet to Ethernet	Transparent
	Token Ring to Token Ring	Source route
Homogeneous environment (remotely)	Ethernet to Ethernet across other media	Remote/encapsulation transparent
	Token Ring to Token Ring across other media	Remote/encapsulation source route
Heterogeneous environment	Ethernet to Token Ring (separate)	Source route transparent
	Ethernet to Token Ring (fully interconnected)	Translational

Two types of bridge are used to interconnect similar media (homogeneous environment):

■ *transparent* – used to interconnect Ethernet segments;
■ *source route* – used to interconnect Token Ring networks.

Both are standardized by the IEEE/ANSI and ISO/IEC and will be described in the following sections.

STANDARDS WATCH   **Bridging standards available from (see also Appendix B):**

IEEE (Institute of Electrical and Electronics Engineers): **http://standards.ieee.org**
ANSI (American National Standards Institute): **http://www.ansi.org**
ISO (International Organization for Standardization): **http://www.iso.ch**

The above two types are not always used to interconnect the relevant media directly or **locally.** We may encounter situations where there is another type of media (e.g. an FDDI or WAN link) between the segments we want to bridge. Therefore, there are also mechanisms that allow for bridged frames to traverse the 'transport' media interconnecting the edge segments. Hence a category of **remote bridges** evolved from this need: they have all the functions of local bridges, plus the need to support **encapsulation**(s) other than Ethernet or Token Ring on the transport media, and the different **performance** characteristics achieved in the network (higher with FDDI, lower with WAN links) (Figure 6.2).

FIGURE 6-2   Example of remote bridging over a WAN link

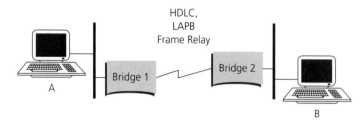

In a situation where it is necessary to put a bridge between the **dissimilar media**, Ethernet and Token Ring segments, a combination of the two basic bridging methods is used. Depending on the complexity of the interconnection we may deploy a simpler method called **source route transparent bridging**, which separates the transparent and source route networks and does not provide complete translation services. However, if there is a need for an overall understanding and support for all types of frame across both types of media, the only option is **translational bridging**. Translational bridges are the most complex devices in the bridging world, as they must handle each individual frame to perform a complete translation between media (where necessary) and between the types of bridging normally used. While source route transparent bridging is standardized, the latter is dealt with on a proprietary basis.

6.1.3 Bridging requirements

The bridging function, according to ISO/IEC 10038, belongs to the MAC sublayer – hence the title of **MAC bridges**. The standard only specifies the use of local bridges as opposed to remote bridging across another media. However, it takes into account not only the standard MAC access method types defined by the IEEE, i.e. Ethernet and Token Ring, but also the FDDI specified by ANSI.

The intention – and at the same time the requirement – for bridged local area networks – is that such networks shall not provide significantly inferior **Quality of Service** (QoS) compared with single LANs. Among the most

STANDARDS WATCH   **MAC bridges**

ISO/IEC 10038 [ANSI/IEEE Std 802.1D, 1993 edition] **Information Technology – Telecommunications and Information Exchange between Systems – Local Area Networks – MAC Bridges**

obvious quality of service parameters a LAN user is mostly interested in and depends on are the following:

- service availability;
- frame loss;
- frame misordering;
- frame duplication;
- transmit delay;
- frame lifetime;
- undetected frame error rate;
- maximum service data unit;
- user priority;
- throughput.

While **service availability** may be both increased or lowered by introducing bridge(s), the other parameters generally are seen as negatively affected by bridges (with the exception of the overall throughput). However, these negative effects relate to the deployment of any type of interconnecting device, not just a bridge. Service availability may be increased by an automatic reconfiguration of the bridged LAN in case of a link or device failure in the data path (if such a bypass is available at all). Bridge failure without any redundancy obviously causes a break in the LAN and thus a partitioning of the network into multiple segments.

With regard to the **loss of frames**, it is necessary to understand under what circumstances a bridge would discard any of the frames received:

- if the size of the service data unit carried by the frame exceeds the maximum allowed by the MAC procedure used in the LAN to which the frame should be relayed (giant frames);
- if the size of the service data unit carried by the frame is below the minimum specified for the MAC procedure used in the LAN from which the frame comes or to which the frame should be relayed (frames called runts);
- if it cannot conform to the set maximum lifetime of the frame;
- if the bridge lacks the necessary capacity in its buffers to allow the processing of the frame;
- if a changed bridged network topology results in a frame relaying disruption.

However, all the above requires that the incoming frame arrives at the bridge uncorrupted. Any corruption in the frame detectable while **checking the FCS value** against the frame content would be handled by the bridge no differently to any other relevant (destination or any interconnection) station on the LAN: it would be discarded. This also means that a bridge interconnecting two LANs and employing dissimilar MAC access methods, thus calculating FCS differently, must handle the recalculation of the FCS field value while relaying the frames. Whatever the reason for frame discarding, a bridge does not have the intelligence to inform the source station about this action and leaves the detection and retransmission of lost frames to the end devices. This is usually achieved by higher (e.g. network and transport) layer protocols.

A bridge has no capability to fragment frames therefore it can handle only frames conforming to the **maximum service data unit size** of the transmission media supporting the minimal size across the network.

Frame misordering or **duplication** should not be introduced by any bridge as no multiple paths may exist in the bridged network topology (see 6.8.1 for load balancing). The order of frames of a given user priority received on the incoming bridge port and transmitted on the outgoing port is preserved.

6.1.4 Bridge operation

Generally any type of bridge performs two main, mutually exclusive, functions:

- **frame filtering;**
- **frame forwarding.**

To support the above functions a bridge must employ procedures to obtain and maintain all the information required to make filtering or relaying decisions. There must also be a mechanism allowing for the management of all bridging operations.

A bridge observes the **appropriate MAC procedures** and protocol for each LAN it is connected to and does **not forward any control frames** (i.e. MAC frames) that govern the operation of the individual LAN.

By definition a bridge provides **filtering** in a case where both sender and receiver stations sit behind the same port of the bridge, i.e. incoming and outgoing bridge ports are the same. Note that the stations do not necessarily sit on the same segment. This implicit form of filtering is inherent to all transparent bridges and is enabled by dynamic learning of the addresses on the LAN segments behind each individual bridge port.

Besides the implicit filtering function, additional filtering may be achieved through the permanent configuration of reserved addresses or the explicit configuration of static filters.

A bridge forwards the frame onto its outgoing port when no filtering applies, the state of the port is forwarding (see section 6.2 below), and the maximum service data unit size of the outgoing LAN does not exceed the current frame size.

bridge relaying of frames

The following **subfunctions** support the **relaying of frames**:

■ **frame reception**;

■ **discarding of selected frames** – frames with errors, frames other than user data frames (control frames), frames depending on filtering conditions, frames with data unit size exceeded, aged frames (to ensure that a maximum bridge transit delay is not exceeded);

■ **forwarding of all other frames** onto outgoing port(s) and selection of outbound access priority;

■ **mapping of data service units** and recalculation on **frame check sequence**;

■ **transmitting of frames**.

Summarized Standards watch

The following standard has been brought to your attention in this chapter:

ISO/IEC 10038 [ANSI/IEEE Std 802.1D, 1993 Edition] **Information technology – Telecommunications and information exchange between systems – Local area networks – MAC bridges**

6.2 Transparent bridging

The transparent bridging specification was initially produced by Digital Equipment Corporation in the early 1980s and then submitted to the IEEE 802.1 subcommittee, under which it was standardized as IEEE 802.1d, with a recent edition under IEEE 802.1h specific for Ethernet version 2.0.

transparent bridges

IEEE 802.1D-1998 IEEE **Standard for Local Area Network MAC (Media Access Control) Bridges** (revision of 802.1D-1990 edition (ISO/IEC 10038; incorporates P802.1p and P802.12e, incorporates and supersedes published standards 802.1j and 802.6k)

IEEE 802.1h-1995 – **ISO/IEC Technical Report 11802-5:** 1997: Local and Metropolitan Area Networks: IEEE Recommended Practice for Media Access Control (MAC) Bridging on Ethernet Version 2.0 in 802 Local Area Networks

IEEE 802.1j-1996 (*superseded by 802.1D*-1998): Supplement to Information Technology – Telecommunications and Information Exchange between Systems – Local Area Networks – Media Access Control (MAC) Bridges: Managed Objects for MAC Bridges

IEEE 802.1p (*superseded by 802.1D*-1998): Standard for Local and Metropolitan Area Networks – Supplement to Media Access Control (MAC) Bridges: Traffic Class Expediting and Dynamic Multicast Filtering

IEEE 802.6k-1992 (*superseded by 802.1D*-1998): Supplement to Media Access Control (MAC) Bridges IEEE Standard 802.6 Distributed Queue Dual Bus (DQDB) Subnetwork of a MAN

IEEE 802.12e (*superseded by 802.1D*-1998): Standard for Information Technology – Local and Metropolitan Area Networks – Part 1D Telecommunications and Information Exchange between Systems – Local Area Networks – Media Access Control (MAC) Bridges – Supplement for support by IEEE 802.12

When IEEE 802.1D(h) is used, bridges are **transparent to the end-stations**, which means that an end-station does not know and does not have to take into account that the end station with which it wishes to communicate may not sit on the same segment. **All the tasks** supporting the correct traversing of segments between source and destination stations are **performed by the participating transparent bridges**. It is the bridge, not the end station, which must learn how to deliver the frame to its destination, or more precisely, which of its ports it should use to forward the frame towards the destination station.

QUICK TIP | **bridge transparency**

A bridge in an Ethernet network is **transparent to end stations**.

Every station is identified by its full **MAC address**, the basic information the bridge looks for in each incoming frame. The key forwarding information for transparent bridge operation is contained in the **decision table** which is referred to as the **filtering database** (according to the standard), or more commonly as the **forwarding database**. Sometimes, unfortunately, the forwarding database is called a routing table. This is rather ambiguous and confusing, especially when both routers and bridges operate in the same network. A bridge does not route, hence the decision table only lists the MAC addresses of end nodes it currently knows about linked with the local outgoing bridge interface behind which the MAC address is assumed.

6.2.1 Forwarding and learning

To support the two main functions of the transparent bridge, two processes are simultaneously invoked and performed (by the relay part of the bridge) after a frame is received, checked for errors, and hence determined as a candidate for transmission:

- **Forwarding process** – forwards or filters a frame on the basis of the information contained in the filtering database, checking it against the **destination MAC address** of the incoming frame, and on the state of the bridge ports.
- **Learning process** – observing the **source MAC addresses** in each incoming frame to update the filtering database (again depending of the state of port on which frame is observed).

A **filtering database** is a container of the forwarding information learned **dynamically** and/or entered **statically**. Each entry in the database specifies:

- **destination MAC address** (it may be an individual or group address, the latter applying to static entries only);
- an associated outgoing **port number** which is to be used to direct a frame towards its destination;
- a **timer** for entry aging is useful for dynamically learned paths. The bridge restarts the timer whenever it detects the relevant source address in incoming frame. If the specified maximum aging time is achieved the entry is removed from the database. Maximum aging time is configurable and its recommended value is 5 minutes. The aging timer has become an issue in the modern mobile network environment (where nomadic computers are attached to bridged networks), in situations when a station is moved from one network segment (or rather from beyond a bridge port) to another within the aging interval.

The bridge checks the **destination MAC address** of each **incoming frame**. If the destination MAC address is found in its **database**, the bridge knows the path to the destination, and submits the frame to the outgoing interface identified in the database, checking at the same time for additional filters. The destination station may be found behind the incoming port in which case the frame is discarded (the action of implicit bridge filtering), otherwise the forwarding is performed.

If the destination MAC **address is unknown**, i.e. not in the forwarding database, the bridge has not seen this address behind any of its ports for significant period of time (or 'never'). Under these circumstances, a bridge will send the **frame to all ports** except the one it was received from. Frames with destination addresses identifying a group (**multicast MAC address**) or all stations (**broadcast MAC address**) are also **flooded** through all outgoing bridge ports (except the incoming one) and thus relayed throughout the whole bridged network.

6.2.2 Requirement for loop-free networks

While the network topology with multiple paths between pair(s) of segments may seem very appealing in terms of **redundancy** since it provides **fault tolerance** in case of a link break, this topology may be very harmful to the bridging operation. Even in the small case shown on Figure 6.3 where two segments are interconnected by two parallel bridges the operation of both segments could easily deteriorate. As we explained earlier, a bridge learns the MAC source addresses of the frames it receives on its ports. If a host A transmits a frame on its Ethernet segment, both bridges will forward it to the destination station sitting on the second connected Ethernet (the correct action, according to their filtering database). However, similarly, as host B receives its frame, each bridge will also receive the frame forwarded to the segment by its companion bridge and would suddenly learn that station A (according to the source MAC address of the frame just received) is no longer behind port 1 but 2 of both bridges. This information is, of course, incorrect and would mean that before the information in the forwarding database reverts to the correct state (through receiving another frame transmitted by host A directly on the right port) the response from host B would never get to host A as both would be deemed to belong to the same segment! Hence, the correct forwarding operation would be disrupted through the incorrect input information for learning process.

FIGURE 6-3   Simple multiple paths topology network

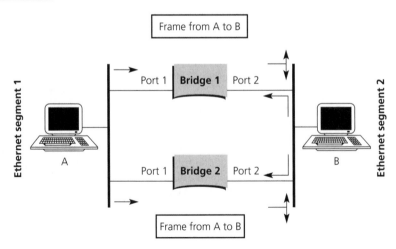

This simple case would become much more serious if the frame initially generated had not been directed to a single station by its unicast destination address but instead to all stations indicated by the broadcast destination address. In that case, within a very short time the bridged network will become flooded by endless **broadcast storms**.

Spanning tree algorithm

To support the proper bridge relaying function there must be a specific protocol deployed with the active participation of all the bridges in the bridged network to learn and handle the network topology so that it keeps the bridged network topology without loops. Transparent bridged networks use the **Spanning Tree Protocol** (STP) which is used to maintain **a loop-free subset of the network's topology dynamically**. To do this, the STP places bridge ports that would create loops when active into a standby, or blocking, condition. **Blocked ports** can be activated if the primary port fails, so they provide **redundant** support.

The spanning tree protocol is **deployed both by bridges and switches** to achieve a loop-free network topology. While we will discuss the STP issue in this Part, it is likewise applicable to LAN switches.

STANDARDS WATCH   Spanning tree protocol

IEEE 802.1D-1998 **IEEE Standard for Local Area Network MAC (Media Access Control) Bridges**

The Spanning Tree Protocol, through its underlying **spanning tree algorithm** (STA), configures the active topology of a bridged LAN of arbitrary topology into a single spanning tree so that there is only a maximum of one data path (best loop-free path throughout a bridged network) between any two end stations, thereby eliminating any network loops. The algorithm deployed is based on the graph theory and its paradigm: 'for every connected graph consisting of nodes (bridges) and edges (segments) there exists a spanning tree of edges which provides for connectivity but does not contain any loop.'

QUICK TIP   spanning tree protocol

Spanning tree protocol is a link management protocol that provides path redundancy while preventing undesirable loops in the network. STP forces all **redundant** data paths into a **standby** (blocked) state.

Bridges send and receive STP frames at regular intervals. They do not forward these frames, but use the frames to construct a loop-free path. The algorithm used provides for fault tolerance by **automatic reconfiguration** of the spanning tree topology as a result of a bridge **failure** or breakdown in a data path. The STA also supports automatic discovery and accommodation of any bridge or bridge port added to the bridged network. The entire active topology must stabilize within a short interval so that the period of time for which the service is unavailable for communication between any pair of end-stations is minimal (usually 30 to 50 seconds with default settings). The protocol operation is transparent to all the end stations and does not introduce high overhead traffic into the bridged network.

QUICK TIP	STP transparency

Spanning-tree operation is **transparent to end stations**.

Spanning tree protocol operation

Each bridge is assigned a group of identifiers, one for the bridge itself and one for each of its ports. The **Bridge ID** (BID) is eight bytes long and contains a **bridge priority** (two bytes) along with one of the bridge **MAC addresses** (six bytes). Each bridge **Port ID** is 16 bits long with two parts, a six bit priority setting and a ten bit port number.

QUICK TIP	bridge's root port and path cost

A **bridge's root port** is the port through which the root bridge can be reached with the **least aggregate path cost**, a value that is called the **root path cost**.

A **path cost** value is given to each port. The cost is typically based on a guideline established as part of 802.1D. According to the original specification, cost is 1000 Mbps (1 Gbps per second) divided by the bandwidth of the segment connected to the port. Therefore, a 10 Mbps connection would have a cost of 100 (1000 divided by 10). To compensate for the increasing speed of networks beyond the gigabit range, the **default cost** has been slightly modified. The new default cost values are shown in Table 6.2. However, interface cost can be an arbitrary value assigned by the network administrator instead of using default cost values.

TABLE 6-2 Modified default values of cost (for STP path cost calculation)

Bandwidth	4 Mbps	10 Mbps	16 Mbps	100 Mbps	155 Mbps	1 Gbps	10 Gbps
Default interface cost	250	100	62	19	14	4	2

Every bridge in the bridged network has its **root path cost** associated with it which is made up of the sum of the least path costs from the root to the bridge. If there are two or more ports with the same value of the root path cost, then first the bridge identifier and then the port identifiers are used as tie-breakers. Only a single bridge port is selected as a designated port for each LAN. The same computation selects the root port of a bridge from all its own ports and the complete active topology of the bridged LAN is determined. The LAN administrator may influence the active topology resulting from the STP operation by specifying (modifying the default value of) bridge priority, port priority, or port cost.

Information on bridges present in the network and their path cost is shared between all the bridges using special frames called **Bridge Protocol Data Units** (BPDU – see below). A **root bridge** is chosen based on the results of the BPDU exchange process between the bridges. Initially, every bridge considers itself the root bridge, i.e. when a bridge powers up on the network, it sends out a BPDU with its own BID as the root BID. When the other bridges receive the BPDU, they compare the BID to the one they already have stored as the root BID. If the new root BID has a lower value, they replace the saved one. But if the saved root BID is lower, a BPDU is sent to the new bridge with this BID as the root BID. When the new bridge receives the BPDU, it realizes that it is not the root bridge and replaces the root BID in its table with the one it has just received. The result is that the bridge that has the lowest BID is elected by the other bridges as the root bridge.

Based on the location of the root bridge, the other bridges determine which of their ports has the lowest path cost to the root bridge. These ports are called **root ports** and each bridge (other than the current root bridge) must have one. The bridges need to determine which will become a **designated bridge** and which port becomes the designated port for a segment. A **designated port** is the connection used to send and receive packets on a specific segment. By having only one designated port per segment, all looping issues are resolved. If a port is determined to have a lower path cost to the root, then it becomes the designated port for that segment. If two or more ports have the same path cost, then the bridge with the lowest BID is chosen.

QUICK TIP   **STP and root**

In a bridged LAN using STP there is one bridge chosen to become a **root** (bridge), i.e. the bridge that serves as the root of the spanning tree. The bridge with the highest **priority** in the network becomes the root (it cannot be deduced from the network topology which of the bridges is the root). The priority has a non-negative integer value within the limits and defaults dictated by the particular STP protocol. The lower the numerical value, the higher the priority.

Once the designated port for a network segment has been chosen, any other ports that connect to that segment become non-designated ports. They block network traffic from taking that path so that it can only access that segment through the designated port. Each bridge has a table of BPDUs that it continually updates. The network is now configured as a single spanning tree with the root bridge as the trunk and all the other bridges as branches. Each bridge communicates with the root bridge through the root ports and with each segment through the designated ports to maintain a loop-free network. In the event that the root bridge begins to fail or have network problems, STP allows the other bridges to immediately reconfigure the network with another bridge acting as root bridge.

SNAPSHOT   **STP operation**

Spanning tree protocol deploys an **exchange of Bridge Protocol Data Units** (BPDUs) to achieve the following situation:

- one bridge is elected as the **root bridge**;
- the **shortest distance to the root bridge** is calculated for each bridge;
- a **designated bridge** is selected (the bridge closest to the root bridge through which frames will be forwarded to the root);
- a **designated port** for each bridge is selected – this is the port providing the best path from the bridge to the root bridge;
- ports included in the spanning tree are selected.

The operation of the spanning tree protocol may be summarized as follows. The spanning tree root bridge is the logical center of the spanning tree topology in a bridged network. All paths that are redundant for reaching the root from anywhere in the network are placed by STP into a blocking mode. Each LAN segment then has one **designated** (bridge) **port** connected to it which forwards frames from that LAN to the root and from the root to the LAN. The **designated port** for each LAN is the bridge port for which the value of the root **path cost** is the lowest. Cost relates to the interface and although it may be derived from the link bandwidth, it may be set differently on the link ends. The bridge whose port is used for this LAN connection is called the **designated bridge** for that LAN. The bridge has a single root port (except the root bridge as all its ports are root ports) and can have designated ports (and blocked ports). Once the designated port for the particular network segment has been chosen, any other ports that connect to that segment become non-designated ports. They block network traffic from taking that path so that it can only access that segment through the designated port.

An example of STP operation is shown in Figure 6.4. Five bridges participate in a single STP operation to create a loop-free topology. To make things more intuitive, bridge 1 has been manually configured to a higher priority than all the other bridges, all having a default priority assigned. Bridge 1 is selected as a root bridge after initial exchange of BPDUs. As bridge 2 has had its default cost manually changed to a smaller value on both its Ethernet ports, it becomes the preferable path for the bottom Ethernet segment (the overall path cost to the root bridge is lower), which could otherwise also be reached by bridge 5. As a result, a port on bridge 5 is blocked to eliminate a loop creation, and will not be used for traffic until bridge 4 or some port on bridge 4 goes down, or a port on bridge 2

FIGURE 6-4 Example of STP creation of loop-free bridge network topology

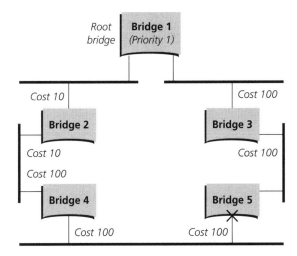

goes down – both situations would prevent communication to stations on the bottom LAN segment, so far possibly reachable via the blocked port on bridge 5.

Port states

Bridge ports may be in one of five defined states as a result of STP or management action (for transitions between the states see Figure 6.6):

- **Blocking** (stand-by) – a port does not forward due to STP decision (another port on this bridge has been identified as a designated port). The blocking state is used to prevent loop creation.
- **Listening** – a port participates in the STP reconfiguration operation. To prevent temporary configuration loops, a port does not forward frames while in the listening state. This state follows the blocking state.
- **Learning** – a port does not forward frames to prevent temporary loops during topology changes and to minimize unnecessary flooding throughout the bridge network (follows the listening state). The port stays in this state only for the necessary predefined period.
- **Forwarding** – a port forwards frames according to the filtering database (follows the learning state), i.e. forwards frames received from the attached segment and frames switched from another port for forwarding, incorporates station location information into its address database, receives BPDUs and directs them to the system module, processes BPDUs received from the system module, and receives and responds to network management messages. (For complete flowchart see Figure 6.5.)
- **Disabled** – a port does not forward frames nor does it participate in STP operation (may follow any of the states specified above due to management action and only such management action may change this state into a blocking state).

FIGURE 6-5   Forwarding states

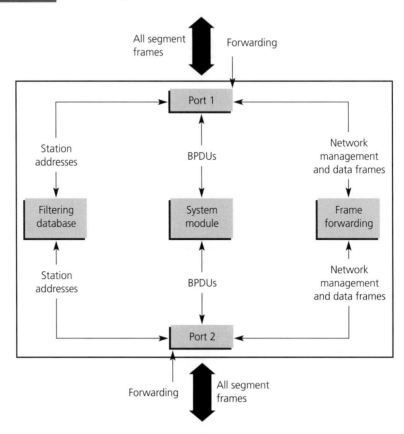

A port moves through these five states as follows:

- from initialization to blocking;
- from blocking to listening or to disabled;
- from listening to learning, to blocking, or to disabled;
- from learning to forwarding, to blocking, or to disabled;
- from forwarding to blocking or to disabled.

QUICK TIP   **bridge port states based on STP**

Bridge ports participating in STP may be in one of five states – **blocking, listening, learning, forwarding, or disabled**.

The flow of port state changes governed by STP is shown in Figure 6.6.

FIGURE 6-6 STP port states flowchart

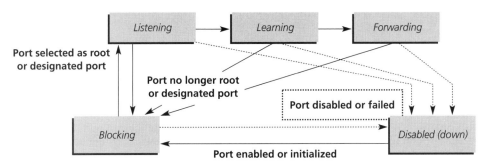

Configuration bridge protocol data units

The STP algorithm is based on the exchange of **configuration bridge protocol data units (BPDUs)** among all the bridges in a single bridged network (see Figure 6.7 for frame format). The bridge group address is used as the MAC destination address to ensure that all the bridges on a single segment receive configuration BPDUs.

STANDARDS WATCH **group MAC addresses**

ISO/IEC TR 11802-2: **Information Technology – Telecommunications and Information Exchange Between Systems – Local and Metropolitan Area Networks – Common Specifications – Part 2: Standard Group MAC Addresses,** 1996

The Spanning Tree Protocol uses two **reserved MAC addresses** for its operation:

- **bridge group address**:   *01-80-C2-00-00-00*
- **all LANs bridge management group address**: *01-80-C2-00-00-10*

Note: Frames with a destination group MAC addresses belonging to the range of reserved addresses hex *<01-80-C2-00-00-00; 01-80-C2-00-00-0F>* shall not be relayed by any bridge (this restriction should be ensured through the use of static entries in the filtering database) and are designated as filtered MAC group addresses; as opposed to MAC group address in the range *<01-80-C2-00-00-10; 01-80-C2-FF-FF-FF>* which may be relayed by MAC bridges if present as the destination address in a frame.

Configuration BPDUs are not directly forwarded by bridges, but may be used for calculating the individual BPDU to transmit. Each **configuration BPDU contains**, among other parameters:

- the unique **identifier** of the bridge which the transmitting bridge assumes to be a **root**;
- the **cost of the path to the root** from the transmitting port;
- the **identifier** of the transmitting **bridge**;
- the **identifier** of the transmitting bridge **port**.

This information allows the receiving bridge to determine whether the transmitting port has a better claim to become a designated port on the LAN on which the configuration BPDU was received than the port currently believed to be the designated one, and to determine whether the receiving bridge should become the root.

The following **mechanisms** are used to determine the **state of all bridge ports** in the bridged LAN:

1 Each bridge initially assumes it is the root until it learns otherwise. A bridge that believes itself to be the root originates a configuration BPDU for each LAN segment to which it is connected at regular intervals (according to a specified Hello timer).

2 When a bridge receives a configuration BPDU on what it decides is its root port, and that BPDU conveys better information (i.e. higher priority root identifier, lower root path cost, higher priority transmitting bridge or port), the bridge passes such information to all the LANs for which it believes itself to be a designated port.

3 When a bridge receives inferior information on a port it considers to be the designated port on the LAN to which it is attached, it transmits its own information in reply for all the other bridges on that LAN rather than the information received.

The spanning tree paths to **the bridge with the highest priority root identifier** are quickly learned in the bridged LAN through the use of the above mechanisms.

To ensure the correctness of the active spanning tree topology, and to allow for possible reconfiguration to the network link or a device failure, the topology information propagated throughout the network has a **bounded lifetime**. A configuration BPDU has an **age** associated with it (i.e. the time elapsed since the configuration BPDU originated from the root). Every bridge stores the configuration information from the designated port on each of the LANs to which it is connected and monitors the age of such information. If the aging timer for the information held for a port expires, the bridge will attempt to become a designated port for the LAN. If the root port of the bridge times out, another port may be selected instead.

The information transmitted on LANs for which a bridge is the designated bridge will be recalculated on the basis of new information received on the newly chosen root port. If there is no information from the current root, the bridge will reconfigure by claiming to be the root itself. In the case of a failure of the current root bridge, all bridges sharing the spanning tree algorithm will start the reconfiguration process anew, and the initialization stage will be repeated.

To ensure the **reliability** of the STP, especially during any topology changes, the configuration BPDUs are transmitted reliably and have to be acknowledged by the designated or root bridge (if information is generated from the spanning tree branches).

The timeout or age value included in every (configuration) *Topology Change Notification* (TCN) BPDU from the root must take into account the propagation delays across all the bridged LANs, i.e. the time it will take to traverse the entire spanning tree.

During **the spanning tree (re)configuration process**, bridge ports are usually **not forwarding** any received user frames from their connected LANs. This period of time is used to clear the dynamic part of the filtering database, if it already exists, to allow for the processing of more up-to-date information through the new learning stage. Clearing of the dynamic part of the filtering database is accomplished by applying a short reconfiguration timeout value on the dynamic database entries (specifically, the value of the forwarding delay is used).

Configuration BPDU format
STP has its standard **reserved LLC service access point** (LSAP) binary value of *01000010* (least significant bit is the leftmost).

STANDARDS WATCH   **LSAP for STP**

ISO/IEC TR 11802-1: **Information Technology – Telecommunications and Information Exchange between Systems – Local and Metropolitan Area Networks – Common Specifications – Part 1: Structure and Coding of LLC Addresses in LANs**

Figures 6.7 and 6.8 show the format of the **configuration** and **topology change bridge PDUs**, respectively, used during the configuration and topology change situations.

FIGURE 6-7   Configuration BPDU

Octets (35 in total):

2	1	1	1	8	4	8	2	2	2	2	2
Protocol ID	Protocol version ID = all 0s	BPDU type = all 0s	Flags	Root ID	Root path cost	Bridge ID	Port ID	Message age	Max. age	Hello time	Forward delay

FIGURE 6-8   Topology change notification BPDU

Octets (four in total):

2	1	1
Protocol ID = 00000000 00000000	Protocol version ID = 00000000	BPDU type = 10000000

Field description for configuration BPDU:

- *Protocol identifier* – all zeros for STP.
- *Protocol version* – all zeros for current STP.
- *BPDU type* – all zeros for configuration BPDU.
- *Flags* – only two bits of this octet are used:
  - the least significant bit, the topology change notification flag, is set to *1* to identify this BPDU as a *Topology Change message* (TC);
  - the most significant bit, the topology change notification acknowledgment flag, is set to *1* to identify the BPDU as a *Topology Change Acknowledgment* (TCA), i.e. a frame used to acknowledge the receipt of a topology change message.
- *Root identifier* – the first two most significant octets of this eight-octet field identify the root priority (a hexadecimal value and settable parameter), followed by the six octets uniquely identifying the root (typically the MAC address of the bridge).
- *Root path cost* – identifies the cost of the complete path between the bridge sending the BPDU to the root bridge.
- *Bridge identifier* (BID) – an eight-octet field that uniquely identifies the sender (by a two-octet configured **priority** and a six-octet **unique identifier**, the recommended value being the MAC address of the lowest numbered bridge port, i.e. port 1).
- *Port identifier* – the hexadecimal value of this field identifies the port from which the BPDU is sent; the identifier consists of two parts: six bits are used for **priority** setting and the remaining ten bits for the **port number**.

■ *Message age* – the time elapsed from the generation of the configuration BPDU by the root (which sets this field to *0* at message generation) and its receipt by the bridge processing the BPDU; it is measured in 1/256 second increments.

■ *Maximum age* – determines the amount of time configuration information received on a port stored by the bridge. When the maximum age of a BPDU is reached, the stored configuration message must be deleted.

■ *Hello time* – identifies the expected period of time that will elapse between the generation of configuration BPDUs by a bridge that assumes itself to be the root.

■ *Forward delay* – this value bounds the time a bridge must remain in each intermediate processing state before transitioning from blocking to forwarding.

Field description for *Topology Change* BPDU (only three fields are used):

■ *Protocol identifier* – all zeros for STP.

■ *Protocol version* – all zeros for current STP.

■ *BPDU type* – value of 128 for topology change BPDU.

QUICK TIP

Configuration BPDUs used by STA help build a spanning tree by providing bridge information to:

■ elect a single bridge to become a **root bridge**;

■ calculate the shortest path to the **root bridge**;

■ choose a **designated bridge** on a LAN which is closest to the **root bridge** (will forward the frames from the LAN to the root bridge);

■ choose one of the ports to become a **root port** (with the shortest distance to the root bridge);

■ select the ports to be included in the spanning tree (to eliminate any potential loops).

Bridge requirements and parameters

STP implementation does not impose particularly high internal computing and memory requirements on bridging devices. **Memory consumption** associated with each bridge port is independent of the total number of bridges and LANs in the bridged network but depends mostly on the total number of stations in the network. From the administrator's perspective, the only requirement for STP operation is the **proper configuration of port addresses** and the **specification of STP choice** (besides standard IEEE 802.1D, the proprietary Digital spanning tree protocol is also popular).

Among the other requirements all bridges must conform to is a common understanding of **reserved group addresses**, unique bridge identification and port identifier assignment. For error-free operation of the protocol all bridge ports across the network must have **unique individual MAC addresses** assigned. To correctly manage STP operation, a method for configuring bridge priority, its port types, and port costs (attached media) must be provided.

There is a handful of **parameters** which have both the impact on the bridge performance and on its participation in the spanning tree protocol operations. The IEEE 802.1D specifies the main transparent bridge parameters values which are described as follows (their values are summarized in Table 6.3):

TABLE 6-3 Transparent bridge parameter values according to IEEE 802.1D

Parameter	Recommended/ default value	Absolute minimum	Absolute maximum	Fixed value	Range
Max. bridge diameter	7 bridges				
Max. bridge transit delay	1 s		4 s		
Max BPDU transmission delay	1 s		4 s		
Max. message age increment	2 s (per hop)		4 s		
Bridge hello timer	2 s				1–10 s
Bridge max. age	20 s				6–40 s
Bridge forward delay	15 s				4–30 s
Hold times				1 s	
Bridge priority	32768				0–65535
Port priority	128				0–255
Path cost		1			0–65535

- *Maximum bridge diameter* = maximum number of bridges in bridged LAN between any two end stations.
- *Maximum bridge transit delay* = maximum time elapsing between reception and transmission by bridge of forwarded frame (frames exceeding this time will be discarded).
- *Maximum BPDU transmission delay* = maximum delay before transmission of BPDU invoked.
- *Maximum message age increment* = message age parameter in transmitted BPDUs or stored Bridge Protocol Message.
- *Path cost* – recommended value is based on following formula: /path cost = 1000 [attached LAN speed in Mbps].

The IEEE 802.1D also recommends that the following two performance parameters should be specified by the manufacturers:

- guaranteed port filtering rate;
- guaranteed bridge relaying rate.

Summary of STA tasks

- Configuring active topology of a bridged system with arbitrary topology into a single spanning tree to eliminate any potential loops.
- Providing for fault tolerance by automatic reconfiguration of the spanning tree topology in case of bridge or link failure, and for the automatic accommodation of any bridge port added to the bridged system without forming any transient data loops.
- Minimizing the unavailability of network service by enforcing the active topology to become stable within a short, known interval (with a high probability), a.k.a. quick convergence of the STP.
- Supporting configuration and performance management by keeping active topology predictable and reproducible.
- Performing transparent operations for end stations.
- Keeping the consumption of communications bandwidth by bridges (during establishing and maintaining the spanning tree) to a minimum (small percentage of the total available bandwidth, independent of the total traffic supported by the bridged system, regardless of the total number of bridges or network segments).
- Keeping the memory requirements associated with each bridge port independent of the number of bridges or network segments in the bridged network.
- Minimizing the initial configuration requirements – each bridge does not have to be individually configured before connecting to the bridged system.

Summary of IEEE 802.1D bridge and bridged network features

- Bridge is not directly addressed by communicating end stations – frames transmitted between end stations carry as the destination address the MAC address of the other communicating station (not the MAC address of any of the bridge's ports, if it has any). NB: The only time the bridge is directly addressed is for management purposes (as an end station).

- All MAC addresses within the bridged network must be unique.
- MAC addresses of end stations are not restricted by the topology and configuration of the bridged system (bridges and networks).
- Key aspects of the bridged network service quality are similar to that of a single LAN.

Extensions to IEEE 802.1D

Support to time-critical traffic and efficient multicast traffic

---

STANDARDS WATCH

IEEE 802.1p: **Standard for Local and Metropolitan Area Networks – Supplement to Media Access Control (MAC) Bridges: Traffic Class Expediting and Dynamic Multicast Filtering** (incorporated into IEEE 802.1D)

To improve support of time critical and multicast intensive applications, including multimedia interactive applications, across bridged LANs, and to reduce the degree to which the level of multicast traffic and the loading levels selected for timely information delivery limit the number of attached stations and the throughput of Bridged Local Area Networks, a new IEEE standard entitled 802.1p was approved. It also helps facilitate bridged LAN support of the 'hierarchical multicast' capabilities developed for internets in a way that is compatible with their emerging network layer protocols.

IEEE 802.1p (currently part of 802.1D) specifies the mechanisms in MAC bridges to **expedite delivery of time-critical traffic** and to limit the extent of high bandwidth multicast traffic within a bridged LAN and specifies the mechanisms to classify traffic as supporting time-critical services or requiring multicast filtering on the basis of MAC frame information. Additionally, it offers the specification of an optional protocol mechanism in MAC bridges to support **dynamic registration** for time-critical delivery or filtering services by end stations, and the specification of optional protocols between MAC bridges to convey registration information in a bridged LAN.

STANDARDS WATCH

New Standard Project IEEE P802.1t: **Standard for Information Technology – Telecommunications and Information Exchange between Systems – Local and Metropolitan Area Networks – Common Specifications – Part 3: Media Access Control (MAC) Bridges: Technical and Editorial Corrections** (*maintenance of the 802.1D-1998 standard*)

Autoconfiguring mechanisms for redundant bridges

STANDARDS WATCH

New Standard Project IEEE P802.1w: **Supplement to ISO/IEC 15802-3 (802.1D): Information Technology – Telecommunications and Information Exchange Between Systems – Local & Metropolitan Area Networks – Common Specifications – Part 3: Media Access Control (MAC) Bridges – Rapid Reconfiguration**

The specification of enhancements to the **autoconfiguring mechanisms** and management controls in that constrain user data frames to all or part of a loop-free topology are to be found in IFEE 802.ID. Where **redundant alternate bridges** and/or connecting LANs are available, these enhancements will provide faster reconfiguration and restoration of the MAC service if LAN component failure occurs.

The purpose is to better support LAN-based applications, including new voice and multimedia solutions, that are increasingly **mission critical** and require much improved network availability and scalability. The specification provides an availability strategy that includes redundant bridges and LAN media, together with rapid failure detection and reconfiguration, and allows the use of currently available cost-effective LAN components. Techniques that are broadly compatible with IEEE 802.1D, but are not interoperable, are now emerging from multiple vendors. The proposed project P802.1w will provide users with interoperable solutions.

6.3 Source-route bridging

The **source-route bridging (SRB) algorithm** was developed by IBM for Token Ring interconnection and subsequently proposed to the IEEE 802.5 where it was standardized as IEEE 802.1D.

STANDARDS WATCH **source-route bridges**

IEEE 802.1D-1998 **IEEE Standard for Local Area Network MAC (Media Access Control) Bridges**

Source-route bridging differs significantly from the algorithm used in transparent bridging. In the bridged Token Ring network it is the task of the source station to determine and specify the route to the destination station. The **route**, i.e. the path across Token Ring networks and bridges, is **'encoded' into every frame** generated **by the source station**. The route is initially inserted one by one by bridges to add to or modify part of the route information. As the frame traverses an interconnected set of Token Ring segments the bridges examine the frame as part of the process of determining the path from the source station to destination station. Once the route is known, it is inserted in the data frame by a source station, and bridges only read and follow the route specified by checking the appropriate part of the Token Ring frame.

IBM introduced SRB using some of the terminology that OSI standards use to describe network layer concepts, but applying these to the data link layer. This has proved to be somewhat confusing. In particular, SRB uses the terms route and packet in the following manner:

- **route** – in SRB this should be understood as a **path** from source to destination end stations within a flat network consisting of Token Ring segments interconnected by bridge(s);
- **packet** – in SRB this means (a specific) Token Ring **frame**.

SNAPSHOT   Source-Route Bridging (SRB)

Source-Route Bridging – enables the connection of two or more **Token Ring** networks at the link layer.

6.3.1 SRB bridge operation

A source route bridge has the following tasks to perform:

- to relay source route data frames;
- to relay and process frames to support the transfer and acquisition of routing information.

In addition to these specific functions the bridge has to follow the **Token Ring operational requirements**, in particular: copying the frame from the local ring, adjusting the frame status field value and awaiting a token to relay the frame onto the connected ring. Unlike in transparent bridging, the source route bridge does not learn the station addresses in the bridged network and relies on the information inserted in every frame to determine whether to forward it and how. This information is provided by the frame source, hence source routing.

QUICK TIP   SRB and end stations

In **Source-Route Bridging**, the major responsibility of finding and capturing the path to the destination lies with the **source station**.

6.3.2 SRB algorithm

To determine the location of the destination station in the network, the source station must first determine whether the destination station sits on the same or a different LAN segment. The source station first tests the local Token Ring by generating a data frame for the destination station. If it learns – by examining the *Frame Status* field value in the frame after its ring rotation – that the destination station does not exist on the local ring (by checking the *Frame Status field* and realizing the data copied bit is not set by the destination station), the source must generate an **explorer packet**.

The **explorer packet** may have the following different characteristics:

- **all-routes explorer packet** – this frame is used to determine all the paths between the source and destination stations;
- **spanning tree explorer packet** – this frame traverses the bridged network over a previously created spanning tree on its way to the destination station, and on the return path, changes its operation to 'all-routes exploring.'

Let's examine the operation of finding all possible paths through the source-route bridged network (see Figure 6.9) using the **all-routes explorer**. When a **source station** generates an explorer packet it must specify that the frame contains (or will contain) routing or path information. The presence of routing information within the frame is indicated by the setting of the most significant bit within the source address field, the **Routing Information Indicator** (RII) bit. This bit is actually the multicast bit of a 48-bit MAC address, but since a source cannot be a multicast address, this bit was conveniently made available for use as a routing information indicator. When set, the bit indicates that additional source routing information is encoded in this frame.

FIGURE 6-9 Determination of the path through an SRB network

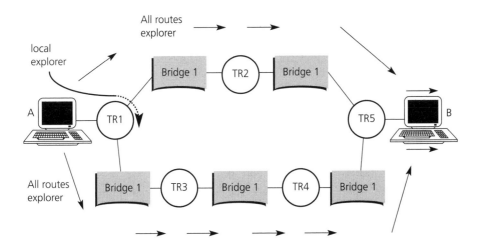

The routing (path) information is inserted immediately following the source address and in front of any data transmitted in the frame (see Figure 6.10), in what is called the **routing information field** (RIF). The RIF is constructed as follows. Every source route bridge which receives the explorer packet inserts its own number and the number of traversed Token Rings into the RIF, and then forwards the explorer packet further by **flooding it through all outgoing ports**. All the bridges connected to the ring copy the explorer packet and check the RIF. If they determine that the route through them (to that ring) has been already included they ignore the packet. In other words source route bridging effectively **eliminates any loops** already at this 'exploring' stage.

QUICK TIP **RIF**

Routing Information Field is derived from explorer packets generated by the source node. RIF contains information about the path the packet has traveled.

However, if the bridge determines that it is 'new' to the path, the bridge must process the explorer packet as though the path through it is valid and should be made known. The bridges not only must adjust the RIF field but also the FCS field (and frame status field, commonly to specify that the frame was copied as if by its destination station) of the frame. Eventually, such a frame is delivered to the destination station on the destination ring. The destination station should receive as many explorer packets as there exist paths to it from the source, each containing a unique path description.

It is now the task for the destination station to return all the explorer packets to the source station. This action is straightforward: the route is already included in every frame so the only requirement on the destination station is to indicate that the **reverse route** should be taken. The destination station thus changes the direction bit to indicate that the path should be read and forwarding performed in the opposite order through the RIF. The station should also change the type indication of the packet from all-route explorer packet to **specific route frame**.

In a fault-free network, where the destination station is active and at least one path exists from the source to the destination, the source station should receive all the explorer packets which were created on the basis of the one originally generated by the source station. When the source has received all the relevant information about the path(s) across the bridged network, it must choose the path which is the best. A station may apply different criteria when determining which path is 'best.' The decision may be based on any of the following:

- **Shortest delay** across the network – the first explorer packet received back gives the indication of the 'quickest' path.

- **Shortest path** through the network – the explorer packet with the shortest route descriptor field (recorded in the **length of route** RIF subfield) describes the path with the fewest number of hops that must be traversed between the source and destination stations.

- **Largest frame** – each explorer packet indicates (in the subfield of the routing control field) the largest frame supported on the particular path; choice of the path with the largest supported frame would allow the use of a frame of that size (with a relatively smaller overhead than in the case of shorter frames) to be generated at the source station without a danger of it being discarded on the way to the destination.

The criterion mostly deployed in source bridged networks is the **minimal delay** of the network traffic.

> **QUICK TIP** route selection in a Token Ring bridged network
>
> The source station, based on the receipt of more than one route explorer packet, usually chooses the first one received as the indicator of the quickest route.

Once the **source station** has chosen the best path to the destination, it will **cache the RIF field** and use this path for any frames that must be forwarded to that destination until a change in the network topology invokes the exploring operation anew.

The all-routes explorer operation requires that all source-route bridges must copy the packet to the next ring. Left unbounded, this operation leads to the generation of an exponentially large number of packets in a large bridged network. For this reason, the **spanning tree route explorer** is more commonly used (sometimes referred to as a single route broadcast). Here, a **single explorer packet** is generated by the source station to each ring. Each ring has a single designated bridge, which is determined by an election process performed by all the bridges on the ring. The designated bridge operates with STP forwarding enabled, and forwards a single copy of the explorer packet to the next ring. When the explorer packet reaches the **destination station**, the route (path) the packet traversed may not have been the optimal route, so the receiving station sends the route explorer packet back to the sender in an **all-routes explorer packet**.

As a result, the source station receives the information on all the routes available through the network. The information the source receives is exactly the same as if an all-routes explorer packet had been used in both directions, but network and bridge resources used for route determination are dramatically reduced.

Since **source-routing stations** maintain their **own forwarding tables** and insert the routing information in every packet they send, **source-routing bridges** maintain **no 'routing' tables** and perform **no look-up functions**. They base the forwarding decision on a simple pattern match function. If a bridge is included in a route, its bridge number and the ring numbers of the rings on both sides of the bridge will be included in the frame RIF. If any of these numbers is missing or incorrect, the bridge will not forward the packet.

In order **to prevent endless circulation** of explorer packets around the ring, bridges check to see that the ring number of the next ring is not already included in the routing information field of the packet. If the bridge determines the explorer packet has already passed through the next ring, it will not forward the packet to that ring.

6.3.3 Routing information field

The RIF consists of two parts (see Figure 6.10):

■ ***Routing control*** – for route specification and follow-up identification, composed of the following subfields:

   – *type* (three bits) – indicates whether the frame should be routed to a single node, a group of nodes that make up a spanning tree of the internet, or all nodes:

   – *specifically routed frame* (can be used as a transit mechanism for multicast frames. It can also be used as a replacement for the all-paths explorer in outbound route queries. In this case, the destination responds with an all-paths explorer) value = *000*;

   – *all-paths explorer* – value = *100*;

   – *spanning-tree explorer* – value = *110*;

   – *length* (five bits) – indicates the total length (in octets) of the RIF which may vary between two (at the source station which creates the explorer packet but does not insert any route descriptor) and 30 octets (with specified path of a maximum length through source bridged network);

   – *direction (D) bit* (one bit) – indicates the direction to the frame, i.e. the direction to follow the route descriptor's sequence of bridges and Token Rings (forward = *0* or reverse = *1*);

   – *largest* (three bits) – indicates the largest frame that can be handled along this route by values identifying popular packet sizes, such as 516, 1500, 2052, 4472, 8144, 11 407, 17 800, 65 535. (The following four bits of the routing control part are not used.)

■ ***Route descriptor*** – consists of one or more **ring number** (12 bits) or **bridge number** (four bits) pairs (maximum 14), sometimes called segments, that uniquely specify a portion of a route, i.e. a sequence of LAN and bridge number pairs (route designators) that start and end with LAN numbers (the last bridge number is left unspecified). Each ring number must be unique across the network while bridge numbers may reuse the same numbers unless there is more than one ring interconnecting two Token Rings. In this case, the parallel bridges must be assigned unique numbers and may provide load balancing.

Limitations

The RIF field has a **maximum length of 30 octets**. This is important, since the maximum length of data in any frame in which the RIF field has been inserted will decrease to conform to the maximum PDU in the Token Ring LANs. This also **limits the maximum span** of the source-route bridged network to a maximum

| FIGURE 6-10 | RIF in Token Ring frame |

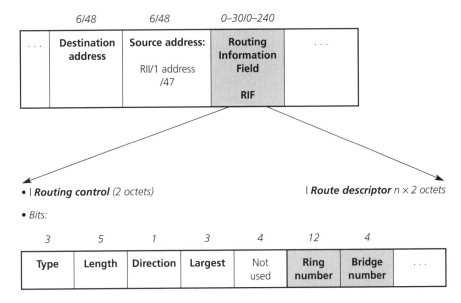

Octets/bits:

of 13 bridges and 14 Token Rings (according to the IEEE standard). However, IBM keeps its limit to only seven bridges and eight rings, a constraint to which some manufacturers adhere rather than to the standard!

IBM required that the source route bridges have only two ports. However, certain implementations allow for the option to use devices with more than two ports, thus allowing the bridge to interconnect more than two rings. This is made possible by operating in a manner similar to the way remote SRB is performed. The limit of two ports to every bridge is preserved by introducing the concept of a **virtual ring** in the bridge itself. The multiport source-route bridge splits into as many virtual bridges connected to the virtual ring as it has ports (see Figure 6.11). However, all the virtual rings count as if they were real so the RIF field length limit may be quickly reached.

| QUICK TIP | **multiport source route bridge** |

A multiport source route bridge has to create an internal **virtual ring** connected to individual virtual internal bridges to adhere to the two-port-bridge-only requirement.

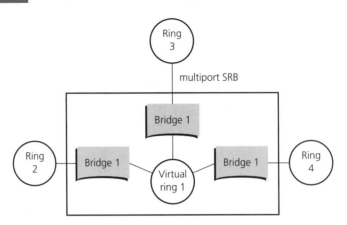

FIGURE 6-11 Multiport source route bridge

6.4 Remote bridging

Whereas local bridges connect LANs in the same physical location, **remote bridges** are used to connect geographically separated LANs via some type of transmission facility. Bridges are available to connect over 100 Mbps FDDI or over WANs, using a wide variety of communications interfaces including EIA/TIA-232C for lower speeds, and V.35 or EIA/TIA-422 for higher speeds, including T1/E1 and T3/E3 dedicated or leased circuits, Frame Relay, and broadband switched services (e.g. ATM or SMDS/CBDS). Broadband fiber optic, infrared, microwave, and satellite transmission capabilities are also available.

The remote bridge has similar characteristics to the bridges previously described, and can be implemented in (potentially) mixed LAN/WAN environments. The distinguishing characteristics of remote bridges include filtering the traffic from the LAN network adapter and reformatting, buffering, and forwarding the traffic destined for the remote LAN over the concrete transport medium.

A standard approach to remote bridging is specified by the IEEE. It models a set of two or more remote bridges interconnected via remote lines into a **remote bridge group**. Within a group, a **remote bridge cluster** is dynamically formed through execution of the spanning tree as the set of bridges that may pass frames among each other. This model bestows on the remote lines the basic properties of a LAN, but does not require a one-to-one mapping of lines to virtual LAN segments.

STANDARDS WATCH   **remote bridging**

ISO/IEC 15802-5 (ANSI/IEEE Std 802.1G, 1998): **Information Technology – Telecommunications and Information Exchange between Systems – Local and Metropolitan Area Networks – Common Specifications – Part 5: Remote Media Access Control (MAC) Bridging**

Most bridges implement some form of **data compression** to maximize the efficiency of the communications link. They also generally implement some type of proprietary protocol across the link to handle error checking and retransmission of bad or incomplete packets (LAN frames transmitted across the WAN link).

To properly interconnect the LANs over another (WAN) medium, one must ensure that the **encapsulation** or **tunneling** of the LAN frame is understood by the equipment (bridges) operating at both edges of the remote bridged network. This can be done at the link layer, where a LAN frame is encapsulated into WAN (e.g. HDLC or PPP, or ATM Adaption Layer) frame. Encapsulation or tunneling may be performed at higher layers (e.g. the LAN frame could be encapsulated into the network layer packet or even the transport layer segment). Bridge ports enabling the remote connection of bridges must participate in the relevant bridging algorithms. The IETF has developed a specific support for bridging by protocol PPP, the **Bridging Control Protocol (BCP),** which is now a proposed standard (RFC 2878). For remote bridging examples see Figures 6.12 and 6.13.

FIGURE 6-12 Example of remote bridging across FDDI

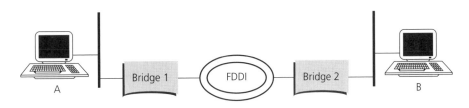

FIGURE 6-13 Example of remote bridging across WAN

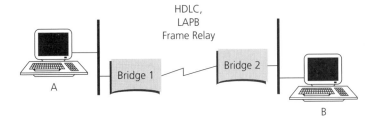

While implementing remote bridging over WAN links, a **performance** mismatch or impedance can be introduced when the WAN link speeds are significantly lower than the interconnected LAN links. The response time to complete an application operation over a remote bridge can be significantly longer than that required on a local LAN segment. If the main transport medium is a slow WAN link, the difference in network bandwidth and throughput must be considered carefully. The low latency, high throughput characteristics associated with local area networks can degrade significantly by introducing a serial line of, for example, 56 kbps between LAN segments. Under heavy load conditions, the increased delay and low capacity of a 56 kbps link could be sufficient to prevent the delay-sensitive traffic (e.g. SNA or banking transactions) from arriving at the destination segment across such media without timing out, and could create significant congestion at the output WAN port of the bridge (which in most cases would cause the bridge to discard frames determined for the destination LAN).

Remote source-route bridging also uses various proprietary encapsulation mechanisms, but in all other respects, still conforms to the SRB requirements. In the IBM terminology, remote bridges are called **half-bridges**.

6.5 Source-route transparent bridging

Moving from the homogeneous bridging environment into the **heterogeneous**, we will first examine an easier method of deploying both source-route and transparent bridging in the same network, at the same bridge. As this form of source-route transparent bridging does not deal completely with all the issues where Token Ring and Ethernet LANs differ, we will concentrate on these basic differences under the translational bridging section below.

Source-route transparent (SRT) bridging connects multiple network segments into a single bridged network (see Figure 6.14). However, SRB does not allow all connected stations to talk to each other. This method of interconnection of the transparent and source-route bridged parts of network is based on simple assumptions: those stations connected to the transparent bridged network will communicate among themselves, and those stations on Token Rings capable of using the RIF field will communicate with each other via source-route bridging. Inevitably, the bridge(s) within the source route transparent bridged network will have to be *bilingual*, i.e. they must operate two bridging modules, one supporting transparent bridging and another supporting forwarding based on the route specified by a source. The determination of when to use either of the two modules is based on detecting the presence of the RIF field in the LAN frame (i.e. determination that the RII bit in the frame is set to one.

FIGURE 6-14   Example of source route transparent bridged network

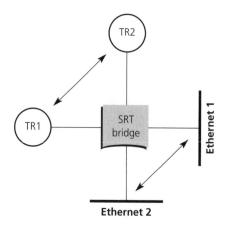

source-route transparent bridging

A **Source-Route Transparent (SRT) bridge** allows both Ethernet and Token Ring segments to be connected. However, the SRT bridge does not perform any translation therefore it supports only communication among Token Ring stations and separately among Ethernet stations.

Frames with an RIF field inserted by the source will be subject to the source-routing operation, while all other frames (both Token Ring and Ethernet frames) will be processed by the **transparent bridging** operation. Ultimately, the network will still be split into two parts, defined by the end-stations, abilities in terms of bridging awareness. However, a **common spanning tree** will be created and end-stations of the same type will be able to communicate over an arbitrary topology network.

The principles of source route transparent bridging have been standardized in IEEE and ISO, currently forming part of ISO standards ISO/IEC 10038 and ISO/IEC 8802-2.

STANDARDS WATCH **source-route transparent bridging**

ISO/IEC 10038 (ANSI/IEEE Std 802.1D, 1993 edition): **Information Technology-Telecommunications and Information Exchange between Systems – Local Area Networks – MAC Bridges**

ISO/IEC 8802-2 (ANSI/IEEE 802.2, 1994 edition): **Information Technology – Telecommunications and Information Exchange between Systems – Local and Metropolitan Area Networks – Specific Requirements – Part 2: Logical Link Control**

IEEE 802.1D-1998 **IEEE Standard for Local Area Network MAC (Media Access Control) Bridges**

6.5.1 LLC route determination entity

Whereas the first attempts to integrate transparent and source-route bridging were made in 1990 by IBM, the standard for SRT bridging was prepared by the IEEE and belongs to the logical link control (LLC) operation definition. This is because not only is the MAC sublayer of the data link layer involved but the LLC sublayer is as well.

The LLC entity supporting SRT bridging is called the **Route Determination Entity** (RDE). The RDE uses the MAC service to discover the route (path) and uses the discovered route for transferring data.

The SRT bridge distinguishes among **four types of frame** a bridge may deal with:

■ Specifically Routed Frames (SRF);

■ Spanning Tree Explorers (STE);

■ All-Routes Explorer frames (ARE);

■ Non-Source Routed frames (NSR).

The first three frame types may appear during the operation of the SRB algorithm, and all of them include the RIF field. The last type, NSR, is relevant to transparent bridging, as it is typically generated by a station having no knowledge of the fact that the destination station is not connected to the same segment.

The RDE frame format is shown in Figure 6.15. The *PType* distinguishes among three types of commands/responses. In addition to the normal LLC Type 1 encapsulation (using unnumbered information data frame), SNAP encapsulation for RDE is available (see Figure 6.16) through the use of the option field in the LLC frame.

FIGURE 6-15 Route Determination Entity PDU

Number of octets:

1	1	6	6	1	1	n
RDE version = 10000000	P-Type	Target MAC	Original MAC	Target SAP	Original SAP	Options

Note:
PType = 10000000 for Route Query Command (RQC) (first left is least significant bit).
PType = 01000000 for Route Query Response (RQR).
PType = 11000000 for Route Selected Command (RSC).

FIGURE 6-16 SNAP encapsulation (option RDE PDU field)

Number of octets:

2	2	5
TAG = 0001	**Length** = 0005	**SNAP PID**

6.6 Translational bridging

The final form of overall communication among all stations of any type requires support for both transparent and source-route bridging. The only way a complete understanding of both Ethernet and Token Ring topologies may be achieved is through the use of a complex translation mechanism. There are numerous fields in the respective bridging frames resulting from the different medium access methods which make the frames incompatible. Therefore, all the discrepancies between the IEEE 802.3 and 802.5 standards must be handled with care while performing translation. Any misunderstanding and possible corruption of frame would lead to its discard.

6.6.1 Differences between Ethernet and Token Ring

The major differences between Ethernet and Token Ring are as follows:

- **Bit ordering** – the internal hardware representation of octets in the frame is incompatible. Token Ring and FDDI consider the first bit encountered to be the high-order bit of an octet (most significant bit). Ethernet, on the other hand, considers the first bit encountered in the octet to be the low-order bit (least significant bit). In other words, Ethernet address is little endian, canonical notation (it transmits least-order bit first) and Token Ring and FDDI addresses are big endian, non-canonical notation (they transmit high-order bit first). For example, the MAC address *00-00-0C-xx-xx-xx* on Ethernet would appear as *00-00-30-yy-yy-yy* on Token Ring since every octet needs to be bit-swapped. Both Ethernet and Token Ring use the first transmitted bit of a frame's destination address to determine whether the frame is unicast or multicast. With no address conversion, a unicast frame (a frame that has only one destination) on one network may appear as a multicast address (an address for more than one station) on another network.

- **Embedded MAC addresses** – in some cases, MAC addresses are actually carried in the data portion of a frame. For example, the Address Resolution Protocol (ARP) used in TCP/IP networks places hardware addresses in the data portion of a link-layer frame. Due to the bit ordering differences between Ethernet and Token Ring (FDDI), the conversion of addresses in the data portion of a frame is difficult because they must be handled on a case-by-case basis. Due to this constraint proprietary solutions usually do not support translational bridging except for non-routable protocols which do not propagate MAC addresses.

- **Maximum data unit sizes** – Token Ring and Ethernet support different maximum frame sizes. Ethernet's maximum is 1518 B, whereas normal Token Ring frames can be three times larger (and extended Token Ring frames even larger). Since bridges are not capable of frame fragmentation and reassembly, frames that exceed the maximum data unit of a given network must be dropped.

- **Handling of exclusive Token Ring functions** – certain Token Ring frame fields have no counterparts in the Ethernet, namely *access control, frame control,* and *frame status* field bits. Ethernet has no priority mechanism, whereas Token Ring does. Other Token Ring bits that must be thrown out when a Token Ring frame is converted to an Ethernet frame include the *token* bit, the *monitor* bit, and the *reservation* bits. Token Ring frames also include three frame status bits: A, C, and E. The purpose of these bits is to inform the source station whether the destination exists (*A* bit set), if it copied the frame (*C* bit set), or found errors in the frame (*E* bit set). Ethernet does not support these bits. The issue of how to deal with these significant bits during translation is not standardized.

- **Handling of explorer frames and RIF** – as explorer frames are exclusively used in source-route bridging, transparent bridges do not understand what to do with SRB explorer frames. Similarly, transparent bridges do not expect any path information to be included in the frame and hence do not understand the RIF field in the Token Ring frame. The problem exists also on the other side: all source-route bridges only accept frames with a RIF field included for processing (as only these are candidates for intersegment forwarding). All other frames, including frames for transparent bridging, will be deemed to belong to the local segment and will be ignored by SRB.

- **Incompatible spanning-tree algorithms** – both transparent bridging and SRB use the spanning-tree algorithm to eliminate any potential bridging loops, but the particular algorithms employed by the two bridging methods are incompatible.

The differences between Ethernet and Token Ring are so significant that they practically eliminate a proper, complete, and comprehensive translation while interconnecting them at the link layer. In fact, a translating bridge has to perform nearly as much work as a router with significantly less flexibility, and robustness. Therefore it is no surprise that few if any translating bridges have been deployed successfully.

Proprietary solutions

As there is no consensus and therefore **no standard solution** of the above problems which could be used in translational bridging, all solutions are **proprietary**. The following describes some aspects of the methods employed for implementing translational bridging.

Translational bridges reorder **source and destination address** bits when translating between Ethernet and Token Ring frame formats. The problem of **embedded MAC addresses** can be solved by programming the bridge to check for various types of MAC addresses, but this solution must be adapted with each new type of embedded MAC address. Some translational bridging solutions simply check for the most popular embedded addresses. **Broadcast, multicast**, and **unknown unicast frames** coming from Ethernet may be handled as explorer packets (spanning tree or all-routes) in the source-route domain.

The RIF field has a subfield that indicates the **largest frame size** that can be accepted by a particular SRB implementation. Translational bridges that send frames from the transparent bridging domain to the SRB domain usually set the **maximum size** field to 1500 bytes to limit the size of Token Ring frames entering the transparent bridging domain. Some hosts cannot correctly process this field, in which case translational bridges are forced to simply drop those frames that exceed Ethernet's maximum frame size.

Bits representing **Token Ring functions** that have no Ethernet corollary are typically thrown out by translational bridges. Token Ring's Priority, Reservation, and *Monitor* bits are discarded. Token Ring's *Frame Status* Bits are treated differently depending on the translational bridge manufacturer. Some manufacturers simply ignore the bits, whereas others have the bridge set the *C* bit (to indicate that the frame has been copied) but not the *A* bit (which indicates that the destination station recognizes its address). In the former case, there is no way for a Token Ring source node to determine whether the frame it sent has become lost, and tracking of lost frames and the resulting retransmission activity is left for implementation in the transport layer. The latter case provides for higher reliability at the Token Ring MAC layer. However, it should be noted that it introduces an otherwise illegal combination of the *AC* bits (binary *01*) in the *Frame Status* field.

The elegant solution to the transparent and source-route bridging understanding and handling by the end stations is to keep their view simple and unambiguous. Translational bridges thus create a software gateway between the two domains. To the SRB end stations, the translational bridge has a ring number and bridge number associated with it, so it looks like a standard SRB. The ring number, in this case, actually reflects the entire transparent bridging domain. To the transparent bridging domain, the translational bridge appears simply as another transparent bridge.

When bridging from the SRB domain to the transparent bridging domain, SRB information is removed. **RIFs** are usually **cached by the bridge** for use by subsequent return traffic. When bridging from the transparent bridging to the SRB domain, the translational bridge can check the frame to see if it has a unicast destination. If the frame has a multicast or broadcast destination, it is sent into the SRB domain as a spanning tree explorer. If the frame has a unicast address, the translational bridge looks up the destination in the RIF cache. If a path is found, it is used, and the RIF information is added to the frame; otherwise, the frame is sent as a spanning tree explorer. Because the two **spanning tree** implementations are **incompatible**, multiple paths between the SRB and the transparent bridging domains are typically not permitted.

Actual frame translation

Various conversion tasks between Token Ring and Ethernet may exist, depending on the actual encapsulations used (some of them are not supported at all by individual vendors). The two most often used are as follows:

- **Between IEEE 802.3 and 802.5, both using LLC encapsulation** – the conversion concentrates specifically on the destination and source MAC addresses, the LLC encapsulated control information (source and destination service access points, and control fields), and user data. Field information is passed to the corresponding fields of the other frame. The destination and source address bits are reordered. When bridging from IEEE 802.3 to Token Ring, the length field of the IEEE 802.3 frame is removed. When bridging from Token Ring to IEEE 802.3, the access control field and RIF field are removed. The RIF can be cached in the translational bridge for use by return traffic.

- **Between Ethernet Type II and Token Ring Subnetwork Access Protocol (SNAP) encapsulation of IEEE 802.5** – frame conversion concentrates again on the destination and source addresses, and protocol type and data. The destination and source address bits are reordered and all the fields are used in the other frame. When bridging from Token Ring SNAP to Ethernet Type II, the RIF information, LLC service access points, control, and vendor code are removed. The RIF can be cached in the translational bridge for use by return traffic. When bridging from Ethernet Type II to Token Ring SNAP, no information is removed.

6.7 FDDI position

Although FDDI was not first included in the standardization activities in terms of bridging, in the course of the work it was added later and it currently forms part of the IEEE/ANSI 802.1i standard (since 1992). The scope and field of application of IEEE 802.1d have been extended to transparent bridging between **Fiber Distributed Data Interface** (FDDI) local area networks (LANs) and between FDDI LANs and IEEE 802 LANs.

STANDARDS WATCH | **FDDI bridging**

IEEE 802.1i-1992 **Standard for Local and Metropolitan Area Network MAC Bridges – Fiber Distributed Data Interface (FDDI)** Supplement to 802.1D-1990

There are two ways to connect to FDDI network via using a bridge:

- **Encapsulation bridging** – sometimes called *transit* bridging because FDDI then forms only a transport, fast backbone LAN in the bridged network (it is one of the forms of remote bridging). The frames which are candidates for forwarding across the FDDI (Token Ring or Ethernet frames) are encapsulated or tunneled directly into the data field of the FDDI frame. Note that the encapsulated frame is neither interpreted by nor understood by the stations directly connected to the FDDI ring. This form of bridging is not standardized and only proprietary solutions exist which preclude the interoperability of bridges of different manufacturers.

- **Translational bridging** – this form allows for the **complete translation of frames** coming from Token Ring or Ethernet onto the FDDI ring which requires addressing all the differences between the relevant media and eventually allows for the FDDI connected stations to be a real part of the bridged network (due to a full understanding of the FDDI frames' content). As with other types of translational bridging the methods used are not standardized and all the solutions are proprietary.

Translational bridging between **Ethernet and FDDI** perpetuates the issue of bit ordering, explained in the previous section, a little further since few protocols work across the FDDI/Ethernet border. One reason for this is the concept of a canonical address above the MAC layer which means that any address that is above the physical dependent sublayer on FDDI should be ordered canonically according to the Ethernet order. IP is a classical example of such a network protocol. Other protocols which may be supported in a similar way are OSI (CLNP), DECnet, and non-routable protocols such as NetBIOS, MOP, and LAT.

6.8 Application and design issues in bridged networks

6.8.1 Load sharing and load balancing

Transparent bridges, based on the spanning tree protocol operation, do not allow for multiple parallel paths between source and destination network segments and thus for load splitting across them. However, this traffic control mechanism may occasionally be very useful (and even more so with remote bridging). As there does not exist any standard mechanism which would provide such a possibility and at the same time ensure the error-free operation of the spanning tree algorithm, each vendor has its own solution.

In case of **remote transparent bridging** where several parallel serial connections exist between a pair of bridges (see Figure 6.17) it should be possible to group the connections in the direction of the STP so that they would exist as a single path (trunk) and the edge bridges would then be able to use them for load balancing on a per destination basis. It means that the frames from the same source and destination MAC address pair will always take the same single path through the transparent bridge (i.e. through the same outgoing port). However, should the path to another destination station from the same source address take the same outgoing port it might use another, parallel port. Eventually each pair of source and destination addresses would be assigned a single path through an outgoing port and the traffic from the same source to various destinations will be balanced across the parallel outgoing bridge ports.

FIGURE 6-17 Parallel paths across WAN

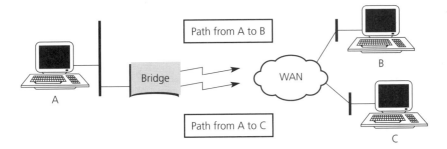

In this case, the initial premise of the spanning tree algorithm, no parallel paths between any two network segments, can be slightly rephrased into: **no parallel paths between any two nodes in the bridged network may exist**.

In the case of **source-route bridging** (both local and remote) the source station would in every case use a **single path to the destination station** on the remote ring (single RIF field in cache) and no load sharing would be offered even if there are multiple parallel paths across bridges or rings (see Figure 6.18). However, some load balancing could be achieved among the parallel paths from the same source to different destination stations on the same destination ring, similar to transparent bridging, and the **load balancing** could be achieved on **per destination basis**.

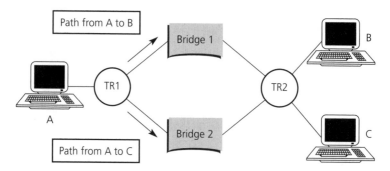

FIGURE 6-18 Load balancing per destination in source route bridged networks

6.8.2 Filtering

Bridges were the first interconnection devices which could be used for filtering the network traffic. However, the criteria on which bridges may base their filtering decisions are limited to data link layer frame fields. Basic filtering is achieved based on:

- **MAC addresses** – source and/or destination;
- **network protocol type**.

More sophisticated filtering may use additional, customer-defined criteria and may perform matching and filtering on specified bit patterns in the data field of the LAN frame.

> **QUICK TIP** **filtering by bridges**
>
> Filtering is based on the link layer information available to bridges in passing frames, such as MAC addresses and network protocol type.

Filtering may be used in its pure form to **forward** or **block** individual frames, or to support sophisticated traffic **prioritizing** and monitoring using various **counters**.

6.8.3 Performance

The performance of the bridge depends on the size of the frames processed. When a frame is received, a bridge checks the relevant fields to resolve forwarding. When incoming frames are large, the bridge has enough time to complete the forwarding decision and switch the frames between incoming and outgoing ports. When the frames are small, the bridge has less time between them to accomplish its functions.

The amount of time the bridge has to process the frames depends not only on the length of the frames but also on the amount of time between them (i.e. the inter-arrival time). In a real-world environment, the time between frames and the frame size emitted by workstations cannot be kept constant because there are an infinite number of types of application traffic of varying sizes, and because at any moment in time, one or many workstations may be emitting traffic over the LAN. This bursty behavior is characteristic of data applications that operate over LANs and complex internetworks.

One important drawback while using bridges should not be forgotten: when a bridge becomes congested or overloaded, it will drop frames without notifying the source station or other bridges in the network about this action. There is no mechanism which would support the generation of error messages whose effect would suppress such congestion. In a congested network, however, generating error messages would also contribute to increased congestion, moreover, the error messages would not necessarily get through.

SNAPSHOT **Bridging advantages**

- High **throughput** at data link layer processing speed (limited by a store-and-forward operation).
- Possibility to interconnect **media** of different **speeds** (e.g. 4 Mbps to 16 Mbps Token Ring).
- Allows a limit to the span of Ethernet collision domains.
- Low **price** (due to limited functionality).
- Easy configuration.
- **Transparency** to network protocols.
- Support to **non-routable protocols** (SNA, LAT, MOP, NetBIOS).

SNAPSHOT **Bridging disadvantages**

- Creates a **flat network** with no logical segmentation or hierarchy.
- **Dependent on the media access control mechanism** (difficult in particular when translation is required in a mixed media environment).
- **Does not eliminate or limit broadcast storms**.
- **Limited filtering** based only on address (source and/or destination MAC addresses) and network protocol type fields in the frame – does not provide full security protection.
- **Limited scalability:** dictated by maximum number of bridges allowed according to standard and by filtering database size (bridge memory limitations).

- **Limited traffic prioritization** mechanisms (based on protocol type).
- **Limited compression** capabilities (required for remote bridging across slow serial lines).
- **Limited load balancing** alternatives.
- Potential for **performance problems** in cases of bridge congestion.
- **No frame fragmentation** capability (common denominator is largest frame across all LANs, i.e. 1518 B).
- **No feedback** to source station in case of frames dropped due to potential bridge overloading.

6.8.4 Design issues

The basis for deciding whether and where to deploy bridging in the corporate network can only be determined by examining the advantages and disadvantages of bridges on a case-by-case basis. Bridging is still useful for segmenting large, flat networks into more manageable small networks, thereby minimizing the individual collision domains. Improving performance following segmentation is only possible by careful analysis of the actual traffic in the LANs, and then ensuring that LAN traffic is kept as local as possible. For example, keeping servers close to or on the same segment as the clients that use them most is an important design consideration. This design rule is a common thread throughout internetwork design, be they bridged, switched, or routed networks.

Bridging is also useful where various network protocols are employed in a relatively small but multiprotocol enterprise network, where segmentation is required and the LAN environment is homogeneous (only Ethernet or Token Ring is deployed), but where multiprotocol routers would be too expensive to purchase or operate.

Bridging, however, is necessary when non-routable protocols are deployed in the network.

Remote transparent bridging should use a single STP across all interconnected LANs. However, using STP on slow WAN transport link(s) is not recommended. On slow WAN links delays can easily exceed the recommended BPDUs timeout of two seconds, which would eventually lead to difficulties among bridges in establishing the root bridge on which the spanning algorithm is based (also known as 'root wars').

Product choice

A network administrator should consider features other than performance when selecting bridging products. Many of the more important features to consider are mentioned above, but an equally important consideration is the network management support embedded in the device: standard agent and MIB support for the SNMP protocol v1/v2 (see Chapter 4), vendor or enterprise-specific extensions to MIBs that provide superior remote diagnostics and more extensive monitoring, terminal (e.g. Telnet) support for remote management, and extended filtering capabilities and security features are available from many products today.

STANDARDS WATCH   MIBs for bridged environment

RFC 1474 **The Definitions of Managed Objects for the Bridge Network Control Protocol of the Point-to-Point Protocol,** 1993 (Proposed Standard)

RFC 1493 **Definitions of Managed Objects for Bridges,** 1993 (Proposed Standard)

RFC 1525 **Definitions of Managed Objects for Source Routing Bridges,** 1993 (Proposed Standard)

RFC 2674 **Definitions of Managed Objects for Bridges with Traffic Classes, Multicast Filtering and Virtual LAN Extensions,** 1999 (Proposed Standard)

Bridges vs. switches

There are many similarities between bridges and LAN switches because both operate at the same layer. **LAN switches** that operate exclusively at Layer 2 (data link) are sometimes referred to as **multiport bridges**, or even **multiport repeaters with bridging**. However, the role of LAN switching in today's networks is considerably different, as we will see after thoroughly investigating the features and qualities of LAN switching in the next Part.

Finally, it should be noted that most routers may be configured for a bridging support. This enables them to combine the functionality of bridging and routing as necessary, depending on the protocol traffic and interfaces to neighboring devices. Routers with bridging capabilities support both functions in a separate regime as a minimum, i.e. a particular protocol would only be bridged while others may be routed. Some routers offer enhanced support: integrating bridging and routing features enabling them to bridge a particular protocol over some of their interfaces while the same protocol is routed on other interfaces. This adds granularity and flexibility in mixed bridged-routed networks (usually in a multivendor environment).

STANDARDS WATCH   Summarized Standards watch

The following standards and RFCs have been brought to your attention in this chapter:

IEE 802.1D-1998 *IEEE Standard for Local Area Network MAC (Media Access Control) Bridges (revision of 802.1D-*1990 edition (ISO/IEC 10038); incorporates P802.1p and P802.12e; incorporates and supersedes published standards 802.1j and 802.6k)

IEEE 802.1h-1995 – *ISO/IEC Technical Report 11802-5: 1997 Local and Metropolitan Area Networks: IEEE Recommended Practice for Media Access Control (MAC) Bridging on Ethernet Version 2.0 in 802 Local Area Networks*

▶

IEEE 802.1i-1992 *Standard for Local and Metropolitan Area Network MAC Bridges – Fiber Distributed Data Interface (FDDI)* Supplement to 802.1D-1990

IEEE 802.1j-1996 (superseded by 802.1D-1998) *Supplement to Information Technology – Telecommunications and Information Exchange between Systems – Local Area Networks – Media Access Control (MAC) Bridges: Managed Objects for MAC Bridges*

IEEE 802.1p (superseded by 802.1D-1998) *Standard for Local and Metropolitan Area Networks – Supplement to Media Access Control (MAC) Bridges: Traffic Class Expediting and Dynamic Multicast Filtering*

IEEE 802.6k-1992 (superseded by 802.1D-1998) *Supplement to Media Access Control (MAC) Bridges IEEE Standard 802.6 Distributed Queue Dual Bus (DQDB) Subnetwork of a MAN*

IEEE 802.12e (superseded by 802.1D-1998) *Standard for Information Technology – Local and Metropolitan Area Networks – Pat 1D: Telecommunications and Information Exchange between Systems – Local Area Networks – Media Access Control (MAC) Bridges – Supplement for Support by IEEE 802.12*

New Standard Project IEEE P802.1t *Standard for Information Technology – Telecommunications and Information Exchange between Systems – Local and Metropolitan Area Networks – Common Specifications – Part 3: Media Access Control (MAC) Bridges: Technical and Editorial Corrections* (maintenance of the 802.1D-1998 standard)

New Standard Project IEEE P801.1w *Supplement to ISO/IEC 15802-3 (802.1D): Information Technology – Telecommunications and Information Exchange between Systems – Local and Metropolitan Area Networks – Common Specifications – Part 3: Media Access Control (MAC) Bridges – Rapid Reconfiguration*

ISO/IEC 8802-2 (ANSI/IEEE 802.2, 1994 edition) *Information Technology – Telecommunications and Information Exchange between Systems – Local and Metropolitan Area Networks – Specific Requirements – Part 2: Logical Link Control*

ISO/IEC 10038 (ANSI/IEEE Std 802.1D, 1993 edition) *Information Technology – Telecommunications and Information Exchange between Systems – Local and Metropolitan Area Networks – MAC Bridges*

ISO/IEC TR 11802-1, 1997 *Information Technology – Telecommunications and Information Exchange between Systems – Local and Metropolitan Area Networks – Common Specifications – Part 1: Structure and Coding of LLC Addresses in LANs*

ISO/IEC TR 11802-2, 1996 *Information Technology – Telecommunications and Information Exchange between Systems – Local and Metropolitan Area Networks – Common Specifications – Part 2:* Standard Group MAC Addresses

ISO/IEC 15802-5 (ANSI/IEEE Std 802.1G, 1998) *Information Technology – Telecommunications and Information Exchange between Systems – Local and Metropolitan Area Networks – Common Specifications – Part 5: Remote Media Access Control (MAC) Bridging*

RFC 1474 *The Definitions of Managed Objects for the Bridge Network Control Protocol of the Point-to-Point Protocol, 1993 (Proposed Standard)*

RFC 1493 *Definitions of Managed Objects for the Bridges 1993* (Proposed Standard)

RFC 1525 *Definitions of Managed Objects for Source Routing Bridges,* 1993 (Proposed Standard)

RFC 2674 *Definitions of Managed Objects for Bridges with Traffic Classes, Multicast Filtering and Virtual LAN Extensions,* 1999 (Proposed Standard)

PART II CONCLUDING REMARKS

This part is dedicated to bridging, one of the oldest ways to extend LAN segments by their interconnection. We realize that bridges directly depend upon the media they interconnect, hence there are two major distinct bridging types: **transparent** for interconnecting **Ethernet** segments and **source-route** for **Token Ring** networks. The two methods differ fundamentally. This is best seen in a situation in which we are forced to interconnect both Ethernet and Token Ring into a **heterogeneous** bridged network using **source-route transparent bridging** or the even more complex **translational bridging**. This situation, due to its complexity, in most cases involves routers instead, unless **non-routable protocols** such as NetBIOS, LAT, SNA, etc. are to be bridged. The more common situation is to keep homogeneous LAN segments apart, in which case we may use **remote bridges** to enable communication over WAN or FDDI.

The most important aspects of **transparent bridging** lie in the **spanning-tree protocol** operation looking after creating and maintaining **loop-free topology** by blocking any redundant bridge ports. On the other hand, source-route bridging relies on the presence of an **RIF field** in the Token Ring frame, where all paths through the bridged network are encoded.

Bridges are internetworking devices operating at **Layer 2** which brings the benefit of lower latency related to forwarding frames, but at the same time diminishes their intelligence such as capabilities of filtering. Bridges invariably forward frames in software, in a **store-and-forward mode**.

Building a bridged network enables us to extend the LANs and segment the network into **collision domains** (in case of Ethernet). However, the result is a flat network encompassing a **single broadcast domain**. In the following Parts the similarities will be shown in Part III dealing with LAN switching, and the significant differences will be depicted in Part IV on routing.

PART III

SWITCHING

It is important to emphasize that the topics covered in the following Parts all have their place in current networks. From the network design point of view, all the following technologies are usually required to build successful campus networks:

- **LAN switching technologies** (covered in Chapter 7 in this Part):
  - **Ethernet switching** – provides Layer 2 switching and offers broadcast domain segmentation using VLANs. This is the base fabric of the network;
  - **Token Ring switching** – offers the same functionality as Ethernet switching but uses Token Ring technology;
  - **Copper Data Distributed Interface** (CDDI) – provides a single-attachment station (SAS) or dual-attachment station (DAS);
  - **Fiber Distributed Data Interface** (FDDI) – provides an SAS or DAS connection to the FDDI backbone network using two multimode, media interface connector (MIC) fiber-optic connections.

  Switched LAN internetworks are also referred to as **campus LANs**.

- **ATM switching technology** – ATM switching offers high-speed switching technology for voice, video, and data. Its operation is similar to LAN switching technologies for data operations. ATM, however, offers superior voice, video, and data integration today. (ATM switching is covered in more detail in Chapter 8 in this Part.)

- **Routing technology** – routing is a key technology for interconnecting LANs in a campus network. It can be either Layer 3 switching or more traditional routing with Layer 3 switching features and enhanced Layer 3 software features. (Routing – in terms of network path determination and packet forwarding – is discussed in detail in Part IV, while its enhancement and combination with switching in one device – with a more elaborate distinction between path determination and packet forwarding – is at the core of Part V.)

Switching technology is currently available in two forms:

- **Frame switches** forward traditional Ethernet or Token Ring LAN frames between end stations (or network segments). Since they forward traditional LAN frames, the appropriate switch can connect to any network device with an Ethernet, a Fast Ethernet, a Gigabit Ethernet, a Token Ring, or an FDDI interface. PCs, workstations, hubs, printers, bridges, and routers can be attached to a frame switch without replacing or reconfiguring a single interface.

- **Cell switching** – used in ATM, is similar to frame switching with one major difference. ATM technology switches fixed-length, 53-byte cells instead of variable-length frames. We will discuss WAN switching in more details in Chapter 18.

Cell switching is connection oriented, like the telephony network. In contrast, frame switching is connectionless; a packet can take any route across a network from its source to its destination. In cell switching, a connection is first negotiated and established across multiple switching points. An appropriate circuit is then set up, based on the amount and duration of data needed to be transported through the network in the form of ATM cells. Depending on the virtual circuit, it is torn down when the transmission is complete (PVC), or after an idle timeout period (SVC). The ATM switch provides dedicated circuits or paths dynamically or 'on the fly' between users at each end of the network.

In Part II on Bridging we have already set the scene for the relatively youngest interconnecting device, the **LAN switch**. We will refer in many instances to the characteristics of bridges which the LAN switch shares, and will enhance it with the additional LAN switch capabilities.

However, as this part deals with switching, we will also have a look at differences in the perception of switching deployed in LANs and WANs. This will clearly show that the terms **switching** and **switch** may have too many meanings to be properly defined and widely understood by means of a single definition. While bridge, router, and gateway are all defined and standardized terms, the term switch causes inevitable confusion among the networking community (like the marketing terms of 'Layer 3 switch,' 'Layer 4 switch,' etc.).

CHAPTER 7

LAN switching

In this chapter we will relate the LAN switch to the MAC bridge and will concentrate on the differences and new possibilities available since the introduction of LAN switching. We will therefore focus on the following issues:

- **shared vs. switched LANs** – various physical media, half/full duplex provision;
- **frame processing in LAN switch**;
- **address learning by LAN switch**;
- **virtual LANs**;
- **interconnecting switches**.

7.1 Reasons for switching

Network congestion became an issue with typical symptoms of variable response times, network timeouts or server disconnects, failure to establish connections, and the slow loading and running of applications. Typical reasons users require **more bandwidth** include larger and more complex LANs, more nodes sharing one LAN segment, and more sophisticated applications. Faced with these demands from their users, network managers must nevertheless also protect heavy investments already made in their existing infrastructure. It is rarely possible to throw out a complete network and replace it with a new model based on one of the newer high-speed technologies. LAN switching, as we will see later in this Part, is an excellent tool to ensure the above mentioned requirements and fulfill the constraints.

Segmenting shared-media LANs divides users into two or more separate LAN segments, reducing the number of users contending for bandwidth. LAN switching technology, which builds upon this trend, employs **microsegmentation**, which further segments the LAN to fewer users and ultimately to a single user with a dedicated LAN segment. Each switch port provides a dedicated Ethernet segment, or dedicated Token Ring segment. Segments are interconnected by internetworking devices that enable communication between LANs while blocking other types of traffic. Switches have the intelligence to monitor traffic and compile address tables, which then allows them to forward packets directly to specific ports in the LAN. Switches also usually provide a non-blocking service, which allows multiple conversations (traffic between two ports) to occur simultaneously.

Switching technology is quickly becoming the preferred solution for improving LAN traffic for the following reasons:

- Unlike hubs and repeaters, switches allow multiple data streams to pass simultaneously.
- Switches have the capability through microsegmentation to support the increased speed and bandwidth requirements of emerging technologies.
- Switches may deliver dedicated bandwidth to users – individually connected stations do not share the bandwidth with another station (private LANs).

SNAPSHOT	Layer 2 switching

Layer 2 switching is **hardware-based bridging** with the frame forwarding handled by specialized hardware, usually application-specific integrated circuits (ASICs).

However, LAN switching is not a universal solution by itself. It needs planning, design, and analysis. Sometimes, an organization might be better off improving the performance level of the server. The implementation of LAN switching should be about **removing complexity** from a network. However, the additional features of sophisticated offerings, such as filtering and media translation, can actually add complexity.

Key issues that must be considered by any organization considering significant switch implementation include:

- the merging of existing routing functionality with switched LAN segments;
- the sharing of information between routers and switches;
- cost per port;
- scalability, both in terms of adding more ports and with a view to expanding networks;
- redundancy and online serviceability;
- the benefits of virtual LANs;
- network management and diagnostic capabilities;
- possible migration to high-speed switches, and WAN connectivity and modularity.

SNAPSHOT	LAN switching place

Network designers integrate switching devices into their existing shared-media networks to achieve the following goals:

- to increase the bandwidth that is available to each user, thereby alleviating congestion in their shared-media networks;

■ to employ the manageability of VLANs by organizing network users into logical workgroups that are independent of the physical topology of wiring closet hubs. This, in turn, can reduce the cost of moves, adds, and changes while increasing the flexibility of the network;

■ to deploy emerging multimedia applications across different switching platforms and technologies, making them available to a variety of users;

■ to provide a smooth evolution path to high-performance switching solutions, such as Fast Ethernet, Gigabit Ethernet, and ATM.

7.2 LAN switch defined

A LAN **switch** is a **multiport bridge that forwards frames from a LAN on one port to one on another port.** (For a sample implementation of an Ethernet switched LAN see Figure 7.1). Switches make their forwarding decisions based on link layer (Layer 2) information, i.e. the destination MAC address in the frame. A switch will ignore a frame that is destined for a node located on the same port as the source node. Switches do not modify frames as they pass through (whereas routers must change the packet to include the MAC address of the next hop and may also increment a hop count field.)

FIGURE 7-1 Sample Ethernet switch implementation

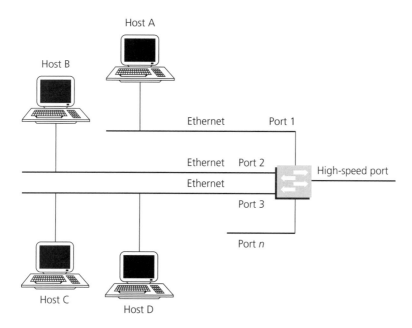

switches transparency to network layer

Switches are **dependent on the physical media** (in a similar way to bridges as Layer 2 interconnecting devices) but are **transparent to networking protocols**, therefore can support communication regardless of differences among network protocols (requiring minimal configuration).

Switches are generally much simpler than routers because they **operate at the link layer**, do not modify frames, and do not need to run complex routing protocols. Switches may also be both cheaper and faster than routers because the switching function is often implemented entirely in Very Large-Scale Integration (VLSI) rather than performed by software running on an expensive high-performance processor.

LAN switching fundamentally segments an Ethernet network into several **collision domains** by separating the physical network segments and at the same time enables increased bandwidth per segment and limiting collisions. The LAN switch task is to **move frames from one segment to another** based on the **destination MAC address**. If the address is unknown, or it is a multicast or broadcast physical address, the LAN switch will flood the frame through all of its ports except for the incoming one. This creates a single **broadcast domain** per switched network (per Virtual LAN, as we will see later). LAN switches, in a similar way to bridges, are not able to segment the network into broadcast domains. Once we need the network segmented into broadcast domains, we have to deploy routers as they operate at the network layer with logical network addresses.

LAN switch defined

A **relay** that forwards (relays) frames based on data link layer information is a bridge. Currently (and some would add unfortunately from a terminology point of view), the high-speed, multiple-port bridges are called **LAN switches**.

As we already noted, LAN switching is fundamentally similar to bridging. Both switches and bridges operate at the link layer and therefore have exactly the same possibilities onto which they may base their operations and decisions. For the sake of proper understanding we will repeat briefly the basic operations.

switch vs. hub

A **hub** repeats all traffic to all ports, regardless of whether the destination is a broadcast address or a specific MAC address. A LAN **switch** learns which MAC addresses are behind which ports, and intelligently forwards frames. A frame with a broadcast address is forwarded to all ports, and a frame with a specific MAC address is only forwarded to a single port. Thus the switch segments the collision domain, and allows for dedicated bandwidth per port.

bridge vs. LAN switch

A LAN switch, like a bridge, is a **Layer 2 network** device that **filters and forwards frames** based upon **Media Access Control (MAC)** layer information.

While bridges are considered **software-based** (higher latency), switches are considered **hardware-based** (Application Specific Integrated Circuit, ASIC).

Broadcast note

Broadcasts can cause problems because they interrupt every device in the broadcast domain, causing a CPU interrupt and requiring processing. On slow CPUs, broadcast storms can be a serious problem. Broadcast storms can wreak havoc on 100 Mbps Ethernet LANs with slow computers, because misbehaving devices have an opportunity to send broadcasts really quickly at 100 Mbps.

Broadcast frames are usually short and do not use much bandwidth. In addition, most normal applications do not broadcast thousands of times in a second. (For a station to use up most of 100 Mbps with 64-byte frames, it would need to send approximately 200 000 times per second, which is obviously abnormal.) So, when broadcasts start to use a lot of available bandwidth in a one-second interval, this probably indicates a serious problem.

Although some switch vendors allow for limiting the broadcasts passed through the switch, configuring the threshold to zero would be the wrong way to suppress broadcasts. The goal of the vendor-specific **broadcast suppression feature** is to prevent broadcast storms, not broadcasts in general. A broadcast storm occurs when bugs in a protocol-stack implementation or in a network configuration cause a station to send hundreds or thousands of broadcasts per second. In the worst case, the broadcasts from one station result in other stations also sending broadcasts, much like a storm that builds upon itself.

The reason for allowing broadcasts (and multicasts) is that they are needed for such important functions as dynamic address assignment (DHCP, BOOTP, or RARP in an IP environment), address and name resolution (ARP and DNS TCP/IP protocols), and service advertisements (SAP in a Novell IPX/SPX environment). Additionally, routing protocols such as RIP, EIGRP, OSPF, group management (IGMP in IP networks), and NetBIOS are some of the other protocols that also use broadcasts and multicasts (see Part IV).

When a **packet-based method** is used to measure broadcast activity, the threshold parameter is the number of broadcast or multicast packets received over a one-second time period. When a **bandwidth-based method** is used, the threshold parameter is the percentage of total available bandwidth used by broadcasts or multicasts. In either case, if the threshold is reached, the switch port cuts off broadcast and multicast packets for the rest of that second. Because packet sizes vary, bandwidth-based measurement is more accurate and more effective than packet-based measurement.

7.2.1 Development of LAN switching to VLANs and Layer 3 switching

In the early 1990s Kalpana (now part of the Catalyst group at Cisco) began to build Ethernet switches. But it was only in 1993–4 that a significant number of vendors came to the market with their Ethernet switches. These early boxes were nothing more than bridges with more than two ports, i.e. multiport bridges, with all of the limitations of bridging. The early switches operated on the same principle as bridges – they would identify which port to forward traffic to based on the destination MAC address.

In essence, all of these products rely on one of two **switching technologies** to boost Ethernet bandwidth over dedicated connections. **Hardware switches** use application-specific integrated circuits to reach wire speed without dropping frames. **Software switches** combine multiport bridging technology with high-speed RISC processors to achieve the same objective. Hardware switches have been shown to be faster than their software counterparts, but performance is not the only issue. They offer little or no **filtering** of bad frames. Software switches, in contrast, typically screen out all errored packets. They also combine Ethernet and FDDI in the same chassis, which suits them in service on the corporate backbone.

As the switches began to grow in size, a new concept emerged. This was the 'bridge group' concept enabling a series of ports to be 'tied' together in the software of the bridge such that they would only bridge between themselves and not the entire switch. This would in essence divide the switch into multiple bridged segments. For example, segment A, comprising four ports, would bridge among those four ports, but not to segment B, comprising of eight ports. To get from segment A to segment B, you still had to traverse a router. These bridge groups were almost always separate IP subnets.

Because there was no way to multiplex (or trunk) multiple bridge groups into a single physical router port, each bridge group had to have its own physical connection to a router port. Cisco Systems developed an **ISL** (Inter-Switch Link) to overcome this shortcoming. At this point in time the 'bridge group' became the **Virtual LAN** (VLAN). The problem was how to identify traffic from one VLAN from all the other traffic on the port. The solution was to explicitly tag the Ethernet frame with a VLAN identifier specified as the **IEEE 802.1Q** protocol standard. ISL, although Cisco-proprietary, is supported also on non-Cisco switches as it operates in a similar way to IEEE 802.1Q.

The other important feature was the concept of **port based VLANs**. As noted earlier, bridges used the MAC address of a station to determine which port to forward traffic to. Some vendors extended this concept and put forward the idea of **MAC address based VLANs**. This was known as implicit tagging, and suffered from some shortcomings. The 802.1Q standard implies port based VLANs. What this means is that the switch looks at the VLAN ID, the explicit tag identifying the VLAN, to see which group of ports the traffic belongs to. Then, from within those ports, it will forward traffic based on the destination MAC address (or multicast/broadcast address). With ISL/802.1Q, the group of ports comprising a VLAN can span multiple switches as well.

The initial solution to inter-VLAN communication was to tie a router to a switch (usually a backbone switch) and terminate all VLANs on that router (usually referred to as a 'router on the stick'). As can probably be deduced, this creates a bottleneck – the physical port on the router. To get around this limitation, protocols were developed to allow for the **forwarding information to be cached from the router onto the switch** itself. The first frame in a flow would be sent to the router, the router would make forwarding determinations based on access lists, routing, etc., and the router would then let the switch know how to forward the traffic from one VLAN to another (or from one subnet to another).

QUICK TIP   **packet flow**

A packet flow is defined as a unidirectional stream of traffic **(series of IP packets)** from a given source address and TCP/UDP port number to a given destination and TCP/UDP Port number such that the synchronization number in the packet header is increasing.

During the same time frame, the concept of **Layer 3 switching** also began to proliferate. This was the concept that the switch would also act as a router, i.e. would add a functionality of path determination to the current functionality of packet forwarding. Some vendors have blended the router and switch code, and others have located Layer 3 devices (routers) in the switch itself. Additional advances in switching are taking place in two areas: the integration of router code and/or hardware on the switch and in flow handling.

The **integration of routing and switching** in a single device has led to routers being increasingly deployed between, not within, high-performance workgroups. Routers are generally slower than switches because they must examine multiple packet fields, make substitutions in packet headers, and compute routes on a packet-by-packet basis. In the process, routers introduce latency and congestion. Switches, in contrast, accept frames, read a simple address header, and move the data along.

7.2.3 Address issues in switching

An Ethernet switch learns on the job in a similar way to a transparent bridge: it examines all the packets which come into its ports, reads the **source MAC address**, and logs that address in its **MAC address table**, building an association of this MAC address with a particular (incoming) switch port. A source address processing flowchart is shown in Figure 7.2. With the introduction of Virtual LANs, discussed later in this chapter, there is an extension of these tables to include information on VLAN membership(s). The switch then forwards frames

FIGURE 7-2   Switch source address processing

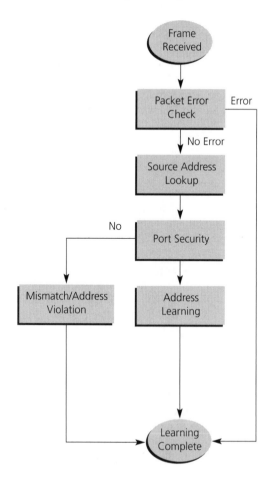

FIGURE 7-3 Example of layer 2 switching table

Destination MAC address	Destination ports
00-00-0C-06-41-7C	3/3
00-00-0C-02-B9-01	3/3
00-80-24-07-8C-60	3/2

between users according to its internal reference table of MAC addresses (an example is shown in Figure 7.3). Once it knows which addresses belong to which port, full switching functions can commence. If no entry is available in the switch table for the destination MAC address **unknown address**, the frame is broadcast to all interfaces to learn the correct destination. When the frame's reply comes back, the switch learns the location of the address and adds an entry in the switching table. If a frame is destined to a **broadcast or multicast** MAC address, the Layer 2 switch broadcasts the frame to all ports, unless the switch supports multicast group registration on its ports, in which case it will flood the multicast frames only out of the ports where group members – identified by the multicast MAC address – reside. The switch forwarding operation is depicted in Figure 7.4.

Usually the size of the table for any one switch port or group of ports is commensurate with the amount of **content-addressable memory (CAM)**. If an end station changes location, the first packet sent from the new location notifies the switch that it has been moved and its old address will be removed from the table. The CAM entries, like bridge forwarding table entries, are aging unless they are seen in frames by the switch. Timeout for a MAC address in CAM is typically 300 s. It is worth repeating that the MAC address table will include the addresses not only of end stations, but also of routers which may exist in the switched network as a CAM table associates MAC addresses with switch ports.

A **managed switch** (in the IP network) needs yet another, separate address table: the ARP table. The ARP table is used only when the switch itself is communicating with other IP devices as the ARP table matches an IP address to a MAC address. The switch itself will send an ARP request and place any responses in the ARP table (for more details on ARP see Section 10.4 in Part IV).

A **private switch** can learn (and serve) only one MAC address through its port and can thus support only dedicated connections (to the server and other switches but not the hub). In this case, the switch connection operates in full duplex. **Full duplex** became possible with the introduction of switching technology. Now the full duplex mode can be deployed in all IEEE 802.3 types.

A **segment switch** can hold **more MAC addresses per port** (as a port connects to the segment where more stations reside) and can be used to boost performance between workgroups. In contrast, a workgroup switch will only support a small number of addresses per port and can be used to boost performance between specific devices on the LAN. Ideally, a workgroup switch can replace a hub shared by power users or in a situation where a server is accessed as a cen-

FIGURE 7-4   Switch forwarding decision flowchart

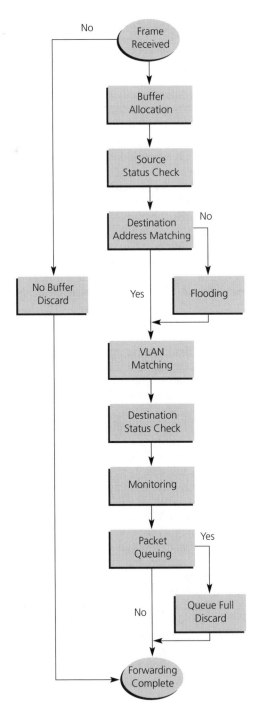

tral resource. On the other hand, a segment switch is most appropriate as a link between workgroup switches and/or hubs.

An **intelligent switching hub** allows multiple LAN segments to communicate with each other. With the definition of a **virtual workgroup**, comprising separate devices on the same or different switched segments, the switching hub can filter the traffic between those end stations, boosting performance and potentially providing an extra layer of security. Such a hub could also serve as a high-performance collapsed backbone, connecting several segments from individual workgroup hubs. This offers benefits in terms of the centralization and simplified management of multiple LANs.

The careful integration of **FDDI** in a switched LAN is another way in which switching can boost performance. Generally, this is achieved via an FDDI module in the switch itself which offers a high-speed connection to servers and high-end workstations. By using the switching hub as a concentrator linking into an FDDI backbone, it is possible to create a switched network without having to invest in any additional LAN infrastructure.

7.2.4 Multicast/broadcast management with switches

Because switches work like bridges, they must **flood all broadcast and multicast traffic**. A potential problem with a large switched network is clear: multicast and broadcast packets are propagated throughout the flat network representing a **single broadcast domain**. This is not a problem in routed networks because routers do not, in general, forward broadcasts. While the volume of multicast/broadcast traffic on any one LAN is generally smaller than specifically addressed traffic (to unicast addresses), the aggregate over a large switched LAN consisting of many separate LANs may be quite substantial.

The accumulation of broadcast and multicast traffic from each device in the network is referred to as broadcast radiation. **Broadcast** packets are of concern because every end node must receive the packet and decide whether it should take any action, on which it can be potentially wasting a great deal of computing resources. As the NIC must interrupt the CPU to process each broadcast or multicast, broadcast radiation affects the performance of hosts in the network. Most often, the host does not benefit from processing the broadcast or multicast: if the host is not the destination being sought, it does not care about the service that is being advertised, or it already knows about the service. High levels of broadcast radiation can noticeably degrade host performance.

Multicasts are less of an issue as most network interface cards can perform simple filtering of multicast packets. A switch should only forward multicast packets to the ports with nodes that are interested in receiving such packets. This is achieved by multicast registration so switches can identify the set of ports that participate in a particular multicast group. Handling multicast traffic is discussed later in this chapter.

Spanning tree protocol

LAN switches need **Spanning Tree Protocol** (STP) operation in the same way as bridges, to discover the Layer 2 topology and to prevent loops and uncontrollable proliferation and looping of packets. Figure 7.5 shows an undesirable network topology with a loop between two routers while Figure 7.6 shows the topology after STP has been deployed and the loop has been broken by blocking one of the switch ports. We have already explained the details of STP in Part II but it is worth including a brief note on STP here too.

FIGURE 7-5 Looped switched network topology

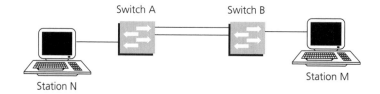

FIGURE 7-6 Looped topology eliminated by STP

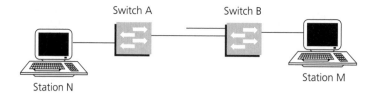

QUICK TIP   **spanning tree algorithm (STA)**

The Spanning tree algorithm defines a **tree** with a root bridge/switch, i.e. it maintains a **loop-free path from the root to all bridges/switches** and between any two non-root **bridges/switches** in the extended Layer 2 network.

STP works as follows. When the switches first come up, they start the **root switch selection process** by each switch transmitting a BPDU to its directly connected switch (on a per-VLAN basis – there will be one root switch identified per VLAN). As the BPDU goes out through the network, each switch compares the BPDU it sent out to the one it received from its neighbors. From this comparison, the switches come to an agreement as to which the root switch is. The switch with the lowest priority in the network wins this election process.

STANDARDS WATCH   spanning tree protocol

IEEE 802.1D-1998 **IEEE Standard for Local Area Network MAC (Media Access Control) Bridges**

After the root switch has been identified, the switches follow the rules defined below:

- **All ports of the root switch must be in forwarding mode** (except for some corner cases where self-looped ports are involved). Next, each switch determines their best path to get to the root. They determine this path by comparing the information in all the BPDUs received on all their ports. The port with the smallest information contained in its BPDU is used to get to the root switch; that port is called the **root port**.
- Once a switch determines its root port, that port must be set to forwarding mode. In addition, for each LAN segment, the switches communicate with each other to determine which switch on that LAN segment is best to use for moving data from that segment to the **root switch** and vice versa. This switch is called the **designated switch**.
- In a given LAN segment, the **designated switch's port** that connects to that LAN segment must be placed in **forwarding mode**.
- All other ports in all the switches (VLAN-specific) must be placed in **blocking mode**.

One drawback of STP is that it is recomputed every time there is a change in topology or there is a link or switch failure resulting in loss of connectivity. In typical networks, the minimum convergence time for the spanning tree is about 50 seconds, based on the default values of spanning-tree timers. Vendors employ various enhancements to the STP to reduce network convergence time, thus increasing the network availability. Some minimize the initialization time for access ports with respect to the STP states, and access ports bypass the listening and learning states and proceed directly to the forwarding state from the blocking state.

7.3 LAN segmentation

Segmentation breaks shared media LANs into several physical segments, and then reassembles them into logical networks using one of several types of network devices. As segmentation is introduced into the network, switches are used to create more and more segments, thus decreasing the number of end users per segment and increasing the effective bandwidth. Therefore, one of the two problems that LANs experience, the bandwidth limitation, is solved.

Using dedicated or 'private' switches takes segmentation to its highest level by placing just one workstation on each segment, thus providing **dedicated con-**

QUICK TIP | **LAN segmentation with switches**

LAN switches help segment LANs into **separate collision domains** creating, however, a switched network as a **single broadcast domain**.
Switches provide **full bandwidth to each port**, such as for IEEE 802.3 10
Mbps for Ethernet and 100 Mbps for Fast Ethernet in **half-duplex mode** (up to
10 or 100 Mbps in each direction), or 20 Mbps for Ethernet and 200 Mbps for Fast
Ethernet in **full-duplex mode** (in this latter case it is also the bandwidth dedicated to a single user).

nectivity to accommodate the individual end user connections. When a server or
workstation is connected directly to a switch, that device has its own private LAN
segment. When a repeater is connected to a switch, all the devices connected to
that repeater are on the same LAN segment and share the bandwidth of that
port. The switch joins these individual LAN segments to form a single LAN with
a bandwidth potential that may be many times that of the original.

QUICK TIP | **why use Layer 2 switching**

LAN switching is used as a method of **increasing bandwidth** use (using it more
effectively by LAN segmentation) and **reducing delay** in existing local networks.
Switches divide the network into several segments, each of which can operate
without interference from traffic local to any of the other segments. LAN switching
is performed at the link layer (Layer 2). Layer 2 switching also offers **dedicated
links** to each node, preserves the LAN infrastructure, and can be used to improve
performance in specific areas within a LAN.

Each port in a switch is connected to a different LAN, and they all operate independently and simultaneously. Only those packets that need to pass from one
LAN segment to another are forwarded by the switch, so a multiport switch might
increase the **aggregate bandwidth** by many times that of a single shared LAN.
The most recent switches can forward frames at the maximum rates, at wirespeed, and do not represent a performance bottleneck, especially with
high-throughput non-blocking internal architecture.

The difference in performance between shared and switched LANs is quite significant. On shared LANs, multiple users contend for shared bandwidth, giving
the end user an unpredictable network response time when time-sensitive information such as compressed motion video or voice is carried across it. By
dedicating a single LAN to each user with each such segment connected to the
switch, each user in effect has access to the full bandwidth available on that LAN

without interference from other users' traffic. In this way, the end user has moved from shared to dedicated bandwidth. These single-node networks are then connected to a much higher capacity backplane which allows the single-node networks to exchange information at the full LAN bandwidth. The result is no contention for transmission media and the end user seeing only the traffic destined for that single, end user LAN segment.

The following are characteristics of the **STP broadcast domain**:

■ Redundant links are blocked and carry no data traffic.
■ Suboptimal paths exist between different points.
■ STP convergence typically takes 30 to 50 seconds.
■ Broadcast traffic within the Layer 2 domain interrupts every host.
■ Broadcast storms within the Layer 2 domain affect the whole domain.
■ Isolating problems can be time consuming.
■ Network security within the Layer 2 domain is limited.

7.4 Switch capabilities

Current switches are equipped with various modern **features** which enable their smoother configuration, better performance and automatic management capabilities. Among the major new features are:

■ **autosensing**;
■ **autonegotiations**;
■ **link aggregation**;
■ **flow control**.

7.4.1 Autosensing

Autosensing capability is available with a switch which supports the full functionality of the **IEEE 802.1aa** (formerly 802.3u) standard on **autonegotiation**. An autosense switch can offer all modes of operation, half-duplex or full duplex, while autosense repeaters or hubs offer only half-duplex because these devices do not operate in full-duplex mode.

STANDARDS WATCH   **switch autonegotiation**

IEEE 802.3aa-1998: **Standard for Information Technology – Local and Metropolitan Area Networks – Part 3: Carrier Sense Multiple Access with Collision Detection (CSMA/CD) Access Method and Physical Layer Specifications – Maintenance Revision #5 (100 BASE-T)**

Autonegotiation allows UTP point-to-point links to establish the best possible common operation mode. Each UTP port on an autosense switch fully supports autonegotiation as defined in this standard. As a consequence of being standardized at the same time as the physical and MAC specifications, most installed 10/100 Mbps NICs support autonegotiation. However, it is not essential that both ends of the link support autonegotiation for the link to work.

For autonegotiation to function, link pulses are transmitted over 10BASE-T and 100BASE-TX links at startup and during idle periods (when there are no packets being transmitted). **Fast Link Pulses** (FLPs) are modulated at link startup to signal the available modes of the technology on each end of the link. The modes are any, or all, of 100BASE-TX full-duplex, 100BASE-TX half-duplex, 10BASE-T full-duplex, and 10BASE-T half-duplex. If both ends of the link support autonegotiation, then each end of the link will select the highest common operation mode. The precedence order (best first) is: 100BASE-TX full-duplex, 100BASE-TX half-duplex, 10BASE-T full-duplex, and, finally, 10BASE-T half-duplex. For example, if the other end of a link supports all types of operation, 100BASE-TX full-duplex will be the selected operation mode after link startup. If the other end of a link supports only half duplex-operation (100BASE-TX half-duplex and 10BASE-T half-duplex are signaled), then 100BASE-TX half-duplex will be selected. If the other end of a link supports only 10BASE-T and supports autonegotiation, then 10BASE-T full-duplex will be selected.

Autonegotiating switch ports listen to the link pulses at startup. The idle signals are different for 10BASE-T and 100BASE-TX. If the autonegotiation signal is not received, the port will select half-duplex operation at either 10BASE-T or 100BASE-TX, depending on which idle signal was detected. Autonegotiation completes its process in less than a second after link startup, so there is no impact on network performance.

QUICK TIP   **autosense switching**

Autosense switching is similar in concept to that of the 10/100 Mbps autosense NIC mentioned in Part I. To accommodate any mix of 10 Mbps and 100 Mbps connections to the switch, autosense switching technology enables the automatic detection of the speed of the attached device and its transmission mode. As a result, each port adapts to one of the following four speeds and modes: 10 Mbps half-duplex, 2x 10 Mbps full-duplex, 100 Mbps half-duplex, or 2x 100 Mbps full-duplex.

Autosense switching eliminates the confusion about which desktop upgrade is the correct strategy, because it evolves automatically to meet the demands of the network. Autosense switching offers hassle-free network operation because the network connection automatically adapts to the port speed of the end user when their NICs are upgraded, without intervention by the network manager.

With an autosense switch installed at the wiring closet, individual end users can upgrade at their convenience when their applications demand more performance. Because end stations automatically receive faster service when they upgrade, no additional hardware purchase is required other than to add greater port capacity for additional end user connections. Autosense switching allows network managers, even in small to mid-size companies, to install a network infrastructure that adapts to the needs and speeds of the business.

7.4.2 Link aggregation

In a typical client/server application, large numbers of users will usually require access to the same server or set of servers. In that case, the segment on which the server resides could become a bottleneck in its own right. Segmentation by itself does not address this problem (even with dedicated switch ports); instead, multiple **high-speed trunk ports** on a switch must be deployed. A useful combination of ports with speeds of different order (e.g. most with 10 Mbps and several with 100 Mbps) can be improved further by the **aggregation** of multiple ports of the same speed to create a fat pipe. For example up to four ports of 100 Mbps could be used to provide a bandwidth up to 400 Mbps – useful before the Gigabit Ethernet became widespread; nowadays even Gigabit Ethernet links get aggregated. The trunks are especially useful for communication between switches.

Link aggregation is a method for achieving **backbone redundancy and bandwidth expansion** by combining the available ports and links. Completed mid-1999, the **IEEE 802.3ad** link aggregation standard defines how two or more Ethernet connections (of any type) can be combined to load share, load balance and provide better resiliency for high-bandwidth network connections. So far vendors have offered their own proprietary **trunking** schemes for 10/100 Mbps Ethernet and FDDI for a few years.

STANDARDS WATCH   **switch link aggregation**

IEEE 802.3ad-2000 **CSMA/CD – Aggregation of Multiple Link Segments**

Port aggregation combines the datastreams from multiple Ethernet ports into a single high-speed virtual workgroup or subnet. Port speeds cannot be typically mixed within a single aggregated channel; the standard applies to 10 Mbps, 100 Mbps, or 1 Gbps Ethernet. The maximum achievable combined bandwidth is 8 Gbps. This increases the options available when there is one remaining gigabit port and three or four 100 Mbps ports available between switches. Link bandwidth can be added incrementally and affordably. Network traffic is dynamically distributed across ports, therefore the administration of the data flowing across a given port is taken care of automatically within the aggregated link.

At the server packets being sent are distributed to multiport NICs. At the switch, the data from each port coming from the server is aggregated into a single high-speed link (see Figure 7.7). In the opposite direction, the data coming over the high-speed aggregated link is split into datastreams by a switch so that it can be forwarded onto individual lower-speed links to the server.

FIGURE 7-7   Link aggregation with IEEE 802.3ad

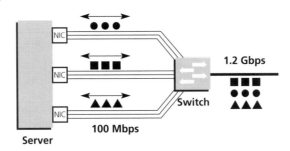

The link aggregation standard provides inherent, automatic redundancy on point-to-point links. If one of the multiple ports used in a link fails, network traffic is dynamically redirected to flow across the remaining good ports in the link. The redirection is fast and triggered when a switch learns that a MAC address has been automatically reassigned from one link port to another in the same link. The switch then sends the data to the new port location, and the network continues to operate with virtually no interruption in service.

The IEEE standard concerns both switches and NICs. There may be several 100 Mbps links from a server to a switch. Using multiple NICs in the server protects against failures of either a single NIC or a single cable connection.

7.4.3 Switch flow control

All switches contain frame buffers to cope with **contention** at a port. Contention occurs when two packets arrive at the same time and are destined for the same output port, so one of them must be stored temporarily. However, buffers can only deal with contention that is very short-lived. If contention persists (the switch is congested), the switch will eventually exhaust its available buffers. The switch must then either discard packets or somehow prevent the sources from sending additional packets. **Flow control** is a mechanism whereby a receiver can tell a source to wait for some period of time before sending any further packets. Flow control is therefore a critical concern for switches in cases of heavily loaded conditions. **IEEE 802.3x** defines the standardized flow control mechanism which is deployed in new switches (requires new chips). This mechanism is set up between the two stations on the point-to-point link. If the receiving station at the end becomes congested, it can send back a frame called a **pause frame** to the source at the opposite end of the connection, instructing that station to stop sending packets for a specific period of time. The sending station waits the requested time before sending more data. The receiving station can also send a frame back to the source with a time-to-wait of zero, instructing the source to begin sending data again.

This flow-control mechanism was developed to match the sending and receiving device throughput. For example, a server can transmit to a client at a rate of 3000 pps. The client, however, may not be able to accept packets at that rate because of CPU interrupts, excessive network broadcasts, or multitasking within the system. In this example, the client sends out a pause frame and requests that the server delay transmission for a certain period of time. This mechanism, though separate from the IEEE 802.3z work, complements Gigabit Ethernet by allowing gigabit devices to participate in this flow-control mechanism.

STANDARDS WATCH	switch flow control

IEEE 802.3x-1997 **IEEE Standards for Local and Metropolitan Area Networks: Specification for 802.3 Full Duplex Operation**

While flow control is a useful mechanism, it may also cause severe problems. The arguments for and against flow control are very interesting. Switch vendors find flow control attractive because it might allow switches of a given performance level to use less memory and hence be cheaper to construct. Many protocol experts, however, believe that flow control is really an end to-end issue which is handled very effectively by transport-layer protocols such as Transmission Control Protocol (TCP), and the best thing the switches could do is simply to notify the sources about congestion.

7.5 Switching modes

There are two different types of core **switch processing mode** used in LAN switches today:

- **cut-through**;
- **store and forward**.

Besides, there are other, hybrid, schemes deployed depending on the vendor. The differences in reading and processing header of the incoming packet are depicted in Figure 7.8.

The switching mode determines how quickly a switch can forward a packet and, therefore, how much latency the packet will experience. **Latency** in general is the delay between the time a packet is received on one port and the time it is transmitted from the appropriate destination port. Selecting a switching mode is often a choice between enhanced error checking and lower latency.

7.5.1 Cut-through regime

The **cut-through processing mode** (also called 'on-the-fly' or fast-forward) is an extremely fast technology that allows a switch to begin the filtering and forward-

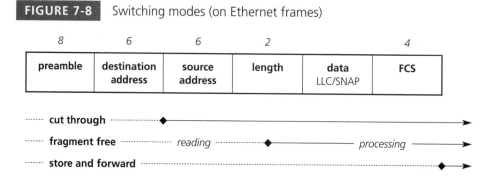

FIGURE 7-8 Switching modes (on Ethernet frames)

ing process (i.e. determine which outbound port the packet should be sent to and send it to the port) just after reading the destination MAC address in the frame header, before the entire packet has been received by the LAN switch. Unicast packets are transferred between ports without the entire frame being read into memory. Instead, when the port receives the first few bytes of a frame, it analyzes the packet header to determine the destination address of the frame, establishes a connection between the input and output ports, and transmits the frame through the determined output port.

QUICK TIP   **cut and through switching mode**

In **cut and through switching mode** the switch begins the filtering and forwarding process, i.e. determines which outbound port the packet should be sent to and sends it to the port, before the entire packet has been received by the LAN switch. It bypasses the buffering process usually associated with most bridge and router technologies (store-and-forward). Low latency is traded off against the inability to perform error correction.

In most cut-through systems, this translates into an inability to perform value-added processing on the packet, including error correction. Genuinely corrupted packets are rare and will not usually cause a problem. Of perhaps greater concern is that the switch propagates 'runt' packets which are smaller than the minimum-size packets allowed for the LAN. This is not uncommon in CSMA/CD LANs where a node may start to send a packet and then stop before it has sent a minimum-size packet because it observes a collision with another node. If the switch has already started to forward the packet, a runt packet will be propagated onto the destination LAN, wasting bandwidth. In a cut-through mode, **latency** is measured as first-bit-received to first-bit-transmitted or FIFO (first-in first-out).

7.5.2 Store-and-forward regime

The **store-and-forward processing regime** is a buffer-based technology where each frame entering a switch is stored in its entirety in a buffer. When in the buffer, error correction and filtering table look-ups are performed. The port adapter reads the entire frame into memory and then determines whether the frame should be forwarded. At this point, the frame is also examined for any errors (frames with errors are not forwarded). If it is determined that the frame should be forwarded and contains no errors, the frame is sent to the destination port for forwarding.

> **QUICK TIP**   **store-and-forward switching mode**
>
> Store-and-forward switching mode is a buffer-based regime where each frame entering a switch is stored in its entirety in a buffer. When in the buffer, error correction and filtering table lookups are performed.

While store-and-forward reduces the amount of error traffic on the LAN, it also causes a delay in frame forwarding that is dependent upon the length of the frame. Typically, this delay is only a problem with certain protocols such as IPX in non-burst mode. IPX in non-burst mode sends a single frame and then waits for an acknowledgment. Most other LAN protocols will send multiple frames before waiting for an acknowledgment. For IPX, the end-to-end delay is important because it will affect the overall throughput. However, for other protocols, the end-to-end delay is typically insignificant because the acknowledgment for the first frame is typically received before the sender would stop transmitting.

In store-and-forward mode, **latency** is measured last-bit-received (whole packet received) to first-bit-transmitted from the output port or LIFO (last-in first-out). This does not include the time it takes to receive the entire packet, which can vary, according to packet size. Store-and-forward is the most error-free form of switching, but the forwarding latency is higher than cut-through switching modes. However, with the advances in high-performance switching fabrics the store-and-forward switch latency difference has diminished. Therefore the store-and-forward mode has become the one most often applied. Moreover, once the switch ports' speeds are mixed, no other regime is applicable.

7.5.3 Hybrid switching regimes

There are other, hybrid switch modes of operation which are proprietary.

In the **fragment-free** regime the switch reads the incoming frame up to its first 64 bytes to filter out collision frames and the majority of packet errors, before forwarding begins. In a properly functioning network, error frames are rarely shorter than 64 bytes. Anything greater than 64 bytes is a valid packet and is usually received without error. Fragment-free switching waits until the received packet has been determined not to be a collision frame before forwarding the packet. In fragment-free mode, latency is measured as FIFO.

7.5.4 Selecting a switching mode

If the attached networks experience a significant number of collisions, the hybrid scheme may be a solution to eliminate the chance of forwarding collision fragments. If the network is experiencing frame check sequence (FCS) or alignment errors, the store-and-forward mode will ensure that packets with errors are filtered and not propagated to the rest of the network.

7.5.5 Adapting the switching regime

What vendors generally deploy on their LAN switches is so called **adaptive cut-through mode**. With adaptive cut-through mode, the user can configure the switch to **automatically use the best forwarding mode** based on user-defined thresholds. In adaptive cut-through mode, the ports operate in cut-through mode unless the number of forwarded frames that contain errors exceeds a specified percentage (they still check frames for errors – but after forwarding them). When this percentage is exceeded, the switch automatically changes the mode of the port to store-and-forward. Then, once the percentage of frames containing errors falls below a specified percentage, the operation mode of the ports is once again set to cut-through.

7.6 Switch technology

Non-blocking architecture supports several simultaneous conversations between local switch ports (reflecting the source and destination pair) without impacting on or interfering with each other. The number of simultaneous connections in a switch generally depends on its architecture which is discussed later. The ultimate need is to guarantee bandwidth availability at all times: with a shared bus the backplane must have a capacity greater than the aggregation of all switch ports; with crossbar switches the non-blocking capability depends on the applied queuing/buffering technology. Most manufacturers claim that their switches can operate on all ports at full **wirespeed**. However, this depends on the allocation of processor power per port. Without sufficient power, it does not matter how many MAC addresses a switch claims to support. Even with sufficient power, bottlenecks are not precluded as data from a number of segments (input ports) could be destined for one output port (see Figure 7.9). Some switches deploy a backpressure mechanism (false **jamming process**) which prevents any more data arriving at the port in the event of a bottleneck; however, in segment switches, this will also prevent communication anywhere else within the segment.

Manufacturers which use **Application-Specific Integrated Circuit** (ASIC) technology claim their products can simultaneously send packets across all ports at wirespeed. Customers should examine this sort of claim very closely, asking if the claimed **aggregate bandwidth** reflects a LAN running at its full specification of traffic. Although a switch allows the creation of a series of individual collision domains (segments), all the domains are still members of the same broadcast domain and should still communicate with each other.

Symmetrical switches offer ports all of the same capacity which may not fit the client-server applications and can lead to bottlenecks in the switch. **Asymmetrical switches** are more common for current workgroups supporting the inherently asymmetrical client–server relationship as they offer higher speed port(s) for usually dedicated connections of servers (uplinks).

FIGURE 7-9   Switch architecture and blocking

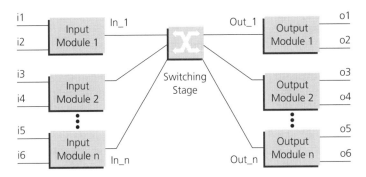

7.6.1 Switch architecture

Not all **chassis-based LAN switches** are made the same way, and the different architectures used may be a factor in your buying decisions. Here are a few basic types of switch architecture:

■ **Shared-bus architectures** use a single backplane to transmit all data moving between modules in a switch. Each module is allocated a time slot for access to the backplane.

■ **Shared-memory architectures** (see Figure 7.10) use a common area of high-speed RAM to store data moving across the switch. Central control reads the control information (to make the forwarding decision) simultaneously with its storage in the memory. This is a relatively simple architecture to design, but

FIGURE 7-10   Switch with shared memory buffering

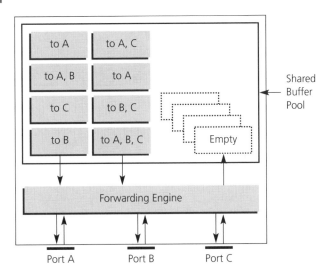

the memory storage operations introduce delay at high speeds, limiting its scalability.

■ In a **star-wired point-to-point architecture**, each module connects to a central switching fabric. This design is less expensive than a crossbar, since switching is moved from the modules to the central switching fabric, but it can still scale to high speeds.

■ **Crossbar (crosspoint) switches** are more expensive than the previous two architectures. In this type, each module is directly wired to every other module in the switch. The arbiter (see Figure 7.11) decides which crosspoint should be activated, based on the input pattern. This allows multiple traffic streams to be processed simultaneously by the switch. However, this is valid only for unicast traffic (see Figure 7.12 for unicast switching across a crossbar switching fabric). Broadcasting or multicasting across a crossbar switch is a weakness: the frame must be replicated with a possible performance loss, and the crossbar fabric must be idle to perform this complex operation (see Figure 7.13 for broadcasting across a crossbar switching fabric). This architecture can scale to high speeds, but it makes the modules more expensive.

FIGURE 7-11 Switch crosspoint architecture

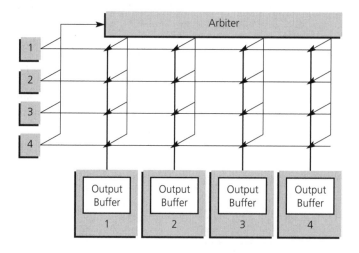

Crossbar switches require sophisticated buffering to avoid contentions for output ports and head-of-line blocking when, with a single input queue served in FIFO mode, a packet for an unavailable output port could block all the other packets behind in the queue from being processed through the available output ports.

Even though a crossbar switch is always internally non-blocking, there are three other types of blocking that can limit its performance. The first is called **head-of-line (HOL) blocking**; the second and third are very closely related to each other and are called input blocking and output blocking respectively. HOL blocking can significantly reduce the performance of a crossbar switch, wasting nearly half of the

FIGURE 7-12 Unicast over crossbar switch

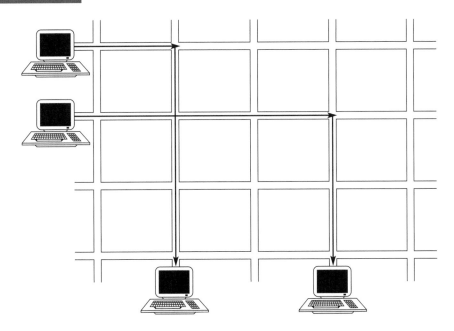

FIGURE 7-13 Broadcast/multicast over crossbar switch

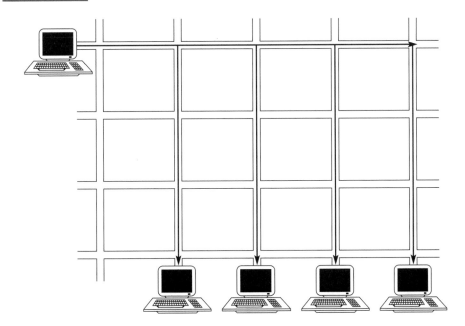

switch's bandwidth. Most routers today that use crossbar switches suffer from HOL blocking. Fortunately, there is a solution for this problem called **Virtual Output Queuing** (VOQ) (see Figure 7.14).

The other types of blocking, **input and output blocking**, are present in all crossbar switches. They arise because of contention for access to the crossbar: each input line and each output line of a crossbar can only transport one cell at a time. If multiple cells wish to access a line simultaneously, only one will gain access while the others will be queued. Fortunately, input and output blocking do not reduce the throughput of a crossbar switch. Instead, they increase the delay of individual packets through the system, and perhaps more importantly make the delay random and unpredictable. We can reduce this problem with two techniques: the first is to use a prioritization mechanism in the crossbar switch for every example and the second is to use a technique called speedup.

Overcoming HOL blocking

In the very simplest crossbar switches, all of the packets waiting at each input are stored in a single FIFO queue. When a packet reaches the head of its FIFO queue, it is considered by the centralized scheduler. The packet contends for its output with packets destined to the same output but currently at the HOL of other inputs. It is the job of the centralized scheduler to decide which packet will go next. Eventually, each packet will be selected and will be delivered to its output across the crossbar switch. Although FIFO queueing is widely used, it has a problem: packets can be held up by frames ahead of them that are destined to a different output. This phenomenon is called HOL blocking. The centralized scheduler only 'sees' the packet at the head of the FIFO queue, and so the HOL packet blocks packets behind it that need to be delivered to different outputs. A good analogy is a traffic light in which traffic turning to the right is allowed to proceed even when the light is red. If there is only a single lane and you wish to turn right, but the car ahead of you wants to go straight ahead, you are blocked: with a single lane you cannot pass the car in front to reach your 'free' output.

Even under benign traffic patterns, HOL blocking limits the throughput to just 60% of the aggregate bandwidth for fixed or variable length packets. When the traffic is bursty, or favors some output ports, the throughput can be much worse. Fortunately, there is a simple fix to this problem known as virtual output queueing (VOQ). At each input, a separate FIFO queue is maintained for each output. After a forwarding decision has been made, an arriving cell is placed in the queue corresponding to its outgoing port.

VOQ eliminates HOL blocking entirely and makes 100% of the switch bandwidth available for transferring packets.

7.6.2 Typology of switches

The following types of LAN switches are commonly available, although in their efforts to grow the market at ever increasing rates, many manufacturers' products overlap. For most purposes, the market can be divided into:

■ **backbone switches** – for linking the LAN into high-speed protocols such Fast or Gigabit Ethernet, ATM, or FDDI;

FIGURE 7-14 Switch architecture with virtual output queuing

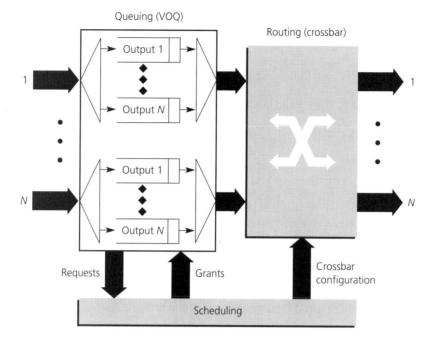

- **workgroup switches** – include **segment switches** for LAN subdivisions;
- **desktop switches** – for dedicated bandwidth.

Backbone switches

Backbone switches, sometimes called enterprise switches, Gigabit Ethernet switches, or campus switches, are implemented at the **core of the network**. They refer to and usually replace backbone or enterprise routers or collapsed backbone hubs ('super hubs'), since they offer higher throughput rates, reduced delay (latency), and greater flexibility in the provision of virtual LANs. Backbone switches typically have the following features:

- dual power supplies;
- modularity with hot-swappable modules;
- uplinks to Fast or Gigabit Ethernet, ATM, or FDDI;
- support for multiple users and VLANs;
- large amounts of buffer memory;
- support for spanning trees, different forwarding methods, and duplex settings on a per port basis.

A backbone switch usually connects to servers, other backbone switches, desktop and workgroup switches, and hubs.

Workgroup switches

Workgroup switches support multiple MAC addresses on some or all ports (often configurable). They can have traditional hubs connected to each port, thus providing greater bandwidth for each user. Multiple 100 Mbps ports may also be configurable. They can either be connected to file servers or provide an uplink to a backbone switch. Some workgroup switches are available in stackable configuration. To provide greater flexibility, these units may also have single or dual Fast Ethernet, Gigabit Ethernet, FDDI, or ATM uplinks. Because several different types of connection may exist on a single switch, a choice of forwarding techniques is usually available on a per port basis, though some units provide a choice of forwarding techniques on a switch-wide basis only.

Desktop switches

A desktop switch is designed to replace a low-end hub. A desktop switch supports a single workstation on most of its ports, supplying each workstation usually with a full 10 Mbps, dedicated connection. Thus, on the majority of ports, the switch needs only support a relatively small number of MAC addresses. However, since at least one port must connect to the backbone, the switch must be capable of supporting a large number of MAC addresses on at least one port. As with other switches, desktop switches must support a per port choice of forwarding techniques. If only one station is supported per port, then cut-through forwarding is the optimum forwarding technique, since no collisions will occur on the segment. However, store and forward or adaptive cut-through should be used for workgroup or backbone connections.

7.6.3 Port and segment switching

Both the dynamic and static switch categories can be subdivided into port and segment switching. In a **dynamic port switch**, each port connects to a single end station or server, making it most suitable for boosting bandwidth economically for users who require access to data-intensive applications. Standard network interface cards, driver software, cabling, and applications can be used without change. In other words, the prevailing LAN infrastructure is protected.

A **dynamic segment switch** works in the same way, but each port can connect to a whole network segment rather than just one end station or server. This allows the network manager to reduce a highly congested LAN to a series of smaller LANs, a function which was traditionally provided by bridges and routers.

A **static port switch** includes software which allows the network manager to move users from one shared LAN bus to another. Individual ports may be selected and assigned to different shared buses, helping to optimize port usage by reducing the number of modules that must be purchased for one hub.

On the other hand, a **static module switch** allows the network manager to move an entire hub module, complete with all its ports, from one shared bus to another.

7.6.4 Stackable switches and switch clusters

Stackable switches (see Figure 7.15) provide for interconnecting multiple switches in a wiring closet to create a single entity with a single IP address. Special cables and connectors provide an independent bus to carry traffic between switches in the stack (cluster).

FIGURE 7-15   Stackable switch

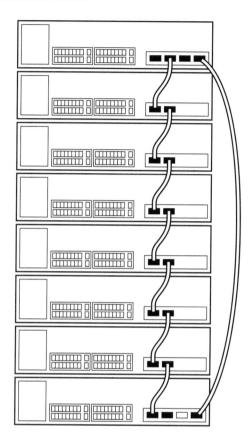

There are two **ways to stack**:

- cascade;
- star wire.

Switch clusters allow for:

- simplified network management;
- geographically dispersed switches to be managed by a single IP address;
- a Web-based interface for easy configuration and management of all clustered switches;
- more efficient port use;
- scaling beyond a single wiring closet;
- more efficient switching fabric use.

Initially the switch clusters offered the following features:

- physical integration;
- limited to single wiring rack;
- proprietary interconnections;
- limited management interface;
- small single IP domain size;
- limited stack citizens;
- no investment protection;
- fixed price/performance point.

Over time **modern clustering capabilities** evolved into the following:

- logical integration;
- location anywhere on a LAN;
- 'open' interconnections;
- embedded integrated management interface;
- larger single IP domain size;
- broad range of cluster members;
- investment protection and future-proofing;
- range of price/performance options.

7.6.5 Note on design

The development of Layer 2 switching in hardware has not only provided a rapid migration to switching but has also made the networks flat, increasing the broadcast or failure domain. The **access layer** is the one to which user computers are attached and workgroups are created. Major considerations for the access layer switches include the following:

- The scalable port density needs to range from small workgroups to about a 1000 node midsized network or enterprise branch. Ten to a hundred autosensing Layer 2 switches suffice for most applications. To support very high bandwidth applications, there may be a need for gigabit speeds at the access layer.
- Superior price/performance is essential as hundreds of users access the network through this layer.
- Multiple, high speed uplinks need to have the ability to connect to the distribution layer in a redundant fashion. Because the access layer can support hundreds of users, redundant uplink configuration is important to the overall network availability.
- Intelligent Layer 2 functions such as VLANs, a fast convergent spanning tree, and other high-availability features are needed. In the event of topology changes, the uplinks should also converge fast enough to not disrupt user access to servers in the network distribution layer or core.

- LAN-edge QoS is needed to prioritize applications such as Voice over IP (VoIP) during congestion and help control both delay and jitter within the access layer. At a minimum, the switches should have at least two queues per port so as to be able to prioritize traffic as high or low priority based on 802.1p/Q Class of Service (CoS).

- Traffic storm control and pruning to prevent flooding is needed in order to send packets only where required.

- The ability to create stacks with a high-performance stacking bus is needed.

- Scalable embedded, Web-based multi-device, management architecture is required for simplified management. The embedded management offers LAN management without requiring any client-side application installation.

- "Plug-and-play" switching is critical in order to minimize configuration and management efforts. Hence, most access layer switches are intelligent Layer 2 switches. In special cases where elaborate application layer filtering and policies need to be applied, Layer 3 switches can be used at the access layer, but this will entail additional network configuration.

The **core layer** forms the backbone for the LAN. All major network services, application servers, and aggregation-layer devices are attached to the core. Virtually all traffic between application servers and clients traverses the core. With the advent of wirespeed Layer 3, gigabit switching devices, LAN backbones have migrated to switched gigabit architectures that provide all the benefits of routing with wirespeed packet forwarding. As an appetizer for later Parts, let us consider what Layer 3 actually has to offer:

- A Layer 3 switching (discussed in Part V) core in a structured design reduces (or terminates) the scope of spanning tree domains. It also provides inter-VLAN and inter-subnet routing, thus offloading the router to focus on critical WAN routing functions.

- A Layer 3 core is not susceptible to loops (due to the time-to-live parameter in IP) unlike the Layer 2 network that is susceptible to loops due to the slow spanning tree convergence.

- Use of Layer 3 routing protocols, such as (Enhanced) Interior Gateway Routing Protocol ((E)IGRP) and Open Shortest Path First protocol (OSPF) help handle difficult tasks such as load balancing, redundancy, and recovery in the backbone (discussed in Part IV).

- Layer 3 designs are highly scalable as they exchange only summary reachability information rather than maintaining path information for every host.

- A Layer 3 switching core also provides a mapping between Layer 2 QoS using CoS and the richer Layer 3 QoS using the Differentiated Service Code Point (DSCP, discussed in Part V). A rich set of QoS policies, packet prioritization and filtering, and permit and deny policies can be created using filters, sometimes called Access Control Lists (ACLs).

General requirements for the **core layer** include the following:

- wirespeed Layer 2 and Layer 3 gigabit switching performance;
- redundancy support with rapid failover to maintain high core availability;

- support for a large number of queues per port (at least four) with intelligent scheduling algorithms to manage congestion and to prioritize traffic;
- intelligent network services such as QoS, security, load balancing, etc.;
- access control lists for rich packet filtering and to easily create permit/deny policies;
- rich Layer 2 to Layer 4 QoS and mapping from downstream Layer 2 QoS to Layer 3 DSCP;
- support for important routing protocols such as RIP, OSPF, EIGRP, and multicast protocols such as PIM.

7.7 Virtual LANs

The arrival of frame and cell switching has been accompanied by the arrival of virtual LANs, the logical grouping of users and corresponding network resources. Traditional networks have the capability to create physical groups of devices separated from the rest of a large network by a router. **Virtual LANs** (VLANs) are **logical groups** of users, servers, and other resources that appear to one another as if they are on the same physical LAN segment, even though they may be spread across a large network. VLANs provide a mechanism for managing broadcasts in large, switched networks. Any device, anywhere on the network, can be a member of any virtual LAN, regardless of where other members of that VLAN are located, though end stations must be connected to switches or hubs that support virtual LANs. Switched LANs form a single broadcast domain, so the network is bogged down by broadcasts from chatty protocols like NetBEUI. Each end station on a particular VLAN and only those end stations would hear broadcast traffic sent by other VLAN members. The concept of VLANs is shown in Figure 7.16.

FIGURE 7-16   Concept of VLANs

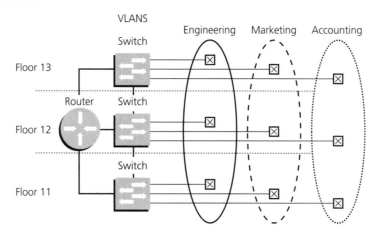

As we explained earlier in this chapter, a switch, like a bridge, builds a MAC address table and an association of MAC addresses with a port. Within the switch architecture these tables extend for VLAN membership(s). For example, in case of port-based VLANs ports 1–5 are in VLAN 1 and 6–12 are in VLAN 2. Any MAC address in ports 1–5 are in VLAN 1 and 6–12 in VLAN 2. Within the switch, VLANs have internal index numbers or IDs to tell the difference between VLANs. Usually these indexes are not configurable by the user, although on some switches you can change the index number.

Virtual LAN technology is one of the most important (and sometimes confusing) topics in switched networking. Virtual LANs are a necessity for switching because they provide an important element in the migration from shared media hub/router network models to fully switched networks. Networks are migrating from shared-media hubs to LAN switches for interconnecting workstations and resources. Switches do not scale well to fit large networks and growing mid-sized networks.

Virtual LANs create **broadcast domains** on switched networks that, in turn, allow them to scale. VLANs represent mechanisms used to determine which end stations should receive broadcast traffic, since it should not be sent arbitrarily to every connected user. This is important because broadcasts are a popular method for establishing communications between servers and groups of end stations. Switches **limit broadcasts** so that they do not propagate across the entire network, causing network failure as a broadcast storm floods the network with spurious messages. VLAN will propagate all broadcasts, i.e. every ARP and BOOTP will traverse the entire VLAN.

> **QUICK TIP**   **VLANs and broadcast domains**
>
> All devices on a switched network hear each other's broadcasts – are in the same broadcast domain – unless VLANs are configured.

VLANs also have other advantages; they make **efficient use of scarce IP addresses**, dramatically **simplify moving devices** around a campus network, and make organizing users a lot easier. With the evolution of switching, a wide variety of virtual LAN implementations have emerged. These implementations have their advantages and drawbacks.

> **QUICK TIP**   **VLANs benefits**
>
> VLANs address the following two problems:
>
> - scalability issues in a flat network topology;
> - simplification of network management by facilitating network reconfigurations (moves and changes).

7.7.1 VLANs defined

A **virtual local area network (VLAN)** is a software-defined group of devices which function as one workgroup, although they do not connect to the same physical LAN segment (conventionally one logical network address pertains to each physical LAN segment and for stations attached to different segments a router is a necessity to communicate). They may well be at various locations and considerable distances apart. Virtual LANs are generally configured by network management software and can be invoked at relatively short notice, for example in response to a sudden need to create interdepartmental project workgroups. These can be adapted and modified dynamically as the project progresses. They also give the network manager improved control over data security, for example by implementing firewalling against server broadcast storms or by limiting access to a departmental server to specific employees. They also offer more effective sharing of applications.

QUICK TIP   **VLAN defined**

A VLAN is a broadcast domain that is not specifically bounded by physical limitations. A single instance of STP may run on each configured VLAN (depends on implementation).

Because virtual LANs link many segments without a bottleneck, they allow extensive LAN segmentation within workgroups, a technique sometimes called **microsegmentation**. The fewer users per segment, the more bandwidth per user. The virtual LAN principle even works when each station has its own dedicated link, as is the case with LAN switches that support only one MAC address per port.

QUICK TIP   **VLAN administrators' benefits**

One of the key aspects of virtual LANs is the way they ease adds, moves, and changes. Users can shift end stations to different physical LAN segments within the virtual LAN without requiring net managers to change IP addresses, reprogram the hub, or shoulder other administrative burdens.

But it must be noted that while virtual LANs ease administrative burdens, they do not eliminate them. As long as end users remain within the virtual LAN there is no problem. Once they move outside the virtual LAN, however, the net manager must manually redefine the network to include the users.

One way to implement virtual LANs within a building puts switches on each floor and uses a router to furnish connections between the LANs (see Figure 7.17). End users on the same virtual LAN are bridged together, whether or not they are on the same switch port.

FIGURE 7-17   Sample VLAN topology

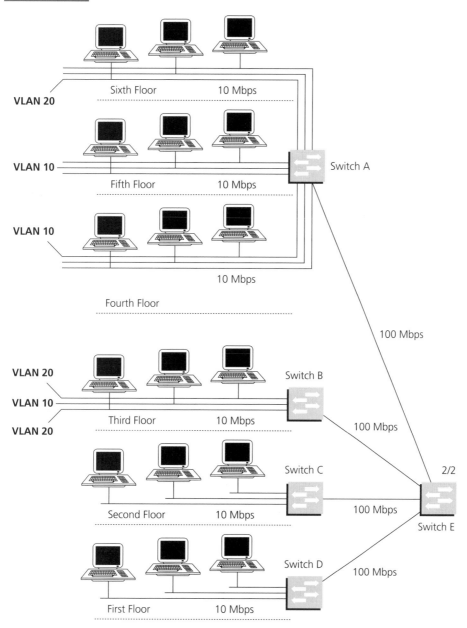

VLANs can be incorporated in a large network using the ATM backbone. Figure 7.18 shows an example of such a network. LANE, the ATM counterpart of VLANs, is then used to interconnect VLANs across the ATM switched backbone, as shown in Figure 7.19. Another possibility is to use bridged PVCs, one PVC per VLAN.

FIGURE 7-18   Example of VLANs across an ATM backbone

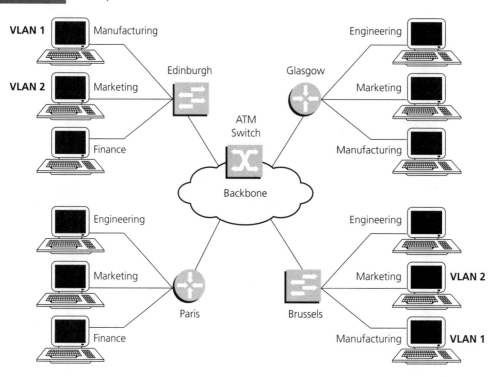

7.7.2 Virtual LANs and addressing issues

A virtual LAN requires only **one subnet address** (for IP; more generally, single subnet address) for all the segments (hosts) it contains. The advantage to this approach is that it makes it possible to consolidate subnetworks by mapping one subnet number to each major workgroup, department, or project. Because subnets can span many physical segments, virtual LANs allow centralized high-performance servers to be seamlessly accessed by end stations anywhere on the local backbone.

Virtual LANs reduce the waste of scarce IP addresses by using a limited number of network addresses very efficiently. In a hub/router-based network, each LAN segment usually needs its own subnet number so that routers can move data between subnets. This quickly becomes inefficient unless there are enough users on a single router port to fill in all of the possible IP addresses. Using variable length subnet masks helps to preserve the IP address space to a certain extent in hub/router-based networks. In a network based on virtual LANs, any number of LAN segments

FIGURE 7-19 VLANs and LANE combination in corporate network

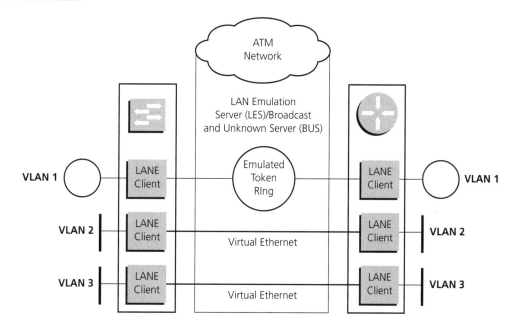

can be combined into a single virtual LAN, allowing administrators to assign IP addresses and subnets more efficiently. A subnet can be one port on one switch, multiple ports on one switch, or multiple ports on multiple switches.

VLANs can complicate **address management** when both VLANs and DHCP servers are used to assign IP addresses to workstations. Many vendor LAN switches permit VLANs to be defined by an Ethernet MAC address, e.g. a VLAN is simply defined as a list of Layer 2 MAC addresses. If a user moves from a port on one LAN switch to a port on another LAN switch, the new switch will recognize the unchanged MAC address – this permits the user's VLAN, IP address, and IP subnet to stay the same.

This may conflict with the operation of DHCP, which will typically try to assign a new IP address to the user when they rejoin the network. This can make it difficult for network managers to determine which IP addresses have been assigned to particular workstations as they are moved about the enterprise network.

7.7.3 VLAN interconnections

Although we are currently discussing the operation of internetworking devices at Layer 2, it is important to note that with the conception of VLANs the Layer 2 devices are simply not enough for the interconnections in a switched network. The **interconnectivity between VLANs** has to be provided by Layer 3 devices, namely routers or multilayer switches. As each VLAN terminates on a Layer 3 device, each VLAN is also assigned its own network subnet from an IP perspective. Regardless of whether a single or multiple VLANs exist within a single switch, Layer 3 devices are used to interconnect them.

Deploying private VLANs (with a single user on the VLAN) means that from a Layer 2 perspective, each customer that is added to such a network requires a new VLAN to be configured and managed. The spanning tree becomes more complicated as more VLANs are added to the topology. In addition, to efficiently manage bandwidth within this environment, you must constantly track each VLAN trunk to ensure it is only transporting necessary VLANs. As new customers are added to the topology, or existing customers span to new switches, the spanning tree becomes a little more complicated.

From a Layer 3 perspective, there are more complications. Because each customer has its **own VLAN**, it must also have its **own IP subnet**. Within such a design, there are likely to be two separate exit points, namely Layer 3 switches (discussed in Part V). Therefore, for each customer added to the network, a separate IP subnet must be allocated. Within each allocated subnet, two addresses are consumed by broadcast addresses, and three addresses are consumed by those addresses associated with connected devices. The complexity is increased by the need to accurately estimate the future address space requirement so that an initial IP subnet can be allocated to accommodate expected growth. Because customers can vary in size, the routing tables within such a design can become cluttered by numerous variable-length subnets.

A multi-VLAN port connected to a router can link two or more VLANs. Intra-VLAN traffic stays within the boundaries of the respective VLANs as shown in Figure 7.20. Connectivity between VLANs is accomplished by using the router connected to the multi-VLAN port. A multi-VLAN port performs normal switching functions in all its assigned VLANs. For example, when a multi-VLAN port receives an unknown MAC address, all the VLANs to which the port belongs learn the address. Multi-VLAN ports also respond to the STP messages generated by the different instances of STP in each VLAN.

FIGURE 7-20 Overlapping VLANs

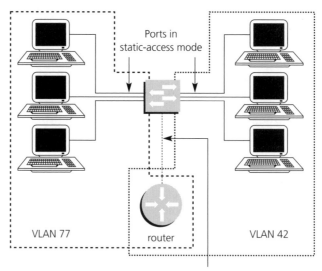

There can be various approaches to interconnecting VLANs with a router:

- **individual router ports for each VLAN** – full wirespeed routing between interfaces is hard to achieve;
- **router on a stick** – using ISL trunking between one switch and the router still limits performance;
- **Layer 3 switch** to perform the routing between VLANs – this additionally requires one link from the Layer 3 switch to the router if external access (WAN or Internet) is required, but can provide very good routing performance under the following conditions:
  - VLANs are isolated with one VLAN per cascaded switch; or
  - aggregate trunks are used between the Layer 3 switch and the Layer 2 switches.

Extensions to VLAN addressing

RFC WATCH	VLAN aggregation

RFC 3069 **VLAN Aggregation for Efficient IP Address Allocation**, 2001 (Informational)

RFC 3069 introduces the concept of Virtual Local Area Network (VLAN) aggregation as it relates to IPv4 address allocation (for IPv4 addressing details see Section 10.3 in Part IV). It introduces a mechanism by which hosts that reside in the same physical switched infrastructure, but separate virtual broadcast domains, are addressed from the same IPv4 subnet and share a common default gateway IP address, thereby removing the requirement of a dedicated IP subnet for each VLAN or Metropolitan Area Network (MAN). Employing such a mechanism significantly decreases IPv4 address consumption in virtual LANs and large switched LANs. It may also ease administration of IPv4 addresses within the network.

If within the switched environment, on the routed side of the network, we introduce the notion of sub-VLANs and super-VLANs, a much more optimal approach to IP addressing can be realized. Essentially, what occurs is that each **sub-VLAN** (customer) remains within a separate broadcast domain. One or more sub-VLANs belong to a super-VLAN, and utilize the default gateway IP address of the super-VLAN. Hosts within the sub-VLANs are numbered out of IP subnets associated with the **super-VLAN**, and their IP subnet masking information reflects that of the super-VLAN subnet.

If desired, the super-VLAN router performs functions similar to a Proxy ARP to enable communication between hosts that are members of different sub-VLANs. This model results in a much more efficient address allocation architecture. It also provides network operators with a mechanism to provide standard default gateway address assignments.

virtual networking and VLANs

Virtual networking is the ability to create logical workgroups of users in their own private and secure network. With VLANs, the network administrator can organize users into **logical groups**, rather than be confined to the physical locations of the user device. This represents a major advance in networking, enabling people to work together more easily and efficiently than ever before.

VLANs have the following key **advantages**:

- VLANs facilitate the easy administration of logical groups of stations that can communicate as if they were on the same LAN.
- VLANs facilitate easier administration of moves, adds, and changes in members of these groups.
- VLANs make more efficient use of scarce network addresses.
- VLANs limit the propagation of multicast and broadcast traffic between VLANs as traffic between VLANs is firewalled. VLANs thus also add security for domain broadcasts.

7.7.4 VLAN components

It is important to recognize that LAN switches are not the only necessary components of a VLAN. Networks that have VLANs contain one or more of the following components.

LAN switches logically segment connected end stations. Switches are the entry points into the switched fabric for end station devices and can group users, ports, or logical addresses into common communities of interest. You can use both a single switch or multiple connected switches to group ports and users into communities. By grouping ports and users together across multiple switches, VLANs can span single-building infrastructures, interconnected buildings, or campus networks. Switches use frame identification, or tagging, to logically group users into administratively defined VLANs. Based on rules you define, tagging determines where the frame is to be sent by placing a unique identifier in the header of each frame before it is forwarded throughout the switch fabric. The identifier is examined and understood by each switch prior to any broadcasts or transmissions to other switches, routers, or end station devices. When the frame exits the switch fabric, the switch removes the identifier before the frame is transmitted to the target end station. Tagging eliminates the dynamic discovery of the paths in the VLAN switches and allows faster forwarding of frames, since the APICs only need to recognize the tags and match them to a small mapping table. Processing of the entire frame (header) is not necessary with tagging.

Routers provide VLAN communications between workgroups. Routers provide policy-based control, broadcast management, and route processing and distribution. They are necessary for communication between VLANs, across the VLAN boundaries. Routers connect to other parts of the network that are either logically segmented into subnets or that require access to remote sites across wide area links. Routers are integrated into the switching fabric by using high-speed backbone connections over Fast Ethernet links, FDDI, or ATM for higher throughput between switches and routers.

Transport protocols carry VLAN traffic across shared LAN and ATM backbones. The VLAN transport protocol enables information to be exchanged between interconnected switches residing on the corporate backbone. The backbone acts as the aggregation point for high-volume traffic. It also carries end user VLAN information and identification between switches, routers, and directly attached servers. Within the backbone, high-bandwidth, high-capacity links carry the traffic throughout the enterprise.

7.7.5 STP and equal cost switching

The existence of VLANs and their proper support by switches again depends on running the Spanning Tree Protocol to avoid switching loops. However, in cases when switches support more parallel high-speed ports or even trunks, there might arise a justified requirement to use them for traffic load balancing. The normal and proper operation of STP will not allow that as anything more than one connection between switches would invariably lead to dangerous loops.

The STP's task is to create a single path to a destination. If there is a need to force the switch to use more paths to one destination, **port channeling** might be deployed which statically load-balances traffic going out of two or more ports. **Static load-balancing** means the creation of a list of source-destination MAC address pairs and these pairs will communicate from a specific port configured to be part of the port channel. This is contrary to **dynamic load-balancing** where each packet can go out of each port of the port channel. Port channeling or link aggregation is standardized in **IEEE 802.3ad** as discussed in Section 7.4.2.

Per VLAN spanning tree

If several VLANs coexist across a set of Layer 2 switches, each individual VLAN has the same characteristics of the associated broadcast domain and spanning tree domain. Some switch vendors already offer a proprietary **Per VLAN Spanning Tree** (PVST) while many switches in the industry offer only a single spanning tree per switch (IEEE works on a standard approach, as discussed later in this chapter). PVST enables load-balancing across the different VLANs for connections from the access layer to the aggregation or distribution layer. In addition, PVST convergence time may be smaller than that for the larger STP topology for the entire switch.

With per VLAN spanning tree a particular switch can belong to **multiple instances of spanning tree,** and in each spanning tree instance it might be acting as a root bridge, while some ports might be in blocking mode or forwarding depending on what VLAN it belongs.

7.7.6 VLAN identification

VLANs are not limited to one switch and may span many switches, even across WAN links. Sharing VLANs between switches is achieved by inserting a **tag** with a VLAN identifier (VID) which is inserted in each frame. A VID must be assigned for each VLAN. By assigning the same VID to VLANs on many switches, one or more VLANs (broadcast domains) can be extended across a large network.

VLANs are uniquely identified throughout the VLAN environment having a consistent representation of VLAN across a VLAN fabric, including across ATM. This shared VLAN knowledge of a particular packet remains the same as the packet travels from one point to another in the VLAN fabric.

IEEE 802.10

The first standardized approach was the **IEEE 802.10** where one of the fields, **Security Association Identifier** (SAID), in the 802.10 header was used as a VLAN ID. The 'coloring' of traffic was achieved by inserting a 16-byte header between the source address and the service access point (SAP) of frames leaving a bridge. This header contains a four-byte VLAN ID or 'color.' A receiving bridge removes the header and forwards the intact frame to interfaces that match that VLAN color.

STANDARDS WATCH	first VLAN tagging approach

IEEE 802.10-1998 IEEE Standard for Interoperable LAN/MAN Security (SILS)

7.7.7 IEEE 802.1Q

The IEEE 802.1Q standard defines the **architecture, protocols,** and **mappings** for bridges/switches to provide interoperability and consistent management of VLANs. Its task was to develop an architecture and bridge/switch protocols for the logical partitioning of a bridged/switched local area network that provides separate instances of the MAC service to administratively defined groups of users, independent of physical location. The architecture and protocols are compatible and interoperable with existing bridged/switched local area network equipment and support a range of implementations.

This IEEE 802.1Q standard has two main goals:

■ to define which are the **capabilities of a VLAN-aware switch;**
■ to add to the standard IEEE 802.1D the **VLAN support**, from which arises the problem of creating devices (switches and bridges) that, while being 802.1Q compliant, can interoperate with VLAN-unaware devices, i.e. devices 802.1D compliant.

The IEEE 802.1Q standard is extremely restrictive as regards untagged frames. The standard provides only a **per-port VLAN solution for untagged frames**. For example, assigning untagged frames to VLANs takes into consideration only the port from which they have been received. Each port has a parameter called a permanent virtual identification (Native VLAN) that specifies the VLAN assigned to receive untagged frames. IEEE 802.1Q assigns frames to VLANs by filtering and assumes the presence of a **single spanning tree** and of an **explicit tagging scheme** with **one-level tagging**.

The role of 802.1Q is to guarantee multi-vendor interoperability. One field where 802.1Q provides added value (over previously used proprietary schemes) is that of the interconnection of high-speed servers: in fact at present there is a lack of NIC cards which can support tagging schemes (i.e. are able to support many VLANs at the same time). The standard provides a **per-port VLAN solution**, i.e. to assign frames to VLANs taking into consideration only the port from which they have been received. Each port has a parameter called the **Port VLAN IDentifier** (PVID) that specifies to which VLAN to assign received untagged frames. The valid range of VLAN PVIDs specified in the IEEE 802.1Q standard is 0–4095.

Figure 7.21 shows the inside of an 802.1Q switch and in particular the so called **relaying function**, the lowest level in the architectural model described in the IEEE 802.1Q standard. The frames are received and filtered by the **ingress rules** (rules relevant to the classification of received frames belonging to a VLAN), that base their decision on the information about the state of ports. The frames are then passed to the **forwarding process** which decides to filter or forward the frame (reads both the information about ingress and egress ports and the information in the filtering database), and then the frames are passed to the **egress rules**. These read the port's state information on the egress port and decide if the frame must be sent tagged or untagged. At the end, the frame is transmitted.

FIGURE 7-21   Relaying function of an 802.1Q switch

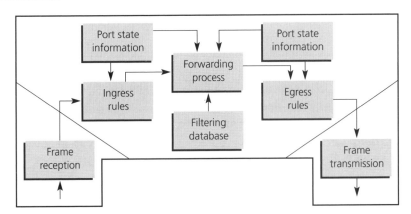

SNAPSHOT   **The main characteristics of IEEE 802.1Q are as follows:**

■ assigning frames to VLANs by filtering, e.g. using Layer 3 information, is allowed but not specified in the standard;

■ the standard assumes the presence of a **single spanning tree** and of an **explicit tagging scheme with one level tagging**.

The VLAN frame tagging principle is shown in Figure 7.22.

FIGURE 7-22 VLAN tagging

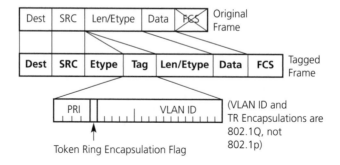

The **IEEE 802.1Q tag** (see Figure 7.23) is stored in the following two octets and it contains:

FIGURE 7-23 IEEE 802.1Q/p encapsulation

7 octets	1 octet	6 octets	6 octets	2 octets	2 octets		4 octets
Preamble	Starting frame delimiter	Destination address	Source address	TAG *3 bits used for COS (user priority)*	Protocol type	Data	FCS

- *user priority* – three bits, used by the standard 802.1p;
- *Canonical Format Identifier (CFI)* – one bit used for compatibility reasons between Ethernet type networks and Token Ring type networks;
- *VLAN Identifier (VID)* – 12 bits representing the identification of the VLAN allow the identification of up to 4096 VLANs.

In the case of a network with an ATM WAN, Ethernet switches with ATM uplinks can have a VLAN-to-ELAN (emulated LAN) mapping feature that matches 802.1Q VIDs to ATM ELAN names. This allows the benefits of VLAN bandwidth optimization and security to be extended between campus buildings or even between remote sites. The second possibility to extend VLANs across an ATM cloud is by using bridged PVCs, where each VLAN is mapped to one PVC.

VLAN trunking

A trunk is a point-to-point link between one or more Ethernet switch ports and another networking device such as a router or a switch. Trunks carry the traffic of multiple VLANs over a single link and allow to extend VLANs across an entire network.

Two trunking encapsulations are available on all Ethernet ports:

- **IEEE 802.1Q** – standard trunking encapsulation;
- **Inter-Switch Link (ISL)** – a proprietary Cisco trunking encapsulation.

802.1Q tunneling

The 802.1Q tunneling feature supports secure **virtual private networks** (VPNs). 802.1Q tunneling enables service providers to keep traffic from different customers segregated in the service provider infrastructure while significantly reducing the number of VLANs required to support the VPNs. 802.1Q tunneling allows multiple customer VLANs to be carried by a single VLAN without losing their unique VLAN IDs.

Traffic to be tunneled comes into the switch from an 802.1Q trunk port on a neighboring device and enters the switch through a port configured to support 802.1Q tunneling (a tunnel port). When the tunnel port receives traffic from an 802.1Q trunk port, it does not strip the 802.1Q tags from the frame header but, instead, leaves the 802.1Q tags intact and puts all the received 802.1Q traffic into the VLAN assigned to the tunnel port. The VLAN assigned to the tunnel port then carries the tunneled customer traffic to the other neighboring devices participating in the tunnel port VLAN. When the tunneled traffic is received by an 802.1Q trunk port on a neighboring device, the 802.1Q tag is stripped and the traffic is removed from the tunnel.

STANDARDS WATCH VLANs

IEEE 802.1Q-1998 **IEEE Standards for Local and Metropolitan Area Networks: Virtual Bridged Local Area Networks**

IEEE P802.1s (New Standard Project) **Standard for Local and Metropolitan Area Networks – Supplement to 802.1Q Virtual Bridged Local Area Networks: Multiple Spanning Trees**

IEEE P802.1u (New Standard Project) **Standard for Virtual Bridged Local Area Networks – Technical and Editorial Corrections**

IEEE P802.1v (New Standard Project) **Supplement to 802.1Q: IEEE Standards for Local and Metropolitan Area Networks: Virtual Bridged Local Area Networks: VLAN Classification by Protocol and Port**

IEEE 802.3ac-1998 **IEEE Standard for Information Technology – Telecommunications and Information Exchange between Systems – Local and Metropolitan Area Networks – Specific Requirements – Part 3: Carrier Sense Multiple Access with Collision Detection (CSMA/CD) Frame Extensions for Virtual Bridged Local Area Networks (VLAN) Tagging on 802.3 Networks**

IEEE 802.1p has two main goals:

- to define expedited traffic capabilities, i.e. to allow user priorities to be defined at the frame level;
- to define a filtering service to support the dynamic use of group MAC addresses.

To achieve the first of these two purposes, 802.1p labels the packets by using the tag and, in particular, it uses the three bits of the *User Priority* at the frame level. The 802.1p tagged frames have an explicit priority which is not computed starting from the MAC address or derived from other information in the frame, but it is explicitly carried. Obviously, a switch, in order to support this type of standard, must have multiple output queues per output port and the output queue selection must be based on the 802.1p tag. 802.1p maintains the order only between frames of the same priority.

This architecture presents information and states already defined in the IEEE 802.1D architectures, for example the filtering database, the state information about the source port and the destination port, the mechanisms to receive, to transmit, or to discard the frames. The ports state information is greatly increased in 802.1p since the presence of protocols like GMRP and GVRP allows state information associated with the ports to be dynamically computed and therefore forwarding or filtering conditions to be created for the frames that arrive or must be transmitted to/from the ports.

GARP

The IEEE 802.1p standard introduced a new protocol, the **Generic Attribute Registration Protocol** (GARP). It is a generic protocol, which means that it is not used directly, but only the applications written by means of this protocol will be used. At present, two **applications based on GARP** have already been defined, **GMRP** and **GVRP**. GARP is defined as registering generic attributes within a LAN. In particular, it is used by participants in **GARP applications** (GARP participants) to register and deregister attribute values with other GARP participants within a bridged LAN.

Attribute types and attribute values are specific to each GARP application. This protocol is designed to **register any type and any value of attribut**e. From the operational point of view, a GARP application makes/withdraws declarations relative to attribute values. This results in registration/deregistration of attribute values in other GARP participants. The registration/deregistration is recorded in a state variable associated to the attribute value itself, and in particular the state variable is located in the **Registrar state machine**. The registration occurs only on the ports that receive the GARP PDU containing the declaration. The registration/deregistration occurs even on ports that are not in the spanning tree forwarding state, which implies that GARP PDUs are received also, for example, on ports that are blocked from the spanning tree point of view.

Attribute values registered on ports belonging to the active topology are propagated to all the other switch ports belonging to the active topology by the **Applicant state machine.**

GARP is suitable for implementing applications where it is desirable to form **reachability trees** that constitute the subset of the active topology that encompasses all registered participants. In each switch the GARP participant consists of a GARP application, a **GARP Information Distribution** (GID) for each port, and of a set of state machines that defines the current registration and declaration state of all attribute values.

Another important entity is represented by the **GARP Information Propagation** (GIP) whose aim is the propagation of information between GARP participants, either within a bridge or between different bridges. In the latter case, GIP uses an LLC Type 1 service.

Figure 7.24 describes GARP's structure on a bridge and on an end station, showing the GARP participants, the GARP applications, the GIDs, and the LLC used to connect the GARP participants through the LAN.

FIGURE 7-24 GARP bridge and end station architecture

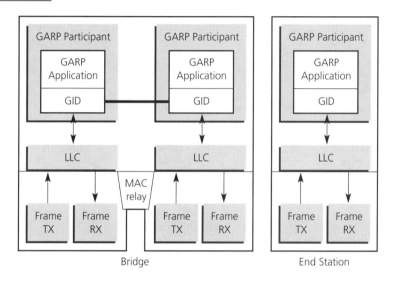

Bridge   End Station

GMRP

The **GARP Multicast Registration Protocol** (GMRP) is a **GARP application**. Its aim is very similar to that of the IGMP (Internet Group Membership Protocol, see Section 11.6), but while IGMP is a protocol for the registration of IP multicast groups at Layer 3, GMRP is a protocol for the **registration of multicast groups at the MAC layer**.

GMRP allows end stations to register for the MAC multicast groups that they want to receive. This improves the network performance, since multicast groups are transmitted by switches only on the ports where it is necessary, i.e. only on the ports that requested to receive that multicast group.

GMRP's existence is complicated by the presence of stations which are not GMRP compliant and therefore by the need, on some ports, to transmit all the multicast groups. GMRP, like all GARP derivation protocols, **registers the attribute values**, and in particular the **Group Membership Information**. It deals with the composition of groups and the attribute type it registers is the 48-bit multicast MAC address.

Another purpose of GMRP is the updating of the **filtering database** to indicate the ports on which the members of the groups have been registered. In GMRP three **default group behaviors** can be selected:

- to **filter** unregistered groups (default), i.e. a switch supporting GMRP by default never sends any frame for multicast group to any port if a station has not registered to receive that multicast group;
- to **forward** all multicast groups;
- to **forward** all unregistered multicast groups.

Figure 7.25 shows how GMRP operates in the presence of stations that belong or not to a multicast group M. In particular, the arrows illustrate the **group registration entries** created by GMRP for a single group (the group registration message propagates in the reverse direction), i.e. they show the direction of propagation of the multicast application data frames toward the end stations.

FIGURE 7-25 Example of GMRP registration

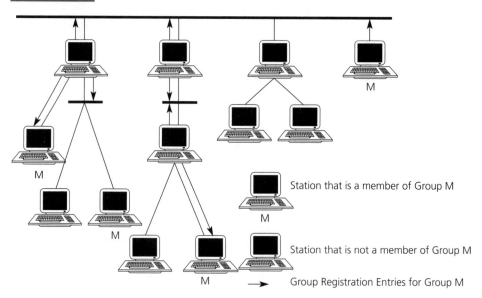

GVRP

The **GARP VLAN Registration Protocol** (GVRP) defined by IEEE 802.1Q is a VLAN membership protocol, where end stations and switches may issue or revoke declarations relating to the membership of VLANs. The attribute type is the 12-bit **VLAN ID** (VID).

Unicast frames propagate only on the desired path. GVRP, as a **pruning protocol**, inhibits the propagation of the multicast frames in the regions of the network that do not need to receive those frames. If in a zone of the network no

SNAPSHOT   GVRP

GVRP is a Generic Attribute Registration Protocol (GARP) application that provides **IEEE 802.1Q-compliant VLAN pruning and dynamic VLAN creation on 802.1Q trunk ports**. With GVRP, the switch can exchange VLAN configuration information with other GVRP switches, prune unnecessary broadcast and unknown unicast traffic, and dynamically create and manage VLANs on switches connected through 802.1Q trunk ports.

station requests to be a member of a given VLAN, the switch connecting the station to that part of the network will not request to be a member of that VLAN and therefore broadcast/multicast frames of the VLAN will not propagate on the switch and will not reach the stations that did not request to receive that VLAN.

GVRP is activated by two service primitives that allow for the registration or deregistration of the VID on a port. We have already seen that the model chosen by 802.1Q is port-based, which provides some **access ports**, untagged ports where frames are assigned to VLANs on the base of the PVID, and some **trunked ports**, hybrid ports where some frames can be tagged and others can be untagged. A **port-based VLANs** model is limited because it does not support user mobility nor decisions based on higher level information.

Figure 7.26 shows a model of port-based VLANs.

FIGURE 7-26   Port-based VLANs

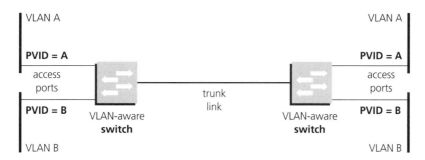

As mentioned before, each physical port has a parameter called PVID. All untagged frames are assigned to the LAN specified in the PVID parameter. When a tagged frame is received by a port, the tag is respected. If the frame is untagged, the value contained in the PVID is considered as a tag. This allows the coexistence, as shown in Figure 7.27, on the same pieces of cable, of VLAN-aware switches and VLAN-unaware station. Let's consider, for example, the two stations connected to the central trunk link in the lower part of Figure 7.27: they are VLAN-unaware and they will be associated to the VLAN C because the PVIDs of the VLAN-aware bridges are equal to C. Since the VLAN-unaware stations will

FIGURE 7-27 Native VLAN

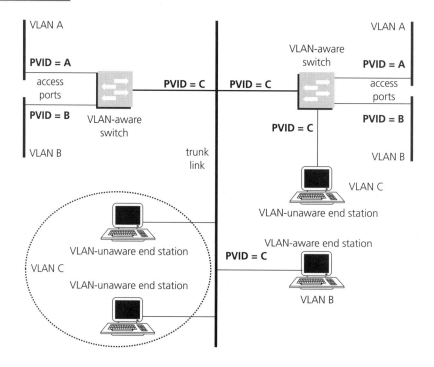

send only untagged frames, when the VLAN-aware switches receive these untagged frames they assign them to the VLAN C.

The mechanism that allows the mixing of VLAN-aware and VLAN-unaware switches presents some problems. One of these problems is related to the **spanning tree**, as shown by Figure 7.28. We can see two servers connected by a VLAN-aware switch S1 and two VLAN-unaware switches S2 and S3, connected to S1 and connecting two VLANs A and B. If port X is spanning tree blocked (remember that there is only one spanning tree shared by the VLAN-aware and the VLAN-unaware switches) there is no problem and the network works properly. If port Y is blocked, the VLAN A is stalled, since while it is true that VLAN A's frames can reach S1 passing through S3, it is also true that, when they reach S1, they are tagged as frames belonging to VLAN B and therefore they are no longer seen by server or VLAN A. This creates an interoperability problem.

Moreover, single spanning tree problems can create partial connectivity or lack of connectivity. The example in Figure 7.29 shows two VLAN-aware switches, each with a port A and a port B; the two ports A are connected together as are the two ports B. There is no connectivity for the VLAN B as in fact when we have two parallel links the spanning tree cuts one of the links independently of the fact that the link would have been assigned to carry a VLAN (B, in this case) which was not active on the other link. This situation is normal and unavoidable in the case of two VLANs implemented with ATM/LANE, where each VLAN uses a VC. VCs of different VLANs are present in parallel and are cut by the spanning tree, causing interoperability and compatibility problems between the standard IEEE 802.1Q

FIGURE 7-28 Spanning tree problem 1

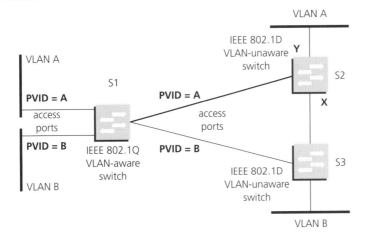

and the backbones in ATM LANE. On the contrary, the problem can be easily solved in the case of two Ethernet switches by defining the two connections as two hybrid connections, which will allow both the VLANs to go on both connections.

FIGURE 7-29 Spanning tree problem 2

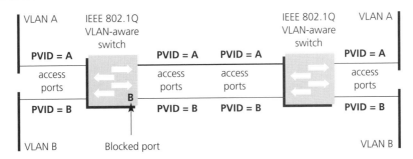

GVRP has functions comparable to those of Cisco's proprietary Virtual Trunking Protocol (VTP) pruning which is discussed briefly later.

Interaction between 802.1p and 802.1Q

The interactions between the two standards can be summarized as follows:

- 802.1Q specifies how to encode the VLAN ID;
- 802.1p specifies how to encode the frame priority;
- 802.1p introduces GARP, the generic protocol used to write applications;
- 802.1p introduces GMRP, a GARP application to control the frame forwarding in a multicast environment;

- 802.1Q adopts GMRP;
- 802.1Q introduces GVRP, a GARP application which specifies how to forward frames in a VLAN environment:
  - on which ports;
  - on which VLANs;
  - tagged or native format.

Adjustment of 802.3 frame format for 802.1Q

Network administrators must ensure that ports with non-802.1Q-compliant devices attached are configured to transmit untagged frames. Many network interface cards for PCs and printers are not 802.1Q-compliant. If they receive a tagged frame, they will not understand the VLAN tag and will drop the frame.

IEEE 802.1Q, the VLAN standard, places a Q-tag in the Ethernet frame header. IEEE 802.1Q-aware devices use Q-tags to differentiate VLANs. This allows the same physical port to host multiple 802.1Q VLANs, each representing a different logical network. Without 802.1Q, physical ports alone define the VLAN. Many older Ethernet devices do not recognize 802.1Q, and because 802.1Q lengthens the Ethernet header, older (non-802.1Q) devices can incorrectly identify the 802.1Q tagged packets as **giants** – an Ethernet frame larger than 1518 bytes – and drop them.

To adjust the 802.3 frame format to align IEEE 802.3 with IEEE 802.1Q is the purpose of approved **IEEE 802.3ac**, the specification of an 802.3 frame when carrying VLAN tag information. Adjustments are necessary to the 802.3 Media Access Control (MAC) parameters, e.g. *maxFrameSize,* to accommodate Virtual Bridged Local Area Network tagged frames to the usual Bridged Local Area Network tag information. The tagging scheme applied to 802.3 frames is specified in IEEE 802.3ac and depicted in Figure 7.30.

FIGURE 7-30   VLAN tagging scheme 802.3ac

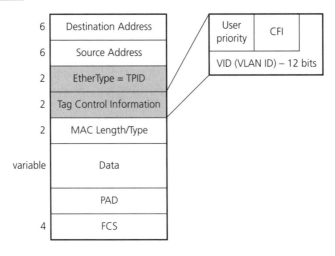

7.7.8 Proprietary Virtual Trunking Protocol

The **Virtual Trunking Protocol** (VTP) is a Cisco Systems proprietary multicast advertisement protocol for dynamically configuring VLAN information across the network regardless of media type (for example Fast Ethernet, ATM, FDDI). VTP enables the automatic creation and mapping of VLANs across different media types with different VLAN tagging schemes. Cisco Systems maps ISL to 802.1Q dynamically with VTP.

SNAPSHOT   **trunk(ing)**

The trunk link carries the traffic of multiple VLANs, as opposed to access links which are part of only one VLAN. Trunking (also called multiplexing) allows more than one signal to be transmitted over a single communications link at (essentially) the same time. Trunking is typically used on switch-to-switch connections (where multiple VLANs are being used). To enable trunking in a networking environment, a **trunking protocol** (ISL, 802.1Q) must be used.

VTP as a Layer 2 messaging protocol maintains consistency throughout the domain and manages the modification of VLANs across multiple switches. VTP handles the addition, deletion, and modification of VLANs at the system level, automatically communicating this information to all the other switches in the network. In addition, VTP minimizes these possible configuration inconsistencies that can result in security violations, such as when VLANs become cross-connected when duplicate names are used, or when VLANs become internally disconnected when they are incorrectly mapped between one LAN type and another. Using VTP enables configuration changes to be made centrally on a single switch. A **VTP management domain** consists of one switch or several interconnected switches under the same administrative responsibility. A switch can be in only one VTP domain.

The VLAN Trunk Protocol provides for each (router or LAN-Circo also uses this server for VTP switch) device to transmit **advertisements** in frames on its trunk ports. These advertisement frames are sent to a multicast address to be received by all neighboring devices (but they are not forwarded by normal bridging procedures). Such an advertisement lists the sending device's management domain, its configuration revision number, the VLANs which it knows about, and certain parameters for each known VLAN. By hearing these advertisements, all devices in the same management domain learn about any new VLANs now configured in the transmitting device. Using this method, a new VLAN needs to be created or configured on only one device in the management domain, and the information is automatically learned by all the other devices in the same management domain.

Once a device learns about a VLAN, it will by default receive all frames on that VLAN from any trunk port and, if appropriate, forward them to each of its other trunk ports, if any. To avoid VLAN traffic being unnecessarily sent to a device pruning the scope of broadcast flooding across trunk links was included in VTP. However, a device's configuration can be modified through management (command-line interface or SNMP) in order to disable one or more known VLANs on individual trunk ports. Ports on a device can be configured to be static ports on any VLAN known to that device.

VTP advertises VLANs configured in one switch to others in the same VLAN domain and other switches check the **revision number** of any update against the current revision number to use the most current revision. VTP uses a configuration revision number to keep all the switches in the VTP domain on the same page. Whenever any change is made to the VLAN configuration or to the VTP domain configuration on a VTP server, the server will increment its revision number by one and send out this number, along with its VLAN information to all the other members of its domain. All domain members will check the configuration revision number and will respond.

The format of a VTP packet encapsulated in ISL frames is shown in Figure 7.31. VTP operates through **VTP messages** (multicast messages) sent to a particular MAC address (*01-00-0C-CC-CC-CC*), with an LLC code of SNAP (*AAAA*) and a type of *2003* (in the SNAP header). VTP advertisements only travel through trunk ports. Therefore, VTP information only flows through the ISL, 802.1Q, 802.10, or LANE port when the trunk is up.

FIGURE 7-31 VTP message format

Number of octets:

26	14	3	3	variable length		
ISL Header	**Ethernet Header** DA: *01-00-0C-CC-CC-CC*	**LLC Header** SSAP: *AA* DSAP: *AA*	**SNAP Header** OUI: cisco Type *2003*	**VTP Header**	**VTP Message**	CRC

If either VTP clients or VTP transparent switches are configured for VLANs, their configurations are not flooded. Every five minutes, VTP servers flood their revision number to the VTP domain. The VTP devices again do a comparison of revision numbers and respond in the above way with one exception. If the received number is greater than the current number for any switch, that switch will request the VTP server to flood its VLAN configuration as described above.

The flooding does not affect the port assignments to VLANs but rather affects whether or not the VLAN is defined on the switch. The one exception to this is that if a VTP server with a higher configuration revision number does not have a certain VLAN defined, that particular VLAN would be deleted from the VTP configuration of all VTP clients and servers. If any of these clients or servers have ports associated with that VLAN, the port will become disabled.

VTP-capable devices can be configured to operate in the following three modes:

■ **VTP server mode** – the server maintains a full list of all VLANs within the VTP domain and advertises local VLANs across trunks, hears other switches' advertisements, adds 'foreign' VLANs to the local switch, and retransmits to any other trunked switches. The server can add, delete, and rename VLANs. When there is a change to the VLAN configuration on a VTP server, the change is propagated to all switches in the VTP domain. VTP advertisements are sent over all trunk connections, including Inter-Switch Link (ISL), IEEE 802.1Q, IEEE 802.10, and ATM LAN Emulation (LANE).

- **VTP client mode** – device maintains a full list of all VLANs. However, this will not be stored in non-volatile memory (will be lost after reloading). The client cannot add, delete, or rename VLANs. Any changes made must be received from a VTP Server advertisement.

- **VTP transparent mode** – does not participate in VTP, i.e. a VTP transparent switch does not advertise its VLAN configuration and does not synchronize its VLAN configuration based on received advertisements. However, transparent switches do forward VTP advertisements that they receive from other switches.

VLAN data packets are typically flooded to all switches while some switches have no ports assigned to some VLANs. VTP pruning is a method of traffic control that reduces unnecessary broadcast, multicast, and flooded unicast packets. This feature restricts flood traffic to only those trunk links that access the appropriate network devices. In a switching fabric, if certain parts of the network do not require the forwarding of flooded traffic on specific VLANs and VTP pruning is enabled, the switch prevents the forwarding of flooded traffic to pruning-eligible VLANs. **VTP pruning** blocks flood traffic to VLANs on trunk ports that are included in the pruning-eligible list. Flooded data traffic for a pruning-eligible VLAN is not sent to switches with no ports in that VLAN, which only affects data for that VLAN and does not affect VTP updates, known unicast or multicast. If the VLANs are configured as pruning-ineligible, the flooding continues.

The major drawback of using VTP is that only one **unique spanning tree** is run for the VLAN in the whole switched domain.

7.7.9 Inter-Switch Link

Inter-Switch Link (ISL) is a Cisco Systems **proprietary protocol** for interconnecting multiple switches and maintaining VLAN information as traffic passes between switches. ISL provides VLAN capabilities while maintaining full wire-speed performance on Fast Ethernet links in full- or half-duplex mode. ISL is designed to interconnect two VLAN capable Ethernet switches using the Ethernet MAC and Ethernet media. The packets on the ISL link contain a standard Ethernet frame and the VLAN information associated with that frame. ISL operates in a point-to-point environment.

ISL uses **'packet tagging'** (see Figure 7.32) to send VLAN packets between devices on the network without impacting switching performance or requiring the

FIGURE 7-32 ISL encapsulation

Number of octets:

26 octets	Max 24 500 octets (8–196 600 bits)	4 octets
ISL header *3 bits used for CoS* *(Class of Service)*	**Encapsulated frame**	**FCS**

use and exchange of complex filtering tables. With ISL, an Ethernet frame is encapsulated with a header that transports VLAN IDs between switches and routers. A 26-byte header that contains a 10-bit VLAN ID is prepended to the Ethernet frame. Figure 7.33 illustrates VLAN packets traversing the shared backbone. Each VLAN packet carries the VLAN ID within the packet header. ISL creates manageable broadcast domains that span the campus, provides load distribution across redundant backbone links and control over spanning tree domains, and substantially reduces the number of physical switch and router ports required to configure multiple VLANs.

FIGURE 7-33   VLAN packets traversing the shared backbone

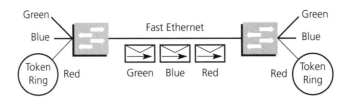

The VLAN field is the **VLAN ID** of the packet. It is a 15-bit value that is used to distinguish different VLANs. However, only 10 bits are actually used for VLAN IDs that therefore range between 1 and 1023. The field is often referred to as the **'color'** of the packet. The additional bit in the two octets is used for BPDU indication.

The ISL frame consists of three primary fields: the **header**, the **original packet**, and the **FCS** at the end. The header is further divided into fields as shown in Figure 7.34.

FIGURE 7-34   ISL header format

Number of bits:

48	4	4	48	16	8	8	8	24	15	1	16	16
DA	type	user	SA	length	*hexAA*	*hexAA*	*hex03*	HSA	VLAN	BPDU	index	res

7.7.10 Overlapping VLANs

The conventional concept of VLANs was that each VLAN represents a separate and exclusive broadcast domain. This meant that each station can belong to only one VLAN. However, current LAN switches allow the configuration of overlapping VLANs enabling each station to belong to one or several VLANs. Broadcasts sent out by a station will be visible to all the members of all the VLANs to which the sending station belongs.

The approach allows for central servers to send to, and receive broadcasts from, multiple workgroups, while preventing the passage of broadcasts between one workgroup and another. The use of overlapping VLANs in this way can substantially reduce the average amount of broadcast traffic that is seen on the individual LAN segments and at the end stations. At the same time, the common resources to which many users need access can be reached directly via switched connections, without having to go through a router. Not only that, but overlapping VLANs can provide a high degree of security, allowing users on many workgroups to access common resources while denying access to local resources for users from other workgroups. Thus we have achieved two of the main aims of router deployment – broadcast control and access security – simply by the intelligent use of switch features.

Overlapping VLANs also help with the connection of routers to the switched LAN. When we connect a router to a LAN switch to provide a link between VLANs, we might expect to have to connect as many physical router ports as there are VLANs to be linked. This would be the case if the VLANs are the conventional, exclusive type. If we define overlapping VLANs, then we can define a single port on a LAN switch to be a member of all the VLANs to be linked, and then connect the router to this port via a single physical connection. Of course, we would need to configure the router to recognize all the relevant subnet IDs on this port.

7.7.11 VLAN membership communication

Switches must have a way of understanding VLAN membership (that is, which stations belong to which VLAN) when network traffic arrives from other switches; otherwise, VLANs would be limited to a single switch. In general, Layer 2-based VLANs (defined by port or MAC address) must communicate VLAN membership explicitly, while VLAN membership in IP-based VLANs is implicitly communicated by the IP address. Depending on the particular vendor's solution, communication of VLAN membership may also be implicit in the case of Layer 3-based VLANs in a multiprotocol environment.

There are two general ways in which VLAN membership information is communicated across multiple switches:

- **Implicit communication** can refer to port-defined VLANs within a single switch. This would be found in smaller networks or networks with large numbers of users on each switch segment. More commonly, however, implicit communication refers to VLANs defined at Layer 3 – the information identifying VLAN membership is found in the packet header.
- **Explicit communication** of VLAN information can be accomplished in three ways, two of which are industry standards. The first standardized method is via an ATM backbone and implementation of the ATM Forum's **LAN Emulation** standard (LANE, see Section 3.8.11). The second standard method of explicit communication of VLAN information is the **IEEE 802.1Q** standard. The third method is **proprietary frame tagging** or encapsulation.

Deploying an ATM backbone also enables the communication of VLAN information between switches, but it introduces a new set of issues with regard to LAN Emulation (LANE). However, for the time being, it should be remembered that with port group-defined VLANs, the LANE standard provides for a non-proprietary method of communicating VLAN membership across a backbone.

7.7.12 VLAN membership types

Port-based

These are the simplest form of virtual LAN. However, port-based VLANs also provide the largest degree of control and security. Devices are assigned to virtual LANs based on the ports to which they are physically attached; VLAN port assignments are static and can be changed only by the MIS staff. However, port-based VLANs do have some limitations. While they are easy to set up, they can support only one virtual LAN per port. Therefore they have limited support for hubs and large servers, which generally need to have access to more than one virtual LAN. In addition, port-based virtual LANs do not make adds, moves, and changes easy since a certain amount of manual configuration is required to change a port's VLAN assignment.

An example of port-based VLANs is:

Port	VLAN
1	1
2	1
3	2

Switching based on ports is simple and efficient because switch indicators or tagging can be applied to all the frames received from the port with minimum overhead. When switching is based on other parameters besides ports, there are some overheads in processing such as protocol and service types matching. Although this processing can be optimized by using hardware, careful compromise needs to be made as to the size of the matching table as well as the flexibility of supporting new parameters. In general, switching indicators or tagging can be applied based on any values or fields inside the link layer frame. Therefore, it is possible to have the switching based not just on Layer 2 parameters but also on higher layer parameters such as protocol and application types.

In a **static port-based VLAN**, ports are statically assigned to a particular virtual LAN by using configuration or management program. Attached to each port can be one host or multiple hosts. The switch associates all frames received on the port with the VLAN configured for the port.

IEEE 802.1Q specifies a single PVID variable (Port VLAN Identifier) for each port of a switch. The configurable value of this single PVID variable specifies the VLAN into which frames untagged at ingress to the port are to be classified. The project will develop a supplement to 802.1Q to specify optional additional classification rules per port based on the protocol (as designated in the frame by 802 family protocol identifiers) in the received untagged frame. The new IEEE **P802.1v** project will consider compatibility and interoperability with existing 802.1Q bridges.

STANDARDS WATCH | **VLANs defined by protocol and port**

IEEE P802.1v (New Standard Project) **Amendment to 802.1Q: IEEE Standards for Local and Metropolitan Area Networks: Virtual Bridged Local Area Networks: VLAN Classification by Protocol and Port**

Classifying multiple protocols into a single VLAN often imposes VLAN boundaries that are inappropriate for some of the protocols, requiring the presence of a non-standard entity to relay between VLANs the frames bearing the protocols for which the VLAN boundaries are inappropriate. The non-standard relay makes the boundaries of the VLANs transparent to the relayed protocols, depriving those protocols of the benefits of the VLANs. The proposed supplementary standard **IEEE P802.1v** will benefit users of multiprotocol LANs by permitting them to specify VLAN structures suitable for each protocol present in a LAN, and removing the need for a non-standard relay function between VLANs.

SNAPSHOT | **port-based VLANs**

Strengths:

- easy to understand and administer;
- common methodology across vendors.

Weaknesses:

- switch reconfiguration necessary upon a station move from one port to another;
- single port cannot pertain to more than one VLAN.

MAC address virtual LANs

Even though they are one of the more simple VLAN types, configuring MAC address VLANs is more complicated than configuring port-based VLANs. A MAC address VLAN is a grouping of MAC addresses which belong to a broadcast domain (VLAN). MAC address identification makes this one of the more secure and controllable VLAN types. MAC address virtual LANs can take a long time to implement – imagine configuring a network with 1000 users and each of these users must be assigned to a VLAN. In addition, MAC addresses are inherently cryptic, making them a bit more difficult to configure.

An example of MAC address-based VLANs is:

MAC address	VLAN
01-23-45-67-89-12	1
02-AB-CD-EF-12	2
00-00-0C-DE-F1-23	2

One of the drawbacks of MAC address-based VLAN solutions is the requirement that all users must initially be configured to be in at least one VLAN. After that initial manual configuration, automatic tracking of users is possible, depending on the specific vendor solution. However, the disadvantage of having to initially configure VLANs becomes clear in very large networks where thousands of users must each be explicitly assigned to a particular VLAN. Some vendors have mitigated the onerous task of initially configuring MAC-based VLANs by using tools that create VLANs based on the current state of the network – that is, a MAC address-based VLAN is created for each subnet.

MAC address-based VLANs that are implemented in shared media environments will run into serious performance degradation as members of different VLANs coexist on a single switch port. In addition, the primary method of communicating VLAN membership information between switches in a MAC address-defined VLAN also runs into performance degradation with larger-scale implementations.

SNAPSHOT **MAC address-based VLANs**

Strengths:

■ no reconfiguration necessary upon station moves as MAC address is embedded in a device.

Weaknesses:

■ slow performance when MAC addresses on a single port belong to different VLANs;
■ VLAN membership tied to a device (burnt in MAC address);
■ all users must be configured to be members of at least one VLAN.

Layer-3 VLANs – protocol-defined

Automatic setup of protocol-based VLANs is different to that of IP. Here, the switch inspects the Ethertype field of each broadcast frame to see which protocol is carried. If there is already a VLAN for that protocol, the source port will be added to that VLAN. Otherwise, the switch will create a new VLAN. Layer 3 VLANs allow network managers to assign traffic with a specific protocol criterion to a corresponding virtual LAN; it is the exact criterion that network managers have been using to create broadcast domains with routers. The protocol could be in the form of an IP subnet or an IPX network number. For example, a network manager could group users into virtual LANs based on the subnet addresses that were assigned by an MIS prior to migrating to a switched solution.

An example of protocol based VLANs is:

Protocol	VLAN
IP	1
IPX	3
AppleTalk	2

The feature set of a switch coupled with its VLAN implementation often determines the flexibility of this type of VLAN. Many Layer-3 virtual LANs extend into multiple switches while others are more limited and exist only on one switch (see Figure 7.35).

FIGURE 7-35 Layer 3 based VLAN

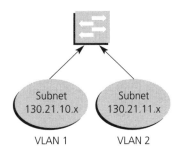

By defining VLANs by IP address, a user who moves from one physical location to another could remain in his or her VLAN (in the case of IP, the term virtual subnet is sometimes used in place of virtual LAN) without having to update the workstation's IP address.

There are several advantages to defining VLANs at Layer 3. First, it enables partitioning by protocol type. This may be an attractive option for network managers who are dedicated to a service- or application-based VLAN strategy. Second, users can physically move their workstations without having to reconfigure each workstation's network address which is a benefit primarily for TCP/IP users. Third, defining VLANs at Layer 3 can eliminate the need for frame tagging in order to communicate VLAN membership between switches, reducing transport overhead.

One of the disadvantages of defining VLANs at Layer 3 (vs. MAC- or port-based VLANs) can be performance. Inspecting Layer 3 addresses in packets is more time consuming than looking at MAC addresses in frames. For this reason, switches that use Layer 3 information for VLAN definition are generally slower than those that use Layer 2 information. It should be noted that this performance difference is true for most, but not all, vendor implementations.

VLANs defined at Layer 3 are particularly effective in dealing with TCP/IP, but less effective with protocols such as IPX, DECnet, or AppleTalk, which do not involve manual configuration at the desktop. Furthermore, Layer 3 defined VLANs have particular difficulty in dealing with non-routable protocols such as NetBIOS. end stations running unroutable protocols cannot be differentiated and thus cannot be defined as part of a network-layer VLAN.

In a **protocol-based VLAN**, VLAN IDs are assigned depending on the protocol type while in application-based VLAN, based on the application's port numbers or service types, different VLAN IDs can be assigned.

SNAPSHOT	layer 3-based VLANs

Strengths:

- partitioning by protocol type;
- partitioning within IP in conjunction with subnet addressing (through subnet masks);
- single port can participate in multiple VLANs;
- no need for frame tagging to communicate VLAN membership.

Weaknesses:

- switch reconfiguration necessary upon a station move from one port to another;
- performance degradation possible due to a need to determine Layer 3 protocol (and network addresses);
- no support to non-routable protocols (such as NetBIOS, LAT).

Protocol policy virtual LANs

These virtual LANs are based on protocol criteria within a frame. A manager could decide that a certain field indicating the protocol type within a frame will be used to determine VLAN membership, and then download this policy to all of the switches in the network. For instance, this could be used to put all users who are using NetBIOS and IP into their own VLAN. Users of this type of VLAN should have thorough knowledge of broadcast frames.

Multicast virtual LANs

Multicasts are unlike broadcasts (which go everywhere on a network) and uni-casts (which are point-to-point). Multicast traffic is point to multipoint or multipoint to multipoint and is rapidly becoming an expected service for data networks. Multicasts can be used for video conferencing, stock quotes, and news feeds to the desktop – users can expect more applications to develop as the benefits of multicasting continue to be realized.

Multicast VLANs are created dynamically by listening to the Internet Group Management Protocol (IGMP – see Part IV). As users open applications which use multicasts, they will dynamically join the multicast VLAN associated with that application, and when they close the application, they will disconnect from the multicast VLAN. Multicasts are generally steady-stream and bandwidth intensive. Therefore it is best to put this type of traffic into its own VLAN to prevent network flooding.

Multicast at Layer 2 is discussed in detail later in this chapter.

Policy-based virtual LANs

This is the most powerful VLAN implementation. It allows network managers to use any combination of VLAN policies to create VLANs that suit their needs. They assign devices to virtual LANs using the policies listed above which will be applied to all switches. Once a policy has been downloaded to a switch, it is applied evenly throughout the network and devices are placed into VLANs. Frames from devices are constantly re-evaluated so that VLAN membership can change based on the type of traffic that a device is generating.

Policy-based virtual LANs can implement a variety of assignment methods including any of the VLAN types listed above: MAC source addresses, Layer 3 addresses, and protocol type field. It is also possible to combine different criteria to make a policy that specifically meets a network manager's needs, even such advanced requirements as time-based policy in security-enhanced environments, so that some ports could only be active during business hours.

Comparison of VLAN types

The overall comparison is shown in Table 7.1. For customers who are moving rapidly to a pure private LAN switching architecture (that is, one user per switch port), the limitations of VLANs defined by the MAC-layer address in a shared media network environment (for example, multiple broadcasts over the same physical segment) become moot. Indeed, for many of these customers, deploying VLANs defined by the MAC-layer address becomes a particularly attractive solution.

With VLANs defined by the MAC-layer address, VLAN membership stays with the user no matter where he or she moves on the network, since the MAC address is hard-wired into the NIC. In this way, initial configuration, as well as moves and changes, can be automated.

Each method is appropriate for meeting different user needs and in different network environments, and there are even situations where it is advantageous to utilize multiple methods within a single network environment. Therefore, it is imperative that a vendor's VLAN solution feature a considerable degree of flexibility.

| **TABLE 7-1** | Comparison matrix of VLAN types |

VLAN based on:	Ports	MAC addresses	Layer 3	Protocol policy	Multicast	Policy
Flexibility	None	Medium	Medium	Medium	Medium	High
Monitoring stations' moves	No	Yes	Yes	Yes	Yes	Automatically
Use of protocol structures	No	No	Yes	No	Yes	Automatically
More VLANs on a port	Not allowed	Allowed	Allowed	Allowed	Allowed	Automatically
Overlapping VLANs	Not allowed	Allowed	Allowed	Allowed	Allowed	Automatically
Security	Minimal	High	Minimal (possibility of spoofing)	Minimal	Minimal	Per choice
Administration	Easy	Difficult	Easy	High	Medium	High

7.7.13 VLAN configuration

For the VLAN administrator the degree of VLAN configuration automation, i.e. the level of control left to the network administrator, is a vital issue. VLAN automation can be described in three levels:

- manual;
- semi-automated;
- fully automated.

In general, these levels represent varying degrees of trade-off between the reduction of administrative effort through automated configuration and the enhancement of administrative control. In each network environment, the equilibrium between these two poles is different. Therefore, as with VLAN definition, the level of automation in configuring VLANs depends on the particular network environment and specific business needs of each customer.

7.7.14 VLAN extensions

Spanning tree consideration

IEEE 802.1Q Virtual LANs provides the equivalent of separate LANs over a single bridged LAN, using a single instance of the spanning tree protocol. IEEE 802.1Q specifies a VLAN frame format and VLAN ID by use of tagging. However, the standard is more than just a tagging mechanism. It also defines a unique spanning tree instance running on the native VLAN for all the VLANs in the network.

Such a **Mono Spanning Tree** (MST) network lacks some flexibility compared to a **Per VLAN Spanning Tree** network (PVST) that runs one instance of STP per VLAN. There exist proprietary solutions to allow the running of several STP instances (even over a 802.1Q network), such as by using a tunneling mechanism. For example Cisco proprietary solution can be briefly described as utilizing a Cisco device to connect an MST zone (typically another vendor's 802.1Q-based network) to a PVST zone (typically a Cisco ISL-based network).

Despite multiple independent implementations employing **multiple instances of the spanning tree protocol**, there is currently no interoperability between different vendors, nor a coherent management framework for different techniques. The IEEE standard (IEEE P802.1s) under development will provide an architecture, protocols, and mappings for bridges to provide that interoperability and consistent management. Its aim is to develop an architecture and protocols for the use of multiple instances of the spanning tree protocol within a network employing VLANs. The architecture and protocols will be compatible and interoperable with existing virtual bridged local area network equipment and will support a range of implementations.

STANDARDS WATCH   **Multiple Spanning Trees**

IEEE P802.1s (New Standard Project) **Standard for Local and Metropolitan Area Networks – Supplement to 802.1Q Virtual Bridged Local Area Networks: Multiple Spanning Trees**

Multiple spanning tree protocols in single VLAN

IEEE 802.1Q specifies a single Port VLAN Identifier (PVID) variable for each port of a switch. The configurable value of this single PVID variable specifies the VLAN into which frames untagged at ingress to the port are to be classified. The new IEEE project (P802.1v) is developing a supplement to 802.1Q to specify optional additional classification rules per port based on the protocol (as designated in the frame by 802 family protocol identifiers) in the received untagged frame. The standard will consider compatibility and interoperability with existing 802.1Q switches.

Classifying multiple protocols in a single VLAN often imposes VLAN boundaries that are inappropriate for some of the protocols, requiring the presence of a non-standard entity to relay between VLANs the frames bearing the protocols for which the VLAN boundaries are inappropriate. The non-standard relay makes the boundaries of the VLANs transparent to the relayed protocols, depriving those protocols of the benefits of the VLANs. The proposed supplement will benefit users of multiprotocol LANs by permitting them to specify VLAN structures suitable for each protocol present in a LAN, and removing the need for a non-standard relay function between VLANs.

Note on security

Virtual LANs offer better network security than regular LANs. Consider a network built with hubs. Anyone can plug a protocol analyzer (or a PC with protocol analyzer software) into any connection on a hub and intercept all of the data that is being sent on that segment. The data being intercepted could easily be confidential. The above applies as well to switched networks without VLANs, where a passive sniffer attached to a port cannot intercept ongoing conversations running on other ports of a switch.

If each device is connected to its own port on a network with switched VLANs, then that is not possible. The only observable information is intended for the device attached to that port. With Policy-Based VLANs MAC and IP addresses can be bound to a port – ensuring that only users with a specific MAC and IP address can operate on a switch port, thus adding to a user's security.

VLANs can enhance security even more by isolating VLANs (i.e. by listing all ports that belong to a VLAN). In this case even active sniffers could not get to the stations/traffic running on foreign ports (ports belonging to protected VLANs). They cannot gain access to the protected VLANs by sending registration packets.

7.8 Multicasting at Layer 2

Multicasting is increasingly used in the area of networked multimedia, where group-based video and audio distribution is growing. But also some routing protocols use multicasting as their way of communicating routing updates. Multicast transmission can be implemented at both the **link layer** (Layer 2) and the **network layer** (Layer 3). To put multicasting in perspective, it is important to first understand the three primary network transmission types: unicast, broadcast, and multicast.

■ **Unicast** – with a unicast design, applications send one copy of each packet to each client's unicast address. Unicast transmission has significant scaling restrictions, especially if the group is large, because the same information has to be carried multiple times, even on shared links.

QUICK TIP   **unicasting**

Unicasting is used to accomplish one-to-one communication.

■ **Broadcast** – in a broadcast design, applications send one copy of each packet and address it to a broadcast address that all devices listen to (the Ethernet broadcast address is a well-known address with the value *FF-FF-FF-FF-FF-FF*). This technique is even simpler than unicast for the application to implement. However, if this technique is used, the network must either stop broadcasts at the LAN boundary (with routers) or transmit the broadcast everywhere. Naturally, transmitting the broadcast everywhere can be inefficient if only a small group actually needs to see the packets.

> QUICK TIP **broadcasting**
>
> Broadcasting is used to accomplish one-to-all communication.

■ **Multicast** – with a multicast design, applications can send one copy of each packet and address it to a group address; the client decides whether or not to listen to the multicast address. Multicasting is helpful in controlling network traffic while also curbing network and host processing by eliminating traffic redundancy.

> QUICK TIP **multicasting**
>
> Multicasting is used to accomplish one-to-many communication.

To understand the benefits of multicasting, consider an MPEG-based video server. Playback of an MPEG stream requires approximately 1.5 Mbps per client viewer, depending on the size (and frame per second (fps) rate) of the MPEG frames, as well as the speed of the client viewer. In a unicast environment, the video server sends $1.5 \times n$ Mbps of traffic to the network (where n = number of client viewers). With a 10 Mbps pipe from the server, approximately six to seven streams can be supported before the network runs out of bandwidth. In a multicast environment, the video server needs to send only one video stream to a multicast address; any number of clients can listen to the multicast address and receive the video stream. In this scenario, the server requires only 1.5 Mbps of bandwidth and leaves the rest of the bandwidth free for other uses.

Multicast transmission can be implemented at the data link layer (Layer 2). Ethernet and Fiber Distributed Data Interface (FDDI), for example, support unicast, multicast, and broadcast addresses. An individual computer can listen to a unicast address, several multicast addresses, and the broadcast address. Token Ring also supports the concept of multicast addressing but uses a different technique. Token Rings have functional addresses that can be used to address groups of receivers.

If the scope of an application is limited to a single LAN, using a data link layer multicast technique is sufficient. However, many multicast applications are valuable precisely because they are not limited to a single LAN.

When a multipoint application is extended to a campus environment consisting of different media types, such as Ethernet, Token Ring, FDDI, Asynchronous Transfer Mode (ATM), Frame Relay, Switched Multimegabit Data Service (SMDS), and other networking technologies, it is best to implement multicast at the network layer (Layer 3) so that the traffic can be restricted to only those segments that request the traffic.

7.8.1 Cisco Group Management Protocol (CGMP)

It is inevitable that the IP multicast traffic will traverse a Layer 2 switch, especially in campus environments. IP multicast traffic maps to a corresponding Layer 2 multicast address, causing the traffic to be delivered to all ports of a Layer 2 switch.

The mapping between IP multicast address and MAC multicast address is depicted at Figure 7.36 (see also Sections 2.1.1 and 11.6.2).

FIGURE 7-36   Ethernet multicast address formation

225	65	15	154
E1	41	0A	9A
1110 0001	0 100 0001	0000 1010	1001 1010

a. Class D IP address representation is decimal, hexidecimal and binary. The last 23 bits are used to form the multicast Ethernet address.

01	00	5E	00	00	00
0000 0001	0000 0000	0101 1110	0 000 0000	0000 0000	0000 0000

b. Host multicast Ethernet address template represented in hexidecimal and binary.

01	00	5E	41	0A	9A
0000 0001	0000 0000	0101 1110	0 100 0001	0000 1010	1001 1010

c. The final multicast Ethernet address is formed by taking the last 23 bits of the IP address and substituting them for the last 23 bits of the ethernet address template.

As an example, consider video server A and video client B. The video client wants to watch a 1.5 Mbps IP multicast-based video feed coming from a corporate video server. The process starts by sending an IGMP join message toward the video server. The client's next hop router logs the IGMP join message and uses some network layer multicast protocol, such as PIM (see Part IV for more details), to add this segment to the PIM distribution tree. At this point the IP multicast traffic is transmitted downstream toward the video client. The switch detects the incoming traffic and examines the destination MAC address to determine where the traffic should be forwarded. Since the destination MAC address is a multicast address and there are no entries in the switching table for where the traffic should go, the 1.5 Mbit video feed is simply sent to all ports, clearly an efficient strategy.

Without any mechanism to efficiently handle multicast traffic, the Layer 2 switch has to deliver the traffic to all ports. Cisco Systems has eliminated such inefficiencies with the **Cisco Group Management Protocol** (CGMP), that allows LAN switches to leverage IGMP information on Cisco routers to make Layer 2 forwarding decisions. The net result is that, with CGMP, IP multicast traffic is delivered only to those switch ports that are interested in the traffic. All other ports that have not explicitly requested the traffic will not receive it.

It is important to note here that the CGMP operation will not adversely affect the Layer 2 forwarding performance. Unlike other solutions that instruct the switch to 'snoop' on Layer 3 information at the port level, CGMP preserves Layer 2 switch operation.

The CGMP messages are shown in Figures 7.37 to 7.40.

FIGURE 7-37 CGMP general message format

<table>
<tr><th>0 3</th><th>4 7</th><th colspan="2">8 23</th><th>24 31</th></tr>
<tr><td>Ver</td><td>Type</td><td colspan="2">Reserved</td><td>Count</td></tr>
<tr><td colspan="5">Group Distribution</td></tr>
<tr><td colspan="3">Address</td><td colspan="2">Multicast</td></tr>
<tr><td colspan="3">Source</td><td colspan="2">Address</td></tr>
</table>

FIGURE 7-38 CGMP join message format

<table>
<tr><th>0 3</th><th>4 7</th><th colspan="2">8 23</th><th>24 31</th></tr>
<tr><td>1</td><td>Join</td><td colspan="2">Reserved</td><td>Count = 1</td></tr>
<tr><td colspan="5">00:00:00:00</td></tr>
<tr><td colspan="3">00:00</td><td colspan="2">Router MAC Address</td></tr>
<tr><td colspan="5">Router MAC Address</td></tr>
</table>

FIGURE 7-39 CGMP leave message format

<table>
<tr><th>0 3</th><th>4 7</th><th colspan="2">8 23</th><th>24 31</th></tr>
<tr><td>1</td><td>Leave</td><td colspan="2">Reserved</td><td>Count = 1</td></tr>
<tr><td colspan="5">01:00:5E:41</td></tr>
<tr><td colspan="3">0A:9A</td><td colspan="2">00:00</td></tr>
<tr><td colspan="5">00:00:00:00</td></tr>
</table>

FIGURE 7-40 CGMP leave-all message format

0	3 4	7 8	23 24	31

1	**Leave**	Reserved	**Count = 1**
00:00:00:00			
00:00		*00:00*	
00:00:00:00			

Without CGMP, multicast traffic is flooded to the entire Layer 2 switch fabric. The upstream router prevents the multicast traffic from hitting the campus backbone, but does nothing to control the traffic in the switch fabric.

7.8.2 IGMP snooping

IP multicast distribution is based on multicast groups. Hosts subscribe to a particular application's transmission via IGMP (see Part IV for details on IGMP). An IGMP subscription indicates that the host is interested in receiving the application's transmissions. IGMP snooping is a technique used within switched environments to mitigate the effect of multicast flooding. It turns off the flooding of switch ports at Layer 2 based on promiscuously monitoring different ports for IGMP messages. On ports where IGMP traffic is found, IP multicast traffic is forwarded; on ports with no IGMP messages, IP multicast is filtered. This technique significantly reduces the impact of flooding at Layer 2 and the potential for congestion leading to frame dropping.

7.9 Token Ring switching

The continued use of MAU-based architectures in smaller corporate outposts, such as remote branch offices, is a clear indication that the tried-and-true approach continues to hold appeal. Still, demand is also building for higher-performance products. And it is that demand that has led to the development of token ring switches.

7.9.1 Token Ring considerations

Although they are sufficient for traditional low-bandwidth applications, today's Token Ring PC bridge backbones cannot support the newer class of high-bandwidth client/server and workgroup applications. Among the factors restricting performance and network growth are:

- seven-hop limit of the SRB network;
- low Token Ring port density of common bridges;
- 16 Mbps Token Ring speed capacity;

- limited packet-forwarding rates and higher latencies of traditional bridges;

- effects of increasing broadcast traffic on network performance.

The traditional method of connecting multiple Token Ring segments is to use a two-port PC bridge to link workgroup rings to a 16 Mbps backbone ring. However, newer applications require better performing bridges and a better performing backbone.

To maintain performance and avoid overloading the backbone, you can locate servers on the same ring as the workgroup that needs to access the server. However, this makes the servers more difficult to back up, administer, and secure than if they are located on the backbone.

One solution is to lobe-extend the servers to the clients while physically placing the servers in a central location. This has the disadvantage of requiring a lot of cable between the central location and the client rings.

Another solution is to use multiport routing or switching platforms to collapse a Token Ring backbone onto the backplane of the internetworking device. **Collapsed backbone** Token Ring networks enhance application performance without impacting current network design.

For larger networks, a high-speed backbone is needed to interconnect multiple collapsed switches or routers. FDDI is the primary technology used to interconnect collapsed Token Rings today, and ATM promises to be an important backbone technology in the future.

Token Ring switching dedicates a single LAN segment (and therefore a token) to one or more stations. This increases server or desktop performance without changes to the server or user's computer. Because it maintains the Token Ring infrastructure, Token Ring switching is easy to install, preserves network investments, and requires minimum network reconfiguration and retraining. VLANs can be used to maintain existing subnets for interconnection with routers. As a local collapsed backbone device, a Token Ring switch offers a lower per-port cost than a router, and it supports the direct connection of workstations and network servers. Alternatively, a Token Ring switch can be used in conjunction with a router, providing a high-capacity interconnection between Token Ring segments while retaining the customer's network policy for filtering and firewalling and taking advantage of the other Layer 3 features provided by the router.

The full-duplex technique, which works on dedicated switch connections to a single network node, involves disabling the token to allow the switch port and the adapter in the attached device to transmit simultaneously, which enables data to be exchanged at 32 Mbps. A **full-duplex Token Ring** can be used not only to connect servers to switches, but to interconnect Token Ring switches without using FDDI or ATM. This is particularly attractive for workgroup environments where a higher-speed backbone may not be available. A full-duplex Token Ring offers significant performance gains while protecting the Token Ring infrastructure investment.

Token ring switches embody what amounts to a third-generation Token Ring design, allowing the full 16 Mbps LAN bandwidth to be dedicated to individual network nodes. Switch vendors say that the main application for their products will be in replacing collapsed backbone hubs or routers, improving performance by segmenting the Token Ring into even smaller LAN segments. Alternatively, Token Ring switches can be used to connect modular hubs.

LAN switching has changed the way that bridged networks are built. In the Token Ring environment, LAN switches can effectively replace old, two-port source-route bridges and provide fewer boxes to manage with improved through-put and latency. LAN switching, when used in a network design with routers, can provide a scalable, robust, campus network for mission-critical applications.

The backbone for Token Ring networks will be any of several high-speed media, such as ATM or FDDI. In the Ethernet market, Fast Ethernet is becoming very popular as backbone and server media. Token Ring does not have an equivalent to Fast Ethernet, so at this point ATM appears to be the most likely high-speed media for Token Ring networks. However, there has been a Token Ring ISL deployed for backbone connections.

7.9.2 First-generation vs. second-generation Token Ring switching

When Token Ring switches first appeared in 1994, Token Ring customers were hopeful that these products would mature quickly and provide rich, strategic solutions to their growing bandwidth needs. However, these first-generation switches have been largely disappointing to many customers. Ethernet customers have a wide range of switches to choose from that are fast, are very inexpensive, come with a variety of high-speed uplinks, provide good management tools, support multiple virtual LANs (VLANs), and scale well in large networks. On the other hand, the first generation of Token Ring switches has many limitations.

There are two basic categories of the first-generation Token Ring switch:

- **Processor-based switches** – these switches use Reduced Instruction Set Computer (RISC) processors to do the switching of Token Ring frames. They typically have high functionality but are slow and relatively expensive. These switches have been deployed mainly as backbone switches because of their high cost.

- **Application-specific integrated circuit (ASIC)-based switches** – these switches are fast and relatively inexpensive but have very limited function. Typically, there is little to no filtering, limited management information, limited support for bridging modes, limited VLAN capability, and a limited choice of uplinks. Today, although these switches are less expensive than processor-based switches, they are still too expensive to justify the cost of widespread deployment of dedicated Token Ring switch ports to the desktop.

What customers really need is a second-generation family of Token Ring switches that are fast, are inexpensive, and provide a lot of function. The second generation should provide ASIC-based switching for high speed and low cost. It should support all the bridging modes, fully **Dedicated Token Ring** (DTR), high port density, high-speed uplinks, filtering, Remote Monitoring (RMON) management, broadcast control, and flexible VLAN implementations. This family of switches could be used for backbone switching, workgroup microsegmentation, and dedicated Token Ring to the desktop.

The second-generation Token Ring switches must support ATM and Fast Gigabit Ethernet uplinks. Typically, this migration is done by installing a Fast

Ethernet or ATM backbone, microsegmenting existing Token Rings, and running Ethernet to the desktop for new clients. This approach requires both routing and translational bridging support between the Token Ring and Ethernet networks.

Use of Token Ring switches

Because Token Ring networks remain critically important to traditional IBM environments, a Token Ring switch vendor who intends to champion a migration path for Token Ring customers needs to bring switched bandwidth relief to the core of the LAN infrastructure and move the switch fabric itself progressively closer to the desktop. For customers with widespread Systems Network Architecture (SNA) environments, SRB allows customers the ability to have duplicate Media Access Control (MAC) addresses on SNA Front-End Processors (FEPs) for redundancy and load balancing. SRB also allows active parallel bridge paths through the network for multiprotocol traffic load balancing from end station to server.

The token priority bits in the frame header allow multimedia streams to be given priority over other types of traffic in the network. Token Ring architecture also permits applications to send data using much larger frame sizes (18 KB versus 1.5 KB for Ethernet, although support to jumbo Ethernet frames has started). Management tools that have been widespread in the Token Ring market for more than a decade facilitate media-level problem determination, isolation, and resolution. For many sites, the installed cable plant consists of IBM Type 1 cable, which supports Token Ring and 25 Mbps ATM. Additionally, legacy devices such as IBM's communication controller family traditionally offer only Token Ring connectivity. Finally, the support staffs of many companies have been trained to support Token Ring implementations, cabling infrastructure, and network designs. For these reasons, most Token Ring customers prefer either to remain firmly in the Token Ring camp or to implement Ethernet only in new LAN projects.

SRB is the traditional bridging implementation found in Token Ring networks (see Section 2.4 in Part II for Token Ring detail). However, with the widespread use of routed protocols such as IPX and IP, in combination with bridged protocols such as NetBIOS and SNA, an alternative bridge mode has become popular. SRT allows the routed traffic to be transparently bridged to the router while the nonroutable traffic can be source-route bridged across the network.

A third switching mode, **source-route switching** (SRS), has become popular for switches that offer microsegmentation. This feature allows multiple switch ports to be given the same logical ring number so that frames are switched either by destination MAC address on the logical ring segment or by the route descriptors carried in source-routed frames.

The Token Ring network infrastructure in most customer environments consists of shared-media hubs that are joined together with bridges. Although some Token Ring customers have implemented Fiber Distributed Data Interface (FDDI) as a high-speed backbone transport, most customers still use 16 Mbps backbone segments. Still others have chosen to collapse their backbone segments across multiport routers and bridges. Until recently, bandwidth pressures have not forced large Token Ring shops to implement switched configurations as quickly as their counterparts in the Ethernet environment.

7.9.3 Token Ring switch features

Token Ring switches feature the following capabilities, which will be described in the text:

■ dedicated Token Ring;
■ filtering;
■ network management, including RMON;
■ uplinks;
■ VLAN support.

Support for automatic speed adaptation and IEEE 802.5r standard

In addition to automatic speed detection and adaptation, second-generation switches must provide direct attachment capabilities for end stations – a function that hubs provide today – as well as the ability to transfer traffic in half- or full-duplex modes via the IEEE's 802.5r standard for Dedicated Token Ring (DTR).

Today's bandwidth requirements may only require that servers have a dedicated switch port, but future needs may demand dedicated 16 or 32 Mbps segments to the desktop. Having a switch in place that supports DTR on every port provides the flexibility to roll out dedicated segments, as required.

STANDARDS WATCH	dedicated Token Ring

IEEE 802.5r-1997 **Token Ring Access Method and Physical Layer Specifications Dedicated Token Ring Operation**

As presently defined, each Token Ring station shares the ring's total available bandwidth. This dedicated attachment extension to 802.5 provides a significant increase in available bandwidth to each station. Additionally, it decouples the operating speed of the concentrator from its attaching stations. The IEEE 802.5r standard defines the dedicated attachment of existing token ring stations and, in addition, it expands the station's capability to simultaneously transmit and receive independent data streams for all frames. It also defines station concentrator functions in sufficient detail to produce an interface between station and concentrator that assures interworking.

Filtering capability

Filters should be implemented in the frame-forwarding ASICs of the switch, which will permit frame filtering at media speed with no impact on performance. The minimum criteria for frame filtering include the ability to filter based on the MAC address of a frame, destination service access point (DSAP), or Ethertype field in a Token Ring Subnetwork Access Protocol (SNAP) header. Filtering by MAC address can provide security on switched ports, while the filtering of broadcast traffic based on protocol information carried in the DSAP and Ethertype fields protects directly attached servers from having to process broadcasts from applications they do not support.

Comprehensive network management

Configuration and management of the switches from a centralized network management system via Simple Network Management Protocol (SNMP) and RMON is a must. In addition, the user should be able to create VLANs by simply dragging and dropping particular ports into customer-defined VLANs.

To facilitate the monitoring and troubleshooting capabilities of the network management system, the switch must have the ability to gather the applicable information either through SNMP or RMON, or for more in-depth analysis, to provide a way to access traffic information on a given port.

Embedded RMON support

Each switch port should collect data for at least the first four groups of RMON: events, alarms, statistics, and history. In addition, the ring station order group should be implemented to allow the switch to 'walk the ring' and report the MAC addresses of stations connected to each of its switch ports, providing media-level visibility from the network management application. The gathering of the RMON information should not affect the frame-forwarding performance or capabilities of the switch.

For more in-depth analysis, or to monitor a port that has a server or other end station directly attached, a **network monitoring port** is required. With this capability, traffic from one Token Ring port on the switch can be mirrored to another Token Ring port on the switch that has been designated as the monitoring port. A Token Ring RMON probe or packet capture analyzer connected to the monitoring port provides the capability for further traffic analysis that is sometimes required for network troubleshooting.

Choice of uplinks

FDDI has traditionally been the high-speed uplink of choice in the Token Ring environment. However, with the advent of Token Ring LANE for ATM and the ability to transport full-length Token Ring frames over Fast Ethernet, many users are looking to these alternatives for scalability and flexibility at a lower price than FDDI. Backbone switches with ATM uplinks should support all the LANE services, LAN Emulation Configuration Server (LECS), LAN Emulation Server (LES)/Broadcast and Unknown Server (BUS), as well as LAN Emulation Client (LEC). The ability to provide redundant LANE services is also important. Desktop switches should support at least an ATM uplink with a LEC.

Transport of Token Ring frames over Fast Ethernet should not restrict the Token Ring frame size to Ethernet's limit of 1500 bytes. Further, the Fast Ethernet links should be able to propagate Token Ring VLAN information across the switch fabric. In the case of a mixed-media chassis that supports both Ethernet and Token Ring, the Fast Ethernet link should support the transport of both Ethernet and Token Ring VLANs simultaneously.

VLAN support

The switch must support VLANs by port with the ability to have a separate spanning tree instance for each VLAN to prevent loops in the network. Configuration of the Token Ring VLANs for each switch in the network should be possible from a single switch interface. When the configuration is completed, the VLAN topology information must be able to be propagated to all the switches in the network. The customer should be able to dynamically create, modify, or delete VLANs graphically by simply dragging and dropping ports.

VTP for Token Ring switching

A proprietary VTP protocol (see Section 7.7.8 for detailed explanation) version 2 is used for creating VLANs in a Token Ring switched environment. There are two types of VLANs:

- **Token Ring Bridge Relay Function** (TrBRF) VLANs – interconnect multiple Token Ring Concentrator Relay Function (TrCRF) VLANs in a switched Token Ring network. The TrBRF can be extended across a network of switches interconnected via trunk links. The connection between the TrCRF and the TrBRF is referred to as a logical port. For source routing, the switch appears as a single bridge between the logical rings. The TrBRF can function as a source-route bridge (SRB) or source-route transparent (SRT) bridge running either the IBM or IEEE STP. If SRB is used, you can define duplicate MAC addresses on different logical rings. The Token Ring software runs an instance of STP for each TrBRF VLAN and each TrCRF VLAN. For TrCRF VLANs, STP removes loops in the logical ring. For TrBRF VLANs, STP interacts with external bridges to remove loops from the bridge topology, similar to STP operation on Ethernet VLANs. To accommodate IBM System Network Architecture (SNA) traffic, a combination of SRT and SRB modes must be deployed. In a mixed mode, the TrBRF considers some ports (logical ports connected to TrCRFs) to operate in SRB mode while others operate in SRT mode.

- **Token Ring Concentrator Relay Function** (TrCRF) VLANs – define port groups with the same logical ring number. Typically, TrCRFs are undistributed, which means each TrCRF is limited to the ports on a single switch. Multiple undistributed TrCRFs on the same or separate switches can be associated with a single parent TrBRF. The parent TrBRF acts as a multiport bridge, forwarding traffic between the undistributed TrCRFs. Within a TrCRF, source-route switching forwards frames based on either MAC addresses or route descriptors. The entire VLAN can operate as a single ring, with frames switched between ports within a single TrCRF. You can specify the maximum hop count for all-routes and spanning-tree explorer frames for each TrCRF. This limits the maximum number of hops an explorer is allowed to traverse. If a port determines that the explorer frame it is receiving has traversed more than the number of hops specified, it does not forward the frame. The TrCRF determines the number of hops an explorer has traversed based on the number of bridge hops in the route information field. A backup TrCRF enables to configure an alternative route for traffic between undistributed TrCRFs located on separate switches that are connected by a TrBRF, in the event that the ISL connection between the switches fails. Only one backup TrCRF for a TrBRF is allowed, and only one port per switch can belong to a backup TrCRF. If the ISL connection between the switches fails, the port in the backup TrCRF on each affected switch automatically becomes active, rerouting traffic between the undistributed TrCRFs through the backup TrCRF. When the ISL connection is reestablished, all but one port in the backup TrCRF is disabled.

7.10 FDDI switches

FDDI switches can offer the full bandwidth of the network to each node in the same manner as Ethernet or Token Ring switches. But because FDDI switches are expensive, they are usually compared to ATM switches despite the difference in bandwidth. Although the switched FDDI's bandwidth of 100 Mbps is less than the 155 Mbps offered by ATM, it is fast enough to satisfy most workgroup applications and backbone connectivity needs.

The one area in which FDDI switches cannot equal ATM is the handling of time-sensitive traffic such as multimedia and interactive video. ATM was designed from the ground up for just such an application, and its 53-byte cells minimize delivery delays. The large frame sizes of FDDI, in comparison, are optimized for asynchronous applications.

It is necessary to consider this additional information in network planning and analysis:

- FDDI uses bandwidth more efficiently than ATM. ATM cells are 53 bytes long, and five of the 53 bytes are used by a header – not data. This leaves ATM with an overhead of 9.5%, while the AAL layer introduces additional overhead to ATM packets. FDDI frames, in contrast, can be as large as 4478 bytes with a 23-byte header – an overhead of only 0.5%.

- The short cells in ATM mean that LAN packets have to be broken up before they travel onto the ATM backbone and then reassembled on the other side. FDDI does not suffer from this overhead because its maximum frame size is larger than that of Ethernet and Token Ring networks. Applications that generate long frames would benefit most from FDDI. Use an analyzer to determine the average frame size on your network.

- An FDDI network may have a frame rate as high as 450 000 frames per second. It is up to the transport layer of the protocol in use to scale back and regulate the traffic flow until both sides can keep up.

7.10.1 LAN switch selection guidelines

LAN switches all share a common set of features:

- support for at least one LAN interface (Ethernet, Token Ring, FDDI);
- bridging support (transparent, translational, IEEE 802.1D spanning trees);
- forwarding technique.

Switching has become very competitive; therefore, enhanced feature sets are the norm to the customer's benefit. However, be wary of vendor marketing hype. Look carefully at the switch's technical specifications and ask vendors specific network questions.

Layer 2, workgroup, and desktop switches are being pushed down to the SOHO level of the market and therefore differ mostly in price and manageability. Layer 3 or backbone switches also seem to blur from vendor to vendor, but look for the following features to distinguish a vendor's switch:

- single element network manager;
- plug and play and autonegotiation;
- redundant switching fabric;
- standby routing protocol (specific to Layer 3 switches);
- Gigabit Ethernet capability;
- load balancing capabilities;
- link aggregation;
- flow control support.

When reading marketing literature, as well as specification sheets, look carefully at the wording. Be aware of phases such as 'will have' or 'will support': this indicates that the product does not have the feature. Also, make sure the vendor is clear on what is standard and what is optional equipment. For example, a redundant power supply is a popular must-have feature on a switch; more often than not, the second power supply must be purchased separately.

In **evaluating alternatives for LAN interconnection**, it is imperative to consider several important issues and features:

- **Network design** – unpredictable effects on network traffic flow at the local level when upgrading to a switched network. Upgrading to a switched virtual network has unpredictable effects on total traffic flow across the enterprise.
- **Connectivity** – physical interconnection options and topological considerations.
- **Transparency** – the extent to which protocol overhead is imposed in mapping dissimilar features and functions of the connected networks.
- **Imposition of delay** – the effect of throughput degradation on different types of traffic scenarios.
- **Ease of implementation** – capability for devices to provide a level of interoperability, facilitating multivendor implementations. Despite the advances made by LAN standards groups, there are no guarantees that internetworking equipment from different vendors will work together. Ask the vendor questions regarding the interoperability and scalability of its products.
- **Standards availability** – the status of standards for various internetworking facilities.
- **Cost** – developing and procuring hardware and software interconnection resources.

7.10.2 Brief comparison of LAN switching and routing

The main points are summarized in Table 7.2.

TABLE 7-2 Summarized comparison of LAN switching and routing

Why use LAN switch	Why use a router
Layer 2 switching offers dedicated links to each node, preserves the LAN infrastructure, and provides for improvement in performance in specific areas within a LAN.	Use a router to provide improved network segmentation, to forward traffic between dissimilar LANs, and to access WANs.
A switch is a Layer 2 network device that filters and forwards frames based upon Media Access Control (MAC) layer information.	A router is a network device that determines the forwarding path, and forwards packets based upon network layer information.

Routed vs. switched/bridged backbone

To reiterate the key issues:

- VLANs must be **consistent with the routed model** (cannot split subnets).
- If subnets must be split, they must be 'glued' together by a bridged path.
- Normal routed behavior must be maintained for end nodes to correctly achieve routing between VLANs.
- Networks must be designed carefully when integrating VLANs; the simplest choice would be not to split VLANs across a routed backbone.

The difference between these two topologies is subtle. Some of the advantages/disadvantages for using one or the other are as follows.

7.11 LAN switching vs. ATM – packets vs. cells

As a transition between LAN switching discussed in this chapter and WAN switching that is the topic for the next, it is interesting to compare the differences in switching as they derive from the inherent different network capabilities and services.

ATM technology, seen by many as the future of networking, is inherently a switched technology which transfers data in small 53-byte cells rather than the large, variable-sized packets used in 802 LANs. Some of the important differences between these technologies are discussed below.

ATM is a connection-oriented service, unlike the connectionless datagram service provided by packet networks. Consequently, its true potential is realized only when ATM is installed from end to end. This requires a substantial investment for most users, and while ATM is achieving notable success as a backbone technology, its success at the desktop has been less evident.

An advantage of ATM is that it can potentially provide a sensible solution to the **flow control** problem. This is possible because the virtual channel identifier in each cell allows a switch to identify each logical flow (datastream) within the sum of flows on a physical link. Consequently, flow control can be imposed on a single logical flow without interfering with other flows on the same link. This is only true provided that the host software is configured such that each logical connection has its own virtual channel.

Another potential advantage of ATM is that it offers a variety of qualities of service, ranging from guaranteed bandwidth through best effort. Packet switches, in contrast, provide the rather primitive service defined for 802 LANs, which is restricted to best-effort service with simple prioritization of traffic. In Part V we will explore advanced switches which are also capable of traffic policing on their ports.

STANDARDS WATCH   **Summarized Standards watch**

The following standards and RFCs have been brought to your attention in this chapter:

IEEE 802.1D-1998 *IEEE Standard for Local Area Network MAC (Media Access Control) Bridges*

IEEE 802.1Q-1998 *IEEE Standards for Local and Metropolitan Area Networks: Virtual Bridged Local Area Networks*

IEEE 802.5r-1997 *Token Ring Access Method and Physical Layer Specifications Dedicated Token Ring Operation*

IEEE P802.1s (New Standard Project) *Standard for Local and Metropolitan Area Networks – Supplement to 802.1Q Virtual Bridged Local Area Networks: Multiple Spanning Trees*

IEEE P802.1u (New Standard Project) *Standard for Virtual Bridged Local Area Networks – Technical and Editorial Corrections*

IEEE P802.1v (New Standard Project) *Amendment to 802.1Q: IEEE Standards for Local and Metropolitan Area Networks: Virtual Bridged Local Area Networks: VLAN Classification by Protocol and Port*

IEEE 802.3x-1997 *IEEE Standards for Local and Metropolitan Area Networks: Specification for 802.3 Full Duplex Operation*

IEEE 802.3aa-1998 *Maintenance Revision #5 (100 BASE-T), Standard for Information Technology – Local and Metropolitan Area Networks – Part 3: Carrier Sense Multiple Access with Collision Detection (CSMA/CD) Access Method and Physical Layer Specifications – Maintenance Revision #5 (100 BASE-T)*

IEEE 802.3ac-1998 *IEEE Standard for Information Technology – Telecommunications and Information Exchange between Systems – Local and Metropolitan Area Networks – Specific Requirements – Part 3: Carrier Sense Multiple Access with Collision Detection (CSMA/CD) Frame Extensions for Virtual Bridged Local Area Networks (VLAN) Tagging on 802.3 Networks*

IEEE 802.3ad-2000 *CSMA/CD – Aggregation of Multiple Link Segments*

IEEE 802.10-1998 *IEEE Standard for Interoperable LAN/MAN Security (SILS)*

RFC 3069 *VLAN Aggregation for Efficient IP Address Allocation,* 2001 (Informational)

CHAPTER 8

WAN switching

As was explained in Part I, WAN communication occurs between geographically separated areas. In enterprise internetworks, WANs connect campuses, branch offices, or telecommuters together. When a local end station wants to communicate with a remote end station (an end station located at a different site), information must be sent over one or more WAN links. WAN links are connected by **switches**, which are devices that relay information through the WAN and dictate the service provided by the WAN. WAN communication is often called a **transport (transmission) service** because the network provider often charges users for the services provided by the WAN (called tariffs).

WAN services are provided through the following three primary switching technologies:

- circuit switching;
- packet switching;
- cell switching.

Each switching technique has advantages and disadvantages. **Circuit-switched networks** offer users dedicated bandwidth that cannot be infringed upon by other users. In contrast, **packet-switched networks** have traditionally offered more flexibility and used network bandwidth more efficiently than circuit-switched networks. **Cell switching**, however, combines some aspects of circuit and packet switching to produce networks with low latency and high throughput. Cell switching is rapidly gaining in popularity. With the deployment of ATM as the most prominent cell-switched technology.

Characteristics of circuit switching:

- uses centralized switching model;
- originally designed and optimized for voice traffic;
- inherently connection-oriented;
- short forwarding delays;
- complete pre-allocation and dedication of network resources.

Characteristics of packet switching:

- uses decentralized switching model;
- designed to carry different data types;
- variable forwarding delays;
- bandwidth (unless some reservation or prioritization enabled) used on FCFS (first-come first-serve) basis.

This chapter will concentrate on the specifics of switching in the WAN environment, specifically:

- **X.25 switching;**
- **Frame Relay switching;**
- **ATM switching;**
- **optical switching.**

We established the basis for understanding different WAN characteristics in Part I, Chapter 3, and we will refer to that as needed. In this chapter we will concentrate on the packet switching specifics and switching/routing capabilities of different WAN types. Additionally we will have a look at the latest major developments in the area of optical switching to be deployed at the network core at the lowest level.

8.1 Advantages of packet switching

Packet-switching techniques are not new; they have been around since the mid-1970s (such as X.25 and the original Arpanet). However, when packet switching was first developed, the packets used variable lengths of information. This variable nature of each packet caused some latency within a network because the processing equipment used special timers and delimiters to ensure that all of the data was enclosed in the packet.

The **X.25** represents a classic (the oldest) packet-switching technique. As a next step to create a faster packet-switching service, the industry introduced the concept of **Frame Relay**. Both of these packet-switching concepts (one a Layer 3 and the other a Layer 2 protocol) used variable length packets. To overcome this overhead and latency, a fixed cell size was introduced. In early 1992, the industry adopted a fast packet or **cell relay** concept adopted in **ATM** that uses a short (53 byte) fixed-length cell to transmit information across both private and public networks. ATM represents a specific type of cell relay that is defined in the general category of the overall broadband ISDN (B-ISDN) standard.

Figure 8.1 shows the packet-switched network operation while, for contrast Figure 8.2 shows the circuit-switched network operation. (ISDN or PSTN are examples of a circuit-switched network.)

Packet switching is considered by many to be the most efficient means of sharing both public and private network facilities among multiple users. Each packet contains all of the necessary control and routing information to deliver the packet across the network. Packets can be transported independently, or as a series of packets that must be maintained and preserved as an entity. The **major advantages of using packet switching** are:

- access shared among multiple users, either in a single company or in multiple organizations;
- full error control and flow control in place to allow for the smooth and efficient transfer of data;
- transparency of the user data;
- speed and code conversion capabilities;

FIGURE 8-1   Switches within the packet-switched network

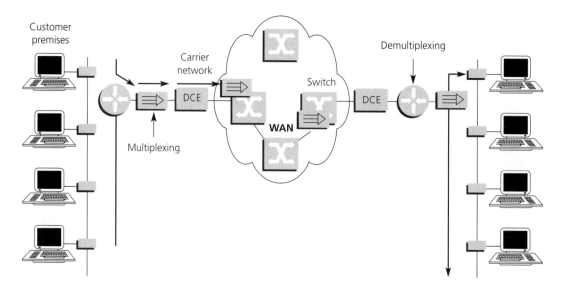

FIGURE 8-2   Switches within the circuit-switched network

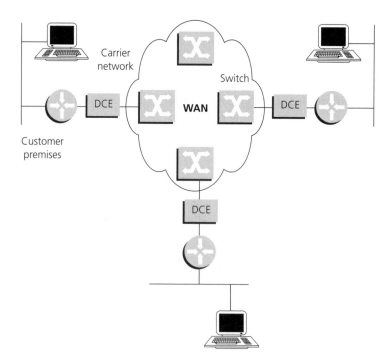

- protection from an intermediate node or link failure;
- pricing advantages – because the network is used by many the prices are based on per packet, rather than cost per minute.

8.2 X.25 packet switching

We start with the classic example of packet-switching technology deployed in X.25 networks a while back. Although it may seem a bit old-fashioned, it is necessary to remember that the packet-switching approach established then is the basis for all further packet-switching types such as frame and cell switching. Therefore the majority of the issues discussed in this section should not be considered as curiosities but, rather as common denominator to all WAN switching issues.

X.25 network devices fall into three general categories: Data Terminal Equipment (DTE), Data Circuit-terminating Equipment (DCE), and Packet Switching Exchange (PSE). **Data terminal equipment** devices are end systems that communicate across the X.25 network. They are usually terminals, personal computers, or network hosts, and are located on the premises of individual subscribers. **Data circuit-terminating equipment** devices are communications devices, such as modems and packet switches, that provide the interface between DTE devices and a PSE. **Packet switching exchanges** are switches that compose the bulk of the carrier's network. They transfer data from one DCE device to another through the X.25 network, with the effect of data transfer from DTE source to DTE sink. DCEs are generally located in the customer premises, but are (generally) owned and administered by the carrier. (DCEs are the endpoints of the network, as far as the carrier is concerned.) The PSEs (and PADs packet assemblers/disassemblers) are located on the carrier's premises.

A local DCE device examines the packet headers to determine which virtual circuit to use and then sends the packets to the closest PSE in the path of that virtual circuit. PSEs (switches) pass the traffic to the next intermediate node in the path, which may be another switch or the remote DCE device. Figure 8.3 illustrates the relationships between the three types of X.25 network devices.

FIGURE 8-3   Components of an X.25 network

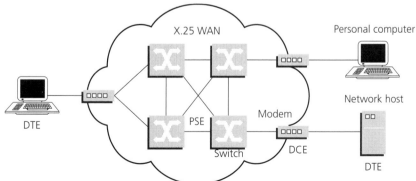

X.25 packet-switched networks are used to interconnect multiple, geographically dispersed computing facilities. They divide data into packets, each of which can be routed to any desired destination. Packet multiplexing permits multiple switch-attached devices to share line bandwidth efficiently (see Figure 8.4). Delays are reduced because messages are broken into smaller segments or packets. Built-in safeguards maintain data integrity. The switches accommodate **retransmission of lost or corrupted data, multiple destinations, flexible alternate routing,** and **built-in redundancy** and **backup facilities**. Unwanted delays produced by error checking and routing functions at each X.25 switch have spurred the development of Frame Relay. However, the X.25 transport service continues to be used in low-speed networks, networking applications that are not highly interactive, and regions of the world lacking error-free fiber optic wide area backbones.

| FIGURE 8-4 | Virtual circuits multiplexed onto a single physical circuit |

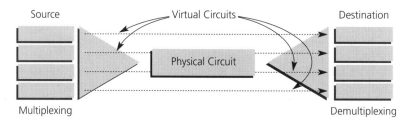

| SNAPSHOT | **X.25 service revisited** |

X.25 can provide a reliable WAN circuit (PVC or SVC) or backbone. An X.25 network also provides transport support for legacy applications.

8.2.1 Switch operation

As a brief reminder we will first look at the functions of the switches or switching nodes in the X.25 network. As already mentioned, X.25 packet switching is a technique that divides data into groups of packets and transmits them individually over the most efficient network paths. Each switching node in the transmission path checks its own **mapping table** to determine where to route the packet, and adds the **routing, control, and error-checking information** needed to successfully transmit the packet through the network. The network transmits the packets from node to node to the correct destination. Packets always travel on a forward path: routing and control information ensures that the packet progresses to the next logical node and is not routed backward.

If a line or component in the transmission route fails, the packet switch automatically routes the packets over an **alternate path**, if one exists, and the user's session continues uninterrupted. Failure of a trunk does not affect calls in progress; the data actually being transmitted is simply rerouted over an alternate path. If there is a main circuit interruption along a route that does not offer an alternate path, the user's session and data are generally maintained intact with a momentary delay in response. New calls are established using the best remaining route. Each node receiving a packet is responsible for detecting and correcting packet errors. The node also stores a copy of the packet before forwarding it to its next destination. The transmitting node retains this copy until it receives a positive acknowledgment from the destination node. The packets are retransmitted automatically if transmission errors are detected. At the last node, the packets are placed in the proper sequence and delivered to the final destination.

Packet switch services and features

Packet switches have two main functionalities:

- **switching** –forwarding the arriving packets to the proper output port;
- **queuing** (buffering) – required since multiple cells arriving at the same time from different input lines may be destined for the same output port. There are three possibilities for queuing (buffer management) in a packet switch:
  - input buffering – buffers packets at the input of the switch;
  - output buffering – buffers packets at the output;
  - shared-memory – buffers packets internally (shared buffer for input and output queues).

The following are some **other important services and features** supported by most packet switches:

- **Dynamic routing** – packet switches make intelligent routing decisions based on realtime information about measured network delays and line availability. Dynamic routing ensures that at any given moment (not just at call setup), each switch routes user traffic to its destination over the fastest available path. Packet switches also automatically route traffic around failed network components without affecting calls in progress, providing a highly reliable network transport service. Service availability for packet switched networks exceeds 99.99%. No predefined or fixed path or reservation of resources exists anywhere in the network. Each successive packet switch in the data path uses its own routing tables to determine the best route for each packet to take toward its final destination. Each packet switch regularly revises its routing tables in a decentralized manner based on line availability and measured delay information, resulting in network capacity that is optimally matched to realtime traffic loading. No central resource or operator intervention is required to define routing paths and tables. This simplifies network management and ensures that no single point of failure will disrupt network operations.
- **Automatic line quality monitoring** – each packet switch in the network continuously monitors trunk quality. When line errors reach a user-defined threshold, the faulty line is removed from service automatically. All switches are notified, routing tables are updated, and traffic is routed transparently around the failed circuit. The switches continue to check the line; when the line quality returns to a predefined level, the circuit is automatically returned

to service. This feature optimizes the use of reliable circuit capacity for the entire network.

- **End-to-end error control** – error control ensures reliable transmission from source to destination. Packet sequencing is verified on an end-to-end basis; a software checksum may also be provided to ensure data integrity. Frame-level Cyclic Redundancy Checks (CRCs) and parity checks provide switch-to-switch error checking. When an error is detected, only the faulty packets are retransmitted.

- **Network monitoring** – packet switches often operate at unattended sites. A centralized Network Operations Center (NOC), therefore, must provide monitoring and control services. Each switch supports the NOC by continuously monitoring hardware, software, and trunk integrity, and providing operational status information to the NOC on a regular basis. All error conditions and status changes are reported through alarms. The packet switch also supports the use of many diagnostic tools, such as loopback facilities, message generators, and packet-tracing capabilities, to monitor and isolate problems in the network. Additionally, each switch participates in a network-wide call accounting facility that measures and records network usage. Each switch collects statistics on call attempts, call duration, packets transmitted, and circuit facilities used. Data is collected, aggregated, and forwarded to the NOC for storage and further processing.

- **Restricted and multiple addressing options** – addressing within a packet switched network conforms to the ITU-T X.121 format. Physical and logical addressing methods facilitate existing and new data processing applications. Logical addressing is independent of the physical locations of the users. When users or hosts move, the move does not impact their network addresses. A multiple addressing facility permits more than one address to be assigned to a single port. For example, when one host provides multiple applications, the user can request connection using an application-specific address. Restricted addressing options promote security for hosts containing sensitive information. The Closed User Group (CUG) option restricts user access to specific ports on the network. This facility provides outgoing or incoming access and outgoing or incoming calls barred within a CUG. Some packet switch manufacturers also offer a Community of Interest (COI) facility, which defines a group of hosts that communicate with each other. The COI feature is transparent to users as no negotiation or subscriber selection is required.

- **Hunt group facilities** – a single address can also be assigned to multiple ports. Hunt group facilities are available on single switches and on a network-wide basis. The 1984 ITU-T X.25 hunt group facility allows a group of ports on the same packet switch to be accessed by a single logical address. Calls are distributed at the switch according to the number of active virtual circuits using each port. A network-wide hunt group capability allows calls to be distributed among several hosts according to one of the following methods: round-robin (provides even distribution of traffic among multiple hosts); closest (provides the fastest communications path); or ordered list (provides backup processing capability).

- **Priority and preemption facilities** – packet switches route traffic according to priority levels that may be negotiated on a per-call basis or assigned as a default. A preemption capability protects priority traffic. For example, if a shortage of switch resources causes the blocking of a high-priority call, lower-priority connections are used to complete the high-priority call.

- **Fast select** – this feature minimizes call-processing overhead. The fast select capability benefits users of transaction-oriented applications.

- **Support to virtual circuits** – WAN connection-oriented services fall into two categories: Permanent Virtual Circuits (PVC) and Switched Virtual Circuits (SVC). In a PVC environment, network connections are established via the service-ordering process and remain in place until another service order is sent to the carrier (analogous to a dedicated line). In an SVC environment, network connections are established dynamically as needed through a signaling process incorporated in the user equipment and supported by the network (analogous to a dialup link).

Delays associated with error checking and routing of data packets prevent the use of X.25 packet switching for transmitting digitized voice. The same limitation makes packet switching less desirable for bandwidth-intensive applications, such as LAN-to-LAN communications, in which fast response time is required. Therefore a newer communications standard, Frame Relay, has evolved to better meet these high-bandwidth requirements. Frame Relay provides higher through-put and lower delay through a simplified transmission process using variable-length frames (packets) and confining error checking to destination nodes. Frame Relay is ideal for highly interactive and delay-sensitive LAN applications.

8.2.2 Switch selection guidelines

Selecting the right type of network (public, private, or hybrid) raises complex issues that can be answered only on an individual basis. Companies that opt for a private packet switched network cite control as the deciding factor. A **private network** provides control over planning; quality, reliability, and availability of facilities; cost; security; growth; geographic coverage; and user-specific technical capabilities that might not be available from the public network. A public network can provide greater economy than a private one, especially when interconnecting multiple sites in a mesh network topology. Functioning as an intelligent hub, the public carrier service minimizes the number of leased access lines needed to establish any-to-any connectivity between all sites. Each corporate site needs only one communications line: the one leading to the public network. The public network can also make transport charges distance insensitive.

   WAN switches vary in size and capabilities, and users can choose from many devices on the market to construct networks that support light to heavy traffic loads; public access, private access, or both; and various types of channel interfaces. Network design and optimization are based on thorough traffic analysis and accomplished through computer-aided design tools.

   Users selecting a packet (frame) switching system should evaluate the system's ease of use and performance specifications as well as the vendor's training and documentation. Important aspects of system **performance** include the following:

- number of communications ports and trunks supported and the ease of expansion;

- interoperability with a range of terminal devices, including LAN bridges and routers, 3270-type communications controllers, and asynchronous hosts;

- the range of physical interfaces supported for device attachment and network access (e.g. RS-232-C, V.35, X.21, X.21bis, T1/E1);
- the maximum data rate per line, and the maximum aggregate throughput;
- network management capabilities provided, including the following:
  - automatic software downloading capability;
  - online configuration capability;
  - hardware tests for remote switches;
  - a variety of reports, including historical event listings with notifications of all major/minor alarms, system usage analysis, and session statistics;
  - support for SNMP and other multivendor network management standards;
  - for Frame Relay networking (see covering section), congestion management features such as support for FECN/BECN, DE bit, sustained bursts above the CIR, and traffic prioritization.

8.3 Switching in Frame Relay networks

As discussed at length in Part I, Frame Relay meets a real need for connecting bursty LAN traffic over a wide area network at fractional or full T1/E1 speeds (see Appendix D). Its streamlined transmission scheme allows users to achieve higher throughput, lower delay, and cost savings compared to traditional X.25 packet switching.

Devices attached to a Frame Relay WAN fall into two general categories:

- **Data Terminal Equipment** (DTE) – generally is considered to be user terminal equipment for a specific network (as opposed to DCEs that are effectively terminating the (public) network, while DTEs attach to DCEs to access that network), and typically is located on the premises of a customer. In fact, they may be owned by the customer. Examples of DTE devices are terminals, personal computers, routers, and bridges.
- **Data Circuit-terminating Equipment** (DCE) – carrier-owned internetworking devices. The purpose of DCE equipment is to provide clocking and switching services in a network, which are the devices that actually transmit data through the WAN. In most cases, these are packet switches.

Figure 8.5 shows the relationship between the two categories of devices.

The connection between a DTE device and a DCE device consists of both a physical-layer component and a link-layer component. The physical component defines the mechanical, electrical, functional, and procedural specifications for the connection between the devices. One of the most commonly used physical-layer interface specifications is the RS-232 specification. The link-layer component defines the protocol that establishes the connection between the DTE device, such as a router, and the DCE device, such as a switch. A virtual circuit can pass through any number of intermediate DCE devices (switches) located within the Frame Relay network.

FIGURE 8-5 Place of DTE and DCE devices in a Frame Relay network

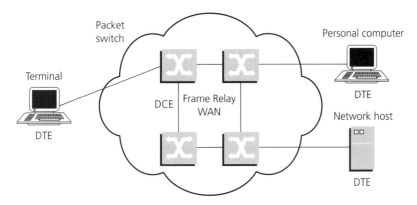

Frame Relay service revisited

Frame Relay provides a cost-effective, **high-speed**, **low-latency mesh topology** between remote sites. It can be used in both private and carrier-provided (public) networks.

The Frame Relay service is very different from other network services in a management sense. Private T1/E1 networks, which most large users are accustomed to managing, are deterministic in most cases. Resources are allocated on a fixed basis for traffic flows, and flow interactions are not a problem. With Frame Relay, network resources are allocated on demand, and only the statistical probability that all users will not demand capacity at once allows them to work.

Congestion management by Frame Relay switches is affected by the following factors:

- the size of **ingress buffers**, which are provided at the point of user access;
- the size of **transit buffers**, which are provided within the network to hold data in the event of collisions while information is being routed about;
- whether **reservation** routing strategy is deployed to minimize information collision within the network.

Switches with significant **buffer capacity** allow users to trade delay for congestion relief. This might not be a bad strategy since forced error recovery is probably more intrusive to performance in the long run. Large buffers can also hide a fundamental problem with switching efficiency of the switch. Queuing has the effect of multiplying basic service times, so these must be kept as low as possible.

Switches that have more transit buffering than ingress buffering will generally be capable of absorbing congestion through delay even when that congestion results from random collisions of data flow within the network. Switches that have primarily ingress buffering will normally need some system to reserve flow capacity through the network to limit collisions once the data has been released. If a switch has little buffering of any type, it is relying on the congestion-control-to-flow-control coupling with the user systems to reduce flow rates. This might be unrealistic in the early stages of network and product deployment.

Reservation routing strategies allow a product to allocate capacity through the network in at least a general sense, prior to actually dispatching the data. The benefit of the strategy is to reduce the risk of discard by reserving capacity forward through the network, which requires either queuing in an ingress buffer or cooperating with the user to manage flows via BECN/FECN.

8.3.1 Congestion in Frame Relay networks and switches role

As multiservice networks become more prevalent, congestion control will gain importance for managing the resulting increased traffic volumes. **Discarding frames** is one legitimate – albeit sometimes self-defeating – way of handling traffic overload. When a network discards a frame, the missing frame will eventually be detected by higher-layer protocols, such as TCP or SNA, at the receiving end, and it will be retransmitted (potentially contributing further to congestion). However, at this juncture, the end system's Layer 3 software might deduce that congestion is occurring – a function called implicit congestion notification – and invoke flow control mechanisms to remedy the situation. For example, the receiver can reduce the window size to throttle back the rate at which frames are sent. One Frame Relay congestion control mechanism is the discard eligible bit (DE-bit) which indicates that the frame with the DE-bit set can be dropped in case of congestion (these frames are thus the first candidates to drop). Applications generally do not want to set the DE-bit, unless the frames can be dropped without prejudice (e.g. voice).

At Layer 2, slowing down the delivery of frames into the network is called explicit congestion notification. Frame Relay specifies two types: **Forward Explicit Congestion Notification** (FECN) and **Backward Explicit Congestion Notification** (BECN). Frame Relay switches invoke these schemes by setting indicator bits in the frame relay header. A **FECN** bit is set to notify the end system that congestion was experienced for traffic in the direction of the frame carrying the FECN indicator. The **BECN** bit is set to notify the end system that congestion may be occurring in the opposite direction of the frame carrying the notification. The problem is that while switches within the carrier's network set these bits (and no subsequent switch may change them), there is no obligation for an end system to act on them.

FECN is the easiest to implement since it indicates that congestion is occurring in the direction the traffic is flowing. As a frame passes through the network, the FECN bit is set to *1* if the frame gets delayed. Any switch can turn the FECN on, but once it is on, it cannot be turned off. The equipment that sees the FECN is at the receiving end, not the transmitting end. So the receiving equipment is supposed to take any possible steps to notify the transmitting equipment to reduce traffic into the network. One action that the receiving equipment can take is to go ahead and set BECN bits in the reverse direction. Just as the FECN bits cannot be reset once they are set, BECN bits must stay set once they are turned on.

8.4 Development of cell-based communication

Packet switching is a standardized multiplexing method. **Cell switching** or **cell relay** is a packet-like multiplexing and switching technology. It handles high-speed (high-bandwidth), low-latency (low-delay), mixed-media communication (voice, data, video) in support of contemporary networking requirements, using short data units of fixed length. Fixed-length cells make the processing associated with switching more efficient; in a way, they make the arrival distribution more predictable. In particular, fixed-length cells allow pipelining of functions, which, in turn, facilitates hardware implementations.

Cell relaying is similar to traditional packet switching but with the following key differences:

- **Simplified protocols** – no error control for the information field (only the header field) and no flow control on the links as the responsibility is moved to the edge of the network. No windowing or processor-intensive protocol tasks are supported. A number of functions of the data-link layer protocol are moved to the edge of the network, while core capabilities are supported directly by the cell switches, in addition to Layer 1 functions such as clocking, bit encoding, and physical-medium connection. The cell header is used for channel identification, in place of the positioned methodology for assigning octets inherent in traditional TDM DS1/DS3 systems (see Appendix D). Cell sequence integrity is thus preserved within a virtual connection.

- **Cells have a fixed, short length** – this framework allows high-speed switching nodes, since the logical decisions are straightforward. Cell length is set to 53 bytes in ATM (48 for user information and five for overhead, a compromise between 32 and 64 bytes). The header identifies cells belonging to the same virtual circuit. Cells are switched by means of the label in the header. For comparison, classic packet switching uses large packets (128 or 256 octets) and, unlike cell relay, requires that every packet be brought entirely into each node and queued for output. As a result, classic packet switching suffers response time and throughput problems.

  The header provides only limited data-link layer functionality and the transmission facility – typically, but not limited to, Synchronous Optical Network (SONET) or Synchronous Digital Hierarchy (SDH) links – provides Layer 1 functionality. Cell relaying does not incorporate higher layer functionality; the responsibility is relegated to the edge of the network. As a result, information is transferred rapidly compared to other protocols. Cell-relay protocols can be implemented in hardware, expediting processing.

Cells associated with a given connection typically arrive in an irregular pattern, since cells are filled according to the actual bursty demand rather than following an inefficient preallocation scheme. Taken as an aggregate, however, cells arriving at a switch can show a statistically stable profile. Cell relay allows bandwidth allocation on demand to each user. The advantages of cell transport (relaying and switching) include the following:

- highly flexible network access due to the cell transport concept and specific cell transfer principles;
- dynamic bandwidth allocation on demand with a fine degree of granularity;

■ flexible-bearer capability allocation and easy provisioning of semipermanent connections due to the virtual path concept;

■ physical facility independence at the physical layer.

8.5 ATM switching

Asynchronous transfer mode (ATM) is based on **cell switching** technology. ATM is the ITU-T (formerly CCITT) standard for accomplishing cell relay. ATM is a connection-oriented network, although it is designed as a basis for supporting both connectionless and connection-oriented services (for more details see Section 1.6). Cell relay in general can also be a connectionless service if each cell is independently made to carry a discrete protocol data unit (PDU).

ATM uses a **fixed-length cell** which is 53 bytes long. The header and the address are also fixed-length which together allow efficient implementation of switching logic in hardware. This is important since, as transmission speeds get faster, there is very little time to do the switching within an ATM switch. When there is a **fix size table** with sequential values it is simple to locate the desired value in the table. ATM has 24-bit addressing for the **User–Network Interface** (UNI) and 28-bit addressing for the **Network–Network Interface** (NNI).

ATM networks are connection-oriented, allowing QoS (Quality of Service) guarantees. The **routing overhead** is performed via connection setup, allowing the per-cell routing to be done easily in hardware as a simple table lookup. Finally, a datagram service can be provided over a permanent connection set overlaid for the purpose.

ATM is specified by the ATM Forum and standardized by the ITU-T, mostly in the form of various interfaces between users and network and network nodes themselves in private and public networks. Figure 8.6 shows the different types of interfaces already widely adopted: UNI (version 4.0), private NNI (PNNI version 1.0), and public NNI. The purpose of the ATM Forum's **Broadband ISDN Inter-Carrier Interface** (B-ICI version 2.1) specification is to provide inter-carrier connectivity between public ATM network providers.

FIGURE 8-6 ATM interfaces for public and private networks

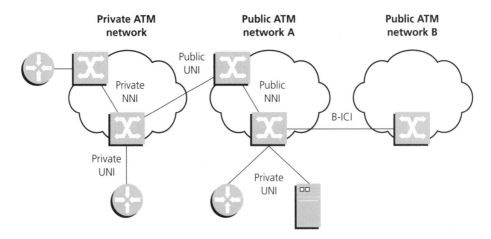

   The ATM network permits an arbitrary **mesh topology** of point-to-point links between switches. This allows the network to be flexible, scalable, and fault tolerant. The switches can be designed to be highly scalable, and growing the network consists of scaling the switches and corresponding links without the constraints of shared medium networks, such as rings or buses. Figure 8.7 shows the physical topology of an ATM network comprising switches and its logical topology as a set of point-to-point virtual links between network edge routers.

FIGURE 8-7   Physical vs. logical topology of an ATM network

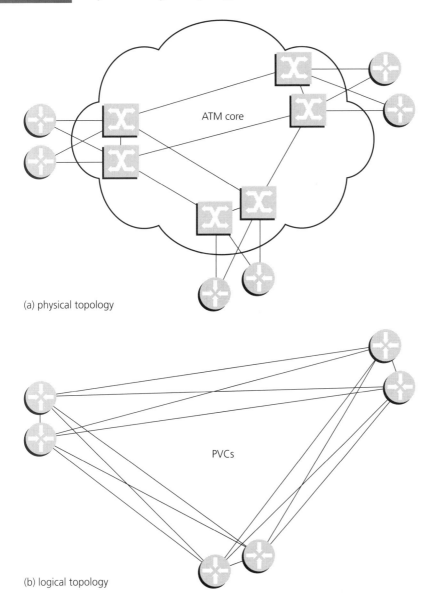

(a) physical topology

(b) logical topology

ATM networks are used to accelerate bandwidth requirements. ATM also provides support for multiple QoS classes for differing application requirements for delay and loss.

8.5.1 ATM switch architectures

ATM switches are fast packet switches designed to move the ATM cells along their respective virtual paths. The prime purpose of an ATM switch is to route incoming cells (packets more generally) arriving on a particular input link to the output link, which is also called the output port, associated with the appropriate route.

A simple ATM switch architecture uses a **central switching engine**, surrounded by I/O modules; while all traffic moves through the central engine. This design usually works very well when lightly loaded. However, as more and more I/O modules are added, the load on the switching engine increases. And central switching creates a possible single point of failure. An example of a shared memory ATM switch is shown in Figure 8.8.

FIGURE 8-8   Shared memory of an ATM switch

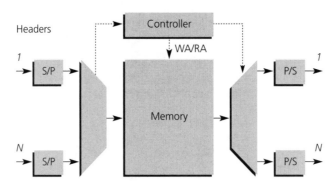

RA = Read address   WA = Write address
S/P = Serial to parallel   P/S = Parallel to serial

The alternative switch architecture is a full **switching matrix** which is more complex to design. It requires that every module be a switching engine, with a full-duplex path to every other module. The interior of the switch is a fully interconnected mesh.

Different types of **switching in hardware** can be implemented by deriving the switch-logic pointers or labels using the fixed-length values such as an ATM address and the link characteristics of nodes. Communication paths can thus be hard-wired into the switch's circuits to enable fast decision. **VLSI or optical switching** technology is therefore applied in ATM switches.

Three basic techniques have been proposed to carry out the switching (routing) function:

- **Space-division** – a basic example for a space-division switch is a crossbar switch, which has also served circuit-switched telephony networks for many years. The inputs and outputs in a crossbar switch are connected at switching points called crosspoints, resulting in a matrix type of structure.

- **Shared-medium** – the operation of a shared-medium switch is based on a common high-speed bus. Cells are launched from input links onto the bus in round-robin fashion, and each output link accepts cells that are destined to it.

- **Shared-memory** – consists of a single dual-ported memory shared by all input and output lines. Packets arriving on all input lines are multiplexed into a single stream that is fed to the common memory for storage; inside the memory, packets are organized into separate output queues, one for each output line. Simultaneously, an output stream of packets is formed by retrieving packets from the output queues sequentially, one per queue; the output stream is then demultiplexed, and packets are transmitted on the output lines. In the shared-memory switch architecture, output links share a single large memory, in which logical FIFO queues are assigned to each link. Although memory sharing can provide a better queuing performance than physically separated buffers, it requires carefully designed buffer management schemes for a fair and robust operation.

Blocking and buffer management

Buffer management is critical to effective switch throughput. An ATM switch can experience two types of **blocking** (see also Sections 7.6 and 13.1.11):

- **Fabric blocking** – occurs when a switch's fabric capacity is less than the sum of its inputs. If so, it is possible for the switch, even when it is lightly loaded, to drop cells. It is more difficult to build a really fast fabric, so most ATM switches are limited to 16 or 32 OC-3c/STM-1 ports (see Appendix D).

- **Head-of-line blocking** – occurs when the queuing structure in the switch is simplistic; generally, that means a single queue in each input port. Imagine such a switch, in which an output on one port is congested, and a cell is sitting at the head of an input queue on another port waiting for that output. All of the cells sitting behind it will also have to wait – even if they are destined for other outputs, even if the cells behind it are CBR or VBR cells, which are supposed to have guaranteed priority. To prevent head-of-line blocking, each input port in the switch should arrange traffic in multiple queues, one for each combination of output port and class of service.

Shared-memory ATM switches gained popularity among switch vendors due to the advantages they bring to both switching and queuing. In fact, both functions can be implemented together by controlling the memory read and write appropriately. As in output buffered switches, shared-memory switches do not suffer from the throughput degradation caused by **Head-of-Line** (HOL) blocking, a phenomenon inherent in input buffered switches. Moreover, modifying the memory read/write control circuit makes the shared-memory switch flexible enough to perform functions such as priority control and multicast. If a shared memory switch is seen from a queuing systems point of view, then the switch has N output ports, and a total buffer space of M. A first-in first-out (FIFO) buffer is allocated to each output port. The sum of the individual buffer allocations may or may not be larger than the size of the memory M. A certain policy of buffer allocation is required in the shared-memory switch to perform its queuing function. There are various buffering methods deployed and proposed. The selection of a queuing strategy is important to minimize the probability of a cell loss. **Cell losses** occur when a cell arrives at a switching node and finds the buffer full. Minimizing cell losses, or reducing them to acceptable levels, is extremely important to support any end-to-end application over networks.

Matrix-based switches bring a fundamental advantage: with more ports added to a switching complex, the **aggregate switching** capacity increases. The general architecture of an $n \times n$ ATM switch (n input and n output ports) is shown in Figure 8.9. Or, the more users the higher switching bandwidth, as opposed to shared media networks.

FIGURE 8-9   General architecture of an $n \times n$ ATM switch

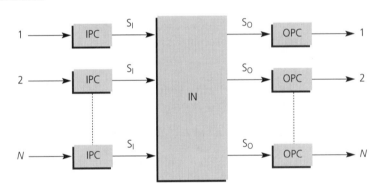

IPC/OPC: Input/output port controller
IN: Interconnecting network

Figure 8.10 shows the non-blocking ATM switching fabric with multiple input queues.

Parallel processing of an ATM switch allows **concurrent switching among many parallel paths**, providing each port full access to the allocated bandwidth. Cell switching breaks up datastreams into very small units that are independently routed through the switch. The routing occurs mostly in the hardware through the switching fabric. The combination of cell switching and scalable switching fabrics are key ingredients of ATM.

The deployment of ATM in the switched backbone is shown in Figure 8.11.

FIGURE 8-10 Non-blocking ATM switching fabric with multiple input queues

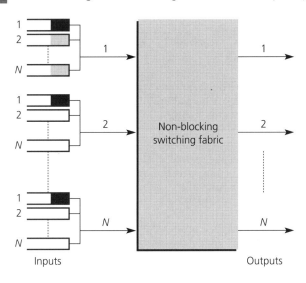

FIGURE 8-11 Switched backbone network based on ATM

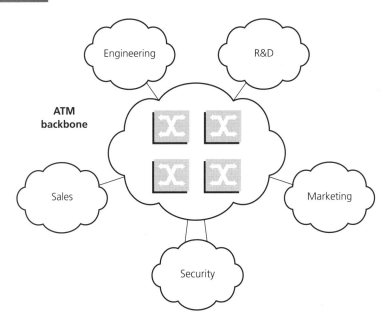

8.5.2 ATM routing – PNNI

Although we are now in a chapter dedicated to switching not routing, shortly we will discover that speaking about ATM switching will directly lead us to routing. The routing basics will be described in the next Part and it will be possible to compare then the ATM routing protocol with those used in a multiprotocol network environment.

The **ATM routing layer** does not directly correlate to the network layer of the OSI model. This is because of the nature of the ATM network's ability to support multiple link layer connections switched through intermediate nodes. Although the **functionality of routing** or forwarding is now done by the **ATM layer**, functions such as route selections, fast topology propagation, and the ability to scale and support large networks are still required like other network protocols such as IP. Therefore, the routing protocol and techniques for ATM reflect similarities in formats and mechanisms of the IP routing protocols such as OSPF.

The ATM Forum **Private Network-to-Network Interface** (PNNI version 1.0) is an interface specification to support **connection routing and connection calls setup** operations among ATM network nodes. The interoperability aspect is important for ATM service providers as they can more readily and easily deploy switches from different vendors within their network.

SNAPSHOT   **PNNI routing and ATM switches**

PNNI is a **dynamic routing protocol** for ATM. It learns the network topology and reachability information with minimal configuration. It automatically adapts to network changes by advertising topology state information. In a PNNI routing domain, the source **ATM switch** computes hierarchically complete routes for connection setups. This route information is included in the call setup signaling message. PNNI provides routes that satisfy Quality of Service (QoS) connection requests.

PNNI specifies two key aspects for the network interface, the routing aspect and the signaling aspect. The PNNI **routing protocol** distributes network topology and route information to participating network nodes. The PNNI routing protocol is based on the traditional **link-state routing protocols** such as OSPF or IS-IS (for details on these protocols see Part IV). As ATM is connection-oriented, there is a need to set up connections across the network before any user information can be sent over the connection. This connection setup requires connection-related information to be relayed along the nodes that are involved to support the connection route. This is done by using the PNNI **signaling protocol**. The ATM PNNI signaling protocol is based on the ITU-T Q.2931 and ATM Forum UNI protocols.

PNNI hierarchical model

One of the key points of PNNI architecture is the ability to scale to a very large network without impacting performance. This is done by logically dividing the network into **multi-level interconnected peer groups.** The peer groups form a routing hierarchy according to the PNNI **hierarchical model** (see Figure 8.12).

FIGURE 8-12   PNNI hierarchy

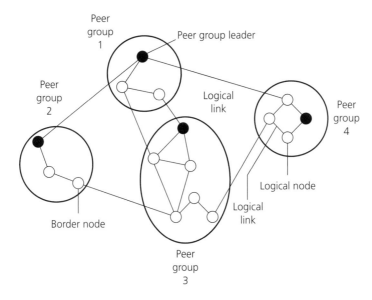

The key components of the PNNI hierarchy follow:

- **Lowest-level nodes** – a logical node in the lowest level of the PNNI hierarchy.
- **Peer group** – a group of logical nodes. Each node exchanges information with other members of the group, and all members maintain an identical view of the group.
- **Peer Group Leader** (PGL) – a logical node within a peer group that summarizes the peer group and represents it as a single logical node at the next level of the PNNI hierarchy.
- **Logical Group Node** (LGN) – a logical node that represents its lower level peer group in the next higher level peer group. Upon becoming a PGL, the PGL creates a parent LGN to represent the peer group as a single logical node at the next level. The PGL is a logical node within the peer group, and the associated LGN is a logical node in the next higher level peer group.

The PNNI hierarchical model can support multiple group levels that potentially will scale to millions of nodes. The multi-level hierarchical routing model supports scalability and at the same time gives better performance compared to a large flat network. The scalability benefit comes indirectly by using address summarization and topology aggregation. In a PNNI hierarchical network, the number of nodes, links, and reachable address prefixes visible from any one ATM switch in the network are reduced exponentially as the flat network is migrated to a hierarchical network.

A disadvantage of the PNNI hierarchy is the loss of information caused by topology aggregation. The PNNI performs route computations based on its view of the network topology. Because a hierarchical view of the network is restricted, compared to a non-hierarchical (flat topology) view, routing decisions are not as effective as in a flat topology. In both cases, a path to the destination is selected; however, in most cases the path selected in a flat topology is more efficient. This trade-off between routing efficiency and scalability is not specific to PNNI; it is a known limitation of any hierarchical routing protocol.

A switch in PNNI network typically supports many ATM nodes. An **ATM node** is an ATM end system or a collection of ATM end systems. Each ATM end system is identified by an ATM address (see Chapter 3 in Part I). ATM switches, nodes, and end systems are identified by their ATM addresses. In PNNI, there can be multiple nodes that a switch supports, and nodes and switch can be seen as logically the same. For end systems that are connected to the switch directly, the switch acts as a logical node.

The **prefix** for a PNNI is the first n number of bits of a system's ATM address. Because prefixes are part of ATM addresses, they represent reachability information to ATM addresses (ATM nodes). The longer the prefix length, the more specific the reachability information is.

Link connection type and routing control channel

Nodes use logical links to exchange PNNI routing control information. As the link as a whole can also be part of a data transfer path, the PNNI routing information is exchanged using a particular **Routing Control Channel** (RCC) between two nodes. This RCC is identified by a **VPI/VCI pair**. Logical links between PNNI nodes can be one of the following connection types depending on the characteristics of the link:

■ physical link connection;
■ Virtual Path Connection (VPC);
■ Switched Virtual Circuit Connection (SVCC).

The Routing Control Channel (RCC) for each of the connection types is as shown in Table 8.1.

TABLE 8-1 RCC for different connection types

	VPI	VCI
Physical connection	0	18
VPC	VPI of the VPC	18
SVCC	Assigned by signaling	Assigned by signaling

Hello protocol

PNNI nodes use a **hello protocol** for **neighbor discovery**, identification, and verification. In addition, the hello protocol is used for checking link integrity. The hello protocol is a common form of neighbor discovery protocol for link-state routing protocols such as OSPF. The hello protocol is run on all the active ports between two neighboring nodes. Hellos are sent between nodes of the lowest level groups using actual physical links. Nodes in the higher level logical groups use SVCC based RCC. Hellos are **sent periodically** based on a configured hello interval time. Hellos are also triggered and sent when certain important events happened such as changes in the node hierarchy, and changes in the link aggregation token. The following summarizes the information exchange based on the hello protocol.

If the nodes belong to the same peer group they exchange and synchronize the topology database. Each node constructs its node and link information. Node and link information is advertised to other nodes in the peer group PNNI packet types:

- Hello;
- PNNI Topology State Packet (PTSP);
- PNNI Topology State Element (PTSE) ACK;
- Database Summary;
- PTSE Request.

Topology database synchronization and distribution

An important part of PNNI is to achieve a synchronized **topology database** in all nodes in a peer group, so that all nodes have the right information for finding the path (routing) as quickly as possible after any change. The topology database synchronization and distribution functions of PNNI use the initial topology database exchange process and flooding to other nodes in the peer group to achieve this goal. **Flooding** is the PNNI advertisement mechanism that provides quick propagation of information to other nodes in the group.

Neighboring nodes first synchronize topology database information after successful Hello exchange. The **synchronization** is done by first doing the database summary exchange and then updating the required **PNNI topology state elements** (PTSEs). The database summary packets contain only the PTSE types and their values. PTSE is like a unit of information that describes a piece of PNNI topology database. The **PNNI topology state packets** (PTSPs) exchanged contain PTSEs.

During the exchange of the PTSE summaries, if a node receives PTSEs which are more recent than those that the node already has, the PTSEs are requested from the sender. The receiving node first updates its database with the more recent PTSEs and then floods the PTSEs to its neighboring nodes. The subsequent receiving nodes continue the flooding to their corresponding neighbor nodes. This procedure can provide a quick convergence of the database (synchronization) within the group. The convergence time depends on the number of nodes in the group as well as the topology structure of the group.

Peer group

A peer group elects a **Peer Group Leader** (PGL) based on the priority configured in each node's nodal information group. The node with the highest priority becomes the peer group leader. If there is a contention because more than one node has the same priority, the node with the highest node identifier becomes the leader. Peer group leader election runs continuously. Therefore, when new nodes are introduced, depending on the priority level, the PGL can change. From an operational perspective of the network, if a stable operating environment is desired, once a node becomes a PGL, its priority should be increased to a value that can maintain it as the leader. PNNI operation does not require a PGL. For a single-level peer group without any hierarchies, selecting a PGL is not necessary. The network hierarchy model according to PNNI is shown in Figure 8.13.

FIGURE 8-13   ATM PNNI network hierarchy model

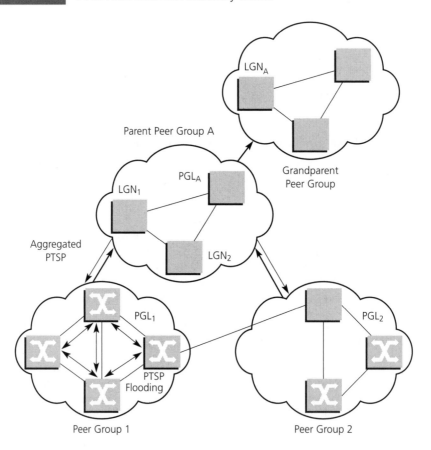

LGN = Logical Group Node
PGL = Peer Group Leader
PTSP = PNNI Topology State Packet

Signaling

PNNI signaling allows call setup over ATM interfaces between two private ATM networks or two private ATM network nodes. PNNI signaling is on the network side as opposed to the user side of UNI signaling. The benefit of interoperability among different vendors' switches for call setups is achieved by using PNNI signaling.

When an ATM device wants to establish a connection with another ATM device, it sends a *signaling request packet* to its directly connected ATM switch. This request contains the ATM address of the desired ATM endpoint, as well as any **QoS parameters** required for the connection. The signaling packet is reassembled by the switch and examined. If the switch has a switch table entry for the destination ATM address, and it can accommodate the QoS requested for the connection, it sets up the virtual connection on the input link and forwards the request out to the interface specified in the switching table for the destination ATM address.

Every switch along the path to the endpoint reassembles and examines the signaling packet and forwards it to the next switch if the QoS parameters can be supported while setting up the virtual connection as the signaling packet is forwarded. If any switch along the path cannot accommodate the requested QoS parameters, the request is rejected, and a *rejection message* is sent back to the originator of the request.

When the signaling packet arrives at the endpoint, it is reassembled and evaluated. If the endpoint can support the desired QoS, it responds with an accept message. As the accept message propagates back to the originator of the request, the switches set up a virtual circuit. The originator of the request receives the **accept message** from its directly connected ATM switch, as well as the VPI/VCI value that the originator should use for cells destined for the endpoint. The result of a call setup using signaling is a **connection path** that satisfied the **call setup parameters**.

> **SNAPSHOT** **ATM signaling**
>
> The ATM connection path computation has two parts: to **find the route** for the connection using the ATM network topology, and to set up the connection path support of each node along the route to **accommodate and support the service category**, traffic types information, and **quality-of-service** requirements, and also simultaneously maintaining network efficiency at all times.

Source routing

In order to ensure that signaling follows a loop-free path, and to allow sources to utilize local policy, the path for a signaling message is specified in the message in the form of a hierarchically complete **source route** known as a **Designated Transit List** (DTL). A DTL consists of the complete path across a peer group based on the node's hierarchical level.

The originating switch examines the full set of maps, as collected by the routing protocol, for the local **peer group**, and all visible higher level peer groups, including the map for the peer group which advertises **reachability** to the called party address. Using this, it then builds a sequence of paths. At the top is a path across the highest necessary level of peer groups to get to the destination from a parent which contains the source. Then, for each intermediate (containing the starting switch, inside the topmost level needed) peer group level, a source route across that containing the peer group is built. The result is a stack of source routes (DTLs) across successively higher levels of peer group.

Every node in the PNNI network maintains its own group's network topology and the hierarchical network topology of the rest of the network. When a UNI signaling request is received by the node, the signaling component requests a route from the routing component which results in a set of DTLs corresponding to a **hierarchically complete source route**. A hierarchically complete source route is a path described by the hierarchical-based DTL of each group across a PNNI routing domain starting from the source node in the group that originates the call and ending at the group that contains the destination. Each border node that generates the complete DTL also saves the DTL in case there is a need to find an alternate path.

The **connection path selection** for a call is computed based on the node's network topology view at the time of selection. Each DTL that a node generates for its own peer group is a complete source route of the nodes that will be traversed to get to the next peer group or the destination node. Because the PNNI protocol is designed to ensure prompt topology convergence when changes happen, every node in the peer group should have a common view of the network topology information. In this context, **common view** implies that each node has all the key information in its network database to decide a common outcome (or the acceptance of the operation by all nodes) of PNNI operations such as generating call setup paths based on the DTLs.

Design issues

This design choice results in low level switches needing a lot of topology information. However, it fully **prevents loops** and allows local switches to make path choices based on **local policy**, and to know that those choices will be obeyed. Additionally, the source routed behavior of the signaling removes one of the significant design difficulties of routing protocols. It is no longer necessary that all switches have the same routing information. Thus, although the routing protocol will converge, quickly, there is no dependence in the signaling on that convergence time.

The PNNI protocol provides a quick convergence of significant change events and thus allows each node to have the key information necessary to make decisions that other nodes will accept. Although this quick convergence of database will ensure a DTL that will be accepted by all nodes, there is still a time window when a DTL originating node might not have received the recent updates from a node in the DTL path and has to generate a DTL. Therefore, in this case, the node that was selected in the DTL might not have sufficient resources to support the connection. The node then cranks back the call setup to the originating node that generated the DTL for the peer group. The originating node will then find an alternate path for this connection. If an alternate path can be computed the call is setup using the new DTL; if not, the call is returned back to the UNI side with an unsuccessful indication.

Cells in Frames (CIF)

The **Cells in Frames** (CIF) specification delivers ATM's quality of service and flow control to the desktop, without the need to replace Ethernet and Token Ring LANs. As a **LAN protocol**, CIF allows ATM communications among workstations and switches in Ethernet or Token Ring nets. In a CIF network, workstations continue to generate Ethernet or Token Ring frames, but the frames contain one ATM header and the payloads of up to 31 ATM cells from the same ATM Virtual Circuit (VC). When the frames reach a CIF edge switch, they are either switched intact to another CIF switch, or they are segmented into cells for transport on an ATM network. Since the workstation still uses a standard Ethernet or Token Ring Network Interface Card (NIC), all that is needed is ATM signaling software and a software 'shim' between the NIC driver and the NDIS (Network Device Interface Specification) layer of the workstation's networking software. The shim adds a four-byte CIF header to frames before they are transmitted or removes the header as frames are received. It also places outgoing data into multiple queues for ATM QoS management and performs ATM explicit rate flow control.

Otherwise, a **CIF workstation** is exactly the same as an ATM workstation. It uses ATM signaling software and runs native ATM applications as well as other applications over IP, IPX, and other protocols. Since CIF has its own Ethernet ID, the workstation can actually mix CIF frames and standard Ethernet frames, but ATM's explicit rate flow control cannot be supported for the non-CIF frames if this is done.

Switches, on the other hand, need more in the way of modification. A **CIF edge switch** differs from Ethernet and Token Ring switches in four ways. First, it interprets the CIF header and ATM virtual path/virtual circuit (VP/VC) information, in addition to other protocols. Second, it supports QoS with multiple queues and uses a weighted fair queuing algorithm to manage delay. (This addition would also be required of switches using TCP/IP's Resource Reservation Protocol.) Third, CIF switches handle congestion by marking ATM Available Bit Rate Resource Management (ABR RM) cells with the maximum rate they can support on a given VC. Finally, switch software must be able to support ATM signaling. Flow control with minimal control delay was always recognized as a necessity for high-speed switched networks. To control the data flow at greatly increased speeds, the ATM Forum developed explicit rate flow control, which is defined in the forum's **traffic management** (TM 4.1) specification. It not only reduces switch buffering requirements (and thus the cost of switches), but also cuts the time required for page accesses like Web requests. With CIF, explicit rate flow control can be extended to the desktop economically over Ethernet or PPP dial-in.

Actually, CIF goes even further in extending the benefits of explicit rate flow control, since it permits true end to-end flow control even over Ethernet or Token Ring LANs. Flow control manages traffic sources so that they do not send too much data onto the network at any one moment. If congestion occurs on any link in a network, all the sources using that link must be told to slow down.

This is absolutely necessary because datastreams will be equally bursty over one second, 10 seconds, or one million seconds. In other words, simply underloading the network will not work. The critical difference among flow control techniques is in how long they take to tell the source about congestion – and to get it under control.

8.5.3 ATM switch operation

In an ATM switch, cell arrivals are not scheduled. The **control processor** resolves contention when it occurs, as well as call setup and tear-down, bandwidth reservation, maintenance, and management. The input controllers are synchronized so that cells arrive at the switch fabric with their headers aligned. The resulting traffic is slotted, and the time to transmit a cell across the switch fabric is called a time slot.

The basic operation of an ATM switch is based on the **VCI/VPI** value of the incoming cell. The switch looks up the connection value in a **local switching table** to determine the outgoing port (or ports) of the connection and the new VPI/VCI value of the connection on that link. The switch then retransmits the cell on that outgoing link with the new appropriate connection identifiers. Because all VCIs and VPIs have only local significance across a particular link, these values are remapped, as necessary, at each switch.

For example, suppose that two cells arrive on port 1 of the ATM switch shown in Figure 8.14. First, the switch examines the VPI and VCI fields of cell 1 and finds that the fields have a value of 6 and 4, respectively. The switch examines the switch table to determine on which port it should send the cell. It finds that when it receives a VPI of 6 and a VCI of 4 on port 1, it should send the cell on port 3 with a VPI of 2 and a VCI of 9. So, for cell 1, the switch changes the VPI to 2 and the VCI to 9 and sends the cell out on port 3.

FIGURE 8-14   ATM switch operation

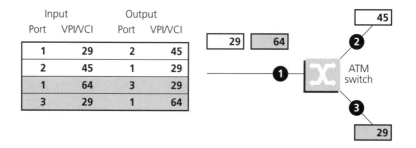

Next, the switch examines cell 2, which has a VPI of 2 and a VCI of 9. The table directs the switch to send out on port 2 cells received on port 1 that have a VPI/VCI of 29, and to change the VPI and VCI to 4 and 5, respectively.

Conversely, when a cell with a VPI and VCI of 2 and 9, respectively, comes in on port 3, the table directs the switch to send the cell out on port 1 with a VPI and VCI of 6 and 4, respectively. When a cell with a VPI and VCI of 4 and 5, respectively, comes in on port 2, the table directs the switch to send the cell out on port 1 with a VPI and VCI of 2 and 9, respectively. Note that VPI and VCI values are significant only to the local interface.

Figure 8.15 shows how the VPI field is used to group virtual channels (identified by their VCI values) into logical groups (different example shown above). By reducing the number of fields that have to be changed as each cell passes through the switch, the performance of the switch increases. In the example shown, cells that enter the ATM switch on port 1 and have a VPI value of 4 are processed through the **VP switch**, which changes the VPI value of each cell to 5, but leaves the VCI value intact, and sends the cell out on port 3. Cells that have a VPI value of 1 are processed through the **VC switch**. For cells that have a VCI value of 1, the VC switch changes the VPI to 3 and the VCI to 3 and sends the cell out on port 2. For cells that have a VCI value of 2, the VC switch changes the VPI to 2 and the VCI to 4.

FIGURE 8-15 Virtual circuit and virtual path switching

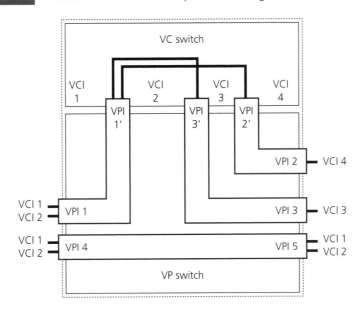

ATM switches and network congestion

Frame discard is a function that can minimize network congestion by discarding frames during congestion or when the network knows certain cells of the frame have been dropped. The **Early Packet Discard** (EPD) will discard the whole AAL-5 frame at the ingress by the switch during related congestion or certain network failure situations. Related congestion means that the network may not have resources for the particular connection category that the connection setup is requesting but may not be in a congested state for a different type of connection category. On the other hand, during some failure conditions the network may be in an overloading state and would not accommodate all connection categories.

Another form of frame discard is when certain cells of the frame have been dropped and therefore the frame has no meaningful value to the receiver. In this frame discard mode, in order to maintain AAL-5 frame delineation, the last cell of the AAL-5 frame is not dropped. Note that AAL-5 frames use an end-of-frame indicator in the last cell. In order for the last cell to have a high probability of getting to the destination, the switch that is doing the frame discard should also change the CLP of the last cell to *0* if it happened to be set to *1*.

Large-capacity ATM switch architecture

The switch fabric is the key component of an ATM switch. A requirement of the ATM switch fabric is to provide cell switching capability at the rated capacity with minimum blocking probability or preferably **non-blocking**. Most switching fabrics of ATM switches are VLSIs-based. Two approaches to switch fabric implementation – as a **single large fabric** and as a **modular set of smaller ones** – is shown in Figure 8.16.

FIGURE 8-16 ATM switch fabric

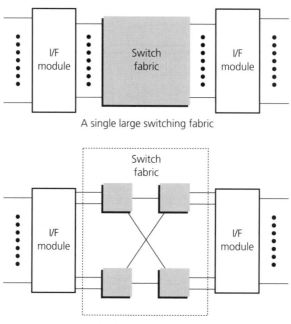

A single large switching fabric

A network of small fabric building blocks
to form a larger switching fabric

Scalability is an important consideration in system development. With anticipated future growth, a carrier or switch user always wants to scale the system to a larger capacity but still preserve the existing installed base as much as possible.

A **buffering mechanism** and queue scheduling are implemented in the ATM switch to support multiple Quality of Service (QoS) class requirements. Depending on the switch architecture, the buffer types used in ATM switches are usually classified as output, input, input-output, or crosspoint (see also Section 7.6.1). The **queue scheduling** structures are generally based on static priority, weighted round-robin scheduling, or weighted fair queuing. These properties will not change in a small- or large-capacity switch. ATM switches require large cell buffers to absorb traffic fluctuation and minimize cell loss. To reduce the cost of the cell buffer in a switch, buffer sharing is always desirable. This is especially true in a large switch. A fully shared cell buffer in the input or output of the switch fabric can minimize the buffer size requirement, improve buffer utilization, and optimize cell loss performance. However, in a large-capacity switch, a fully shared buffer over the whole switch, although efficient, makes the buffer size too large and too complex to be easily implemented.

Call processing capability is developed to support broadband signaling in Switched Virtual Services (SVC). The need for call processing capacity increases as the number of users increases. For a large-capacity switch with a large number of users having SVC capability, the call processing capability will easily translate into hundreds of calls per second for the system. This means that the switch call processor will have to scale to meet the call processing requirements.

Depending on the architecture, the **call processor design** can be either centralized or distributed. A **centralized design** (see Figure 8.17) has a group of processors to handle the call processing needs of the whole switch. Any call setup message received at the interface will be directed to the central processors. In this centralized architecture, the system designer only needs to consider the overall

FIGURE 8-17 Centralized ATM switch design

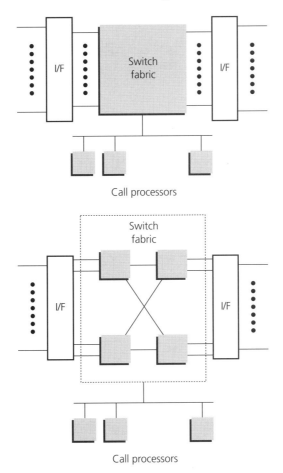

Call processors

Call processors

call setup load. The call setup load distribution among user interfaces has no impact on the design of call processor capacity. A **distributed processor architecture** (see Figure 8.18) usually has dedicated call processors to handle the call processing needs of a group of user ports. The call setup message received at the interface will be directed to a dedicated processor. In the distributed architecture, the local processor has to be able to handle the signaling load from the supported ports, where the load could be dramatically different from port to port, depending on the user application. In this design, the call processor is likely to be over- or under-engineered. As the port number increases when the switch capacity grows, the number of call processors will also grow linearly. The call processing resources cannot be deployed efficiently.

FIGURE 8-18 Distributed ATM switch processor design

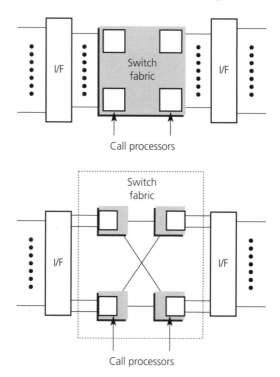

ATM switch typology

ATM provides scalable bandwidth that spans both LANs and WANs. It also promises Quality of Service (QoS) guarantees – bandwidth on demand – that can map into and support higher-level protocol infrastructures for emerging multimedia applications and provide a common, multiservice network infrastructure.

ATM switches are one of the key components of ATM technology. Not all ATM switches, however, are alike. Even though all ATM switches perform cell relay, ATM switches differ markedly in the following capabilities:

- variety of interfaces and services that are supported;
- redundancy;
- depth of ATM internetworking software;
- sophistication of traffic management mechanism;
- blocking and non-blocking switching fabrics;
- SVC and PVC support.

Just as there are routers and LAN switches available at various price/perform-
ance points with different levels of functionality, ATM switches can be segmented
into several categories reflecting the needs of particular applications and markets. There exists various methods of distinguishing different types of ATM
switches. The method which seems closely related to the modern hierarchical network design divides the ATM switches into the following categories:

- **Workgroup ATM switches** – designed to interconnect workstations in a high-
  speed cluster, and optimized for deploying ATM to the desktop over low-cost ATM
  desktop interfaces, with ATM signaling interoperability for ATM adapters and
  QoS support for multimedia applications. These usually support an uplink for
  connecting the cluster to an ATM backbone. Some workgroup switches can also,
  or alternately, be used to link an ATM workgroup with one or more legacy LANs.

- **Campus ATM switches** – generally used for small-scale ATM backbones (for
  example, to link ATM routers or LAN switches). This use of ATM switches can
  alleviate current backbone congestion while enabling the deployment of such
  new services as VLANs. Campus switches need to support a wide variety of
  both local backbone and WAN types but to be price/performance optimized for
  the local backbone function. In this class of switches, ATM routing capabilities
  that allow multiple switches to be tied together is very important. Congestion
  control mechanisms for optimizing backbone performance is also important.

- **Backbone ATM switches** – sophisticated multiservice devices to form the
  core backbones of large, enterprise networks. They are intended to complement
  the role played by today's high-end multiprotocol routers. Backbone ATM
  switches, much as campus ATM switches, are used to interconnect workgroup
  ATM switches and other ATM-connected devices, such as LAN switches.
  Enterprise-class switches, however, can act not only as ATM backbones but can
  serve as the single point of integration for all of the disparate services and
  technology found in enterprise backbones today. By integrating all of these
  services onto a common platform and a common ATM transport infrastructure,
  network designers can gain greater manageability while eliminating the need
  for multiple overlay networks.

8.6 Optical switching

There is a growing interest in optical (photonic) switching and signal processing.
Much of the stimulus comes from the worldwide installation of optical fiber communication systems and the rapidly increasing demand for broadband services. In
the late 1990s, optical switching became an attractive alternative to electronic

switching. An optical switch has the advantage of transmission channel data rate independence and can handle throughput far in excess of a conventional electronic switch.

8.6.1 Optical MAN switches

IP Metropolitan Area Networks (MANs) are attractive to application service providers and Web-caching service providers that are looking for a fast, flexible, inexpensive way to deliver Internet, intranet, and extranet services to their corporate customers. Gigabit Ethernet-based MANs offer several advantages over traditional SONET rings, including the following:

- The connection between the LAN and WAN is easy because Ethernet is running on both sides of the WAN access device.
- Prices are significantly lower than comparable bandwidth on a SONET/ATM network.
- Bandwidth can be turned up in 1 Mbps increments within minutes of a customer request, compared with having to wait weeks for an additional 1.5 Mbps T-1 line.

Carrier-class gigabit switches, also known as **aggregation switches**, differ from enterprise switches in that they provide connectivity to optical core networks, including SONET, and they provide access to customers.

Wavelength Division Multiplexing (WDM) plays a major role in this scheme by complementing Gigabit Ethernet technology. Full-duplex Gigabit Ethernet requires a fiber pair – one for transmitting and the other for receiving. This can become economically unsound when running numerous gigabit channels to points of presence (POP). Using WDM substantially reduces the number of fiber pairs required to connect to POPs. In the MAN backbone, Dense WDM (DWDM) is now replacing traditional SONET switches to provide a substantial increase in bandwidth and dramatically reduce the time it takes to provision a circuit.

SDH/SONET position

A telecommunications industry technology for highly scalable, large-bandwidth traffic requirements, SONET/SDH, is a time-division multiplexing transport technology (see also Section 3.9 and Chapter 16). It was developed in the 1980s for high-volume voice traffic, and although it can support any kind of traffic, it is optimized for voice. SONET is a hierarchical digital transport technology for transmission over fiber and is organized into 64 kbps (digital service, level zero) voice channels. The SONET hierarchy is relevant to the North American marketplace, while most of the rest of the world is adopting SDH technology. The two technologies are closely related, similar in functionality, and offer similar in transmission rates, but in reality there are interoperability issues between SDH and SONET, particularly at higher data rates.

SONET has serious drawbacks for packet-oriented traffic. SDH/SONET does not directly accommodate the bandwidth variability essential to the evolving networks (public or private) which carry voice, bursty data, and video. SDH/SONET transmit all information at standard transmission rates. ATM allows an organization of the SDH/SONET payload so that varying bandwidth signals can be effectively carried. When cells between two users are assigned statistically, dynamic bandwidth results; if the cells are assigned in a periodical manner, a fixed-bandwidth channel is obtained. This allows ATM/AAL to support both continuous bit rate services, such as voice, video, and multimegabyte file transfer, and variable rate services, such as bursty data transactions. SDH/SONET represent physical layer standards, which are oblivious to what occurs beyond a single physical link and so do not take an end-to-end routing view. SDH/SONET are synchronous standards in the sense that the information's position within the frame determines who owns that information. ATM is asynchronous in the sense that the position of the information does not establish ownership.

SONET frame format contains large and expanding payload capacities. The payload portion of a NET frame, called the Synchronous Payload Envelope, is organized into a byte format that expands from 87 octets for OC-1 (see Appendix D) to 16 704 octets for OC-192. This large payload format can be a limitation because any unused channel capacity is wasted. Packets must be mapped to a SONET frame format, then stripped from the SONET frame on arrival at their destinations. Data must be packed into these rigid channels, resulting in wasted channel capacity where packets do not exactly fit the channel. This inefficiency becomes more pronounced with increased data traffic on the network.

Gigabit Ethernet *vis-à-vis* SONET

By contrast, Gigabit Ethernet technology addresses data-intensive traffic and is highly scalable. It also supports Layer 3 through Layer 7 IP packet processing required for developing value-added services, and bandwidth management and provisioning. Gigabit Ethernet switches are an order of magnitude lower in cost than SONET. By using WDM, Gigabit Ethernet can duplicate the robust dual-ring architecture of SONET by provisioning multiple Gigabit Ethernet channels over WDM fiber to create a scalable, robust, data-optimized optical ring. The deployment of 10 Gbps Ethernet will flexibly aggregate native data traffic across high-speed optical MANs, providing an end-to-end Ethernet network.

Gigabit Ethernet technology is becoming the technology of choice for today's data-intensive MANs. It is an economically sound, large-bandwidth solution that provides access flexibility and connectivity with SONET or emerging DWDM-optic networks.

SONET rings can be replaced with Gigabit Ethernet switches using DWDM to provide an end-to-end Ethernet network that supports voice, video, and data. Alternatively the switches can be positioned on the edge of a core SONET network, enabling MANs and service providers to provision network services to subscribers, while maintaining the SONET core for high-volume traffic.

8.6.2 Optical switches

The advancement in optical technology is at the core of optical multiplexers, cross-connect and photonic switches, all supporting the high-speed networks. The advent of fiber optic signaling and switching equipment capable of transmitting at several gigabits per second over long distances and with low error rates through optical fiber proves that gigabit and even terabit networks are feasible.

Advances in optical components are opening up new possibilities for network architectures. In particular, optical switches and amplifiers, and multi-wavelength techniques have important roles in these developments. In addition, both radio and microwaves are also capable of providing gigabit bandwidth.

There are optical switches that rely on bubble-jet printer technology and a vapor bubble to switch light signals from one optical fiber to another without first converting the signals to electrical impulses. The alternative approach is to use microscopic mirrors. Optical switching will be discussed on more detail in the final chapter of Part V.

8.7 WAN design

Traditionally, WAN communication has been characterized by relatively low throughput, high delay, and high error rates. WAN connections are mostly characterized by the cost of renting media (wire) from a service provider to connect two or more campuses together. Because the WAN infrastructure is often rented from a service provider, WAN network designs must optimize the cost of bandwidth and bandwidth efficiency.

All technologies and features used to connect campuses over a WAN are developed to meet the following design requirements:

■ to optimize WAN bandwidth;
■ to minimize the tariff cost;
■ to maximize the effective service to the end users.

Recently new network requirements have appeared:

■ the necessity to connect to remote sites;
■ the growing need for users to have remote access to their networks;
■ the explosive growth of corporate intranets;
■ the increased use of enterprise servers.

Network designers are turning to WAN technology to support these new requirements. WAN connections generally handle mission-critical information, and are optimized for price/performance bandwidth. The routers connecting the campuses, for example, generally apply traffic optimization, multiple paths for redundancy, dial backup for disaster recovery, and QoS for critical applications.

8.7.1 Packet-switching network topologies

Packet-switching network topology appears to the external world as a set of physical **point-to-point links** which are in fact usually represented only by virtual circuits. The outer view of any type of packet-switching network – not only X.25 – is shown in Figure 8.19. The routers at the edges are the boundary between the network for which they are DTEs, and the user to which they represent an entry point connecting them to a usually unknown internal network switching infrastructure (in the case of a public network).

FIGURE 8-19   Packet-switching network

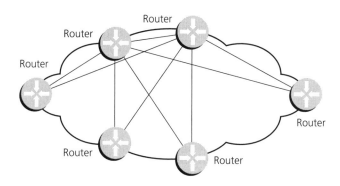

The actual topology of the network may take one of the following
forms:

■ **Star** (hub-and-spoke) – consists of a single internetworking hub providing
access from leaf internetworks into the backbone and access to each other only
through the core router. The advantages of a star approach are simplified
management and minimized tariff costs. However, the disadvantages are
significant. First, the core router represents a single point of failure. Second,
the core router limits overall performance for access to backbone resources
because it is a single pipe through which all traffic intended for the backbone
(or for the other regional routers) must pass. Third, this topology is not
scalable. (For an example of the star topology see Figure 8.20.)

FIGURE 8-20   Star topology network

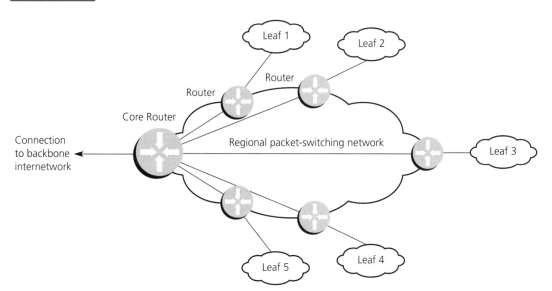

■ **Fully meshed** – requires that each routing node on the periphery of a given packet-switching network has a direct path to every other node on the cloud. The key rationale for creating a fully meshed environment is to provide a high level of redundancy. Although a fully meshed topology facilitates the support of all network protocols, it is not tenable in large packet-switched internetworks. Key issues are the large number of virtual circuits required (one for every connection between routers), problems associated with the large number of packet/broadcast replications required, and the configuration complexity for routers in the absence of multicast support in non-broadcast environments. By combining fully meshed and star approaches into a partially meshed environment, you can improve fault tolerance without encountering the performance and management problems associated with a fully meshed approach (see Figure 8.21). The major drawback of fully meshed networks is that they do not scale, as $O(n^2)$ circuits are needed. Therefore they are generally reserved for high-speed backbones that consist of a small number of core routers.

FIGURE 8-21   Full mesh topology network

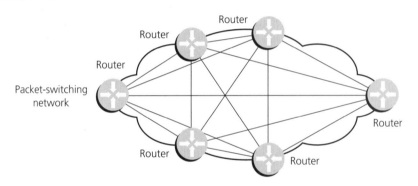

■ **Partially meshed** – reduces the number of routers within a region that have direct connections to all other nodes in the region. All nodes are not connected to all other nodes. For a non-meshed node to communicate with another non-meshed node, it must send traffic through one of the collection point routers. There are many forms of partially meshed topologies. In general, partially meshed approaches are considered to provide the best balance for regional topologies in terms of the number of virtual circuits, redundancy, and performance (see Figure 8.22).

While the logical network topology shown above may not have any particular significance to the internal physical packet-switching network structure, it is extremely important for the network access routers. Their configurations will differ in relation to the particular topology which would derive from a different neighbor approach significant for routing protocols. However, routing is the topic of the next part, Part IV.

FIGURE 8-22   Partial mesh topology network

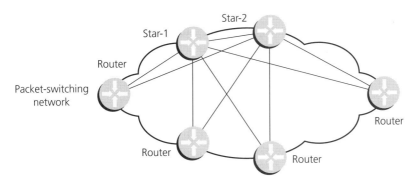

PART III CONCLUDING REMARKS

Part III concentrated on **switching principles**, switch **architectures**, and switch deployment in the networks. The two major categories of switching, **circuit and packet switching**, are introduced here, with subsequent finer division into currently used methods of packet switching: **packet switching** at Layer 3, **frame switching** at Layer 2, and **cell switching** at Layer 1/2.

Frame switches are switching devices primarily used in local area networks where they were introduced to overcome the disadvantages of shared media. Their operation is mostly similar to that of **bridges**, as both interconnecting devices reside at Layer 2. **LAN switches** also help segment networks into collision domains, while keeping the whole switched network in **one broadcast domain**. Again, **STP** must be used in a switched Ethernet network to eliminate loops which could lead to broadcast flooding and eventual disruption of the network. LAN switches bring new features compared to bridges which distinguish their position in the network. Their **forwarding** is done mostly **in hardware**, hence they introduce less latency, and with advances in the internal switching fabric they achieve high throughput even in the store-and-forward mode of operation, although they may be even faster in the cut-through mode.

The major benefit of LAN switches, however, is the introduction of **virtual LANs** (VLANs) which allow the formation of logical groups of users into a LAN regardless of their physical network connection. Thus the **broadcast domains** become controlled within the borders of a VLAN. While for communication between VLANs it is necessary to deploy **routers**, switches support a VLAN's span across more switches with the use of VLAN identifiers tagged to the particular frames (supported by IEEE 802.1Q protocol or proprietary solutions).

The implementation of **WAN switches** depends largely on the network type: X.25 switches are much different from Frame Relay or ATM switches. Again, the internal architecture in most advanced ATM switches is built so that it supports high-performance, **non-blocking cell switching** in hardware.

The development in both **switch fabrics** and **congestion management** methods has opened a new era in building **high-performance switches, multilayer switches, and high-speed routers** which are the topic of the final Part V. However, each of these solutions would not be complete without the **routing** mechanisms operated in the network, discussed next in Part IV.

PART IV

Routing

In Part I, the basic differences between the different network interconnection methods, including routing, were described. In Parts II and III we encountered main features of Layer 2 interconnecting devices. However, now we are going to concentrate fully on the routing principles and the importance of routers in networks.

This Part will be fully dedicated to **routing** and **routers** with the aim of providing an overview of:

- **routing principles** and **types**;
- **routing algorithms**;
- **routing IP** (including IPv6 and multicast protocols);
- **routing in proprietary network architectures** (AppleTalk, Novell, XNS, Banyan VINES, DECnet);
- **routing in standard OSI architecture**;
- **multiprotocol routing**.

As the various **network architectures** are introduced we will look more closely at their protocol hierarchy, namely the network layer and lower layers, to understand the network address formats and addressing principles, and the relationship between the network address and the physical address.

Besides general routing protocol issues we will also consider **router architecture**, **performance**, and **benchmarking**, and security issues while deploying routers.

C H A P T E R 9

Routing principles

SNAPSHOT	routing

Routing is the act of **selecting a path and moving packets across that path** from a source to a destination. Routing devices (routers) **connect networks** by means of physical attachments to either LANs or WANs. A routing device can be used to connect only LANs together, only WANs together, or any combination of the two. Routing involves two basic activities: determining optimal routing paths and forwarding packets. A routing device's **attachment to a LAN or a WAN** is called an **interface** (port).

With reference to Part I it is necessary to re-emphasize the two aspects of routing (see Figure 9.1):

FIGURE 9-1   Elements of a routing system

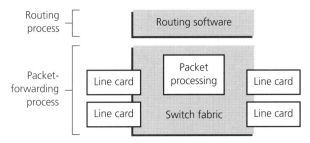

Packet processing may be distributed to each line card, executed in a centralized fashion, or performed by both the line cards and a centralized processor

- **Path determination** (the leading theme throughout this chapter: see Figure 9.2) – may be based on a variety of criteria to determine the optimal route where there are a number of available paths to the destination. Software implementations of routing algorithms calculate the appropriate criteria

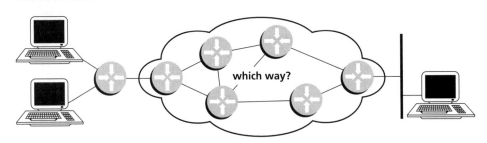

FIGURE 9-2 Path determination task

values for each available (known) path to determine the optimal route(s) to a destination. To aid the process of path determination, routing algorithms initialize and maintain routing tables which contain route information. Route information varies depending on the routing algorithm used. Path determination may require a quite complex process.

The path determination function may consist of one or more routing protocols that provide exchange of routing information among routers, as well as the procedures (algorithms) that a router uses to convert this information into a routing table. In the case of IP routing, OSPF, BGP, and PIM are examples of such routing protocols.

■ **Packet forwarding** – when we start looking at different routing mechanisms in various network architectures, we will need to look at the way Layer 2 and Layer 3 addresses are mapped. To summarize the process background, upon examining the packet's destination protocol address, the router determines that it either knows or does not know how to forward the packet to the next hop. In the case where the router does not know how to forward the packet, the packet is typically dropped. In the former case, the router sends the packet to the next hop by changing the destination physical address to that of the next hop and transmitting the packet. The next hop may or may not be the ultimate destination host. If not, the next hop is usually another router, which executes the same switching decision process. As the packet moves through the internetwork, its physical address changes, but its protocol address remains constant. Packet forwarding is relatively straightforward and is described in detail for IP routing in Chapter 11.

The forwarding function consists of a set of procedures (algorithms) that a router uses to make a forwarding decision on a packet. The algorithms define the information from the packet that a router uses to find a particular entry in its routing (forwarding) table, as well as the exact procedures that the router uses for finding the entry. For **unicast forwarding**, the information from a packet that a router uses to find a particular entry in the forwarding table is the network layer destination address, and the procedure that the router uses for finding the entry is the longest match algorithm. For **multicast forwarding**, the information from a packet that a router uses to find a particular entry in the forwarding table is a combination of the network layer source and destination addresses and the incoming interface (the interface that a packet arrives on), and the procedure that the router uses for finding the entry uses both the longest and the exact match algorithms. For **unicast forwarding with Types of Service** (in the IP case), the information from a packet that a router uses to find a particular entry in the forwarding table is the network layer destination address and the Type of Service value, and the procedure that the router uses for finding the entry is the longest match algorithm on the destination address and the exact match algorithm on the Type of Service value.

SNAPSHOT	router defined

The device capable of the functions discussed in this chapter is a **relay** (intermediate, internetworking system) that forwards (relays) **network protocol data units** (PDUs) based on network-layer information. This relay is more commonly called a **router** (formerly *gateway*).

9.1 Evolution of routing theory

The topic of routing has been covered in the literature of computer science for more than two decades, but routing achieved commercial popularity only as late as the mid-1980s. The primary reason for this time lag is that networks in the 1970s were fairly simple, homogeneous environments.

From the beginning of routing theory it could be understood that routing as such was never seen as completely separate from some other network tasks. It is not possible to 'guarantee' the optimum path through the network just by looking at the obvious criteria, like path length, which are static and can be deduced purely from the topology. Network traffic should be also taken into account, and this is no static value at all. While the chosen path may be the shortest in the topology graph, in reality the traffic may be so heavy on it that the factual delay makes the route quite poor. Therefore initial research in routing theory depicted the close relationship between **flow control** and **routing**. However, as we will see in the following, the first widely deployed routing mechanisms were too simple to provide a reasonable link and balance between flow control and routing.

9.1.1 Static or dynamic routing

Currently we distinguish between the two different types of routing, **static** (fixed) and **dynamic** (adaptive). However, in the 1960s and 1970s there were more than these two extremes to be considered:

■ **Static routing** (non-adaptive, fixed, deterministic, or explicit) – the path between source and destination is predetermined in the packet origin node and fixed for all relevant packets unless administratively changed, with no protocol required to exchange up-to-date routing information. Static routing as we know it today does not allow the packet origin node or a router to specify the path directly in the packet, hence the static route must be configured manually in all routers (unless the static route is distributed with the help of a routing protocol).

■ **Quasi-static routing** – a node in the network is designated to make all routing decisions on behalf of all the other nodes. The central node periodically gets information from the others on traffic requirements and uses it to solve current routing problems. Protocol is required to support communication between the central 'routing' node and other 'listening' nodes. The central node is a single point of failure. An example of such routing was delta routing.

■ **Dynamic routing** (adaptive, stochastic) – the complete route is not selected at the packet origin node nor at any intermediate node. The routing decision of the packet is entirely up to an intermediate node whose routing table is updated when changes in traffic and topology occur; therefore all nodes participate in a common routing algorithm (protocol) allowing them to find the optimal path to the destination (if one exists) based on the given criteria, taking into account not only the quality of available paths but also the instantaneous states of the queues for the individual links. The route to the furthest hop on the path depends on each intermediate node as no complete route exists across the network.

■ **Hot potato passing** – a form of *ad hoc* routing, using the shortest transmission queue in each router. The strategy ensures the quickest packet forwarding (not delivery) without regard to where it goes. It definitely does not strive for the optimal path and therefore it is not accepted in current internets. Obviously, routing loops may easily occur.

Once the routes have been constructed, the route information must be stored so that it can be used to forward packets. The route information can be put either in each individual packet to be forwarded – **source routing** (originating host choses the route) – with quite easy packet forwarding in each intermediate node. In source-routing systems, routers merely act as store-and-forward devices, mindlessly sending the packet to the next stop. **Entry-to-exit routing** is based on a mechanism whereby each intermediate node forwards the packet according to the route selected not by the source of the packet but rather by its entry point into the network (edge router). Entry-to-exit routing is transparent to the hosts and can more easily adapt to changes in topology or network load.

Alternatively, the route information is stored in the **routing tables** at the nodes along the route. Then either hop-by-hop routing is deployed. **Hop-by-hop routing** is based on the individual intermediate nodes making their decisions on forwarding the packet while they pay no attention to its source and history (suitable for best-effort delivery).

Another classification of routing, closer to how we see different routing types today, is as follows:

■ **fixed routing**:
  – single routes between any source and destination;
  – multiple routes between any source and destination with a predetermined fraction of traffic using each (load balancing);

- **adaptive routing**:
  - routing based on locally available parameters and decided on a local basis;
  - routing based on network-wide parameters but implemented on a local basis;
  - routing based on network-wide parameters and imposed by a central controller on the local nodes.

Modern routing theories basically distinguish between the two routing types: static and dynamic routing (for their comparison, see Table 9.1).

TABLE 9-1   Comparison of static and dynamic routing

Feature	Static routing	Dynamic routing
Automatic reaction to internet changes	No	Yes
Administrator's involvement in (re)configuration	High	Low
Administrative (human) supervision of available routes	High	Low
Exchange of routing information	None	Necessary
Impact on router's processing capacity	Low	High
Memory consumption	Low	Medium to high
Network routing overhead load	None	Medium (regular operation) to high (initial bursts or periodically)

    Static routing requires the network administrator to determine and then configure manually the routes to destination networks and thus create a static routing table. Once configured, the network paths will not change automatically. The router will use the predetermined route even if it is down (a link within the path or another router has gone down), because it does not have a mechanism to automatically reconfigure the routing table to reroute the traffic around the disabled link (if an alternative exists). In that case all packets will be sent to a black network hole. Only if the broken link is detected by the router (i.e. a directly attached link), will the packets not be sent by the route to a static route.

    A good reason for deploying static routing is in cases where there is a single path to the network with no possible alternative paths. In such circumstances, dynamic routing would not provide any added value – on the contrary, it would bother the particular network and its attached routers with routing updates and occasional recalculation of the dynamic routing table. An example of static routing is shown in Figure 9.3.

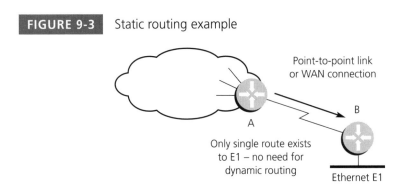

FIGURE 9-3 Static routing example

Point-to-point link or WAN connection

B

A

Only single route exists to E1 – no need for dynamic routing

Ethernet E1

Dynamic routing, on the other hand, automatically updates the routing table and recalculates the best path when a change is noticed in the network topology. Routers exchange information about the network's topology with other participating routers. A router starts with a very limited view of the network, as it just gets from the network administrator information about directly connected segments. The rest is left to the routing protocol: the mechanism of routing information exchange, update periods, building and modifying the routing table, choosing the best route, and, if that goes down, replacing it with an existing (second best) alternative. Dynamic routing can adapt to changing conditions in the interconnected network (links go up and down, new links and routers are added) without any intervention from the administrator (provided the routing protocol configuration on the routers in the internet is right).

An example of a dynamic routing operation is shown in Figure 9.4. The network initially works well with one chosen optimal path between the two indicated hosts (actually between the source network segment and the destination one (a)). However, once a link on the used path gets broken (b), the dynamic routing quickly detects the existence of an alternative path and after all routers converge the other path will replace the unavailable path in all routing tables (c).

QUICK TIP **dynamic routing defined**

Routing that dynamically, automatically, adjusts to network topology changes. Requires a **routing protocol** configured on routers. A.k.a. **adaptive routing**.

Routing theory in the 1970s realized that dynamic routing may increase throughput when trunks are moderately loaded but may reduce throughput at heavily loaded trunks when uniform loading is in question. The main problem was to

FIGURE 9-4 Dynamic routing operation

(a) operational network

(b) network with link down

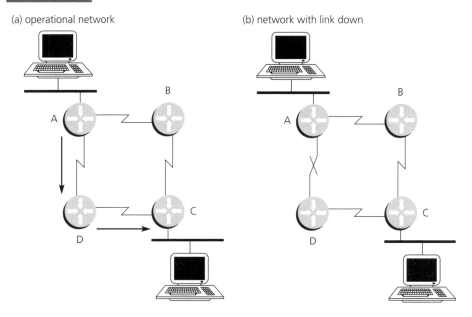

(c) dynamic routing detects and uses alternate path

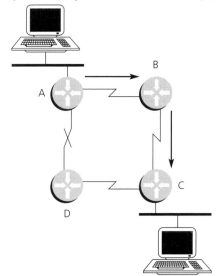

decide when the routing information should be exchanged and how often, because there arises a conflict: the period should be small enough to base a decision on recent information, and at the same time the period should be large enough to minimize the overhead associated with the updates.

Dynamic routing can coexist in networks that also use static routing on certain routers. Stub portions of an organization's network could use static routes to move packets onto the organization's backbone internet. The backbone internet could then use dynamic routing among its routers. However, it must be taken into account that in the majority of cases cooperation between the routing protocol and static routing is not automatic and requires additional configuration support from the administrator (on relevant routers).

Link and system failures

Static and dynamic routing differ mostly in terms of their reaction to failures. **Dynamic routing** allows for detecting problems with both links and routers on the particular route (missing Hello, keepalive messages or 'purely' missing routing updates), and after that deal with chasing another route, if available.

Static routing, as it does not involve exchange of messages among routers, not only does not have any mechanism to solve a lost route but is not even, in many cases, able to detect such a problem with the particular route, be it a link or system failure. It is important to realize the impact of this behavior on the network users. If host X (see Figure 9.5) sends packets to Y, they first reach router A. It has in its routing table a static route configured for subnet 10 via router B.

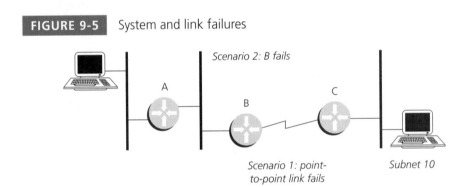

FIGURE 9-5   System and link failures

Where a segment connecting B and C fails, a point-to-point **link failure** causes the static route to become invalid. However, the packets will be forwarded by A, according to its routing table, to B. Router B has detected the link failure and will generate an ICMP message *Destination unreachable* (in IP environment; see also Section 10.5).

However, in the situation where router B fails, instead of a link failure, a **system failure** occurs and the static route again becomes invalid. In this scenario a **black hole** is created, as the packets are sent to an undetectable dead end: packets forwarded by A would not be accepted by router B which, in turn, means that no router will send an ICMP message *Destination unreachable* and packets will be inadvertently lost.

Convergence

Convergence as the status of common understanding of the network topology shared by all routers is a major benchmark of routing protocols. Loss of convergence, leading to network downtime, can be caused by either a change in the status of a router or a change in the status of a link. The process of (re)gaining convergence may require reconfiguring the routing tables in cases of topology change. Therefore routers must converge quickly before those routers with incorrect information misroute data packets into dead ends.

SNAPSHOT   **network convergence**

Convergence is the process of agreement, by all routers, on network topology (and in effect optimal routes). When a network event causes routes to either halt operation or become available, routers distribute routing update messages. **Routing update messages** permeate networks, stimulating the recalculation of optimal routes and eventually causing all routers to agree on these routes. Routing algorithms that converge slowly can cause **routing loops** or **network outages**.

Factors determining protocol convergence are:

- network size;
- hop count limitations;
- peering arrangements (edge, core);
- topology design;
- routing information compatibility;
- port and switch-level addressing;
- path selection.

QUICK TIP   **causes of network convergence loss**

Loss of convergence, leading to network downtime, can be caused by:

- a change in the status of a router;
- a change in the status of a link.

Multicast routing

Routing theory also studies the situation in which there is not a single destination station but multiple stations. Initially the problem was called **Multiple Destination Routing** (MDR) while currently it is referred to as multicast routing. Modern applications that take advantage of multicast include video conferencing, corporate communications, distance learning, and the distribution of software, stock quotes, and news.

There is an inherent difference to **unicast routing**, the common routing regime, when every packet is routed individually. The distribution of a number of the same packets among the group requires the generation of a number of packet copies to be routed individually. Obviously, this unnecessarily adds to network and router processing load.

Multicast routing, instead, sends only a single copy of the particular packet destined for a group of stations (to the multicast address) over every network link and, in more sophisticated cases, only over the links to the multicast routers or end stations which are members of that particular addressed group. Multicast is based on the concept of a group. An arbitrary group of receivers expresses an interest in receiving a particular datastream. This group does not have any physical or geographical boundaries – the hosts can be located anywhere on the routed network.

Figures 9.6 and 9.7 provide a comparison between unicast and multicast routing for a typical multicast application such as videoconferencing.

FIGURE 9-6   Unicast routing

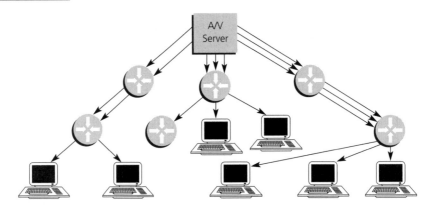

FIGURE 9-7   Mulitcast routing

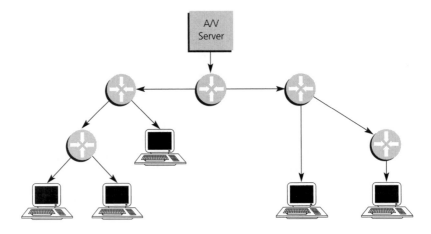

Multicast is thus a bandwidth-conserving technology that reduces traffic by simultaneously delivering a single stream of information to thousands of corporate recipients and homes. Multicast delivers source traffic to multiple receivers without adding any additional burden to the source or the receivers while using the least network bandwidth.

9.1.2 Routed, routable, and routing protocols

While considering routing, it is necessary to define some basic terminology relating to protocols.

Routed protocols are protocols that are routed over an internet, generally **network protocols**. Examples of such protocols are the Internet Protocol (IP), DDP of AppleTalk, IPX of NetWare, CLNP of OSI or VIP of Banyan VINES, and Xerox Network System (XNS). Routed protocols are **routable protocols**, i.e. they implement network layer and network addressing, the prerequisites of routing. Compare these with the non-routable protocols in Part II which cannot be routed due to their non-hierarchical network addressing structure and which must therefore only be bridged in the internet. Alternatively, they can be tunneled using some routable (network) protocol as a carrier, using its respective routing mechanism. Thus the non-routable data units would be 'encapsulated' into different (carrier protocol) packets (i.e. not an understandable payload for the carrier protocol).

Routing for network protocols may be provided by static or dynamic means. Dynamic routing is based on **routing protocols** that implement **routing algorithms**. Put simply, they help route routed protocols through an internet. The routing protocols do not really route routed protocols; they contribute to the distribution of routing updates and to the convergence of the routing tables. Routers route routed protocols based on their (current) routing tables, and these routing tables are continuously updated by a routing protocol.

Examples of routing protocols include the Routing Information Protocol (RIP), Open Shortest Path First (OSPF), Exterior Gateway Protocol (EGP), Border Gateway Protocol (BGP), OSI Routing, and Intermediate System to Intermediate System (IS-IS). Both routed and their related routing protocols are discussed in detail later in this Part.

A **routed network**, consequently, is an internet deploying routers as interconnecting devices. Again, the network is not routing by itself – hence it is not a routing network. Instead, its traffic is routed with the support of routers as internetworking devices and static/dynamic routing processes. (Compare this with the bridged and switched networks discussed in Parts II and III, respectively.)

9.1.3 Broadcast domains

As we saw in previous parts, broadcast frames or packets on an internet may cause an unprecedented and undesirable increase in network traffic, even broadcast storms. While at the link layer very limited or no remedy exists to handle broadcasts by bridges and switches, routing can handle them effectively. In general, routers having more intelligence than Layer 2 devices; do not allow broadcasts to proliferate on the internet and therefore block them (they discard them before they are forwarded from the outgoing interfaces). However, there are several types and many more applications of broadcasting in the internet which we will consider later. Some broadcasting is very useful for routers themselves; other broadcasting is necessary for end stations and servers. And routers must be capable enough and ready to handle these appropriately.

Some of the routing protocols generate heavy broadcast traffic themselves which is generally intended only for their neighbors. However, developments are following the trend of continuously lowering the routing overhead, overhead created partially by broadcasting. Table 12.6 on p. 674 at the end of Part IV summarizes the relative broadcast traffic among the various routing protocols.

QUICK TIP | **neighbor**

Neighbor = any router that can be reached directly (i.e. connects to the same network), without passing via another router.

9.2 Routers – complex devices

Before we start discussing the routing algorithms and individual routable protocol architectures and their available routing schemes, it is necessary to look more closely at the device performing all routing tasks – the router. We will consider the router requirements, tasks, and architectures first.

9.2.1 Router requirements

The router must be able to cope with a variety of differences among networks, including the following:

■ **Addressing schemes** – there is a variety of addressing structures used across the LAN/MAN/WAN networking world. And it is not only logical addressing that the router must be able to fully comprehend and support (through its routing tables and mapping tables), but also the physical addressing (maintaining the ARP cache).

■ **Maximum data (transmission) unit sizes** – data units from one network may have to be broken into smaller pieces to be transmitted on another network, using a process of fragmentation.

■ **Interfaces** – the hardware and software interfaces to various networks differ in terms of frame/packet encapsulation/decapsulation and communication control at implemented layers, but this should not have an impact on the internal operation structure of the router.

■ **Reliability** – various network services may provide anything from a reliable end-to-end virtual circuit to an unreliable service. The operation of the routers should not depend on an assumption of network reliability.

Besides dynamically finding paths for datagrams to their destinations – packet forwarding as discussed above – routers perform a variety of additional functions and offer other capabilities:

- **Broadcast and multicast control** – routers offer broadcast-limiting functions that reduce network traffic and minimize broadcast storms (the simultaneous transmission of many broadcasts across all network segments) and can be configured to control multicast traffic.
- **Network segmentation** – to limit unnecessary traffic by dividing the internet into broadcast segments (such as setting up IP subnets in the case of IP networks). This limits traffic on a given segment to local broadcasts or to traffic intended for another router. By distributing hosts and clients carefully, this simple method of dividing up a network may be used to reduce overall network congestion.
- **Packet tracing** – supporting RMON MIB.
- **Statistics collection** – packets and bytes per source and destination for future network planning.
- **Security** – routers help ensure that users can perform only the tasks they are authorized to perform, can obtain information only they are authorized to have, and cannot damage the data, applications, or operating environment of a system. In the context of internetworking, security also means protecting against attacks by outsiders and controlling the effects of errors and equipment failures. Routers may function as packet firewalls with the help of filters, and for dial-in purposes with the use of RADIUS.
- **Quality of Service** (QoS) – refers to the capability of a network to provide a better service to selected network traffic over various technologies, such as Ethernet and IP-routed networks. The primary goals of QoS include dedicated bandwidth, controlled jitter and latency (required by some real-time and interactive traffic), and improved loss characteristics. Current routers are capable of handling issues surrounding QoS requirements set up by users. The different methods of QoS deployment in a routed network are discussed in Part V.
- **Congestion control** and **queuing (link scheduling)** – these mechanism support better network throughput and are discussed in Part V.

To summarize, it is quite important to realize that a router device has much more to do than merely looking up a routing table. There are other router **tasks**, some mandatory, others optional or dependent on the vendor, which are performed (and which use a CPU processing capacities):

- memory management;
- network management support;
- console and telnet;
- interrupt scanning;
- dynamic routing;
- filtering;
- traffic shaping;

- debugging;
- packet rewriting;
- accounting;
- encryption, tunneling, compression.

An abstract overview of router software is shown in Figure 9.8.

FIGURE 9-8   Components of routing software

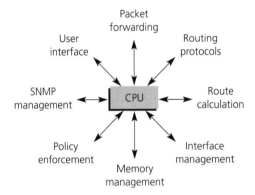

It should be noted that route lookup is not too CPU expensive, especially if it uses an enhancement algorithm such as the **Expedited Forwarding**, discussed in Part V. Rewriting packet headers (e.g. for fragmentation) is much more CPU expensive, and filtering can also require CPU capacity (and memory).

SNAPSHOT   **router services summarized**

Routers offer the following services (in comparison to switches):

- broadcast firewalling;
- hierarchical addressing;
- fast convergence;
- policy routing;
- QoS routing;
- security;
- redundancy and load balancing;
- traffic flow management.

9.2.2 Router architectures

The evolution in the architecture of routers is illustrated in Figure 9.9 (a)–(d). The original routers were built around a conventional computer architecture, as shown in Figure 9.9 (a): a **shared central bus, with a central CPU, memory and peripheral line cards**. Each line card performs the MAC layer function, connecting the system to each of the external links. Packets arriving from a link are transferred across the shared bus to the CPU, where a forwarding decision is made. The packet is then transferred across the bus again to its outgoing line card, and onto the external link.

The main limitation of the architecture in Figure 9.9 (a) is that the central CPU must process every packet, ultimately limiting the throughput of the system. This limitation prompted the architecture in Figure 9.9 (b), in which **multiple CPUs process packets in parallel**. Incoming packets are forwarded to a CPU as before, but this time there is a choice. For example, the packet could be sent to the first available CPU, or packets with the same destination address could always be sent to the same CPU. The advantage is clear: parallelism can increase the system throughput, or allow the use of lower-cost CPUs.

FIGURE 9-9   Evolution of router architecture

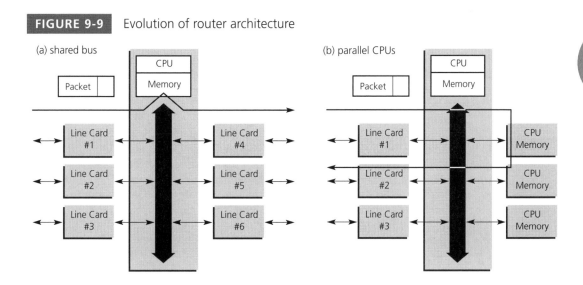

FIGURE 9-9   Evolution of router architecture (Continued)

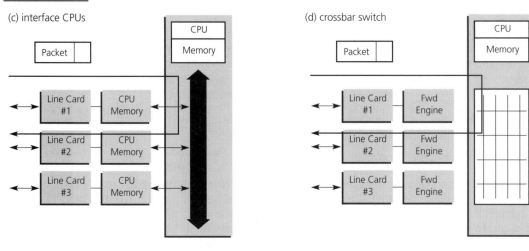

The architecture in Figure 9.9 (c) takes parallelism one stage further, placing a **separate CPU at each interface.** A local forwarding decision is made in a **dedicated CPU**, and the packet is immediately forwarded to its outgoing interface. This has the additional benefit that each packet need only traverse the bus once, thus increasing the system throughput. The central CPU is needed to maintain the forwarding tables in each of the other CPUs, and for centralized system management functions.

The performance of the architecture in Figure 9.9 (c) is ultimately limited by two factors. First, forwarding decisions are made in software, and so are limited by the speed of a general-purpose CPU. But general-purpose CPUs are not well suited to applications in which the data (packets) flow through the system; CPUs are better suited to applications in which data is examined multiple times, thus allowing the efficient use of a cache. Carefully designed, special-purpose ASICs can readily outperform a CPU when making forwarding decisions, managing queues, and arbitrating access to the bus. Hence, CPUs are being replaced increasingly by specialized ASICs. The second factor that limits the performance is the use of a shared bus – only one packet may traverse the bus at a time between two line cards.

Performance can be increased if multiple packets can be transferred across the bus simultaneously. This is the reason that a **crossbar switch** is increasingly used in place of a shared bus. In a crossbar switch, multiple line cards can communicate with each other simultaneously greatly increasing the system throughput. So, by introducing a hardware forwarding engine and replacing the bus with a crossbar switch, we reach the architecture shown in Figure 9.9 (d). Today, the very highest performance routers are designed according to this architecture.

If all of the line cards wish to transfer datagrams simultaneously, a backplane will need to support an aggregate bandwidth of the number of ports times their bandwidth. If the backplane cannot keep up, the shared bus becomes congested and buffers overflow. However, it is impractical today to build **shared backplanes** operating at tens of Gbps. But fortunately, switched backplanes provide a simple and efficient alternative and can easily operate at these rates. When the highest performance is required, shared backplanes are impractical for two reasons.

The first is congestion: the bandwidth of the bus is shared among all the ports, and contention leads to additional delay for packets. If the arrival rate of packets exceeds the bus bandwidth for a sustained period, buffers will overflow and data will be lost. Second, high-speed shared buses are difficult to design. The electrical loading caused by multiple ports on a shared bus, the number of connectors that a signal encounters, and reflections from the end of unterminated lines lead to limitations on the transfer capacity of a bus. State-of-the-art shared buses today can achieve a maximum capacity of about 20 Gbps. This is more than adequate for bridges and routers with a few 100 Mbps Ethernet ports. But for the high-end router with line-rates of 2.4 Gbps, an aggregate bandwidth of 40 Gbps is needed, which a shared backplane cannot sustain. The limitations of a shared backplane are being increasingly overcome by use of a **switched backplane**. Figures 9.10 and 9.11 make a simplified comparison between a conventional shared backplane and a switched backplane comprised of multiple line cards arranged around a central **crossbar switch**. Crossbar switches are widely used for switched backplanes because of their simplicity. They can support multiple bus transactions simultaneously – all inputs and outputs can transfer packets simultaneously – therefore crossbar switches are inherently non-blocking. The simple structure of a crossbar switch allows it to be readily implemented in silicon. Furthermore, using multiple crossbar switches in parallel increases the performance.

To keep up with faster links, each router lookup should take a few hundred nanoseconds. IP addresses are 32-bit strings, and each prefix length can vary from 1 to 32 bits. Most current implementations are based on bitwise branching tries. Thus, each possible length is tested sequentially, requiring up to the number of address bits memory accesses; this is too slow for high-speed routers.

FIGURE 9-10 Router based on shared backplane

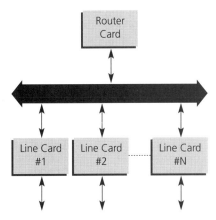

FIGURE 9-11   Router based on switched backplane

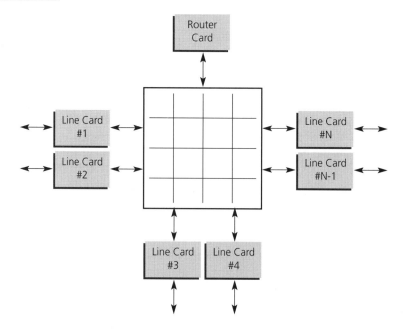

9.2.3 Router switching types

Related to the discussion above is what available options the router actually has to optimize its internal processing speeds for the given architecture. Now we have to introduce the term **switching** again. But although it means something similar to what was discussed in a previous Part, it should not confuse anyone who automatically links switching to Layer 2 operation. We are really talking about the operations of a device residing at Layer 3.

Here we are exclusively referring to the internal work of a router whose most important job is to **switch packets from incoming interfaces to outgoing interfaces**. Naturally, switching involves receiving a packet, determining how to forward the packet based on the routing topology, QoS, and policy requirements, and switching the packet to the right outgoing interface or interfaces for forwarding them further. The speed at which a router can perform this task is a major factor in determining network performance in a routed network.

Depending on various router architectures the router vendors offer different switching types which may also differ in terminology. Below are some of the details on the common switching types (the terminology used is Cisco's).

The first generation of routing equipment used process switching to look up all the associated best-path information in each routing table for every packet processed. To improve upon the performance of **process-switched** systems, solutions known as **fast switching** and **optimum switching** were designed. These switching designs yield higher throughput by switching a packet using a cache that is created by the initial packet sent to a particular destination prefix. Destination prefixes are stored in the high-speed cache to speed information lookup and forwarding.

Process switching is the slowest of the switching methods. With process switching, when a packet arrives at an interface, the system processor is interrupted for the time it takes to copy the packet from the interface buffer to system memory. The processor looks up the Layer 3 destination address for the packet in the routing table to determine the exit interface. The packet is rewritten with the correct header for that interface and copied to the interface. At this time, an entry is also placed in the fast-switching cache so that subsequent packets for the destination address can use the same header. The first packet to a destination is always process switched. Packets which are subject of complex filters are usually also process switched (therefore the filters may have a negative impact on performance).

Fast switching allows higher throughput by switching a packet using an entry in the fast-switching cache that was created when a previous packet to the same destination was processed. With fast switching, a packet is handled immediately, without scheduling an interrupt of the system processor. The fast-switched packets do go through the CPU, but their destination is looked up in a cache that is faster for lookup than the main routing table. Fast switching, for other reasons, reduces the CPU load. Changes in network topology require invalidating the entry/entries in the fast-switching cache.

Optimum switching is similar to fast switching, but is faster, due to an enhanced caching algorithm, and the optimized structure of the optimum switching cache. Optimum switching is only available on routers equipped with a Route Switch Processor (RSP).

When fast- or optimum-switched, packets are copied to packet memory, and the destination network or host is found in the fast-switching cache. This approach means that each time a packet is forwarded, it does not have to wait to be processed until the CPU finishes its previous task. The frame is rewritten and sent to the exit interface that services the destination. Subsequent packets for the same destination use the same switching path. The interface processor computes the Cyclic Redundancy Check (CRC).

The difference between fast switching and optimum switching is that optimum switching uses a more efficient tree structure in its forwarding table to enable faster lookups. In addition, optimum switching takes advantage of the pipelining characteristics of RISC processors, which are used on more recent routing platforms.

Both fast switching and optimum switching are prone to latency and jitter during the processing of the first packet in a flow – before a cache has had a chance to be created. Express Forwarding (CEF), which is the latest development (discussed in Part V), overcomes this issue by using a more consistent amount of CPU resources to process each packet. In the CEF scenario, packets do not queue up for process switching, so routers maintain performance even under high-bandwidth loads.

Autonomous switching is available on routers with an autonomous-switching cache located on the interface processors. Autonomous switching provides faster packet switching by allowing the bus controller to switch packets independently, without having to interrupt the system processor.

Distributed switching is supported on routers that include processor cards or other interface cards that can receive route information from the master RSP to make their own autonomous, multilayer switching decisions. Distributed switching supports very fast throughput because the switching process occurs on the interface card.

Flow-based switching is a switching mode optimized for environments where services must be applied to packets to implement security, QoS features, and traffic accounting. An example of such an environment is the boundary between an enterprise network and the Internet. This type of switching identifies traffic flows between hosts, and then quickly switches packets in these flows at the same time that it applies services. More on flow-based switching is to be found in Part V.

All types of switching get at least some of the forwarding out of the main processor. Typically, the first packet to a destination goes through the main processor and creates a cache entry that will be used for subsequent packets. The only exception is advanced **express forwarding** (discussed in Part V on high-speed routing) when a forwarding table is built based on the routing information beforehand, according to which the first packet is switched thus bypassing the main processor.

9.2.4 Router fault tolerance

The degree to which a system is fault tolerant (able to operate properly even when there are errors) depends mainly on the following two interrelated concepts:

- **Reliability** – the total number of system failures, whether or not the failures resulted in system downtime.

- **Availability** – the percentage of time that a system is operating (that is, the total time the system is operational divided by the total time elapsed since the product was installed or since the last failure). Availability rates for hardware are calculated as follows:

  - *Step 1.* Calculate the Mean Time Between Failure (MTBF) – the amount of time that typically elapses between failures, based on historical data.

  - *Step 2.* Calculate the Mean Time to Repair (MTTR) – how long it typically takes to fix a hardware problem.

  - *Step 3.* Divide the MTBF by the sum of MTBF and MTTR: MTBF / (MTBF + MTTR).

QUICK TIP   **fault**

Fault with regards to router fault tolerance means **hardware or software related system failures** in the router, and not link failures which are normal in regular operations.

There are the following ways how to improve availability:

- **Increase MTBF** – replacing components with high failure rates or by adding redundant components.

■ **Decrease MTTR** – by training on-site technicians in system maintenance and troubleshooting, by contracting with technical experts through a service plan, and by ensuring that there are sufficient spare hardware components on hand.

9.3 Dynamic routing

As introduced above, dynamic routing is based on routing protocols to support routing user data for routed protocols, i.e. to provide a **path determination** function. The main characteristic of every routing protocol, no matter if for IP or IPX, is the underlying **routing algorithm** it uses to exchange the routing information, and build and maintain the routing table. A similarly important feature of the routing protocol is the measurement of route quality and optimality, the **metric**.

9.3.1 Metrics

As mentioned above, one of the characteristic of routing protocols is the way of measuring the **quality** of each possible (alternative) route to the destination network. The criterion or set of criteria is commonly called a **metric**. Routing algorithms have used many different metrics to determine the best route. Sophisticated routing algorithms can base route selection on multiple metrics, combining them in a single (hybrid) metric. All of the following metrics have been used:

■ **Path length (hop count)** – the oldest metric used with protocols measured in number of hops (routers) on the route to the destination; the best route according to the path length metric means the path with the lowest number of hops (routers) on it.

■ **Delay** – the length of time required to move a packet from source to destination through the internet. The delay depends on the bandwidth of the intermediate network links, the port queues at each router along the way, and network congestion on all intermediate network links. (In a simple case delay is derived statically from the network topology without monitoring operational network.) The best route according to the delay metric means the lowest cumulative path delay.

■ **Bandwidth** – available traffic capacity of a link, i.e. the maximum attainable throughput on a link which equals to the lowest bandwidth on the particular route. Paths are compared according to their minimum throughput ('thinnest link') and the best route is the path with the highest value of the minimum throughput across the whole path.

■ **Load** – how network resources are busy on the route to the destination throughput of links and CPU utilization of routers). The load needs to be measured through continuous network monitoring. The best route according to the load metric means the path with the lowest load on the path.

■ **Reliability** – usually described in terms of the bit-error rate of each network link comprising the route, and is monitored continuously. The best route according to the reliability metric means the route with the highest reliability.

■ **Cost** – an arbitrary value (but one usually derived from other 'fix' criteria like bandwidth) assigned to each network segment (router's interface). The best route according to the cost metric means the path with the lowest sum of the costs associated with each link traversed.

QUICK TIP **metric**

A **metric** is a standard of measurement, such as path length, that is used by routing algorithms to determine the optimal path to a destination (routers compare metrics to determine optimal routes). To aid the process of path determination, routing algorithms initialize and maintain **routing tables**, which contain route information including the path metric. Route information and metric varies depending on the routing algorithm used.

Each of these metrics has its advantages and disadvantages. Metrics which are easily derived from the network topology and physical structure are deployed in routing protocols without additional overhead. Metrics which reflect (quasi) momentary network status, like load, require additional reliable monitoring resources. Currently the 'golden middle way' opts for metrics like delay or bandwidth, or cost reflecting those values. Hop count is not a well accepted metric in today's large internets mixing various types of media, nor are the metrics requiring some monitoring. However, some protocols use not a single criterion, but a combination of criteria instead. The result is a more appropriate metric but higher computational overhead and more routing information pieces to exchange.

9.4 Routing algorithms

To aid the process of path determination, routing algorithms initialize and maintain **routing tables**, which contain route information. **Route information** varies depending on the routing algorithm used. Routing algorithms fill routing tables with a variety of information. Destination/next hop associations shown in Figure 9.12 tell a router that a particular destination can be gained optimally by sending the packet to a particular router representing the 'next hop' on the way to the final destination.

When a router receives an incoming packet, it checks the destination address and attempts to associate this address with a next hop. The next hop may be either the ultimate destination host or another router, which executes the same path determination decision process.

Routing tables can also contain other information, such as data about the desirability of a path. Routers compare metrics to determine optimal routes, and these metrics differ depending on the design of the routing algorithm used.

Routers communicate with one another to create and maintain their **routing tables** using the transmission of a variety of messages. The **routing update mes-**

FIGURE 9-12   Destination/next hop association routing table

To reach network	Send to:
27	Node A
57	Node B
17	Node C
24	Node A
52	Node A
16	Node B
26	Node A
–	–
–	–
–	–

sage is one such message that generally consists of all or a portion of a routing table. By analyzing routing updates from all other routers, a router can build a detailed picture of the network topology. A **link-state advertisement**, another example of a message sent between routers, informs other routers of the state of the sender's links. Link information also can be used to build a complete picture of the topology to enable routers to determine optimal routes to network destinations.

Some routing algorithms fill routing tables with **destination/next hop associations** (see Figure 9.12). These associations tell a router that a particular **destination** (usually a particular network, or subnet, but can also be a group of networks or stations, or an individual station) can be gained optimally by sending the packet to the node identified in **next hop**. Other algorithms provide **destination/metric associations**. These associations tell a router that a particular **destination** is some **metric** (sometimes referred to as distance) away. The router compares metrics to determine optimal routes. Metrics differ depending on the design of the routing algorithm that is being used. A variety of common metrics will be introduced and described later in this chapter.

Still other routing algorithms provide **destination/path associations**. These associations relate destinations to the path to be taken to reach that destination. Routers simply forward packets along this path until the destination is achieved.

They are the means by which routers communicate path information with one another. Armed with path information from other routers, routers can determine optimal routes. Routing updates may be sent on a regular basis, or when a network topology change affects route paths, or both.

Routing algorithms can be differentiated based on several key characteristics. First, the particular **goals** of the algorithm designer affect the operation of the resulting routing protocol. Second, there are various **types of routing algorithm**. Each algorithm has a different impact on network and router resources. Finally, routing algorithms use a variety of **metrics** that affect the calculation of optimal routes. The following sections analyze these routing algorithm attributes.

9.4.1 Routing algorithm design goals

Routing algorithms often have one or more of the following design goals (which should also be understood in the case of individual routing protocols):

- **Optimality** – to select the 'best' route, i.e. it must use appropriate criteria to evaluate the quality of each possible route-to-destination network (the metric(s) and metric weightings used to make the calculation).
- **Simplicity** – low overhead and minimal network bandwidth requirements, minimal impact on router's processing and memory resources.
- **Flexibility, robustness, and stability** – capable of functioning well in unusual or unforeseen circumstances such as hardware failures, high load conditions, even incorrect implementations; the ability to quickly and accurately adapt to a variety of network circumstances.
- **Rapid convergence** – fast process of agreement, by all routers, on optimal routes and the recreation and recalculation of routing tables based on the quick dispersion of the new and correct routing information (routing algorithms that converge slowly can cause routing loops).
- **Routing loop avoidance** – arrangement for routing information to get only to the relevant routers and not cause incorrect understanding of the network situation.

9.4.2 Types of routing algorithms

In the beginning there was only one single routing algorithm deployed in routing protocols, distance vector. Further developments have led to the design of more granular algorithms. Today we can choose between two leading algorithms used both in the *de facto* and *de jure* standard routing protocols which will be discussed in subsequent chapters:

- **distance vector** – used in RIP (IP, IPX, and XNS), IGRP (non-standard Cisco Systems protocol for IP), RTP (Banyan VINES), and RTMP (AppleTalk);
- **link states** – used in OSPF (IP) and IS-IS (OSI).

As we will see later, the BGP protocol uses a vector-based algorithm too, but using the path vector instead of a distance vector. The most recent development in distance vector routing algorithms is the **Diffusing Update Algorithm** (DUAL) used in the proprietary routing protocol of Cisco Systems, Enhanced IGRP.

Distance vector algorithm

Distance vector routing was the original form of dynamic routing, but it is still used for routing by many protocols. **RIP** is the routing protocol used initially in XNS (discussed in Chapter 12, section 12.3, where a comparison of all the different approaches to RIP implementation is presented), then adopted for Novell (Chapter 12, section 12.2) and also IP (Chapter 11). However, there are other routing protocols using the distance vector algorithm sharing numerous characteristics with the classical RIP, such as **RTMP** for AppleTalk (Chapter 12, section 12.1) and **RTP** for VINES (Chapter 12, section 12.4), and the proprietary routing protocol for IP, **IGRP**.

Distance vector algorithms, also referred to as **Bellman-Ford**-style routing, require that a router maintain a single routing table of routes from itself to the destination network associated with their metric and forwarding path (denominated by router's outgoing port and/or neighbors' incoming port addresses). The algorithm uses a principle of advertising everything known to all directly connected neighbors and choosing the path with the best metric.

For a high-level view of a distance vector algorithm operation see Figure 9.13.

FIGURE 9-13 Distance vector operation

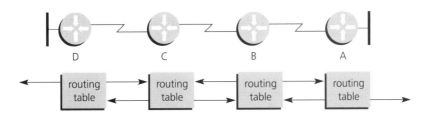

SNAPSHOT	**distance vector algorithm**

In distance vector routing protocols **each node advertises** (usually in form of broadcasting) **all the destinations** it knows about **to its directly attached neighbors**.

The **reachability information** is announced in the form of:

- **distance** – the cost of reaching the particular destination; and
- **vector** – the direction packets should take to reach that destination.

The router begins (when powered up) just with the information provided by the administrator, i.e. on the directly connected segments. Hence the very first routing table reflects only the limited knowledge of the outside world (with the minimum metric for connected links). Once the routing protocol has started, the initial routing information of this new router will be **broadcast** to its neighbors. At the same time the routing information broadcast by the **neighbor**(s) is received. The router compares this new information with its routing table and updates it accordingly: adds newly learned routes (increases the metric received from the neighbor by the distance to the neighbor, or in hops it increases it by 1); ignores routes with the same or worse metrics. This process continues with all the routing information received.

The steps in building the routing table upon the router's start are shown in Figure 9.14. First, the three participating routers in the distance vector routing process will have their initial routing tables manually built by their administrator. These initial routing tables contain only the information about the routes to directly connected networks. With the proper configuration for the particular routing protocol, in the next step the routers perform the first exchange of routing tables by broadcasting its table to its neighbors. The situation after the first exchange is shown in Figure 9.15. Only after the next exchange of routing tables will all the routers in this simple network get to know about all the reachable networks and will know what neighbor to use for forwarding the packets with that particular destination address. The complete routing tables are shown in Figure 9.16. After that the routers will periodically exchange routing tables to be kept up to date about the reachable networks and available neighbors.

At a certain moment the router will 'know' the network, but only from the point of view that it will know it can get to the destination networks via its neighbors. However, it will have no idea about the network topology as the only information gathered and computed reveals what neighbor shall be contacted to forward packets to the destination and how long the route is. The router is therefore capable of routing while knowing only its neighbors and routes through them. Due to this way of passing on the routing information the distance vector based routing is colloquially called *routing by rumor*.

FIGURE 9-14 Distance vector routing: initial stage – basic configuration of routing tables

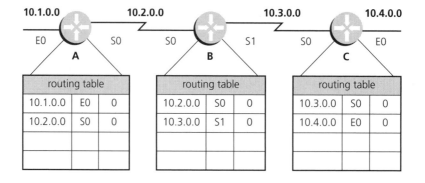

FIGURE 9-15 Distance vector routing: after the first exchange of routing tables

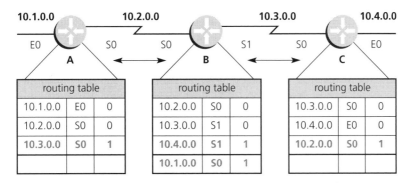

FIGURE 9-16 Distance vector routing: all tables exchanged and routers converge

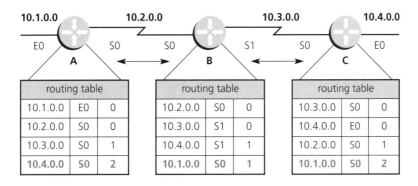

The process of passing on the updated information and the steps required before routers converge is shown in Figure 9.17.

FIGURE 9-17 Distance vector routing: steps after a change in topology

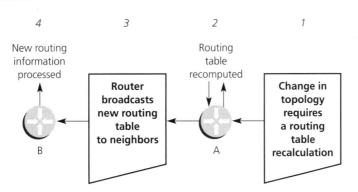

Upon receipt of different metric information included in the routing update from its neighbor, the router has to decide how to handle it: unless the current router's information about the network was 'unreachable,' it will always prefer the new route if it is shorter (with a better metric) and will replace the older information. If the newly announced metric is equal to the one in the routing table, it will ignore it (if it is exactly the same path, through the same neighbor, as was in routing table) or will add it to the routing table for possible load balancing (only some protocols will effectively use more than one route). If the advertised metric is worse, it will have to be taken into account when the route is received from the same neighbor as the routing table says, and the routing table record will be updated, or it will be ignored in cases when the advertised route is an alternative to the currently used one.

In the initial versions of distance vector routing protocols only **periodic exchange** of routing information was used no matter if changes in the network occurred (denominated as routing by propaganda). Later the possibility of sending **triggered updates** upon a change in the situation in the network (link added or down, etc.) was added. Also, as **broadcasting** in current networks is not the behavior of choice, in newer protocols it has been replaced by more selective **multicasting** of the routing information. The routing updates are then sent to the reserved multicast address specifying the routers participating in the routing protocol operation within the network. (For concrete examples of reserved IP multicast addresses deployed in routing protocols see Table 11.11 on page 543.

Once a router calculates each of its distance vectors, it sends the information to each of its neighbor routers on a regular basis, such as each 30 to 90 seconds. If any changes have occurred in the network, the receiving router will modify its routing table and transmit it to each of its neighbors. Typical distance vector routing protocols will send the whole routing table. Advanced distance vector protocols will send just incremental updates. This process will continue until all routers have converged on the new topology.

A good discussion of the general distance vector routing algorithm, its operation, and solutions to problems, is given in RFC 2453.

RFC WATCH	Distance vector routing

RFC 2453 **RIP Version 2**, 1998 (Standard)

Characteristics of distance-vector protocols

- Simple implementation and well proven in internet history.
- Simple metric (usually with some limit in terms of path length).
- Broadcast of routing information (routing table) which could be wasteful of bandwidth.
- Susceptible to routing loops.
- Slow topology convergence in large networks.

Distance vector algorithm problems – routing loops

Distance vector routing is extremely simple; however, with this simplicity comes many potential problems. Due to periodical exchange of routing tables between neighbors the routing information spreads through the network very slowly, step by step, which contributes to slow network convergence.

Unless a remedy is provided inherently by the protocol, a routing loop might easily occur, not allowing some packets to be routed properly due to the incorrect routing information circulating in the network. The symptom of such a routing loop is counting to infinity: while routing updates on the unreachable network are incorrectly replaced by the older routing information, the metric when passed from router to router gradually increases. Unless some limit is given to the metric, which means that network is unreachable (in case of IP RIP it is 16 hops), the routing loop would be infinite. However, this infinity determines the maximum allowed diameter of the particular network and the network administrator should carefully check whether this limit fits the network reality.

A simple example of the potential danger of creating a routing loop (without the preventive action discussed below) is shown in Figure 9.18. All three routers have initially correct information about routes in the simple internet in their routing tables, until router C's E0 interface is detected as down. Router C correctly changes the information about the reachability of subnet 10.4.0.0 (i.e. to non-reachable, down); however, before its periodic update timer forces router C to broadcast all its modified routing table to its neighbors, router B's is quicker (its update timer times out earlier – they are not synchronized in the network). This results in spreading the wrong information about the reachability of subnet 10.4.0.0. Router C thinks that the subnet is reachable via router B and includes this incorrect information in its routing table. This results in a ping-pong of subsequent routing tables exchanged between the two routers, each pointing to the other for reaching subnet 10.4.0.0 while continuously increasing the metric of the path to subnet 10.4.0.0. Unless there is some limit on path length, this process will continue for ever (the routers will count the hops on the path to subnet 10.4.0.0 to infinity). Moreover, the wrong and ever changing information about the route proliferates throughout the network and forces all the routers to change their routing tables with each update cycle.

FIGURE 9-18   Danger of routing loops with distance vector

(a) routers converged

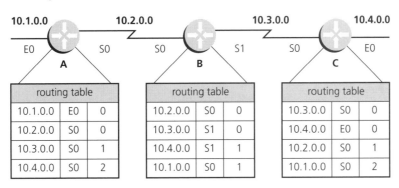

FIGURE 9-18 (Continued)

(b) 10.1.0.0 detected as down to router C

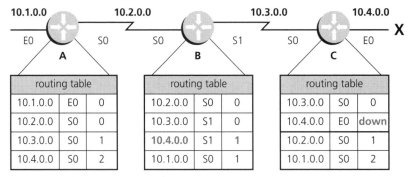

(c) router C gets old information about how to get to 10.1.0.0

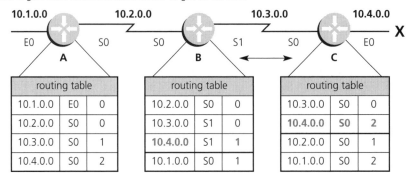

(d) router C advertises the wrong information to 10.1.0.0. as reachable

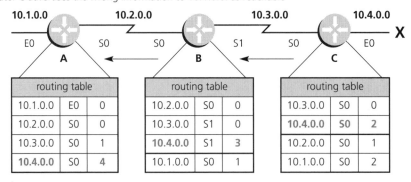

QUICK TIP **network diameter defined**

Network diameter = shortest distance between the two most distant nodes in a network.

Three modifications to the distance vector protocol have been developed in an attempt to reduce the chance of routing loops:

- **Split horizon** – to prevent loops between adjacent routers. **Rule**: Never advertise a route out of the interface through which you learned it!
- **Poisoned reverse** – to prevent larger loops. **Rule**: Once you learn of a route through an interface, advertise it as unreachable back through that same interface.
- **Hold-down timer** – to prevent incorrect route information from entering routing tables.

Split horizon is one of the techniques used to reduce the chance of routing loops. Split horizon states that it is never useful to send information about a route back in the direction from which the information came and therefore routing information should not be sent back to the source from which it came. This technique omits from routing update messages any information about destination routed on the link. The split horizon rule helps prevent two-node routing loops, as well as improving the performance by eliminating unnecessary updates. Split horizon means that an usually incomplete routing table will be advertised out of any interface (not taking into account potential routing filters), and that the routing updates might differ interface by interface when sent by the router.

> **QUICK TIP**   **split horizon**
>
> **Split horizon** prevents loops between adjacent routers (tight loops) by not advertising the routes on the same interface from which they were learned.

Whereas split horizon should prevent routing loops between adjacent routers, reverse poisoned updates are intended to defeat larger routing loops. While the simple split horizon scheme omits routes learned from one neighbor in updates sent to that neighbor, split horizon with **poisoned reverse** includes such routes in updates, but sets their metrics to infinity.

Poisoned reverse thus establishes a single direction through which routes can be reached. An interface should not be traversed in the opposite direction to reach a particular destination. Poisoned reverse ensures this single direction by blocking the other way (by poisoning it with a high cost). Its effect is best seen in the following situation: once a router discovers it has lost contact with a neighboring router, it will immediately forward a routing update with the inoperable route metric set to infinity. Additionally, the router will broadcast the route, with an infinite metric, for several regular routing update periods to ensure all other routers on the internet have received the information and gradually converge. Poisoned reverse is intended to stop large routing loops between multiple routers and is used in conjunction with hold-down timers.

Hold-down is a process in which a router, after receiving destination unreachable information regarding a route from a neighbor router, will not accept new routing information from that router for a specified period of time, to prevent regular update messages from inappropriately reinstating a route that has gone bad. This is due to the possibility that a device that has yet to be informed of a network failure may send a regular update message (indicating that a route that has just gone down is still good) to a device that has just been notified of the network failure. In this case, the latter device now contains (and potentially advertises) incorrect routing information.

Hold-down timer tells routers to hold down for some period of time any changes that might affect routes that went down recently. The hold-down period is usually calculated to be just greater than the period of time necessary to update the entire network with a routing change. Hold-down prevents the count-to-infinity problem. An additional benefit of hold-down is that it prevents a situation where routers begin thrashing, i.e. attempting to converge. This is a common occurrence where a link is flapping from operable to inoperable in a short period of time.

Hold-down timers help in the handling of new routing updates for recently announced unreachable network (marked as such in the routing table) in the following way:

- If at any time before the timer expires an update is received from the same neighbor who sent the unreachable information, indicating that the network is accessible again, the router marks the network as accessible and stops the hold-down timer.

- If an update arrives from a different neighboring router with a better metric than originally recorded for the network (before it became unreachable), the router removes the network from unreachable state, uses the new metric for the route, and stops the hold-down timer.

- If an update is received from a neighbor other than the originating neighbor with a poorer metric, it is ignored (this could be the routing information looped in the internet before all routers converge).

Hold-down timers must be used even when a **triggered updating** regime is used by the protocol alongside the periodic updates. As triggered updates do not happen instantaneously, routers which have not received them yet might issue in the meantime a regular update causing the wrong route to be reinserted in a neighbor's table. With the hold-down timer the neighbor would not accept such information as valid.

While hold-down helps inhibit the formation of routing loops, it may have an adverse impact on convergence. Due to this side effect hold-down is not used in all distance vector routing protocols: for example, IP RIP does not use it, while IGRP does.

Timers

Besides the hold-down timer, distance vector protocols utilize other timers to allow for network convergence and for accurate routing tables:

- **Routing update timer** – period after which each router will send a complete copy of its routing table to all its neighbors.

■ **Route invalid (expiration) timer** – determines how much time must expire without a router having heard about a particular route before that route is considered invalid. When a route is marked invalid, neighbors are notified of this fact.

■ **Route flush timer** – after it expires, the route is removed from the routing table (a process sometimes referred to as garbage collection).

Expiration and garbage collection timers must be chosen to achieve a trade-off between the rapid recognition of a failed router and the prevention of spurious failure indications which can generate extra routing traffic. If the expiration timer is too small, after a single routing update is missed, routing messages are broadcast into the network on a dead route. On the other extreme, too long an expiration timer may result in an undetected dead router and potential black hole in the network.

Link-state routing algorithm

Link-state algorithm is newer than distance vector and was designed to provide fast convergence even in large and complex networks. Routing protocols using the link-state algorithm are, for example, **OSPF** for IP (discussed in Chapter 11), **NLSP** for Novell (described in Chapter 12, section 12.2), and **IS-IS** for OSI CLNP, sections 12.6 and 12.7, and **Integrated IS-IS** for both IP and OSI (discussed in Chapter 12).

Routers using these protocols update each other and learn the **topology** of the internetwork by **flooding** the network with **link-state information**. Link-state data include the cost and identification of only those networks directly connected to each router. Routers send link-state data to all routers on a LAN which in turn use the data to build a complete table of routers and network connections. Hence, gathering the link-state information leads first to the building of a **topology database**. The algorithm employs a replicated distributed database approach.

Routers then have a complete overview of the network topology and may use this information to run the **Shortest Path First** (SPF) algorithm to create a **tree** with a root in the local router and branches reflecting the reachable networks (with nodes being an abstraction of other routers). The SPF algorithm computes network reachability, determining the shortest path to each other reachable network. The router then uses the tree information for its **routing table** where all the best (shortest) paths are listed.

Figure 9.19 shows the high-level overview of the link-state algorithm operation. Link-state protocols exchange routing information via **Link-State Packets** (LSPs) or **Link-State Advertisements** (LSA). An LSP is sent when a link to a neighboring router goes down or comes up, when the cost of a link changes (perhaps due to congestion), or when a new router is inserted into the network. LSPs are sent to reserved multicast addresses dedicated to all SPF routers. Thus other nodes or routers not participating in the protocol do not need to bother about the LSPs.

Once the router receives an update in the form of an LSP, it first compares the information in the packet with its topology database. If the information differs, it has to recompute its routing table and runs the SPF algorithm to do so. At the same time the router has to pass the new information further and forwards the LSP to its neighbors. LSP flooding is a higher priority than SPF calculation. Thus in a short time the routing update may quickly proliferate throughout the

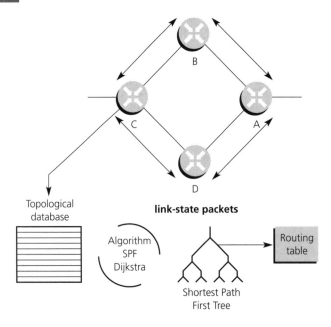

FIGURE 9-19   Overview of link-state algorithm

SNAPSHOT   **link-state algorithms**

Routers running the link-state routing protocol **advertise only their local information** (on the states of the links they are directly attached to) to all the routers in the network (in the form of **multicasting**). The **updates** are **incremental**, with potential periodic refresh, and are **flooded** throughout the network.

---

complete internet. As this operational issue resembles propaganda, sometimes the link-state protocols are referred to as providing *routing by propaganda*. On the other hand, when the LSP received contains information equal to that already included in the topology database (it may be due to the enforced periodic updating mechanism which link-state protocols sometimes use), there is no need to run the SPF algorithm nor forward the LSP further. In other words, when a topology change occurs **every router receives an original or a copy of the LSP** with the information on that change.

After any link-state change, each node has to do an SPF calculation to compute the new topology. This calculation can take a lot of time (seconds) and has poor scaling properties ($n\log n$ to n^2). This has a serious impact on convergence (because the SPF calculation is in series with the LSP propagation) and on overall network stability (because of router CPU saturation). Since the SPF calculation can take a significant amount of time, router implementations impose a limit on how frequently the calculation can be done. In some implementations this limit is fixed (5 seconds) and in some it is changeable but with a granularity of 1 second. This limit essentially adds to the propagation time.

QUICK TIP   **link-state routing updates**

A link-state packet is generated at the point of detection then flooded, unmodified, through the network. It should propagate at near the speed of light plus one store-and-forward delay per hop. (*Note*: in practice, signals propagate at only a fraction of the speed of light – propagation speed varies between (2/3)c (copper) and ~c (fiber).)

Routers have to keep track of all their neighbors, therefore they keep current also their **neighbor database** listing the neighbors' names, their status and metric of the link to the neighbor. The link-state routing algorithm is loop tolerant as loops are eliminated by the SPF algorithm.

LSP distribution is crucial to the correct performance of the link-state protocols. Missing or outdated LSPs create a disagreement among routers as their topology databases are not synchronized and the resulting path decisions are inconsistent. To avoid this undesirable situation, LSPs use time stamps, sequence numbers and acknowledgments, and aging schemes so that they are consistently sent and received. In large-scale internets the topology is better managed through a hierarchical approach and division into areas, for which link-state protocols are particularly suitable while achieving better performance through route aggregation.

Shortest path algorithm

An algorithm invented by Dijkstra (almost 40 years old) is used as the basis for the route calculation by link-state algorithm. It has a computational complexity of the square of the number of nodes, which can be decreased to the number of links in the domain times the log of the number of nodes for sparse networks (networks which are not highly connected). A number of additional optimizations are possible:

- If the routing metric is defined over a small finite field, the factor of $\log n$ may be removed by using data structures which maintain a separate list of systems for each value of the metric rather than sorting the systems by logical distance.

- Updates can be performed incrementally without requiring a complete recalculation. However, a full update must be done periodically to ensure recovery from data corruption, and studies suggest that with a very small number of link changes (perhaps two) the expected computation complexity of the incremental update exceeds the complete recalculation. Thus this annex specifies the algorithm only for the full update.

More recent algorithms can compute changes to SPF trees in time proportional to $\log n$ rather than $n\log n$. This allows a net to scale up to virtually any size while bringing the calculation time down from seconds to microseconds.

Database organization

Database **PATHS** represents an acyclic directed graph of shortest paths from the system S performing the calculation. It is stored as a set of triples of the form <N,d(N),{Adj(N)}>, where

- *N* is a system identifier;
- d(N) is N's distance from S (i.e. the total metric value from N to S);
- {Adj(N)} is a set of valid adjacencies that S may use for forwarding to N.

When a system is placed on PATHS, the path(s) designated by its position in the graph is guaranteed to be the shortest path.

Database **TENT** is a list of triples of the form <N,d(N),{Adj(N)}>, where N, d(N), and {Adj(N)} are as defined above for PATHS. TENT can intuitively be thought of as a tentative placement of a system in PATHS. In other words, the triple <N,x,{A}> in TENT means that if N were placed in PATHS, d(N) would be x, but N cannot be placed on PATHS until it is guaranteed that no path shorter than x exists. Similarly, the triple <N,x,{A,B}> in TENT means that if N were placed in PATHS, then d(N) would be x via either adjacency A or B.

Internal metrics are not comparable to **external metrics**. For external routes (routes to destinations outside of the routing domain), the cost d(N) of the path from N to S may include both internal and external metrics. d(N) may therefore be maintained as a two-dimensional vector quantity (specifying internal and external metric values).

d(N) is initialized to [internal metric = 0, external metric = 0]

In incrementing d(N) by 1, if the internal metric value is less than the maximum value MaxPathMetric, then the internal metric value is incremented by 1 and the external metric value left unchanged; if the internal metric value is equal to the maximum value MaxPathMetric, then the internal metric value is set to 0 and the external metric value is incremented by 1. Note that this can be implemented in a straightforward manner by maintaining the external metric as the high order bits of the distance.

The **basic algorithm**, which builds PATHS from scratch, starts out by putting the system doing the computation on PATHS (no shorter path to SELF can possibly exist). TENT is then pre-loaded from the local adjacency database.

Note that a system is not placed on PATHS unless no shorter path to that system exists. When a system N is placed on PATHS, the path to each neighbor M of N, through N, is examined, as the path to N plus the link from N to M. If <M,*,*> is in PATHS, this new path will be longer, and thus ignored.

If <M,*,*> is in TENT, and the new path is shorter, the old entry is removed from TENT and the new path is placed in TENT. If the new path is the same length as the one in TENT, then the set of potential adjacencies {Adj(M)} is set to the union of the old set (in TENT) and the new set {Adj(N)}. If M is not in TENT, then the path is added to TENT. Next the algorithm finds the triple <N,x,{Adj(N)}> in TENT, with minimal x. When the list of triples for distance Dist is exhausted, the algorithm then increments Dist until it finds a list with a triple of the form <*,Dist,*>.

N is placed in PATHS. We know that no path to N can be shorter than x at this point because all paths through systems already in PATHS have already been considered, and paths through systems in TENT still have to be greater than x because x is minimal in TENT.

When TENT is empty, PATHS is complete.

Any route utilizing an entry with an external metric will always be considered to be less desirable than any entry which uses an internal metric. This implies that in the addition of systems to PATHS, all systems reachable via internal routes are always added before any system reachable via external routes.

Intra- and inter-area routers

Link-state algorithms, due to their complexity and requirements, lead to the deployment of a hierarchy to routing in the network. Building a hierarchy basically reduces the number of link-state advertisements and therefore saves bandwidth and time to compute the Dijkstra algorithm. The reason is that the number of links in a network/domain is $O(n^2)$, and building hierarchies reduces n, and therefore $O(n^2)$ significantly. The hierarchy for link state routing is created by dividing a complex routed network into **areas**. Within each area there are Level 1 routers which will know and share the same topology database for the networks in the particular area. The areas are interconnected by Level 2 routers which will have a topological database for each connected area and will run separate SPF processes for each connected area.

The **decision process algorithm** must be run once for each supported routing metric (i.e. for each supported type of service). A **Level 1 router** (intra-area router) runs the algorithm using the Level 1 LSP database to compute Level 1 paths (for those Level 1 routers which are not Level 2 routers, this includes the path to the nearest attached Level 2 router). Level 2 routers (inter-area routers) also separately run the algorithm using the Level 2 LSP database to compute Level 2 paths. IP-capable Level 2 routers must keep Level 2 internal IP routes separate from Level 2 external IP routes. This implies that routers which are both Level 1 and Level 2 routers, and which support all four routing metrics, must run the SPF algorithm eight times (assuming partition repair is not implemented).

Routing loops with link state algorithms?

In distance vector routing protocols such as RIP in which each node does not have an entire topological view of the network, there is a well-known situation – counting to infinity – where a metric for a looping route is repeatedly incremented and advertised among two or more nodes until it reaches its maximum value.

Even in link-state-type routing protocols such as OSPF in which each node maintains the entire topological database of its routing area or domain, there is a possibility of transient routing loop if synchronization of the database update is not achieved upon topological change.

The more heterogeneous the processing power and/or link speed in the network, the more the routing loop forms and the longer it stays. In addition, if static routing is used in some portion of the network, the routing loop will be less transient.

Comparing distance vector and link-state routing algorithms

A comparison of distance vector and link-state routing algorithms is summarized in Table 9.2.

characteristics of link-state protocols

- Flooding information on link states immediately upon the occurrence of change ensuring fast convergence.
- No or little periodic updates sent.
- Low routing overheads through multicasting of routing information (but heavy load in the internet at the initial routing discovery process).
- Intense CPU utilization (SPF algorithm cycles) and memory requirements (databases) for the router.
- Suitable for rules-based routing, security functions, and support of type of service (ToS) or quality of service (QoS).
- Resistant to forming routing loops.
- Router-to-router authentication.

TABLE 9-2   Comparison of distance vector and link-state routing algorithms

	Distance vector	*Link state*
To whom	Neighbors	All routers
When	Periodically	Immediately after change
How	By broadcast	By multicast
What	(Almost complete) routing table	Information on changed connected links
How much	Proportional to number of network addresses (aggregates) routed within the network	Proportional to topology change

QUICK TIP   **distance vectors vs. link-state routing**

Distance vector protocols exchange their routing tables (subject to split horizon) with their neighbors, add their incremental link costs to the routes received, and pick the best routes.

Link state protocols exchange information about routers and directly connected links, including accurate copies of this information from non-neighboring routers, and independently create routing tables from their topology databases using the Dijkstra algorithm for the computation of the shortest path.

Diffusing update algorithm

The **Diffusing Update Algorithm** (DUAL) was developed at SRI International by Dr J. J. Garcia-Luna-Aceves. It is the algorithm used to obtain loop-freedom at every instance throughout a route computation. This allows all routers involved in a topology change to synchronize. Routers that are not affected by topology changes are not involved in the recomputation. The convergence time with DUAL rivals that of any other existing routing protocol.

The **DUAL finite state machine** embodies the decision process for all route computations. It tracks all routes advertised by all **neighbors**. The distance information, known as a metric, is used by DUAL to select efficient loop-free paths. DUAL selects routes to be inserted into a routing table based on **feasible successors.** A successor is a neighboring router used for packet forwarding that has a least-cost path to a destination that is guaranteed not to be part of a routing loop. When there are no feasible successors but there are neighbors advertising the destination, a **recomputation** must occur. This is the process where a new successor is determined. The amount of time it takes to recompute the route affects the convergence time. Even though the recomputation is not processor-intensive, it is advantageous to avoid recomputation if it is not necessary. When a topology change occurs, DUAL will test for feasible successors. If there are feasible successors, it will use any it finds in order to avoid any unnecessary recomputation.

The routing table keeps a list of the computed costs of reaching networks. The topology table keeps a list of all routes advertised by neighbors. For each network, the router keeps the real cost of getting to that network and also keeps the advertised cost from its neighbor. In the event of a failure, convergence is instant if a feasible successor can be found. A neighbor is a feasible successor if it meets the feasibility condition set by DUAL. DUAL finds feasible successors by performing the following computations:

- Determines membership of *V1* – the set of all neighbors whose advertised distance to network x is less than Feasible Distance (FD – defined as the best metric during an active-to-passive transition).

- Calculates *Dmin* – the minimum computed cost to network x.

- Determines membership of *V2* – the set of neighbors that are in V1 whose computed cost to network x equals **Dmin**. The feasibility condition is met when **V2** has one or more members. The concept of feasible successors is illustrated in Figure 9.20. Consider Router A's topology table entries for Network 7. Router B is the successor with a computed cost of 31 to reach Network 7, compared to the computed costs of Router D (230) and Router H (40).

If Router B becomes unavailable, Router A will go through the following three-step process to find a feasible successor for Network 7:

- **Step 1**. Determining which neighbors have an advertised distance to Network 7 that is less than Router A's feasible distance (FD) to Network 7. The FD is 31 and Router H meets this condition. Therefore, Router H is a member of **V1**.

- **Step 2.** Calculating the minimum computed cost to Network 7. Router H provides a cost of 40, and Router D provides a cost of 230. **Dmin** is, therefore, 40.

- **Step 3.** Determining the set of neighbors that are in V1 whose computed cost to Network 7 equals **Dmin** (40). Router H meets this condition.

FIGURE 9-20 DUAL feasible successor

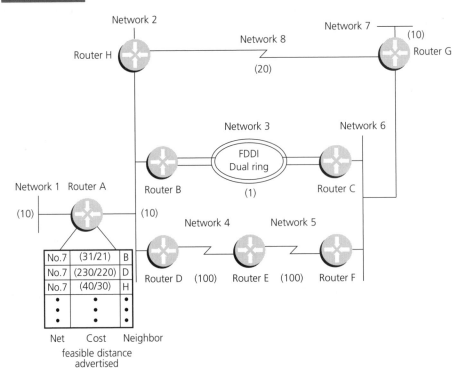

The feasible successor is Router H which provides a least cost route of 40 from Router A to Network 7. If Router H now also becomes unavailable, Router A performs the following computations:

- **Step 1**. Determines which neighbors have an advertised distance to Network 7 that is less than the FD for Network 7. Because both Routers B and H have become unavailable, only Router D remains. However, the advertised cost of Router D to Network 7 is 220, which is greater than Router A's FD (31) to Network 7. Router D, therefore, cannot be a member of **V1**. The FD remains at 31 – the FD can only change during an active-to-passive transition, and this did not occur. There was no transition to active state for Network 7; this is known as a local computation.

- **Step 2**. Because there are no members of **V1**, there can be no feasible successors. Router A, therefore, transitions from passive to active state for Network 7 and queries its neighbors about Network 7. There was a **transition to active**; this is known as a **diffusing computation**.

The following example and graphics further illustrate how DUAL supports virtually instantaneous convergence in a changing internetwork environment. In Figure 9.21, all routers can access one another and Network N. The computed cost to reach other routers and Network N is shown. For example, the cost from Router E to Router B is 10. The cost from Router E to Network N is 25 (cumulative of 10 + 10 + 5 = 25).

FIGURE 9-21 DUAL example: (a) initial network connectivity

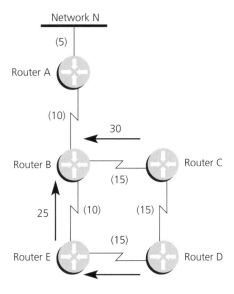

In Figure 9.22, the connection between Router B and Router E fails. Router E sends a multicast query to all of its neighbors and puts Network N into an active state.

FIGURE 9-22 DUAL example: (b) sending queries

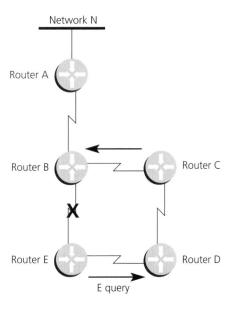

Next, as illustrated in Figure 9.23, Router D determines that it has a feasible successor. It changes its successor from Router E to Router C and sends a reply to Router E.

FIGURE 9-23 DUAL example: (c) switching to a flexible successor

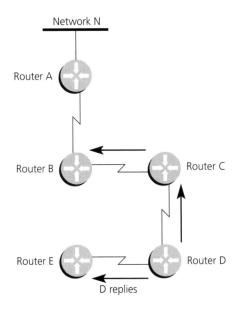

Router A, Router B, and Router C were not involved in route recomputation. Router D recomputed its path to Network N without first needing to learn new routing information from its downstream neighbors.

9.4.3 The choice is yours

Some of a network manager's goals in choosing and configuring a routing protocol include the following:

- achieving optimal path selection for traffic;
- fast convergence – or the rate at which routers are able to make decisions based on network changes;
- scalability;
- minimizing update traffic among devices in order to keep network overhead low.

There is no single best protocol (if there are alternatives) or best algorithm to use for routing each network protocol. The final choice relies on many aspects, including protocol **performance, scalability, implementation and operation requirements**, and **type of environment** (multivendor, multiprotocol, etc.). Therefore we need to understand the differences not only between the two leading routing algorithms, but individual protocols which are using them.

9.5 Scalability of routing protocols

Routing protocols scale well if their resource use grows less than linearly with the growth of the network. Three critical resources are used by routing protocols:

■ **Memory** – routing protocols use memory to store routing tables and topology information. Route summarization cuts memory consumption for all routing protocols. Keeping routed network areas small reduces the memory consumption for hierarchical routing protocols.

■ **CPU usage** – protocol-dependent. Some routing protocols use CPU cycles to compare new routes to existing routes. Other protocols use CPU cycles to regenerate routing tables after a topology change. In most cases, the latter technique will use more CPU cycles than the former. For link-state protocols, keeping areas small and using summarization reduces CPU requirements by reducing the effect of a topology change and by decreasing the number of routes that must be recomputed after a topology change.

■ **Bandwidth usage** – also protocol-dependent. Three key issues determine the amount of bandwidth (together with CPU) a routing protocol consumes:
  – *when* routing information is sent – periodic updates are sent at regular intervals while flash updates are sent only when a change occurs;
  – *what* routing information is sent – complete updates contain all routing information while partial updates contain only changed information;
  – *where* routing information is sent – flooded updates are sent to all routers while bounded updates are sent only to routers that are affected by a change.

Distance vector protocols such as RIP and IGRP broadcast their complete routing table periodically, whether or not the routing table has changed. When the network is stable, distance vector protocols behave well but waste bandwidth because of the periodic sending of routing table updates, even when no change has occurred. When a failure occurs in the network, distance vector protocols do not add excessive load to the network and do not consume excessive amounts of CPU resources, but on the other hand they take a long time to reconverge to an alternative path or to flush a bad path from the network.

Link-state routing protocols such as OSPF were designed to address the limitations of distance vector routing protocols (slow convergence and unnecessary bandwidth usage). Link-state protocols are more complex than distance vector protocols, and running them adds to the router's overhead. The additional overhead (in the form of memory utilization and bandwidth consumption when link-state protocols first start up) constrains the number of neighbors that a router can support and the number of neighbors that can be in an area (a logical set of network segments and their attached devices).

When the network is stable, link-state protocols minimize bandwidth usage by sending updates only when a change occurs. A hello mechanism ascertains accountability of neighbors. When a failure occurs in the network, link-state protocols flood link-state advertisements (LSAs) throughout an area. LSAs cause every router within the failed area to recalculate routes. The fact that LSAs need to be flooded throughout the area in a failure situation, and the fact that all routers recalculate routing tables subsequently, constrains the number of routers that can be in an area.

9.6 Security

Controlling access to network resources is a primary concern in today's internets. Some routing protocols provide techniques that can be used as part of a security strategy. With some routing protocols, you can insert a filter on the routes being advertised so that certain routes are not advertised in some parts of the network.

Some routing protocols can authenticate routers that run the same protocol. Authentication mechanisms are protocol specific. Authentication can increase network stability by preventing unauthorized routers or hosts from participating in the routing protocol, whether those devices are attempting to participate accidentally or deliberately.

9.7 Load-sharing and load-balancing

The majority of modern routing protocols support multiple paths to the same destination. These **multi-path algorithms** permit traffic multiplexing over multiple lines; single-path algorithms do not. The advantages of multi-path algorithms are obvious; they can provide substantially better throughput and redundancy.

Load-balancing is more difficult than load-sharing over available parallel paths to the destination. Over equal cost paths, it ensures that an equal amount of traffic flows over each path. At best, this can be controlled in the outward direction only, and still may not be very precise. Per-packet load-balancing among different autonomous systems (exterior IP routing) is likely to cause terrible out-of-sequence effects. Per-destination load-balancing works well only to the extent that the essentially identical amount of traffic goes to each destination. Per-source-destination-pair is probably the best available method.

Load sharing does not pretend to be as precise as load balancing, and thus is more likely to be realistic. The easiest way to add bandwidth in a backbone network is to implement additional links. Routers provide built-in **load-sharing** (sometimes even load-balancing) for multiple links and paths. In some rare routing protocol cases, the paths need not be of equal cost.

Within IP, routers provide load-balancing on both a per-packet and a per-destination basis, as well as on a per-source-destination-pair basis. **Per-packet load-balancing** distributes the packets across the possible routes in a manner proportional to the route metrics. With equal-cost routes, this is equivalent to a round-robin scheme. One packet or destination (depending on switching mode) is distributed to each possible path. **Per-destination load-balancing** distributes packets across the possible routes based on destination. Each new destination is assigned the next available route. This technique tends to preserve packet order. For per-destination load-balancing, each router uses its route cache to determine the output interface. **Per-source-destination-pair** load-balancing balances the paths taken based on each communication between the source and destination.

Very few routing protocols provide for **unequal-cost load-balancing**. The router uses metrics to determine which paths the packets will take; the amount of load-balancing can be adjusted by the user. The router will try to 'balance' the traffic over the individual paths based on their proportional throughput.

9.8 Hierarchical routing

Some routing algorithms operate in a flat space, while others utilize and/or impose routing hierarchies, creating a logical topology (over the physical network topology) related to the protocol operation (for example, OSPF). In a **flat routing system**, all routers are peers of all others. In a **hierarchical routing system**, some routers form what amounts to a routing backbone. Packets from non-backbone routers travel to the backbone routers, where they are sent through the backbone until they reach the general area of the destination. At this point, they travel from the last backbone router through zero or more non-backbone router(s) to the final destination.

Routing systems often designate logical groups of nodes called domains, autonomous systems, or areas. In **hierarchical systems**, some routers in a domain can communicate with routers in other domains, while others can only communicate with routers within their domain. In very large networks, additional hierarchical levels may exist. Routers at the highest hierarchical level form the routing backbone.

The primary advantage of **hierarchical routing** is its ability to limit the pervasiveness of routing exchanges. Hierarchical routing limits routing exchanges because it mimics the organization of most companies and therefore supports their traffic patterns very well. Most network communication occurs within small company groups (domains). **Intra-domain routers** only need to know about other routers within their domain, so their routing algorithms may be simplified. Depending on the routing algorithm being used, routing update traffic may be reduced accordingly.

Routing protocol strategy within a network should balance choosing a protocol that successfully handles the particular type of network with simplicity of installation and minimal overhead. From there, it is up to the network manager to remain alert when making configuration changes to optimize performance so as to ensure that routers remain in continual and consistent communication.

CHAPTER 10

TCP/IP overview

TCP/IP history dates back to the 1960s and 1970s, the very beginning of the networking history, when the first packet switched network, ARPANET, started. The core TCP/IP protocols became standards in the Internet community in 1980–81 and have remained unchanged since then. (There are numerous publications devoted completely to TCP/IP which provide a detailed history and complete overview. See Appendices B and E for related links, and the numerous IETF informational documents on the Internet, its architecture, tools, e.g. RFC 1180, 1958, 2151.)

RFC WATCH	TCP/IP and Internet basics

RFC 1180 **TCP/IP Tutorial**, 1991 (Informational)

RFC 1958 **Architectural Principles of the Internet**, 1996 (Informational)

RFC 2151 **A Primer On Internet and TCP/IP Tools and Utilities**, 1997 (Informational)

Before we fully concentrate on the routing in the most deployed protocol stack in the world, **Transmission Control Protocol/Internet Protocol** (TCP/IP), we will first discuss the protocol stack with the emphasis on IPv4 and IPv6 addressing.

10.1 TCP/IP architecture

TCP/IP comprises four layers (see Figure 10.1 for a comparison with the OSI reference model):

■ **application layer** – performing the functions of the RM-OSI session, presentation and application layers;

■ **transport layer** – providing similar services as the OSI transport layer (offers two transport protocols: TCP or UDP);

■ **internet layer** – performing similar functions to the OSI network layer, but, only through a single, unreliable connectionless network protocol (IP) accompanied by a number of supporting protocols (ARP, RARP, ICMP, IRDP) and routing protocols;

FIGURE 10-1 Comparison of TCP/IP architecture with OSI reference model

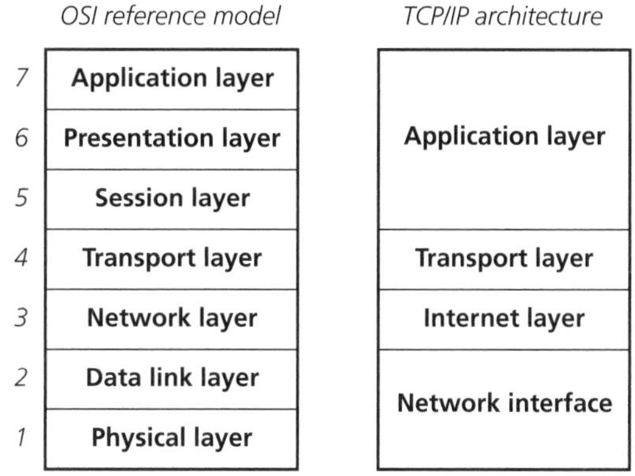

	OSI reference model	TCP/IP architecture
7	Application layer	Application layer
6	Presentation layer	
5	Session layer	
4	Transport layer	Transport layer
3	Network layer	Internet layer
2	Data link layer	Network interface
1	Physical layer	

■ **network interface** – providing the lower layers' services (those of the physical and link layers) of the OSI model.

All TCP/IP protocol specifications and related supportive information is publicly available in the form of **Request for Comments** (RFC), published on-line by the IETF (for details on the standardization process within the Internet community see Appendix B), to which references will be made frequently in the following text. Only some of the protocols specified have become Internet **standards** (*de facto* standards from the official international standardization point of view). Of the remaining vast majority of RFCs some are proposed or draft standards which are at some stage of the Internet community acceptance process (the current RFC 3000 describes the standardization process, various types of RFC states and status, and lists all standard, network-specific standard, draft, and proposed standard protocols). Due to the speed at which internetworking evolves draft proposals will also sometimes be referred to. Caution must be taken as this reference information may change and become obsolete or updated, while only the latest approved information is valid at all times.

RFC WATCH   **TCP/IP standards**

RFC 3000 **Internet Official Protocol Standards**, 2001 (Standard)

The RFCs of the standard protocols are shown in Figure 10.2 which describes the relationships between the major protocols within the TCP/IP protocol stack and the position of the routing protocols as for their encapsulation and underlying service dependence (routing is inherently a layer 3 service). Besides providing RFC numbers Figure 10.2 serves as a summary of other well known reference information. (For a list of well known reference numbers and their explanation see Appendix E.)

FIGURE 10-2 TCP/IP protocol stack

HTTP RFC 2616 port #80	FTP RFC 959 port #20/21	TELNET RFC 854 port #23	SMTP RFC 2821 port #25	DNS RFC 2821 port #53	TFTP RFC 1350 port #69	DHCP RFC 2131 port #546/547	RPC RFC 1831 port #111	BOOTP RFC 2132 port #67/68	SNMP RFC 1157 port #161/162

Border Gateway Protocol (**BGP**) RFC 1771 (port #179)	Routing Information Protocol (**RIPv2**) RFC 2453 (port #520/521)
TRANSMISSION CONTROL PROTOCOL (**TCP**) RFC 793 (protocol #6)	**USER DATAGRAM PROTOCOL** (**UDP**) RFC 768 (protocol #17)

Open Shortest Path First (**OSPFv2**) RFC 2328 (protocol #89)	**INTERNET CONTROL MESSAGE PROTOCOL** (**ICMP**) RFC 792 (protocol #1)	Internet Group Management Protocol (**IGMP**) RFC 2236 (protocol #2)	(Enhanced) Interior Gateway Routing Protocol (**IGRP**) (protocol #88)

INTERNET PROTOCOL (**IP**) RFC 791

ADDRESS RESOLUTION PROTOCOL (**ARP**) RFC 826	**REVERSE RESOLUTION PROTOCOL** (**RARP**) RFC 903

Ethernet RFC 894 802 networks RFC 1042 FDDI RFC 1188, NetBIOS RFC 1088 Arcnet RFC 1201 X.25 RFC 1356

In the following we will discuss primarily the internet layer but will also consider the principles of the transport layer and its protocols. Briefly we will have a look at some of the commonly used application protocols. As regards the bottom layer, the network interface, IP can run on all widely spread networks and transmission media (Figure 10.2 shows some of the possibilities with related RFCs specifying the IP issues above a particular medium). We have discussed these topics in Part I and will not revisit them again here.

Multicast and mobile issues will be discussed in Chapter 11 on IP routing.

10.2 Internet layer

The **internet layer** comprises the following protocols:

■ **network protocol** (IP) – for transferring user data (IP packets called datagrams by the Internet community);

■ **control protocol** (ICMP) – for control messages supporting the best-effort network service provision;

■ **mapping protocols** (ARP and RARP) – for dynamic mapping between logical (network) addresses and physical (MAC) addresses;

■ **group management protocol** – for enabling the effective communication within groups of TCP/IP stations;

■ **routing protocols** (OSPF, IGRP) – for supporting the routing function of IP datagrams. (Note that as a hangover from the beginning of the Internet and TCP/IP development, the term **gateway** might be still heard – or read – in place of router.)

The **Internet protocol** (IP) provides a connectionless best-effort **datagram** (a packet) delivery service that performs **addressin**g, routing, and **control functions** for transmitting and receiving datagrams over a network. IP encapsulates the TCP or UDP segments (or other payload type, as will be discussed later) into datagrams. Each datagram includes its **source and destination addresses**, control information, and any actual data passed from or to the host layer. IP relies on the upper layer protocols and network applications to provide retransmissions if needed (therefore mostly it is work for end systems to recover rather than routers in the network, unless they are configured slightly differently, e.g. as X.25 switches). IP also has the ability to **fragment** a datagram if it is determined that it is too large for the particular network. This might result in a costly process as the sending device has to fragment the packet and the receiving device must reassemble the fragmented packet before passing it up to the transport layer. Fragmentation done on the way through the network (by routers) requires the **reassembly** of datagrams at the receiving end. Routers never reassemble IP datagrams. In fact IP datagrams may get (increasingly) fragmented traversing the network, but are never reassembled in the network itself, only by the destination end stations.

The standard version 4 of IP is documented in RFC 791 and is the primary network-layer protocol in the Internet protocol suite. IP version 6, which is still at the stage of proposed standard and is waiting broader deployment, will be discussed later in this chapter.

RFC WATCH	IP protocol

RFC 791 **Internet Protocol**, J. Postel, 1981 (Standard)

10.3 IP version 4 addressing

All the Internet-connected networks use a consistent, global addressing scheme. Each host, or server, must have a globally unique IP address. In the case of a large number of network interfaces, each interface should have its own, unique IP address (although exceptions in terms of unnumbered interfaces do exist). Within

IP it is thus interfaces that get addresses, not the network devices as a whole. All (inter)network devices with more than one port (such as routers and possibly servers) will have more than one IP address assigned. Interfaces may have multiple IP addresses, but each IP address must be assigned to only one interface (worldwide), with the exception of non-routed (reserved) addresses and multicast addresses (see below).

Global IP addresses are assigned on a hierarchical basis; worldwide this function used to be undertaken by InterNIC (Network Information Center) which distributed the responsibility to regional (continental) centers such as the American Registry for Internet Numbers (ARIN), Réseaux IP Européens (RIPE), and the Asia Pacific Network Information Center (APNIC). These are responsible for assigning unique address space to Internet Service Providers (ISPs) and large corporations within the region of their responsibility. See Appendix B for their Web site addresses.

RFC WATCH IP address management

RFC 1166 **Internet Numbers**, 1990 (Informational)

RFC 2050 **Internet Registry IP Allocation Guidelines**, 1996 (Best Current Practice)

RFC 1917 **An Appeal to the Internet Community to Return Unused IP Networks (Prefixes) to the IANA**, 1996 (Best Current Practice)

Each device's interface supporting IP is assigned a **single and unique IP address,** usually administratively unless DHCP, BOOTP, or RARP is used. Even when DHCP is used, IP addresses are administratively assigned to tables (IP to MAC). There may be exceptions to this: in the case of point-to-point lines unnumbered interfaces (without IP addresses) may be supported depending on vendor implementation, or more than one IP address is assigned to the single interface (routers sometimes connect to the IP segment which bears two IP network addresses and the interface must be assigned two distinct addresses each belonging to the individual network).

SNAPSHOT IP version 4 addressing

IP version 4 addresses uniquely all network interfaces with a 32-bit logical address that is divided into two main parts: the **network number** and the **host number**. The IP address is usually expressed in **decimal dotted notation**. IP addresses may generally be of five classes, A–E; however, valid IP addresses for network interfaces are always of **class A, B or C** only. The specific address for the network has all zeros in the host portion of the address, while all ones in the host part of the address signifies the broadcast address within the network.

Private TCP/IP networks may not follow the rule of global uniqueness; however, where there is a high possibility of future connection to the Internet several IP address ranges will be dedicated for this purpose as will be mentioned below.

The **IP address** consists of 32 bits usually displayed in so-called **decimal dotted notation**, i.e. 32 bits divided into four fields of one octet each (in decimal notation) delimited by dots (the official description of IP addresses is found in RFC 1166). However, binary or hexadecimal presentation of IP addresses is also used but less frequently.

An IP address has two parts:

- **network number**;
- **host number**.

10.3.1 IPv4 address classes

There is no constant rule on how many bits are always used for the network and host portions of the address. Instead, IP from its inception has applied a concept of address classes where each has a unique address format made up from the 32 bits. There are five **IP address classes** which specify the structure and use of the addresses. The address classes are as follows (see also Table 10.1):

TABLE 10-1 IP address classes reference

IP address class	Address format	High-order bits (binary)	First-address octet range (decimal)	Range of network address (decimal)	Number of networks/ number of hosts
A	N.H.H.H	0...	1–126 (127)	1.0.0.0– 126.0.0.0	$126/(2^{(24)} - 2)$
B	N.N.H.H	10..	128–191	128.0.0.0– 191.255.0.0	$2^{14}/(2^{(16)} - 2)$
C	N.N.N.H	110.	192–223	192.0.0.0– 223.255.255.0	$2^{21}/254$
D (multicast)	N/a	1110	224–239	224.0.0.0– 239.255.255.255	N/a
E (experimental)	N/a	1111	240–254	240.0.0.0– 254.255.255.255	N/a

Notes: N = Network number, H = Host number. Number of hosts is restricted by reserving two addresses: one is reserved for the broadcast address (all ones in host portion), and one address is reserved for the network (all zeros).

■ **Class A** – uses the first octet for the network number and the remaining three octets for the host number. The first octet ranges in decimal value from 1 to 127 (the unique sign for a class A address is that the first octet starts with binary *0*), which allows up to 126 regular class A networks (network 127.0.0.0 is reserved for loopback address) and up to ($2^{(24)} - 2$) hosts per network.

■ **Class B** – dedicates the first two octets for the network number and the last two octets for the host number. The first octet ranges in decimal value from 128 to 191 (the first octet starts with binary *10*), which allows up to 2^{14} networks and up to ($2^{(16)} - 2$) hosts per network.

■ **Class C** – uses the first three octets for the network number and the last octet for the host number. The first octet ranges in decimal value from 192 to 223 (the first octet starts with binary *110)*, which allows up to 2^{21} networks, and 254 hosts per network.

■ **Class D** – reserved for group addressing (for multicast), as described formally in RFC 1112. In class D addresses, the four highest-order bits are set to *1110* hence in decimal the first octet ranges from 224 to 239.

■ **Class E** – reserved for future use, with the four highest-order bits are set to *1111* and therefore the first octet noted in decimal ranges from 240 to 255.

RFC WATCH   IP multicasting

RFC 1112 **Host extensions for IP multicasting**, 1989 (Standard)

Of the five address classes described above, only IP addresses of class A, B, and C are valid for addressing individual interfaces. More precisely yet, source IP addresses in the IP datagrams in regular TCP/IP networks and the Internet may be only of class A to C. Destination IP addresses may additionally be of class D, the multicast type address.

Not all possible addresses in the host part of the IP address are valid interface addresses. The host part with all binary *0*s is reserved to address the **network**, while all *1*s specifies the **broadcast** address for the network, i.e. the highest available IP address for the particular segment determines the broadcast address.

Several early IP implementations do not use the current broadcast address standard. Instead, they use the old standard, which calls for all zeros instead of all ones to indicate broadcast addresses. Many of these implementations do not recognize an all-ones broadcast address and fail to respond to the broadcast correctly. Others forward all-ones broadcasts, which causes a serious network overload known as a broadcast storm. Implementations that exhibit these problems include systems based on versions of BSD UNIX prior to version 4.3.

The router support for Internet broadcasts generally complies with RFC 919 and RFC 922; however, it does not support multisubnet broadcasts as defined in RFC 922.

RFC WATCH   **IP broadcasting**

RFC 919 **Broadcasting Internet Datagrams**, 1984 (Standard)

RFC 922 **Broadcasting Internet Datagrams in the Presence of Subnets**, 1984 (Standard)

Private IP addresses and NAT

There are several reserved addresses (address ranges) in classes A to C. RFC 1918 sets aside three address blocks for use solely in **private networks**:

- class A network **10.0.0.0** (10/8 using CIDR notation explained later);
- class B networks **172.16.0.0 through 172.31.0.0** (172.16/12 using CIDR notation);
- class C networks **192.168.0.0 through 192.168.255.0** (192.168/16 using CIDR notation).

Originally, these reserved address blocks were intended for use in networks not connected to the Internet, or for isolated test or experimental networks. But the shortage has prompted networkers to use these blocks, hiding the private addresses behind firewalls or packet-filtering routers.

The key is **network address translation** (NAT), which is defined in RFC 3022. A firewall using NAT essentially takes all private addresses of outbound traffic (traffic from the internal network to the Internet) and converts the source address to that of the router or firewall's external interface (or to a series of addresses if there are multiple external interfaces). For inbound traffic, the process works in reverse: the NAT box converts destination addresses to those used by the private network. But address conversion is just one of the advantages of NAT. Security is perhaps the more important one as attackers cannot reach machines they do not see (the private addresses are invisible in the public Internet).

NAT on a router is configured on inside/outside boundaries such that the outside (usually the Internet) sees one or a few registered addresses while the inside could have any number of hosts using a private addressing scheme. To maintain the integrity of the address translation scheme, NAT must be configured on every boundary router between the inside (private) network and the outside (public) network. One of the advantages of NAT from a security standpoint is that the systems on the private network cannot receive an incoming IP connection from the outside network unless the NAT gateway is specifically configured to allow the connection. The disadvantage is that the whole 'hidden' internet is seen as a single address.

RFC WATCH   private addressing and NAT

RFC 1918 **Address Allocation for Private Internets**, 1996 (Best Current Practice)

RFC 3022 **Traditional IP Network Address Translator** (Traditional NAT), 2001 (Informational)

10.3.2 Subnetting

Due to obvious limitations in the IP version 4 addressing space (32 bits with reserved formats for global addressing) so-called subnetting was introduced. IP networks can be divided into smaller networks called **subnets** whose addressing uses a continuous set of bits from the left side of the host portion of the IP address (the network portion stays untouched). Subnetting provides the network administrator with several benefits, including extra flexibility, more efficient use of network addresses, and the capability of containing broadcast traffic (a broadcast will not cross a router). Subnets are under local administration.

Without subnetting, the IP address could be easily decoded by its format (number of bits used for the network and the rest for the host) by just looking at its first octet. However, with subnetting the individual IP address is not complete without an additional number – a **subnet mask** – indicating how many bits are used to address the network and subnet. The subnet mask is a 32-bit number where all the (contiguous) bits in the network and subnet portion are set to one and all the bits in the host number are set to zero. Without subnetting the network mask of the address is the default for each class. The default subnet mask for an address of class A that has no subnetting is 255.0.0.0, for a class B address it is 255.255.0.0, while the default subnet mask for class C addresses is 255.255.255.0.

The common current notation of a subnet mask is to specify a number of bits used both for the network and subnet portions of the address after a slash following the concrete IP address. For example, 132.23.67.5/21 means that IP address 132.23.67.5 belongs to the network 132.23.0.0 which is subnetted by five bits of the third octet, i.e. the IP address sits in the subnet 132.23.64.0.

RFC WATCH   subnetting

RFC 950 **Internet Standard Subnetting Procedure**, 1985 (Standard)

Subnetting (standard procedure defined in RFC 950) provides for better usage of the address space; however, it is still limited by the address class boundaries. In order to avoid conflict with reserved addresses for the network itself and a broadcast in it, the following regime is used for **subnetting**:

- **Class A** – the first octet is reserved for the network number (bits 1–8); bits 10–30 of the IP address may then be used for subnetting, and the rest for host addressing. Each class A address provides for up to 2^{21} subnet numbers.
  - Default subnet mask: 255.0.0.0
  - Range of (used) subnet masks: (255.192.0.0–255.255.255.252) or (/10–/30)

- **Class B** – two octets are reserved for the network number (bits 1–16); bits 18–30 may then be used for subnetting, and the rest for host addressing. (Note that if we want to use the maximum pool of subnet addresses, we can expect only two hosts addressed per each subnet!) Each class B address provides for up to 2^{13} subnet numbers.
  - Default subnet mask: 255.255.0.0
  - Range of (used) subnet masks: (255.255.192.0–255.255.255.252) or (/18–/30)

- **Class C** – three octets are reserved for the network number (bits 1–24), bits 26–30 may then be used for subnetting, and the rest for host addressing. Each class C address provides for up to 2^{5} subnet numbers.
  - Default subnet mask: 255.255.255.0
  - Range of (used) subnet masks: (255.255.255.192–255.255.255.252) or (/26–/30).

The number of bits for subnetting and the resulting address space for addressing subnets and hosts within them is shown in Table 10.2. Note that the table offers all the options for subnetting class B (from two bits used for subnetting up to the maximum 14 bits). For classes A and C the subnet masks will be similar to the number of hosts available within a subnet, but the number of available subnets will differ.

As some, especially older, routing protocols are quite peculiar about under-standing and advertising network and subnet addresses with masks, we will strictly use the distinction between the IP **network** (of a certain address class) and **subnet address** (within a network of a certain address class).

As we noted earlier, IPv4 addresses network segments and interfaces connect-ing to them. Due to a lack of addresses some interfaces sometimes stay unnumbered, i.e. they do not have an address assigned. It is possible to do this only on point-to-point links where assigning an individual subnet address (espe-cially when no variable length subnet mask is used) may be quite a luxury for addressing just two end stations. IP unnumbered interfaces require both ends of the point-to-point link to be unnumbered, and similarly the whole physical net-work segment. At the same time, for troubleshooting and management purposes the routing device must have at least one interface properly addressed (to which the unnumbered interface might refer).

The opposite extreme to not having any IP address assigned within an IP net-work is to have more addresses per network segment or even interface. An example would be a single Ethernet segment which for security reasons needed to 'separate' two groups of stations attached to it. This could be done by using two (or more) IP subnet addresses per the segment to which each of the stations has an IP address assigned belonging to one of the IP subnets. This mechanism is sometimes called **multinetting**. Multiple addresses appearing on a segment require all routers to have per the connecting interface assigned addresses belonging to all subnet numbers deployed so that they might route between the subnets.

TABLE 10-2 Subnetting reference chart (class B)

Number of bits	Subnet mask	Number of subnets available	Number of hosts available within subnet
/18	255.255.192.0	2	16382
/19	255.255.224.0	6	8190
/20	255.255.240.0	14	4094
/21	255.255.248.0	30	2046
/22	255.255.252.0	62	1022
/23	255.255.254.0	126	510
/24	255.255.255.0	254	254
/25	255.255.255.128	510	126
/26	255.255.255.192	1022	62
/27	255.255.255.224	2046	30
/28	255.255.255.240	4094	14
/29	255.255.255.248	8190	6
/30	255.255.255.252	16382	2

Multiple IP addresses on a single segment should be used with caution because they add an overhead. The traffic between the two stations belonging logically to different subnets will always be run through the router despite the fact that they are connected to the same physical segment. (Recall what a station usually does when it needs to send data to a distant station – checks its IP address, and if it is on a different subnet uses the default gateway.) In terms of routing, the IP distance vector routing protocols such as RIP or IGRP will broadcast routing tables from all addresses assigned to the RIP or IGRP running router interfaces.

Routers use the network mask to route IP packets by:

■ extracting the destination network number from the datagram received;
■ performing logical AND with the destination IP address and related subnet mask;
■ comparing the result of this operation with the routing information in the routing table;
■ taking the most precise longest match to choose the most appropriate best route to the destination.

QUICK TIP **IP address mask**

A **mask** is a bit combination used to describe which portion of an IP address refers to the network or subnet and which part refers to the host.

Mirror image counting

There was another scheme of subnet numbering proposed called **mirror image counting** (RFC 1219) which turned upside down (mirrored) the bits in the subnet address portion which would have been assigned systematically (from least significant bit towards the most significant). An example is shown in Figure 10.3.

FIGURE 10-3 Example of mirror-image counting used in addressing

Base network number: 11000001.00000001.00000001.00000000 = 193.1.1.0/24

The regular and systematic assignment of subnet numbers as per classic RFC 950:

Subnet #1:	11000001.00000001.00000001.***0001***0000 = 193.1.1.16/28
Subnet #2:	11000001.00000001.00000001.***0010***0000 = 193.1.1.32/28

Subnet numbers assigned as per mirror image counting:

Subnet #1:	11000001.00000001.00000001.***10*** ***00***0000 = 193.1.1.128/28
Subnet #2:	11000001.00000001.00000001.***01*** ***00***0000 = 193.1.1.64/28

The reason for this approach was to leave the boundary between subnet and host numbers quite flexible for any future changes in the subnet mask (in the case of regular subnetting as per RFC 950 any change to the subnet mask requires complete host and subnet renumbering, while in this case it may be possible not to renumber each node but only change the accompanying subnet mask). However, as this scheme does not work with a Variable Length Subnet Mask (VLSM), it has been abandoned.

RFC WATCH **mirror image counting**

RFC 1219 **On the Assignment of Subnet Numbers**, 1991 (Informational)

Broadcast handling by routers

Caution must be taken with respect to **broadcast** addresses. It is clear that the router will keep in its routing table the records which typically specify the network (or subnet) addresses of all reachable networks. Therefore any broadcast address within the network (or subnet) is not recognized as broadcast by the router (the sending station wishes to get someone on the destination segment, knowing the segment address, of course) and datagrams will be forwarded as indicated by the routing table. This type of broadcasting is called **directed network/subnet broadcast** (RFC 1027).

On the other hand, a broadcast to all (IP address 255.255.255.255) without knowing any particular network address will be recognized and implicitly blocked by the router. As this type of broadcast will not leave the segment where it originated, it is called a **local broadcast**.

> **RFC WATCH**   broadcasts and routers
>
> RFC 919 **Broadcasting Internet Datagrams**, 1984 (Standard)
>
> RFC 922 **Broadcasting Internet Datagrams in the Presence of Subnets**, 1984 (Standard)
>
> RFC 1027 **Using ARP to Implement Transparent Subnet Gateways**, 1987

Security issues – address spoofing

An **IP spoofing attack** occurs when an attacker outside your network pretends to be a trusted computer either by using an IP address that is within the range of IP addresses for your network or by using an authorized external IP address that you trust and to which you wish to provide access to specified resources on your network.

Normally, an IP spoofing attack is limited to the injection of data or commands into an existing stream of data passed between a client and server application or a peer-to-peer network connection. To enable bidirectional communication, the attacker must change all routing tables to point to the spoofed IP address. If an attacker changes the routing tables to point to the spoofed IP address, he or she can receive all the network packets addressed to the spoofed address and reply just as any trusted user can. Like packet sniffers, IP spoofing is not restricted to people who are outside the network.

Spoofing IP addresses indicates a security threat, particularly leading to a denial of service attack. Therefore there is a best current practice deployed in the Internet defeating this particular case of denial of service attacks. The method uses a network ingress filtering.

RFC WATCH **defense against address spoofing**

RFC 2827 **Network Ingress Filtering: Defeating Denial of Service Attacks which Employ IP Source Address Spoofing**, 2000 (Best Current Practice)

10.3.3 VLSM and prefix routing

When subnetting was first defined in RFC 950, it prohibited the use of the **all-zeros** and the **all-ones subnet**. The reason for this restriction was to eliminate situations that could potentially confuse a classful router (understanding the IP addresses only with the relationship to their classes and their boundaries). Note that today a router can be both classless and classful at the same time – it could be running RIPU1 (a classful protocol) and BGP-4 (a classless protocol) at the same time.

QUICK TIP **IP address prefix**

Address in **decimal dotted notation/number of bits used for network and subnet** portion of that address (e.g. 10.5.6.7/16 – network 10.0.0.0 with second octet bits used for subnetting).

With respect to the **all-zeros subnet** (subnet zero), a router requires that each routing table update includes the **route/<prefix-length>** pair to differentiate between a route to the all-zeros subnet and a route to the entire network. For example, when using RIPU1 which does not supply a mask or prefix-length with each route, the routing advertisements for subnet 193.1.1.0/27 and for network 193.1.1.0/24 are identical – 193.1.1.0. Without somehow knowing the prefix length or mask, a router cannot tell the difference between a route to the all-zeros subnet and the route to the entire network. This is illustrated in Figure 10.4.

FIGURE 10-4 Differentiating between a route to the all-zero subnet and the entire network

Network route (24-bit prefix):	193.1.1.0/24	***11000001.00000001.00000001***.00000000
Subnet route (27-bit prefix):	193.1.1.0/27	***11000001.00000001.00000001.000***00000

Regarding the **all-ones subnet,** a router requires each routing table entry to include the **prefix-length** so that it can determine if a broadcast (directed or all-subnets) should be sent only to the all-ones subnet or to the entire network (if that is allowed). For example, when the routing table does not contain a mask or prefix-length for each route, confusion can occur because the same broadcast address (193.1.1.255) is used for both for the entire network 193.1.1.0/24 and the all-ones subnet 193.1.1.224/27. This is illustrated in Figure 10.5.

FIGURE 10-5   Identifying a broadcast to the all-ones subnet and the entire network

```
Broadcast to network with 24-bit prefix:

193.1.1.0/24        11000001.00000001.00000001.11111111

Broadcast to subnet with 27-bit prefix:

193.1.1.224/27      11000001.00000001.00000001.111 11111
```

As a final note on all-zeros and all-ones subnets, while they were not recommended some time ago and some older routers do not understand them by default, they are now regularly used in the general Internet (which means that it might be useful if routers understand them properly).

Variable length subnet masks

Initially it was expected to have a single subnetting mechanism used in a single network (if necessary at all); however, due to a lack of addresses it was allowed to use various subnet masks in a single network address called **Variable Length Subnet Masks** (VLSM) to more effectively work with the numbers of subnets and hosts within them.

VLSM supports more efficient use of an organization's assigned IP address space. One of the major problems with the earlier limitation of supporting only a single subnet mask across a given network prefix was that once the mask was selected, it locked the organization into an available number of fixed-sized subnets. For example, assume that a network administrator decided to configure the network 130.5.0.0/16 with a /22 extended network prefix (see Figure 10.6).

FIGURE 10-6   130.5.0.0/16 with /22 prefix

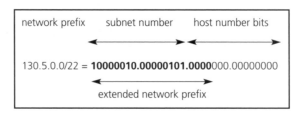

network prefix   subnet number   host number bits

130.5.0.0/22 = **10000010.00000101.0000000**.00000000

extended network prefix

A /16 network with a /22 extended network prefix permits 64 subnets (2^6 including all ones and all zeros), each of which supports a maximum of 1022 hosts ($2^{10} - 2$). This is fine if the organization wants to deploy a number of large subnets, but less useful for small subnets containing only 20 or 30 hosts. Since a subnetted network could have only a single mask, the network administrator was still required to assign the 20 or 30 hosts to a subnet with a 22-bit prefix. Such an assignment would waste approximately 1000 IP host addresses for each small subnet deployed. Limiting the association of a network number with a single mask did not encourage the flexible and efficient use of an organization's address space.

The solution to this problem is to allow a subnetted network to deploy more than one subnet mask. Assume that in the previous example, the network administrator is also allowed to configure the 130.5.0.0/16 network with a /26 extended network prefix. A /16 network address with a /26 extended network prefix permits 1024 subnets (2^{10}), each of which supports a maximum of 62 hosts ($2^6 - 2$). The /26 prefix would be ideal for small subnets with less than 60 hosts, while the /22 prefix is well suited for larger subnets containing up to 1000 hosts.

VLSM addressing allows the recursive division of an organization's address space so that it can be reassembled and aggregated to reduce the amount of routing information at the top level. Conceptually, a network is first divided into subnets, some of the subnets are further divided into sub-subnets, and some of the sub-subnets are divided into sub-sub-subnets (see example in Figure 10.7). This allows the detailed structure of routing information for one subnet group to be hidden from routers in another subnet group.

FIGURE 10-7   Division of network prefix in VLSM – example

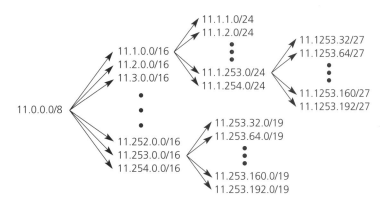

10.3.4 Classless interdomain routing

While classful routing distinguishes IP addresses by the class they belong to and automatically aggregates the addresses belonging to the particular network into a single route at the network boundary, classless routing does not bother with classes at all. All that is important is the address prefix which may or may not correspond to the address class but which is guiding the router for more and less specific routes to particular destinations. **The longer the prefix, the more specific the route**.

classful vs. classless network

A **classful network** uses traditional IP network addresses within a class A, B, or C. In a classful addressing system, each host field has the same number of bits.

A **classless network** defines instead the **network boundary** using a prefix indicating the number of bits used for the network/subnet portion.

While in the case of classful routing the router would have a single routing entry in its routing table for how to get to the particular distant network, e.g. 143.23.0.0 (or more entries for load balancing but all for the network 143.23.0.0), a classless router could have many more routes to the network because the routes would have different prefixes. For example, the router might know the route to 143.23.0.0/16, 143.23.64.0/18, and 143.23.64.132/30. Should an IP datagram arrive with the destination address 143.23.64.134, the longest match rule will apply and the route for 143.23.64.132/30 will be used. If another datagram is destined for 143.23.201.66, the longest route available would be the route for 143.23.0.0/16.

The formats for distinction between classful and classless addressing are shown in Figure 10.8.

FIGURE 10-8 Comparison of classful and classless addressing formats

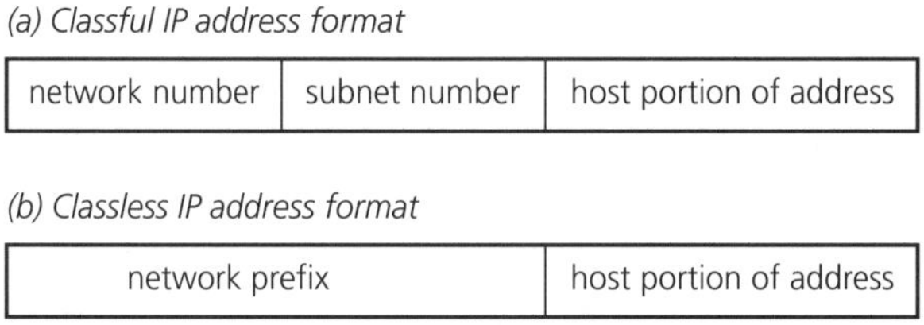

(a) Classful IP address format

network number	subnet number	host portion of address

(b) Classless IP address format

network prefix	host portion of address

An example of classless routing in the Internet is shown in Figure 10.9. The networks are not advertised by their class boundaries but by their identifying address prefix instead.

Extending IP addresses through CIDR

IP version 4, although in full use to date in the current Internet, has been accused of having too small, unnecessarily limited address space and rigid structure rules. To overcome this problem, several schemes have been suggested and some are widely used. Besides IP version 6 which is discussed later, the main improvement to IPv4 is the use of a prefix rather than a subnet mask for network address assignment and routing.

FIGURE 10-9 Classless routing example

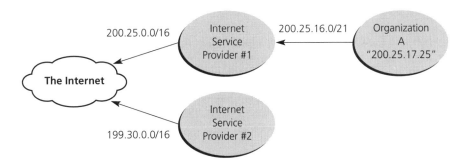

In 1992, the Internet Engineering Steering Group (IESG) determined that class B addresses assigned to hosts were rapidly becoming exhausted and inefficiently used. This problem demanded a quick solution, which resulted in the development of an Internet standard track protocol, called the **Classless Inter-Domain Routing** (CIDR) approach (RFCs 1517–15.19).

CIDR is supported by all newer IP interior routing protocols, such as RIPv2, OSPF, EIGRP and exterior routing protocol BGP-4, while older RIPv1 or IGRP are typical classful protocols that do require a single mask deployed within a network and do summarize the routing information for the network at its boundary. As we will see later in the next chapter, this also has an impact on the fact that discontiguous networks are difficult to handle by the classful routing protocols.

RFC WATCH evolution of classless routing

Classless routing was first introduced under the term **supernetting**:

RFC 1338 **Supernetting: an Address Assignment and Aggregation Strategy,** 1992

The broader **CIDR** effort was a little later, and the main documents are:

RFC 1517 **Applicability Statement for the Implementation of Classless Inter-Domain Routing** (CIDR), 1993 (Proposed Standard)

RFC 1518 **An Architecture for IP Address Allocation with CIDR,** 1993 (Proposed Standard)

RFC 1519 **Classless Inter-Domain Routing (CIDR): an Address Assignment and Aggregation Strategy**, 1993 (Proposed Standard)

RFC 1520 **Exchanging Routing Information Across Provider Boundaries in the CIDR Environment**, 1993 (Informational)

QUICK TIP | **subnetting vs. supernetting**

The goal of **supernetting** is to group routes together so that a router **reduces the number of routes** it advertises to other routers.

The goal of **subnetting** is to **subdivide the network number** (to cope with lack of addresses) assigned from outside by ISP or RIPE/ARIN/APNIC.

CIDR or supernetting is a new way of looking at IP addresses. There is no longer any reference to classes (class A, B, or C), instead, only an address prefix matters (bits counted from the far left of the IP address). Prior to CIDR, IP address prefixes were forced into a small number of fixed-size lengths based on address class. CIDR replaces address classes with **address prefixes**, which must accompany the address and can be of arbitrary length. This strategy conserves address space and slows the increasing growth of routing tables. In a classless environment, prefixes are viewed as bitwise contiguous blocks of the IP address space. For example, all prefixes with a /20 prefix represent the same amount of address space. Furthermore, a /20 prefix can be linked with a traditional class A, class B, or class C network number.

SNAPSHOT | **CIDR**

Classless Inter-Domain Routing supercedes the notion of implicit address masks based on IP address classes; instead, it requires that explicit masks be passed in inter-domain routing protocols.

QUICK TIP | **differences between VLSM and CIDR**

VLSM is an arbitrary prefix length technique, but its applicability lies inside enterprises rather than among providers. VLSM can contain different numbers of network + subnet bits.

CIDR was specifically intended to solve the problems of address exhaustion and routing table size in the public Internet. CIDR includes administrative procedures for global address assignment. CIDR does not consider the 'subnetting a subnet' or VLSM approach.

Aggregates are used to minimize the size of routing tables. **Aggregation** is the process of combining the characteristics of several different routes in such a way that a single route can be advertised. For example, CIDR can aggregate an IP address, which is called a **supernet** address, in the form of 192.24.0.0/13, where 192.24.0.0 represents the address prefix, and 13 is the prefix length in bits. This represents the block of 2048 class C network numbers from the range between 192.24.0.0. and 192.31.255.0.

CIDR in action

Consider an ISP that services 254 class C network addresses, starting with 204.36.0.0. The addresses start with network 204.36.1.0 and run to 204.36.255.0. The CIDR notation for all of the networks in this block is 204.36.0.0/16, where /16 is the CIDR prefix notation. The first 16 bits of the 32-bit IP address – 204.36 – identify the starting network number of the CIDR block. The remaining bits identify what were formerly considered separate Class C networks.

Eliminating class distinctions gives ISPs more flexibility in handing out addresses. For example, an ISP could elect to subdivide the /16 CIDR block into two /17 CIDR blocks, each with 128 contiguous networks, or into four /18 CIDR blocks, each with 64 contiguous networks. Note that adding a bit to the CIDR mask reduces by a power of two the number of contiguous networks in the block – 254 networks with a /16 mask, 128 networks with a /17 mask, and so on.

Regardless, the ISP has just one routing table entry as far as the top-level routers are concerned; the ISP announces only one entry (204.36.0.0/16) to its upstream providers. There is no longer any need to know exactly where all of the networks in the 204.36.0.0 address block are located. So when a router sees an IP datagram bound for any address that starts with 204.36.x.x, it locates the single routing table entry for that CIDR block. Then it can leave delivery up to the provider.

CIDR may not solve IP address exhaustion, but when it comes to allocating the right number of addresses the scheme is a big help. If a network manager needs network addresses for 10 000 hosts, it normally means applying for a class B address – a request likely to be denied given how scarce class B networkers are. Even if a class B were granted, more than 55 000 addresses would go unused (class B network supports more than 65 000 hosts). But with CIDR, a net manager can apply to an ISP for a block of 64 class Cs. The CIDR scheme offers plenty of room for growth – a block of 64 class C addresses supports more than 16 000 hosts – without unduly draining the pool of available addresses.

Longest match algorithm

All routers must implement a consistent forwarding algorithm based on the **longest match** algorithm. A route with a longer extended network prefix describes a smaller set of destinations than the same route with a shorter extended network prefix. As a result, a route with a longer extended network prefix is more specific while a route with a shorter extended network prefix is less specific. Routers must use the route with the longest matching extended network prefix (most specific matching route) when forwarding traffic.

For example, if a packet's destination IP address is 11.1.2.5 and there are three network prefixes in the routing table (11.1.2.0/24, 11.1.0.0/16, and 11.0.0.0/8), the router would select the route to 11.1.2.0/24. The 11.1.2.0/24 route is selected because its prefix has the greatest number of corresponding bits in the destination IP address of the packet. This is illustrated in Figure 10.10.

FIGURE 10-10   Best match with the route having the longest prefix (most specific)

```
Destination 11.1.2.5    = 00001011.00000001.00000010.00000101
*Route #1 11.1.2.0/24   = 00001011.00000001.00000010.00000000
Route #2 11.1.0.0/16    = 00001011.00000001.00000000.00000000
Route #3 11.0.0.0/8     = 00001011.00000000.00000000.00000000
```

There is a very subtle but extremely important issue here. Since the destination address matches all three routes, it must be assigned to a host which is attached to the 11.1.2.0/24 subnet. If the 11.1.2.5 address is assigned to a host that is attached to the 11.1.0.0/16 or 11.0.0.0/8 subnet, the routing system will *never* route traffic to the host since the longest match algorithm assumes that the host is part of the 11.1.2.0/24 subnet. This means that great care must be taken when assigning host addresses to make sure that every host is reachable!

QUICK TIP   **all ones and all zeros**

The term *all zeros* stands for the **default network** (IP address of all bits set to *0*). This is used when creating a default route by specifying the 0.0.0.0 network out of a specific interface.

The term *all ones* means the **broadcast address** which is in the case of IP 255.255.255.255 (IP address of all bits set to *1*).

Router aggregation with prefix routing

The class C network numbers allocated following the CIDR strategy are contiguous and share the same prefixes. This makes it more important to allocate addresses intelligently, usually grouping networks by region so that all network numbers within a given region share the same prefix and could be represented by a single entry in the routing tables of other regions, i.e. **routing table aggregation**. If addresses for devices in a given region are not allocated contiguously, then routing table aggregation cannot be performed and routers would be forced to store larger routing tables, leading to impaired performance of routers in the core network. An example of route aggregation is shown in Figure 10.11.

FIGURE 10-11 Route aggregation – example

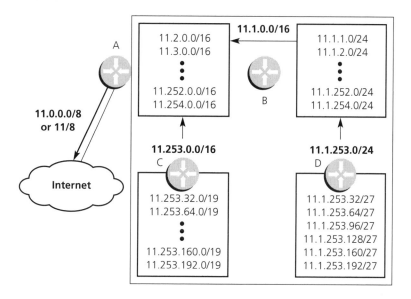

Rules for route advertisement summarized

1 Routing to all destinations must be done on a **longest-match basis** only. This implies that destinations which are multi-homed relative to a routing domain must always be explicitly announced into that routing domain – they cannot be summarized. (This makes intuitive sense – if a network is multi-homed, all of its paths into a routing domain which is higher in the hierarchy of networks must be known to the higher network.)

2 A routing domain which performs a summarization of multiple routes must discard packets which match the summarization but do not match any of the explicit routes which make up the summarization. This is necessary to prevent routing loops in the presence of less-specific information (such as a default route). One simple way to implement this rule would be for the border router to maintain a sink route for each of its aggregations. By the rule of longest match, this would cause all traffic destined to components of the aggregation which are not explicitly known to be discarded. An arbitrary network number and mask are accepted for all routing destinations, and the mask must be left contiguous. The degenerate route *0.0.0.0* mask *0.0.0.0* is used as a **default**

route and must be accepted by all implementations. In global Internet operations, no one should allow for automatic summarization. Summarization needs to be planned.

Just like VLSM, the successful deployment of **CIDR has three prerequisites**:

■ The routing protocols must carry network prefix information with each route advertisement.

■ All routers must implement a consistent forwarding algorithm based on the longest match.

■ For route aggregation to occur, addresses must be assigned so that they are topologically significant.

After the introduction of CIDR, the router must forward a packet based on the most specific forwarding entry (longest prefix) that the router has for the packet's destination address in its routing table. The longest match rule does not allow for any overlapping prefixes of different lengths.

Hierarchical routing

Hierarchical routing, introduced with some routing protocols, requires that addresses be assigned to reflect the actual network topology. This reduces the amount of routing information by taking the set of addresses assigned to a particular region of the topology, and aggregating them into a single routing advertisement for the entire set. Hierarchical routing allows this to be done recursively at various points within the hierarchy of the routing topology. If addresses do not have a topological significance, aggregation cannot be performed and the size of the routing tables cannot be reduced.

OSPF and integrated IS-IS convey the extended network prefix information with each route, therefore the VLSM subnets can be scattered throughout an organization's topology. However, to support hierarchical routing and reduce the size of an organization's routing tables, addresses should be assigned so that they are topologically significant.

Renumbering

There are also occasions when networks need to be renumbered for more effective and smooth routing deployment. For example, if a corporation obtains a series of class C addresses and uses CIDR, the regions of the network should be carefully planned to allow for routing table aggregation to avoid excessive demands on network routers.

Distributing the new addresses and manually reconfiguring all network devices, including routers, gateways, servers, and workstations, undoubtedly consumes a great deal of time and manpower. Automating the processes of address distribution is not only a definite timesaver but lowers the cost of renumbering. Also, if a company is connected to the Internet, it might chose to change its ISP (Internet Service Provider), forcing the company to use a different set of addresses for all of its computing equipment.

RFC WATCH	renumbering

RFC 1900 **Renumbering Needs Work**, 1996 (Informational)

RFC 1916 **Enterprise Renumbering: Experience and Information Solicitation**, 1996 (Informational)

Special prefixes for point-to-point links

Given the scarce address space with IPv4 many ways of improving the effectiveness of assigning IP addresses have been studied. Even today when some advocate the transition to IPv6 many feel that the currently widely deployed IPv4 may still serve their purposes – with sophistication in assigning addresses and working with them through aggregation etc.

Point-to-point links have been seen as one of the networks where the waste of IP addresses was painful (with only two stations attached the point-to-point link commonly requires a separate subnet address). However, opportunities have been discovered regarding how to change the way that point-to-point links are numbered. One option, which is used today on some parts of the Internet, is simply to not number point-to-point links between routers. While this practice may seem, at first, to handily resolve the problem, it causes a number of problems of its own, including the inability to consistently manage the unnumbered link or reach a router through it, difficulty in management and debugging of those links, and the lack of standardization (RFC 1812).

RFC WATCH	IP addressing in point-to-point links

RFC 3021 **Using 31-Bit Prefixes on IPv4 Point-to-Point Links**, 2000 (Proposed Standard)

In current practice, numbered Internet subnets do not use a longer than 30-bit subnet mask (in most cases), which requires four addresses per link – two host addresses, one all-zeros network, and one all-ones broadcast. This is unfortunate for point-to-point links, since they can only possibly have two identifying endpoints and do not support the notion of broadcast – any packet which is transmitted by one end of a link is always received by the other.

A third option is to use host addresses on both ends of a point-to-point link. This option provides the same address space savings as using a 31-bit subnet mask, but may only be used in links using PPP encapsulation (RFC 1332). The use of host addresses allows for the assignment of IP addresses belonging to different networks at each side of the link, rendering link and network management not straightforward.

RFC WATCH	point-to-point links

RFC 1332 **The PPP Internet Protocol Control Protocol (IPCP),** 1992 (Proposed Standard)

RFC 3021 is based on the idea that conserving IP addresses on point-to-point links (using a longer than 30-bit subnet mask) while maintaining manageability and standard interaction is possible. The savings in address space resulting from this change is easily seen: each point-to-point link in a large network would consume two addresses instead of four. In a network with 500 point-to-point links, for example, this practice would amount to a saving of 1000 addresses (the equivalent of four class C address spaces).

<Host-number> represents the unmasked portion of the address and it should be at least one bit wide. If a 31-bit subnet mask is assigned to a point-to-point link, it leaves the <Host-number> with only one bit taking the value of either *0* or *1*. These addresses have historically been associated with network and broadcast addresses. In a point-to-point link with a 31-bit subnet mask, the two addresses above must be interpreted as host addresses.

The recommendations for 31-bit subnet addressing have been implemented by several router vendors in beta code. The implementation has been tested by at least three ISPs with positive results (i.e. no problems have been found). Among the routing protocols tested successfully are OSPF, IS-IS, BGP, and EIGRP.

10.3.5 IP datagram

IP routing is based on the **destination network address** of each datagram. However, the router must also deal with other information in the IP datagram.

An IP datagram is of variable length and consists of the following fields (see Figure 10.12):

■ *Version* – indicates the version of IP currently used (version 4). (*Note*: IP version 6 uses a different datagram format – see later – therefore an appearance of other than version number 4 in the datagram means the datagram is corrupted.)

■ *IP header length* (IHL) – indicates the datagram header length in 32-bit words.

■ *Type of service* – specifies how a particular upper-layer protocol would like the current datagram to be handled. Datagrams can be assigned various levels of **precedence** (three P bits) and importance through this field; the **type of service** defined (four bits) means the requirement for **lowest delay (D)**, **highest throughput (T)**, **highest reliability (R)**, or **lowest cost (C)**. (However, a requirement of more than two such service criteria would be quite impossible for networking systems to achieve.)

FIGURE 10-12 IP datagram format

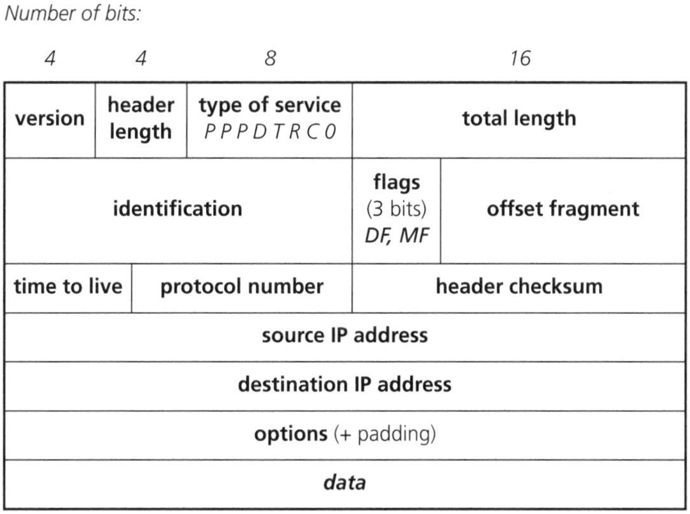

Number of bits:

4	4	8	16

version	header length	type of service *P P P D T R C 0*	total length	
identification			flags (3 bits) *DF, MF*	offset fragment
time to live	protocol number		header checksum	
source IP address				
destination IP address				
options (+ padding)				
data				

- **Total length** – specifies the length of the entire IP datagram, including data and header, in octets (maximum IP packet length is limited to 65 535 octets).

- **Identification** – contains an integer that identifies the current datagram. This field is used to help in reassembling datagram fragments and identifying duplicate packets on the network.

- **Flags** – three-bit field of which the low-order two bits control the **fragmentation** of datagrams due to maximum transmission unit (MTU) limits on a particular network. (For example, an Ethernet network sets MTU of 1500 octets which means that no frame can be transmitted onto the Ethernet if it is larger than 1500 octets or it will not be processed correctly. The MTU of a Token Ring network defaults to 4500 octets. Therefore, if a device sends a frame onto a Token Ring network and the frame has to traverse an Ethernet network, the frame would likely have to be fragmented before it could enter the Ethernet segment.)
  One bit in flags specifies whether the packet can be fragmented: bit set to *1* means '*do not fragment*,' **DF**; the second bit specifies whether the packet is the **last fragment** in a series of fragmented packets: bit set to *1* means '*more fragments*,' **MF**. (The fragmented datagram is reassembled at the destination. The receiving station will know in which order to put the frames using the identification field and flag field indicating the last frame – MF bit set to *0*.)

- **Fragment offset** (13 bits) – indicates where in the datagram this fragment belongs. The fragment offset is measured in units of 8 octets (64 bits). The first fragment has offset zero. The Internet **fragmentation and reassembly** procedure needs to be able to break a datagram into an almost arbitrary number of pieces that can be reassembled later by the destination station. *Identification, MF* bit and *fragment offset* are used for final reassembly. The first fragment will have the fragment offset zero, and the last fragment will have the more-fragments flag reset to zero. Fragments from different datagrams may arrive out of order and still be sorted out.

- *Time to live* (TTL) – maintains a counter that gradually decrements at each traversed router by one (initially by number of seconds) down to zero, at which point the datagram is discarded. This keeps packets from looping endlessly. The initial measurement in seconds was replaced by the number of hops, which is used in **traceroute** (for more details see Section 10.5 on ICMP).

- *Protocol* – indicates which upper-layer protocol receives incoming packets after IP processing is complete. (This is information for IP regarding which port to use at the destination station when decapsulating the data and sending it up to the transport layer.) The interfaces (SAPs) between the internet and transport layer are called **protocol numbers** (standardized in RFC 1700: e.g. TCP's protocol number is *6*, UDP's *17*, and ICMP's *1*) – not to be confused with port numbers identifying the interlayer interfaces one layer up the TCP/IP stack.

- *Header checksum* – helps ensure IP header integrity: the checksum does a calculation to determine that the datagram's header has not been changed since it was transmitted from the sender. If the header checksum does not calculate the same checksum as contained inside the packet, the packet will be discarded.

- *Source address* – specifies the IP address of sending node, which might only be a unicast IP address.

- *Destination address* – specifies the IP address of receiving node(s), which might be a unicast, multicast, or broadcast IP address. (*Note*: The source and destination IP addresses will remain the same except for NAT – inside the datagram as it traverses the network to reach its destination, as opposed to hardware (link-layer) addresses that always identify the direct neighbors.)

- *Options* – allows IP to support various options, such as security.

- *Data* – contains upper-layer information of different length (max. 65 535 octets less header length).

RFC WATCH	TCP/IP numbers

RFC 1700 **Assigned Numbers**, 1994 (Standard)

All the datagrams with local addresses are delivered directly by the IP through the network interface layer (encapsulated with the proper destination physical address), and the external datagrams are forwarded to their next destination based on the routing table information.

IP also monitors the **size** of a datagram it receives from the host layer. If the datagram size exceeds the maximum length the physical network is capable of sending, then IP will break up the datagram into smaller fragments according to the capacity of the underlying network hardware. These fragments are then reassembled at the datagram's destination.

Note on error handling: IP is not an error-correcting service, merely a very simple error-**detecting** service. IP only detects errors in the IP datagram header, not in the payload (CRC is computed only across the header). It is the responsibility of carried protocols like UDP or TCP to error-check the payload. Most error detecting is still the responsibility of the data link service. With regard to the upper (transport) layer service, TCP is intended to be responsible for reliable error correction, while UDP is intended to be error detecting only.

While in modern implementations the data link protocols have a frame-checking sequence for error detection implemented in hardware and generating a 32-bit checksum, IP and TCP use the simple Fletcher algorithm, with a smaller field, so they do not have the same error-detection power. The error detection/correction of the upper layers may thus seem redundant. It is there due to the fact that IP was introduced long before the advanced data link layer's error-checking was perfected, and because IP can also be used with the less powerful underlying Layer 2 protocols.

How the router 'processes' every passing datagram is discussed in detail in the next chapter.

10.4 Address mapping protocols

On some media (such as IEEE 802 LANs), media addresses and IP addresses are dynamically discovered through the use of two other members of the TCP/IP protocol suite: the **Address Resolution Protocol** (ARP) and the **Reverse Address Resolution Protocol** (RARP). ARP uses broadcast messages to determine the MAC address corresponding to another IP address. ARP is sufficiently generic to allow the use of IP with virtually any type of underlying media-access mechanism. RARP uses broadcast messages to determine the IP address associated with the local hardware address. RARP is particularly important to diskless nodes, which may not know their IP address when they boot.

10.4.1 Address resolution protocol

The **Address Resolution Protocol** (ARP), defined in RFC 826, is a method for finding a host's physical address from its Internet address. The ARP allows the dynamic resolution between network and physical addresses.

RFC WATCH   **ARP**

RFC 826 **Ethernet Address Resolution Protocol: or Converting Network Protocol Addresses to 48-bit Ethernet Address for Transmission on Ethernet Hardware**, 1982 (Standard)

A device on the network is assigned an IP address and network mask identifying the network the device is on, and a MAC address (burnt in hardware (BIA) and not subject to change – only using software to overwrite). The IP address is determined by the network administrator in charge of the network topology. A network device must know the MAC address of the device it wants to communicate with to encapsulate the IP datagram into a LAN frame. To determine that MAC address, the device must use the dynamic protocol ARP to map the destination device's IP address to its associated MAC address. The sender broadcasts an ARP request (frame) containing the IP address of the receiving host and asks it to send back its MAC address. The destination device with the corresponding IP address will send back a reply directly to the sending device containing its MAC address. ARP operation is depicted in Figure 10.13.

FIGURE 10-13 ARP operation overview – stations on the same network segment

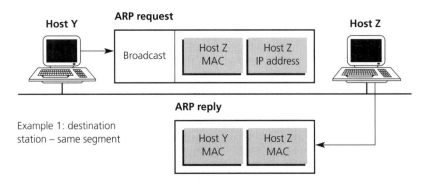

The sender then stores the obtained pair of network and physical addresses in its ARP cache. The destination host will also use the ARP request to update its ARP cache, this time on the sending station (the ARP request contains the IP address and MAC address of the source). Each host maintains an **ARP cache** of address translations (IP address to MAC address associations) to reduce delay and loading (the entries in the ARP cache usually expire in the order of hours). The ARP cache layout is shown in Figure 10.14. The next time the device needs to send data to the receiving device it will reference its ARP cache to determine if the IP address of the receiving device has an associated MAC address. If it does, it will put the MAC address into the destination address field of the frame and send

FIGURE 10-14 ARP cache layout

	IF index	Physical address	IP address	Type
Entry 1				
Entry 2				
Entry 3				
Entry n				

it off. The process of referencing the ARP cache is faster and much more efficient than having to send out an ARP broadcast every time it needs to communicate with a device.

As it is defined on RFC 826, a router and host must be attached to the same network segment to accomplish ARP as the broadcasts cannot be forwarded by another router to a different network segment. When this is not the case (i.e. if the destination station does not reside on the same segment as the sender), the router will generate a response on behalf of the distant station as its proxy. If the router knows the path to the destination network through a port other than the segment the inquiring station is connected to, any communication with the destination station must pass through the router. Therefore the router will respond to the ARP request with a reply containing the MAC address of its incoming port for the local segment. This procedure is referred to as **proxy ARP** (RFC 1027). If there are multiple routers attached to the network segment, all will respond to the broadcast and the sending station will use the first reply received. If the router does not have the remote network in its routing table, it does not respond to the initial broadcast. If no routers have the remote network in their routing tables, then the packet is dropped.

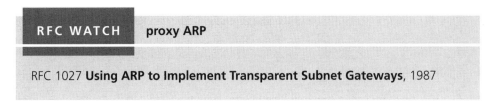

RFC WATCH   **proxy ARP**

RFC 1027 **Using ARP to Implement Transparent Subnet Gateways**, 1987

An overview of proxy ARP operation is shown in Figure 10.15.

FIGURE 10-15 ARP operation – destination station resides on a different network segment

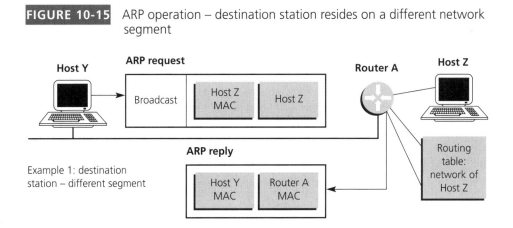

A concrete example of proxy ARP operation is shown at Figure 10.16. A host 199.19.8.5 (on a subnet 199.19.8.0/24) needs to send a packet to 199.19.90.9/24, but is not configured with default gateway information and therefore does not

know how to reach a router. The host will issue an ARP request for the destination IP address 199.19.90.9/24. The local router, upon receiving this ARP request and knowing how to reach network 199.19.90.0, will issue an ARP reply with its own MAC address (of the interface attached to the local network 199.19.8.0/24, i.e. 199.19.8.1/24). Thus the router informs the sending host about its own MAC address as if it were the destination's MAC address: the ARP reply will contain the destination IP address for the host 199.19.90.9/24 linked with the MAC address of router's E0 interface, 199.19.8.1/24. All packets destined for that address will then be sent to the router. This does not replace the default gateway configuration because the host would need to run ARP for every single station with which it wants to communicate. It will not be able to assume that the router's local MAC address could actually be a gateway to the outer world.

FIGURE 10-16 Proxy ARP in action

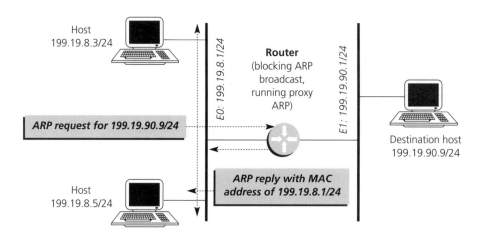

A more granular view of the host operation is as follows. The sending host looks at its own IP address and subnet mask and compares it to the destination host IP address to determine whether they both reside on the same subnet. If this is so, an ARP request for the destination host is issued.

But if the hosts are not part of the same subnet, the sending host looks for its default gateway and issues an ARP request for it. End stations may also be manually configured with their **default gateway**, so that the router address is known and the proxy ARP is not used. The station sends all non-local packets to the default router, which either routes them appropriately or sends an **ICMP redirect message** back to the station telling it of a better route. The ICMP redirect message indicates which local router the host should use. The software caches the redirect messages and routes each packet thereafter as efficiently as possible. The limitations of this method are that there is no means of detecting when the default router has crashed or is unavailable and no method of picking another router if one of these events should occur. The station then loses connectivity to everything beyond that router.

If the end station is configured for the **ICMP Router Discovery Protocol** (IRDP – see Section 10.5), however, the workstation knows when the router went down and finds an alternate router through the hello messages that the routers send. In all cases, the routers terminate broadcasts and reduce traffic on the network.

If there is no default gateway setup for the sending host, it will not even attempt to do an ARP request because it would indicate the destination host is unreachable. The only exception to this is if the default gateway for a device is its own IP address. In this case, the machine will issue an ARP request for all destinations.

> **QUICK TIP**   **ARP in action**
>
> If the subnet mask for the destination station indicated that the originator and destination stations were not on the same subnet, the sending station would not initiate an ARP request for the other station. Instead, it would use an ARP request for the **default gateway**.

The **router** keeps in its ARP cache (as a maximum) the address mapping information acquired through ARP on the stations on directly connected segments and MAC addresses of its neighbor routers. As we saw above, the ARP cache is created dynamically (once the first datagram is to be passed to the IP address of the destination station or to the neighbor router), and cache records, unless used, age to the point that they may be dropped from the cache (typically it takes hours of no usage for the address mapping to be deleted).

ARP message format

Figure 10.17 shows the format of ARP messages (requests and replies). Ethertype for ARP is hex*0806*. Note that both ARP and RARP messages are carried directly inside an Ethernet (IEEE 802 × frame in general) frame; none uses IP datagrams.

FIGURE 10-17   ARP message format

Number of bits:

16	16	8	8	16	16(48)	32	16(48)	32
Hardware type	Protocol type	Layer 2 address length	Layer 3 address length	Operation (message code) **1 = REQ** **0 = RPLY**	Source Layer 2 address	Sources Layer 3 address	Destination Layer 2 address	Destination Layer 3 address

10.4.2 *Reverse address resolution protocol*

The **Reverse Address Resolution Protocol** (RARP), as defined in RFC 903, provides the reverse function of ARP discussed above. RARP maps a local hardware MAC address to an IP address. RARP is primarily used by diskless nodes, when they first initialize, to find their Internet address. Its function is very similar to BOOTP which is a TCP/IP application protocol.

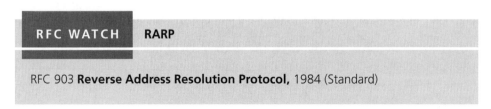

RFC WATCH	RARP

RFC 903 **Reverse Address Resolution Protocol,** 1984 (Standard)

RARP operation is depicted in Figure 10.18.

FIGURE 10-18 RARP operation

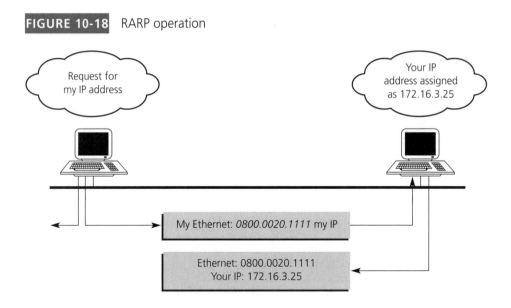

Routers may use the RARP (or BOOTP) during automatic configuration when they need to download configuration from the network. On the other hand, they may provide a repository for the information required by the serverless segments, in which case they will act as BOOTP or RARP servers.

Both RARP and BOOTP have been gradually replaced by the DHCP application protocol discussed later on in Section 10.7.1.

10.5 Internet control message protocol

The **Internet Control Message Protocol** (ICMP), as defined in RFC 792, is a part of IP that handles error and system level messages and sends them to the offending router or host. It uses the basic support of IP as if it were a higher level protocol; however, ICMP is actually an integral part of IP, and must be implemented by every IP module. ICMP performs a number of tasks within an IP internet. The principal reason it was created was to report routing failures back to the source.

RFC WATCH	ICMP

RFC 792 **Internet Control Message Protocol**, 1981 (Standard)

Control or error messages are sent in various situations (ICMP message types and their explanation are summarized in Table 10.3):

TABLE 10-3 ICMP message types and their meaning

ICMP message type	Message contents
0	*Echo reply* = reply to *Echo request*
3	*Destination unreachable* = destination network, station, protocol, or port is unreachable due to its unavailability, that there is no knowledge of it, or that fragmentation was needed but not allowed (*DF* bit was set to *1*) (for codes see Table 10.4)
4	*Source quench* = flow control mechanism informing the source station about the overflowing buffers dropping packets in router
5	*Redirect* = informing source station about another router with a better route to the destination (for codes see Table 10.4)
8	*Echo request* = request for reply
9	*Router advertisement* = router advertises its address
10	*Router solicitation* = station requests a router's address
11	*Time exceeded* = packet lifetime reached 0 (TTL field in IP datagram reached 0)
12	*Parameter problem* = some of the bits or fields in the IP datagram header not complete or correct, other than problems invoking other ICMP messages

▶

TABLE 10-3 continued

ICMP message type	Message contents
13	*Timestamp request* = request for time information for synchronization, or for finding out the route time length
14	*Timestamp reply* = reply to *Timestamp request*
15	*Information request* = request for network address (obsolete due to protocols such as RARP, BOOTP, or DHCP)
16	*Information reply* = reply to *Information request*
17	*Address mask request* = request for IP subnet mask
18	*Address mask reply* = reply to *Address mask request*

TABLE 10-4 ICMP destination unreachable message types

Code	ICMP destination unreachable types
0	*Network unreachable*
1	*Host unreachable*
2	*Protocol unreachable*
3	*Port unreachable*
4	*Fragmentation needed and don't fragment (DF) bit set*
5	*Source route failed*
6	*Destination network unknown*
7	*Destination host unknown*
8	*Source host isolated*
9	*Communication with destination net administratively forbidden*
10	*Communication with destination host administratively forbidden*
11	*Network unreachable for specified type of service*
12	*Host unreachable for specified type of service*

- **Destination unreachable** – sent when a datagram does not reach its destination, e.g. due to a missing path to the destination (sub)network (generated by the first router on the path which notices it has no information about how to get to the destination – message subtype *Network unreachable*); due to missing information on the destination node (message subtype *Host unreachable* generated by the last router on the path with the directly attached network segment where the destination host should reside if it cannot get its MAC address using ARP); due to a missing application on the destination host (message subtype *Protocol* or *Port unreachable*); due to forbidden fragmentation (set by the originating host in the DF flag bit) if fragmentation is detected by a router as needed to pass the datagram over the next medium (the MTU is smaller than the datagram size – message subtype *Fragmentation needed and DF set*).

- **Echo request** and **echo reply messages** – to test node reachability across an internet (used in Packet Internet Groper, PING – for details see later in this section).

- **Redirect messages** to stimulate more efficient routing (for details see later in this section).

- **Time exceeded messages** to inform sources that a datagram has exceeded its allocated time to exist within the internet (based on checking the TTL field).

- **Router advertisement** and **router solicitation messages** to determine the addresses of routers on directly attached subnets.

Among the traffic originated by routers, ICMP messages are the most frequent besides routing information. However, routers must be careful with sending ICMP messages not to adversely affect network performance. Therefore a router does not generate an ICMP message in response to IP broadcast or multicast datagrams or datagrams received encapsulated in Layer 2 frames sent to a multicast or broadcast Layer 2 address. Routers also do not react to errored ICMP messages, with the exception of *Echo request* or *Echo reply* messages encountering problems. *Source quench* ICMP messages, which were initially intended for routers to notify hosts on congestion, are no longer in use due to their harmful consequences to network performance.

ICMP messages are intended mainly for **diagnostic purposes** and generally should not cause the host to take specific actions, such as in the case of receiving a *Destination unreachable* message to reset the TCP connection. However, they may sometimes be used as diagnostic tools (within PING or Traceroute) or to implement network functionality (MTU discovery for hosts via receiving *Destination unreachable* message with subtype *Fragmentation needed and DF set*).

10.5.1 ICMP message format

The ICMP protocol uses IP datagrams to transport its messages as shown in Figure 10.19. The ICMP message format, later encapsulated in IP datagram, is shown in Figure 10.20.

FIGURE 10-19 ICMP message encapsulation

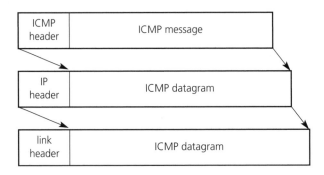

FIGURE 10-20 ICMP message format

Number of bits:

8	8	16
message type *(see Table 10.3)*	**code – parameters**	**checksum**
message body *(depends on message type)*		

10.5.2 Ping

The **Packet Internetwork Groper** (PING) is one of the most widely available tools bundled with TCP/IP software packages. PING uses a series of ICMP echo messages to determine if a remote host is active or inactive, and to determine the round-trip delay in communicating with it. PING is the basic diagnostic to be used for connection verification on routers (for destinations contained in the routing table). However, it should be borne in mind that even successful PING does not ensure that an application could be run on the remote device. PING, using ICMP messages, operates at the Internet layer and therefore cannot verify the operation of any of the layers above (transport and application).

A common form of the PING command, showing some of the more commonly available options that are of use to general users, is

> *ping [-q] [-v] [-R] [-c Count] [-i Wait] [-s PacketSize] Host*

where:

- -q **Quiet output** – nothing is displayed except summary lines at startup and completion;
- -v **Verbose output** – lists ICMP packets that are received in addition to Echo replies;
- -R **Record route option** – includes the *RECORD_ROUTE* option in the Echo request packet and displays the route buffer on returned packets;

- -c **Count** – specifies the number of Echo requests to be sent before concluding test (default is to run until interrupted with a control-C);

- -i **Wait** – indicates the number of seconds to wait between sending each packet (default = 1);

- -s **PacketSize** – specifies the number of data octets to be sent; the total ICMP packet size will be PacketSize+8 octets due to the ICMP header (default = 56, or a 64-octet packet);

- **Host** – IP address or host name of target system.

The PING result shows the round-trip delay of each *Echo* message returned to the sending host; at the end of the test, summary statistics are displayed. For example (from RFC 2151):

> *--- thumper.bellcore.com ping statistics ---*
>
> *6 packets transmitted, 5 packets received, 16% packet loss*
>
> *round-trip min / avg / max = 482.1 / 880.5 / 1447.4 ms*

RFC WATCH	TCP/IP diagnostics

RFC 2151 **A Primer on Internet and TCP/IP Tools and Utilities**, 1997 (Informational)

10.5.3 Traceroute

Traceroute is based on the effective use of the TTL field of an IP datagram and is a common TCP/IP tool allowing users to learn about the detailed route that packets take from their local host to a remote host. Although often used by network and system managers as a simple, yet powerful, debugging tool, traceroute can be also used by end users to learn something about the ever-changing structure of the Internet.

Traceroute does exactly what its title says: it traces the route across all the path hops. When generated by a network device, the datagram first uses the smallest TTL possible, i.e. 1 (single hop), and sends several queries to the destination station (to its not well known UDP port). If the destination is more than one hop away, the first router on the route will return back the ***ICMP TTL exceeded*** message. In the next step the IP datagram will be sent to the destination with TTL increased by one and this process will continue until the destination station responds (*ICMP destination unreachable* message due to unreachable port), or the last router on the route returns back an ICMP *host unreachable message*, or some router on the path has reason to indicate the destination network as unreachable. Hence, either the whole route for communicating with the destination station is revealed, or a problem on the route for which the communication does not work all along the way.

The classic traceroute command has the following general format (where '#' represents a positive integer value associated with the qualifier):

> ***traceroute [-m #] [-q #] [-w #] [-p #] {IP_address | host_name}***

where

- -m is the **maximum allowable TTL** value, measured as the number of hops allowed before the program terminates (default = 30);
- -q is the **number of UDP packets** that will be sent with each time-to-live setting (default = 3);
- -w is the **timeout**, in seconds, to wait for an answer from a particular router before giving up (default = 5);
- -p is the **invalid port address** at the remote host (default = 33 434).

When discussing IP addressing, we mentioned the important issue of private IP addresses. Because **private IP** addresses as per RFC 1918 have no global meaning, routing information about private networks will not be propagated on inter-enterprise links, and packets with private source or destination addresses will not be forwarded across such links. It is interesting to know, for example, what happens in the case of the **traceroute**. The *ICMP TTL exceeded* messages that define the traceroute responses have the source address of the router interfaces that generated them. If these interfaces are numbered according to RFC 1918, and the address originating the traceroute is in registered space, only two situations may occur: either packets with private source addresses have to enter registered space, or there will be no response to the traceroute.

PING and traceroute represent the most capable IP network diagnostic tools. Their relevant place in relation to the TCP/IP layered architecture is shown in Figure 10.21 and compared to the application layer virtual terminal protocol, Telnet.

FIGURE 10-21 TCP/IP network diagnostics

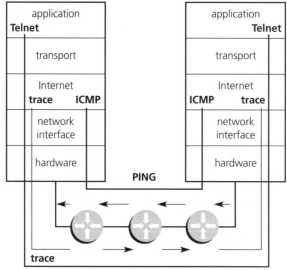

PING and traceroute may not sometimes provide the intended results. One problem is that some administrations block the ICMP Echo request/reply in their filters for whatever reason so PING is not able to get through. And traceroute does not work properly if tunnels (namely in VPNs, as discussed in Part V) are being used. One hop may very well represent all the intermediate networks that the tunnel spans.

10.5.4 ICMP redirect

Routes can sometimes become less than optimal. For example, it is possible for the router to be forced to resend a packet through the same interface on which it was received. If this happens, the router sends an *ICMP Redirect* message to the packet's originator telling it that it is on a subnet directly connected to the router, and that it must forward the packet to another system on the same subnet. It does so because the originating host presumably could have sent that packet to the next hop without involving the router at all.

ICMP redirect messages are only generated when at least two routers are attached to the same subnet and the sending host has chosen the suboptimal router for routing a packet. Generally, this situation does not occur frequently in practice, where most subnets with hosts are connected to a single router. Of course, there are exceptions to this rule.

The *ICMP Redirect* message instructs the sender to remove the router from the route and substitute a specified device representing a more direct path. The codes of *ICMP Redirect* message are shown in Table 10.5.

TABLE 10-5 ICMP redirect message codes

Code	Meaning
0	Redirect datagrams for the net
1	Redirect datagrams for the host
2	Redirect for the type of service and net
4	Redirect for the type of service and host

10.5.5 ICMP router discovery protocol

Before a host can send IP datagrams beyond its directly-attached subnet, it must discover the address of at least one operational router on that subnet. Typically, this is accomplished by reading a list of one or more **default router** addresses from a (possibly remote) configuration file at startup time. On broadcast links, some hosts also discover router addresses by listening to routing protocol traffic. Both of these methods have serious drawbacks: configuration files must be maintained manually which constitutes a significant administrative burden, and are unable to track dynamic changes in router availability; eavesdropping on routing traffic requires that hosts recognize the particular routing protocols in use, which vary from subnet to subnet and which are subject to change at any time.

The **ICMP Router Discovery Protocol** (IRDP) uses *ICMP Router advertisement* and *ICMP Router solicitations* (RFC 1256) to discover the addresses of routers on directly attached subnets (router discovery messages do not constitute a routing protocol). IRDP offers several advantages over other methods of discovering the addresses of neighboring routers. It eliminates the need for manual configuration of router addresses and is independent of any specific routing protocol. It enables hosts to discover the existence of neighboring routers, but not which router is best to reach a particular destination.

If the router supports multicasting on that particular interface, *ICMP router advertisements* are sent to the IP multicast address 224.0.0.1 (*All systems on the subnet*). Otherwise, the local broadcast address is used 255.255.255.255. ICMP solicitation messages are multicast to the address 224.0.0.2 (*All routers on the subnet*), alternatively to 255.255.255.255. (For reserved multicast addresses see Appendix E and for multicasting in general see Chapter 11.)

RFC WATCH   **ICMP Router Discovery Protocol (IRDP)**

RFC 1256 **ICMP Router Discovery Messages**, 1991 (Proposed Standard)

The way IRDP works is that each router periodically multicasts *ICMP Router advertisement* messages (Figure 10.22 shows the message format) from each of its interfaces, announcing the IP address(es) of that interface. Hosts discover the addresses of routers on the directly attached subnet by listening for these mes-

FIGURE 10-22   Router advertisement message format

Number of bits:

8	8	16
Type (9)	**Code** (0)	**Checksum**
Number of addresses (≥1)	**Address entry size** (2)	**Lifetime** (s)
1st router address		
1st preference level		
2nd router address		
2nd preference level		
. . .		

sages. It allows hosts to discover the existence of neighboring routers, but not which router is best to reach a particular destination. If a host uses a poor first-hop router to reach a particular destination, it receives an *ICMP Redirect message* identifying a better choice in terms of another router address.

Hosts can use router solicitation messages to request immediate advertisements rather than wait for unsolicited messages. When a host attached to a multicast link starts up, it may multicast a *ICMP Router solicitation* to ask for immediate advertisements rather than wait for the next periodic ones to arrive; if (and only if) no advertisements are forthcoming, the host may retransmit the solicitation a small number of times, but then must refrain from sending any more solicitations. Any routers that subsequently start up, or that were not discovered because of packet loss or temporary link partitioning, are eventually discovered by the reception of their periodic (unsolicited) advertisements. (Links that suffer high packet loss rates or frequent partitioning are accommodated by increasing the rate of advertisements, rather than increasing the number of solicitations that hosts are permitted to send.)

10.6 Transport layer

The transport layer offers a choice between two protocols:

- the **User Datagram Protocol** (UDP) – offers unreliable transport service;
- the **Transmission Control Protocol** (TCP) – offers reliable transport service.

The interfaces (SAPs) of the transport layer to the application layer are commonly referred to as **port numbers**, and numbers smaller than 1024 have well-known, specified associations with concrete application protocols (known numbers are released in specific RFCs, the latest being RFC 1700 see also Appendix E) while higher numbers are of local (user's) significance.

10.6.1 Transmission control protocol

The **Transmission Control Protocol** (TCP) provides a connection-oriented (full-duplex, acknowledged, and flow-controlled) transport service to upper-layer protocols. It moves data in a continuous, unstructured octet stream where octets are identified by sequence numbers. TCP can also support numerous simultaneous upper-layer conversations.

Using a **handshaking scheme**, this protocol provides the mechanism for **establishing, maintaining, and terminating logical connections** between hosts. Additionally, TCP provides numerous ports (transport service access points with common numbers) to distinguish multiple applications executing on a single device by including the destination and source port number with each message. TCP also provides **reliable transmission** of octet streams, data flow definitions, data acknowledgments, data retransmission, and multiplexing multiple connections through a single network connection. The TCP segment format with all control fields is shown in Figure 10.23.

FIGURE 10-23 TCP segment format

Number of bits:

| 16 | | | | 16 |

source port			destination port	
sequence number				
acknowledgment number				
header length – *multiple 32 bits* (4 bits)	reserved = 0 (6 bits)	**control function** (6 bits) *U A P R S F* *R C S S Y I* *G K H T N N*	**window size**	
checksum			**urgent pointer**	
options (padding)				
data				

The **TCP segment fields** are as follows:

■ *Source port* – describes the connection to the specific upper-layer protocol when a sending device sends the packet down the TCP/IP protocol stack; the upper-layer protocol is identified by the port number (well-known numbers within the range 1–1023 identify the most common application layer protocols – see Appendix F – while numbers above are user assigned).

■ *Destination port* – describes the upper-layer protocol that TCP will transfer its data up to the protocol stack on a receiving station.

■ *Sequence number* – number assigned to every byte (octet) of data within the TCP segment (only 32 bits wide) to support reliable delivery of segments by identification of each correctly received byte (see RFC 1323 for ways to work around the sequence number limitation for high-speed links). The sending station uses sequence numbers to tag bytes sent out to the receiving station. The receiving station uses them to organize the bytes in the same order as they were sent. Sequence numbers uniquely identify every segment (the first byte therein) which helps eliminate duplicity, missing segments (in conjunction with acknowledgments), and also reassembly in the case of data segments received out of order. A receiving station will process TCP packets in this manner because on multi-homed links, bytes sent to the receiving station may arrive out of order. This can occur because one link may be slower than the other link. The sequence numbers can start at any arbitrary value and are incremented with the number of bytes sent. Therefore, the sequence number is not incremented in steps of one for each TCP segment, but in steps of the number of payload octets (starting with an arbitrary value).

- *Acknowledgment number* – used for establishing the reliability of the TCP communication together with sequence numbers: each station acknowledges the receipt of correctly delivered segments identified by their sequence number. The most common acknowledgment scheme is **positive acknowledgment** when the recipient station acknowledges receipt of all correctly received segments (bytes therein) by stating the sequence number of the next expected first byte of the segment. A more elaborate version of acknowledgment is **negative (or selective) acknowledgement** (SACK) which allows the recipient station to identify not the last segment (actually first byte of that segment) in a row received properly but to identify more granularly those segments (bytes) not received properly in the communication. This latter method eliminates the need to retransmit all the bytes in a row starting from the number identified in positive acknowledgment (as some might already be stored in the recipient's buffer), and instead permits the sending of just those not delivered or corrupted. The method used for the acknowledgment process is agreed between the communicating stations during connection establishment.

- *Header length* – describes where the actual data begins.

- *Reserved* – six bits which may be used in the future if such a need exists.

- *Control* – six code bits which distinguish session management messages from the data. This is where the *ACK* (acknowledgment) or *SYN* (synchronization) bits are flagged, besides *URG* (pointer to urgent data), *PSH* (push), *RST* (reset connection), and *FIN* (terminate the connection).

- *Window* – specifies the amount of traffic sent (number of segments) at one time before waiting for acknowledgment. The acknowledgment will be sent after the segment set is sent (in other words, the window relates to the necessary size of both the sender buffers). The TCP **sliding window** allows multiple packets to be sent before waiting for individual acknowledgment. The initial size of the TCP window is established at the beginning of the TCP session and can vary during the data transfer based upon network congestion and other variables. This is also referred to as flow control. A TCP window size of zero equals 'send no data.' The initial TCP three-way handshake (see below) is the point at which the receiving station specifies the TCP window size. After the sending station sends a SYN, the receiving station will respond with a SYN ACK segment and in that segment the window size will be indicated.

- *Checksum* – when a packet arrives at the destination, the receiving device calculates the Cyclic Redundancy Check (CRC) across the segment plus a so-called TCP/UDP pseudo-header (see Figure 10.27) to determine if the packet arrived intact. If not, the receiving device will ask for the packet to be retransmitted.

- *Urgent pointer* – specifies last octet of urgent data.

- *Options* – utilized by specific vendors to enhance their protocol services. The field may contain no bits, or up to 32 bits.

- *Data* – data handed down from the upper layer protocols.

The **three-way handshake** used by TCP for **connection establishment** is shown in Figure 10.24. The first synchronization (*SYN*) TCP message request opens the connection while setting up the startup sequence number for the byte flow from the source station. Once the *SYN* is received by the destination station,

FIGURE 10-24 Establishment of TCP connection

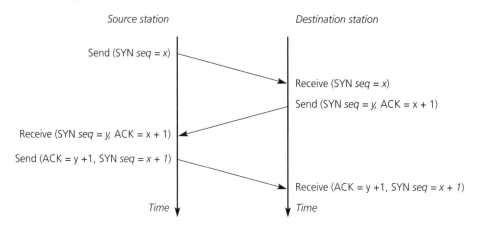

FIGURE 10-25 Reliable TCP communication with sequence numbers, acknowledgments, and windowing

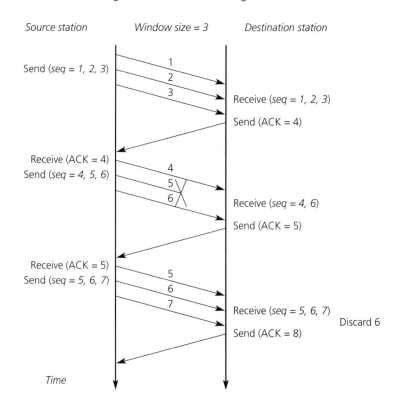

its transport layer generates an acknowledgment for the *SYN* message. Besides acknowledging the receipt of *SYN* by specifying the next expected sequence number, it also specifies the starting sequence number for the flow of bytes from the destination station to the source. This *SYN ACK* message still needs to be acknowledged by the source station. Once the three messages are successfully exchanged, the connection is established and user data communication may start.

10.6.2 TCP reliable transmission

RFC 2018 specified the use of the SACK option for acknowledging out-of-sequence data not covered by TCP's cumulative acknowledgment field (compared with traditional TCP operations as depicted in Figure 10.25). RFC 2883 is an extension of the **Selective Acknowledgement** (SACK) Option for TCP **for acknowledging duplicate packets**. When duplicate packets are received, the first block of the SACK option field can be used to report the sequence numbers of the packet that triggered the acknowledgment. This extension to the SACK option allows the TCP sender to infer the order of packets received at the receiver, allowing the sender to infer when it has unnecessarily retransmitted a packet. A TCP sender could then use this information for more robust operation in an environment of reordered packets, *ACK* loss, packet replication, and/or early retransmit timeouts. The advantage of *SACK* becomes apparent when large windows are being used in the sliding window protocol. Examples are fat pipes, fast links, and links where a large amount of data is transient (e.g. satellite links).

RFC WATCH   **TCP reliable transmission**

RFC 1323 **TCP Extensions for High Performance**, 1992 (Proposed Standard)

RFC 2018 **TCP Selective Acknowledgment Options**, 1996 (Proposed Standard)

RFC 2883 **An Extension to the Selective Acknowledgment (SACK) Option for TCP**, 2000 (Proposed Standard)

RFC 2988 **Computing TCP's Retransmission Timer**, 2000 (Proposed Standard)

RFC 3042 **Enhancing TCP's Loss Recovery Using Limited Transmit**, 2001 (Proposed Standard)

In TCP, each connection has a set of **states** associated with it. Such states are reflected by a set of variables stored in the **TCP Control Block** (TCB) of both ends. Such variables may include the local and remote socket number, precedence of the connection, security level, and compartment, etc. Both ends must agree on the setting of the precedence and security parameters in order to establish a connection and keep it open. There is no field in the TCP header that indicates the precedence of a segment. Instead, the precedence field in the header of the IP packet is used as the indication. The security level and compartment are likewise carried in the IP header, but as IP options rather than a fixed header field.

TCP requires that the **precedence** (and security parameters) of a connection must remain unchanged during the lifetime of the connection. Therefore, for an established TCP connection with precedence, the receipt of a segment with different precedence indicates an error. The connection must be reset. With the advent of DiffServ the understanding of the precedence field has changed and an extension to TCP has been proposed (see Section 10.6.4 below).

10.6.3 TCP flow control and congestion management

RFC WATCH	congestion management

RFC 896 **Congestion Control in IP/TCP Internetworks**, 1984

RFC 2581 **TCP Congestion Control**, 1999 (Proposed Standard)

RFC 2914 **Congestion Control Principles**, 2000 (Best Current Practice)

The original specification of TCP (RFC 793) included **window-based flow control** as a means for the receiver to govern the amount of data sent by the sender. This flow control was used to prevent overflow of the receiver's data buffer space available for that connection. Segments could be lost due either to errors or to network congestion, but there was no dynamic adjustment of the flow-control window in response to congestion.

When the receiver receives a data segment, it checks that data segment's four octet (32-bit) sequence number against the number the receiver expected, which would indicate that the data segment was received in order. If the numbers match, the receiver delivers all of the data that it holds to the target application, then it updates the sequence number to reflect the next number in order, and finally it either immediately sends an acknowledgment (*ACK*) packet to the sender or it schedules an *ACK* to be sent to the sender after a short delay. The *ACK* notifies the sender that the receiver received all bytes up to but not including the one marked with the new sequence number.

Receivers usually try to send an *ACK* in response to alternating data segments they receive; they send the *ACK* because for many applications, if the receiver waits out a small delay, it can efficiently include its reply acknowledgment on a normal response to the sender (so-called piggybacking). However, when the receiver receives a data segment out of order, it immediately responds with an *ACK* to direct the sender to resend the lost data segment.

When the sender receives an *ACK*, it determines if any data is outstanding. If no data is outstanding, the sender determines that the *ACK* is a keepalive, meant to keep the line active, and it does nothing. If data is outstanding, the sender determines whether the *ACK* indicates that the receiver has received some or none of the data. If the *ACK* indicates receipt of some data sent, the sender determines if new credit has been granted to allow it to send more data. When the *ACK* indicates receipt of none of the data sent and there is outstanding data, the sender interprets the *ACK* to be a repeatedly sent *ACK*. This condition indicates that some data was received out of order, forcing the receiver to remit the first *ACK*, and that a second data segment was received out of order, forcing the receiver to remit the second *ACK*. In most cases, the receiver would receive two segments out of order because one of the data segments had been dropped.

When a TCP sender detects a dropped data segment, it resends the segment. Then it adjusts its transmission rate so that it is half of what it was before the drop was detected. This is the **TCP back-off** or **slow-down** behavior. Although this behavior is appropriately responsive to congestion, problems can arise when multiple TCP sessions are carried on concurrently with the same router and all TCP senders slow down transmission of packets at the same time.

The original fix for Internet meltdown was provided by Van Jacobson. Beginning in 1986, Jacobson developed the congestion avoidance mechanisms that are now required in TCP implementations (RFC 2581). These mechanisms operate in the hosts to cause TCP connections to back off during congestion. We say that TCP flows are responsive to congestion signals (i.e. dropped packets) from the network. It is these TCP congestion avoidance algorithms that prevent the congestion collapse of today's Internet, particularly as TCP makes up 95% of current Internet traffic making it the dominant data transport.

Considerable research has been done on Internet dynamics since 1988, and the Internet has grown. It has become clear that the available TCP congestion avoidance mechanisms, while necessary and powerful, are not sufficient to provide good service in all circumstances. In addition to the development of new congestion control mechanisms, **router-based mechanisms** are in development that complement the endpoint congestion avoidance mechanisms.

A major issue that still needs to be addressed is the potential for future collapse through congestion of the Internet due to flows that do not use responsible end-to-end congestion control. RFC 896 suggested in 1984 that gateways (routers) should detect and squelch misbehaving hosts: 'Failure to respond to an *ICMP Source Quench* message, though, should be regarded as grounds for action by a gateway to disconnect a host. Detecting such failure is non-trivial but is a worthwhile area for further research.' Current papers still propose that routers detect and penalize flows that are not employing acceptable end-to-end congestion control.

In addition to a concern about congestion collapse, there is a concern about **fairness for best-effort traffic**. Because TCP backs off during congestion, a large number of TCP connections can share a single, congested link in such a way that bandwidth is shared reasonably equitably among similarly situated flows. The equitable sharing of bandwidth among flows depends on the fact that all flows are running compatible congestion control algorithms. For TCP, this means congestion control algorithms in conformance with the current TCP specification.

The issue of fairness among competing flows has become increasingly important for several reasons. First, using **window scaling** (RFC 1323), individual TCPs can use high bandwidth even over high-propagation-delay paths. Second, with the growth of the Web, Internet users increasingly want high-bandwidth and low-delay communications. The growth of best-effort traffic that does not use TCP underscores this concern about fairness between competing best-effort traffic in times of congestion.

The popularity of the Internet has caused a proliferation in the number of TCP implementations. Some of these may fail to implement the TCP congestion avoidance mechanisms correctly because of poor implementation (RFC 2525). Others may be deliberately implemented with congestion avoidance algorithms that are more aggressive in their use of bandwidth than other TCP implementations; this would allow a vendor to claim to have a *faster* TCP. The logical consequence of such implementations would be a spiral of increasingly aggressive TCP implementations, or increasingly aggressive transport protocols, leading back to the point where there is effectively no congestion avoidance and the Internet is chronically congested.

RFC WATCH   **TCP problems**

RFC 2525 **Known TCP Implementation Problems**, 1999 (Informational)

There is a well-known way to achieve more aggressive performance without even changing the transport protocol, but by changing the level of granularity: open **multiple connections** to the same place, as has been done in the past by some Web browsers. Thus, instead of a spiral of increasingly aggressive transport protocols, we would instead have a spiral of increasingly aggressive Web browsers, or increasingly aggressive applications.

There exist further proposals for TCP congestion control, such as a modification to the way TCP increases its **congestion window**. Rather than the traditional method of increasing the congestion window by a constant amount for each arriving acknowledgment, the increase could be based on the number of previously unacknowledged bytes each *ACK* covers. This change improves the performance of TCP, as well as closing a security hole TCP receivers can use to induce the sender into increasing the sending rate too rapidly.

However, it is important to realize that TCP does not distinguish packet loss caused by **network transmission error** from that caused by **network congestion**. The congestion control and avoidance mechanism makes TCP drop its **transmit window** upon detecting a packet loss, thus lowering the transmission rate even if the loss is caused by a physical link transmission error. As a result there may occur an unnecessary reduction in link bandwidth utilization. But in general, even on noisy lossy lines, some 90% of lost packets are due to router congestion rather than actual mangling of bits on the wire. In the environment of wireless physical links, a **selective acknowledgment** (RFC 2018) may be deployed to allow recovery without losing the window.

Queuing mechanisms in the router

The basic **queue mechanism** on the router works in the following way: the output interface queues fill when the bandwidth of the output link cannot keep up with the amount of traffic scheduled to go out of that link. If the traffic continues to pass through the router at a rate that exceeds the speed of the output link, it is possible for the queue system to fill to its maximum capacity. When this happens, the router has no choice but to drop all subsequent packets until the queue has more room. This result is called a **tail drop** condition (some packets are in the queue, but trailing packets are dropped). Tail drops are undesirable because packets from all flows are dropped at the same time and continue to drop until the queue system gets below its maximum capacity. The downside of this condition is that applications that cannot tolerate much packet loss, such as voice, will degrade.

In addition, **retransmission** of dropped packets must be handled, causing network congestion as its side effect. This is because TCP flows make up the majority of the traffic in current networks (WWW, File Transfer Protocol, Telnet, and many other client/server applications use the TCP protocol). When these TCP flows experience a tail drop, all of the senders associated with the flows trigger retransmission at the same time. This global synchronization of retransmissions congests the network further.

The TCP protocol deploys a unique mechanism for packet retransmission. TCP senders retransmit packets and subsequently resume their flows using a process called TCP **slow start**. In TCP slow start, an end station starts with a window size of one byte, i.e. sending one byte for which it expects an acknowledgment. The station then keeps increasing the window (the number of bytes) until delay or congestion limits performance.

Global synchronization combined with TCP slow start can lead to some very undesirable results. When many TCP flows have one or more packets dropped in a tail drop, they all go through TCP slow start at the same time. This means all these flows slow down at the same time, and traffic on the network as a whole drops abruptly. The network gets significantly quieter than it was before the tail drop. Next, because the flows are synchronized, they all start to speed up at the same time. This acceleration continues until the aggregate rate of the flows once again climbs to a maximum rate, at which time congestion causes another tail drop and the cycle repeats.

The behavior of TCP depends on a large number of factors, such as the congestion on the path from the client to server, the transmission window negotiated at connection establishment, maximum segment size, round-trip time estimation, and protocol version (Reno, Tahoe, Vegas), which provide different implementations of delayed *ACK* and window recovery mechanisms. Furthermore, users navigate the Internet in a random manner.

TCP connections do not generate bursts of packets, as could be expected from the slow start behavior. Rather than following a predetermined pattern imposed by TCP dynamics, the connection packet arrival process exhibits more randomness due to a number of contributions (loss, jitter, etc.) in the network segments from client to server.

The manner in which TCP responds to **packet loss** is both its biggest strength and its greatest source of unpredictability. TCP can adapt to any environment or line speed, because a small number of drops caused by local congestion signal to TCP that it should reduce its transmission rate.

When several message segments are lost simultaneously, though, TCP cannot determine how to recover, and it waits for a timeout before trying. Because timeouts can last for a matter of seconds, TCP operating in such environments tends to move data very slowly. The way to avoid these slowdowns is to use a drop policy such as **Random Early Detection** (RED), which distributes drops over different TCP sessions. RED drops random packets based on the number of packets queued on an interface. As a queue reaches its maximum capacity, RED drops packets more aggressively to avoid a tail drop. RED throttles back flows and takes advantage of TCP slow start. Rather than tail-dropping all packets when the queue is full, RED manages queue depth by randomly dropping some packets as the queue fills (past a certain threshold). As packets drop, the applications associated with those dropped packets slow down and go through TCP slow start. This process reduces the traffic destined for the link and provides relief to the queue system.

10.6.4 TCP and QoS

The TCP functionality may be usefully enhanced by specific mechanisms enforcing and ensuring the QoS levels which we discuss in more detail in Part V.

RFC 2873 describes a conflict between TCP and **Differentiated Services** (DiffServ – see Part V) on the use of the three leftmost bits in the TOS octet of an IPv4 header. In a network that contains DiffServ-capable nodes, such a conflict can cause failures in establishing TCP connections or can cause some established TCP connections to be reset undesirably. Because the IPv6 traffic class octet does not have any defined meaning except what is defined by DiffServ, and in particular does not define precedence or security parameter bits, there is no conflict between TCP and DiffServ on the use of any bits in the IPv6 traffic class octet.

RFC WATCH **TCP and IP precedence**

RFC 2873 **TCP Processing of the IPv4 Precedence Field**, 2000 (Proposed Standard)

The proposed modification to TCP is that TCP must ignore the precedence of all received segments. More specifically, in TCP's synchronization process, the TCP modules at both ends must ignore the precedence fields of the *SYN* and *SYN ACK*. The TCP connection will be established if all the conditions specified by RFC 793 are satisfied except the precedence of the connection. After a connection is established, each end sends segments with its desired precedence. The precedence picked by one end of the TCP connection may be the same or may be different from the precedence picked by the other end (because precedence is ignored during connection setup time). The precedence fields may be changed by the intermediate nodes too. In either case, the precedence of the received packets will be ignored by the other end. The TCP connection will not be reset in either case.

To ensure that each application gets the level of service it requires from the network, a classification system is employed that relies on **Differentiated Services Code Point** (DSCP) to limit some class of traffic to some rate or to guarantee some application or community of users a certain rate. As a mechanism for QoS (discussed at length in Part V), RED drops low-precedence packets before high-precedence packets. This means applications with specific timing demands – such as voice – that are less tolerant of a packet drop (and TCP slow start) than other applications stand a better chance of receiving the resources they need. RED achieves QoS by maintaining thresholds at various queue depths – one threshold for each precedence level. As a queue fills and exceeds a threshold, the precedence level associated with that threshold is eligible for random drops. A high-precedence level correlates to a high threshold in that queue. This combination of RED and DSCP is known as **Weighted Random Early Detection** (WRED, see Part V).

10.6.5 User datagram protocol

User Datagram Protocol (UDP), as specified in RFC 768, provides an unreliable, connectionless transport service for IP. Therefore, this protocol is usually used for transaction-oriented utilities such as the IP standard Simple Network Management Protocol (SNMP) and Trivial File Transfer Protocol (TFTP), and BOOTP. All of these applications rely on UDP for its fast and efficient delivery. (See Figure 10.2 for protocols using UDP as a transport protocol.)

RFC WATCH	UDP

RFC 768 **User Datagram Protocol**, 1980 (Standard)

UDP uses the underlying IP protocol (through SAP or protocol number 17) to transport messages to a destination and provides a transport service through the port numbers (for well-known UDP port numbers see Appendix F) to distinguish between software applications executing on a single host. However, UDP avoids the overhead of a reliable data transfer mechanism by not protecting against datagram loss or duplication, unlike TCP. UDP supports broadcast to 255.255.255.255, unlike TCP which has to open a connection to a concrete destination address.

UDP is a much simpler protocol than TCP and is useful in situations where the reliability mechanisms of TCP are not necessary. UDP does not support fragmentation of data into an IP datagram, hence there is a one-to-one mapping between the UDP segment and IP datagram. The UDP header has only four fields: *source port, destination port, length* (of UDP segment in 32-bit words), and *UDP checksum*. The source and destination port fields serve the same functions as they do in the TCP header (see Section 10.6.1). The length field specifies the length of the UDP header and data, and the checksum field allows packet integrity checking. (For the UDP segment format see Figure 10.26.)

FIGURE 10-26 UDP segment format

Number of bits:

16	16
source port	destination port
length	checksum
data	

A **pseudo-header** is used for checksum (fictively attached before the real header), both in TCP and UDP. A pseudo-header is shown in Figure 10.27.

FIGURE 10-27 Pseudo-header of TCP/UDP segment

Number of bits:

8	8	16
source IP address		
destination IP address		
0... ...0	protocol number	segment length *(without pseudo-header)*

10.7 New internet protocols

There is a handful of newer TCP/IP **application layer protocols** related to multimedia and other widely available Internet features. Some applications such as stream media or interactive TV do not require the reliability that TCP provides, but need to preserve data transmission order and the connection state for a considerable duration of packet exchange or transmission. We will briefly discuss several protocols supporting the current internetworking requirements, including IP stations' autoconfiguration, multimedia support, and quality of service support (the QoS issues are discussed at length in Part V).

10.7.1 Dynamic host configuration protocol

As IP address management has become very difficult with the ever growing number of attached stations, subnets, and networks, and as stricter rules have been imposed on IP address assignment due to lack of address space and Internet routers' capacity, a move from inherent statically assigned addressing has led to the development of a dynamic protocol: **Dynamic Host Configuration Protocol** (DHCP) was developed in 1997 (RFC 2131).

RFC WATCH DHCP

RFC 2131 **Dynamic Host Configuration Protocol**, 1997 (Draft Standard)

RFC 3004 **The User Class Option for DHCP**, 2000 (Proposed Standard)

RFC 3011 **The IPv4 Subnet Selection Option for DHCP**, 2000 (Proposed Standard)

RFC 3046 **DHCP Relay Agent Information Option**, 2001 (Proposed Standard)

The DHCP is designed to provide a centralized approach to the configuration and maintenance of an IP address space. It allows the network administrator to configure various clients on the network from a single location. DHCP permits IP address leases to be dynamically assigned to workstations, eliminating the need for static IP address allocation by network and systems management staff. Pools of available IP addresses are maintained by servers that implement DHCP server functionality (DHCP servers have permanent IP addresses).

DHCP supports three mechanisms for IP address allocation: dynamic allocation, automatic allocation, and manual allocation. With **automatic allocation**, DHCP assigns a **permanent** IP address to a host. With **dynamic allocation**, DHCP assigns an IP address to a host for a **limited period of time**. Using **manual allocation**, the network administrator assigns the host's IP address, and DHCP is used to convey the assigned address to the host.

When a **DHCP client** workstation boots, it broadcasts a **DHCP request** asking for any **DHCP server** on the network to provide it with an IP address and configuration parameters. A DHCP server on the network that is authorized to configure this client will offer an IP address by sending a reply to the client. Upon receiving this offer, the client may decide to accept it or it may wait for additional offers from other servers on the network. At the end, the client decides on a particular offer and sends a request to accept the offer made by the server. Knowing that it has been chosen, the server will then send back an acknowledgment with the offered IP address and any other configuration **parameters** that the client might have requested. The server does not force any parameters on the client and it is up to the client to request the parameters that it is willing to accept.

Under the **dynamic allocation** scheme the IP **address** offered to the client has an associated **lease time**. The lease time dictates for how long the IP address is valid. During the lifetime of the lease, the client will repeatedly ask the server to renew. If the client chooses not to renew or if the client machine is shut down, the lease will eventually expire. Once the lease expires, the IP address returns to the pool of available IP addresses and may be given to another machine. DHCP dynamic allocation works well for stations that stay temporarily connected to the network.

Besides dynamic assignment of addresses, DHCP servers can assign **static IP addresses** to clients. In this case, addresses are assigned **with an infinite lease**. Net managers need a way to keep the same IP address from being issued to more than one user on the network. DHCP servers commonly verify addresses by using a PING to determine if an IP address is already in use.

10.7.2 Real-time transport protocol

Real-time Transport Protocol (RTP, RFC 1889) supports end-to-end delivery of broadcast packetized multi-party interactive video and audio. While most implementations of RTP use the UDP protocol, it was not designed to be dependent on this. RTP provides for timing information to synchronize and display audio and video data and to determine if packets are lost or misordered. RTP can support multiple data and compression types.

The minimal 12 octets of the RTP header, combined with 20 octets of IP header and eight octets of UDP header, create a 40-octet IP/UDP/RTP header. The RTP packet has a payload of approximately 20 to 150 octets for audio applications that use compressed payloads. It is very inefficient to transmit the IP/UDP/RTP

RFC WATCH   **real-time transport protocol (RTP)**

RFC 1889 **RTP: A Transport Protocol for Real-Time Applications**, 1996
  (Proposed Standard)
RFC 3016 **RTP Payload Format for MPEG-4 Audio/Visual Streams**, 2000
  (Proposed Standard)

header without compressing it. The RTP header compression feature compresses the IP/UDP/RTP header in an RTP data packet from 40 octets down to approximately two to five octets. It uses a hop-by-hop compression scheme, **Compressed Real-Time Protocol** (CRTP), similar to RFC 1144 for TCP header compression.

10.7.3 Real-time transport control protocol

The **Real-time Transport Control Protocol** (RTCP) works alongside TCP, supports RTP, and provides mechanisms for reporting reception quality (needed to allow adaptive behavior on the sender's part), for diagnosing distribution faults, for identifying and tracking the receivers, and for controlling the rate at which participants transmit RTCP packets.

RTCP sends multicast feedback, not only to the sender but to all other recipients of the multicast stream. This helps to determine if the reported problem is a local or network-wide problem. RTCP also provides feedback on who has subscribed to a given group at any time.

10.7.4 Real-time streaming protocol

The **Real-Time Streaming Protocol** (RTSP) is an application level protocol for control over the delivery of data with realtime properties. It provides an extensible framework to enable controlled, on-demand delivery of realtime data (such as audio or video). Sources of data can include live feeds and stored clips. This protocol is intended to control multiple data delivery sessions, provide a means for choosing delivery channels such as UDP, multicast UDP, and TCP, as well as delivery mechanisms based on RTP. RTSP uses the Stream Control Transmission Protocol to allow the use of a single TCP connection between the client and server for controlling the delivery of one or more streams of data.

RFC WATCH   **RTSP**

RFC 2326 **Real-Time Streaming Protocol** (RTSP), 1998 (Proposed Standard)
RFC 2960 **Stream Control Transmission Protocol,** 2000 (Proposed Standard)

10.7.5 Resource reservation protocol

The **Resource ResSerVation Protocol** (RSVP, RFC 2205) is a **receiver-oriented signaling protocol** used to allow each receiver operation to reserve bandwidth in a network required for **delay-sensitive traffic**, like voice and video. Hosts and routers use RSVP to deliver these requests to the routers along the paths of the data flow and to maintain the router and host state to provide the requested service. RSVP specifies that each router between network end-points participate in the RSVP signaling sessions to reserve, tear down, and manage appropriate resources. This model provides end-to-end, fine-grained resource control but leads to serious scalability difficulties in large, high-speed networks (such as the ISP backbone). It provides the mechanism for creating and maintaining flow-specific state information in the end point hosts and in routers along the data-flow path.

RSVP defines a way for applications on end stations to request priority, a specific quality of service. It require forwarding decisions to be made about routing at each intermediate node along the RSVP path based on RSVP-controlled packets carrying the 'abstract handle,' or session ID, for the TCP/IP session to which they belonged. Each intermediate router has to maintain a dynamically updated table containing abstract handles and reservation information set up by RSVP exchanges. When the router receives a packet belonging to an RSVP session, it has to look up the packet's abstract handle in its local table to know what to do with the packet.

RSVP was designed to **meet a number of requirements**: support for **heterogeneous service** needs; flexible control over the way reservations are shared along branches of multicast delivery trees; **scalability** to large multicast groups; and the ability to **preempt resources to accommodate advance reservations**. RSVP allows multimedia streaming applications to receive the highest priority and ensure the service quality they need, while coexisting with existing bursty applications on the same network.

RFC WATCH   **RSVP**

RFC 2205 **Resource ReSerVation Protocol (RSVP) – Version 1 Functional Specification**, 1997 (Proposed Standard)

RSVP permits end systems to request **Quality of Service** (QoS) guarantees from the network. (See Part V for more details on QoS and RSVP.)

10.8 Internet Protocol version 6

IP version 6, the Next-Generation Internet Protocol (IPng), was specified in RFC 2460. IPv6 provides a framework for solving some critical problems that currently exist inside and between enterprises. On the global scale, IPv6 should allow Internet backbone designers to create a highly flexible and open-ended global routing hierarchy. At the level of the Internet backbone it is necessary to maintain a hierarchical addressing system.

RFC WATCH   **IPv6**

RFC 2460 **Internet Protocol, Version 6 (IPv6) Specification**, 1998 (Draft Standard)

Without an address hierarchy, backbone routers would be forced to store routing table information on the reachability of every network in the world which is not feasible. With a hierarchy, backbone routers can use IP address prefixes to determine how traffic should be routed through the backbone. As we saw in Section 10.3.4 above, IPv4 uses a technique called Classless InterDomain Routing (CIDR), which allows flexible use of variable-length network prefixes. With this flexible use of prefixes, CIDR permits considerable route aggregation at various levels of the Internet hierarchy, which means backbone routers can store a single routing table entry that provides reachability to many lower-level networks.

But the availability of CIDR routing does not guarantee an efficient and scalable hierarchy. In many cases, legacy IPv4 address assignments that originated before CIDR do not facilitate summarization. In fact, much of the IPv4 address space was formed before the current access provider hierarchy was developed. The lack of uniformity in the current hierarchical system, coupled with the rationing of IPv4 addresses, means that Internet addressing and routing increasingly are fraught with complications at all levels. These issues affect high-level service providers and individual end users in all types of businesses.

For compatibility purposes of the two IP versions and for co-existence within an internet, RFC 3056 was specified.

RFC WATCH   **IPv6 over IPv4 cloud**

RFC 3056 **Connection of IPv6 Domains via IPv4 Clouds**, 2001 (Proposed Standard)

10.8.1 IPv6 addressing

To meet the strict extended and hierarchical addressing needs, IPv6 uses 128-bit addresses. The IPv6 addressing architecture is specified in RFC 2373. A single interface may have multiple unique **unicast** addresses. Any of the unicast

SNAPSHOT **IPv6 benefits**

- Extended address space allowing hierarchical prefix-based routing (smaller routing tables) to overcome future address shortages.
- A standardized header format and size making it easier to process packets in modern 64-bit hardware architectures.
- Header and payload compression.
- QoS and DiffServ features.
- Mandated security (authentication, integrity, confidentiality, and key management).
- Mandated autoconfiguration in both stateful and stateless modes.
- Updated routing protocols (RIPv6, OSPFv6, BGP4+, IDRPv6).
- Multi-homing possibilities.
- Dual stack migration strategy ensuring interoperability with the installed base of IPv4 devices.
- Simplified mobility supporting mobile and nomadic scenarios.

addresses associated with a node's interface may be used to uniquely identify that node. Besides **multicast** addresses IPv6 also introduces a new, **anycast** type of address.

RFC WATCH **IPv6 addressing**

RFC 2373 **IP Version 6 Addressing Architecture**, 1998 (Proposed Standard)

The combination of long addresses and multiple addresses per interface enables improved routing efficiency of IPv6 over IPv4. Longer addresses allow for aggregating addresses by hierarchies of network, access provider, geography, corporation, and so on. Such aggregation should make for smaller routing tables and faster table lookups. The allowance for multiple addresses per interface would allow a subscriber using multiple access providers across the same interface to have separate addresses aggregated under each provider's address space.

Unicast address

A **unicast address** is an identifier for a single interface. It may be structured in a number of ways. The following types have been identified:

■ **Provider-based global unicast address** – provides for global addressing across the entire universe of connected hosts. The address has five fields after the format prefix:

– *Registry ID* – identifies the registration authority which assigns the provider portion of the address.

– *Provider ID* – a specific internet service provider which assigns the subscriber portion of the address.

– *Subscriber ID* – distinguishes among multiple subscribers attached to the provider portion of the address.

– *Subnet ID* – a topologically connected group of nodes within the subscriber network.

– *Interface ID* – identifies a single node interface among the group of interfaces identified by the subnet prefix.

The IPv6 aggregatable global unicast address format is shown in Figure 10.28.

FIGURE 10-28 IPv6 aggregatable global unicast address

Number of bits:

3	13	8	24	16	64
Format Prefix (001)	Top-Level Aggregation Identifier	Reserved	Next-Level Aggregation Identifier	Site-Level Aggregation Identifier	Interface Identifier

IPv6 accommodates **local-use unicast addresses**. Packets with such addresses can only be routed locally, that is within a subnet or set of subnets of a given subscriber. Two types of local-use addresses have been defined:

■ **Link-local addresses** – used for addressing on a single link or subnet. They cannot be integrated into the global addressing scheme (e.g. for neighbor discovery).

■ **Site-local addresses** – for local use but formatted in such a way that they can later be integrated into the global address scheme. The advantage of such addresses is that they can be used immediately by an organization that expects to make the transition to the use of global addresses.

The structure of these addresses is such that the meaningful portion of the address is confined to the low-order bits not used for global addresses. The remaining bits consist of a local-use format prefix – *1111 1110 10* for link-local, or *1111 1110 11* for site-local address – followed by a zero field. When an organization is ready for global connection, these remaining bits can be replaced with a global prefix (e.g. *010 + Registry ID + Provider ID + Subscriber ID*).

IPv4-compatible IPv6 addresses provide for a period of coexistence. This form of address consists of a 32-bit IPv4 address in the lower-order 32 bits prefixed by 96 zeroes. The IPv4-compatible IPv6 address supports tunneling of an IPv6 packet over an IPv4 network. With the use of an IPv4-compatible IPv6 address for the destination node, the tunneling may be automated in the sense that the destination IPv4 address may be derived from the IPv6 address, avoiding the need to explicitly configure the mapping from an IPv6 address to an IPv4 address.

The **loopback address** (*0:0:0:0:0:0:0:1*) is the last type of unicast address. It may be used by a node to send an IPv6 packet to itself; such packets are not to be sent outside a single node.

Anycast address

Anycast addresses, a completely new address type, are identifiers for a set of interfaces (typically belonging to different nodes). A packet sent to an anycast address is delivered to only one of the interfaces identified by that address (the 'nearest' according to the routing protocol's measure of distance). An example of the use of an anycast address is within a routing header to specify an intermediate address along a route. The anycast address could refer to the group of routers associated with a particular provider or particular subnet, thus dictating that the packet be routed through that provider or internet in the most efficient manner.

QUICK TIP	anycast vs. multicast address

A packet destined to an **anycast address** will be delivered to just **one member** of the anycast group. A packet destined to a **multicast address** would be delivered to **every member** of the group.

One example of effective anycast address usage is querying a pool of DNS servers (implementing, for example, a root DNS server with heavy traffic). Since DNS queries are short enough to fit in a single UDP packet, this packet could be sent to an anycast address representing the DNS pool. Just one DNS server would get that request, and if the router implements a round-robin or other load balancing scheme among the anycast group members, the load would be evenly distributed among the DNS servers. Another use is a random router chosen with an anycast address in a fan-out setting (multi-link, where the routers at the other end are members of the same anycast group).

Anycast addresses are allocated from the same address space as unicast addresses. Thus, members of an anycast group must be configured to recognize that address, and routers must be configured to be able to map an anycast address to a group of unicast interface addresses.

One particular form of anycast address, the **subnet-router anycast address**, is predefined. The subnet prefix field identifies a specific subnet. For example, in a provider-based global address space, the subnet prefix is of the form (*010 + Registry ID + Provider ID + Subscriber ID + Subnet ID*). Thus the anycast address is identical to a unicast address for an interface on this subnet, with the interface ID portion set to zero. Any packet sent to this address will be delivered to one router on the subnet; all that is required is to insert the correct interface ID into the anycast address to form the unicast destination address.

Multicast address

Multicast addresses serve as identifiers for a set of interfaces (typically belonging to different nodes). A packet sent to a multicast address is delivered to all interfaces identified by that address. IPv6 includes the capability to address a predefined group of interfaces with a single multicast address. A packet with a multicast address is to be delivered to all members of the group. A multicast address consists of an eight-bit format prefix of all ones (*11111111*), a four-bit flag field (indicating a permanent or transient assigned multicast address), a four-bit scope field (link, site, organization, or global), and a 112-bit group ID (identifying a multicast group, either permanent or transient, within the given scope). (See Table 10.6 for reserved multicast addresses.)

TABLE 10-6	Reserved IPv6 multicast addresses
All nodes addresses:	*FF01:0:0:0:0:0:0:1*
	FF02:0:0:0:0:0:0:1
All routers addresses:	*FF01:0:0:0:0:0:0:2*
	FF02:0:0:0:0:0:0:2
	FF05:0:0:0:0:0:0:2
Solicited-node address:	*FF02:0:0:0:0:1:FFXX:XXXX*

Multicasting is a useful capability in a number of contexts (some will be discussed in relation to IPv4 multicast applications in the next chapter). For example, it allows hosts and routers to send neighbor discovery messages only to those machines that are registered to receive them, removing the necessity for all other machines to examine and discard irrelevant packets. As another example, most LANs provide a natural broadcast capability. A multicast address with link-local scope can be assigned to all LAN nodes with a group ID to be a subnet broadcast address.

10.8.2 Address autoconfiguration in IPv6

IPv6 supports an automatic method of client address configuration, using protocols known from IPv4 as ICMP and DHCP, and adding one protocol. The process of auto-configuration under IPv6 starts with the **Neighbor Discovery** (ND) protocol (RFC 2461). ND combines and refines the services provided in the IPv4 environment by ARP and ICMP. Although it has a new name, ND is actually just a set of complementary ICMP messages that allow IPv6 nodes on the same link to discover link-layer addresses and to obtain and advertise various network parameters and reachability information. In a typical scenario, a host starts the process of autoconfiguration by self-configuring a link-local address to use temporarily. This address can be formed by adding a **generic local address prefix** to a **unique address** (typically the host's MAC address). Once this address is formed, the host sends out an ND message to the address, to ensure that it is unique. If no ICMP message comes back, the address is unique. If a message comes back indicating that the link-local address is already in use, then a different base is used (e.g. an administratively created or a randomly generated one). IPv6 neighbor discovery and stateless auto-configuration is quite similar to the ES-IS (End System to Intermediate System) protocol operation in an OSI/CLNP routed environment (see Section 12.6).

RFC WATCH **discovery in IPv6**

RFC 2461 **Neighbor Discovery for IP Version 6 (IPv6)**, 1998 (Draft Standard)

RFC 3019 **IP Version 6 Management Information Base for the Multicast Listener Discovery Protocol**, 2001 (Proposed Standard)

Using the new link-local address as a source address, the host then sends out an ND **router solicitation** request. The solicitation is sent out using the IPv6 multicast service (see Table 10.6). Unlike the broadcasted ARPs of IPv4, IPv6 ND multicast solicitations are not necessarily processed by all nodes on the link, which can conserve processing resources in hosts. IPv6 defines several permanent multicast groups for finding resources on the local node or link, including an all-routers group, an all-hosts group, and a DHCP server group. Routers respond to the solicitation messages from hosts with a unicast router advertisement that contains, among other things, prefix information that indicates a valid range of addresses for the subnet. Routers also send these advertisements out periodically to local multicast groups, whether or not they receive solicitations.

Using the **router advertisement** message, the router can control whether hosts use stateless or stateful autoconfiguration methods. In the case of **stateful** autoconfiguration, the host will contact a DHCP or similar address server, which will assign an address from a manually administered list.

With the **stateless** approach (defined in RFC 2462), a host can automatically configure its own IPv6 address without the help of a stateful address server or any human intervention. The host uses the globally valid address prefix information in the router advertisement message to create its own IPv6 address. This process involves the concatenation of a valid prefix with the host's Layer 2 address or a similar unique token. As long as the base part of the address is unique and the prefix received from the router is correct, the newly configured IP address should provide reachability for the host that extends to the entire enterprise and the Internet at large.

RFC WATCH **IPv6 address autoconfiguration**

RFC 2462 **IPv6 Stateless Address Autoconfiguration**, 1998 (Draft Standard)

RFC 3041 **Privacy Extensions for Stateless Address Autoconfiguration in IPv6**, 2001 (Proposed Standard)

The advantages of stateless autoconfiguration are many. For instance, if an enterprise changes service providers, the prefix information from the new provider can be propagated to routers throughout the enterprise, and hence to all stateless autoconfiguring hosts. Hypothetically, if all hosts in the enterprise use IPv6 stateless autoconfiguration, the entire enterprise could be renumbered without the manual configuration of a single host. At a more modest level, workgroups with substantial move/change activity also benefit from stateless autoconfiguration because hosts can receive a freshly configured and valid IP number each time they connect and reconnect to the network. The IP address autoconfiguration helps support the station mobility under IP. With the IP forwarding features, DNS entries can remain essentially untouched, even if a host moves to another part of the world.

10.8.3 IPv6 routers performance

Although the IPv6 header is longer than the mandatory portion of the IPv4 header (40 octets versus 20 octets), it contains fewer fields (8 versus 12). Thus, routers have less processing to do per header, which should speed up routing.

Three aspects of IPv6 design contribute to meeting current LAN–WAN interconnect performance requirements:

■ the number of fields in the IPv6 packet header is reduced from IPv4;

■ a number of the IPv6 options are placed in separate optional headers located between the IPv6 header and the transport-layer header – most of these optional headers are not examined or processed by any router on the packet's path;

■ the IPv6 packet header is fixed length as opposed to the IPv4 header, which simplifies processing;

■ packet fragmentation is not permitted by IPv6 routers, only by the source.

RFC WATCH	router renumbering in IPv6
	RFC 2894 **Router Renumbering for IPv6**, 2000 (Proposed Standard)

10.8.4 IPv6 datagram

Beyond the streamlined datagram format, IPv6 features improve support for **header extensions and options**, changing the way IP header options are encoded to allow more efficient forwarding. Optional IPv6 header information is conveyed in independent extension headers located after the IPv6 header and before the transport-layer header in each packet (typically they do not require router processing). IPv6 header extensions are now variable in length and have less stringent length limits. IPv6 gives network software designers a very straightforward technique for introducing new header options in the future.

Option fields have already been defined for carrying explicit routing information created by the source node, as well as facilitating authentication, encryption, and fragmentation control. At the application level, header extensions are available for specialized end-to-end network applications that require their own header fields within the IP packet.

The IPv6 header has a fixed length of 40 octets (compared to 20 octets for the mandatory portion of the IPv4 header), consisting of the following fields (see Figure 10.29):

FIGURE 10-29 IPv6 datagram format

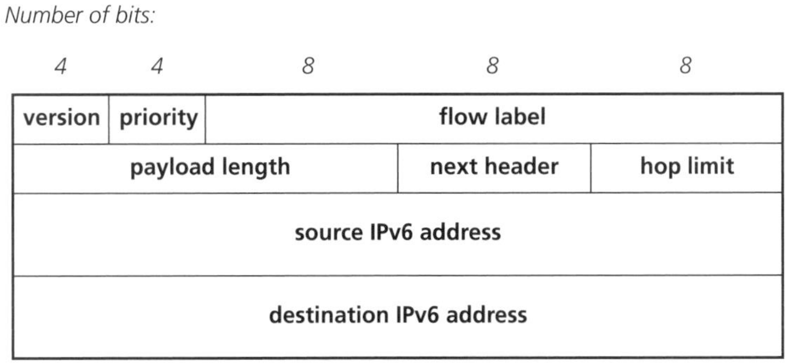

Number of bits:

version (4)	priority (4)	flow label (8 · 8 · 8)		
payload length		next header	hop limit	
source IPv6 address				
destination IPv6 address				

- *Version* (four bits) – IP version number; the value is *6*.

- *Priority* (four bits) – the four-bit priority field enables a source to identify the desired two-part transmit and delivery priority of each packet relative to other packets from the same source (first, packets are classified as being part of the traffic for which the source is either providing congestion control or not; second, packets are assigned one of eight levels of relative priority within each classification).

- *Flow label* (24 bits) – may be used by a host to label those packets for which it is requesting special handling by routers within a network. (Hosts or routers that do not support the flow label field must set the field to zero when originating a packet, pass the field unchanged when forwarding a packet, and ignore the field when receiving a packet.) The IPv6 standard defines a flow as a sequence of packets sent from a particular source to a particular (unicast or multicast) destination for which the source desires special handling by the intervening routers. A flow is uniquely identified by the combination of a source address and a non-zero 24-bit flow label which is the same for all packets that are part of the same flow.

  From the router's point of view, a **flow** is a sequence of packets that share attributes which affect how they are handled by the router, including path, resource allocation, discard requirements, accounting, and security attributes. The router may treat packets from different flows differently in a number of ways, including allocating different buffer sizes, giving different precedence in terms of forwarding, and requesting different qualities of service from subnets. As there is no special significance to any particular flow label, the special handling to be provided for a packet flow must be declared beforehand in some other way, e.g. using the RSVP protocol, and the router must save flow requirement information about each flow. However, to build a general table for all possible flow labels and even to have only one entry in the table per active flow would require the router to search the entire table each time a packet is encountered. This imposes an unnecessary processing burden on the router. Instead, most routers are likely to use some sort of hash table approach. With this approach a moderate-sized table is used, and each flow entry is mapped into the table using a hashing function on the flow label.

- *Payload length* (16 bits) – length of the remainder of the IPv6 packet following the header, in octets. In other words, this is the total length of all the extension headers plus the transport PDU.

- *Next header* (eight bits) – identifies the type of header immediately following the IPv6 header.

- *Hop limit* (eight bits) – the remaining number of allowable hops for this packet. The hop limit is set to some desired maximum value by the source, and decremented by 1 by each node that forwards the packet. The packet is discarded if the hop limit is decremented to zero (similar to the currently used IPv4 TTL field).

- *Source address* (128 bits) – the address of the originator of the packet.

- *Destination address* (128 bits) – the address of the intended recipient of the packet. This may not in fact be the intended ultimate destination if a routing header is present.

Six **extension headers** have been defined which may or may not appear after the standard IPv6 header in the following order:

- **Hop-by-hop options header** – defines special options that require hop-by-hop processing (by each router along the path).

- **Destination options header** – contains optional information to be examined by the destination node (appears as second optional header for options to be processed by the first destination that appears in the IPv6 destination address field plus subsequent destinations listed in the routing header, or last for options to be processed only by the final destination of the packet).

- **Routing header** (next header type 43) – provides extended routing, similar to IPv4 source routing. It contains a list of one or more intermediate nodes to be visited on the way to a packet's destination. All routing headers start with a 32-bit block consisting of four eight-bit fields (next header, header extension length, routing type, segments left) followed by routing data specific to a given routing type. In addition to this general header definition, a Type 0 routing header exists which includes a 24-bit strict/loose bit map. The bits of the field are considered to be numbered from left to right (bit 0 through bit 23), with each bit corresponding to one of the hop. Each bit indicates whether the corresponding next destination address must be a neighbor of the preceding address (1 = strict, must be a neighbor; 0 = loose, need not be a neighbor). When using the Type 0 routing header, the source node does not place the ultimate destination address in the IPv6 header. Instead, that address is the last address listed in the routing header, and the IPv6 header contains the destination address of the first desired router on the path. The routing header will not be examined until the packet reaches the node identified in the IPv6 header. At that point, the packet IPv6 and routing header contents are updated, and the packet is forwarded. The update consists of placing the next address to be visited in the IPv6 header and decrementing the segment's left field in the routing header. The protocol requires an IPv6 node to reverse routes in a packet it receives containing a routing header in order to return a packet to the sender.

- **Fragment header** – contains fragmentation and reassembly information. In IPv6, fragmentation may only be performed by source nodes, not by routers along a packet's delivery path. To take full advantage of the internetworking environment, a node must perform a path discovery algorithm that enables it to learn the smallest Maximum Transmission Unit (MTU) supported by any subnet on the path. In other words, the path discovery algorithm enables a node to learn the MTU of the bottleneck subnet on the path. With this knowledge, the source node will fragment, as required, for each given destination address. Otherwise, the source must limit all packets to 576 octets, which is the minimum MTU that must be supported by each subnet.

- **Authentication header** – provides packet integrity and authentication.

- **Encapsulating security payload header** – provides privacy.

The IPv6 header and each extension header include a next header field. This field identifies the type of the header immediately following. If the next header is an extension header, then this field contains the type identifier of that header; other-wise, this field contains the protocol identifier of the upper-layer protocol using IPv6 (typically a transport-level protocol), using the same values as the IPv4 protocol field.

IPv6 does not have a header length field as does IPv4. Instead, it has a fixed basic header with a pointer to optional fixed-length extended headers, or a null pointer that says there are no more header fields. This was very carefully considered as a necessary step to ensure high-performance routing.

10.8.5 ICMP version 6

The accompanying protocol for IPv6 is ICMPv6 with the same operations and general message format as ICMPv4 (see Section 10.5 above). It uses the error and informational messages (RFC 2463) listed in Table 10.7.

TABLE 10-7 ICMP version 6 message types

Message type	Error message	Message type	Informational messages
1	Destination unreachable	128	Echo request
2	Packet too big	129	Echo reply
3	Time exceeded	130	Group membership query
4	Parameter problem	131	Group membership report
		132	Group membership reduction

RFC WATCH   ICMPv6

RFC 2463 **Internet Control Message Protocol (ICMPv6) for the Internet Protocol Version 6 (IPv6) Specification**, 1998 (Draft Standard)

10.9 Next hop resolution protocol

Routers and hosts can use **Next Hop Resolution Protocol** (NHRP) to discover the addresses of other routers and hosts connected to a Non-Broadcast, Multi-Access (NBMA) network (typically WAN). In the past, partially meshed NBMA networks had to be configured with overlapping LIS (logically independent IP subnets). In such configurations, packets might have had to make several hops over the NBMA network before arriving at the exit router (the router nearest the destination network). In addition, such NBMA networks (whether partially or fully meshed) have typically required static configurations of mapping between network layer addresses (such as IP) and NBMA addresses (such as X.121 addresses for X.25).

NHRP provides an ARP-like solution that alleviates these NBMA network problems. With NHRP, systems attached to an NBMA network can dynamically learn the NBMA address of the other systems that are part of that network. These systems can then directly communicate without requiring traffic to use an intermediate hop.

The NBMA network can be considered to be non-broadcast either because it technically does not support broadcasting (for example, an X.25 network) or because broadcasting is not feasible (too large).

RFC WATCH   NHRP

RFC 2332 **NBMA Next Hop Resolution Protocol** (NHRP), 1998 (Proposed Standard)

RFC 2333 **NHRP Protocol Applicability Statement**, 1998 (Proposed Standard)

RFC 2335 **A Distributed NHRP Service Using Server Cache Synchronization Protocol** (SCSP), 1998 (Proposed Standard)

RFC 2336 **Classical IP to NHRP Transition**, 1998 (Informational)

RFC 2520 **NHRP with Mobile NHCs**, 1999 (Experimental)

RFC 2603 **ILMI-Based Server Discovery for NHRP**, 1999 (Proposed Standard)

RFC 2677 **Definitions of Managed Objects for the NBMA Next Hop Resolution Protocol** (NHRP), 1999 (Proposed Standard)

RFC 2735 **NHRP Support for Virtual Private Networks**, 1999 (Proposed Standard)

With NHRP, once the NBMA next hop is determined, the source can either start sending IP packets to the destination (in a connectionless NBMA network such as SMDS) or first establish a connection to the destination with the desired bandwidth and QoS characteristics (in a connection-oriented NBMA network such as ATM).

Other address resolution methods can be in use while NHRP is deployed. Hosts that can use only the LIS model might require ARP servers and services over NBMA networks, and deployed hosts might not implement NHRP but might continue to support ARP variations. NHRP is designed to eliminate the suboptimal routing that results from the LIS model, and can be deployed with existing ARP services without interfering with them.

NHRP can be used to facilitate the building of a Virtual Private Network (VPN). In this context, a virtual private network consists of a virtual Layer 3 network that is built on top of an actual Layer 3 network. The VPN topology can be largely independent of the underlying network, and the protocols run over it can be completely independent of it.

Connected to the NBMA network are one or more **next hop servers**, which implement NHRP. Each next hop server serves a set of destination hosts, which might or might not be directly connected to the NBMA network. Next hop servers cooperatively resolve the NBMA next hop addresses within their NBMA network. In addition to NHRP, next hop servers typically participate in protocols used to disseminate routing information across (and beyond the boundaries of) the NBMA network, and might support ARP service also.

A next hop server maintains a **next-hop resolution cache**, which is a table of IP-to-NBMA address mappings. The table is created from information gleaned from NHRP register packets, extracted from NHRP request or reply packets that traverse the next hop server as they are forwarded, or through other means such as ARP and preconfigured tables.

NHRP modes of operation

NHRP supports two modes of operation: fabric and server modes. The modes differ in the way the next hop server updates the destination address in the IP packet containing the NHRP Request.

- **Fabric mode** – all routers within the NBMA network are NHRP-capable. A Next Hop Server serving a destination must lie along the routed path to that destination. In practice, this means that all egress routers must double as Next Hop Servers serving the destinations beyond them, and that hosts on the NBMA network are served by routers that double as next hop servers.

- **Server mode** – few next hop servers exist in an NBMA network. This might occur in networks having routers that do not support NHRP or networks that have many directly attached hosts and relatively few routers. Server mode requires static configuration of next hop server identity in the client stations (hosts or routers). The client station must be configured with the IP address of one or more next hop servers, and there must be a path to that Next Hop Server (either directly, in which case the next hop server's NBMA address must be known, or indirectly, through a router whose NBMA address is known). If there are multiple next hop servers, they must be configured with each other's addresses, the identities of the destinations they each serve, and a logical

NBMA network identifier. (This static configuration requirement, which might also involve authentication, tends to limit the number of next hop servers.)

Hosts attached directly to the NBMA network have no knowledge of whether NHRP is deployed in server or fabric mode and host configuration is the same in each case. Regardless of which mode is used, NHRP clients must be configured with the IP address and NBMA address of at least one next hop server. In practice, a host's default router should also be its next hop server.

If the NBMA network offers a group addressing or multicast feature, the client station can be configured with a group address assigned to the group of next hop servers. The client might then submit NHRP requests to the group address, eliciting a response from one or more next hop servers, depending on the response strategy selected.

The servers can also be configured with the group or multicast address of their peers, and a next hop server might use this address to forward NHRP requests it cannot satisfy to its peers. This might elicit a response. The next hop server would then forward the NHRP reply to the NHRP request originator. The purpose of using group addressing or a similar multicast mechanism in this scenario is to eliminate the need to preconfigure each next hop server in a logical NBMA network with both the individual identities of other next hop servers and the destinations they serve. It reduces the number of next hop servers that might be traversed to process an NHRP request (in those configurations where next hop servers either respond or forward via the multicast, only two next hop servers would be traversed) and allows the next hop server that serves the NHRP request originator to cache next hop information associated with the reply.

10.10 Broadcasts and multicasts in IP networks revisited

There are three **sources of broadcasts and multicasts** in IP networks:

- **Workstations** – an IP workstation broadcasts an Address Resolution Protocol (ARP) request every time it needs to locate a new IP address on the network. For example, the command *telnet mumble.com* translates into an IP address through a Domain Name System (DNS) search, and then an ARP request is broadcast to find the actual station. Generally, IP workstations cache 10 to 100 addresses for about two hours. The ARP rate for a typical workstation might be about 50 addresses every two hours or 0.007 ARPs per second. Thus 2000 IP end stations produce about 14 ARPs per second.

- **Routers** – an IP router is any router or workstation that runs RIP. Some administrators configure all workstations to run RIP as a redundancy and reachability policy. Every 30 seconds, RIP uses broadcasts to retransmit the entire RIP routing table to other RIP routers. If 2000 workstations were configured to run RIP and if 50 packets were required to retransmit the routing table, the workstations would generate 3333 broadcasts per second. Most network administrators configure a small number of routers, usually five to 10, to run RIP. For a routing table that requires 50 packets to hold it, 10 RIP routers would generate about 16 broadcasts per second.

■ **Multicast applications** – IP multicast applications can adversely affect the performance of large, scaled, switched networks. Although multicasting is an efficient way to send a stream of multimedia (video data) to many users on a shared-media hub, it affects every user on a flat switched network. A particular packet video application can generate a several Mbps stream of multicast data that, in a switched network, would be sent to every segment, resulting in severe congestion.

When broadcast and multicast traffic peak due to 'storm' behavior, peak CPU loss can be orders of magnitude greater than average. Broadcast 'storms' can be caused by a device requesting information from a network that has grown too large. So many responses are sent to the original request that the device cannot process them, or the first request triggers similar requests from other devices that effectively block normal traffic flow on the network.

RFC WATCH	Summarized RFC watch

The following RFCs have been brought to your attention in this chapter (ordered by number):

RFC 768 *User Datagram Protocol*, 1980 (Standard)

RFC 791 *Internet Protocol*, J. Postel, 1981 (Standard)

RFC 826 *Ethernet Address Resolution Protocol: or Converting Network Protocol Addresses to 48-Bit Ethernet Address for Transmission on Ethernet Hardware*, 1982 (Standard)

RFC 903 *Reverse Address Resolution Protocol*, 1984 (Standard)

RFC 919 *Broadcasting Internet Datagrams*, 1984 (Standard)

RFC 922 *Broadcasting Internet Datagrams in the Presence of Subnets*, 1984 (Standard)

RFC 950 *Internet Standard Subnetting Procedure*, 1985 (Standard)

RFC 1027 *Using ARP to Implement Transparent Subnet Gateways*, 1987

RFC 1112 *Host Extensions for IP Multicasting*, 1989 (Standard)

RFC 1166 *Internet Numbers*, 1990 (Informational)

RFC 1180 *TCP/IP Tutorial*, 1991 (Informational)

RFC 1219 *On the Assignment of Subnet Numbers*, 1991 (Informational)

RFC 1256 *ICMP Router Discovery Messages*, 1991 (Proposed Standard)

RFC 1323 *TCP Extensions for High Performance*, 1992 (Proposed Standard)

RFC 1332 *The PPP Internet Protocol Control Protocol (IPCP)*, 1992 (Proposed Standard)

RFC 1338 *Supernetting: an Address Assignment and Aggregation Strategy*, 1992

▶

RFC 1517 *Applicability Statement for the Implementation of Classless Inter-Domain Routing* (*CIDR*), 1993 (Proposed Standard)

RFC 1518 *An Architecture for IP Address Allocation with CIDR*, 1993 (Proposed Standard)

RFC 1519 *Classless Inter-Domain Routing (CIDR): an Address Assignment and Aggregation Strategy*, 1993 (Proposed Standard)

RFC 1520 *Exchanging Routing Information Across Provider Boundaries in the CIDR Environment*, 1993 (Informational)

RFC 1700 *Assigned Numbers*, 1994 (Standard)

RFC 1889 *RTP: a Transport Protocol for Real-Time Applications*, 1996 (Proposed Standard)

RFC 1917 *An Appeal to the Internet Community to Return Unused IP Networks (Prefixes) to the IANA*, 1996 (Best Current Practice)

RFC 1958 *Architectural Principles of the Internet*, 1996 (Informational)

RFC 2018 *TCP Selective Acknowledgment Options*, 1996 (Proposed Standard)

RFC 2050 *Internet Registry IP Allocation Guidelines*, 1996 (Best Current Practice)

RFC 2131 *Dynamic Host Configuration Protocol*, 1997 (Draft Standard)

RFC 2151 *A Primer on Internet and TCP/IP Tools and Utilities*, 1997 (Informational)

RFC 2205 *Resource ReSerVation Protocol (RSVP) – Version 1 Functional Specification*, 1997 (Proposed Standard)

RFC 2326 *Real Time Streaming Protocol (RTSP)*, 1998 (Proposed Standard)

RFC 2332 *NBMA Next Hop Resolution Protocol* (*NHRP*), 1998 (Proposed Standard)

RFC 2333 *NHRP Protocol Applicability Statement*, 1998 (Proposed Standard)

RFC 2335 *A Distributed NHRP Service Using Server Cache Synchronization Protocol* (*SCSP*), 1998 (Proposed Standard)

RFC 2336 *Classical IP to NHRP Transition*, 1998 (Informational)

RFC 2373 *IP Version 6 Addressing Architecture*, 1998 (Proposed Standard)

RFC 2460 *Internet Protocol, Version 6 (IPv6) Specification*, 1998 (Draft Standard)

RFC 2461 *Neighbor Discovery for IP Version 6 (IPv6)*, 1998 (Draft Standard)

RFC 2463 *Internet Control Message Protocol (ICMPv6) for the Internet Protocol Version 6 (IPv6) Specification*, 1998 (Draft Standard)

RFC 2520 *NHRP with Mobile NHCs*, 1999 (Experimental)

RFC 2525 *Known TCP Implementation Problems*, 1999 (Informational)

RFC 2603 *ILMI-Based Server Discovery for NHRP*, 1999 (Proposed Standard)

RFC 2677 *Definitions of Managed Objects for the NBMA Next Hop Resolution Protocol* (*NHRP*), 1999 (Proposed Standard)

RFC 2735 *NHRP Support for Virtual Private Networks*, 1999 (Proposed Standard)

RFC 2800 *Internet Official Protocol Standards*, 2001 (Standard)

RFC 2827 *Network Ingress Filtering: Defeating Denial of Service Attacks which Employ IP Source Address Spoofing*, 2000 (Best Current Practice)

RFC 2873 *TCP Processing of the IPv4 Precedence Field*, 2000 (Proposed Standard)

RFC 2883 *An Extension to the Selective Acknowledgment (SACK) Option for TCP*, 2000 (Proposed Standard)

RFC 2894 *Router Renumbering for IPv6*, 2000 (Proposed Standard)

RFC 2960 *Stream Control Transmission Protocol*, 2000 (Proposed Standard)

RFC 2988 *Computing TCP's Retransmission Timer*, 2000 (Proposed Standard)

RFC 3004 *The User Class Option for DHCP*, 2000 (Proposed Standard)

RFC 3011 *The IPv4 Subnet Selection Option for DHCP*, 2000 (Proposed Standard)

RFC 3016 *RTP Payload Format for MPEG-4 Audio/Visual Streams*, 2000 (Proposed Standard)

RFC 3019 *IP Version 6 Management Information Base for the Multicast Listener Discovery Protocol*, 2001 (Proposed Standard)

RFC 3021 *Using 31-Bit Prefixes on IPv4 Point-to-Point Links*, 2000 (Proposed Standard)

RFC 3042 *Enhancing TCP's Loss Recovery Using Limited Transmit*, 2001 (Proposed Standard)

RFC 3046 *DHCP Relay Agent Information Option*, 2001 (Proposed Standard)

RFC 3056 *Connection of IPv6 Domains via IPv4 Clouds*, 2001 (Proposed Standard)

CHAPTER 11

Routing IP

Once we have overviewed the TCP/IP protocol suite, namely the characteristics of the IP protocol and its supportive protocols at the network layer, and have explored how to discover routers in the TCP/IP environment, we may move on to the routing of IP datagrams. IP supports both static and dynamic routing. While static routing was described in Chapter 10, **dynamic routing** will be the topic of this chapter.

Let us remind ourselves that the **key actions for the router**, when using a dynamic routing protocol, comprise the following:

- **identifying neighbors;**
- **discovering routes;**
- **selecting a route;**
- **maintaining routing information.**

We will explore the different methods deployed in the **IP routing protocols** depending on their perception of autonomous systems:

- **interior routing protocols:**
  - **Routing Information Protocol** (RIP);
  - **Open Shortest Path First** (OSPF);
  - **Integrated Intermediate System-to-Intermediate System** (IS-IS) (discussed after the explanation of the standard IS-IS in Chapter 12, section 12.7);
  - **Interior Gateway Routing Protocol** (IGRP);
  - **Enhanced Interior Gateway Routing Protocol** (EIGRP);
- **exterior routing protocols:**
  - **Exterior Gateway Protocol** (EGP);
  - **Border Gateway Protocol** (BGP).

Besides, we will also look at the related non-routing protocols optionally used by routers, such as the **Virtual Router Redundancy Protocol** (VRRP) and **Hot Standby Router Protocol** (HSRP).

To be able to route a packet, a **router needs to know**:

- the final destination of the packet/datagram;
- the source from which the router learned the paths to the given destination;
- possible paths (routes) to the destination;
- best path to that destination.

11.1 Path determination and packet forwarding

Once again we should remind ourselves that the IP router generally has two major operational tasks:

- **path determination** – we will discuss how the IP routing protocols help deal with this task;
- **packet forwarding** – there is much more the IP router has to deal with when 'processing' the datagram than just to determine the destination IP address. We will look at various subissues the router's Layer 2 and Layer 3 are obligatorily or optionally involved in.

11.1.1 IP datagram forwarding under the microscope

Let's have a look at datagram forwarding in more detail to understand all the actions a router must perform to complete the task successfully. In our example an Ethernet frame would be received on the Ethernet port of a router. The router's Layer 2 first checks the Ethernet header. If no mistakes in the frame are detected, the protocol field is checked to determine the upper layer protocol.

Upon finding out that the particular frame belongs to IP (Ethertype *0x800*), the IP header is checked in the next step. But before definitely stripping off the Ethernet header, the router has to note the length of the frame and has to find out whether the frame is broadcast or multicast (by checking the first bit in the destination MAC address). In some cases the router will not forward Layer 2 multicast or broadcast frames.

At this moment the Layer 3 operation within the router starts with the number of tasks before it. If the router supports IP routing, the **IP header** of a datagram (for details on TCP/IP see Chapter 10 in this Part) is checked for **protocol version, header length** (must be greater than minimum IP header size, i.e. five 32-bit words), **length** (must not be smaller than the header length), and **header checksum**. The IP datagram length is checked against the size of the received Ethernet frame to determine whether a complete datagram has been received. The **header checksum** computation serves to verify all the header fields against corruption. In the case of failure of at least one of these initial IP datagram checks, the router sees the datagram as malformed and discards it even without sending out an error notification to the datagram originator.

If the above checking was successful, as the next step, the router checks the value of the **time-to-live** (TTL) field. The TTL field has two functions: to limit the lifetime of IP datagrams and to terminate Internet routing loops. Although TTL initially indicated time in seconds, it now has the attribute of a hop-count, since each router is required to reduce the TTL field by one. TTL expiration is intended to cause datagrams to be discarded by routers, but not by the destination host. Hosts that act as routers by forwarding datagrams must therefore follow the router's rules for TTL.

The TTL value should be greater than one because the router has to decrement it by one before further forwarding the datagram to the next hop. Any datagram with zero value of TTL must be discarded (unless addressed to the particular router) and the ICMP *TTL Exceeded* message generated. TTL is checked first but not decremented before actually checking the destination IP address. Note in particular that a router must not modify the TTL of a packet except when forwarding it. A router must not originate or forward a datagram with a TTL value of zero (RFC 1812).

RFC WATCH	IP routers' requirements

RFC 1812 **Requirements for IP Version 4 Routers**, 1995 (Proposed Standard)

The **destination IP address** is the next field the router has to look at within the datagram. As the address may be unicast, multicast, or broadcast, various scenarios may be invoked here. **Unicast datagrams** are discarded in case they were received as Layer 2 broadcast or multicast. Otherwise, the unicast IP address of the destination network node is used for routing table lookup: the best-matching routing table entry is returned indicating to which router's outgoing interface the datagram should be internally switched. In the case that no match is found, including the default route, the datagram cannot be forwarded and is discarded instead, with the ICMP *Destination unreachable* message generated.

Routers must not forward a local **broadcast** (datagram with destination IP address of 255.255.255.255) but receive and forward **directed broadcasts** (broadcast directed to the specified network prefix). RFC 1812 specifies that routers must have an option to disable this feature, and that this option must default to permit the receiving and forwarding of directed broadcasts. While directed broadcasts have purposes, their current use on the Internet backbone appears to be comprised entirely of malicious attacks, such as Smurf Attacks where by permitting directed broadcasts these systems become Smurf Amplifiers on other networks. Therefore RFC 2644 has changed the required default for routers to help ensure new routers connected to the Internet do not add to the problems already present. Therefore currently, a router may have a configuration option to allow it to forward directed broadcast packets; however, this option must be disabled by default, and thus the router must not receive network directed broadcast packets unless specifically configured by the end user.

RFC WATCH   **broadcast handling by routers**

RFC 2644 **Changing the Default for Directed Broadcasts in Routers (BCP0034)** (Best Current Practice)

If the route through an outgoing interface is determined, the datagram TTL is decremented by one and datagram header checksum recomputed. However, a **fragmentation** may be needed in case the particular interface media MTU is smaller than the datagram length (see Figure 11.1). As fragmentation can affect performance, the originating host may disallow fragmentation of the datagram (by setting the *Don't Fragment (DF)* bit in the *Flag* field). In this case the router will not fragment the datagram, but will discard it and generate an ICMP *Destination unreachable* message (specifying the *Fragmentation needed and DF bit set*). The originating host may, based on these ICMP messages, determine the minimum MTU on the route to the destination and use it from that point on.

FIGURE 11-1   IP datagram fragmentation

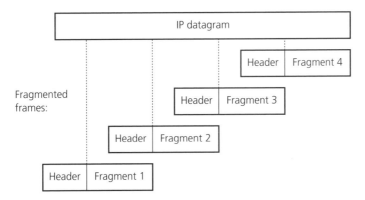

There might be an additional task introduced in the forwarding process: **filtering**. Depending on the position of configured filters, the router may discard a datagram without going through all the steps depicted above. This would happen in case of configuring the filter on the incoming router interface. Then the IP datagram header will be checked for a match against the filter conditions before bothering the routing table. Only datagrams which are permitted will get involved in further internal router processing. On the other hand, in the case of filters attached to the outgoing interface, all steps mentioned above will be performed with the datagram header but the datagram may still be dropped just before final Layer 2 encapsulation if the filter says so.

After the optional fragmentation described above is performed, if needed, the **datagram** (or fragments) need to be **encapsulated** according to the particular outgoing interface – the router's Layer 2 operation at the outgoing interface starts. The IP datagram gets a Layer 2 header and trailer appended. The destination Layer 2 address must be found by mapping the next hop IP address on it. Generally the ARP cache or ARP protocol operation is invoked at this moment. In the case of WAN interconnections the mapping between the destination IP and WAN addresses may be configured manually on the router or may be achieved dynamically by using a protocol, such as Inverse ARP in Frame Relay. The Layer 2 frame is then forwarded to the next hop through the outgoing interface.

To summarize, it is useful to realize that more than just the destination IP address among the IP datagram fields is important for an IP router, and recognize the operations required within a process of packet forwarding. It is also important to note that some operations are never done by router, such as packet **reassembly**. Reassembling previously fragmented datagrams is valid only in cases when the router is the intended recipient, otherwise the reassembly is performed by the receiving end node.

Fast packet forwarding is a requirement in today's interconnecting devices. Every nanosecond added to a packet in the main data path is significant, especially at gigabit speeds. A router's basic operation includes extracting the destination field, masking it, and looking up the next hop, decrementing the TTL field and recomputing the header checksum, adding whatever internal headers are needed, and sending it to the next hop. While fragmentation is less and less a requirement in current IP networks, there are more and more needs to conduct traffic shaping and other QoS mechanisms. Lots of carriers want accounting in the fast path. Protection against denial of service – either filtering or reverse path verification – is somewhat more scalable but still bothers routers CPU.

Finally, it is worth remembering that in the **conventional routing architecture** (compared to those discussed in the final Part V), different functionality provided by the path determination function (e.g. unicast routing, multicast routing, unicast routing with types of service) requires **multiple forwarding algorithms**. For example, in IP forwarding of unicast packets requires the longest match based on the network layer destination address; forwarding of multicast packets requires the longest match on the source network layer address plus the exact match on both source and destination network layer addresses, whereas unicast forwarding with types of service requires the longest match on the destination network layer address plus the exact match on the type of service bits carried in the network layer header.

11.1.2 Loop detection and prevention

While IP routing protocols attempt to establish loop-free routes, almost all protocols can lead to looping during transient conditions, for example during the period immediately following the failure of a link. There are two basic ways to tackle loops:

■ **loop prevention** – prevent the formation of a looping path before any packets are sent on it;

■ **loop mitigation** – take steps to minimize the negative effects of loops.

Since most IP routing protocols cannot prevent the formation of transient loops, IP forwarding uses the mitigation approach. The TTL field in a packet is decremented at every IP hop; if it reaches zero, the packet is assumed to be looping and is discarded. By discarding packets that are stuck in loops, the routers in the looping path are not overwhelmed with packets that must be forwarded, and they can devote their resources to updating the routing tables. Once the routing tables are stable, the loop should be broken (unless a configuration error has been made in one of the routers).

11.2 IP interior and exterior gateway protocols

Dynamic IP routing currently offers a variety of routing protocols which may be effectively deployed in different environments. Before choosing any of the protocol options, careful thought is always required as to whether or not there is a real need for a routing protocol. Static routes, possibly with backup static routes, may be much simpler.

Routing protocols are sometimes used to provide a **keepalive function** rather than conveying routing information. For example, if an individual PVC fails in frame, ATM, etc., and a router system and carrier do not support recognition of down interfaces, it is not uncommon to use a routing protocol with hellos to detect the failure and trigger backup.

IP defines an **autonomous system**, AS (similar to the administrative domain in OSI) as a set of routers under a single technical administration, using an interior gateway protocol and common metrics to route packets within the AS and using an exterior gateway protocol to route packets to other ASs. RFC 1930 describes an AS as a set of addresses (and, by association, routers) under one or more administrations that present a common routing policy to the Internet. Since this classic definition was developed, it has become common for a single AS to use several interior gateway protocols and sometimes several sets of metrics within an AS. The use of the term autonomous system currently stresses the fact that, even when multiple IGPs and metrics are used, the administration of an AS appears to other ASs to have a **single coherent interior routing plan** and presents a consistent picture of which destinations are reachable through it.

One more observation may be made at this point on the perception of autonomous system existence among different routing protocols. OSPF and EIGRP consider an AS as a set of addresses and routers under a single administration (which may be called a routing domain). IGRP and EIGRP have the notion that, even though routing domains may be under the control of the same adminis-

---

RFC WATCH **autonomous systems**

RFC 1930 **Guidelines for Creation, Selection, and Registration of an Autonomous System (AS)**, 1996 (Best Current Practice)

RFC 2270 **Using a Dedicated AS for Sites Homed to a Single Provider**, 1998 (Informational)

RFC 2769 **Routing Policy System Replication**, 2000 (Proposed Standard)

trator, the domains will not automatically exchange routing information unless they have the same AS number.

Autonomous Systems (AS) are assumed to be administered by a **single administrative entity**, at least for the purposes of representation of routing information to systems outside of the AS. The Internet consists of uniquely addressed autonomous systems. AS numbers, 16 bits long, are allocated by the same source as IP network addresses – from the regional registry or from the ISP (provider-assigned address space).

There are **reserved private AS numbers** alongside **public AS numbers** (mostly for ISPs offering transit services). The Internet Assigned Numbers Authority (IANA) has reserved the following block of AS numbers for private use (not to be advertised on the global Internet): 64512 through 65535. The provider can give the customer an AS number from the private range of ASNs (RFC 2270).

> *Note*: One can get the provider independent AS number with the proper justification, although there is no guarantee that this prefix will propagate through the Internet as a whole and the prefix will be reachable. In general, it is necessary to demonstrate to the registry that there is a plan to multihome, that there exist contracts with at least two upstream providers, and that the routing policy has been documented.

The design may be scrutinized, and questions are likely to be asked why this cannot be achieved with provider-assigned address space. The registry might evaluate whether the links are fast enough to support the number of routes in plan to receive. AS numbers are an increasingly scarce resource. At the present rate of allocation, we will run out of 16-bit AS numbers around 2004. There are active efforts underway to develop an upwardly compatible extension to 32-bit AS numbers, so this probably will not be a crisis.

As there is a strong distinction between the internal structure of the autonomous systems (AS) and the external relationship between ASs, there are two principal routing protocol groups (see Figure 11.2):

- **Interior Gateway Protocols** (IGPs) – operate within an autonomous system (RIP, IGRP, EIGRP, OSPF, IS-IS): the requirement for interior protocols is to calculate efficient routes and recalculate them quickly after any network topology change;
- **Exterior Gateway Protocols** (EGPs) – operate between autonomous systems (EGP, BGP): the requirement for exterior protocols is different – to express particular routing policies and to aggregate routing information.

QUICK TIP   IGPs *vis-à-vis* EGPs

IGPs should calculate efficient routes and recalculate them quickly after any network topology change.

EGPs should be able to express particular routing policies and to aggregate routing information.

FIGURE 11-2 Relationship between interior and exterior routing

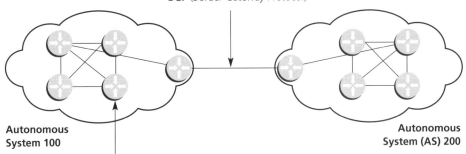

Exterior Gateway Protocols *(EGP)*
- **EGP** (*Exterior Gateway Protocol*)
- **BGP** (*Border Gateway Protocol*)

Autonomous System 100

Autonomous System (AS) 200

Interior Gateway Protocols *(IGP)*
- **RIP** (*Routing Information Protocol*)
- **IGRP/EIGRP** (*Enhanced Interior Gateway Routing Protocol*)
- **OSPF** (*Open Shortest Path First*)

The difference in the requirements for IGP and EGP determines also the choice of the routing algorithm (we discuss the routing algorithms in Chapter 9 of this Part): while modern IGPs are more dependent on the link-state algorithm, EGPs are based on the distance vector.

Although IGPs and EGPs have to collaborate for global routing, there are certain strict rules concerning how this collaboration is governed. We will see later what external information is understood by individual routing protocols as valid, which takes precedence as more trustworthy. Mutual exchange of routes between the exterior and interior protocols is not reasonable and feasible, as it would destroy the hierarchical approach to global routing maintained by distinguishing interior and exterior routing. It is rarely a good idea to inject any external routes into an IGP. This may make sense as part of a traffic engineering strategy, but it always requires extreme caution and a thorough understanding of what is going on.

SNAPSHOT **exterior routing protocols**

Exterior protocols convey routing information among network domains, such as the Internet. They are intended to protect one system of networks (a domain) against errors or intentional misrepresentation by other domains.

OSPF and IS-IS are not explicitly concerned with AS numbers, but both have a concept of **external routes**. External routes are those not generated by the local dynamic routing domain (i.e. a backbone and a set of subordinate areas). OSPF and IS-IS need to know what is external to them, but not what number is associated with the externals. OSPF and IS-IS do have additional concepts of the scope of internal routes. Conceptually, an internal route stays in its own area. In actuality, OSPF intra-area routes will propagate outside the originating area to other non-stub areas and area 0.0.0.0. OSPF's external relationships are not particularly associated with areas. OSPF assumes that an AS is a set of areas (i.e. a single area, or an area 0.0.0.0 and some number of non-zero areas), which exchange routing information. Externals come from redistribution or default information origination.

11.2.1 Logical network topology

The **physical topology** of an internetwork is described by the complete set of routers and the networks that connect them. Networks also have a logical topology. Different routing protocols establish the logical topology in different ways.

Some routing protocols do not use a logical hierarchy. Such protocols use addressing to segregate specific areas or domains within a given internetworking environment and to establish a logical topology. For such non-hierarchical, or flat, protocols, no manual topology creation is required.

Other protocols require the creation of an **explicit hierarchical topology** through the establishment of a backbone and logical areas. The OSPF and IS-IS protocols are examples of routing protocols that use a hierarchical structure. A general hierarchical network scheme is illustrated in Figure 11.3. The explicit topology in a hierarchical scheme takes precedence over the topology created through addressing.

FIGURE 11-3 Hierarchical logical network

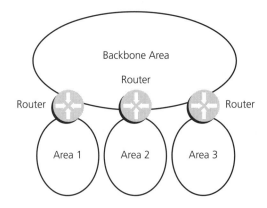

If a hierarchical routing protocol is used, the **addressing topology** should be assigned to reflect that hierarchy. If a flat routing protocol is used, the addressing implicitly creates the topology. There are two recommended ways to assign addresses in a hierarchical network. The simplest way is to give each area (including the backbone) a unique network address. An alternative is to assign address ranges to each area.

Areas are logical collections of contiguous networks and hosts. Areas also include all the routers having interfaces on any one of the included networks. Each area runs a separate copy of the basic routing algorithm. Therefore, each area has its own topological database.

11.2.2 Choice of right routing protocol

Choosing the best fitting routing protocol for the particular network scenario depends on numerous variables which all have to be considered to search for the best trade-off:

- internetwork size and complexity;
- need to support Variable-Length Subnet Masks (VLSM) – only some of the protocols are classless (protocols that carry subnet masks on their route advertisements, such as RIPv2, EIGRP, and OSPF);
- internetwork traffic levels;
- security needs;
- reliability needs;
- internetwork delay characteristics;
- organizational policies;
- organizational acceptance of change.

Among the **network manager's goals** in choosing and configuring an **interior routing protocol** the following dominate:

- achieving optimal path selection for traffic;
- fast convergence – or the rate at which routers are able to make decisions based on network changes;
- scalability;
- minimizing update traffic among devices in order to keep network overhead low.

Comparison of various important characteristics of routing algorithms to help match the routing requirements in a particular network and the routing protocol is shown in Table 11.1. For introductory comparison of characteristics of all IP routing protocols see Table 11.2.

The characteristics with respect to each routing protocol will be discussed in detail later in the text. The path vector routing algorithm will be introduced in the BGP section. One additional important characteristic is worth remembering: the possibility and prevention of routing loops. In Chapter 9 of this Part we discussed the danger of routing loops in the case of distance vector routing algorithms. Prevention is built into the routing protocols in the form of split horizon, and poison reverse mechanisms, and the hold-down timer. Link-state routing protocols compute loop-free routes. This is guaranteed because all routers calculate their routing tables based on the same information from the link-state database. DUAL algorithm provides also for loop-free routing.

TABLE 11-1 Comparison of routing algorithms deployed in IP routing protocols

	Distance vector (RIP, IGRP)	Advanced distance vector (EIGRP)	Link state (OSPF)	Path vector (BGP)
Scalability	Low	High	Good	Excellent
Bandwidth usage	High	Low	Low	Low
Memory usage	Low	Moderate	High	High
CPU usage	Low	Low	High	Moderate
Convergence	Slow	Fast	Fast	Moderate
Configuration	Easy	Easy	Moderate	Difficult

TABLE 11-2 Comparison of characteristics of all IP routing protocols

Protocol	Algorithm	IETF standard	Interior/ exterior	Updates	Metric	VLSM/ CIDR support	Summarization
RIPv1	DV	Yes	Interior	30 s	Hops	No	Automatic
RIPv2	DV	Yes	Interior	30 s	Hops	Yes	Automatic
IGRP	DV	No (Cisco)	Interior	90 s	Composite	No	Automatic
EIGRP	Advanced DV (DUAL)	No (Cisco)	Interior	Triggered	Composite	Yes	Automatic/ manual
OSPF	LS	Yes	Interior	Triggered	Cost	Yes	Manual
IS-IS	LS	Yes	Interior	Triggered	Cost	Yes	Automatic
BGP	Path vector	Yes	Exterior	Incremental		Yes	Automatic

Note: DV = distance sector; LS = link state

evolution of routing protocols

First generation (IP RIP, AppleTalk RTMP, XNS RIP): characterized by hop count metric, periodic plus optional triggered updates, loop prevention through split horizon and hold-down, loop detection through count to infinity, unreliable transfer of routing updates.

Second generation (IP IGRP, IPX RIP): characterized by bandwidth/delay metric, periodic plus optional triggered update, loop prevention through split horizon and basic hold-down, loop detection through sensing monotonically increasing metric or count to infinity, unreliable transfer of routing updates.

Third generation (IP/IPX/AppleTalk EIGRP): characterized by bandwidth/delay metric, updates on change only, loop-free route computation algorithm, reliable transfer of routing updates. Loop avoidance is achieved principally by a reliable update (i.e. no old or bad information), and following the (simplified) premise that a route with lower cost than your current one cannot form a loop. Although applicable in enterprise networks, EIGRP does not support hierarchical routing, hence is not used in ISPs.

Fourth generation (IP OSPF, IS-IS, IPX NLSP): characterized by link-state algorithms used with metric related to the path bandwidth or arbitrary link cost, with immediate updates on changes and fast convergence. These protocols support hierarchical routing and therefore are best suited to current general Internet service providers.

QUICK TIP **convergence**

The capability and efficiency (in terms of speed) of a group of routers, running a particular routing protocol to agree on the network topology after it has changed.

Additional capabilities

While discussing the IP routing protocols, we will have a look at capabilities additional to those described earlier. The additions derive either from the IP characteristics or from the network topology:

■ **IP ToS field** – five ToS values have been defined: normal service (default setting), minimal cost, minimal delay, maximal throughput, maximal reliability. To implement ToS, the router would need to keep different routing tables for different ToS requirements. Although the ToS option within IP sounds tempting, e.g. for routing over high-bandwidth satellite links with high delay, ToS routing has been very rarely used in reality. Two routing protocols offered support for ToS routing, OSPF and IS-IS, but OSPF has removed this support from the spec. Also IPv6 discontinued support to ToS.

- **IP options** – among the variety of IP options, the following help the application to control the packet's path:
  - **strict-source route** – specifies the exact path the packet should take, router by router, with a maximum number of nine hops (due to the maximum size of the IP header);
  - **loose-source route** – specifies the set of intermediate routers through which the packet should pass (does not have to form a continuous route but only requires certain hops to be there). This option has been used for troubleshooting network problems, and also as a mechanism for tunneling in the past.

  Again, IP options as an additional field to the standard IP datagram header create a processing overhead for routers which are optimized for fast datagram forwarding based on a certain constant set of criteria. Therefore IP options have never been used extensively in operational IP networks.
- **Multipath routing** – across alternative routes to allow for load balancing.

While discussing IP routing, it is worth re-emphasizing that IP routers nowadays route to prefixes rather than to end node network segment addresses. We discussed prefix routing and route aggregation in the previous chapter. Instead of containing every existing network segment IP address in a routing table, IP routers use aggregates of these addresses in shorter prefixes. For example, a router may connect to subnets 130.80.1.0/24, 130.80.2.0/24, and 130.80.3.0/24, but instead of advertising each subnet individually in the direction of the Internet, it would aggregate this address information into a shorter prefix: 130.80.0.0/16. It means that all packets coming from the Internet for anyone residing within the address range of 130.80.0.0/16 would be forwarded to this router. It, in turn, will then be responsible for finding the proper way to the actual destination segment, without disturbing any other router with irrelevant and redundant routing information.

Default routes et al.

Before we speak in detail about the routing protocols and their routing tables, it should be noted that there is a special entry for 0.0.0.0. called the **default route**. This is the entry with a zero prefix, *0/0* according to the CIDR notation in the case of IP. The default route thus matches every destination but it is not chosen as the best match if there are more specific prefixes. The default route may be statically configured on the router or may be chosen by a particular routing protocol. The concept of a default route helps the router **minimize the size of their routing tables** to the absolutely necessary set of entries relevant to the relatively smaller network in comparison to the Internet, such as a corporate network.

QUICK TIP   **default route**

The default route is a route in the routing table to direct packets for a destination not specified in any other routing table entry. The default route may be configured manually (for RIP or OSPF) or is chosen directly by a routing protocol (e.g. IGRP). If no default route is defined, all packets to unknown destinations are dropped.

The Internet is organized in a **hierarchical structure** as a collection of autonomous systems (a core with downstream attached ASs). The core routers (Level 1 tier ISPs) of the Internet maintain a complete routing table (with effective use of prefixes) and do not use default routes (so-called **default-free zone**). All other autonomous systems' routers use a default route pointing up the hierarchy, while maintaining only a subset of the Internet's routes.

To put **default** issues in the right perspective, we will describe all the 'defaults' we may use in the network with respect to routing:

- **Default route** – by convention shown as the routing table entry to network address *0.0.0.0/0*, understood by the router as the **least specific possible route** to be taken when there is no other route option to take. The default route may be either configured manually (similar to a static route), or it can be learned dynamically from routing protocols. There may be multiple static default routes – with different weights – for backup purposes. Static default routes can be redistributed into a routing protocol (see section 11.10.1 on redistribution later in this chapter).
- **Default gateway** – used in situations when no IP routing is enabled (on a switch, or a router box that is only doing bridging) to make getting beyond the local segment possible (e.g. for booting from a network server or to reach network management servers not on the same subnet). It has the specific next hop address of the gateway router.
- **Default network** – used by some routing protocols, such as IGRP and EIGRP (they flag a candidate default route), involving only a network or subnet prefix, so unless internal assumptions are made, there's no way of knowing the specific next hop address.
- **Gateway of Last Resort** (GOLR) – router selected by the process that actually installs routes in the routing table. The GOLR represents the default destination that comes from the source of default that is perceived as the most trustworthy.

Underlying service

As will be noted later on, different routing protocols use different TCP/IP protocols as their support, providing the underlying network service. Routing protocols may run over the following types of underlying protocols, i.e. to get a routing update encapsulated in a frame, datagram, or segment:

- **Over Layer 2 protocol** – direct encapsulation into frames which would not support fragmentation and reassembly (this feature should be embedded in the routing protocol itself), requiring a specific protocol code for each link layer the protocol would run over (such as *Ethertype* for use over Ethernet).
- **Over IP** – encapsulation within IP datagrams allows the use of all network layer services provided by IP (including the underlying independent infrastructure support, fragmentation, and reassembly), the only pitfall is the possibility of creating a deadlock in terms of mutual dependencies: the routing protocol depending on the forwarding services, while the forwarding in turn depends on data supplied by the routing protocol. An example of a protocol designed for running over IP is OSPF.

- **Over UDP** – encapsulation in unreliable transport segment, with additional benefits of checking routing packet integrity, implementation easiness (UDP services open on all systems without restrictions while direct IP usage may require certain privileges), UDP port availability (16-bit value for port numbers allows for more assigned numbers than IP protocol numbers using only eight bits). An example of a protocol designed for running over UDP is RIP.

- **Over TCP** – encapsulation in a reliable transport segment offers additional reliability of transport service to that provided by UDP, but with a larger overhead (compare the header lengths of UDP and TCP segments discussed in the previous chapter). An example of a protocol designed for running over IP is BGP.

It should be noted, however, that no matter what the underlying protocol, routing is a network (layer 3) service.

11.3 Interior routing protocols

Interior Gateway Protocols (IGP) are protocols designed to distribute routing information to the routers within a single autonomous system. There exist the following IP IGPs:

- **open – Routing Information Protocol** (RIP), derived from Xerox Corporation's XNS for IP networks, specified by IETF;

- **open – Open Shortest Path First** (OSPF) from the IETF for IP networks;

- **open – Integrated Intermediate System-to-Intermediate System** (IS-IS) for OSI and IP networks, initially standardized by ISO and then adopted and adjusted by IETF (discussed after the explanation of the standard IS-IS in Chapter 12, section 12.7);

- **proprietary – Interior Gateway Routing Protocol** (IGRP) from Cisco Systems for IP (Cisco devices only);

- **proprietary – Enhanced Interior Gateway Routing Protocol** (EIGRP), from Cisco Systems for IP, IPX, and AppleTalk networks (Cisco devices only).

QUICK TIP   **IP interior routing protocol preferences**

Among the existing IP interior routing protocols, link state protocols such as integrated IS-IS and OSPF dominate in current (large and complex) networks, followed by proprietary EIGRP in a Cisco environment. There is a significant use of RIP in small networks.

The IGPs do not work in a vacuum unless the particular internet they work on does not extend any further. Usually there is a world behind the boundary as seen by the IGP in terms of served networks. Therefore it is important to understand how the particular IGP will work with the routing policies, protocols, and routing information which is in the external world. We will discuss redistribution, i.e. way of collaboration of various routing styles, later in this chapter. But a word of caution should be repeated: it is rarely a good idea to inject any external routes into an IGP. This may make sense as part of a traffic engineering strategy, but requires careful insight.

QUICK TIP   **terminology**

Route flapping – an instability associated with a prefix when the route for the prefix may come and go frequently over a short time.

Dampen (suppress) a route – not to advertise a route that has shown instability until the route has been stable for a minimum amount of time.

11.3.1 Routing information protocol

The **Routing Information Protocol** (RIP) is the oldest routing protocol originally designed for Xerox PARC Universal Protocol (where it was called GWINFO) and used in the Xerox Network Systems (XNS) protocol suite. RIP became associated with both UNIX and TCP/IP in 1982 when the Berkeley Software Distribution (BSD) version of UNIX began shipping with a RIP implementation referred to as 'routed'. RIP, which is still a very popular routing protocol in the Internet community, was formally defined in the XNS Internet Transport Protocols publication (1981) and in RFC 1058 (1988, now historic). The initial version of RIP was extended by **version 2** as a proposed standard in 1994 (RFC 1723) but since 1998 it has been a **full Internet Standard** (RFC 2453).

RFC WATCH   **RIP**

RFC 1058 **Routing Information Protocol**, 1988 (Historic)

RFC 2453 **RIP Version 2**, 1998 (Standard)

RIP has been widely adopted by personal computer (PC) manufacturers for use in their networking products. RIP was the basis for the routing protocols of AppleTalk, Novell, 3Com, Ungermann-Bass, and Banyan (see Chapter 12). For a comparison of all RIP-derived protocols see Table 12.1 in the next chapter.

The main features of RIP version 1 and version 2 are summarized in Table 11.3.

TABLE 11-3	Comparison of RIP versions 1 and 2	
Characteristic	*RIP Version 1*	*RIP Version 2*
Routing algorithm	Distance vector algorithm	Distance vector algorithm
Routing updates	Regularly (each 30 s)	Regularly and on change
Broadcast/multicast	Broadcast to IP address 255.255.255.255 (mapped onto a broadcast MAC address *FF-FF-FF-FF-FF-FF*)	Multicast to IP address 224.0.0.9 (mapped onto a multicast MAC destination address *01-00-5E-00-00-09*)
Metric	Hop count	Hop count
Load balancing over equal cost paths	No	Yes
Support to VLSM	No	Yes
Authentication	No	Yes
Main limitation	Scalability (15 hop maximum path)	Scalability

Routing operation

RIP is based on the **distance vector routing algorithm** which provides only a limited view of the internet topology to each router running RIP. RIPv1 operation follows step by step the operation of the distance vector algorithm as described in Chapter 9. Only periodic updates, in the form of (almost) **complete routing tables**, are broadcast between neighbor routers. RIPv1 generally uses the destination broadcast IP address 255.255.255.255 which translates at the data link layer to a broadcast MAC address *FF-FF-FF-FF-FF-FF*. Some RIP implementations, however, send routing tables to the destination IP address 0.0.0.0 or to the network address, but all the implementations use a broadcast address *FF-FF-FF-FF-FF-FF* at the MAC layer.

There are **triggered updates** included in the protocol specification used to help converge the routers much more quickly and thus support more reliable and less overhead routing, namely for use of RIP for dial on demand (DDR) routing (RFC 1582 and 2091). Version 2 of the RIP protocol is based on the same operational background but adds some new features.

An extension to the distance vector algorithm allows for an immediate reaction to any topology change (a route added, changed, expired) in the form of a **triggered update**. To reduce a related overhead with triggered updates there is a

RFC WATCH   **RIP extensions**

RFC 1582 **Extensions to RIP to Support Demand Circuits**, 1994 (Proposed Standard)

RFC 2091 **Triggered Extensions to RIP to Support Demand Circuit**s, 1997 (Proposed Standard)

certain delay after the actual change which allows for multiple changes to occur. Triggered updates are introduced with the following characteristics and impact:

- updates are sent independent of periodic updates and do not affect their timing;
- updates include only the routes which have changed since the last update;
- there must exist some mechanism to limit the frequency of triggered updates to prevent network disfunctioning.

RIP uses UDP as the underlying protocol to provide unreliable transport service (its designated port number is 520).

Each entry in a **RIP routing table** provides a variety of information, including the ultimate destination, the next hop on the way to that destination, and a metric. The metric indicates the distance in number of hops to the destination with no merit for the link bandwidth, path delay, or load. Other information can also be present in the routing table, including various timers associated with the route.

RIP maintains only the **single best route** to a destination. When new information provides a better route, this information replaces the old route information. Network topology changes can provoke changes to routes, causing, for example, a new route to become the best route to a particular destination. When network topology changes occur, they are reflected in routing update messages. For example, when a router detects a link failure or a router failure, it recalculates its routes and sends routing update messages. Each router receiving a routing update message that includes a change updates its tables and propagates the change.

The special address *0.0.0.0* is used to describe a **default route**. A default route is used when it is not convenient to list every possible network in the RIP updates, and when one or more closely connected routers in the internet are prepared to handle traffic to the networks that are not listed explicitly. These routers should create RIP entries for the address *0.0.0.0*, just as if it were a network to which they are connected. The entries for *0.0.0.0* are handled by RIP in exactly the same manner as if there were an actual network with this address. However, the entry is used to route any datagram whose destination address does not match any other network in the table. Routes involving *0.0.0.0* should generally not leave the boundary of an autonomous system, as each AS would generally have a single default route. Typically, only one router will have the default route configured, while all other routers will get the default route through routing updates propagation with their respective added metric.

RIP version 1 packet format

FIGURE 11-4   RIPv1 message format

Number of bits:

8	8	8	8
Command	Version (1)	zero	
Address Family Identifier		zero	
IP Address			
zero			
zero			
Metric			

Figure 11.4 shows the RIP packet format for IP, as specified by RFC 1058. The fields of the RIPv1 packet are as follows:

- **Command** – indicates that the packet is a request or a response. The *request command* requests the responding system to send all or part of its routing table. Destinations for which a response is requested are listed later in the packet. The *response command* represents a reply to a request or, more frequently, an unsolicited regular routing update. In the *response* packet, a responding system includes all or part of its routing table. Regular routing update messages include the entire routing table.

- **Version number** – specifies the RIP version being implemented. With the potential for many RIP implementations in an internet, this field can be used to signal different, potentially incompatible, implementations.

- **Address family identifier** – follows a 16-bit field of all zeros and specifies the particular address family being used. On the Internet, this address family is typically IP (value = 2), but other network types may also be represented.

- **Address** – follows another 16-bit field of zeros. In Internet RIP implementations, this field typically contains an IP address.

- **Metric** – follows two more 32-bit fields of zeros and specifies the hop count. The hop count indicates how many hops (routers) must be traversed before the destination can be reached.

Up to 25 occurrences of the address family identifier field through the metric field are permitted in any single IP RIP packet, as the maximum length of a RIP packet is 512 octets. In other words, **up to 25 destinations** may be listed in any single RIP packet. Multiple RIP packets are used to convey information from larger routing tables.

As there is no place in the RIP message to specify the destination network address mask it has no mechanism to advertise the subnets beyond the IP network boundary, hence we get classful routing not supporting the address aggregation by address prefix. For the same reason no support to VLSM can be expected from RIP. Caution must be taken in cases where the network (classful) is not contiguous, as the routers in another network could receive two or more pieces of information on the route to the particular network each of which would in fact not provide access to all the network subnets.

Like other routing protocols, RIP uses certain timers to regulate its performance. The RIP **routing update timer** is generally set to 30 seconds, ensuring that each router will send a complete copy of its routing table to all neighbors every half a minute. The update interval is not exactly 30 seconds, but is instead plus or minus a random factor to prevent routers from synchronizing. The route **invalid (expiration) timer**, which determines how much time must expire without a router having heard about a particular route before that route is considered invalid, is set to 180 seconds for RIP. When a route is marked invalid, neighbors are notified of this fact. This notification must occur prior to expiration of the route **garbage collection (flush) interval**. If there is no update after 240 seconds, the router removes all routing table entries for the non-updating router.

These intervals might be changed in router configurations, but it is highly recommended to set all the routers with the same values. Otherwise a problematic routing update may occur: a router with a shorter update interval expects to receive updates from its neighbors within the same interval. Hence, it can easily expire routes from neighbors with longer update intervals, perhaps even upon a single routing update packet loss.

Stability features

RIP specifies a number of features designed to make its operation more stable in the face of rapid network topology changes. These include a hop count limit, holddowns, split horizons, and poison reverse updates, explained in Chapter 9. RIP permits a maximum hop count of 15. Any destination greater than 15 hops away is tagged as unreachable. RIP's maximum hop count greatly restricts its use in a large internet, but prevents the problem of counting to infinity from causing endless network routing loops.

RIP operates with two types of user devices: active and passive. **Active** users, typically routers, advertise their routes via a broadcast over their networks. **Passive** users, typically hosts, listen and update their routes based on the RIP information, but do not advertise routes.

An active RIP user advertises routes about every 30 seconds (the update interval is not exactly 30 seconds to prevent routers from sychronizing). Within a RIP broadcast is a paired listing of every IP network the sender of the RIP message can reach and the distance, in hops, to that network. Within RIP, a router is defined to be one hop away from directly connected networks, two hops from networks that are reachable from one other router, and so on.

As RIP is a **standalone routing protocol** not using any separate hello protocol (unlike OSPF or EIGRP), it may sometimes be susceptible to incorrect assumptions about (even) the connected network. Typically this may occur with an FDDI backbone which, due to a single 'break,' becomes partitioned into two FDDI rings. There persists the notion that one router can be happily used to access the FDDI which is no longer true for a couple of stations! As there is no feedback on the current situation all routers will persistently use the invalid route to the FDDI and datagrams will end up in the black hole.

SNAPSHOT	RIP version 1 at a glance

A **distance vector routing protocol** with **hop count metric**, periodically **broad-casting** routing table every 30 s. The longest route (RIP-routed network diameter) is **limited to 15 hops** – a metric of 16 hops indicates an unreachable network. **No support for VLSM, prefix routing, authentication, or multiple-path routing** is provided.

RIPv1 and subnet masks

RIPv1 allows only a single subnet mask to be used within each network number because it does not provide subnet mask information as part of its routing table update messages. In the absence of this information, RIPv1 is forced to make very simple assumptions about the mask that should be applied to any of its learned routes.

If the router has a subnet of the same network number assigned to a local interface, it assumes that the learned subnet was defined using the same mask as the locally configured interface. However, if the router does not have a subnet of the learned network number assigned to a local interface, the router has to assume that the network is not subnetted and applies the route's natural classful mask.

QUICK TIP	subnet masks within RIP

RIPv1 is limited to a single subnet mask for each network number.

Consider the following example: assume that Port 1 of a router has been assigned the IP address 130.24.13.1/24 and that Port 2 has been assigned the IP address 200.14.13.2/24. If the router learns about network 130.24.36.0 from a neighbor, it applies a /24 mask since Port 1 is configured with another subnet of the 130.24.0.0 network. However, when the router learns about network 131.25.15.0 from a neighbor, it assumes a default /16 mask since it has no other masking information available.

How does a RIPv1 based router know if it should include the subnet number bits in a routing table update to a RIPv1 neighbor? A router executing RIPv1 will only advertise the subnet number bits on another port if the update port is configured with a subnet of the same network number. If the update port is configured with a different subnet or network number, the router will only advertise the network portion of the subnet route and 'zero-out' the subnet-number field (classful routing).

For example, assume that Port 1 of a router has been assigned the IP address 130.24.13.1/24 and that Port 2 has been assigned the IP address 200.14.13.2/24. Also, assume that the router has learned about network 130.24.36.0 from a neighbor. Since Port 1 is configured with another subnet of the 130.24.0.0 network, the router assumes that network 130.24.36.0 has a /24 subnet mask. When it comes to advertise this route, it advertises 130.24.36.0 on Port 1, but it only advertises 130.24.0.0 on Port 2. Classful routing protocols summarize routes automatically as network borders.

RIP version 2

There are several advantages to be gained if more than one subnet mask can be assigned to a given IP network number:

■ multiple subnet masks permit more efficient use of an organization's assigned IP address space;
■ multiple subnet masks permit route aggregation which can significantly reduce the amount of routing information at the 'backbone' level within an organization's routing domain.

Multiple subnet masks are achieved through VLSM and advanced routing protocols support it, including RIPv2 but not RIPv1.

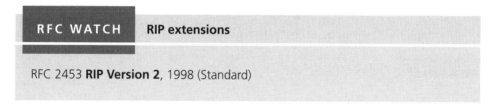

RFC WATCH   **RIP extensions**

RFC 2453 **RIP Version 2**, 1998 (Standard)

RIP version 2 (RFC 2453) builds on RIPv1 and enhances it with the following features:

■ **Subnet masks** – the inclusion of subnet masks was the original intent of opening the RIP protocol for improvement. As long as the subnet mask was fixed for a network, and well known by all the nodes on that network, a heuristic approach could be used to determine if a route was a subnet route or a host route. With the advent of VLSM, CIDR, and supernetting, it was no longer possible to reasonably distinguish between network, subnet, and host routes. By using the 32-bit field immediately following the IP address in a RIP routing entry, it became possible to positively identify a route's type. In fact, one could go so far as to say that the inclusion of the subnet mask effectively creates a 64-bit address which eliminates the network/subnet/host distinction. RIPv2 can therefore be used, as opposed to RIPv1, in an environment with VLSM.
■ **Alternate next hop addresses** – support for next hop addresses allows for optimization of routes in an environment which uses multiple routing protocols. For example, if RIPv2 were being run on a network along with another IGP, and one router ran both protocols, then that router could indicate to the other RIPv2 routers that a better next hop than itself exists for a given destination. Note that this is not a recursive algorithm; it only works to eliminate a single extra hop from the path.

- **Authentication** – RIPv2 represents a significant improvement over RIPv1. Essentially, it is the same extensible mechanism provided by OSPF. A plain text password was initially defined for authentication. While the authentication mechanism specified in RIPv2 is less than ideal, it does prevent anyone who cannot directly access the network (i.e. someone who cannot sniff the routing packets to determine the password) from inserting bogus routing information. The specification does allow for additional types of authentication to be incorporated into the protocol, e.g. MD5 authentication is proposed in RFC 2082 and further security enhancements are drafted. **MD5 authentication**, used also with OSPF and BGP, is similar to plain text authentication but the key is never sent over the wire. Instead, the router uses the MD5 algorithm to produce a message digest of the key which is then sent over. The amount of space available for providing authentication information with RIP is only 16 bits.

- **Multicasting** – RIPv2 packets may be multicast instead of being broadcast. The use of an IP multicast address reduces the load on hosts which do not support routing protocols. It also allows RIPv2 routers to share information which RIP-1 routers cannot hear. This is useful since a RIPv1 router may misinterpret route information because it cannot apply the supplied subnet mask. The multicast address used by RIPv2 is *224.0.0.9* which is translated at the link layer to the destination multicast MAC address *01-00-5E-00-00-09*.

- **External route tags** – may be used to propagate information acquired from an EGP (for example, an EGP AS number). The use to which the EGP puts the information is transparent to RIPv2. RIPv2 is required only to store the received information in the routing table and to include it in the update messages.

FIGURE 11-5   RIPv2 message format

8	8	8	8
Command	Version	unused	
Address Family Identifier		Route Tag	
IP Address			
Subnet Mask			
Next Hop			
Metric			

Figure 11.5 depicts the format of a RIPv2 message. The fields of the RIPv2 packet are as follows:

- *Command* – indicates whether the packet is a request or a response. The *request* asks that a router send all or a part of its routing table. The *response* can be an unsolicited regular routing update or a reply to a request. Responses contain routing table entries. Multiple RIP packets are used to convey information from large routing tables.

- **Version** – specifies the RIP version used. In a RIP packet implementing any of the RIPv2 fields or using authentication, this value is set to 2.
- **Unused** – value set to zero.
- **Address family identifier** (AFI) – specifies the address family used. RIP is designed to carry routing information for several different protocols. Each entry has an address family identifier to indicate the type of address specified. The address family identifier for IP is 2. If the AFI for the first entry in the message is *hexFFFF*, the remainder of the entry contains authentication information. Currently, the only authentication type is a simple password.
- **Route tag** – provides a method for distinguishing between internal routes (learned by RIP) and external routes (learned from other protocols).
- **IP address** – specifies the IP address for the entry.
- **Subnet mask** – contains the subnet mask for the entry. If this field is zero, no subnet mask has been specified for the entry.
- **Next hop** – indicates the IP address of the next hop to which packets for the entry should be forwarded.
- **Metric** – indicates how many hops (routers) have been traversed in the trip to the destination. This value is between 1 and 15 for a valid route, or 16 for an unreachable route.

Up to 25 occurrences of the AFI, address, and metric fields are permitted in a single IP RIP packet. That is, up to 25 routing table entries can be listed in a single RIP packet. If the AFI specifies an authenticated message, only 24 routing table entries can be specified.

QUICK TIP   **RIP version 2**

A **distance vector routing protocol with hop count metric, multicasting** routing table every 30 s or at change. The longest route (RIP-routed network diameter) is **limited to 15 hops** – a metric of 16 hops indicates unreachable network. Support for **VLSM, prefix routing, authentication, multiple-path routing** is provided.

RIPv1 and RIPv2 coexistence

UDP port number of 520 and packet formats are identical for RIPv1 and RIPv2 as for number of fields and their lengths but RIPv1 routers are not capable of handling the additional information in RIPv2 packets (the files which are by default filled with zero). Fortunately RIPv1 routers, thanks to protocol **forward compatibility**, simply **ignore the information** they cannot understand in packets with a version number higher than 1. It means that RIPv1 routers process the relevant (comprehensible) information of RIPv2 instead of totally ignoring all updates.

The problem with the difference in understanding of **subnetting** between the two versions persists: the RIPv1 router has to make an assumption on the subnet mask of a route (the subnet mask is the same as the subnet mask of the interface over which the update was received). RIPv1 makes this assumption obviously even in the case of receiving RIPv2 updates. If that assumption is not correct, routing loops and black holes may occur.

RIPv2 specification allows network administrators to control what version of the protocol is supported and how using **version control parameters** per interface:

■ **Send version:**

  – *1* to indicate that RIPv1 packets should be sent to the broadcast address;
  – *2* to indicate that RIPv2 packets should be sent to the RIPv2 multicast address;
  – *compatibility* (deprecated) to indicate that RIPv2 packets should be sent to the broadcast address.

■ **Receive version:**

  – *1* to indicate that only RIPv1 packets should be accepted;
  – *2* to indicate that only RIPv2 packets should be accepted;
  – *both* to indicate that both RIPv1 and RIPv2 packets should be accepted.

When a RIPv1 packet is received, the 'must be zero' fields are checked for zero. If they do not equal zero, the entry is ignored. In RIPv2 packets these fields are checked for validity.

Some router implementations also allow **equal-cost multipath** (ECMP) **routing** usage with RIP (while inherently part of other protocols such as OSPF). The effect of multipath routing on a forwarder is that the forwarder potentially has several next-hops for any given destination and must use some method to choose which next-hop should be used for a given data packet. There is more on ECMP issues valid generally later in this chapter.

RFC WATCH	RIP authentication and multipath routing

RFC 2082 **RIP-2 MD5 Authentication**, 1997 (Proposed Standard)
RFC 2992 **Analysis of an Equal-Cost Multi-Path Algorithm**, 2000 (Informational)

It should be noted that RIPv2 is not intended to be a substitute for OSPF in large autonomous systems; the restrictions on AS diameter and complexity which applied to RIPv1 similarly apply to RIPv2. Rather, RIPv2 allows the smaller, simpler, distance vector protocol to be used in environments which require authentication or the use of variable length subnet masks, but are not of a size or complexity which require the use of the larger, more complex, link-state protocol.

RIP next generation

To support IP version 6 the RIP next generation (RIPng) protocol was proposed in RFC 2080. RIP is a simple extrapolation of RIPv2 and has nothing conceptually new. In essence, the IPv4 address was expanded into an **IPv6 address**, the IPv4 subnet mask was replaced with an IPv6 **prefix length**, and the **next-hop** field was eliminated but the functionality has been preserved. **Authentication** was removed from RIPng as IPv6, which carries the RIPng packets, has built-in security which IPv4 did not have. The **route tag** field has been preserved. The maximum diameter of the network (the maximum metric value) is 15; 16 still means infinity (unreachable network).

The basic RIP header is unchanged. However, the size of a routing packet is no longer arbitrarily limited. Because routing updates are never forwarded, the routing packet size is now determined by the physical media and the sizes of the headers which precede the routing data (i.e. media MTU minus the combined header lengths). The number of routes which may be included in a routing update is the routing data length divided by the size of a routing entry.

RFC WATCH   **RIP next generation (for IPv6)**

RFC 2080 **RIPng for IPv6**, 1997 (Proposed Standard)
RFC 2081 **RIPng Protocol Applicability Statement**, 1997 (Informational)

RIPng will efficiently support networks of moderate complexity and topologies without too many multi-hop loops. RIPng also efficiently supports topologies which change frequently because routing table changes are made incrementally and do not require the computation which link-state protocols require to rebuild their maps.

Server-based routing scenarios

While RIP is much less used nowadays as a base routing protocol, it is still used in server-based routing scenarios because it enables servers to make dynamic routing decisions while incurring little CPU and network overhead. To further complicate matters in some organizations, the personnel in charge of servers (and configuring RIP) might be a different group of people from those configuring the internetwork infrastructure and associated interior routing protocols. Metrics set by different groups can therefore be inconsistent. This situation, if gone unnoticed, can adversely affect network performance.

Servers might be set up running RIP to find optimal routes for servers – but know nothing about finding a best path across a complex internetwork. A router running RIP will believe anything it is told via RIP, including information from RIP-based servers. This could result in less than optimal paths being chosen through the network.

Network managers, then, can configure routers to ignore RIP advertisements emanating from servers or to accept them as secondary information. This way, RIP can still make good decisions for server connectivity but not adversely affect the rest of the network by propagating inappropriate information.

RIP strengths

- **Router interworking** – some routers do not support OSPF, and RIP may be the only common dynamic discovery protocol in a heterogeneous environment. This often applies to workstations, Unix machines, or PC file servers used as routers.

- **Router discovery** – many end user devices listen to RIP traffic to discover the local router interface(s).

- **Simplicity** – RIP is simple to set up, and if a router has no complex choices to make on alternate paths, then RIP is good enough. Note that some of these 'advantages' cause problems in real networks. Misconfiguration of a Unix machine may generate illegal routes, and RIP will propagate these through the internet unless route filters are used. RIP's easy administration is a plus even in modern implementations, such as in MPLS/VPN Provider Edge – Customer Edge (PE-CE) routing (see Part V for detailed discussion on MPLS and VPNs) where the PE router may support several hundreds of routing processes (one for each VPN), or in the case of ADSL or cable concentrators where RIP behaves better than OSPF or BGP.

RIP weaknesses

- **Slow convergence** – RIP does not find and advertise new routes quickly when known routes fail. In addition, more complex topologies with resilient routers can produce count to infinity problems, where a spurious route is used and not discovered for several minutes.

- **Poor metrics** – RIP only supports a hop count metric, with a maximum value of 15 hops. It is not practical to cost different speed links to bias traffic towards better routes unless the network is simple and small.

- **Limited network diameter** – due to a maximum hop count of 15, RIP networks have limited diameters. Very complex networks may well span more than 15 hops, hence rendering RIP unsuitable in such situations (if networks are so large, a distance vector routing algorithm would not be a good choice anyway).

- **Trust** – the RIP protocol does not support checking for common faults and errors. All routes sent by a router to others are assumed correct, even if no traffic can flow on the return path.

11.3.2 Interior Gateway Routing Protocol – proprietary

The **Interior Gateway Routing Protocol** (IGRP) is a routing protocol developed in 1986 by Cisco Systems, Inc. Cisco's principal goal in creating IGRP was to provide a robust protocol for routing within an autonomous system having arbitrarily complex topology and consisting of media with diverse bandwidth and delay characteristics.

IGRP was developed to overcome the main RIP's limits: a small hop-count limit (16) which restricted the size of internets, and its single metric of hop count that did not allow for much routing flexibility in complex environments. The goals with which IGRP was designed were summarized by its authors as follows:

- provide stable routing in complex or very large networks with no routing loops;
- provide fast responses to topology changes;
- create low overhead;
- split traffic among several parallel routes of approximately equal desirability;
- take into account error rates and level of traffic on different paths;
- handle multiple types of service.

IGRP operation

In IGRP, the general Bellman-Ford algorithm is modified in three critical aspects. First, instead of a simple metric, a **vector of metrics** is used to characterize paths. Second, instead of picking a single path with the smallest metric, traffic is **split among several paths** equal- or unequal-cost load balancing (metrics fall into a specified range). Third, several features are introduced to provide stability in situations where the topology is changing. IGRP uses IP protocol number 88. IGRP requires for its operation the notion of an **autonomous system** for which it supports the interior routing. The AS number must be configured manually on the router and then is contained in every update routing message.

IGRP uses a **combined metric** (vector of metrics) in the routing decision consisting of:

- **delay**;
- **bandwidth**;
- **reliability**;
- **load**.

Network administrators can set the weighting factors for each of these metrics. IGRP uses either the administrator-set or the default weightings to automatically calculate optimal routes. IGRP provides a wide range for its metrics. For example, **reliability** and **load** can take on any value between 1 and 255 – in fact these are measured as a fraction of 255 which is deemed as 100% (desirable for reliability, unacceptable for load). **Bandwidth** can take on values reflecting speeds from 1200 bps to 10 Gbps. The bandwidth is a normalized value (with respect of 10^7) of the minimum bandwidth (in kbps) on the path to the destination. The **delay** is the sum of delays (in ms) in the path and can take on any value from 1 to 2^{24}.

Wide metric ranges allow satisfactory metric setting in internets with widely varying performance characteristics. Most importantly, the metric components are combined in a user-definable algorithm. As a result, network administrators can influence route selection in an intuitive fashion. The best path is selected based on the following **formula of a composite metric**:

$$M = [(K1 * B + K2 * B) / (256 - L) + K3 * D] * [K5 / (R + K4)]$$

where:

- M = metric (quality of a particular path – the lower the value, the better the route);
- K1, K2, K3, K4, K5 = constants;
- B = vertical bandwidth;
- L = load;
- D = topological delay;
- R = reliability.

Default values for constants are: K1 = K3 = 1 and K2 = K4 = K5 = 0.

If K5 is set to 0, the algebra is turned on its head because instead of M becoming zero, the reliability portion is simply not taken into account (the [K5 / (Reliability + K4)] term is not used), and the formula is simplified to:

M = [K1 * BW + (K2 * BW) / (256 – Load) + K3 * Delay] only if K5 = 0

For the default metric (the majority of real-life network cases) the formula may be simplified more intuitively into:

$$M = (10^7 / \textbf{Bandwidth}) + \Sigma \textbf{ Delays}$$

K1 and K2 indicate the weight to be assigned to bandwidth and delay. These would depend upon the required type of service. For example, interactive traffic would normally place a higher weight on delay, and file transfer on bandwidth.

The path having the smallest composite metric will be the best path. Where there are multiple paths to the same destination, the router can use **load splitting** over more than one path.

IGRP can perform load balancing over an asymmetric set of paths for a given destination. This feature is known as **unequal-cost load balancing**. Unequal-cost load balancing allows traffic to be distributed among multiple (up to four) unequal-cost paths to provide greater overall throughput and reliability. The alternate path **variance** V (that is, the difference in desirability between the primary and alternate paths) is used to determine the feasibility of a potential route. The variance is set up by the network administrator (default is one, i.e. equal-cost load balancing), and V multiplied by the best metric would result in the worst metric path used for load balancing. An alternate route is feasible if the next router in the path is closer to the destination (has a lower metric value) than the current router and if the metric for the entire alternate path is within the variance (their metric is lower than $(V * M)$). Only paths that are feasible can be used for load balancing and included in the routing table. These conditions limit the number of cases in which load balancing can occur, but ensure that the dynamics of the network will remain stable.

Load balancing is done in accordance with the composite metric for each data path. For instance, if one path has a composite metric of 1 and another path has a composite metric of 3, the proportion will be 1:3 between the two paths, i.e. three times as many packets will be sent over the data path having the composite metric of 1. However, only paths whose composite metrics are within a certain range of the smallest composite metric will be used.

The general rules applicable to IGRP unequal-cost load balancing can be summarized as follows:

- IGRP will accept **up to four paths** for a given destination network.
- The local best metric must be greater than the metric learned from the next router, that is the next-hop router must be closer (have a smaller metric value) to the destination than the local best metric.
- The alternative path metric must be within the specified variance of the local best metric. The multiplier V times the local best metric M for the destination must be greater than or equal to the metric through the next router.

If these conditions are met, the route is deemed feasible and can be added to the routing table.

SNAPSHOT	IGRP at a glance

IGRP is a **proprietary** IP **distance vector routing protocol** to be implemented in Cisco-based routed networks. It uses a **composite metric** dependent mostly on minimum path link **bandwidth** and sum of path links **delay**. The routing tables are **periodically broadcast** every 90 s. IGRP provides for **equal- and unequal-load balancing** but does not support VLSM.

Stability features

IGRP provides a number of features that are designed to enhance its stability and convergence. These include flash updates, hold-downs, split horizons, and poisoned reverse updates. For default routers see Table 11.4).

TABLE 11-4   IGRP timers

Update	Invalid = 3 * update	Hold-down	Flush = 7 * update
90 s	270 s	280 s	630 s

By default, a router running IGRP broadcasts an **update** every 90 seconds. It declares a route inaccessible if it does not receive an update from the first router in the route within three update periods (270 seconds, invalid timer). After seven update periods (630 seconds), the route is removed from the routing table (flush timer).

IGRP uses flash update and poisoned reverse updates to speed up the convergence of the routing algorithm. **Flash update** is the sending of an update sooner than the standard periodic update interval of notifying other routers of a metric change. **Poisoned reverse** updates are intended to defeat larger routing loops caused by increases in routing metrics. The poisoned reverse updates are sent to remove a route and place it in **hold-down**, which keeps new routing information from being used for a certain period of time. The IGRP default for **hold-time** is three times the update timer period plus ten seconds (280 s).

Hold-down is a state in which the route is placed so that routers will neither advertise nor accept the advertisements for the route for a certain period of time. A typical reason for a route to be placed in a hold-down is that a link on the route has gone down. Hold-down is an effective mechanism to prevent spreading wrong routing information throughout the network.

IGRP also advertises three types of routes: interior, system, and exterior, as shown in Figure 11.6:

FIGURE 11-6 Interior, system, and exterior routes within IGRP

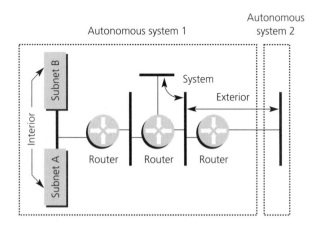

- **Interior routes** – routes between subnets in the network attached to a router interface. If the network attached to a router is not subnetted, IGRP does not advertise interior routes.

- **System routes** – routes to networks within an autonomous system. The router derives system routes from directly connected network interfaces and system route information provided by other IGRP-speaking routers. System routes do not include subnet information.

- **Exterior routes** – routes to networks outside the autonomous system that are considered when identifying a **gateway of last resort**. The router chooses a gateway of last resort from the list of exterior routes that IGRP provides. The router uses the router of last resort if it does not have a better route for a packet and the destination is not a connected network. If the autonomous system has more than one connection to an external network, different routers can choose different exterior routers as the gateway of last resort.

IGRP has a different approach to the **default route**, the collection route for all the datagrams destined for networks not individually listed in the routing table. It is for all traffic for destinations outside the organization or generally in the Internet, which can be sent to just one of a few boundary routers. Those boundary gateways may have more complete information. The default route is the route to the best boundary router. RIP, and some other routing protocols, circulate information about the default route as if it were a real network. IGRP takes a different approach. Rather than a single fake entry for the default route, IGRP allows real networks to be flagged as **candidates** for being a default. This is implemented by placing information about those networks in a special exterior section of the update message. However, it might as well be thought of as turning on a bit associated with those networks. Periodically IGRP scans all the candidate default routes and chooses the one with the lowest metric as the actual default route.

The router enforces a maximum diameter to the IGRP network. Routes whose hop counts exceed this diameter will not be advertised. The default maximum diameter is 100 hops. The **maximum diameter** is 255 hops.

11.3.3 Enhanced Interior Gateway Routing Protocol

The **Enhanced Interior Gateway Routing Protocol** (EIGRP) is an enhanced version of IGRP. Cisco developed Enhanced IGRP in the early 1990s to improve further the operating efficiency of IGRP, namely by supporting not only IP, but AppleTalk and IPX (independently in a ships-in-the-night mode, not integrated mode), and using the DUAL routing algorithm (advanced distance vector). There are two major revisions of EIGRP, versions 0 and 1. As EIGRP is not an open protocol, there are no RFCs available for it but there is a fair amount of detail available at the Cisco Web site related to the particular EIGRP configuration on Cisco routers. EIGRP uses protocol number 88.

From a technical standpoint, EIGRP is an advanced distance vector routing protocol. From a marketing standpoint, Cisco has called it 'hybrid,' which has no accepted technical meaning. 'Hybrid' is an attempt to differentiate EIGRP, and its DUAL algorithm, from the problems of first- and second-generation DV protocols. J. J. Garcia-Luna-Aceves, the inventor of DUAL, has always called it an advanced DV protocol. EIGRP has legitimately fixed some of the problems of earlier DV protocols, such as the lack of a hello subprotocol and a reliable update mechanism. Without these mechanisms, periodic update becomes necessary, and the protocol cannot be loop-free.

A router running Enhanced IGRP stores all its **neighbors' routing tables** so that it can quickly adapt to **alternate routes**. If no appropriate route exists, Enhanced IGRP queries its neighbors to discover an alternate route. These queries propagate until an alternate route is found (see Section 9.4 for DUAL operation).

Enhanced IGRP does not make periodic updates. Instead, it sends **partial updates** only when the metric for a route changes. Propagation of partial updates is automatically bounded so that only those routers that need the information are updated. EIGRP uses for hellos a reserved IP multicast address 224.0.0.10 which maps onto the multicast MAC address *01-00-5E-00-00-0A*). As a result of these two capabilities, Enhanced IGRP consumes significantly less bandwidth than IGRP.

EIGRP combines advanced decision-making based on a **composite metric** (in the same way as IGRP based on minimum path bandwidth and available path delay, optionally on reliability and load) with schemes that also reduce the overhead required for inter-router communication. The minimum bandwidth taken into account for the EIGRP metric is set to the minimum bandwidth of the entire path, and does not reflect how many hops or low bandwidth links are in the path. Delay is a cumulative value which increases by the delay value of each segment in the path. The metric is calculated according to the following formula:

$$M = [10^7/(\text{Min. bandwidth on the path}) + \sum (\text{Delays on the path})] * 256$$

Load sharing is enabled in EIGRP by default for equal-cost routes, and configurable variance enables **unequal load balancing** over routes of suboptimal metrics. However, unequal load balancing may result in out-of-order packets in end nodes creating significant overhead which cancels out the advantage of network load sharing (see Section 11.3.2 for more details on load balancing).

QUICK TIP   **hybrid protocols**

Hybrid routing protocol is a marketing term rather than a technical one. Initially it was an attempt to differentiate EIGRP from the older distance vector and standards-based link-state protocols.

The Distributed Update Algorithm (DUAL) is the algorithm used to obtain loop-freedom at every instant throughout a route computation (for details see Chapter 9). It allows all routers involved in a topology change to synchronize at the same time. Routers that are not affected by topology changes are not involved in the recomputation. The convergence time is very short.

QUICK TIP   **EIGRP metric**

The metric calculation for IGRP and Enhanced IGRP are the same. By default, the composite metric is the sum of the segment delays and the minimum bandwidth (scaled and inverted) for a given route ((10^7 / BW + Delay) * 256).

The main EIGRP features include the following:

- **Fast convergence** – Enhanced IGRP uses DUAL to achieve convergence quickly. A router running Enhanced IGRP stores all of its neighbors' routing tables so that it can quickly adapt to alternate routes. If no appropriate route exists, Enhanced IGRP queries its neighbors to discover an alternate route. These queries propagate until an alternate route is found.

- **Route aggregation and VLSM** – Enhanced IGRP includes full support for VLSM. Subnet routes are automatically summarized on a network boundary, but in addition, Enhanced IGRP can be configured to summarize on any bit boundary at any interface.

- **Limited bandwidth utilization** – Enhanced IGRP does not make periodic updates. Instead, it sends **incremental (partial) updates** only when the metric for a route changes. The multicast address *224.0.0.10* is used. Propagation of partial updates is automatically bounded so that only those routers that need the information are updated. As a result of these two capabilities, Enhanced IGRP consumes significantly less bandwidth than IGRP. Regarding processor utilization, the feasible successor technology greatly reduces the total processor utilization of an AS by requiring only the routers that were affected by a topology change to perform the route recomputation. Furthermore, the route recomputation only occurs for routes that were affected.

- **Multiple network-layer support** – Enhanced IGRP includes support for AppleTalk, IP, and Novell NetWare.
- **Scaling** – enhanced IGRP scales to large networks; the largest possible network width supported by EIGRP is 224 hops.

SNAPSHOT   **EIGRP**

EIGRP is a **proprietary** IP **routing protocol**, using the DUAL routing algorithm, to be implemented in Cisco-based routed networks. It uses a **composite metric** dependent mostly on minimum path link **bandwidth** and sum of path links **delay**, similar to IGRP. The **partial and incremental updates** are multicast only to affected routers immediately after any change which reduces bandwidth utilization. Only when a topology change occurs do routers exchange updates, sending the changes only, rather than automatically exchanging complete routing tables at regular intervals. IGRP provides for **equal- and unequal-load balancing** and supports VLSM. Additionally, EIGRP may support AppleTalk and IPX routing alongside IP routing.

EIGRP operation

EIGRP has the following basic **components**:

- **Neighbor discovery/recovery** – process that routers use to dynamically learn of other routers on their directly attached networks. When a router discovers a new neighbor, it records the neighbor's address and interface as an entry in the neighbor table. One neighbor table exists for each protocol-dependent module. When a neighbor sends a hello packet, it advertises a hold time, which is the amount of time a router treats a neighbor as reachable and operational. If a hello packet is not received within the hold time, the hold time expires and DUAL is informed of the topology change. Unlike IGRP or RIP, EIGRP sends hello packets in order to form and sustain neighbor adjacencies. Without a neighbor adjacency, EIGRP cannot exchange routes with a neighbor.
- **Reliable transport protocol** – responsible for guaranteed, ordered delivery of EIGRP packets to all neighbors. It supports intermixed transmission of multicast or unicast packets. Some EIGRP packets must be transmitted reliably and others need not. For efficiency, reliability is provided only when necessary. For example, on a multi-access network that has multicast capabilities, such as Ethernet, it is not necessary to send hellos reliably to all

neighbors individually. EIGRP sends a single multicast hello to 224.0.0.10 with an indication in the packet informing the receivers that the packet need not be acknowledged. Other types of packets, such as updates, require acknowledgment and this is indicated in the packet. The reliable transport has a provision to send multicast packets quickly when there are unacknowledged packets pending. This helps ensure that convergence time remains low in the presence of varying speed links.

■ **DUAL finite state machine** – embodies the decision process for all route computations. It tracks all routes advertised by all neighbors. The distance information, known as a metric, is used by DUAL to select efficient loop-free paths. DUAL selects routes to be inserted into a routing table based on feasible successors. A successor is a neighboring router used for packet forwarding that has the least cost path to a destination that is guaranteed not to be part of a routing loop. When there are no feasible successors but there are neighbors advertising the destination, a recomputation must occur. This is the process where a new successor is determined. The amount of time it takes to recompute the route affects the convergence time. Even though the recomputation is not processor-intensive, it is advantageous to avoid recomputation if it is not necessary. When a topology change occurs, DUAL will test for feasible successors. If there are feasible successors, it will use any it finds in order to avoid any unnecessary recomputation.

SNAPSHOT   **EIGRP DUAL algorithm concept**

It is mathematically possible to determine whether any route is loop-free, based on the information provided in standard distance vector routing.

■ **Protocol dependent modules** – responsible for network layer, protocol-specific requirements. For example, the IP-EIGRP module is responsible for sending and receiving EIGRP packets that are encapsulated in IP. IP-EIGRP is responsible for parsing EIGRP packets and informing DUAL of the new information received. IP-EIGRP asks DUAL to make routing decisions the results of which are stored in the IP routing table. IP-EIGRP is responsible for redistributing routes learned by other IP routing protocols.

■ **Intelligent bandwidth control** – the latest optimization made to EIGRP includes the bandwidth consumption control. EIGRP takes into account the available bandwidth when determining the rate at which to transmit updates (by default EIGRP does not use more than up to 50% of link bandwidth). Also, it allows configuration of the maximum bandwidth percentage per interface to use for routing updates so that even in periods of topology change followed by heavy routing recomputations, a defined portion of the link remains available for data traffic.

Neighbor table

Neighbor table – based on the hellos received from adjacent EIGRP routers and maintained with a HoldTime (3 × Hello timer) for each of the router's neighbors.

Each router keeps information on the state of **adjacent neighbors**. When newly discovered neighbors are learned, the address and interface of the neighbor is recorded. This information is stored in the **neighbor table**. There is one neighbor table for each protocol-dependent module. When a neighbor sends a hello, it advertises a hold time. The hold time is the amount of time a router treats a neighbor as reachable and operational. In other words, if a hello packet isn't heard within the hold time, then the hold time will expire. When the hold time expires, DUAL is informed of the topology change.

Routing devices periodically send **hello packets** to each other to dynamically learn of other routers on their directly attached networks. This information is used to discover who their neighbors are, and to learn when their neighbors become unreachable or inoperative. By default, hello packets are sent every five seconds. The exception is on low-speed, non-broadcast, multi-access (NBMA) media, where the default hello interval is 60 seconds. Low speed is considered to be a rate of T1 (see Appendix D) or slower. The default hello interval remains five seconds for high-speed NBMA networks.

NBMA is a network that supports the **connection of multiple routers** but at the same time **does not support delivery of broadcast or multicast packets**, such as Frame Relay or X.25.

The neighbor table entry also includes information required by the reliable transport mechanism. **Sequence numbers** are employed to match **acknowledgments** with data packets. The last sequence number received from the neighbor is recorded so out of order packets can be detected. A transmission list is used to queue packets for possible retransmission on a per neighbor basis. Round trip timers are kept in the neighbor data structure to estimate an optimal retransmission interval.

Topology table

The **topology table** is populated by the **protocol dependent modules** and acted upon by the **DUAL finite state machine**. It contains all destinations advertised by neighboring routers. Associated with each entry is the destination address and a list of neighbors that have advertised the destination. For each neighbor, the advertised metric is recorded. This is the metric that the neighbor stores in its routing table. If the neighbor is advertising this destination, it must be using the route to forward packets. This is an important rule that all distance vector protocols must follow.

QUICK TIP   **topology table**

Topology table – the topology table contains the information needed to build a set of distances and vectors to each reachable network: the lowest bandwidth on the path to this destination as reported by the upstream neighbor, total delay, path reliability, path loading, MTU, feasible distance, reported advertised distance, and route source (external routes are marked). DUAL acts on the topology table to determine successors and feasible successors.

Also associated with the destination is the metric that the router uses to reach the destination. This is the sum of the best advertised metric from all neighbors plus the link cost to the best neighbor. This is the **metric** that the router uses in the routing table and to advertise to other routers.

EIGRP also stores MTU, link reliability, and link load in its topology table and can be configured to use this information for calculating the best path. However, none of these optional metrics can trigger an update and composite route metric recalculation.

Feasible successors

QUICK TIP   **successors**

Successor – a neighbor that has been selected as the next hop for a destination based on the feasibility condition.

Feasible successor (FS) – a neighbor that has satisfied the feasibility condition and has a path to the destination.

Feasibility condition (FC) – a condition that is met when the lowest of all the neighbors' costs plus the link cost to that neighbor is found, and the neighbor's advertised cost is less than the current successor's cost.

A destination entry is moved from the topology table to the routing table when there is a feasible successor. All minimum cost paths to the destination form a set of **feasible distances**. From this set, the neighbors that have an advertised metric less than the current routing table metric – **reported distance** – are considered feasible successors. Where the reported distance is less than feasible distance, the path is considered loop-free.

Feasible distance – the current best distance (metric) to a destination. In other words, the metric through the successor.

Reported advertised distance – the distance from the successor to the destination network.

Feasible successors are viewed by a router as neighbors that are downstream with respect to the destination. These neighbors and the associated metrics are placed in the forwarding table.

When a neighbor changes the metric it has been advertising or a topology change occurs in the network, the set of feasible successors may have to be re-evaluated. However, this is not categorized as a route recomputation.

Route states

Routes that have a **valid successor** are said to be in a **passive state**. If for some reason a router loses a route through its successor, and it does not have a feasible successor for that route, the route transitions to an **active state**. In the active state a router sends queries out to its neighbors requesting a path to the lost route. Table 11.5 shows the queries related to the route states and actions required.

When there are no feasible successors, a route goes into the active state and a route recomputation occurs. A route recomputation commences with a router sending a *Query* packet to all neighbors. Neighboring routers can either *Reply* if they have feasible successors for the destination or optionally return a *Query* indicating that they are performing a route recomputation. While in Active state, a router cannot change the next-hop neighbor it is using to forward packets. Once all replies are received for a given Query, the destination can transition to the passive state and a new successor can be selected. When a link to a neighbor which is the only feasible successor goes down, all routes through that neighbor commence a route recomputation and enter the active state.

Active state – a router's state for a destination when it has lost its successor to that destination and has no other feasible successor available. The router is forced to compute a route to the destination through the query process.

Passive state – a router's state after losing its successor when it has a feasible successor to the destination available in its topology table.

TABLE 11-5 Rules for processing a query from a neighbor

Query from	Route state	Action
Neighbor (not the current successor)	Passive	Reply with current successor information
Successor	Passive	Attempt to find new successor; if successful, reply with new information; if not successful, mark destination unreachable and query all neighbors except the previous successor
Any neighbor	No path through this neighbor before query	Reply with best path currently known
Any neighbor	Not known before query	Reply that the destination is unreachable
Neighbor (not the current successor)	Active	If there is no current successor to this destination (normally this would be true), reply with an unreachable; if there is a good successor, reply with the current path information
Successor	Active	Attempt to find new successor; if successful, reply with new information; if not successful, mark destination unreachable and query all neighbors except the previous successor

When an **EIGRP neighbor receives a query for a route** it behaves as follows:

- If the EIGRP topology table does not currently contain an entry for the route, the router immediately replies to the query with an unreachable message, stating that there is no path for this route through this neighbor.
- If the EIGRP topology table lists the querying router as the successor for this route and a feasible successor exists, the feasible successor is installed and the router immediately replies to the query.

■ If the EIGRP topology table lists the querying router as the successor for this route and a feasible successor does not exist, the router queries all of its EIGRP neighbors except those which sent out the same interface as its former successor. The router will not reply to the querying router until it has received a reply to all queries it originated for this route.

■ If the query was received from a neighbor that is not the successor for this destination, the router replies with its successor information.

DUAL example

The topology in Figure 11.7 will illustrate how the DUAL algorithm converges. The example will focus on destination N only. Each node shows its cost to N (in hops). The arrows show the node's successor. So, for example, C uses A to reach N and the cost is 2.

FIGURE 11-7 Example of DUAL topology

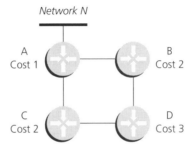

If the link between A and B fails, B will send a *Query* informing its neighbors that it has lost its feasible successor. D receives the *Query* and determines if it has any other feasible successors. If it did not, it would have to start a route computation and enter the active state. However, in this case, C is its feasible successor because its cost (2) is less than D's current cost (3) to destination N. D can switch to C as its successor. Note A and C did not participate because they were unaffected by the change.

Now let's cause a route computation to occur. In this different scenario, let's say the link between A and C fails. C determines that it has lost its successor and has no other feasible successors. D is not considered a feasible successor because its advertised metric (3) is greater than C's current cost (2) to reach destination N. C must perform a route computation for destination N. C sends a *Query* to its only neighbor D. D Replies because its successor has not changed. D does not need to perform a route computation. When C receives the *Reply* it knows that all neighbors have processed the news about the failure to reach N. At this point, C can choose its new feasible successor D with a cost of (4) to reach destination N. Note that A and B were unaffected by the topology change and D needed to simply reply to C.

EIGRP

EIGRP menages uses five packet types:

- *Hello* – are **multicast** (224.0.0.10) for neighbor discovery/recovery and sent every five seconds on high bandwidth links and every 60 seconds on low bandwidth multipoint links (multipoint circuits with T1 bandwidth or slower, such as Frame Relay multipoint interfaces, ATM multipoint interfaces, ATM switched virtual circuits, and ISDN BRIs). The hold time is the amount of time that a router will consider a neighbor alive without receiving a hello packet. The hold time is typically three times the hello interval, by default, 15 seconds and 180 seconds. Both the hello interval, and hold-time interval can be adjusted per interface. It is possible for two routers to become EIGRP neighbors even though the hello and hold timers do not match because hold time is included in the hello packets so each neighbor should stay alive even though the hello interval and hold timers do not match. Hellos do not require acknowledgment as they are sent unreliably. A hello with no data is also used as an *Acknowledgment*.

- *Acknowledgments* – always sent unreliably using a **unicast** address and contain a non-zero acknowledgment number.

- *Updates* – convey the reachability of destinations. *Updates* are sent in the following instances: when a neighbor first comes up, when a router transitions from active to passive for a destination, or when there is a metric change for a certain destination. When a new neighbor is discovered, update packets are sent so the neighbor can build up its topology table. In this case, update packets are **unicast**. In other cases, such as a link cost change, updates are **multicast**. *Updates* are always transmitted reliably.

- *Queries* – sent when destinations go into the active state and the router is asking for information on that destination. Unless it receives replies back from all its neighbors, the router will remain in the active state and not start the computation for a new successor. *Queries* enable EIGRP converge quickly but may involve a significant overhead activity, particularly in cases of major network topology changes. *Queries* may cascade throughout the network until either an alternative path is found or the end of network is reached, or if the information about the network that is subject of the query is unknown *Queries* are always **multicast** unless they are sent in response to a received query. In this case, it is unicast back to the successor that originated the query. They are transmitted reliably.

- *Replies* – sent by every EIGRP neighbor which receives a *Query*. If the neighbor does not have the information, it queries its neighbors. *Replies* are **unicast** to the originator of the *Query*. *Replies* are transmitted reliably.

- *Requests* – used to get specific information from one or more neighbors. Request packets are used in route server applications. They can be **multicast** or **unicast**. *Requests* are transmitted unreliably.

The format of EIGRP packets is shown in Figure 11.8:

FIGURE 11-8 EIGRP message format

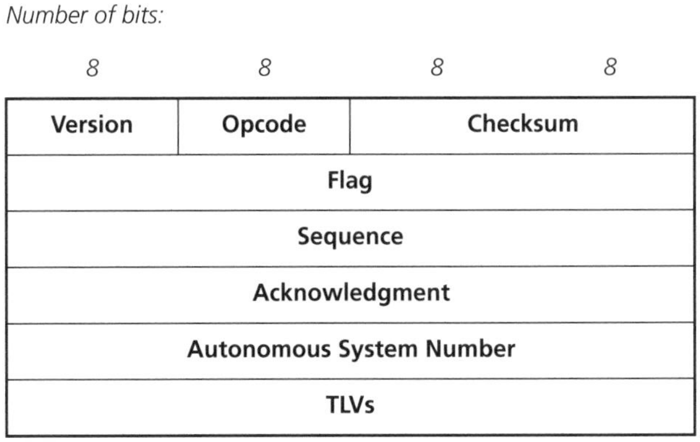

Number of bits:

Version	Opcode	Checksum

(8, 8, 8, 8)

Version	Opcode	Checksum
Flag		
Sequence		
Acknowledgment		
Autonomous System Number		
TLVs		

EIGRP message contains the following fields:

- **Version** – EIGRP version.
- **Opcode** – *1* for update, *2* for query, *3* for reply, *4* for hello, *5* for IPX SAP.
- **Checksum** – standard IP checksum over the entire packet, excluding IP header.
- **Flags** – values of *hex00000001* (Init), *hex00000002* (conditional receive bit).
- **Sequence** – 32-bit sequence number.
- **Acknowledgment** – 32-bit sequence number.
- **Autonomous system number** – ID number of the IP EIGRP domain.
- **TLVs** (Type, Length, Value):
  - *hex0001* EIGRP parameter;
  - *hex0003* sequence;
  - *hex0005* next multicast sequence;
  - IP specific: *hex0102* IP internal route, *hex0103* IP external route;
  - AppleTalk specific: *hex0202* Appletalk internal route, *hex0203* Appletalk external route, *hex0204* Appletalk cable configuration;
  - IPX specific: *hex0302* IPX internal route, *hex0303* IPX external route.

Route tagging

Enhanced IGRP uses three kinds of **routes**:

- **internal routes** – routes learned from Enhanced IGRP;
- **external routes** – routes learned from another protocol and then redistributed into Enhanced IGRP;
- **summary routes** – routes that Enhanced IGRP may dynamically create due to auto summarization, or due to an explicit summary route configuration.

Internal routes are ones that have been originated within an EIGRP Autonomous System (AS). Therefore, a directly attached network that is configured to run EIGRP is considered an internal route and is propagated with this information throughout the EIGRP AS.

External routes are those that have been learned by another routing protocol or reside in the routing table as static routes. These routes are tagged individually with the identity of their origination. **External routes** are tagged with the following information:

- the router ID of the EIGRP router that redistributed the route;
- the AS number where the destination resides;
- a configurable administrator tag;
- protocol ID of the external protocol;
- the metric from the external protocol;
- bit flags for default routing.

As an example, suppose there is an AS with three border routers. A border router is one that runs more than one routing protocol. The AS uses EIGRP as the routing protocol. Let's say two of the border routers, BR1 and BR2, use OSPF and the other, BR3, uses RIP. Routes learned by one of the OSPF border routers, BR1, can be conditionally redistributed into EIGRP (more on redistribution in Sections 11.10.1 and 12.8). This means that EIGRP running in BR1 will advertise the OSPF routes within its own AS. When it does so, it will advertise the route and tag it as an OSPF learned route with a metric equal to the routing table metric of the OSPF route. The router-ID will be set to BR1. The EIGRP route will propagate to the other border routers. Let's say that BR3, the RIP border router, also advertises the same destinations as BR1. Therefore BR3 redistributes the RIP routes into the EIGRP AS. BR2, then, has enough information to determine the AS entry point for the route, the original routing protocol used, and the metric. Further, the network administrator could assign tag values to specific destinations when redistributing the route. BR2 can use any of this information to use the route or readvertise it back out into OSPF.

Using EIGRP route tagging can give a network administrator flexible policy controls and help customize routing. Route tagging is particularly useful in transit ASs where EIGRP would typically interact with an inter-domain routing protocol that implements more global policies. This combines for very scalable policy-based routing.

EIGRP provides compatibility and seamless interoperation with IGRP routers. There is an **automatic redistribution** mechanism used so IGRP routes are imported into EIGRP and vice versa. Since the metrics for both protocols are directly translatable, they are easily comparable as if they were routes that originated in their own AS. In addition, IGRP routes are treated as external routes in EIGRP so the tagging capabilities are available for custom tuning. IGRP routes will take precedence over EIGRP routes by default. This can be changed with a configuration command that does not require the routing processes to restart.

Design considerations

Note that for the purposes of Enhanced IGRP, Frame Relay and SMDS networks may or may not be considered to be NBMA. These networks are considered NBMA if the interface has not been configured to use physical multicasting; otherwise they are not considered NBMA.

The hold time is advertised in hello packets and indicates to neighbors the length of time they should consider the sender valid. The default **hold time** is three times the hello interval, or 15 seconds. For slow-speed NBMA networks, the default hold time is 180 seconds. On very congested and large networks, the default hold time might not be sufficient for all routers to receive hello packets from their neighbors. In this case, the hold time should be increased.

The hold timer is reset when any packet is received from a neighbor. The hello and hold timers on both ends of a link do not need to match for a neighbor relationship because hold time is included in the hello packet itself. It is important to note that on diversion from the default timers' values, a manual change of a value for one timer will not automatically affect the other.

There is no such binding limit of a maximum route length as with RIP. When IP Enhanced IGRP is enabled, the network diameter is up to 224 hops.

A new EIGRP feature, **stub routing**, improves network stability, reduces resource utilization, and simplifies stub router configuration. Stub routing is commonly used in a hub and spoke network topology. In a hub and spoke network, one or more end (stub) networks are connected to a remote router (the spoke) that is connected to one or more distribution routers (the hub). The remote router is adjacent only to one or more distribution routers. The only route for IP traffic to follow into the remote router is through a distribution router.

This type of configuration is commonly used in WAN topologies where the distribution router is directly connected to a WAN. The distribution router can be connected to many more remote routers. Often, the distribution router will be connected to 100 or more remote routers. In a hub and spoke topology, the remote router must forward all non-local traffic to a distribution router, so it becomes unnecessary for the remote router to hold a complete routing table. Generally, the distribution router need not send anything more than a default route to the remote router.

IGRP and EIGRP integration

EIGRP provides for smooth and easy migration from the IGRP and may be deployed in the IGRP-routed network in several phases. The key considerations for integrating Enhanced IGRP into an IP network running IGRP are as follows:

- **Metric handling** – the metric calculation and default metric value for IGRP and Enhanced IGRP are the same. By default, the composite metric is the sum of the segment delays and the lowest segment bandwidth (scaled and inverted) for a given route.

- **Redistribution** – there is an automatic redistribution between the two protocols (both ways) but only if they operate in a single AS. Otherwise, manual redistribution is required, as in the case of integrating EIGRP with another routing protocol (with RIP caution must be taken so that no advertised routes from one 'routing zone' are advertised back).

- **Route summarization** – with IGRP, routing information advertised out of an interface is often automatically summarized at the network boundaries. Specifically, this automatic summarization occurs for those routes whose network number differs from the network number of the interface to which the advertisement is being sent. The remaining routes, which are part of the network number of the interface, are advertised without summarization.

  EIGRP also supports automatic summarization of network addresses at major network borders. But unlike IGRP, EIGRP allows much needed summarization and aggregation at any point in the network. EIGRP supports aggregation to any bit. This allows properly designed EIGRP networks to scale exceptionally well without the use of areas. Although not a hierarchical routing protocol, EIGRP can use summarization to create a hierarchy as information can be filtered and aggregated at any interface boundary to bound the propagation of routing information.

Strengths of EIGRP

- **Convergence** – incremental updates and a query process based on the DUAL algorithm help achieve very quick convergence even in networks of large span.
- **Bandwidth consumption** – EIGRP solves the problem of bandwidth consumption in case of converging network by setting up the limit for bandwidth use. EIGRP cannot consume more than 50% of available bandwidth (by default), while the administrator may configure this limit differently. It is recommended that the bandwidth value for a link, especially in the case of serial links with clock rate differing from signal rate, be configured manually to reflect reality as part of the composite metric.

  Implementing EIGRP in NMBA packet-switched networks requires a lot of care. There are certain rules in terms of the bandwidth EIGRP consumes on the virtual circuits: the traffic that EIGRP is allowed to send on a single VC cannot exceed the capacity of that virtual circuit; the total EIGRP traffic for all virtual circuits cannot exceed the access line speed of the interface; and the bandwidth allowed for EIGRP on each virtual circuit must be the same in each direction.

  A word of caution should be added, as EIGRP uses the configured bandwidth to determine a pacing interval between EIGRP packets. Therefore, if for some reason the bandwidth is changed to a very small value (to force the choice of an alternate route), it may affect the exchange of EIGRP messages (determined to use only up to 50% of configured bandwidth) and even the establishing of a neighbor relationship.

- **Classless protocol** – EIGRP supports VLSM and CIDR thus is not bound by network boundaries. Filtering and summarization of routing information is therefore possible at any router within the EIGRP network. Automatic summarization, however, is performed as in RIP or IGRP, with the exception of external routes that are not autosummarized. Automatic summarization represents a migration from classful routing protocols – summarizing to classful network addresses any time a network boundary is crossed. To support discontiguous subnets the autosummarization must be manually turned off.

QUICK TIP   **discontiguous network**

An **addressing scheme** in which the components of a **major classful network** are **physically or logically separated** by addresses corresponding to a different major classful network. In other words, a discontiguous network is a network in which not all the subnets/segments may be reached via links that are also part of the same network.

- **Route summarization and filtering** – help minimize the query scope in a network. This is needed in the case of large networks where queries may sometimes not get replies, generating **Stuck in Active** (SIA) routes. The most basic SIA routes occur when it simply takes too long for a query to reach the other end of the network and for a reply to travel back before the router that issued the query gives up and clears its connection to the router that is not answering, effectively restarting the neighbor session. The reason the router on the network cannot answer a query may be one of the following: the router is too busy to answer the query (generally due to high CPU utilization); the router is having memory problems and cannot allocate the memory to process the query or build the reply packet; the circuit between the two routers is not good – enough packets are getting through to keep the neighbor relationship up, but some queries or replies are getting lost between the routers; unidirectional links (a link on which traffic can only flow in one direction because of a failure). To avoid an SIA situation the best approach is to make the paths to certain networks unknown to minimize the number of routers involved in the convergence process. Route summarization and route filtering achieve the hiding of the networks as needed.

- **Load balancing** – EIGRP puts up to four routes of equal cost in the routing table, which the router then load balances. The type of load balancing (per packet or per destination) depends on the type of switching being done in the router. Additionally, EIGRP can also load balance over unequal cost links (based on variance as explained in section on IGRP).

- **Extensions** – for reducing the query range in a network with a lot of dual-homed remotes, some routers may be effectively configured as stub routers.

- **Multiprotocol support** – EIGRP can be used for routing IP, IPX, and AppleTalk. However, in terms of multiprotocol support it is necessary to remember that EIGRP is not an integrated routing protocol (such as integrated IS-IS), instead it operates in **ships-in-the-night mode** running separate routing processes for all routed protocols supported. The individual routing processes then share a common algorithm (hence similar configuration and easier troubleshooting), and routing protocol name. EIGRP is quite robust and easy to configure (compared, for example, to OSPF), especially when more than IP routing is in question (IPX and/or AppleTalk routing).

Weaknesses of EIGRP

The obvious limit of EIGRP is that it is **not an open protocol** and thus may only be used exclusively in networks based on Cisco devices. As for other limits follow:

- **No hierarchy supported** – EIGRP is easy to configure, even in a large network, which may adversely result over time in an unmanageable network with the only remedy being redesign and painful renumbering. EIGRP is therefore of no use in an ISP network and enterprise networks are more and more built on OSPF. With regard to its deployment in multiprotocol label switching (MPLS), discussed in Part V, EIGRP lacks enough support from Cisco to become important.

- **Split horizon** – a necessary precaution against routing loops which may actually become an obstacle for EIGRP. In some cases DUAL cannot find an alternative loop-free path even if one exists. EIGRP uses split horizon or advertises a route as unreachable when:
  - two routers are in startup mode (exchanging topology tables for the first time) – when two routers first become neighbors, they exchange topology tables during startup mode. For each table entry a router receives during startup mode, it advertises the same entry back to its new neighbor with a maximum metric (poison route);
  - advertising a topology table change;
  - sending a query – queries result in a split horizon only when a router receives a query or update from the successor it is using for the destination in the query.

11.3.4 Open Shortest Path First

Open Shortest Path First (OSPF) was the first routing protocol based on the shortest path first (SPF) algorithm (discussed in Chapter 9). OSPF has two primary characteristics. The first is that it is open, in that its specification is in the public domain. The second principal characteristic is that it is based on the SPF algorithm, which is sometimes referred to as the Dijkstra algorithm, named after the person credited with its creation. OSPF uses IP protocol number 89.

OSPF was derived from several research efforts, including the following:

- Bolt, Beranek, and Newman's (BBN's) SPF algorithm developed in 1978 for the ARPANET (a landmark packet-switching network developed in the early 1970s by BBN);
- Dr Perlman's research on fault-tolerant broadcasting of routing information (1988) and BBN's work on area routing (1986);
- an early version of OSI's Intermediate System-to-Intermediate System (IS-IS) routing protocol.

OSPF has developed from its initial specification and **version 2** of the protocol is now a standard (RFC 2328). OSPF has been reworked to include better security and a more easily adaptable architecture, hence a proposed new version of OSPF is on its way, **OSPF Version 3** (more details are given below).

The requirements for designers of OSPF, as a successor to RIP, were the following:

- to use a more descriptive metric than RIP;
- to provide for equal-cost multipath routing for load balancing;
- to introduce a hierarchy to support routing within large domains;
- to separate internal and external routes;
- to support flexible addressing schemes (subnetting, VLSM);
- to ensure security;
- to allow for ToS routing.

Technology basics

OSPF is a link-state routing protocol. As such, it calls for the sending of **link-state advertisements** (LSAs) to all other routers within the same hierarchical **area**. An LSA contains fundamentally information on the router's interface states, i.e. physical condition of the interface, is it up or down, the IP address of the interface, the subnet mask assigned to the interface, the network to which the interface is connected, and the associated cost for using the router's network connection. The LSAs are propagated (flooded) throughout the OSPF network until every OSPF router has a complete and identical link-state database. As OSPF routers accumulate link-state information, each router can build a tree (with itself as the root, and the branches representing the shortest, or least cost, routes to all the networks in the AS). Each OSPF router will use the SPF algorithm to calculate the shortest path to each node to build the routing table.

As a link-state routing protocol, OSPF contrasts with RIP and IGRP, which are distance vector routing protocols. Routers running the distance vector algorithm send all or a portion of their routing tables in routing update messages, but only to their neighbors.

▶

RFC 1585 **MOSPF: Analysis and Experience**, 1994 (Informational)

RFC 1586 **Guidelines for Running OSPF Over Frame Relay Networks**, 1994 (Informational)

RFC 1587 **The OSPF NSSA Option**, 1994 (Proposed Standard)

RFC 1745 **BGP4/IDRP for IP-OSPF Interaction**, 1994 (Historic)

RFC 1765 **OSPF Database Overflow**, 1995 (Experimental)

RFC 1793 **Extending OSPF to Support Demand Circuits**, 1995 (Proposed Standard)

RFC 1850 **OSPF Version 2 Management Information Base**, 1995 (Draft Standard)

RFC 2154 **OSPF with Digital Signatures**, 1997 (Experimental)

RFC 2328 **OSPF Version 2**, 1998 (Standard)

RFC 2329 **OSPF Standardization Report**, 1998 (Informational)

RFC 2370 **The OSPF Opaque LSA Option**, 1998 (Proposed Standard)

RFC 2676 **QoS Routing Mechanisms and OSPF Extensions**, 1999 (Experimental)

RFC 2740 **OSPF for IPv6**, 1999 (Proposed Standard)

RFC 2844 **OSPF over ATM and Proxy-PAR** (PNNI Augmented Routing), 2000 (Experimental)

The flooding algorithm is one of the most important parts of any link-state routing protocol. It ensures that all routers within a link-state domain converge on the same topological information within a finite period of time. To ensure reliability, typical implementations of the flooding algorithm send new information via all interfaces other than the one the new piece of information was received on. This redundancy is necessary to guarantee that flooding is performed reliably, but implies considerable overhead of utilized bandwidth and CPU time if neighboring routers are connected with more than one link. There exist proposals for methods reducing this overhead.

The **metric** OSPF uses is, as with other link-state protocols, **cost**. It is an arbitrary value (with values of 1 to 65 535 inclusive, i.e. a 16-bit positive integer value); however, in many cases it is by default derived from the bandwidth on the particular link between two neighbors. The cost of a path is a sum of the path's constituent links. The cost is assigned to the outgoing interfaces of a router, so in the case of a metric assigned by the administrator the link may bear different costs in different directions.

OSPF uses two different types of external metrics establishing two distinct routing levels but using different semantics:

- **Type 1 metric** – takes the internal (path to AS boundary router advertising AS-external-LSA) and external component of the external metric as of the same quality;
- **Type 2 metric** – understands the external part of the path as more significant (hence Type 2 metric cost is the external part).

Routing hierarchy

Unlike RIP or (E)IGRP, OSPF can operate within a hierarchy. The largest entity within the hierarchy is the **Autonomous System** (AS). OSPF is an intra-AS (interior gateway) routing protocol, although it is capable of receiving routes from and sending routes to other ASs.

QUICK TIP **OSPF area**

An **area** is a logical set of network segments and their attached devices. The inter-connection between the areas is performed by routers, in OSPF called **area border routers**. Areas are built in order to reduce the $O(n^2)$ complexity of the number of links, therefore greatly cutting down the overhead (both in terms of bandwidth and CPU) incurred by the SPF algorithm.

An AS can be divided into a number of areas. An **area** is a group of contiguous networks and attached hosts. Single backbone area is a mandatory area always present in OSPF network design. Area 0 represents a backbone area providing for all inter-area routing. OSPF's external relationships are not particularly associated with areas. OSPF assumes that an **AS is a set of areas** (i.e. a single area, or an area *0.0.0.0* and some number of non-zero areas), which exchange routing information. Externals come from redistribution or default information origination. The OSPF routing hierarchy is shown in Figure 11.9.

FIGURE 11-9 OSPF routing hierarchy

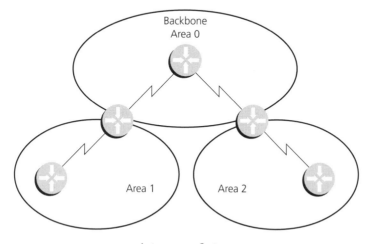

An area's topology is invisible to entities outside the area. By keeping area topologies separate, OSPF passes less routing traffic than it would if the AS were not partitioned. **Area partitioning** creates two different types of OSPF routing, depending on whether the source and destination are in the same or different areas:

- **intra-area routing** – occurs when the source and destination are in the same area;
- **inter-area routing** – occurs when they are in different areas (between backbone area and non-backbone area, or between two non-backbone areas, yet always with Area 0).

QUICK TIP   **intra- and inter-area routing**

Intra-area routing – routing between networks in the same area. Routes are based only on information received from within the area.

Inter-area routing – routing between two different OSPF areas. The inter-area path between two different OSPF non-backbone areas consists of three parts: the intra-area path from the area to the ABR of the source area; the backbone path from the source ABR to the destination ABR; and finally from the destination ABR to the destination network.

Routers with multiple interfaces can participate in multiple areas. These routers, which are called area border routers, maintain separate topological databases for each area.

OSPF defines four **types of routers** (OSPF speakers – see Figure 11.10):

- **Backbone routers** – interface only in Area 0 and can connect to other backbone or area border routers.
- **Internal routers** – interface only to non-zero area, connect to other interior routers or area border routers.
- **Area border routers** (ABR) – with interfaces in two or more areas, one of which should be area 0 (the upper limit should be two non-zero areas). ABRs perform the inter-area routing and route summarization of routes from within the AS but not of external routes injected into OSPF via redistribution.
- **Autonomous system border router** (ASBR) – interconnects OSPF routing domains (not necessarily ASs), most frequently in Area 0 but it is not a fixed requirement. Ignoring the case of default information origination, an ASBR must redistribute something. ASBRs running OSPF learn about external routes through exterior gateway protocols (EGPs) such as Exterior Gateway Protocol (EGP) or Border Gateway Protocol (BGP), or through configuration information. ASBRs can perform external route summarization of external routes that are injected into OSPF via redistribution.

FIGURE 11-10 Types of OSPF router

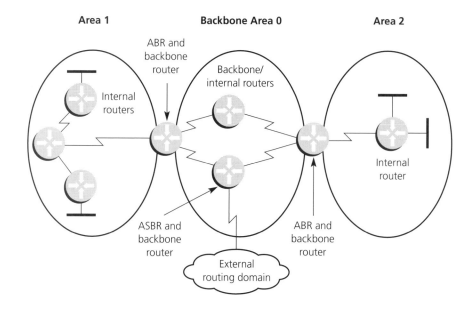

Area 1   Backbone Area 0   Area 2

ABR and backbone router

Backbone/ internal routers

Internal routers

Internal router

ASBR and backbone router

ABR and backbone router

External routing domain

QUICK TIP   **external OSPF routes**

Routes learned from another AS or from another routing protocol can be injected into OSPF as external routes. There are **two types of external routes**. A **type 1** external route has a cost that includes the OSPF cost plus the cost from the ASBR to the network. A **type 2** external route has a cost equal only to the cost from the ASBR to the external network.

As we said earlier, all OSPF areas must be connected to an Area 0, or backbone area. If there is a break in backbone continuity (which is most certainly not recommended), a **virtual link** can be established. The two end points of a virtual link are area border routers. The virtual link must be configured in both routers. The configuration information in each router consists of the other virtual endpoint (the other ABR), and the non-backbone area that the two routers have in common – the **transit area**. Virtual links then cannot be configured through stub areas.

Topological database

A **topological database** (link-state database, LSDB) is essentially an overall picture of networks in relationship to routers. Unlike the distance vector routing protocols, OSPF as a link-state protocol needs to know the topology of the routed network. The topological database contains the collection of LSAs received from all routers in the same area. Because routers within the same area share the same information, they have identical topological databases.

LSDB synchronization in OSPF is achieved via two methods: initial LSDB synchronization when an OSPF router has just been connected to the network, and asynchronous flooding that ensures continuous LSDB synchronization in the presence of topology changes after the initial procedure was completed. It may sometimes be necessary for OSPF routers to resynchronize their LSDBs. The OSPF standard, however, does not allow routers to do so without actually changing the topological view of the network. A mechanism to perform such a form of out-of-band LSDB synchronization was proposed in IETF.

Router ID

A **router ID** is necessary for OSPF communication to identify each individual router participating in the OSPF protocol. OSPF uses the **largest IP address** configured on the interfaces as its router ID. If the interface associated with this IP address is ever brought down, or if the address is removed, the OSPF process must recalculate a new router ID and resend all its routing information out of its interfaces.

QUICK TIP   **OSPF router ID**

A router ID is a 32-bit number used to identify each router. Typically it is the **highest IP address** assigned to the router's physical interfaces, unless **loopback** interfaces are used when the router ID is the highest IP address of the loopback interfaces regardless of the value of the IP address for the physical interfaces.

If a **loopback** interface is configured with an IP address, it will become a router ID. Since loopback interfaces never go down, greater stability in the routing table is achieved. OSPF automatically prefers a loopback interface over any other kind, and it chooses the highest IP address among all loopback interfaces. If no loopback interfaces are present, the highest IP address in the router is chosen. You cannot tell OSPF to use any particular interface.

Neighbors and adjacencies

Once a router is assured that its interfaces are functioning, it uses the **OSPF hello protocol** to learn about neighbors. OSPF distinguishes two levels of inter-relationship between routers: neighbors and adjacencies. **Neighbors** are routers with interfaces to a common network. The router sends **hello** packets to its neighbors and receives their hello packets. In addition to helping acquire neighbors, hello packets also act as keepalives to let routers know that other routers are still functional and, similarly, are used on multi-access networks to choose the designated router. Hellos are sent within prespecified intervals which must be equal for the two neighbors. The same applies to the so-called **dead interval** which specifies the time elapsing without any hello packets from the neighbor before declaring it down (dead for routing).

SNAPSHOT | **OSPF hello protocol**

The part of the OSPF protocol used to **establish and maintain neighbor relationships**. On broadcast networks the hello protocol can also dynamically **discover neighboring routers**.

When the link-state databases of two neighboring routers are synchronized, the routers are said to be **adjacent**. On multi-access networks, the **designated router** (DR and its backup, BDR) determines which routers should become adjacent – the designated router is adjacent to all other attached routers on the multi-access network. Topological databases are synchronized between pairs of adjacent routers. Adjacencies control the distribution of routing protocol packets. These packets are sent and received only on adjacencies. On point-to-point networks the two neighbors become automatically adjacent (there is no concept of DR and BDR).

QUICK TIP | **adjacency**

The relationship formed between selected neighboring routers for the purpose of exchanging routing information, i.e. not all neighboring routers necessarily become adjacent.

Building the adjacencies is quite a complex process involving numerous states:

1 **Down** – no information received from anyone on the segment.

2 **Attempt** – on NBMA networks (X.25 or Frame Relay) this means that no recent information has been received from the neighbor therefore an attempt should be made to contact the neighbor using a hello packet (at reduced interval).

3 **Init** – the interface has detected a hello packet from a neighbor but bi-directional communication has not yet been established,

4 **Two-way** – bi-directional communication with a neighbor has been established (router has seen itself in the hello packet coming from the neighbor). At the end of this stage DR and BDR election shall be completed on multi-access networks and adjacency relationships shall be resolved (depending on the type of the link – point-to-point, virtual link, and DR or BDR function).

5 **Exstart** – with routers trying to establish the initial sequence number for the following routing information exchange, one router will become primary and other secondary in the adjacent relationship (primary will poll secondary for information).

6 **Exchange** – routers describe the entire database by sending database description packets.

7 **Loading** – routers finalize the information exchange by building link-state request lists and retransmission lists. (Information which looks outdated or incomplete will be put on request list, and any update sent is put on the retransmission list before it becomes acknowledged.)

8 **Full** – adjacency complete and adjacent routers have synchronized databases.

On **multi-access networks** (networks supporting more than two routers), the hello protocol elects a **designated router** and a **backup designated router** to effectively use up the adjacency relationship and to limit the exchange of LSAs. The designated router is responsible, among other things, for generating LSAs for the entire multi-access network. Designated routers allow a reduction in network traffic and in the size of the topological database. All other routers on the multi-access network become **adjacencies** to the designated router. Designated router (DR) election uses the hello protocol and is based on the **OSPF priority** of the connected routers. In the case of a tie, the router with a highest ID wins. The router with the highest priority becomes DR, followed by the router with the second highest priority which becomes the BDR. The default priority is 1 while a higher priority is configurable by the administrator to force the router to become DR. On the other hand, priority 0 removes the router from the group of eligible DR or BDR candidates. The DR and BDR do not change even if a new router attaches with a higher priority or ID until a network or routers go down. DR and BDR use the reserved multicast address *224.0.0.6* (*AllDRouters* address which maps onto multicast MAC address *01-00-5E-00-00-06*).

QUICK TIP	designated router

An OSPF router generating network LSAs for **multi-access network** and being responsible for other routers attached to the same network. The designated router reduces the number of adjacencies required in a multi-access network environment, also reducing as a consequence the routing traffic and size of the topological database. The designated router is selected based on the **OSPF hello protocol**.

It is important to understand the meaning of the (backup) designated router in relation to a particular subnet it interfaces. A physical router can have multiple interfaces, each of which has an independent status as DR, BDR, or non-(B)DR. The DR acknowledges updates and sends the appropriate LSAs to *AllSPFRouters* on single subnets. Flooding has nothing to do with DR status. *AllSPFRouters* uses reserved multicast IP address *224.0.0.5* which maps onto multicast MAC address *01-00-5E-00-00-05*. Flooded LSA information goes out of interfaces on the router other than the interface to the subnet on which the LSA was originated. A physical router (actually each OSPF process) must flood the LSA Type 1 information (see Table 11.7) that affects its LSDB to all other directly connected routers in the same area. However, the DR makes sure that all OSPF routers on a multi-access broadcast network have the same LSDB. The DR is responsible for generating LSA Type 2. Not every router will generate a Type 2, only the DR will.

QUICK TIP   **OSPF designated routers**

There must be a single **designated router** (DR) selected for each multi-access network (physical or virtual – the network/subnet address matters), together with an optional **backup designated router** (BDR).

Link-state advertisements

Each router is responsible for flooding an LSA on its connected networks (links). LSAs are sent when a router's state changes (OSPF routers are not allowed to update their self-originated LSAs more than once every five seconds, in the absence of errors). In the case of stable networks, LSAs still need to be generated and flooded through the network (every 30 minutes). LSAs include information on a router's adjacencies. By comparing established adjacencies to link states, failed routers can be quickly detected and the network's topology altered appropriately. From the topological database generated from LSAs, each router calculates a shortest-path tree, with itself as root. The shortest-path tree, in turn, yields a routing table.

There are **five OSPF packet types** (see Table 11.6):

TABLE 11-6   OSPF packet types

Type	Packet name	Protocol function
1	**Hello**	Discover/maintain neighbors
2	**Database description**	Summarize database contents
3	**Link state request**	Database download
4	**Link state update**	Database update
5	**Link state ack**	Flooding acknowledgment

- **Hello** – sent at regular intervals to establish and maintain neighbor relationships.
- **Database description** – describes the contents of the topological database, and is exchanged when an adjacency is being initialized.

■ **Link-state request** – requests pieces of a neighbor's topological database. Requests are exchanged after a router has discovered (through examination of database description packets) that parts of its topological database are out of date.

■ **Link-state update** – responses to link-state request packets. They are also used for the regular dispersal of LSAs. Several LSAs may be included within a single packet.

■ **Link-state acknowledgment** – acknowledges link-state update packets. Link-state update packets must be explicitly acknowledged to ensure that link-state flooding throughout an area is a reliable process.

QUICK TIP | **exchange of OSPF messages summarized**

Hello packets are sent to the multicast destination *AllSPFRouters* (IP multicast address *224.0.0.5* mapped onto multicast MAC address *01-00-5E-00-00-05* at link layer). The designated router and its backup send both **link-state update packets** and **link-state acknowledgment packets** to the multicast address *AllSPFRouters*, while all other routers send both their **link-state update** and **link-state acknowledgment packets** to the multicast address *AllDRouters* (IP multicast address *224.0.0.6* mapped onto multicast MAC address *01-00-5E-00-00-06*).

There are **five standard LSA types** (Types 1 through 5, see Table 11.7):

TABLE 11-7 Standard OSPF LSA types

Type	LSA name	LSA description
1	Router-LSAs	Originated by all routers. Describes the collected states of the router's interfaces to an area. Flooded throughout a single area only.
2	Network-LSAs	Originated for broadcast and NBMA networks by the designated router. Contains the list of routers connected to the network. Flooded throughout a single area only.
3, 4	Summary-LSAs	Originated by area border routers, and flooded throughout the LSA's associated area. Each summary-LSA describes a route to a destination outside the area, yet still inside the AS (i.e. an inter-area route). Type 3 summary-LSAs describe routes to networks. Type 4 summary-LSAs describe routes to AS boundary routers.

TABLE 11-7 Continued

Type	LSA name	LSA description
5	AS-external-LSAs	Originated by AS boundary routers, and flooded throughout the AS. Each AS-external-LSA describes a route to a destination in another Autonomous System. Default routes for the AS can also be described by AS-external-LSAs.

- **Router Links Advertisements** (RLAs) – describe the collected states of the router's links to a specific area. A router sends an RLA for each area to which it belongs. RLAs are flooded throughout the entire area, and no further.

- **Network Links Advertisements** (NLAs) – sent by the designated routers. They describe all the routers that are attached to a multi-access network, and are flooded throughout the area containing the multi-access network.

- **Summary Links Advertisements** (SLAs) – summarize routes to destinations outside an area, but within the AS. They are generated by area border routers, and are flooded throughout the area. Only intra-area routes are advertised into the backbone. Both intra-area and inter-area routes are advertised into the other areas.

- **AS external links advertisements** – describe a route to a destination that is external to the AS. AS external links advertisements are originated by AS boundary routers. This type of advertisement is the only type that is forwarded everywhere in the AS; all others are forwarded only within specific areas.

QUICK TIP **OSPF Link-State Database features**

- A router has a separate LSDB for each area to which it belongs.
- All routers belonging to the same area have an identical LSDB.
- SPF calculation is performed separately for each area and its associated LSDB.
- LSA flooding occurs only within the area sending the advertisement.

Topology change

OSPF as a typical link-state protocol dictates that an immediate routing update be generated after any topology change. Fault detection by OSPF can differ slightly depending upon the media type. OSPF uses two mechanisms to detect **topology changes**.

Interface status changes (such as carrier failure on a serial link) deletion is the first mechanism. The second mechanism is the failure of OSPF to receive a **hello** packet from its neighbor within a timing window called a **dead timer**. After this timer expires, the router assumes the neighbor is down. The default value of the dead timer is four times the value of the hello interval, which results in a dead timer default of 40 seconds for broadcast networks and two minutes for non-broadcast networks, but the dead timer can be configured by the administrator. Table 11.8 shows hello and dead interval default values for different types of networks.

TABLE 11-8 Default OSPF hello and dead timers

Network type	Default hello interval	Default dead interval
Non-broadcast	30 s	120 s
Point-to-point	10 s	40 s
Broadcast	10 s	40 s

OSPF hellos have a **scope** of a single subnet as they do not propagate beyond the local medium. Type 1 LSAs (router LSA) have a scope of a single area. In the absence of summarization and stubbiness, Types 2 through 5 LSAs have a scope of the entire OSPF routing domain.

In general, the failure of a hello packet can supersede the failure of keepalive packets. The media type will affect how OSPF detects a failure:

■ **Ethernet** is detected after the keepalive packet fails two to three times.
■ **Token Ring and FDDI** – detected immediately.
■ **Serial interface** – faults detected in one of two ways:
  – immediate detection of carrier (LMI) loss;
  – two to three times the time of the keepalive packet (default 10 seconds).

After a failure has been detected, the router that detected the failure floods an LSA packet with the change information to all routers to which it is directly connected. The detecting router will continue to flood this information until each router to which it is directly connected acknowledges its receipt.

The current behavior of OSPF requires that all LSAs be refreshed every **30 minutes** regardless of the stability of the network except for *Do Not Age* (DNA) LSAs. Stable topologies may require an extension to the OSPF protocol to optimize flooding of Link State Advertisements (LSA). Some proposals exist in this respect in IETF.

QUICK TIP | **OSPF types of routing information (depositories)**

■ **LSDBs.**
■ **Transient routing tables** for OSPF (i.e. the output of the enhanced Dijkstra process, which is sent to the routing table manager but not otherwise retained).
■ **Main routing table**.
■ **Routing information** redistributed into OSPF from **external sources**.

Stub areas and not-so-stubby areas

Stub areas are areas into which information on external routes is not sent. Instead, there is a default external route generated by the area border router, into the stub area for destinations outside the autonomous system.

A **stub router** can be thought of as a spoke router in a hub-and-spoke network topology, where the only router to which the spoke is adjacent is the hub router. In such a network topology, the IP routing information required to represent this topology is fairly simple. These stub routers commonly have a WAN connection to the hub router, and a small number of LAN network segments (*stub networks*) are directly connected to the stub router.

These stub networks might consist only of end systems and the stub router, and thus do not require the stub router to learn any dynamic IP routing information. The stub routers can then be configured with a default route that directs IP traffic to the hub router. To provide full connectivity, the hub router can be statically configured to know that a particular stub network is reachable via a particular stub router. However, if there are multiple hub routers, many stub networks, or asynchronous connections between hubs and spokes, statically configuring the stub networks on the hub routers becomes a problem.

Not-so-stubby areas (NSSAs) are similar to OSPF stub areas. NSSAs were introduced in OSPF later on (proposed standard RFC 1587). An NSSA does not flood Type 5 external link-state advertisements (LSAs) from the core into the area, but it has the ability to import AS external routes in a limited fashion within the area. Figure 11.11 provides an example. If Area 1 is defined as a stub area, IGRP routes cannot be propagated into the OSPF domain because redistribution is not allowed in the stub area. However, if Area 1 becomes an NSSA, IGRP

FIGURE 11-11 NSSA example in an OSPF network

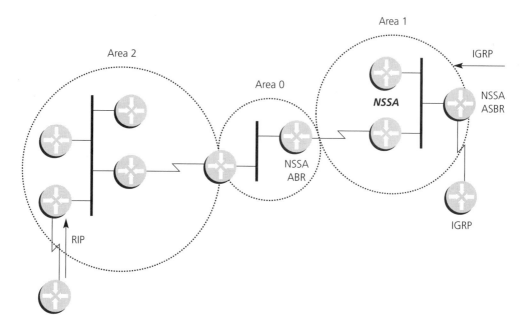

routes can be injected into the OSPF NSSA domain by creating Type 7 LSAs. Redistributed RIP routes will not be allowed in Area 1 because NSSA is an extension to the stub area. The stub area characteristics still exist, including the condition that no Type 5 LSAs are allowed.

RFC WATCH　　**OSPF NSSA**

RFC 1587 **The OSPF NSSA Option**, 1994 (Proposed Standard)

NSSA allows the importing of new **Type 7 AS external routes** within an NSSA area by redistribution. These Type 7 LSAs are translated into Type 5 LSAs by the NSSA ABRs and are flooded throughout the whole routing domain. Summarization and filtering are supported during the translation. NSSAs are used to simplify administration in cases where an Internet Service Provider (ISP) or a network administrator must connect a central site using OSPF to a remote site that is using a different routing protocol.

Prior to NSSA, the connection between the corporate site border router and the remote router could not be run as an OSPF stub area because routes for the remote site cannot be redistributed into the stub area. A simple protocol like RIP is usually run to handle the redistribution. This meant maintaining two routing protocols. With NSSA, you can extend OSPF to cover the remote connection by defining the area between the corporate router and the remote router as an NSSA.

Figure 11.12 shows an example of NSSA use: the central site and branch office are interconnected through a slow WAN link. The branch office is not using OSPF, but the central site is. Rather than define an RIP domain to connect the sites, you can define an NSSA.

FIGURE 11-12　OSPF NSSA operation

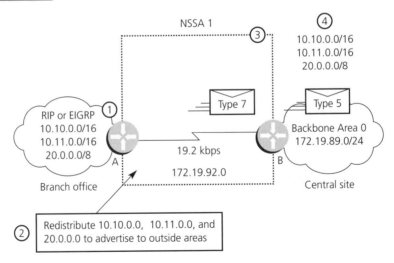

In this scenario, Router A is defined as an ASBR (autonomous system border router). It is configured to redistribute any routes within the RIP/EIGRP domain to the NSSA. The following lists what happens when the area between the connecting routers is defined as an NSSA:

1 Router A receives RIP or EGRP routes for networks 10.10.0.0/16, 10.11.0.0/16, and 20.0.0.0/8.

2 Because Router A is also connected to an NSSA, it redistributes the RIP or EIGRP routers as Type 7 LSAs into the NSSA.

3 Router B, an ABR between the NSSA and the backbone Area 0, receives the Type 7 LSAs.

4 After the SPF calculation on the forwarding database, Router B translates the Type 7 LSAs into Type 5 LSAs and then floods them throughout Backbone Area 0. It is at this point that Router B could have summarized routes 10.10.0.0/16 and 10.11.0.0/16 as 10.0.0.0/8, or could have filtered one or more of the routes.

Before implementing NSSA, the following considerations should be evaluated:

■ A Type 7 default route can be used to reach external destinations. When configured, the router generates a Type 7 default into the NSSA by the NSSA ABR.

■ Every router within the same area must agree that the area is an NSSA; otherwise, the routers will not be able to communicate with each other. If possible, using explicit redistribution on NSSA ABR should be avoided because confusion may result over which packets are being translated by which router.

QUICK TIP   **LSA Type 7**

Type 7 LSAs have the following characteristics:

■ They are originated only by ASBRs that are connected between the NSSA and the autonomous system domain.

■ They include a forwarding address field. This field is retained when a Type 7 LSA is translated as a Type 5 LSA.

■ They are advertised only within an NSSA.

■ They are not flooded beyond an NSSA. The ABR that connects to another non-stub area reconverts the Type 7 LSA into a Type 5 LSA before flooding it.

■ NSSA ABRs can be configured to summarize or filter Type 7 LSAs into Type 5 LSAs.

■ NSSA ABRs can advertise a Type 7 default route into the NSSA.

■ Type 7 LSAs have a lower priority than Type 5 LSAs, so when a route is learned with a Type 5 LSA and Type 7 LSA, the route defined in the Type 5 LSA will be selected first.

OSPF packet format

All OSPF packets begin with a 24-octet header, as shown in Figure 11.13.

FIGURE 11-13 OSPF packet header format

Number of bits:

8	8	8	8
Version number	Type	Packet length	
Router ID			
Area ID			
Checksum		Authentication type	
Authentication			

The fields of the **OSPF header** are as follows:

■ *Version number* – identifies the particular OSPF implementation being used.

■ *Type* – specifies one of five OSPF packet types.

■ *Packet length* – specifies in octets the packet's length, including the OSPF header.

■ *Router ID* – identifies the packet's source.

■ *Area ID* – identifies the area to which the packet belongs. All OSPF packets are associated with a single area. Most packets travel a single hop only. Packets traveling over a virtual link are labeled with the backbone area ID of 0.0.0.0.

■ *Checksum* – checks the entire packet contents (excluding authentication) for potential damage suffered in transit.

■ *Authentication type* – contains an authentication type. A simple password is an example of an authentication type. All OSPF protocol exchanges are authenticated. The authentication type is configurable on a per area basis.

■ *Authentication* – contains authentication information and is 64 bits in length.

QUICK TIP **OSPF packets**

- OSPF runs directly above IP, using protocol type 89. (It does not use TCP or UDP.)
- OSPF packets have an IP TTL of 1.
- OSPF packets are sent to a reserved IP multicast address, either *AllSPFRouters* (224.0.0.5) or *AllDRouters* (224.0.0.6).
- Each OSPF packet type begins with an OSPF packet header.
- There are five OSPF packet types, all but **OSPF hello** carrying one or more **Link-State Advertisements (LSA)**. One of the packet types is **Link-State Acknowledgement (LSAck** – to avoid confusion with LSA). An LSAck can carry one or more LSA headers (LSAs have both fixed-length headers and variable-length specific information).
- There are more than five LSA types – Types 1 through 5 are mandatory, while others are optional and used based on the vendor type (e.g. Type 7); newer types (Type 9 and above) are still experimental or used in new technologies such as OSPF traffic engineering.

All LSA start with 20-octet header (see Figure 11.14):

FIGURE 11-14 LSA header

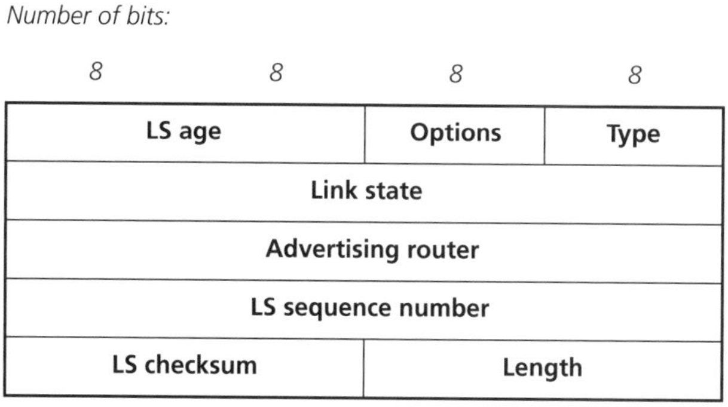

Number of bits:

- **LS age** – time in seconds since the LSA was originated.
- **Options** – optional capabilities supported by the described portion of the routing domain.
- **LS type** – specifies one of the OSPF LSA types (having separate formats).
- **Link state ID** – uniquely distinguishes the LSA, often carrying addressing information (depends on LS type).

■ *Advertising router* – originating router's OSPF router ID.

■ *LS sequence number* – serves to identify the most recent LS instance (detects old and duplicate LSAs).

■ *LS checksum* – Fletcher checksum of the complete contents of the LSA, including the LSA header but excluding the LS age field. Once LS instance is originated, the checksum is not altered (therefore does not include LS age as it is modified during flooding).

■ *Length* – length of header plus contents (although the size of this field would allow for two 16 bit-long LSAs, in bytes, it is very unlikely to happen in reality – LSAs are small and usually do not exceed several kB).

Additional OSPF features

Additional OSPF features include **equal-cost multipath routing** (ECMP). The effect of multipath routing on a forwarder is that the forwarder potentially has several next-hops for any given destination and must use some method to choose which next-hop should be used for a given data packet. OSPF, however, cannot use multiple equal-cost external paths. (More is given on ECMP later in this chapter.)

OSPF also supported routing based on upper-layer **Type of Service** (TOS) requests. TOS-based routing supports those upper-layer protocols that can specify particular types of service. For example, an application might specify that certain data is urgent. If OSPF has high-priority links at its disposal, these can be used to transport the urgent datagram.

IP subnet masks are included with each advertised destination, enabling **variable-length subnet masks**.

As was already explained in the section on link-state protocols, OSPF does not have problems with **routing loops**. Therefore it does not deploy the loop prevention mechanisms of distance vector protocols, such as split horizon or poison reverse. However, there is a mechanism that OSPF can use with a similar effect as poison reverse. When a router desires to withdraw an LSA it originated, it sets the age field to a maximum and refloods it.

OSPF design

OSPF is an efficient IP interior gateway protocol yet quite complex to implement. The complexity lies in the fact that it needs some prerequisites to become really efficient. In other words OSPF requires a proper design. The two design activities that are critically important to a successful OSPF implementation are **defining area boundaries** and **assigning addresses**. The following important characteristics apply to OSPF:

■ **A hierarchical routing structure** must exist or be created.

■ **A contiguous backbone area (Area 0)** must be present and all areas must have a connection to the backbone so that all inter-area traffic goes through it. Grouping all routers into Area 0 is justifiable in a very small internet. OSPF will provide fast convergence and fine routing but its full capabilities are shown only in a hierarchical design with more than Area 0.

■ **All non-zero areas** should have a border with Area 0 as it is not recommendable to use virtual links with Area 0 via a transit area.

■ **Explicit topology has precedence** whatever IP addressing schemes might have been applied. **Route summarization** is the consolidation of advertised addresses. This feature causes a single summary route to be advertised to other areas by an ABR. In OSPF, an ABR will advertise networks in one area into another area. If the network numbers in an area are assigned in a way such that they are contiguous, you can configure the ABR to advertise a summary route that covers all the individual networks within the area that fall into the specified range.

Several important items to consider when designing the **topology** for an OSPF network are as follows:

- **Number of routers in an area** – the larger and more unstable the area, the greater the likelihood for performance problems associated with OSPF routing recalculation (due to running the CPU-intensive SPF algorithm); it is recommended that an area should have no more than 200–250 routers depending on the network stability, while areas with unstable, slower links and/or older routers should be smaller. RFC 2329 gives some hints as to the design recommendations based on tested implementations along the standardization process (see Table 11.9).

TABLE 11-9 OSPF domain sizes deployed

Parameter	Min.	Mode	Mean	Max.
Max. routers in domain	20	350	510	1000
Max. routers in single area	20	100	160	350
Max. areas in domain	1	15	23	60
Max. AS-external -LSAs	50	1000	2000	5000

- **Area border routers** – none should interface with more than three areas. Additionally, each area should have more than one area border router for redundancy, avoiding a single point of failure.
- **Number of areas connected to an area border router** (ABR) – the more areas are attached per ABR, the lower its performance because each ABR keeps a copy of the database for all areas it is attached to. To maximize stability, one router should not be in more than three areas.
- **Number of neighbors for any one router** – routers with many neighbors have the most work to do when link-state changes occur because OSPF floods all link-state changes to all routers in an area. In general, any one router should have no more than 60 neighbors. The number of routers connected to the same LAN is also important because each LAN has a DR and BDR that build adjacencies with all other routers, therefore the fewer neighbors that exist on the LAN, the smaller the number of adjacencies a DR or BDR has to build.

- **Addressing design** – very important for controlling routing advertisements between the areas, to reduce the amount of routing traffic, and for maintaining stability (which increases with decreases in the number of routing table recomputations). The whole domain, i.e. all areas, may not use the same tactics.

- **Selecting the designated router** (DR) – DR and BDR on a LAN have the most OSPF work to do. It is a good idea to select routers that are not already heavily loaded with CPU-intensive activities to be the DR and BDR. If DR selection is based on the highest router ID, then one router could accidentally become a DR over all segments to which it is connected. This router would be doing extra effort while other routers are idle; if possible, it should be avoided having the same router as the DR on more than one segment. The OSPF priority to select the DR is configurable on the routers.

- **Non-broadcast multi-access** (NBMA) networks (such as Frame Relay or X.25) – OSPF runs in one of two modes over non-broadcast networks. The first mode, called non-broadcast multi-access or NBMA, simulates the operation of OSPF on a broadcast network. The second mode, called point-to-multipoint, treats the non-broadcast network as a collection of point-to-point links. Non-broadcast networks are referred to as NBMA networks or point-to-multipoint networks, depending on the OSPF's mode of operation over the network.

RFC WATCH   **OSPF implementation tested**

RFC 2329 **OSPF Standardization Report**, 1998 (Informational)

Operationally, OSPF networks should be designed so that **areas** do not need to be split to accommodate growth. Address space should be reserved to permit the addition of new areas. **Scalability** should always be taken into consideration when designing the network. As the network grows, routers will eventually reach a point where their link-state database becomes too large, resulting in inefficiency in network routing. Additionally, the LSAs will be flooded throughout the network, resulting in a congestion problem. The capability of the OSPF network to scale properly is determined by a multitude of factors, including the following:

- **CPU requirements** – the SPF computation is very CPU-intensive and as it must be performed any time the link-state database changes (a new LSP is received), it may have an adverse impact on the router's performance.

- **Router memory requirements** – total memory used by OSPF is the sum of the memory used for the routing table and the memory used for the LSDB, where each entry in the routing table will consume between approximately 200 and 280 bytes plus 44 bytes per extra path, and each LSA will consume a 100-byte overhead plus the size of the actual LSA, possibly another 60 to 100 bytes (for router links, this depends on the number of interfaces on the router). While memory could be a constraint in older routers *vis-à-vis* the OSPF implementation, it is no longer an issue with larger and extendable memories deployed in newer routers.

- **Available bandwidth** – bandwidth is a concern in case of unstable links and large areas, particularly when an unintentionally synchronized LSP flooding occurs (many routers restart at once).

OSPF security

All OSPF protocol exchanges are authenticated. OSPF supports multiple types of authentication; the type of authentication in use can be configured on a per network segment basis. One of OSPF's authentication types, namely the **cryptographic authentication** option, is believed to be secure against passive attacks and to provide significant protection against active attacks. When using the cryptographic authentication option, each router appends a message digest to its transmitted OSPF packets. Receivers then use the shared secret key and received digest to verify that each received OSPF packet is authentic.

The quality of the security provided by the cryptographic authentication option depends completely on the strength of the message digest algorithm (MD5), the strength of the key being used, and the correct implementation of the security mechanism in all communicating OSPF implementations. It also requires that all parties maintain the secrecy of the shared secret key.

OSPF on-demand circuit

The OSPF on-demand circuit is an enhancement to OSPF that allows efficient operation over demand circuits, e.g. ISDN, X.25 SVCs, or dial-up lines (RFC 1793). The OSPF typically requires the link to be open for any routing information exchanges, which is not appropriate usage of heavily charged lines on demand. The OSPF on-demand circuit feature avoids OSPF hellos and routing information refreshes to invoke the line; instead the reachability is presumed.

RFC WATCH	overview of OSPF RFCs

RFC 1793 **Extending OSPF to Support Demand Circuits**, 1995 (Proposed Standard)

Prior to this feature, OSPF periodic hello and link-state advertisement updates would be exchanged between routers that connected the on-demand link, even when no changes occurred in the hello or LSA information. With this feature, periodic hellos are suppressed and the periodic refreshes of LSAs are not flooded over the demand circuit. These packets bring up the link only when they are exchanged for the first time, or when a change occurs in the information they contain. This operation allows the underlying datalink layer to be closed when the network topology is stable.

This feature is useful when you want to connect telecommuters or branch offices to an OSPF backbone at a central site. In this case, OSPF for on-demand circuits allows the benefits of OSPF over the entire domain, without excess connection costs. Periodic refreshes of hello updates, LSA updates, and other protocol overhead are prevented from enabling the on-demand circuit when there is no 'real' data to transmit.

Overhead protocols such as hellos and LSAs are transferred over the on-demand circuit only upon initial setup and when they reflect a change in the topology. This means that critical changes to the topology that require new SPF calculations are transmitted in order to maintain network topology integrity. Periodic refreshes that do not include changes, however, are not transmitted across the link.

OSPF new generation – OSPF version 3

A new version of the protocol, OSPF version 3, has been worked on but there is no standard RFC available yet, only drafts. OSPF version 3 allows complex networks to be changed – to add things such as multicast support – and includes enhancements to ensure that upgrades integrate safely and easily. In an IP version 6 environment, OSPF version 3 messages can be authenticated and encrypted, which previously required the addition of separate and complex protocols.

OSPF version 3 permits routers to forward IPv6 data across networks. OSPF version 3 boosts versatility so networks can be adapted to changing requirements. It allows complex networks to be simplified and includes enhancements to ensure that upgrades integrate safely and easily. OSPFv3 has also been streamlined, and its security has been increased.

A main goal of OSPFv3 was to create a routing protocol independent of any specific network layer. To accomplish this, OSPFv3's inter-router messages have been redesigned. Unlike past versions, OSPFv3 does not insert IP-based data in the headers that begin its packets and link-state advertisements (LSAs). To perform critical tasks that used to require IP header data, such as identifying LSAs which distribute routing data, OSPFv3 utilizes network protocol-independent information.

In addition to changing header data, OSPFv3 redefines the roles its LSAs play. In OSPFv3, the tasks of advertising the network topology and IPv6 data are divided among new and existing LSAs. For example, OSPFv3's network and router LSAs no longer distribute IP data; routers use them solely to discern network design. To advertise the data removed from these LSAs, OSPFv3 introduces two dedicated IPv6 messages, termed the *Intra-Area-Prefix* and *Link LSAs*. By reducing dependency on IPv6, OSPFv3's packet and LSA improvements enable easy support for new network protocols.

OSPFv3 is versatile enough to transcend IPv6 with minor network upgrades instead of major protocol migrations. To supplement its versatility, OSPFv3 increases the number of optional capabilities, such as multicast OSPF, that can be implemented. To achieve this, OSPFv3 expands the **Options** data field, which is used by network devices to advertise enabled capabilities. The Options field is contained in most OSPFv3 inter-router messages. Running OSPFv3, devices can support as many as 24 optional capabilities. Previous versions supported only eight. To simplify the construction of complex fault-tolerant networks, OSPFv3 introduces Instance IDs and the R-bit option. As a component of every OSPFv3 packet header, Instance IDs can control communication between routers sharing a physical network and OSPF area, without relying on complex authentication schemes or access lists as needed in the past. In addition to Instance IDs, OSPFv3 can bring effective redundancy to end systems, such as servers, with the R-bit. The R-bit is a way for hosts to wiretap the routing protocol safely, participating in OSPFv3 without attracting non-local traffic.

OSPFv3 ensures that future upgrades integrate smoothly with new mechanisms, including flooding scopes and handling options. Like a passport for LSAs, routers use flooding scopes to permit or deny travel across the net. The flooding scope's range limits every LSA (and, therefore, its effect on the network) to the local link, an area, or the entire OSPFv3 network. Because routers can only enforce the flooding scope of readable LSAs, handling options are also incorporated into these messages. Handling options instruct routers to contain or forward undecipherable LSAs.

In OSPFv3, less security is definitely more. To simplify message structure, OSPFv3 breaks from the past by providing no inherent security. By relying on IPv6's integrated system of packet security subheaders, OSPFv3 messages can be authenticated and encrypted, a feat that previously required the addition of separate and complex protocols. OSPFv3 offers increased capabilities, and it is so versatile that new network protocols can be easily supported. New features simplify network design and operation. With OSPFv3, the integration of updates will be less worrisome. Finally, outdated portions of OSPFv3 have been removed, and its security has been boosted.

SNAPSHOT   **OSPF features summarized**

- No limit on hop count.
- Support to VLSM and route aggregation.
- Fast convergence through immediate link-state information flooding through the network.
- Support to load balancing.
- Use of routing authentication (simple password for specific area or MD5 cryptographic authentication, the latter allows for uninterrupted transitions between keys).
- Support to transfer and tagging of external routes injected into the autonomous system by exterior gateway protocols.

OSPF strengths

- **Low traffic overhead** – OSPF is economical of network bandwidth on links between routers.
- **Fast convergence** – OSPF routers flood updates to changes in the network around the internet, so that all routers quickly agree on the new topology after a failure.

- **Larger network metrics** – this gives a network planner the freedom to assign costs for each path around the network, to maintain fine control over routing paths.

- **Area-based topology** – large OSPF networks are organized as a set of areas linked by a backbone. Routing within each area is isolated to minimize cross-area discovery traffic. OSPF sustains up to about 250 routers in one area. (In this respect IS-IS is even a better choice with its capability to hold about 1000 routers in a single area.)

- **Route summaries** – OSPF can minimize the routes propagated across an area boundary by collapsing several related subnet routes into one. This reduces routing table sizes, and increases the practical size of a network.

- **Support for complex address structures** – OSPF allows variable size subnetting within a network number, and subnets of a network number to be physically disconnected. This reduces waste of address space, and makes changing a network incrementally much easier.

- **Authentication** – OSPF supports the use of passwords for dynamic discovery traffic, and checks that paths are operational in both directions. The main use for this is to prevent misconfigured routers from poisoning the routing tables throughout the internet. In practice this is not a serious problem, as almost all end user devices do not support OSPF.

OSPF weaknesses

- **Memory overhead** – OSPF uses a link-state database to keep track of all routers and networks within each attached area. With a complex topology, this database can be much larger than the corresponding routing pool, and may limit the maximum size of an area.

- **Processor overhead** – during steady-state operation the OSPF CPU usage is low, mainly due to the traffic between routers. However, when a topology change is detected, there is a large amount of processing required to support flooding of changes and recalculation of the routing table.

- **Configuration** – OSPF can be complex to configure and design into a network.

11.3.5 Comparison of IP interior routing protocols

As we mentioned earlier, there are three protocols widely understood as sufficiently advanced and suitable for today's networks. The **advanced IGPs** are **OSPF, EIGRP, and IS-IS** (for the latter see Chapter 12, section 12.7).

OSPF and IS-IS require a structured network topology from the very beginning, while EIGRP is much more tolerant but it has its limits too.

The biggest argument against **EIGRP** is that it is Cisco **proprietary**. Being proprietary has implications beyond the multivendor question. Because some of the EIGRP mechanisms have not been published by Cisco, there is not the external knowledge base about EIGRP that there is about OSPF and IS-IS. Protocol and network architects have a very deep understanding of how OSPF and IS-IS will behave and what their strengths and weaknesses are, but no one who has not been a Cisco employee can have the same sort of insight concerning EIGRP.

For similar topologies, EIGRP generally needs less processing than OSPF. On the other hand, with ever-faster processors, this may not be a significant constraint. In a fair test, with equivalent timers set to equivalent values, both converge very quickly, and convergence time should not be an issue with any protocol (assuming a reasonable network topology). EIGRP may be able to find an alternate path faster when that path goes through a neighbor, but OSPF is faster if the alternate path might be several hops away. If it is necessary to run Appletalk or IPX routing, there is a definite advantage to using EIGRP. EIGRP also can bring incremental updating to a Netware 3.x environment that cannot be upgraded.

In Table 11.10 the major differences among all the existing interior routing protocols for IP are summarized.

TABLE 11-10 Comparison of RIP, OSPF, (E)IGRP, and Integrated IS-IS

Protocols/ criteria	RIP	RIPv2	IGRP	EIGRP	OSPF	IS-IS
Algorithm	Distance vector	Distance vector	Distance vector	DUAL (distance vector)	Link state	Link state
Metric	Hop count	Hop count	Composite: based on bandwidth and delay	Composite: bandwidth and delay	Cost: based on bandwidth	Arbitrary cost
Updates	Complete RT periodically broadcasted (30s) to 255.255.255.255 (to MAC address FF-FF-FF-FF-FF-FF)	Complete RT periodically multicast to 224.0.0.9 (30s) (to MAC address 01-00-5E-00-00-09)	Complete RT periodically broadcasted (90s) to 255.255.255.255 (to MAC address FF-FF-FF-FF-FF-FF)	Incremental updates multicast to 224.0.0.10 (to multicast MAC address 01-00-5E-00-00-0A)	Updates flooded upon change (or after 30 min) to multicast address 224.0.0.5 (AllSPF Routers, MAC address 01-00-5E-00-00-05) 224.0.0.6 (AllDRouters, multicast MAC address 01-00-5E-00-00-06)	Updates flooded upon change (or after configurable period, default 15 min)

▶

| TABLE 11-10 | continued | | | | |

Protocols/ criteria	RIP	RIPv2	IGRP	EIGRP	OSPF	IS-IS
Loop prevention	Split horizon Hold-down	Split horizon Hold-down	Split horizon Hold-down	Split horizon and DUAL	Complete topology knowledge	Complete topology knowledge
Convergence	Slow: waiting for alternative paths to be advertised and hold-down timers	Slow: waiting for alternative paths to be advertised and hold-down timers	Slow: waiting for alternative paths to be advertised and hold-down timers	Fast: based on DUAL potential alternative routes known or neighbors queried	Fast: based on recomputing Dijkstra algorithm	Fast: based on recomputing Dijkstra algorithm
Classful and summaries	Classful, summarization on network boundaries	Classless	Classful, summarization on network boundaries	Classless, summarization possible anywhere	Classless, summarization at ABRs and ASBRs	Classless, summarization possible at router injection into network or at level boundary

11.4 Exterior gateway protocols

The other group of protocols important for IP routing between autonomous systems is called **exterior routing protocols** which used to be represented by two protocols:

- **exterior gateway protocol** (deprecated);
- **border gateway protocol** (widely used).

> **QUICK TIP** **exterior protocols**
>
> **Exterior protocols** convey routing information among autonomous systems (network domains). They are intended to protect one system of networks (a domain) against errors or intentional misrepresentation by other domains.

11.4.1 Exterior gateway protocol

The **Exterior Gateway Protocol** (EGP) is (or more precisely was) the IP interdomain reachability protocol (historic RFC 904, 1984). As the first exterior gateway protocol to gain widespread acceptance in the Internet, EGP served a valuable purpose. Unfortunately, the weaknesses of EGP have become more apparent as the Internet has grown and matured. Among the weaknesses two are not acceptable: it has no metric, only reachability sorted out for routing decisions; and no alternate interconnections between autonomous systems are allowed (no loops in physical topology required). Because of these weaknesses, EGP is currently being phased out of the Internet, and has been fully replaced by other exterior gateway protocols such as the Border Gateway Protocol (BGP) and the Interdomain Routing Protocol (IDRP), and is not seen in action in live networks any more. However, for the purpose of an introduction to exterior routing protocols (and for comparison with a truly workable BGP), in the following the EGP basics will be laid down.

RFC WATCH	EGP

RFC 904 **Exterior Gateway Protocol Formal Specification**, 1984 (Historic)

Technology basics

EGP was originally designed to communicate reachability to and from the Advanced Research Projects Agency Network (ARPANET) core routers. Information was passed from individual source nodes in distinct ASs up to the core routers, which passed the information through the backbone until it could be passed down to the destination network within another AS.

Although EGP is a dynamic routing protocol, it uses a very simple design. It does not use metrics and therefore cannot make intelligent routing decisions. EGP routing updates contain **network reachability** information. In other words, they specify that certain networks are reachable through certain routers.

EGP defines the manner in which two or more autonomous systems exchange routing information. When a router uses EGP to communicate with another autonomous system, it is called an **exterior gateway**.

SNAPSHOT	EGP

EGP is the oldest protocol used for **interconnection between ASs** for IP communication. However, it acts more like a **reachability** than a routing protocol, checking only whether networks are reachable regardless of distance (or other metric). EGP require a **tree internet topology** without any loops. Due to its **weaknesses**, EGP is no longer in use.

EGP has three main **functions**:

- **Neighbor acquisition** – allows two exterior routers to agree to exchange reachability information. Neighbors are simply routers with which an EGP router wishes to share reachability information; there is no implication of geographic proximity.
- **Testing for neighbor response** – an EGP router periodically polls its neighbors to check if they are responding.
- **Exchange of reachability information** – EGP routers send update messages containing information about the reachability of networks within their ASs.

Packet format

An EGP packet is shown in Figure 11.15.

FIGURE 11-15 EGP message format

Number of bits:

EGP Version (2)	Type	Code	Status
8	8	8	8
Checksum		Autonomous system number	
Sequence			

The fields of the EGP packet are as follows:

- *EGP version number* – identifies the current EGP version and is checked by recipients to determine whether there is a match between the sender and recipient version numbers.
- *Type* – identifies the message type. EGP defines five separate **message types**: neighbor acquisition (establishes/de-establishes neighbors), neighbor reachability (determines if neighbors are alive), poll (determines reachability of a particular network), routing update (provides routing updates), error (indicates error conditions).
- *Code* – distinguishes among message subtypes.
- *Status* – contains message-dependent status information. Status codes include insufficient resources, parameter problems, protocol violations, and others.
- *Checksum* – used to detect possible problems that may have developed with the packet in transit.
- *Autonomous system number* – identifies the AS to which the sending router belongs.
- *Sequence number* – allows two EGP routers exchanging messages to match requests with replies. The sequence number is initialized to zero when a neighbor is established and incremented by one with each request-response transaction.

Additional fields follow the EGP header. The contents of these fields vary depending on the **message type** (as specified by the type field):

- *Neighbor acquisition message* – includes a hello interval field and a poll interval field. The hello interval field specifies the interval period for testing whether neighbors are alive. The poll interval field specifies the routing update frequency.

- *Neighbor reachability message* – adds no extra fields to the EGP header. These messages use the code field to indicate whether the message is a hello message or a response to a hello message. Separating the reachability assessment function from the routing update function reduces network traffic because network reachability changes usually occur more often than routing parameter changes. Only after a specified percentage of reachability messages have not been received does an EGP node declare a neighbor to be down.

- *Poll message* – allows EGP routers to acquire reachability information about the networks on which these hosts reside. These messages only have one field beyond the common header: the IP source network field. This field specifies the network to be used as a reference point for the request.

- *Routing update messages* – provide a way for EGP routers to indicate the locations of various networks within their ASs. In addition to the common header, these messages include many additional fields. The number of interior gateways field indicates the number of interior gateways appearing in the message. The number of exterior gateways field indicates the number of exterior gateways appearing in the message. The IP source network field provides the IP address of the network from which reachability is measured. Following this field is a series of gateway blocks. Each gateway block provides the IP address of a gateway and a list of networks and distances associated with reaching those networks.

  Within the gateway block, EGP lists networks by **distances**. In other words, at distance three, there may be four networks. These networks are then listed by address. The next group of networks may be those that are distance four away, and so on. However, EGP does not interpret the distance **metrics** that are contained within the routing update messages. In essence, EGP uses the distance field to **indicate whether a path exists**; the distance value can only be used to compare paths if those paths exist wholly within a particular AS. For this reason, EGP is more of a **reachability protocol** than a routing protocol.

  This restriction also places topology limitations on the structure of the internet. Specifically, an EGP portion of the internet must be a **tree structure** in which a core gateway is the root, and there are no loops among other ASs within the tree. This restriction is a primary limitation of EGP, and provides an impetus for its gradual replacement by other, more capable exterior gateway protocols.

- *Error messages* – identify various EGP error conditions. In addition to the common EGP header, EGP error messages provide a reason field, followed by an error message header. Typical EGP errors (reasons) include bad EGP header format, bad EGP data field format, excessive polling rate, and the unavailability of reachability information. The error message header consists of the first three 32-bit words of the EGP header.

EGP strengths

- Use of point-to-point communication (not broadcast).
- Requests and confirmation of the acquisition of a neighbor.
- Use of hello messages to test neighbor reachability.
- Poll function to force net reachability updates.
- Generally uses a single router in each autonomous system.
- Logical, not necessarily topologically proximate neighbors.

EGP weaknesses

- Only forwards reachability information (not real distance metric) or advertises nets pertinent to its own autonomous system.
- Does not make any routing decisions.
- Requires a tree topology as it cannot decide about the quality of routes in case of alternate paths in a network with loops.

11.4.2 Border gateway protocol

The Border Gateway Protocol (BGP) addressed the most serious of EGP's problems and allowed the protocol to scale to a much larger network. Unlike EGP, BGP was designed to detect routing loops. To fix the problem of processing time for EGP updates, BGP exchanges the full routing table only at initialization; afterwards, it simply exchanges information about what has changed at each update. To fix the problem of IP fragmentation, BGP uses a TCP connection (port 179), which guarantees in-order delivery without loss or duplication.

QUICK TIP	BGP

BGP is an **IP exterior (inter-domain) routing protocol** with current **version 4** (BGP-4). BGP's **path vector algorithm** is a variant on the distance vector. BGP supports classless inter-domain routing, allows the aggregation of routes, and provides for **policy-based routing**. It uses a reliable transport protocol (TCP) for incremental updates upon a topology change.

BGP is currently the widely used **IP exterior routing protocol** between ASs. The BGP specification (RFC 1771) states:

> *The classic definition of an Autonomous System is a set of routers under a single technical administration, using an interior gateway protocol and common metrics to route packets within the AS, and using an exterior gateway protocol to route packets to other autonomous systems. Since this classic definition was developed, it has become common for a single AS to use several interior gateway protocols and sometimes several sets of metrics within an AS. The use of the term Autonomous System here stresses the fact that, even when*

multiple IGPs and metrics are used, the administration of an AS appears to other autonomous systems to have a single coherent interior routing plan and presents a consistent picture of what destinations are reachable through it.

Mainly for the purposes of exterior routing it is wise to understand an **AS** as a **connected group of one or more IP prefixes** run by one or more network operators that has a **single and clearly defined routing policy**.

RFC WATCH   **BGP**

RFC 1771 **A Border Gateway Protocol 4 (BGP-4)**, 1995 (Draft Standard)

RFC 1772 **Application of the Border Gateway Protocol in the Internet**, 1995 (Draft Standard)

RFC 1773 **Experience with the BGP-4 protocol**, 1995 (Informational)

RFC 1774 **BGP-4 Protocol Analysis**, 1995 (Informational)

The network reachability information exchanged via BGP provides sufficient information to detect routing loops and enforce routing decisions based on performance preference and policy constraints as outlined in RFC 1104. In particular, BGP exchanges routing information containing full AS paths and enforces routing policies based on configuration information.

RFC WATCH   **policy-based routing**

RFC 1104 **Models of Policy Based Routing**, 1989

As the Internet has evolved and grown in recent years, it has become painfully evident that it is soon to face several serious scaling problems, including:

- exhaustion of the Class B network address space – one fundamental cause of this problem is the lack of a network class of a size which is appropriate for mid-sized organization; Class C, with a maximum of 254 host addresses, is too small while Class B, which allows up to 65 534 addresses, is too large to be densely populated;
- the growth of full routing tables (with all global routes) in Internet routers is beyond the ability of current software (and people) to effectively manage;
- eventual exhaustion of the 32-bit IP address space.

It has become clear that the first two of these problems are likely to become critical within the next one to three years. Classless inter-domain routing (CIDR) attempts to deal with these problems by proposing a mechanism to slow the growth of the routing table and the need for allocating new IP network numbers. It does not attempt to solve the third problem, which is of a more long-term nature, but instead endeavors to ease enough of the short- to mid-term difficulties to allow the Internet to continue to function efficiently while progress is made on a longer-term solution.

BGP-4 (RFC 1771, 1995) is an extension of BGP-3 (having historic status as versions 1 and 2) that provides support for **routing information aggregation**. One of the main enhancements of BGP-4 over BGP-3 is CIDR support. Version 2 of BGP removed from the protocol the concept of up, down, and horizontal relations between autonomous systems that were present in version 1 and introduced the concept of path attributes. Version 3 of BGP lifted some of the restrictions on the use of the *NEXT_HOP* path attribute and added the *BGP Identifier* field to the BGP *OPEN* message. It also clarified the procedure for distributing BGP routes between the BGP speakers within an autonomous system.

BGP uses TCP port 179 to ensure delivery of inter-autonomous system information. **Update** messages are generated only if a **topology change** occurs and contain information only about the change. This reduces network traffic and bandwidth consumption used in maintaining consistent routing tables between routers. Passing on only differences to previous routes in BGP was only possible because of the TCP connection scheme used. Thanks to TCP, routing update messages cannot be lost unnotified, and their delivery is guaranteed in the right order. A BGP process has to maintain a (quite limited) list of BGP neighbors (corresponding to the TCP connections). The BGP process therefore knows exactly what it has already sent to each of these neighbors and so is able to generate appropriate incremental updates.

Path vector algorithm

The BGP protocol does not use either the distance vector or link-state algorithm. Instead a **path vector algorithm** is deployed which is in many ways similar to the distance vector, but not quite the same. Path vector has no concept of cost in the basic routing algorithm. It maintains a traceroute-like **path vector** indicating how the route was created and propagated. Routes that contain their own AS, by definition, show looping behavior and are rejected. Loops could be very large, spanning multiple ASs. Incidentally, path vector is demonstrably loop-free only when unconstrained by policies. In classical path vector, a route is either acceptable or not while routes containing their own AS number are unacceptable. Each BGP speaker adds (prepends) its own AS to the path vector, if not already present.

What makes BGP underlying routing algorithm difficult, thinking in terms of the distance vector metric (summing costs – hops, delays, etc. – to get the route metric), is that BGP does not have sum-of-costs concepts. BGP attributes come into question, such as MEDs and local preferences (see further on) that are not end-to-end with respect to the destination as they affect next-hop decisions.

BGP uses a **Routing Information Base** (RIB) term for the routing table. Actually there are many RIBs deployed in BGP operation:

- **Adj-RIB-In** – represents a repository for prefixes learned from a particular neighbor (as many Adj-RIB-Ins as peers);
- **Loc-RIB** – contains prefixes selected to use (only one per system);
- **Adj-RIB-Out** – stores prefixes to be advertised to a particular neighbor (one for each peer).

Incoming BGP updates, before filtering, go into the **Adj-RIB-In**. After filtering, which is primarily on a per-peer basis, the remaining updates go into a **Loc-RIB**.

This table contains all the BGP potential routes that passed acceptance filtering and is router-wide. It also indicates which are the best BGP routes to a given destination. All the best routes from the Loc-RIB are sent to the main IP **routing table**, where they compete with potential routes from all other sources.

BGP neighbor relationship

Although BGP was designed as an inter-AS protocol, it can be used both within AS (for local traffic) and between ASs (for transit traffic). Two **BGP neighbors** communicating between ASs must reside on the same physical network. There can be as many BGP speakers as deemed necessary within an AS. Usually, if an AS has multiple connections to other ASs, multiple BGP speakers are needed. All BGP speakers representing the same AS must give a consistent image of the AS to the outside. BGP routers within the same AS communicate with one another to ensure that they have a consistent view of the AS and to determine which BGP router within that AS will serve as the connection point to or from certain external ASs. These routers can communicate with each other via BGP or by other means.

QUICK TIP	BGP neighbor relationship

BGP is a protocol working between two routers: while at any time instance a network may have a number of BGP sessions occurring, and a router may be participating in many BGP sessions, only two routers are involved in an individual BGP session.

Routers that belong to the same AS and exchange BGP updates are **internal BGPs** (IBGPs), and routers that belong to different ASs and exchange BGP updates are running **external BGPs** (EBGPs) – see Figure 11.16. IBGP requires full mesh logical topology of IBGP connections (independent of physical connectivity). Therefore loopback interfaces are often used by IBGP peers. The advantage

FIGURE 11-16   IBGP and EBGP position in the network

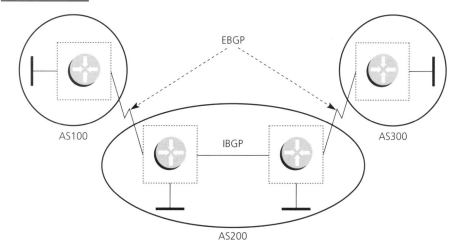

of using loopback interfaces is that it eliminates a dependency that would otherwise occur when you use the IP address of a physical interface to configure BGP. Instead EBGP sessions depend on physical links, therefore a physical interface is used for connectivity, not loopback. If the EBGP peers are not directly connected, they may use EBGP multihop to exchange routing information.

SNAPSHOT   neighbors and IBGP/EBGP

BGP must completely understand the relationships it has with its neighbors. BGP supports two kinds of neighbors: internal and external. **Internal neighbors** are in the same autonomous system; **external neighbors** are in different autonomous systems. Normally, external neighbors are adjacent to each other and share a subnet, while internal neighbors may be anywhere in the same autonomous system.

Internal BGP (IBGP) exchanges BGP updates learned from other sources (EBGP or static routes) within an AS. IBGP peers may use loopback interfaces to eliminate a dependency that would otherwise occur with the use of an IP address of a physical interface.

External BGP (EBGP) exchanges routing information between different ASs.

IBGP and EBGP share the same message types, attribute types, and state machine, **but** have **different rules about advertising prefixes**: prefixes learned from EBGP may be advertised to an IBGP neighbor; prefixes learned from IBGP cannot be advertised to another IBGP neighbor (to prevent routing loops).

When a router advertises a **prefix** to one of its BGP neighbors, this information is considered **valid** until the originating router advertises that the information is no longer valid or until the particular BGP session is lost (such as the TCP connection goes down). Besides, the recipient router may be certain that the path advertised is an **active path** (i.e. the originating router actively uses the particular path to reach the destination in question).

QUICK TIP   BGP using TCP connections and keepalives

Two BGP routers exchanging routing information establish a **TCP connection** between themselves and then use it to pass BGP messages over reliably. Additionally, to identify a link failure, BGP must introduce periodic **keepalive** messages to confirm the active connection.

One of the practical limits of scaling a BGP implementation is the number of neighbors with which it peers. There is no single factor involved here, but the challenges include:

- maintaining TCP sessions and BGP keepalives;
- the more peers, the more likely an update, so the more likely there is to be a frequent need to filter route updates and recompute the BGP Loc-RIB.

Different strategies are involved in reducing the workload for IBGP and EBGP peers. For IBGP, the basic approach is to reduce the number of peers by splitting the AS into smaller sub-topologies. Route reflectors are the most common way of doing so, although confederations also can serve a similar function.

There is evolving interest in building ISP topologies that have an intra-provider core that runs little or no BGP. Edge routers run the BGP, and create MPLS tunnels across the core. The core may run a fast-converging IGP to help MPLS (see Part V) find alternate paths.

To reduce the EBGP peering workload, one strategy, historically used at multi-lateral exchange points, is to peer with a route server (i.e. typically a UNIX box that runs route computation code only with no forwarding). While this technique is less popular than it once was, you essentially create an eBGP reflector cluster, with the route server acting as the reflector.

Other measures help scale EBGP by limiting the amount and frequency of routes that can hit the router. These include flap dampening, maximum received prefix limits, etc.

In the global Internet, things are going to get worse before they get better, so appropriately scalable implementation is important. At the IETF meeting last week, there were both public and private discussions about the global routing system. Some of the trends we are seeing are:

- exponential growth in prefixes, especially more-specifics of existing prefixes that primarily are being advertised for multihoming and traffic engineering;
- more non-transit AS (because more enterprises have their own policy);
- more instances of paths to a given destination (i.e. there might be 10 different AS paths to a given destination, where four to five were typical not long ago);
- shorter AS paths (hierarchy is tending to disappear).

The short- and medium-term fixes are not going to be pretty. One of the problems is that scalability tends to demand hierarchy and structure, while the free market and lack of clue tends to more chaotic routing.

BGP metric and attributes

BGP update messages consist of **network number/AS path pairs**. The AS path contains the string of ASs through which the specified network can be reached. These update messages are sent over the TCP transport mechanism to ensure reliable delivery.

The initial data exchange between two routers is the entire BGP routing table. Then, only **incremental updates** are sent out as the routing tables change. Unlike some other routing protocols, BGP does not require a periodic refresh of the entire routing table. Instead, routers running BGP retain the latest version of each peer routing table. Although BGP maintains a **routing table** with **all feasible paths** to a particular network, it **advertises only the primary (optimal) path** in its update messages.

When a BGP speaker receives updates from multiple ASs that describe different paths to the same destination, it must choose the single best path for reaching that destination. The decision over the quality of path is based on the **BGP metric** which is an arbitrary unit number specifying the **degree of preference of a particular path**. Criteria for assigning a degree of **preference to a path** are specified as the value of **BGP attributes** (such as next hop, administrative weights, local preference, the origin of the route, and path length) that the update contains and other BGP-configurable factors. Once chosen, BGP propagates the best path to its neighbors. The best path is advertised for a particular address **prefix** (group of reachable destination addresses) and accompanied by a set of **attributes**.

> ## QUICK TIP   BGP prefixes and attributes
>
> Attributes and their values carry even more important information than prefixes in BGP routing information exchange, such as which prefixes are exchanged, and which one of the multiple paths for a prefix is used.

The following **attributes** and factors are used by BGP in the **decision-making process** (attribute type code is assigned by IANA):

- *AS_path attribute* – sequence of AS path segments. Each AS path segment is represented by a triple *<path segment type, path segment length, path segment value>*. The *path segment type* is a one-octet long field with the following values defined: AS_SET (unordered set of ASs a route in the UPDATE message has traversed), AS_SEQUENCE (ordered set of ASs a route in the UPDATE message has traversed). The *path segment length* is a one-octet long field containing the number of ASs in the path segment value field. The *path segment value* field contains one or more AS numbers, each encoded as a two-octets long field. Paths with a smaller AS count are generally shorter, hence better. Whenever an update passes through an AS, BGP prepends its AS number to the update. The AS_path attribute is the list of AS numbers that an update has traversed in order to reach a destination. Currently the Autonomous System number is encoded in BGP as a two-octet field (an extension to BGP to carry the Autonomous System number as a four-octet field is currently proposed as an Internet Draft).

- *Origin attribute* – a path learned entirely from BGP (i.e. whose endpoint is internal to the last AS on the path) is generally better than one for which part of the path was learned via EGP or some other means providing information about the origin of the route. Prefixes are learned from some other source of information and only then injected into BGP. The origin of a route can be one of three values:

 - **IGP** – the route is interior to the originating AS. This value is set when the network router configuration command is used to inject the route into BGP.
 - **EGP** – the route is learned via the Exterior Gateway Protocol (EGP).
 - **Incomplete** – the origin of the route is unknown or learned in some other way. An origin of Incomplete occurs when a route is redistributed into BGP, such as for manually configured static routes.

■ *Next_Hop attribute* – the IP address of the next hop that is going to be used to reach a certain destination. Fundamentally, a BGP router will never install a prefix into the routing table that it cannot resolve a route to the NEXT_HOP for. There is no way to turn this feature off as doing so would very likely create huge black holes. If the NEXT_HOP attribute of a BGP route depicts an address to which the local BGP speaker does not have a route in its Loc-RIB, the BGP route should be excluded from the decision function.

■ *Multi-exit discriminator attribute* (MED) – is a hint to external neighbors about the preferred path into an AS when there are multiple entry points. (However, MED is not sufficient for path selection among multiple path options, when local preference attribute is used. A lower MED value is preferred over a higher MED value. The default value of the MED attribute is 0. (In BGP-3, MED was known as *Inter-AS_Metric*). Unlike local preference, the MED attribute is exchanged between ASs, but a MED attribute that comes into an AS does not leave the AS. When an update enters the AS with a certain MED value, that value is used for decision making within the AS. When BGP sends that update to another AS, the MED is reset to 0.

■ *Local preference attribute* – when there are multiple paths to the same destination, the local preference attribute indicates the preferred path. The preference might be governed by the **presence or absence of certain AS(s) in the path** when, by means of information outside the scope of BGP, an AS may know some performance characteristics (e.g. bandwidth, MTU, intra-AS diameter) of certain ASs and may try to avoid or prefer them. Also a BGP speaker may be aware of some **policy constraints** (both within and outside of its own AS) and carry out appropriate path selection. Paths that do not comply with policy requirements are not considered further. The path with the higher preference is preferred (the default value of the local preference attribute is 100). The local preference attribute is part of the routing update and is exchanged among routers in the same AS.

> **QUICK TIP** **MED vs. local preference attribute**
>
> **MEDs** are advertised to a neighbor-AS (non-transitively) [EBGP-Attribute], whereas **local preference** is advertised only inside AS [IBGP-Attribute].

■ *Atomic aggregate* – is used by a BGP speaker to inform other BGP speakers that the local system selected a less specific route without selecting a more specific route which is included in it. A prefix with this attribute set cannot be deaggregated into more specific entries upon receipt.

■ *Community attribute* – provides a way of grouping destinations (called communities) to which routing decisions (such as acceptance, preference, and redistribution) can be applied. A BGP community is a group of destinations that share some common property. A community is not restricted to one network or one AS; it has no physical boundaries, for example, groups of networks that belong to the educational or government communities. These networks can belong to any AS. Communities are used to simplify routing policies by identifying routes based on a logical property rather than an IP prefix or an AS number. *Community Attribute* (type code 8) is an optional transitive attribute that is of variable length and consists of a set of four-byte values. *hex00000000–hex0000FFFF* and *hexFFFF0000–hexFFFFFFFF* are reserved. Well known communities are *hexFFFFFF01* (*NO_EXPORT*), *hexFFFFFF02* (*NO_ADVERTISE*). An often used practice is to concatenate one's own AS number with an arbitrary community value; for example, AS256, my-peer-routers, could use the community value 256:1.

QUICK TIP **BGP community**

A **community** is a group of destinations that share some common attribute. Each destination can belong to multiple communities. Autonomous system administrators can define to which communities a destination belongs. By default, all destinations belong to the general Internet community. The community is carried as the Community attribute.

If a given router does not understand or use the community attribute, the route is not dropped and the community is passed along in updates sent to other BGP neighbors. Any given router need not use the community attribute, but that information must remain intact so that other routers might make use of it should they decide to do so. A BGP community is strictly an administrative attribute. It has zero effect on routing if the router is not configured to use that information. However, the router needs to forward that information intact to other neighbors in case they need it to enforce whatever routing or filtering policies they have implemented.

Summary of the BGP path selection process

BGP selects only one path as the best path. When the path is selected, BGP puts the selected path in its routing table and propagates the path to its neighbors. BGP uses the following **decision algorithm** with different **criteria**, in the order presented, to select a path for a destination:

1 If the path specifies a **next hop** that is inaccessible, drop the update.

2 Prefer the path with the largest **weight**.

3 If the weights are the same, prefer the path with the largest **local preference**.

4 If the local preferences are the same, prefer the path that was **originated** by BGP running on this router.

5 If no route was originated, prefer the route that has the **shortest AS_path**.

6 If all paths have the same AS_path length, prefer the path with the **lowest origin type** (where IGP is lower than EGP, and EGP is lower than Incomplete).

7 If the origin codes are the same, prefer the path with the lowest **MED** attribute.

8 If the paths have the same MED, prefer the **external path over the internal path**.

9 If the paths are still the same, prefer the path through the **closest IBGP neighbor**.

10 Prefer the path with the **lowest IP address**, as specified by the BGP router ID.

QUICK TIP **BGP decision algorithm**

The **BGP decision algorithm** comes into play when a BGP speaker receives updates that describe different paths to the same destination. After choosing the best path, BGP propagates the path to its neighbors based on attributes such as next hop, local preference, and administrative policies.

Currently there does not exist a mechanism in BGP-4 to dynamically request a re-advertisement of the *Adj-RIB-Out* from a BGP peer. When the inbound routing policy for a peer changes, all prefixes from that peer must be somehow made available and then re-examined against the new policy. To accomplish this, a commonly used approach, known as soft reconfiguration, is used to store an unmodified copy of all routes from that peer at all times, even though routing policies do not change frequently (typically no more than a couple of times a day). Additional memory and CPU are required to maintain these routes.

RFC WATCH **route refresh for BGP**

RFC 2911 **Route Refresh Capability for BGP-4**, 2000 (Proposed Standard)

RFC 2918 proposes an alternative solution that avoids the additional maintenance cost. More specifically, it defines a new BGP capability termed **Route Refresh Capability**, which would allow the dynamic exchange of a route refresh request between BGP speakers and subsequent re-advertisement of the respective *Adj-RIB-Out*. To advertise the Route Refresh Capability to a peer, a BGP speaker uses a BGP Capabilities Advertisement. By advertising the Route Refresh Capability to a peer, a BGP speaker conveys to the peer that the speaker is capable of receiving and properly handling the *ROUTE-REFRESH* message from the peer.

Synchronization

If the local autonomous system will be passing traffic through it from another autonomous system to a third autonomous system, it is very important that the local autonomous system be consistent about the routes that it advertises. For example, if BGP were to advertise a route before all routers in your network had learned about the route through the local IGP, the local autonomous system could receive traffic that some routers cannot yet route. To prevent this from happening, BGP must wait until the IGP has propagated routing information across your autonomous system. This causes BGP to be synchronized with the IGP.

Synchronization means that, by rule, a BGP router should not advertise to external neighbors destinations learned from IBGP neighbors unless those destinations are also known via an IGP. If a router knows about these destinations via an IGP, it assumes that the route has already been propagated inside the AS and internal reachability is ensured.

Synchronization is relevant when a transit AS (one that passes traffic for which it is neither the source nor destination) chooses not to use a full IBGP mesh, i.e. not all routers within an AS run BGP (otherwise the IBGP requires a full mesh within an AS unless router reflectors are deployed). Hence, if routers A, B, C, and D were connected in series, consider that only A and D are IBGP peers and are providing transit between multiple ISPs. For this to work, an IGP would have to have full prefix awareness, or put another way, the IGP table and the BGP tables would need to contain the same routes. Hence, it could be said that the tables would need to be synchronized. For protection, the BGP routers will not advertise a prefix outbound via EBGP to other ASs until their internal IGP table has the prefix installed. This means that it is likely the other IGP routers in the domain will also have the prefix and thus traffic will not be black holed. In practice, no one does this.

Synchronization was designed for transit networks that have transit providing routers which do not run BGP. Back when the Internet was smaller some network designs had the IGP in an AS carry the full table, or parts of it, and hence it was relevant to make sure BGP and IGP were synchronized to ensure there were no black hole routes. Currently this is not an issue.

Today, BGP is run fully meshed with all transit providing routers in an AS peering with IBGP and hence synchronization is a complete non-issue. Full mesh, of course, has its scalability issues, and we deal with IBGP scalability measures such as route reflectors. There is a trend to have the main BGP at the edge, and to have principally an IGP in the provider core. As a note related to the topics covered in Part V, it is possible to build a BGP-free core with multiprotocol label switching (MPLS). The core is stupid, and is traversed by MPLS tunnels. The role of the IGP is to establish reachability for these LSPs, which run between BGP speakers on the edges.

BGP packet format

The BGP packet format is shown in Figure 11.17. BGP packets have a common 19-octet header consisting of the following three fields:

FIGURE 11-17 BGP packet format

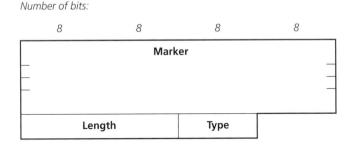

- **Marker** – contains a value that the receiver of the message can predict. This field is used for authentication.
- **Length** – contains the total length of the message, in octets.
- **Type** – specifies the message type. Four message types are specified:
  - **Open** – after a TCP connection is established, the first message sent by each side is an *open* message. If the *open* message is acceptable to the recipient, a keepalive message confirming the *open* message is sent back. Upon successful confirmation of the *open* message, updates, keepalives, and notifications may be exchanged.
    In addition to the common BGP packet header, open messages define several fields. The version field provides a BGP version number, and allows the recipient to check that it is running the same version as the sender. The autonomous system field provides the AS number of the sender. The hold-time field indicates the maximum number of seconds that may elapse without receipt of a message before the transmitter is assumed to be dead. The authentication code field indicates the authentication type being used (if any). The authentication data field contains actual authentication data (if any).
  - **Update** – provides routing updates to other BGP systems. Information in these messages is used to construct a graph describing the relationships of the various ASs. In addition to the common BGP header, *update* messages have several additional fields. These fields provide routing information by listing path attributes corresponding to each network.
  - **Notification** – sent when an error condition has been detected, and one router wishes to tell another why it is closing the connection between them. Aside from the common BGP header, *notification* messages have an error code field, an error subcode field, and error data. The error code field indicates the type of error and can be one of the following: *Message header error, Open message error, Update message error, Hold time expired*.

– **Keepalive** – sent often enough to keep the hold-time timer from expiring, but does not contain any additional fields beyond those in the common BGP header.

Security

As far as security is concerned, BGP provides a flexible and extensible mechanism for authentication and security. The mechanism allows it to support schemes with various degrees of complexity. As part of the BGP authentication mechanism, the protocol allows BGP to carry an encrypted digital signature in every BGP message. All authentication failures result in the sending of notification messages and immediate termination of the BGP connection. Since BGP runs over TCP and IP, BGP's authentication scheme may be augmented by any authentication or security mechanism provided by either TCP or IP, such as port filtering.

Routing policies

BGP provides the capability for enforcing policies based on various routing preferences and constraints. Policies are not directly encoded in the protocol. Rather, policies are provided to BGP in the form of configuration information.

Routing policies are related to political, security, or economic considerations. For example, if an AS is unwilling to carry traffic to another AS, it can enforce a policy prohibiting this. A number of performance-related criteria can be controlled with the use of BGP: number of transit ASs, quality of transit ASs (bandwidth, tendency to become congested, etc.), preference of internal routes over external routes.

BGP enforces policies by affecting the **selection of paths** from multiple alternatives and by controlling the **redistribution of routing information**. To put BGP routing and routing policies in a real-world perspective, the BGP protocol itself imposes no restriction on prefix length, but the policies of the ISPs involved do (an example is shown in Figure 11.18). Policies are determined by the AS administration. Routing policies may be configured and activated without clearing the BGP session, i.e. without invalidating the forwarding cache. This enables policy reconfiguration without causing short-term interruptions to traffic being forwarded in the network.

FIGURE 11-18   Example of routing policy imposed by filters

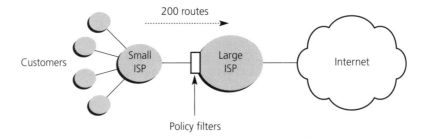

Route aggregation

The global BGP default-free routing table has around 100 000 routes in it. A tier 1 ISP will have an additional 30 000 or so customer and internal routes. Many of these routes (in the BGP view, a route is a destination) will have four potential paths to use but. Depending on the number of peers, there may be appreciably sized views that differ per peer or per peer group. Full routes are not always necessary but, depending on the policies in effect, only customer routes of your provider, or routes belonging to some community.

A conformant BGP-4 implementation is required to have the ability to specify when an aggregated route may be generated out of partial routing information. For example, a BGP speaker at the border of an autonomous system (or group of autonomous systems) must be able to generate an aggregated route for a whole set of destination IP addresses over which it has administrative control (including those addresses it has delegated), even when not all of them are reachable at the same time. In BGP-4 terminology such a set is called the **Network Layer Reachability Information** (NLRI).

QUICK TIP   **NLRI**

BGP routers exchange **network layer reachability information** (NLRI) which includes the **full route** (BGP AS numbers) to reach the destination network.

BGP does not carry subnet information in routing updates. Therefore, when supporting ASs with classless IGP, multiple subnet routes for a subnetted network in AS are collapsed into one network route when exported into BGP (e.g. RFC 1403 for BGP-OSPF interworking). Routes learned via BGP from peers within the same AS must not be imported back into that IGP.

Note that one cannot aggregate an address (externally) if there is not a more specific route of that address in the BGP routing table. The more specific route could be injected into the BGP table via incoming updates from other ASs, from redistributing an IGP or static route into BGP, or via manual configuration.

RFC WATCH   **BGP-OSPF**

RFC 1403 **BGP OSPF Interaction**, 1993 (Historic)

QUICK TIP   **BGP proxy aggregation**

Type of aggregation in which the autonomous system with aggregatable address space depends on another autonomous system to perform the aggregation.

Route flap dampening

Route dampening (or damping – the terminology is not used consistently) (see RFC watch on page 534) is a mechanism to minimize the instability caused by **route flapping** and **oscillation** over the network, i.e. to minimize the propagation of flapping routes across an internetwork. A route is considered to be flapping when it is repeatedly available (up), then unavailable (down), then available, then unavailable. Flaps are single events: the cycle of announce/withdraw/announce over a short period of time. Various timing parameters influence the point at which flaps become flapping. Some providers have additional conditional elements – they are less tolerant of flapping on long prefixes – they would put up with more flapping on a /19 than on a /24.

When BGP route flap dampening is enabled in a router the router starts to collect **statistics** about the **announcement and withdrawal of prefixes**. Route flap dampening is governed by a set of parameters with vendor-supplied default values which may be modified by the router manager. The names, semantics, and syntax of these parameters differ between the various implementations; however, the behavior of the dampening mechanism is basically the same.

Route dampening uses the criteria defined to identify poorly behaved routes. If a threshold of the **number of pairs of withdrawals/announcements** (flap) is exceeded in a given time frame (cutoff threshold) the prefix is held down for a calculated period (penalty). A route that is flapping receives a penalty of 1000 for each flap. The penalty is further incremented with every subsequent flap. When the accumulated penalty reaches a configurable limit, BGP suppresses advertisement of the route even if the route is up. The penalty is then decremented by using a half-life parameter until the penalty is below a re-use threshold. Therefore, after being stable and up for a certain period the hold-down is released from the prefix and it is re-used and re-advertised.

Routes external to an AS learned via IBGP will not be dampened. This is to avoid the IBGP peers having a higher penalty for routes external to the AS.

There exist recommended values by RIPE of route-flap dampening parameters which should be applied by all ISPs in the Internet and should be deployed as new default values by BGP router vendors. The mechanism now significantly helps with keeping severe instabilities more local. There is a second benefit: it is raising the awareness of the existence of instabilities because severe route/line flapping problems lead to permanent suppression of the unstable area by means of holding down the flapping prefixes. Route flap dampening is most valuable and most consistent and helpful if applied as near to the source of the problem as possible. Therefore flap dampening should not only be applied at peer and upstream boundaries but even more so at customer boundaries.

BGP topology

All BGP speakers within an AS must establish a **peer relationship** with each other. That is, the IBGP speakers must be **fully meshed logically**. The result is that for n BGP speakers within an AS ($n * (n - 1)/2$) unique IBGP sessions are required. This full mesh requirement clearly does not scale when there are a large number of IBGP speakers within the autonomous system, as is common in many networks today.

BGP-4 provides two techniques that alleviate the requirement for a logical full mesh: confederations and route reflectors. The policy constraints applied to all BGP speakers within an AS must be consistent. Techniques such as using a tagged IGP may be employed to detect possible inconsistencies.

One way to eliminate the need for fully meshed BGP communication is to divide an autonomous system into multiple parts called **confederations**. Splitting a single AS into confederations allows the same AS to speak EBGP, although to all external ASs the entire confederation grouping looks like a single AS. Each autonomous system is fully meshed within itself, and has a few connections to other autonomous systems in the same confederation. Even though the peers in different autonomous systems have EBGP sessions, they exchange routing information as if they were IBGP peers. Specifically, the *next-hop, MED,* and *local preference* information is preserved. This enables us to retain a single IGP for all of the autonomous systems.

SNAPSHOT   **confederations defined**

An AS confederation is a collection of autonomous systems advertised as a single AS number to BGP speakers that are not members of the confederation.

RFC 3065 (revision of RFC 1965) specifies an extension to BGP which may be used to create a confederation of autonomous systems that is represented as a single autonomous system to BGP peers external to the confederation, thereby removing the full mesh requirement. The intention of this extension is to aid in policy administration and reduce the management complexity of maintaining a large autonomous system.

RFC WATCH   **BGP confederations**

RFC 3065 **Autonomous System Confederations for BGP**, 2001 (Proposed Standard)

An example of the benefits of a confederation is shown in Figure 11.19: AS 500 consists of nine BGP speakers (although there might be other routers that are not configured for BGP). Without confederations, BGP would require that the routers in AS 500 be fully meshed. That is, each router would need to run IBGP with each of the other eight routers, and each router would need to connect to an external AS and run EBGP for a total of nine peers for each router.

Instead of configuring a confederation, another way to reduce the IBGP mesh is to configure a route reflector. **Route reflectors** are designed to provide

FIGURE 11-19 Example of BGP confederations

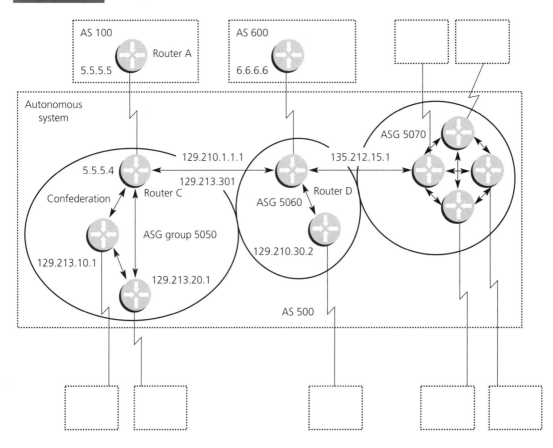

additional control by allowing a router to advertise (reflect) IBGP learned routes to other IBGP peers without requiring a full network mesh. A BGP speaker does not advertise a route learned from another IBGP speaker to a third IBGP speaker. Route reflectors ease this limitation and allow a router to advertise (reflect) IBGP-learned routes to other IBGP speakers, thereby reducing the number of IBGP peers within an AS. An example of route reflector is shown in Figure 11.20.

FIGURE 11-20   Simple case of BGP with route reflector

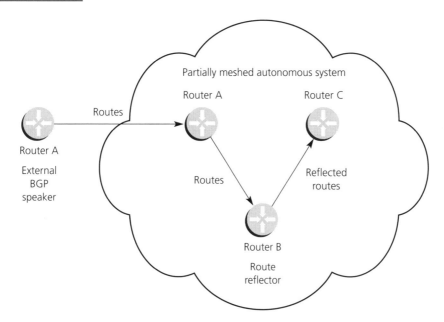

Some configurations are required to have multiple reflectors. However, network operators can run into problems if they do not have proper connectivity, that is the clients have been set up improperly. A typical symptom of a route reflector problem is a missing route from at least one router in the network. Other causes may include routers not sending or receiving routes because route filters have been activated.

RFC WATCH   **BGP route reflection**

RFC 1966 **BGP Route Reflection – An Alternative to Full Mesh IBGP**, 1996 (Experimental)

RFC 2796 **BGP Route Reflection – An Alternative to Full Mesh IBGP**, 2000 (Proposed Standard)

In addition to missing routes, common BGP problems involving route reflectors include **routing loops** and close calls. Routing loops occur when traffic is recursively forwarded over the same link or links without ever reaching its destination. This situation can occur if routing policies are not consistently deployed throughout the network. **Close calls** occur when the best path is not being followed to an external destination, which, of course, can be nettlesome. For example, all the EBGP peers are configured with their interface addresses, and while the *next_hop* is expected in a network trace, it does not show up. Verifying the configuration and checking for alternate routes is the first step in sorting out the problem. The problem could be a result of the fact that a router is a route reflector with two clients, and one of them is not physically attached to the reflector but has another router in the path.

Since a full **AS path** provides an efficient and straightforward way of **suppressing routing loops** and eliminates the count-to-infinity problem associated with some distance vector algorithms, BGP imposes no topological restrictions on the interconnection of ASs. An AS may be placed into one of the following **categories:**

- **Stub AS** – an AS that has only a single connection to one other AS. Naturally, a stub AS only carries local traffic.

- **Multi-homed AS** – an AS that has connections to more than one other AS, but refuses to carry transit traffic (see subsection on multi-homing later in this chapter).

- **Transit AS** – an AS that has connections to more than one other AS, and is designed (under certain policy restrictions) to carry both transit and local traffic. Some ASs are merely pass-through channels for network traffic, i.e. they carry network traffic that did not originate within the AS and is not destined for the AS. BGP must interact with whatever intra-AS routing protocols exist within these pass-through ASs.

The overall Internet topology may be viewed as an arbitrary interconnection of transit, multi-homed, and stub ASs. In order to minimize the impact on the current Internet infrastructure, stub and multi-homed ASs need not use BGP. These ASs may run other protocols (e.g. EGP) to exchange reachability information with transit ASs. Transit ASs using BGP will **tag** this information as having been learned by some method other than BGP. The fact that BGP need not run on stub or multi-homed ASs has no negative impact on the overall quality of inter-AS routing for traffic that is either destined to or originated from the stub or multi-homed ASs in question. Stub ASs may use static or default routing instead of BGP saving the unnecessary dynamic routing overhead.

QUICK TIP   **BGP multi-homing**

Internet subscriber procures not only a link to the Internet but also a tool to increase **reliability** (conection redundancy) and/or **performance** (load sharing).

However, it is recommended that BGP be used for multi-homed ASs as well, particularly when multi-homing with more ISPs. In these situations, BGP will provide an advantage in bandwidth and performance over some of the currently used protocols (such as EGP). In addition, this would reduce the need for the use of default routes and result in better choices of inter-AS routes for multi-homed ASs.

Multi-homing

In the broadest sense, **multi-homing** is an approach to increase the availability of the network. There are numerous technologies for achieving multi-homing as we will see later on. The most common way, however, is when an enterprise wishes to acquire its Internet connectivity from more than one ISP for several reasons. Maintaining connectivity via more than one ISP can be viewed as a way to increase the reliability of Internet connectivity. Such multiply connected enterprises are referred to as being **multi-homed**. When connectivity through one of the ISPs fails, connectivity via the other ISP(s) enables the enterprise to preserve its connectivity to the Internet. In addition to providing more reliable connectivity, maintaining connectivity via more than one ISP also enables the enterprise to distribute load among multiple connections. For enterprises that span wide geographical areas, this could also enable better (less suboptional) routing.

The above considerations, combined with the decreasing cost of Internet connectivity, motivate more and more enterprises to become multi-homed. At the same time, the routing overhead that such enterprises impose on the Internet routing system becomes more and more significant. Scaling the Internet, and being able to support a growing number of such enterprises, demands scalable mechanism(s) to contain this overhead. We assume that an approach where routers in the default-free zone (without any default routes in their routing tables) of the Internet would be required to maintain a route for every multi-homed enterprise that is connected to multiple ISPs does not provide an adequate scaling.

RFC 2260 describes an address allocation and routing scheme for multi-homed enterprises that has fairly good scaling properties. However, the scheme proposed is not without its own drawbacks. To begin with, it requires **renumbering** part of an enterprise when the enterprise changes one of its ISPs. In addition, it requires renumbering part of an enterprise when the enterprise first becomes multi-homed. In addition, the ability of an enterprise to distribute load across multiple connections to ISPs is determined largely by the address assignment inside an enterprise. This could be viewed as making load distribution fairly rigid and inflexible. Controlling load distribution via address assignment also adds complexity to addressing schemes used inside an enterprise.

RFC WATCH   **multi-homing**

RFC 2260 **Scalable Support for Multi-homed Multi-provider Connectivity**, 1998 (Informational)

A multi-homed enterprise connected to a set of ISPs is allocated a **block of addresses** (address prefix) by each of these ISPs (e.g. an enterprise connected to N ISPs would get N different blocks). These addresses are referred to as '**inside global addresses**.' The allocation of inside global addresses from the ISPs to the enterprise could be based on the '**address-lending' policy** as described in RFC 2008. Such addresses would be allocated out of a block of addresses that the ISP would use for lending to its customers.

Network Address Translators (NATs) can be used to address various problems including facilitating scalable routing for multi-homed multi-provider connectivity. This method does not require enterprise host renumbering when changing ISPs, and allows load distribution that does not depend on the address assignment scheme inside an enterprise.

A NAT that connects an enterprise to an ISP uses BGP to advertise to the ISP direct reachability to the inside global addresses obtained from that ISP. The ISP aggregates this reachability information for all of its customers into a single route, thus eliminating the need to carry within the default-free zone of the Internet a route for each multi-homed enterprise. A NAT acts as an enterprise border router: it has an EBGP peering session with one or more of the ISP's routers, as well as IBGP peering sessions with other NATs inside the enterprise.

RFC WATCH   addressing

RFC 2008 **Implications of Various Address Allocation Policies for Internet Routing**, 1996 (Best Current Practice)

RFC 3022 **Traditional IP Network Address Translator** (Traditional NAT), 2001 (Informational)

The concept of a Network Address Translator (NAT) is described in RFC 3022. NAT can perform translation of both source and destination IP addresses in a packet. The translation is performed by using the address translation table maintained by the NAT. The address translation table maintained by a NAT consists of two types of entries: inside address translation, and outside address translation. Each entry consists of two components: local address and global address.

The situation with advertising prefixes and their aggregates to ISPs would be handled differently if the address space was allocated directly (i.e. provider independent), or if it was sub-assigned by one of the providers (i.e. provider assigned).

With **provider independent space** (PI), if multi-homing serves fault tolerance as well as load distribution, the enterprise must:

■ announce the less-specific aggregate to both ISPs;

■ announce the more-specific prefixes to the preferred ISP (to have traffic to that block come into its own AS).

With **provider assigned space** (PA), the enterprise must:

- announce the less-specific aggregate to both ISPs;
- announce the more-specific prefixes to the preferred ISP to have traffic to that block come into AS;
- be sure that the assigning AS advertises its own more-specific as well as its aggregate prefixes;
- be sure that the other AS coordinates with its own AS so that it can announce a more-specific from another AS's space (a must in Europe, and strongly recommended elsewhere);
- be sure that all three ASs (the enterprise and the two ISPs) register the routing policies with a public routing registry.

Load-balancing/sharing and BGP

When a BGP speaker learns two identical EBGP paths for a prefix from a neighboring AS, it will choose the path with the lowest *route-ID* as the best path. This best path is installed in the IP routing table. If BGP **multipath support** is enabled and the EBGP paths are learned from the same neighboring AS, instead of picking one best path, multiple paths are installed in the IP routing table. But by default, BGP will install only **one path in the IP routing table**.

Per packet load balancing among different ASs is likely to cause terrible out-of-sequence effects. Per destination load balancing works well only to the extent that an essentially identical amount of traffic goes to each destination. Per source destination pair is probably the best available method.

Load-sharing does not pretend to be as precise as load balancing, and thus is more likely to be realistic. Nevertheless, the BGP routing system was never designed to carry out either load-balancing or load-sharing. There is an increasing tendency to inject more-specific routes into it for load-sharing/traffic control, backup, etc., and it is this injection of additional state that is raising serious concerns about the overall scalability of this routing system.

RFC WATCH   **multi-homing and BGP**

RFC 1998 **An Application of the BGP Community Attribute in Multi-home Routing**, 1996 (Informational)

RFC 2260 **Scalable Support for Multi-homed Multi-provider Connectivity**, 1998 (Informational)

RFC 2270 **Using a Dedicated AS for Sites Homed to a Single Provider**, 1998 (Informational)

However, BGP does not equate to multi-homing. Multi-homing itself is a technical architectural matter, subordinate to the larger business requirements of availability, performance, and budget. Depending on what the target is to accomplish, it may be necessary to employ multiple technologies at multiple layers to meet those requirements:

- TCP load distribution within server farms;
- RAID mirroring within server farms, with hot failover;
- DNS redistribution and/or intelligent tunneling among multiple server farms;
- multi-homed routing, both BGP and IGP;
- multilinking at data link and below (MLPPP, FastEtherChannel, SONET, etc.);
- local loop diversity (e.g. wireless and wired).

A basic way to tell which technology(ies) are applicable is to ask oneself whether the functional requirement is defined in terms of multi-homing to specific hosts, or to specific networks. If the former, some type of application or transport technology is needed, because only these technologies have awareness of specific hosts.

Technologies in this category may involve referring a client request to different instances of the endpoint represented by a single name. Another aspect of application/name multi-homing may work at the level of IP addressing, but specifically is constrained to endpoint (i.e. server) activities that redirect the client request to a different endpoint.

- **Application-level firewall proxy services** can provide this functionality, although their application protocol modification emphasizes security while a multi-homing application service emphasizes availability and quality of service.
- **Transport-based technologies** are based on maintaining tunnels through an underlying network or transmission system. The tunnels may be true end to end, connecting a client host with a server host, or may interconnect between proxy servers or other gateways. Virtual private networks are based on tunneling.
- **Network-based approaches** to multi-homing are router-based. They involve having alternative next-hops, or complete routes, to alternative destinations.
- **Data link layer methods** may involve coordinated use of multiple physical paths, as in multilink PPP or X.25. If the underlying WAN service has a virtual circuit mechanism, as in Frame Relay or ATM, the service provider may have multi-homed paths provided as part of the service. Such functions blur between data link and physical layers.
- **Physical multi-homing** strategies can use diverse media, often of different types such as a wire backed up with a wireless data link. They also involve transmission media which have internal redundancy such as SONET.

> **QUICK TIP** **BGP capabilities**
>
> ■ Exchange of reachability information only with other BGP systems.
>
> ■ Use of an **authentication** method to protect against unauthorized updates to routing tables.
>
> ■ Support for **policy-based routing**.
>
> ■ Maintenance of a **virtual connection** between two hosts and use of this connection to exchange entire BGP routing table and table updates.
>
> ■ **Multipath support** over multiple EBGP sessions to provide **load balancing** and redundancy.
>
> ■ Filtering of routing information based on *prefix*, *AS_path*, or *community*.

ISP issues

We introduced in a discussion above the notion of ISP. So far we have spoken about BGP usage for external routing from the end customer perspective but the ISP view is more valid because they are responsible for proper BGP configuration, following their policies (in relation to their partners and paying customers) and following the policies of the global Internet (i.e. advertise as few yet well specified routes to the outer world as possible using route aggregation hence proper addressing). It is also important to recognize that ISPs do not exist in vacuum and that they are just part of an **overall Internet routing design**.

The ISP routing issues are very complex because they involve routing policies which do not necessarily having very clear links with the technicalities of routing, rather with internet (and Internet) design. There are issues related to:

■ **address** justification and registration;

■ defining **policies** for multi-homing, interprovider **peering**, etc.;

■ understanding the addressing, registration, etc., requirements;

■ single provider **multi-homing**;

■ hot and cold potato designs for provider networks;

■ defining **service level agreements** (SLAs) and then carrying out the **traffic engineering** to implement them;

■ denial of service protection.

In terms of **routing information**, the customer network can receive from the ISP one of the following:

■ **Default routes** – 0.0.0.0 routes from the provider with the result that there are no specific routes in the customer network routers, except for the customer network or subnets.

- **Customer and default routes** – 0.0.0.0 routes and all other routes that originate from the provider's AS (provider's internal routes). This will route traffic coming from customers of this provider back to the provider.
- **Full routes** – all known routes. This provides the best routing outbound for customer connections, but requires a great deal of memory because of the number of routes (hundreds of thousands) in the tables.

Core routers of the Internet and full routing tables

It is misleading to think that all ISP routers need to be **core routers**. Arguably, the highest-bandwidth **core routers inside an ISP** may not need to run full **BGP**, but have more stringent demands on **OSPF, IS-IS, and/or MPLS**. Think of provider routers (RFC 2547 P routers, discussed in Chapter 15 in Part V. Depending on the design of the core, the routers at the edge of the core will use full routes to set up MPLS LSPs from one side of the core to the other, but routers internal to the core may not need it if they are under LDP or RSVP-TE control from the edge routers.

An ISP POP access router might have the greatest number of BGP routes and paths, but not as much bandwidth requirements. If the POP router primarily deals with customers, it will advertise only default and partial routes to many of them. Only a small proportion of customers want full routes. A POP router will also generally accept only a small number of routes from customers.

In the core of interconnected POP/access and server sites inside an ISP or an enterprise, there is a good deal of interest in subsecond reconvergence times. This probably is achievable with link-state IGPs, using millisecond or microsecond hellos (or relying on hardware failure detection on optical links), and more advanced algorithms than the 40-year-old Dijkstra. In the short to moderate term, there is no foreseeable way to get convergence times this fast with exterior routing. Actually, superfast convergence in the global Internet may be a really bad idea with respect to Internet stability.

If the customers want to multi-home to multiple providers, or even to multiple POPs of the same provider, BGP is really the only option. Single-homed customers do not need it, and, for some situations, multiple defaults will work at the cost of suboptimal routing.

Interprovider routers at **tier 1** are unlikely to need to exchange full routes. Such routers are bandwidth-intense, but the definition of a tier 1 is that you exchange only customer routes (this is perhaps an oversimplification but it is close) with other tier 1 providers.

The **number of routes in the core** is not a simple number, but there are proposals for ways of estimating the load. Let's say the number of routes in a **default-free table** is D. Actually, this number will vary depending on where you measure it: the weekly CIDR reports probe routers in Tokyo and London and come up with slightly different sizes. In a large provider, there are **customer routes** that are aggregated at the edges, as well as **infrastructure routes**. The working number for the number of routes a large provider's internal number is in the order of 1.3 to 1.5 D.

Another consideration is the **number of paths per route** – in other words, how many potential paths there are from which BGP will select one (ignoring complex policies). An informal rule of thumb is that there are an **average of four**

paths per route. The number of routes in the **Default Free Zone** (DFZ) has returned to exponential growth.

With regard to ISPs and the Internet backbone, the terms previously used for network design are modified somewhat:

- **access** – customer site routers, which may either be customer provided (CPE) or carrier provided at the customer location;
- **collection** – the broadband access network (DSL, cable, etc.), which may aggregate into VLANs, etc.;
- **distribution or edge** – POP, possibly interprovider interconnect, at least some servers (e.g. cache);
- **core** – intraprovider backbone.

The distinction between core and edge ISP routers is not clearly specified but the suggested heuristic distinction is as follows:

- The **ISP core router** has lots of bandwidth, perhaps lots of MPLS paths, perhaps a big forwarding table (as distinct from the routing table), but limited filtering or policy controls and limited traffic conditioning. Additionally, all its interfaces tend to be the same general speed.
- In contrast, an **ISP edge router** has lots of logical interfaces, extensive filtering, policy, and traffic shaping. It has the most extensive routing (including the 'border' function here). It may be asymmetrical with respect to interfaces (e.g. 10/100/1000 Ethernet toward the customer, OC-48 (see Appendix D) or better toward the core).

BGP extensions

RFC WATCH	multiprotocol extensions to BGP

RFC 2858 **Multiprotocol Extensions for BGP-4**, 2000 (Proposed Standard)

Multiprotocol extensions

The only three pieces of information carried by BGP-4 that are IPv4 specific are: the *NEXT_HOP* attribute (expressed as an IPv4 address), *AGGREGATOR* (contains an IPv4 address), and *NLRI* (expressed as IPv4 address prefixes). To enable BGP-4 to support routing for multiple network layer protocols the only two things that have to be added to BGP-4 are the ability to associate a particular network layer protocol with the next-hop information, and the ability to associate a particular network layer protocol with NLRI.

The next-hop information (the information provided by the *NEXT_HOP* attribute) is meaningful (and necessary) only in conjunction with the advertisements of reachable destinations – in conjunction with the advertisements of unreachable destinations (withdrawing routes from service) the next-hop information is meaningless. This suggests that the advertisement of reachable destinations should be grouped with the advertisement of the next hop to be used for these destinations, and that the advertisement of reachable destinations should be segregated from the advertisement of unreachable destinations.

To provide backward compatibility, as well as to simplify introduction of the multiprotocol capabilities into BGP-4, two new attributes have been introduced: ***Multiprotocol Reachable NLRI*** *(MP_REACH_NLRI)*, used to carry the set of reachable destinations together with the next-hop information to be used for forwarding to these destinations; and ***Multiprotocol Unreachable NLRI*** *(MP_UNREACH_NLRI)*, used to carry the set of unreachable destinations. Both of these attributes are optional and non-transitive. This way a BGP speaker that does not support the multiprotocol capabilities will just ignore the information carried in these attributes, and will not pass it to other BGP speakers.

Cooperative route filtering capability

Currently it is not uncommon for a BGP speaker to receive and then filter out some unwanted routes from its peers based on its local routing policy. Since the generation and transmission of routing updates by the sender, as well as the processing of routing updates by the receiver, consume resources, it may be beneficial if the generation of such unwanted routing updates can be avoided in the first place. A BGP-based mechanism that allows a BGP speaker to send to its BGP peer a set of **Outbound Route Filters** (ORFs) is currently a proposed Internet Draft. The BGP peer would then apply these filters, in addition to its locally configured outbound filters (if any), to constrain/filter its outbound routing updates to the speaker.

RFC WATCH	capabilities advertisement with BGP

RFC 2842 **Capabilities Advertisement with BGP-4**, 2000 (Proposed Standard)

Route dampening is a BGP feature designed to minimize the propagation of flapping routes across an internetwork. A route is considered to be flapping when it is repeatedly available, then unavailable, then available, then unavailable, and so on.

RFC WATCH	BGP route dampening

RFC 2439 **BGP Route Flap Dampening**, 1998 (Proposed Standard)

A route that is flapping receives a penalty of 1000 for each flap. When the accumulated penalty reaches a configurable limit, BGP suppresses advertisement of the route even if the route is up. The accumulated penalty is decremented by the half-life time. When the accumulated penalty is less than the re-use limit, the route is advertised again (if it is still up).

Troubleshooting BGP

Generally problems in networks with BGP routing are not protocol problems but configuration-related. Some of the biggest challenges with maintaining successful BGP deployments arise from seemingly trivial configuration errors which can easily become magnified as the size of IP networks expands. The gurus for BGP deployment thus invariably suggest to avoid difficulties that might arise down the road by paying close attention to proper configuration details up front, and keeping BGP configurations as simple as possible to make it easier later to isolate any trouble spots that do occur. Simplicity with the aim of network stability is key to avoid tiresome troubleshooting exercises (this applies, of course, far beyond BGP).

BGP might seem difficult to deploy at the inter-domain level. The reason is that the more detailed an organization's routing policies are, the more complex the configuration appears to be. **Routing policies** are set by network administrators to dictate network behavior, such as which network paths traffic should take under certain conditions, which traffic should take priority, and how much bandwidth a flow should receive. Policies can be based on application, user group, IP address, or other criteria.

The basic recommendations are the following:

- maintain a consistent policy;
- promote stable networks by nailing down routes and using loopback interfaces;
- ease network growing pains by using peer groups and route reflectors for scalability.

A systematic approach is necessary also at the point of performing the necessary troubleshooting. With the available router commands the administrator can get real-time displays of the protocol messages and events that will help resolve a problem. This important data may describe routes with non-natural masks, routes that match the communities, path information, peer group information, or routes sent to a BGP neighbor. Detailed information about a BGP neighbor is vital to the BGP well-being, hence the reason for the last session reset and any changes in a BGP neighbor should be carefully logged.

After running through the basic troubleshooting commands, the next task is to work through common problems with establishing peer sessions such as no IP reachability, incorrect configurations, wrong peering addresses, and failed open parameters, for example. First, **IP connectivity** should be verified by checking the routing table. Next, PING/trace utilities may be used to verify **two-way reachability**; any filters should be also be inspected in the path to the neighbor.

The first attempt to solve the **peer session establishment** problem involves making sure that both routers source the information from the appropriate interface. The basic points to keep in mind are that TCP sessions are always sourced from the IP address closest to the destination, and if redundant paths exist, loopback interfaces should be used to establish the session. The advantages of a **loopback** interface are that it is always up, and multiple physical paths may exist to reach it. This setup means that alternate paths may be available if a physical link should fail. On the downside, a physical-link failure may take somewhat longer to detect. Still, the benefits outweigh this shortcoming.

It is recommended that EBGP peers be directly connected by default so that network managers can constantly gather information that could point to a physical interface failure. If an error is still present after verifying the physical and logical connectivity, it is likely that the remote routers have an inconsistent configuration (the open message parameters such as AS number or hold times may be mismatched). The available **optional parameters** are used for capabilities: to specify multiprotocol support, route refresh, or outbound route filtering (ORF) support. Once the connectivity issues are rectified, customers will not need to go through this exercise again.

Once a session has been established, **updates** are exchanged to provide all the locally known routes with only the best path advertised. Incremental update messages are exchanged later. If the best path is received from an EBGP peer, then it is advertised to all peers. If the best path comes from an Internal BGP (IBGP) peer, then it should be advertised only to EBGP peers. As a result, a full IBGP mesh should be created. If a full mesh is not created, missing routes and other troubles can arise. The lack of a full IBGP mesh may be the easiest of these problems to solve. In general, the state of the connection will not be established, if configured at all.

The **update filters** may be the cause of route problems. *Prefix filters, AS_path* filters, and *community filters* may be used and applied to any incoming or outgoing updates. To determine which filters are applied to the BGP session, the route (and its relevant attributes) should be compared against the filters. If there is no match, a route should be refreshed to isolate the problem. Such detective work may pay off by indicating why a route is not advertised or the reason that it is being denied by the receiving router.

Slow convergence can be far more difficult to pinpoint. Possible causes may be an unhealthy remote router, or a problem in the lower layer of the network, such as with a maximum time-to-live within an IP datagram. For example, if routers A and B are EBGP peers (see Figure 11.21) and the longest path between A and B involves more than two hops it is necessary to use a higher TTL setting on that path. The lower-level issues should be tackled and eliminated before checking higher-layer variables.

QUICK TIP **multihop BGP**

A border gateway protocol between two routers in different autonomous systems that are more than one hop away from each other.

FIGURE 11-21 An issue in BGP and TTL – slow convergence

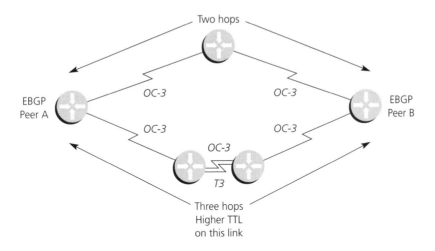

Two hops

EBGP
Peer A

OC-3

OC-3

EBGP
Peer B

OC-3

OC-3

OC-3

T3

Three hops
Higher TTL
on this link

Route selection is another perennial area of confusion in the BGP arena. A common policy should be maintained across the AS to guarantee loop-free operation. Filters may be used to modify or add attributes, affecting the route selection algorithm. For example, difficulties may arise when these steps lead to an inconsistent decision or policy that prevents important information about communities from being propagated. One symptom of this trouble is that the best path changes each time the peering is reset in the network. This situation occurs when the prefixes are compared in the order of their arrival, and the attributes yield a different result each time. The problem can be avoided by using *bgp deterministic-med*. The paths are ordered by peer-AS. The best path for each group is selected, and collectively they create an overall best path.

TROUBLESHOOTING TIPS

- A consistent policy should be enforced throughout the AS.
- IP reachability must exist for sessions to be established.
- The source and destination addresses should match the configuration.
- Loopback interfaces should be used for stability and where multiple paths exist.
- Common and simple filters should be deployed.
- *deterministic-med* should be used.
- The physical topology should be followed when using route reflectors.
- A *bgp cluster-id* with route reflectors should be defined only if administratively needed.

11.5 Routing in IPv6/IPv4 networks

Routers running both IPv6 and IPv4 can be administered in much the same fashion that IPv4-only networks are currently administered. IPv6 versions of popular routing protocols, such as Open Shortest Path First (OSPF) and Routing Information Protocol (RIP), are already under development. In many cases, administrators will choose to keep the IPv6 topology logically separate from the IPv4 network, even though both run on the same physical infrastructure. This will allow the two to be administered separately. In other cases, it may be advantageous to align the two architectures by using the same domain boundaries, areas, and subnet organization. Both approaches have their advantages. A separate IPv6 architecture can be used to abolish the chaotic, inefficient IPv4 addressing systems from which many of today's enterprises suffer. An independent IPv6 architecture presents the opportunity to build a fresh, hierarchical network address plan that will greatly facilitate connection to one or more ISPs. This lays a foundation for efficient renumbering, route aggregation, and the other goals of an advanced internetwork routing hierarchy.

In most organizations where IPv6 is deployed incrementally, there is the strong possibility that all IPv6 hosts will not have direct connectivity to each other via IPv6 routers. In many cases there will be islands of IPv6 topology surrounded by an ocean of IPv4. Fortunately, IPv6 designers have fashioned transition mechanisms that allow IPv6 hosts to communicate over intervening IPv4 networks. The essential technique of these mechanisms is IPv6 over IPv4 tunneling, which encapsulates IPv6 packets in IPv4 packets. **Tunneling** allows early IPv6 implementations to take advantage of existing IPv4 infrastructure without any change to IPv4 components. A dual-stack router or host on the 'edge' of the IPv6 network simply appends an IPv4 header to each IPv6 packet and sends it as native IPv4 traffic through existing links. IPv4 routers forward this traffic without knowledge that IPv6 is involved. On the other side of the tunnel, another dual-stack router or host de-encapsulates the IPv6 packet and routes it to the ultimate destination using standard IPv6 protocols. For tunnelling, see also Section 12.5.

To accommodate different administrative needs, IPv6 transition mechanisms include two types of tunneling: automatic and configured. To build configured tunnels, administrators manually define IPv6-to-IPv4 address mappings at tunnel endpoints. On either side of the tunnel, traffic is forwarded with full 128-bit addresses. At the tunnel entry point, a router table entry is defined manually to dictate which IPv4 address is used to traverse the tunnel. This requires a certain amount of manual administration at the tunnel endpoints, but traffic is routed through the IPv4 topology dynamically, without the knowledge of IPv4 routers. The 128-bit addresses do not have to align with 32-bit addresses in any way.

11.5.1 Automatic tunneling

Automatic tunnels use IPv4-compatible addresses, which are hybrid IPv4/IPv6 addresses. Compatible addresses are created by adding leading zeros to the 32-bit IPv4 address to pad them out to 128 bits (see also Section 10.8.1). When traffic is forwarded with compatible addresses, the device at the tunnel entry point can automatically address encapsulated traffic by simply converting the IPv4-compatible 128-bit address to a 32-bit IPv4 address. On the other side of the tunnel, the IPv4 header is removed to reveal the original IPv6 address. Automatic tunneling allows IPv6 hosts to dynamically exploit IPv4 networks, but it does require the use of IPv4-compatible addresses, which do not bring the benefits of the 128-bit address space.

IPv6 nodes using IPv4-compatible addresses cannot take advantage of the extended address space, but they can exploit the other IPv6 enhancements, including flow labels, authentication, encryption, multicast, and anycast. Once a node is migrated to IPv6 with IPv4-compatible addressing, the door is open for a fairly painless move to the full IPv6 address space (hopefully with the help of an IPv6-based autoconfiguration service). IPv4-compatible addressing means that administrators can add IPv6 nodes while initially preserving their basic addressing and subnet architecture. Automatic tunnels are available when needed, but they may not be necessary in cases where major backbone routers are upgraded all at once to include the IPv6 stack. This is something that can be achieved quickly and efficiently when backbone routers support full remote configuration and upgrade capabilities.

The **OSPF** protocol, the cornerstone of high-performance, standards-based internetworking, is the IETF recommended interior gateway protocol for IPv6. OSPF is being updated with full support for IPv6, allowing routers to be addressed with 128-bit addresses. The 32-bit link-state records of current OSFP will be replaced by 128-bit records. In general, the OSPF IPv6 link-state database of backbone routers will run in parallel with the database for IPv4 topologies. In this sense, the two versions of OSPF will operate as 'ships in the night,' just as the routing engines for NetWare, DECnet, AppleTalk, and other protocols coexist in the same router without major interaction. Given the limited nature of the OSPF IPv6 upgrade, those engineers and administrators who are proficient in OSPF for IPv4 should have no problems adapting to the new version. An updated version of RIP is also available, referred to as **RIPng**.

As with the interior gateway protocols, work is underway to create IPv6-compatible versions of the *exterior gateway protocols* that are used by routers to establish reachability across the Internet backbone between large enterprises, providers, and other autonomous systems. *BGP* is known by providers and enterprises and has a large installed base. Consequently, BGP has the inside track for IPv6. Currently, work is underway to define BGP extensions that will allow it to be used to exchange reachability information based on the new IPv6 hierarchical address space.

From a routing protocol standpoint, *tunnels* appear as a single IPv6 hop, even if the tunnel is comprised of many IPv4 hops across a number of different media. IPv6 routers running OSPF can propagate link-state reachability advertisements through tunnels, just as they would across conventional point-to-point links. In the IPv6 environment, OSPF will have the advantage of flexible metrics for tunnel routes, to ensure that each tunnel is given its proper weight within the topology. In general, routers make packet-forwarding decisions in the tunneling environment in the same way that they make decisions in the IPv6-only network. The underlying IPv4 connections are essentially transparent to IPv6 routing protocols.

11.6 IP multicast protocols

11.6.1 Multicasting introduction

Multicasting is used for a variety of purposes in today's networks. The Enhanced Interior Gateway Routing Protocol (EIGRP) and Open Shortest Path First (OSPF), as we saw above, use multicast packets to send updates to neighboring routers. And increasingly, more desktop applications are relying on IP multicasting for group, or multipoint, computing. The best examples are in the area of networked multimedia, where group-based video and audio distribution is very user attractive.

To understand the fundamentals of any type of multicast routing, it can be viewed as a sort of 'upside down routing.' While in normal unicast routing the concern is about getting from a source to a destination, in multicast routing it is the exact opposite. Destinations are multicast clients and they are trying to find a path to the source or sources of the multicast streams.

The network layer must define several parameters in order to support multicast communications:

- **Multicast addressing** – there must be a Layer 3 address that is used to communicate with a group of receivers rather than a single receiver. In addition, there must be a mechanism for mapping this address onto Layer 2 (physical) multicast addresses where they exist.

- **Dynamic registration** – there must be a mechanism for the station to communicate to the network that it is a member of a particular group and thus announce its expectations for a particular multicast traffic.

- **Multicast routing** – the network must be able to build packet distribution trees that allow sources to send packets to all receivers in a group. A primary goal of these packet distribution trees is to ensure that each packet exists only one time on any given network (that is, if there are multiple receivers on a given branch, there should be only one copy of the packets on that branch).

An overview of the network operations involved to support multicast is shown in Figure 11.22.

11.6.2 IP multicast address

IP multicasting is based on the concept of the **host group**, a dynamic set of hosts identified by a single **Class D address**, which can be joined or left at any time.

RFC WATCH	scoped multicast

RFC 2365 **Administratively Scoped IP Multicast**, 1998 (Best Current Practice)

RFC 2776 **Multicast-Scope Zone Announcement Protocol** (MZAP), 2000 (Proposed Standard)

FIGURE 11-22 Multicast-enabled network

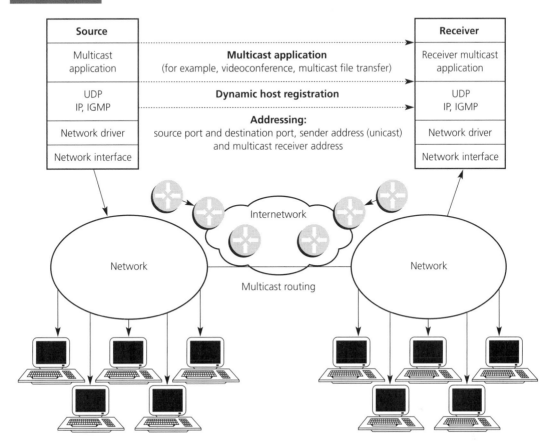

The use of an **administratively scoped IP multicast**, as defined in RFC 2365, allows packets to be addressed to a specific range of multicast addresses (e.g. 239.0.0.0 to 239.255.255.255 for IPv4) such that the packets will not cross configured administrative boundaries, and also allows such addresses to be locally assigned and hence are not required to be unique across administrative boundaries. This property of logical naming not only allows for address reuse, but also provides the capability for infrastructure services such as address allocation, session advertisement, and service location to use well-known addresses which are guaranteed to have local significance within every organization.

The range of administratively scoped addresses can be subdivided by administrators so that multiple levels of administrative boundaries can be simultaneously supported. As a result, a **multicast scope** is defined as a particular range of addresses which has been given some topological meaning. To support such usage, a router at an administrative boundary is configured with one or more per-interface filters, or multicast scope boundaries. Having such a boundary on an interface means that it will not forward packets matching a configured range of multicast addresses in either direction on the interface.

A specific area of the network topology which is within a boundary for a given scope is known as a **multicast scope zone**. Since the same ranges can be reused within disjoint areas of the network, there may be many multicast scope zones for any given multicast scope. A scope zone may have zero or more textual names (in different languages) for the scope, for human convenience.

Administrative scope zones may be of any size, and a particular host may be within many administrative scope zones (for different scopes, i.e. for non-overlapping ranges of addresses) of various sizes, as long as scope zones that intersect topologically do not intersect in address range.

Applications and services are interested in various aspects of the **scopes** within which they reside:

- Applications which present users with a choice of which scope in which to operate (e.g. when creating a new session, whether it is to be confined to a corporate intranet, or whether it should go out over the public Internet) are interested in the textual names which have significance to users.

- Services which use relative multicast addresses in every scope are interested in the range of addresses used by each scope, so that they can apply a constant offset and compute which address to use in each scope.

- Address allocators are interested in the address range, and whether they are allowed to allocate addresses within the entire range or not.

- Some applications and services may also be interested in the nesting relationships among scopes. For example, knowledge of the nesting relationships can be used to perform expanding-scope searches in a similar, but better behaved, manner to the well-known expanding ring search where the TTL of a query is steadily increased until a replier can be found. Studies have also shown that nested scopes can be useful in localizing multicast repair traffic.

Two **barriers** currently make administrative scoping difficult to deploy and use:

- Applications without any possibility of dynamically discovering information on scopes relevant to them – this makes it difficult to use administrative scope zones, and hence reduces the incentive to deploy them.

- Easy misconfiguration – difficulty of detecting scope zones that have been configured so as to not be convex (the shortest path between two nodes within the zone passes outside the zone), or to leak (one or more boundary routers were not configured correctly), or to intersect in both area and address range.

These two barriers are addressed in RFC 2776. It defines the **Multicast Scope Zone Announcement Protocol** (MZAP) which allows an entity to learn what scope zones it is within. Typically servers will cache the information learned from MZAP and can then provide this information to applications in a timely fashion upon request using other means. MZAP also provides diagnostic information to the boundary routers themselves that enables misconfigured scope zones to be detected.

The **local scope** is defined in RFC 2365 and represents the smallest administrative scope larger than link-local, and the associated address range is defined as 239.255.0.0 to 239.255.255.255 inclusive (for IPv4, FF03::/16 for IPv6).

A multicast scope **Zone Boundary Router** (ZBR) is a router that is configured with a boundary for a particular multicast scope on one or more of its interfaces. Any interface that is configured with a boundary for any administrative scope zone must also have a boundary for the local scope zone, as described above. **Zone ID** means the lowest IP address used by any ZBR for a particular zone for sourcing MZAP messages into that scope zone. The combination of this IP address and the first multicast address in the scope range serve to uniquely identify the scope zone. Each ZBR listens for messages from other ZBRs for the same boundary, and can determine the zone ID based on the source addresses seen. The zone ID may change over time as ZBRs come up and down.

Multicast IP addressing in local scope reserves Class D addresses which are allocated dynamically. The set of hosts listening to a particular IP multicast address is called a host group. A **host group** can span multiple networks. Membership in a group is dynamic, i.e. hosts may join and leave host groups. Some multicast group addresses are assigned as well-known addresses by the Internet Assigned Numbers Authority (IANA). These groups are called permanent host groups, similar in concept to the well-known TCP and UDP port numbers. Table 11.11 shows some of the well-known Class D addresses.

TABLE 11-11   Well-known IP multicast (Class D) addresses (as per RFC 1700)

Well-known Class D address	Purpose
224.0.0.1	All hosts on a subnet
224.0.0.2	All routers on a subnet
224.0.0.4	All DVMRP routers
224.0.0.5	All (M)OSPF routers
224.0.0.6	OSPF designated and backup designated routers
224.0.0.9	Routing Information Protocol (RIP) Version 2 routers
224.0.0.10	EIGRP routers
224.0.0.11	Mobile-agents
224.0.0.12	DHCP server/relay agent
224.0.0.13	All PIM routers

▶

| TABLE 11-11 | Continued |

Well-known Class D address	Purpose
224.0.0.22	IGMP
224.0.1.1	Network Time Protocol (NTP)
224.0.1.2	SGI Dogfight
224.0.1.7	Audio news
224.0.1.11	IETF audio
224.0.1.12	IETF video

In addition to the reserved Class D addresses, the IANA owns a block of Ethernet addresses, which in hexadecimal start with *0000.5E*. This block is the high-order 24 bits of the Ethernet address, meaning that this block includes addresses in the range *0000.5E00.0000* through *0000.5EFF.FFFF*. The IANA allocates half of this block for multicast addresses. The first octet of any Ethernet address must be *01* to specify a multicast address (see Part I), then the Ethernet addresses corresponding to IP multicasting are in the range *0100.5E00.0000* through *0100.5E7F.FFFF*.

This allocation allows for 23 bits in the Ethernet MAC address to correspond to the IP multicast group ID (RFC 1112). The mapping places the low-order 23 bits of the multicast group ID into these 23 bits of the Ethernet address (see Figure 11.23). When a station sends a frame to an IP group that is identified by a Class D address, the station inserts the low-order 23 bits of the Class D address into the low-order 23 bits of the MAC-layer destination address. The top nine bits of the Class D address are not used. The top 25 bits of the MAC address are *0100.5E* followed by a zero, or, in binary: *00000001 00000000 01011110 0*.

FIGURE 11-23   Network layer to link layer multicast address mapping

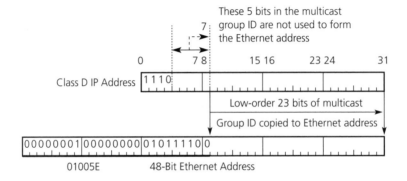

RFC WATCH   IP multicasting

RFC 1112 **Host Extensions for IP Multicasting**, 1989 (Standard)

Since the upper five bits of the multicast address are ignored in this mapping, the mapping is not unique. Thirty-two different multicast group IDs map to each Ethernet address. Since the mapping is not unique, the device driver or the IP modules must perform filtering, as it may receive multicast frames in which the host is really not interested.

Slightly different mapping occurs in the case of mapping an IP multicast address on a Token Ring MAC address. It would be highly desirable if Token Ring could use the same mapping as Ethernet and FDDI for IP multicast to hardware multicast addressing. However, current implementations of Token Ring controller chips cannot support this. As a reminder from Part I, Chapter 2 on LANs, a special subtype of group addresses are called functional addresses and are indicated by a Functional Address Indicator bit in the destination MAC address. There are a limited number of functional addresses, 31 in all, and therefore several unrelated functions must share the same functional address. Because there is a shortage of Token Ring functional addresses, all IP multicast addresses have been mapped to a single Token Ring functional address (RFC 1469). In canonical form, this address is *03-00-00-20-00-00*. In non-canonical form, it is *C0-00-00-04-00-00*. It should be noted that since there are only 31 possible functional addresses there may be other protocols that are assigned this functional address as well. Therefore, just because a frame is sent to the functional address *03-00-00-20-00-00* does not mean that it is an IP multicast frame.

RFC WATCH   IP multicast over Token Ring

RFC 1469 **IP Multicast over Token Ring Local Area Networks**, 1993 (Proposed Standard)

Using a MAC-layer multicast address optimizes network performance by allowing network interface cards (NICs) that are not part of a group to ignore a data stream that is not for them.

IP multicasting on a single physical network is simple. The sending process specifies a destination IP address that is a multicast address, and then the device driver converts this address to the corresponding Ethernet address and sends it. The receiving processes must notify their IP layers that they want to receive datagrams destined for a given multicast address, and the device driver must enable reception of these multicast frames. This process is handled by joining a multicast group.

When a multicast datagram is received by a host, it must deliver a copy to all the processes that belong to that group. This scenario is different from UDP, where a single process receives an incoming unicast UDP datagram. With multicast, it is possible for multiple processes on a given host to belong to the same multicast group.

The most important **requirements for supporting network multicast** are the following:

■ **Group establishment:**
  - **Multicast group address assignment mechanism** – before transmitting information to a group, there must be mechanisms that allow some hosts to be grouped under the same group identifier without conflict.
  - **group set-up** – apart from the unambiguous identification of a group, there must be other protocols allowing the allocation of an address for setting up a group. They should also allow the members of a group to know the address of the group they wish to join.

■ **Membership management** – allows hosts wishing to be part of a given group to join it, hosts wishing to end their membership to leave it or to switch from one group to another. Once the communication has been finished, some protocol must be defined to end the group communication, i.e. to carry out group tear-down. When extending multicasting beyond a single physical network, routers do not inherently forward multicast traffic, therefore a specific protocol must be implemented to instruct routers when to forward and when not to forward multicast traffic. This function is handled by the Internet Group Management Protocol IGMP (see next Section), which tells the router if any hosts on a given physical network belong to a given multicast group.

■ **Transport reliability** – depending on the characteristics of the information transmitted to the group, reliability will take the form of error recovery at the receivers or retransmissions in case of losses. When retransmission is not possible due to time constraints, error recovery mechanisms will use redundant information to recover some losses. On the other hand, retransmission will be used when the focus is on the correctness of the information transmitted regardless of the time it takes to be transmitted.

■ **Flow control** to adapt to network load – controls the information placed in the network per unit time and may therefore increase network efficiency by reducing the number of losses and consequent retransmissions.

■ **Efficient packet forwarding strategies** at network nodes – must be developed to allow all the above requirements to be fulfilled.

There are four **requirements for IP multicast implementations:**

■ both **sender and receiver** (operating systems and TCP/IP protocol stack) must support multicast and the IGMP protocol;
■ each host's network **adapter** drive must implement multicast;
■ **routers** and **switches** in the network must be multicast-capable;
■ **applications** must be multicast-enabled.

Internet group management protocol

IP dynamic registration is based on the **Internet Group Management Protocol** (IGMP, version 2, RFC 2236) which specifies how the host should inform the network that it is a member of a particular multicast group. IGMP, considered part of the IP layer, uses IP datagrams to transmit data. IGMP messages may be longer than eight octets, especially future backwards-compatible versions of IGMP, and are encapsulated in an IP datagram (see Figure 11.24). IGMP messages are specified in the IP datagram with a protocol value of 2.

FIGURE 11-24 IP datagram with IGMP messages

20 octets *≥ 8 octets*

IP header	IGMP message

RFC WATCH **IGMP**

RFC 2236 **Internet Group Management Protocol, Version 2**, 1997 (Proposed Standard)

RFC 2933 **Internet Group Management Protocol MIB**, 2000 (Proposed Standard)

A snapshot of router function in enabling network multicasting follows with more details later on. When a user starts an application that requires a host to **join a multicast group**, the host transmits a ***membership-report message*** to inform routers on the segment that traffic for the group should be multicast to the host's segment. In addition to allowing hosts to join groups, IGMP specifies that a multicast router should send an IGMP ***query*** out every interface at regular intervals to see if any hosts belong to the group. A host responds by sending an IGMP *membership-report* message for each group in which it is still a member. The main feature of IGMPv2 is the ability for a router to more quickly learn that the last host has left a group, which is important for high-bandwidth multicast groups and subnets with highly volatile group membership. The IGMP communication is shown in Figure 11.25.

In addition to determining which local network segments should receive traffic for particular multicast groups, a router must also learn how to route multicast traffic across an internet. Multicast routing protocols, such as DVMRP, MOSPF, and PIM (discussed in the next section), provide this function.

FIGURE 11-25 Overview of IGMP communication

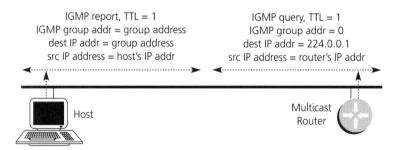

Like ICMP, IGMP is an integral part of the internet layer. It is required to be implemented by all hosts wishing to receive IP multicasts. All IGMP messages described here are sent with IP TTL 1, and contain the IP Router Alert option (RFC 2113) in their IP header.

RFC WATCH   **router alert**

RFC 2113 **IP Router Alert Option**, 1997 (Proposed Standard)

All IGMP messages of concern to hosts have the format shown in Figure 11.26.

FIGURE 11-26   IGMP message format

Number of bits:

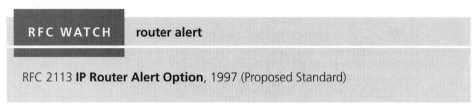

The fields in IGMPv2 message are as follows:

- *Types* – three message types are of concern to the host-router interaction:
  - hex11 = *Membership Query*. There are two sub-types of Membership Query messages: *General Query*, used to learn which groups have members on an attached network; and *Group-Specific Query*, used to learn if a particular group has any members on an attached network.
  - hex16 = *Version 2 Membership Report*.
  - hex17 = *Leave Group*.
  - There is an additional type of message, for backwards-compatibility with IGMPv1: bex12 = *Version 1 Membership Report*.

- *Maximum response time field* – only in *Membership Query* messages, this field specifies the maximum allowed time before sending a responding report in units of 1/10 second. In all other messages, it is set to zero by the sender and ignored by receivers.

- *Checksum* – 16-bit 1s complement of the 1s complement sum of the whole IGMP message (the entire IP payload). For computing the checksum, the checksum field is set to zero. When transmitting packets, the checksum must be computed and inserted into this field. When receiving packets, the checksum must be verified before processing a packet.

- *Group address* – in a *Membership Query message*, the field is set to zero when sending a *General Query*, and set to the group address being queried when sending a *Group-Specific Query*. In a *Membership Report* or *Leave Group* message, the group address field holds the IP multicast group address of the group being reported or left.

Fundamental to multicasting is the concept of a process joining a multicast group on a given interface on a host. Membership in a multicast group on a given interface is dynamic (that is, it changes over time as processes join and leave the group). Thus end users can dynamically join multicast groups based on the applications they execute.

Multicast routers use IGMP to learn which groups have members on each of their attached physical networks. A multicast router keeps a list of multicast group memberships for each attached network, and a timer for each membership. **Multicast group memberships** means the presence of at least one member of a multicast group on a given attached network, not a list of all of the members.

With respect to each of its attached networks, a multicast router may assume one of two roles: Querier or Non-Querier. There is normally only one **Querier** per physical network. All multicast routers start up as a Querier on each attached network. If a multicast router hears a *Query* message from a router with a lower IP address, it must become a **Non-Querier** on that network. If a router has not heard a *Query* message from another router for some time (*Other Querier Present Interval*), it resumes the role of Querier. Routers periodically send a *General Query* on each attached network for which this router is the Querier, to solicit membership information. On startup, a router should send *General Queries* spaced closely together in order to quickly and reliably determine membership information. A *General Query* is addressed to the all-systems multicast group (224.0.0.1), has a Group Address field of *0*, and has a *Maximum Response Time*.

IGMP messages are used by multicast routers to keep track of group membership on each of the router's physically attached networks. The following rules apply:

- Host sends an *IGMP report* when the first process joins a group. If multiple processes on a given host join the same group, only one report is sent the first time a process joins the group. This report is sent out on the same interface on which the process joined the group.

- Host does not send a *report* when processes leave a group, even when the last process leaves a group. The host knows that there are no members in a given group, so when it receives the next query, it will not report the group.

- Multicast router sends an IGMP query at regular intervals to see if any hosts still have processes belonging to any groups. The router must send one query out on each interface. The group address in the query is 0 since the router expects one response from a host for every group that contains one or more members on the host.

- Host responds to an IGMP query by sending one IGMP report for each group that still contains at least one process.

Using these queries and reports, a multicast router keeps a table (forwarding cache) of which of its interfaces have one or more hosts in a multicast group. When the router receives a multicast datagram to forward, it forwards the datagram (using the corresponding multicast link layer address) out only the interfaces that still have hosts with processes belonging to that group. Specifically, a router forwards packets received on its upstream interface to each downstream interface based upon the downstream interface's subscriptions and whether or not this router is the IGMP Querier on each interface. A router forwards packets received on any downstream interface to the upstream interface, and to each downstream interface other than the incoming interface based upon the downstream interface's subscriptions and whether or not this router is the *IGMP Querier* on each interface. A router may use a forwarding cache in order not to make this decision for each packet, but must update the cache using these rules any time any of the information used to build it changes.

Since only the *Querier* forwards packets, the IGMP Querier election process may lead to black holes if a non-forwarder is elected *Querier*. An attacker on a downstream LAN can cause itself to get elected Querier resulting in no packets being forwarded.

The Time-to-Live (TTL) field of the reports and queries is set to 1, referring to the normal TTL field in the IP header. A multicast datagram with an initial TTL of 0 is restricted to the same host. By default, multicast datagrams are sent with a TTL set to 1, restricting the datagram to the same subnet. Higher TTLs can be forwarded by multicast routers. By increasing the TTL, an application can perform an expanding search for a particular server. The first multicast datagram is sent with a TTL of 1. If no response is received, a TTL of 2 is tried, then 3, and so on. In this way the application locates the closest server, in terms of hops. The special range of addresses 224.0.0.0 through 224.0.0.255 is intended for applications that never need to multicast further than one hop. A multicast router should never forward a datagram with one of these addresses as the destination, regardless of the TTL.

There exists a proposal for Version 3 of the Internet Group Management Protocol, **IGMPv3**. Version 3 of IGMP adds support for source filtering, that is the ability for a system to report interest in receiving packets only from specific source addresses, or from all but specific source addresses, sent to a particular multicast address. That information may be used by multicast routing protocols to avoid delivering multicast packets from specific sources to networks where there are no interested receivers.

11.6.3 IP multicast routing protocols

IP multicast traffic flows from the source to the multicast group over a **distribution tree** that connects all of the sources to all of the receivers in the group. This tree may be shared by all sources (a shared tree), or a separate distribution tree can be built for each source (a source tree). The shared tree may be one-way or bidirectional. Applications send one copy of each packet using a multicast address, and the network forwards the packets to only those networks, LANs, that have receivers.

Source trees are constructed with a single path between the source and every LAN that has receivers. They build an optimal shortest-path tree rooted at the source. Each source/group pair requires its own state information, so for groups with a very large number of sources, or networks that have a very large number of groups with a large number of sources in each group, the use of source-based trees can stress the storage capability of routers.

Shared trees are constructed so that all sources use a common distribution tree. Shared trees use a single location in the network to which all packets from all sources are sent and from which all packets are sent to all receivers. Shared distribution trees are formed around a central router, called a **rendezvous point** or core, from which all traffic is distributed regardless of the location of the traffic sources. The advantage of shared distribution trees is that they do not create lots of source/group states in the routers. The disadvantage is that the path from a particular source to the receivers may be much longer, which may be important for delay-sensitive applications. The rendezvous router may also be a traffic bottleneck if there are many high data rate sources.

The distribution trees are obviously (as graph theory dictates) **loop-free**. Messages are replicated only when the tree branches. Members of multicast groups can join or leave at any time, so the distribution tree must be dynamically updated. Branches with no listeners are discarded (pruned). The type of distribution tree used and the way multicast routers interact depend on the objectives of the routing protocol, including receiver distribution, number of sources, reliability of data delivery, speed of network convergence, shared path or source path, and if shared path, direction of data flow.

Distribution of receivers

One criterion to determine what type of tree to use relates to whether receivers are sparsely or densely distributed throughout the network (for example, whether almost all of the routers in the network have group members on their directly attached subnetworks). If the network has receivers or members on every subnet or the receivers are closely spaced, they have a dense distribution. If the receivers are on only a few subnets and are widely spaced, they have a sparse distribution. The number of receivers does not matter; the determining factor is how close the receivers are to each other and the source.

Sparse-mode protocols use **explicit join messages** to set up distribution trees so that tree state is set up only on routers on the distribution tree and data packets are forwarded to only those LANs that have hosts who join the group. Sparse-mode protocols are thus also appropriate for large internets where dense-mode protocols would waste bandwidth by flooding packets to all parts of the internet and then pruning back unwanted connections. Sparse-mode protocols may build either shared trees or source trees or both types of distribution trees. Sparse-mode protocols may be best compared to a magazine subscription since the distribution tree is never built unless a receiver joins (subscribes) to the group.

Dense-mode protocols build only **source-distribution trees**. Dense mode protocols determine the location of receivers by **flooding data** throughout the network and then explicitly **pruning** off branches that do not have receivers, therefore creating a distribution state on every router in the network. Dense-mode protocols may use fewer control messages to set up a state rather than sparse-mode protocols, and they may be able to guarantee better delivery of data to at least some group members in the event of some network failures. Dense-mode protocols may be compared to junk mail in that every network will receive a copy of the data whether they want it or not.

> QUICK TIP   **dense-mode multicast routing protocols**
>
> Dense-mode routing protocols assume that the multicast group members are densely distributed throughout the network and bandwidth is plentiful, i.e. almost all hosts on the network belong to the group. Dense-mode routing protocols are Distance Vector Multicast Routing Protocol (DVMRP), Multicast Open Shortest Path First (MOSPF), and Protocol-Independent Multicast – Dense Mode (PIM-DM).

Multicast routing protocols

IP multicast routing is supported by several protocols (compared in Table 11.12 on p. 559 in various stages of the IETF standardization process), all using UDP, with a common goal to establish paths in the network so that multicast traffic can effectively reach all group members:

- **Distance Vector Multicast Routing Protocol** (DVMRP) (RFC 1075) – multicast routing protocol based on the distance vector algorithm.
- **Multicast OSPF (MOSPF) Protocol** (RFC 1584) – an extension to OSPF that allows it to support IP multicast.
- **Protocol Independent Multicast** (PIM) sparse mode (RFC 2362) – a multicast protocol that can be used in conjunction with all unicast IP routing protocols, PIM dense mode operation is currently drafted.
- **Core Based Tree** (CBT) (RFC 2201) – distribution tree multicast protocol.

Latest proposals (still in the form of Internet Drafts) for multicast routing are:

- **Pragmatic General Multicast (PGM);**
- **Multicast Border Gateway Protocol (MBGP);**
- **Multicast Source Discovery Protocol (MSDP);**
- **Source Specific Multicast (SSM);**
- **Internet Protocol Multicast (IPM).**

RFC WATCH   **multicast routing protocols**

RFC 1075 **Distance Vector Multicast Routing Protocol**, 1988 (Experimental)

RFC 1584 **Multicast Extensions to OSPF**, 1994 (Proposed Standard)

RFC 2201 **Core Based Trees (CBT) Multicast Routing Architecture**, 1997
(Experimental)

RFC 2362 **Protocol Independent Multicast – Sparse Mode (PIM-SM): Protocol
Specification**, 1998 (Experimental)

RFC 2909 **The Multicast Address-Set Claim (MASC) Protocol**, 2000 (Experimental)

Reverse path forwarding

Reverse Path Forwarding (RPF) is an algorithm used for forwarding multicast
datagrams. The algorithm works as follows:

- The packet has arrived on the RPF interface if a router receives it on an
  interface that it uses to send unicast packets to the source.
- If the packet arrives on the RPF interface, the router forwards it out the
  interfaces that are present in the outgoing interface list of a multicast routing
  table entry.
- If the packet does not arrive on the RPF interface, the packet is silently
  discarded to avoid loop-backs.

If a PIM router has source tree state, it does the RPF check using the source IP
address of the multicast packet. If a PIM router has shared tree state, it uses the
RPF check on the rendezvous point's (RP) address (which is known when members join the group). Sparse-mode PIM uses the RPF lookup function to determine
where it needs to send *Joins* and *Prunes*. Shared-tree state *Joins* are sent towards
the RP. Source-tree state *Joins* are sent towards the source.

DVMRP and PIM-DM groups use only source-rooted trees and make use of
RPF forwarding as described above. MOSPF does not necessarily use RPF since it
can compute both forward and reverse shortest path source-rooted trees by using
the Dijkstra computation.

Distance vector multicast routing protocol

The Distance Vector Multicast Routing Protocol (DVMRP, RFC 1075) uses a technique known as **Reverse Path Forwarding**. When a router receives a packet, it
floods the packet out of all paths except the one that leads back to the packet's
source. Doing so allows a datastream to reach all LANs (possibly multiple times).
If a router is attached to a set of LANs that do not want to receive a particular
multicast group, the router can send a *prune* message back up the distribution
tree to stop subsequent packets from traveling where there are no members.

DVMRP periodically repeats floods in order to reach any new hosts that want
to receive a particular group. There is a direct relationship between the time it
takes for a new receiver to get the datastream and the frequency of flooding.

DVMRP implements its own **unicast routing protocol** in order to determine which interface leads back to the source of the datastream. This unicast routing protocol is very much like Routing Information Protocol (RIP) and is based purely on hop counts. As a result, the path that the multicast traffic follows may not be the same as the path that the unicast traffic follows.

DVMRP has significant **scaling problems** because of the necessity to flood frequently, a limitation that is exacerbated by the fact that early implementations of DVMRP did not implement pruning. As a result, DVMRP typically uses tunneling mechanisms to control flooding (tunnels are a way of short-cutting through a potentially large tree towards the destination) and, in some cases, the lack of pruning. Fixed tunnels are used also to traverse non-multicast areas. The tunnel source and destination are multicast routers which encapsulate/decapsulate multicast datagrams within unicast IP datagrams. The tunnel, a virtual link, supports regular IP traffic transparent to intervening non-multicast routers. Since the virtual link is a single hop long, multicast routers forward multicast datagrams via it only if their TTL values exceed a certain threshold (to limit their scope).

SNAPSHOT	Distance Vector Multicast Routing Protocol (DVMRP)

The first protocol developed to support multicast routing and used extensively on the MBONE. The approach used by DVMRP is to assume initially that every host on the network is part of the multicast group. Multicast messages are transmitted over every possible router interface as they proceed across the network, forming a spanning tree to all possible members of the multicast group. DVMRP maintains a current image of the network topology using a distance vector routing protocol such as the RIP. The distance metric used for RIP and DVMRP is the number of hops in the path. DVMRP uses source-routed trees.

DVMRP has been used to build the **MBONE** (a multicast backbone across the public Internet – see below) by building tunnels between DVMRP-capable machines. Networks that wish to participate in the MBONE dedicate special hosts to the MBONE. The hosts establish tunnels to each other over the IP Internet and run DVMRP over the tunnels. The MBONE is a very high consumer of bandwidth both because of the nature of the traffic (audio and video) and because it is implemented with host-based tunnels. Host-based tunnels tend to result in packet duplication, which the backbone networks transmit unnecessarily. The MBONE is used widely in the research community to transmit the proceedings of various conferences and to permit desktop conferencing.

Multicast extensions to OSPF

Multicast Extensions to OSPF (MOSPF), a proposed IETF standard (RFC 1584), was defined as an extension to the OSPF unicast routing protocol (and works only in OSPF routed internets). MOSPF includes multicast information in OSPF link-state advertisements. An MOSPF router learns which multicast groups are active on which LANs.

MOSPF builds a **distribution tree** for each source/group pair and computes a tree for active sources sending to the group. The tree states are cached on all routers, because MOSPF uses source-routed trees, not shared trees. The trees must be recomputed when a link-state change occurs or when the cache times out. The tree recomputation is also necessary when parts of the tree get pruned. This eventuality in turn can hinder multicast performance, depending upon the size of the network and the volatility of the multicast groups.

SNAPSHOT **Multicast Open Shortest Path First (MOSPF)**

The MOSPF routing protocol is the IP Multicast extension of the Open Shortest Path First (OSPF) unicast routing protocol. OSPF routes messages along least-cost paths, where cost is expressed in terms of a link-state metric, as opposed to hops, used by RIP and DVMRP. Each router can calculate a spanning tree with the multicast source at the root and the group members as leaves. This tree is the path that is used to route multicast traffic from the source to each of the group members.

With MOSPF, datagrams are only propagated when actually needed, as opposed to DVMRP. MOSPF is best suited for environments that have relatively few source/group pairs active at any given time. It will work less well in environments that have many active sources or environments that have unstable links.

When mixing MOSPF and non-multicast routers on a LAN, a MOSPF router should become a designated router. Otherwise multicast datagrams will not be forwarded on the LAN, nor will group membership be monitored, nor will the group membership LSA be flooded over the LAN. This can be arranged by assigning the priority 0 to non-multicast routers attached to the multi-access broadcast network, so that they are disqualified as DR candidates.

QUICK TIP **MOSPF**

MOSPF complements OSPF's capability to develop a link-state database that describes a network topology. MOSPF supplements the database with an additional type of link-state record for group memberships.

Protocol independent multicast protocol

Unlike MOSPF, which is OSPF-dependent, the **Protocol Independent Multicast** protocol (PIM) was designed to work with all existing IP unicast routing protocols. And unlike DVMRP, which has inherent scaling problems, PIM offers **two different types of multipoint traffic distribution patterns** to address multicast routing scalability: dense mode and sparse mode. Sparse-mode PIM has become an experimental protocol, while dense-mode PIM operation is still in the drafting phase.

SNAPSHOT	Protocol Independent Multicast (PIM)

The PIM collaborates with IGMP and is not dependent on the unicast routing protocols such as OSPF, RIP, and Enhanced IGRP. PIM has two modes: dense mode and sparse mode. The denomination 'dense' and 'sparse' refer to the density of group members.

PIM **dense mode** is most useful when:

- senders and receivers are in close proximity to one another;
- there are few senders and many receivers;
- the volume of multicast traffic is high;
- the stream of multicast traffic is constant.

Dense-mode PIM uses **reverse path forwarding** and operates in a similar way to DVMRP. The most significant difference between DVMRP and dense-mode PIM is that PIM works with whatever unicast protocol is being used; PIM does not require any particular unicast protocol. In dense mode (see Figure 11.27), PIM floods the network and prunes back based on multicast group member information. In a LAN TV multicast environment, for instance, dense mode would be effective because there is a high probability that there will be group members off all subnets. Flooding the network thus will be effective because little pruning would have been necessary. In the example shown in Figure 11.27, the bottom middle router sends prune to its right parent because the router already gets a feed from its left parent. In a second stage, the middle-right router would prune the tree from the upper router completely, since it does not require any kind of multicast traffic then.

QUICK TIP	PIM dense mode

- Broadcast and joins.
- Senders and receivers in close proximity.
- Few senders, many receivers.

FIGURE 11-27 PIM dense-mode operation

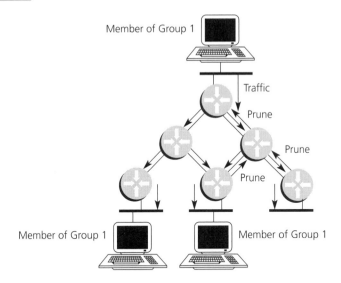

Member of Group 1

Traffic

Prune

Prune

Prune

Prune

Member of Group 1

Member of Group 1

PIM **sparse mode** (**PIM-SM**) (experimental RFC 2362) is most useful when:

- there are few receivers in a group;
- senders and receivers are separated by WAN links;
- the type of traffic is intermittent.

Sparse-mode PIM (see Figure 11.28) is optimized for environments where there are many multipoint datastreams and each multicast stream goes to a relatively small number of the LANs in the internet. For these types of groups, Reverse Path Forwarding techniques make inefficient use of the network bandwidth. Sparse-mode PIM works by defining a **Rendezvous Point**. When a sender wants to send data, it first sends it to the Rendezvous Point and when a receiver wants to receive data, it registers with the Rendezvous Point. Once the datastream begins to flow from sender to Rendezvous Point to receiver, the routers in the path optimize the path automatically to remove any unnecessary hops. Sparse-mode PIM assumes that no hosts want the multicast traffic unless they specifically ask for it.

PIM-SM is centered on a single, unidirectional shared tree. The root of the tree is the RP. In a shared tree, sources must send the multicast traffic to the root (RP) for the traffic to reach all receivers.

PIM sparse mode can be used for any combination of sources and receivers, whether densely or sparsely populated, including topologies where senders and receivers are separated by WAN links, and/or when the stream of multicast traffic is intermittent. Among the strengths of PIM-SM are the following:

- **Independent of unicast routing protocols** – PIM can be deployed in conjunction with any unicast routing protocol.
- **Explicit-join** – PIM-SM assumes that no hosts want the multicast traffic unless they specifically ask for it. It creates a shared distribution tree centered

FIGURE 11-28 PIM sparse-mode operation

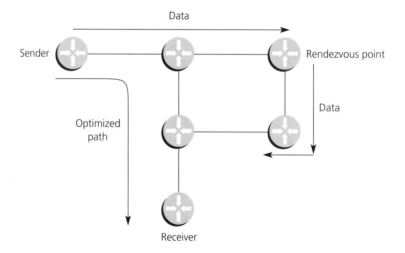

on a defined 'rendezvous point' (RP) from which source traffic is relayed to the receivers. Senders first send the data to the RP, and the receiver's last-hop router sends a join message toward the RP (explicit join).

■ **Scalable** – PIM-SM scales well to a network of any size including those with WAN links. PIM-SM domains can be efficiently and easily connected together using MBGP and MSDP to provide a native multicast service over the Internet.

■ **Flexible** – a receiver's last-hop router can switch from a PIM-SM shared tree to a source tree or shortest-path distribution tree whenever conditions warrant it, thus combining the best features of explicit-join, shared-tree and source-tree protocols.

QUICK TIP   **PIM sparse mode**

■ Explicit join.
■ Few receivers in multicast group.

Core based tree

Core Based Tree (CBT) multicasting (experimental RFC 2201) is similar to sparse-mode PIM. It builds a single distribution tree with one focal router, the core router. Multicast traffic for the entire group is sent and received over the same tree, regardless of the source. The use of shared tree can provide significant savings for applications that have many active senders.

> **QUICK TIP** **core based tree protocols**
>
> Unlike DVMRP or MOSPF, which construct spanning trees for each source/group pair, the CBT protocol constructs a single tree that is shared by all members of the group. Multicast traffic for the entire group is sent and received over the same tree, regardless of the source. A CBT shared tree has a small number of core routers (called cores) that are used to construct the tree. Other routers may join the tree by sending a join message to the core.

11.6.4 Comparison of major IP multicast routing protocols

Table 11.12 compares the characteristics of each routing protocol when handling multicast traffic.

TABLE 11-12 Comparison of multicast routing protocols

Multicast routing protocol	Unicast routing protocol requirements	Flooding algorithm	Tree type	Network application environment
DVMRP	RIP	Reverse path flooding	Source	Small
MOSPF	OSPF	Shortest path first	Source	Few senders, stable links
PIM dense mode	Any	Reverse path flooding	Source	Dense distribution pattern
PIM sparse mode	Any	None	Both	Sparse distribution pattern

Note on multicast scalability

There are certain **scalability** issues with multicast. However, the solution to this is to have a very good inter-domain multicast routing as well as intra-domain multicast routing protocols. With that the problem of the host affecting the entire routing core is greatly reduced. The protocols like CBT and PIM-SM were developed because it was found that protocols like DVMRP and PIM-DM cannot scale. It is also necessary to note the fact that PIM-SM is only efficient for sparsely distributed hosts and it is a receiver-initiated protocol. This has significant advantage over flood and prune protocols like DVMRP.

11.6.5 Multicast extensions

There are various new proposals for multicast routing, all only in drafts, therefore the following text should be treated as related to work in progress.

PIM extension

Source-Specific Multicast (SSM) addresses concern several aspects of multicast services such as IP-based TV and *n*-party conferences. SSM has been proposed to overcome the deployment limitations of PIM-SM such as handling of well-known sources, access control, and address allocation. IP addresses in the 232/8 (232.0.0.0 to 232.255.255.255) range are (currently) designated as source-specific multicast (SSM) destination addresses and are reserved for use by source-specific applications and protocols. The semantics of source-specific multicast addresses and the policies governing their use is proposed. The draft defines an extension to the Internet network service that applies to datagrams sent to SSM addresses and defines the host and router requirements to support this extension.

SSM breaks with traditional concepts: an IP-based TV-broadcast's delivery tree will be identified by the source address S and a multicast-ID provided by S. The same shall apply to each from n well-correlated point-to-$(n-1)$ point delivery trees of a small n-party conference. Consequently, a TV-host may send out more than one program and any user-host may participate in more than one conference.

Mapping to a globally unique multicast group address is not needed, would be complex, and does not work. QoS/Policy-Routing, the degree of state (Layer 3, Layer 3 plus MPLS-label, or no state), and several more aspects need to be respected homogeneously all over the entire delivery tree. This cannot be provided by reverse path setup while depending on each receiver's guesses. Therefore the tree (i.e. an initial tree as well as additional branches at a later time) must be established in the downstream direction. No RP routers are required. However, current SSM work seems to neglect some other deployment issues such as the construction of the shortest-path tree especially in inter-domain. The routing table entries for constructing the SSM tree proportionally increase depending on the number of sources and groups.

PIM interconnect

The **Multicast Source Discovery Protocol** (MSDP) describes a mechanism to **connect multiple PIM-SM domains** together. Each PIM-SM domain uses its own independent RP(s) and does not have to depend on RPs in other domains. MSDP connects multiple PIM-SM domains. The RP in each domain establishes an MSDP peering session using a TCP connection with the RPs in other domains or with border routers leading to the other domains.

When the RP learns about a new multicast source within its own domain (through the normal PIM register mechanism), the RP encapsulates the first data packet in a Session Advertisement (SA) and sends the SA to all MSDP peers. The SA is forwarded by each receiving peer using a modified RPF check, until it reaches every MSDP router in the internet. If the MSDP peer is an RP, and the RP has a (*,G) entry for the group in the SA, the RP will create (S,G) state for the source and join to the shortest path for the source. The encapsulated packet is decapsulated and forwarded down that RP's shared tree. When the packet is received by a receiver's last hop router, the last hop may also join the shortest path to the source. The source's RP periodically sends SAs which include all sources within that RP's own domain. MSDP peers may be configured to cache SAs to reduce join latency when a new receiver joins a group within the cache.

Inter-domain multicast routing protocol

The **Multicast Border Gateway Protocol** (MBGP) is a protocol for **inter-domain multicast routing**. MBGP builds shared trees for active multicast groups, and allows receiver domains to build source-specific, inter-domain, distribution branches where needed. Building upon concepts from CBT and PIM-SM, MBGP requires that each multicast group be associated with a single root (in MBGP it is referred to as the root domain). It offers a method for providers to distinguish which prefixes they will use for performing multicast reverse path forwarding (RPF) checks. The RPF check is fundamental in establishing multicast forwarding trees and moving multicast content successfully from source to receiver(s). MBGP assumes that at any point in time, different ranges of the class D space are associated (e.g. with MASC) with different domains. Each of these domains then becomes the root of the **shared domain trees** for all groups in its range. Multicast participants will generally receive better multicast service if the session initiator's address allocator selects addresses from its own domain's part of the space, thereby causing the root domain to be local to at least one of the session participants. MBGP is a basic way to carry two sets of routes: one set for unicast routing and one set for multicast routing. MBGP provides the control necessary to decide where multicast packets are allowed to flow. The routes associated with multicast routing are used by PIM to build data distribution trees. MBGP provides the RPF path, not the creation of multicast state. PIM is still needed to forward the multicast packets.

Reliable multicast

Pragmatic General Multicast (PGM) is a **reliable multicast transport protocol** for applications that require ordered or unordered, duplicate-free, multicast data delivery from multiple sources to multiple receivers. PGM guarantees that a receiver in the group either receives all data packets from transmissions and repairs, or is able to detect unrecoverable data packet loss. PGM is specifically intended as a workable solution for multicast applications with basic reliability requirements. Its central design goal is simplicity of operation with due regard for scalability and network efficiency.

Reliable multicast protocols overcome the limitations of unreliable multicast datagram delivery and expand the use of IP multicast. IP multicast is based on UDP in which no acknowledgments are returned to the sender. The sender therefore does not know if the data it sends are being received, and the receiver cannot request that lost or corrupted packets be retransmitted. Multimedia audio and video applications generally do not require reliable multicast, since these transmissions are tolerant of a low level of loss. However, some multicast applications require reliable delivery.

Some elements that are relevant to deciding whether reliable multicast is applicable include the degree of reliability required, requirements for bandwidth and for ordered packet delivery, the burstiness of data, delay tolerance, timing (realtime vs. non-realtime), the network infrastructure (LAN, WAN, Internet, satellite, dial-up), heterogeneity of links in the distribution tree, router capabilities, number of senders and size of multicast group, scalability, and group setup protocol.

Implementation of PGM uses negative-acknowledgments to provide a reliable multicast transport for applications that require ordered, duplicate-free, multicast data delivery from multiple sources to multiple receivers. PGM guarantees that a receiver in the group either receives all data packets from transmissions and retransmissions, or is able to detect unrecoverable data packet loss. PGM is specifically intended as a workable solution for multicast applications with basic reliability requirements. Its central design goal is simplicity of operation with due regard for scalability and network efficiency.

Reliable multicast will be useful in areas where loss is not tolerated or where a high-degree of fidelity is required, as for example in such areas as bulk data transfer, inventory updates, financial stock quotes, data conferencing, hybrid broadcasting (whiteboard), software distribution, push (webserver content), data replication, caching, and distributed simulation. Reliable multicast applications are also frequently deployed over satellite networks with terrestrial (e.g. Internet) back channels.

Internet protocol multicast

Internet Protocol Multicast (IPM) is an extension of internet routing that permits efficient many-to-many communications and is used extensively for multimedia conferencing. Multicast traffic tends to fall into one of two categories: traffic that is intended for almost all LANs (known as dense) and traffic that is intended for relatively few LANs (known as sparse).

11.6.6 The multicast backbone

The **Multicast backbone** (MBONE – http://www.mbone.com) is a very important component when transmitting audio and video over the Internet. The MBONE is a virtual network layered on top of portions of the physical Internet to support routing of IP multicast packets since that function has not yet been integrated into many production routers.

IP multicast packets are encapsulated for transmission through tunnels, so that they look like normal unicast datagrams to intervening routers and subnets. A multicast router that wants to send a multicast packet across a tunnel will prepend another IP header, set the destination address in the new header to be the unicast address of the multicast router at the other end of the tunnel, and set the IP protocol field in the new header to be 4 (which means the next protocol is IP). The multicast router at the other end of the tunnel receives the packet, strips off the encapsulating IP header, and forwards the packet as appropriate.

MBONE originated from the first two IETF 'audiocast' experiments with live audio and video multicast from the IETF meeting site to destinations around the world. The whole concept is to construct a semi-permanent IP multicast testbed to carry the IETF transmissions and support continued experimentation between meetings, which, by the way, is a cooperative, volunteer effort.

Topologically, the MBONE network is composed of islands linked by virtual point-to-point links, or tunnels. The tunnel endpoints are typically workstation-class machines having operating system support for IP multicast and running the *mrouted* multicast routing daemon.

To join the MBONE is not complicated: provide one IP multicast router to connect with tunnels to users and other participants. This multicast router will usually be separate from the main production router, as most of these routers do not support multicast. Workstations will need to have the *mrouted* program running. A dedicated workstation should be allocated for the multicast routing function. This will prevent other activities from interfering with the multicast transmission.

11.7 Mobile IP issues

The main idea behind mobile IP development is the need to preserve the IP address of the mobile host, by having other clients go through a home base station, which will relay all the traffic to the (tracked) mobile station, i.e. to a possibly frequently changing care-of address. Mobile IP can be thought of as the cooperation of three major subsystems. First, there is a **discovery mechanism** defined so that mobile computers can determine their new attachment points (new IP addresses) as they move from place to place within the Internet. Second, once the mobile computer knows the IP address at its new attachment point, it registers with an agent representing it at its home network. Lastly, mobile IP defines simple mechanisms to deliver datagrams to the mobile node when it is away from its home network. The IETF proposed two linked standards (RFC 2002 and 2005) with respect to IP mobility issues.

IP MOBILITY	multihoming and BGP

RFC 2002 **IP Mobility Support**, 1996 (Proposed Standard)

RFC 2005 **Applicability Statement for IP Mobility Support**, 1996 (Proposed Standard)

Some attempts have been made to manage the movement of Internet stations by less functional methods. It is possible with deployment of DHCP for a mobile node to get an IP address at every new point of attachment. This will work fine until the mobile node moves somewhere else. Then the old address will no longer be of use, and the node will have to get another one. Unfortunately, this approach usually also means that every established IP client on the mobile node will stop working, so the mobile node will have to restart its Internet subsystems.

Mobile IP is a way of performing three related functions:

■ **agent discovery** – mobility agents advertise their availability on each link for which they provide service;

■ **registration** – when the mobile node is away from home, it registers its care-of address with its home agent;

■ **tunneling** – in order for datagrams to be delivered to the mobile node when it is away from home, the home agent has to tunnel the datagrams to the care-of address.

Mobility agents make themselves known by sending *agent advertisement* messages. An impatient mobile node may optionally solicit an agent advertisement message. After receiving an *agent advertisement*, a mobile node determines whether it is on its home network or a foreign network. A mobile node basically works like any other node on its home network when it is at home. When a mobile node moves away from its home network, it obtains a care-of address on the foreign network, for instance by soliciting or listening for *agent advertisements*, or contacting a Dynamic Host Configuration Protocol (DHCP) server. While away from home, the mobile node registers each new care-of address with its home agent, possibly by way of a **foreign agent**. Datagrams sent to the mobile node's home address are intercepted by its **home agent**, tunneled by its home agent to the care-of address, received at the tunnel endpoint (at either a foreign agent or the mobile node itself), and finally delivered to the mobile node. In the reverse direction, datagrams sent by the mobile node are generally delivered to their destination using standard IP routing mechanisms, not necessarily passing through the home agent. This is a typical example of **asymmetric routing**. The mobile host must be careful not to use its temporary care-of address as a source address when sending datagrams to others. It should use its regular (home-base) address, so that replies can reach it, even if it has moved in the meantime to yet another care-of address. The receiving node should never see the care-of address of the mobile host, only its home-base address. The routers in the guest-domain should route datagrams with foreign source addresses as well (should not block them), so that the above mechanism works.

An example of a tunnel from a home router (home agent) to the current location of a mobile node (foreign agent) is shown in Figure 11.29. A mobile IP datagram flow is shown in Figure 11.30.

FIGURE 11-29 Mobile IP – tunnel between home and foreign agent

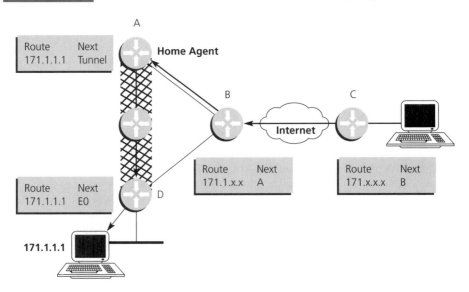

FIGURE 11-30 Mobile IP datagram flow

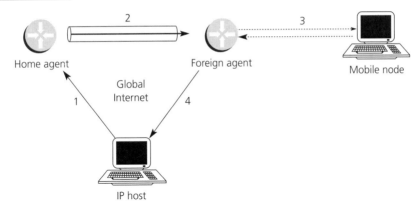

Figure 11.30 illustrates the routing of datagrams to and from a mobile node away from home, once the mobile node has registered with its home agent. The mobile node is presumed to be using a care-of address provided by the foreign agent:

1 Datagram to the mobile node arrives on the home network via standard IP routing.
2 Datagram is intercepted by the home agent and is tunneled to the care-of address, as depicted by the arrow going through the tube.
3 Datagram is taken from the tunnel and delivered to the mobile node.
4 For datagrams sent by the mobile node, standard IP routing delivers each to its destination. In Figure 11.30 the foreign agent is the mobile node's default router.

When the home agent **tunnels** a datagram to the care-of address, the inner IP header destination (i.e. the mobile node's home address) is effectively shielded from intervening routers between its home network and its current location. At the care-of address, the original datagram exits from the tunnel and is delivered to the mobile node. It is the job of every home agent to attract and intercept datagrams that are destined to the home address of any of its registered mobile nodes. The home agent basically does this by using a minor variation on the proxy

---

SNAPSHOT   **mobile IP operation**

- Mobile node discovers agent.
- Mobile node obtains care-of address.
- Mobile node registers with home agent.
- Home agent tunnels packets from correspondent node to mobile node.
- Foreign agent forwards packets from mobile node to correspondent node.

Address Resolution Protocol (ARP), and to do so in the natural model it has to have a network interface on the link indicated by the mobile node's home address. However, the latter requirement is not part of the mobile IP specification.

When foreign agents are in use, in a similar way the natural model of operation suggests that the mobile node should be able to establish a link to its foreign agent. Other configurations are possible, however, using protocol operations not defined by (and invisible to) the mobile IP. Notice that, if the home agent is the only router advertising reachability to the home network but there is no physical link instantiating the home network, then all datagrams transmitted to mobile nodes addressed on that home network will naturally reach the home agent without any special link operations.

11.7.1 Mobile IP routing and tunneling

The home agent, after a successful registration, will begin to attract datagrams destined for the mobile node and tunnel each one to the mobile node at its care-of address. The tunneling can be done by one of several encapsulation algorithms, but the default algorithm that must always be supported is simple IP-within-IP encapsulation (RFC 2003). Encapsulation is a very general technique used for many different reasons, including multicast, multiprotocol operations, authentication, privacy, defeating traffic analysis, and general policy routing.

RFC WATCH	IP in IP

RFC 2003 **IP Encapsulation within IP**, 1996 (Proposed Standard)

In the case of mobile IP, the values of the fields in the new IP header are selected naturally, with the care-of address used as the destination IP address in the tunnel header. The encapsulating IP header indicates the presence of the encapsulated IP datagram by using the value 4 in the outer protocol field. The inner header is not modified except to decrement the TTL by 1.

Alternatively, minimal encapsulation can be used as long as the mobile node, home agent, and foreign agent (if present) all agree to do so. IP-within-IP uses a few more octets per datagram than minimal encapsulation, but allows fragmentation at the home agent when needed to deal with tunnels with smaller path maximum transmission units (MTUs). The minimal encapsulation header fits in the same relative location within the encapsulated payload, as indicated by the old IP header. The presence of the minimal encapsulation header is indicated by using protocol number 55 in the encapsulating IP header protocol field. The length of the minimal header is either 12 or 8 octets, depending on whether the original source IP address is present, and it includes the following fields:

- *Protocol* – copied from the protocol field in the original IP header.
- *Original source address present* (S) – if 1, the original source address field (below) is present; otherwise, it is not.

- **Reserved** – sent as zero; ignored on reception.
- **Header checksum** – the 16-bit 1s complement of the 1s complement sum of all 16-bit words in the minimal forwarding header. For purposes of computing the checksum, the value of the checksum field is 0. The IP header and IP payload (after the minimal forwarding header) are not included in this checksum computation.
- **Original destination address** – copied from the destination address field in the original IP header.
- **Original source address** – copied from the source address field in the original IP header. This field is present only if the original source address present (S) bit is set.

11.7.2 Route optimization

As noted above, datagrams going to the mobile node have to travel through the home agent when the mobile node is away from home, but datagrams from the mobile node to other stationary Internet nodes can instead be routed directly to their destinations. This asymmetric routing, called **triangle routing** (see Figure 11.31), is generally far from optimal, especially in cases when the correspondent node is very close to the mobile node.

FIGURE 11-31 Mobile IP – triangle routing

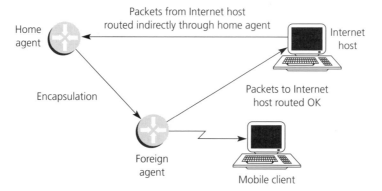

The advantages of route optimization are clear. The disadvantage is that, for the first time, and in major distinction to the base mobile IP protocol, changes are required in the correspondent nodes. The basic idea underlying route optimization is that the routes to mobile nodes from their correspondent nodes can be improved if the correspondent node has an up-to-date mobility binding for the mobile node in its routing table. Most of the proposed protocol described below is geared toward providing such an updated mobility binding (usually shortened to just binding) to correspondent nodes that need them. With an updated binding, the correspondent node will be able to send encapsulated datagrams directly to the mobile node's care-of address instead of relying on a possibly distant home agent to do so.

Every aspect of the design is influenced by the need to allow the correspondent nodes to be sure of the **authenticity** of the updates. Mobile computer users would not be very satisfied if their traffic were easily hijacked, and their very mobility increases the likelihood that aspects of network security at their point of attachment may be inadequate. We also have to keep in mind that a majority of such nodes, today, will not be able to understand the protocol.

The current unsatisfactory state of security within the Internet, and especially the lack of key distribution protocols, has determined several further aspects of the design of the route optimization protocols. Correspondent nodes seem more likely to maintain security relationships with home agents than with individual mobile nodes. The protocol is designed so that the home agent is responsible for providing binding updates to any concerned correspondent nodes at foreign enterprises. Briefly, the protocol operates in as many as four steps:

- a binding warning control message may be sent to the home agent, indicating a correspondent node that seems unaware of the mobile node's care-of address;
- the correspondent node may send a binding request;
- the home agent (typically) may send an authenticated binding update containing the mobile node's current care-of address;
- for smooth handoffs (sixth section), the mobile node transmits a binding update and has to be certain that the update was received. Thus it can request a binding acknowledgment from the recipient.

The sending agent must be careful not to blindly send the messages without regard to past history. If the message has been sent recently, and seemingly has had no effect, the natural conclusion can be drawn that the intended recipient does not understand route optimization protocol messages. Therefore, the sender is obligated to send those messages less frequently in the future, or perhaps not at all. The protocol specifies a random exponential backoff mechanism for retransmitting these messages. All messages are transmitted by way of UDP. As with the basic mobile IP protocol, there is no need for the additional features of TCP.

11.7.3 Routing in mobile ad hoc networks

Mobile IP technology aims to support nomadic host roaming, where a roaming host may be connected through various means to the Internet other than its well known fixed-address domain space. The host may be directly physically connected to the fixed network on a foreign subnet, or be connected via a wireless link, dial-up line, etc. Supporting this form of host mobility (or nomadicity) requires address management, protocol interoperability enhancements, and the like, but core network functions such as hop-by-hop routing still presently rely upon pre-existing routing protocols operating within the fixed network.

In contrast, the goal of **mobile ad hoc networking** is to extend mobility into the realm of autonomous, mobile, wireless domains, where a set of nodes – which may be combined routers and hosts – themselves form the network routing infrastructure in an ad hoc fashion.

A **Mobile ad hoc Network** (MANET) is an **autonomous system of mobile routers** (and associated hosts) connected by wireless links – the union of which forms an arbitrary graph. The technology of mobile ad hoc networking is somewhat synonymous with mobile packet radio networking. The routers are free to move randomly and organize themselves arbitrarily; thus the network's wireless topology may change rapidly and unpredictably. Such a network may operate in a standalone fashion, or may be connected to the larger Internet.

The primary focus of the IETF working group is to develop and evolve MANET routing specification(s) with the goal of supporting networks scaling up to hundreds of routers. If this proves successful, future work may include development of other protocols to support additional routing functionality. The working group will also serve as a meeting place and forum for those developing and experimenting with MANET approaches.

Some of the various proposals (all at the stage of Internet Drafts) for routing protocols in mobile networks are discussed below.

The **Optimized Link State Routing** (OLSR) protocol for mobile ad hoc networks is an optimization of the pure link state algorithm tailored to the requirements of a mobile wireless LAN. The key concept used in the protocol is that of **multipoint relays** (MPRs). MPRs are the selected nodes which forward the broadcast packets during the flooding process. This technique substantially reduces the packet overhead as compared to a pure flooding mechanism where every node retransmits the packet when it receives the first copy. In the OLSR protocol, the information flooded in the network through these multipoint relays is also about the multipoint relays. Hence, a second optimization is achieved here by minimizing the contents of the control packet flooded in the network. Contrary to the classic link-state algorithm, only a small subset of links with the neighbor nodes are declared instead of all the links. This information is then used by the OLSR protocol for route calculation, and therefore the routes contain only the MPRs as the intermediate nodes from source to destination. It results in providing the optimal routes (in terms of number of hops), and hence another optimization. The protocol is particularly suitable for large dense networks as the technique of multipoint relays works well in this context.

Topology Broadcast based on Reverse-Path Forwarding (TBRPF) is a proactive, link-state routing protocol designed for use in mobile ad hoc networks. TBRPF has two modes: Full Topology (FT) and Partial Topology (PT).

RFC WATCH	MANET

RFC 2501 **Mobile Ad hoc Networking (MANET): Routing Protocol Performance Issues and Evaluation Considerations**, 1999 (Informational)

11.8 Equal-cost multipath routing

Equal-cost multipath (ECMP) is a routing technique for routing packets along multiple paths of equal cost (informational RFC 2991). The forwarding engine identifies paths by next-hop. Using equal-cost multipath means that if multiple equal-cost routes to the same destination exist, they can be discovered and used to provide load balancing among redundant paths. When forwarding a packet the router must decide which next-hop (path) to use. The forwarder potentially has several next-hops for any given destination and must use some method to choose which next-hop should be used for a given data packet.

RFC WATCH   multipath

RFC 2991 **Multipath Issues in Unicast and Multicast Next-Hop Selection**, 2000 (Informational)

ECMP can be achieved in various ways. This is sometimes done naively via **round-robin**, where each packet matching a given destination route is forwarded using the subsequent next-hop in a round-robin fashion. This does provide a form of load balancing, but there are several problems with approaches such as round-robin or random:

- **Variable path MTU** – since each of the redundant paths may have a different MTU, this means that the overall path MTU can change on a packet-by-packet basis, negating the usefulness of path MTU discovery.

- **Variable latencies** – since each of the redundant paths may have a different latency involved, having packets take separate paths can cause packets to always arrive out of order, increasing delivery latency and buffering requirements. Packet reordering causes TCP to believe that loss has taken place when packets with higher sequence numbers arrive before earlier ones. When three or more packets are received before a 'late' packet, TCP enters a 'fast-retransmit' mode which consumes extra bandwidth (which could potentially cause more loss, decreasing throughput) as it attempts to unnecessarily retransmit the delayed packet(s). Hence, reordering can be detrimental to network performance.

- **Debugging** – common debugging utilities such as PING and traceroute are much less reliable in the presence of multiple paths and may even present completely wrong results.

In multicast routing, the problem with multiple paths is that multicast routing protocols prevent loops and duplicates by constructing a single tree to all receivers of the same group address. Multicast routing protocols deployed today (DVMRP, PIM-DM, PIM-SM) construct shortest-path trees rooted at either the source, or another router known as a core or rendezvous point. Hence, the way they ensure that duplicates will not arise is that a given tree must use only a single next-hop towards the root of the tree.

The following **requirements** apply **for efficient multipath routing**:

- Ensure that packets for the **same flow always use the same path**.
- Maintain **minimal disruption**. When multipath is used, meaning that multiple routes contribute valid next-hops, the chances are higher of routes

being added to and deleted from consideration than when only the 'best' route is used (in which case metric changes in alternate routes have no effect on traffic paths). Since a higher number of routes may actually be used for forwarding when multipath is in use, the potential for packet reordering and packet loss due to route flaps can be much greater than when not using multipath. Hence, it is desirable to minimize the number of active flows affected by the addition or deletion of another next-hop.

■ Provide for **fast implementation**. The amount of additional computation required to forward a packet should be small. For example, when doing round-robin, this computation might consist of incrementing (modulo the number of next-hops) a next-hop index.

Possible solutions are as follows:

■ **Modulo-N hash** – to select a next-hop from the list of N next-hops, the router performs a modulo-N hash over the packet header fields that identify a flow. This has the advantage of being fast, at the expense of $(N-1)/N$ of all flows changing paths whenever a next-hop is added or removed.

■ **Hash-threshold** RFC 2992 – the router first selects a key by performing a hash over the packet header fields that identify the flow. The N next-hops have been assigned unique regions in the hash function's output space. By comparing the hash value against region boundaries the router can determine which region the hash value belongs to and thus which next-hop to use. This method has the advantage of only affecting flows near the region boundaries (or thresholds) when next-hops are added or removed. For ECMP hash-threshold's lookup can be done with a simple division *(hash_value/fixed_region_size)*. When a next-hop is added or removed, between a quarter and a half of all flows change paths.

RFC WATCH   **multi-homing and BGP**

RFC 2992 **Analysis of an Equal-Cost Multi-Path Algorithm**, 2000
(Informational)

■ **Highest Random Weight** (HRW) – the router computes a key for each next-hop by performing a hash over the packet header fields that identify the flow, as well as over the address of the next-hop. The router then chooses the next-hop with the highest resulting key value. This has the advantage of minimizing the number of flows affected by a next-hop addition or deletion (only $1/N$ of them), but is approximately N times as expensive as a modulo-N hash.

The applicability of these three alternatives depends on (at least) two factors: whether the forwarder maintains per-flow state, and how precious the CPU is to a multipath forwarder.

11.9 Virtual router redundancy protocol

There are a number of methods that an end host can use to determine its first hop router towards a particular IP destination. These include running (or snooping) a dynamic routing protocol such as RIP or OSPF version 2, running an ICMP router discovery client, or using a statically configured default route.

Running a dynamic routing protocol on every end host may be infeasible for a number of reasons, including administrative overhead, processing overhead, security issues, or lack of a protocol implementation for some platforms. Neighbor or router discovery protocols may require active participation by all hosts on a network, leading to large timer values to reduce protocol overhead in the face of a large numbers of hosts. This can result in a significant delay in the detection of a lost (i.e. dead) neighbor, which may introduce unacceptably long 'black hole' periods.

The use of a statically configured default route is quite popular; it minimizes configuration and processing overhead on the end host and is supported by virtually every IP implementation. This mode of operation is likely to persist as dynamic host configuration protocols are deployed, which typically provide configuration for an end host IP address and default gateway. However, this creates a single point of failure. Loss of the default router results in a catastrophic event, isolating all end hosts that are unable to detect any alternate path that may be available.

The **Virtual Router Redundancy Protocol** (VRRP) (RFC 2338) is designed to eliminate the single point of failure inherent in the static default routed environment. VRRP specifies an **election protocol** that dynamically assigns responsibility for a **virtual router** to one of the VRRP routers on a LAN. The VRRP router controlling the IP address(es) associated with a virtual router is called the **master** that is assuming the responsibility of forwarding packets sent to the IP address(es) associated with the virtual router, and answering ARP requests for these IP addresses. Virtual router as an abstract object managed by VRRP acts as a **default router** for hosts on a shared LAN. It consists of a **Virtual Router Identifier** (VRID) and a set of associated IP address(es) across a common LAN. A VRRP router may back up one or more virtual routers.

RFC WATCH　　**VRRP**

RFC 2338 **Virtual Router Redundancy Protocol**, 1998 (Proposed Standard)
RFC 2787 **Definitions of Managed Objects for the Virtual Router Redundancy Protocol**, 2000 (Proposed Standard)

The election process provides dynamic failover in the forwarding responsibility should the master become unavailable. Any of the virtual router's IP addresses on a LAN can then be used as the default first hop router by end hosts. The advantage gained from using VRRP is a higher availability default path without requiring configuration of dynamic routing or router discovery protocols on every end host.

The VRRP router that has the virtual router's IP address(es) as real interface address(es) is the so-called **IP address owner**. As such, when it is up it will respond to packets addressed to one of these IP addresses. If the IP address owner is available, then it will always become the Master. An IP address selected from the set of real interface addresses is a **primary IP address**. One possible selection algorithm is to always select the first address. VRRP advertisements are always sent using the primary IP address as the source of the IP packet. Virtual Router Backup is the set of VRRP routers available to assume forwarding responsibility for a virtual router should the current Master fail.

VRRP provides a function similar to a Cisco Systems, Inc. proprietary protocol named **Hot Standby Router Protocol** (HSRP) (informational RFC 2281) and to a Digital Equipment Corporation, Inc. proprietary protocol named **IP Standby Protocol**. VRRP is intended for use with IPv4 routers only. VRRP is only relevant in situations, where multiple routers are attached to the same shared-media LAN. As long as the master is available and responding, other VRRP routers will refrain from adopting the address. Neither HSRP nor VRRP is very critical for carrier oriented routers. In most cases, there will not be large numbers of hosts defaulting to them, which is the major application for these protocols – fault tolerance in finding a default gateway. Backup static routes and/or load balancing over multiple paths can be done as the primary alternatives. HSRP/VRRP can do that with multiple groups/VRIDs but more resources. HSRP/VRRP are meant for redundancy for the host's default gateway settings.

11.9.1 Hot standby router protocol

The idea behind the **Hot Standby Router Protocol** (HSRP) is to establish a **virtual router** (with its own IP address and MAC address) as the default router for the hosts on a LAN. One or more routers (with their own IP and MAC interface addresses) then pool as the standby group for this virtual router. One of the routers in the pool is active at any time, actually forwarding packets sent to the virtual router's MAC address. If that active router disappears, another router in the pool takes over. The advantage is that the host computer never knows that different routers are involved. It just sends packets to the virtual router, oblivious to the actual router that forwards the packets. And it only has to ARP once, to get the MAC address associated with the virtual router's IP address. So this saves all the ARP traffic that comes with proxy ARP. It also accommodates host implementations that ignore ARP table changes, a problem with moving a MAC address from one IP address to another (one real router's address to another's).

RFC WATCH	Hot standby router protocol (HSRP)

RFC 2281 **Cisco Hot Standby Router Protocol (HSRP)**, 1998 (Informational)

Using HSRP, a set of routers work together to present the illusion of a single virtual router to the hosts on the LAN. This set is known as an **HSRP group** or a

standby group. A single router elected from the group is responsible for forwarding the packets that hosts send to the virtual router. This router is known as the **active router**. Another router is elected as the standby router. In the event that the active router fails, the standby assumes the packet forwarding duties of the active router. Although an arbitrary number of routers may run HSRP, only the active router forwards the packets sent to the virtual router.

SNAPSHOT   HSRP

The **Hot Standby Router Protocol** (HSRP) is a solution that allows network topology changes to be transparent to the host. HSRP typically allows hosts to reroute in approximately 10 seconds. HSRP is supported on Ethernet, Token Ring, FDDI, Fast Ethernet, and ATM (and is compatible with IPX, AppleTalk, and Banyan VINES). An HSRP group can be defined on each LAN. All members of the group know the standby IP address and the standby MAC address. One member of the group is elected the leader. The lead router services all packets sent to the HSRP group address. The other routers monitor the leader and act as HSRP routers. If the lead router becomes unavailable, the HSRP router elects a new leader who inherits the HSRP MAC address and IP address.

HSRP (and VRRP) share a virtual IP address among the devices participating. Hosts point their default gateway to this virtual IP address. This allows the hosts to still forward traffic when the primary router/switch interface goes down and the standby router/switch changes over to active. This is the function of HSRP/VRRP – to provide a shared IP address among multiple interfaces on the same network. If the interface is in standby mode for HSRP then the standby IP address is not active on this interface, but the primary IP is active and IP-helper, routing, and all the other IP features that have been configured, are active unless the interface is down.

At any one time, **HSRP-configured routers** are in one of the following **states**:

- **Active** – the router is performing packet-transfer functions.
- **Standby** – the router is prepared to assume packet-transfer functions if the active router fails.
- **Speaking and listening** – the router is sending and receiving hello messages.
- **Listening** – the router is receiving hello messages.

To minimize network traffic, only the **active** and the **standby routers** send **periodic HSRP messages** once the protocol has completed the election process. If the active router fails, the standby router takes over as the active router. If the standby router fails or becomes the active router, another router is elected as the standby router.

HSRP-configured routers exchange **three types of multicast messages:**

- *Hello* – the hello message conveys to other HSRP routers the router's HSRP priority and state information. By default, an HSRP router sends hello messages every three seconds.

- *Coup* – when a standby router assumes the function of the active router, it sends a coup message.

- *Resign* – a router that is the active router sends this message when it is about to shut down or when a router that has a higher priority sends a hello message.

The HSRP **pre-emption** feature enables the router with highest priority to immediately become the active router. **Priority** is determined first by the priority value configured manually, and then by the IP address. In each case a higher value is of greater priority. When a higher priority router pre-empts a lower priority router, it sends a *Coup* message. When a lower priority active router receives a *Coup* message or *Hello* message from a higher priority active router, it changes to the Speak state and sends a *Resign* message.

QUICK TIP	**default gateway**

The purpose of HSRP is to **provide a default gateway in the event of router failure**. HSRP is not a routing protocol.

Each router has an IP address on an interface (HSRP works at the LAN interface level) and there is a virtual router (IP address) created between them. Routers that are running HSRP send and receive multicast UDP-based hello packets to detect router failure and to designate active and standby routers. HSRP detects when the designated active router fails because of the lack of hello packets, at which point a selected standby router assumes control of the Hot Standby group's MAC and IP addresses. A new standby router is also selected at that time.

HSRP operates on the **edge** of the network. It is symmetric between edge routers, and does not involve any protocol interaction with end hosts. HSRP can be viewed as a management protocol of single medium scope, with the additional constraint that this is intended as an edge medium. The scope of its knowledge (as distinct from the scope of its propagation) includes the interfaces of the routers in an HSRP group, but not the routing tables of those routers. Interface tracking fits into this model, but knowing whether a given ISP is reachable over an interface is a function beyond the HSRP scope.

On a particular LAN, **multiple hot standby** (MHSRP) **groups** may coexist and overlap. Each standby group emulates a single virtual router. This further enables redundancy and load-sharing within networks, and allows redundant routers to be more fully utilized. While a router is actively forwarding traffic for one HSRP group, it can be in Standby or Listen state for another group. For each standby group, a single well-known MAC address is allocated to the group, as well as an IP address. The IP address should belong to the primary subnet in use on the LAN, but must differ from the addresses allocated as interface addresses on all routers and hosts on the LAN, including virtual IP addresses assigned to other HSRP groups. If multiple groups are used on a single LAN, load splitting can be achieved by distributing hosts among different standby groups.

The protocol protects against the failure of the first hop router when the source host cannot learn the IP address of the first hop router dynamically. The protocol is designed for use over multi-access, multicast or broadcast capable LANs (e.g. Ethernet). For reserved MAC addresses see Table 11.13. HSRP is not intended as a replacement for existing dynamic router discovery mechanisms and those protocols should be used instead whenever possible. A large class of legacy host implementations that do not support dynamic discovery are capable of configuring a default router. HSRP provides failover services to those hosts.

TABLE 11-13 Cisco Reserved (virtual) MAC addresses for HSRP

Medium	MAC addresses
Ethernet	0000.0c07.ac** (** – HSRP grp #)
FDDI	0000.0c07.ac** (** – HSRP grp #)
Token Ring	c000.0001.0000

HSRP works well with all routing protocols without any modifications. While running HSRP, it is important to prevent the host from discovering the primary MAC addresses of the routers in its standby group. Thus any protocol that informs a host of a router's primary address should be disabled. Therefore routers participating in HSRP on an interface must not send **ICMP redirects** on that interface. If an HSRP router is configured to support **proxy ARP** with HSRP, then the router must specify the HSRP virtual MAC address in any proxy ARP responses it generates. These proxy ARP responses must not be suppressed based upon the HSRP state. Suppression based upon state could result in the lack of any proxy ARP response being generated, since these proxy ARP responses may be suppressed due to other reasons, such as split-horizon rules.

HSRP for IP is currently an RFC but, in general, the protocol is not limited to IP and may support other network protocols. Newly it can run also across the ISL links and thus may support the VLAN interconnections and router redundancy (see Part III for discussion of VLANs). An example of HSRP use in a hierarchical redundant topology with VLANs is shown at Figure 11.32. As the HSRP deployment in ATM LANE requires its support on LAN switching with ATM LANE uplinks, its usage is basically limited to Cisco devices.

FIGURE 11-32 Hierarchical redundant topolgy with HSRP and VLANS

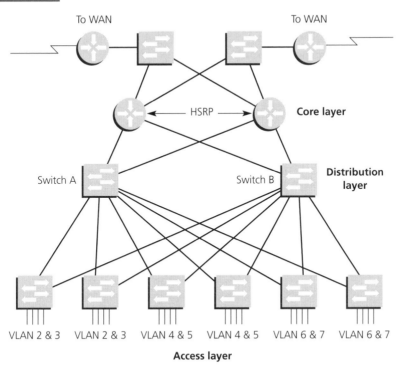

To WAN   To WAN

HSRP

Core layer

Switch A   Switch B   Distribution
                              layer

VLAN 2 & 3   VLAN 2 & 3   VLAN 4 & 5   VLAN 4 & 5   VLAN 6 & 7   VLAN 6 & 7

Access layer

11.10 Passing IP datagrams through routers revisited

Routers are often overlooked when dealing with network security. They are the lifeblood of an Internet connection. They provide all the data on a network a path to the outside world. This also makes them a wonderful target for attacks. Since most sites have one router to connect to the outside world, all it takes is one attack to destroy that connection.

Router vendors recommend you always keep up with the latest version of the router's software. The newer releases can fix a great deal of the denial-of-service attacks that have recently emerged. These attacks are often trivial to execute and require only a few packets across the connection to trigger. A router upgrade will sometimes mean further expense in memory or firmware upgrades, but as a critical piece of equipment, it should not be neglected.

Other than updating the software, disabling remote management is often the key to preventing both denial-of-service attacks and remote attacks to try to gain control of the router. With a remote management port open, attackers have a way into the router. Some routers fall victim to brute-force attempts against their administrative passwords. Quick scripts can be written to try all possible password combinations, accessing the router only once per try to avoid being detected. If there are so many routers that manual administration is a problem, then perhaps investigating network switch technology would be wise.

11.10.1 Redistribution

Redistribution of information among different routing protocols might be needed in the following situations:

- transitioning from one routing protocol to another;
- having a mix of devices supporting various routing protocols in the network;
- merging companies with different routing policies;
- having a bad network design.

Routing information redistribution may take the form of:

- one-way redistribution;
- mutual redistribution at one point in the network;
- mutual redistribution at multiple points between two networks;
- mutual redistribution at multiple points among multiple networks.

Redistribution is revisited in Chapter 12, section 12.8.1

Summary of recommendations on routing protocols migration and coexistence

Routing protocol changes are major changes for a production network. Migration changes should be scheduled and implemented during downtime hours and not attempted during production hours. They should also be carefully planned and a number of recommendations followed:

- Migrate to advanced IGPs when possible.
- Keep the number of IGPs used in a network to an absolute minimum (ideally one).
- Run only a single IGP on a given segment or link if possible.
- The migration plan should generally be implemented in as short a time period as possible.
- Use techniques to eliminate or minimize the occurrence of routing loops.
- Analyze how different destinations will be reached from all parts of the network considering the redistribution scenario and topology.
- Do not run dynamic routing protocols on end systems if possible.
- Redistribution and filtering should be used to tightly control all mutual redistribution points especially when multiple mutual redistribution points are present.
- Understand the IGPs with their different convergence properties.

Addressing and route summarization

With the expanding nature of the Internet and private intranets, the number of entries in the IP routing tables can make troubleshooting and managing the network an extremely difficult task. With increased routing tables, routers require more time to process routing table lookups which may in turn have an adverse affect on their performance.

Route summarization procedures condense routing information. Without summarization, each router in a network must retain a route to every subnet in the network. With summarization, routers can reduce some sets of routes to a single advertisement, reducing both the load on the router and the perceived complexity of the network. The importance of route summarization increases with network size.

Figure 11.33 provides an example of route summarization. In this environment, Router R2 maintains one route for all destination networks beginning with B, and Router R4 maintains one route for all destination networks beginning with A. This is the essence of route summarization. Router R1 tracks all routes because it exists on the boundary between A and B.

FIGURE 11-33 Route summarization example

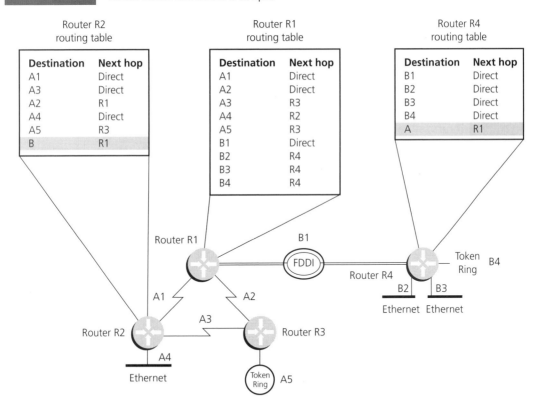

The reduction in route propagation and routing information overhead can be significant. Without summarization, each router in a network with 1000 subnets must contain 1000 routes. With summarization, the picture changes considerably. If you assume a Class B network with eight bits of subnet address space, each router needs to know all of the routes for each subnet in its network number (250 routes, assuming that 1000 subnets fall into four major networks of 250 routers each) plus one route for each of the other networks (three) for a total of 253 routes. This represents a nearly 75 percent reduction in the size of the routing table.

The preceding example shows the simplest type of route summarization: collapsing all the subnet routes into a single network route. Some routing protocols also support route summarization at any bit boundary (rather than just at the major network number boundaries) in a network address. A routing protocol can summarize on a bit boundary only if it supports variable-length subnet masks (VLSMs), for example RIPU2, EIGRP, or OSPF.

Some routing protocols summarize automatically such as RIP or IGRP. Other routing protocols require manual configuration to support route summarization for example OSPF. Route summarization reduces the size of routing tables by allowing routes to collections of subnets or collections of networks to be identified by a single routing entry. With classful protocols, summarization occurs by default on collections of subnets, with advertised routes being those of the classful addressing boundaries (i.e. class A, B, and C network numbers). Conversely, classless routing protocols allow collections of networks to be advertised with a single routing entry. With both methods, there are some basic rules that govern when and how summarization occurs. **Address aggregation** means the same thing as route summarization. The alternative terminology is used to identify groups of IP class networks that are summarized into a single route that causes the multiple network class addresses to be aggregated into a single route advertisement.

Overview of individual IGP summarization principles

RIP is a typical **classful** IP routing protocol that summarizes addresses at the class boundary (to an exact Class A, B, or C address). Routes advertised by RIP may be either **default, network**, or **subnet routes**. Subnet routes are subnets of a specific class address, and the only subnet routes that are advertised are those routes that match the standard fixed subnet mask used throughout the class address. For example, if Class B address 160.18.0.0 has a subnet mask of 255.255.255.0 applied, only subnets that match that specific subnet mask are sent to other RIP neighbors. Network routes are classful addresses, and only addresses that are Class A, B, or C, are sent to RIP neighbors. Exterior routes can be injected into our autonomous system from external autonomous systems. These exterior routes are treated as network routes and are sent to RIP neighbors as if they were part of our autonomous system with no indication that they are external. Default routes are treated like network routes.

The primary difference between RIP version 1 and **RIP version 2** is that in version 2 the subnet routes have their associated subnet mask included in the routing update. In RIP version 1, only global subnet mask is used; in RIP version 2, **variable prefix** subnets are permitted and advertised.

IGRP is again a typical **classful** routing protocol. Routes advertised by IGRP are of three types – **interior, system**, and **exterior routes**. Interior routes are subnets of a classful address, and the only interior routes that are advertised are those routes with the standard fixed subnet mask used throughout the classful address. For example, if Class B address 140.55.0.0 has a subnet mask of 255.255.255.0 applied, only subnets that match that specific subnet mask are sent to other IGRP neighbors. System routes are classful addresses, and only addresses that are Class A, B, or C are sent to IGRP neighbors. Exterior routes can be injected into our autonomous system by setting default networks or setting up default routes. These exterior routes are treated the same as system routes and are sent to IGRP neighbors as if they were part of our autonomous system. *Note on redistribution*: IGRP automatically mutually redistributes routing information with RIP within a single network. IGRP automatically mutually redistributes routing information with EIGRP within an autonomous system.

OSPF as a link-state protocol deals with IP in a **classless** manner. OSPF uses both the subnetwork and the subnet mask to calculate pathways through the IP cloud. Because the network or subnet and the subnet mask are used, all networks and subnets are maintained in the routing table. In order to process the information in the routing table, the routes within a single classful address are sorted by descending subnet prefix length. This places the more specific routes at the top of the table, and properly sends traffic to the most specific destination.

EIGRP is a composite routing protocol that, by default, deals with IP in a **classless** manner, but automatically summarizes routes based on the classful addresses A, B, and C. Within a classful address, EIGRP uses the network or subnet in combination with the subnet mask to maintain detailed pathways within directly connected networks. Optionally, EIGRP can be configured without the default classful address summarization by manually defining a summary route to be advertised on each active interface. *Note on redistribution*: EIGRP automatically mutually redistributes routing information with IGRP within an autonomous system.

Automatic summarization is generally not recommended as summarization needs to be planned.

11.10.2 IGP convergence

With new and emerging technologies like Gigabit Ethernet, or 10 Gigabit Ethernet, some may wonder how scalable or well suited today's IP routing protocols (like OSPF, IGRP, EIGRP) are to be managed effectively. However, the ability to have precise metrics is less and less essential to routing protocols. There are, however, other limiting factors for conventional IGPs. Therefore they will continue to be evolved rather than replaced by new paradigms.

Bandwidth is often cheap, as in campus or photonic networks. Fine distinctions based on physical segment bandwidth are not that important. Where there is a bandwidth limitation (e.g. wireless), there is a whole range of relevant techniques at all OSI layers. Traffic engineering extensions to OSPF and IS-IS, or strategies like Optimized Multipath (OSPF-OMP, IS-IS-TE) take a more reasoned view of reservation and utilization. Topology in well designed networks is usually more important than metric.

Now, there are issues – and controversial ones – with **convergence time**. Current IGP's typically reconverge in tens of seconds, which is too slow for certain services such as voice call setup. In other services, nothing is broken. Fast response to convergence may be fine in an IGP, but, in the context of the global Internet, may contribute to instability. There is much controversy and theoretical work going on in global BGP convergence. Some of the complexities being explored in the research community deal variously with BGP's path vector algorithm itself, with the issue of constraint-based BGP routing (the path vector can be guaranteed to converge only when additional constraints, such as AS path length and MED, are not considered), and operational use of constraints and policies.

For solving convergence problems, in modern IP interior routing protocols like IS-IS or OSPF it is necessary to look closely at the steps required for re-routing, i.e. finding whether an alternative path exists and spreading the word throughout the network:

- Detect a local topology change (link up/down or peer reachability).
- Flood a Link State Packet (LSP) to tell adjacent peers about the change.
- Compute new routes by running a Dijkstra Shortest Path First (SPF) algorithm on the changed topology.

One of the issues having quite great impact on the efficiency of the protocol and the convergence time is the algorithm for the calculation of new routes. New computing algorithms exist now which are considered replacements for Dijkstra's algorithm.

11.10.3 Packet retransmission and routers

What is the task of the routers in the internet when packet retransmission is needed for some reason (e.g. due to lost or corrupted packets)? In an IP environment it is the hosts which are architecturally responsible for the retransmission for a reliable communication hence routers do not retransmit (RFC 1812 and 1958). However, hosts – which support the full TCP/IP protocol stack as opposed to routers – will look after reliability only when using reliable transport/application protocols. It means, that in Telnet communication the end hosts may be required to retransmit packets which get lost or corrupted; but hosts running a UDP-based application such as streaming video will be never required to take care of retransmission as the nature of such communication does not require anyone to retransmit to achieve reliability.

RFC WATCH	router requirements based on Internet architecture

RFC 1812 **Requirements for IP Version 4 Routers**, 1995 (Proposed Standard)

RFC 1958 **Architectural Principles of the Internet**, 1996 (Informational)

Generally, however, there is no absolute rule for what hosts do and what routers do in this respect, because it depends a great deal on the protocol run across the link and/or internet. While X.25 deals with error checking at each network node, routers specifically configured to support the set of X.25 protocols would need to deal with packet retransmission.

In summary, routers retransmit only when they are using data link protocols that specifically retransmit (e.g. SDLC and LAP-B but not HDLC), or when they are acting as a host (e.g. as a protocol converter or the end point of a reliable tunnel).

It is good to remember that reliable and unreliable protocols either have error detection mechanisms or have expectations that a layer below them will have such mechanisms. It determines their reaction once they detect an error:

■ either they do not pass the data to the upper layer and, if there is a need for retransmission, let the sender detect the need and act on it (e.g. IP approach);

■ or they do not pass the data to the upper layer and send a request for retransmission.

RFC WATCH   **Summarized RFC watch**

The following RFCs have been brought to your attention in this chapter:

RFC 1058 *Routing Information Protocol*, 1988 (Historic)

RFC 1075 *Distance Vector Multicast Routing Protocol*, 1988 (Experimental)

RFC 1245 *OSPF Protocol Analysis*, 1991 (Informational)

RFC 1246 *Experience with the OSPF Protocol*, 1991 (Informational)

RFC 1370 *Applicability Statement for OSPF* (Proposed Standard)

RFC 1403 *BGP OSPF Interaction*, 1993 (Historic)

RFC 1469 *IP Multicast over Token-Ring Local Area Networks*, 1993 (Proposed Standard)

RFC 1582 *Extensions to RIP to Support Demand Circuits*, 1994 (Proposed Standard)

RFC 1584 *Multicast Extensions to OSPF*, 1994 (Proposed Standard)

RFC 1585 *MOSPF: Analysis and Experience*, 1994 (Informational)

RFC 1586 *Guidelines for Running OSPF Over Frame Relay Networks*, 1994 (Informational)

RFC 1587 *The OSPF NSSA Option*, 1994 (Proposed Standard)

RFC 1745 *BGP4/IDRP for IP-OSPF Interaction*, 1994 (Historic)

RFC 1765 *OSPF Database Overflow*, 1995 (Experimental)

RFC 1771 *A Border Gateway Protocol 4 (BGP-4)*, 1995 (Draft Standard)

RFC 1772 *Application of the Border Gateway Protocol in the Internet*, 1995 (Draft Standard)

RFC 1773 *Experience with the BGP-4 protocol*, 1995 (Informational)

RFC 1774 *BGP-4 Protocol Analysis*, 1995 (Informational)

RFC 1793 *Extending OSPF to Support Demand Circuits*, 1995 (Proposed Standard)

RFC 1812 *Requirements for IP Version 4 Routers,* 1995 (Proposed Standard)

▶

RFC 1850 *OSPF Version 2 Management Information Base*, 1995 (Draft Standard)

RFC 1930 *Guidelines for Creation, Selection, and Registration of an Autonomous System (AS)*, 1996 (Best Current Practice)

RFC 1958 *Architectural Principles of the Internet*, 1996 (Informational)

RFC 1998 *An Application of the BGP Community Attribute in Multi-home Routing*, 1996 (Informational)

RFC 2002 *IP Mobility Support*, 1996 (Proposed Standard)

RFC 2005 *Applicability Statement for IP Mobility Support*, 1996 (Proposed Standard)

RFC 2008 *Implications of Various Address Allocation Policies for Internet Routing*, 1996 (Best Current Practice)

RFC 2080 *RIPng for IPv6*, 1997 (Proposed Standard)

RFC 2081 *RIPng Protocol Applicability Statement*, 1997 (Informational)

RFC 2082 *RIP-2 MD5 Authentication*, 1997 (Proposed Standard)

RFC 2091 *Triggered Extensions to RIP to Support Demand Circuits*, 1997 (Proposed Standard)

RFC 2154 *OSPF with Digital Signatures*, 1997 (Experimental)

RFC 2201 *Core Based Trees (CBT) Multicast Routing Architecture*, 1997 (Experimental)

RFC 2236 *Internet Group Management Protocol, Version 2*, 1997 (Proposed Standard)

RFC 2260 *Scalable Support for Multi-homed Multi-provider Connectivity*, 1998 (Informational)

RFC 2270 *Using a Dedicated AS for Sites Homed to a Single Provider*, 1998 (Informational)

RFC 2281 *Cisco Hot Standby Router Protocol (HSRP)*, 1998 (Informational)

RFC 2328 *OSPF Version 2*, 1998 (Standard)

RFC 2329 *OSPF Standardization Report*, 1998 (Informational)

RFC 2338 *Virtual Router Redundancy Protocol*, 1998 (Proposed Standard)

RFC 2362 *Protocol Independent Multicast-Sparse Mode (PIM-SM): Protocol Specification*, 1998 (Experimental)

RFC 2365 *Administratively Scoped IP Multicast*, 1998 (Best Current Practice)

RFC 2370 *The OSPF Opaque LSA Option*, 1998 (Proposed Standard)

RFC 2439 *BGP Route Flap Dampening*, 1998 (Proposed Standard)

RFC 2453 *RIP Version 2*, 1998 (Standard)

RFC 2501 *Mobile Ad hoc Networking (MANET): Routing Protocol Performance Issues and Evaluation Considerations*, 1999 (Informational)

RFC 2644 *Changing the Default for Directed Broadcasts in Routers (BCP0034)* (Best Current Practice)

RFC 2676 *QoS Routing Mechanisms and OSPF Extensions*, 1999 (Experimental)

RFC 2740 *OSPF for IPv6*, 1999 (Proposed Standard)

RFC 2769 *Routing Policy System Replication*, 2000 (Proposed Standard)

RFC 2776 *Multicast-Scope Zone Announcement Protocol* (MZAP), 2000 (Proposed Standard)

RFC 2787 *Definitions of Managed Objects for the Virtual Router Redundancy Protocol*, 2000 (Proposed Standard)

RFC 2842 *Capabilities Advertisement with BGP-4*, 2000 (Proposed Standard)

RFC 2844 *OSPF over ATM and Proxy-PAR (PNNI Augmented Routing)*, 2000 (Experimental)

RFC 2858 *Multiprotocol Extensions for BGP-4*, 2000 (Proposed Standard)

RFC 2909 *The Multicast Address-Set Claim (MASC) Protocol*, 2000 (Experimental)

RFC 2918 *Route Refresh Capability for BGP-4*, 2000 (Proposed Standard)

RFC 2933 *Internet Group Management Protocol MIB*, 2000 (Proposed Standard)

RFC 2992 *Analysis of an Equal-Cost Multi-Path Algorithm*, 2000 (Informational)

RFC 3022 *Traditional IP Network Address Translator (Traditional NAT)*, 2001 (Informational)

RFC 3065 *Autonomous System Confederations for BGP*, 2001 (Proposed Standard)

C H A P T E R   1 2

Routing in a non-IP environment

12.1 AppleTalk routing

Although TCP/IP has been rolled out all over the world, there are still several protocol architectures which are worth mentioning to compare the networking and routing approaches. One is definitely AppleTalk of Apple Computer, which applies an interesting user-friendly approach to networking: the user is not supposed to do much in terms of administering his or her access to the AppleTalk internetwork as addressing is done in the background dynamically, and all services that are available are nicely advertised (and divided into geographic and/or functional areas for the user's benefit).

12.1.1 AppleTalk protocol architecture

Apple Computer developed its proprietary protocol architecture in the 1980s under the name of AppleTalk. AppleTalk was developed to be a general-purpose network system that pays special attention to the needs of personal computers and their users. AppleTalk was designed as a client-server distributed network system and initial AppleTalk implementation strictly distinguished between clients and servers from the addressing point of view.

The original implementation of AppleTalk, which was designed for local workgroups, is now commonly referred to as **AppleTalk Phase 1**. The enhanced protocol, known as **AppleTalk Phase 2**, improved the addressing and routing capabilities of AppleTalk and allowed AppleTalk to run successfully in larger networks. The hierarchical protocol architecture is shown in Figure 12.1 in comparison to the OSI reference model.

From the following it should be noted that routers supporting the AppleTalk environment have to implement not only Layers 1 to 3 but also have to understand some other protocols residing above the network layer. In the following we will have a brief look at all AppleTalk layers with the emphasis on the protocols related to the AppleTalk routing.

12.1.2 Lower layers

Apple designed AppleTalk to be link-layer independent and therefore it supports a variety of link-layer implementations, including Ethernet, Token Ring, Fiber Distributed Data Interface (FDDI), and LocalTalk. **LocalTalk** is Apple's proprietary media-access system. It is based on contention access, bus topology, and baseband signaling, and runs on shielded twisted-pair media at 230.4 kbps. LocalTalk segments can span up to 300 meters and support a maximum of 32

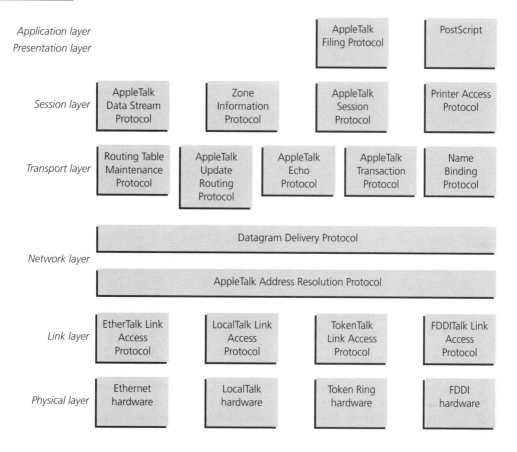

FIGURE 12-1 AppleTalk and the OSI reference model

nodes. The **physical interface** is EIA/TIA-422 (formerly RS-422), a balanced electrical interface supported by EIA/TIA-449 (formerly RS-449).

Apple refers to AppleTalk over Ethernet as **EtherTalk**, to AppleTalk over Token Ring as **TokenTalk**, and to AppleTalk over FDDI as **FDDITalk**. The link-layer protocols that support AppleTalk over these media are EtherTalk Link Access Protocol (ELAP), LocalTalk Link Access Protocol (LLAP), TokenTalk Link Access Protocol (TLAP), and FDDITalk Link Access Protocol (FLAP).

12.1.3 Network layer

While discussing the AppleTalk network layer, we will concentrate on addressing issues, the network (routed) protocol, and supporting routing protocols.

Dynamic addressing

AppleTalk is a plug and play (and foolproof) architecture (as opposed to TCP/IP or NetWare) which does not require the users (or administrators) to configure the node's addresses manually. To ensure minimal network administrator overhead, AppleTalk node **addresses are assigned dynamically**. When a station running AppleTalk starts up, it chooses a protocol (network-layer) address (starts usually with the latest it used before a shut-down, if one exists), and checks to see whether that address is currently in use through broadcasting a probe with the chosen address. If no response is received (the address is not used in the network by another node) the new node has successfully assigned itself an address. If the address is currently in use, the node with the conflicting address sends a message indicating a problem, and the new node chooses another address (sequentially higher than the one used before) and repeats the process until it gets a currently available AppleTalk address.

The **AppleTalk Address Resolution Protocol** (AARP) is used to associate AppleTalk addresses with particular media addresses. The AARP operation is similar to that of IP ARP. Unlike the IP ARP, AARP has the additional purpose to guarantee that the network-layer address is unique. The AppleTalk **ARP cache** maintained with routers collects and maintains the following information: address, age of record, type of address (hardware or dynamic), hardware address, and encapsulation used on the interface.

AppleTalk addresses network segments (wires) and interfaces attaching to them. AppleTalk **network addresses** are 24-bits long and consist of two components, separated by a period:

- **16-bit network number** expresses in decimal way;
- **8-bit node number** written as decimal number.

Additionally a socket number is defined as an eight-bit number that uniquely identifies a specific logical point at which upper-layer AppleTalk software processes and the network-layer protocol interact running on a network node.

AppleTalk Phase 1 used a single and unique network number for each AppleTalk segment, while it divided the node address into two intervals: one for servers and the rest for clients. Such networks started to be called **non-extended networks**.

AppleTalk Phase 2 enhances the addressing process by introducing **extended networks**. It no longer distinguishes between clients and servers in terms of node numbering, but also allows for multiple network addresses on single wire. Although it is still restricted by the 16 and eight bits for network and node address parts, respectively, it no longer has problems with lack of address space. Each segment may have as many (unique) network addresses assigned (sometimes referred to as the cable range) so that all nodes can be addressed within them and all attached nodes are then uniquely addressed within the segment.

Network entities

AppleTalk identifies several network entities. The most elemental is a **node**, which is simply any device connected to an AppleTalk network.

The next entity defined by AppleTalk is the **network**. An AppleTalk network is simply a single logical cable. Although the logical cable is frequently a single physical cable, some sites use bridges to interconnect several physical cables.

Finally, an AppleTalk **zone** is a logical group of networks. Zones are identified by their (unique) names and each node in an AppleTalk network belongs to, at least one single, specific zone. Extended networks can reside in multiple zones and nodes on extended networks can belong to any zone associated with the extended network.

All AppleTalk entities are shown in Figure 12.2.

FIGURE 12-2   AppleTalk nodes, extended networks, and zones

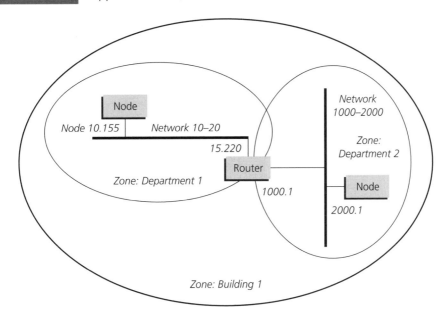

Datagram delivery protocol

AppleTalk's primary network-layer protocol is the **Datagram Delivery Protocol** (DDP). DDP provides a **connectionless** network service between network sockets. Sockets can be assigned either statically or dynamically.

The DDP packet format has two forms:

■ **Short DDP Packet** – the short format is used for transmissions between two nodes on the same network segment in a non-extended network only. This format is seldom used in new networks;

■ **Extended DDP Packet** – the extended format is used for transmissions between nodes with different network numbers (in a non-extended network), and for any transmissions in an extended network.

Figure 12.3 shows the format of the extended DDP packet. An extended DDP packet consists of 13 fields among which the following are non-zero:

FIGURE 12-3 DDP packet format

Number of bits:

1	1	4	10	16	16	16	8	8	8	8	8	0–4688
0	0	Hop count	Length	Checksum	Destination network	Source network	Destination node ID	Source node ID	Destination socket	Source socket	Type	Data

- ***Hop count*** – counts the number of intermediate devices through which the packet has passed. At the source, this field is set to zero. Each intermediate node through which the packet passes increases the value of this field by one. The maximum number of hops is 15.
- ***Length*** – indicates the total length, in bytes, of the DDP packet.
- ***Checksum*** – contains a checksum value used to detect errors. If no checksum is performed, the bits in this optional field are set to zero.
- ***Destination network*** – indicates the 16-bit destination network number.
- ***Source network*** – indicates the 16-bit source network number.
- ***Destination node ID*** – indicates the 8-bit destination node ID.
- ***Source node ID*** – indicates the 8-bit source node ID.
- ***Destination socket*** – indicates the 8-bit destination socket number.
- ***Source socket*** – indicates the 8-bit source socket number.
- ***Type*** – indicates the upper-layer protocol to which the information in the data field belongs.
- ***Data*** – contains data from an upper-layer protocol.

12.1.4 Transport layer

AppleTalk's transport layer is implemented by several **transport protocols**:

- **AppleTalk Echo Protocol** (AEP) – simple protocol that generates packets that can be used to test the reachability of various network nodes.
- **AppleTalk Transaction Protocol** (ATP) – provides such classical transport-layer functions, as data acknowledgment and retransmission, packet sequencing, and fragmentation and reassembly (it limits message segmentation to eight packets, and packet length to 578 octets). ATP is suitable for transaction-based applications (transactions occur between two socket clients).
- **Name Binding Protocol** (NBP) – protocol supporting association of node names to their logical location (addresses). Name binding can be done when the user node is first started up, or dynamically, immediately before first use. NBP orchestrates the name binding process, which includes name registration, name confirmation, name deletion, and name lookup. Zones allow name lookup in a group of logically related nodes.
- **Zone Information Protocol** (ZIP) – protocol supporting NBP to identify nodes in various zones. ZIP maintains network number to zone name

mappings in zone information tables (ZITs). ZITs are stored in routers, which are the primary users of ZIP, but end nodes use ZIP during the startup process to choose their zone and to acquire internetwork zone information. ZIP uses RTMP routing tables to keep up with network topology changes. When ZIP finds a routing table entry that is not in the ZIT, it creates a new ZIT entry.

12.1.5 Upper-layer protocols

To complete the discussion of AppleTalk basic information on the top layers is as follows. AppleTalk supports several upper-layer protocols:

- **AppleTalk Data Stream Protocol** (ADSP) – establishes and maintains full-duplex data streams between two sockets in an AppleTalk internet. ADSP is a reliable protocol which numbers each data octet to keep track of the individual elements of the datastream and specifies a flow-control mechanism.
- **AppleTalk Session Protocol** (ASP) – establishes and maintains sessions (logical conversations) between an AppleTalk client and a server.
- **AppleTalk's Printer Access Protocol** (APAP) – is a connection-oriented protocol that establishes and maintains connections between clients and servers. (The use of the term printer in this protocol's title is purely historical.)
- **AppleTalk Filing Protocol** (AFP) – helps clients share server files across a network.

12.1.6 Multicasting in AppleTalk networks (instead of broadcasting)

An important aspect of AppleTalk (compared to IP, for example) is that it does not support network layer broadcasts: nothing like an AppleTalk broadcast address exists. Instead, AppleTalk uses data link-layer multicasts. When there are no zones, AppleTalk nodes send multicasts to the *09-00-07-FF-FF-FF* MAC destination address. For example, when a station tries to find a printer, it sends a name binding protocol multicast looking for all printers. Note that to support this way of 'broadcasting' in a switched network the switches must be able to forward AppleTalk multicasts.

AppleTalk uses **multicasting** extensively to advertise services, request services, and resolve addresses. On startup, an AppleTalk host transmits a series of at least 20 packets aimed at resolving its network address (a Layer 3 AppleTalk node number) and obtaining local 'zone' information. Except for the first packet, which is addressed to itself, these functions are resolved through AppleTalk multicasts.

In terms of overall network traffic, the AppleTalk **Chooser** is particularly broadcast intensive. The Chooser is the software interface that allows the user to select shared network services. It uses AppleTalk multicasts to find file servers, printers, and other services. When the user opens the Chooser and selects a type of service (for example, a printer), the Chooser transmits 45 multicasts at a rate of one packet per second. If left open, the Chooser sends a five-packet burst with a progressively longer delay. If left open for several minutes, the Chooser reaches its maximum delay and transmits a five-packet burst every 270 seconds. By itself, this does not pose a problem, but in a large network, these packets add to the total amount of broadcast radiation that each host must interpret and then discard.

Among other AppleTalk protocol the **Router Discovery Protocol**, a RIP implementation that is transmitted by all routers and listened to by each station, is broadcast intensive.

12.1.7 Routing possibilities

In terms of currently supported routing protocols, AppleTalk may use the following:

- **Routing Table Maintenance Protocol** (RTMP) – inherent AppleTalk routing protocol based on the distance vector algorithm and derived from RIP.
- **AppleTalk Update-based Routing Protocol** (AURP) – a specific protocol allowing tunneling AppleTalk through other network types, such as IP.
- **Simple Multicast Routing Protocol** (SMRP) – a single routing protocol supporting AppleTalk multicasting.
- **Enhanced Interior Gateway Routing Protocol** (EIGRP) – Cisco Systems' proprietary routing protocol for AppleTalk networks (for details see Chapter 11). Note that EIGRP automatically redistributes the RTMP routing information.

In a similar way to other network (routed) protocols, AppleTalk can be also supported by static routing.

Routing table maintenance protocol

The oldest, classical, routing protocol supporting AppleTalk internetworking is the **Routing Table Maintenance Protocol** (RTMP). It is no surprise that RTMP is distance vector based, the simple routing protocol using a single metric (mostly hop-count). Although it was derived from RIP (see Table 12.1 on page 620 for a comparison of all RIP-derived protocols), RTMP reflects AppleTalk's addressing scheme and other unique AppleTalk protocol features. RTMP works with Apple's DDP to ensure that messages can traverse AppleTalk networks. DDP delivers the datagrams; RTMP maintains the routing tables.

The accuracy of the routing information is maintained by having each router **periodically broadcast its routing table** to all neighboring routers (i.e. routers directly reachable over one of the router's AppleTalk-enabled interfaces) every 10 seconds. All routers upon receiving this information compute the least cost path to all destination networks. Like other routing protocols, RTMP entries time out when they become too old. RTMP entries become invalid if an update has not been received for 20 seconds. The bad entry is eventually deleted from the routing table.

RTMP routing tables (see Figure 12.4) include an entry for each network a datagram can reach. Each entry includes the destination network, the interface over which packets for this destination are to be forwarded, the next-hop node address, the hop count to the destination, and the route state (good, suspect, or bad). The periodic exchange of routing tables allows the routers in an AppleTalk internet to ensure that they supply current and consistent information.

 **FIGURE 12-4**   RTMP routing table

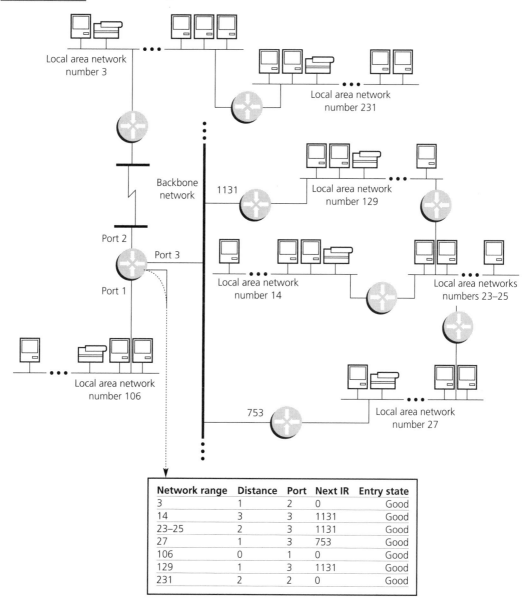

Network range	Distance	Port	Next IR	Entry state
3	1	2	0	Good
14	3	3	1131	Good
23–25	2	3	1131	Good
27	1	3	753	Good
106	0	1	0	Good
129	1	3	1131	Good
231	2	2	0	Good

There are the following types of **RTMP packets**:

- *Data packets* – contain routing update information. Routing updates consist of the entire routing table and are distributed every 10 seconds to AppleTalk address <network.255> which at the link layer maps onto the MAC multicast destination address *09-00-07-FF-FF-FF*. The split horizon update technique is used.

- *Request and response packets* – provide the means for newly initialized AppleTalk nodes to acquire their network number and the node ID of a nearby router.

- *Route data request* – used by nodes that wish to have routing information sent to a socket other than the standard RTMP socket. They are also used to obtain information from distant routers.

The RTMP **metric** is typically hop count, but sometimes an arbitrary metric is allowed (weighted cost value to AppleTalk interfaces). In all cases the maximum path length or cost is 15.

Each **router** periodically broadcasts *ZIP Query* packets requesting zone list information to all routers in the network, and constructs a local zone information table from the replies it receives. This information is used by end nodes for zone selection and resource location. Routers also assist in name-to-address processing on behalf of end nodes by listening for an *NBP Broadcast Request* packet for a named entity from an AppleTalk node, and either broadcasting an *NBP Lookup Request* packet across the local zone or issuing an *NBP Forward Request* packet toward the router connected to the destination zone. See Figure 12.5 for a router model of the relationship of RTMP with ZIP and NBP protocols.

FIGURE 12-5   AppleTalk routing model with RTMP

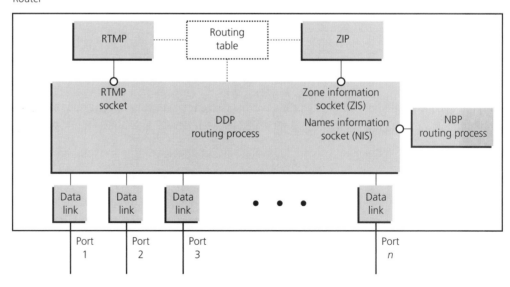

Enhanced Interior Gateway Routing Protocol

AppleTalk is one of three network protocols, besides Novell IPX and IP, which can be 'handled' by Cisco's proprietary EIGRP protocol. (For details on EIGRP operation see Chapter 11.) Where the AppleTalk metric for route determination is based on hop count only, AppleTalk Enhanced IGRP uses a combination of configurable metrics, such as delay, bandwidth, reliability, and load.

Redistribution between AppleTalk RTMP and Enhanced IGRP, and vice versa, is automatic by default. Redistribution involves converting the Enhanced IGRP metric back into an RTMP hop count metric. AppleTalk Enhanced IGRP routes are preferred over Routing Table Maintenance Protocol (RTMP) routes. The formula for converting RTMP metrics to AppleTalk Enhanced IGRP metrics is hop count multiplied by 252524800. This is a constant based on the bandwidth for a 9.6-kbps serial line and includes an RTMP factor. An RTMP hop distributed into Enhanced IGRP appears as a slightly worse path than an Enhanced IGRP-native, 9.6-kbps serial link. The formula for converting Enhanced IGRP to RTMP is the value of the Enhanced IGRP external metric plus 1.

AppleTalk update-based routing protocol

The **AppleTalk Update-based Routing Protocol** (AURP) allows a network administrator to connect two or more AppleTalk networks through another transport network (most commonly an IP network, specified in RFC 1504) to form an AppleTalk wide area network. Apple Computer designed the AURP to address concerns their customers had about the amount of traffic caused by RTMP, particularly on WAN links. AURP reduces routing traffic because it sends only updates after its initial sending of the route table.

The AURP connection is called a **tunnel**, which functions as a single, virtual data link between the AppleTalk networks, as shown in Figure 12.6. The tunnel can connect two or more non-contiguous AppleTalk internets that are separated by a non-AppleTalk network (such as an IP network).

FIGURE 12-6 AppleTalk tunnel using AURP

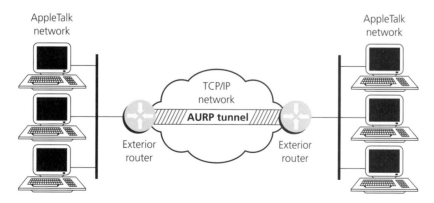

RFC WATCH   AURP

RFC 1504 **Appletalk Update-Based Routing Protocol: Enhanced Appletalk Routing**, 1993 (Informational)

A router that connects an AppleTalk internet to a tunnel (that is a router that runs AURP) is called an **exterior router**. Each exterior router functions both as an AppleTalk router within its local internet and as an end node of the transport network that interconnects the AppleTalk networks. The exterior router sends AppleTalk packets and routing information through the transport network by encapsulating the packets with the header information required by the network system. The receiving exterior router removes the protocol header and sends the packets out of the appropriate interface. Packets are encapsulated in UDP headers.

Tunnel connection may be point-to-point or multipoint with only two or more peers, respectively. If all exterior routers connected to a multipoint tunnel can send packets to each other, the tunnel is **fully connected**. If one or more exterior routers are not aware of other exterior routers, the tunnel is only **partially connected**. Exterior routers forming a tunnel provide for **encapsulation** and **decapsulation** of the packets transported according to the transport 'media.'

The main function of AURP is to maintain accurate routing tables for the entire AppleTalk WAN by the exchange of routing information between exterior routers. AURP uses the principle of **split horizon** to limit the propagation of routing updates. For that reason, an exterior router sends routing information about only the networks that comprise its local environment to other exterior routers connected to the tunnel.

When an exterior router becomes aware of another exterior router on the tunnel, the two exterior routers exchange their lists of network numbers and associated zone information. Thereafter, an exterior router sends routing information only when the following events occur:

- a network is added to the routing table;
- a change in the path to a network causes the exterior router to access that network through its local internet rather than through the tunnel or to access that network through the tunnel rather than through the local internet;
- a network is removed from the routing table;
- the distance to a network is changed.

AURP converts RTMP and ZIP packets into AURP packets and vice versa.

AURP is preferable to RTMP for the core of the network because AURP sends fewer routing packets than RTMP. In addition, a router running AURP can reset the hop count field in the DDP header to zero for traversal across the non-AppleTalk network. This permits the creation of very large AppleTalk internets where the hop-count limit of 15 would be a problem.

> **QUICK TIP**   **AURP**
>
> The **AppleTalk Update-Based Routing Protocol** (AURP) is a distance-vector tunneling protocol, but it sends changes only and supports summarization. It remaps remote network numbers to resolve numbering conflicts and resets the hop count so that there is no restriction to 15 hops. It supports tunneling AppleTalk through an IP backbone.

Simple multicast routing protocol

The **Simple Multicast Routing Protocol** (SMRP) is a new routing protocol to support multicast AppleTalk traffic, such as QuickTime Conferencing (QTC). SMRP routes AppleTalk packets to all members of a multicast group so that packets are not replicated on a link. Instead, a single copy of a packet is sent over the physical network. Group membership services determine which hosts need to receive multicast traffic. SMRP allows a host to register dynamically for the multicast sessions in which it decides to participate. The protocol dynamically establishes unique shortest path distribution trees to restrict traffic propagation to only relevant parts of network and provides just-in-time packet duplication upon encountering a branch in the distribution tree.

SMRP addressing is based on the local network of a creator endpoint. An SMRP address consists of two parts: a three-byte network number and a one-byte socket number. Each local network is configured with a range of unique network numbers. In the case of multicast address mapping, SMRP multicast addresses must be mapped to network-layer multicast addresses, and these in turn are mapped to data link-layer multicast addresses. For each network-layer type, a block of multicast addresses must be obtained for SMRP. In the best case, these addresses will map directly. In most cases, a direct mapping is not possible, and more than one SMRP multicast address is mapped to a single network-layer multicast address.

The manner in which multicast addresses are mapped to network-layer addresses is network-layer dependent. When SMRP **transport-layer multicast addresses** do not map directly to network-layer multicast addresses, filtering of the SMRP multicast addresses is required. When network-layer multicast addresses do not map directly to data link layer multicast addresses, the network layer is expected to filter out multicast addresses that have not been subscribed.

SMRP involves a **multicast transaction protocol** (MTP) that provides for three transaction types: node, endpoint, and simultaneously node/endpoint. Communications between adjacent nodes and between nodes and endpoints occurs through request/response transactions. Responses are always unicast. MTP provides for the retransmission of requests and/or responses in case of network errors. Only hello and designated node-request packets are sent as multicast messages; all others are unicast.

Endpoint-to-node requests are sent as multicasts, while node-to-endpoint requests are sent either as unicasts or multicasts. SMRP relies on a spanning tree-based forwarding scheme to determine routing paths for multicast traffic. This route-determination process relies on the use of a distance vector algorithm. A node sends distance vector request packets to adjacent nodes at startup time and when routes change. The distance specified in the vector is the number of hops needed to reach a particular network number range.

Nodes contain a vector for each entry in the network route table and send as many packets as necessary to send all the vectors. When routes change, each node sends distance vector request packets to every adjacent node. SMRP data forwarding involves nodes forwarding multicast datagrams on active paths of the source tree for a particular group. An active path has member endpoints on it for the group, or is a path needed as a transit path to reach other active paths. The subset of active paths for the source tree is the distribution tree for the group.

AppleTalk router responsibilities summarized

In addition to supporting AARP and a routing protocol (RTMP, AURP, or EIGRP), AppleTalk routers must support the ZIP to map network numbers to zone names on the network, and the NBP to bind names of network visible entities (e.g. printers or file servers) to AppleTalk addresses. Each router periodically broadcasts *ZIP Query packets* requesting zone list information to all routers in the network, and constructs a local zone information table from the replies it receives. This information is used by end nodes for zone selection and resource location. Routers also assist in name-to-address processing on behalf of end nodes by listening for an *NBP Broadcast Request* packet for a named entity from an AppleTalk node, and either broadcasting an *NBP Lookup Request* packet across the local zone or issuing an *NBP Forward Request* packet toward the router connected to the destination zone.

Misconceptions about AppleTalk

Sometimes it is thought that AppleTalk is a quite chatty protocol suite. RTMP with its **periodic updates** every 10 seconds is a very chatty protocol indeed, but for a reason. The advantage to a small update timer is quick convergence. Also, end stations learn very quickly who their new router is. There is no need for HSRP as in IP. The other case where AppleTalk is chatty is the AppleTalk Transaction Protocol (ATP) which sends **keepalives** to the other side every 10 seconds. Although zoning is an inherent feature in AppleTalk, it does not advertise zones. The request to learn the zones associated with a network is sent as a unicast frame.

Besides, AppleTalk does not use link-layer broadcasts, it **multicasts** instead. A well-behaved NIC in a PC should not bother the CPU with AppleTalk multicasts.

Moreover, Apple fixed the excessive traffic caused by leaving the **Chooser** open in System 7 (1989). It caused a lot of traffic only if the user had also highlighted an object type (printer, server) and zone name. It was never really a serious problem.

AppleTalk was designed as a user-oriented protocol architecture therefore we should value it properly for its easy configuration, dynamic addressing, easy resource location, and other features that alleviate users' work.

12.2 Novell NetWare routing

Novell's IPX/SPX protocol stack (here interchangeably referred to as NetWare architecture) is another proprietary architecture that used to reign in local area networking – before the wide spread of TCP/IP. Until recently, NetWare was the preferred enterprise networking system but recently it has merged with or been replaced by TCP/IP protocols. However, it is useful to see how IPX/SPX protocols work in the network, how IPX routing is performed, and what else is required from routers to perform it properly.

12.2.1 NetWare architecture: IPX/SPX

NetWare is a **network operating system** (NOS) and related support services environment created by Novell, Inc. and introduced to the market in the early 1980s. Much of NetWare's networking technology was derived from Xerox Network Systems (XNS) (see Section 12.3).

NetWare is based on a client-server architecture. Originally, NetWare **clients** were small PCs, while **servers** were slightly more powerful PCs. As NetWare became more popular, it was ported to other computing platforms. Currently, NetWare clients and servers can be represented by virtually any kind of computer system, from PCs to mainframes. A primary characteristic of the **client-server** system is that remote access is transparent to the user. This is accomplished through remote procedure calls, a process by which a local computer program running on a client sends a procedure call to a remote server. The server executes the remote procedure call and returns the requested information to the local computer client.

Figure 12.7 illustrates a simplified view of NetWare's best-known protocols and their relationship to the OSI reference model. NetWare runs on various physical media and LAN types.

FIGURE 12-7 NetWare in comparison with the OSI reference model

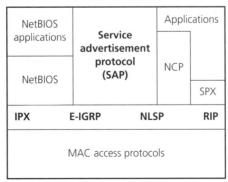

12.2.2 Lower layers – IPXWAN protocol

Although IPX was derived from XNS, it has several unique features. From the standpoint of routing, the **encapsulation** mechanisms of these two protocols are the most important difference. Whereas for Ethernet, XNS uses standard Ethernet encapsulation, IPX packets are encapsulated in Ethernet Version 2.0 or IEEE 802.3 without the IEEE 802.2 information that typically accompanies these frames (raw IPX packet in Ethernet encapsulation). With reference to Part I it is therefore possible to encounter up to four different encapsulations on a single Ethernet/IEEE 802.3 segment: raw (exclusively found in the Novell environment), Ethernet v 2.0, IEEE 802.3 with encapsulated LLC (currently default in latest NetWare releases) or SNAP information. See Figure 12.8 for a comparison of the four Ethernet encapsulation types for IPX.

FIGURE 12-8   IPX encapsulation types for Ethernet

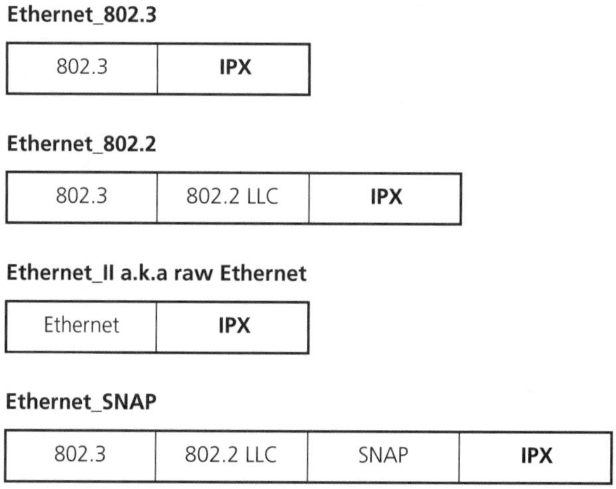

Ethernet_802.3

802.3	IPX

Ethernet_802.2

802.3	802.2 LLC	IPX

Ethernet_II a.k.a raw Ethernet

Ethernet	IPX

Ethernet_SNAP

802.3	802.2 LLC	SNAP	IPX

Hex8137 and *8138* are used to indicate the Novell IPX protocol as an EtherType number; *E0* indicates the Novell IPX LSAP.

One of the newest protocols incorporated into the Novell NetWare stack is IPXWAN protocol. It was developed to treat consistently various WAN links. Once an appropriate media-dependent link is available, the routers at each side of the WAN link use a hello process to begin the IPXWAN connection. One of the neighbor routers acts as the primary requester while the other has a secondary role responding to the requests.

The two routers have to agree on the protocol to use: RIP/SAP, unnumbered RIP, NLSP, or on-demand routing. The requester proposes a network number to assign the link. In the final stage, the routers negotiate the configuration parameters, like calculated link delay measured in microseconds (expressed in ticks, approximately 1/18 s) and throughput for IPX packets measured in packets per second. IPXWAN adds very little overhead on the IPX network (typically 12 packets to set up a serial link). Once the negotiation process completes, IPXWAN is no longer involved in IPX or the routing operation.

12.2.3 Network layer

The NetWare network layer consists of the following routed and routing protocols:

- **Internet Packet Exchange** (IPX) – supports connectionless network service to upper layers: IPX had been the default communications method used between NetWare servers and clients until NetWare 5 was introduced.
- **Routing Information Protocol** (RIP) – traditional routing protocol for Novell internets.
- **NetWare Link Services Protocol** (NLSP) – newer routing protocol enabling a dynamic routing protocol choice in Novell internets.
- **Enhanced Interior Gateway Routing Protocol (EIGRP)** – Cisco System's proprietary routing protocol, supporting also AppleTalk and IP (more details are given in Chapter 11).

Novell addressing

Novell addresses network segments and device interfaces connecting to them. IPX addresses are unique. These addresses are represented in **hexadecimal** format and consist of the following parts in the form of **<network.node.socket>**:

- **IPX network number** – assigned by the network administrator and 32 bits long;
- **node number** – usually the MAC address for one of the system's network interface cards (NICs) and 48 bits long;
- **socket number** – a two-octet number identifying the server process.

IPX's use of a MAC address for the node number makes the mapping between network and physical addresses straightforward without any need for an additional protocol, such as ARP with IP or AARP with AppleTalk.

QUICK TIP   IPX addresses vs. IP addresses

IPX addresses are much simpler than IP addresses:

- they do not have to be assigned to each workstation administratively;
- they are essentially unlimited;
- they are static hence do not require ARP to do network-to-hardware address mapping;
- they have fixed lengths of the network and node portions of the address.

Internet packet exchange

Internet Packet Exchange (IPX) is Novell's original network-layer protocol. IPX is used for the majority of NetWare client-to-server communications. It is a connectionless protocol that operates at Layer 3 providing no guaranteed delivery mechanism (similar to best-effort service with IP).

The fields of the IPX packet are as follows (see Figure 12.9):

FIGURE 12-9 IPX packet format

Number of octets:

2	2	1	1	4	6	2	4	6	2	0-546
Checksum	Packet length	Transport control	Packet type	Destination network	Destination node	Destination socket	Source network	Source node	Source socket	Data

- *Checksum* – 16-bit field that is set to all ones.
- *Packet length* – 16-bit field that specifies the length, in octets, of the complete IPX datagram. IPX packets can be any length up to the media maximum transmission unit (MTU) size. There is no packet fragmentation.
- *Transport control* – eight-bit field that indicates the number of routers the packet has passed through. When the value of this field reaches 15, the packet is discarded under the assumption that a routing loop might be occurring.
- *Packet type* – eight-bit field that specifies the upper-layer protocol to receive the packet's information. Three common values for this field are 5, which specifies Sequenced Packet Exchange (SPX), 17, which specifies the NetWare Core Protocol (NCP), and 20, specifying IPX NetBIOS broadcast.
- *Destination network, destination node, and destination socket* – specify destination information.
- *Source network, source node, and source socket* – specify source information.
- *Data* – contains information for upper-layer processes.

Novell provides a list of well-known **socket** numbers to software developers (starting at *8000*). Dynamic sockets are in the range *4000-7FFF*.

12.2.4 Transport layer

At the Novell NetWare transport layer two major protocols operate:

- **Sequenced Packet Exchange** (SPX) – reliable transport protocol.
- **Service Advertising Protocol** (SAP) – protocol for spreading the information on available services and their servers.

Sequenced packet exchange

Sequenced Packet Exchange (SPX) is the most commonly used NetWare transport protocol. Novell derived this protocol from the XNS Sequenced Packet Protocol (SPP). As with the Transmission Control Protocol (TCP) and many other transport protocols, SPX is a reliable, connection-oriented protocol that supplements the datagram service provided by Layer 3 protocols.

SNAPSHOT   SPX

Sequenced Packet Exchange is a connection-oriented protocol (equivalent of TCP) that is used for NetWare communications that require the additional security of acknowledged transmission of data.

The SPX packet is identical to the IPX packet except that is adds 12 bytes to the header. The IPX look-alike portion has only minor differences including a special value in the packet type field indicating an SPX packet, and the destination address is restricted so that broadcasts are not allowed.

The **connection control field** is one byte in size containing four bits which control data flow. The bits represent an *End of Message*, *Request for Acknowledgment*, *Attention Message*, or *System Packet*. This is followed by a second byte called the *datastream type field*. This field identifies what type of data is contained in the frame. It can also carry data that creates and tears down connections.

The **source connection ID** follows with an identification of a specific connection number (required to create a virtual connection) at the source and the same for the destination follows. These connection numbers are analogous to mailboxes with a specific address. The sender may transmit data from its mailbox to the mailbox connection of the receiver. The receiver can then reply to the specific mailbox number of the original sender. If the server was the sender, it may be maintaining virtual connections with several workstations at once. The destinations would all be different, but the source would be the same.

A **sequence number** follows uniquely identifying each packet. This field is two bytes in length. This field is followed by a two-byte **acknowledgment number** field that contains the sequence number of the next packet that the receiver should expect.

Since each node only has a limited amount of memory resources available to accommodate incoming packets, an **allocation field** is necessary to help keep the sender apprised of available receiving buffers (memory locations for holding received packets). The allocation field is two bytes in length and follows the acknowledgment number.

Finally, the data field rounds out the SPX frame providing data for the higher levels of the OSI model.

Novell also offers Internet Protocol (IP) support in the form of User Datagram Protocol (UDP)/IP encapsulation of other Novell packets, such as SPX/IPX packets. IPX datagrams are encapsulated inside UDP/IP headers for transport across an IP-based internet.

Service advertising protocol

Service Advertising Protocol (SAP) allows network resources, including file and print servers, to advertise their network addresses and the services they provide. Services are identified by a number, called a SAP identifier (for example, hex*4* = file server and hex*7* = print server; for useful SAP numbers see Appendix F). SAP updates are sent every 60 seconds.

Intermediate network devices, such as routers, listen to the SAP updates and build a table of all known services and associated network addresses. When Novell clients request a particular network service, the router responds with the network address of the requested service. The client can then contact the service directly.

SNAPSHOT   **SAP**

The **Service Advertising Protocol** allows devices that provide network services (such as file servers, print servers, or backup servers) to announce their availability on the network.

One of the limiting factors in the operation of large IPX internets is the amount of bandwidth consumed by the large, periodic Service Advertisement Protocol (SAP) updates. The SAP is very efficient on a LAN environment where workstations do not need to be configured to find servers, as they simply wait for the SAP announcements to arrive. Novell servers periodically (every 60 s) broadcast information about their services to their clients. Routers are required to propagate SAP through an IPX network so that all clients can see the service messages. The cumulative effect of hundreds of servers announcing themselves every minute can overwhelm a WAN circuit and can impact on performance on a LAN as well. In addition, servers read and store all the SAPs they receive, and processing and storing all this information can also affect server performance.

It is possible to reduce SAP traffic on Novell IPX networks by the following means:

■ **Filtering SAP updates** – SAP updates can be filtered by prohibiting routers from advertising services from specified Novell servers; this completely eliminates the service advertisements. SAP filtering is also a recommended way of handling IPX over WANs (namely ISDN in dial-on-demand routing) or any other backbone network (see example in Figure 12.10).

FIGURE 12-10 SAP filtering recommended

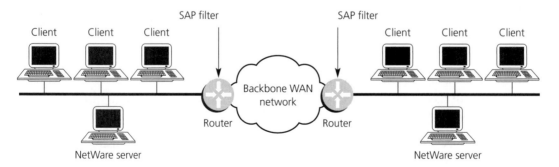

■ Using **Enhanced IGRP** routing protocol – provides **incremental SAP updates** for a finer granularity of control. Complete SAP updates are sent periodically on each interface only until an IPX Enhanced IGRP neighbor is found. Thereafter, SAP updates are only sent when there are changes to the SAP table. In this way, bandwidth is conserved, and the advertisement of services is reduced without being eliminated. Incremental SAP updates are automatic on serial interfaces and can be configured on LAN media. Enhanced IGRP also provides partial routing updates and fast convergence for IPX networks. Administrators may choose to run only the partial SAP updates or to run both the reliable SAP protocol and the partial routing update portion of Enhanced IGRP.

12.2.5 Upper-layer protocols

NetWare supports a wide variety of upper-layer protocols, but several are somewhat more popular than others. The NetWare shell runs in clients (often called workstations in the NetWare community) and intercepts application I/O calls to determine whether they require network access for satisfaction. If so, the NetWare shell packages the requests and sends them to lower-layer software for processing and network transmission. If not, they are simply passed to local I/O resources. Client applications are unaware of any network access required for completion of application calls. **NetWare Remote Procedure Call** (NetWare RPC) is another more general redirection mechanism supported by Novell.

The **NetWare Core Protocol** (NCP) is a series of server routines designed to satisfy application requests coming from, for example, the NetWare shell. Services provided by NCP include file access, printer access, name management, accounting, security, and file synchronization. NetWare also supports the **Network Basic Input/Output System** (NetBIOS) session-layer interface specification from IBM and Microsoft. NetWare's NetBIOS emulation software allows programs written to the industry-standard NetBIOS interface to run within the NetWare system.

NetWare application-layer services include **NetWare Message Handling Service** (NetWare MHS), Btrieve, NetWare Loadable Modules, and various IBM connectivity features. NetWare MHS is a message delivery system that provides electronic mail transport. **Btrieve** is Novell's implementation of the binary tree (btree) database access mechanism. **NetWare Loadable Modules** (NLM) are implemented as add-on modules that attach into the NetWare system. NLMs for alternate protocol stacks, communication services, database services, and many other services are currently available from Novell and third parties. With the release of NetWare 4.x, Novell introduced **Novell Directory Services** (NDS), a distributed directory service that reduces the need for SAP. However, SAP is still used by NetWare 4.x clients when they boot up to locate an NDS server.

12.2.6 Broadcasts in Novell networks

Novell poses the following unique **scaling problems**:

■ NetWare servers use broadcast packets to identify themselves and to advertise their services and routes to other networks.

■ NetWare clients use broadcasts to find NetWare servers.

- Version 4.0 of Novell's SNMP-based network management applications, such as NetExplorer, periodically broadcasts packets to discover changes in the network.

An idle network with a single server with one shared volume and no print services generates one broadcast packet every four seconds. A large LAN with high-end servers might have up to 150 users per PC server. If the LAN has 900 users with a reasonably even distribution, it would have six or seven servers. In an idle state with multiple shared volumes and printers, this might average out to four broadcasts per second, uniformly distributed. In a busy network with route and service requests made frequently, the rate would peak at 15 to 20 broadcasts per second.

Peak traffic load and CPU loss per workstation can be orders of magnitude greater than with average traffic loads. A common scenario is that at 9 a.m. on Monday, when everyone starts their computers. Normally, in circumstances with an average level of utilization or demand, the network can handle a reasonable number of stations. However, in circumstances in which everyone requires service at once (a demand peak), the available network capacity can support a much lower number of stations. In determining network capacity requirements, **peak demand levels** and duration can be more important than average serviceability requirements.

12.2.7 Routing in NetWare internets

To route packets in an internet, IPX can use static or dynamic routing. **Dynamic routing** is supported by three possible routing protocols:

- **Routing Information Protocol** (RIP) – distance vector protocol derived from XNS RIP.
- **NetWare Link Services Protocol** (NLSP) – link-state routing protocol. NLSP and IPX RIP automatically redistribute routing information in IPX internets.
- **Enhanced Interior Gateway Routing Protocol** (EIGRP) – non-standard and non-native routing protocol developed by Cisco Systems (see Chapter 11). Note that there is automatic redistribution from IPX RIP to EIGRP, and from NLSP to EIGRP (one way only).

Routing information protocol

IPX **Routing Information Protocol** (RIP) provides a basic solution for networking Novell LANs together. IPX RIP is directly derived from the oldest distance vector routing protocol, XNS RIP (see Table 12.1 on page 620 for comparison among all RIP-derived protocols). Two major extensions were made to improve the original protocol: split horizon and metric of delay. IPX RIP should not be confused with IP RIP. Although the two routing protocols have the same origins and thus use the distance vector routing algorithm, they differ in many ways, notably the metric and update period.

IPX RIP sends **routing updates** every 60 seconds. Routing updates are sent to IPX destination address <network.FF-FF-FF-FF-FF-FF> which is mapped onto a broadcast MAC address *FF-FF-FF-FF-FF-FF*. RIP uses **network delay** and **hop count** as its routing metrics; the best route is the path with the lowest cumulative delay; in the case of a tie, the path with the lowest hop count is chosen. The delay is measured in **ticks**. A tick is a time measurement in which 18.21 ticks equals 1 second. Length of route is limited to a total of 16 hops (passage of a packet through an intermediate network device). There are the following default values for media (router interfaces) delays:

- any LAN – 1 tick delay;
- any WAN – 6 ticks delay.

Default values can be overwritten by the administrator (to distinguish between, for example, Token Ring and Gigabit Ethernet), or more appropriate values may be agreed for WAN links using the IPXWAN protocol (in the range between 108 ticks for a 9600 kbps line down to 6 ticks, minimum, per 2 Mbps line).

IPX RIP deploys all remedies to distance vector routing algorithms' problems: *split horizon*, *hold-down time*, and *poison reverse*. The difference is, however, that split horizon cannot be disabled in those cases where it becomes an undesirable action. A typical example is a WAN environment, when connectivity in NBMA will be limited only to the routers directly connected by the virtual circuit. In such cases other IPX routing protocols would be a better choice (even EIGRP allows split horizon to be disabled in particular cases on the router).

IPX RIP has a **network-diameter** limit of 15 hops; whereas enhanced IGRP supports a limit up to 224 hops and NLSP 127 hops.

The frequent periodic routing table exchanges between neighbors causing slow convergence when the network topology changes and the 16-hop count limitation of RIP make it a poor choice for larger networks or networks connected via WAN links. Since NetWare version 4.x **incremental RIP/SAP updates** are allowed which may significantly reduce the routing information overhead exchanged periodically between neighbors.

Enhanced IGRP

Proprietary EIGRP supports IP, IPX, and AppleTalk routing, in the ships-in-the-night mode, based on the DUAL routing algorithm. It was extensively discussed in section 11.3.3 in Chapter 11. With reference to that discussion, only basic features will be mentioned on EIGRP for IPX. It provides the following features compared to classical IPX RIP:

- **Increased network width** – with IPX RIP, the largest possible width of the network is 15 hops. When IPX EIGRP is enabled, the largest possible width is 224 hops. Since the EIGRP metric is sufficiently large enough to support thousands of hops, the only barrier to expanding the network is the transport layer hop counter. Cisco works around this problem by only incrementing the transport control field when an IPX packet has traversed 15 routers and the next hop to the destination was learned via EIGRP. When a RIP route is being used as the next hop to the destination, the transport control field is incremented as usual.

- **Incremental SAP updates** – complete SAP updates are sent periodically until an EIGRP neighbor is found and thereafter only when there are changes to the SAP table. This works by taking advantage of EIGRP's reliable transport mechanism so an IPX EIGRP peer must be present for incremental SAPs to be sent. If no peer exists on a particular interface, then periodic SAPs will be sent on that interface until a peer is found. This functionality is usually automatic on serial interfaces and may be configured on LAN media if desired.

NetWare link services protocol

To address the limitations of RIP, Novell added a new routing protocol to NetWare 3.12 and 4.x servers, the **NetWare Link Services Protocol** (NLSP). NLSP is a link-state protocol, derived from the OSI Intermediate System-to-Intermediate System (IS-IS) routing protocol.

NLSP shares all the advantages (and disadvantages) of the **link-state** underlying algorithm with IS-IS or OSPF protocols: very fast convergence through immediate flooding information on network topology changes and less network bandwidth consumption for routing information, but is more demanding of router performance and may require additional router memory.

The **metric** used in NLSP is **cost** ranging in value from 1 to 63. Metric may be either default for interface or manually configured by administrator. There is an upper limit on the length of the route allowed: 1023 hops (the difference in hop count limit between NLSP and RIP must be taken into account when combining the two in the same internet).

NLSP uses a **hello** protocol to identify the routers themselves and to get information on the neighbor routers. Hello packets help in building the first database required for NLSP operation, the adjacency database.

NLSP maintains three types of **database**:

- **adjacency database** (containing information on the immediate neighbors);
- **link-state database** (containing information on the available links and services);
- **forwarding database** (containing for each destination network the following information: destination address, next hop to use, link cost, and outgoing interface).

NLSP takes a step-by-step approach to learning about the routers and services on the network. NLSP routers on the same network must exchange **hello** packets to learn about **adjacent routers** before a link can be established. Once this information is known, it is added to an **adjacency database**. The adjacency database stores information accumulated about a router's immediate neighbors and the status of the attached links (see Figure 12.11). Adjacency is a record that a router keeps about the state of its connectivity with a neighbor and the attributes of the neighboring router. Hello packets are issued every 14–20 s, the exact timing being determined by jitter algorithm which limits the possibility of transmiting two packets simultaneously between the two routers.

FIGURE 12-11 Overview of NLSP operation

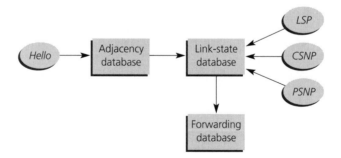

> **QUICK TIP**   **adjacency**
>
> Relationship formed between selected neighboring routers for the purpose of exchanging routing information, i.e. not all neighboring routers become necessarily adjacent. Adjacencies are established based on the information the router receives from hello packets (sent by routers on the same physical network).

Establishing router **adjacency over a WAN** involves first establishing the underlying data-link connection (details depend upon the medium). The routers then exchange identities by using the IPX WAN Version 2 protocol and determine certain operational characteristics of the link. Hello packets are exchanged and the routers update their adjacency databases. The routers exchange both link-state packets (LSPs) describing the state of their links and IPX data packets over the link. To maintain a WAN link, the router maintains a state variable indicating whether the link is up, down, or initializing for each adjacency. If the router does not hear from a neighbor within the time specified in a holding timer, the router generates a message indicating that the link is down and deletes the adjacency.

For establishing the **adjacency relationship on an LAN**, the router begins sending and accepting hello packets from other routers on the LAN and starts the **Designated Router** election process. The Designated Router (DR) represents the LAN as a whole in the link-state database, makes routing decisions on behalf of the whole, and originates LSPs on behalf of the LAN. This ensures that the size of the link-state databases that each router must construct and manage will stay within reasonable limits. Periodically, every router sends a multicast Hello packet on the LAN. The router with the highest priority (a configurable parameter) becomes the Level 1 Designated Router on the LAN. In the case of a tie, the router with the higher MAC address wins.

Once the adjacency database is established, the next step is to create some representation of the network as a whole. First, portions of the adjacency database that describe a router's immediate neighbors are combined with similar information learned from all other routers. This information is shared in the form of **Link-State Packets** (LSPs). These newly detected LSPs are flooded to other routers in the area, then merged into the receiving router's **link-state database**. As a result, the link-state database is a collection of two types of LSP packets, packets derived from the router's own link-state database and LSP packets received from other routers.

The link-state database is synchronized by reliably propagating LSPs throughout the routing area when a router observes a **topology change**. Two methods ensure that accurate topology change information is propagated: flooding and receipt confirmation. **Flooding** is instigated when a router detects a topology change. When such a change is detected, the router constructs a new LSP and transmits it to each of its neighbors. Such LSPs are directed packets on a WAN and multicast packets on an LAN. Upon receiving an LSP, the router uses the sequence number in the packet to decide whether the packet is newer than the current copy stored in its database. If it is a newer LSP, the router retransmits it to all its neighbors (except on the circuit over which the LSP was received). The **receipt confirmation** process is different for LANs and WANs. On WANs, a router receiving an LSP replies with an acknowledgment. On LANs, no explicit acknowledgment occurs, but the Designated Router periodically multicasts a packet called a **Complete Sequence Number Packet** (CSNP) that contains all the LSP identifiers and sequence numbers it has in its database for the entire area. This ensures that other routers can detect whether they are out of synchronization with the Designated Router.

Synchronization is an important function in NLSP. Every router within the local routing area must have an identical version of the link-state database. Short transitional periods can occur during which versions differ when a topology changes; part of the NLSP function is to make them converge again. To efficiently convey the topology changes to the many routers connected to one LAN segment and have each of them process the information to make routing decisions, NLSP provides the concept of a **pseudonode** that represents the LAN as a whole in the link-state database. Each router represents itself as being directly connected to the pseudonode. This process significantly reduces the size of the adjacencies in the router's link-state database.

The pseudonode does not physically exist, so a physical device (router) must represent the pseudonode for the link-state exchanges. This physical device is called a **designated router**, and it maintains an LSP database that includes the pseudonode's link to each router on the network. The designated router transmits packets on behalf of the pseudonode. It is elected using a **priority** value included in the hello packets; the router with the highest priority value and address is elected. Each router that receives the packet adds an entry to its link-state database so that when the exchanges are finished, each router has an identical link-state database. The designated router takes charge of sending out complete sequence number packets with a summary of the link-state database and also handles the translation and propagation of RIP/SAP information from non-NLSP sources.

The link-state database provides the router's view of the network topology. After this information is available, the next step is to determine the best route to a particular network and thus create a **routing table** or **forwarding database**. The NLSP decision process selects the best route based on a computation using Dijkstra's algorithm, which determines the shortest distance (best metric) from the local node to every other node. Each router has a unique version of the forwarding database, a table that maps a destination network into a next-hop address. The decision process rebuilds the forwarding database only when the router detects a change in the link-state database. In fact the router waits a little (5 seconds) before recomputing the link-state database. This holds down unnecessary computing and allows the router to act on several accumulated changes it receives during the 'waiting' period.

Routers exchange **LSPs** only when a change occurs in available links, services, or external routes. Otherwise an LSP will be retransmitted after its timer expires (typically after two hours). There are four types of packets used in NLSP:

- **Hello** – type *15*.
- **LSP** – type *18*, sent by all routers indicating their directly connected links. Each LSP is numbered (LSP ID), sequenced, and synchronized. The receiver does not acknowledge LSPs on LAN but it does on WAN links.

- **Complete sequence number packet** (CSNP) – type *24*, generated by the designated router every 30 s (for networks where DR exists). The CSNP does not leave the segment.

- **Partial sequence number packet** (PSNP) – type *26*, issued by adjacent routers on multiaccess LANs (non-DR) as a request for completing their link-state knowledge (issued, for example, in cases of failed checksum, or when having a newer LSP), or on WAN to acknowledge LSPs. PSNP does not leave the particular segment.

Over a WAN the NLSP operation is as follows: one router sends a CSNP across a **WAN link** to synchronize its database with the neighbor. For adjusting their communication parameters they might use also the IPXWAN protocol which also sets the NLSP delay and throughput for the WAN link. There is no DR, pseudonode, or IPX network number representing the WAN link which is treated as pure pipe. This situation of having the NLSP routers on both ends is preferable. However, if one of the two routers is a RIP/SAP router, than the NLSP router automatically becomes the DR and creates a pseudonode to absorb the RIP/SAP information.

NLSP supports **load balancing** and **splitting** over multiple equal-cost paths (maximum of eight).

NLSP hierarchical routing

NLSP supports hierarchical routing with **area, domain, and global IPX internet** components. An **area** is a collection of connected networks that all have the same area address. A **domain** is a collection of areas that belong to the same organization. A **global internet** is a collection of domains that usually belong to different organizations but with an arm's length relationship. Areas can be linked to create routing domains, and domains can be linked to create a global internet.

NLSP supports three **levels of hierarchical routing: Level 1, Level 2**, and **Level 3** routing. A Level 1 router connects network segments within a given routing area. A Level 2 router connects areas and also acts as a Level 1 router within its own area. A Level 3 router connects domains and also acts as a Level 2 router within its own domain. Figure 12.12 illustrates the three routing levels.

FIGURE 12-12 NLSP hierarchical routing

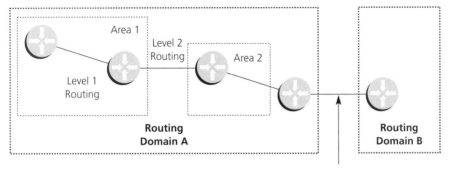

Level 3 Routing

Hierarchical routing simplifies the process of enlarging a network by reducing the amount of information that every router must store and process to route packets within a domain. A Level 1 router is required to keep detailed information only about its own area instead of storing link-state information for every router and network segment in its domain. To exchange traffic with other areas, a Level 1 router must only find the nearest Level 2 router. Between areas, Level 2 routers advertise the area address(es) only for their respective areas, not their entire link-state databases. Level 3 routers perform similarly between domains.

Route aggregation

NLSP route aggregation provides several important benefits to users of large IPX networks. The first is the ability to divide IPX networks into multiple **NLSP areas**. Previously, NLSP was specified as a single area routing protocol, meaning that individual NLSP areas had to use IPX RIP to communicate routing information between areas. Support to multiple NLSP areas allows multiple instances of NLSP to run on the same router, with routing information shared or 'leaked' between areas. Thus much larger internets can be created using just NLSP, even with only a single router.

In well-designed, hierarchically addressed networks, NLSP route aggregation allows routing information to be shared more efficiently. When possible, ranges of addresses within an area can be aggregated (or summarized) into a single, much smaller route entry. By minimizing the size of the routing databases and reducing the amount of update traffic, aggregation produces a more efficient routing process.

Route aggregation offers the following:

- **Segmentation of very large NLSP networks** (typically with more than 400 network addresses) into two or more smaller NLSP areas, which are then connected with a router that can communicate with both areas. Before, in NLSP 1.0, two areas had to use IPX RIP to exchange routing information.

- **Sharing and redistribution of routing information** directly between areas. (Novell refers to this process as 'route leaking.') It is also now possible to redistribute NLSP routing information through the EIGRP.

- **Reduction in routing overhead** through NLSP summarization to eliminate excessive routing updates and reduce network overhead and CPU utilization. Routing traffic between areas is reduced because the addresses for each area can be summarized at the backbone and routed to other areas in an efficient form. Many IPX network numbers may be advertised using a small amount of information.

- **Improved network performance** as route summaries do not require the router to recalculate the forwarding table unless the aggregated route is created or removed, thus reducing the processor load. In addition, because routes are summarized, less system memory is required to store routing information.

- **Enhanced management capabilities** allow the use of access control policies between NLSP areas. It also allows such filtering at boundaries where NLSP connects to Routing Information Protocol (RIP)/Service Advertisement Protocol (SAP) or Enhanced IGRP networks.

The IPX network is divided into areas by assigning **area addresses** that uniquely identify each NLSP area. An area address is configured on each router to define the areas to which the router belongs. Up to three area addresses are allowed per NLSP area on the router. Adjacencies are formed only between routers that share at least one common area address.

Each configured area address is identified by two 32-bit quantities that specify a network address and a **mask**. The mask indicates how much of the area number identifies the area and how much identifies individual networks in the area. For example, the area address pair *12345600 FFFFFF00* describes an area composed of 256 networks in the range *12345600* to *123456FF*. To derive the maximum benefit from NLSP Route Aggregation, it is important that IPX network addresses be assigned in a structured, **hierarchical** manner.

One of two metrics is used to determine the value of paths to destinations included in an aggregated route or in an explicit route, depending on whether the destination is within the area or in another area. The **route aggregation metric** is thus calculated as follows:

- the best path to destinations within an area is determined using the cost metric;
- the best path to destinations in another NLSP or non-NLSP area (external route) is determined using the tick metric.

When the router is configured to send an address summary into an NLSP area, by default, the delay in ticks is equal to *1* and the area count is equal to *6*. The **area count** is the number of areas through which the information is allowed to propagate. The tick value of an address summary increases and the area count decreases as the address summary is passed from area to area.

Together, the tick and cost metrics allow the initial sending router to control the spread of information and ensure that if a summary ceases to exist, the routing mechanism will eventually purge the summary. As the aggregated route circulates to different areas, each router that connects the areas increases the tick value. If a router that interconnects multiple areas receives several route summaries that have equal ticks for a destination, the router selects the aggregated route with the least cost value to that destination.

When an NLSP 1.1 router receives an explicit route to a destination and an aggregated route that subsumes the same destination's address, the router selects the explicit route as the best path. In addition, if the router receives two aggregated routes that subsume the same destination address, the router selects the aggregated route that is more specific (longest match approach applies). For example, if the router receives an aggregated route of *A0000000 F0000000* and then receives an aggregated route of *AAAA0000 FFFF0000*, it chooses the *AAAA0000 FFFF0000* aggregated route as having the best path if the destination is *AAAA0123*. It chooses *A0000000 F0000000* if the destination is A*1234567*.

A **route summary** defines a set of explicit routes that the router uses to generate an aggregated route. Route summaries can be used within and between NLSP 1.1 areas to transmit routing information. However, because IPX RIP, NLSP 1.0, and Enhanced IGRP routers cannot interpret route summaries, the **default route** must be used to reach any destination for which no explicit route is known. The default route is a reserved network (−2) that is used to route packets to any destination for which a more explicit route is not known. It is assumed that eventually the packet will reach a router with more complete routing information such that the packet will either be delivered to its destination or dropped.

When route summarization is enabled while running **multiple instances** of NLSP, the router performs **route summarization by default** based on the area address configured in each NLSP area. Explicit routes that match the area address in a given area are not redistributed individually into neighboring NLSP areas; instead, the router redistributes a single aggregated route that is equivalent to the area address into neighboring areas.

Redistributing route information

Previously, when IPX networks grew to the point where RIP and SAP were no longer able to adequately support them, users were forced to choose between Enhanced IGRP and NLSP in order to gain the scalability benefits inherent to these protocols. Through the use of route redistribution, users may now select the routing protocol, or a **combination of routing protocols**, that best meets their needs. For example, an IPX network can be built that uses a combination of RIP and NLSP on the NetWare servers and uses Enhanced IGRP as the single, integrated backbone protocol.

NLSP and Enhanced IGRP support the traditional IPX network by supporting RIP by default. Route redistribution should be disabled between instances of NLSP Version 1.1 and Enhanced IGRP to minimize the possibility of routing loops in certain topologies.

NLSP route aggregation features the ability to redistribute route information between NLSP areas. This feature allows network managers to connect a combination of Enhanced IGRP, NLSP, and IPX RIP/SAP routing areas into a single, comprehensive IPX internet. Depending on the vendor's support, routers redistribute routes between multiple NLSP areas, between NLSP and RIP, and between Enhanced IGRP and RIP. Unless otherwise specified, all routes are redistributed as individual, explicit routes.

The redistribution of routing information is automatic between NLSP and RIP and ensures routing loop avoidance (although it may lead to suboptimal routing). Also between NLSP and EIGRP automatic redistribution works while it assigns the value of 2 ticks per any backbone network (WAN).

IPX RIP routes are automatically redistributed into EIGRP, and IPX EIGRP routes are automatically redistributed into RIP.

Filtering works independently of route summarization; however, since filtering occurs before the aggregation algorithm is applied, filtering could indirectly affect route summarization. It is possible to filter all explicit routes that could generate aggregated routes, making the router unable to generate aggregated routes even when it has been explicitly configured.

IPX watchdog and SPX keepalive spoofing

NetWare includes an **IPX watchdog protocol** that periodically queries for inactive workstation connections and transmits updates to the server when a connection fails to respond appropriately. The server closes connections that the IPX watchdog reports as unavailable. Both ends of an SPX connection send **keepalive** requests to keep the connection established when no data is being transmitted. Like excessive RIP and SAP updates, the IPX watchdog packets and SPX keepalives can bring up and keep up WAN circuit-switched links, making their use extremely expensive. The intervals between these packets can be increased to reduce the amount of traffic they generate. Also, if spoofing both of these protocols is supported on routers, it eliminates most of this traffic altogether, and especially over WAN it prevents these packets from bringing up DDR links.

Misconception about IPX

Not just AppleTalk is unjustifiably sometimes called chatty; at times IPX is also given this label. Let us summarize what is going on in the IPX/SPX network:

- **SAP** broadcasts every 60 seconds – may be too much but could be easily filtered;
- **IPX RIP** broadcasts every 60 seconds – longer interval than RTMP's 10-second timer or IP RIP with 30 seconds;
- **NLSP** or **EIGRP** are alternatives to IPX RIP and SAP – as link-state protocols do not (generally) contribute to network congestion;
- NCP keepalives – every 5 seconds but router vendors offer some remedies such as a watchdog feature mainly for dial-on-demand.

If we compare IPX with IP it is first of all necessary to realize that IP was designed with different goals in mind. IPX, like to AppleTalk, was designed to be easy for the user. A tradeoff is that things like service location are easy, but they cause extra traffic. IP has more options for routing and the newer options such as OSPF are not chatty. For file sharing, you would have to use NFS or SMB over NetBIOS over UDP/IP, which can be chatty, depending on the configuration. Last but not least, the static relationship between IPX addresses and MAC addresses reduces the need for a dynamic address mapping protocol, such as ARP in IP, which may be unpleasant particularly due to its broadcast nature.

12.3 Xerox Network Systems routing

The **Xerox Network Systems** (XNS) is probably unlikely to operate in more than a few locations around the world (if any at all). The reason why I decided to include a note on XNS routing here is that XNS is one of the oldest networking architectures and its routing protocol, RIP, has been used as a base for all distance vector routing protocols used ever since.

12.3.1 XNS architecture

The Xerox Network Systems (XNS) protocols were created by Xerox Corporation in the late 1970s and early 1980s. They were designed to be used across a variety of communication media, processors, and office applications.

Because of its availability and early entry into the market, XNS was adopted by most of the early LAN companies, including Novell, Inc., Ungermann-Bass, Inc. (now a part of Tandem Computers), and 3Com Corporation. Each of these companies has since made various changes to the XNS protocols. Novell added the Service Advertising Protocol (SAP) to permit resource advertisement and modified the OSI Layer 3 protocols (which Novell renamed IPX, for Internetwork Packet Exchange) to run on IEEE 802.3 rather than Ethernet networks. Ungermann-Bass modified RIP to support delay as well as hop count and made other small changes.

12.3.2 Technology basics

Although the XNS design objectives are the same as the OSI reference model, the XNS concept of a protocol hierarchy is somewhat different from that provided by the OSI reference model. A rough comparison is shown in Figure 12.13.

FIGURE 12-13 XNS and the OSI reference model

OSI reference model	XNS protocol architecture
Application layer	*Level 4* **Application protocols**
Presentation layer Session layer	*Level 3* **Printing, Filing, Clearinghouse, Echo Protocols, Courier Protocol**
Transport layer	*Level 2* **Sequenced Packet Protocol Packet Exchange Protocol Error Protocol**
Network layer	*Level 1* **Internet Datagram Protocol Routing Information Protocol**
Link layer Physical layer	*Level 0* **Media access**

Xerox provided a **five-level model** of packet communications. **Level 0** corresponds roughly to OSI Layers 1 and 2, handling link access and bit-stream manipulation. **Level 1** corresponds roughly to the portion of OSI Layer 3 that pertains to network traffic. **Level 2** corresponds roughly to the portion of OSI Layer 3 that pertains to internetwork routing, and to OSI Layer 4, which handles interprocess communication. **Levels 3 and 4** correspond roughly to the upper two layers of the OSI model, handling data structuring, process-to-process interaction and applications. XNS has no protocol corresponding to OSI Layer 5 (the session layer).

12.3.3 Media access

Although XNS documentation mentions X.25, Ethernet, and High-Level Data Link Control (HDLC), XNS does not expressly define what it refers to as a Level 0 protocol. Like many other protocol suites, XNS leaves media access an open issue, implicitly allowing any such protocol to host the transport of XNS packets over a physical medium.

12.3.4 Network layer

The network layer offers a single connectionless network protocol with simple dynamic routing performed by RIP.

XNS addressing

XNS addresses uniquely network segments and all node interfaces. XNS **addresses** are 80 bits long and consist of the following parts in the form of **<network.node>**:

■ **network address** – 32 -bit unique network segment identification in decimal notation;

■ **node address** – 48-bit identification of a node on the network, expressed in hexadecimal notation (usually derived from the MAC address of a single interface);

■ **(socket** – additional part specification of upper-layer process (in hexadecimal format).)

The network address is unique for each network segment; the node address is uniform across a station's interfaces. (Only one MAC address of the lowest numbered interface automatically becomes the node part of XNS address; if there is no MAC address on a router then a bogus node address must be configured manually.) As the MAC address is part of the XNS address, the mapping between physical and logical addresses is static (without a need for a dynamic protocol). XNS provides for multicast and broadcast addresses.

Network protocol

The XNS network-layer protocol is called the **Internet Datagram Protocol** (IDP). IDP performs standard Layer 3 functions, including logical addressing and end-to-end datagram delivery across an internetwork. The format of an IDP packet is shown in Figure 12.14.

FIGURE 12-14 IDP packet format

Number of octets:

2	2	1	1	4	6	2	4	6	2	0–546
Checksum	Length	Transport control	Packet type	Destination network number	Destination host number	Destination socket number	Source network number	Source host number	Source socket number	Data

The fields of the IDP packet are as follows:

■ *Checksum* – 16-bit field that helps gauge the integrity of the packet after it traverses the internetwork.

■ *Length* – 16-bit field that carries the complete length (including checksum) of the current datagram.

- ***Transport control*** – eight-bit field that contains *hop count* and *maximum packet lifetime* (MPL) subfields. The *hop count* subfield is initialized to zero by the source and incremented by one as the datagram passes through a router. When the hop count field reaches 16, the datagram is discarded on the assumption that a routing loop is occurring. The *MPL* subfield provides the maximum amount of time, in seconds, that a packet can remain on the internetwork.

- ***Packet type*** – eight-bit field that specifies the format of the data field.

- ***Destination network number*** – 32-bit field that uniquely identifies the destination network in an internetwork.

- ***Destination host number*** – 48-bit field that uniquely identifies the destination host.

- ***Destination socket number*** – 16-bit field that uniquely identifies a socket (process) within the destination host.

- ***Source network number*** – 32-bit field that uniquely identifies the source network in an internetwork.

- ***Source host number*** – 48-bit field that uniquely identifies the source host.

- ***Source socket number*** – 16-bit field that uniquely identifies a socket (process) within the source host.

IEEE 802 addresses are equivalent to the numbers, so devices that are connected to more than one IEEE 802 network have the same address on each segment. This makes network numbers redundant, but nevertheless useful for routing. Certain socket numbers are well known, meaning that the service performed by the software using them is statically defined. All other socket numbers are reusable.

XNS supports Ethernet Version 2.0 encapsulation for Ethernet and three types of encapsulation for Token Ring: 3Com, SubNet Work Access Protocol (SNAP), and Ungermann-Bass.

XNS supports unicast (point-to-point), multicast, and broadcast packets. Multicast and broadcast addresses are further divided into directed and global types. Directed multicasts deliver packets to members of the multicast group on the network specified in the destination multicast network address. Directed broadcasts deliver packets to all members of a specified network. Global multicasts deliver packets to all members of the group within the entire internetwork, whereas global broadcasts deliver packets to all internetwork addresses. One bit in the host number indicates a single versus a multicast address. All ones in the host field indicate a broadcast address.

12.3.5 Transport layer

OSI transport-layer functions are implemented by several protocols. Each of the following protocols is described in the XNS specification as a Level 2 protocol. The **Sequenced Packet Protocol** (SPP) provides reliable, connection-based, flow-controlled packet transmission on behalf of client processes. It is similar in function to the TCP/IP suite's Transmission Control Protocol (TCP) and the OSI protocol suite's Transport Protocol 4 (TP4, see Section 12.6.4). Each SPP packet includes a sequence number, which is used to order packets and to determine if any have been duplicated or missed.

SPP packets also contain two 16-bit **connection identifiers**. One connection identifier is specified by each end of the connection. Together, the two connection identifiers uniquely identify a logical connection between client processes. SPP packets cannot be longer than 576 octets. Client processes can negotiate the use of a different packet size during connection establishment, but SPP does not define the nature of this negotiation.

The **Packet Exchange Protocol** (PEP) is a request-response protocol designed to have greater reliability than a simple datagram service (as provided by IDP, for example), but less reliability than SPP. PEP is functionally similar to the TCP/IP suite's User Datagram Protocol (UDP). PEP is single-packet based, providing retransmissions but no duplicate packet detection. As such, it is useful in applications where request-response transactions can be repeated without damaging data, or where reliable transfer is executed at another layer.

The **Error Protocol** (EP) can be used by any client process to notify another client process that a network error has occurred. This protocol is used, for example, in situations where an SPP implementation has identified a duplicate packet.

The Level 2 **Echo Protocol** is used to test the reachability of XNS network nodes and to support functions such as that provided by the PING command found in UNIX and other environments.

12.3.6 Upper-layer protocols

XNS offers several upper-layer protocols. The **Printing Protocol** provides print services. The Filing Protocol provides file-access services. The **Clearinghouse Protocol** provides name services. Each of these three protocols runs on top of the **Courier Protocol**, which provides conventions for data structuring and process interaction.

XNS also defines Level 4 protocols. These are application protocols but, because they have little to do with actual communication functions, the XNS specification does not include any pertinent definitions.

12.3.7 Routing solution

To route packets in an internetwork, XNS uses a single dynamic routing protocol, **Routing Information Protocol** (RIP). XNS RIP is the most basic implementation of a distance vector algorithm encompassing only the functionality to determine the path between two nodes that contain the fewest hops. As was mentioned earlier, RIP has been adopted (with some changes – see Table 12.1) by other network protocols as the fundamental and oldest routing solution in the form of:

- **Routing Information Protocol** (RIP) for IP;
- **Routing Information Protocol** for IPX (IPX RIP);
- **Routing Table Maintenance Protocol** (RTMP) for AppleTalk;
- **Routing Table Protocol** (RTP) for Banyan Vines.

| TABLE 12-1 | Comparison of all RIP derived protocols |

Routing protocol name	RIP	RTP	RTMP	RIP	RIPv1/2
Protocol architecture	XNS	VINES	AppleTalk	IPX	TCP/IP
Routing algorithm	Distance vector	Distance vector	Distance vector	Distance vector	Distance vector
Metric	Hop count	Delay	Hop count	Delay (ticks); in case of tie – hops	Hop count
Periodic updates	30 s	90 s	10 s	60 s	30 s
Support to equal-cost multipath	No	No	Yes	Yes	No (RIPv1)/ Yes (RIPv2)

XNS supports **two types of routers**:

■ information suppliers;
■ information requestors.

During start-up, each type of RIP router broadcasts a request for routing information. Information suppliers respond directly to the requestor and also send periodic advertisements (every 30 seconds). When an information supplier is shut down gracefully, it broadcasts an advertisement to indicate that all routes via it have become invalid.

An **invalid router** is detected by aging routes in the routing table. After 90 seconds without an update for a route, it is believed to have expired. An expired route is marked with a **metric of infinity**, i.e. 16, and stays in the routing table for another 60 seconds (to be advertised twice to the neighbors) before it is deleted from the table.

| QUICK TIP | **XNS RIP timers** |

Update timer = 30 s

Expiration timer = 90 s

Garbage collection timer = 150 s

For details on different vector routing, see Section 9.4.2; for details on RIP see Section 11.3.1.

12.4 Banyan VINES routing

The **Virtual Integrated Network Service** (VINES) of the Banyan company is another 'old-fashioned' representative of proprietary networking implementations. However, it is interesting to see what addressing approach has been used in VINES compared to other approaches that are around. In terms of routing, VINES is one of the first followers of XNS RIP in its adopted RTP distance vector routing protocol.

12.4.1 VINES architecture

The Banyan Virtual Integrated Network Service (VINES) implements a distributed network operating system based on a proprietary protocol family derived from Xerox Corporation's Xerox Network Systems (XNS) protocols. VINES uses a **client-server** architecture.

The VINES protocol stack is shown in Figure 12.15.

FIGURE 12-15 VINES protocol stack

OSI reference model	Banyan Vines protocol stack
Application layer	*Application layer* **StreetTalk, file, print services**
Presentation layer / Session layer	*Remote procedure call* **NetRPC**
Transport layer	*Transport layer* **Interprocess Communications Protocol Sequenced Packet Protocol**
Network layer	*Level 1* **VINES Internet Protocol VINES ARP, ICP, RTP**
Link layer / Physical layer	*Medium access*

12.4.2 Media access

The lower two layers of the VINES stack are implemented with a variety of well-known media-access mechanisms, including High-Level Data Link Control (HDLC), X.25, Ethernet, and Token Ring.

12.4.3 Network layer

The network layer of the VINES architecture comprises the following protocols:

- **VINES Internetwork Protocol** (VIP) – performs Layer 3 activities;
- **VINES Address Resolution Protocol** (ARP) – dynamically maps physical and logical addresses;
- **Routing Table Protocol** (RTP) – provides routing services;
- **Internet Control Protocol** (ICP) – provides exception handling and special routing cost information.

ARP, ICP, and RTP packets are encapsulated in a VIP packet.

VINES dynamic addressing

The VINES approach to addressing is very interesting. First, it does not address physical network segments (the wire); instead it uniquely addresses servers/routers. Second, in principal it distinguishes between **servers** (including routers) and **clients**. Each server has an assigned VINES network address through a hardware key. Clients get their addresses from a server dynamically.

VINES network-layer addresses are 48-bit entities, expressed in hexagonal format, subdivided into two parts in the form of <**network:subnetwork**>:

- **network** – 32 bits, rather a **server** number as it is derived directly from the server's key (a hardware module that identifies a unique number and the software options for that server);
- **subnetwork** – 16 bits, a **host** number (in range of hex*8000* to *FFFF*) because it is used to identify hosts on VINES networks (servers are globally assigned *1* as the subnetwork address portion).

Examples of VINES address are: *1A5B:1* (server or router with its network address 1A5B), *1A5B:8000* (client who was the first one acquiring the address from server 1A5B).

The network number identifies a VINES logical network, which is represented as a two-level tree with the root at a service node. Service nodes, which are usually servers, provide address resolution and routing services to clients, which represent the leaves of the tree. The service node, which has a hardware derived network address, assigns VIP addresses to clients.

The addressing is provided dynamically by servers without any need to administratively assign addresses to client stations (see Figure 12.16). When a client is powered on, it broadcasts a request for servers. All servers that hear the request respond. The client chooses the first response and requests a subnetwork (host) address from that server. The server responds with an address consisting of its own network address (derived from its special hardware key), concatenated with a subnetwork (host) address of its own choice. Eventually there are as many network addresses per wire as there are servers attached, each keeping a record of 'its clients.' Every node in a VINES internet has a unique address, single in the case of a station, single or multiple in the case of servers. All servers with multiple interfaces are essentially routers.

FIGURE 12-16 VINES address selection process

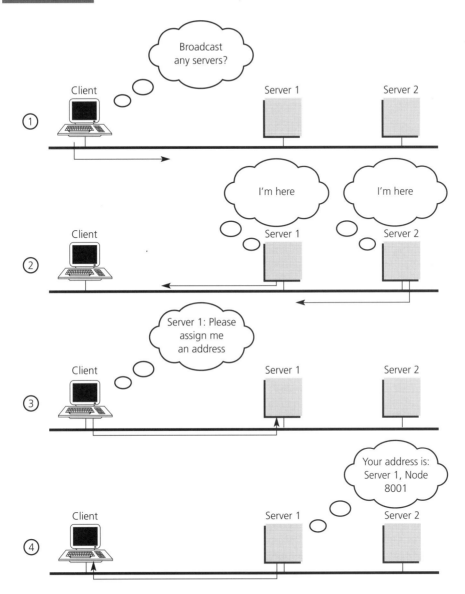

VINES internetwork protocol

The VIP packet format is shown in Figure 12.17. The fields of a VIP packet are as follows:

- ■ *Checksum* – used to detect packet corruption.
- ■ *Packet length* – indicates the length of the entire VIP packet (maximum length is 1500 octets).

FIGURE 12-17	VIP packet format

Number of octets:

2	2	1	1	4	2	4	2	var
Checksum	Packet length	Transport control	Protocol type	Destination network number	Destination subnetwork number	Source network number	Source subnetwork number	Data

- **Transport control** – consists of several subfields. If the packet is a broadcast packet, two subfields are provided: *class* (bits 1 through 3) and *hop count* (bits 4 through 7). If the packet is not a broadcast packet, four subfields are provided: *error*, *metric*, *redirect*, and *hop count*. The class subfield specifies the type of node that should receive the broadcast. For this purpose, nodes are broken into various categories having to do with the type of node and the type of link the node is on. By specifying the type of nodes to receive broadcasts, the class subfield reduces the disruption caused by broadcasts. The *hop count* subfield represents the number of hops (router traversals) the packet has been through. The *error* subfield specifies whether the ICP protocol should send an exception notification packet to the packet's source if a packet turns out to be unroutable. The *metric* subfield is set to one by a transport entity when it needs to learn the routing cost of moving packets between a service node and a neighbor. The *redirect* subfield specifies whether the router should generate a redirect (when appropriate).

- **Protocol type** – indicates the network- or transport-layer protocol for which the metric or exception notification packet is destined.

- **Destination network number, destination subnetwork number, source network number,** and **source subnetwork number** – provide VIP address information.

Address resolution protocol

VINES Address Resolution Protocol (VARP) entities are classified as either **address resolution clients** or **address resolution services**. Address resolution clients are usually implemented in client nodes, whereas address resolution services are typically provided by service nodes. ARP packets have an eight-octet header consisting of a two-octet packet type, a four-octet network number, and a two-octet subnetwork number. There are four packet types: a **query request**, which is a request for an ARP service; a **service response**, which is a response to a **query request**; an **assignment request**, which is sent to an ARP service to request a VINES internetwork address; and an **assignment response**, which is sent by the ARP service as a response to the assignment request. The network number and subnet number fields only have meaning in an **assignment response** packet.

ARP clients and services implement the following algorithm when a client starts up. First, the client broadcasts *query request* packets. Then, each service that is a neighbor of the client responds with a *service response* packet. The client then issues an **assignment request** packet to the first service that responded to its query request packet. The service responds with an **assignment response** packet containing the assigned internetwork address.

Internet control protocol

The **Internet Control Protocol** (ICP) defines exception notification and metric notification packets. Exception notification packets provide information about network-layer exceptions; metric notification packets contain information about the final transmission used to reach a client node. Exception notifications are sent when a VIP packet cannot be routed properly and the error subfield in the VIP header's transport control field is enabled. These packets also contain a field identifying the particular exception by its error code. ICP entities in service nodes generate metric notification messages when the metric subfield in the VIP header's transport control field is enabled and the destination address in the service node's packet specifies one of the service node's neighbors.

12.4.4 Transport layer

VINES provides three transport-layer services:

- **unreliable datagram service** – sends packets that are routed on a best-effort basis but not acknowledged at the destination;
- **reliable message service** – a virtual-circuit service that provides reliable sequenced and acknowledged delivery of messages between network nodes. A reliable message can be transmitted in a maximum of four VIP packets;
- **datastream service** – supports the controlled flow of data between two processes. The datastream service is an acknowledged virtual circuit service that supports the transmission of messages of unlimited size.

12.4.5 Upper-layer protocols

As a distributed network, VINES uses the Remote Procedure Call (RPC) model for communication between clients and servers. RPC is the foundation of distributed service environments. The NetRPC protocol (Layers 5 and 6) provides a high-level programming language that allows access to remote services in a manner transparent to both the user and the application.

At Layer 7, VINES offers file-service and print-service applications, as well as StreetTalk, which provides a globally consistent name service for an entire internetwork. VINES also provides an integrated applications development environment under several operating systems, including DOS and UNIX. This development environment allows third parties to develop both clients and services that run in the VINES environment.

12.4.6 Routing in VINES

Clients always choose their own server as a first-hop router, even if another server on the same cable provides a better route to the ultimate destination. Clients can learn about other routers by receiving **redirect messages** from their own server. Since clients rely on their servers for first-hop routing, VINES servers maintain routing tables to help them find remote nodes. VINES supports both static routing and dynamic routing.

Because the clients rely on their servers for first-hop routing, VINES servers maintain **routing tables** to help them find remote nodes. VINES routing tables consist of client/metric pairs, where the client corresponds to a reachable network node, and the metric corresponds to a delay in reaching that node, expressed in milliseconds. The protocol that helps VINES servers find neighboring clients, servers, and routers is the **Routing Table Protocol** (RTP).

Periodically, all clients broadcast both their network and MAC-layer addresses with **hello** packets. Hello packets indicate that the client is still operating and the network is ready. Broadcasts alert other routers to changes in node addresses and network topology. VINES uses a routing update scheme that helps diminish the number of broadcast storms, a common problem in other network environments.

Altogether the VINES messages that support routing are:

- **hellos** – sent by clients and servers;
- **routing updates** – sent by servers and routers (thus routers notify the network devices about their presence).

When a VINES server receives a packet, it checks to see if the destination IP address is that of another server or if the packet is a broadcast packet. If the current server is the destination, the server passes the request to the correct transport layer and handles the request appropriately. If another server is the destination, the current server either forwards the packet directly (if the server is a neighbor) or routes it to the next server or router in line. If the packet is a broadcast packet, the server checks to see if it came from the least-cost path. If not, the packet is discarded. If the packet did come from the least-cost path, it is forwarded to all interfaces except the one on which it was received.

VINES broadcast packets include several modifier bits that control the types of media on which broadcasts are propagated. Setting the modifier bits allows network managers to keep broadcast traffic at a minimum level. The ideal is to minimize the amount of bandwidth allocated to broadcast traffic so that just enough broadcast traffic gets through to maintain an efficient network topology.

Routing table protocol

The **Routing Table Protocol** (RTP) is a distance vector based routing protocol, derived from XNS RIP (see Table 12.1 on p. 620 for a comparison among all RIP-derived protocols), using **delay** as a metric. RTP distributes network topology information. Routing update packets are broadcast periodically (every 90 s) by both routers and service nodes. These packets inform neighbors of a node's existence and also indicate whether the node is a client or a service node. Service nodes also include, in each routing update packet, a list of all known networks and the cost factors associated with reaching those networks.

Two **routing tables** are maintained, a table of all known networks and a table of neighbors. For service nodes, the **table of all known networks** contains an entry for each known network except the service node's own network. Each entry contains a network number, a routing metric, and a pointer to the entry for the next hop to the network in the table of neighbors. The table of **neighbors** contains an entry for each neighbor service node and client node. Entries include a network number, a subnetwork number, the media type (for example, Ethernet) used to reach that node, a LAN address (if the medium connecting the neighbor is a LAN), and a neighbor metric.

RTP specifies four packet types:

- **routing update** – issued periodically to notify neighbors of an entity's existence;
- **routing request** – exchanged by entities when they need to learn the network's topology quickly;
- **routing response** – contains topological information and is used by service nodes to respond to routing request packets;
- **routing redirect** – provides better path information to nodes using inefficient paths.

RTP packets have a four-octet header consisting of the following one-octet fields:

- *operation type* – indicates the packet type;
- *node type* – indicates whether the packet came from a service node or a non-service node;
- *controller type* – indicates whether the controller in the node transmitting the RTP packet has a multi-buffer controller;
- *machine type* – indicates whether the processor in the RTP sender is fast or slow. Both the controller type and the machine type fields are used for pacing.

RTP supports load balancing across the routes with the same metric.

Native RTP operation may be improved depending on the router vendor support. For example, lengthening the interval between RTP updates can save bandwidth while maintaining optimum service to users. If the timers on different interfaces can be configured independently, administrators can modify wide-area updates without any impact on timers or on the convergence time for routing in local environments. An option to configure a partial routing update scheme for LAN and WAN interfaces may give administrators another way to reduce the bandwidth used for routing updates without degrading convergence time.

Sequenced RTP

With VINES Release 5.50, Banyan introduced a routing protocol called **Sequenced RTP** (SRTP). This protocol is significantly more efficient than Banyan's older RTP routing protocol, because it does not require the periodic exchange of complete routing tables. Instead, a router running SRTP sends a short message containing a sequence number every 90 seconds. This sequence number references the state of the routing table when the last change occurred.

Sequenced RTP sends new routing information only when there is a change in the network, and then such updates contain only the changed information. The use of Sequenced RTP can significantly improve the bandwidth efficiency of the VINES environment, because less traffic is devoted to broadcasts. This is especially important with costly WANs.

12.5 DECnet routing

Digital was one of the first companies in the world to start developing a networking architecture. Their DNA used to be well-known and widely used at the time in large DEC (Digital Equipment Corporation) mainframes (VAX machines). DECnet, the set of networking protocols, introduced several interesting issues to networking, including: hierarchical routing (although based on the distance vector algorithm) supported by dividing the network into areas whose numbers form part of DECnet addressing, only that devices are addressed, not network segments.

12.5.1 DECnet architecture

Digital Equipment Corporation (then Digital, now acquired by Compaq) developed the DECnet protocol family to provide a well thought-out way for its computers to communicate with one another. The first version of DECnet was released in 1975, while the latest developments put an equal sign between DECnet and OSI architectures. DECnet is used in its fourth and fifth product releases, called Phases.

Phase IV is a typical proprietary networking architecture while the later Phase V was referred to as **DECnet/OSI** (alternatively DECnet Plus). DECnet **Phase V** is a superset of the OSI protocol suite and supports almost all OSI protocols as well as several other proprietary and standard protocols that were supported in previous versions of DECnet, backward compatible with Phase IV. There are certain incompatibilities, however, between Phase V and OSI architectures (such as management protocol CMIP) which prevent the taking of Phase V as a copy of OSI.

12.5.2 Digital network architecture

Contrary to popular belief, DECnet is not a network architecture at all but is, rather, a series of products conforming to Digital's **Digital Network Architecture** (DNA). Like most comprehensive network architectures from large systems vendors, DNA supports a large set of both proprietary and standard protocols. The list of DNA-supported technologies grows constantly as Digital implements new protocols. Figure 12.18 illustrates an incomplete snapshot of DNA and the relationship of some of its components to the OSI reference model. While in Phase IV there was no name service (the mapping between names and addresses was performed manually), Phase V introduced a dynamic mapping.

12.5.3 Media access

As Figure 12.18 shows, DNA supports a variety of media and link implementations. Among these are well-known standards such as Ethernet, Token Ring, Fiber Distributed Data Interface (FDDI), IEEE 802.2, and X.25. DNA also offers its own point-to-point link-layer protocol called **Digital Data Communications Message Protocol** (DDCMP).

FIGURE 12-18 DNA and the OSI reference model

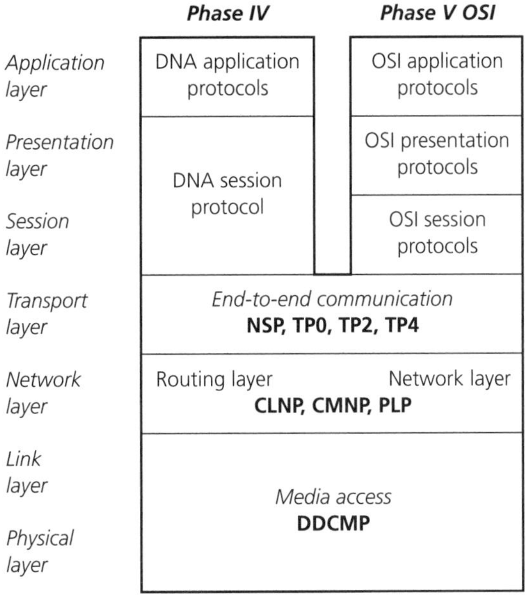

12.5.4 Network layer

DECnet supports both connectionless and connection-oriented network services implemented by OSI protocols. The connectionless implementation uses the **Connectionless Network Protocol** (CLNP)/ **Connectionless Network Service** (CLNS) – see section 12.6 below on OSI for more details. The connection-oriented network layer uses the X.25 **Packet-Level Protocol** (PLP), which is also known as X.25 Level 3, and the **Connection-Mode Network Protocol** (CMNP).

DECnet Phase IV routing was not very similar to OSI routing; a distance vector based routing was used. Phase V DNA routing, on the other hand, consists of OSI routing (ES-IS and IS-IS), plus continued support for the DECnet Phase IV routing protocol.

Addressing

DECnet addresses nodes by their residence in administratively created **areas**. DECnet addresses neither interfaces, nor network segments (wires). DECnet locates hosts using **<area.node> address pairs** as a network address:

■ **area address** – six-bit value ranging from 1 to 63, expressed in decimal;

■ **node address** – 10-bit value between 1 and 1023, expressed in decimal.

Hence, each area can have 1023 nodes, and approximately 65 000 nodes can be addressed in the whole DECnet internet. If a node has several network interfaces, it uses the same area.node address for each interface. Areas can span many routers, and a single cable can support many areas (contrary to other approaches, such as OSPF areas, it is the node which belongs to the area, not the segment). The area must not be discontiguous (exceptionally, in Phase V under certain provisions, this may occur).

Figure 12.19 shows a sample DECnet network with several addressable entities.

FIGURE 12-19 DECnet addresses

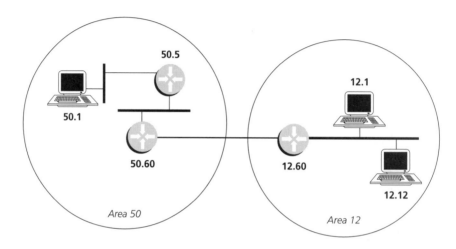

DECnet has one not very pleasant feature related to mapping physical and network addresses. It does not need a dynamic protocol because it provides a **static mapping** between the two address types. However, contrary to the approaches we see in Novell IPX or OSI where the physical address is statically mapped into the network address as part of it, DECnet uses this approach the other way round: it maps the administratively assigned network addresses **<area.node>** and uses them to change the physical burned-in MAC addresses in the software.

Thus, network-level addresses are embedded in the MAC-layer address according to an algorithm that multiplies the area number by 1024 and adds the node number to the product. The resulting 16-bit decimal address is converted to a hexadecimal number and appended to the address prefix of hex*AA00.0400* in octet-swapped order, with the least significant octet first. For example, DECnet address *5.17* (area 5, node 17) becomes *0001010000010001* in binary concatenation, which is hex*1411*. After this octet-swapped address is appended to the standard DECnet MAC address prefix, the resulting MAC address is hex*AA00.0400.**1114***.

12.5.5 Transport layer

The DNA transport layer is implemented by a variety of transports, both proprietary and standard. OSI **transport protocols** TP0, TP2, and TP4 are supported (see Section 12.6.4). Digital's own **Network Services Protocol** (NSP) is functionally similar to TP4 in that it offers a connection-oriented, flow-controlled service with message fragmentation and reassembly. Two subchannels are supported: one for normal data and one for expedited data and flow control information. Two **flow control** types are supported: a simple start/stop mechanism (the receiver tells the sender when to terminate and resume data transmission) and a more complex flow control technique where the receiver tells the sender how many messages it can accept. NSP can also respond to congestion notifications from the network layer by reducing the number of outstanding messages it will tolerate.

12.5.6 Upper-layer protocols

Above the transport layer, DECnet supports its own proprietary upper-layer protocols as well as standard OSI upper-layer protocols. DECnet application protocols use the DNA session control protocol and the DNA name service. OSI application protocols are supported by OSI presentation- and session-layer implementations.

12.5.7 DECnet routing overview

DECnet distinguishes between two types of nodes: **end nodes** and **routing nodes**. The difference is that, while both end nodes and routing nodes can send and receive network information, only routing nodes can provide routing services for other DECnet nodes. Among routing nodes belong not only routers but also VAX mainframes. It is not even necessary for routing nodes to be multi-interface. For example, when two (inter-area) routing nodes belonging to different areas connect to the same Ethernet segment, they perform inter-area routing for nodes belonging to their areas, respectively.

DECnet routing occurs at the routing layer of the DNA in DECnet Phase IV and at the network layer of the OSI model in DECnet/OSI. DECnet Phase IV routing is implemented by the **DECnet Routing Protocol** (DRP) which is **distance vector** based while it also provides for **hierarchical routing**. Routing updates are sent periodically every 40 s, while hello messages have a period of 15 s.

The **hello protocol** supports up-to-date knowledge about the existing end nodes and usable routers in the DECnet network. Routers send hellos to each other and at least one router per data link sends hellos to all end nodes. End nodes also send hellos to all routers so the routers learn who is on their networks. Hello messages are sent to data link-layer multicast addresses.

DECnet routing decisions are based on a **cost** metric, an arbitrary measure assigned by the network administrators to be used in comparing various paths through an internetwork environment. DECnet costs are typically based on media bandwidth, or alternatively on other measures. The lower the cost, the better the path. When network faults occur, DECnet uses cost values to recalculate the best paths to each destination. Routing updates contain cost information to all reachable nodes within each router's area. Each router's interface has an outgoing cost associated with it and routing decisions are based on total path cost.

DECnet **routing nodes** are referred to as either Level 1 or Level 2 routers (similar to OSI CLNP routing). A **Level 1 router** communicates with end nodes, with other Level 1 routers only within its particular area, and with Level 2 routers in its area. **Level 2 routers** provide for inter-area routing as they communicate with Level 1 routers in the same area and with Level 2 routers in different areas. To perform proper routing across a DECnet internet, there must exist a continuous physically connected chain of Level 2 routing nodes (see Figure 12.20). Hence, besides the Level 2 routers residing at the boundaries of areas there may occasionally be needed Level 2 routers inside areas to support the physical connectivity across the area. Together, Level 1 and Level 2 routers form a **hierarchical routing scheme**.

FIGURE 12-20 DECnet hierarchical routing

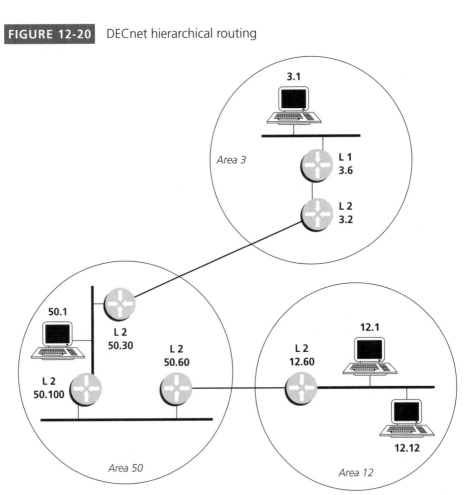

The routing in a DECnet internetwork works as follows: end systems send hello messages to notify the (designated) Level 1 router about its existence. On the LAN, the Level 1 router with the highest priority is elected to be the **desig-**

nated router. If two routers have the same priority, the one with the larger node number becomes the designated router. A router's priority can be manually configured to force it to become the designated router. The designated router builds adjacencies with all nodes attached to the LAN. All traffic from the end nodes is sent to designated router which periodically advertises their services.

As shown in Figure 12.20 above, multiple Level 2 routers can exist in any area. When a Level 1 router wishes to send a packet outside its area, it forwards the packet to a Level 2 router in the same area. In some cases, the Level 2 router may not have the optimal path to the destination, but the mesh network configuration offers a degree of fault tolerance not provided by the simple assignment of one Level 2 router per area. This concept is known as area partitioning.

DECnet Phase IV routing frame format

The DECnet Phase IV **routing protocol** includes the following fields:

- ■ *Routing flags* – consisting of:
  - – *return-to-sender bit* – if set, indicates that the packet is returning to the source;
  - – *return-to-sender-request bit* – if set, indicates that request packets should be returned to the source if they cannot be delivered to the destination;
  - – *intraLAN bit* – on by default. If the router detects that the two communicating end systems are not on the same subnetwork, it turns the bit off;
  - – other bits that indicate header format, whether padding is being used, and other functions.
- ■ *Destination node and source node* fields – identify the network addresses of the destination nodes and the source node.
- ■ *Nodes traversed* field – shows the number of nodes the packet has traversed on its way to the destination. This field allows implementation of a maximum hop count so that obsolete packets can be removed from the network.

12.6 OSI routing

While the **OSI reference model** (see Part I) was approved as an international standard in 1984, the concrete OSI architecture and layer protocols have been developed gradually since then. While OSI implementations are not unheard of, the OSI protocols stopped to be the final goal of network developers and implementors. (Long ago even Internet community expressed publicly its aim to converge to OSI architecture in the future but this is no longer true as TCP/IP became a worldwide *de facto* standard.)

The full OSI architecture with the names of the major protocols is shown in Figure 12.21.

FIGURE 12-21 OSI architecture

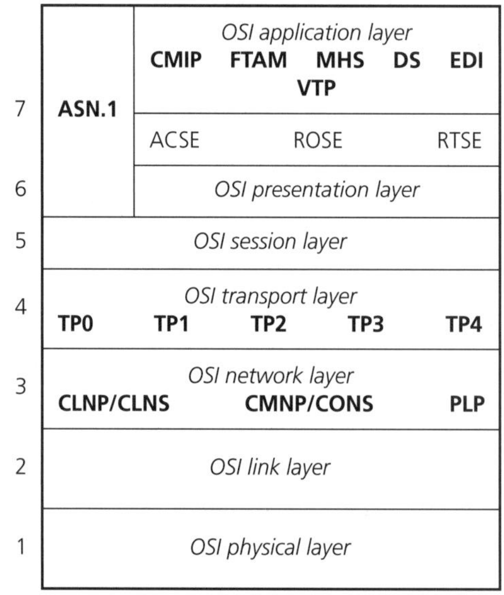

		OSI application layer				
		CMIP	FTAM	MHS	DS	EDI
			VTP			
7	ASN.1	ACSE		ROSE		RTSE
6		OSI presentation layer				
5		OSI session layer				
4		OSI transport layer				
		TP0	TP1	TP2	TP3	TP4
3		OSI network layer				
		CLNP/CLNS		CMNP/CONS		PLP
2		OSI link layer				
1		OSI physical layer				

12.6.1 OSI terminology

The world of OSI networking has a unique (albeit standardized) terminology. The two types of nodes in OSI network, the smallest pieces in the network routing hierarchy, are:

- **end system** (ES) – refers to any non-routing network device; all end systems in a particular routing area have full access to all other end systems in the area;
- **intermediate system** (IS) – refers to a router.

The OSI network topology defines hierarchical structure, which is then efficiently used for routing by longest prefixes:

- **area** – group of contiguous networks and attached hosts that are specified to be an area by a network administrator or manager;
- **administrative domain** – collection of connected areas. Routing domains provide full connectivity to all end systems within them.

12.6.2 Lower layers

The OSI stack may run over many of today's popular media-access protocols, including IEEE 802.2, IEEE 802.3, IEEE 802.5, FDDI, X.21, V.35, X.25, and others.

12.6.3 Network layer

The **OSI network service definition** (ISO 8348) describes the connection-oriented and connectionless services provided by the OSI network layer. Network layer addressing is also defined in this document. Unlike any other protocol stack, OSI offers both a **connectionless** and a **connection-oriented network layer service:**

■ **ConnectionLess Network Service/Protocol** (CLNS/CLNP) – provides connectionless network service (ISO 8473).
■ **Connection-mode Network Service** (CONS) – provides connection-oriented network layer service (ISO 8878 and 9574).

STANDARDS WATCH   OSI protocols

ISO/IEC 8208:2000 **Information Technology – Data Communications – X.25 Packet Layer Protocol for Data Terminal Equipment**

ISO/IEC 8348:1996 **Information Technology – Open Systems Interconnection – Network Service Definition**

ISO/IEC 8348:1996/Amd 1:1998 **Addition of the Internet Protocol Address Format Identifier**

ISO/IEC 8473-1:1998 **Information Technology – Protocol for Providing the Connectionless-mode Network Service: Protocol Specification**

ISO/IEC 8473-2:1996 **Information Technology – Protocol for Providing the Connectionless-mode Network Service – Part 2: Provision of the Underlying Service by an ISO/IEC 8802 Subnetwork**

ISO/IEC 8473-3:1995 **Information Technology – Protocol for Providing the Connectionless-mode Network Service: Provision of the Underlying Service by an X.25 Subnetwork**

ISO/IEC 8473-4:1995 **Information Technology – Protocol for Providing the Connectionless-mode Network Service: Provision of the Underlying Service by a Subnetwork that Provides the OSI Data Link Service**

ISO/IEC 8473-5:1997 **Information Technology – Protocol for Providing the Connectionless-mode Network Service: Provision of the Underlying Service by ISDN Circuit-switched B-Channels**

ISO/IEC 8602:1995 **Information Technology – Protocol for Providing the OSI Connectionless-mode Transport Service**

ISO/IEC 8878:1992 **Information Technology – Telecommunications and Information Exchange between Systems – Use of X.25 to Provide the OSI Connection-mode Network Service**

ISO/IEC 9574:1992 **Information Technology – Provision of the OSI Connection-mode Network Service by Packet Mode Terminal Equipment to an Integrated Services Digital Network (ISDN)**

Connectionless network service and protocol

The **connectionless network service** (CLNS) is supported by the **connectionless network protocol** (CLNP), a connectionless datagram protocol used to carry data and error indications. It has no facilities for error detection or correction, relying on the transport layer to provide these services as appropriate. It has only one phase, called data transfer. Each invocation of a service primitive is independent of all other invocations, requiring all address information to be completely contained within the service primitive.

While CLNP defines the actual protocol performing typical network-layer functions, the **connectionless network service** (CLNS) describes a service provided to the transport layer in which a request to transfer data receives 'best effort' delivery similar to that of IP. Such delivery does not guarantee that data will not be lost, corrupted, misordered, or duplicated. Connectionless service assumes that the transport layer will correct such problems as necessary. CLNS does not provide any form of connection information or state, and connection setup is not performed.

Connection-oriented network service and protocol

The OSI **connection-oriented network service** (CONS) uses the X.25 Packet-Level Protocol (PLP) for connection-oriented data movement and error indications. Six services are provided to transport-layer entities: one for **connection establishment**, one for **connection release**, and four for **data transfer**. Services are invoked by some combination of four primitives: request, indication, response, and confirmation.

At time t-1, the transport layer of end system 1 (ES 1) sends a request primitive to ES 1's network layer. This request is placed onto ES 1's subnetwork by lower-layer subnetwork protocols, and is eventually received by ES 2, which sends the information up to the network layer. At time t-2, ES 2's network layer sends an indication primitive to its transport layer. After the required upper-layer processing for this packet is complete, ES 2 initiates a response to ES 1 by using a response primitive sent from the transport layer to the network layer. The response, which occurs at time t-3, travels back to ES 1, which sends the information up to the network layer where a confirm primitive is generated and sent to the transport layer at time t-4.

Addressing

OSI addresses network devices using their hierarchical placement in the network topology: **domain, area, node identifier**. Therefore, within OSI, domain, area, and node are uniquely addressed while there is no address assigned to network segments. The hierarchical addressing is used for routing by the longest prefixes. OSI uses two different approaches to addressing (having similar formats):

- **network service access point** (NSAP);
- **network entity title** (NET).

The OSI network service is provided to the transport layer through a conceptual point on the network/transport layer boundary known as a **network service access point** (NSAP). There is one NSAP per transport entity. Each NSAP can be individually addressed in the global OSI internet through its NSAP address. An OSI end system can have multiple NSAP addresses, in which case the addresses usually differ only in the last octet, known as the **n-selector**.

It is also useful to address a system's network layer without being associated with a specific transport entity (e.g. when a system participates in routing protocols or when addressing an intermediate system). Such addressing is done via a special network address called a **network entity title** (NET). A NET is structurally identical to an NSAP address, but uses the special n-selector value *00* (no concrete SAP is identified). Most end systems and ISs have only a single NET. However, an intermediate system that is participating in multiple areas or domains can choose to have multiple NETs.

NETs and NSAP addresses are **hierarchical addresses**. Addressing hierarchies facilitate both administration (by allowing multiple levels of address administration) and routing (by encoding network topology information). An NSAP address (see Figure 12.22) is first separated into two parts:

FIGURE 12-22 OSI address format (NSAP)

Initial Domain Part IDP		*Domain Specific Part DSP*		
Authority and Format Identifier **AFI**	Initial Domain Identifier **IDI**	High-order DSP **HO–DSP**	System Identifier ID	NSAP Selector **SEL**

- **initial domain part** (IDP) – consisting of:
  - **authority and format identifier** (AFI) – provides information about the structure and content of the IDI and DSP fields, including whether the IDI is of variable length and whether the DSP uses decimal or binary notation (different standard AFI types are shown in Table 12.2);
  - **initial domain identifier** (IDI) – specifies an entity that can assign values to the DSP portion of the address.

- **Domain specific part** (DSP) – further subdivided by the authority responsible for its administration. Typically, another administrative authority identifier follows, allowing address administration to be further delegated to subauthorities. Following that comes information used for routing, such as the **area** within the routing domain, the **station ID** (usually MAC address) within the area, and the **selector** within the station.

NSAP addresses can take several forms, depending on the requirements of the organization. The encoding is always hexadecimal and can range from eight octets to twenty octets in length. NSAP addresses do not have a fixed structure; instead, the format is specified in the first field of each address (AFI). A node can have more links in that area all with the same address, but physically only exist in one area. The system ID must be unique within the network. NSAP addressing is used also beyond OSI, e.g. in ATM (see Part I, section 3.8).

TABLE 12-2   Major AFI identifiers in OSI addresses

AFI	Use	Standard	Maximum IDP length	Maximum DSP length
37, 53	X.25 numbering	X.121	8	12
39	Geographical assignment	ISO DDC	3	17
41, 55	Telex	F.69	5	15
43, 57	Phone	E.163	7	13
45, 59	ISDN	E.164	9	11
47	Organization assignment	ISO	3	17
49	Local		1	19

12.6.4 OSI transport layer

As with the OSI network layer, both connectionless and connection-oriented transport services are offered. There is only one formal standard for the transport layer defined by the ISO, but it has five classifications (see Table 12.3 for their comparison):

■ **Transport protocol 0** (TP0) – the simplest OSI connection-oriented transport protocol. Of the classical transport layer functions, it performs only segmentation and reassembly. This means that TP0 will note the smallest maximum size protocol data unit (PDU) supported by the underlying

TABLE 12-3   Comparison of OSI transport protocols

	TP0	TP1	TP2	TP3	TP4
Segmentation and reassembly	Yes	Yes	Yes	Yes	Yes
Error control	No	Yes	No	Yes	Yes
Flow control	No	No	Yes	Yes	Yes
(De)multiplexing	No	No	No	Yes	Yes
Reliable service	No	No	No	No	Yes

subnetworks, and will break the transport packet into smaller pieces that are not too big for network transmission.

■ **Transport protocol 1** (TP1) – in addition to segmentation and reassembly, it offers basic error recovery. It numbers all PDUs and resends those that are not acknowledged. TP1 can also reinitiate connections when excessive unacknowledged PDUs occur.

■ **Transport protocol 2** (TP2) – can multiplex and demultiplex datastreams over a single virtual circuit. This capability makes TP2 particularly useful over public data networks (PDNs), where each virtual circuit incurs a separate charge. Like TP0 and TP1, TP2 also segments and reassembles PDUs.

■ **Transport protocol 3** (TP3) – combines the features of TP1 and TP2.

■ **Transport protocol 4** (TP4) – the most popular OSI transport protocol. TP4 is similar to the TCP. In addition to TP3's features, TP4 provides reliable transport service. It assumes a network in which problems are not detected. TP4 works with both connection-oriented and connectionless services.

12.6.5 Upper-layer protocols

The **session layer protocol** turns the datastreams provided by the lower four layers into sessions by implementing various control mechanisms. These mechanisms include accounting, conversation control (that is, determining who can talk when), and session parameter negotiation. Session conversation control is implemented by use of a token, the possession of which provides the right to communicate. The token can be requested, and ESs can be given priorities that provide for unequal token use.

The **presentation layer** is typically just a pass-through protocol for information from adjacent layers. Abstract Syntax Notation 1 (ASN.1) standardized by ISO is used for expressing data formats in a machine-independent format. This allows communication between applications on diverse end systems in a manner transparent to the applications.

The **application layer** includes actual applications as well as **application service elements** (ASEs). ASEs allow easy communication from applications to lower layers. The three most important ASEs are:

■ **Association Control Service Element** (ACSE) – associates application names with one another in preparation for application-to-application communication.

■ **Remote Operations Service Element** (ROSE) – implements a generic request-reply mechanism that permits remote operations in a manner similar to that of remote procedure calls (RPCs).

■ **Reliable Transfer Service Element** (RTSE) – aids reliable delivery by making session-layer constructs easy to use.

Five OSI application services and protocols receive the most attention:

■ **Common Management Information Protocol** (CMIP) – supports OSI network management (see Part 1, Chapter 4) allowing exchange of management information between OSI managed nodes and management station(s) (ITU-T X.700 series).

- **Directory Services** (DS) – derived from the ITU-T X.500 recommendation series, this service provides distributed database capabilities useful for upper-layer node identification and addressing.
- **File Transfer, Access, and Management** (FTAM) – provides file transfer service with numerous options.
- **Message Handling Systems** (MHS) – provides an underlying transport mechanism for electronic messaging applications and other applications desiring store-and-forward services (ITU-T X.400 series).
- **Virtual Terminal Protocol** (VTP) – provides terminal emulation.

12.6.6 OSI routing

Due to the hierarchical topology of OSI internets, the routing hierarchy was also built into the following levels (see Figure 12.23):

FIGURE 12-23   Hierarchical routing in OSI

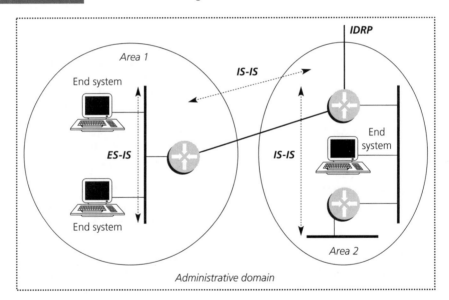

- **End system to intermediate system** (ES-IS) communication supports the basic exchange of addressing information from routers (IS) to end systems and thus provides the end systems with information about the available intermediate system (ISO 9542), and describes how ESs communicate with ISs in a connectionless environment (CLNP).
- **Intermediate system to intermediate system** (IS-IS) is a true intra-domain routing protocol providing for routing within an area and between areas belonging to the single administrative domain (ISO 10589).
- **Inter-domain routing protocol** (IDRP) supports routing between different domains of the OSI internet (ISO 10747).

OSI routing (note: the spelling is correct, as endorsed)

ISO/IEC TR 9575:1995 **Information Technology – Telecommunications and Information Exchange between Systems –** *OSI Routeing Framework*

ISO 9542:1988 **Information Processing Systems – Telecommunications and Information Exchange between Systems –** *End System to Intermediate System Routeing Exchange Protocol* for Use in Conjunction with the Protocol for Providing the Connectionless-mode Network Service (ISO 8473)

ISO/IEC 10030:1995 **Information Technology – Telecommunications and Information Exchange between Systems –** *End System Routeing Information Exchange Protocol* for Use in Conjunction with ISO/IEC 8878

ISO/IEC 10589:1992 **Information Technology – Telecommunications and Information Exchange between Systems –** *Intermediate System to Intermediate System Intra-domain Routeing Information Exchange Protocol* for Use in Conjunction with the Protocol for Providing the Connectionless-mode Network Service (ISO 8473)

ISO/IEC 10747:1994 **Information Technology – Telecommunications and Information Exchange between Systems –** *Protocol for Exchange of Inter-domain Routeing Information among ISs to Support Forwarding of ISO 8473 PDUs*

12.6.7 *End system to intermediate system protocol*

The **End System to Intermediate System Protocol** (ES-IS) is more a discovery protocol than a routing protocol. Through ES-IS, end systems and intermediate systems learn about each other. ES-IS accomplishes this through **hello** packets. ESs discover the nearest IS by listening to **IS hello messages**. Hello packets convey subnetwork- and network-layer address information. Through these exchanges, all ESs and ISs on a particular subnetwork can learn the physical (subnetwork) address and the network address of all attached network devices. Configuration information is discarded when it becomes too old.

ES-IS distinguishes between three different types of subnetworks:

- point-to-point subnetworks – e.g. PPP link;
- broadcast subnetworks – e.g. Ethernet, IEEE 802.3, IEEE 802.5;
- general topology subnetworks – support an arbitrary number of systems. However, unlike broadcast subnetworks, the cost of an n-way transmission scales directly with the subnetwork size on a general topology subnetwork. X.25 is an example of a general topology subnetwork.

Configuration information is transmitted at regular intervals through two types of messages to convey the subnetwork and network-layer addresses of the systems that generate them:

- **ES hello messages** (ESHs) – generated by ESs and sent to every IS on the subnetwork;

- **IS hello messages** (ISHs) – generated by ISs and sent to all ESs on the subnetwork.

Where possible, ES-IS attempts to send configuration information to many systems simultaneously. On broadcast subnetworks, ES-IS hello messages are sent to all ISs through a special MAC multicast address (see Table 12.4 – communication runs directly over the link layer). ISs send hello messages to a special multicast address designating all end systems. When operating on a general topology subnetwork, ES-IS generally does not transmit configuration information because of the high cost of multicast transmissions.

TABLE 12-4   Reserved multicast addresses used in OSI

Use	Type of address	MAC address (hexadecimal)
All End System Network Entities Address (ISO/IEC 9542)	Reserved MAC group address	09-00-2B-00-00-04
	Locally administered MAC group address (IEEE 802.5 functional address)	03-00-00-00-02-00
All Intermediate System Network Entities Address (ISO/IEC 9542)	Reserved MAC group address	09-00-2B-00-00-05
	Locally administered MAC group address (IEEE 802.5 functional address)	03-00-00-00-01-00
All Multicast Capable End Systems Address (ISO/IEC 9542)	Reserved MAC group address	01-80-C2-00-00-1B
All Multicast Announcements Address (ISO/IEC 9542)	Reserved MAC group address	01-80-C2-00-00-1C
All Multicast Capable Intermediate Systems Address (ISO/IEC 9542)	Reserved MAC group address	01-80-C2-00-00-1D
All Level 1 Intermediate Systems Address (ISO/IEC 10589)	Reserved MAC group address	01-80-C2-00-00-14
All Level 2 Intermediate Systems Address (ISO/IEC 10589)	Reserved MAC group address	01-80-C2-00-00-15

ES-IS conveys both network-layer addresses (NSAP and NET) and subnetwork addresses. OSI subnetwork addresses, **subnetwork point of attachment addresses** (SNPA), are the points at which an ES or IS is physically attached to a subnetwork. The SNPA address uniquely identifies each system attached to the subnetwork. In an Ethernet network, for example, the SNPA is the 48-bit Media Access Control (MAC) address. Part of the configuration information transmitted by ES-IS is the NSAP-to-SNPA or NET-to-SNPA mapping.

ESs maintain two **caches**: an **IS cache** that contains data link-layer addresses for all ISs on the LAN and a **destination cache** that contains the network layer/data link-layer address mappings for all destination ESs. The **communication** between end systems works as follows. When an ES needs to transmit a packet to another ES, it first checks its **destination cache**. If the destination ES is listed in the cache, the source ES addresses and sends the packet accordingly. If the destination ES is not in the destination cache, the source ES looks in its **IS cache**. If the IS cache is not empty, the source ES selects an IS from the cache and addresses its packet to that IS. In other words, the ES sends the packet to any directly connected IS in its area. The IS may or may not be the first step along the optimal path to the destination. If the IS determines that the next hop is another IS on the ES's LAN, it forwards the packet to that IS and sends the ES a redirect message. If the IS determines that the destination ES is on the source ES's LAN, it forwards the packet to the destination ES and sends a redirect message to the source ES.

If the IS cache is empty and there is no appropriate entry in the destination cache, the ES sends the packet to a multicast address indicating all ESs. All ESs on the LAN receive the multicast and examine the network-layer address. If an ES sees a network-layer address matching its own, it accepts the packet and sends an ESH to the source ES. All ESs without a matching network-layer address discard the packet.

SNAPSHOT   **ES-IS for end system and intermediate system discovery**

The end system to intermediate system protocol (ES-IS) is dedicated to the exchange of information between intermediate systems (routers) and end systems (hosts). ESs send **ES hello** messages to all ISs on the local subnetwork. In turn, **IS hello** messages are sent from all ISs to all ESs on the local subnetwork. Both types of message convey the addresses of the systems that generate them. Using this protocol, end systems and intermediate systems can locate one another.

12.6.8 Intermediate system to intermediate system

IS-IS is based on work originally done at Digital Equipment Corporation for Phase V DECnet. Although IS-IS was created to route in OSI Connectionless Network Protocol (CLNP) networks, an integrated version has since been created to support both CLNP and Internet Protocol (IP) networks (see Section 12.7 below).

IS-IS is quite similar to the Open Shortest Path First (OSPF) routing protocol. Both are **link-state protocols** (see Section 9.4) flooding the network with link-state information in order to build a complete, consistent picture of network topology. Both offer a variety of features, including routing hierarchies, path splitting, authentication, support for multiple network-layer protocols, and (with Integrated IS-IS) support for variable length subnet masks. Additionally, IS-IS offers type-of-service (TOS) which was discontinued for IP routing in OSPFv2.

IS-IS uses SAP identifier hex*FE* (CLNP), and reserved MAC multicast addresses for hello packets are 0x*0180.C200.0014* (OSI Route level 1 IS hello) and *0180.C200.0015* (OSI Route level 2 IS hello), see Table 12.4 above.

Routing hierarchy

As IS-IS is designed to route within a single domain, it does have an inherent hierarchy:

- **Level 1 routing** operates within an area. **Level 1 ISs** know how to communicate with other Level 1 ISs in the same area. For extra area routing Level 1 ISs only need to know how to get to the nearest Level 2 IS.
- **Level 2 routing** is performed between different areas. **Level 2 ISs** know how to communicate with ISs in other areas. Level 2 ISs form a **routing backbone**. Level 2 ISs can get to other Level 2 ISs by traversing only Level 2 ISs. The backbone simplifies design because Level 1 ISs now only need to know how to get to the nearest Level 2 IS. An additional benefit is that the backbone routing protocol can change without impacting the intra-area routing protocol.

With regard to designing IS-IS areas, it is useful to be aware of the following issues:

- **Area partitioning** –when a break occurs in the network that causes the routers within an area to be partitioned into multiple groups, no routes will exist from one group to any destination in another group. Comparing this with OSPF, if the two area partitions are connected to the backbone and no summarization is performed, it may not cause any problem. Otherwise OSPF needs virtual links for alternate backbone paths. With IS-IS, Level 2 routers can be anywhere, not just in the backbone. The resulting flexibility removes the need for virtual links. However, IS-IS network designers are encouraged to include backup paths, often in the form of a loop.
- **Area limitations** – IS-IS has very few limitations with regard to the use of areas. Most of the large ISPs operate a single area encompassing tens or hundreds of routers. Single-area networks of over 400 routers have been built (even more with Integrated IS-IS discussed later). The number of areas is quite large. The address uses 16-bits for the area ID, resulting in over 65 000 different areas. Normally, each router will be within one Level 1 area and may have Level 2 connectivity as well, resulting in two copies of the Dijkstra algorithm running.

Exchange of routing information

Each IS generates an update specifying the ESs and ISs to which it is connected, as well as the associated metrics. The **update** in the form of a **link-state packet** (LSP) is sent to all neighboring ISs, which forward (flood) it to their neighbors, and so on. Sequence numbers terminate the flood and distinguish old updates from new ones. Because all ISs receive link-state updates from all other ISs, each IS can build a complete full topology database. When the topology changes, new updates are sent. An IS-IS LSP contains a lot of information in the form of TLV (type, length, value) objects.

ISs send **LSAs at regular intervals** and when the following **special events** occur:

- when an IS discovers that its link to a neighbor is down;
- when an IS discovers that it has a new neighbor;
- when an IS discovers that the cost of a link to an existing neighbor has changed.

Once LSAs have been distributed appropriately, an algorithm must be run to compute optimal paths to each ES. The algorithm most often chosen for this task is the Dijkstra algorithm. The Dijkstra algorithm iterates on the length of a path, examining the LSAs of all ISs working outward from the host IS. At the end of the computation, a connectivity tree yielding the shortest paths (including all intermediate hops) to each IS is formed.

IS-IS path selection is similar to that in an OSPF network. If the destination address is an ES in the same area, the IS will know the correct route and will forward the packet appropriately. The Level 1 routers know about all ESs within the area. Intra-area paths are always preferred over inter-area paths. The Level 1 routers use the area ID portion of the NET to determine which neighboring routers are Level 1 routers within the same area.

If the destination address is an ES in another area, the Level 1 IS sends the packet to the nearest Level 2 IS. Forwarding through Level 2 ISs continues until the packet reaches a Level 2 IS in the destination area. Within the destination area, ISs forward the packet along the best path until the destination ES is reached.

Link-state detect

The IS-IS spec allows for two **link-state change detection mechanisms**: link-level notification and peer-to-peer **hello packets**. Link-level detection should be fastest but it is not always possible (e.g. in switched Ethernet) and seems to be inconsistently implemented by vendors. The spec says that adjacent routers should send hello packets to each other at a fixed interval (default 10 s, minimum even below 1 s) and declare the adjacency lost if no hellos are received for three intervals (or other configured value of the so-called multiplier). This works for any interconnect but constrains the repair time to be three times the hello interval.

Since the protocol's ultimate limit on the hello interval is set by the bandwidth used by hello packets, extending the spec to allow sub-second intervals would allow sub-second detection on almost all links. This does not mean that the detection time can be made arbitrarily small, only that detection should be limited by the physical constraints of links, not by arbitrary clock granularity choices made by protocol designers. In general, detection time should be limited by the transient error spectrum on a particular link. For example, a link that takes 30 ms noise hits should have at least a 30 ms hello interval.

For either event-triggered or hello-driven detection, there are network-wide stability issues if the routing tries to follow rapid link transients (i.e. a link that goes down and up several times a second). The usual way of dealing with this is to treat 'bad news' differently from 'good news' so routing is quick to find an alternative path on any failure but slow to switch back when the link comes up. The current IS-IS spec treats bad news and good news the same but it should be possible to change the spec to allow different filtering constants for 'down' and 'up' state changes.

Metrics

IS-IS uses **cost** as its metric with a maximum path value of 1024. The metric is **arbitrary** and is typically assigned by a network administrator. Any single link can have a maximum cost of 64 (six-bit value). Path costs are calculated by summing path link values. Maximum metric values were set at these levels to provide the granularity to support various link types, while at the same time ensuring that the shortest path algorithm used for route computation would be reasonably efficient. There is no rule on equating the metric with link bandwidth. Each organization typically develops its own relationships between the metric values and the link bandwidths. The range of speeds in large networks has increased to the point where the metric values cannot adequately represent the range of speeds which allows the routing protocol to select the optimum path.

The result of the compressed metric range is that two high-speed links in series will often have a higher metric than one much slower link. For example, a path over two 10 Mbps Ethernets will have a higher metric than a single 56 kbps link. This is clearly not desirable and may require a network redesign or the use of the wide metric described below. To solve the problem of small metric values, the IS-IS development community has come up with a wide metric which is represented in 24-bits. The large range of link metrics can now be represented and routers can make optimum routing decisions on these new metrics. With metrics this large, it is now reasonable to create a formula similar to that used by OSPF to represent the bandwidth of each link.

IS-IS also defines three **additional metrics** (costs) as an option for those administrators who feel they are necessary. The **delay cost** reflects the amount of delay on the link. The **expense cost** reflects the communications cost associated with using the link. The **error cost** reflects the error rate of the link. IS-IS maintains a mapping of these four metrics to the **quality of service** (QoS) option in the CLNP packet header. Using these mappings, IS-IS can compute routes through the internetwork.

IS-IS packet formats

IS-IS uses three basic packet formats:

- **IS-IS hello packets:**
  - **Level 1 LAN hellos and Level 2 LAN hellos** – used to elect a **designated router** (DR) on LAN media, just as with OSPF. However, there is no backup DR. If the DR fails, a new DR is elected. The router with the highest priority determines the DR and in the case of a tie, the router with the highest system ID becomes the DR. The priority values range from 0 to 127. A value of zero

makes a router ineligible to become a DR. The DR is also pre-emptable. If a new router on a LAN segment has a higher priority or higher system ID, it will become the new DR. By setting the priority, the control of which routers are eligible to become the DR on each segment is enabled. And because there are separate Level 1 and Level 2 hello packets, the DR for Level 1 on a given LAN may be different than the Level 2 DR on the same LAN.

- **Point-to-point links' hellos** – NBMA networks do not have special treatment within IS-IS. Instead, they must be presented to IS-IS by the IOS as a set of point-to-point links.

■ **Link-State Packets** (LSPs) – link-state information is flooded throughout each area in which the router is a member. Each LSP must be refreshed periodically, 15 minutes by default. Each LSP is acknowledged by information in a sequence number packet.

■ **Sequence Number Packets** (SNPs) – on point-to-point links, each LSP is acknowledged by a **Partial Sequence Number PDU** (PSNP), which contains information unique to the LSP. On LANs, the DR originates a **Complete Sequence Number PDU** (CSNP) which contains identifying information about every LSP from all routers on the LAN. If any router finds an entry within the CSNP that is newer than its corresponding LSP, it purges the out-of-date LSP. The purge is propagated to the adjacent routers and the originating router will originate a new LSP. The LSPs support variable length subnet mask addressing, an important requirement for modern networks.

Each of the three IS-IS packets has a complex format with three different logical parts (see Figure 12.24):

FIGURE 12-24 IS-IS packet header format

Number of octets:

8	Fixed	Variable
Common header	Packet-type-specific header	Packet-type-specific

■ The **first part** is an eight-octet fixed header shared by all three packet types. (The format of the common header of IS-IS packets is shown in Figure 12.25.)

■ The **second part** is a packet-type-specific portion with a fixed format.

■ The **third logical part** is also packet-type-specific, but is of variable length.

FIGURE 12-25 Common header in IS-IS packets

Number of octets:

1	1	1	1	1	1	1	1
Protocol identifier	Header length	Version	ID length	Packet type	Version	Reserved	Maximum area addresses

The **fields of the IS-IS common header** are as follows:

- *Protocol identifier* – identifies the IS-IS protocol. This field contains a constant (131).
- *Header length* – contains the fixed header length. The length is always equal to eight octets, but is included so that IS-IS packets do not differ significantly from CLNP packets.
- *Version* – contains a value of 1 in the current IS-IS specification.
- *ID length* – specifies the size of the ID portion of an NSAP address. If the field contains a value between 1 and 8 inclusive, the ID portion of an NSAP address is that number of octets. If the field contains a value of zero, the ID portion of an NSAP address is six octets. If the field contains a value of 255 (all ones), the ID portion of an NSAP address is zero octets.
- *Packet type* – specifies the type of IS-IS packet (hello, LSP, or sequenced numbered packet, SNP).
- *Version* – repeated after the packet type field.
- *Reserved* – ignored by the receiver and is equal to zero.
- *Maximum area addresses* – specifies the number of addresses permitted in this area.

Following the common header, each packet type has a different additional fixed portion, followed by a variable portion.

IS-IS timers

The following timers play critical roles in the link state database synchronization process:

- *isis hello-interval* – point-to-point hellos are sent out every 10 seconds by default. The same value is used by non-designated routers on broadcast links. The DIS uses a value of 3.33 seconds for default.
- *isis hello-multiplier* – determines how many hellos would be lost before an adjacency is torn down. It is used to calculate the neighbor holdtime in the following manner: holdtime = hello interval × hello multiplier; the default multiplier is 3.
- *max-lsp-lifetime* (*Maxage*) – refers to the maximum lifetime of an LSP (limits its validity) with the default of 20 minutes,
- *lsp-refresh-interval* – specifies the period for regeneration of all locally originated LSPs and provides a means for refreshing the link-state database in case there is no change; default value is 15 minutes, but mostly this timer is set to its maximum value, i.e. 65535 s (about 18 hours), while at the same time it is necessary to keep (*lsp-refresh-interval* < *max-lsp-lifetime*).
- *spf-interval* – default minimum interval between two consecutive SPF runs is 5 seconds.

- *CSNP timer* – refers to the periodic transmission of CSNPs by the designated IS on a broadcast medium; the default is 10 seconds.

- *isis lsp-interval* – specifies the minimum interval between transmitting two consecutive LSPs; the default is 33 ms.

- *isis retransmit-interval* – specifies the wait between periodic resending of an LSP to a point-to-point neighbor until a PSNP acknowledgment is received from that neighbor; the default is 5 seconds.

SNAPSHOT   **IS-IS characteristics**

- Supports multiple circuit load balancing.
- Converges very quickly to network topology changes.
- Not susceptible to routing loops.
- Single metric with a maximum value of 1024. This metric is the sum of all link metrics in a path. The link metric, assigned by the network administrator, cannot exceed 64.
- Optionally IS-IS allows three additional metrics to be used for route calculations: delay, expense, and error.
- IS-IS (similarly to OSPF) explicitly allows **equal-cost multipath** (ECMP) **routing**. The effect of multipath routing on a forwarder is that the forwarder potentially has several next hops for any given destination and must use some method to choose which next hop should be used for a given data packet. (More details on ECMP are given in Chapter 11 on IP routing.)

Target address resolution protocol

The **Target Address Resolution Protocol** (TARP) is just a mechanism to map a name to an CLNS address, like DNS maps names to IP addresses. Unlike DNS which has a client/server model with unicast queriers and replies, TARP is **broadcast**, and all the devices are servers.

When a device knows the name but needs the CLNS address of a device, it originates a TARP query. These queries are broadcast out on all interfaces. A device which receives a query will reply if it has the CLNS address which maps to the name in the query (any device can reply, if it knows the answer to the query). Otherwise it forwards the query on all of its interfaces, except the incoming interface. Duplicate queries are discarded, since each device maintains a cache of recently received queries. **Reverse lookups** are also possible, e.g. if we know a CLNS address and want to know the corresponding name. Reverse lookups are sent directly to the queried device.

For a conventional IS-IS configuration with a single Level 1 and a Level 2 area (or configuration with a single Level 1 area or a Level 2 area), the **Target**

Address Resolution Protocol (TARP) continues to work without any change in the previous behavior.

If multiple Level 1 areas are defined, the **router resolves addresses using TARP** in the following way:

- The router obtains the Network Service Access Point (NSAP) of the Level 2 area, if present, from the locally assigned target identifier.

- If only Level 1 areas are configured, the router uses the NSAP of the first active Level 1 area as shown in the configuration at the time of TARP configuration ('tarp run'). (Level 1 areas are sorted alphanumerically by tag name, with capital letters coming before lower case letters. For example, AREA-1 precedes AREA-2, which precedes area-1.) Note that the target identifier NSAP could change following a reload if a new Level 1 area is added to the configuration after TARP is running.

- The router continues to process all Type 1 and 2 protocol data units (PDUs) that are for this router. Type 1 PDUs are processed locally if the target identifier is in the local target identifier cache. If not, they are propagated (routed) to all interfaces in the same Level 1 area. (The same area is defined as the area configured on the input interface.)

- Type 2 PDUs are processed locally if the specified target identifier is in the local target identifier cache. If not, they are propagated via all interfaces (all Level 1 or Level 2 areas) with TARP enabled. If the source of the PDU is from a different area, the information is also added to the local target identifier cache. Type 2 PDUs are propagated via all static adjacencies.

- Type 4 PDUs (for changes originated locally) are propagated to all Level 1 and Level 2 areas (because internally they are treated as 'Level 1-2').

- Type 3 and 5 PDUs continue to be routed.

- Type 1 PDUs are only propagated (routed) via Level 1 static adjacencies if the static NSAP is in one of the Level 1 areas in this router.

12.6.9 Interdomain routing protocol

The **InterDomain Routing Protocol** (IDRP) is the higher routing level in the routing hierarchy in OSI networks designed to move information between routing domains. As such, it is designed to operate seamlessly with CLNP, ES-IS, and IS-IS. IDRP is based on the Border Gateway Protocol (BGP) for IP.

IDRP introduces several new terms, including the following:

- **border intermediate system** (BIS) – IS that participates in interdomain routing. As such, it uses IDRP;

- **routing domain** (RD) – group of ESs and ISs operating under the same set of administrative rules, including the sharing of a common routing plan;

- **routing domain identifier** (RDI) – unique RD identifier;

- **routing information base** (RIB) – routing database used by IDRP. RIBs are built by each BIS from information received from within the RD and from other BISs. A RIB contains the set of routes chosen for use by a particular BIS;

- **confederation** – group of RDs. The confederation appears to RDs outside the confederation as a single RD. A confederation's topology is not visible to RDs outside the confederation. Confederations help reduce network traffic by acting as internetwork firewalls and may be nested within one another.

SNAPSHOT   **IDRP concepts compared to BGPs**

- **Routing domain = autonomous system**
- **Routing domain identifier = autonomous system number**
- **Border intermediate system = EBGP speaker**

An IDRP route is a sequence of RDIs. Some of these RDIs can be confederations. Each BIS is configured to know the RD and confederations to which it belongs, and learns about other BISs, RDs, and confederations through information exchanges with each neighbor. As with distance vector routing, routes to a particular destination accumulate outward from the destination. Only routes that satisfy a BIS's local policies and have been selected for use will be passed on to other BISs. Route recalculation is partial and takes place when one of three events occurs: an incremental routing update with new routes is received; a BIS neighbor goes down; or a BIS neighbor comes up.

IDRP features include the following:

- support for CLNP **quality of service**;
- **loop suppression** by keeping track of all RDs traversed by a route;
- **reduction of route information** and processing by using confederations, the compression of RD path information, and other means;
- **reliability** by using a built-in reliable transport;
- **security** by using cryptographic signatures on a per-packet basis;
- route servers;
- RIB refresh packets.

SNAPSHOT   **route server**

Route server is a process that collects routing information from **border ISs** and distributes this information to **client routers**, i.e. routers that peer with a route server in order to acquire routing information. A server's client can be a router or another route server.

The IDRP is not extensively discussed here for a legitimite reason: it is not used in practice. However, some of its concepts are being examined in the IRTF for next-generation routing.

12.7 Integrated IS-IS

Integrated IS-IS (I-IS-IS) or Dual IS-IS is an implementation of the IS-IS protocol for supporting CLNP and IP protocols and it is the development of IETF (proposed standard RFC 1195) to introduce the OSI routing protocol into TCP/IP networks.

RFC WATCH	Integrated IS-IS

RFC 1142 **OSI IS-IS Intra-domain Routing Protocol**, 1990 (Informational)

RFC 1195 **Use of OSI IS-IS for routing in TCP/IP and dual environments**, 1990 (Proposed Standard)

RFC 2763 **Dynamic Hostname Exchange Mechanism for IS-IS**, 2000 (Informational)

RFC 2966 **Domain-wide Prefix Distribution with Two-Level IS-IS**, 2000 (Informational)

RFC 2973 **IS-IS Mesh Groups**, 2000 (Informational)

Integrated IS-IS uses an alternative approach to **ships in the night** (completely independent routing protocols for each of the two protocol suites), which makes use of a **single integrated protocol** for interior routing (i.e. for calculating routes within a routing domain) for both protocol suites. The integrated protocol design is based on the OSI Intra-domain IS-IS routing protocol (ISO 8473), with IP-specific functions added (RFC 1195).

By supporting both IP and OSI traffic, this integrated protocol design supports traffic to IP hosts, OSI end systems, and dual end systems. This approach is 'integrated' in the sense that the IS-IS protocol can be used to support pure IP environments, pure OSI environments, and dual environments. In addition, this approach allows interconnection of dual (IP and OSI) routing domains with other dual domains, with IP-only domains, and with OSI-only domains. The integrated IS-IS provides a single routing protocol which can simultaneously provide an efficient routing protocol for TCP/IP, and for OSI. This design makes use of the OSI IS-IS routing protocol, augmented with IP-specific information. This design provides explicit support for IP subnetting, variable subnet masks, TOS-based routing, and external routing. There is provision for authentication information, including the use of passwords or other mechanisms. The precise form of authentication mechanisms (other than passwords) is not specified.

Both OSI and IP packets are forwarded 'as is,' i.e. they are transmitted directly **over the underlying link-layer services** without the need for mutual encapsulation. The integrated IS-IS is a dynamic routing protocol, based on the SPF (Dijkstra) routing algorithm.

The integrated approach does not change the way that IP packets are handled nor the way that OSI packets are handled. There is no change at all to the contents or to the handling of ISO 8473 data packets and error reports, or to ISO

9542 redirects and ES hellos. ISO 9542 IS hellos transmitted on LANs are similarly unchanged. ISO 9542 IS hellos transmitted on point-to-point links are unchanged except for the addition of IP-related information. Similarly, other OSI packets (specifically those involved in the IS-IS intra-domain routing protocol) remain unchanged except for the addition of IP-related information.

The dual approach makes use of the existing IS-IS packets, with IP-specific fields added:

- **authentication information** may be added to all IS-IS packets;
- the **protocols supported** by each router, as well as each router's IP addresses, are specified in ISO 9542 IS hello, IS-IS hello, and link-state packets;
- **internally reachable IP addresses** are specified in all link-state packets;
- **externally reachable IP addresses**, and external routing protocol information, may be specified in Level 2 link-state packets.

12.7.1 Overview of the integrated IS-IS

The integrated IS-IS allows a single routing protocol to be used to route both IP and OSI packets. This implies that the same two-level hierarchy is used for both IP and OSI routing.

An **IS-IS routing domain – an autonomous system** running IS-IS – can be partitioned into multiple Level 1 (L1) areas, and a Level 2 (L2) connected subset of the topology that interconnects all of the L1 areas. Within each L1 area, all routers exchange link-state information. L2 routers also exchange L2 link-state information to compute routes between areas.

Each area needs to be specified to be either IP-only (only IP traffic can be routed in that particular area), OSI-only (only OSI traffic can be routed in that area), or dual (both IP and OSI traffic can be routed in the area).

Within an IP-only or dual area, the amount of knowledge maintained by routers about specific IP destinations will be as similar as possible as for OSI. For example, IP-capable Level 1 routers will maintain the topology within the area, and will be able to route directly to IP destinations within the area. However, IP- capable Level 1 routers will not maintain information about destinations outside of the area. Just as in normal OSI routing, traffic to destinations outside of the area will be forwarded to the nearest Level 2 router. Since IP routes to subnets, rather than to specific end systems, IP routers will not need to keep or distribute lists of IP host identifiers (note that routes to hosts can be announced by using a subnet mask of all ones).

Within an area, **Level 1 routers** exchange link-state packets which identify the IP addresses reachable by each router. Specifically, zero or more (IP address, subnet mask, metric) combinations may be included in each link-state packet. Each Level 1 router is manually configured with the <IP address, subnet mask, metric> combinations which are reachable on each interface. A Level 1 router routes as follows:

- If a specified destination address matches an <IP address, subnet mask, metric> reachable within the area, the packet is routed via Level 1 routing.
- If a specified destination address does not match any <IP address, subnet mask, metric> combination listed as reachable within the area, the packet is routed towards the nearest Level 2 router.

Integrated IS-IS supports both **VLSM** and **prefix routing** (longest match routing). The integrated IS-IS provides optional Type of Service (TOS) routing, through use of the QoS feature from IS-IS.

Level 2 routers include in their Level 2 LSPs a complete list of (IP address, subnet mask, metric) specifying all IP addresses reachable in their area. This information may be obtained from a combination of the Level 1 LSPs (obtained from Level 1 routers in the same area), and/or by manual configuration. In addition, Level 2 routers may report external reachability information, corresponding to addresses which can be reached via routers in other routing domains (autonomous systems).

Default routes may be announced by use of a subnet mask containing all zeros. Default routes should be used with great care, since they can result in 'black holes.' Default routes are permitted only at Level 2 as external routes. Default routes are not permitted at Level 1.

RFC 1195 also specifies the **semantics and procedures for interactions between levels**. Specifically, routers in an L1 area will exchange information within the L1 area. For IP destinations not found in the prefixes in the L1 database, the L1 router should forward packets to the nearest router that is in both L1 and L2 (i.e. an L1L2 router) with the 'attached bit' set in its L1. An L1L2 router should be manually configured with a set of prefixes that summarizes the IP prefixes reachable in that L1 area. These summaries are injected into L2. RFC 1195 specifies no further interactions between L1 and L2 for IPv4 prefixes.

Type, Length, and Value (TLV) tuples are used by IS-IS to transport IPv4 routing information in IS-IS. RFC 1195 defines two TLVs for carrying IP prefixes:

- **TLV 128** – defined as *IP Internal Reachability Information* should be used to carry IP prefixes that are directly connected to IS-IS routers;

- **TLV 130** – defined as *IP External Reachability Information* should be used to carry routes learned from outside the IS-IS domain. The original specification documents TLV type 130 only for Level 2 LSPs.

IS-IS uses two types of metrics. Metrics of the **internal metric-type** should be used when the metric is comparable to metrics used to weigh links inside the IS-IS domain. Metrics of the **external metric-type** should be used if the metric of an IP prefix cannot be directly compared to internal metrics. The external metric-type can only be used for external IP prefixes. A direct result is that metrics of external metric-type should never be seen in TLV 128.

The RFC 1195 definition states that L1L2 routers can advertise IP routes that were learned via L1 routing into L2. These routes can be regarded as inter-area routes. The RFC 1195 definition also states that these L1→L2 inter-area routes must be advertised in L2 LSPs in the *IP Internal Reachability Information TLV* (TLV 128). Intra-area L2 routes are also advertised in L2 LSPs in an *IP Internal Reachability Information TLV*. Therefore, L1→L2 inter-area routes are indistinguishable from L2 intra-area routes. RFC 1195 does not define L2→L1 inter-area routes. A simple extension would be to allow an L1L2 router to advertise routes learned via L2 routing in its L1 LSP. However, to prevent routing loops, L1L2 routers must never advertise L2→L1 inter-area routes that they learn via L1 routing back into L2. The extensions to the original specification are proposed by a recently endorsed RFC 2966 discussed in section below.

There are several **ways of advertising IP routes** in IS-IS. There are four variables involved:

- the **level of the LSP** in which the route is advertised – there are currently two possible values: Level 1 and Level 2;
- the **route-type**, which can be derived from the type of TLV in which the prefix is advertised – internal routes are advertised in IP Internal Reachability Information TLVs (TLV 128), and external routes are advertised in IP External Reachability Information TLVs (TLV 130);
- the **metric-type**: internal or external – the metric-type is derived from the internal/external metric-type bit in the metric field (bit 7);
- whether or not this route is leaked down in the hierarchy, and thus cannot be advertised back up – this information can be derived from the newly defined up/down bit in the default metric field (RFC 2966, see below).

Unfortunately IS-IS cannot depend on metrics alone for route selection. Some types of routes must always preferred over others, regardless of the costs that were computed in the Dijkstra calculation. One of the reasons for this is that inter-area routes can only be advertised with a maximum metric of 63. Another reason is that this maximum value of 63 does not mean infinity (e.g. like a hop count of 16 in RIP denotes unreachable). Introducing a value for infinity cost in IS-IS inter-area routes would introduce counting-to-infinity behavior via two or more L1L2 routers, which would have a bad impact on network stability.

IP routes learned via Level 1 routing are advertised by default into Level 2. Even when multiple Level 1 processes are configured on the same unit, this fact is still true. No additional configuration is required to redistribute all Level 1 IP routes into the Level 2 process.

In CLNP routing there is no redistribution of Level 1 host routes into Level 2. Only Level 1 addresses are advertised into Level 2. Redistribution of all area addresses of all Level 1 areas into Level 2 is implicit in IS-IS.

12.7.2 Support of mixed routing domains

Integrated IS-IS allows for three **types of routing domain**: pure IP, pure OSI, and dual.

In a pure **IP routing domain**, all routers must be IP-capable. IP-only routers may be freely mixed with dual routers. Some fields specifically related to OSI operation may be included by dual routers, and will be ignored by IP-only routers. Only IP traffic will be routed in a pure IP domain. Any OSI traffic may be discarded (except for the IS-IS packets necessary for the operation of the routing protocol).

In a pure **OSI routing domain**, all routers must be OSI-capable. OSI-only routers may be freely mixed with dual routers. Some fields specifically related to IP operation may be included by dual routers, and will be ignored by OSI-only routers. Only OSI traffic will be routed in a pure OSI domain. Any IP traffic may be discarded.

In a **dual routing domain**, IP-only, OSI-only, and dual routers may be mixed on a per-area basis. Specifically, each area may itself be defined to be pure IP, pure OSI, or dual.

- In a pure IP area within a dual domain, IP-only and dual routers may be freely mixed. Only IP traffic can be routed by Level 1 routing within a pure IP area.

- In a pure-OSI area within a dual domain, OSI-only and dual routers may be freely mixed. Only OSI traffic can be routed by Level 1 routing within a pure OSI area.

- In a dual area within a dual routing domain only dual routers may be used. Both IP and OSI traffic can be routed within a dual area. Within a dual domain, if both IP and OSI traffic are to be routed between areas then all Level 2 routers must be dual.

As the routers may not understand all types of routing information supported by dual IS-IS it is necessary that hello packets and LSPs carry an identifier indicating the supported routed protocol. The network protocol discriminator is an eight-bit long field with value of *83* for IP. Through hello packets the routers inform their neighbors whether they support IP, CLNP, or both. This prevents the routers from getting (spreading) routing information in a foreign format pertaining to another, not supported and thus non-comprehensible, protocol.

SNAPSHOT Integrated IS-IS configurations on routers

Most internetworks running Integrated IS-IS support three **different IS configurations**: those running only IP, those running only CLNP, and those running both IP and CLNP.

ISs running only one of the two protocols ignore information concerning the other protocol. In fact, such ISs will refuse to recognize other ISs as neighbors unless they have at least one protocol in common. ISs running both protocols can and will become neighbors with the other IS types.

Address independence and integrated protocol

IS-IS was developed to be **independent of any specific address family**. Therefore it is easy to extend the protocol to handle other address types. Using this extension mechanism is how IP addresses are handled within IS-IS and is how IPv6 addresses will be routed within IS-IS. Because of the protocol independence, IS-IS uses the data-link layer as its communications mechanism between adjacent routers.

In an IP-only network it is best to set it to some representation of an IP address of an interface in the router. It is a good idea to configure a loopback interface with an IP address to use for this purpose. The 12 digits of an IP address will map directly into the 12 digits in the system ID field.

With Integrated **IS-IS**, for inclusion of support to IP, the premise of a node residing in a single area could no longer apply since a node has a different address for each interface. But even for CLNP, it was possible to implement what looked to the rest of the world like two nodes by having a **router run multiple**

instances of IS-IS, one for each (Level 1) area, and then the router could exist in both areas, and even pass routing summaries between them. This was implemented in NLSP, a variant of IS-IS for IPX. Such an implementation is straightforward and completely compatible with current IS-IS routers, that would not be able to tell the difference between such a device and two routers. But the specification states that a router be in (at most) one Level 1 area, while it might also be a level 2 router.

Like all integrated routing protocols, Integrated IS-IS calls for all routers to run a single routing algorithm. LSAs sent by routers running Integrated IS-IS include all destinations running either IP or CLNP network-layer protocols. Protocols such as the Address Resolution Protocol (ARP) and the Internet Control Message Protocol (ICMP) for IP and the ES-IS protocol for CLNP must still be supported by routers running Integrated IS-IS.

Standard **IS-IS packets** must be modified to support multiple network-layer protocols. IS-IS packet formats were designed to support the addition of new fields without a loss of compatibility with non-integrated versions of IS-IS. The **fields** that are added to IS-IS to support integrated routing follow:

- which network-layer protocols are supported by other ISs – the first byte of an IS-IS packet contains an intra-domain routing protocol discriminator, where the IP protocol identifier assigned is 83 decimal;

- whether end stations running other protocols can be reached;

- any other required network-layer, protocol-specific information.

12.7.3 Advantages of using integrated IS-IS

Use of the **Integrated** IS-IS protocol, as a single protocol for routing both IP and OSI packets in a dual environment, has significant advantages over using separate protocols for independently routing IP and OSI traffic. With the **ships-in-the-night** approach (with different types of routing information passing like ships in the night), completely separate routing protocols are used for IP and for OSI. For example, OSPF may be used for routing IP traffic, and IS-IS may be used for routing OSI traffic. With ships in the night the two routing protocols operate more or less independently. However, dual routers will need to implement both routing protocols, and therefore there will be some degree of competition for resources.

Note that the operation of two routing protocols with the ships-in-the-night approach are not really independent, since they must share common resources. However, with integrated IS-IS, the interactions are explicit (defined in the protocol and software interactions), whereas with ships in the night the interactions are implicit. Since the interactions are explicit, it may be easier to manage and debug dual routers. An advantage of the integrated IS-IS is that, since it requires only one routing protocol, it uses fewer resources. In particular, less implementation resources are needed (since only one protocol needs to be implemented), less CPU and memory resources are used in the router (since only one protocol needs to be run), and less network resources are used (since only one set of routing packets needs to be transmitted).

The primary benefit of dual IS-IS is **reduced CPU utilization**. Link-state algorithms are CPU intensive. With dual IS-IS, the routing algorithm is only run one time, and only one set of routing updates (with both IP and OSI information) is sent. While it is difficult to rationalize the different 'network views,' held by IP and OSI protocols (for example, IP considers 'networks'; OSI considers 'areas'), dual IS-IS is of utility in mixed environments. It is particularly useful on backbones where both types of traffic are common.

The use of a single **integrated routing protocol** similarly reduces the likely frequency of software upgrades. Specifically, if you have two different routing protocols in your router, then you have to upgrade the software any time either of the protocols change. If you make use of a single integrated routing protocol, then software changes are still likely to be needed, but less frequently. Integrated IS-IS is the only truly integrated routing protocol around as proprietary EIGRP uses the suboptimal ships-in-the-night approach.

Another advantage of integrated IS-IS relates to the network management effort required. Since Integrated IS-IS provides a single routing protocol, within a single coordinated routing domain using a single backbone, this implies that there is less information to configure. This combined with a single coordinated MIB simplifies network management.

12.7.4 Differences between IS-IS and OSPF

As we refer frequently to IP OSPF for IS-IS operation characteristics, it is useful to realize there are differences between these two link-state routing protocols. Among the major differences are the following:

- **IS-IS packets are encapsulated directly in link layer frames**, while OSPF uses encapsulation in IP datagrams.
- IS-IS requires a **continuous chain of Level 2 routers**, while OSPF allows a virtual link between a discontiguous backbone area.
- IS-IS makes Level 1 routers use the **closest Level 2 router** for inter-area communication which may not be the optimal route, while OSPF allows the internal routers to choose among available area border routers and find the best for a particular communication.
- Standard IS-IS Level 1 routes only propagate into the backbone. There are new extensions that allow controlled leakage of IS-IS Level 2 routes into non-backbone areas, but otherwise, IS-IS non-backbone areas behave like OSPF not-so-stubby areas.
- IS-IS is able to support up to 1000 routers in a single area while with the OSPF the experience is that the number of routers gathered in an area tops at about 200–250 routers.

12.7.5 New extensions for IS-IS routing in IP environment

Recently, new extensions have been designed and implemented for the IS-IS routing protocol to serve multiple purposes. The goals are the following:

- to remove the six-bit limit on link metrics;
- to allow for inter-area IP routes;

- to enable IS-IS to carry different kinds of information for the purpose of traffic engineering.

To meet these goals, two new **type, length, and value** objects (TLVs) have been defined:

- **TLV 22** describes links or adjacencies, serving the same purpose as the 'IS neighbor option' in ISO 10589 (TLV 2).

- **TLV 135** describes reachable IP prefixes similar to IP neighbor options from RFC 1195. RFC 1195 defines TLVs 128 and 130 as containing IP routes. TLVs 128 and 130 have a metric field that consists of four TOS metrics. The first metric, the so-called default metric, has the high-order bit reserved (bit 8). Routers must set this bit to zero on transmission, and ignore it on receipt.

Both new TLVs have a fixed-length part, followed by optional sub-TLVs. The metric space in these new TLVs has been enhanced from six bits to 24 or 32 bits. The sub-TLVs allow managers to add new properties to links and prefixes. Traffic engineering is the first technology to make use of this ability to describe new properties of a link.

RFC WATCH	IS-IS extensions

RFC 2763 **Dynamic Hostname Exchange Mechanism for IS-IS**, 2000 (Informational)

RFC 2966 **Domain-wide Prefix Distribution with Two-Level IS-IS**, 2000 (Informational)

Dynamic hostname exchange mechanism for IS-IS

IS-IS uses a 1–8 byte system ID (normally six bytes as in MAC address) to represent a node in the network. For management and operational reasons, network operators need to check the status of IS-IS adjacencies, entries in the routing table, and the content of the IS-IS link state database. It is obvious that, when looking at diagnostics information, hexadecimal representations of system IDs and LSP identifiers are less clear than symbolic names.

One way to overcome this problem is to define a name-to-system ID mapping on a router. This mapping can be used bidirectionally, e.g. to find symbolic names for system IDs, and to find system IDs for symbolic names. One way to build this table of mappings is by static definitions. Among network administrators who use IS-IS as their IGP it is current practice to define such static mappings. Thus every router has to maintain a table with mappings between router names and system IDs. These tables need to contain all names and system IDs of all routers in the network.

There are several ways one could build such a table. One is via static configurations. The obvious drawback of static configuration of mappings is the issue of scalability and maintainability. The network operators have to maintain the name tables. They have to maintain an entry in the table for every router in the network. They have to maintain this table on each router in the network. The effort to create and maintain these static tables grows with the total number of routers on the network. Changing the name or system ID of one router, or adding one new router will affect the configurations of all the other routers on the network. This will make it very likely that those static tables are outdated.

Another scheme that could be implemented is via DNS lookups. A drawback is that for the duration of network problems, the response time of DNS services might not be satisfactory or the DNS services might not even be available. Another possible drawback might be the added complexity of DNS.

A third way to build dynamic mappings would be to use the transport mechanism of the routing protocol itself to advertise symbolic names in an IS-IS link-state PDU. RFC 2763 defines a new TLV which allows the IS-IS routers to include the name to system ID mapping information in their LSPs. This will allow simple and reliable transport of name mapping information across the IS-IS network. The **dynamic hostname TLV** is defined as *TLV type 137*. The dynamic hostname TLV is optional. When originating an LSP, a router may decide to include this TLV in its LSP. Upon receipt of an LSP with the dynamic hostname TLV, a router may decide to ignore this TLV, or to install the symbolic name and system ID in its hostname mapping table. A router may also optionally insert this TLV in its pseudo node LSP for the association of a symbolic name to a local LAN.

Domain-wide prefix distribution with two-level IS-IS

RFC 2966 specifies the extensions to the IS-IS protocol to support optimal routing within a **two-level domain**. The original IS-IS specification (RFC 1195) does not define L2→L1 inter-area routes. The distribution of IP prefixes between Level 1 and Level 2 and vice versa requires certain restrictions to ensure that persistent forwarding loops do not form. The goal of this domain-wide prefix distribution is to increase the granularity of the routing information within the domain.

One major reason for distributing more **prefix information** is to improve the quality of the resulting routes. A well known property of prefix summarization or any abstraction mechanism is that it necessarily results in a loss of information. This loss of information in turn results in the computation of a route based upon less information, which will frequently result in routes that are not optimal.

A simple example can serve to demonstrate this adequately. Suppose that an L1 area has two L1L2 routers that both advertise a single summary of all prefixes within the L1 area. To reach a destination inside the L1 area, any other L2 router is going to compute the shortest path to one of the two L1L2 routers for that area. Suppose, for example, that both of the L1L2 routers are equidistant from the L2 source, and that the L2 source arbitrarily selects one L1L2 router. This router may not be the optimal router when viewed from the L1 topology. In fact, it may be the case that the path from the selected L1L2 router to the destination router may traverse the L1L2 router that was not selected. If more detailed topological information or more detailed metric information was available to the L2 source router, it could make a more optimal route computation.

This situation is symmetric in that an L1 router has no information about prefixes in L2 or within a different L1 area. In using the nearest L1L2 router, that L1L2 is effectively injecting a default route without metric information into the L1 area. The route computation that the L1 router performs is similarly suboptimal.

Besides the **optimality** of the routes computed, there are other significant drivers for the domain-wide distribution of prefix information. When a router learns multiple possible paths to external destinations via BGP, it will select only one of those routes to be installed in the forwarding table. One of the factors in the BGP route selection is the IGP cost to the BGP next hop address. Many ISP networks depend on this technique, which is known as 'shortest exit routing.' If an L1 router does not know the exact IGP metric to all BGP speakers in other L1 areas, it cannot do effective shortest exit routing. Another driver is the current practice of using the IGP (IS-IS) metric as part of the BGP Multi-Exit Discriminator (MED). The value in the MED is advertised to other domains and is used to inform other domains of the optimal entry point into the current domain. Current practice is to take the IS-IS metric and insert it as the MED value. This tends to cause external traffic to enter the domain at the point closest to the exit router. Note that the receiving domain may, based upon policy, choose to ignore the MED that is advertised. However, current practice is to distribute the IGP metric in this way in order to optimize routing wherever possible. This is possible in current networks that are only a single area, but becomes problematic if a hierarchy is to be installed into the network. This is again because the loss of end to-end metric information means that the MED value will not reflect the true distance across the advertising domain. Full distribution of prefix information within the domain would alleviate this problem as it would allow accurate computation of the IS-IS metric across the domain, resulting in an accurate value presented in the MED.

The disadvantage to performing the domain-wide prefix distribution described above is that it has an impact on the scalability of IS-IS. Areas within IS-IS help scalability in that LSPs are contained within a single area. This limits the size of the link-state database that in turn limits the complexity of the shortest path computation.

Further, the summarization of the prefix information aids scalability in that the abstraction of the prefix information removes the sheer number of data items to be transported and the number of routes to be computed. The distribution of prefixes on a domain-wide basis impacts on the scalability of IS-IS in the second respect. It will increase the number of prefixes throughout the domain. This will result in increased memory consumption, transmission requirements, and computation requirements throughout the domain. However, the domain-wide distribution of prefixes has no effect on the existence of areas and the limitation of the distribution of the link-state database.

The introduction of domain-wide prefix distribution into a formerly flat, single area network is a clear benefit to the **scalability** of that network. However, it is a compromise and does not provide the maximum scalability available with IS-IS. Domains that choose to make use of this facility should be aware of the trade-off that they are making between scalability and optimality and provision and monitor their networks accordingly. Normal provisioning guidelines that would apply to a fully hierarchical deployment of IS-IS will not apply to this type of configuration.

The RFC 2966 encoding is an **extension of the encoding** in RFC 1195 as it redefines this high-order bit in the *default metric field* in TLVs 128 and 130 to be the **up/down bit**. L1L2 routers must set this bit to one for prefixes that are derived from L2 routing and are advertised into L1 LSPs. The bit must be set to zero for all other IP prefixes in L1 or L2 LSPs. Prefixes with the up/down bit set that are learned via L1 routing must never be advertised by L1L2 routers back into L2. The external metric-type can only be used for external IP prefixes. A direct result is that metrics of the external metric-type should never be seen in TLV 128.

IS-IS routers must give the same preference to IP routes advertised in an *IP Internal Reachability Information TLV* and IP routes advertised in an *IP External Reachability Information TLV* when executing the Dijkstra calculation. However, routers that implement multiple IGPs are free to use this distinction between internal and external routes when comparing routes derived from different IGPs for inclusion in their global routing table.

With the extensions specified in RFC 2966, the **preferences** for route selection by IS-IS are as follows:

1 L1 intra-area routes with internal metric.

L1 external routes with internal metric.

2 L2 intra-area routes with internal metric.

L2 external routes with internal metric.

L1→L2 inter-area routes with internal metric.

L1→L2 inter-area external routes with internal metric.

3 L2→L1 inter-area routes with internal metric

L2→L1 inter-area external routes with internal metric.

4 L1 external routes with external metric.

5 L2 external routes with external metric.

L1→L2 inter-area external routes with external metric.

6 L2→L1 inter-area external routes with external metric.

It should be noted that the proposed solution in RFC 2966 is not fully compatible with the original IS-IS specification (RFC 1195); instead, it is an extension to it.

IS-IS mesh groups

RFC 2973 describes a mechanism to reduce redundant packet transmissions – flooding of LSPs – for the IS-IS, as described in ISO 10589.

In a full mesh topology, where every pair of ISs is connected by a point-to-point link, IS-IS protocol operation leads to redundant transmission of certain PDUs due to the flooding operation because when an IS gets a new LSP, it stores it, and prepares to flood it out every circuit except the source circuit. The net effect of the mechanism proposed in RFC 2973 is to engineer a flooding topology for LSPs which is a subset of the physical topology.

RFC WATCH	IS-IS mesh groups

RFC 2973 **IS-IS Mesh Groups**, 2000 (Informational)

Final note on IS-IS

IS-IS is a powerful protocol for routing IP. It is a link-state protocol, providing fast convergence and a flexible, two-level hierarchy. Each IS-IS Level 1 area operates like an OSPF NSSA. If you are deciding between running OSPF and running IS-IS in a network, there are other factors than the protocol upon which to base your decision. The most important factor is the knowledge base of the network design and operations team.

12.8 Multiprotocol routing

Today's routers are mostly multiprotocol routers. This means they can route multiple network protocols simultaneously (see Figure 12.26). However, separate routing protocols are used to route each protocol suite. That means that if a router is routing three protocols, it will use three routing protocols, one for each protocol suite unless an integrated protocol.

FIGURE 12-26 Example of multiprotocol routing

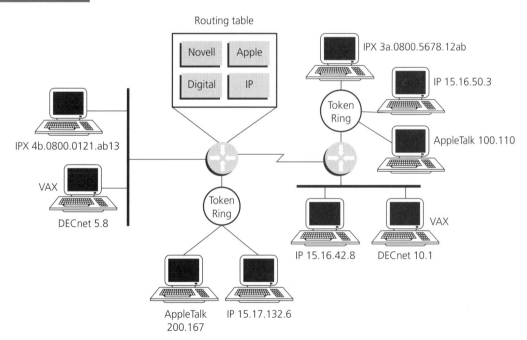

Routing protocols generally do not interact or share routing information. This strategy is termed '**ships in the night,**' because routing information passes much like the way cargo ships pass one another on the high seas. Ships in the night has an advantage in that a change to a protocol does not affect any other protocol being routed, because they all stand alone. A significant disadvantage of ships in the night is wasted bandwidth and increased router processing. Routing table updates for multiple separate routing protocols could consume significant bandwidth on a large internetwork.

Integrated routing addresses this situation by providing a single routing protocol for all protocol suites. The first steps in that direction are Integrated IS-IS protocol which can support both CLNP (OSI) and IP. Note that Cisco Systems' EIGRP is not an integrated protocol because it runs separate routing processes for all network protocols it may support (IP, IPX, and AppleTalk). Effectively, it uses the ships-in-the-night approach.

Regardless of the reasons driving the use of multiple protocols, a solid knowledge of each protocol's capabilities, limitations, features, and operations is essential for optimum network routing. Armed with this knowledge, enterprises can develop a solid strategy that enhances – rather than impedes – a network's performance.

12.8.1 Redistribution of routing information

It is increasingly common for enterprises to use multiple routing protocols in their networks. There are several circumstances in which an intranet might have to operate with more than one protocol, even though doing so adds to the complexity of the network and often increases the overhead burden on the infrastructure.

For example, organizations migrating from an older routing protocol to a newer one in planned stages – such as one network segment at a time – will find themselves concurrently running two Interior Gateway Protocols (IGPs) for at least some period of time. Similarly, installing two or more connections to diverse Internet Service Provider (ISP) networks for redundancy may necessitate adding Border Gateway Protocol (BGP), the standard, to the protocol mix. BGP enables the network to make optimal IP routing decisions across multiple administrative domains. Mixed-routing environments are common also with the mergers and acquisitions that dictate the unification of previously separate network infrastructures.

When supporting multiple routing protocols for a single network protocol within a single autonomous system, it is important to the integrity of the network to make sure that the exchange of information among disparate routing protocols – redistribution of routing information – is handled properly.

Redistribution is the process of collaboration between routing protocols to route the same protocol suite through a way of translating and introducing relevant routing information. A router that performs redistribution must implement both routing protocols and have a scheme to translate one metric to another. Route redistribution has to be considered carefully as it introduces susceptibility to non-optimal routing and may create a danger of routing loops, but it may be necessary in certain circumstances when two distinct protocols must be used in neighbor internets and must still talk to each other. The redistribution process can become complicated where routing metrics must be converted and yet ensure that optimal routes are still selected.

Redistribution may also be enabled so that static routes are known in a routed network. Among the major issues to take into account while considering redistribution are:

- **routing protocol metric** – types, single or combined, ranges;
- **route limits** – the maximum metric per route allowed;
- **default route understanding** – if it is necessary to advertise it or will candidates be found automatically (e.g. the RIP default route *0.0.0.0* should not be advertised to other protocols);
- **address summarization** – automatic only on network boundary or manually allowed;
- **VLSM or prefix routing understanding** – allowed or not (e.g. RIP does not allow VLSM, although it does allow the insertion of it through static route redistribution);
- **possibility to use routing information filtering** – to avoid routing loops and impose further restrictions on information type and volume distributed into other routed internets.

Each routing protocol determines the best-path or least-cost routes to a network or subnet differently. As such, each routing protocol creates its own database of connected devices, links, and the metrics associated with those links. Employing multiple routing protocols can be confusing for routers and the people who manage them.

The **metrics** of one routing protocol do not necessarily translate into the metrics of another. For example, the RIP metric is a hop count and the IGRP metric is a composition value. In such situations, an artificial metric has to be assigned to the redistributed route. Because of this unavoidable tampering with dynamic information, carelessly exchanging routing information between different routing protocols can create routing loops, which can seriously degrade network operation.

While each protocol uses its own metric or set of metrics to determine best paths through the network, there is no algorithmic way to translate or compare one protocol's metric to another metric. The answer to this problem is to use **weights** on the sources of the routing information. Each source, dynamic protocol, or static route, may be assigned a particular value (arbitrary as per router vendor and potentially modifiable to a certain extent by an administrator) which would clearly allow the router to choose among routes sourced differently. We can view these weights as a measure of trustworthiness of each routing information source, and the degree to which a source recommending a route should be believed. Network managers may be able, depending on the particular routing software, to tune the distance factors to optimize traffic flows across their networks. For example, they can assign believability weights to individual source IP addresses or to source IP address ranges. They can even assign a weight to an individual route advertisement.

One way to work around **incompatibilities** in routing protocols is to implement them redundantly. This approach can be undertaken in varying degrees, depending on needs. At one extreme, for example, it might seem an easy solution to implement two routing protocols on every router in the internetwork. This action would result in each router having two sets of routing tables, performing two sets of table updates, and converging twice after topology changes. This option would work; however, each router would have twice the work to do in addition to the usual responsibility of forwarding packets on behalf of end systems. Therefore, using redundant routing protocols is unavoidably resource-intensive and is not an advisable approach.

A more efficient alternative is to **partition off** just the segments of the inter-network that require a specific protocol and use a single protocol on each segment. This approach improves the operational efficiency of the routers, as well as the overall network. Enterprises may elect, for example, to create routing protocol-specific segments within their internetworks. Each segment could use a single IGP such as RIP, RIPv2, OSPF, or EIGRP. In such a scenario, only the border routers between the two protocol-specific segments would have to support both protocols.

Redistribution requires care when **configuring**. When a misconfigured router makes decisions based on inconsistent metrics, some links might become congested while utilization on others remains unnaturally low. Performance-monitoring tools will ultimately expose the lopsided distribution of traffic. Unfortunately, though, loud user complaints about slow response times and failed connection attempts will likely come to a network manager's attention first.

12.8.2 Filtering routing updates

Routers may allow the filtering of incoming and outgoing routing updates. Network managers might use route filters when they want to advertise selected routes only, such as a default route (and none of the other routes usually advertised by the router). Conversely, routers can be configured not to accept advertisements for selected routes, most often for default routes.

Routing protocol information can be filtered by performing the following tasks:

- Suppress the sending of routing updates on a particular interface. Doing so prevents other systems on an interface from learning about routes dynamically.

- Suppress networks from being advertised in routing updates. Doing so prevents other routers from learning a particular interpretation of one or more routes.

- Suppress a routing protocol from both sending and receiving updates on a particular interface.

- Suppress networks listed in updates from being accepted and acted upon by a routing process. Doing so keeps a router from using certain routes.

- Filter on the source of routing information. To prioritize routing information from different sources, because the accuracy of the routing information can vary. Some rating of the trustworthiness of a routing information source, such as an individual router or a group of routers, may be deployed. In a large network, some routing protocols and some routers can be more reliable than others as sources of routing information. Also, when multiple routing processes are running in the same device for IP, the same route may be advertised by more than one routing process.

- Apply an offset to routing metrics. Doing so provides a local mechanism for increasing the value of routing metrics.

The **route filtering process** employed on a router works, in general, as follows:

1 The router receives a routing update or is getting ready to send an update about one or more networks.

2 The router looks at the interface involved with the action. On an incoming update, for example, the configuration for the interface on which the update has arrived is checked. Conversely, if it is an update that must be advertised, the configuration of the outbound interface is checked.

3 Filters can be associated with all interfaces running a specific routing protocol and impose further restrictions on information type and are called global filters. Filters can also be associated with an interface (interface filters). If a filter is associated with the interface, the router views the filter to learn if there is a match for the given routing update. If a filter is not associated with the interface, the packet is processed normally.

4 If there is a match, the route entry is processed as configured.

5 It is inadvisable to filter internal (vs. external) routing updates with link-state protocols – such as OSPF and IS-IS – because doing so may cause unexpected and undesirable routing behavior in the network.

12.9 Snapshot routing

Snapshot routing provides an efficient and cost-effective routing solution in a **Dial-on-Demand Routing** (DDR) environment. Snapshot routing only works with distance vector routing protocols, such as IP RIP, IGRP, RIP for IPX, etc. For link-state routing protocols like OSPF, IS-IS, or EIGRP with hello packet exchanges with neighbors, snapshot routing will not work over ISDN or PSTN with neighbors across the network.

Snapshot routing is a routing update mechanism that answers two key customer concerns:

- It eliminates the need for configuring and maintaining large static tables (dynamic routing protocols can now be used on DDR lines).
- It cuts down the overhead of these routing updates.

ISDN is the primary target for snapshot routing, but other media, such as dedicated leased lines, can also benefit from the reduction of periodic updates. Snapshot routing allows dynamic routing protocols to run over DDR lines. Usually, routing broadcasts (routes and services) are filtered out on DDR interfaces and static definitions are configured instead. With snapshot, normal updates are sent across the DDR interface for a short duration of time called an **active period**. After this, routers enter a **quiet period** during which the routing tables at both ends of the link are frozen. Snapshot is therefore a 'triggering' mechanism that controls routing update exchange in DDR scenarios.

Only in the active period do routers exchange dynamic updates. During the quiet period, no updates go through the link (up or down) and the routing information previously collected is kept unchanged (frozen) in the routing tables. The lengths of the active period and quiet period are user configurable. By default, each DDR connection (triggered by user data) starts an active period during which routers update their tables. Afterwards, routers freeze the received information, enter the quiet period and stop sending routing updates – until the next data connection or the expiration of the quiet period. If, during the quiet period, no connection has been triggered, the snapshot mechanism triggers a call to update its information at the end of the quiet period interval.

SNAPSHOT   **snapshot routing components**

- *Active period* – duration of snapshot routing exchange.
- *Quiet period* – maximum time between the routing exchanges period.
- *Client router* – determines the frequency at which the routing information is being exchanged. In other words, it fixes the quiet period.
- *Server router* – accepts incoming snapshot connections from several client routers.

Moreover, the snapshot routing principle is to let normal routing protocols update naturally their routing tables. The routing protocol timers remain unchanged when snapshot is used. Therefore, in order for the received information to reliably represent the network topology, the active period needs to last long enough to let several routing updates come through the link. The active period's minimum duration is five minutes. As an option, snapshot routing can be prevented from using data connections as active periods. Snapshot routing will then update its routing table regularly after each quiet period.

Snapshot can be used with all distance vector routing protocols for all supported network protocols on DDR lines. The options are:

- RIP and IGRP for IP;
- RTMP for Appletalk;
- RIP and SAP for IPX;
- RTP for VINES.

Snapshot routing brings the following benefits:

- It allows the use of dynamic routing protocols (like RIP, IGRP, IPX RIP/SAP, VINES RTP, Apple's RTMP, etc.) in DDR environments. Information about network changes is spread automatically at the other end of DDR links.
- It allows the elimination of static routes, and as such, it eases the network administration. Administering static routes can be very cumbersome. With snapshot routing there is no need to add, suppress, or modify static routes; with snapshot routing, the network adapts transparently as the topology changes.
- Snapshot routing's key advantages include easy evolution and manageability.

Snapshot is meant to take advantage of data transfers and exchange the routing information. Routing information is exchanged during active periods. Snapshot expects the active period to last at least three times the routing updates interval. At the end of this period, the routers take a snapshot of the entries in the routing table. These entries remain frozen during the quiet period. At the end of the quiet period, another active period starts during which routing information is again exchanged. If the line is not available when the router transitions from the quiet to the active period, it enters a retry period, when the router will repeatedly attempt to connect until an active period is successfully entered.

Contrary to distance vector protocols, link-state routing protocols send periodic 'hellos' to the neighbors, as well as link-state packets. The hellos are exchanged between the neighbors every 5 or 10 seconds. They are inherent in the operation of link-state protocols as they allow the discovery of routing neighbors. They would trigger the link-up every 5 or 10 seconds. Therefore the link-state routing protocols (NLSP, OSPF, IS-IS) are not usable in dial-on-demand environments. EIGRP also relies on the exchange of hellos between neighbors and, for that reason, should not be used with snapshot either.

12.10 Tunneling

Tunneling, as described in Section 11.5 in the particular case of IPv4–IPv6 collaboration, is a method of taking packets or frames from one network system and placing them inside frames from another network system. This method is sometimes – wrongly – referred to as encapsulation. Encapsulation instead is a proper way of passing data units through all the communication system layers before they are transmitted (for more details see Part I). Tunneling may put a Layer 2 frame into a Layer 3 packet or even a Layer 4 segment for transmission.

Tunneling may be effectively used for allowing the non-routable traffic to pass through a routed network (e.g. IBM traffic), or to effectively deploy a single routed backbone, typically IP, for interconnecting multiprotocol enterprise environments (see Figure 12.27 for an example). However, as tunneling requires handling of the packets, it is generally faster to route protocols natively than to use tunnels (this is, of course, applicable only to routable protocols). Performance depends on the passenger protocol, broadcasts, routing updates, and bandwidth of the physical interfaces. It is also difficult to debug the physical link if problems occur. This problem can be mitigated in several ways. In IPX environments, route filters and SAP filters cut down on the size of the updates that travel over tunnels. In AppleTalk networks, keeping zones small and using route filters can limit excess bandwidth requirements.

FIGURE 12-27 Tunneling multiprotocol traffic through IP backbone

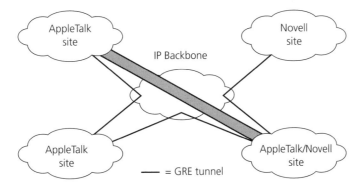

IP tunneling also provides communication between subnetworks that have invalid or discontiguous network addresses. With tunneling, virtual network addresses are assigned to subnetworks, making discontiguous subnetworks reachable. Figure 12.28 illustrates that with Generic Route Encapsulation (GRE) tunneling it is possible for the two subnetworks of network 131.108.0.0 to talk to each other even though they are separated by another network.

FIGURE 12-28   Connecting discontiguous networks with tunnels

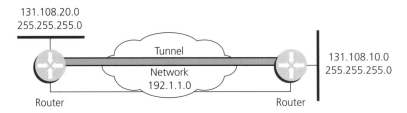

Tunneling can disguise the nature of a link, making it look slower, faster, or more or less costly than it may actually be in reality. This can cause unexpected or undesirable route selection. Routing protocols that make decisions based only on hop count will usually prefer a tunnel to a real interface. This may not always be the best routing decision because an IP cloud can comprise several different media with very disparate qualities; for example, traffic may be forwarded across both 100 Mbps Ethernet lines and 9.6 kbps serial lines. When using tunneling, attention must be paid to the media over which virtual tunnel traffic passes and the metrics used by each protocol.

Moreover, it is not only the qualities of the media involved in the tunnel that are relevant, but also its varying behavior in time. The tunnel virtual link has (due to the cloud) throughput and error characteristics that can continuously vary in time. This usually tends to confuse metric computations that assume relative stability of link characteristics over time.

If a network has sites that use protocol-based packet filters as part of a firewall security scheme, be aware that because tunnels encapsulate unchecked passenger protocols, you must establish filtering on the firewall router so that only authorized tunnels are allowed to pass. If tunnels are accepted from unsecured networks, it is a good idea to establish filtering at the tunnel destination or to place the tunnel destination outside the secure area of your network so that the current firewall scheme will remain secure.

Tunneling IP within IP (see also Section 11.7) must be carefully thought ahead to avoid inadvertently configuring a recursive routing loop. A routing loop occurs when the protocol carried and the underlying transport protocol are identical. The routing loop occurs because the best path to the tunnel destination is via the tunnel interface. To avoid recursive loops, carried and transport routing information should be kept separately either by using separate routing protocol identifiers or by using different routing protocols. Alternatively, the metric for using the tunnel should be set very high so as not to take precedence as a route. Also it is recommended to use different IP addresses for tunnels from those in the actual IP network. Keeping the address ranges distinct also aids in debugging because it is easy to identify an address as the tunnel network instead of the physical network and vice versa.

12.11 Routing protocol scalability revisited

For a comparison of the various characteristics of different routing protocols across network architectures, see Table 12.5. All the characteristics have a certain impact on the network scalability they support:

■ **hierarchical routing** is particularly scalable in cases of good addressing structure;

■ link-state protocols are more scalable than distance vector protocols due to their minimal network load in cases of stable topology;

■ some metric types limit the scalability of a protocol, as in the case of RIP where due to count to infinity problems the longest path – and thus the network diameter – is set a limit of 15 hops.

TABLE 12-5 Summary of dynamic routing protocol characteristics

Routing protocols	RIP	IGRP	OSPF	ISO IS-IS	ISO ES-IS	EGP	BGP	RTMP	DECnet
Flat vs. hierarchical	F	F	H	H	F	F	F	F	H
Intra- vs. inter-domain	Intra	Intra	Intra	Both	Intra	Inter	Inter	Inter	Both
Link state vs. distance vector	DV	DV	LS	LS	Neither	Neither	Neither (path vector)	DV	DV
Metric	Hop count	Delay bandwidth load reliability	Cost	Arbitrary	N/a	None	Arbitrary	Hop count	Arbitrary
Single vs. multipath	S	M	M	M	S	S	M	S	M

Distance vector protocols such as Routing Information Protocol (RIP), Interior Gateway Routing Protocol (IGRP), Internetwork Packet Exchange (IPX) RIP, IPX Service Advertisement Protocol (SAP), and Routing Table Maintenance Protocol (RTMP), broadcast their complete routing table periodically, regardless of whether the routing table has changed. This periodic advertisement varies from every 10 seconds for RTMP to every 90 seconds for IGRP. When the network is stable, distance vector protocols behave well but waste bandwidth because of the periodic sending of routing table updates, even when no change has occurred. When a failure occurs in the network, distance vector protocols do not add excessive load to the network, but they take a long time to reconverge to an alternative path or to flush a bad path from the network.

Link-state routing protocols, such as Open Shortest Path First (OSPF), Intermediate System-to-Intermediate System (IS-IS), and NetWare Link Services Protocol (NLSP), were designed to address the limitations of distance vector routing protocols (slow convergence and unnecessary bandwidth usage). Link-state protocols are more complex than distance vector protocols, and running them adds to the router's overhead. The additional overhead (in the form of memory utilization and bandwidth consumption when link-state protocols first start up) constrains the number of neighbors that a router can support and the number of neighbors that can be in an area.

When the network is stable, link-state protocols minimize bandwidth usage by sending updates only when a change occurs. A hello mechanism ascertains the reachability of neighbors. When a failure occurs in the network, link-state protocols flood link-state advertisements (LSAs) throughout an area. LSAs cause every router within the failed area to recalculate routes. The fact that LSAs need to be flooded throughout the area in failure mode and the fact that all routers recalculate routing tables constrain the number of neighbors that can be in an area.

Enhanced IGRP is an advanced distance vector protocol in that it addresses the limitations of conventional distance vector routing protocols (slow convergence and high bandwidth consumption in a steady-state network). When the network is stable, Enhanced IGRP sends updates only when a change in the network occurs. Like link-state protocols, Enhanced IGRP uses a hello mechanism to determine the reachability of neighbors. When a failure occurs in the network, Enhanced IGRP looks for feasible successors by sending messages to its neighbors. The search for feasible successors can be aggressive in terms of the traffic it generates (updates, queries, and replies) to achieve convergence. This behavior constrains the number of neighbors that is possible.

The scalability of routing protocols is also directly connected to their use of broadcasting in the internet. For comparison, look at Table 12.6 where the routing protocols are compared for each network protocol.

TABLE 12-6   Comparison of broadcast traffic generated by routing protocols

Network protocol	Relatively high broadcast traffic	Relatively low broadcast traffic
IP	RIP	OSPF
	IGRP	EIGRP
		Integrated IS-IS
Novell	RIP	EIGRP
	SAP	NLSP

TABLE 12-6	Continued	

Network protocol	Relatively high broadcast traffic	Relatively low broadcast traffic
AppleTalk	RTMP	EIGRP
DECnet	IS-IS (Phase V)	Level 1/2 routing
XNS	RIP	
Banyan VINES	RTP	Sequenced RTP
OSI	IS-IS	

To summarize the features that are important for a proper decision on their deployment in the network:

- standard vs. proprietary;
- internal vs. external use;
- metrics;
- non-integrated vs. integrated;
- what information is exchanged as updates and how often – convergence;
- other timers;
- in-built features avoiding routing loops, low convergence and inconsistency, split horizon, counting to infinity, poison updates, time stamps;
- support for autonomous systems/administrative domains;
- support to hierarchical internetwork design (areas);
- support to VLSM/CIDR (IP), authentication;
- trustworthiness;
- scalability and reliability issues.

STANDARDS WATCH   Summarized Standards watch

The following standards have been brought to your attention in this chapter:

ISO/IEC 8208:2000 *Information Technology – Data Communications – X.25 Packet Layer Protocol for Data Terminal Equipment*

ISO/IEC 8348:1996 *Information Technology – Open Systems Interconnection – Network Service Definition*

ISO/IEC 8348:1996/Amd 1:1998 *Addition of the Internet Protocol Address Format Identifier*

ISO/IEC 8473-1:1998 *Information Technology – Protocol for Providing the Connectionless-Mode Network Service: Protocol Specification*

ISO/IEC 8473-2:1996 *Information Technology – Protocol for Providing the Connectionless-Mode Network Service – Part 2: Provision of the Underlying Service by an ISO/IEC 8802 Subnetwork*

ISO/IEC 8473-3:1995 *Information Technology – Protocol for Providing the Connectionless-Mode Network Service: Provision of the Underlying Service by an X.25 Subnetwork*

ISO/IEC 8473-4:1995 *Information Technology – Protocol for Providing the Connectionless-Mode Network Service: Provision of the Underlying Service by a Subnetwork that Provides the OSI Data Link Service*

ISO/IEC 8473-5:1997 *Information Technology – Protocol for Providing the Connectionless-Mode Network Service: Provision of the Underlying Service by ISDN Circuit-switched B-Channels*

ISO/IEC 8602:1995 *Information Technology – Protocol for Providing the OSI Connectionless-Mode Transport Service*

ISO/IEC 8878:1992 *Information Technology – Telecommunications and Information Exchange between Systems – Use of X.25 to Provide the OSI Connection-Mode Network Service*

ISO/IEC 9574:1992 *Information Technology – Provision of the OSI Connection-Mode Network Service by Packet Mode Terminal Equipment to an Integrated Services Digital Network (ISDN)*

ISO/IEC TR 9575:1995 *Information Technology – Telecommunications and Information Exchange between Systems – OSI Routeing Framework*

ISO 9542:1988 *Information Processing Systems – Telecommunications and Information Exchange between Systems – End System to Intermediate System Routeing Exchange Protocol for Use in Conjunction with the Protocol for Providing the Connectionless-mode Network Service (ISO 8473)*

ISO/IEC 9542:1994 *Information Technology – Telecommunications and Information Exchange between Systems – Protocol for Exchange of Inter-domain Routeing Information among ISs to Support Forwarding of ISO 8473 PDUsISO/IEC 10030*:1995 *Information Technology – Telecommunications and Information Exchange between Systems – End System Routeing Information Exchange Protocol for Use in Conjunction with ISO/IEC 8878*

ISO/IEC **10589**:1992 *Information Technology – Telecommunications and Information Exchange between Systems – Intermediate System to Intermediate System Intra-domain Routeing Information Exchange Protocol for Use in Conjunction with the Protocol for Providing the Connectionless-mode Network Service (ISO 8473)*

RFC WATCH   **Summarized RFC watch**

The following RFC have been brought to your attention in this section:

RFC 1142 *OSI IS-IS Intra-domain Routing Protocol*, 1990 (Informational)

RFC 1195 *Use of OSI IS-IS for Routing in TCP/IP and Dual Environments*, 1990 (Proposed Standard)

RFC 1504 *Appletalk Update-Based Routing Protocol: Enhanced Appletalk Routing*, 1993 (Informational)

RFC 2763 *Dynamic Hostname Exchange Mechanism for IS-IS*, 2000 (Informational)

RFC 2966 *Domain-wide Prefix Distribution with Two-Level IS-IS*, 2000 (Informational)

RFC 2973 *IS-IS Mesh Groups*, 2000 (Informational)

PART IV CONCLUDING REMARKS

Part IV represents the core section of the book for a very good reason: routing is as essential for today's networks as it will be in the future. However, its evolution is clear:

- from routing **proprietary** network protocols, such as IPX or AppleTalk, to **routing IP** which now supports the majority of networks (not only the Internet but in enterprises too);
- from simple routing algorithms to algorithms providing routing updates instantly after topology changes and providing them accurately, hence enabling the much needed fast convergence in today's vital networking environment;
- from older **distance vector protocols** (such as RIP and IGRP) to robust **link-state protocols** (such as OSPF and IS-IS) which are more complex for administration but bring excellent results;
- from **unicast** traffic routing to mixed unicast and **multicast** routing, requiring new protocols to be deployed.

In-depth knowledge of the routing protocols themselves and of their behavior in different situations is an essential virtue for all network and router administrators. Therefore this Part has not only presented straight facts but also hints and experience relating to a variety of scenarios, including situations requiring the **coexistence** of more than one routing protocol, the **filtering** of routing information, or **tunneling** one type of traffic via a different protocol. Methods limiting the routing **overhead** where needed (e.g. across dial-up links) are also presented.

Current requirements for routing protocols are primarily **fast convergence, robustness, and scalability**. Although there are preferred routing protocols based on these criteria, there is no single routing protocol of choice recommendable for every situation.

The **architecture** of routers has also significantly evolved, particularly in the high-end, core routers for the ISPs forming the Internet backbone. Their high-performance internal switching fabrics and internal switching processes tend to continuously increase in speed by eliminating the lookups made in the central processor. However, the high performance required can only be achieved by deploying **advanced mechanisms** such as **label switching**. This is discussed in detail in Part V.

PART V

Getting up to speed

Internetworking has come a great distance over the past couple of years in terms of technological advancements and new devices introduced. Current networks, with the view into the future, need both to support new and coming applications (real-time, voice, multicast, etc.) and to sustain the growth in the passing traffic. Obviously, internetworking devices must not become bottlenecks in an internet and so we will look at the latest ways of speeding up packet processing in routers and switches, and how they may be enabled to serve the user traffic in a differentiated manner.

In particular our focus will concentrate upon:

- **high-speed networking requirements** (Chapter 13);
- **high-end advanced router architectures**;
- **effective routing and switching combinations**, Layer 3+ switching, and multilayer switching solutions;
- the evolution of **label switching**, in particular the proprietary proposals: *Cell switch router* (CSR) from Toshiba, *IP switching* from Ipsilon, *Aggregated route-based IP switching* (ARIS) from IBM, and *Tag switching* from Cisco Systems;
- **quality of service** support through integrated and differentiated services (Chapter 14), and **multiprotocol label switching** (MPLS) (Chapter 15);
- **optical switching** (Chapter 16).

CHAPTER 13

High-speed networking

Both local area networks and wide area networks have been evolving in the direction of supporting **increased bandwidth**. This is in line with the new bandwidth-intensive applications including motion video and realtime interactive traffic. These applications are not only hungry for bandwidth but have at the same time different requirements in terms of packet loss, delay, and delay variation sensitivity. Hence the increased bandwidth is only part of the solution to the current networking requirements. The other part vests in the guaranteed **quality of service** (QoS). Then there are more options available in terms of reserved bandwidth and other resources necessary (e.g. RSVP protocol). However, in many cases it is still not the network that can guarantee actual and reliable packet delivery. Even in connection-oriented networks packet loss may result in dropping the connection which requires upper-layer protocols in end systems to take care of recovery, i.e. requesting retransmission (in many cases of complete sets of packets, not just the lost ones which may be difficult to identify).

High-speed networks currently deployed reach the maximum bandwidth of Gbps, both in local and wide area network forms: 1–10 Gbps with (10) Gigabit Ethernet and 2.5 Gbps with ATM. Further increases in both arenas are being researched, exclusively concentrating on the optical fiber infrastructure and devices, and optical signal processing methods. High capacity in backbone networks is achieved by using many individual channels, much more than are used today. This motivates continuous research in **multichannel network** solutions, such as multiplexing in the wavelength and space domains.

The **challenges** to be dealt with in high-speed networks are manifold:

- **distributed switching** – signaling protocols, addressing, routing, and clock distribution needed for distributed switching; network structures suitable for interconnecting switching elements; the advantages and disadvantages with using circuits, cells, and packets as the basis for switching; variable length packet switching provision in cell-based networks;

- **fault-tolerance** – network organization in terms of resiliency to link and node failures; the best ways to reconfigure high-speed networks after faults, to detect and locate faults in optical networks;

- **high-speed switching** – switching fabric, optical interfaces and circuit architectures moving from current low and medium rate switching systems towards tens of Gbps per port;

- **protocols** – medium access and switching techniques best suited for multi-wavelength distribution techniques; protocols best designed for cost-efficient use of optical switches and amplifiers;

■ **multicasting** – techniques used to efficiently implement logical channels for multicast switching in a network with many subscribers in order to support applications ranging from selective distribution to dynamically reconfigurable group communications;

■ **resource management and routing** – traffic control policies, feedback schemes, cost-efficient reservation-based policies.

IP has now clearly become the *de facto* standard for carrying data, but at the same time, scalability for use across high-speed backbones has not been easy. As an alternative, many carriers and enterprise-level networks have chosen ATM technology in the core of their networks to carry IP traffic within fixed TDM cells that can be transported in a much faster circuit-switched mode, as it is much simpler to route ATM cells than IP because of their fixed size (53 bytes) and simple routing via a single path.

To carry IP over ATM significantly limits scalability, especially when the backbone network becomes larger and more complex. The extra overhead involved with encapsulating IP packets into ATM cells is now becoming a major burden on large-scale network efficiency, especially considering that many larger IP packets have to be segmented and spread across multiple ATM cells, and then reassembled at the end of the ATM switched circuit. In addition, the complexity of ATM control protocols that are required for maintaining point-to-point virtual switched connections in today's dynamic internet environment makes these protocols unwieldy at best. Although Gigabit Ethernet has provided something of a viable alternative to ATM at the enterprise level, it also lacks the inherent scalability needed.

The complexity of the Layer 3 software necessary for maintaining routing protocols has been a major challenge when scaling the Internet backbone, since these backbone routers must constantly exchange IP accessibility information through routing updates in order to build and maintain accurate routing tables. In addition, gateways to the Internet are increasingly multiplying everyday, which is demanding a very complex mesh of IP subnets controlled through routing protocols, such as Border Gateway Protocol (BGP), that are essentially used to build TCP sessions between neighboring routers and therefore must exchange IP prefixes for subnets throughout the Internet.

The challenge of scaling up inter-router and ATM circuit control protocols is becoming especially problematic, when IP prefixes are growing at such a fast pace, adding to the complexity of the global topology of the Internet backbone. The combination of physical internal and external connections plus the complexity of Layer 3 software protocols required to implement Internet point-of-presence (POP) installations represents an extremely intricate challenge. Current routers are interconnected via line cards which is not only a very expensive practice but also limits the overall transit throughput of the POP to the speed of the router port. No matter how big the individual router backplanes become, the bandwidth on links between separate routers and ATM switches may quickly become a bottleneck. Because today's POPs must be pieced together out of such disparate components, the results are generally suboptimal throughput, with degraded Quality of Service (QoS), reduced fault-tolerance, and a complete lack of scalability.

Furthermore, besides higher overall bandwidth within the campus/building network, enterprise networks now need to provide different levels of service to applications and end users. Enterprises are building general-purpose utility networks that must support the requirements of all applications. However, from a business point of view, and from a network manager's, not all applications are created equal.

Therefore, the main challenge for very high-speed systems is to enable the inherent capacity to cost-effectively terminate the maximum number of ports within each box as well as to be able efficiently to expand the overall system to encompass additional capacity. Very high-speed technology requires transitioning from the concept of a single responsible box to a system where all the components can be mutually optimized and smoothly scaled.

Formerly, the ISP community adapted **general-purpose equipment** for use in the core of the Internet. The explosive growth of the Internet has created a market for networking equipment that is specially built to solve the unique problems confronting Internet backbone providers. This new class of equipment is required to scale the Internet not only in terms of aggregate bandwidth and raw throughput, but also in terms of software richness and control.

To achieve the objectives of providing **increased bandwidth** and software richness, the designers of new routing systems must achieve the forwarding performance previously found only in switches. However, delivering **wirespeed performance** for **variable-sized packets** with **longest-match lookups** is considerably more complex than the relatively straightforward switching goal of supporting wirespeed performance for fixed-sized cells with fixed-length lookups. In particular, packet processing can no longer remain a microprocessor-based or microprocessor-assisted function, but must transition to an ASIC-based approach that supports the evolution of routing software as the Internet environment changes.

13.1 The challenges to be met

It is worthwhile to make a link between the high-speed networking requirements and resulting requirements placed upon internetworking devices, mainly switches and routers, compared to their current architectures and capabilities. The requirements closely relate to the major drivers of current networking: speed and **scalability** (performance of routers and switches), **quality of service support**, and **feasible cost** (price/performance ratio).

As we already know all routers must perform two fundamental tasks, routing (path determination) and packet forwarding (Figure 13.1). The routing process collects information about the network topology and creates a forwarding table. The packet-forwarding process copies a packet from an input interface of the router to the proper output interface based on information contained in the forwarding table.

FIGURE 13-1 Routing and packet forwarding processes

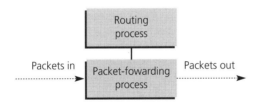

Any routing system requires four essential elements to implement the routing and packet-forwarding processes: routing software, packet processing, a switch fabric, and line cards (Figure 13.2). For any system that is designed to operate in the core of the Internet, all four elements must be equally powerful because a high-performance router can be only as strong as its weakest element.

FIGURE 13-2   Elements of a routing system

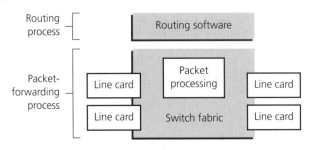

The **routing software** is the part of the system that performs the path determination function. It is responsible for maintaining peer relationships, running the routing protocols, building the routing table, and creating the forwarding table that is accessed by the packet-forwarding part of the system. The software also provides system control features including traffic engineering, the user interface, policy, and network management.

Regardless of a router's architecture, each packet entering the system requires a certain amount of **packet processing** that is completely independent of the packet's length. The incoming encapsulation must be removed, a longest-match route lookup needs to be performed, the packet needs to be queued on the output port, and the outgoing encapsulation must be provided. The tasks of performing longest-match lookups and the related packet processing at a high rate are the most difficult challenges to overcome when developing a high-performance routing system. Packet processing may be distributed to each line card, executed in a centralized fashion, or performed by both the line cards and a centralized processor.

The internal **switch fabric** provides the infrastructure for moving packets between router line cards. Designers have been working with switch fabrics for a number of decades, and the issues are well understood by the vendor community. There even are a number of off-the-shelf chip sets available to router vendors to build a switch fabric. These solutions might be crossbar switches, or some other types not discussed here (e.g. banyan networks, perfect shuffle networks).

A **line card** terminates circuits of different physical media types, implementing the Layer 1 and Layer 2 technologies such as DS-3 (see Appendix D), ATM, SONET, Frame Relay, and PPP. Issues involving the design and development of router line cards also are well understood by the vendor community. Line cards simply have to be built according to the prevailing standards that define physical interface types, optical characteristics, electrical levels, and so forth.

13.1.1 High-speed interfaces

The common user interface to the Internet has shifted from analog modems operating at a few kbps to xDSL or cable modems operating at a few Mbps. Therefore, it is essential that the backbone connection speed should also grow from common speeds ranging between a few Mbps to 155 Mbps to multiple Gbps and beyond. The port speeds of high end routers are more commonly 622 Mbps (OC12) and 2.5 Gbps (OC48) and will gradually climb up towards tens of Gbps (OC192+, see Appendix D). These **high speeds** imply the use of optical physical interfaces and very wide parallel electrical buses operating at high speeds. Optical interfaces offer even higher speeds as Wave Division Multiplexing (WDM) technology is developed that will allow multiple optical bit streams to be transmitted on a single fiber.

The most popular network **infrastructures** are Gigabit Ethernet, ATM, and Packet Over SONET (POS). The latter enables transmission of IP packets directly over a SONET fiber without an intermediate ATM layer. Therefore, POS uses the link more efficiently than ATM. IP routers can be connected to an ATM interface through IP/ATM or MPOA interfaces. By definition, a router will not forward ATM cells. Instead, IP packets coming from an ATM network will be reassembled from cells, routed, and then segmented back into cells before transmission to an ATM network.

The system challenges facing this new class of Internet backbone router also are complex. New routing systems must be deployed into existing OC-3 and OC-12 based cores with their related intra-POP infrastructure, and they also must support the transition to OC-48 based cores with OC-12 and Gigabit Ethernet based intra-POP infrastructures. In addition, new routing systems must accelerate the evolution of the Internet from a best-effort service to a fundamentally reliable service. With the Internet emerging in its role as the new public network, users are demanding and expecting increased reliability and stability to support mission-critical applications. The Internet cannot continue to provide erratic best-effort service that generally works but at other times fails. As they have come to expect with the Plain Old Telephone Service (POTS), Internet users want to 'hear the dial-tone' and receive quality service whenever they wish to communicate.

13.1.2 Line capacity vs. total switching capacity

The discussion about necessary improvements to the internetworking service and the devices providing it is mostly about the speed of operation – and then its diversification with relation to the particular traffic type. While discussing the processing speed of interconnecting devices, it is useful to define the measures used to understand how various types of scalable Gigabit and Terabit level systems are applicable to the Internet's edge and core routing environments. There are differences between line capacity and total switching capacity. The real switching (internal) capacity depends on the architecture used (the architecture was discussed in Parts III and IV with reference to switches and routers, respectively).

Line capacity consists of the **effective input/output bandwidth that is available to a subscriber via the line card ports**. For example, a line card that has four port OC-48s at 2.5 Gbps each would deliver 10 Gbps of line capacity. Invariably line capacity represents only a percentage of the overall switching capacity; however, it is also a key factor because it dictates the size of the pipes that can be connected into the system.

Gigabit routing devices typically can provide total line capacity of up to tens of gigabits per second, while providing line capacity performance to support multiple port interface speeds up to OC-48 (2.5 Gbps) or OC-192 (10 Gbps) in next-generation devices.

Terabit routing devices are designed with the aggregate line capacity to handle thousands of gigabits per second (1000 gigabits = 1 terabit) and to provide ultra-scalable performance and high port density. These routers can support port interface speeds as high as OC-192 (10 Gbps) and beyond. Terabit devices are typically designed to handle core applications within the carriers' networks. By using matrix architectures, terabit systems can maximize their total switching capacity to meet core bandwidth demands.

The **switching capacity** of a system consists of the **total bandwidth for all line card connections and internal switching connections throughout the system**. The switching capacity could be substantially higher than the line capacity in order to provide non-blocking switching between any input to any output line card port. Additional switching is also needed in order to provide active redundancy and a higher level of fault-tolerance. Switching capacity includes:

- bandwidth used for line card connections;
- bandwidth available to modular expansion of line card connections;
- bandwidth for non-blocking switching;
- aggregate bandwidth needed to support redundancy and fault tolerance.

High-speed router general architecture is shown in Figure 13.3.

FIGURE 13-3   General high-speed router architecture

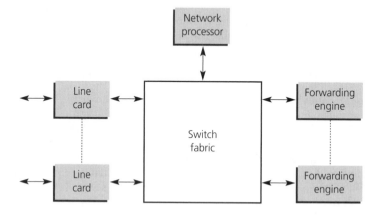

All of the high-speed router designs use the same functional components illustrated in Figure 13.3. The **line card** contains the physical layer components necessary to interface the external data link to the switch fabric. The **switch fabric** is used to interconnect the various components of the gigabit router. A switch fabric is used for interconnection as it offers a much higher aggregate capacity than is available from the more conventional backplane bus.

The **forwarding engine** inspects packet headers, determines to which outgoing line card they should be sent, and rewrites the header. The forwarding engine may be a physically separate component or may be integrated with either the line card or the network processor. If the forwarding engine is a separate component, the packet forwarding rate may be varied independently from the aggregate capacity by adjusting the ratio of forwarding engines to line cards. Currently, the high-end routers with the top performance deploy forwarding engines directly on line cards. The **network processor** runs the routing protocols and computes the routing tables that are copied into each of the forwarding engines. It handles network management and housekeeping functions and may also process unusual packets that require special handling.

13.1.3 Packet forwarding

To remind ourselves, the two main functions of an internetworking device is path determination and packet forwarding. **Packet forwarding** is the process of moving packets from incoming interfaces to outgoing interfaces. In order to make a **forwarding decision**, the router must process the headers of the incoming IP packets. These headers are essentially a key to a forwarding table that returns the outgoing interface the packets should be forwarded to. The forwarding table does not hold a separate entry for every possible destination address; instead, the table holds entries for a subset of address **prefixes**, and an incoming packet is forwarded to the port corresponding to the longest prefix that matches its destination address. This type of lookup is generally known as a best-match lookup that is clearly more difficult than a simple table lookup.

Classic router architectures perform the forwarding table **lookup in software** using either a central CPU or several CPUs positioned at the incoming interfaces. Either way, using general purpose CPUs for the forwarding task is good if, at the most, hundreds of thousands of packets per second need to be forwarded. However, even an OC-12 POS interface may transmit up to 1.5 million packets per second. A router with 128 such interfaces would need to cope with 200 million forwarding decisions per second – a task too heavy for any existing CPU.

Therefore, a high-end router must perform forwarding by **dedicated hardware**. The contents of the forwarding table depends on a database held by every router that reflects either the topology of the network or at least what the next hop router is for every destination. This database is usually referred to as the routing table. The routing table is built upon the information received through routing protocols such as RIP, OSPF, or BGP. The size of the routing table and the frequency at which it must be updated depend heavily on the size of the network.

To ensure wire-rate service delivery, separation of the path determination and packet forwarding functions is necessary in high-speed routers. This separation ensures that stress experienced by one component does not adversely affect the performance of another since there is no overlap of required resources. Routing fluctuations and network instability do not limit the forwarding of packets. Nor does packet forwarding affect the router's ability to handle routing updates.

13.1.4 Queuing

Every router or switch must be able to store packets in order to deal with multiple packets destined for the same output, and so that high priority packets can leapfrog low priority packets. Basically, **packet buffers** (or queues) can be placed near the inputs, near the outputs, or at both ends of the router. Placing buffers at the output enables exact shaping of the traffic transmitted from the router. However, implementing output queues requires the switching fabric to be able to forward traffic to a single output at the aggregate speed of all inputs (in the case where all inputs receive a packet intended for the same output simultaneously). Clearly, for Gbps speed ports, this kind of architecture is not feasible. On the other hand, placing the queues near the inputs creates difficulties in shaping the traffic at the outputs and can cause head of line (HOL) blocking (discussed in Section 7.6.1).

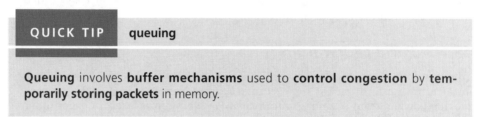

QUICK TIP   queuing

Queuing involves **buffer mechanisms** used to **control congestion** by **temporarily storing packets** in memory.

Input queuing (see Figure 13.4):

- packets buffered at the inbound port;
- reduces throughput to 60% maximum;
- results in head of line blocking not allowing the traffic behind the block to enter the switching fabric.

FIGURE 13-4   Input queuing

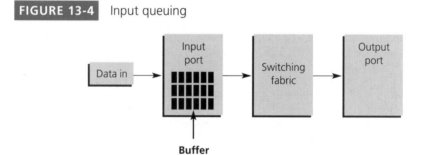

HOL blocking occurs when the packet at the head of a queue cannot be transmitted to an output due to a contending packet from another input, while at the same time, a packet further back in the queue is blocked although its destination port is free to receive a packet (see Figure 13.5). The HOL blocking problem can limit the throughput of an input buffered router to approximately 60% of the maximum aggregate input rate under certain traffic patterns. In order to overcome HOL blocking, multiple queues must be used at the inputs. This type of queuing is called Virtual Output Queuing (VOQ), introduced in Part IV. When intelligently managed, VOQ can perform as well as output queuing. The key factor is the arbitration algorithm used to choose which queue to send a packet from at every given time.

FIGURE 13-5 Head of line blocking

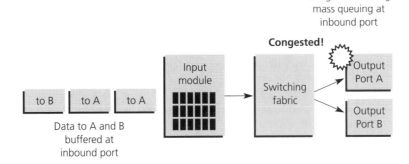

QUICK TIP **throughput**

Throughput is the **highest rate in packets per second** through a device in which **no frame loss** occurs.

Output queuing (see Figure 13.6):

■ buffers at the output port;
■ no head of line blocking.

FIGURE 13-6 Output queuing

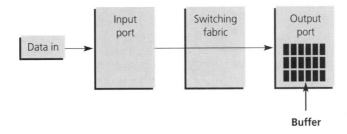

Output queuing with shared buffers (see Figure 13.7):

■ central pool of buffers shared between all ports;
■ maximum throughput with fewest buffers;
■ no head of line blocking;
■ if there are no QoS requirements, the amount of buffer can be dynamically allocated per port to handle traffic;
■ if QoS is a requirement, buffers are typically fixed per port and per queue.

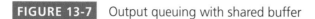

FIGURE 13-7   Output queuing with shared buffer

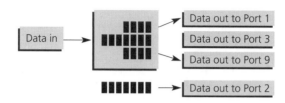

Multiple queues per port can be implemented for output queuing or shared memory architectures. A scheduling and/or congestion mechanism is needed.

The **size of the queues** is another important characteristic. If, during a given time frame, traffic destined to one of the outputs surpasses its capacity, the superfluous traffic is stored in the queues. The queues may be emptied gradually as the temporary congestion declines. Therefore, the larger the queues, the better the router can cope with such traffic bursts. If the queues of a router are too small to hold a burst of traffic, some packets may be discarded. Although this is considered acceptable router behavior, it will cause degradation of the quality of connections going through it.

A major bottleneck in queue design is the bandwidth of the **memory** in which the queues are implemented. If queues are designed per input port, the memory bandwidth needed is at least double the port bandwidth (every packet must be written and later read from the queues). However, if several ports share the same buffers, a multiple of this bandwidth is needed. Conventional memory chips (i.e. SRAM or SDRAM) usually operate at frequencies around 100 Mhz. Even at this frequency, board design is not trivial. Given a 64-bit wide bus, the bandwidth of such memory is no more than 6.4 Gbps and thus only a 3.2 Gbps port can be supported. This implies that no more than one OC-48 port can be connected to a single buffer. In any case, it is clear that a central memory that holds all queues is out of the question for high-end routers.

In the case of higher speed ports, such as an OC-192 port (operating at 10 Gbps), either a very wide memory bus would be required or more exotic memory technologies would be needed. Even with these technologies at hand, efficient memory management is needed in order to achieve the desired bandwidth. Packets may be as short as 40 bytes (or 320 bits) long, and a consecutive packet may need to be written to arbitrarily different memory locations. This means that the memory needs to be randomly accessed every five clocks for a 64-bit wide bus, every three clocks for a 128-bit bus, or less for wider buses. Random access is no problem for SRAM, but DRAM-based technologies, such as SDRAM or RAMBUS, are optimized only for burst access. When used for random access, their bandwidth deteriorates rapidly. A solution to the above problems usually combines SRAM and DRAM technologies and incorporates a memory allocation scheme that optimizes memory access time.

13.1.5 The switching fabric

The **interconnect fabric** is a critical design component in all high-performance switching systems. With the exception of line cards able to switch locally, all switched traffic crosses the switching fabric. Obviously, under heavy network loads, interconnect capacity can easily become the bottleneck limiting overall throughput. We have discussed switch and router architectures in previous Parts, but here we summarize the three basic architectures commonly used for switches and routers (see more details in Part III).

The **bus architecture** is the most simple of the three. With this architecture, all inputs are connected to all outputs through a common bus. Therefore, the bandwidth of this interconnect fabric is exactly the bandwidth of the bus. Using the same arguments from the above discussion concerning memory bandwidth, it is clear that a bus architecture is not sufficient for more than a very few Gbps speed ports.

The **shared memory architecture** is similar to the bus architecture except that traffic coming from the inputs is first stored in a central memory before being read out towards the outputs. Here, the bandwidth achieved is half the bandwidth of the data bus to the memory since every packet must be written to memory and read from it.

The **crossbar architecture** enables multiple inputs to be connected to multiple outputs simultaneously, as long as different inputs are connected to different outputs. The bandwidth of a crossbar is the sum of the bandwidths of its inputs. Therefore, it is very suitable for building high-performance switching fabrics. It is possible to connect several crossbars together in order to achieve even greater bandwidth and larger numbers of inputs. The internal crossbar speed is clocked several times faster than the interface to the fabric which is useful in cases of multicasting (the frame is copied onto multiple output interfaces in one step). The high clocking helps avoid head of line blocking and generally prevents the crossbar become a bottleneck in the system.

An important parameter of the switching fabric is its non-blocking bandwidth. This is defined as the maximum of the minimal aggregate bandwidth of all possible connections from inputs to outputs. As opposed to non-blocking bandwidth, aggregate bandwidth can be achieved by connecting multiple non-blocking fabrics.

Some vendors' products are built around a scalable, multi-gigabit non-blocking switching fabric that eliminates backbone interconnect bottlenecks and delivers continuous wirespeed throughput.

The majority of routers in use today are based on shared-memory architectures that are often designed with a single, centralized CPU. As traffic demands escalate and forwarding table information continues to grow larger, packet-forwarding speeds and system performance must increase as well. So router and switch designs are evolving particularly in how they divide up CPU cycles among tasks – to accommodate the added processing burden. Shared-memory architectures have been enhanced, and other types of designs such as crossbar switches have been created, that are rendering system performance much more predictable under the large traffic loads generated by Gigabit Ethernet, Packet over SONET (POS), and other new high-speed networks.

ASIC-based architectures with single-stage buffering significantly reduce latency by requiring only one write to and one read from shared memory. Unlike traditional methods where the entire packet is moved from input buffer to output buffer to output queue, current high-speed routers leave the packet in the non-blocking shared memory and move only a packet pointer through the queues. When packets arrive they are immediately placed in distributed shared memory where they remain until being read out of memory for transmission.

Conceptually the best approach to enhancing system performance – which we will revisit several times in this chapter – has proved to be to **logically isolate the packet forwarding from control functions** that take place within a device's centralized CPU (or in CPUs residing on distributed line cards in certain router platforms). Routing functions are processor-intensive, but are performed on a relatively infrequent basis. Packet-forwarding functions, on the other hand, require little processing, but must be performed at wirespeed. This design keeps the two sets of functions from interrupting one another, thus avoiding unpredictable latency during packet forwarding while a control function takes place.

The impact of latency has been compounded in recent years by the shift in the nature of Internet traffic patterns. Today's Hypertext Transfer Protocol (HTTP) traffic, for example, tends to constitute a large volume of short-duration flows, contrasted with once-prevalent FTP and Telnet sessions, which were fewer in number but of longer duration. Supporting more flows of shorter duration generates more latency in some switching architectures, because the first packet in the flow must be process-switched. Using this mechanism, all the associated best-path information in each routing table from source to destination must be looked up as the packet is processed.

Without isolating functions on a shared CPU, random latency occurs and can cause jitter or variability in packet delays. Jitter is the biggest culprit in application performance degradation – particularly that of realtime traffic such as voice – so minimizing jitter has become a significant payoff associated with separating the control and forwarding functions within a device's CPU(s) in newer switching designs.

QUICK TIP   **flow**

A flow is defined as a packet stream from a unique source IP address to a unique destination address:

■ destination flow – based on destination IP;

■ source/destination flow – based on source and destination IP;

■ full flow – based on source/destination and TCP/UDP port number.

Express forwarding

One of the proprietary technologies that allows for increased scalability and performance is **Cisco Express Forwarding** (CEF), topology-based switching. CEF has evolved to meet the ever-changing traffic patterns of today's networks. These networks are frequently characterized by an increasing number of short-duration flows. Shorter flows are very common in environments with a high degree of Web-based or other highly interactive types of traffic. As these types of applications continue to proliferate, a higher-performing and more scalable forwarding methodology is required to meet the needs in the largest of these environments.

High-speed routers use a route-cache model to maintain a fast lookup table for destination network prefixes. The route-cache entries are traffic-driven in that the first packet to a new destination is routed via routing table information, and as part of that forwarding operation a route-cache entry for that destination is then added. This allows subsequent packets flows to that same destination network to be switched based on an efficient route-cache match. These entries are periodically aged out to keep the route cache current and can be immediately invalidated if the network topology changes. This 'demand-caching' scheme – maintaining a very fast access subset of the routing topology information – is optimized for scenarios whereby the majority of traffic flows are associated with a subset of destinations. However, given that traffic profiles at the core of the Internet (and potentially within some large enterprise networks) are no longer resembling this model, a new switching paradigm was required that would eliminate the increasing cache maintenance resulting from growing numbers of topologically dispersed destinations and dynamic network changes.

With a CEF-based mechanism, the challenges presented by flow-caching models are greatly reduced and scalability is greatly increased. With flow-cached models, a complete forwarding table must be maintained for the proper handling of first packets by the CPU or packets that for some other reason cannot be processed in hardware. After the CPU makes a forwarding decision (part of which involves a lookup against the routing table), an entry is made into the flow cache table, and subsequent packets are handled in hardware.

With a CEF-based forwarding model, all packets, including the first packet in a given flow, are handled in hardware. A **routing table** is still maintained by the router CPU, but two additional tables are created in the CEF-based model. These tables are populated before any actual user traffic is present in the network, such as would be the case with a cache-based model. The first of these tables is actually a copy of the relevant forwarding data points from the routing table, the **forwarding information base** (FIB). The FIB is conceptually similar to a routing table. It contains a subset of the forwarding information contained in the IP routing table that defines best paths only. When routing or topology changes occur in the network, the IP routing table is automatically updated, and the FIB reflects those changes. The FIB maintains next-hop address information based on the information in the IP routing table. CEF uses the FIB to make IP destination prefix-based switching decisions. Because there is a direct relationship between FIB entries and routing table entries, the FIB contains all needed routes and eliminates the need for the route cache maintenance that is associated with other types of switching mechanisms. CEF systems, then, do not have to wait for traffic to generate an entry in a cache to forward packets and can thus switch traffic more efficiently.

The second table is called the **adjacency table**, which defines the next-hop forwarding information. Nodes in the network are considered adjacent if they can reach one another in a single hop across a link layer. The adjacency table maintains a database of node adjacencies, and their associated Layer 2 MAC rewrite or next-hop information. The adjacency table maintains Layer 2 next-hop addresses for all FIB entries (similar to the ARP table). The adjacency table is used to pre-process Layer 2 addressing information. The adjacency table is populated as adjacencies are discovered. Each time an adjacency entry is created, a link-layer header for that adjacent node is precomputed and stored in the adjacency table.

Once a route is determined, it points to a next hop and corresponding adjacency entry. It is subsequently used for encapsulation during CEF switching of packets. The method of CEF operation is shown in Figure 13.8.

Cisco's CEF in action

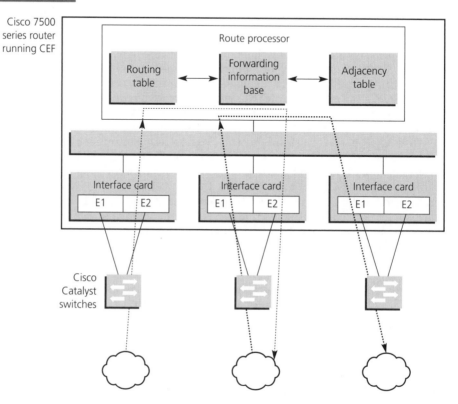

By performing a high-speed lookup in FIB and adjacency tables, a forwarding decision, along with the appropriate rewrite information, can be accessed in a highly efficient and consistent manner while also providing a mechanism that offers a high degree of scalability.

CEF is enhanced for router architectures with route processors distributed among interface processors (line cards). This method is called **distributed CEF** (dCEF). The router architecture with dCEF deployed is shown in Figure 13.9.

Cisco Express Forwarding also delivers additional functionality with respect to **load balancing** of traffic across multiple equal-cost parallel paths. Traditionally, routing protocols such as OSPF and EIGRP have limited equal-cost load-balancing paths to four paths. With CEF, this has been increased to six equal-cost parallel paths. Moreover, CEF provides for load-balancing both in per destination mode, and per packet mode. Before, the latter always called for the slowest possible internal switching.

FIGURE 13-9 Distributed CEF

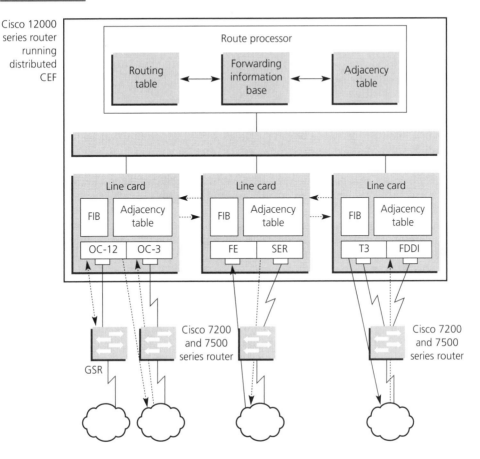

With routing protocols, more than four parallel paths can exist, but a maximum of four can be installed in the actual routing table. Routing protocols such as EIGRP and OSPF support the concept of a **Routing Information Base** (RIB). If a route cannot be installed into the routing table, it can be maintained in the RIB. Because CEF relies upon an FIB and an adjacency table for forwarding decisions, it is not limited to that which is actually present in the routing table, and, in fact, can reference the RIB, which enables CEF to install a greater number of parallel paths (with entries gleaned from the RIB). For each path, a pointer is added for the adjacency corresponding to the next-hop interface for that path.

CEF is a little different to other types of switching in that it creates FIBs that mirror the RIB. Hence, once routing protocols or other mechanisms put a destination into the RIB, the FIBs change in response. There is no need to wait for a first packet going to a particular destination.

High-perfomance router design note

Many traditional routers are designed for a stable network, i.e. the packet-forwarding function of these routers is designed for a network operating in a steady state. Moreover, the packet forwarding performance goals are often arrived at by calculating an arithmetic mean on IP traffic characteristics to derive the average packet size (sum total size of all packets transmitted divided by the number of packets).

Designs based on such principles fail in three areas. First, they do not simulate a realistic Internet environment, which is one of routing fluctuations, large bursts of traffic, and congestion. Second, IP traffic characteristics are not at all well described by averages because the packet size distribution is actually multi-modal. Finally, these designs do not reflect the fact that roughly 50 percent of all Internet packets are smaller than 45 bytes long. But performance is important for all packet sizes. As evidenced by the multi-modal nature of Internet traffic, there are large volumes and bursts of small packets; traffic is not a constant average size.

As the Internet continues to expand and diverse applications emerge, wire-rate forwarding performance becomes even more imperative. Many of these new applications that are based on small packets, such as VoIP, must be forwarded smoothly at wire rate even during network instability. Such traffic cannot tolerate packet loss, the result of which is choppy and incoherent service.

Demands on the network are increasing because of broader use of the Internet and the deployment of richer services. Customers expect the deterministic performance they already receive from voice or private data networks; hence, tolerance for variable performance is decreasing. Performance must remain constant regardless of packet size; otherwise, performance can impede your flexibility in offering new services. Performance is important in unstable networks.

Using a router designed for **exceptional conditions** means you can be assured of:

- **wire-rate forwarding performance**, regardless of the network state;
- **router stability** while keeping up with large bursts of control information, such as routing protocol messages.

The ability to forward large volumes of packets becomes more important as circuit speeds continue to increase.

Routers must be able to keep up with the forwarding decisions they make. Otherwise, packets are dropped and end devices must retransmit, possibly intensifying network congestion. Routers designed for an average network state may not be able to maintain performance during fluctuations in the network. Moreover, deploying routers that are not designed for exceptional conditions means more upgrades, shorter network lifecycles, and more wholesale changes as the network grows.

High-performance routers must keep pace with peaks and fluctuations to ensure network reliability. During heavy loads and rapid fluctuations in the network topology, routers must maintain their forwarding process just as under normal conditions. They must maintain peer relationships, transmit and process routing update messages, apply policies, calculate a new shortest-path-first tree, and modify the forwarding table. Furthermore, routers must rapidly perform these processes so the network can quickly converge to a consistent view of routing. This stability ensures that when the forwarding process moves traffic to different interfaces, the links and routers carrying the additional traffic continue to function at wire-rate speed. By carrying the increased traffic load, a relatively simple local failure does not cascade across and seriously affect the entire network.

A high-performance router does not arbitrarily drop packets because of insufficient resources within the router. Rather, it operates at peak aggregate load because the packet load does not exceed its processing ability and because the router can handle the influx of packets (caused by rerouted traffic) on individual ports or circuits.

Since the TCP user traffic is sensitive to loss, routers must maintain their forwarding speed so that end devices do not adjust their internal operating parameters to send packets less frequently. This forwarding ability results in fewer packets being dropped, thereby increasing the users' perceptions of faster response time, even if they are running interactive applications.

Finally, since control packets describe the network to other routers, it is imperative that routers effectively forward them even during times of network instability and large routing fluctuations. The result of high-performance forwarding of control packets is an increased ability to manage router adjacencies and, consequently, to maintain only valid routing information. Since routers that effectively handle control packets do not miss updates, they continue to route traffic with up-to-date routing and forwarding entries, thereby keeping traffic away from internal forwarding loops that may otherwise never reach their destination.

As the Internet matures, operators are evaluating value-added services, such as Class of Service (CoS) and multicasting, that require more than best-effort delivery. Infrastructures must transmit packets at wire rate when delivering advanced services even during congestion. For example, today's CoS requirements dictate that premium customers get priority access to bandwidth during periods of congestion. With wire-rate performance, forwarding never becomes a bottleneck, and you maintain the ability to offer CoS because there is no contention for processing cycles to execute both forwarding and CoS queue management.

Since Internet usage is evolving to include VoIP, streaming video, and interactive gaming applications, all of which increase the volume of small packets, it would be highly undesirable to be forced to change your infrastructure once this trend becomes an everyday reality. The costs of adding nodes is significant enough, but the hidden costs of designing, testing, deploying, and maintaining infrastructures can be overwhelming, and can even prevent you from growing at the rate you need to keep up with the competitive Internet market.

Key attributes for an internet backbone router

The next generation of Internet backbone routers must be specifically designed to deliver Internet scale, Internet control, and unparalleled performance over an optical infrastructure. The key attributes supported by any Internet backbone router must include:

- stable and complete routing software that has been written by Internet experts and has successfully passed extensive interoperability testing in large ISP networks;

- traffic engineering features that offer fundamentally new and sophisticated control to support the efficient utilization of available resources in large ISP networks;
- packet processing capable of performing incoming decapsulation, route lookup, queuing, and outgoing encapsulation at wirespeed, regardless of packet size or system configuration;
- a switch fabric that has been oversized to provide an effective aggregate bandwidth;
- a wide variety of interface types capable of delivering wire-rate performance;
- a chassis capable of providing a port density of at least one slot per rack-inch;
- mechanicals, serviceability, and management that make the system very deployable in the core of a large ISP network.
- an ability to maintain overall network stability and adapt to a highly fluctuating environment without impacting other parts of the network.

13.2 High-speed internetworking devices

All the previous Parts dealt with the major types of internetworking devices operating at different layers. For a brief reminder see the Snapshot below.

SNAPSHOT	internetworking devices revisited

Hubs (concentrators): used to connect multiple users to a single physical device, which connects to the network. Hubs and concentrators act as repeaters by regenerating the signal as it passes through them.

Bridges: used to logically separate network segments within the same network. They operate at the OSI data-link layer (Layer 2), hence they forward data based on Layer 2 information and are dependent on Layer 2, while they are independent of higher-layer protocols.

LAN switches: similar to bridges but usually have more ports. Switches provide a unique network segment on each port, thereby separating collision domains. Today, network designers are replacing hubs in their wiring closets with switches to increase their network performance and bandwidth while protecting their existing wiring investments. Switches are dependent on the particular Layer 2 protocol(s) they support and use Layer 2 information for forwarding frames. As their decision-making is mostly done in hardware, they are faster than devices making decisions in software.

Routers: separate broadcast domains and are used to connect different networks. Routers direct network traffic based on the destination network layer address (Layer 3) rather than the workstation data-link layer or MAC address. More generally, routers forward traffic based on Layer 3+ information. Routers are Layer 3 protocol dependent.

We have not delved too much in the previous discussion into distinguishing the interconnecting devices by their relevant processing speeds or performance levels. Generally, if processing is done by hardware (switches) it is quicker than processing done by software (bridges and classic routers). The router as a Layer 3 device has always had more work than the other devices: it has to discard a Layer 2 header from the incoming frame, examine the Layer 3 header, and create a new Layer 2 header.

There is one additional important distinction between the interconnecting devices and routers of the lower layers. None of the devices in both Layer 2 (switches and bridges) and Layer 1 (hubs, repeaters) is **explicitly referenced** by the sender in the frame. A **switch, bridge, or repeater** is transparent to both the sender and receiver, whereas a **router** is not. We discussed in Part IV that while Layer 3 source and destination addresses in packets do not change in the ordinary routing process, the Layer 2 addresses change with each link the packet traverses. The sender directs a packet to a router for forwarding. The destination station will then receive a packet from a distant sender with the source physical address of the final router on the path, its outgoing interface.

An important note before we move on to Layer 2/3 switches and other rather more marketing than technical terms: 'switch' does not have a clear enough definition. We have to be careful to distinguish between an LAN switch (multiport bridge), and a WAN switch (device forming up the WAN network switching packets). The term 'switch' without qualification is essentially meaningless unless the context is clear. As we view switches (in general) as very fast operating devices, we could use the following note as a guide: 'Layer 2 switch' means 'fast bridge' and 'Layer 3 switch' means 'fast router.'

13.2.1 Layer 2 and Layer 3 switching

Switching is the process of taking an incoming frame from one interface and delivering it out through another interface. **Routers** use Layer 3 switching to route a packet, and **switches** (Layer 2 switches) use Layer 2 switching to forward frames. The difference between Layer 2 and Layer 3 switching is the type of information inside the frame that is used to determine the correct output interface. With Layer 2 switching, frames are switched based on MAC address information. With Layer 3 switching, frames are switched based on network-layer information.

Layer 2 switching does not look inside a packet for network-layer information as does Layer 3 switching. Layer 2 switching is performed by looking at a destination MAC address within a frame. It looks at the frame's destination address and sends it to the appropriate interface if it knows the destination address location. Layer 2 switching builds and maintains a switching table that keeps track of which MAC addresses belong to each port or interface. If the Layer

SNAPSHOT	Layer 2 switching

Layer 2 switching is hardware-based bridging.

2 switch does not know where to send the frame, it broadcasts the frame out all its ports to the network to learn the correct destination. When the frame's reply is returned, the switch learns the location of the new address and adds the information to the switching table. Layer 2 addresses assume a flat address space with universally unique addresses.

Layer 3 switching operates at the network layer. It examines packet information and forwards packets based on their network-layer destination addresses. Layer 3 switches attempt to combine Layer 2 switching with routing by integrating switching and routing in hardware.

SNAPSHOT	Layer 3 switching

Layer 3 switching is hardware-based routing.

As routers operate at Layer 3 of the OSI model, they can adhere to and formulate a hierarchical addressing structure dependent on the network topology. Therefore, a routed network can tie a logical addressing structure to a physical infrastructure, for example through TCP/IP subnets or IPX networks for each segment. Traffic flow in a switched (flat) network is therefore inherently different from traffic flow in a routed (hierarchical) network. Hierarchical networks offer more flexible traffic flow than flat networks because they can use the network hierarchy to determine optimal paths and contain broadcast domains.

Layer 3 switches are also known as **routing switches, switching routers**, or **multilayer switches**. A Layer 3 switch can forward packets faster than classical routers but does not usually have multiprotocol functionality or the extensive filtering capabilities of a router. Advance filtering and flow control features are proliferating in switching technology. A Layer 3 switch, as well as acting on MAC addresses, can also examine the IP address and forward a packet appropriately. Such switches are now used within LANs to take the place of routers, leaving the router to handle WAN connectivity. As Layer 3 switches add functionality, they will take the place of routers in more situations.

While there has been a hype in the trade press and industry concerning the multitude of apparently dissimilar Layer 3 switching technologies, they can be divided into three classes:

■ **ASIC-based routing**;
■ **cut-through routing**:
  – flow-based;
  – address-based;
■ **label switching**.

All mechanisms make the following basic assumptions:

- The edge is still an LAN – the desktop connection, in almost all cases, is still a legacy LAN. It might be fully switched, full duplex Ethernet, Fast Ethernet, or Token Ring but it still uses protocol stacks and access mechanisms which have been in use for years.
- The edge of the switched Layer 3 domain is still conventional routing – traffic forwarded over the switched Layer 3 domain is done so using conventional, but hopefully very high speed, routing mechanisms.
- The backbone is ATM – most Layer 3 switching mechanisms are designed to operate over ATM networks.

Besides **speed**, the big benefit to Layer 3 switching is **cost**. In essence, vendors are giving away supersonic routing with their boxes. It is important to realize that not all vendors are basing their Layer 3 schemes on conventional routing protocols like RIP (Routing Information Protocol) and OSPF (Open Shortest Path First). Some rely on route servers that implement the IETF's Next Hop Routing Protocol (NHRP is discussed in Part I, Chapter 3 on WANs). While it is true that NHRP is a standard, there is no guarantee that other vendors will implement it.

SNAPSHOT   Layer 2/3 switching vs. routing

Layer 2 switching has the following characteristics:

- performs data-link layer forwarding;
- forwards packets based upon MAC-layer address;
- functions as wirespeed multiport bridge;
- is transparent to upper layers.

Layer 3 switching has the following characteristics:

- forwards packets using ASICs based upon the network layer (IP, IPX) address;
- performs wirespeed routing for the LAN;
- provides network reachability learned by routing protocols, such as RIP, EIGRP, OSPF, BGP.

Routing characteristics are as follows:

- performs network-layer forwarding;
- forwards packets using CPU processing based upon the network layer address;
- fundamental building block of Layer 3 switching;
- network reachability learned by routing protocols such as RIP, EIGRP, OSPF, BGP;
- routers generally process far more protocols than Layer 3 switches.

Routing is compared to Layer 3 switching in Table 13.1. Wire-speed interconnecting devices are aimed at minimizing the latency caused by internal packet switching, but the latency will always be greater than zero.

TABLE 13-1	Routing vs. Layer 3 switching	
	Routing	*Layer 3 switching*
Advantages	Rich set of protocols, applications and functionality: VPN, security, and multiservice capabilities.	Combination of expandable memory and special purpose ASIC(s), and faster path determination.
Disadvantages	Combination of memory and general-purpose CPU(s). Path determination calculations slow down the router.	Limited set of protocols and applications supported.

SNAPSHOT   **when to use a router, and when to use a Layer 3 switch**

Use a traditional router to:

■ provide better WAN aggregation;

■ route multiprotocols;

■ in a multiservice network with high functionality such as VoIP, VPN, security, and robust QoS.

Use a Layer 3 switch to:

■ scale Layer 3 performance to handle changing traffic patterns;

■ when the network has one or more of the following characteristics:

   – campus environment;

   – multiple network segments;

   – multiple application-specific servers.

13.2.2 Layer 4 to 7 switches

Some vendors are marketing what they call **Layer 4 switches** able to examine what application the datastream belongs to and offer an appropriate class of service. Layer 4 is the transport layer of the OSI model and uses TCP/UDP application port numbers to transmit data packets. The term Layer 4 switch is misleading just like the term Layer 3 switch since true switching occurs at Layer 2. Besides, today's routers already look at transport layer information, e.g. TCP or

UDP port numbers, to enable or disable selected services (if filters are configured). It is worth noting, however, that some TCP/IP higher-layer protocols like RTP do not use well-known ports, and other protocols like HTTP are not forced to use their well-known port and may use other ports.

Adding complex Layer 4+ support to the existing router and switch concepts may increase some of the major bottlenecks of the forwarding task. Performance loss due to even more complex search and update operations may be the result. The fact that the switch-router now needs to access the encapsulated data whereas classic routers and switches do not need to care about the payload and its encoding may add to the problems. Another challenge is the handling of encrypted data, which inhibit the switch-router from accessing the transferred data.

Support for Layer 4 port number handling increases the sizes of search/routing tables dramatically, since for every entry additional information has to be stored whereas standard IP routers need to hold only one entry per destination address. Since a Layer 4+ switch-router handles different protocols separately, such a switch-router needs to store one entry for each protocol used on each destination machine. As the routing table lookup is a bottleneck for standard IP routers, fast lookup will become an even more important issue with Layer 4(+) switching. Furthermore the length of the lookup keys is increased by the source address (which is not used in IP routers, but is needed to identify a TCP connection), the port numbers of source and destination, and additional information extracted from Layer 4+ information.

The information derived from Layer 4 and above needs to be mapped to the QoS parameters or classes of the respective network QoS model used, like IP Differentiated Services, IP Integrated Services or ATM, or other future QoS architectures (see Chapter 14). This requires a translation of implicit priorities and service requests given by the information extracted from Layer 4 and above, and explicit priorities and requests given by applications or extracted from information of Layers 4 and above to the service parameters and classes of the respective target model. In addition, signaling for explicit reservations may be included to allow some applications to reserve dedicated resources for a stream.

The Layer 4 switches, called '**content-based**' or '**application-aware**' switches, are able to look at the payload itself to get an idea of where to send the packet. This is a capability that is probably a bit too advanced for most users but many vendors do support it nowadays.

These switches form an integral part of policy networking as they allow for **load balancing among servers**. Load balancing is where several servers are connected to a switch, all of the servers are given the same virtual IP address, and the switch distributes requests among the available servers. The technique is becoming popular because it lets the servers handle high loads and it gives the server farm a degree of resiliency.

A final note on terminology: the term **load balancing** has rightly replaced Layer 4 switching, just as the term **application-aware switching** has mostly replaced Layer 7 switching. Therefore fortunately we are back with the term network switching in its proper place: the link layer (while we all know that even routers do also switch – internally – packets between their ports).

The first Layer 4 switches simply looked at the TCP port in the initial TCP connection packet (TCP SYN) to determine the application and used that information to prioritize traffic. Layer 4 switches evolved further to include address translation, enabling server load balancing. In any case all the required information was available in the initial TCP SYN packet, including source/destination IP address and TCP port number. When a new TCP connection is created, the Layer 4 switch sets up a new session, and uses this information to make a policy or server selection decision, then switches all of the subsequent packets for that session. By looking at the TCP port, for instance, a Layer 4 switch can distinguish a Telnet session from an FTP request or an HTTP request. However, to a Layer 4 load balancer all Web applications appear to use TCP port 80 (typical port for HTTP), making them indistinguishable from one another. Therefore, a CGI request looks no different from a Web-enabled SAP application or streaming audio request, even though all of these requests have very different QoS requirements. Performance measurements for Layer 4 switches include the speed with which the switch can set up new TCP sessions (new flows per second), including latency for the flow setup, and the speed of data transfer in the packet forwarding mode (pps).

While Layer 4 switches are optimized for the transport layer, they are completely unaware of the application layer, mainly HTTP. Then **Web switches** must be used as networking devices that provide high-speed switching of traffic, using information in the TCP and HTTP request header to make policy and routing decisions based on the actual content (e.g. URL) being requested, and manage request/response flows and transactions from beginning to end.

The first significant difference in the nature of Web switch traffic is that they use information in the HTTP header to make routing and policy decisions. With this knowledge, the Web switch uses both user-defined and/or pre-set policies to provide Web site security, eliminating denial of service attacks and enforcing high-speed filters. The Web switch also determines which QoS requirements are needed for specific content or user groups, and finally routes the request to the best site and the best server. The ability to use cookies embedded in the HTTP request header enables sticky connections and user authentication – two critical requirements for e-commerce.

The HTTP request header comes from the client browser and includes the URL and the cookie among other things, but the client does not send this until the TCP connection is set up. The Web switch sits between the client and the Web servers, and in order to obtain the HTTP request header, the Web switch performs delayed binding. Delayed binding means that the Web switch, after receiving the initial TCP SYN, sends the SYN ACK prior to establishing the TCP session, thus 'tricking' the client browser into sending its HTTP request. The Web switch now has all of the information it needs to make a policy or routing decision based on the content being requested, and can select the best site and server to service the request at that given moment. The Web switch then initiates a new TCP connection to that server and sends the HTTP request, and the Web server responds back to the client via the Web switch. In the flow switching stage the Web switch is providing network address translation and wirespeed forwarding of packets for all traffic going between the Web server and the client browser. In the final stage, the Web switch tears down the connection, freeing the resources allocated and aggregating statistics for the flow.

13.2.3 Multilayer switching

Although we are using here the widely recognized terms such as Layer 3 switch or multilayer switch, we should always bear in mind that these devices try to perform some part of the routing responsibilities. Routers are responsible for path determination and packet forwarding. Multilayer switching is a way in which the packet forwarder (a client) can get a forwarding table from the path determination process (a server). Layer 3 switching is really no more than emphasizing that there is a separate path determination process and a forwarder, the latter of which has a hardware-assisted destination lookup.

The idea behind **multilayer switching** (MLS) is that the packet-forwarding function is performed by a switching device whenever a partial or complete switched **path** exists between two hosts. Packets that do not have a known path to reach their destinations are still forwarded in software by routers. Standard routing protocols, such as OSPF, EIGRP, or IS-IS, are used for route determination.

Layer 3 protocols are (in the main) connectionless; however, actual network traffic consists of many end-to-end conversations, or flows, between users or applications. A **flow** is a unidirectional sequence of packets between a particular source and destination that share the same protocol and transport-layer information. Communication from a client to a server and from a server to a client are separate flows.

Flows are based not only on Layer 3 addresses, but other specifics of the particular communication. As this requires looking into the header of an upper layer data unit (Layer 4 and above), multilayer switching is sometimes called Layer 4+ switching.

Both switching and routing processing engines are necessary for multilayer switching.

Layer 3 switching table

A **Layer 3 switching table, or MLS cache**, for Layer 3 switched flows includes entries for traffic statistics that are updated in tandem with the switching of packets. After the MLS cache is created, packets identified as belonging to an existing flow can be Layer 3-switched based on the cached information. The MLS cache maintains flow information for **all active flows**.

An **MLS cache entry** is created for the **initial packet of each flow**. Upon receipt of a packet that does not match any flow currently in the MLS cache, a new IP MLS entry is created. The state and identity of the flow are maintained while packet traffic is active; when traffic for a flow terminates, the entry ages out. If an entry is not used for the specified period of time, the entry ages out and statistics for that flow can be exported to a flow collector application.

The switching engine uses **flow masks** to determine how MLS entries are created. The flow mask is realized with the help of the filters configured on the router interfaces. The switching engine learns the flow mask through **Multilayer Switching Protocol** (MLSP) messages from each MLS route processor for which the switching engine is performing Layer 3 switching. MLSP is the protocol running between the switching engine and route processor to enable MLS.

A switching engine supports only one flow mask (the most specific one) for all MLS route processors that are Layer 3 switched by that switching engine. If the switching engine detects different flow masks from different MLS route processors for which it is performing Layer 3 switching, it changes its flow mask to the most specific flow mask detected. When the switching engine flow mask changes, the entire MLS cache is purged. When a switching engine exports cached entries, flow records are created based on the current flow mask. Depending on the current flow mask, some fields in the flow record might not have values. The three flow masks, for IP, are as follows (although MLS is not aimed only at IP):

- **destination-ip** – one MLS entry for each destination IP address represents the least-specific flow mask. All flows to a given destination IP address use this MLS entry;

- **source-destination-ip** – one MLS entry for each source and destination IP address pair. All flows between a given source and destination use this MLS entry regardless of the IP protocol ports;

- **ip-flow** – for every IP flow there is a separate MLS cache entry representing the most-specific flow mask. An ip-flow entry includes the source IP address, destination IP address, protocol, and protocol ports. This mode is used if there is a complex filter on any of the MLS route processor interfaces. When a packet is Layer 3 switched from a source host to a destination host, the switch (switching module) performs a packet rewrite based on information learned from the router (routing module) and stored in the MLS cache.

If Host A and Host B are on different VLANs and Host A sends a packet to the route processor to be routed to Host B, the MLS switching engine recognizes that the packet was sent to the Media Access Control (MAC) address of the route processor. The switching engine checks the MLS cache and finds the entry matching the flow in question. The switching engine rewrites the Layer 2 frame header, changing the destination MAC address to the MAC address of Host B and the source MAC address to the MAC address of the route processor (these MAC addresses are stored in the MLS cache entry for this flow). The Layer 3 IP addresses remain the same, but the IP header Time to Live (TTL) is decremented and the checksum is recomputed. The MLS switching engine rewrites the switched Layer 3 packets so that they appear to have been routed by a router. The MLS switching engine forwards the rewritten packet to Host B's VLAN (the destination VLAN is stored in the MLS cache entry) and Host B receives the packet.

Figure 13.10 shows a simple IP MLS network topology. In this example, Host A is on the Sales VLAN (IP subnet 171.59.1.0), Host B is on the Marketing VLAN (IP subnet 171.59.3.0), and Host C is on the Engineering VLAN (IP subnet 171.59.2.0). When Host A initiates an FTP file transfer to Host B, an MLS entry for this flow is created (this entry is the first item in the MLS cache shown in Figure 13.10). The switching engine stores the MAC addresses of the MLS route processor and Host B in the MLS entry when the MLS route processor forwards the first packet from Host A through the switch to Host B. The switching engine uses this information to rewrite subsequent packets from Station A to Station B. Similarly, a separate MLS entry is created in the MLS cache for the HTTP traffic from Host A to Host C, and for the HTTP traffic from Host C to Host A. The destination VLAN is stored as part of each MLS entry so that the correct VLAN identifier is used when encapsulating traffic on trunk links.

FIGURE 13-10	Example of IP MLS topology

Source IP Address	Destination IP Address	Application	Rewrite Src/Dst MAC Address	Destination VLAN
171.59.1.2	171.59.3.1	FTP	Dd:Bb	Marketing
171.59.1.2	171.59.2.2	HTTP	Dd:Cc	Engineering
171.59.2.2	171.59.1.2	HTTP	Dd:Aa	Sales

13.3 Shortcut routing a.k.a. label switching

Forwarding performance needs to keep pace with growing bandwidth requirements. A way to relax this requirement is to forward more Layer 3 traffic directly at Layer 2, thus shifting to a more connection-oriented hardware-driven forwarding mode. This approach is called **shortcut routing**, referring to its **ability to shortcut Layer 3 routers in the forwarding process**. Shortcut routing most directly affects the Internet Protocol/asynchronous transfer mode (IP/ATM) routing paradigm. The key issue is how to **provide the connectivity of Layer 3 with the performance of Layer 2**. The IP/ATM routing paradigm must satisfy the requirements of both unicast and multicast traffic. The major trade-off for providing high-performance solutions is complexity. The key to efficient IP/ATM routing is a good balance between complexity and performance.

Shortcut routing refers to the ability to forward network-layer packets (Layer 3) directly at the link layer (Layer 2), regardless of the existing network boundaries. Shortcut routing is particularly applicable in non-broadcast multiple access (NBMA) networks, where direct connectivity can be provided between any two NBMA nodes.

For **Layer 2/3 routing** to achieve the performance of layer-dedicated routing protocols, interworking complexity will have to be traded off against the complexity of integrating heterogeneous environments (mixed node types, mixed connection-oriented/connectionless forwarding, etc.). Integration can be achieved either by concentrating all routing intelligence in one of the two layers or by designing a single multilayer routing protocol.

The first option corresponds to the **multiprotocol label switching** (MPLS), currently deployed open approach of shifting control over ATM routing to the IP layer by means of **label switch routers** (LSR). IP switches (Ipsilon), tag switches (Cisco), or integrated switch-routers (IBM), for example, belong to this family. In MPLS, a single Layer 3 routing protocol determines the forwarding path through a mixed Layer 2/Layer 3 topology. MPLS requires Layer 2 switches, whether or not enhanced with Layer 3 forwarding capabilities, to run the same routing protocol as Layer 3 routers.

In the specific case of IP/ATM, routing is performed by traditional IP routing protocols (e.g. OSPF), while the routes are translated to the ATM layer by MPLS-dedicated lightweight signaling protocols such as **Ipsilon Flow Management Protocol** (IFMP) or **Tag Distribution Protocol** (TDP). These protocols replace the traditional ATM Forum UNI/NNI signaling and interface with IP routing. The result is that ATMF signaling or routing is no longer needed in ATM to support IP traffic. If other than IP/ATM traffic (e.g. native ATM) is to be carried over the same ATM infrastructure, it must be performed in parallel with separate signaling and routing protocols (in ships-in-the-night mode).

The second option corresponds to the ATM Forum approach, where the ATM routing protocol (PNNI, see Section 3.8.9) is extended with a hop-by-hop routing mode to become a true multilayer routing protocol: **Integrated-PNNI** (I-PNNI). Routing both at Layer 2 (ATM) and Layer 3 (IP) is controlled by the same I-PNNI routing protocol. IP and ATM nodes both have a full topology map of the two layers.

A comparison of the classic routing model components with MPLS and I-PNNI is depicted in Figure 13.11.

FIGURE 13-11 Route selection procedure using different models – classic, MPLS, and I-PNNI

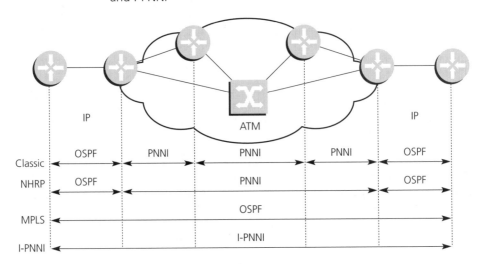

In the following text we will concentrate on different label switching approaches, in particular:

- **Proprietary proposals** (before MPLS development):
  - **Cell Switch Router** (CSR) from Toshiba;
  - **IP Switching** from Ipsilon (now part of Nokia);
  - **Aggregated Route-Based IP Switching** (ARIS) from IBM;
  - **Tag Switching** from Cisco Systems.

- *De facto* **standard**:
  - **Multiprotocol Label Switching** (MPLS).

13.3.1 Label switching overview

Shortcut routing is based on **label switching** technologies. A **label** is a short, fixed-length identifier, with no internal structure, that is used to forward packets. A label does not directly encode any of the information from the network-layer header. For example, a label does not directly encode network-layer addresses (either source or destination addresses). Label values are normally local to a single link (more precisely, a single data-link layer subnet) and thus have no global significance. They are also unstructured, that is they are not made up of distinct components. A label switching device will usually replace the label in a packet with some new value before forwarding it to the next hop. For this reason we call the forwarding algorithm label swapping. **Forwarding decisions** based on labels use the exact match algorithm to decide where to send the packets. A device capable of label switching, called a **label switching router** (LSR), runs standard IP control protocols (e.g. routing protocols, RSVP, etc.) to determine where to forward packets.

The first approach of shortcut routing to gain significant attention in the marketplace (although not the first to be publicly disclosed) was called **IP Switching** by its inventors at the start-up company Ipsilon. Toshiba had previously described a similar scheme, implemented in their **Cell Switching Router** (CSR), and several other approaches were soon published, notably Cisco's **Tag Switching** (introducing the Tag Switching Router (TSR) and tag switch) and IBM's **Aggregate Route-based IP Switching** (ARIS, introducing the Integrated Switch Router (ISR)).

One can think of an edge **Label Switching Router** (LSR) as a device that implements the control and forwarding components of both the label switching and conventional routing. When an edge LSR receives a packet without a label, the LSR uses the conventional forwarding component to determine the **Forwarding Equivalence Class** (FEC) that this packet belongs to and the next hop that the packet should be sent to. FEC refers to all the packets to which a specific label is being applied so that they are forwarded to the same next hop or along the same path through the network.

If the next hop is an LSR, then the LSR uses the label switching forwarding component to determine the label that should be added to the packet. Likewise, when an edge LSR receives a packet with a label, the LSR uses the label switching forwarding component to determine the FEC that this packet belongs to and the next hop that the packet should be sent to. If the next hop is not an LSR, then the LSR just strips the label from the packet and hands the packet to its conventional forwarding component, which, in turn, sends the packet to the next hop.

The fact that both LSRs and conventional routers use the same set of routing protocols makes interworking between the conventional and the label switching control components of little concern. The only thing that is required of the label switching control component is the ability to determine whether a particular (next hop) router is an LSR or not.

Forwarding and path determination tasks

With reference to Part III, network layer routing can be separated into two basic components: path determination (control) and packet forwarding. The **forwarding** component is responsible for the actual forwarding of packets from input to output across a switch or router. To forward a packet the forwarding component uses two sources of information: a forwarding table maintained by a router and the information carried in the packet itself. The **path determination** component is responsible for construction and maintenance of the routing (forwarding) table. Each router in a network implements both components while actual network-layer routing is realized in a distributed fashion by the set of routers that forms the network.

The two functions with relation to the internal router architecture are shown in Figure 13.12.

FIGURE 13-12 Control and forwarding functions

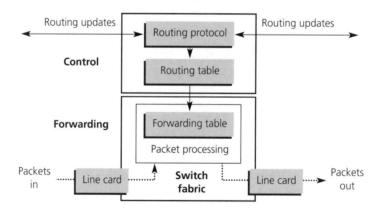

From a forwarding point of view, it is useful to view procedures used by the forwarding component as a way of partitioning the set of all possible packets that a router can forward into a finite number of disjoint subsets. Packets within each subset are treated by the router in the same way (e.g. they are all sent to the same next hop), even if the packets within the subset differ from each other with respect to the information in the network layer header of these packets. Hence the subsets are called **Forwarding Equivalence Classes** (FECs). The reason a router forwards all packets within a given FEC the same way is that the mapping between the information carried in the network layer header of the packets and the entries in the forwarding table is many-to-one (with one-to-one as a special case). That is, packets with different network-layer headers could be mapped into the same entry in the forwarding table, where the entry describes a particular FEC.

One example of an FEC is a set of unicast packets whose destination address matches a particular IP address prefix. A set of multicast packets with the same source and destination network-layer addresses is another example of an FEC. A set of unicast packets whose destination addresses match a particular IP address prefix and whose Type of Service bits are the same is yet another example of an FEC.

An essential part of a forwarding entry maintained by a router is the address of the next hop router. A packet that falls into an FEC associated with a particular forwarding entry is forwarded to the next hop router specified by the entry. Therefore, the construction of a forwarding table by the path determination function means constructing a set of FECs and the next hop for each of these FECs.

One important characteristic of an FEC is its forwarding granularity. For example, in the simplest case an FEC could include all the packets whose network-layer destination address matches a particular address prefix. This type of FEC provides coarse forwarding granularity. In a more specific and complex example, an FEC could include only the packets that belong to a particular application running between a pair of computers, thus including only the packets with the same source and destination network-layer addresses (these addresses identify the computers), as well as the transport-layer port numbers (these ports identify a particular application within a computer). This type of FEC provides fine forwarding granularity.

Consistent mapping of packets into FECs, combined with the consistent forwarding tables across multiple routers, provides a correctly functioning routing system.

Before we move on to label switching development it may be useful to look at Figure 13.13 to see how these functions are implemented currently in ATM switches and IP routers, and how they are reflected in general multilayer switch architecture based on label swapping.

FIGURE 13-13 Control and forwarding functions in ATM switch, IP router, and multilayer switch

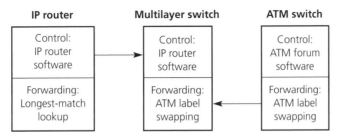

The **label switching forwarding** component defines a **label** carried in a packet as the information that an LSR uses to find a particular entry in its **forwarding table**. The label switching forwarding component defines the exact match on the label as the procedure for finding an entry in a forwarding table.

> **SNAPSHOT**   label switching: forwarding function
>
> The forwarding function is based on a simple **label swapping algorithm** and uses fixed-length labels. These labels are used as an **index to the label switching table**, which identifies where a packet should be forwarded and may include some local resource assignment. In contrast to conventional routing, the label switching routers use the same algorithm no matter what control components are in use.

The following summarizes other key properties of the label switching forwarding component:

- The label switching forwarding component uses a single forwarding algorithm based on label swapping.
- The label carried in a packet is a short, fixed-length unstructured entity that has both forwarding and resource reservation semantics.
- The label switching forwarding component by itself does not place any constraints on the forwarding granularity that could be associated with a label.
- The label switching forwarding component can support multiple network-layer protocols as well as multiple link-layer protocols.

Essential to the label switching forwarding component is the ability to **carry a label in a packet**. This can be accomplished in several ways. Certain link-layer technologies, most notably ATM and Frame Relay, can carry a label as part of their link-layer header. Specifically, with ATM the label could be carried in either the VCI and/or VPI fields of the ATM header. Likewise, with Frame Relay the label could be carried in the DLCI field of the Frame Relay header. Using the option of carrying the label as part of the link-layer header allows the support of label switching with some but not all link-layer technologies. Constraining label switching to only the link-layer technologies that could carry the label as part of their link-layer header would severely limit the usefulness of label switching (as it would immediately exclude the use of label switching over such media as Ethernet or point-to-point links).

A way to support label switching over link-layer technologies where the link-layer header can't be used to carry a label is to carry the label in a small 'shim' label header. This shim label header is inserted between the link layer and the network-layer headers and thus could be used with any link-layer technology.

An entry in a **label switching forwarding table** is created by a combination of the following (see Figure 13.14):

FIGURE 13-14   Example of a forwarding table entry

Incoming label	First subentry	Second subentry
Incoming label	Outgoing label Outgoing interface Next hop address	Outgoing label Outgoing interface Next hop address

- **Next hop** – provided by routing protocols as an FEC to next hop mapping.
- **Incoming label** – with downstream binding this is provided by creating a local binding between an FEC and the label; with upstream binding this is provided by receiving a remote binding between an FEC and the label.
- **Outgoing label** – with downstream binding this is provided by a remote binding between an FEC and the label; with upstream binding this is provided by creating a local binding between an FEC and the label.

SNAPSHOT   **label switching forwarding table**

A forwarding table is maintained by an LSR and contains a sequence of entries, where each entry consists of an incoming label, and one or more subentries, where each subentry consists of an outgoing label, an outgoing interface, and the next hop address.

The **forwarding algorithm** used by the forwarding component of label switching is based on **label swapping**. The algorithm works as follows: when an LSR receives a packet, the router extracts the label from the packet and uses it as an index in its **forwarding table**. Once the entry indexed by the label is found (this entry has its incoming label component equal to the label extracted from the packet), for each subentry of the found entry the router replaces the label in the packet with the outgoing label from the subentry and sends the packet over the outgoing interface specified by this subentry to the next hop specified by this subentry. If the entry specifies a particular outgoing queue, the router places the packet on the specified queue.

Because a label carried in a packet uniquely determines a particular entry in the forwarding table maintained by an LSR, and because that particular entry contains information about where to forward a packet as well as what local resources (e.g. outgoing queue) the packet may use, the label determines both where the packet will be forwarded, as well as what local resources the packet can use. The ability to obtain both forwarding and resource reservation information in just one memory access makes label switching suitable as a technology for high forwarding performance.

The simplicity of the forwarding algorithm used by the label switching forwarding component facilitates inexpensive implementations of this algorithm in hardware, which, in turn, enables faster forwarding performance without requiring expensive hardware.

It is important to understand that the use of label swapping forwarding combined with the ability to carry labels on a wide range of link-layer technologies means that many different devices can be used to implement LSRs. For example, carrying the label inside the VCI field of ATM cells enables unmodified ATM switch hardware to function as an LSR, given the addition of suitable control software. Similarly, the shim header described above appears in packets in a place where most conventional routers can process it in software. Thus, with the addition of suitable software, a conventional router can also become an LSR.

The label-swapping forwarding algorithm requires packet classification at the ingress edge of the network to assign an initial label to each packet. In Figure 13.15, the ingress label switch receives an unlabeled packet with a destination address of 192.4.2.1. The label switch performs a longest-match routing table lookup and maps the packet to an FEC – 192.4/16. The ingress label switch then assigns a label (with a value of 5) to the packet and forwards it to the next hop in the label-switched path (LSP).

FIGURE 13-15 Packet traversing LSP

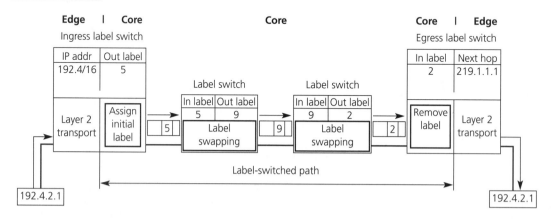

SNAPSHOT   label switching forwarding

Properties of label switching forwarding:

■ The label switching forwarding component uses a **single forwarding algorithm** based on **label swapping**.

■ The **label** carried in a packet is a **short, fixed-length** unstructured entity that has both forwarding and resource reservation semantics.

■ The label switching forwarding by itself does not place any constraints on the forwarding granularity that could be associated with a label.

■ The label switching forwarding can support **multiple network layer protocols** as well as **multiple link layer protocols**.

The **label switching control** (equivalent to the path determination function in classic routers) component uses both local and remote bindings to populate its forwarding table with incoming and outgoing labels. The first method is when labels from the local binding are used as incoming labels, and labels from the remote binding are used as outgoing labels. The second is exactly the opposite – labels from the local binding are used as outgoing labels, and labels from the remote binding are used as incoming labels.

- **Downstream label binding** – binding between a label carried by a packet and a particular FEC that the packet belongs to is created by an LSR that is downstream (with respect to the flow of the packet) from the LSR that places the label in the packet. Observe that with downstream label binding, packets that carry a particular label flow in the direction opposite to the flow of the binding information about that label.

- **Upstream label binding** – binding between a label carried by a packet and a particular FEC that the packet belongs to is created by the same LSR that places the label in the packet; that is, the creator of the binding is upstream with respect to the flow of packets. Observe that with upstream label binding, packets that carry a particular label flow in the same direction as the label binding information about this label.

Note: The denotations upstream and downstream seem to have caused considerable confusion; it helps to consider the flow of data packets – they flow toward the downstream end of the link – and then ask the question 'At which end of the link were the bindings created: upstream or downstream?'

Label binding information must be distributed throughout the network. This could be achieved through piggybacking label binding information with deployed routing protocols. But as this way would not always be feasible, a separate **label distribution protocol** is introduced into the label switched network.

SNAPSHOT   label switching: control function

The control function (path determination) of label switching consists of **conventional network-layer routing protocols** and a **label binding mechanism**. It is in the area of creating and distributing label bindings that the various approaches show the most diversity. **Label bindings** may be created by **upstream or downstream LSRs**; they may be created either in ordered or in independent fashion; they may be created in response to data or control traffic; and the bindings may be distributed in a standalone protocol or piggybacked on an existing one.

Flow- and topology-driven shortcuts

The criteria for establishing a **shortcut path** and the classification of traffic that will be placed on the shortcut path is dependent on the type of flow switching solution and protocol. There are two types of IP switching solutions: **traffic-driven** (also flow-driven, or data-driven) and **topology-driven**.

The **flow-driven model** (data or traffic driven) for label switching acts upon a particular flow which is defined as a sequence of packets with the same source IP address, destination IP address, and port numbers. The basic operation of flow-driven label switching consists of the following steps:

- The first N packets of a flow are routed hop by hop through one or more IP routing entities to the destination. The routing entities are the routing components of a label switch or virtual IP switch or they may be actual routers that are connected to each other by ATM connections.

- Based on the characteristics of the IP flow (e.g. traffic type, port number, source/destination IP address, arrival rate, etc.), the IP routing entity (either at the edge or middle of the network) will trigger the initiation of a redirect process. The redirect process involves the actions required to build a shortcut path and to redirect the IP flow over the shortcut path so that hop-by-hop router processing is bypassed. This is accomplished by assigning a new label to the packets belonging to the IP flow and then having the label switching tables updated within the label switch. Once the IP flow is redirected over the shortcut path, the remaining packets of the flow are switched.

Flow-driven label switching has several interesting properties. First of all, it may not and should not be necessary to switch all flows. Some flows such as ICMP Pings and best-effort e-mail may not warrant or derive any benefit from a faster switched path. Secondly the redirect process is performed individually for each flow that qualifies to flow over a shortcut path. What qualifies a particular flow as a candidate to be switched depends on implementation-specific policies and heuristics. There is no standard that says this flow identified by these header fields will be switched. And finally observe that the first few packets of the flow are routed through the network and only after the redirect process has completed will the 'tail' of the flow traverse the shortcut path.

The basic **functional characteristics of flow-driven label switching** are as follows:

- The appearance of specific IP flows may trigger the establishment of a shortcut path where a flow is defined as application-to-application or host-to-host traffic. A flow is identified by a sequence of packets that share common IP header information such as source and destination IP addresses and TCP or UDP port numbers.

- Packets can be routed through the network or placed on a shortcut path on a per-flow basis.

- The redirect process is performed independently for each flow that is to be placed on a shortcut path. The scope of the redirect process may be limited to a pair of adjacent IP switches or it could be end-to-end between ingress and egress.

- Each label switch may perform the redirect process on an individual basis for each flow. In other words the decision to relabel a flow and hence update a switch's connection tables will not be dependent on what another IP switch does with the same flow.

- Some flows may not qualify to be switched based on the shortcut path decision criteria and policies implemented in the label switching system.

- A flow-based ingress component may place some flows on a shortcut path and route others.

■ If a shortcut path does not exist or it suddenly disappears then packets can be routed to the destination.

■ The entire flow is generally not switched. The first few packets are routed so that the IP switches have an opportunity to classify a flow and decide to initiate the redirect process. After the shortcut path is established, the remaining packets of the flow are switched.

Operating a flow-driven label switching solution does incur some overhead. First of all there are the redirect or flow-setup messages that must be exchanged and processed on a per-flow basis with the participating components in the network. Secondly the switching elements in this scheme must allocate per-connection resources (e.g. labels, buffers) for each flow that will be switched. The arrival of a large number of switch-qualified flows could introduce some delays in routing normal IP traffic and setting up shortcut paths as well as imposing resource constraints on switch resources.

SNAPSHOT **flow-driven (data- or traffic-driven) label switching**

The flow-driven approach is based on investigating Layer 3 packets on the fly. If these packets meet some criteria, a shortcut is initiated. Because it is the **data flow** that triggers the establishment of shortcut paths, these techniques are called **flow-driven**, or data-driven.

Ipsilon IP switching (IFMP protocol) is an example of the flow-based shortcut method.

Topology-driven label switching techniques learn about the network topology by looking at the Layer 3 routing information base maintained by routing protocols (e.g. OSPF, BGP). Shortcut paths to well-known destinations are pre-established. If the network topology changes, new shortcut paths are established and the older ones are released. Occasionally, control messages can be used to trigger the establishment of shortcut paths. For example, in the case of RSVP: if the label switch router (LSR) sees a reservation request it can establish the shortcut path as part of the resource reservation process. Shortcut paths are established by explicit requests, not by looking at the data or the topology.

New labels associated with destination IP prefix(es) reflecting a destination network(s) are generated and distributed to the other label switches in the routing domain. All traffic destined for a particular destination network follows a switched path based on the new labels.

■ Label switches converge on a network topology based on the exchange of routing protocol messages between the IP routing entities.

■ New labels associated with destination IP prefixes in the form of *<destination prefix, label>* are generated and distributed to the switching components of the IP switches in the routing domain.

- The ingress label switch checks the destination prefix of the packets entering the network. Instead of forwarding packets to the next hop IP address, the ingress IP switch places the packets on a switched path to the network egress. All traffic to that destination flows over a switched path from the network ingress to the network egress.

- The egress IP switch receives the packets over the switched path and forwards at Layer 3 to the destination.

The topology-driven approach to IP switching offers several performance and scalability enhancements when compared with the flow-driven approach. Firstly, all traffic consisting of one or more flows going to a common destination network will be switched. In other words, the entire flow is switched, not just the tail as is the case with flow-driven IP switching. Secondly, the run time overhead is much lower for topology-driven IP switching because switched paths are built only after a change in topology. If the topology is stable, then switched paths have been setup and traffic will flow over them. And finally, from the perspective of scalability, the topology-driven approach is superior. This is because the number of switched paths in a routing domain is proportional to the number of routes or the size of the network. In addition, an even higher level of aggregation is possible by creating multipoint-to-point shortcut paths (e.g. using VC merge) that lead to a shared collection of destination networks.

Of course the better scaling and performance properties available to all flows comes with a cost. Topology-driven label switching builds shortcut paths whether traffic flows over them or not. This means that switch resources are consumed as a result of control traffic (e.g. routing protocol updates) and not data traffic. Another possible issue to consider is that fact that it might be difficult to provide QoS to a flow that is traveling over a topology-driven shortcut. This is because you may have a mix of realtime and best-effort IP flows destined for resources on a common destination network flowing over a topology-driven best-effort shortcut path. Of course the best-effort flows will not be affected but the realtime flows may experience less than satisfactory performance. And finally, until a network converges inaccurate routing table updates can cause the formation of transient loops which can lead to a set of labels being generated that form a switched loop. IP routers can limit the damage caused by transient loops by decrementing the TTL field to zero and then discarding the packet. Layer 2 (e.g. ATM) switches may not have such a mechanism so a loop in this case could be problematic.

The basic characteristics of topology-driven IP switching are:

- Shortcut paths are established based on the existence of destination networks and are established only after a change in topology.

- All traffic bound for a destination will be switched.

- Ingress IP switches will receive a new per destination label (VPI/VCI). Normal IP forwarding will be performed but instead of directing the packet to the next hop IP address, the ingress IP switch will append the new label and place the packet on the switched path.

- At each intermediate switching component, the packets (or cells) will be label-swapped.

- Egress IP switches will receive the packet over the switched path, remove the label and then forward the packet using normal Layer 3 procedures.

- Packets may be routed to the destination if a shortcut path suddenly disappears.
- Transient loops at Layer 2 may be caused.

Examples of topology-driven IP switching solutions are Tag Switching and ARIS, so MPLS is based on topology, too, as closely derived from these two proprietary solutions.

SNAPSHOT   **topology-driven label switching**

Topology-driven techniques look at the **network topology to pre-establish shortcut paths**. Shortcut paths are established before the data begins to flow. This eliminates the setup latency and improves performance when the data flows are highly dynamic. The network topology is learned by looking at the **routing information base**. The topology-driven techniques are closely interrelated with but **independent of the routing protocols**. They merely require the routing protocols to update the routing information base and sometimes carry piggybacking control messages. Instead of allocating one label per flow, topology-driven techniques **allocate one label per egress router or per destination prefix**.

There is a fundamental difference between the label semantics of traffic (flow) driven and topology-driven techniques. With traffic-driven techniques, the label is an abbreviation for the packet header (or a set of packet headers). All packets belonging to the same flow carry the same label value. With topology-driven techniques, the label is an abbreviation for a piece of routing information. Conceptually all packets heading towards the same destination carry the same label value (assuming all switches are merge capable).

Label switched path establishment – independent control vs. ordered control

Tag Switching is an example of the **independent control** of the establishment of the label switched path (LSP). When label switching is used in support of destination-based routing, each label switching router (LSR) may make an independent decision to assign a label to a **Forwarding Equivalence Class** (FEC) and to advertise that assignment to its neighbors. In this way, the establishment of an LSP follows the convergence of routing almost immediately.

The alternative to independent LSP control is **ordered control**. This technique was used in the ARIS approach to label switching. In ordered control, label assignment proceeds in an orderly fashion from one end of an LSP to the other. Under ordered control, LSP setup may be initiated by the head (ingress) or tail (egress) end of an LSP. For example, ARIS required ordered control and egress initiation of LSPs. In such an environment, the only LSRs that can initiate the process of LSP establishment are the egress LSRs, that is the edge LSRs that are at the tail end of one or more LSPs. An LSR knows that it is an egress for a given FEC if its next hop for that FEC is not an LSR. It would then assign a label to the

FEC and advertise the assignment to its neighbor LSRs. Any neighbor that believes the egress LSR is the next hop for that FEC would then proceed to assign a label for that FEC and advertise the assignment to *its* neighbors, and so on. In this way the assignment of labels would proceed in an orderly fashion from egress to ingress.

An example of this process is shown in Figure 13.16. In Figure 13.16 (a), node E has identified itself as an egress for the address prefix 192.69/16, to which it has a direct route. It allocates a label for this FEC (6) and advertises the binding of that label to the FEC to its only LSR neighbor, D. Upon receiving the advertisement (Figure 13.16 (b)), D then allocates a label (14) and advertises the binding to its LSR neighbors, A and C. In this way LSP establishment proceeds in an orderly fashion from egress to ingress.

FIGURE 13-16   Ordered LSP establishment:

(a) Label is advertised by egress

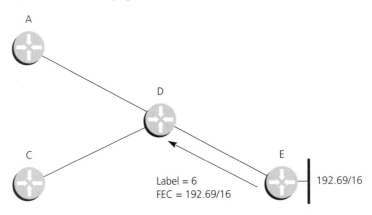

(b) LSR D assigns label and advertises it to neighbours after receiving advertisement from E

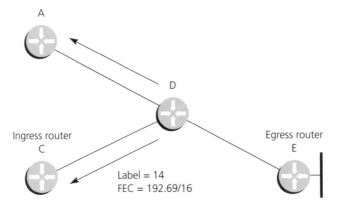

Label switching vs. conventional routing – differences revisited

One of the most easily understood claims made for label switching is that it improves **performance** and does so at a lower cost than conventional approaches. Because there are conventional routers on the market with comparable performance to ATM switches, the performance claim can be called into question. Some recent advances in algorithms to implement the longest match algorithm also suggest that very high speed longest match implementation is possible. The cost angle is harder to figure out, because vendor list prices are not necessarily a good indication of the real cost of a device. **Cost** is driven by a mixture of technical and economic factors, and the latter are largely beyond the scope of this book. However, there are a few observations we can make about cost.

First, label switching only reduces the **cost of the header lookup and forwarding decision**. Even if this could be driven to zero (clearly the best case, albeit an unlikely one), the impact on the cost of the whole system remains modest. The reason is that there are many other costs in building a device that can forward packets at many gigabits per second, such as the cost of the switching fabric itself and, very importantly, the cost of buffering. Buffering can be a large part of the cost of a high-performance router, because high-speed links increase both the required speed of the buffer memory and the total buffering requirements for good application performance.

Thus, there are limits to how much cost label switching can save, as a percentage of the total cost of a router. With lots of vendors making ATM switches with near identical functionality (a situation that does not pertain to routers today), the price (as opposed to the cost of parts) of these devices will drop because of competition. Furthermore, if enough ATM switches are made using common chip technology, the cost of chipsets needed for ATM switches might also drop, just as PC chipsets have done.

Label switching enables various pieces of new **functionality** that were either unavailable or inefficient with conventional routing. A good example of this is explicit route support. Because the decision to send a packet down an explicit route is made only at the beginning of the explicitly routed path, explicit route support is more efficient than prior schemes, such as the source route option in IP. Also, policies that could not be implemented in IP (e.g. because they depend on information that is only available to the router at the start of the explicit path) can be implemented using label switching.

13.3.2 Cell switch router

The Toshiba **Cell Switch Router** (CSR) and IBM's **Integrated Switch Router** (ISR) had similar configurations and used special control protocols, similar to IP switching in Ipsilon's proposal, but they also included specific support for and coexistence with ATM Forum protocols. The CSR/FANP approach was the first label switching technique to be publicly specified. It was realized on ATM: unlike the other approaches, CSR was designed to operate in conjunction with standard ATM and classical IP over ATM subnets. It was the only approach to enable label switching devices to communicate over standard ATM VCs.

The **Cell Switch Router** (CSR) uses as a label binding protocol its **Flow Attribute Notification Protocol** (FANP). CSR was presented to the IETF IP over ATM working group in spring 1994 and to the ATM Forum's Service Aspects and Applications working group in the summer of that year. The CSR was presented again at an IETF BOF (Birds of a Feather) session in spring 1995. When the effort to charter the MPLS working group began in late 1996, the CSR was presented as one of the candidate approaches to label switching (along with Tag Switching and ARIS). The CSR was initially proposed as a solution to the IP/ATM integration problem.

SNAPSHOT	Cell Switch Router (CSR)

- The IP switches and the technology are both called **Cell Switch Router**. CSR is multiprotocol at Layer 2, so the underlying switches need not be ATM switches.
- The shortcut path is called an **ATM bypass-pipe**.
- **Flow Attribute Notification Protocol** (FANP) is the current bypass-pipe control protocol.
- Unlike Ipsilon switching, not all the switches in the network are CSRs. In fact, most of the switches are not. A CSR is only needed between different IP clouds.

Like all the label switching approaches described, CSR uses label swapping forwarding combined with IP control protocols and a label distribution mechanism. Unlike the other approaches, it does not try to do away with standard ATM signaling and RFC 1577. CSRs were originally conceived as the default routers required by RFC 1577 for the interconnection of logical IP subnets. CSR is attached to the ATM cloud via UNI, not via NNI. A CSR can be attached with a single UNI to connect multiple IP clouds within a single ATM cloud or via multiple UNIs to connect IP clouds in different ATM clouds.

Unlike the other IP switching approaches which try to take over the entire ATM network, ignoring much of the ATM Forum and ITU-T efforts, CSR had only minimal impact on an existing ATM network. The conceptual integrity of ATM was left intact as CSR was non-disruptive, both to IP and to ATM.

CSR looks – from the path determination point of view – very much like a router therefore it can interconnect subnets in the classical model. However, from a forwarding point of view, it behaves just like an ATM switch, since a CSR can be built using standard ATM switch hardware.

The CSR specifications defined three types of VC: default, dedicated, and cut-through. In the initial state, a pair of CSRs communicate over the **default VC** and all traffic between them – routing protocols, data traffic – flows over this VC. Flows are identified (according to some local criteria) from it with the intention of providing cut-through paths for them (see Figure 13.17). A **dedicated VC** is one that carries an individual flow only (e.g. traffic belonging to a single application, which could be identified by <source address, destination address, protocol, source port, destination port>). A **cut-through VC** is one that is made by splicing together, at a CSR, two dedicated VCs.

FIGURE 13-17 Achieving cut-through in CSRs

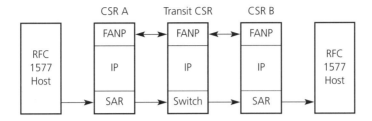

CSR uses the **Flow Attribute Notification Protocol** (FANP) to tell the next hop CSR about the association between flows and the VCs on which they will arrive. FANP operates in two phases. The first phase is called **VCID negotiation**. VCID is a unique number within a single network. A unique value is constructed by appending a locally unique six-octet value (generated by the system creating the VCID) to its own six-octet **end system identifier** (ESI). In the VCID negotiation phase, a *PROPOSE* message containing a VCID is sent down a certain VC. The message associates the particular VCID with the VC on which it arrived. In the second phase, the *OFFER* messages are used to indicate the particular flow that will be sent over the VC. (The message contains bindings of the form <VCID, FLOWID>.) The two-phase nature of FANP also illustrates the use of both in band and out of band signaling. FANP uses an upstream, data-driven, and independent model of label allocation. The decision to allocate a label is made locally in response to data traffic and is passed to the downstream neighbor.

SNAPSHOT   **FANP (CSR protocol)**

The **Flow Attribute Notification Protocol** (FANP) is the protocol that is used both to identify the dedicated VCs between CSRs and to establish the association between individual flows and individual dedicated VCs identified in the protocol by VCID. VCID is designed to allow the unique identification of VCs within a network and it also allows PVCs and SVCs in both public and private networks to be used as cut-through VCs.

Once a CSR is receiving a certain flow over a dedicated VC and transmitting the same flow onto its next hop over a dedicated VC, it can then set up the cell switching hardware to forward cells from the flow at the ATM level, thereby creating a cut-through VC (bypass pipe in CSR terminology). A point to note is that there may be standard ATM switches between the CSRs. It is a key feature of the CSR approach that neighboring CSRs may communicate over standard ATM virtual circuits. On the other hand, merging and aggregation, two important issues in scalability, were hardly addressed by CSR.

It is fair to acknowledge that MPLS and the label switching effort in general owe a great debt to the early work done by Toshiba. In fact, as we will see later, the IP Switching proposal from Ipsilon, which generated interest in label switching, bears significant similarities to the CSR/FANP approach. The differences between all four leading proposals for label switching technologies, pieces of which were later deployed in MPLS, are summarized in Table 13.2 on p. 742.

13.3.3 IP switch

Ipsilon's IP switching was introduced in early 1996 and protocol specifications were made public by Ipsilon in several informational RFCs (see p. 728). The **Ipsilon IP switch** consisted of an **IP switch controller** (e.g. a router) attached to a separate ATM switching fabric running the **Ipsilon Flow Management Protocol** (IFMP) and **General Switch Management Protocol** (GSMP).

Unlike MPOA, IP switching is Internet protocol-focused and does not support other protocols such as IPX, SNA, NetBIOS, or DECnet. IP switching is based on the recognition that ATM hardware is excellent but that the standard is complex. ATM software is unnecessary since IP routing is an already ubiquitous and open protocol. IP switching integrates ATM hardware with IP routing software by using IP routing intelligence to control ATM switching and enable switches to better support IP protocol. The architecture uses an IP switch controller which is essentially a router added to the switch. The router exchanges topology information with other IP switches and provides routing information while the ATM switch forwards cells at full ATM speeds. Unlike CSR, IP switching was not designed to allow label switches to communicate over standard ATM VCs.

SNAPSHOT	IP switch

An IP switch is a device or system that can forward IP packets at Layer 3 and possesses a switching component(s) that enables packets to be switched at Layer 2 as well. An IP switch possesses mechanisms to classify which packets will be forwarded at Layer 3 and which will be switched at Layer 2 and then to redirect some or all packets over a Layer 2 switched path. Most IP switches utilize an ATM switching fabric but other Layer 2 switching technologies can be used as well.

An IP switch maps the forwarding functions onto a hardware switch such as an ATM switch. A similar idea occurred independently, at about the same time, to three groups. The devices based upon this idea were called: IP/ATM, the IP switch, and the Cell Switch Router (CSR).

The proposals of **IP switch** and **cell switch router** (CSR) were based on similar hybrid ATM switch/IP router designs which allow the coexistence of hop-by-hop IP forwarding with direct VC cut-through modes of service in order to provide each flow with the most suitable mode of service while maintaining desirable network conditions such as a manageable number of VCs. Both IP switch and CSR rely on a signaling protocol to inform neighboring nodes of any chosen flow-specific VCs.

The IP switch and CSR hybrid switch/routers contain all the usual functionality of conventional IP routers and thus are capable of providing a connectionless IP forwarding service. However, the valid topological configurations vary according to the type of hybrid switch/router. The IP switch did not support the ATM user-network interface (UNI) standards, so it was incapable of interfacing with conventional ATM devices. Instead, the IP switch would typically be used to replace each conventional ATM switch in existing ATM network (see its architecture in Figure 13.18).

FIGURE 13-18 IP switch architecture

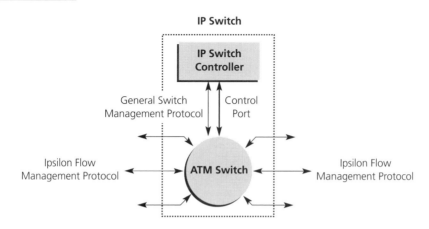

To construct an IP switch the hardware of an ATM switch is used without any modification, but the software resident in the control processor above AAL-5 is completely removed. Thus we remove the signaling, any existing routing protocol, and any LAN emulation server or address resolution servers, etc. In place of the ATM software we load a simple, low-level control protocol, called the **General Switch Management Protocol** (GSMP), to give the IP switch controller access to the switch hardware. The IP switch controller is a high-end processor running standard IP router software with extensions that allow it to make use of the switching hardware. These extensions include the **Ipsilon Flow Management Protocol** (IFMP) to associate IP flows with ATM virtual channels, a flow classifier to decide whether to switch each flow, and GSMP to control the switch hardware.

The basic operation of IP switching is as follows. Initially packets are forwarded hop by hop. At a certain moment, the flow classifier inside the switch controller decides the packets belong to a persistent (long-lived) flow. When a flow is thought to be persistent enough to create a shortcut path, the Ipsilon switch sends an IFMP redirect message to its upstream neighbor telling it to send packets belonging to that flow on a new VC. Thus far there is no performance gain; the packets are still being forwarded hop by hop. Some time later the downstream neighbor might also decide that the packets belong to a persistent flow, and send its own IFMP redirect message upstream. Having received the redirect message from downstream and sent the redirect message upstream is the trigger for the

> SNAPSHOT   IP switching components
>
> The three major **components** of the **Ipsilon IP switching technology** are:
>
> - **Ipsilon Flow Management Protocol** (IFMP) – used to exchange control information between neighboring Ipsilon switches.
> - **Generic Switch Management Protocol** (GSMP) – used to exchange control information between the switch controller and the switch.
> - The **flow classifier** inside the switch controller – this is where the real intelligence in Ipsilon switching is located.

switch controller to send a GSMP message to the switch, telling it to concatenate the incoming and outgoing VCs, thereby creating the shortcut path. It should be clear that Ipsilon switching uses downstream allocation. The downstream node selects the VC and reports it upstream.

IP switching relies on IP routing protocols to establish a routing information base from which the next hop for a packet can be determined. Only after this has been done, that is only after the next hop has been identified, does the separate process of negotiating label bindings with that next hop take place. IP switching is depicted in Figure 13.19.

FIGURE 13-19   IP switch architecture

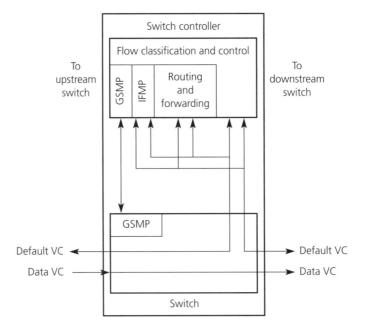

The important functions of IP switching ingress and egress (at the network edges) comprise the following:

- provides normal default IP forwarding for traffic entering and exiting the network;
- provides media translation (e.g. Ethernet-to-ATM) services where necessary;
- participates in the control procedures for establishing, maintaining, and removing a Layer 2 switched path between the appropriate ingress and egress;
- at the ingress, classifies eligible packets and forwards them over the Layer 2 switched path;
- at the egress, receives packets over the Layer 2 switched path and performs standard IP forwarding procedures.

Flow switching

IP switching flow classification is performed by inspecting the IP traffic arriving at the switch with the aim of selecting from it flows that are likely to benefit from being label switched. Classification policies are local so the network administrator can select and tune the algorithms according to local conditions.

Flow redirection is the process of binding labels to flows and establishing label switched paths. One IP switch tells another to redirect a particular flow to it. The semantics are simply 'use label x to send traffic from flow y to me.' A label is just a locally significant identifier that is used to switch some class of packets. Because IP switching is designed to run on ATM hardware, labels represent VPI/VCI values.

IP switching uses **low-level switching of flows** (equivalent to cached routing decisions) and includes a cooperative protocol to allow the explicit use and management of this cached information, on a link-by-link basis, throughout an IP switching network. In an IP switch, all flows are classified. The **flow classification** process dynamically selects flows to be forwarded in the switch fabric while the remaining flows are forwarded hop by hop. This flow classification allows an IP switch to intrinsically support multicast, quality of service differentiation, simple firewall filtering, and complex policy-based routing decisions for each switched flow. These features can be difficult to support in a gigabit router with the fast forwarding path optimized for only destination address lookup. The forwarding engine in an IP switch is optimized for flow classification and for forwarding packets on those flows that are decided should not be cut-through the switch fabric.

When a packet is received across a default channel it is reassembled and submitted to the IP switch controller for forwarding. The controller forwards the packet in the normal manner but it also performs a **flow classification** on the packet to determine whether future packets belonging to the same flow should be switched directly in the ATM hardware or continue to be forwarded hop by hop by the IP switch controller. Flow classification is a local policy decision. The flow classifier inspects the contents of the fields that characterize the flow and makes its decision based upon a local policy expressed in a table. For example, by looking for well known source or destination port numbers one can identify the application. Flows belonging to FTP data connections may be configured to be switched, but DNS queries could be forwarded as datagrams.

IP switching distinguishes **two types of flows** (sequence of IP datagrams):

- **Type 1 flows** – identified by *<source address, source port, destination address, destination port>*, enabling different applications between the same pair of machines to be distinguished.
- **Type 2 flows** – identified by an ordered pair of the form *<source address, destination address>*, a.k.a. host-to-host flow.

IP switching is an example of flow-based tagging. A tag is allocated based on the arrival of new data packets on a flow. This scheme is less scalable than those used by tag switching, and is sensitive to the specific traffic patterns in a network. Traffic-driven approaches set up individual flows only after some number of packets from the same source to the same destination pass by, resulting in many more flows (not scalable) and some packets taking a slower non-switched path (lower performance). Flow-based schemes also only switch long-lived flows at high speed, meaning that short-lived flows take a much lower performance path. Lastly, control-driven schemes are a better match to protocols like RSVP than are traffic-driven methods.

IP switching is a **flow-driven** (sometimes called traffic-driven or even data-driven) solution based on defining flow classification depending on the characteristics of the network traffic. A flow is defined as a continuous stream of packets between the same source and destination and the same protocol type such as UDP or TCP. Flows are handled in cell streaming mode in which only the first cell is routed and subsequent cells are moved using cut-through switching in the ATM hardware. The switching achieved in IP switching following flow redirect looks a lot like the cut-through switching of the CSR. Short-lived traffic such as DNS queries receive the default store and forward routing treatment and incur conventional router delays. Using IP switching, Internet applications such as FTP and Web downloads bypass the IP routing software and its associated processing overhead resulting in less delays and achieving considerable throughput increase. With performance in the tens of millions of packets per second, IP switching provides performance levels similar to ATM and far better than conventional routing.

> **SNAPSHOT**   **IP switching concept**
>
> IP switching is a flow-driven approach to label switching specified for use over ATM hardware and links.

Switch and flow management protocols

Before any IP switching can be performed, there has to be a way to get control traffic, including routing protocols and IFMP messages, between switches. A default VC is defined for this. It uses a well-known VCI/VPI value, so that two adjacent IP switches will be able to communicate without first signaling for a VC. It is a VC in the sense that it connects a pair of adjacent IP switch controllers through their attached ATM switches, but no ATM procedures (e.g. signaling) are used to establish it. Traffic that flows on the default VC was encapsulated in accordance with RFC 1483 (using LLC/SNAP, as is common for data on ATM VCs) and was sent to the switch controller and reassembled. The default VC is also used for data that does not yet have a label associated with it. Such data is forwarded in software by the switch controller.

IFMP runs on a point-to-point link between two IP switches and is designed to communicate flow to label binding information between them. The protocol operates using the downstream label allocation model. Decisions on how and when to assign labels is a matter of local policy, in the sense that each switch can make its own assignment decisions. However, it makes sense for all the switches in a domain, or at least for ones adjacent to each other, to have a coherent view of what this policy is to enable the establishment of switched paths.

IFMP is a soft state protocol, meaning that the state that it installs will automatically timeout (i.e. be deleted after some interval) unless refreshed. Flow binding information has a limited life once it is learned by an upstream switch and must be refreshed periodically as long as it is required.

The control protocol used in IP switching between the switch and the controller is the **General Switch Management Protocol** (GSMP) (RFC 1987) which has been designed to give the IP switch controller full control of an ATM switch. It is useful to re-emphasize that from a technology perspective, IP switching is essentially independent of GSMP, and vice versa. GSMP is used solely to control an ATM switch and the VC connections made across it.

GSMP is a rather simple master/slave protocol, with the slave running on the ATM switch and the master running on an IP switch controller (which is really a general-purpose computing engine with an ATM interface to allow it to talk to the switch). Only the slave portion has to know anything that is specific to the ATM switch hardware.

The protocol allows the master to:

- establish and release VC connections across the switch;
- add and delete leaves to point-to-multipoint connections;
- perform port management (*Up, Down, Reset, Loopback*);
- request data (configuration information, statistics).

As GSMP has also been adopted in MPLS, it will be discussed in that regard in the next chapter.

The **Ipsilon Flow Management Protocol** (IFMP) (RFC 1953) is the flow-forwarding-cache distribution protocol. It runs between the IP switch controller and its peers across each external link. In comparison with general high-speed router architecture, the line cards are part of the ATM switch and the forwarding engine is implemented in software within the IP switch controller.

Although IP switching allows for considerable improvement in performance, its shortcoming is, however, that as yet it still cannot take advantage of the end-to-end QoS capability of ATM. Some other fast IP approaches are tackling the QoS issue and when they become fully available they should become more tempting solutions to carriers. With QoS capabilities, service providers are able to set service parameters and usage thresholds at different levels and bill users accordingly. The main critics of IP switching models are, however, focused on their use of virtual circuits (VCs) for each individual flow which could result in exhausting VC tables in cases of large networks like the Internet. While efforts were under way to solve this issue by allowing the traffic between two networks to be lumped together in a common flow, another approach, tag switching, resolved this issue.

RFC WATCH   IP switch

RFC 1953 **Ipsilon Flow Management Protocol Specification for IPv4 Version 1.0**, 1996 (Informational)

RFC 1954 **Transmission of Flow Labelled IPv4 on ATM Data Links Ipsilon Version 1.0**, 1996 (Informational)

RFC 1987 **Ipsilon's General Switch Management Protocol Specification Version 1.1**, 1996 (Updated by RFC 2297) (Informational)

RFC 2297 **Ipsilon's General Switch Management Protocol Specification Version 2.0**, 1998 (Updates RFC 1987) (Informational)

IP switching contribution

One of the significant innovations of the Ipsilon approach was to define not only a label distribution protocol (which all the label switching approaches do) but also a switch management protocol. GSMP allows an ATM switch to be controlled by an IP switch controller and thus be turned into an IP switch. GSMP protocol took the separation of control and forwarding to its logical conclusion: it enabled control and forwarding to reside in separate physical boxes connected by a link, over which GSMP runs.

GSMP was a general-purpose technique for controlling ATM switches with third-party software, thus enabling a large number of vendors' switches to easily become IP switches. GSMP may also be used by any other software that can control an ATM switch, for example software to support standard ATM signaling. GSMP provides a range of technical, business, and economic benefits. In particular, at the time that Ipsilon was founded, ATM switches with capacities of around 2.5 Gbps were becoming commodity items. In such an environment, an approach that could turn any vendor's ATM switch into something with the capabilities of a router with only a modest increase in total cost was likely to have considerable market appeal. This is exactly what GSMP enabled Ipsilon to do.

In addition to GSMP, Ipsilon also defined a label binding protocol, called Ipsilon Flow Management Protocol (IFMP).

Alone among initial label switching proposals, IP switching offered some protection against the dangers of incorrect flows being submitted on a label switched path. It is also unique in enabling label switched paths to extend all the way to hosts, provided they have ATM interfaces and suitable software.

The differences between all four leading proposals for label switching technologies, pieces of which were later deployed in MPLS, are summarized in Table 13.2 on p. 742.

13.3.4 Aggregated route-based IP switching

Aggregated Route-Based IP Switching (ARIS) (with no RFC) and Cisco's **Tag Switching** architecture (RFC 2105) are approaches to run IP over ATM in which VC association is completely topology-driven, unlike the hybrid switch/router models discussed in the previous section, where setup of VCs is either topology-driven for default-VCs or traffic-driven for flow-specific VCs. Unlike the hybrid switch/router approaches, both ARIS and Tag Switching use VC cut-through for all traffic, including best-effort. ARIS and Tag Switching are able to do this without causing VC explosion since the cut-through VCs of both ARIS and Tag Switching can have a coarser granularity than the per-flow cut-through VCs of the hybrid switch/routers (see Figure 13.20). In fact, both ARIS and Tag Switching offer a choice of granularities according to the network environment.

Both proposals rely on some ideas that had been published previously, such as the notion of threaded indices described by Varghese in 1995. The naming of ARIS, Aggregate Route-based IP switching, suggests something about its origins: unlike Ipsilon's IP switching, ARIS binds labels to aggregate routes (or groups of address prefixes), rather than to flows.

FIGURE 13-20   Cut-through service of a hybrid switch/router

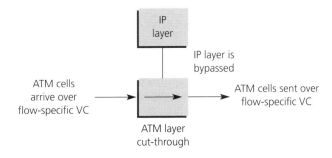

ARIS (an IBM technology), is a control-driven approach which sets up label bindings and label switched paths in response to control traffic, such as routing updates. Routers and switches that are able to participate in label switching are in ARIS referred to as **Integrated Switch Routers** (ISRs).

ARIS introduces the concept of the **egress identifier** type to define granularity. In the simplest case, an egress ID represents the identity of the ISR at the egress end of a label switched path. However, an egress ID might represent any number of things, such as a prefix carried in a distance vector protocol or a multicast tree. The egress ID must be unique to the network. The routers in a region all need to agree on how egress IDs are chosen. The upstream neighbors are, in the case of an egress ISR, all ISRs to which it is directly connected.

For each value of the egress identifier the ARIS protocol establishes a **multipoint-to-point tree** that originates at the routing domain ingress **Integrated Switch Routers** (ISRs) and terminates at the routing domain egress ISR for that particular egress identifier (see Figure 13.21). Thus, if the egress identifier represents IP destination prefixes, a separate multipoint-to-point tree is set up per IP destination prefix. When a packet arrives at one of the ingress ISRs, the forwarding table is consulted to determine the outgoing interface and virtual path identifier/VC identifier (VPI/VCI) label to be used. Cells from the packet are then switched along the tree completely at the ATM layer until they reach the egress ISR, where the datagram is again reassembled at the IP layer.

FIGURE 13-21 ARIS multipoint-to-point tree

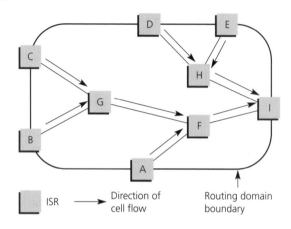

The ARIS protocol is a peer-to-peer protocol that runs between ISRs directly over IP. The protocol includes an initialization phase, in which peers determine their neighbors' capabilities and establish an adjacency, followed by the active phase in which label bindings may be exchanged, requested, and deleted. Because it runs directly over IP, the protocol requires its own reliability mechanisms.

The establishment of **label switched paths** for destination-based routing in the ARIS architecture is originated by the egress ISR. As with all label switching approaches, it is assumed that all label switching routers are running conventional routing protocols. The operation of ARIS, and the usage of egress IDs in particular, is dependent on the type of routing protocol used. ARIS ISRs need to determine what type of egress ID is being used based on the routing protocol being used and perhaps some local configuration. We begin this discussion by assuming that a link-state protocol (such as OSPF) is being used, and furthermore that all the ISRs in the region in question are in the same routing area. The consequence of these assumptions is that all ISRs in the region have a complete database of the topology of the region. This in turn means that an ISR can determine not just the next hop for any entry in its routing table, but also the egress ISR for that entry. To begin the establishment of a label switched path, an egress ISR advertises a binding between a label and its own egress ID to its upstream ISR neighbors.

SNAPSHOT **ARIS label distribution**

A controlled approach to label distribution which begins at the egress and propagates in an orderly fashion toward the ingress.

Upon receiving an advertisement from a neighboring ISR, the recipient ISR checks to see whether the message came from the expected next hop for that egress ID by checking the routing table entry for the route to the ISR with that egress ID. If the message did not come from the appropriate next hop, then it is discarded. (The recipient may also perform some loop prevention procedures.) If the message did come from the appropriate next hop, then the ISR records the **binding** between t**he egress ID and the advertised label**. It now knows that this label can be used as the outgoing label for all routes in its routing table that have that egress ID.

Once the ISR has processed the received message, it generates a **new label binding** between a locally assigned label and the egress ID of the received message. It stores this as the incoming label for those routes in the routing table that match the egress ID and then advertises the binding to its neighbors. Those neighbors in turn process the advertisement in exactly the same way, so that eventually the advertisement propagates all the way to the ingress of the ISR region. At this point, every ISR in the region that uses the egress ISR in question for any routes at all will have incoming and outgoing label bindings for those routes and can forward packets toward that egress ISR using label switching.

Example of ARIS operation

In the example network shown in Figure 13.22, the major network area consists of interconnected ISRs. On the right is a network with the address prefix 171.69.210, which is connected to both ISR A and ISR B. Let's assume for this example that all the ISRs except ISR B have chosen a route to 171.69.210 that passes through ISR A. Thus they all have a routing table entry for 171.69.210 that includes an egress ID corresponding to ISR A.

FIGURE 13-22   Example of ARIS operation

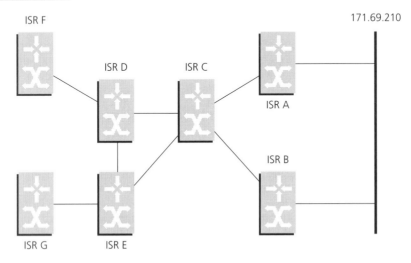

Assume that ISR A advertises a binding between its egress ID and a label. (ISR A will typically do this as soon as it learns that it has any neighbors who are ISRs, e.g. when it is booted or when it first establishes that it is connected to ISR C.) The binding advertisement is sent within an *ESTABLISH* message. The first thing ISR C has to do when it receives the advertisement from A is to determine whether this message has arrived from the correct next hop. In this case, it is pretty obvious that A is the next hop for A, but in the general case, an ISR would check the routing table entry that corresponds to the router identified in the egress ID. For example, if ISR A had an IP address of 171.69.244, then C would look in its routing table to find the next hop for that address. It would, of course, be ISR A, so C would accept the message.

Suppose that the advertisement from A contains a binding between the label 17 and the egress ID for ISR A. Then ISR C would update its forwarding information base as follows:

Prefix	Next hop	Egress ID	Remote label
171.69.210	ISR A	ISR A	17

Note that when ISR B advertises bindings to ISR C, ISR C performs exactly the same steps. It first checks to see whether B is the next hop to B, which, of course, it is, and thus C decides to accept the message. It then looks to see whether ISR B is the egress router for any routes in its routing table. In this simple example, it may be that B is not the egress for any routes, so the message is discarded.

Having processed the advertisement from ISR A, ISR C creates a **local label binding**. Let's suppose it allocates the label 10. Although we could add that as another column to the table we have used so far, the ARIS documents talk about a separate table called the **Virtual Circuit Information Base** (VCIB). Note that the term virtual circuit is used in ARIS to refer to a label switched path, which is not exactly the same as a conventional VC, notably because it may be multipoint-to-point. The VCIB contains information that is used to forward label switched packets, which would include the incoming label, outgoing label, and outgoing interface.

ISR C now advertises a binding between the egress ID for ISR A and the label 10 to all of its neighbors except ISR A. ISR B, we may assume, does not believe that ISR C is the next hop toward ISR A, because B can reach A directly over the 171.69.210 network. Thus ISR B discards the advertisement. Both ISRs D and E, however, believe that C is the next hop to A, and accept the advertisement. They process it just as C did, storing the label 10 as the outgoing label for routes corresponding to this egress ID and assigning new labels, which they in turn advertise to their neighbors.

When ISR F receives an advertisement from ISR D, it processes the message and stores the outgoing label provided by D. However, ISR F has no more ISR neighbors aside from D and thus does not need to assign a locally generated label or make any further advertisements. It should be clear that the overall effect of the propagation of label assignments from egress to ingress is to build up a multipoint-to-point tree rooted at the egress.

ARIS label encapsulation

ARIS introduced two methods for carrying labels, one for ATM and one for shared media LANs. As in every other label switching approach, the label must be placed where an ATM switch can use it, that is in the VCI or VPI field. ARIS's LAN encapsulation is very different from the Tag Switching approach (the only other approach that has a LAN encapsulation). The ARIS team has proposed carrying the label inside the destination address field of the MAC header. The label is put inside the destination address field of the MAC header, as shown in Figure 13.23. The first 24 bits are a standard Ethernet OUI, which indicates that this in fact is not a normal MAC address but a label. The next 20 bits are the actual **label**, followed by three bits of Class of Service (CoS) and a stack bit. The CoS bits enable packets to receive different 'class of service' treatment in the network and are similar to the precedence field in the IP header. The stack bit is used to enable multiple tags, when hierarchical tags are used. The encapsulation has no TTL field, which means that it evokes the looping and TTL adjustment issues of the ATM encapsulation.

FIGURE 13-23 ARIS label encapsulation for LAN

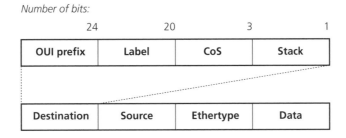

A notable characteristic of the ARIS approach is that it puts the label in a place where an existing piece of hardware, such as a LAN switch, might expect to find it. This is, in some sense, analogous to putting labels in the VCI field of an ATM switch. The problem with the analogy is that ATM switches are label swapping devices and LAN switches are not. Thus, whereas putting labels in the VCI field of an ATM cell leverages the capabilities of existing switch hardware, the same claim cannot be made for this LAN encapsulation. Any device that is to act as an LSR using this encapsulation will need to have label switching capability.

One might expect that the ARIS LAN encapsulation might be able to utilize existing router hardware, but this turns out not to be the case. The problem is that an ISR might in principle receive a packet with any value in the destination address. Devices that are able to receive such a range of packets are said to operate in promiscuous mode. Conventional bridges, for example, operate in this mode but do not perform label swapping. Making a host or router operate in promiscuous mode is costly – sometimes prohibitively so – because it needs to receive every packet that arrives at its network interface card and decide (usually in software) whether the packet is relevant to the recipient or not. Thus neither standard router hardware nor standard bridge hardware can easily use this encapsulation.

Another potentially significant issue with this scheme arises when we consider how label switching might be deployed. When deploying LSRs in a WAN environment, one only needs to replace the two devices at the ends of a link (or perhaps install some new software) to enable label switching across that link. However, in the LAN environment, deployment issues are different. In particular, the link between a pair of routers usually contains numerous bridges and LAN switches.

It will often be desirable to be able to upgrade the routers to label switches without having to worry about any bridges or LAN switches that are between the routers. Such incremental deployment is more difficult when labels are carried in the MAC header, for reasons we now describe.

Consider what happens if a pair of ISRs using this encapsulation attempt to communicate over an LAN that includes some bridges or switches. These devices expect the address fields in the MAC header to have a particular meaning, which is different from that used by the ARIS scheme. To deal with this, the ARIS *ESTABLISH* messages that advertise a binding to a certain label place that label in the source address field of the message. By doing this, the bridges and switches are fooled into thinking that a device with that address is located where the advertising ISR is. They will thus forward packets containing that label in the destination address field toward the advertising LSR.

Because ISRs are in effect creating MAC addresses on the fly each time they advertise a new binding, care needs to be taken to make sure that two ISRs on the same LAN do not allocate the same label at the same time. This is different from the ATM-LSR case, where all links are point-to-point; it also differs from the LAN encapsulation used by Tag Switching, where the uniqueness of a label is assured by the fact that it is carried in a frame with the real MAC addresses of the sender and receiver. The ARIS approach deals with the problem by partitioning the label space among all the ISRs on an LAN, using either static or dynamic means. Such partitioning is likely to be administratively complex.

Another potential problem for bridges in this environment is that the dynamic allocation of labels may create many more MAC addresses for the bridges to store in their tables than they are designed to handle. When these tables overflow, excessive flooding of packets can occur on the LAN. Thus, there were serious difficulties to using this scheme with either existing bridge hardware or with existing devices such as routers, preventing ARIS from being widely deployed.

VC merging

The ARIS protocol mechanisms for setting up the tree vary depending on whether or not VC merging is used. **VC merging** is when cells arriving on separate incoming links of an ISR are routed onto the same VC of an outgoing link of the ISR. With ATM adaptation layer type 5 (AAL5), which has no intra-VC multiplexing identifier, VC merging is only possible provided no interleaving of cells from different AAL5 frames occurs. Otherwise, it is not possible to reconstruct each AAL5 frame at the destination since there is no simple way to determine which cells belong to which frames.

Switches that support VC merging do so by **buffering cells** of each incoming AAL5 frame until the full frame has arrived, storing the full frame for a period of time determined by the scheduler, and then transmitting the frame so that it occupies a contiguous sequence of cells on the output link. VC merging reduces the number of consumed VCs but adds latency due to buffering of AAL5 frames. However, this increase in latency will still be less than for the case of IP forwarding, while the switching speed will be close to that attainable without VC merging. If VC merging is not used by the ISRs, buffering of AAL5 frames is unnecessary since mapping each input VC to a separate output VC allows cells of frames from different input VCs to be interleaved on the output link while still being able to reconstruct each frame at the destination.

ARIS vs. Tag Switching

The ARIS and Tag Switching mechanisms are similar in other respects apart from those already mentioned. For example, both mechanisms provide support for multicast and explicit routes. In addition, both use default VCs between the hybrid switch/routers in order to implement hop-by-hop forwarding for their control protocols as well as for the IP routing protocols. Furthermore, the ARIS and Tag Switching architectures include protocol mechanisms to prevent the setup of switched path loops. Another common feature between the two mechanisms is that they are both able to correctly implement time-to-live (TTL) decrements for cut-throughs. In other words, when a packet is reassembled at the egress router following VC cut-through, its TTL value will be the same as if it had undergone hop-by-hop IP forwarding instead. Apart from the throughput improvement obtained by ARIS and Tag Switching through bypassing the IP layer, the use of underlying ATM technology also makes them very suitable for offering QoS support, although to date Tag Switching has made more progress in this respect.

However, there are many significant differences between ARIS and Tag Switching in spite of their architectural similarity. The differences between all four leading proposals for label switching technologies, pieces of which were later deployed in MPLS, are summarized in Table 13.2 on p. 742.

13.3.5 Tag Switching

Cisco Systems proprietary **Tag Switching** was introduced as multilayer switching technology combining the performance and traffic management capabilities of Layer 2 (data link layer) switching with the scalability and flexibility of Layer 3 (network layer) routing. Tag Switching enables routers at the edge of a network to apply simple tags to packets, while devices in the core of the network (tag switches) switch packets according to these tags. The process starts with edge device applying a tag to a packet, then the tag switches forward according to label swapping tables, and finally the edge device removes the tag and forwards the packet. The whole process occurs at the link layer; it does not use network-layer information.

Tag Switching focused on adding functionality (such as explicit routes) and improving scalability (e.g. through the use of a hierarchy of routing knowledge). **High performance** was just one among many goals for Tag Switching. It also aimed at being **link-layer independent**, thus allowing operation over virtually any media type, not just ATM.

QUICK TIP   **Tag Switching terminology**

- A router that supports Tag Switching is called a **Tag Switching Router** (TSR).
- **Labels** are called **tags**, hence the technology name.
- A **label switching forwarding table** is called a **Tag Forwarding Information Base** (TFIB).

Tag Switching allows **Forwarding Equivalence Classes** (FECs) to be identified with **address prefixes** or even whole groups of prefixes, which is essential for providing scalable routing. Tag Switching also allows FECs to be associated with a source/destination address pair. This is essential for supporting multicast with Tag Switching. By associating FECs with a combination of source address, destination address, transport protocol, source port, and destination port, Tag Switching provides support for RSVP (for more details on RSVP, see Chapter 14) and application flows. Finally, Tag Switching allows association with FECs based on purely local rules in order to support explicit routes according to local policy.

Tag Switching in the core can be performed by switches, such as ATM switches, or by existing routers. These systems will run Tag Switching software, which communicates with tag routers on the edge using a **Tag Distribution Protocol**. A tag is 16 bits when used with ATM, and 19 bits for PPP and LAN applications. The tag header used in Tag Switching incorporates the **IP precedence** information used to indicate class of service or priority.

Tag Switching uses a **tag information base** (TIB) in each **Tag Switch Router** (TSR) in order to provide the mapping between an incoming interface and the tag (VPI/VCI value) of an incoming cell to the outgoing interface and outgoing tag of the cell. The TIB entries can be installed either explicitly or using the **Tag Distribution Protocol** (TDP). In the latter case a separate TIB entry is created for each route in the **tag forwarding information base** (TFIB). In addition, the FIB is extended to include a tag entry for each route. Then when a packet first arrives at the ingress TSR for the Tag Switching network, the FIB forwards the packet to the next hop while labeling the outgoing cells with the indicated tag value.

Destination-based routing

To support destination-based routing, a TSR, just like an ordinary router, participates in unicast routing protocols and uses the information provided by these protocols to construct its mapping between destinations (expressed as address prefixes) and their corresponding next hops. However, in contrast with an ordinary router, a TSR does not use this mapping for the actual packet forwarding – this mapping is used by the Tag Switching control component only for the purpose of constructing its Tag Forwarding Information Base (TFIB). That is the TFIB which is used for the actual packet forwarding.

Once a TSR has constructed a mapping between a particular FEC and its next hop, the TSR is ready to construct an entry in its TFIB. The information needed to construct the entry is provided from three sources:

■ a local binding between the FEC and a tag;
■ a mapping between the FEC and the next hop for that FEC (provided by the routing protocol(s) running on the TSR);
■ a remote binding between the FEC and a tag that is received from the next hop.

Tag Switching addresses the need for scalability via the notion of a **hierarchy** of routing knowledge. TSRs can be either interior or border routers to a particular domain. Interior TSRs – within a routing domain – participate in a common intra-domain routing protocol. The TFIB of an **interior TSR** contains entries for FECs corresponding only to the intra-domain routes, whereas the TFIB of a

border TSR contains entries for FECs corresponding to both inter- and intra-domain routes.

Tag Switching's support of a hierarchy of routing knowledge is shown in Figure 13.24. Routing domain A consists of two border TSRs, TSR T and TSR W, and two interior TSRs, TSR X and TSR Y. There is a set of destinations (an address prefix) in routing domain C that is reachable through the border TSR of that domain (TSR Z). TSR Z distributes the routing information about these destinations to TSR W, which in turn distributes it to TSR T, which in turn distributes it to TSR V.

FIGURE 13-24   Tag Switching hierarchy of routing knowledge

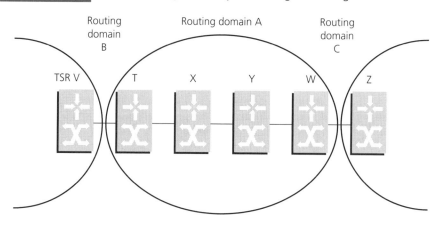

To support forwarding in the presence of a hierarchy of routing knowledge, Tag Switching allows a packet to carry not one, but several tags organized as a **tag stack**. When a packet is forwarded from one routing domain to another, the tag stack carried by the packet contains just one tag. However, when a packet is forwarded through a transit routing domain, the tag stack contains not one, but two tags. For the purpose of finding a TFIB entry that should be used for forwarding, a TSR always uses the tag at the top of the stack. When a packet carries a stack of tags, a TSR, in addition to swapping the tag at the top of the stack, could also push or pop a tag onto/off the stack. Pushing tags onto and popping tags off the stack occur at the domain boundaries. At the ingress a tag is pushed onto the tag stack, and at the egress a tag is popped off the stack.

RFC WATCH   **Tag Switching**

RFC 2105 **Cisco Systems' Tag Switching Architecture Overview**, 1997 (Informational)

Tag Switched network components

A Tag Switching internetwork consists of the following elements:

- **Tag edge routers** – as devices located at the boundaries of the core of a network, tag edge routers perform value-added network layer services and apply tags to packets. Tag edge routers are full-function Layer 3 routing devices located at the edge of a tag switching network. They examine incoming packets and apply the proper tag to the packet before forwarding the packet.

- **Tag switches** – devices that switch tagged packets or cells based on the tags. They implement the lookup and forwarding capabilities using fast hardware techniques. Tag switches may also support full Layer 3 routing or Layer 2 switching, in addition to tag switching.

- **Tag Distribution Protocol** (TDP) – protocol that is used, in conjunction with standard network layer routing protocols, to distribute tag information between devices in a tag switched network. TDP provides the means by which tag switches exchange tag information with other tag switches and with tag edge routers. The tag edge routers and tag switches build their routing databases using standard routing protocols. Neighboring tag switches and edge routers then distribute tag values to each other using TDP. Unlike standard ATM, there is no call setup procedure. The Tag Distribution Protocol uses a downstream tag maintenance scheme (such as a tag router advertising to its neighbor a binding, combining a tag and an IP prefix). The downstream approach can be driven off routing tables (when the routing table changes, it triggers TDP information) and creates routes in advance of need.

A key difference between Tag Switching and ATM is that standard ATM uses a connection setup procedure to allocate virtual circuits and program the ATM switching hardware, whereas Tag Switching uses standard routing protocols and TDP. The result is that ATM switches that perform Tag Switching have no call setup overhead for IP traffic.

Tag Switching provides great flexibility in the algorithms and techniques it supports for **mapping tags** to packets, such as:

- **Destination prefix** – tags are based on the routes in the routing tables. This technique allows traffic from multiple sources, going to the same destination, to share the same tag (in addition, multiple destination prefixes can share the same tag value) and avoids the label explosion problem of IP switching.

- **Class of service** – similar to the destination prefix method, except that the IP precedence field and the Type of Service (ToS) byte in the standard IP packet header is used to select the tag to use for the packet. This scenario enables different packets to be placed in differentiated IP service classes in a tag network.

- **Application flows** – depends on both the source and destination addresses, as well as other Layer 3 or Layer 4 information used to provide finer granularity in processing the tagged packets and to maintain a given QoS through the network for a specific source/destination flow of packets.

- **Multicast** – uses the Protocol Independent Multicast (PIM, see Section 11.6.3) protocol to define the paths for multicast flows and to distribute the tags for multicast packets. Unique to the Tag Switching approach is the capability to enable ATM switches to directly support PIM and to become fully integrated into the IP infrastructure to support IP multicast services, even within an IP VPN.

- **Explicit routing** – packets can be tagged so that they flow along specified routes, allowing network managers to balance the load across trunk circuits between nodes or cope with unbalanced network topologies during a node outage. This scenario is analogous to the use of VCs in pure Layer 2 devices for Internet traffic engineering, and can be implemented on Layer 3 routers using Tag Switching.

- **Virtual Private Networks** (VPN) – tag switching can also be used to support multiple overlapping IP address spaces on a common IP infrastructure. By tagging a packet based on both its destination IP address and its VPN, multiple private IP networks can be accommodated, and customers can subscribe to multiple VPNs.

Tag Switching, when performing destination-based routing, will generally assign the same number of label switched paths as ARIS. However, this is done by binding the same tag to different prefixes (which can be done in a single message) as opposed to a redefinition of the egress ID.

For ATM, the tag is placed in the ATM cell header in the Virtual Path Identifier/Virtual Channel Identifier (VPI/VCI) field. For use with the Point-to-Point Protocol (PPP), the tag is placed between the Layer 2 and Layer 3 headers. In an LAN, the tag is placed after the MAC header.

Tag switching is topology-based and control-driven because the creation of tag binding is driven by the creation of a mapping between a particular FEC and its next hop, which, in turn, is driven by routing updates. Specifically, **tag bindings** can be created in two basic ways:

- **Topology-based** – assigns tags based on the routes or topology of the network (i.e. a course level of granularity), while flow-based schemes assign tags for each conversation between a source and a destination (i.e. fine-grained granularity).

- **Traffic-driven** – uses protocols that are triggered by the receipt of data packets to set up tags or labels for packets. In contrast, control-driven schemes use explicit protocols for establishing these tags. Orthogonal to this is the issue of what a tag is bound to, or its level of granularity.

Tag Switching uses **downstream label binding**: whereas the binding between an incoming tag and an FEC is created locally by a TSR (local binding), the binding between an outgoing tag and the FEC is created as a result of receiving the tag binding information (remote binding) from the next-hop TSR associated with that FEC.

Tag distribution protocol

The **Tag Distribution Protocol** (TDP) is used to assign and distribute tags, and these tags are based on the topology of the network. This provides a highly scalable, low-overhead means of assigning tags, and one that is not sensitive to specific traffic patterns. This topology-based approach means that all packets of a flow of packets can be tag switched, and that even packets on short-lived flows can be tag switched. In the RSVP case, tag switching uses RSVP to distribute the tags on a per-flow basis, so in this case is an example of control-driven, flow-based tagging.

Information exchanged via TDP consists of a stream of messages, where each message consists of a fixed header followed by one or more **Protocol Information Elements** (PIEs). The fixed header consists of the Version field, followed by the *Length* field, followed by the TDP Identifier field. The *Version* field identifies a specific version of TDP. The *Length* field specifies the total length of a message. The TDP Identifier field identifies the TSR that sends the message. Each PIE is encoded as a *<Type, Length, Value>* (TLV) structure, where the *Type* field defines the semantics of the *Value* field, and the *Length* field defines the length of the *Value* field. All the information carried within a PIE is encoded as *<Type, Length, Value>* as well.

The exchange of tag binding information via TDP is based on the technique of **incremental updates**, where only changes to the tag binding information (e.g. creation of a new binding, deletion of an existing binding) are communicated via the protocol. Use of incremental updates requires **reliable, in-order delivery** of information. To meet this requirement TDP uses TCP as a transport to carry all the TDP messages. This design choice was largely based on the positive experience gained with BGP, where routing information is exchanged via incremental updates and TCP is used as a transport to carry the change of the routing information. This approach has very low overhead in the presence of a stable topology because there is no need to refresh any information that has not changed.

Tag Switching vs. IP Switching

The differences between all four leading proposals for label switching technologies, pieces of which were later deployed in MPLS, are summarized in Table 13.2 on p. 742.

The main difference between the two major pioneer technologies in high-speed packet switching is that Tag Switching provides the aggregation-disaggregation capability, which allows the bundling of multiple flows under a single tag and potentially provides more scalability. While IP Switching eliminates the need for separate routers, Tag Switching is understandably a router-based solution. Tag Switching is topology driven and handles all traffic at Layer 2, based on pre-configured routes. It is based on assigning tags to packets traversing packet or cell-based networks. The architecture is based on tag edge-routers located at the boundaries of an Internet, and tag switches which support both Layer 3 routing and Layer 2 switching.

As packets enter the network, tag routers handle Layer 3 routing and assign each packet a tag using the data tag distribution protocol (TDP) based on routing information exchanged using standard routing protocols. At subsequent nodes, Layer 3 processing is bypassed, and packets are forwarded based solely on their tags without re-analyzing the network layer header. At the egress point of the network, the tag edge router strips off the tag and delivers the packet to its destination. In an ATM network, VCIs are used as tags, and ATM switches supporting the tag distribution protocol will perform the switching as usual. Since tags correspond to destinations rather than source destination entries, this solution promises to improve scalability to large-scale networks like the Internet.

Although IP Switching and Tag Switching are architecturally different, both technologies provide ultimately the same benefits. The common purpose in all the efforts was to reduce to a minimum routing in favor of switching, and replace Layer 3 hops with efficient Layer 2 connections. These techniques allow the Internet to be scaled economically through the use of ATM switching to support legacy Internet traffic. In an IP Internet built, for example, from a core of ATM switches surrounded by edge routers which are connected by VCIs through the switches, scalability problems arise with the routing protocols when the number of routers increases.

These techniques of switching and routing integration enable a solution of the scalability problem by limiting the number of peers through the participation of the switches in the hierarchical routing protocols and eliminating the limitations of pure, flat Layer 2 networks. Connection-oriented routing provides various advantages in handling very high-speed flows and flexibility in routing through different paths for traffic splitting or according to QoS parameters.

Tag Switching is a control-driven, topology-based approach, which couples its destination prefix algorithm to standard routing protocols, supports much more efficient use of tags than traffic-driven per-flow schemes like IP switching, and avoids flow-by-flow setup procedures altogether. This yields the scalability required for public Internet networks and large enterprise networks.

By pre-establishing tag mappings at the same time as routing tables are populated, Tag Switching can tag switch both short lived flows and the initial packets of long-lived flows, avoiding bottlenecks in high-performance applications. IP switching can only switch flows classified as long lived.

Tag Switching is designed from the ground up to support both packet and cell interfaces. In contrast, IP switching is focused on turning an ATM switch into a router, and has not defined how it will work over non-ATM interfaces or on devices other than ATM switches.

Being topology-based, Tag Switching can tag switch all packets, not just long-lived flows, and hence Tag Switching is not sensitive to traffic flow patterns. Since IP Switching uses a traffic-driven flow-based approach, simulation is required to determine if IP Switching will improve performance. Should flow patterns change in the future to include a higher percentage of short-lived flows, the performance of IP Switching will decrease, while that of Tag Switching will not.

Tag Switching's TDP protocol only sends messages when the network topology changes, and only to those nodes that need to recompute tags. IP Switching's protocol (IFMP), on the other hand, sends messages whenever a source host wants to communicate with a destination host, resulting in far higher overhead.

Comparison of main label switching approaches

All label switching approaches have certain characteristics in common, such as the ability to run on standard ATM hardware and the use of IP routing protocols to determine paths through the network to the destination. All use some sort of new protocol to distribute bindings between labels and FECs. However, there are many significant differences, some of which are fundamental to the respective architectures, some of which simply reflect the priorities of the design teams in picking features to address. (See Table 13.2 for a comparison of all four approaches discussed in this chapter.) The most important difference between schemes is the choice between a **data-driven** or **control-driven** approach. The biggest drawback to a data-driven approach seems to be the difficulty in predicting performance because it depends so much on the detailed characteristics of the

TABLE 13-2 Comparison of four major label switching proprietary proposals

	CSR	IP Switching	ARIS	Tag Switching
Supported link types	ATM	ATM	ATM, Ethernet	ATM, PPP, Ethernet
Data- or control-driven	Data-driven	Data-driven	Control-driven	Control-driven
Binding creation	Independent	Independent	Ordered (from egress)	Independent (except explicit routes)
Binding distribution	Upstream	Downstream	Downstream	Downstream
Label distribution protocol	Separate	Separate	Separate	Separate/ Piggybacked
Hierarchy of labels	No	No	Yes	Yes
Loop prevention	Unspecified	Supported	Supported	Supported (on ATM only)
Soft or hard state	Soft	Soft	Soft	Hard/Soft
Multicast support	Unspecified	Yes	Partial	Yes
RSVP support	Yes	Yes	Yes	Yes

offered traffic. A small change in the length or number of flows passing through a point may cause a large change in the percentage of traffic that can be switched, resulting in overload of the control processor.

Ipsilon's IP Switching and Toshiba's CSR are **data-driven approaches**. They rely on the identification of a flow and some heuristics to decide when to assign a label to a flow. They bear some resemblance to caching algorithms. Both use a soft state model for label binding distribution. IP Switching has a number of features absent from CSR, such as TTL handling and loop prevention. The most notable feature provided by CSR not found in the other schemes is a way to interoperate with standard ATM SVCs, using the VCID mechanism.

Tag Switching and ARIS are **control-driven approaches**. A key difference is in the approach to looping: ARIS prevents the establishment of looping label switched paths, whereas Tag Switching uses TTL mechanisms to mitigate the effect of loops, just as conventional IP does. ARIS uses ordered label distribution; Tag Switching uses an independent approach. The result of both these choices is that there are more situations where ARIS cannot label switch packets for some period of time and must either resort to Layer 3 forwarding or dropping. However,

ARIS can create label switched paths through points of routing aggregation, at the cost of loss of scalability. Tag Switching and ARIS also differ in their LAN encapsulations and in the details of their label binding distribution protocols. The notable protocol differences are the decision to build reliability into ARIS rather than run over TCP as Tag Switching's protocol does and the fact that ARIS requires refreshing of bindings, making it a soft state approach.

13.3.6 Other proprietary technologies

Several related technologies have been proposed by other vendors for Layer 2/Layer 3 integration but did not gain enough attention.

Newbridge's **CSI architecture** leveraged MPOA to provide a way to support IP across a standard ATM backbone. CSI uses edge devices based on Newbridge's VIVID LAN products and on separate route servers to provide the routing functionality in the network. Because MPOA, as a standard, was designed for LAN environments and because MPOA had some VC scalability issues, Newbridge was modifying MPOA to create the proprietary CSI protocol set (for example, removing support for LAN Emulation, adding multipoint-to-point VC support, and so forth). The key concerns expressed within the industry regarding this approach included scalability and the closed nature of the solution (no publicly disclosed technical details of CSI were available). Besides, the CSI architecture did not have a sensible way of allocating bandwidth to particular IP services and would require inefficient use of network resources. The CSI approach was ATM-centric and did not implement an end-to-end IP model.

Ascend's **IP Navigator technology** was also a Layer 2/Layer 3 integration technique. Like CSI, it used a proprietary protocol – **Virtual Network Navigator** (VNN) – within the IP Navigator network (hence all components within the network had to be a limited set of Ascend products). It was targeted at providing IP-based VPN capabilities on an Ascend ATM backbone, not at supporting public Internet service. Like CSI, it supported ATM only in the backbone (the Ascend GRF router did not support IP Navigator).

Nortel's **Virtual Network Switching** (VNS) (RFC 2340) was a multiprotocol switching architecture aimed at providing COS-sensitive packet switching, reducing the complexity of operating protocols like PPP and Frame Relay, provide the logical networks and traffic segregation for Virtual Private Networks (VPNs), security and traffic engineering, enabling efficient WAN broadcasting and multicasting, and reducing address space requirements. VNS reduced the number of routing hops over the WAN by switching packets based on labels. VNS made a network of point-to-point links appear to be a single LAN (broadcast, multiple access) media. The network used by a particular instance of VNS is called a Logical Network (LN). Label distribution in VNS was based on a distributed serverless topology-driven approach. VNS labels were treated as MAC addresses by the network layer. This means that labels were distributed by the same means network layers use to distribute MAC addresses. Thus VNS leveraged existing Layer 2/Layer 3 mapping techniques and did not require a separate Label Distribution Protocol. VNS supported both unicasting and multicasting.

13.3.7 Evolution of shortcut routing

Of all the proposed multilayer switching technologies, Tag Switching has provided the best match with the requirements for such a technology. The Tag Switching topology-driven approach, which couples its destination prefix algorithm to standard routing protocols, supports much more efficient use of labels than traffic-driven per-flow schemes, and avoids flow-by-flow setup procedures altogether.

Tag Switching allows any number of different FECs to coexist in a single tag switch router (TSR), as long as these FECs provide unambiguous (with respect to that TSR) partitioning of the universe of packets that could be seen by the TSR.

One of the key innovations of Tag Switching is the use of a hierarchy of tags, organized as a **tag stack**. This enables enhancements to routing scalability by allowing FECs to form a hierarchy that reflects the hierarchy in the underlying routing system.

In Tag Switching the creation of tag binding information is driven mostly by control, rather than data traffic. Tag Switching uses downstream tag binding. Distribution of tag binding information, whenever practical, is accomplished by piggybacking this information on top of routing protocols. To cover the cases where piggybacking is impractical, Tag Switching provides a separate protocol, TDP, for distributing tag binding information.

Notably, Tag Switching has paid more attention to non-ATM links than any other approach. This is reflected both in the encapsulation for frame-based links and in the attention to issues such as tag partitioning on multi-access media. Tag Switching also provides direct support for advanced IP services, such as CoS, RSVP, IP VPNs, and multicast on ATM switches, and brings the benefits of explicit routing and VPNs to gigabit routers. The MPLS standard has used the TDP protocol in the widely accepted label switching specification.

Following the publication of the first set of Tag Switching Internet drafts, an IETF Birds of a Feather (BOF) session was held in December 1996, with presentations made by Cisco, IBM, and Toshiba (who had, by this time, produced a new set of Internet drafts on the CSR approach). The BOF session was one of the most attended in IETF history. The level of interest in the BOF, and the fact that so many companies had produced fairly similar proposals to solve a problem, made it clear that a standardization effort was in order. Even though some doubt existed as to whether the problem being solved was an important one (e.g. some people made the argument that faster routers would make the whole problem irrelevant), there was no doubt that, without a standards group, there would be a proliferation of incompatible label switching techniques.

Thus an effort to charter a working group began, and a charter was successfully accepted by the IETF in early 1997. The first meeting of the working group was held in April 1997. The name **Multiprotocol Label Switching** was adopted primarily because the names IP Switching and Tag Switching were each associated with the products of a single company, and a vendor-neutral term was required.

It may be quite interesting to compare the terminology and view the shift from Tag Switching to MPLS (see Table 13.3) before we actually move on to MPLS in detail (after discussing QoS in Chapter 15). The resemblance between the two approaches will then become clear.

TABLE 13-3   Tag Switching/MPLS terminology

Tag Switching	MPLS (Multiprotocol Label Switching)
Tag (item or packet)	Label
TDP (Tag Distribution Protocol)	LDP (Label Distribution Protocol)
TFIB (Tag Forwarding Information Base)	LFIB (Label Forwarding Information Base)
TSR (Tag Switching Router)	LSR (Label Switching Router)
TSC (Tag Switch Controller)	LSC (Label Switch Controller)
TVC (Tag VC, Tag Virtual Circuit)	LVC (Label VC, Label Virtual Circuit)

RFC WATCH   **Summarized RFC watch**

The following RFCs have been brought to your attention in this chapter:

RFC 1953 *Ipsilon Flow Management Protocol Specification for IPv4 Version 1.0*, 1996 (Informational)

RFC 1954 *Transmission of Flow Labelled IPv4 on ATM Data Links Ipsilon Version 1.0*, 1996 (Informational)

RFC 1987 *Ipsilon's General Switch Management Protocol Specification Version 1.1*, 1996 (Updated by RFC 2297) (Informational)

RFC 2105 *Cisco Systems' Tag Switching Architecture Overview*, 1997 (Informational)

RFC 2297 *Ipsilon's General Switch Management Protocol Specification Version 2.0*, 1998 (Updates RFC1987) (Informational)

RFC 2340 *Nortel's Virtual Network Switching (VNS) Overview*, 1998 (Informational)

CHAPTER 14

Quality of service

14.1 Background to QoS

In the simplest sense, **Quality of Service** (QoS) means providing a **consistent, predictable data delivery service** – in other words, satisfying customer application requirements. It means providing a network that is transparent to its users. QoS is the ability of a network element (e.g. an application, host, or router) to have some level of assurance that its traffic and service requirements can be satisfied. To enable QoS requires the cooperation of all network layers from top to bottom, as well as every network element from end to end. Any QoS assurances are only as good as the weakest link between sender and receiver. By no means does QoS create bandwidth.

Network quality of service refers to the ability of a network to **differentiate** and provide better service to selected network traffic over various underlying technologies including Frame Relay, Asynchronous Transfer Mode (ATM), local networks, SONET, and IP-routed networks. By better service we also mean the ability of a network element (e.g. an application, a host, or a router) to provide some level of assurance for consistent network data delivery.

SNAPSHOT	QoS

Quality of Service may be defined as a classification of packets for the purpose of treating certain classes or flows of packets in a particular way compared to other packets. Quality of Service enables differentiation of traffic – individual flows, as well as aggregates – and it requires policy definition and enforcement to manage who gets good service and who gets bad service.

In more concrete terms, the QoS of a wide-area network is a measure of how well it does its job, i.e. how quickly and reliably it transfers various kinds of data, including digitized voice and video traffic, from source to destination. The contracts that specify QoS, **service level agreements** (SLAs), are becoming more and more common, at least between service providers and their largest customers. Obviously, QoS requires developing **enterprise policies** and configuring related features to reflect them across a network to achieve an end-to-end QoS level.

In the past, when networks supported mostly exclusively voice telephony, the subject hardly ever came up because the circuit-switched telephone system was designed specifically to satisfy needs of the human conversation over the phone. Nowadays, with the advent of packet switching and the proliferation of many kinds of communications traffic (time-sensitive financial transactions, still images, large data files, voice, video, and so on), there are more than one set of criteria to satisfy. The data rate needed for satisfactory voice communication may take an intolerable time to transfer high-resolution images. Conversely, the degree of network latency acceptable in transferring some files may not be adequate for realtime voice.

14.1.1 QoS alternative – overprovisioning

The obvious solution – an alternative to QoS – to how to handle peak periods is to **overprovision the network**, to provide surplus bandwidth capacity in anticipation of these peak data rates during high-demand periods. Equally obvious, however, is that this is not economically viable. Since peak data rates and the network regions on which they might occur are seldom possible to predict, this is not a realistic alternative anyway. Besides, each application requires different service from the network and behaves in different ways. Even generous overprovisioning may not provide the assurance that the network will handle the specific demands of certain applications adequately.

For instance, some applications such as enterprise resource planning (ERP) systems can tolerate peak bursts but they cannot be sustained if the average round-trip time of a packet exceeds a certain threshold. At that point, the applications go into excessive retransmit mode and flood the network. To ensure the performance of these applications, then, an enterprise would need to provision network capacity that exceeds an application's average round-trip time. On the other hand, realtime data transactions are sensitive both to average round-trip time and to peak rates. Voice, as yet another important application in today's networks, requires network services with low latency and minimal jitter and packet loss. Voice traffic in and of itself does not require much bandwidth (a conversation can be compressed to 8 kbps).

New technologies for the **WAN backbone**, such as **wave division multiplexing** (WDM), are emerging for ISP networks which could solve the congestion problem with huge capacity. WDM as a multiplexing scheme based on channels of light extends the capacity of a SONET transmission network. Hence if the inherent problem in the network were only capacity (bandwidth, throughput, delay), it could be solved once these technologies are widely deployed in the transport infrastructure.

However, the complex problem of network usage policy enforcement may not be solved by a simple solution, basically because it consists of different tasks, involves different types of network devices at different layers, and fulfills a trade-off of different requirements. Therefore, there is hardly going to be a single product, or a single protocol, that will provide all forms of policy management and support all types of QoS levels. Therefore we will discuss different solutions to different issues involved in QoS in the following.

why not network overprovision?

Increasing network capacity so that it is not a bottleneck – i.e. 'throwing bandwidth at the problem' – has the following disadvantages:

■ the expense of increasing bandwidth throughout the entire network to meet the needs of the busiest segment;

■ the inability of telecommunications providers and ISPs to provide all the bandwidth needed;

■ the inability to control or grade traffic by type or source, either through technological solutions (e.g. greatly reducing the priority of undesirable traffic) or social measures (e.g. discouraging the use of applications through prohibitions or by making their performance poor enough that users give up);

■ the inability of these solutions to work with voice over IP (it does not require excessive bandwidth);

■ the continuing nature of the problem – additional bandwidth gets very quickly exhausted, while any reserve bandwidth (not available to users outside peak periods) would be wasteful.

14.1.2 QoS performance criteria

Technically, QoS refers to the **performance metrics**. The five most important of these are as follows:

■ **Availability** – ideally, a network is available 100% of the time. Criteria are quite strict. Even so high-sounding a figure as 99.8% translates into about an hour and a half of down time per month, which may be unacceptable to a large enterprise. Serious carriers strive for 99.9999% availability, which they refer to as 'six nines,' and which translates into a downtime of 2.6 seconds a month.

■ **Throughput** – the effective data transfer rate measured in bits per second. It is not the same as the maximum capacity, or wirespeed, of the network, often erroneously called the network's bandwidth. Sharing a network lowers the throughput realizable by any user, as does the overhead imposed by the extra bits included in every packet for identification and other purposes. A minimum rate of throughput is usually guaranteed by a service provider.

■ **Packet loss** – network devices, like switches and routers, sometimes have to hold data packets in buffered queues when a link gets congested. If the link remains congested for too long, the buffered queues will overflow and data will be lost. The lost packets must be retransmitted, adding to the total transmission time. In a well-managed network, packet loss will typically be less than 1% averaged over, say, a month.

■ **Latency** – the time taken by data to travel from the source to the destination, also known as **propagation delay**. This encompasses delay in a transmission path or in a device within a transmission path. In a router, latency is the amount of time between when a data packet is received and when it is retransmitted. For the public Internet, a voice call may easily exceed 150 ms of latency because of delays, such as those caused by signal processing (digitizing and compressing the analog voice input) and congestion (queuing).

The three major contributors to **packet delivery delays** are the following:

- **Queuing delays** – introduced by a packet sitting in a queue behind other packets waiting for transmission. Queuing delays increase with network load and are usually the longest of the three delays. (Only queuing delays are managed through QoS.)

- **Transmission delays** – account for the time necessary to serialize a packet onto a link. Transmission delays are inversely proportional to link speeds, and they can vary widely. For example, a 532-byte packet is serialized onto a DS-1 link in under 3 milliseconds, whereas on an OC-12/STM-4 (see Appendix D) link it will take under 7 microseconds.

- **Propagation delays** – the time necessary for a packet to travel a given distance over a specific media. The speed of light in fiber is not the same as in a vacuum; instead a reference commonly used is $(0.6)*c$.

■ **Jitter** (latency variation) – the distortion of a signal as it is propagated through the network, where the signal varies from its original reference timing. In packet-switched networks, jitter is a distortion of the interpacket arrival times compared to the interpacket times of the original transmission. This distortion is particularly damaging to multimedia traffic. Jitter has many causes including: variations in queue length; variations in the processing time needed to reorder packets that arrived out of order because they traveled over different paths; and variations in the processing time needed to reassemble packets that were segmented by the source before being transmitted.

Altogether the performance characteristics mean some measure of **predictability** over the network traffic and how it is served. To ensure that the network provides enough end-to-end services for a particular traffic type, the network must have some intelligence. It may vest in the network itself (intelligent network) or the network nodes. However, as it may be counterproductive to have too much intelligence in every piece of the network, the answer is to have just enough **intelligence in every network component** (router, switch, and host).

Predictability – of traffic amount in the network and traffic delay – means that it has a mean value, statistical distribution, and upper bound. A predictable amount of traffic in the network requires that the source must pace traffic initiation so that standing queues are bounded. Queues form when the arrival rate exceeds the departure rate. When congestion (too many messages in one queue) sets in, sources must not increase their rate; instead, sources should decrease their rate.

14.1.3 Service level agreements

We need to mention **Service Level Agreements** (SLAs) here again (they were first discussed in Part I, Chapter 3) because they are inherently linked to the required level of service a provider has to provide to the user. SLAs are one part technical, one part contracting, and three parts negotiation. Carriers have a vested interest in minimizing their exposure to penalties; end users have an equally vested interest in maximizing it. In order for both sides to maximize their gains, a clear understanding of one's own business objectives is critical when drawing up an SLA.

A well-crafted SLA should include the metrics of QoS and factors such as availability, maintenance scheduling, and mean time to repair. The client has the right to know about the time needed for network recovery after a power outage or equipment failure. The client also should be cognizant of the provider's ability to proactively detect and correct problems that may be looming. Automatic generation of QoS reports, alarms, and trouble tickets, and the issuing of credits for the vendor's non-compliance should be an integral part of an SLA. The deployment of QoS-based services is challenged by the ability to monitor and bill for such services.

Other key questions are what type of QoS reports should be generated, and how often should QoS metrics be taken and reported. If a service provider's report bases average availability on measurements taken over 24 hours, it may hide the problems that occur during the hours of peak usage. Generating billing and credit records as per SLAs have not yet reached a high degree of automation.

Another challenge to delivering good QoS arises when a **virtual private network** (discussed in more detail in Section 15.4) crosses the administrative and technical domains of many providers, perhaps incumbent operators and competitive providers, who may not all adhere to the same transmission and QoS technologies. Without uniform technologies and standards, service providers must negotiate individual operating agreements on a network-by-network basis. The associated cost can be prohibitive and limit service footprints, diluting the business promise of the Internet.

The more diverse and important a client's communications traffic becomes, the more crucial it is that the carrier maintains a high QoS. Throughput, availability, packet loss, latency, and jitter must all be spelled out in SLAs, along with how each is to be measured and reported. It is not uncommon for carriers to track QoS but not report the results to the client unless an extra fee is paid. A carrier can hardly be expected to generate credits automatically unless obliged to under the SLA.

14.2 IP quality of service

As we noted in Part IV while discussing TCP/IP architecture, IP-based networks provide **best-effort** data delivery by default. Best-effort IP allows the complexity to stay in the end hosts, so the network can remain relatively simple (based on end-to-end reliability responsibilities).

IP as a best-effort protocol does not guarantee delivery of data packets. Confirmation of the arrival of data packets at the destination is the responsibility of the upper layer protocol, first of all TCP. If any packet is not delivered (as determined by checking the sequence numbers of packets at the destination), TCP requests a retransmission of the missing packet, thereby ensuring that all packets eventually get to the destination. This is effective, but slow. Therefore, TCP is generally used by applications that are not time-sensitive.

The default service offering associated with the Internet is thus characterized as a **best-effort variable service response**. Within this service profile the net-

RFC WATCH — IP QoS architecture

RFC 2386 **A Framework for QoS-based Routing in the Internet**, 1998
(Informational)

RFC 2676 **QoS Routing Mechanisms and OSPF Extensions**, 1999
(Experimental)

RFC 2990 **Next Steps for the IP QoS Architecture**, 2000 (Informational)

work makes no attempt to actively differentiate its service response between the traffic streams generated by concurrent users of the network. Best-effort service is based on first-come, first-served (FCFS) processing (and, similarly, first-in, first-out, FIFO, queuing). As the load generated by the active traffic flows within the network varies, the network's best-effort service response will also vary.

QoS is largely about priorities. At network aggregation points, like routers, multiplexers, and switches, datastreams with different QoS needs are combined for transport over a common infrastructure, based on their priorities. Satisfactory QoS has two main requirements: a means for **labeling flows** with respect to their priorities, and network mechanisms for recognizing the labels and acting on them. Some networks, such as ATM, have extensive provisions of this kind. Unfortunately, the IP networks do not have the inherent means to achieve that task. So, ensuring adequate QoS comes down to devising a means for labeling data flows and recognizing and acting on those labels.

QUICK TIP — flow

A set of packets traversing a network element, all of which are covered by the same request for control of quality of service.

The objective of various Internet Quality of Service (QoS) efforts is to augment its base service with a number of selectable service responses. These service responses may be distinguished from the best-effort service by some form of superior service level, or they may be distinguished by providing a predictable service response which is unaffected by external conditions such as the number of concurrent traffic flows, or their generated traffic load.

14.2.1 Real-time applications

Let's have a look at some applications which require different service levels from the underlying IP network, and the caveats they might need to overcome even with QoS. **Real-time applications** cannot take advantage of TCP. Obviously, the time needed for keeping track of missing packets and retransmitting them is not acceptable in such cases. So these applications rely on UDP, which runs faster than TCP by omitting some of its functionality. Applications that run over UDP must either have those missing capabilities built into them or else do without.

While TCP flows are easy to detect (core to QoS support) due to their connection-oriented nature, UDP traffic imposes several problems when the detection of a certain kind of flows is intended. UDP is a connectionless protocol, where the data is sent in (unrelated) datagrams over the network. No obvious relationship between the packets of one single flow exists at the UDP level.

Voice over IP

Voice over IP (VoIP) is one of the applications which requires the QoS processing the most in current networks. This is due to the inherent characteristics that voice distinguishes from data, summarized in Table 14.1. For encapsulated voice into IP see Figure 14.1. In the case of voice communications, where retransmitting packets takes too long to be of any value anyway, missing packets are simply lost. Fortunately the voice (generally sound) transmissions show low sensitivity to packet loss as opposed to data; hence the major issue in voice transmission is the requirement for constant available bandwidth and low delay.

TABLE 14-1 Data vs. voice features

	Data	Voice
Bandwidth consumption	Variable – bursty	Constant
Bandwidth required	High	Low
Sensitivity to packet loss	High	Low
Sensitivity to delay	Low	High

FIGURE 14-1 VoIP packet format

Number of octets:

depends on medium	20	8	12	variable
link header	IP header	UDP header	RTP header	voice payload

Video

Key issues with video communication are that all packets that comprise a video frame must arrive during the same frame interval (any time within that interval) and audio and video must be synchronized when shown to user. The **fundamen-**

tal problems with voice/video traffic are that it does not slow down in response to delay or loss and that it requires **minimal variation in delay**.

Therefore the QoS definition for video needs to be all of the measures below:

- low loss rate;
- low absolute delay in two-way situations;
- low variation in delay.

14.2.2 Network service and network resources

Any **network service response** is an outcome of the **resources** available to service a load, and the level of the load itself. To offer such distinguished services there is not only a requirement to provide a differentiated service response within the network, there is also a requirement to control the service-qualified load admitted into the network, so that the resources allocated by the network to support a particular service response are capable of providing that response for the imposed load. This admission control function is undertaken by a traffic conditioner (an entity which performs traffic conditioning functions and which may contain meters, markers, droppers, and shapers), where the actions of the conditioner are governed by explicit or implicit admission control agents.

> **QUICK TIP**   **Admission control**
>
> A policy decision applied initially to QoS requests for controlling the admission of network traffic from outside a given administrative domain. Admission control is closely tied to accounting, and relies on source authentication. Contrast with Policing, which occurs after a request is accepted and data is flowing.

As a general observation of QoS architectures, the **service load control aspect** of QoS is perhaps the most troubling component of the architecture. While there is a wide array of well understood service response mechanisms that are available to IP networks, matching a set of such mechanisms within a controlled environment to respond to a set of service loads to achieve a completely consistent service response remains an area of weakness within existing IP QoS architectures. The control elements span a number of generic requirements, including end-to-end application signaling, end-to-network service signaling and resource management signaling to allow policy-based control of network resources. This control may also span a particular scope, and use edge-to-edge signaling, intended to support particular service responses within a defined network scope.

One way of implementing this control of imposed load to match the level of available resources is through an application-driven process of **service level negotiation** (also known as application signaled QoS). Here, the application first signals its service requirements to the network, and the network responds to this request. The application will proceed if the network has indicated that it is able to carry the additional load at the requested service level. If the network indicates that it cannot accommodate the service requirements the application may proceed in any case, on the basis that the network will service the application's data on a best-effort basis. This negotiation between the application and the network can take the form of explicit negotiation and commitment, where there is a single negotiation phase, followed by a commitment to the service level on the part of the network.

This application-signaled approach can be used within the **Integrated Services architecture**, where the application frames its service request within the **resource reservation protocol** (RSVP), and then passes this request into the network. The network can either respond positively in terms of its agreement to commit to this service profile, or it can reject the request. If the network commits to the request with a resource reservation, the application can then pass traffic into the network with the expectation that as long as the traffic remains within the traffic load profile that was originally associated with the request, the network will meet the requested service levels.

There is no requirement for the application to periodically reconfirm the service reservation itself, as the interaction between RSVP and the network constantly refreshes the reservation while it remains active. The reservation remains in force until the application explicitly requests termination of the reservation, or the network signals to the application that it is unable to continue with a service commitment to the reservation. There are variations to this model, including an aggregation model where a proxy agent can fold a number of application-signaled reservations into a common aggregate reservation along a common sub-path, and a matching deaggregator can re-establish the collection of individual resource reservations upon leaving the aggregate region. The essential feature of this Integrated Services model is the 'all or nothing' nature of the model. Either the network commits to the reservation, in which case the requestor does not have to subsequently monitor the network's level of response to the service, or the network indicates that it cannot meet the resource reservation.

An alternative approach to load control is to decouple the network load control function from the application. This is the basis of the **Differentiated Services architecture**. Here, a network implements a load control function as part of the function of admission of traffic into the network, admitting no more traffic within each service category as there are assumed to be resources in the network to deliver the intended service response. Necessarily there is some element of imprecision in this function given that traffic may take an arbitrary path through the network.

In terms of the interaction between the network and the application, this takes the form of a service request without prior negotiation, where the application requests a particular service response by simply marking each packet with a code to indicate the desired service. Architecturally, this approach decouples the end systems and the network, allowing a network to implement an active admission function in order to moderate the workload that is placed upon the network's resources without specific reference to individual resource requests from end systems. While this decoupling of control allows a network's operator a greater ability to manage its resources and a greater ability to ensure the integrity of its services, there is a greater potential level of imprecision in attempting to match applications' service requirements to the network's service capabilities.

QoS categorization

The approaches to QoS enforcement may be different as shown above. The following two **mechanisms** are the results of the standardization work within IETF:

- **Reservation Based: Integrated Services** (IntServ) – intended to transition the Internet into a robust integrated-service communications infrastructure that can support the transport of audio, video, realtime, and classical data traffic. Network resources are apportioned according to an application's QoS request, and subject to bandwidth management policy. RSVP provides the mechanisms to do this, as a part of the IntServ architecture.

- **Prioritization** (reservation-less): **Differentiated Services** (DiffServ) – intended to meet the need for relatively simple and coarse methods of providing differentiated classes of service for Internet traffic, to support various types of applications, and specific business requirements. The differentiated services approach to providing quality of service in networks employs a small, well-defined set of building blocks from which a variety of services may be built. A small bit-pattern in each packet, in the IPv4 TOS octet or the IPv6 Traffic Class octet, is used to mark a packet to receive a particular forwarding treatment, or per-hop behavior, at each network node. Network traffic is classified and apportioned network resources according to bandwidth management policy criteria. To enable QoS, classifications give preferential treatment to applications identified as having more demanding requirements. DiffServ provides this service.

SNAPSHOT   **IP QoS mechanisms**

There are two types of QoS mechanism:

- **Resource reservation** (integrated services): network resources are apportioned according to an application's QoS request, and subject to bandwidth management policy. The resource reservation mechanism is used in RSVP and IntServ.

- **Prioritization** (differentiated services): network traffic is classified and apportioned network resources according to bandwidth management policy criteria. To enable QoS, network elements give preferential treatment to classifications identified as having more demanding requirements. DiffServ uses this mechanism.

These types of QoS can be applied to individual application **flows** or to flow **aggregates**, hence there are two other ways to characterize types of QoS:

- **Per flow** – a flow is defined as an individual, unidirectional, datastream between two applications (sender and receiver), uniquely identified by source address and destination address as a minimum, but also may be more specifically identified by transport protocol, source port number, and destination port number.

■ **Per flow aggregate** – an aggregate is simply two or more flows. Typically the flows will have something in common (e.g. any one or more of their identifying parameters, a label or a priority number, or perhaps some authentication information). Applications, network topology, and policy dictate which type of QoS is most appropriate for individual flows or aggregates.

SNAPSHOT   **IP Quality of Service (QoS) preview**

At a high level of abstraction, **Quality of Service** (QoS) refers to the ability to deliver network services according to the parameters specified in a Service Level Agreement (service contract between a network provider and the customer). **Quality** is characterized by **service availability, delay, jitter, throughput, and packet loss ratio**. At a network resource level, QoS refers to a set of capabilities that allow a service provider to prioritize traffic and control bandwidth and network latency.

There are two different approaches to QoS on IP networks: Integrated Services and Differentiated Service. **Integrated Services** require policy control over the creation of signaled reservations, which provide specific quantitative end-to-end behavior for a (set of) flow(s). In contrast, **Differentiated Services** require policy to define the correspondence between codepoints in the packet's DS-field and individual per-hop behaviors (to achieve a specified per-domain behavior). A maximum of 64 per-hop behaviors limits the number of classes of service traffic that can be marked at any point in a domain. These classes of service signal the treatment of the packets with respect to various QoS aspects, such as flow priority and packet drop precedence. Policy controls the set of configuration parameters for each class in Differentiated Service, and the admission conditions for reservations in Integrated Services.

State-based and stateless QoS

The two approaches to load control can be characterized as state-based and stateless approaches respectively. The architecture of the **Integrated Services** model equates the cumulative sum of honored service requests to the current reserved resource levels of the network. In order for a resource reservation to be honored by the network, the network must maintain some form of remembered state to describe the resources that have been reserved, and the network path over which the reserved service will operate. This is to ensure the integrity of the reservation. In addition, each active network element within the network path must maintain a local state that allows incoming IP packets to be correctly classified into a reservation class. This classification allows the packet to be placed into a packet flow context that is associated with an appropriate service response consistent with the original end-to-end service reservation. This local state also extends to the function of metering packets for conformance on a flow-by-flow basis, and the additional overheads associated with maintenance of the state of each of these meters.

The state-based Integrated Services architectural model admits the potential to support a greater level of accuracy, and a finer level of granularity on the part of the network to respond to service requests. Each individual application's service request can be used to generate a reservation state within the network that is intended to prevent the resources associated with the reservation to be reassigned or otherwise pre-empted to service other reservations or to service best-effort traffic loads. The state-based model is intended to be exclusionary, where other traffic is displaced in order to meet the reservation's service targets.

With regard to concerns of **per-flow service scalability**, the resource requirements (computational processing and memory consumption) for running per-flow resource reservations on routers increase in direct proportion to the number of separate reservations that need to be accommodated. By the same token, router forwarding performance may be impacted adversely by the **packet-classification** and scheduling mechanisms intended to provide differentiated services for these resource-reserved flows. This service architecture also poses some challenges to the queuing mechanisms, where there is the requirement to allocate absolute levels of egress bandwidth to individual flows, while still supporting an unmanaged low priority best-effort traffic class.

In the **Differentiated Services** model, the packet is marked with a code to trigger the appropriate service response from the network elements that handle the packet, so that there is no strict requirement to install a per-reservation   state on these network elements. Also, the end application or the service requestor is not required to provide the network with advance notice relating to the destination of the traffic, nor any indication of the intended traffic profile or the associated service profile. In the absence of such information any form of per-application or per-path resource reservation is not feasible. In this model there is no maintained per-flow state within the network, hence it is a **stateless approach**.

The stateless approach to service management is more approximate in the nature of its outcomes. There is no explicit negotiation between the application's signaling of the service request and the network's capability to deliver a particular service response. If the network is incapable of meeting the service request, then the request simply will not be honored. In such a situation there is no requirement for the network to inform the application that the request cannot be honored, and it is left to the application to determine if the service has not been delivered.

The major attribute of the stateless approach is that it can possess excellent scaling properties from the perspective of the network. If the network is capable of supporting a limited number of discrete service responses, and the router uses per-packet marking to trigger the service response, then the processor and memory requirements in each router do not increase in proportion to the level of traffic passed through the router. Of course this approach does introduce some degree of compromise in that the service response is more approximate as seen by the end client, and scaling the number of clients and applications in such an environment may not necessarily result in a highly accurate service response to every client's application.

14.2.3 QoS architecture

The following three components are necessary to deliver QoS across a heterogeneous network:

- QoS within a single network element – includes **queuing, scheduling, and traffic shaping features;**
- coordinating QoS from end-to-end between network elements – requires specific QoS **signaling techniques;**
- control and administration of end-to-end traffic across a network – needs QoS **policing and management functions**.

The end-to-end principle is the primary focus of QoS architects. As a result, the fundamental principle of 'Leave complexity at the "edges" and keep the network "core" simple' is a central theme among QoS architecture designs. However, depending largely on the type of the vendor, the actual device which should be responsible for different facets of QoS differs. Router vendors strictly suggest that the router is the right place for dealing with QoS requirements while some non-router vendors claim that the DSU/CSU should handle it.

They claim that the router is responsible for sending traffic on the best route through the network, LAN or WAN, hence the router's job is to route, and all other functions are of secondary importance. Routers are cost-optimized for the function of routing. While it is true that you can activate additional network services in a router, it cannot support them without incurring a performance penalty on its primary function, which is to forward packets to their destination along the optimal network path.

Not all QoS techniques are appropriate for all network routers. Because edge routers and backbone routers in a network do not necessarily perform the same operations, the QoS tasks they perform might differ as well. To configure an IP network for realtime voice traffic, for example, you would need to consider the functions of both edge and backbone routers in the network, then select the appropriate QoS feature or features.

In general, **edge routers** perform the following QoS functions:

- packet classification;
- admission control;
- configuration management.

In general, **backbone routers** perform the following QoS functions:

- congestion management;
- congestion avoidance.

Finally, before going into the detail of QoS mechanisms and protocols, it is worth summarizing what implementing QoS in the network promotes:

- **control over resources** – network owners have control over which resources (bandwidth, equipment, wide-area facilities) are being used (and may make easy any changes for the provision of more preferable services by their prioritization within the overall network traffic);

- **tailored services** – for ISPs, the control and visibility provided by QoS enables them to offer carefully tailored grades of service differentiation to their customers;
- **coexistence of mission-critical applications** – ensures that bandwidth and minimum delays required by time-sensitive multimedia and voice applications are available and that other applications using the link get their fair service without interfering with mission-critical traffic.

14.3 Resource reservation protocol

The **Resource Reservation Protocol** (RSVP) is a **signaling protocol** (part of the IETF **integrated services architecture**, ISA), that provides reservation setup and control to enable the **integrated services** (IntServ), intended to provide the closest thing to circuit emulation on IP networks. RSVP works with both unicast and multicast applications. It is a signaling protocol not a routing protocol; instead it uses its parameters and information. It must be supported by routers and switches in the internet. The dependence on the routing protocol is more visible in complex topologies and in the case of asymmetric or policy-based routing. RSVP supports both IPv4 and IPv6. However, RSVP does not allow IP fragmentation and supports datagram length only up to the minimum MTU on the path.

> **SNAPSHOT**   **RSVP defined**
>
> Resource reSerVation Protocol (RSVP) is a **setup protocol** designed for an Integrated Services Internet, to reserve network resources for a path, and a **signaling mechanism** for managing an application traffic's QoS in a Differentiated Service network. Although typically used on a per-flow basis, RSVP is also used to reserve resources for aggregates.

The need for network resource reservations differs as follows for **data traffic** versus **realtime traffic**:

- **Data traffic** seldom needs reserved bandwidth (resource guarantees) since internetworks provide datagram services for data traffic. This asynchronous packet switching does not need guarantees of service quality. Routers can operate in a first-in, first out (FIFO) manner for data traffic packets. End-to-end control between data traffic senders and receivers helps ensure adequate transmission of bursts of information.
- **Realtime traffic** (voice or video) experiences problems when operating over datagram services. Since realtime traffic involves an almost constant flow of information being sent and received, the network pipes must be consistent. Some guarantee must be provided that service between realtime hosts will not vary. Routers operating on a FIFO basis risk unrecoverable disruption of the realtime information that is being transmitted.

Realtime traffic (unlike data traffic) requires a **guaranteed network consistency**. Without consistent QoS, realtime traffic faces the following problems we mentioned among the QoS measures above:

- **jitter** – a slight time or phase movement in a transmission signal can introduce loss of synchronization or other errors;
- **insufficient bandwidth** – voice calls use a digital signal level 0 (DS0 at 64 kbps); video conferencing uses T1/E1; higher-fidelity video uses much more;
- **delay variations** – if the wait time between when signal elements are sent and when they arrive varies, the realtime traffic will no longer be synchronized and may fail;
- **information loss** – when signal elements drop or arrive too late, lost audio causes distortions with noise or crackle sounds. The lost video causes image blurring, distortions, or blackouts.

RSVP mechanisms enable realtime traffic to reserve the resources necessary for consistent latency. A video conferencing application can use settings in the router to propagate a request for a path with the required bandwidth and delay for video conferencing destinations. RSVP will check and repeat the reservations at regular intervals. By this process, RSVP can adjust and alter the path between RSVP end-systems to recover from router changes.

RFC WATCH   **RSVP**

RFC 2205 **Resource ReSerVation Protocol (RSVP) – Version 1 Functional Specification**, 1997 (Proposed Standard)

RFC 2206 **RSVP Management Information Base using SMIv2**, 1997 (Proposed Standard)

RFC 2207 **RSVP Extensions for IPSEC Data Flows**, 1997 (Proposed Standard)

RFC 2208 **Resource ReSerVation Protocol (RSVP) – Version 1 Applicability Statement Some Guidelines on Deployment**, 1997 (Informational)

RFC 2209 **Resource ReSerVation Protocol (RSVP) – Version 1 Message Processing Rules**, 1997 (Informational)

RFC 2379 **RSVP over ATM Implementation Guidelines**, 1998 (Best Current Practice)

RFC 2380 **RSVP over ATM Implementation Requirements**, 1998 (Proposed Standard)

RFC 2746 **RSVP Operation Over IP Tunnels**, 2000 (Proposed Standard)

RFC 2747 **RSVP Cryptographic Authentication**, 2000 (Proposed Standard)

RFC 2750 **RSVP Extensions for Policy Control**, 2000 (Proposed Standard)

RFC 2752 **Identity Representation for RSVP**, 2000 (Proposed Standard)

14.3.1 RSVP operation

RSVP mandates that a resource reservation be initiated by the receiver rather than by the sender. While the sender knows the properties of the traffic stream it is transmitting, sender-initiated reservation scales poorly for large, dynamic multicast delivery trees and for heterogeneous receivers. **Receiver-initiated reservation** deals with this by having each receiver request a reservation appropriate to itself; differences among heterogeneous receivers are resolved within the network by RSVP.

QUICK TIP	characteristics of the RSVP mechanism

- Reservations are **receiver-based**, in order to efficiently accommodate large heterogeneous (multicast) receiver groups.

- Reservations in each router are 'soft,' which means they need to be **refreshed periodically** by the receiver(s).

- RSVP is neither a transport, nor routing protocol, but an application (session, from OSI perspective) protocol instead. As such, it does not carry data, but works in parallel with TCP or UDP data flows; it does not find the path through the network, but works alongside the routing protocol.

- Applications require **APIs** to specify the flow requirements, initiate the reservation request, and receive notification of reservation success or failure after the initial request and throughout a session. To be useful, these APIs also need to include RSVP error information to describe a failure during reservation setup or anytime thereafter during the lifetime of a reservation as conditions change.

- Although RSVP traffic can traverse non-RSVP routers, this creates a weak link in the QoS chain where the service falls back to best effort (i.e. there is no resource allocation across these links).

After learning the sender's flow specifications via a higher level out-of-band mechanism, the **receiver** generates its own desired flow specification and propagates it to the senders, making reservations in each router along the way. The first **RSVP router** that receives the request informs the requesting host whether the requested resources are available or not. Interaction between an RSVP capable node and an RSVP capable router is shown in Figure 14.2. Note that the admission control module is present in both host and router; however, they look after different resources. A router's task is to control admission to network resources, while the host performs a control only over its own internal resources. The packet classifier and packet scheduler modules on every node are responsible for the QoS given to a flow for which a reservation has been made. The classifier looks at every data packet to determine whether the appropriate flow has a reservation and which QoS the flow should get.

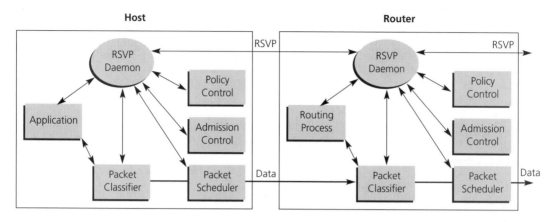

FIGURE 14-2   Interaction between an RSVP capable node and an RSVP capable router

Flows are identified in one of several formats. The simplest format contains the sender IP address and sender port together with the destination address and port. In this case, the **classifier** has to look at the IP and UDP/TCP headers. The **packet scheduler** then makes the forwarding decision according to the QoS class. For example, the packet scheduler decides in which queue to put the packet. The packet scheduler is a key component of the architecture because it actually gives different services to different flows. To ensure that flows receive their requested QoS, the packet schedulers on all nodes must support the distinction between different services.

The **resource reservation request** is forwarded to the next router, towards the sender of a traffic stream. If the reservations – hop by hop – are successful, an end-to-end pipeline of resources is available for the application to obtain the required quality of service. The reservation is valid for **one-way traffic** only. If reservation is required for both end-to-end directions, then two independent reservation processes must be involved.

RSVP uses a connectionless approach to multicast distribution. The reservation state is cached in the router and **periodically refreshed** by the end station. If the route changes, these refresh messages automatically install the necessary state along the new route. This approach was chosen for the simplicity and robustness associated with IP and other connectionless protocols.

The major advantage of RSVP is the ability to reject calls that would, if admitted, receive unacceptable QoS and also degrade the QoS of other calls in progress. For example, in the case of voice over IP (VoIP) in the event of the call rejection, the VoIP gateway may opt to reroute the call over an alternative path, while the previously established calls proceed without interruption. This capability is the result of RSVP sending messages along the path that VoIP packets will travel if the call proceeds, so that it is able to accurately determine the resource availability along the path, no matter how many gateways are deployed or how complex the topology is.

RSVP messages

There are two types of **messages** involved in RSVP, *RESV* and *PATH*:

- *RESV* (Reserve) **message** – request for reservation, or its modification, or cancel. To make a resource reservation for a particular communication across the network, the receiver sends a *RESV* (reservation request) message upstream. In addition to the *traffic specification (TSpec)*, the **RESV message** includes a *request specification (Rspec)* that indicates the type of Integrated Services required (either Controlled Load or Guaranteed – see below) and a *filter specification (filter spec)* that characterizes the packets for which the reservation is being made (e.g. the transport protocol and port number). Together, the *RSpec* and *filter spec* represent a **flow-descriptor** that routers use to identify each reservation (a flow or a session).

  When each **RSVP router** along the upstream path receives the RESV message, it uses the admission control process to **authenticate the request** and **allocate the necessary resources**. If the request cannot be satisfied (due to lack of resources or authorization failure), the router returns an error back to the receiver. If accepted, the router sends the *RESV* upstream to the next router. When the last router – either closest to the sender or at a reservation merge point for multicast flows – receives the *RESV* and accepts the request, it sends a confirmation message back to the receiver.

- *PATH* **message** – contains information from sender or intermediate router, including the possible reservation parameters, acknowledgment of the reservation request or its refusal, a request for reservation refreshment, and error messages. Senders characterize outgoing traffic in terms of the upper and lower bounds of bandwidth, delay, and jitter. RSVP sends a *PATH* **message** from the sender that contains this *traffic specification (TSpec)* information to the (unicast or multicast receiver(s)) destination address. Each RSVP-enabled router along the downstream route establishes a **path-state** that includes the previous source address of the *PATH* message (i.e. the next hop upstream towards the sender).

RFC 2961 describes a number of mechanisms that can be used to reduce the processing overhead requirements of refresh messages, eliminate the state synchronization latency incurred when an RSVP message is lost and, when desired, refresh state without the transmission of whole refresh messages. The same extensions also support reliable RSVP message delivery on a per hop basis. These extensions present no backwards compatibility issues.

RFC 2747 assigns RSVP Message Type 12 to an Integrity Response message, while RFC 2961 assigns the same value to a Bundle message. Recently released RFC 3097 resolves the conflict over RSVP Message Type 12 by assigning a different value to the Message Type of the Integrity Response Message in RFC 2747. Message Types defined in the RSVP Integrity extension (RFC 2747) are changed by RFC 3097 as follows: *Challenge message* has Message Type 25, and *Integrity Response message* has Message Type 25+1.

RFC WATCH **RSVP Refresh Overhead Reduction Extensions**

RFC 2961 **RSVP Refresh Overhead Reduction Extensions**, 2001 (Proposed Standard)

RFC 3097 **RSVP Cryptographic Authentication – Updated Message Type Value**, 2001 (Proposed Standard)

There are three possibilities for specifying the **data flow – filter specification**:

■ **wildcard filter** (WF) – reservation for concrete receiver from any sender (identified by unicast receiver IP address and port number, or multicast address);

■ **shared – explicit filter** (SE) – reservation for concrete receiver and group of senders;

■ **fixed filter** (FF) – reservation for unique receiver–sender pair.

QUICK TIP **Filter spec**

Part of the RSVP (Resource Reservation Protocol) that is used by senders in a PATH message to identify themselves, and by recipients in RESV messages to select which senders they are interested in receiving messages from.

There are several reservation models proposed, **control-load** (priority, RFC 2211) and **guaranteed service** (RFC 2212):

■ **Guaranteed** (quantitative QoS, reserved bandwidth) – emulating a dedicated virtual circuit. It provides firm (mathematically provable) bounds on end-to-end queuing delays by combining the parameters from the various network elements in a path, in addition to ensuring bandwidth availability according to the *TSpec* parameters (IntServ Guaranteed).

■ **Controlled load** – equivalent to best-effort service under unloaded conditions. Hence, it is 'better than best-effort,' but cannot provide the strictly bounded service that Guaranteed service promises (IntServ Controlled).

Token-bucket model

A **token-bucket** is designed to smooth the flow of outgoing traffic, but unlike a leaky-bucket model used for example in ATM (which also smoothes the outflow), the token-bucket model allows for data bursts (higher send rates that last for short periods). The token-bucket parameters – bucket rate, bucket depth, and peak rate – are part of the RSVP *TSpec* and *RSpec* (and used by IntServ to

QUICK TIP	leaky and token buckets

Leaky bucket – a traffic-shaping mechanism in which only a fixed amount of traffic is admitted to the network. The traffic is 'leaked' into the network. Excess traffic is held in a queue until either it can be accommodated or must be discarded.

Token bucket – a traffic-shaping mechanism in which a predetermined amount of tokens in a bucket represent the capacity allowed to each class of traffic. Packets are forwarded until they exhaust their supply of tokens. When the token supply is exhausted, packets may be discarded or delayed until the bucket is replenished. This controls the transmit rate and accommodates bursty traffic. In some systems, a customer's token supply might correspond to a service fee.

characterize its input/output queuing algorithm). The token-bucket algorithm used is more effective for regulating the long-term average transmission rate while handling bursts of traffic.

The following lists the **parameter descriptions** (for both Guaranteed and Controlled Load service, non-conforming – out-of-spec – traffic is treated like non-QoS, i.e. best-effort traffic):

■ **Token rate (r)** – the continually sustainable bandwidth (bps) requirements for a flow. This reflects the **average data rate into the bucket**, and the **target shaped data rate out of the bucket**.

■ **Token-bucket depth (b)** – the extent to which the data rate can exceed the sustainable average for short periods of time. More precisely, the amount of data sent cannot exceed $rT + b$ (where T is any time period).

■ **Minimum policed size (m)** – the length of the smallest packet (data payload only) generated by the sending application. This is not an absolute number, but in cases where the percentage of small packets is small, this number should be increased to reduce the overhead estimate for this flow (which can affect reservation acceptance). All packets smaller than m are treated as size m and policed accordingly.

■ **Maximum packet size (M)** – the biggest packet (in bytes). This number should be considered an absolute, since any packets of larger size are considered out of spec and may not receive QoS-controlled service as a result.

■ **Peak rate (p)** – maximum send rate (bps) if known and controlled, or a positive infinity if not known. For all time periods (T), the amount of data sent cannot exceed $M + pT$.

RSVP is implemented today on both switches and routers. RSVP can work closely with mechanisms deployed in IntServ (discussed later), such as **Random Early Detect** (RED) to maintain the end-to-end QoS during peak traffic loads. **Weighted Random Early Detect** (WRED) provides preferential treatment for appropriate RSVP flows in the network backbone during periods of congestion and is used in conjunction with queuing mechanisms.

We will discuss the RED mechanism later but it is worth noting that without such a mechanism, when the queue on the router fills up, all packets that arrive are dropped (tail drop). With RED, as opposed to doing a tail drop, the router monitors the average queue size and uses randomization to choose connections to notify that a congestion is impending.

There is an extension to WRED – **Flow Weighted Random Early Detect** – which penalizes flows that do not respond to drops (e.g. UDP), while adaptive flows get a fair share of resources. Flow-WRED ensures that no single flow can monopolize all the buffer resources.

14.3.2 SBM – subnet bandwidth management

QoS assurances are only as good as their weakest link. The QoS chain is end-to-end between sender and receiver, which means every router along the route must have support for the QoS technology in use, as we have described with the previous QoS protocols. The QoS chain from top to bottom is also an important consideration, however, in two respects.

Sender and receiver hosts must enable QoS so that applications can enable it explicitly or the system can enable it implicitly on behalf of the applications. Each layer below the application must also support QoS to assure that high-priority send and receive requests receive high-priority treatment from the host's network system.

The Local Area Network (LAN) must enable QoS so that high-priority frames receive high-priority treatment as they traverse the network media (e.g. host-to-host, host-to-router, and router-to-router). LANs are Layer 2 services, whereas other QoS technologies described are Layer 3 (DiffServ) or above (RSVP).

Some Layer 2 technologies have always been QoS-enabled, such as Asynchronous Transfer Mode (ATM). However, other more common LAN technologies such as Ethernet were not originally designed to be QoS-capable. As a shared broadcast medium or even in its switched form, Ethernet provides a service analogous to standard best-effort IP Service, in which variable delays can affect realtime applications.

SNAPSHOT **RSVP for Ethernet LANs: Subnet Bandwidth Manager (SBM)**

- Enables categorization and prioritization at Layer 2 on shared and switched LANs.
- RSVP in switch or router controlling LAN segment.
- Controls rate promises made on a shared/switched LAN DSBM (designated SBM).
- Works with IEEE 802.1p.
- DSBM does admission control for segment bandwidth.

The IEEE 802.1p, 802.1Q, and 802.1D standards (discussed in Parts II and III) define how Ethernet switches can classify frames in order to expedite delivery of time-critical traffic. The IETF Integrated Services over Specific Link Layers (ISSLL) Working Group is chartered to define the mapping between upper-layer QoS protocols and services with those of Layer 2 technologies like Ethernet.

RFC WATCH   **SBM**

RFC 2814 **SBM (Subnet Bandwidth Manager): A Protocol for RSVP-based Admission Control over IEEE 802-style Networks**, 2000 (Proposed Standard)

Among other things, this has resulted in the development of the **Subnet Bandwidth Manager** (SBM) for shared or switched 802 LANs such as Ethernet, FDDI, and Token Ring. SBM is a **signaling protocol** that allows communication and coordination between network nodes and switches in the SBM framework and enables mapping to higher-layer QoS protocols. A fundamental requirement in the SBM framework is that all traffic must pass through at least one SBM-enabled switch. Aside from the QoS-enabled application and Layer 2, the primary (logical) components of the SBM system are as follows:

- **Bandwidth Allocator (BA)** – maintains state about allocation of resources on the subnet and performs admission control according to the resources available and other administrator-defined policy criteria (see Figure 14.3 showing two forms of SBM with distributed and centralized bandwidth allocator).
- **Requestor Module (RM)** – resides in every end station, not in any switches. The RM maps between Layer 2 priority levels and the higher-layer QoS protocol parameters according to the administrator-defined policy. For example, if used with RSVP it could perform mapping based on the type of QoS (guaranteed or controlled load) or specific *Tspec, Rspec,* or *Filter-spec* values. The location of the BA determines the type of SBM architecture in use: centralized or distributed. Whether there is only one or more than one BA per network segment, only one is the **Designated SBM** (DSBM).

QUICK TIP   **Designated Subnet Bandwidth Manager (DSBM)**

A device on a managed subnetwork that acts as the Subnet Bandwidth Manager for the subnetwork to which it is attached. This is done through an election process specified in the IETF SBM protocol specification.

FIGURE 14-3 Forms of subnet bandwidth manager – centralized and distributed bandwidth allocator (centralized BA must know LAN topology)

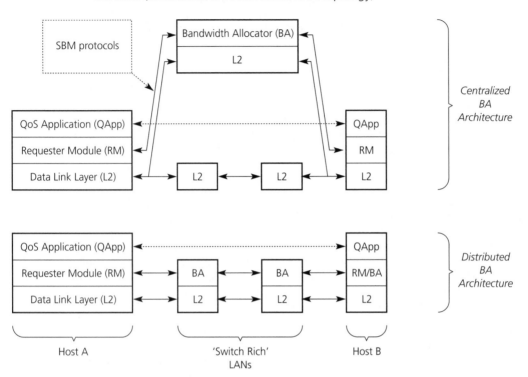

The SBM protocol provides an RM-to-BA or BA-to-BA signaling mechanism for initiating reservations, querying a BA about available resources, and changing or deleting reservations. The SBM protocol is also used between the QoS-enabled application (or its third-party agent) and the RM, but this involves the use of a programming interface (API) rather than the protocol, so it simply shares the functional primitives.

A simple summary of the **admission control procedure** of the SBM protocol follows:

1 **Designated Subnet Bandwidth Manager** (DSBM) initializes: gets resource limits.

2 **DSBM Client** (any RSVP-capable host or router) looks for the DSBM on the segment attached to each interface (done by monitoring the *AllSBMAddress*, the reserved IP multicast address 224.0.0.17).

3 When sending a *PATH* message, a DSBM client sends it to the *DSBMLogicalAddress* (reserved IP Multicast address, 224.0.0.16) rather than to the destination RSVP address.

4 Upon receiving a *PATH* message, a DSBM establishes the PATH state in the switch, stores the Layer 2 and Layer 3 addresses from which it came, and puts

its own Layer 2 and Layer 3 addresses in the message. DSBM then forwards the PATH message to the next hop (which may be another DSBM on the next network segment).

5 When sending an RSVP *RESV* message, a host sends it to the first hop (as always), which would be the DSBM(s) in this case (taken from the PATH message).

6 DSBM evaluates the request and if sufficient resources are available, forwards to the next hop (else returns an error).

The above scenario looks very much like standard RSVP processing in a router; however, some details were omitted for the sake of simplicity. Additionally, there is the *TCLASS* object that either a sender or any DSBM can add to a RSVP *PATH* or *RESV* message. It contains a preferred 802.1p priority setting and allows a default setting to be overridden, although any DSBM may change the value after receiving it. Routers must save the *TCLASS* in the *PATH* or *RESV* state, and remove it from the message to avoid forwarding it on the outgoing interface, but then they must put it back into incoming messages.

IEEE 802.1p uses a three-bit value (part of an 802.1Q header) which can represent an eight-level **priority value**. The default service-to-value mappings defined in **SBM mapping** are as follows:

- Priority 0: Default, assumed to be best-effort service.
- Priority 1: Reserved, 'less-than' best-effort service.
- Priority 2–3: Reserved.
- Priority 4: Delay Sensitive, no bound.
- Priority 5: Delay Sensitive, 100 ms bound.
- Priority 6: Delay Sensitive, 10 ms bound.
- Priority 7: Network Control.

The flexibility that mapping provides allows for a wide variety of possibilities capable of supporting a wide range of QoS assurances and granularity.

14.4 Integrated services

Integrated Services (IntServ) is a multiple service model that can accommodate multiple QoS requirements. In this model the application requests a specific kind of service from the network before sending data. The request is made by explicit signaling: the application informs the network of its traffic profile and requests a particular kind of service that can encompass its bandwidth and delay requirements. The application is expected to send data only after it gets a confirmation from the network. It is also expected to send data that lies within its described traffic profile. The network performs admission control, based on information from the application and available network resources. It also commits to meeting the QoS requirements of the application as long as the traffic remains within the profile specifications. The network fulfills its commitment by maintaining per-flow state and then performing packet classification, policing, and intelligent queuing based on that state.

The term **integrated services** refers to an overall QoS architecture that was produced by an IETF working group in the mid-1990s. In a closely related effort, another working group created RSVP, a signaling protocol that can be used within the IntServ architecture but is not a required part of it.

RFC WATCH   IntServ

RFC 2210 **The Use of RSVP with IETF Integrated Services**, 1997 (Proposed Standard)

RFC 2211 **Specification of the Controlled-Load Network Element Service**, 1997 (Proposed Standard)

RFC 2212 **Specification of Guaranteed Quality of Service**, 1997 (Proposed Standard)

RFC 2998 **A Framework for Integrated Services Operation over Diffserv Networks**, 2000 (Informational)

RFC 3006 **Integrated Services in the Presence of Compressible Flows**, 2000 (Proposed Standard)

There are two major components of the Integrated Services architecture: **signaling** and **admission control** (accomplished by RSVP). Other components of the architecture include **packet classification**, **policing**, **and scheduling**.

The IntServ router performs **admission control** and **resource allocation** based on the information contained in an RSVP *TSpec* (among other things). As currently defined, *TSpecs* convey information about the data rate (using a token bucket explained above), and range of packet sizes of the flow in question. However, the *TSpec* may not be an accurate representation of the resources needed to support the reservation if the router is able to compress the data at the link level. RFC 3006 describes an extension to the *TSpec* which enables a sender of potentially compressible data to provide hints to IntServ routers about the compressibility they may obtain. Routers which support appropriate compression take advantage of the hint in their admission control decisions and resource allocation procedures; other routers ignore the hint. An initial application of this approach is to notify routers performing Real-time Transport Protocol (RTP) header compression that they may allocate fewer resources to RTP flows.

Packet classification is the process of identifying packets that belong to **flows** for which reservations have been made, so that they can receive the appropriate QoS. IntServ classification may examine up to five fields in the packet: the source address, destination address, protocol number, source port, and destination port. Based on this information, packets can be given the appropriate policing and scheduling treatment.

Policing is the function applied to packets in a reserved flow to ensure that it conforms to the **traffic specification** (*TSpec*) that was used to make the reservation. If a flow does not conform because the source is sending more bytes per second than it advertised or for other reasons, then it is likely to interfere with the service provided to other flows, and corrective action is needed. Options include **dropping excess packets** or giving them a lower priority in the scheduler. Admission control takes place at call setup time to see if a reservation can be allowed, while policing is applied to each packet at forwarding time to ensure that the flow is behaving correctly.

The final IntServ part is **scheduling**. Many scheduling algorithms can be used to support IntServ. **Queuing** is one popular algorithm that can provide a guaranteed service rate to each reserved flow. One possibility is to place all the packets from reserved flows in a single high-priority queue to ensure that they are transmitted ahead of best-effort packets.

One important issue to note in any discussion of IntServ is the role of **policy.** RSVP-capable routers may use the **Common Open Policy Service** (COPS) protocol to obtain policy information from a centralized policy server. COPS extensions have also been developed for DiffServ environments.

14.4.1 Common open policy service

The IETF has developed the **Common Open Policy Service** (COPS) to provide a common way for policy servers to communicate with devices that apply priority to traffic. There are two versions: COPS for dynamic QoS and COPS for device provisioning (COPS-PR). COPS is defined in RFC 2748, and COPS-PR in RFC 3084.

SNAPSHOT   **Common Open Policy Service defined**

A simple query and response TCP-based protocol that can be used to exchange policy information between a **Policy Decision Point** (PDP) and its clients, Policy Enforcement Points (PEPs).

COPS is a **query/response protocol** that supports two common models for policy control:

- **Outsourcing model** – addresses the kind of events at the **Policy Enforcement Point** (PEP) that require an instantaneous policy decision (authorization). In the outsourcing scenario, the PEP delegates responsibility to an external policy server – **Policy Decision Point** (PDP) to make decisions on its behalf. For example, in COPS Usage for RSVP (RFC 2749) when an RSVP reservation message arrives, the PEP must decide whether to admit or reject the request. It can outsource this decision by sending a specific query to its PDP, waiting for its decision before admitting the outstanding reservation.

- **Provisioning model** (a.k.a. **configuration model**) – makes no assumptions of such direct 1:1 correlation between PEP events and PDP decisions. The PDP may proactively provision the PEP reacting to external events (such as user input), PEP events, and any combination thereof (N:M correlation). Provisioning may be performed in bulk (e.g. entire router QoS configuration) or in portions (e.g. updating a DiffServ marking filter).

Network resources are often provisioned based on relatively static SLAs (Service Level Agreements) at network boundaries. While the outsourcing model is dynamically paced by the PEP in realtime, the provisioning model is paced by the PDP in somewhat flexible timing over a wide range of configurable aspects of the PEP.

RFC 3084 describes the use of the COPS protocol for support of policy provisioning. This specification is independent of the type of policy being provisioned (QoS, security, etc.). Rather, it focuses on the mechanisms and conventions used to communicate provisioned information between PDPs and PEPs. The data model assumed is based on the concept of **Policy Information Bases** (PIBs) that define the policy data. There may be one or more PIBs for a given area of policy and different areas of policy may have different sets of PIBs.

In COPS-PR, policy requests describe the PEP and its configurable parameters (rather than an operational event). If a change occurs in these basic parameters, an updated request is sent. Hence, requests are issued quite infrequently. Decisions are not necessarily mapped directly to requests, and are issued mostly when the PDP responds to external events or PDP events (policy/SLA updates).

COPS-PR has been designed within a framework that is optimized for efficiently provisioning policies across devices: it allows for efficient transport of attributes, large atomic transactions of data, and efficient and flexible error reporting. Second, as it has a single connection between the policy client and server per area of policy control identified by a COPS *Client-Type*, it guarantees only one server updates a particular policy configuration at any given time. Such a policy configuration is effectively locked, even from local console configuration, while the PEP is connected to a PDP via COPS. COPS uses reliable TCP transport and, thus, uses a state sharing/synchronization mechanism and exchanges differential updates only. If either the server or client are rebooted (or restarted) the other would know about it quickly. Last, it is defined as a realtime event-driven communications mechanism, never requiring polling between the PEP and PDP.

RFC WATCH   COPS

RFC 2748 **The COPS (Common Open Policy Service) Protocol**, 2000 (Proposed Standard)

RFC 2749 **COPS usage for RSVP**, 2000 (Proposed Standard)

RFC 2753 **A Framework for Policy-based Admission Control**, 2000 (Informational)

RFC 3084 **COPS Usage for Policy Provisioning** (COPS-PR), 2001 (Proposed Standard)

Policy

The requirements and the rules for allocation of system resources, **policies**, are decided in advance. The objective is to specify a service in unequivocal terms and to allocate the resources required to deliver that service. Policy information is stored in a **policy server** from where it is shared with other network devices using COPS. The rules follow an **if, what, when, then** logic. As an example, a sequence of events could be:

- **if** – the user belongs to the computer-aided design group # 003 and
- **what** – the application is the design of a rocket engine and
- **when** – the time is between 0800 and 1400 hours on Monday through Friday
- **then** – the user is entitled to a **service level**, S, that gives a throughput of X kbps with an end-to-end latency of no more than Y ms.

The service level could also specify other parameters, such as constant-bit-rate service. Once a user has put such a policy in place, it becomes easier for the client's network administrator to configure and adapt the system to the company's changing circumstances.

The three principal elements of such a **policy-based traffic management** system are: **policy creation and storage, interpretation, and enforcement**. When a data packet arrives at the input port of the enforcement device, the device first determines the classification of the data by some predefined criteria. Then, using the COPS protocol and the simple network management protocol (SNMP), it checks with the policy interpreter as to the QoS to which the packet is entitled. The policy interpreter, in its turn, verifies the status of the data by pulling the policy rules using the Lightweight Directory Access Protocol (LDAP), a protocol commonly used for exchanging information among directory databases.

With the help of the information thus retrieved, the interpreter determines the rights of that particular data packet. On receipt of information on these rights, the enforcement device sends the packet, properly tagged, onward to a router. If the same type of data, such as a request to a specific Web site, is found to be repeating often, the rules could be temporarily cached in the enforcement device itself.

SNAPSHOT	**Classes and policies**

Classes allow traffic types with common QoS requirements to be grouped together.

Policies define what QoS each class will get.

14.5 Differentiated services

Differentiated Services (DiffServ) evolved from integrated services (IntServ), the IETF service classification standard that relies on RSVP to set up and tear down resource reservations along the intended path of a flow of packets. But DiffServ effectively eliminates the need to use RSVP across the wide area.

DiffServ is a generic lightweight QoS architecture: a limited number of simple components are defined, and it is generic in the sense that the limited set of architectural components can be combined in a large number of ways to get a specific behavior.

As a QoS architecture, DiffServ offers a predictable expectation which is better than best effort but softer than IntServ. DiffServ is not a service by itself. DiffServ is a generic framework for defining new services. By combining the architectural components in specific ways, a large number of services can be defined.

SNAPSHOT   **Differentiated Services (DiffServ):**

Provides a coarse and simple way to categorize and prioritize network traffic **flow** aggregates. It is based on the IP header field, called the DS-field. In IPv4, it defines the layout of the ToS (Type of Service) octet; in IPv6, it is the traffic class octet. Differentiated Services is also an 'area of use' for QoS policies. It requires policy to define the correspondence between codepoints in the packet's DS-field and individual per-hop behaviors (to achieve a specified per-domain behavior).

DiffServ operates strictly at Layer 3 – it can run without modification on any Layer 2 infrastructure that supports IP, and it makes no assumptions about the underlying transport. DiffServ relies on traffic conditioners sitting at the edge of the network to indicate each packet's requirements, and capability can be added via incremental firmware or software upgrades.

Like RSVP, DiffServ expects advance reservation to have occurred at intermediate nodes. It also relies on the same type of fundamental buffer, queue, and scheduling reservations at intermediate nodes, but it uses simple markings in each packet that routers can examine without reference to session lookups. Routing determinations can thus be made on a per-packet rather than a per-session basis.

QoS will be assured for a range of service classes by combining admission control functions, such as traffic policing (dropping traffic in excess of allowable levels), and core functions, such as provisioning (supplying needed bandwidth).

Traffic conditioners will mark packets; they sit at the boundaries of the network, where unclassified traffic meets DiffServ-capable devices, and make use of primitives, or policy sets, against which they evaluate all traffic. Primitives outlined in the current DiffServ draft include classification, policing, marking, and shaping. **Classification primitives** let the traffic conditioner steer packets marked with the same DS byte to the same queues for transmission. **Policing primitives** will let the traffic conditioner monitor the behavior of packets it receives and mark or drop them according to the behavioral requirements set for the packet. **Marking primitives** will let the traffic conditioner set the DS byte to a particular bit pattern and add marked packets to a stream of packets slated for a specified service. **Shaping primitives** will let a traffic conditioner enforce conformance to preconfigured traffic properties by smoothing burst rates and reallocating buffer space.

Ultimately, DiffServ-capable routers will store information to control how packets are scheduled onto an output interface. This interface may have queues with different rates, queue lengths, round-robin weights, drop preference weights, and other thresholds. There is no requirement that different IP networks use the same router mechanisms or service configurations.

Unlike in case of IntServ, which provides a well-defined, end-to-end service between hosts for both point-to-point and point-to-multipoint applications, the objective of DiffServ is not to provide an end-to-end service for the host/application. Rather, the goal is to create a set of building blocks that provide a foundation for building end-to-end services throughout the network. DiffServ takes an approach similar to IPv4 Type of Service (ToS) but is better targeted to meet the needs of today's applications. DiffServ is sufficiently scalable that it can be supported in routers at the core of the Internet since it avoids per-session states. Instead, each packet carries information about the service class.

The simplicity of DiffServ to prioritize traffic belies its flexibility and power. When DiffServ uses RSVP parameters or specific application types to identify and classify constant-bit-rate (CBR) traffic, it will be possible to establish well-defined aggregate flows that may be directed to fixed bandwidth pipes. As a result, resources could be shared efficiently and still provide guaranteed service.

Differentiated services code points

Unlike the integrated service model, an application using differentiated service does not explicitly signal the router before sending data. For differentiated service, the network tries to deliver a particular kind of service based on the QoS specified by each packet. The IETF has decided to take the **Type of Service** (ToS) byte from the IP header, which has not been widely used in an original way, and redefine it (RFC 2474) into a DS byte. Six bits of this byte (providing for a total of eight classes of service) have been allocated for **Differentiated Services Code Points** (DSCPs). Each DSCP is thus a six-bit value that identifies a particular behavior to be applied in each node to a packet. The other two bits are for **Explicit Congestion Notification** (ECN). Traffic might be identified by one or more DSCPs. Traffic without a DSCP identifier requires another classifier to be used.

The node at the ingress edge of the DiffServ domain must ensure that the DS field is set appropriately in each packet. This is just part of the role of **traffic conditioning**. Since the behavior definition can specify the admissible traffic profiles, the ingress node of the DiffServ domain actually provides more functions than simply marking the DS byte. All of the functions that are combined in the role of traffic conditioning are then examined in turn. Since the bearer service class is dependent on the individual Service Level Agreement (SLA), the traffic conditioning is performed independently for each logical access.

DiffServ assumes the existence of an SLA between networks that share a border. The SLA establishes the policy criteria, and defines the traffic profile. It is expected that traffic will be policed and smoothed at egress points according to the SLA, and any traffic 'out of profile' (i.e. above the upper-bounds of bandwidth usage stated in the SLA) at an ingress point have no guarantees (or may incur extra costs, according to the SLA). The policy criteria used can include time of day, source and destination addresses, transport, and/or port numbers (i.e. applications). Basically, any context or traffic content (including headers or data) can be used to apply policy.

The structure of the original IPv4 ToS octet in a datagram is depicted in Figure 14.4 and has the following fields:

FIGURE 14-4 Classic ToS field in IPv4 datagram

Bits:

0	1	2	3	4	5	6	7
IP precedence			Type of service				0

- **Precedence Field** – the three leftmost bits in the ToS octet of an IPv4 header. Note that in DiffServ, these three bits may or may not be used to denote the precedence of the IP packet. There is no precedence field in the traffic class octet in IPv6.
- **ToS Field** – bits 3–6 in the ToS octet of an IPv4 header (identifying delay, throughput, and reliability, discussed in Chapter 10 in Part IV, defined in RFC 1349, and made obsolete by DS definition RFC 2474).

SNAPSHOT **Codepoint**

Codepoint markings are made in a new implementation of the IPv4 Type of Service (ToS) header called the DiffServ (DS) field (six bits, reserving two for congestion notification) and are used to select a per hop behavior (PHB). This marking takes place on the host or on a boundary or edge device.

The ToS octet of an IPv4 header is renamed the ***Differentiated Services (DS) Field*** by DiffServ. The structure of the DS field is shown in Figure 14.5.

FIGURE 14-5 ToS field used for DiffServ as DS field

Bits:

0	1	2	3	4	5	6	7
Differentiated Services Codepoint (DSCP)						Currently unused	

The differentiated service model is used for several mission-critical applications and for providing end-to-end QoS. Typically, this service model is appropriate for aggregate flows because it performs a relatively coarse level of traffic classification.

RFC 1349 **Type of Service in the Internet Protocol Suite**, 1992 (made obsolete by RFC 2474)

RFC 1812 **Requirements for IP Version 4 Routers**, 1995 (Proposed Standard)

RFC 2474 **Definition of the Differentiated Services Field (DS Field) in the IPv4 and IPv6 Headers**, 1998 (Proposed Standard)

IntServ combined with DiffServ

The solution to a complex QoS problem seems to lie in combining the methods: solid QoS guarantees of Integrated Services (IntServ) with the scalable architecture of Differentiated Services (DiffServ). IntServ handles individual application flows, while DiffServ deals with large aggregates of traffic. The challenge is to extend IntServ QoS to deal with numerous traffic flows across DiffServ sections of the network.

QUICK TIP DiffServ vs. IntServ

DiffServ is a coarse-grained approach, providing QoS to aggregated traffic, while IntServ is a fine-grained approach that provides QoS to individual applications or flows.

The proposed solution to this problem is an **Aggregate RSVP**. The IETF is about to issue a standards-track RFC that will specify extensions to RSVP, the signaling protocol for IntServ QoS. Aggregate RSVP will make a single reservation on behalf of a large number of individual flows across a DiffServ network.

Integrated Services (IntServ) and **Differentiated Services** (DiffServ) are two approaches representing the endpoints of what can be seen as a continuum of control models, where the fine-grained precision of the per application invocation reservation model can be aggregated into larger, more general and potentially more approximate aggregate reservation states, and the end-to-end element-by-element reservation control can be progressively approximated by treating a collection of subnetworks or an entire transit network as an aggregate service element. There are a number of **work in progress** efforts which are directed towards these aggregated control models, including **aggregation of RSVP**, the **RSVP DCLASS Object** to allow Differentiated Services Code Points (DSCPs) to be carried in RSVP message objects, and the operation of **integrated services over differentiated services** networks.

RFC WATCH RSVP DCLASS

RFC 2996 **Format of the DCLASS Object**, 2000 (updates RFC 2205) (Proposed Standard)

RFC 3175 **Aggregation of RSVP for IPU4 and IPU6 Reservation,** 2001 (Proposed Standard)

14.5.1 Per hop behaviors

Differentiated Services introduces the notion of **Per Hop Behaviors** (PHBs) that define how traffic belonging to a particular behavior aggregate is treated at an individual network node. PHBs define the behavior of individual routers rather than end-to-end services. The packet treatment includes selection of the queue and scheduling discipline to apply at the egress interface and congestion thresholds.

QUICK TIP	Per Hop Behavior (PHB)

Per hop behavior is the forwarding treatment given to a specific class of traffic, based on criteria defined in the DiffServ field. Routers and switches use PHBs to determine priorities for servicing various traffic flows.

The packets are marked to identify the treatment that the packets must receive using the DS byte. There are only 64 possible DSCP values, but there is no such limit on the number of PHBs. In a given network domain, there is a locally defined mapping between DSCP values and PHBs. Standardized PHBs recommend a DSCP mapping, but network operators may choose alternative mappings.

The DiffServ model divides traffic into a small number of classes (see Figure 14.6). One way to deploy DiffServ is simply to divide traffic into two classes. Such an approach makes good sense. If you consider the difficulty that network operators experience just trying to keep a best-effort network running smoothly, it is logical to add QoS capabilities to the network in small increments.

Suppose that a network operator has decided to enhance a network by adding just one new service class, designated as premium. Clearly, the operator needs some way to distinguish premium (high-priority) packets from best-effort (lower-priority) packets. Setting a bit in the packet header as a one could indicate that the packet is a premium packet; if it is a zero, the packet receives best-effort treatment.

RFC WATCH	DiffServ and per hop behaviors

RFC 2475 **An Architecture for Differentiated Service**, 1998 (Informational)

RFC 2597 **Assured Forwarding PHB Group**, 1999 (Proposed Standard)

RFC 2598 **An Expedited Forwarding PHB**, 1999 (Proposed Standard)

RFC 3086 **Definition of Differentiated Services Per Domain Behaviors and Rules for their Specification**, 2001 (Informational)

RFC 3140 **Per Hop Behavior Identification Codes**, 2001 (Proposed Standard)

FIGURE 14-6 Creation of DiffServ classes on router

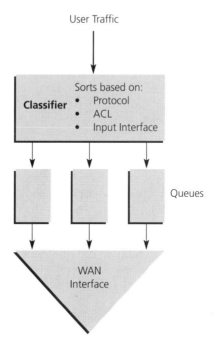

There are currently two specific **Per Hop Behaviors** (PHBs) and one default PHB defined that effectively represent two **service levels** (traffic classes):

■ **Expedited Forwarding** (EF) – specified in RFC 2598, EF has a single codepoint (DiffServ value). EF **minimizes delay, loss,** and **jitter** (useful for voice applications) and provides the highest level of aggregate quality of service. The dominant causes of **delay** in packet networks are fixed propagation delays (e.g. those arising from speed-of-light delays) on wide area links and queuing delays in switches and routers. Since propagation delays are a fixed property of the topology, delay and jitter are minimized when queuing delays are minimized. In this context, **jitter** is defined as the variation between maximum and minimum delay. The intent of the EF PHB is to provide a PHB in which suitably marked packets usually encounter short or empty queues. Furthermore, if queues remain short relative to the buffer space available, packet loss is also kept to a minimum.

Any traffic that exceeds the traffic profile (which is defined by local policy) is discarded. To provide the low delay, the EF handling further defines that the maximum aggregated reception rate of data for this PHB at any time must be no greater than the minimum transmission rate available for this PHB per egress. This requirement ensures that there is no queue buildup occurring for this service within the node (apart from synchronous data arrival compared to the packet transmission period), which minimizes the delay and the delay variation. The recommended codepoint for EF PHB is *101110* (Bis version of RFC 2598 for Expedited Forwarding is to become proposed standard at time of writing).

- **Assured Forwarding** (AF) – To manage packet discard in IP networks in such a way that service providers can deliver a CIR-like guarantee with their IP services, the IETF has designed the Assured Forwarding (AF) service (RFC 2597). AF defines n independent forwarding classes (four defined currently) denoted as $AF1$ to AFn. Within each of these forwarding classes, there are also M subclasses (3 defined currently) for probability of delivery. The higher level of delivery probability should have a greater probability than the second level of getting data through in times of congestion. Likewise, the second level should have a better probability for delivery than the third level. Each forwarding class within this group is configured independently for resources such as buffer space and minimum egress capacity that should be ensured by the scheduling mechanism.

  Within each AF class, an IP packet can be assigned one of three different levels of **drop precedence** to manage which traffic gets discarded in a congestion situation. Each AF class is allocated a certain amount of forwarding resources (buffer space and bandwidth), based on the service class to which a customer has subscribed. The idea is to make sure that each application gets the resources it requires to perform properly. Excess AF traffic is not delivered with as high probability as the traffic within profile, which means it may be demoted but not necessarily dropped. AF ensures the forwarding of packets at a guaranteed rate over IP networks. It is specified for IP networks that use TCP at Layer 4.

- **Best Effort** (BE) – default behavior. The definition of this behavior states that the node will deliver as many of these packets as possible, as soon as possible. As other defined behaviors have greater requirements for timeliness of delivery, the BE definition of 'as many as possible' and 'as soon as possible' allows deference to those other behaviors.

QUICK TIP   **per hop behaviors currently defined**

Expedited Forwarding (EF) – appropriate to voice/video and requires undersubscribed traffic classes, reservation of bandwidth, and policing.

Assured Forwarding (AF) – divides IP packets into four separate per-hop behavior (PHB) classes. Using these classes, a provider may offer different levels of service for IP packets received from a customer domain. Each Assured Forwarding class is allocated a specified amount of buffer space and bandwidth. AF is designed for TCP; drop controls trace effects back to sources, implemented using committed access rate, Random Early Detection, queuing.

Best Effort (BE) – default behavior

PHBs are applied by the conditioner to traffic at a network ingress point (network border entry) according to predetermined policy criteria. The traffic may be marked at this point, and routed according to the marking, then unmarked at the network egress (network border exit). Originating hosts can also apply the DiffServ marking, and there are a number of advantages in doing so. RFC 3140 defines a binary encoding to uniquely identify PHBs and/or sets of PHBs in protocol messages. This encoding must be used when such identification is required.

> **SNAPSHOT** **differentiated services framework**
>
> The differentiated services framework enables **quality-of-service provisioning within a network domain** by **applying rules at the edges** to create **traffic aggregates** and coupling each of these with a **specific forwarding path treatment in the domain** through use of a **codepoint** in the IP header.

Per-domain behavior

The DiffServ has focused on the forwarding path behavior required in routers, PHBs, and functionality required at DiffServ domain edges to select (classifiers) and condition (e.g. policing and shaping) traffic according to the rules. Short-term changes in the QoS goals for a DS domain are implemented by changing only the configuration of these edge behaviors without necessarily reconfiguring the behavior of interior network nodes.

The next step is to formulate examples of how forwarding path components (PHBs, classifiers, and traffic conditioners) can be used to compose traffic aggregates whose packets experience specific forwarding characteristics as they transit a differentiated services domain. **Per-domain behavior** (PDB) describes the behavior experienced by a particular set of packets as they cross a DS domain. A PDB is characterized by specific metrics that quantify the treatment a set of packets with a particular DSCP (or set of DSCPs) will receive as it crosses a DS domain. A PDB specifies a forwarding path treatment for a traffic aggregate and, due to the role those particular choices of edge and PHB configuration play in its resulting attributes, it is where the forwarding path and the control plane interact. The measurable parameters of a PDB should be suitable for use in service level specifications at the network edge. Per-domain behaviors are specified in detail in RFC 3086.

Behavior aggregates

DiffServ services are expected to be supported over various underlying technologies, or link layers. For the transport of IP packets, some of these link layers (such as ATM and MPLS) make use of connections or logical connections where the forwarding behavior supported by each link layer device is a property of the connection. In particular, within the link layer domain, each link layer node will schedule traffic depending on which connection the traffic is transported in.

For efficient support of DiffServ over these link layers, one model is for different **Behavior Aggregates** (BAs) (or sets of behavior aggregates, RFC 2597) to be transported over different connections so that they are granted different (and appropriate) forwarding behaviors inside the link layer cloud. When those connections are dynamically established for the transport of DiffServ traffic, it is very useful to communicate at connection establishment time what forwarding behavior(s) is (are) to be granted to each connection by the link layer device so that the BAs transported experience consistent forwarding behavior inside the link layer cloud. This can be achieved by including the encoding of the corresponding PHB, or set of PHBs, in the connection establishment signaling messages.

14.5.2 Traffic conditioning and network congestion

Consideration of the **behavior of congested systems** is not easy and cannot be dealt with in a simplistic manner, as traffic rates do not just rise to a level, stay there a while, then subside. Periods of traffic congestion can be quite long, with losses that are heavily concentrated. In contrast to Poisson traffic models, linear increases in buffer size do not result in large decreases in packet drop rates; a slight increase in the number of active connections can result in a large increase in the packet loss rate. This understanding of the behavior of congested networks suggests that because the level of busy period traffic is not predictable, it would be difficult to efficiently size networks to reduce congestion adequately. Observers of network congestion report that, in reality, traffic 'spikes,' which causes actual losses, ride on longer-term ripples, and they in turn ride on still longer-term swells.

There are two different sets of tools to deal with network congestion:

- **Congestion management tools** – operate to control congestion once it occurs. One way that network elements handle an overflow of arriving traffic is to use a queuing algorithm to sort the traffic, then determine some method of prioritizing it onto an output link (scheduling). Each queuing algorithm was designed to solve a specific network traffic problem and has a particular effect on network performance. Examples of congestion management techniques are First-In, First-Out (FIFO) queuing (provides basic store and forward capability), or Weighted Fair Queuing (WFQ).

- **Congestion avoidance tools** – monitor network traffic loads in an effort to anticipate and avoid congestion at common network and internetwork bottlenecks before it becomes a problem. These techniques are designed to provide **preferential treatment** for premium (priority) class traffic under congestion situations while concurrently maximizing network throughput and capacity utilization and minimizing packet loss and delay. An example of a congestion avoidance technique is Random Early Detection (RED), with many variants of RED now proposed such as **Weighted RED** (WRED), **Fair RED** (FRED), **RED with In-Out** (RIO), and **adaptive RED**.

Traffic conditioning functions within DiffServ are applied at the network edge (an example is shown in Figure 14.9 on page 790:

- classifying;
- metering;
- marking;

- shaping;
- dropping.

Mechanisms deployed for the individual functions under traffic conditioning are shown in Table 14.2.

TABLE 14-2 DiffServ traffic conditioning components and mechanisms

Traffic conditioner	Mechanism	Network effect
Policing	CAR (Committed Access Rate)	Enforce a maximum transmission rate Conform or exceed thresholds
Marking	CAR (Committed Access Rate), policy routing, DSCP (DiffServ),	Sets IP precedence/DSCP By application, protocol, address
Scheduling	Queuing (WFQ): LLQ (Low Latency Queuing), WRR (Weighted Round-Robin), MDRR (Modified Deficit Round-Robin)	Bandwidth management: traffic Set servicing sequence
Shaping	GTS (Generic Traffic Shaping), FRTS (Frame Relay Traffic Shaping)	Conforms traffic to committed bandwidth Interworks with Layer 2 notification (FECN)
Dropping	RED (Random Early Detect), WRED (Weighted RED), Flow RED	Avoids congestion by source notification Prioritizes which traffic is told to reduce

SNAPSHOT   **DiffServ traffic conditioning components plus PHB**

- **Conditioners** are located on the edges of the network, on inter-provider boundary points, and in fact at any point in the network where a customer–provider relationship exists. Conditioners can be very flexible and may be somewhat complex since conditioning happens only once in each cloud. The DiffServ architecture defines four kinds of conditioners:
  - *Markers* mark incoming packets with a set of information bits. For instance, a marker could mark packets as either IN-profile or OUT-of-profile. A priority

▶

marker can indicate a drop priority or a delay priority or a queuing priority, etc. In general, markers add information to each packet to influence the per-hop behavior.

– *Shapers* shape incoming packets to try and make them as much IN-profile as possible.

– *Policers* drop incoming packets according to some criterion.

– *Classifiers* select packets based on some portion of their packet header and steer packets matching some classifier rule to another traffic conditioner for further processing.

■ The **per hop behavior** (PHB) describes the behavior of the interior nodes in the network. Unlike conditioners, PHB implementations should be simple and efficient since each node must invoke the appropriate PHB for each packet.

Classifier

The data has to be classified for the PHB at the boundary of the DiffServ domain in a classifier function. The classification typically considers information from the IP header such as protocol, source and destination IP address, and source and destination port, although it can go even further into the protocol if required to identify an application. The classifier applies a filter to each packet. This filter defines the conditions that the IP header must match to be accepted. If the filter accepts the traffic, then the profile attached to that filter is applied to that traffic.

> **QUICK TIP**   **QoS traffic**
>
> *Classification can be generally based on:*
>
> ■ Layer 1 – physical port;
>
> ■ Layer 2 – MAC destination address in a VLAN and CoS based on 802.1Q/p;
>
> ■ Layer 3 – for TCP/IP networks it may use IP precedence (for differentiated services), IP source and destination addresses (filters), protocol number;
>
> ■ Layer 4 – a source and destination port number.

Classification is where the policy is defined and the routers informed how to recognize what traffic belongs to which class of service. This is typically done at the edges of a network, leaving the backbone or core to do more in the way of queuing and efficient routing. The classification might be based on the incoming interface (e.g. which customer of a service provider, which department of a company) or on the source or destination address, or other characteristics.

QoS Policy Propagation via BGP (QPPB) allows the classification of packets based on packet filters, BGP community lists, and BGP AS paths. The classification can then set either IP precedence (a global tagging scheme), or internal QoS group identifier (internal to the router). The BGP community can also contain both AS and IP precedence information. After classification, other QoS features such as CAR and WRED can then be used to enforce business policy.

This mechanism allows a policy to be set up at one BGP speaking router, and propagated to other routers via BGP. This means that at the service provider router connecting to a site, a policy can be set up so that inbound traffic elsewhere is classified into the right class of service (IP precedence bits). This can then interact with MPLS.

Committed Access Rate (CAR) as a mechanism for traffic policing and marking has two functions:

- **packet classification** – using IP precedence and QoS group setting;
- **access bandwidth management** – through rate limiting.

So CAR is basically the input side of traffic shaping. Traffic is sequentially classified using pattern matching specifications, or filters, on a first-match basis. The pattern matched specifies what action policy rule to use, based on whether the traffic conforms. That is, if traffic is within the specified rate, it conforms, and is treated one way. Non-conforming (excess) traffic can be treated differently, usually either by giving it lower priority or by dropping it. If no rule is matched, the default is to transmit the packet. This allows you to use rules to rate limit some traffic, and allow the rest to be transmitted without any rate controls.

The possible action policy rules are:

- transmit;
- drop;
- continue (go to next rate-limit rule on the list);
- set IP precedence bits and transmit;
- set IP precedence bits and continue;
- set QoS group and transmit;
- set QoS group and continue.

The **rate-limiting feature** of CAR provides the network operator with the means to define Layer 3 aggregate or granular access, or egress bandwidth rate limits, and to specify traffic handling policies when the traffic either conforms to or exceeds the specified rate limits. Aggregate access or egress matches all packets on an interface. Granular access or egress matches a particular type of traffic based on precedence. One can designate CAR rate-limiting policies based on physical port, packet classification, IP address, MAC address, application flow, and other criteria specifiable by filters. CAR rate limits may be implemented either on input or output interfaces including Frame Relay and ATM. An example of the use of CAR's rate-limiting capability is application-based rates limiting HTTP World Wide Web traffic to 50% of link bandwidth, which ensures capacity for non-Web traffic including mission-critical applications.

Meter

After the data has passed the classifier, it passes through a metering engine. The metering engine calculates the traffic level, which is compared against the customer 's contract/SLA profile. The traffic profile can include such aspects as the agreed average data rates, maximum data rate, and the maximum data burst at the maximum rate. The metering engine polices the traffic level for each service-class agreement and can take one of a number of actions if the level exceeds the agreed parameters. Note that service agreements may contain multiple clauses for different applications, so the meter may examine the same data in the IP header as the classifier.

Marker

When the data has been classified and the rate has been determined, the selected PHB is marked into the DS byte. The reason that the PHB is not marked directly from the classifier is that the PHB is dependent on the data rate. There are groups of related PHBs that can be applied to data that do not result in packet reordering. Although the timeliness of the delivery cannot be varied (because it would cause reordering), these groups of related PHBs provide different levels of delivery probability. The probability for delivery is dependent on the level of network congestion, and the various classes are impacted differently by that congestion. For example, traffic rates up to a first threshold would all be marked as class 1. Traffic making up the data rate between the first and second threshold would be marked as class 2, while traffic in excess of the second threshold would be marked as class 3. Under network congestion, traffic in class 3 is more likely to be discarded than traffic in class 2, which is likewise more likely to be discarded than traffic in class 1. The AF service classes have multiple levels of drop preference that can be used in this manner.

However, it is not until the data has passed the metering engine that the final PHB can be determined. Customers can choose to perform most of the traffic conditioning function in their own networks, rather than in the provider's network. However, the network must still verify the marking and shaping by the customer, and hence much of the same functionality is still required in the provider's network.

To summarize, the marker's task is to measure the rate of arriving or departing traffic and mark it with one or another DSCP based on conformance at a network edge with a simple classifier. An external shaper or policer is required, such as Weighted RED.

QUICK TIP   **marking traffic at edge**

A useful technique is to mark traffic at a network edge with a **simple classifier** and to allow all routers in a domain to use the mark. This allows the network to do the right thing without having to fully classify everywhere and to use more effective markings.

Scheduler

The node must decide how packets from different PHBs are to be scheduled out on the link. The scheduling mechanism may consider priority order between classes, but it must control access to the link bandwidth for each class. A strict priority mechanism between two or more classes aims to provide the lowest possible delay for the highest priority class. This mechanism sends the data from the highest priority class before sending data for the next class.

As it could lead to starvation of lower priority classes, the traffic level must be shaped to limit the used bandwidth. **Weighted Round-Robin** (WRR) aims to give a weighted access to the available bandwidth to each class, ensuring a minimum allocation and distribution. The scheduling services each class in a round-robin manner according to the weights. If one or more classes is not using its full allocation, then the unused capacity is distributed to the other classes according to their weighting. A class can be given a lower effective delay by giving it a higher weighting than the traffic level it is carrying.

Class-Based Queuing (CBQ) is a more general term for any mechanism that is based on the class. CBQ can allow the unused capacity to be distributed according to a different algorithm than a minimum bandwidth weighting. For example, there could be a different weighting which is configured for this excess capacity, or it could be dependent on the traffic load in each class, or some other mechanism such as priority.

Weighted Fair Queuing (WFQ) aims to distribute available bandwidth over a number of weighted classes. Packets are sorted in weighted order of arrival of the last bit, to determine transmission order. Using order of arrival of last bit emulates the behavior of Time Division Multiplexing (TDM), hence is fair. In Frame Relay, FECN, BECN, and DE bits will cause the weights to be automatically adjusted, slowing flows if needed.

WFQ classifies sessions as high- or low-bandwidth. Low-bandwidth traffic gets priority, with high-bandwidth traffic sharing what is left over. If the traffic is bursting ahead of the rate at which the interface can transmit, new high-bandwidth traffic gets discarded after the configured or default congestive-messages threshold has been reached. However, low-bandwidth conversations, which include control-message conversations, continue to enqueue data.

The scheduling mechanism uses a combination of weighting and timing information to select which queue to service. The weighting effectively controls the ration of bandwidth distribution between classes under congestion and can also indirectly control delay for underutilized classes. There are two implementations of weighted fair queuing (WFQ): flow-based WFQ and class-based WFQ.

In **flow-based WFQ**, packets are classified by flow. Each flow corresponds to a separate output queue. When a packet is assigned to a flow, it is placed in the queue for that flow. During periods of congestion, WFQ allocates a portion of the available bandwidth to each active queue.

Class-based WFQ aims at providing weighted fair queuing functionality among traffic classes defined by the user. A user could create traffic classes using mechanisms like filters and then assign a fraction of the output interface bandwidth to each of these traffic classes.

The primary difference between flow-based WFQ and class-based WFQ is the fact that in flow-based WFQ bandwidth allocation is relative to other flows. But in class-based WFQ bandwidth allocation is absolute. Class-based WFQ allows the user to assign bandwidth to a class based upon a percentage of the available bandwidth or a fixed kbps value.

Low Latency Queuing (LLQ – see Figure 14.7) is based on the class definition that sets the minimum bandwidth. Queue servicing (metering) controls latency with unused capacity shared among the other classes.

FIGURE 14-7 Low latency queuing

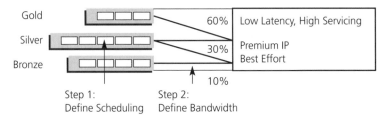

Shaper

Once the data has been metered and marked, the router enforcing the policy knows whether the data rate is within the allowed traffic profile or whether the traffic profile has been exceeded. If the data rate is within the profile, then the data can be routed and scheduled toward the destination along with other traffic. If, on the other hand, the data rate is in excess of the profile, then there are two possible actions. The first of these is to shape the traffic. The data is forwarded on to the normal routing/scheduling processes at a rate defined by the customer's traffic profile. Since this rate is lower than the rate at which data has been received, it is necessary to buffer this excess data and then send it on later as the profile permits. This can be used to smooth out small rate excesses if any previous traffic shaping is not sufficiently accurate or if traffic delay variation has changed the timing. The shaper's task is to shape traffic to some rate description such as leaky bucket (CBR) or dual leaky bucket (simple VBR).

QUICK TIP   **Policing**

Policing is the packet-by-packet monitoring function at a network border (ingress point) that ensures a host (or peer or aggregate) does not violate its promised traffic characteristics. Policing means limiting the amount of traffic flowing into or out of a particular interface to achieve a specific policy goal. Policing typically refers to actions taken by the network to monitor and control traffic to protect network resources such as bandwidth against unintended or malicious behavior. Traffic shaping may be used to achieve policing goals or to carry out congestion management.

The difference between **traffic policing** and **traffic shaping** is shown in Figure 14.8.

FIGURE 14-8 **FIGURE 14-8** Traffic policing vs. shaping

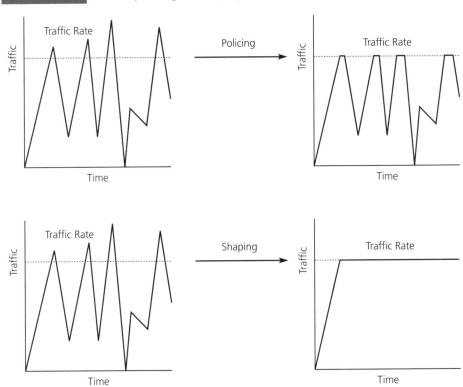

There exist various **traffic shaping** features which manage traffic and congestion on the network. Among them are the following:

- **Generic Traffic Shaping** (GTS) – provides a mechanism to control the flow of outbound traffic on a particular interface. It reduces outbound traffic flow to avoid congestion by constraining specified traffic to a particular bit rate. Traffic adhering to a particular profile can be shaped to meet downstream requirements, eliminating bottlenecks in topologies with data rate mismatches.

- **Frame Relay Traffic Shaping** (FRTS) – provides parameters, such as the following, that are useful for managing network traffic congestion:
  - committed information rate (CIR);
  - forward and backward explicit congestion notification (FECN/BECN);
  - the discard eligible (DE) bit.

Dropper

The dropper performs the other action that can be applied for traffic in excess of the profile. The excess data can simply be discarded. This occurs if the buffering for the shaper is full. In some cases, the service itself may not tolerate any excess data rate; therefore, the allocation of buffers to the service may be very low. This would result in almost all data in excess of the profile being discarded immediately. While this action appears drastic, it may be necessary for some PHBs such as EF, for which there are strict requirements on the traffic levels throughout the internal network. (These concepts are illustrated in Figure 14.9.)

FIGURE 14-9 Example of traffic conditioning for QoS

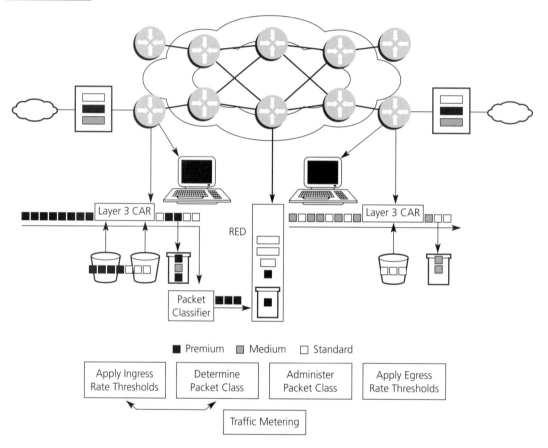

Random Early Detection (RED) is a high-speed **congestion avoidance mechanism**. We introduced RED while discussing its usage with relation to the TCP (see Chapter 10 in Part IV). RED is not intended as a congestion management mechanism in the way the queuing techniques are. It is also more appropriate for long-haul trunks with many traffic flows, e.g. trans-oceanic links, rather than campus networks.

RED allows the router to drop packets before queues become full. Without such congestion-avoidance mechanisms in place, transmission queues begin dropping packets once they are full, which has some negative effects. One of the biggest issues is that the packets delivered are often the oldest packets, for which retransmits may have already been requested. The result is even more congestion. Another consequence is global synchronization, which is the phenomenon of all TCP sessions sharing a common link going into slow start at approximately the same time. Slow start refers to the small initial size of the sliding window that controls the number of TCP packets that can be transmitted without receiving an ACK. If a link employs FIFO that results in tail dropping; once the queue becomes congested, all TCP sessions using that link detect the congestion at the same time.

QUICK TIP   **tail drop**

Tail drop is a fundamental FIFO management technology and thus represents the standard network behavior. It causes session synchronization when waves of traffic experience correlated drops.

RED anticipates a link being congested prior to it happening and takes action by dropping packets in a random manner from the front of the queue. The randomness of RED ensures that no specific session is consistently affected, thereby introducing a fairness in which sessions drop packets. By configuring policing at the network edge, packets that exceed a threshold can either be discarded or tagged. If tagged, they have a higher probability of being dropped in the event of congestion. It is necessary to simply configure separate drop profiles for packets with the packet loss priority (PLP) bit set and for packets with the PLP clear.

QUICK TIP   **Random Early Detection (RED)**

RED performs random drops used to desynchronize TCP sessions and control rates. The effect of random drops is to distribute drops over various sessions.

The RED mechanism was proposed by Sally Floyd and Van Jacobson in the early 1990s to address network congestion in a responsive rather than reactive manner. Underlying the RED mechanism is the premise that most traffic runs on data transport implementations that are sensitive to loss and will temporarily slow down when some of their traffic is dropped. TCP, which responds robustly to traffic drop by slowing down its traffic transmission, effectively allows the traffic-drop behavior of RED to work as a congestion-avoidance signaling mechanism.

TCP constitutes the most heavily used network transport. Given the ubiquitous presence of TCP, RED offers a widespread, effective congestion-avoidance mechanism. In considering the usefulness of RED when robust transports such as TCP are pervasive, it is important to consider also the seriously negative implications of employing RED when a significant percentage of the traffic is not robust in response to packet loss. Neither Novell NetWare nor AppleTalk is appropriately robust in response to packet loss. RED aims to control the average queue size by indicating to the end hosts when they should temporarily slow down transmission of packets. However, currently the major trouble is caused by the interaction of RED and IP-based realtime traffic like, for example, VoIP or streaming video that do not necessarily use TCP (because they cannot tolerate the delays incurred by retransmission). Here, RED would not have any positive effect on the senders (which would not slow down); instead, RED would only gratuitously degrade the quality of the streams. Of course, RED should be applied to the TCP-only traffic or, more precisely, to the traffic that responds accordingly to packet loss by reducing the packet rate temporarily.

Router behavior allows output buffers to fill during periods of congestion, using **tail drop** to resolve the problem. During tail drop, a potentially large number of packets from numerous connections are discarded because of lack of buffer capacity. This behavior can result in waves of congestion followed by periods during which the transmission link is not fully used. RED improves this situation proactively by providing congestion avoidance. That is, instead of waiting for buffers to fill before dropping packets, the router monitors the buffer depth and performs early discards on selected packets transmitted over selected connections.

RED takes advantage of the congestion control mechanism of TCP. By randomly dropping packets prior to periods of high congestion, RED tells the packet source to decrease its transmission rate. RED distributes losses in time and maintains a normally low queue depth while absorbing spikes. The packet drop probability is based on the minimum threshold, maximum threshold, and mark probability denominator. When the average queue depth is above the **minimum threshold**, RED starts dropping packets. The rate of packet drop increases linearly as the average queue size increases until the average queue size reaches the **maximum threshold**.

The **mark probability denominator** is the fraction of packets dropped when the average queue depth is at the maximum threshold. For example, if the denominator is 512, one out of every 512 packets is dropped when the average queue is at the maximum threshold. The minimum threshold value should be set high enough to maximize the link utilization. If the minimum threshold is too low, packets may be dropped unnecessarily, and the transmission link will not be fully used.

The difference between the maximum threshold and the minimum threshold should be large enough because if the difference is too small, many packets may be dropped at once, resulting in global synchronization. This is what RED is primarily supposed to avoid, because generally when the TCP packets are discarded, the TCP scheduling algorithm responds by lowering its transmission rate, then building it up again. When core routers overload, they drop packets from many hosts, leading to many TCP sessions backing off and ramping up their transmission rates synchronously again. This can lead to a sawtooth pattern of underutilization and congestion.

Assuming the packet source is using TCP, after packets are dropped it will decrease its transmission rate until all the packets reach their destination, indicating that the congestion is cleared. TCP not only pauses, but it also restarts quickly and adapts its transmission rate to the rate that the network can support.

RED works in conjunction with TCP to intelligently avoid network congestion by implementing algorithms which:

- distinguish between temporary traffic bursts which can be accommodated by the network and excessive offered load likely to swamp network resources;
- work cooperatively with traffic sources to avoid TCP slow start oscillation which can create periodic waves of network congestion;
- provide fair bandwidth reduction to reduce traffic sources in proportion to the bandwidth being utilized. Thus RED works with TCP to anticipate and manage congestion during periods of heavy traffic to maximize throughput via managed packet loss. RED also provides the network operator with considerable flexibility, including parameters to set minimum and maximum queue depth thresholds as well as packet drop probability, and MIBs for network management visibility into packet switching and packet dropping behavior.

14.5.3 *Frame Relay: DiffServ considerations*

By using separate permanent virtual circuits to serve different applications, traffic flows can be guaranteed appropriately differentiated service levels. The downside for customers is that this approach costs more than combining a mix of traffic types on a single PVC.

However, service providers are testing an option for delivering different quality of service levels using priority queuing for IP-over-frame traffic. Switch manufacturers are starting to offer 'IP-aware' Frame Relay capabilities, in which the frame switch actually looks inside Frame Relay frames and makes queuing decisions based on IP parameters. This technology would allow customers of service providers to merge multiple traffic types on a single PVC but still make sure certain traffic takes priority.

Switches may examine the Differentiated Services setting in each IP packet to make egress queuing decisions for various traffic types within a single PVC. This can be particularly effective when used in conjunction with the overbooking of an output port to ensure that critical traffic does not suffer an adverse impact from other, less critical, traffic.

For instance, consider a common situation where a given 768 kbps port can accept traffic from up to five PVCs, each with a committed information rate of 384 kbps and a burst rate of up to 768 kbps – a reasonable oversubscription ratio. A challenge arises when some of the traffic within each PVC is more critical than other traffic. That is where the ability to look at IP-based priorities pays off.

In an IP-aware Frame Relay service the egress queue is managed by the Differentiated Services – marked priorities of the various traffic flows, not just by PVC. The major advantage to this approach is that a particular port can be oversubscribed while ensuring that critical flows are not delayed too much. If there are two flows within an IP stream – a high-priority customer service application and low-priority Web browsing, and if both are in the same PVC, a traditional Frame Relay cannot distinguish the higher-priority traffic from the lower-priority traffic.

When the switches are able to manage the output queues, based on the DiffServ bits, the various flows may be assigned different priorities. Thus, traffic generated by the business-critical application on any PVC would always leave the queue ahead of Web-browsing traffic.

This technology has particularly strong implications for voice over IP and voice over Frame Relay. Making DiffServ-based queuing work for voice over IP also brings up the question of whether the traffic is being fragmented – and, if so, where. The frame-based (FRF.12) fragmentation needs careful attention when deployed in conjunction with DiffServ-based queuing.

14.6 QoS support for multicast

IP multicast is a requirement, not an option, if the Internet is going to scale. It is a natural complement to QoS for support of one-to-many audio and video multicasts over the Internet, so support for multicast has always been a fundamental requirement in the design of QoS protocols. However, due to its complexity full multicast support within QoS has not been standardized yet.

14.6.1 RSVP/IntServ support for multicast

The initial design for RSVP and Integrated Services took IP multicast support into consideration by making the reservations receiver-based. One aspect of multicast that makes it a challenge to support is that the receivers that comprise a multicast group may vary widely in their capabilities with regard to the downstream bandwidth available to them. This **heterogeneous receivership** is likely to have a wide variety of reservation requests, specific to the path their data will flow downstream.

Generally two approaches are proposed: either **full trees** for each service class will be constructed with the effect that the sender has to send its traffic twice across the network (e.g. one best-effort and one QoS tree); or **one tree** is constructed with the best-effort users connected to the QoS tree. Hence, it is essential that each receiver be allowed to specify a different reservation according to its needs.

Another aspect of the Integrated Services design relevant to multicast in general and heterogeneous receivers specifically is the ability to set filter specifications. By allowing this, hierarchical data may be possible. **Hierarchically encoded datastreams** are designed so that when less bandwidth is available, receivers can still get a usable signal, though with lower fidelity. Filter specifications could reserve bandwidth for the portion of the stream a lower-bandwidth receiver is capable of receiving.

14.6.2 DiffServ support for multicast

The relative simplicity of differentiated services makes it a better (easier and more scalable) fit for multicast support, but there are still challenges involved. Specifically, estimating the traffic is a challenge due to the dynamic nature of group memberships and to the fact that although a multicast distribution tree may have a single ingress point, it will often have multiple egress points (which can change as membership changes).

The **subnet bandwidth manager** has explicit support for multicast, and, as described previously, SBM utilizes IP multicast as part of the protocols. There are no issues with SBM multicast support assuming support for IGMP in SBM-enabled switches, so multicast traffic is only forwarded to segments where group members reside.

RFC WATCH   **Summarized RFC watch**

The following RFCs have been brought to your attention in this chapter:

RFC 1349 *Type of Service in the Internet Protocol Suite,* 1992 (made obsoleted by RFC 2474)

RFC 1812 *Requirements for IP Version 4 Routers*, 1995 (Proposed Standard)

RFC 2205 *Resource ReSerVation Protocol (RSVP) – Version 1 Functional Specification*, 1997 (Proposed Standard)

RFC 2206 *RSVP Management Information Base using SMIv2*, 1997 (Proposed Standard)

RFC 2207 *RSVP Extensions for IPSEC Data Flows*, 1997 (Proposed Standard)

RFC 2208 *Resource ReSerVation Protocol (RSVP) – Version 1 Applicability Statement Some Guidelines on Deployment*, 1997 (Informational)

RFC 2209 *Resource ReSerVation Protocol (RSVP) – Version 1 Message Processing Rules*, 1997 (Informational)

RFC 2210 *The Use of RSVP with IETF Integrated Services*, 1997 (Proposed Standard)

RFC 2211 *Specification of the Controlled-Load Network Element Service*, 1997 (Proposed Standard)

RFC 2212 *Specification of Guaranteed Quality of Service*, 1997 (Proposed Standard)

RFC 2379 *RSVP over ATM Implementation Guidelines*, 1998 (Best Current Practice)

RFC 2380 *RSVP over ATM Implementation Requirements*, 1998 (Proposed Standard)

RFC 2474 *Definition of the Differentiated Services Field (DS Field) in the IPv4 and IPv6 Headers*, 1998 (Proposed Standard)

RFC 2475 *An Architecture for Differentiated Service*, 1998 (Informational)

RFC 2597 *Assured Forwarding PHB Group*, 1999 (Proposed Standard)

RFC 2598 *An Expedited Forwarding PHB*, 1999 (Proposed Standard)

▶

RFC 2746 *RSVP Operation Over IP Tunnels*, 2000 (Proposed Standard)

RFC 2747 *RSVP Cryptographic Authentication*, 2000 (Proposed Standard)

RFC 2748 *The COPS (Common Open Policy Service) Protocol*, 2000 (Proposed Standard)

RFC 2749 *COPS usage for RSVP*, 2000 (Proposed Standard)

RFC 2750 *RSVP Extensions for Policy Control*, 2000 (Proposed Standard)

RFC 2752 *Identity Representation for RSVP*, 2000 (Proposed Standard)

RFC 2753 *A Framework for Policy-based Admission Control*, 2000 (Informational)

RFC 2814 *SBM (Subnet Bandwidth Manager): A Protocol for RSVP-based Admission Control over IEEE 802-style Networks*, 2000 (Proposed Standard)

RFC 2961 *RSVP Refresh Overhead Reduction Extensions*, 2001 (Proposed Standard)

RFC 2996 *Format of the DCLASS Object*, 2000 (updates RFC 2205) (Proposed Standard)

RFC 2998 *A Framework for Integrated Services Operation over DiffServ Networks*, 2000 (Informational)

RFC 3006 *Integrated Services in the Presence of Compressible Flows*, 2000 (Proposed Standard)

RFC 3084 *COPS Usage for Policy Provisioning* (COPS-PR), 2001 (Proposed Standard)

RFC 3086 *Definition of Differentiated Services Per Domain Behaviors and Rules for their Specification*, 2001 (Informational)

RFC 3097 *RSVP Cryptographic Authentication – Updated Message Type Value*, 2001 (Proposed Standard)

RFC 3140 *Per Hop Behavior Identification Codes*, 2001 (Proposed Standard)

RFC 3175 *Aggregation of RSVP for IPv4 and IPv6 Reservations*, 2001 (Proposed Standard)

CHAPTER 15

Multiprotocol label switching

15.1 Background to MPLS

The most promising approach to speeding the transit of data through a network is **Multiprotocol Label Switching** (MPLS), developed by the IETF and based on some of the aspects seen in proprietary label switching approaches discussed in Chapter 13 of this Part. MPLS was specifically designed to address the most significant issues facing service providers today: the need for a highly scalable foundation to deliver value-added IP business services. The innovative label-based forwarding mechanism of MPLS both simplifies IP traffic routing in complex networks and enables very scalable value-added IP services.

SNAPSHOT   **Multiprotocol Labeling Switching (MPLS)**

MPLS is an approach to achieving the simplified forwarding characteristics of Layer 2 switching technologies while retaining the equally desirable flexibility and scalability of Layer 3 routing. MPLS accomplishes this through **label switching**, strictly distinguished from **network-layer routing.** The basic label switching idea involves assigning short **fixed-length labels** to packets at the **ingress** to an MPLS cloud. Throughout the interior of the MPLS domain, the labels attached to packets are used to make forwarding decisions.

The work on MPLS specification started already during Birds of a Feather (BOF) at the 37th IETF in December 1996. The MPLS architecture document has been the work of a design team formed after the Memphis IETF meeting in April 1997. The team consisted of representatives from Cisco Systems, IBM, and Ascend Communications. Given the composition of the team (which reflected the most active players in the working group as a whole), it should come as no surprise that the emerging architecture is close to a union of the Tag Switching and ARIS proposals.

MPLS is about gluing connectionless IP to connection-oriented networks, not only ATM but also optical networks. Normally, under IP, packet headers are examined at every transit point (multiplexer, router, or switch) in a network, which takes time and contributes to the overall data delay. A more efficient

> QUICK TIP **MPLS rationale**
>
> - **Mechanism combining the best features of WANs and IP networks** – privacy and QoS of ATM, flexibility of Frame Relay, and scalability of IP.
> - **Foundation for IP business services** – flexible grouping of users and value-added services.
> - **Low-cost managed IP services** – scaling both small and large networks.

approach would be to label the packets in such a way as to make it unnecessary for each IP packet header to be analyzed at points intermediate between the source and destination.

> SNAPSHOT **MPLS fundamentals**
>
> MPLS is based on the **combination of Layer 3 routing with label switching and forwarding:**
>
> - **Traditional destination-based routing** – each router maintains a routing table and forwards to the next hop – multiple routing paradigms.
> - A single forwarding paradigm – **label swapping:**
> - The forwarding information – **label** – is separate from the content of the IP header. As a packet enters an MPLS network, it gets a label associated with its **Forwarding Equivalence Class** (FEC) as determined at the edge of the MPLS network (ingress router). Then the label is used throughout the MPLS network for all forwarding decisions, bypassing routing tables (no routing table lookup is needed). A forwarding hierarchy is enabled via **label stacking.**
> - **Multiple link-specific realizations** of the label swapping forwarding paradigm – 'shim,' virtual connection/path identifier (VCI/VPI), frequency slot (wavelength), time slot.

At the edge of the MPLS network, a **label** is added to a packet containing information that alerts the next hop MPLS router to the packet's predefined path or to a set of predefined paths it may travel. MPLS is using labels to move packets quickly along a pre-established path, without any deep analysis at each intermediate node. **Packet forwarding** in an MPLS network is **based on the simple labeling scheme, not on IP headers**. As the packet traverses the network, it may be relabeled to travel a more efficient path. MPLS adds labels with specific routing information to packets, which lets routers assign explicit paths to various classes of traffic.

MPLS also provides more deterministic, or predictable, performance by eliminating the latency caused by Internet traffic moving through routers where
message headers are read and then re-encrypted before moving to the next hop –
a latency that keeps realtime data, such as voice and video traffic, from having a
smooth and uninterrupted transmission.

MPLS is critical to a unified, multiservice network. It combines IP to ATM in a
simple and resilient manner, economically delivers VPNs with the privacy and
security that customers demand today, and efficiently offers quality of service
(QoS) across a service provider's network or multiple networks.

SNAPSHOT   **MPLS benefits**

MPLS is a strategic solution for minimizing congestion and meeting reliability
objectives so customers receive predictable performance, specifically aimed to:

- decrease the number of packets dropped during network instability;
- increase service reliability under all network conditions;
- offer preferential service for priority traffic without negatively affecting other
  traffic;
- offload traffic from a congested IGP route while delaying expensive upgrades to
  the physical topology;
- control operational costs;
- meet customers' performance demands;
- quickly adjust to changing traffic flows;
- rapidly bring new customers online;
- develop new revenue-generating services without performance degradation
  and without major upgrades to the network infrastructure.

The separation of forwarding information from the content of the IP header allows
MPLS to be used with devices such as optical crossconnects (OXCs), whose data
plane cannot recognize the IP header.

15.1.1 MPLS origins

MPLS is based on technologies such as **IP switching** from Ipsilon Networks Inc.
(since purchased by Nokia) and **Tag Switching** from Cisco Systems Inc.,
both discussed in Chapter 13 of this Part. Although the industry's focus is on
MPLS, it recognizes that without interaction with routing protocols, the value
of MPLS is limited.

Ordered versus independent control

While defining MPLS, a discussion on the respective merits of independent and local control considered in Chapter 13 of this Part emerged. The MPLS architecture eventually settled on allowing both. Ordered control and independent control are fully interoperable, and the choice between the two is a local matter. Since the two methods interwork, a given Label Switching Router (LSR) need support only one or the other. The choice of independent versus ordered control does not appear to have any effect on the label distribution mechanisms (discussed below). A less apparent consequence of the choice between ordered and independent approaches is that it affects the way Forwarding Equivalent Classes (FECs) are selected for label bindings. With the **independent approach**, each LSR makes its own choice about how it will partition the set of possible packets into FECs. For example, it might decide that each prefix in its routing table will represent an FEC. If neighboring LSRs make different decisions about the FECs they will use, then it will not be possible to establish label switched paths for some of those FECs. Normally, the neighboring LSRs are configured so that this does not happen. However, this situation may arise when an LSR aggregates routes at an area boundary.

QUICK TIP	control over label mapping

In **independent control** each Label Switching Router (LSR) can take the initiative to conduct a label mapping. In **ordered control** an LSR only maps a label when it has already received a label from its next hop.

If one wants to ensure that traffic in a particular FEC follows a path with some specified set of properties (e.g. that the traffic does not traverse any node twice, that a specified amount of resources are available to the traffic, that the traffic follows an explicitly specified path, etc.) **ordered control** must be used. With **independent control**, some LSRs may begin label switching traffic in the FEC before the Label Switched Path (LSP) is completely set up, and thus some traffic in the FEC may follow a path which does not have the specified set of properties.

Ordered control also needs to be used if the recognition of the FEC is a consequence of the setting up of the corresponding LSP. Ordered LSP setup may be initiated either by the ingress or the egress.

In the ordered approach, the selection of FECs can be made at the LSR that initiates the LSP. As path setup proceeds along the LSP, all LSRs use the same FEC as was chosen by the initiator – there is no chance of different choices being made by different LSRs. All that is required is that the LSRs are able to determine the next hop for the FEC in question, so that they can determine whether the binding came from the correct next hop.

The ordered approach may also be advantageous in a network that is undergoing a transition from conventional routing to MPLS. In such a network, a network administrator may want to have very tight control over which packets are forwarded via MPLS. With the ordered approach, this control can be obtained by configuring filters at the edge LSRs that initiate LSP setup. By contrast, to achieve the same control using the independent approach, it would be necessary to configure each LSR in the network.

The downside of the ordered approach is an increase in the amount of time it takes to set up a label switched path. In general, the ordered approach requires that bindings propagate across an entire region of LSRs before a label switched path is established. During the period when this is going on, packets must either be dropped or processed using longest match in the control processor, neither of which is desirable. By contrast, the independent approach allows every LSR to establish and advertise label bindings at any time, without the delay of waiting for messages to propagate in order from one side of the network to the other. Furthermore, the fact that LSRs can remember label bindings from neighbors who were not next hops at the time of advertisement enables almost instantaneous establishment of new label switched paths when routing changes. Thus, the overall effect of independent control is to provide faster convergence times than would occur with ordered control.

Unless all LSRs in an LSP are using ordered control, the overall effect on network behavior is largely that of independent control, since one cannot be sure that an LSP is not used until it is fully set up.

Every LSR needs to know (by configuration) what granularity to use for labels that it assigns. Where ordered control is used, this requires each node to know the granularity only for FECs which leave the MPLS network at that node. For independent control, best results may be obtained by ensuring that all LSRs are consistently configured to know the granularity for each FEC. However, in many cases this may be done by using a single level of granularity which applies to all FECs (such as one label per IP prefix in the forwarding table, or one label per egress node).

15.2 MPLS architecture

SNAPSHOT   **MPLS terminology**

Label Switching Router (LSR) – the core device that switches labeled packets according to precomputed switching tables. This device can be a switch or a router.

Label – a fixed-length header used by an LSR to forward packets. The header format depends upon network characteristics. In router networks, the label is a separate, 32-bit header. In ATM networks, the label is placed into the Virtual Path Identifier/Virtual Channel Identifier (VPI/VCI) cell header. In the core, LSRs read only the label, not the network layer packet header. One key to the scalability of MPLS is that labels have only local significance between two devices that are communicating.

▶

Edge Label Switching Router (ELSR) – the provider-edge device that performs initial packet processing and classification so that it may apply the first label accordingly. This device can be either a router or a switch with built-in routing.

Label Switched Path (LSP) – path defined by all labels assigned between end points. An LSP can be dynamic or static. Dynamic LSPs are provisioned automatically using routing information. Static LSPs are explicitly provisioned.

Label Virtual Circuit (LVC) – a hop-by-hop connection established at the ATM transport layer to implement an LSP. Unlike ATM VCs, LVCs are not implemented end to end and do not result in wasted bandwidth.

Label Distribution Protocol (LDP) – protocol for communicating labels and their meaning among LSRs. It assigns labels in edge and core devices to establish LSPs in conjunction with routing protocols such as Open Shortest Path First (OSPF), Intermediate System-to-Intermediate System (IS-IS), Routing Information Protocol (RIP), Enhanced Interior Gateway Routing Protocol (EIGRP), or Border Gateway Protocol (BGP).

15.2.1 Separation of control and forwarding

The key architectural principle of MPLS is a clean separation of control and forwarding we have discussed already in relation with the industry proposals for label switching. This separation enables effective service integration including QoS transparency between service layers. MPLS has a simple label-switching paradigm that applies to all traffic. Various applications using MPLS can directly manipulate label bindings to effect the desired behavior of the forwarding elements.

Label semantics are completely up to the control plane. A label may represent a fine-grained micro flow, or a coarse-grained macro flow. It can represent **unicast** or **multicast** traffic. Labels can be used to **implicitly route packets** as in native IP forwarding or they can be used to **explicitly route packets** in the same way as an ATM VC.

The **forwarding** component of MPLS is designed to be simple and efficient. While this is motivated by a desire to allow the forwarding to occur in hardware, it also makes the forwarding algorithm independent of the control module. As a result, all of the control modules share a single QoS paradigm. Label lookups

QUICK TIP   **IP and ATM integration with MPLS**

The IP and ATM integration based on MPLS deployment enables **internal routing scalability** (limited number of adjacencies, no full mesh required), **external routing scalability** (full BGP4 support with enhancements), and **VC merge** for large networks (limited by VPI/VCI space available on routers).

determine both the output queue and drop priority. What is unique with MPLS is that the same QoS mechanisms are invoked regardless of which control plane assigned the labels: the QoS mechanisms available to IP traffic engineering, as well as any layered services such as virtual private networks, are the same. No complex, possibly incomplete QoS translation occurs as it often does when mapping IP onto ATM.

Many possible **control planes** can operate in an MPLS environment. These include unicast routing, multicast, RSVP, virtual private networks, frame relay, and traffic engineering. Multiple control planes can manipulate labels on a single packet; combinations of control planes allow many services. In fact, MPLS could stand for *multipurpose label switching*. **Traffic engineering**, discussed later, is an important control component.

RFC WATCH   **core MPLS standardization status**

RFC 3031 **Multiprotocol Label Switching Architecture**, 2001 (Proposed Standard)

RFC 3032 **MPLS Label Stack Encoding**, 2001 (Proposed Standard)

RFC 3034 **Use of Label Switching on Frame Relay Networks Specification**, 2001 (Proposed Standard)

RFC 3035 **MPLS using LDP and ATM VC Switching**, 2001 (Proposed Standard)

RFC 3036 **LDP Specification**, 2001 (Proposed Standard)

RFC 3037 **LDP Applicability**, 2001 (Informational)

RFC 3063 **MPLS Loop Prevention Mechanism**, 2001 (Experimental)

15.2.2 MPLS routing

MPLS routing is used to establish fixed bandwidth pipes analogous to ATM or Frame Relay virtual circuits. MPLS routing is shown in comparison with traditional routing in Figures 15.1 and 15.2.

MPLS operation is straightforward (see Figure 15.3):

- **Step 1.** The network automatically builds routing tables while routers throughout the service provider network participate using interior gateway protocols such as OSPF or IS-IS. Interior gateway protocols such as OSPF or IS-IS support routing throughout the service provider network. The **Label Distribution Protocol** (LDP) distributes labels assigned to routes in the routing table. This operation creates LSPs, i.e. preconfigured maps between destination end points. Unlike ATM permanent virtual circuits (PVCs), which require manual assignment of VPIs/VCIs, labels are assigned automatically.

- **Step 2**. A packet enters the ingress **Edge LSR** (ELSR) where it is examined to determine which Layer 3 services it requires (based on the packet's source address, destination address, and priority level) in terms of QoS and bandwidth

FIGURE 15-1 Traditional routing: route distribution

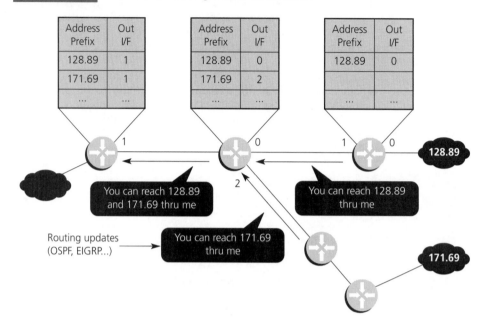

FIGURE 15-2 Traditional routing: packet routing

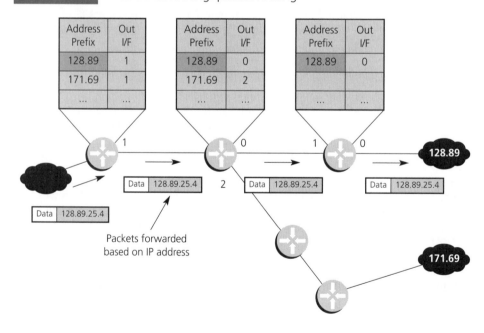

FIGURE 15-3 MPLS operation

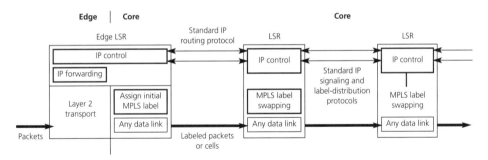

management. Based on routing and policy requirements, the Edge LSR selects and applies a label to the packet header and forwards the packet to the next hop. The appropriate label value is determined by the packet classification based on the **Forwarding Equivalence Class (FEC)**. The MPLS label contains such information as whether the packet should be treated as MPLS traffic or routed as an ordinary IP packet, the packet's TTL, and, of course, what its next hop should be. The edge router then forwards the packet to the next hop router. Labels have local significance only. The labeling process is shown in Figure 15.4.

FIGURE 15-4 MPLS labeling principle

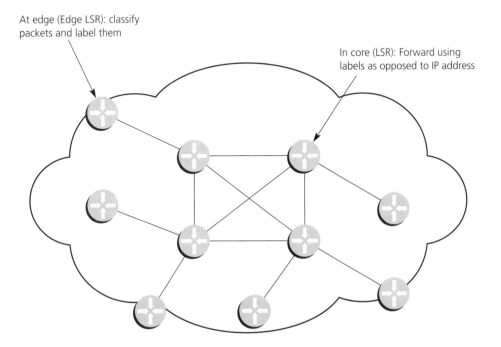

■ **Step 3.** At the next hop, the LSR in the core reads the label of incoming packets and uses its value as an index into a table that specifies the next hop and a new label. The two labels are swapped before the packet is forwarded to the next hop. The LSR attaches the new label, then forwards the packet to the next hop. This action is repeated at all core hops.

The route taken by an MPLS-labeled packet is called the **Label Switched Path (LSP).** The idea behind MPLS is that by using a label to determine the next hop, routers have less work to do and can act more like simple switches. The label represents the route and by using policy to assign the label, network managers have more control for more precise traffic engineering.

The MPLS label is compared to **precomputed switching tables** in core LSRs that contain Layer 3 information, allowing each router to automatically apply the correct IP services to each packet. Tables are precalculated, so there is no need to reprocess packets at every hop. This not only makes it possible to separate types of traffic, such as best-effort traffic from mission-critical traffic, it also renders an MPLS solution highly scalable.

■ **Step 4.** Once the packet reaches the **egress ELSR** via an LSP, the egress ELSR strips the label, and forwards the packet to its final destination, based on that label. The most significant benefit of MPLS is the ability to assign labels that have special meanings: sets of labels distinguish routing information as well as application type or service class. Traffic may actually bear **multiple labels** or a stack of labels. Only the outermost (last) label is used for forwarding. The MPLS label contains enough information as for what the egress ELSR should do with the packet, unless it is an aggregate label. Therefore the router does not need to look for a destination IP address in the IP header.

Label Switch Paths (LSPs) are created between pairs of nodes in the network. The LSPs are initiated based on the routing information within the nodes; therefore, the path to the destination address will be the same for the LSP as for routed packets. If the network consists of router nodes at the edge and a core of MPLS ATM switches, then MPLS LSPs are established between each pair of routers at the edge through the ATM switches. These paths then create direct connections between the MPLS domain edge routers (which are not directly connected).

By looking up the inbound interface and label in the Local Forwarding Information Base (LFIB), the outbound interface and label are determined. The LSR can then substitute the outbound label for the incoming, and forward the frame. This is analogous to, if not exactly the same, way Frame Relay and ATM behave as they send traffic through a virtual circuit. The labels are locally significant only, meaning that the label is only useful and relevant on a single link between adjacent LSRs. The adjacent LSR label tables, however, should end up forming a path through some or all of the MPLS network, i.e a Label Switch Path (LSP), so that when a label is applied, traffic transits multiple LSRs (see Figure 15.5). If traffic is found to have no label (only possible in an IP MPLS network, not in Frame Relay or ATM), a routing lookup is done, and possibly a new label applied.

The internal structure of an LSR is shown in Figure 15.6.

The path through the network created by MPLS can be controlled using the path selection capability of **explicit routing**. With explicit routing, the path does not need to follow the normal routing path for that destination. Instead, the path to be taken by the LSP is specified in the signaling. In **strict explicit routing**, each node the LSP passes through is identified. In **loose explicit routing**, only selected nodes are explicitly identified. The route is 'pinned' at a node through

FIGURE 15-5 Label switched path across MPLS network

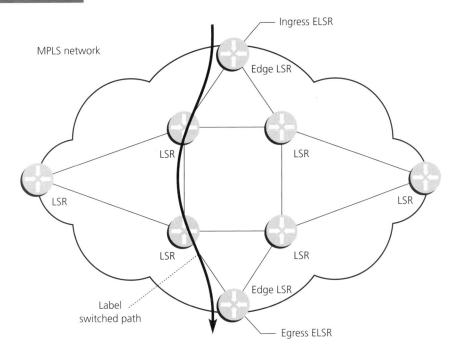

FIGURE 15-6 MPLS LSR structure

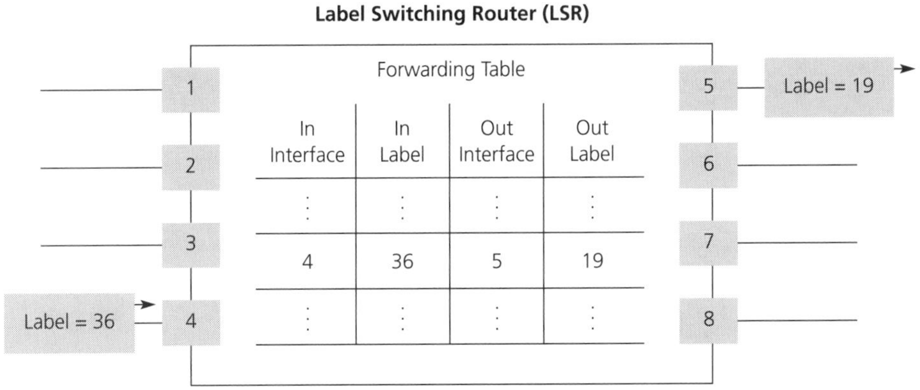

which it must pass, but the LSP may pass through other nodes between the pinned points. Service providers can leverage the combination of the explicit routing and LSP characteristics to provide traffic engineering and dedicated service usage. Traffic engineering enhances the service delivery across the network by optimizing the usage of network resources. For example, traffic can be diverted around network congestion 'hot spots' and through other nodes that are not congested.

The **Forwarding Equivalency Class** (FEC) refers to the idea that all sorts of different packets might need to be forwarded to the same next hop or along the same MPLS path. The FEC is given to all the packets to which a specific label is being applied. This might be all the packets bound for the same egress LSR, or for a service provider, all packets with a given **Class of Service** (CoS) bound for a certain AS boundary router, or matching certain CIDR prefixes. CoS is roughly similar to the DiffServ codepoint but has only eight values, not 64 as in DSCP. It implements similar drop/delay management within labeled tunnels, therefore MPLS networks have fundamental TCP QoS support.

QUICK TIP   **Label Forwarding Information Base**

The **Label Forwarding Information Base** (LFIB) is a data structure used in MPLS to hold information about incoming and outgoing labels and associated Forwarding Equivalence Class (FEC) packets.

MPLS forwarding example

MPLS forwarding is shown in the example in the sequence of Figures 15.7(a)–(e) depicting the starting process of building the label switching tables through assigning frame-based MPLS labels and their use for packet forwarding, to assigning cell-based MPLS labels and their use for packet forwarding.

FIGURE 15-7 (a)   MPLS forwarding

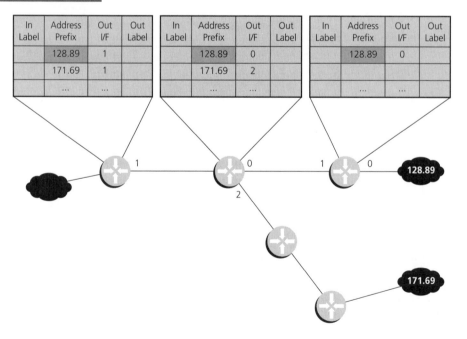

FIGURE 15-7 (b) Frame-based MPLS – assigning labels

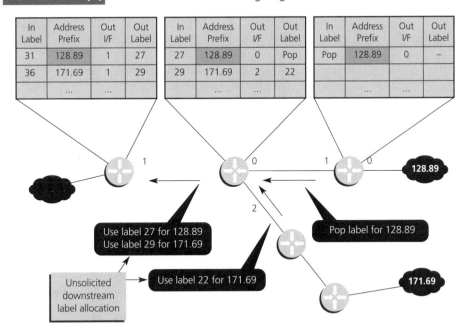

FIGURE 15-7 (c) Frame-based MPLS – packet forwarding

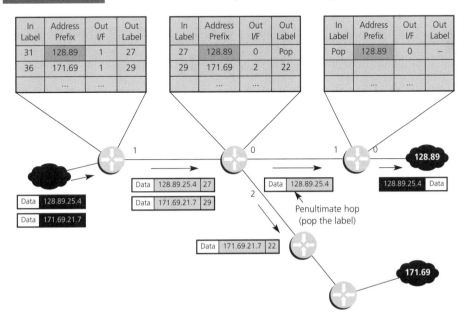

FIGURE 15-7 (d) Cell-based MPLS – assigning labels

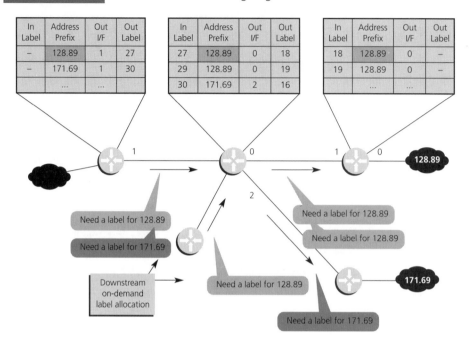

FIGURE 15-7 (e) Cell-based MPLS – cell forwarding

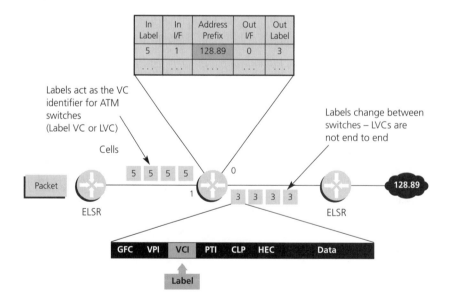

Label Switched Path (LSP)

The MPLS specifications are flexible regarding how traffic is mapped to an LSP and can be used to avoid congestion in the transit network. In particular, MPLS allows rich tools for handling LSP redundancy to protect traffic, including a standby secondary LSP and a fast reroute feature.

15.2.3 MPLS – label switching

Multiprotocol Label Switching is similar to DiffServ in some respects, as it also marks traffic at ingress boundaries in a network, and unmarks it at egress points. But unlike DiffServ, which uses the marking to determine priority within a router, MPLS markings (20-bit labels) are primarily designed to determine the next router hop. MPLS is not application-controlled (no MPLS APIs exist), nor does it have an end host protocol component. Unlike some other QoS protocols, MPLS resides only on routers. MPLS is protocol-independent both at Layer 3 and at Layer 2. In practice, however, IP is the primary considered Layer 3 protocol. As for Layer 2 independence, MPLS can run on top of several Layer 2 technologies (PPP/SONET, Ethernet, ATM, Frame Relay).

Label encapsulation

Figure 15.8 shows the different types of frames (and underlying services) in which an MPLS label is encapsulated. For ATM encapsulation, the cell format is shown as a VPI/VCI value and used as a label with a necessary shim header. When a labeled packet is transmitted on a Label Switching Controlled ATM (LC-ATM) interface, where the VPI/VCI (or VCID) is interpreted as the top label in the label stack, the packet must also contain a **shim header** consisting of label stack entries (shown below). If the packet has a label stack with n entries, it must carry a shim with n entries. The actual value of the top label is encoded in the VPI/VCI field. The label value of the top entry in the shim must be set to 0 upon transmission, and must be ignored upon reception. The packet's outgoing TTL, and its CoS, are carried in the TTL and CoS fields respectively of the top stack entry in the shim. If a packet has a label stack with only one entry, this requires it to have a single-entry shim (four bytes), even though the actual label value is encoded into the VPI/VCI field. This is done to ensure that the packet always has a shim. Otherwise, there would be no way to determine whether it had one or not, i.e. no way to determine whether there are additional label stack entries.

Figure 15.9 depicts the **label stack entry** (frame based) which consists of the following fields:

- *Label* (20 bits) – actual value of the label (0–15 are reserved values) which includes information on:
  - the **next hop** to which the packet is to be forwarded;
  - the **operation** to be performed on the label stack before forwarding (such as to replace the top label stack entry with another, or to pop an entry off the label stack, or to replace the top label stack entry and then to push one or more additional entries onto the label stack).

FIGURE 15-8   MPLS frame and cell format

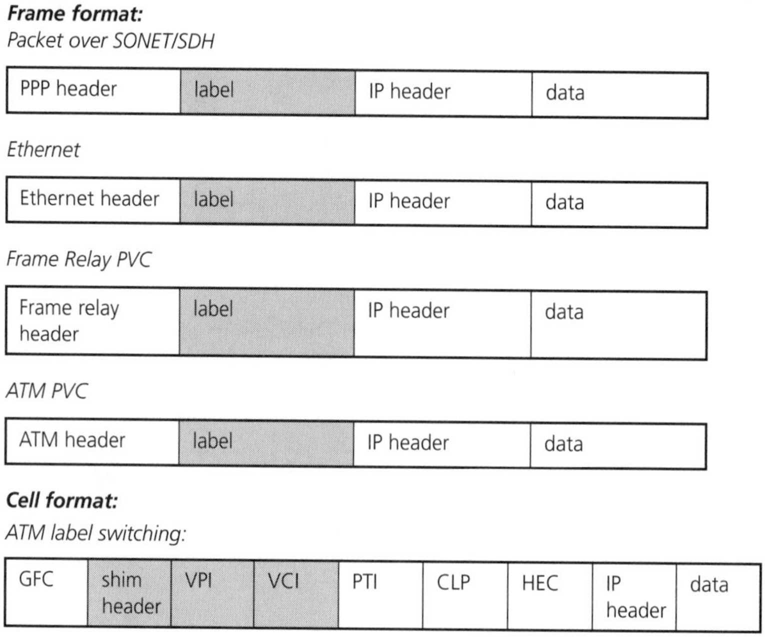

Frame format:
Packet over SONET/SDH

PPP header	label	IP header	data

Ethernet

Ethernet header	label	IP header	data

Frame Relay PVC

Frame relay header	label	IP header	data

ATM PVC

ATM header	label	IP header	data

Cell format:
ATM label switching:

GFC	shim header	VPI	VCI	PTI	CLP	HEC	IP header	data

FIGURE 15-9   Label header format

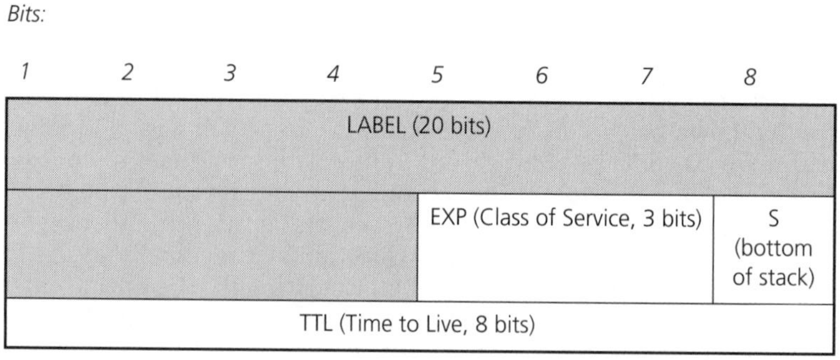

Bits:

1	2	3	4	5	6	7	8
LABEL (20 bits)							
				EXP (Class of Service, 3 bits)			S (bottom of stack)
TTL (Time to Live, 8 bits)							

- *Experimental* (EXP, class of service) – three-bit field reserved for experimental use.
- *Bottom stack* (S) – one bit indicating whether this label is at the bottom of the label stack. This bit is set to one for the last entry in the label stack (i.e. for the bottom of the stack), and zero for all other label stack entries.
- *Time to live* (TTL) – used to encode a time-to-live value.

The **label stack entries** appear after the data link layer headers, but before any network layer headers.

| SNAPSHOT | label switching controlled ATM (LC-ATM) |

A **label switching controlled ATM** (LC-ATM) interface is an ATM interface controlled by the label switching control component. When a packet traversing such an interface is received, it is treated as a labeled packet. The packet's top label is inferred either from the contents of the VCI field or the combined contents of the VPI/VCI fields. Any two LDP peers which are connected via an LC-ATM interface will use LDP negotiations to determine which of these cases is applicable to that interface.

An ATM-LSR is an LSR with a number of LC-ATM interfaces which forwards **cells** between these interfaces, using labels carried in the VCI or VPI/VCI field, without reassembling the cells into frames before forwarding. A **frame**-based LSR is an LSR which forwards complete frames between its interfaces. Note that such an LSR may have zero, one or more LC-ATM interfaces.

TTL and label stacking

Label processing is a relatively simple aspect of MPLS, yet it is actually slightly more involved than described in Step 3 above: labels can be stacked (a **label stack** is represented as a sequence of label stack entries as shown in Figure 15.9) and labeled packets have a **time-to-live value** (TTL). The TTL works essentially the same way TTL in an IP header works: each router hop decrements the value by one until it hits zero.

The purpose of label stacking is to provide a capability comparable to IP-in-IP **tunneling** or **loose source routing**. Stacking essentially maintains the identity of several streams when they are aggregated into a single LSP. This enables packets to be switched at the de-aggregation point. For ease of visualization, this concept can be likened to be a generalization of the Virtual Path tunnels in ATM, the main difference being that the ATM has only dual hierarchy, where as MPLS provides multilevel hierarchy.

Consider an MPLS/VPN network (Virtual Private Networks, VPNs, are discussed later in this section) that uses an aggregated LSP to an exit node E (Figure 15.10). Ingress nodes A and B send packets on the LSP terminating at E. Now E must forward the IP packets destined to different networks shown in the figure. If E supplies A and B with a specific label for each of the networks behind it (label L2 for destination 128.2), ingress nodes A and B can stack the appropriate label before sending packets on the LSP terminating at E. Thus packets originating at ingress node A have two label encapsulations: the top label is that of the LSP that terminates at E (L1) and the next encapsulation has the label supplied by E for the destination prefix in the packet header (L2 for destination 128.2). The packet is switched based on the top level encapsulation (L1). When E receives such packets from LSP terminating at E it can pop the top label (L1) and switch the packet based on the next label in the stack (L2). Note that the label (L1) can also be popped by the penultimate router. Thus stacking avoids the need

FIGURE 15-10 Example of label stacking

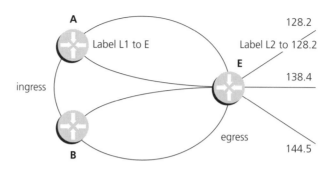

to forward the packet at E based on IP header. For example, such FEC-specific stack labels can be piggybacked in BGP. Ingress LSRs A and B learn about the stack label along with route updates through their BGP peering with E.

Unlike Frame Relay which has a single label (DLCI), or ATM which has two (VPI/VCI), MPLS allows an **arbitrary number of labels** which are simply stacked. A field in the label encapsulation indicates whether this label is the bottom of the stack. There are three **label operations**:

- **swap operation** – analogous to VCI or VPI switching: it represents the movement of the packet through a device at a single control level;
- **push operation** – adds a new label to the top of the stack: usually this represents a new control element taking action on the packet;
- **pop operation** – removes one label from the stack: this usually represents the return of the previous control element.

The power of the label stack is that it allows **multiple control components** to act on a packet. Further, this can occur with little or no coordination between the control planes, making it simple to combine services in useful ways. For example, traffic engineering can be applied independent of any other services that use labels. Additionally, the QoS semantics can easily be carried through the stack, allowing consistent QoS to be applied even as traffic engineering is choosing the path that the traffic will take.

15.3 Label distribution protocol

The Label Distribution Protocol (LDP) specification is the work of a design team that included authors from Cisco, Bay Networks, Ericsson, and IBM, and was formed after the 39th IETF meeting in Munich. The MPLS architecture is based on a control-driven model therefore as a consequence the proposal for an LDP is based on a union of the (control-driven) TDP and ARIS protocols discussed in Chapter 13.

A **Label Distribution Protocol** is how MPLS nodes communicate and bind labels. **Binding** is the process of assigning labels to FECs. After the LDP has run hop by hop, the MPLS network should have LSPs from ingress to egress LSRs, along which only labels are used.

The LDP provides an **LSR discovery mechanism** to enable LSR peers to find each other and establish communication. It defines **four classes of messages:**

- *DISCOVERY* messages;
- *ADJACENCY* messages – dealing with initialization, keepalive, and shutdown of sessions between LSRs;
- *LABEL ADVERTISEMENT* messages – dealing with label binding advertisements, requests, withdrawal, and release;
- *NOTIFICATION* messages – used to provide advisory information and to signal error information.

The LDP runs over TCP to provide reliable delivery of messages (with the exception of *DISCOVERY* messages).

The LDP **message format** (shown in Figure 15.11) consists of the following fields:

FIGURE 15-11 LDP message format

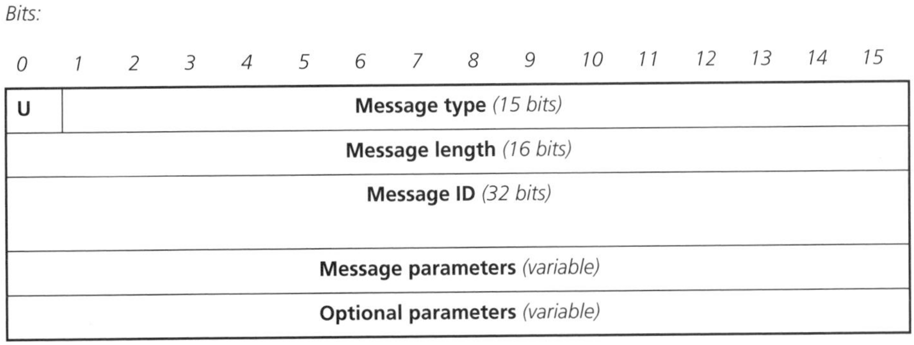

Bits:

- *Unknown message* (*U bit*) – upon receipt of an unknown message, if *U* is clear (= *0*), a notification is returned to the message originator; if *U* is set (= *1*), the unknown message is silently ignored. The sections following that define messages specify a value for the U-bit.
- *Message type* – identifies the type of message.
- *Message length* – specifies the cumulative length in octets of the message ID, mandatory parameters, and optional parameters.
- *Message ID* – 32-bit value used to identify this message. Used by the sending LSR to facilitate identifying notification messages that may apply to this message. An LSR sending a notification message in response to this message should include this Message ID in the Status TLV carried by the notification message.

- *Mandatory parameters* – variable length set of required message parameters. Some messages have no required parameters. For messages that have required parameters, the required parameters must appear in the order specified by the individual message specifications in the sections that follow.
- *Optional parameters* – variable length set of optional message parameters. Many messages have no optional parameters. For messages that have optional parameters, the optional parameters may appear in any order.

The LDP is designed to be easily extensible, using messages specified as collections of **TLV** (type, length, value) encoded objects (see Figure 15.12). The TLV encoding means that each object contains a type field to say what sort of object it is (e.g. a label binding), a length field to say how long the object is, and a value field, the meaning of which depends on the type. New capabilities are added with new type definitions. The first two fields are of constant length and are at the start of the object, which makes it easy for an implementation to ignore object types that it does not recognize. The value field of an object may itself contain further TLV encoded objects.

FIGURE 15-12 TLV encoding

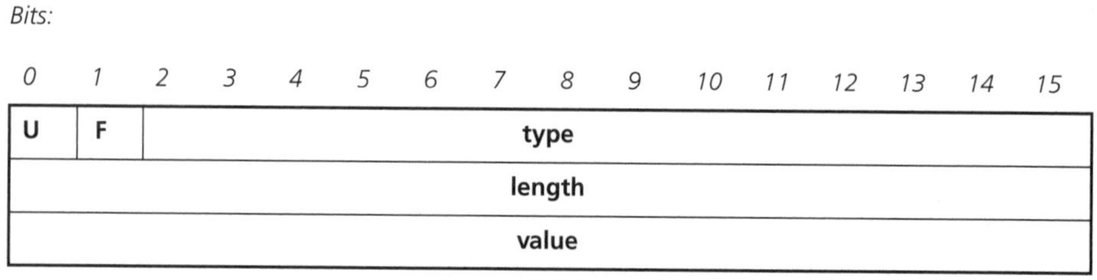

TLV encoding consists of the following fields:

- *Unknown TLV bit* (*U bit*) – upon receipt of an unknown TLV, if $U = 0$, a notification must be returned to the message originator and the entire message must be ignored; if $U = 1$, the unknown TLV is silently ignored and the rest of the message is processed as if the unknown TLV did not exist. The sections following that define TLVs specify a value for the U-bit.
- *Forward unknown TLV bit* (*F bit*) – applies only when the U bit is set and the LDP message containing the unknown TLV is to be forwarded. If $F = 0$, the unknown TLV is not forwarded with the containing message; if $F = 1$, the unknown TLV is forwarded with the containing message. The sections following that define TLVs specify a value for the F-bit.
- *Type* – encodes how the *value* field is to be interpreted.
- *Length* – specifies the length of the *value* field in octets.
- *Value* – octet string of *length* octets that encodes information to be interpreted as specified by the *type* field (variable length field).

15.3.1 *LSR neighbor discovery*

LDP's discovery protocol runs over UDP and works as follows. An LSR periodically multicasts a *HELLO* message to a well-known UDP port on the multicast group identifying all routers on this subnet. All LSRs listen on this UDP port for the *HELLO* messages. Thus at some point an LSR will learn about all the other LSRs to which it has direct connections.

When an LSR learns the address of another LSR by this mechanism, it establishes a TCP connection to that LSR. At this point an LDP session can be established between the two LSRs. An LDP session is bidirectional, that is the LSR at each end of the connection can advertise and request bindings to and from the peer at the other end of the connection.

An additional discovery mechanism enables LSRs to discover each other even when they are not directly connected to a common subnet. In this case an LSR periodically unicasts *HELLO* messages to the well-known UDP port at a specific IP address, which it must have learned by some other means (e.g. configuration). The recipient of this message may respond to the *HELLO* with another *HELLO* that is unicast back to the original LSR, and session establishment then proceeds as before. A typical situation in which this discovery mechanism might be useful is when a traffic engineering LSP is configured between two LSRs, and it is desired to send already labeled packets over that LSP. In this case the LSR at the head of the LSP needs to learn what labels to put on the packets that it will send to the LSR at the far end of the LSP.

Reliable transport

The decision to run LDP over TCP was a somewhat controversial one. The need for reliability is clear: if a label binding or a request for a binding is not successfully delivered, then traffic cannot be label-switched and will have to be handled by the control processor or dropped. It is also easy to find examples where the order of message delivery is important: a binding advertisement followed by a withdrawal of that binding, for example, will have a very different effect if the messages are received in the reverse order. The issue, therefore, was whether to use TCP to provide reliable, in-order delivery or to build that functionality into LDP itself.

Building reliability into LDP had some attraction. The idea was to provide exactly the level of functionality needed, and no more. For example, TCP provides a congestion avoidance mechanism that may not be strictly necessary for a neighbor-to-neighbor control protocol, and the complete ordering of messages that it provides is more strict than required for label distribution.

The advantages of building reliability into the Label Distribution Protocol, however, were outweighed by the drawbacks. For example, because every label binding message must be acknowledged, a timer would be needed for every unacknowledged message. By contrast, LDP delegates the timer function to TCP, which can use a single timer for the whole session. The overhead of managing large numbers of timers can be significant.

TCP provides a wealth of useful functions that LDP is able to use for free, such as efficient packing of higher layer messages into IP packets, piggybacking of ACKs on data packets, and flow control. Unlike congestion control, flow control (making sure that a sender does not overrun the capacity of a receiver) is necessary for a control protocol.

Transport protocol design is notoriously difficult, and there have been plenty of efforts to 'improve' on TCP that have ultimately failed to do so. There are many details to get right and special cases to consider, such as ensuring that old messages from closed sessions are not accepted erroneously by new sessions. This argued in favor of using a well-tested protocol rather than reinventing the wheel.

LDP messages

The most commonly used LDP messages are as follows:

- *INITIALIZATION* – sent at the beginning of an LDP session to enable two LSRs to agree on various parameters and options for the session. These include the label allocation mode (discussed below), timer values (e.g. for *KEEPALIVES*), and the range of labels to be used on the link between these two LSRs. Both LSRs may send *INITIALIZATION* messages, and the receiving LSR responds with a *KEEPALIVE* if the parameters are acceptable. If any parameters are not acceptable, the LSR responds with an error notification, and session initialization is terminated.

- *KEEPALIVE* – sent periodically in the absence of any other messages to ensure that each LDP peer knows that the other peer is still functioning correctly. In the absence of a *KEEPALIVE* or some other LDP message within the appropriate time interval, an LSR concludes that its peer, or the connection to it, has gone down and terminates the session.

- *LABEL MAPPING* – at the heart of label distribution. These are the messages that are used to advertise a binding between an FEC (e.g. an address prefix) and a label.

- *LABEL WITHDRAWAL* – message that reverses the process as it is used to revoke a previously advertised binding. Reasons for withdrawing a binding include the removal of an address prefix from the routing table of the advertising LSR due to a routing change, or a change in configuration of the LSR that causes it to cease label switching packets on that FEC.

- *LABEL RELEASE* – message used by an LSR that previously received a label mapping and no longer has a need for that mapping. This typically happens when the releasing LSR finds that the next hop for this FEC is not the advertising LSR. An LSR releases bindings in this way when it is operating in conservative label retention mode, which we discuss (along with other modes) in the following section.

- *LABEL REQUEST* – recall that LSRs may operate in unsolicited downstream or downstream-on-demand label assignment modes. In the latter mode, LSRs request label mappings from their downstream neighbors using *LABEL REQUEST* messages.

- *LABEL REQUEST ABORT* – if a *LABEL REQUEST* message needs to be revoked before it has been satisfied (e.g. because the next hop for the FEC in question has changed), the requesting LSR aborts the request with a *LABEL REQUEST ABORT* message.

Label distribution modes

Label distribution and assignment may be performed in a number of different modes. All of these alternative modes are negotiated by LSRs during LDP session initialization. One such alternative is unsolicited downstream versus downstream-on-demand label assignment. The MPLS architecture allows an LSR to explicitly request a label binding for that FEC from its next hop for a particular FEC. This is known as **downstream-on-demand label distribution**. The MPLS architecture also allows an LSR to distribute bindings to LSRs that have not explicitly requested them. This is called **unsolicited downstream label distribution.**

It is expected that some MPLS implementations will provide only downstream-on-demand label distribution, and some will provide only unsolicited downstream label distribution, and some will provide both. Which one is provided may depend on the characteristics of the interfaces which are supported by a particular implementation. However, both of these label distribution techniques may be used in the same network at the same time. On any given label distribution adjacency, the upstream LSR and the downstream LSR must agree on which technique is to be used.

Another choice is between liberal and conservative label retention. When an LSR operates in **conservative label retention mode**, it retains only those label-to-FEC mappings that it needs at the current time. Any other mappings are released. By contrast, in **liberal mode**, an LSR retains all mappings that have been advertised to it, even if some of them were not directly useful at the time of advertisement. The common usage of liberal retention mode is as follows. LSR1 advertises a mapping between some FEC and a label to one of its neighbors, LSR2. LSR2 observes that LSR1 is not currently the next hop for that FEC, so it cannot use the mapping for forwarding purposes at this time, but it stores the mapping anyway. At some later time there is a change in routing, and LSR1 becomes LSR2's next hop for this FEC.

LSR2 can now update its label forwarding table accordingly and begin forwarding labeled packets to LSR1 along their new route. This all happens without any new LDP signaling or allocation of labels. The chief advantage of liberal retention mode is quicker response to changes in routing. Its main drawback is waste of labels. This can be particularly important in devices that store label forwarding information in hardware, notably ATM-LSRs. Thus it is common to see conservative label retention used on ATM-LSRs.

15.3.2 Traffic engineering

Traffic Engineering (TE) is the process of administratively selecting the paths through the network in order to balance the traffic load on the various links, routers, and switches. Traffic engineering allows the network operator to manually distribute the load across the entire network for better utilization of the available bandwidth. MPLS is more of a traffic engineering protocol than a QoS protocol, *per se*.

QUICK TIP	traffic engineering is not QoS

Traffic engineering and QoS have opposite objectives:

- **Traffic engineering** optimizes the utilization of the available bandwidth in a network.
- **QoS** deploys needed bandwidth to applications or traffic classes.

Can be used together to optimize application behavior in optimally utilized network.

MPLS traffic engineering automatically **establishes and maintains LSPs** across the backbone by using RSVP. The path that an LSP uses is determined by the LSP resource requirements and network resources, such as bandwidth. Available resources are flooded by means of extensions to a link-state based IGP.

QUICK TIP   **traffic engineering (TE) basics**

Goal of traffic engineering – to optimize link utilization, to specify path by customer or class, to balance traffic load.

Traffic engineering impacts – traffic follows pre-specified path, different from normally routed path, and packet flows are controlled across Layer 2/3 infrastructure.

As current network routing protocols deliver topology-driven routes with shortest-path calculations, there is a high potential that the shortest paths of multiple streams may converge to specific link(s) or router interface(s), which may or may not have the system performance necessary for that aggregate of flows (such as bandwidth and latency).

When network resources are insufficient or inadequate to accommodate the offered network load, traffic flows are inefficiently mapped onto available resources, causing subsets of network resources to become overutilized while others remain underutilized. **Routing with Resource Reservation** (RRR) or **constraint-based routing** delivers the traffic engineering functionality necessary to overcome these service-affecting inefficiencies.

QUICK TIP   **traffic engineering**

- Tunnels are unidirectional.
- Tunnels use explicit routes (different to those discovered by IGP – other path(s) than the shortest one are calculated, using the SPF algorithm).
- Tunnels work only with link-state IGPs (OSPF or IS-IS).
- No routing protocol is run over TE tunnels.
- Unequal load sharing is enabled (better link utilization).

Traffic engineering algorithms calculate **explicit routes** to one or more nodes in the network based on a fit between required and available resources (constraint-based routing). The originating router views these explicit routes as logical interfaces. The explicit routes are represented by LSPs and referred to as **traffic engineering tunnels** (TE tunnels). These tunnels use explicit routes, and the path taken by a TE tunnel is controlled by the router that is the head-end of the tunnel. In the absence of errors, TE tunnels are guaranteed not to loop, but routers must agree on how to use the TE tunnels. Otherwise, traffic might loop through two or more tunnels.

MPLS traffic engineering automatically **establishes and maintains tunnels** across the backbone using the **Resource Reservation Protocol** (RSVP, see Section 14.3). Using RSVP, an MPLS traffic-engineered network defines a physical pathway used by the tunnel at any point in time based on how much bandwidth is required and where that bandwidth is available. The path used by a given tunnel is determined based on the tunnel resource requirements and network resources, such as bandwidth. **Assigning Traffic to Tunnels** can be done statically or dynamically based on modified SPF calculation.

SNAPSHOT   **extended RSVP for MPLS**

Extended RSVP delivers all of the functionality required to support signaling for MPLS/traffic engineering applications. It permits the establishment of explicitly routed LSPs, performs the label distribution function, supports resource reservations or class of service along an LSP, and delivers information about the physical route traversed by an LSP. Extended RSVP elegantly supports the concept of make before break when rerouting an existing LSP, allows the reassignment of previously allocated network resources when establishing a new LSP, and performs loop-prevention/detection during LSP setup. Finally, extended RSVP overcomes the scalability, latency, and reliability concerns of the conventional RSVP soft state model.

Traffic engineering components

The MPLS **traffic engineering** (control plane) includes the following **components** (separable and independent of each other):

- **Resource discovery**.
- **State information dissemination** – is used to distribute relevant information concerning the state of the network, including topology and resource availability information. In the MPLS context, this is accomplished by extending conventional IP link-state routing protocols to carry additional information in their link-state advertisements.
- **Path selection** – used to select an appropriate route through the MPLS network for explicit routing. It is implemented by introducing the concept of constraint-based routing, which is used to compute paths that satisfy certain specifications subject to certain constraints, including constraints imposed by the operational environment.

■ **Path management** – includes **label distribution, path placement, path maintenance,** and **path revocation.** These are used to establish, maintain, and tear down LSPs in the MPLS context. The label distribution, path placement, and path revocation functions are implemented through a signaling protocol, such as the Resource Reservation Protocol (RSVP) extensions or constraint routed label distribution protocol (CR-LDP see next section).

QUICK TIP   **TE components**

■ Information distribution – distributes constraints (such as available bandwidth) pertaining to links.

■ Path selection algorithm – selects paths that obey the constraints.

■ Route setup – uses RSVP for signaling LSPs.

■ Link admission control – decides which tunnels may have resources.

■ Traffic engineering control – establishes and maintains tunnels.

■ Forwarding data.

The relationship among the elements discussed above required for MPLS traffic engineering is shown in Figure 15.13.

FIGURE 15-13   Relationship between MPLS signaling and routing for traffic engineering

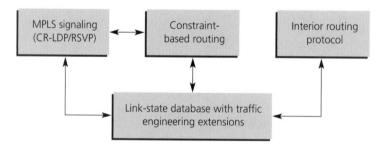

15.3.3 Constraint-based routing

Because MPLS integrates traffic engineering capabilities into Layer 3, providers can optimize the routing of IP traffic even across switched cores. MPLS traffic engineering routes traffic flows across the network by aligning the resources required by a given traffic flow with actual backbone capacity and topology. The **constraint-based routing** (CR) approach lets the network route traffic down one or more pathways, preventing congestion and enabling recovery from link or node failures.

> **SNAPSHOT**   **constraint-based routing**
>
> **Constraint-based routing (CR)** refers to the computation of traffic paths that simultaneously satisfy label-switched path attributes and current network resource limitations. CR is realized through a combination of **extensions** to existing IP **link-state routing protocols** (e.g. OSPF and IS-IS) with RSVP or CR-LDP as the MPLS control plane, and the **Constraint-based Shortest-Path-First** (CSPF) algorithm.

MPLS runs a **Constraint-based Shortest Path First** (CSPF) algorithm based on information distributed by the link-state IGP. The CSPF calculation performs link admission and accounting of resource information flooded into the core. Each router maintains a list of all its traffic-engineered tunnels.

The extensions to OSPF and IS-IS allow nodes to exchange information about network topology, resource availability, and even policy information. This information is used by the CSPF heuristic to compute paths subject to specified resource and/or policy constraints. For example, either RSVP-TE or CR-LDP is used to establish the label forwarding state along the routes computed by a CSPF-based algorithm: this creates the LSP.

Enhancement to the SPF computation

During each step of the SPF computation, a router discovers the path to one node in the network.

- If that node is directly connected to the calculating router, the first-hop information is derived from the adjacency database.
- If the node is not directly connected to the calculating router, the node inherits the first-hop information from the parent(s) of that node. Each node has one or more parents, and each node is the parent of zero or more downstream nodes.

For traffic engineering purposes, each router maintains a list of all TE tunnels that originate at this head-end router. For each of those TE tunnels, the router at the tail-end is known to the head-end router. During the SPF computation (for details see Section 9.4.2), the *TENT* (tentative) *list* stores paths that are possibly the best paths and the *PATH list* stores paths that are definitely the best paths. When it is determined that a path is the best possible path, the node is moved from *TENT* to *PATH*. *PATH* is thus the set of nodes for which the best path from the computing router has been found. Each *PATH* entry consists of ID, path cost, and forwarding direction.

The router must **determine the first-hop information**. There are several ways to do this:

- Examine the list of tail-end routers directly reachable by a TE tunnel. If there is a TE tunnel to this node, use the TE tunnel as the first hop.
- If there is no TE tunnel and the node is directly connected, use the first-hop information from the adjacency database.
- If the node is not directly connected and is not directly reachable by a TE tunnel, copy the first-hop information from the parent node(s) to the new node.

As a result of this computation, traffic to nodes that are the tail end of TE tunnels flow over the TE tunnels. Traffic to nodes that are downstream of the tail-end nodes also flows over the TE tunnels. If there is more than one TE tunnel to different intermediate nodes on the path to destination node X, traffic flows over the TE tunnel whose tail-end node is closest to node X.

If the SPF algorithm finds **equal-cost parallel paths** to destinations, the enhancement above does not change this. Traffic can be forwarded over any of the following:

- one or more native IP paths;
- one or more traffic engineering tunnels;
- a combination of native IP paths and traffic engineering tunnels.

MPLS traffic-engineered tunnels can actually tune their own bandwidth requirements to increase or decrease their RSVP reservations, as warranted by changing network conditions. At the tunnel ingress, an **Edge Label Switching Router** (ELSR) calculates the tunnel pathway by correlating what resources are needed with what's available – performing **constraint-based routing**. An interior gateway protocol (IGP) automatically routes traffic into the tunnel. The IGP must be a link-state protocol, either Open Shortest Path First (OSPF) or Intermediate System-to-Intermediate System (IS-IS), with extensions for global flooding of resource information as needed.

The control plane for MPLS traffic engineering utilizes the Resource Reservation Protocol (RSVP) as a soft state protocol. Path setup establishes the forwarding state (routes) for traffic trunks based on the RSVP path message. This establishes an explicit route, while the RSVP *RESV* messages establish the label. RSVP maintains the state by sending a refresh message.

In the case of an MPLS fast reroute for link protection, the first level label is used for a backup tunnel/LSP and the second level label is the original next-hop LSP. As illustrated in Figure 15.14, the link protection, the first-level label, would start at R2 and traverse to R6. The second-level label would identify R2 to R4, or the original LSP. In the case of the physical interface outbound on R2 being placed in a down state the alternate path is selected locally, meaning no notification back to the head-end router is required. This link protection is established for 1000 LSP in less than 20 ms.

FIGURE 15-14   MPLS fast reroute with traffic engineering

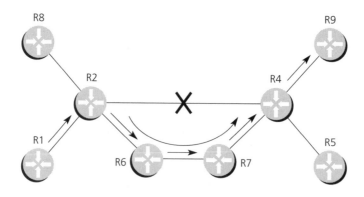

With reference to the discussion on connectionless and connection-oriented networks in Part I, it is interesting to note the following: MPLS- and RSVP-based networks support both connectionless and packet-switched connection-oriented modes. This is because all MPLS label switching routers (LSRs) are also IP routers, and RSVP is added to IP routers to support a connection-oriented mode. Therefore RSVP routers and any other IP router that provides connection-oriented services at the IP layer can be referred to as IP switches.

Constraint-based routing LDP

One of the most important services that LDP offers (RFC 3036) is support for constraint-based routing of traffic across the routed network. **Constraint-based routing** offers the opportunity to extend the information used to set up paths beyond what is available for the routing protocol. For instance, an LSP can be set up based on explicit route constraints, QoS constraints, and other constraints. Constraint-based routing is a mechanism used to meet traffic engineering requirements that have been proposed in RFC 3031 and RFC 2702. These requirements may be met by extending LDP for support of **constraint-based routed label switched paths** (CR-LSPs). Other uses for CR-LSPs include MPLS-based VPNs (RFC 2764).

Constraint-based routing LDP (CR-LDP) is a simple, scalable, open, non-proprietary, traffic engineering signaling protocol for MPLS IP networks, defined as extensions to LDP. CR-LDP provides mechanisms for establishing explicitly routed LSPs. Because LDP is a **peer-to-peer protocol** based on the establishment and maintenance of TCP sessions, the following natural benefits exist:

- CR-LDP messages are **reliably delivered** by the underlying TCP, and state information associated with explicitly routed LSPs does not require periodic refresh;
- CR-LDP messages are **flow controlled** (throttled) through TCP.

CR-LDP is defined for the specific purpose of establishing and maintaining explicitly routed LSPs. Additional optional capabilities included have minimal impact on system performance and requirements when not in use for a specific explicitly routed LSP. Optional capabilities provide for negotiation of LSP services and traffic management parameters over and above best-effort packet delivery including bandwidth allocation, setup, and holding priorities. CR-LDP optionally allows these parameters to be dynamically modified without disruption of the operational (in-service) LSP.

CR-LDP allows the specification of a set of parameters to be signaled along with the LSP setup request. Moreover, the network can be provisioned with a set of edge traffic conditioning functions (which could include marking, metering, policing, and shaping). This set of parameters along with the specification of edge conditioning functions can be shown to be adequate and powerful enough to describe, characterize, and supply parameters for a wide variety of QoS scenarios and services including IP DiffServ (RFC 2495 – see in Chapter 14), IntServ (RFC 2215), ATM service classes, and Frame Relay.

CR-LDP is designed to adequately support the various media types that MPLS was designed to support (ATM, FR, Ethernet, PPP, etc.). Hence, it will work equally well for multi-service switched networks, router networks, or hybrid networks. In particular CR-LDP and RSVP-TE, extensions to RSVP for LSP tunnels (work in progress), are two signaling protocols that perform similar functions in MPLS networks.

RFC WATCH   **CR-LDP**

Internet Drafts pending approval at time of writing:

Constraint-Based LSP Setup using LDP <draft-ietf-mpls-cr-ldp-05.txt> as a Proposed Standard.

LSP Modification Using CR-LDP <draft-ietf-mpls-crlsp-modify-03.txt> as a Proposed Standard.

Applicability Statement for CR-LDP <draft-ietf-mpls-crldp-applic-01.txt> as an Informational RFC.

LDP State Machine <draft-ietf-mpls-ldp-state-04.txt> as an Informational RFC.

15.3.4 DiffServ-aware traffic engineering

DiffServ-aware Traffic Engineering (DS-TE, work in progress) extends MPLS traffic engineering to enable constraint-based routing of guaranteed traffic, which satisfies a more restrictive bandwidth constraint than that satisfied by constraint-based routing for regular traffic, so called **sub-pool** (or class type). This ability to satisfy a more restrictive bandwidth constraint translates into an ability to achieve higher QoS performance (in terms of delay, jitter, or loss) for the guaranteed traffic.

SNAPSHOT   **DiffServ-aware traffic engineering**

The bandwidth reservable on each link for constraint-based routing purposes can be managed through two **bandwidth pools**: a global pool and a sub-pool. The sub-pool can be limited to a smaller portion of the link bandwidth. MPLS tunnels using the sub-pool bandwidth can then be used in conjunction with MPLS QoS mechanisms to deliver **guaranteed bandwidth services end to end** across the network. Simultaneously, tunnels using the global pool can convey DiffServ traffic.

For example, DS-TE can be used to ensure that traffic is routed over the network so that, on every link, there is never more than an assigned percentage of the link capacity of guaranteed traffic (e.g. voice), while there can be up to 100% of the link capacity of regular traffic. Assuming QoS mechanisms are also used on every link to queue guaranteed traffic separately from regular traffic, it then becomes possible to enforce separate overbooking ratios for guaranteed and regular traffic. In fact, for the guaranteed traffic it becomes possible to enforce **no overbooking** at all — or even an underbooking — so that very high QoS can be achieved end to end for that traffic, even while for the regular traffic a significant overbooking continues to be enforced.

QUICK TIP   **bandwidth sub-pool and global pool**

The **sub-pool bandwidth** is a more restrictive bandwidth in an MPLS traffic engineering link. The sub-pool is a portion of the link's overall **global pool bandwidth** which in turn is the total bandwidth allocated to an MPLS traffic engineering link.

Additionally, through the ability to enforce a **maximum percentage of guaranteed traffic** on any link, the network administrator can directly control the end-to-end QoS performance parameters without having to rely on over-engineering or on expected shortest path routing behavior. This is essential for transport of applications that have very high QoS requirements (such as realtime voice, virtual IP leased line, and bandwidth trading), where over-engineering cannot be assumed everywhere in the network. DS-TE involves extending OSPF so that the available sub-pool bandwidth at each pre-emption level is advertised in addition to the available global pool bandwidth at each pre-emption level. And DS-TE modifies constraint-based routing to take this more complex advertised information into account during path computation.

DiffServ-aware traffic engineering enables service providers to perform **separate admission control and separate route computation** for discrete subsets of traffic (for example, voice and data traffic).

Therefore, by **combining DS-TE with other QoS features**, the service provider can:

■ develop QoS services for end customers based on **signaled QoS** rather than provisioned QoS;

■ build the higher revenue-generating **strict-commitment QoS services,** without overprovisioning;

■ offer virtual IP leased-line, Layer 2 service emulation, and point-to-point **guaranteed bandwidth services** including voice-trunking;

■ utilize the scalability properties offered by MPLS.

15.3.5 Multicast and MPLS

The following limitations, related to mapping label switching on Layer 2 switching capabilities, can impact on the implementation of multicast in MPLS:

■ **limited label space** – either the standardized or the implemented number of bits available for a label can be small (e.g. VPI/VCI space, DLCI space), limiting the number of LSPs that can be established;

■ **merging** – some Layer 2 technologies or implementations of these technologies do not support multipoint-to-point and/or multipoint-to-multipoint 'connections,' obstructing the merging of LSPs.

■ **TTL** – Layer 2 technologies do not support a 'TTL-decrement' function.

When native MPLS is deployed the above limitations vanish. Moreover, on PPP and Ethernet links the same label can be used at the same time for a unicast and a multicast LSP because different EtherTypes for MPLS unicast and multicast are defined. Therefore, the assignment of labels for unicast routes is completely independent from the assignment of labels for multicast routes. For example, the same label value could be allocated for a unicast route and for a multicast route, without any possibility of ambiguity. MPLS on a **label switching controlled ATM** (LC-ATM) interface uses VPI/VCI as the top label. There is no VPI/VCI range specifically reserved for multicast or for unicast.

The advantage of using **shared trees**, when label switching is applied, is that shared trees consume less labels than source trees (one label per group versus one label per source and per group). However, mapping a shared tree end to end on Layer 2 implies setting up **multipoint-to-multipoint LSPs**. In practice shared trees are often only used to discover new sources of the group and a switchover to a source tree is made at very low bit rates.

If MPLS used in conjunction with DiffServ, a sender can construct one or more trees with different DSCPs. These *(S, G, DSCP)* or *(*, G, DSCP)* trees can be mapped very easily onto LSPs when the traffic-driven trigger is used. In this case one can create LSPs with different attributes for the various DSCPs. Note, however, that these LSPs still use the same route as long as the tree construction mechanism itself does not take the DSCP as an input.

Using PIM to distribute MPLS labels for multicast routes

Work is in progress to specify a method of distributing MPLS labels for multicast routes (for more details see the discussion on multicast routing in Part IV). This design for using PIM to distribute MPLS labels for multicast routes has the following goals:

■ If an interface attaches to a network with data-link broadcast capability, an LSR should never have to send more than one copy of a given multicast data packet out of that interface. However, it is not a goal for that LSR to be able to send the same packet, with the same label, out of multiple interfaces. When an interface supports data-link multicasting, it must be possible for the receiver of a labeled packet to interpret the label without knowing who the transmitter is.

■ When a LAN contains multiple label distribution peers, it should be possible to use data-link multicast to distribute the label distribution control packets themselves. Other aspects of label distribution methodology should remain as consistent with unicast label distribution as possible.

■ Multicast label distribution procedures should not depend on the media type. (However, it has been necessary to compromise this goal in the case of ATM-

LSRs which do not have multipoint-to-multipoint capability.)

■ Once the label for a particular multicast tree on a given LAN has been assigned, unicast routing changes should not cause redistribution or reassignment of the label for that group on that LAN.

■ When a multicast routing table change requires a label distribution change, the latency between the two should be minimized, both to improve performance and to minimize the possibility of race conditions.

■ The procedures should work with either dense-mode or sparse-mode operation.

The **labels** are distributed in the same **PIM messages** that are used to create the corresponding routes. The method is media-type independent, and therefore works for multi-access/multicast capable LANs, point-to-point links, and NBMA networks. PIMv1 and PIMv2 are used to combine MPLS label distribution with the distribution of $(*,G)$ join state, (S,G) join state, or (S,G) RP-tree bit (RPT-bit) prune state. Labels and multicast routes are sent together in one message.

An LSR that supports multicast sends *PIM Join/Prune messages* on behalf of hosts that join groups. It sends *Join/Prune messages* to upstream neighboring LSRs toward the RP for the shared tree $(*,G)$ or toward a source for a source tree (S,G). Labels are distributed by being associated with addresses in the join list or the prune list (hence are piggybacked with multicast routes).

Only one copy of a given multicast data packet is sent downstream. On an LAN, this packet will be received by all the LSRs on the LAN. The **label** it carries is used, by the receiving LSRs, to find the packet's **multicast distribution tree**. The label must have a unique association, on that LAN, with a multicast distribution tree. Therefore, once an LSR assigns a label to a particular multicast distribution tree on a particular LAN, all other LSRs on that LAN are prohibited from making any other use of that label. The prohibition remains in effect as long as the distribution tree in question exists. In order to meet this requirement, the LSRs on an LAN must **partition the label space**, such that each LSR has a particular unique range of labels which it may distribute.

PIM Hello messages, sent periodically by all PIM-capable routers, will indicate if the router is MPLS-capable. An upstream router on an LAN will therefore know if all routers on the same LAN are LSRs or not. If there are any **MPLS-incapable routers** which are interested in a particular group, the upstream router will transmit to the LAN only **unlabeled multicast packets** for that group. If there are any group members on an LAN, only unlabelled multicast data for that group will be transmitted onto that LAN.

15.3.6 MPLS extensions

MPLS is still in progress and numerous extensions to currently approved core specifications already exist – some accepted as an RFC, others existing in Internet drafts only at the time of writing.

MPLS loop prevention mechanism

RFC 3063 presents a simple mechanism, based on 'threads,' which can be used to prevent MPLS from setting up LSPs which have loops. The mechanism is compatible with, but does not require, VC merge. The mechanism can be used with either the ordered downstream-on-demand allocation or ordered downstream allocation. The amount of information that must be passed in a protocol message is tightly bounded (i.e. no path-vector is used). When a node needs to change its next hop, a distributed procedure is executed, but only nodes which are downstream of the change are involved.

MPLS and ICMP

There is an Internet draft describing extensions to ICMP that permit LSRs to append MPLS header information to ICMP messages. These ICMP extensions support an MPLS aware traceroute application that network operators can use to trace paths through the MPLS user plane. When a router receives an undeliverable IP datagram, it can send an ICMP message to the host that originated the datagram. The ICMP message indicates why the datagram could not be delivered. It also contains the IP header and leading payload octets of the user datagram. MPLS LSRs also use ICMP to convey control information to source hosts.

When an LSR receives an undeliverable MPLS encapsulated datagram, it removes the entire MPLS label stack, exposing the previously encapsulated IP datagram. The LSR then submits the IP datagram to a network-forwarding module for error processing. Error processing can include ICMP message generation. The ICMP message indicates why the original datagram could not be delivered. It also contains the IP header and leading octets of the original datagram. The ICMP message, however, includes no information regarding the MPLS label stack that encapsulated the original datagram when it arrived at the LSR. This omission is significant because the LSR would have routed the original datagram based upon information contained by the MPLS label stack.

The proposed extensions to ICMP permit an LSR to append MPLS label stack information to ICMP messages. ICMP messages regarding MPLS encapsulated datagrams can include the MPLS label stack, as it arrived at the router that sent the ICMP message. The ICMP message must also include the IP header and leading payload octets of the original datagram. These ICMP extensions support an MPLS aware traceroute application that network operators can use to trace paths through the MPLS user plane and troubleshoot routing problems.

15.3.7 General switch management protocol

The **General Switch Management Protocol** (GSMP, work in progress) provides an interface that can be used to separate the data forwarder from the routing and other control plane protocols such as LDP. As such it allows service providers to move away from monolithic systems that bundle the control plane and data plane into a single tightly coupled system – usually in a single chassis. Separating the control components from the forwarding components and using GSMP for switch management enables service providers to create multi-service systems composed of various vendors' equipment. It also allows for a more dynamic means of adding services to their networks.

The IETF GSMP working group was established in the routing area because GSMP was being seen as an optional part of the MPLS solution. In an MPLS system, it is possible to run the routing protocols and label distribution protocols on one system while passing data across a generic switch, e.g. an ATM switch. GSMP provides the switch resource management mechanism needed in such a scenario.

The General Switch Management Protocol (GSMP) has been available to the IETF community for several years now as informational RFCs – **GSMPv1.1** (RFC 1987), and **GSMPv2.0** (RFC 2297) – intended only for use with ATM switches. Several vendors have implemented GSMPv1.1. The work on GSMP has undergone major revisions and currently version 3 is in the form of an Internet Draft.

RFC WATCH   **GSMP**

RFC 1987 **Ipsilon's General Switch Management Protocol Specification Version 1.1**, 1996 (Informational)

RFC 2297 **Ipsilon's General Switch Management Protocol Specification Version 2.0**, 1998 (Informational)

GSMP has also been selected by the **Multiservice Switching Forum** (MSF) as its protocol of choice for the switch control interface identified in their architecture. The MSF is an industry forum, which among its activities establishes their members' requirements and then works with the appropriate standards bodies to foster their goals. In the case of GSMP, the MSF presented the IETF GSMP Working Group with a set of requirements for GSMP. The working group has made a determined effort to comply with those requirements in its specifications.

The GSMP protocol has been defined to handle communications between a controller and the label-based packet or cell switch under control. Extensions to the GSMP label formats for optical, SONET/SDH, TDM, and spatial switching are proposed. Where possible, the GMPLS label formats and methods are reused (see next chapter).

GSMP description

The **General Switch Management Protocol version 3** (GSMP) is a general purpose **protocol to control a label switch**. GSMP allows a controller to establish and release connections across the switch; add and delete leaves on a multicast connection; reserve resources; manage switch ports; request configuration information; and request statistics. It also allows the switch to inform the controller of asynchronous events such as a link going down. The GSMP protocol is asymmetric, the controller being the master and the switch being the slave. GSMP may be transported in three ways: across an IP network, across an ATM virtual channel as specified, and across an Ethernet link. Other encapsulations are possible, but have not been defined.

A **label switch** is a frame or cell switch that supports connection-oriented switching using the exact match-forwarding algorithm based on labels attached to incoming cells or frames. A label switch may support multiple label types; however, each switch port can support only one label type. The label type supported by a given port is indicated in a port configuration message. Connections may be established between ports supporting different label types using the adaptation methods. There are two forms of label support; short 28-bit labels which are sufficient for many purposes, and TLV labels which are defined for labels that do not fit into 28 bits. Examples of the label types that can use the short form include ATM, Frame Relay, and MPLS generic labels. Examples of labels which are defined to use the TLV form include DS1, DS3, E1, E3 (see Appendix D), and MPLS FECs.

A connection across a switch is formed by connecting an incoming labeled channel to one or more outgoing labeled channels. Connections are generally referenced by the input port on which they arrive and the label values of their incoming labeled channel. In some messages connections are referenced by the output port.

GSMP supports **point-to-point** and **point-to-multipoint** connections. A multipoint-to-point connection is specified by establishing multiple point-to-point connections each of which specifies the same output label. A multipoint-to-multipoint connection is specified by establishing multiple point-to-multipoint connections each of which specifies a different input label with the same output labels.

In general a connection is established with a certain **quality of service** (QoS). The latest version of GSMP includes a **default QoS configuration** and additionally allows the negotiation of alternative, optional QoS configurations. The default QoS configuration includes three QoS models: a default service model, a simple priority model, and a QoS profile model. This version of GSMP also supports the reservation of resources when the labels are not yet known. This ability can be used in support of MPLS.

GSMP contains an **adjacency protocol**. The adjacency protocol is used to synchronize state across the link, to negotiate which version of the GSMP protocol to use, to discover the identity of the entity at the other end of a link, and to detect when it changes.

Switch partitioning

A **physical switch** can be **partitioned in many virtual switches**. GSMP does not provide support for defining switch partitions. GSMP treats a virtual switch as if it was a physical switch. In the third version of GSMP switch partitioning is static and occurs prior to running GSMP. The partitions of a physical switch are isolated from each other by the implementation and the controller assumes that the resources allocated to a partition are at all times available to that partition and only to that partition. A partition appears to its controller as a physical label switch.

The resources allocated to a partition appear to the controller as if they were the actual physical resources of a physical switch. For example if the bandwidth of a port is divided among several partitions, each partition would appear to the controller to have its own independent port with its fixed set of resources.

GSMP controls a partitioned switch through the use of a partition identifier that is carried in every GSMP message. Each partition has a one-to-one control relationship with its own logical controller entity and GSMP independently maintains adjacency between each controller-partition pair. Multiple switches may be controlled by a single controller using multiple instantiations of the protocol over separate control connections. Alternatively, multiple controllers can control a single switch. Each controller would establish a control connection to the switch using the adjacency protocol. The adjacency mechanism maintains a state table indicating the control connections that are being maintained by the same partition. The switch provides information to the controller group about the number and identity of the attached controllers. It does nothing, however, to coordinate the activities of the controllers, and will execute all commands as they are received. It is the controller group's responsibility to coordinate the use of the switch. This mechanism is most commonly used for controller redundancy and load sharing.

15.4 MPLS in VPNs

A **Virtual Private Network** (VPN) is an autonomous network deployed as an alternative to the wide-area network (WAN) infrastructure to replace or augment existing private networks, employing the same security, management, and throughput policies as leased-line or enterprise-owned Frame Relay/ATM networks. A VPN comprises a set of sites that can communicate with each other and belong to a closed user group (see the example in Figure 15.15). A VPN is defined with a set of administrative policies. These policies determine both connectivity and QoS among sites.

FIGURE 15-15   VPN overview

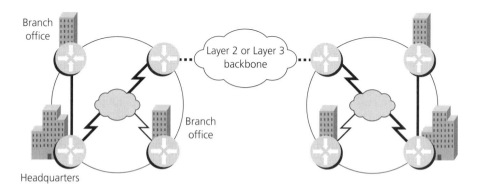

The policies established by VPN customers can now be implemented completely by VPN service providers using Border Gateway Protocol (BGP)/MPLS VPN mechanisms to connect remote and branch offices to the central site. As the term suggests, this solution is based on a combination of two technologies, BGP and MPLS. VPN customers can migrate to a flexible inter-site connectivity ranging from full to partial mesh. These sites may be either within the same (intranet) or in different (extranet) organizations. VPN customers can also be in more than one VPN and may overlap. Not all sites have to be connected to the same service-provider VPN. A VPN can span multiple service providers.

Private IP connectivity services are built using **IP VPN** – a private network that is built within a public or shared IP infrastructure. Virtual refers to the fact that customers share the infrastructure rather than using dedicated private lines to build their networks. The shared network could be the public Internet or a specially managed, shared network that is built exclusively for VPN customers. Private reflects the need to address security issues, because IP was designed as an open protocol. Customers and network service providers must take measures to protect data within the customer's company walls and while in transit across the network.

VPNs come in three different forms: **access VPNs** for remote dial access, **intranet VPNs** for interconnecting networks between different sites within a company, and **extranet VPNs** for interconnecting networks between companies. Historically, remote access has been the strongest of the three drivers for VPN adoption, but this situation is changing. While remote access remains at the top of the list for VPN implementers, the goals of establishing extranets and building site-to-site intranets have emerged.

15.4.1 IP VPNs solutions

VPNs may be realized by different methods, not only by the effective use of an MPLS service provider network. Here we will briefly overview the different types of underlying VPN infrastructure in use, before we move on to the MPLS/VPN related issues.

The **taxonomy of VPNs** is as follows:

- **Dial** – via dial-up, xDSL, mobile IP, cable modem:
  - client-initiated – IPSec, L2TP, PPTP, IPSec (see below);
  - network access server (NAS)-initiated – L2TP.
- **Dedicated:**
  - **IP tunnel – point-to-point tunnels** among routers at the edge of the service provider's network. The customer and provider networks use IP and each provider router must maintain complete routing information about all customer networks. Every edge router must exchange addresses and link and device status information with every other router. The volume of routing information that each router must maintain increases geometrically as new sites are added, which is where the scalability challenge arises (and the routers' CPU consumption grows). The typical tunnel mechanisms are GRE and IPSec. (Tunneling was introduced in Part IV, Section 11.7.)
  - **Virtual circuit** – point-to-point network within the carrier network at Layer 2 using **Frame Relay or ATM PVCs**. This approach requires mapping a unique identifier to each site in the closed user group and managing which sites can exchange communications. The need to establish and manage a full mesh of virtual circuits within the provider's WAN makes it difficult to add large volumes of new sites quickly, because each one must connect to a growing population of locations.
  - **VPN-aware networks** – MPLS/BGP VPNs.

SNAPSHOT   **VPN**

A **Virtual Private Network** (VPN) is a network implemented using a shared network infrastructure but providing the security and privacy of a private leased-line network. VPNs connect branch offices and remote users through a **shared or public network**, such as the Internet, and provide the same security and availability as a private network. Because VPNs use an existing shared WAN infrastructure, costs are lower and deployment is faster than is the case with traditional private networks. A VPN can consist of sites (or systems) that are all from the same enterprise (intranet) or from different enterprises (extranet); it can consist of sites (or systems) that all attach to the same service provider backbone or to different service provider backbones.

Tunnels

Encrypted tunnels are a popular VPN solution to protect data from being intercepted and viewed by unauthorized entities and to perform multiprotocol encapsulation, if necessary. **Tunnels** provide logical, point-to-point connections across a connectionless IP network, enabling the application of advanced security features. **Encryption** is applied to the tunneled connection to scramble data, thus making data legible only to authorized senders and receivers. In applications where security is less of a concern, tunnels can be employed without encryption to provide multiprotocol support without privacy.

    IP Security (IPSec), **Point-to-Point Tunneling Protocol** (PPTP), **Layer 2 Tunneling Protocol** (L2TP) or alternatively the Microsoft-proprietary **Point-To-Point Encryption** (MPPE), and **generic routing encapsulation** (GRE) are alternatives deployed for tunnel support. For additional security, the strongest standard encryption technologies are available, such as **Data Encryption Standard** (DES).

RFC WATCH   **tunneling protocols and their security options**

RFC 2341 **Cisco Layer Two Forwarding Protocol (L2F)**, 1998 (Historic)

RFC 2419 **The PPP DES Encryption Protocol, Version 2** (DESE-bis), 1998 (Proposed Standard)

RFC 2420 **The PPP Triple-DES Encryption Protocol (3DESE),** 1998 (Proposed Standard)

RFC 2516 **A Method for Transmitting PPP Over Ethernet (PPPoE),** 1999 (Informational)

RFC 2637 **Point-to-Point Tunneling Protocol,** 1999 (Informational)

RFC 2661 **Layer Two Tunneling Protocol (L2TP),** 1999 (Proposed Standard)

RFC 2809 **Implementation of L2TP Compulsory Tunneling via RADIUS,** 2000 (Informational)

RFC 2888 **Secure Remote Access with L2TP**, 2000. (Informational)

RFC 2983 **Differentiated Services and Tunnels**, 2000 (Informational)

RFC 3070 **Layer Two Tunneling Protocol (L2TP) over Frame Relay,** 2001 (Proposed Standard)

RFC 3077 **A Link-Layer Tunneling Mechanism for Unidirectional Links,** 2001 (Proposed Standard)

RFC 3078 **Microsoft Point-To-Point Encryption (MPPE) Protocol,** 2001 (Informational)

Client- and NAS-initiated scenarios

When implementing a remote access VPN architecture, an important consideration is where to initiate tunneling and encryption – on the dialup client PC or on the Network Access Server (NAS). In a **client-initiated model**, the encrypted tunnel is established at the client using IPSec, L2TP, or PPTP, thereby making the service provider network solely a means of transport to the corporate network. An advantage of a client-initiated model is that VPN intelligence resides in the customer premises equipment (CPE), enabling VPN functionality to be delivered over any network infrastructure, including the Internet. Furthermore, in the client-initiated model, the last mile service provider access network used for dialing to the point of presence (POP) is secured.

In an **NAS-initiated scenario**, a remote user dials into a service provider's POP using a Point-to-Point Protocol/Serial Line Internet Protocol (PPP/SLIP) connection, is authenticated by the service provider, and, in turn, initiates a **secure tunnel** to the corporate network from the POP using L2TP, which is then authenticated by the enterprise. With an NAS-initiated architecture, VPN intelligence resides in the service provider network – there is no end user client software for the corporation to maintain, thus eliminating client management issues associated with remote access. The drawbacks, however, are lack of security on the local access dial network connecting the client to the service provider network and the need to utilize a single service provider end to end, a scenario that eliminates the Internet as a transport network. In a remote access VPN implementation, these security/management trade-offs must be balanced.

RFC WATCH   **IP Security**

RFC 2401 **Security Architecture for the Internet Protocol,** 1998 (Proposed Standard)

RFC 2402 **IP Authentication Header**, 1998 (Proposed Standard)

RFC 2406 **IP Encapsulating Security Payload (ESP),** 1998 (Proposed Standard)

RFC 2407 **The Internet IP Security Domain of Interpretation for ISAKMP,** 1998 (Proposed Standard)

RFC 2408 **Internet Security Association and Key Management Protocol** (ISAKMP), 1998 (Proposed Standard)

RFC 2409 **The Internet Key Exchange (IKE),** 1998 (Proposed Standard)

RFC 2410 **The NULL Encryption Algorithm and Its Use With IPsec,** 1998 (Proposed Standard)

RFC 2411 **IP Security Document Roadmap,** 1998 (Informational)

Generic routing encapsulation tunneling

Generic Routing Encapsulation (GRE) tunnels provide a specific pathway across the shared WAN and encapsulate traffic with new packet headers to ensure delivery to specific destinations. The network is private because traffic can enter a tunnel only at an end point. Although primarily used for IP traffic, GRE tunneling can also be used to encapsulate non-IP traffic, such as Novell IPX and AppleTalk, into IP and send it over the Internet or IP network. Tunnels do not provide true confidentiality (encryption does) but can carry encrypted traffic.

RFC WATCH	Generic Routing Encapsulation (GRE)

RFC 2784 **Generic Routing Encapsulation (GRE),** 2000 (Proposed Standard)

RFC 2890 **Key and Sequence Number Extensions to GRE,** 2000 (Proposed Standard)

Data encryption methods operate on top of GRE tunneling. To that end a GRE tunnel must be configured before encryption is applied to the connection. IPSec encryption supports 56-bit, 128-bit, and 256-bit encryption algorithms in IPSec client software. IPSec also supports certificate authorities and **Internet Key Exchange** (IKE) negotiation. IPSec encryption can be deployed in standalone environments between clients, routers, and firewalls, or used in conjunction with L2TP tunneling in access VPNs. IPSec is supported in Windows and UNIX and can be used between these clients.

The **Point-to-Point Tunneling Protocol** (PPTP) was developed by Microsoft and is widely deployed in Windows 95, Windows 98, and Windows NT client software to enable voluntary VPNs.

Microsoft Point-to-Point Encryption (MPPE) is Microsoft-proprietary encryption that uses RC4-based encryption. MPPE is part of Microsoft's PPTP client software solution and is useful in voluntary-mode access VPN architectures. PPTP/MPPE is supported only on certain platforms.

The **Layer 2 Tunneling Protocol** (L2TP) incorporates the best attributes of Microsoft-proprietary PPTP and Cisco Layer 2 Forwarding (L2F). L2TP tunnels are used primarily in dialup access VPNs for both IP and non-IP traffic.

PPP over Ethernet (PPPoE) is primarily deployed in DSL environments. PPPoE leverages existing Ethernet infrastructures to allow users to initiate multiple PPP sessions within the same LAN. This technology enables Layer 3 service selection, an emerging application that lets users simultaneously connect to several destinations through a single remote access connection.

Table 15.1 shows characteristics for different VPN platforms, showing clearly the benefits of MPLS-based VPNs. Security as a major issues is not included as a decision feature in the table because all three types of VPNs provide similarly high security to customers. **Quality of Service** (QoS) is another VPN challenge. Frame Relay and ATM PVCs enable the delivery of varied service levels using mechanisms such as per-PVC buffering. However, managing multiple service

	Layer 2 – virtual circuits	Layer 3 – tunnels	Layers 2/3 – MPLS
Setup and management	Complex Limited scalability	Medium complex Limited scalability Each router maintains full routing information about all customer networks	Easy High scalability Routing tables contain only edge devices connected to each VPN
QoS	High	Not included	High
Cost	High	Medium	Low

TABLE 15-1 Comparison of VPN platforms

levels across multiple PVCs for each VPN can be an administrative stumbling block as network sizes increase. In the tunneling scenario, the IP Security (IPSec) and Generic Route Encapsulation (GRE) technologies used to provision VPNs do not support QoS on their own.

The requirements for an effective VPN are:

- **Privacy** – all IP VPN services offer privacy over a shared (public) network infrastructure, the most well known solution of which is an encrypted tunnel. An IP VPN service must offer private addressing, where addresses within a customer private network do not need to be globally unique.
- **Scalability** – IP VPN services must scale to serve hundreds of thousands of sites and users. An IP VPN service should also serve as a management tool for service providers to control access to services, such as closed user groups for data and voice services.
- **Flexibility** – IP VPN services must accommodate any-to-any traffic patterns and be able to accept new sites quickly, connect users over different media, and meet transport and bandwidth requirements of new intranet applications.
- **Predictable performance** – intranet applications supported by an IP VPN service require different classes of service. The service level performance between customer sites must be guaranteed. Examples include widespread connectivity required by remote access for mobile users and sustained performance required by interactive intranet applications in branch offices.

15.4.2 MPLS VPN components

The high-level structure of MPLS VPN is shown in Figure 15.16 showing the traffic passing through the MPLS network within a VPN, going from Customer Edge (CE), entering the MPLS network at the PE and going through Provider Core (PC) to the far end Provider Edge (PE) to leave the MPLS network at the customer edge.

FIGURE 15-16   Example of traffic crossing MPLS VPN

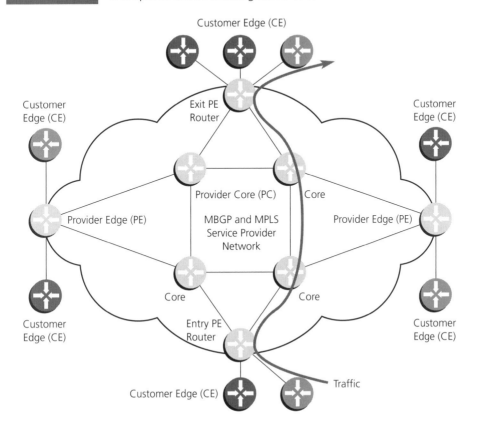

MPLS VPN terminology

Provider network (P-network) – network under the control of a service provider.

Customer network (C-network) – network under the control of the customer.

Provider Edge (PE) router – a router in the service provider network (part of P-network) to which customer edge routers connect (all MPLS VPN processing occurs in the PE router).

Customer Edge (CE) router – a router at a customer site (part of C-network) that connects to the service provider (via one or more provider edge routers).

Provider Core (P) router – a router in the service provider network interconnecting provider edge routers but, generally, not itself a provider edge router and without knowledge of the VPN.

▶

Entry/exit PE routers – the PE routers by which a packet enters and exits the service provider network.

Route distinguisher – an eight-octet value that is concatenated with an IPv4 prefix to create a unique VPN-IPv4 prefix.

VPN-IPv4 addresses – a prefix that consists of a customer VPN address that has been made unique by the addition of an eight-octet route distinguisher.

VPN-aware network – a provider backbone where MPLS-VPN is deployed.

MPLS VPN network architecture

The components that make up an MPLS VPN network are shown in Figure 15.17. At the edges of the network are **Customer Edge (CE) routers**. CE routers are part of the customer network and are not VPN aware. **Provider Edge (PE) routers** are where most VPN-specific configuration and processing occurs. PE routers receive routes from CE routers and transport them to other PE routers across a service-provider MPLS backbone. In the middle of the network are **Provider Core (P) routers**, or LSRs, which implement a pure Layer 3 MPLS transport service.

SNAPSHOT   **MPLS VPN features**

Connectionless service — with no requirements for tunnels or encryption to ensure network privacy.

Centralized service — flexible delivery of customized services to the user group represented by a VPN. VPNs deliver IP services such as multicast, QoS, and telephony support within a VPN, and centralized services like content and Web hosting. Combinations of services can be customized for individual customers.

Scalability — MPLS-based VPNs use Layer 3 connectionless architecture and are highly scalable.

Security — traffic belonging to individual VPNs remains separate.

Flexible addressing — MPLS VPNs provide a public and private view of addresses, enabling customers to use their own unregistered or private addresses. Customers can freely communicate across a public IP network without network address translation (NAT).

Straightforward migration — MPLS VPNs can be built over multiple network architectures, including IP, ATM, Frame Relay, and hybrid networks. There is no requirement to support MPLS on the customer edge (CE) router.

FIGURE 15-17 VPN/MPLS components

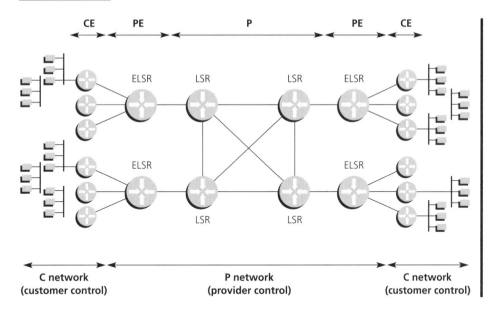

An important point to note is that P routers in the backbone are not VPN aware, hence do not have to carry customer routes, preventing routing tables in P routers from becoming unmanageable. VPN information is required only at PE routers, and can be partitioned between PE routers. PE routers need to know VPN routing information only for VPNs in which there are direct connections. The connection model and protocols used in MPLS VPNs are shown in Figure 15.18.

In MPLS VPNs, **the service provider backbone** is composed of **edge and core Label Switch Routers** (LSRs). Edge routers link to customer premise routers running standard routing software, and the devices communicate with one another via IP. They exchange routing information through dynamic routing (any routing protocol) and static routing.

In the provider network, the edge routers use MPLS and the Multiprotocol Interior Border Gateway Protocol (MP-IBGP) to communicate with one another and distribute VPN information. The routers in the core of the provider's MPLS network share a common interior gateway protocol with the edge routers, but do not run BGP and cannot distinguish one VPN from another. Since the core routers do not have to carry VPN addresses, provider networks scale to support more and bigger VPNs. Core LSRs do not mind how many VPNs are configured, only how many PE routers are in the core.

The provider's edge routers maintain separate routing tables for global and VPN routing. The global routing table contains all edge and core routes and is populated by IGP running across the VPN backbone. A **VPN routing and forwarding** (VRF) table is associated with each VPN and can include information about one or more directly connected customer sites. Overlapping IP addresses are enabled by the IP VPN addressing scheme in a way that still guarantees

FIGURE 15-18 MPLS VPN network

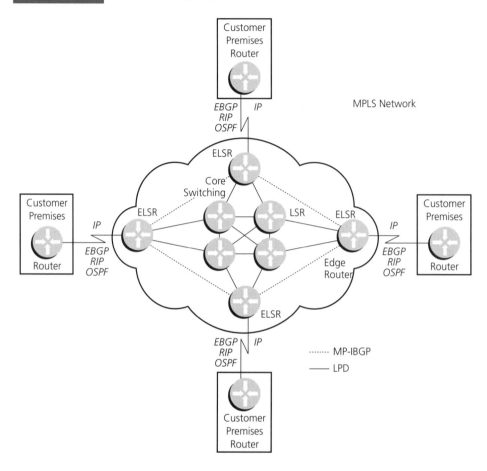

global uniqueness. Per-VPN segregation of routing information can take place in a single edge router, allowing that router to support multiple customer VPNs.

Based on the routing information stored in each VRF's IP routing, extended VPN-IPv4 addresses are used to forward packets to their destinations. To achieve this, an MPLS label is associated with each customer route. The PE router assigns the route originator's label and directs data packets to the correct CE router. Label forwarding across the provider backbone is based on dynamic IP paths or traffic engineered paths.

A customer data packet has two levels of labels attached when it is forwarded across the backbone:

■ **top label** – directs the packet to the correct PE router (VPN egress point) and is derived from an IGP route;

■ **second label** – indicates how that PE router should forward the packet and corresponds to the actual VPN route.

Figure 15.19 shows an MPLS/VPN forwarding example.

FIGURE 15-19 Example of MPLS VPN forwarding

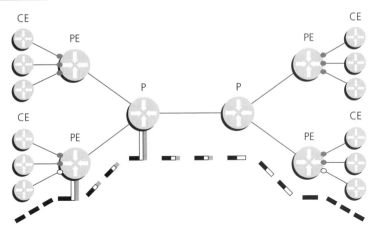

The PE router associates each CE router with a forwarding table that contains only the set of routes that are available to that CE router.

QUICK TIP   **VRF table**

The VPN routing and forwarding (VRF) table includes the routing information that defines a customer VPN site that is attached to a PE router. A VRF table consists of the following elements:

■ IP routing table;

■ derived forwarding table;

■ set of interfaces that use the forwarding table;

■ set of rules and routing protocols that determine what goes into the forwarding table.

VPN-IP forwarding tables contain labels that correspond to VPN-IP addresses. These labels route traffic to each site in a VPN. Because labels are used instead of IP addresses, customers can keep their **private addressing schemes**, within the corporate Internet, without requiring Network Address Translation (NAT) to pass traffic through the provider network. Traffic is separated between VPNs using a logically distinct forwarding table for each VPN. Based on the incoming interface, the switch selects a specific forwarding table, which lists only valid destinations in the VPN (thanks to BGP).

Any two non-intersecting VPNs (i.e. VPNs with no sites in common) may have overlapping address spaces; the same address may be reused, for different systems, in different VPNs. As long as a given end system has an address which is

SNAPSHOT   **VPN-IPv4 address**

A VPN-IPv4 address is a 12-byte quantity, beginning with an eight-octet Route Distinguisher (RD) and ending with a 32-bit IPv4 address.

unique within the scope of the VPNs that it belongs to, the end system itself does not need to know anything about VPNs. If two VPNs use the same IPv4 address prefix, the PEs translate these into unique VPN-IPv4 address prefixes. This ensures that if the same address is used in two different VPNs, it is possible to install two completely different routes to that address, one for each VPN.

Instead of peering with every other VPN site, the **customer premises router** peers only with the router in the service provider's local point of presence (POP). That router receives and holds routing information only for the VPNs directly connected to it. Consequently, customers who are managing their own VPNs will find that routing under the MPLS model is quite simple. Instead of dealing with complex networks consisting of cores of PVCs at Layer 2 or huge routing tables at Layer 3, they can employ the service provider backbone as the default route to all their sites.

Many customers have used private rather than global IP **addressing schemes**, so service providers need an efficient way to deal with the overlap of non-unique addresses: they append a **route distinguisher** (RD) to the IP address of each customer. Service providers are making such assignments independently of one another, but they can ensure the global uniqueness of each RD by including their own exclusive autonomous system (AS) number as part of the RD. With this approach, customers do not have to renumber their nodes, and service providers do not have to deal with address translation.

Two labels are associated with the VPN-IP address: a **VPN label** that identifies the VPN and an **IGP label** that directs the next hop across the appropriate IGP route in the provider's core network. Within the core, the forwarding is all done using hop-to-hop MPLS, which mimics regular hop-to-hop IP forwarding but does lookups based on the labels instead of the IP addresses. Any type of router or ATM switch that supports the Label Distribution Protocol (LDP) can be used.

The packet comes in through one access edge router (ingress), which uses the VPN label to forward it to another edge router (egress). One hop before the packet gets to the egress router, at the penultimate LSR, the IGP label is removed, and the BGP label tells the router which route associated with the FEC (i.e. which VPN) to send the packet across. This use of two levels of labeling increases the scalability of MPLS VPNs. The backbone LSRs carry only IGP routes, not VPN routes; only the edge routers carry the VPN routes.

The global routing table is not aware of the customer routes and the edge router/customer router, but a static route pointing to the interface is installed in the global table. This route is redistributed into the BGP-4 global table and advertised to the Internet gateway. The Internet gateway specified in the default route does not have to be directly connected, and different Internet gateways can be used for different VRF tables. A customer site can receive and announce routes to

SNAPSHOT   **MPLS VPNs**

Members of each VPN are identified as belonging to a closed user group through the use of MPLS labels. These labels carry next-hop switching information for packet forwarding as well as a VPN identifier to keep communications within a VPN private. Labels can indicate packet routes, user group, and service attributes. At the ingress into the provider network, incoming packets are processed and labels are selected and applied using VPN routing and forwarding (VRF) instance tables. The core devices merely forward packets based on labels, replacing traditional switching or routing tables.

or from the Internet by using a dedicated EBGP session over a separate interface. The service provider's edge router imports the customer-site routes into the global routing table and advertises them to the Internet. It also exports the default route or Internet routes to the customer premise router.

Peer vs. overlay VPNs

BGP/MPLS VPNs use the peer model, which will eventually replace the overlay model (see Figure 15.20). Although VPN solutions based on the **overlay model** are common today, these types of solutions have several major problems that limit large-scale VPN service deployment. Overlay model VPNs are based on creating connections and not networks. Each site has a router that is connected via point-to-point links to routers in other sites. This increases the amount of configuration changes required when adding a new site to an existing VPN. For VPNs that require full-mesh connectivity among sites, it involves changes to the configuration on all the existing sites, because each one needs an additional point-to-point connection to the new site and an additional routing peer with the router in the new site. VPNs built on connection-oriented, point-to-point overlays, Frame Relay, or ATM virtual connections (VCs) without fully meshed connections between customer sites simply do not scale well.

MPLS-based VPNs instead use the peer model and Layer 3 connectionless architecture to take advantage of a highly scalable VPN solution. The peer model requires a customer site to peer with only one PE router, as opposed to all other CPE or customer edge (CE) routers in the same VPN. The connectionless architecture allows the creation of VPNs in Layer 3, eliminating the need for tunnels or VCs, as shown in Figure 15.21.

MPLS solves these scalability problems by enabling service providers to deploy multiple VPN services across one very large physical network without the manual labor of configuring full logical point-to-point meshes for each customer's VPN. Rather, MPLS makes use of information in IP addresses for building any-to-any linkages in a Layer 3 connectionless network.

The peer-oriented model of MPLS-based VPNs requires a customer site to directly exchange routing information with just one provider edge router, as opposed to all other CPE routers that are members of the VPN. This connection-

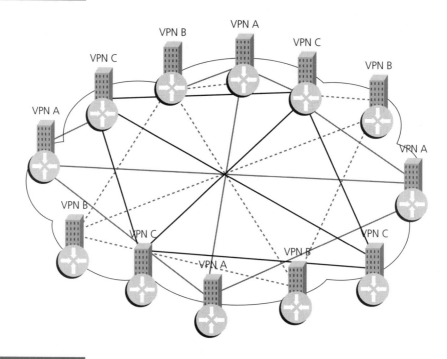

FIGURE 15-20 VPN overlay network

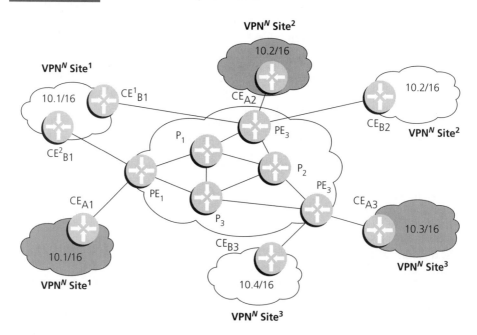

FIGURE 15-21 BGP/MPLS VPN peer model

less architecture allows the creation of VPNs in Layer 3, eliminating the need for Layer 2 tunnels or virtual circuits.

RFC WATCH   **MPLS VPN standardization status:**

RFC 2547 **BGP/MPLS VPNs**, 1999 (Informational)

RFC 2702 **Requirements for Traffic Engineering Over MPLS**, 1999 (Informational)

RFC 2917 **A Core MPLS IP VPN Architecture**, 2000 (Informational)

Multiprotocol extension to BGP-4

BGP uses VPN-IPv4 addresses to distribute network reachability information for each VPN within a service provider network. In building and maintaining routing tables, BGP sends routing messages within domains using interior BGP (iBGP) or between IP domains using exterior BGP (eBGP).

BGP propagates VPN information using BGP **multiprotocol extensions** for handling extended addresses (RFC 2858). BGP propagates reachability information (expressed as VPN-IPv4 addresses) among PE routers; reachability information for a given VPN is propagated only to members of that VPN. BGP multiprotocol extensions identify valid recipients of VPN routing information.

RFC WATCH   **BGP+**

RFC 2858 **Multiprotocol Extensions for BGP-4**, 2000 (Proposed Standard)

The distribution of VPN routing information is controlled through the use of VPN **route-target communities**, implemented by BGP **extended communities**. Distribution works as follows:

- When a VPN route is injected into BGP, it is associated with a list of VPN route-target communities. This list is set through an export list associated with the VRF from which the route was learned.

- Associated with each VRF is an import list of route-target communities, which defines values to be verified by the VRF table before a route is deemed eligible for import into the VPN routing instance. For example, if a given VRF's import list includes community-distinguishers A, B, and C, then any VPN route carrying A, B, or C is imported into the VRF.

A PE router learns an IP prefix from a CE router through static configuration, a BGP session, RIP, or OSPF. The PE then generates a VPN-IPv4 prefix by linking an eight-byte route distinguisher to the IP prefix. The VPN-IPv4 address uniquely identifies hosts within each VPN site, even if the site uses globally non-unique (unregistered private) IP addresses. The route distinguisher used to create the VPN-IPv4 prefix is specified by a configuration command on the PE router.

Note that among the suitable routing protocols mentioned for PE-CE routing is also RIP. This is because of its simplicity and easy implementation, namely in situations when PE router may support several hundreds of routing processes (one for each VPN).

QUICK TIP   **routing and label distribution protocols used in MPLS VPNs**

- Any IGP – provides reachability between all Label Switching Routers (PE-P-PE).
- LDP – distributes label information for IP destinations in core.
- MP-BGP-4 – used to distribute VPN routing information between PEs.
- RIPv2/BGP/OSPF/EIGRP/Static – can be used to route between PE and CE.

Routing information distribution steps (see Figure 15.22) are as follows:

FIGURE 15-22   MPLS VPN routing information distribution example

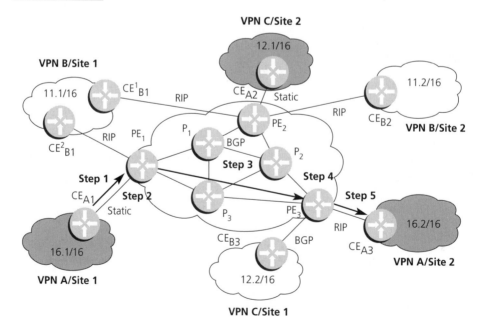

- Step 1: From site (CE) to service provider (PE), e.g. via RIP, OSPF, static routing, or BGP.
- Step 2: Export to provider's BGP at ingress PE.
- Step 3: Within/across service provider(s) (among PEs), e.g. via BGP.
- Step 4: Import from provider's BGP at egress PE.
- Step 5: From service provider (PE) to site (CE), e.g. via RIP, or static routing, or BGP.

QUICK TIP **MPLS VPN benefits**

- Private connectionless IP VPNs.
- Excellent scalability.
- IP addressing based on customers.
- Multiple QoS classes.
- Secure intranets/extranets.
- Simplified VPN provisioning.
- Support over any backbone technology.

15.4.3 MPLS/VPN extensions

MPLS VPNs are quite new and a quickly evolving topic, namely in conjunction with BGP deployment. There are many extensions and new features proposed, among which the following two (at least) are worth noting.

Carrier supporting carrier

Carrier supporting carrier is a term used to describe a situation where one service provider allows another service provider to use a segment of its backbone network. The service provider that provides the segment of the backbone network to the other provider is called the **backbone carrier**. The service provider that uses the segment of the backbone network is called the **customer carrier**. There is a work in progress on supporting this extension for a backbone carrier offering BGP/MPLS VPN services to a customer carrier in the form of ISPs or, again, BGP/MPLS VPN service provider.

When a backbone carrier and the customer carrier both provide BGP/MPLS VPN services, the method of transporting data is different from when a customer carrier provides only ISP services:

- When a customer carrier provides BGP/MPLS VPN services, its **external routes** are VPN-IPv4 routes. When a customer carrier is an ISP, its external routes are IP routes.

■ When a customer carrier provides BGP/MPLS VPN services, every site within the customer carrier must use **MPLS**. When a customer carrier is an ISP, the sites do not need to use MPLS.

Implementing the MPLS VPN carrier supporting carrier feature enables the **backbone carrier** to realize the following benefits:

■ **Effectiveness** – the backbone carrier can accommodate many customer carriers and give them access to its backbone. The backbone carrier does not need to create and maintain separate backbones for its customer carriers. Using one backbone network to support multiple customer carriers simplifies the backbone carrier's VPN operations. The backbone carrier uses a consistent method for managing and maintaining the backbone network.

■ **Scalability** – carrier supporting carrier can change the VPN to meet changing bandwidth and connectivity needs. The feature can accommodate unplanned growth and changes. The carrier supporting carrier feature enables tens of thousands of VPNs to be set up over the same network, and it allows a service provider to offer both VPN and Internet services.

■ **Flexibility** – the backbone carrier can accommodate many types of customer carriers. The backbone carrier can accept customer carriers who are ISPs or VPN service providers or both. The backbone carrier can accommodate customer carriers that require security and various bandwidths.

Benefits to the customer carrier are also numerous:

■ The MPLS VPN carrier supporting carrier feature removes from the customer carrier the burden of configuring, operating, and maintaining its own backbone. The customer carrier uses the backbone network of a backbone carrier, but the backbone carrier is responsible for network maintenance and operation.

■ Customer carriers who use the VPN services provided by the backbone carrier receive the same level of security that Frame Relay or ATM-based VPNs provide. Customer carriers can also use IPsec in their VPNs for a higher level of security; it is completely transparent to the backbone carrier.

■ Customer carriers can use any Layer 2 technology (SONET, DSL, Frame Relay) to connect the CE routers to the PE routers and the PE routers to the P routers. The MPLS VPN carrier supporting carrier feature is link-layer independent. The CE routers and PE routers use IP to communicate, and the backbone carrier uses MPLS.

■ The customer carrier can use any addressing scheme and still be supported by a backbone carrier. The customer address space and routing information are independent of the address space and routing information of other customer carriers or the backbone provider.

Inter-autonomous systems for MPLS VPNs

Some VPNs need to extend across multiple service providers. Regardless of the complexity and location of the VPNs, the connection between autonomous systems must be seamless to the customer. The **inter-autonomous systems for**

MPLS VPNs extension (work in progress) provides that seamless integration of autonomous systems and service providers. Separate autonomous systems from different service providers can communicate by exchanging IPv4 network layer reachability information (NLRI) in the form of VPN-IPv4 addresses. The autonomous systems' border edge routers use EBGP to exchange that information. Then, an IGP distributes the network layer information for VPN-IPv4 prefixes throughout each VPN and each autonomous system. An EBGP allows a service provider to set up an inter-domain routing system that guarantees the loop-free exchange of routing information between separate autonomous systems.

An MPLS VPN with inter-autonomous system support allows a service provider to provide to customers scalable Layer 3 VPN services, such as Web hosting, application hosting, interactive learning, electronic commerce, and telephony service. A VPN service provider supplies a secure, IP-based network that shares resources on one or more physical networks.

The primary function of an EBGP is to exchange network reachability information between autonomous systems, including information about the list of autonomous system routes. The autonomous systems use EGBP border edge routers to distribute the routes, which include label switching information. Each border edge router rewrites the next-hop and MPLS labels.

The inter-autonomous system MPLS VPN feature provides for a VPN to cross more than one service provider backbone and for a VPN to exist in different areas. Additionally it supports **confederations** to optimize IBGP meshing; in other words it allows a service provider to offer MPLS VPNs across the confederation because it supports the exchange of labeled VPN-IPv4 NLRI between the sub-autonomous systems that form the confederation.

15.4.4 Putting it all together – RSVP, DiffServ, and MPLS

A certain set of conflicts may arise when taking into account only the current (*de facto*) standards:

- How far is MPLS different from DiffServ? (Are they not both ways of doing the same thing?) Both are standards efforts from the IETF and use tagging packets to prioritize them. But DiffServ works at the network layer, while MPLS works at the lower link layer, meaning the efforts should be mutually exclusive of each other. MPLS can work fine with or without DiffServ, and vice versa; DiffServ networks can make use of MPLS underlying networks, and MPLS devices could assign switching labels after reading DiffServ instructions in IP headers.

- What type of protocol is used to distribute MPLS? At an IETF meeting in August 1998, a proposal was passed to use RSVP, though more members of the group wanted to use the Label Distribution Protocol (LDP) or its extension Constraint-based Routing-LDP (CR-LDP). While members were swayed by Cisco's argument that RSVP was further along, there was some concern that Cisco had used its muscle to pass the decision. Cisco has since committed to supporting LDP.

Note: Standard efforts are supported by related vendor (industry) forums which are dedicated both to specification preparation and also interoperability testing. One of the latest created is the **MPLS Forum** (initiated in 2000).

RSVP provisions resources for network traffic, whereas DiffServ simply marks and prioritizes traffic. RSVP is more complex and demanding than DiffServ in terms of router requirements, so can negatively impact on backbone routers. This is why the best common practice says to limit the use of RSVP on the backbone, and why DiffServ can exist there.

DiffServ is a perfect complement to RSVP as the combination can enable end-to-end quality of service (QoS). End hosts may use RSVP requests with high granularity (e.g. bandwidth, jitter threshold, etc.). Border routers at backbone ingress points can then map those reservations to a class of service indicated by a DS-byte (or the source host may also set the DS-byte accordingly). At the backbone egress point, the RSVP provisioning may be honored again, to the final destination. Ingress points essentially do traffic conditioning on a customer basis to assure that service level agreements (SLAs) are satisfied.

RSVP provisioning for aggregates

By classifying traffic flows, DiffServ and MPLS create what are effectively pipes for aggregates. For these pipes to provide any service quality better than standard best-effort, traffic on these virtual pipes must not exceed capacity. The problem is that neither DiffServ nor MPLS have specific protocol mechanics for detecting how much bandwidth they need and then allocating the necessary resources for dedicated usage. Only RSVP is designed to do that. Hence, although RSVP was originally designed to allocate bandwidth for individual application flows, it is very important for allocating bandwidth to accommodate the needs of traffic aggregates as well.

This need highlights the challenge, however, for network engineers using DiffServ or MPLS to know the bandwidth demands in anticipation, so they can make the appropriate resource reservation request. Additionally, senders and receivers at both ends of the virtual pipes must make these reservation requests so the appropriate *PATH* and *RESV* messages can be sent from and to the appropriate unicast locations. A key problem in the design of RSVP version 1 is, as noted in its applicability statement, that it lacks facilities for the aggregation of individual reserved sessions into a common class. The use of such aggregation is required for scalability. So, in addition to using RSVP to provision for QoS aggregates, another consideration is using RSVP to provision for **RSVP aggregates** (discussed in Chapter 13 in relation to IntServ and DiffServ interoperation).

MPLS for DiffServ

As might be expected, because DiffServ and MPLS are similar with respect to the qualitative QoS they enable (i.e. classification), mapping DiffServ traffic on MPLS LSPs is relatively simple, but there are still DiffServ-specific considerations. To support DiffServ's per-hop model, an MPLS network operator needs to allocate a set of aggregate forwarding resources for each DiffServ forwarding class in each MPLS router (LSR) and assign labels. Additionally an LSR may need to associate the packet with a particular drop-precedence (which could be stored in the experimental (*Exp*) field of the MPLS header).

Further considerations relate to the complexity of the policy setting and interoperability across the Internet. Policies need to be defined, set up, and maintained, which may be beyond the scope of some organizations. In addition, network administrators may discover that they need to **upgrade** their internetworking hardware or software to provide QoS. Another potential risk is that of **incompatibility**. Due to lack of specificity in protocol definitions, as well as vendors' desire to add value by extending a protocol, it is possible for products from two vendors to each be compatible with a standard and yet not be able to interwork with each other. Users should also carefully verify what a particular vendor means by policy management deployed at its products.

15.4.5 MPLS: the reality vs. the misconceptions

Multiprotocol Label Switching (MPLS) is the latest step in the evolution of routing/forwarding technology for the core of the Internet. However, there are still a number of misconceptions concerning the role of MPLS in the core of the Internet. Some in the Internet community believe that MPLS was developed to provide a standard that allowed vendors to transform ATM switches into high-performance Internet backbone routers. While this might have been one of the original goals of proprietary multilayer switching solutions in the mid-1990s, recent advances in silicon technology allow ASIC-based IP route lookup engines to run just as fast as MPLS or ATM VPI/VCI lookup engines. Although MPLS can enhance the forwarding performance of processor-based systems, accelerating packet forwarding performance was not the primary force behind the creation of the MPLS working group.

Others in the Internet community believe that MPLS was designed to completely eliminate the need for conventional, longest-match IP routing. This never was an objective of the MPLS working group because its members understood that traditional Layer 3 routing would always be required in the Internet. MPLS is not independent of routing: it offers some alternatives in the packet-forwarding part of routing, but still depends on path determination. MPLS hence can only work after the routing protocols or static routing has been implemented and become functional. Packet filtering at firewalls and ISP boundaries is a fundamental component of supporting security and enforcing administrative policy. Because packet filtering requires a detailed examination of packet headers, conventional Layer 3 forwarding is still required for these applications.

It is unlikely that a large number of host systems will implement MPLS. This means that each packet transmitted by a host still needs to be forwarded to a first-hop Layer 3 device where the packet header can be examined prior to forwarding it towards its ultimate destination. The first-hop router can then either forward the packet using conventional longest-match routing or assign a label and forward the packet over an LSP.

If a Layer 3 device along the path examines the IP header and assigns a label, the label represents an aggregate route because it is impossible to maintain label bindings for every host on the global Internet. This means that, at some point along the delivery path, the IP header must be examined by another Layer 3 device to determine a finer granularity to continue forwarding the packet. This router can elect to either forward the packet using conventional routing or assign a label and forward the packet over a new label switched path.

At the last hop before the destination host, the packet must be forwarded using conventional Layer 3 routing because it is not practical to assign a separate label to every host on the destination subnetwork.

The reality about MPLS is that it delivers a solution that seamlessly integrates the control of IP routing with the simplicity of Layer 2 switching. Furthermore, MPLS provides a foundation that supports the deployment of advanced routing services because it solves a number of complex problems:

- MPLS addresses the scalability issues associated with the currently deployed IP-over-ATM overlay model.
- MPLS significantly reduces the complexity of network operation.
- MPLS facilitates the delivery of new routing capabilities that enhance conventional IP routing techniques.
- MPLS offers a standards-based solution that promotes multivendor interoperability.

As a reminder let's mention again that the fundamental building blocks MPLS shares with all multilayer switching solutions are:

- separation of the control and forwarding components;
- label-swapping forwarding algorithm.

A summary of the actual **sequence** of events in MPLS network deployment is as follows:

- Layer 3 path determination, either dynamic or static, works out the connectivity.
- Application of additional mechanisms, which may be no more than additional constraints on path determination, select **Label Switched Paths** (LSP). LSPs are associated with **Forwarding Equivalence Classes** (FEC), which are ways to leave your cloud (i.e. interface, output QoS, etc.) Think of these as hop-by-hop specifications of MPLS tunnels through an IP or other cloud that can map labels onto a cloud-specific forwarding lookup mechanism (label between Layer 2/Layer 3 headers, lambda – see Chapter 16).
- Use a **label distribution mechanism** (LDP, RSVP-TE, CR-LDP) to distribute information to **Label Switching Routers** (LSR) on how to handle the next-hop forwarding for a specific incoming label. The scope of a label is a single link. There is a relationship between a label and an FEC, but it is not a one-to-one relationship. Loosely, an FEC is operationally defined by sets of labels. LSRs do not know much about the traffic they carry.
- Use **Edge Label Switching Routers** (ELSR) at the **ingress** and **egress** to the cloud, to apply the rules to recognize the FEC to which traffic belongs, and tag the traffic with a label. In practical terms, the ELSR may have a rule that identifies traffic and puts it on a particular path (i.e. LSP with ingress label). LSRs forward the traffic given them by ingress ELSR or other LSRs.

The following RFCs have been brought to your attention in this chapter:

RFC 2341 *Cisco Layer Two Forwarding Protocol (L2F),* 1998 (Historic)

RFC 2401 *Security Architecture for the Internet Protocol, 1998* (Proposed Standard)

RFC 2402 *IP Authentication Header,* 1998 (Proposed Standard)

RFC 2406 *IP Encapsulating Security Payload (ESP),* 1998 (Proposed Standard)

RFC 2407 *The Internet IP Security Domain of Interpretation for ISAKMP,* 1998 (Proposed Standard)

RFC 2408 *Internet Security Association and Key Management Protocol* (ISAKMP), 1998 (Proposed Standard)

RFC 2409 *The Internet Key Exchange (IKE),* 1998 (Proposed Standard)

RFC 2410 *The NULL Encryption Algorithm and Its Use With IPsec,* 1998 (Proposed Standard)

RFC 2411 *IP Security Document Roadmap,* 1998 (Informational)

RFC 2419 *The PPP DES Encryption Protocol, Version 2* (DESE-bis), 1998 (Proposed Standard)

RFC 2420 *The PPP Triple-DES Encryption Protocol (3DESE),* 1998 (Proposed Standard)

RFC 2516 *A Method for Transmitting PPP Over Ethernet (PPPoE),* 1999 (Informational)

RFC 2637 *Point-to-Point Tunneling Protocol,* 1999 (Informational)

RFC 2661 *Layer Two Tunneling Protocol (L2TP),* 1999 (Proposed Standard)

RFC 2784 *Generic Routing Encapsulation (GRE),* 2000 (Proposed Standard)

RFC 2809 *Implementation of L2TP Compulsory Tunneling via RADIUS,* 2000 (Informational)

RFC 2888 *Secure Remote Access with L2TP,* 2000 (Informational)

RFC 2890 *Key and Sequence Number Extensions to GRE,* 2000 (Proposed Standard)

RFC 2983 *Differentiated Services and Tunnels,* 2000 (Informational)

RFC 3031 *Multiprotocol Label Switching Architecture,* 2001 (Proposed Standard)

RFC 3032 *MPLS Label Stack Encoding,* 2001 (Proposed Standard)

RFC 3034 *Use of Label Switching on Frame Relay Networks Specification,* 2001 (Proposed Standard)

▶

RFC 3035 *MPLS using LDP and ATM VC Switching,* 2001 (Proposed Standard)

RFC 3036 *LDP Specification,* 2001 (Proposed Standard)

RFC 3037 *LDP Applicability,* 2001 (Informational)

RFC 3063 *MPLS Loop Prevention Mechanism,* 2001 (Experimental)

RFC 3070 *Layer Two Tunneling Protocol (L2TP) over Frame Relay,* 2001 (Proposed Standard)

RFC 3077 *A Link-Layer Tunneling Mechanism for Unidirectional Links,* 2001 (Proposed Standard)

RFC 3078 *Microsoft Point-To-Point Encryption (MPPE) Protocol,* 2001 (Informational)

C H A P T E R   1 6

Optical networking

16.1 Background to optical networking

Currently the largest segment of network and Internet traffic growth stems from applications based on the set of IP/RTP/HTTP protocols. The recent trend has been to offer routing and switching for IP layers in Application-Specific Integrated Circuits (ASICs). The internetworking performance need, coupled with the requirement for IP quality of service (QoS), multicast applications has led to a new trend: IP over optical internetworking infrastructure. The underlying communications architectures that support the portfolio of IP services and applications are usually **layered** upon one another.

16.1.1 Typical four-layer network

Today's data networks may have four layers (see Figure 16.1): IP for carrying applications and services, asynchronous transfer mode (ATM) for traffic engineering, SONET/SDH for transport, and Dense Wavelength Division Multiplexing (DWDM) for capacity.

  The Asynchronous Transfer Mode (ATM) layer (see also Section 3.8):

- performs segmentation and reassembly of variable length packets to fixed sized cells (53 bytes);
- creates class of service based on elements such as delay, jitter, and loss;
- creates connections from source to destination (either PVC or SVC);
- scales bandwidth beyond DS3/E3 (see Appendix D) rates to optical carrier rates.

The SONET/SDH layer (see also Section 3.9):

- interfaces the electrical and optical layers;
- delivers highly reliable ring-based topologies;
- performs mapping of time-division multiplexing (TDM) time slots from digital hierarchical levels;
- defines strict jitter bounds.

The Dense Wavelength Division Multiplexing (DWDM) layer:

- multiplexes electrical signals onto specific wavelengths (by color) in a point-to-point topology to maximize the bandwidth out of available fiber runs;

FIGURE 16-1 Multilayer physical topologies

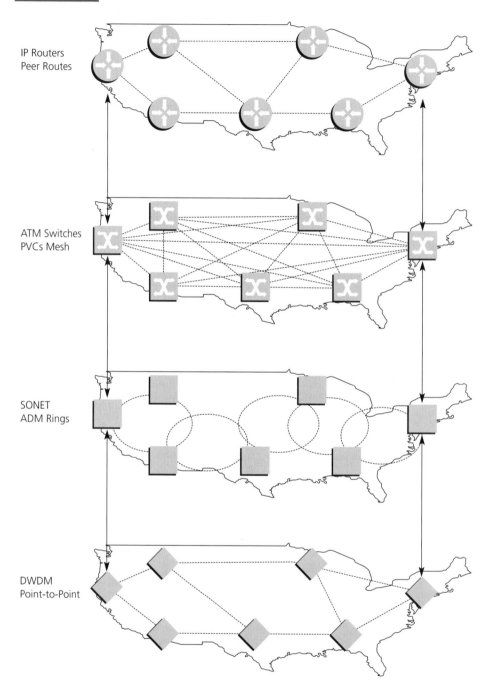

IP Routers
Peer Routes

ATM Switches
PVCs Mesh

SONET
ADM Rings

DWDM
Point-to-Point

- creates multiple virtual fibers, each carrying multigigabits of traffic per second, on a single fiber;
- interfaces the electrical and optical layers.

The main roles of the router are still perceived as being to:

- maintain available IP path or routing information (such as how to get from source to destination);
- forward IP packets (possibly with MPLS labels);
- provide other services such as encryption, compression, packet-based QoS, address translation, and tunneling.

16.1.2 *Advanced two-layer network*

However, due to the continuous striving for more network bandwidth, the typical four-layer architecture is converging into a two-layer communication infrastructure (see Figure 16.2 for the evolution of layering into communications architectures): **packet-by-packet IP routers supported by an optical transport layer.** The ATM function of traffic engineering (e.g. quality of service, QoS, DiffServ) is being absorbed into the **IP layer**, and the transport capabilities of SONET/SDH (e.g. protection and accommodation of the various bit rates through tributaries) is being absorbed by the **optical layer.** Therefore, what has been four layers converges to two. For nomadic situations, the physical layer would be wireless, but we will concentrate on optical networking here.

FIGURE 16-2 Evolution of multiplayer architecture

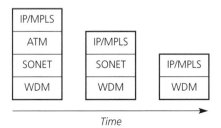

Time

Dense and **Ultra Dense Wavelength Division Multiplexing** (DWDM and UDWDM) is proposed for the physical layer. The denser the packing of hundreds and thousands of lightwaves, each carrying 40 Gbps, the more can be gained from a dozen or more fiber strands. Each network end point port would still be terminated with the self-healing, extremely reliable SONET/SDH protocol on the network side. WDM, via DWDM and UDWDM, will become the major technology operating in the core. WDM will likely become the technology of choice for an **all-optical network** (AON) in long-distance applications.

The DWDM system basic building blocks (see Figure 16.3):

FIGURE 16-3 DWDM system

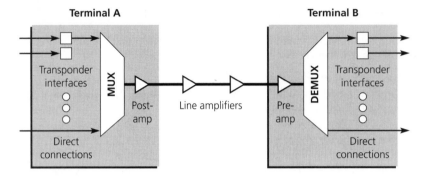

- optical amplifiers;
- optical multiplexers;
- stable optical sources;
- transponders (one transponder required per wavelength).

Optical cross-connects (OXCs) are likely to emerge as the preferred option for switching multigigabit or even terabit datastreams, since electronic per-packet processing is avoided. It is widely expected that the predominant traffic carried over data networks will be IP-based, which suggests that the development of fast router technologies is essential for the aggregation of slower datastreams into streams suitable for OXCs. Likewise, IP packet-based statistical multiplexing is likely to be the predominant multiplexing technology for data streams smaller than those suitable for DWDM. As the capabilities of both routers and OXCs grow rapidly, the high data rates of optical transport suggest the distinct possibility of bypassing the SONET/SDH and ATM layers. In order to bypass these layers their necessary functions must move directly to the routers, OXCs, and DWDMs. In the end, this results in a simpler, more cost-efficient network that will transport a wide range of datastreams and very large volumes of traffic.

16.2 Different flavors of optical networks

Optical networks are those in which the dominant physical layer technology for transport is **optical fiber.** They can be opaque or all-optical, and can be single-wavelength or based on **dense wavelength division multiplexing** (DWDM). In **opaque networks** the path between end users is interrupted at intermediate nodes by **optical-electronic-optical** (OEO) conversion operations. When this introduces dependencies on bit rate and even bit pattern syntax, any hope of transparency to these attributes is lost. The traditional SONET/SDH is an **opaque single-wavelength system.** Today's widely installed WDM systems are opaque too, the intermediate nodes being either electronic add-drop multiplexers or digital crossconnects (optical add-drop multiplexers, OADMs, or optical crossconnects, OXCs) that actually have electronic bit handling in the signal path. None of these opaque systems have the versatility and power of the all-optical network.

SNAPSHOT lightpath

The **lightpath** is a **circuit-switched connection** consisting of the **same wavelength allocated on each link** along the path. It may consist of **different wavelengths** along the path if **converters** are present.

An optical packet network consists of optical packet switches interconnected with fibers running WDM. In **all-optical networks,** each circuit-switched connection – **lightpath** – is totally optical, or at least totally transparent, except at the end nodes. In other words, an all-optical WDM lightpath is characterized by its complete lack of protocol dependency.

The switches may be adjacent or connected by lightpaths. The user data is transmitted in optical packets switched within each **optical packet switch** entirely in the optical domain. Thus, the user data remains as an optical signal in the entire path from source to destination eliminating the optical-to-electrical or electrical-to-optical conversions.

The dominant role assumed by the all-optical approach applies not only in wide area Telco networks, where the lightpaths can be hundreds to thousands of kilometers in length, but also in the metropolitan environment (tens to several hundreds of kilometers in length) and to some extent the access (1–10 km). There is some question whether LANs (0–1 km) will ever go all-optical.

At the technical level, the recent decade of **progress in optical networking** has been mainly due to advances in six areas:

- improved architectural understanding;
- developments in purely optical crossconnects;
- more channels of higher bit rate;
- new kinds of fiber and amplifiers;
- longer lightpaths;
- lower technology costs.

Although optical switching is viewed as a breakthrough in the direction of high-speed networking and has been accordingly researched over the past decade, the optical technologies have not yet been widely used in actual products. Among the most often quoted reasons for this situation are the following inadequacies:

- the lack of deep and fast optical memories – preventing the implementation in optics of the same router architectures as in electronics;
- the poor level of integration – due to some intrinsic limitations and also the limited effort devoted to the subject compared to the mature silicon industry.

Recent technical advancements and proper network design can now make the optimal use of optics and electronics. It is also important to point out that the legendary longer time to market of optical technology compared to electronics is becoming less and less an argument since the recent explosion worldwide of activity around optical technologies.

16.2.1 Standardization activities

Underscoring the importance of versatile networking capabilities in the optical domain, a number of standards organizations have initiated work items to study the requirements and architectures for reconfigurable optical networks. ITU-T Recommendation G.872 speaks of an **optical transport network** (OTN) as a transport network bounded by optical channel access points. IP over OTN is shown in Figure 16.4.

FIGURE 16-4 Optical transport network

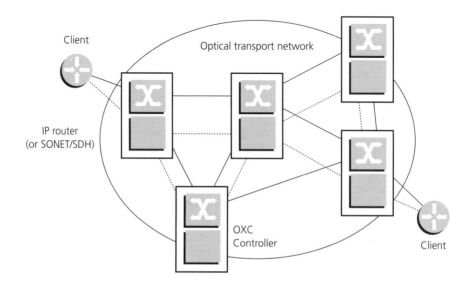

The OTN architecture is based on a layered structure, which includes:

- **optical channel layer network** – supports end-to-end networking of optical channel trails between access points. The optical channel layer network provides the following functions: routing, monitoring, grooming, and protection and restoration of optical channels;
- **optical multiplex section layer network;**
- **optical transmission section layer network.**

Other standards organizations and interoperability forums actively pursuing projects related to dynamically configurable optical networks include the ANSI T1X1.5 committee, the **Optical Internetworking Forum** (OIF), the **Optical Domain Service Interconnect** (ODSI) coalition, and the IETF, namely in the area of MPLS in optical networks (see below).

16.2.2 The place of SONET and WDM in high-speed network infrastructures

Today's fiber optic transport networks are primarily constructed with SONET/SDH terminals and **add/drop multiplexers** (ADMs) using TDM technology. The long-distance networks rely mostly on SONET/SDH technology for its reliability and richness of bandwidth. However, SONET/SDH high-performance capabilities are far from being a contender to terabit routers. The current bandwidth demands are being aggregated in thousands of Gbps to quench the enormous Internet thirst for data transport.

SNAPSHOT   **SONET pros and cons**

SONET is the standard for optical transport built on the multiplexing hierarchy based on DS0 with fast protection switching for all traffic. SONET has two parts:

- protocol – framing structure, signaling;
- architecture – self-healing rings.

Pros:

- very high performance;
- guaranteed low delay;
- excellent Layer 1 resilience;
- dynamic allocation of bandwidth (SRP and DPT);
- for OC-3c OC-12c and above (more than 9.6 Gbps).

Cons:

- high cost (but prices falling);
- not always available.

Packet over SONET

Packet over SONET (PoS) provides a method for efficiently carrying data packets in SONET/SDH frames. High-bandwidth capacity coupled with efficient link utilization make PoS largely preferred for building the core of data networks. PoS overhead, which averages about 3%, is significantly lower than the 15% average for the ATM cell overhead. The current IETF PoS specification is RFC 2615 (PPP over SONET), which renders obsolete RFC 1619.

RFC WATCH *Packet over SONET*

RFC 2615 **PPP over SONET/SDH,** 1999 (Proposed Standard)

PoS overview:

■ Either cells or frames within a switch and SONET/SDH payload at egress of switch.

■ PoS is serial transmission of multiprotocol packets over SONET/SDH frames – efficient high-speed transport with low overhead.

■ Available bandwidth is dynamically allocated.

■ Any application can burst up to the entire available bandwidth capacity – packet-based infrastructure.

■ Switching delay is low, as is the variability in delay.

Packet over SONET (PoS) cons:

■ More suited towards packet-based applications – direct mapping of packets over transport SONET/SDH media.

■ QoS evolving from best-effort to guaranteed approach – efforts underway to include differentiated service mechanisms.

■ Not suitable for low speed links – typically used over high-speed fiber-based infrastructures.

PoS pros:

■ Dynamic allocation of bandwidth – bandwidth is available to any application that needs it.

■ Scalable – underlying technology can scale in speeds with increase in traffic volume.

■ Efficiency-overhead – direct mapping of packets over SONET payload increases efficiency by removing overhead.

■ Fault-tolerant, reliable carrier class redundancy with automatic protection switching (APS) – very fast switchovers in case of failure.

■ Underlying transport flexibility – can be used with different underlying transport-SONET/SDH, DWDM equipment.

SONET and PoS differences

SONET/SDH is a high-speed TDM physical-layer transport technology, inherently optimized for voice. PoS provides a means for using the speed and excellent management capabilities of SONET/SDH to optimize data transport. A SONET/SDH **frame** is 810 bytes and is normally represented as a two-dimensional byte-per-cell grid of 9 rows and 90 columns. The SONET/SDH frame is divided into transport overhead and payload bytes. The transport overhead bytes consist of section and line overhead bytes, while the payload bytes are made up of the payload capacity and some more overhead bytes, referred to as path overhead. The overhead bytes are responsible for the rich management capabilities of SONET/SDH.

PoS specifies STS-3c/STM-1 (155 Mbps) as the basic data rate, and it has a usable data bandwidth of 149.760 Mbps. PoS frames are mapped into SONET/SDH frames and they sit in the payload envelope as octet streams aligned on octet boundaries. RFC 2615 recommends payload scrambling. The addition of **payload scrambling** when inserting the HDLC-like framed PPP packets into the SONET STS- SPE/SDH Higher Order VC remedies the RFC 2615. It was operationally found to permit malicious users to generate packets with bit patterns that could create SONET/SDH-layer low transition density synchronization problems, emulation of the SDH set-reset scrambler pattern, and replication of the STM-N frame alignment word. The use of the $x^{43} + 1$ self-synchronous scrambler was introduced to alleviate these potential security problems.

RFC 2615 also recommends a safeguard against bit **sequences**, a known security issue of bandwidth reduction by intentional transmission of characters or sequences requiring transparency processing by including flag and/or escape characters in user data. A user may cause up to a 100% increase in the bandwidth required for transmitting his or her packets by filling the packet with flag and/or escape characters.

16.2.3 Optical switching

A **WDM optical packet switch** consists of four parts: the input interface, the switching fabric, the output interface, and the control unit. The input interface is mainly used for packet delineation and alignment, packet header information extraction, and packet header removal. The switch fabric is the core of the switch and is used to switch packets optically. The output interface is used to regenerate the optical signals and insert the packet header. The control unit controls the switch using the information in the packet headers. Because of synchronization requirements, optical packet switches are typically designed for fixed-size packets.

When a packet arrives at a WDM optical packet switch, it is first processed by the input interface. The header and payload of the packet are separated, and the header is converted into the electrical domain and processed by the control unit electronically. The payload remains an optical signal throughout the switch. After the payload passes through the switching fabric, it is recombined with the header, which is converted back into the optical domain at the output interface.

Packet coding techniques

Several optical packet coding techniques have been studied. There are three basic categories: bit serial, bit parallel, and out-of-band signaling. Bit serial coding can be implemented using **optical code-division multiplexing** (OCDM), optical pulse interval, or mixed-rate techniques. In OCDM, each bit carries its routing information, while in the latter two techniques, multiple bits are organized into a packet payload with a packet header that includes routing information. The difference between the latter two techniques is that in optical pulse interval, the packet header and payload are transmitted at the same rate, whereas in the **mixed-rate technique**, the packet header is transmitted at a lower rate than the payload so that the packet header can easily be processed electronically. In bit parallel coding, multiple bits are transmitted at the same time but on separate wavelengths.

Out-of-band signaling coding includes **subcarrier multiplexing** (SCM) **and dual-wavelength coding**. In SCM, the packet header is placed in an electrical subcarrier above the baseband frequencies occupied by the packet payload, and both are transmitted in the same time slot. In dual-wavelength coding, the packet header and payload are transmitted in separate wavelengths but in the same time slot.

Contention resolution

Contention resolution is necessary in order to handle the case where more than one packet is destined to go out of the same output port at the same time. This is a problem that commonly arises in packet switches, and is known as external blocking. It is typically resolved by buffering all the contending packets, except one which is permitted to go out. In an optical packet switch, techniques designed to address the external blocking problem include optical buffering, exploiting the wavelength domain, and using deflection routing. Whether these will prove adequate to address the external blocking problem is still highly doubtful. Below we discuss each of these solutions.

Optical buffering

Currently, optical buffering can only be implemented using **optical delay lines** (ODLs). An ODL can delay a packet for a specified amount of time, which is related to the length of the delay line. Thus, optical buffering is the Achilles' heel of optical packet switches. Delay lines may be acceptable in prototype switches, but are not commercially viable. The alternative, of course, is to convert the optical packet to the electrical domain and store it electronically. This is not an acceptable solution, since electronic memories cannot keep up with the speeds of optical networks. There are many ways an ODL can be used to emulate an electronic buffer.

For instance, a buffer for N packets with a FIFO discipline can be implemented using N delay lines of different lengths. Delay line i delays a packet for i time slots. A counter keeps track of the number of packets in the buffer. It is decreased by 1 when a packet leaves the buffer, and increased by 1 when a packet enters the buffer. Suppose that the value of the counter is j when a packet arrives at the buffer; then the packet will be routed to the j-th delay line. Limited by the length of the delay lines, this type of buffer is usually small, and does not scale up.

Exploiting the wavelength domain

In WDM, several wavelengths run on a fiber link that connects two optical switches. This can be exploited to minimize external blocking. If two packets are destined to go out of the same output port at the same time they can be still transmitted out, but on two different wavelengths. This method may have some potential in minimizing external blocking, particularly since the number of wavelengths that can be coupled together onto a single fiber continues to increase.

Deflection routing

Deflection routing is ideally suited to switches that have little buffer space. When there is a conflict between two packets, one will be routed to the correct output port, and the other to any other available output port which may lead to greater than minimum distance routing. Hence, for each source–destination pair the number of hops taken by a packet is no longer fixed. In this way, little or no buffer is needed. The deflected packet may end up following a longer path to its destination. As a result, the end-to-end delay for a packet may be unacceptably high. Also, packets will have to be reordered at the destination since they are likely to arrive out of sequence.

Deflection routing plays a prominent role in many optical network architectures, since it can be implemented with no or modest optical buffering. Asynchronous (unslotted) deflection routing combined with limited buffering can help avoid complex synchronization schemes and provide decent performance with careful design.

Monitoring the number of hops a packet has taken is essential to avoid congestion, which can be caused by too many packets wandering in the network. Having a time-to-live field in the packet header (as in IP packets) is hard to implement because it requires the header to be rewritten at every node. One possible solution is to have the source node put a time stamp on each packet and the other nodes compare it with the local time when the packet is in transit, provided all the nodes have a globally synchronized clock.

16.3 Optical switches

Today, **optical switches** are being built in two fundamentally different ways:

- **OEO** (Optical-Electrical-Optical) architectures – convert optical signals into electrical signals and back to optical. This enables extraction and manipulation of the control plane information and enables the data itself to be manipulated, assuming the components can keep up with line speed. However, the opto-electrical converters cannot operate at the extreme high speed of pure optical switches.

- Pure **photonic switches** – use emerging technologies, such as MEMS (micro-electromechanical) tilting mirrors, to concentrate and switch individual **lambdas** (DWDM wavelengths) without converting the signals to the electrical domain. While this may offer very fast lightwave switching, it has substantial implications for signaling and routing and for the control plane, in terms of extracting information embedded in a lightwave. The control plane either consumes an entire lambda, which must then be converted to an electrical signal, or an alternative out-of-band mechanism must be used to transmit signaling and routing information. Photonic switching, where traffic is rerouted based at the high-speed stream level rather than the packet or cell level, is coming rapidly. However, photonic switching will complement, not replace, routing.

Recent technology developments that are now making the all-optical solution quite workable include particularly the invention of practical **all-optical cross-connects** (OXCs) and **all-optical add-drop multiplexers** (OADMs) that enable the evolution from just point-to-point WDM links to full networks.

An OXC is simply a large photonic switch having N full-duplex ports, each of which can connect to any other, and also itself. For WDM service, the OADM is a 2×2 degenerate form of the $N \times N$ OXC that extracts and reinserts certain lightpaths for local use and expresses the others through. At each wavelength, the OADM has two full-duplex ports on the facilities side and two on the local side. Usually, for the passthrough state at a given wavelength, the two line-side ports are connected to each other, and for the add-drop state each line-side full-duplex port terminates locally. In general, with the OXC, any one of N full-duplex ports can connect to any other one or to itself, and any of the ports can play the role of a line side or local side port.

MEMS

Recently, there has been a surge in interest in the use of silicon-based **micro-electromechanical systems** (MEMS) for a variety of optical networking applications. This interest is due to a convergence of market needs for specific types of devices which can only be made possible through the use of MEMS technology, coupled with the rapid maturing of optical MEMS technology itself from a research curiosity to an enabler of key applications in optical networks.

One of the key application areas for MEMS technology is large-scale optical switches. MEMS technology is also finding its way into small-scale switches, variable optical attenuators, and tunable lasers, all of which are key elements of an optical network.

Using silicon microfabrication to produce optical components provides some compelling advantages. First, the silicon surface when treated properly can provide an optical surface of extremely high quality (i.e. flat and scatter-free). Second, the excellent mechanical properties of single-crystal silicon allow the fabrication of fatigue-free devices. Since single-crystal silicon has no dislocations, it has virtually no fatigue and is a perfect elastic material – a property that is extremely desirable for precision mechanics applications. Third, the electrical properties of silicon allow for the integration of sensors and detectors with extraordinarily high precision, often required in optical work. Since optics is 'light work,' the required forces are low and can often be provided by microactuators which have very limited force capabilities, typically the case with micromachined parts. Often the required displacements in many applications are also quite small, in the order of a wavelength (a few microns), which again provides a good match for the capabilities of MEMS.

Additional optical components such as gratings and lenses may be integrated in the devices. Silicon is also totally transparent at the wavelengths used in optical communication, a useful property for some applications. Finally, the lithographic batch fabrication of these devices, driven and made possible by the infrastructure of the IC industry, provides a relatively inexpensive fabrication method.

16.3.1 Optical packet switch approach

Optical Packet Switching has the potential to reconcile the optimization of resource utilization and service differentiation from packet switching with direct application of MPLS techniques, and the scalability of wavelength crossconnects, where IP routers are interconnected to a Layer 1/2 optical system performing both traffic aggregation and core switching in a much more flexible way than a crossconnect, but at a lower cost than an IP router. IP packets are concatenated into **optical bursts** at edge nodes, and are then routed as a single entity through the network within core **optical packet routers.**

Optical switches provide a more economical and efficient means of supporting isochronous or realtime time division multiplexing (TDM) traffic over an optical core, while terabit switch/routers are optimized to support the explosive growth of IP data packets and society's future communication needs.

Terabit switch routing (T-routers)

MPLS routers are now reaching capacities in the subterabit-per-second throughput range, with 10 Gbps line cards. Label switching at Layer 2 runs over Layer 1 WDM infrastructure. Reaching multiterabits-per-second throughputs requires massive parallelism and complex interconnection, which are not likely to drive the cost down significantly. However, this approach has the merit of being completely IP-driven, and therefore obviously compatible with traffic engineering and distributed management techniques developed for IP networks. The challenge for **terabit router** technology is to make sure OC-768/STM-256 (40 Gbps) technology is viable.

Optical packet switch (OPS)

The advantage of this optical packet switching is to process only one header for multiple IP packets, relaxing drastically the forwarding speed required from core routers, and to scale up their forwarding capability by at least one order of magnitude, well within the multiterabits-per-second range. In addition, with this approach, it becomes possible to consider WDM ports as a single resource (typically 300–600 Gbps of capacity), and therefore to improve the logical performance and/or decrease the memory requirements with respect to IP routers with single-wavelength processing capabilities. Cooperation between an OXC and optical packet switch is shown in Figure 16.5.

Burst switching also offers the advantage compared to crossconnects of direct compatibility of IP management techniques. There is much debate going on worldwide about having either a fixed or variable burst frame length: variable length is more future-proof and adapted to IP traffic, whereas fixed length offers better switching performance and simpler optical implementation.

Optical burst switching is a technique for transmitting bursts of traffic through an optical transport network by setting up a connection and reserving resources end to end only for the duration of a burst. Optical burst switching is an adaptation of an ITU-T standard for burst switching in ATM networks known as **ATM Block Transfer** (ABT, see Appendix D). There are two versions of ABT: ABT with delayed transmission and ABT with immediate transmission. In the first case, when a source wants to transmit a burst, it sends a packet to the ATM

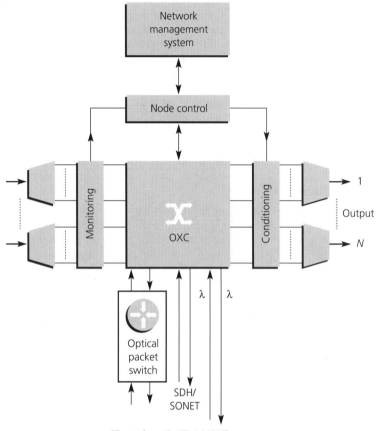

FIGURE 16-5   OPS and OXC

switches on the path of the connection to inform them that it wants to transmit a burst. If all the switches on the path can accommodate the burst, the request is accepted and the source is allowed to go ahead with its transmission.

Otherwise, the request is refused, and the source has to send another request later. In ABT with immediate transfer, the source sends the request packet, and then immediately after it, without receiving a confirmation, transmits its burst. If a switch along the path cannot carry the burst due to congestion, the burst is dropped. These two techniques have been adapted to optical networks. The **Tell-and-Go** (TAG) scheme is similar to the ABT with immediate transmission, and the **Tell-and-Wait** (TAW) scheme is similar to ABT with delayed transmission. An intermediate scheme known as **Just-Enough-Time** (JET) was also proposed.

An optical burst switching network consists of optical burst switches interconnected with WDM links. An optical burst switch transfers a burst coming in from an input port to its destination output port. Depending on the switch architecture, it may or may not be equipped with optical buffering. The fiber links carry multiple wavelengths, and each wavelength can be seen as a channel. A burst is dynamically assigned to a channel. The control packet associated with a burst may also be transmitted over a channel, or over a non-optical network. The burst may be fixed to carry one or more IP packets. Currently, optical burst switching networks do not exist.

The burst switching principle is in addition very optics-friendly, since fast optical switching technology requires some specific framing to avoid the loss of any payload data. Optical switching also offers the perspective of large scalability (current research has demonstrated up to 10 Tbps). It is also less sensitive to an increase in line rate, which is very important in view of the oncoming evolution toward 40 Gbps transmission.

Although the ultimate target could be to reach an **all-optical implementation** of such a network, and although some other key functions, such as buffering or regeneration, have been demonstrated in the laboratory using optical means (optical fiber delay lines and non-linear optical elements), these functions could also be realized using electronics, depending on cost/performance trade-offs, and reducing the time to market.

16.4 Label switching and optical networking

The concepts developed in MPLS and the application of IP routing techniques are viewed as technologies to meet optical networking challenges. They are becoming tried and trusted mechanisms in the Internet core, and **optical extensions to MPLS** (MPλS) and routing protocols, such as OSPF, will enable the characteristics particular to optical/TDM networks to become metrics in the signaling and routing process. In these evolving networks, equipment becomes more than simple optical nodes; advanced control plane software develops these devices into **Optical Label Switched Routers** (OLSRs).

SNAPSHOT   **lambda**

DWDM wavelength = lambda

The MPLS concepts are totally foreign in a TDM/optical environment. Paths through these networks are generally bidirectional, and the concept of a label must be abstracted to the particular technology being signaled. The concept of traffic engineering is replaced by parameters specific to TDM/optical networks and the bandwidth inherent in the technology. Factors such as delay still play a role, but error rates and signal attenuation become issues, along with restrictions on how paths can be signaled and routed based on the network technology (e.g. OEO vs. pure photonic).

A hybrid IP-centric **optical internetworking environment** would consist of both **label switching routers** (LSRs) and **optical crossconnects** (OXCs), where the OXCs are programmable and support wavelength conversion/translation. Architecturally, both LSRs and OXCs emphasize problem decomposition by decoupling the control plane from the data plane. The structure of an optical transport network is shown in Figure 16.6.

FIGURE 16-6 Optical transport network with optical packet switches (OPS)

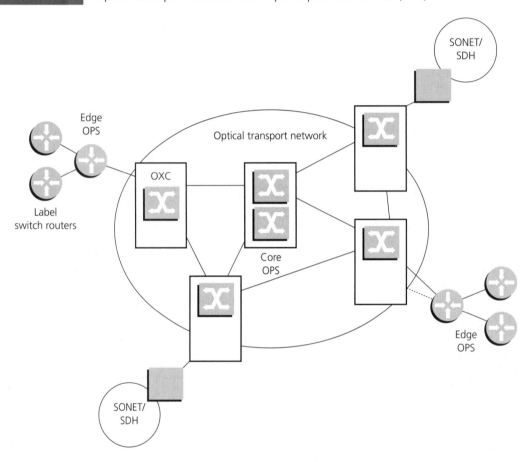

Essentially, there are two extreme architectural options for the deployment of LSRs and OXCs:

- **Overlay option** – uses different instances of the control plane in the OTN (OXC) and IP (LSR) domains. In this situation, each instance of the control plane will operate independently of the other. Interworking (including control coordination) between the two domains can be established through static configuration or through some other procedures. This partitioned and explicitly decoupled deployment option allows maximal control isolation between the OTN and IP domains. This scheme is conceptually similar to the model in use today, whereby the OTN simply provides point-to-point channels between IP network elements with very minimal control interaction between the two domains (see Figure 16.7).

MPLS over an optical network

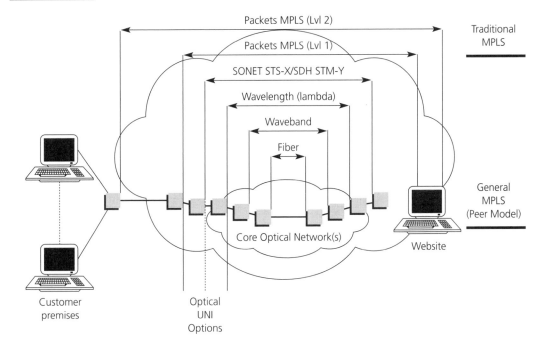

- **Peer option** – uses a single instance of the control plane that subsumes and spans LSRs and OXCs. In such an environment an LSP could traverse an intermix of routers and OXCs, or span just routers or just OXCs.

The separation of forwarding information from the content of the IP header allows MPLS to be used with devices such as OXCs, whose data plane cannot recognize the IP header. LSRs forward data using the label carried by the data. This **label**, combined with the port on which the data was received, is used to determine the output port and outgoing label for the data. A wavelength could be viewed as an implicit label. The concept of a forwarding hierarchy via label stacking enables interaction with devices that can support only a small label space. This property of MPLS is essential in the context of OXCs and DWDMs since the number of wavelengths (which act as labels) is not very large.

There are several emerging synergies between LSRs and photonic switches, and between an LSP and an optical trail. An **optical trail** is an end-to-end path composed exclusively of photonic elements without optical-electronic conversions. Analogous to switching labels in an LSR, a photonic switch toggles wavelengths from an input to an output port. Establishing an LSP involves configuring each intermediate LSR to map a particular input label and port to an output label and port. Similarly, the process of establishing an optical trail involves configuring each intermediate photonic switch to **map** a particular input **lambda and port** to an output lambda and port. As in LSRs, photonic switches need routing protocols like OSPF or IS-IS to exchange link-state topology and other optical resource availability information for path computation. They also need signaling protocols like RSVP and LDP to automate the path establishment process. In the remainder of this chapter we discuss the routing enhancements and link management.

Explicit LSPs and **optical channel trails** are both fundamentally unidirectional point-to-point path connection abstractions. An explicit LSP provides a parameterized packet-forwarding path (traffic trunk) between an ingress LSR and an egress LSR. Correspondingly, an optical channel trail provides a (possibly parameterized) optical channel between two end points for the transport of client digital signals. The **payload** carried by both LSPs and optical trails are transparent to intermediate nodes along their respective paths. Both LSPs and optical trails can be parameterized to stipulate their performance, behavioral, and survivability requirements from the network. A **constraint-based routing** scheme can be used to select appropriate paths for both LSPs and optical trails. Generally, such paths may satisfy some demands and policy requirements subject to some constraints imposed by the operational environment. A subset of the MPLS traffic engineering capabilities can be mapped onto an OTN by substituting the term optical channel trail for the term **traffic trunk.**

The MPLS traffic engineering control plane (with some minor extensions) would be very suitable as the control plane for OXCs. An OXC that uses the MPLS traffic engineering control plane would effectively become an IP addressable device, which solves the problem of addressing for OXCs. The distribution of topology state information, establishment of optical channel trails, OTN traffic engineering functions, and protection and restoration capabilities would be facilitated by the MPLS traffic engineering control plane.

SNAPSHOT   optical layer control plane

The **optical layer control plane** is the software used to determine routings and establish and maintain connections.

The functions of the **control plane** – for both LSRs and OXCs – include resource discovery, distributed routing control, and connection management. In particular, the control plane of the LSR is used to discover, distribute, and maintain relevant state information associated with the MPLS network, and to instantiate and maintain label switched paths under various MPLS traffic engineering rules and policies. The control plane of the OXC, on the other hand, is used to discover, distribute, and maintain relevant state information associated with the optical transport network, and to establish and maintain optical channel trails under various optical traffic engineering rules and policies. An optical channel trail provides a point-to-point optical connection between two access points. At each intermediate OXC along the route of an optical channel trail, the OXC switch fabric connects the trail from an input port to an output port.

OXCs, contrary to LSRs, do not perform packet-level processing in the data plane, while LSRs are datagram devices which may perform certain packet-level operations in the data plane. A significant conceptual difference is that with LSRs the forwarding information is carried explicitly as part of the labels appended to data packets, while with OXCs the switching information is implied from the wavelength or optical channel.

16.4.1 MPλS

One of the exciting aspects of two-layer networking is that both the optical networking community and the IP router community have begun to agree that the way to control both layers is by MPLS or, in the case of the optical layer, a slightly modified version, **multiprotocol lambda switching** (MPλS). The control phases of these two emerging standards – MPLS and MPλS – provide a unified, agreed-upon way for the nodes in the IP and optical layers to set up and take down their portions of virtual point-to-point IP packet connections between end users. There are a number of reasons for MPλS to replace the many variants in current practice in the lower communication layers (especially SONET/SDH) and the IP layer.

The only serious MPLS vs. MPλS disagreement seems to be whether the control entity within each set of IP routers forming the IP layer will be topologically aware of just what pattern of OXC traversals constitutes the lightpath across an optical island, or whether the optical layer will set these up autonomously and tell the IP layer where the endpoints are without saying which sequence of OXCs constitutes the lightpath.

Protection switching, the millisecond-scale substitution of a new lightpath for a failed one, usually requires precanned algorithms akin to the SONET/SDH protection switching algorithms, and invokes only a very localized part of the network, usually no more than a single span, string, or ring of nodes. Whereas conventional protection switching is often triggered by some bit-level process, in optical protection switching the trigger can be loss of optical signal-to-noise ratio (OSNR).

Restoration, the replacement of the failed optical path, providing a new backup for the former one, is now playing the role of the service path. Since one can allow minutes or even longer to do this, it is possible not only to have realtime software do the job, but to involve much larger portions of the network in the process than can be tolerated for protection switching.

Provisioning or **reconfiguration,** in which one relieves stranded bandwidth conditions, arranges for the brokering of bandwidth between service providers using the optical facility or even setting up rent-a-wavelength conditions. Provisioning/reconfiguration can involve optimization over the entire optical network island or even several of them, since minutes or hours are allowable for their completion.

16.4.2 Generalized MPLS

Work has been progressing in the Multiprotocol Label Switching (MPLS) working group on the application of MPLS technology to non-packet switching networks.

Specifically, development of the **Generalized MPLS** (GMPLS) signaling draft has allowed for optical, SONET/SDH, and spatial switching to be controlled by IP protocols. GMPLS, also referred to as **multiprotocol lambda switching,** supports not only devices that perform packet switching, but also those that perform switching in the time, wavelength, and space domains. The development of GMPLS requires modifications to current signaling and routing protocols.

GMPLS identifies that the multiplexing hierarchy that exists in transport networks (fiber in a bundle, lambda on a fiber, STS/STM on a lambda, etc.) can be modeled as a set of nested tunnels, with the larger container consisting of a number of lower order containers, such as a specific fiber in a bundle with a label to identify it, a specific lambda on the fiber with another label, or the STS within the lambda with a third label identifying it. Since the nested lower order containers inherit the context of the higher order container that they are subordinate to, it is possible to use the MPLS label stack to reference the subordinate signal.

The **Generalized Multiprotocol Label Switching** (GMPLS) vision aims at providing a common control plane architecture for setting up the swapping of input to output forwarding labels within any kind of node. For IP routers the labels designate principally input and output ports. For optical networks they designate input and output port, and wavelength or band of wavelengths for each OXC. For the time-division world of SONET/SDH ADMs and digital crossconnects, they designate input and output time slots. For some purely space-division switches they designate input and output ports. Thus GMPLS is a framework that promises unified point-and-click control of packets (including cells), circuits, wavelengths, and ports.

Some modifications and additions are required to the MPLS routing and signaling protocols to adapt to the peculiarities of photonic switches. These are being standardized by the IETF under the umbrella of generalized MPLS, which can be summarized as follows:

- a new **Link Management Protocol** (LMP) designed to address issues related to link management in optical networks using photonic switches;
- **enhancements to the OSPF/IS-IS** routing protocols to advertise availability of optical resources in the network (e.g. the generalized representation of various link types, bandwidth on wavelengths, link protection type, fiber identifiers);
- **enhancements to the RSVP/constraint-based routing LDP** signaling protocols for traffic engineering purposes that allow a label-switched path to be explicitly specified across the optical core;
- **scalability enhancements** such as hierarchical LSP formation, link bundling, and unnumbered links.

Constraint-based routing is used today for two main purposes: traffic engineering and fast reroute. With suitable network design, the constraint-based routing of IP/MPLS can replace ATM as the mechanism for traffic engineering. Likewise, fast reroute offers an alternative to SONET as a mechanism for protection/restoration. Both traffic engineering and fast reroute are examples of how enhancements provided by MPLS to IP routing make it possible to bypass ATM and SONET/SDH by migrating functions provided by these technologies to the IP/MPLS control plane.

While the MPLS label space is comparatively large (one million per port), there are a relatively limited number of lambdas and TDM channels. MPLS LSPs that enter the optical transport domain at the same node and leave the domain at the same node may be aggregated and tunneled within a single optical LSP. This aggregation helps to conserve the number of lambdas used by the MPLS domain. The LSP hierarchy (LSPs can be nested inside other LSPs, giving rise to a **hierarchy** of LSPs, achieved by considering an LSP as a link in the IS-IS or OSPF link state database) also helps deal with the discrete nature of optical bandwidth.

MPLS LSPs can be allocated bandwidth from a continuous spectrum, whereas optical/TDM bandwidth allocation is from a small discrete set of values. When an optical LSP is set up, it gets a discrete bandwidth. However, when this optical LSP is treated as a link, that link's bandwidth need no longer be discrete. A 100 Mbps MPLS LSP that crosses the optical transport domain can be tunneled through the optical LSP, leaving the rest of bandwidth for other MPLS LSPs.

The overall number of links in an optical/TDM network can be several orders of magnitude larger than that of an MPLS network. The link state database consists of all the nodes and links in a network, along with the attributes of each link. Hence the link state database for an optical network can easily be several orders of magnitude bigger than that for an MPLS network. To address this issue, the link attributes of several parallel links of similar characteristics can be aggregated, and these **aggregated attributes** assigned to a single bundled link. In doing so, the size of the link-state database is reduced by a large factor, leading to vastly improved scaling of the link-state protocol. By summarizing the attributes of several links into one bundled link, some information is lost; for example, with a bundle of SONET links the switching capability of the link interfaces (OC-12, OC-48, OC-192) are flooded; however, the number of such interfaces and the exact time slots used are not announced. It seems that the benefit of improved scalability will significantly outweigh the value of the information lost. In addition, while the link state protocol carries a single bundled link, signaling requires that individual component links be identified.

All the links in an MPLS network are typically assigned IP addresses. When a path is computed through the network, the links that constitute the path are identified by their IP addresses and this information is conveyed to the signaling protocol, which then sets up the path. Thus, it would seem that every link must have an IP address. However, assigning IP addresses to each fiber, lambda, and TDM channel would create a serious problem, because of both the scarcity of IP addresses and the management burden. Unnumbered links are used to resolve this problem; however, if an IP address is not used to identify a link, an alternative must be substituted.

What is required is a **unique means of identifying links** in a network; the task may be broken down into two steps. First, a mechanism is required to uniquely identify each node in the network; then each link emanating from that node is identified. Each node in the network is identified by a unique router ID; what remains is the latter problem of identifying the links emanating from a particular node. Identifying which port on a network element is connected to which port on a neighboring network element is also a major management burden and is highly error-prone. Each network node numbers its interfaces locally. The tuple <router ID, link number> serves as the identification for a link. The reduction of management effort in configuring IP addresses, tracking allocated IP addresses, and dealing with the occasional duplicate address allocation brings significant savings, especially in the context of optical networks with their large numbers of links.

Link management protocol

A consequence of generalizing MPLS is that a **label** is no longer an abstract identifier, but must now be able to map to time slots, wavelengths, and physical resources such as the ports of a switch. This requires that the association of these physical labels be created between adjacent nodes. For IGP scaling purposes, multiple links between nodes may be combined into a single bundled link as described above. The **Link Management Protocol** (LMP) runs between adjacent nodes and is used for both link provisioning and fault isolation. A key service provided by LMP is the associations between neighboring nodes for the component link IDs that may in turn be used as labels for physical resources. These associations do not have to be configured manually, a potentially error-prone process. A significant improvement in manageability accrues because the associations are created by the protocol itself.

Within a bundled link, the component links and associated control channel need not be transmitted over the same physical medium. LMP allows for decoupling of the control channel from the component links. For example, the control channel could be transmitted along a separate wavelength or fiber, or over a separate Ethernet link between the two nodes. A consequence of allowing the control channel for a link to be physically diverse from the component links is that the health of a control channel of a link does not correlate to the health of the component links, and vice versa. Furthermore, due to the transparent nature of photonic switches, traditional methods can no longer be used to monitor and manage links.

Standards development and focus

The adaptation of MPLS concepts into the optical world is being driven by three major organizations. The IETF is developing electrical MPLS standards and is using its wealth of experience to produce a set of standards that will enable the overall integrated model described above, encompassing new generalized MPLS signaling standards, the mechanisms to hierarchically create the LSPs, and additional functionality specific to optical networks.

The OIF (Optical Interworking Forum) and the ODSI (Optical Domain Services Interconnect) have focused on a more specific area: the interface between edge devices and the network core. As the standards forum for the optical market space, the OIF has the expertise to identify those aspects that are significant to establishing LSPs through optical networks. The OIF is working closely with the IETF. Although the specific focus of each organization is different, the MPLS protocol standards themselves are in broad alignment, and the expertise of these two organizations can be leveraged to streamline the standardization process.

ODSI has taken a different tack, using the concepts of MPLS, including the structural approach of the LDP/CR-LDP (Label Distribution Protocol/Constraint Based-Label Distribution Protocol) to produce a new standard, the **Optical Gateway Protocol** (OGP). The challenge for ODSI is to gain acceptance for its alternative solution in the face of the combined efforts of the IETF and the OIF.

Other standards bodies are also active in the MPLS area. The MPLS Forum is closely monitoring progress in all areas, with a current goal of overall market education and a focus on areas that are inadequately addressed by other standards bodies. The ITU is also becoming active in MPLS.

SNAPSHOT   *MPλS*

Labels in MPLS can be viewed as analogous to optical channels in optical networks. LSRs are then viewed as analogous to OXCs. Each **OXC** has an IP-based processor that is used to transmit messages over a signaling network between neighboring OXCs. MPλS then adds additional information to IGPs (e.g. OSPF) to propagate information about the optical network topology and resource availability. A **constraint-based routing** algorithm uses the network topology and state information to compute routes through the network for optical connections. Once a route is selected, MPλS uses a similar message set to that of explicit routing in an MPλS signaling protocol (RSVP and/or CR-LDP) to effect cross-connects along the chosen route.

PART V CONCLUDING REMARKS

In Part V the main themes discussed are the hot topics of today:

- quality of service support in the network to enable proper handling of different types of traffic;
- high-performance network interconnecting using fast (optical) switching fabrics and methods to bypass the traditional lookups (adding latency) in the routing tables of each intermediate node.

We can appreciate the standardization effort in favour of multiprotocol label switching, the technology benefiting from clearly distinguishing between **path determination** processes required for finding routes across the network (done with help of traditional routing protocols) and packet forwarding. Routing protocols will not stop their evolution; they will change with the use of new routing algorithms, both distance vector and link state, which are under development.

While path determination stays in the hands of routing protocols, **packet forwarding** has gradually reached a simplified form using labels to identify the path through the special label switching routers. The whole process of packet forwarding is very fast as once the packet is labeled at the network edge, it quickly traverses the network, only requiring the label switching routers to perform the fixed-length label processing without actually performing any lookup in the routing tables. Packet forwarding will be getting faster in the future with the recent advances in optical networking and developments in optical switches which could operate within MPLS networks.

A P P E N D I X A

Abbreviations

The following list decodes all the abbreviations used in the text, except for abbreviations used for protocol messages and/or the fields within.

10 GEA	10 Gigabit Ethernet Alliance
AAL	ATM Adaptation Layer
AARP	Appletalk Address Resolution Protocol
ABM	Asynchronous Balanced Mode
ABR	Area Border Routers
ABR	Available Bit Rate
ABR RM	Resource Management
ABT	ATM Block Transfer
ACK	ACKnowledgment
ACR	Allowed Current Rate
ACR	Automatic Call Routing
ACSE	Association Control Service Element
ADMs	Add/Drop Multiplexer
ADSP	Appletalk Data Stream Protocol
AEP	Appletalk Echo Protocol
AF	Assured Forwarding
AFI	Authority and Format Identifier
AFP	Appletalk Filing Protocol
ANSI	American National Standards Institute
AON	All-Optical Network
APAP	Appletalk Printer Access Protocol
APNIC	Asia Pacific Network Information Center
APPN	Advanced Peer-to-Peer Networking
APS	Automatic Protection Switching
ARE	All Routes Explorer
ARIN	American Registry for Internet
ARIS	Aggregated Route-Based IP Switching
ARM	Asynchronous Response Mode
ARP	Address Resolution Protocol
ASBR	Autonomous System Border Router
ASIC	Application-Specific Integrated Circuits
ASN.1	Abstract Syntax Notation One
ASP	Appletalk Session Protocol
ATM	Asynchronous Transmission Mode
ATP	Appletalk Transaction Protocol
AURP	Appletalk Update-based Routing Protocol
AWG	American Wire Gauge

BA	Bandwidth Allocator
BACP	Bandwidth Allocation Control Protocol
BAP	Bandwidth Allocation Protocol
Bc	committed Burst
BCP	Best Current Practice
BCP	Bridging Control Protocol
BDR	Backup Designated Router
Be	excess Burst
BECN	Backward Explicit Congestion Notification
BER	Basic Encoding Rules
BGP	Border Gateway Protocol
BIA	Burnt In Address
B-ICI	Broadband Isdn Inter-Carrier Interface
BID	Bridge Identifier
BIS	Border Intermediate System
B-ISDN	Broadband ISDN
BLSR	Bidirectional Line-Switched Ring
BPDU	Bridge Protocol Data Unit
BRI	Basic Rate Interface
BS	Burst Size
BSD	Berkeley Software Distribution
BUS	Broadcast and Unknown Server
BWIF	Broadband Wireless Internet Forum
CAC	Call Admission Control
CAM	Content-Addressable Memory
CAR	Committed Access Rate
CBDS	Connectionless Broadband Data Service
CBQ	Class Based Queuing
CBR	Constant Bit Rate
CBT	Core Based Tree
CCITT	International Telephone and Telegraph Consultative Committee
CCP	Compression Control Protocol
CCS	Common Channel Signaling
CDDI	Copper Data Distributed Interface
CDVT	Cell Delay Variation Tolerance
CE	Customer Edge
CEF	Cisco Express Forwarding
CEN	Comité Européen de Normalisation
CENELEC	Comité Européen de Normalisation Electrotechnique
CHAP	Challenge Handshake Authentication Protocol
CIDR	Classless Inter-Domain Routing
CIF	Cells in Frames
CIR	Committed Information Rate
CLIP	Classical IP over ATM
CLNP	ConnectionLess Network Protocol
CLNS	ConnectionLess Network Service
CLP	Cell Loss Priority
CLR	Cell Loss Ratio
CMIP	Common Management Information Protocol
CMIS	Common Management Information Services
CMNP	Connection-Mode Network Protocol

COI	Community Of Interest
CONS	Connection-Oriented Network Service
COPS	Common Open Policy Service
CoS	Class of Service
CPE	Customer Premises Equipment
CR	Constraint-Based Routing
CRC	Cyclic Redundancy Check
CR-LDP	Constraint Routed Label Distribution Protocol
CS	Convergence Sublayer
CSMA/CA	Carrier Sense Multiple Access with Collision Avoidance
CSMA/CD	Carrier Sense Multiple Access with Collision Detection
CSNP	Complete Sequence Number Packet
CSPF	Constraint-based Shortest Path First
CSR	Cell Switch Router
CUG	Closed User Group
DAC	Dual Attached Concentrator
DAS	Dual Attached Station
DCC	Data Country Code
DCE	Data Circuit-Terminating Equipment
dCEF	Distributed Cisco Expert Forwarding
DDCMP	Digital Data Communications Message Protocol
DDP	Datagram Delivery Protocol
DDR	Dial-on-Demand Routing
DB	Default Behavior
DE	Discard Eligibility
DES	Data Encryption Standard
DNIC	Data Network Identification Code
DQDB	Distributed Queue Dual Bus
DR	Designated Router
DRAM	Dynamic Random Access Memory
DRP	DECnet Routing Protocol
DS	Directory Services
DSAP	Destination Service Access Point
DSBM	Designated Subnet Bandwidth Manager
DSCP	Differentiated Services Code Point
DSP	Domain Specific Part
DS-TE	DiffServ-aware Traffic Engineering
DSU	Digital Service Units
DTE	Data Terminal Equipment
DTL	Designated Transit Lists
DUAL	Diffusing Update Algorithm
DVMRP	Distance Vector Multicast Routing Protocol
DWDM	Dense Wavelength-Division Multiplexing
DXI	Digital eXchange Interface
EA	Extended Address
EBGP	External Border Gateway Protocol
ECMP	Equal-Cost MultiPath
ECMPR	Equal-Cost MultiPath Routing
ECP	Encryption Control Protocol

EF	Expedited Forwarding
EFCI	Explicit Forward Congestion Indication
EGP	Exterior Gateway Protocol
EIA	Electronics Industry Association
EIGRP	Enhanced Interior Gateway Routing Protocol
EIR	Excess Information Rate
ELAP	Ethertalk Link Access Protocol
ELSR	Edge Label Switching Router
EP	Error Protocol
EPD	Early Packet Discard
ERC	Explicit Rate Control
ERP	Enterprise Resource Planning
ES	End System
ESI	End System Identifier
ES-IS	End System to Intermediate System
ETSI	European Telecommunications Standards Institute
FAI	Functional Address Indicator
FANP	Flow Attribute Notification Protocol
FC	Fiber Channel
FCAPS	Fault, Configuration, Accounting, Performance, Security
FCFS	First-Come First-Served
FCIA	Fibre Channel Industries Association
FCS	Frame Check Sequence
FDDI	Fiber Distributed Data Interface
FDM	Frequency Division Multiplexing
FDR	Full-Duplex Repeater
FEC	Forwarding Equivalence Class
FECN	Forward Explicit Congestion Notification
FF	Fixed Filter
FIB	Forwarding Information Base
FIFO	First-In First-Out
FLAP	Fdditalk Link Access Protocol
FLP	Fast Link Pulse
FPS	Frames per second
FRAD	Frame Relay Access Device
FRF	Frame Relay Forum
FRTS	Frame Relay Traffic Shaping
FTAM	File Transfer, Access, and Management
FUNI	Frame User-Network Interface
GARP	Generic Attribute Registration Protocol
GCRA	Generic Cell Rate Algorithm
GFC	Generic Flow Control
GFI	General Format Identifier
GIP	GARP Information Propagation
GMPLS	Generalized MPLS
GMRP	GARP Multicast Registration Protocol
GOLR	Gateway Of Last Resort
GRE	Generic Routing Encapsulation
GSMP	General Switch Management Protocol

GTS	Generic Traffic Shaping
GVRP	GARP VLAN Registration Protocol
HDLC	High-Level Data Link Control
HEC	Header Error Control
HOL	Head Of Line
HRW	Highest Random Weight
HSRP	Hot Standby Router Protocol
HSTR	High-Speed Token Ring
HSTRA	High-Speed Token Ring Alliance
HTTP	HyperText Transfer Protocol
IAB	Internet Architecture Board
IBGP	Internal BGP
ICD	International Code Designator
ICMP	Internet Control Message Protocol
ICP	Internet Control Protocol
IDI	Initial Domain Identifier
IDN	International Data Numbers
IDP	Initial Domain Part
IDP	Internet Datagram Protocol
IDRP	Inter-Domain Routing Protocol
IE	Information Element
IEC	International Electrotechnical Commission
IEEE	Institute of Electrical and Electronics Engineers
IESG	Internet Engineering Steering Group
IETF	Internet Engineering Task Force
IFMP	Ipsilon Flow Management Protocol
IGMP	Internet Group Management Protocol
IGP	Interior Gateway Protocol
ISP	Internet Service Provider
ILMI	Interim Local Management Interface
IPM	Internet Protocol Multicast
I-PNNI	Integrated-PNNI
IPX	Internet Packet exchange
IRDA	InfraRed Data Association
IRDP	ICMP Router Discovery Protocol
IRTF	Internet Research Task Force
ISDN	Integrated Services Data Network
IS-IS	Intermediate System-to-Intermediate System
ISL	Inter-Switch Link
ISO	International Organization for Standardization
ISOC	Internet Society
ISP	Internet Service Provider
ISR	Integrated Switch Router
ISUP	ISdn User Part
ITU-T	International Telecommunications Union – Telecommunications Standardization Sector
IWF	InterWorking Function
IWU	InterWorking Unit

JET	Just-Enough-Time
L2TP	Layer 2 Tunneling Protocol
LAG	Local Address Group
LAN	Local Area Network
LANE	LAN Emulation
LAP	Link Access Procedure
LAPB	Link Access Procedure, Balanced
LAPD	Link Access Protocol on D-Channel
LAT	Local Area Transport
LCI	Logical Channel Identifier
LCP	Link Control Protocol
LDP	Label Distribution Protocol
LEC	LAN Emulation Client
LECS	LAN Emulation Configuration Server
LES	LAN Emulation Server
LIFO	Last-In First-Out
LIS	Logical IP Subnets
LLAP	Localtalk Link Access Protocol
LLC	Logical Link Control Sublayer
LLQ	Low Latency Queuing
LMI	Local Management Interface
LMP	Link Management Protocol
LSA	Link-State Advertisements
LSAP	LLC Service Access Point
LSDB	Link-State DataBase
LSP	Label Switched Path
LSP	Link-State Packet
LSR	Label Switching Router
LVC	Label Virtual Circuit
MAC	Media Access Control
MAN	Metropolitan Area Netywork
MANET	Mobile Ad Hoc NETwork
MARS	Multicast Address Resolution Server
MBGP	Multicast Border Gateway Protocol
MCR	Minimum Cell Rate
MDR	Multiple Destination Routing
MED	Multi-Exit Discriminator attribute
MEMS	Micro-ElectroMechanical Systems
MHS	Message Handling Systems
MHSRP	Multiple Hot Standby Router Protocol
MIB	Management Information Base
MLPPP	MultiLink Point-to-Point Protocol
MLS	MultiLayer Switching
MOP	Maintenance Operations Protocol
MOSPF	Multicast OSPF
MPC	MPOA Clients
MPLS	MultiProtocol Label Switching
MPλS	MultiProtocol Lambda Switching
MPOA	Multi-Protocol Over ATM
MPPE	Microsoft Point-to-Point Encryption
MPR	MultiPoint Relay

MPS	MPOA Server
MSAU	MultiStation Access Unit
MSDP	Multicast Source Discovery Protocol
MSF	Multiservice Switching Forum
MST	Mono Spanning Tree
MLPPP	MultiLink PPP
MZAP	Multicast scope Zone Announcement Protocol

NANP	North American Numbering Plan
NAS	Network Access Server
NAT	Network Address Translation
NAUN	Nearest Active Upstream Neighbor
NBMA	Non-Broadcast, Multi-Access
NBP	Name Binding Protocol
NCP	Network Control Protocol
NCP	Netware Core Protocol
NET	Network Entity Title
NetBEUI	NetBIOS Extended User Interface
NetBIOS	Network Basic Input/Output System
NIC	Network Information Center
NHC	Next Hop Client
NHRP	Next Hop Resolution Protocol
NHS	Next Hop Server
NIC	Network Interface Card
NLM	Netware Loadable Module
NLRI	Network Layer Reachability Information
NLSP	Netware Link-State Protocol
NNI	Network-to-Network Interface
NOS	Network Operating System
NRM	Normal Response Mode
NRT	Non-Real Time
NSAP	Network Service Access Point
NSO	National Standards Organization
NSP	Network Services Protocol
NSR	Non-Source Routed frame
NSSA	Not-So-Stubby Area
NT	Network Termination
NTN	National Terminal Number

OADM	Optical Add-Drop Multiplexer
OC	Optical Carrier
OCDM	Optical Code-Division Multiplexing
ODL	Optical Delay Line
ODSI	Optical Domain Services Interconnect
OEO	Optical-Electrical-Optical
OFDM	Orthogonal Frequency Division Multiplexing
OGP	Optical Gateway Protocol
OIF	Optical Interworking Forum
OLSR	Optical Label Switched Router
OLSR	Optimized Link-State Routing
OPS	Optical Packet Switching

OSI	Open Systems Interconnection
OSNR	Optical Signal-to-Noise Ratio
OSPF	Open Shortest Path First
OTN	Optical Transport Network
OXC	Optical cross-Connects

P	Provider core
PAD	Packet Assembler/Disassembler
PARC	Palo Alto Research Center
PCI	Protocol Control Information
PCM	Pulse-Code Modulation
PCR	Peak Cell Rate
PDB	Per-Domain Behavior
PDN	Public Data Network
PDU	Protocol Data Unit
PE	Provider Edge
PEP	Packet Exchange Protocol
PGL	Peer Group Leader
PGM	Pragmatic General Multicast
PHB	Per Hop Behavior
PIE	Protocol Information Element
PIM-DM	Protocol Independent Multicast Dense Mode
PIM-SM	Protocol Independent Multicast Sparse Mode
PING	Packet Internetwork Groper
PLCP	Physical Layer Convergence Procedure
PLP	Packet-Level Protocol
P-NNI	Private Network-to-Network Interface
POP	Point-Of-Presence
POS	Packet Over Sonet
POS	Personal Operating Space
PPS	Point-to-Point Protocol
PPPoE	PPP over Ethernet
PPS	Packet Per Second
PPTP	Point-to-Point Tunneling Protocol
PRI	Primary Rate Interface
PSE	Packet Switching Exchange
PSNP	Partial Sequence Number Packet
PT	Payload Type
PTI	Packet Type Identifier
PTSE	PNNI Topology State Element
PTSP	PNNI Topology State Packet
PVC	Permanent Virtual Circuit
PVID	Port VLAN IDentifier
PVST	Per-VLAN Spanning Tree

QoS	Quality of Service
QOSF	QoS Forum
QPPB	QoS Policy Propagation via BGP
QTC	QuickTime Conferencing

RAID	Redundant Array of Independent Disks
RARP	Reverse Address Resolution Protocol
RD	Route Distinguisher
RD	Routing Domain
RDE	Route Determination Entity
RDI	Routing Domain Identifier
RED	Random Early Detect
RIB	Routing Information Base
RIF	Routing Information Field
RIO	RED with In-Out
RIP	Routing Information Protocol
RIPE NCC	Réseaux IP Européens Network Coordination Center
RM	Requestor Module
RMON	Remote MONitoring
ROSE	Remote Operations Service Element
RPC	Remote Procedure Call
RPF	Reverse Path Forwarding
RPR	Resilient Packet Ring
RSP	Router Switch Processor
RSVP	Resource Reservation Protocol
RT	Real Time
RTCP	Real-time Transport Control Protocol
RTMP	Routing Table Maintenance Protocol
RTP	Real-time Transport Protocol
RTP	Routing Table Protocol
RTSE	Reliable Transfer Service Element
RTSP	Real Time Streaming Protocol
SAC	Single Attached Concentrator
SAID	Security Association IDentifier
SAN	Storage Area Networks
SAP	Service Access Point
SAP	Service Advertising Protocol
SAPI	Service Access Point Identifier
SAR	Segmentation And Reassembly
SAS	Single Attached Station
SCCP	Signaling Connection Control Part
SCM	Subcarrier Multiplexing
SCR	Sustainable Cell Rate
SCSI	Small Computer Systems Interface
SDH	Synchronous Digital Hierarchy
SDLC	Synchronous Data Link Control
SDRAM	Synchronous Dynamic Random Access Memory
SE	Shared-Explicit filter
SIP	SMDS Interface Protocol
SLA	Service Level Agreements
SLIP	Serial Line Internet Protocol
SMDS	Switched Multimegabit Data Service
SMI	Structure of Management Information
SMON	Switch MONitoring
SMRP	Simple Multicast Routing Protocol
SNAP	SubNetwork Access Protocol

SNI	Subscriber-Network Interface
SNIA	Storage Networking Industry Association
SNMP	Simple Network Management Protocol
SNP	Sequence Number Protection
SNPA	SubNetwork Point of Attachment
SONET	Synchronous Optical NETwork
SPF	Shortest Path First
SPP	Sequenced Packet Protocol
SPX	Sequenced Packet exchange
SRB	Source-Route Bridging
SRF	Specifically Routed Frame
SRT	Source Route Transparent
SS7	Signaling System #7
SSM	Source Specific Multicast
STA	Spanning Tree Algorithm
STE	Spanning Tree Explorer
STP	Shielded Twisted Pair
STP	Spanning Tree Protocol
STS	Synchronous Transport Signal
SVC	Switched Virtual Circuits
SVCC	Switched Virtual Circuit Connection

TA	Terminal Adapter
TAG	Technical Advisory Group
TAG	Tell-And-Go
TARP	Target Address Resolution Protocol
TAW	Tell-And-Wait
TAXI	Transmitter/Receiver Interface
TCAP	Transaction CAPability
TCB	TCP Control Block
TCN	Topology Change Notification
TCP/IP	Transmission Control Protocol/Internet Protocol
TDM	Time Division Multiplexing
TDP	Tag Distribution Protocol
TE	Terminal Equipment
TE	Traffic Engineering
TEI	Terminal End-point Identifier
TFIB	Tag Forwarding Information Base
TIA	Telecommunications Industries Association
TIB	Tag Information Base
TLAP	Tokentalk Link Access Protocol
TLV	Type, Length, and Value
ToS	Type of Service
TP	Transport Protocol
TrBRF	Token Ring Bridge Relay Function
TrCRF	Token Ring Concentrator Relay Function
TTL	Time-to-Live

UBR	Unspecified Bit Rate
UDP	User Datagram Protocol
UDWDM	Ultra Dense Wavelength Division Multiplexing

UNI	User-to-Network Interface
UPC	Usage Parameter Control
UPSR	Unidirectional Path-Switched Ring
UTP	Unshielded Twisted Pair

VAN	Value-Added Network
VARP	VINES Address Resolution Protocol
VBR	Variable Bit Rate
VC	Virtual Circuit
VCC	Virtual Channel Connection
VCI	Virtual Channel Identifier
VCIB	Virtual Circuit Information Base
VID	VLAN IDentifier
VINES	Virtual Integrated Network Service
VIP	VINES Internetwork Protocol
VLAN	Virtual LAN
VLSI	Very Large-Scale Integration
VLSM	Variable Length Subnet Mask
VNN	Virtual Network Navigator
VNS	Virtual Network Switching
VoIP	Voice over Internet Protocol
VOQ	Virtual Output Queuing
VPC	Virtual Path Connection
VPI	Virtual Path Identifier
VPN	Virtual Private Network
VRF	VPN Routing and Forwarding
VRRP	Virtual Router Redundancy Protocol
VTP	Virtual Terminal Protocol
VTP	Virtual Trunking Protocol

WAN	Wide Area Network
WDM	Wave Division Multiplexing
WECA	Wireless Ethernet Compatibility Alliance
WF	Wildcard Filter
WFQ	Weighted Fair Queuing
WG	Working Group
WLANA	Wireless LANs Association
WPAN	Wireless Personal Area Network
WRED	Weighted Random Early Detection
WRR	Weighted Round-Robin

XNS	Xerox Network Systems

ZBR	Zone Boundary Router
ZIP	Zone Information Protocol
ZIT	Zone Information Table

APPENDIX B

Network standardization overview

Why are international standards so important? International standards facilitate world trade by, effectively, removing technical barriers to trade, leading to new markets and economic growth. International technology standards provide industry and users with the framework for economies of design, greater product and service quality, more interoperability, and better production and delivery efficiency. At the same time, standards also encourage an improved quality of life by contributing to safety, human health and the protection of the environment.

A **standard** (as defined in IEC/ISO Guide 2) is a document, established by consensus and approved by a recognized body, that provides, for common and repeated use, rules, guidelines or characteristics for activities or their results, aimed at the achievement of the optimum degree of order in a given context. An international standard is a standard adopted by an international standardizing/standards organization and made available to the public (usually for a not negligible fee).

A standard means a definition or description of a technology. The purpose of developing standards is to help vendors build components that will function together or that will facilitate use by people by providing consistency with other products. There are two kinds of standards: *de facto* and *de jure*.

De facto means in fact. If more than one vendor 'builds to' or complies with a particular technology, one can reasonably refer to that technology as a standard. *De jure* means in law, although standards do not generally have the force of law. In some parts of the world, when a standard is set, it in fact becomes law. If a user or vendor violates the rules, the penalties can be quite severe. But a standard is a *de jure* standard if an independent standards body (i.e. one not solely vendor-sponsored) successfully carries it through a more or less public standards-making procedure and announces that it is now a standard. It is necessary to emphasize that the IETF, the Internet community body producing Internet standards, has not been approved internationally as a standards body and hence still produces 'only' *de facto* standards.

Standardization organizations

The international organizations having a direct relationship with standardization activities in telecommunications and data communications generally fall into two categories:

- **Recognized organizations** – with the following characteristics:
  - they perform *de jure* **standardization**;

- they produce standards (specifications or recommendations) that are further on sold and that are prepared by expert groups administered and paid by the organization (i.e. from membership fees);
- their members are mainly individual countries (represented by designated national bodies) and/or private companies;
- their approval process is based on majority voting after the document is submitted to public inquiry in the member country;
- their standardization work is not usually or fully open to the public;
- comments on standards are usually done after they are published and implementations verified;
- they can have global or regional span (including *National Standards Organization* NSO);
- among the recognized major international standardization bodies in the communications area belong:

  - **ITU-T** (*International Telecommunications Union – telecommunications standardization sector*)
    http://www.itu.int
  - **ISO** (*International Organization for Standardization*)
    http://www.iso.ch
  - **ANSI** (*American National Standards Institute*)
    http://www.ansi.org
  - **IEC** (*International Electrotechnical Commission*)
    http://www.iec.ch
  - **IEEE** (*Institute of Electrical and Electronics Engineers*)
    http://standards.ieee.org
  - **ETSI** (*European Telecommunications Standards Institute*)
    http://www.etsi.org
  - **CEN/CENELEC** (*Comité Européen de Normalisation / Comité Européen de Normalisation Electrotechnique*)
    http://www.cenorm.be; http://www.cenelec.be

- **non-recognized organizations** – with the following characteristics:
  - they perform ***de facto* standardization**;
  - they produce specifications that are publicly available (usually beyond their membership) and that are prepared by expert groups administered and paid by the member organizations;
  - their members are companies or individuals but not countries;
  - their approval process is usually based on consensus;
  - their standardization work is open to public;
  - comments on standards are incorporated during the standardization process and implementations are verified before the specification is published;
  - the resulting specifications serve as a basis for standards mostly adopted without further work by the recognized standardization bodies with whom collaboration is close;

    – among the major international non-recognized standardization bodies in the communications area belong:

- **ATM Forum**
  http://www.atmforum.com
- **BWIF** (*Broadband Wireless Internet Forum*)
  http://www.bwif.org/
- **EIA** (*Electronics Industry Association*)
  http://www.eia.org
- **FCIA** (*Fibre Channel Industries Association*)
  http://www.fibrechannel.com
- **FRF** (*Frame Relay Forum*)
  http://www.frforum.com
- **10 GEA** (*10 Gigabit Ethernet Alliance*)
  http://www.10gea.org
- **HSTRA** (*High-Speed Token Ring Alliance*)
  http://www.hstra.com
- **IRDA** (*Infrared Data Association*)
  http://www.irda.org
- **MPLS** Forum
  http://www.mplsrc.com
- **Multiservice Switching Forum** (*MSF*)
  http://www.msforum.org
- **Optical Interworking Forum** (*OIF*)
  http://www.oiforum.com/
- **Optical Domain Services Interconnect** (*ODSI*)
  http://www.odsi-coalition.com
- **OFDM** (*Orthogonal Frequency Division Multiplexing*) **Forum**
  http://www.ofdm-forum.com/
- **QOSF** (*QoS Forum*)
  http://www.qosforum.com/
- **TIA** (*Telecommunications Industries Association*)
  http://www.tiaonline.org
- **WLANA** (*Wireless LANs Association*)
  http://www.wlana.com
- **IAB** (*Internet Architecture Board*)
  http://www.iab.org
- **IESG** (*Internet Engineering Steering Group*)
  http://www.ietf.org/iesg.html
- **IETF** (*Internet Engineering Task Force*)
  http://www.ietf.org
- **IRTF** (*Internet Research Task Force*)
  http://www.irtf.org
- **ISOC** (*Internet Society*)
  http://www.isoc.org

ITU-T

The first **International Telegraph Convention** was signed by the 20 participating countries on May 17, 1865 and the **International Telegraph Union** as an inter-governmental organization was set up to enable subsequent amendments to this initial agreement to be agreed upon. ITU is the most important organization devoted fully to international standardization in telecommunications. Since 1947 it has worked as a specialized body of the UN.

In 1927 the **International Radio Consultative Committee** (CCIR) was established. The **International Telephone Consultative Committee** (CCIF) was set up in 1924, and the **International Telegraph Consultative Committee** (CCIT) in 1925. In 1956, the CCIT and the CCIF were amalgamated to give rise to the **International Telephone and Telegraph Consultative Committee** (CCITT). (*Note*: These older well-known abbreviations for the bodies come from their French names.) In 1992 the CCITT went through a major reorganization which led to the change of name to the **International Telecommunications Union** (ITU) with three sectors: **Telecommunications standardization sector** (ITU-T), **Radio-communications sector** (ITU-R), and **Development sector** (ITU-D).

Study groups (SG) are the core working bodies in standardization activities (see Table B.1 for their current list). The major results of their work are **recommendations** (not standards). Recommendations adopted before 1993 bear the title of CCITT origin, while since then the recommendations bear the title ITU-T. For recommendation series categorization see Table B.2. Recommendations used to be published in books (blue, red, yellow, etc.) every four years but since 1988 they have been published separately after their individual adoption.

The ITU-T may be contacted as follows:

- **http://www.itu.int**

TABLE B-1 ITU-T study groups

- SG 2 – Operational aspects of service provision, networks, and performance
- SG 3 – Tariff and accounting principles including related telecommunications economic and policy issues
- SG 4 – Telecommunication management, including TMN
- SG 5 – Protection against electromagnetic environment effects
- SG 6 – Outside plant
- SG 7 – Data networks and open system communications
- SG 9 – Integrated broadband cable networks and television and sound transmission
- SG 10 – Languages and general software aspects for telecommunication systems
- SG 11 – Signalling requirements and protocols
- SG 12 – End-to-end transmission performance of networks and terminals
- SG 13 – Multi-protocol and IP-based networks and their internetworking
- SG 15 – Optical and other transport networks
- SG 16 – Multimedia services, systems, and terminals
- SSG – Special Study Group 'IMT-2000 and Beyond'

| TABLE B-2 | Series of ITU-T recommendations |

- A series – Organization of the work of ITU-T
- B series – Means of expression: definitions, symbols, classification
- C series – General telecommunication statistics
- D series – General tariff principles
- E series – Overall network operation, telephone service, service operation, and human factors
- F series – Non-telephone telecommunication services
- G series – Transmission systems and media, digital systems and networks
- H series – Audiovisual and multimedia systems
- I series – Integrated services digital network (ISDN)
- J series – Transmission of television, sound program, and other multimedia signals
- K series – Protection against interference
- L series – Construction, installation, and protection of cables and other elements of outside plant
- M series – TMN and network maintenance: international transmission systems, telephone circuits, telegraphy, facsimile, and leased circuits
- N series – Maintenance: international sound program and television transmission circuits
- O series – Specifications of measuring equipment
- P series – Telephone transmission quality, telephone installations, local line networks
- Q series – Switching and signaling
- R series – Telegraph transmission
- S series – Telegraph services terminal equipment
- T series – Terminals for telematic services
- U series – Telegraph switching
- V series – Data communication over the telephone network
- X series – Data networks and open system communications
- Y series – Global information infrastructure and Internet protocol aspects
- Z series – Languages and general software aspects for telecommunication systems

ISO

The **International Organization for Standardization** (ISO) plays a key role in the standardization activities across different industries, including telecommunications: mainly physical interfaces and OSI (in the case of local networking the ISO adopts the IEEE standards as the international standards). ISO as a nongovernmental organization was founded in 1947 and represents today about 100 member countries.

Each standard takes the following cycle:

- Working Paper (WP);
- Committee Draft (CD, formerly Draft Proposal, DP);
- *Draft International Standard* (**DIS**);
- *International Standard* (**IS**).

Alongside the standards, the ISO also produces Technical Reports (TR) and Standard profiles (ISP).

The ISO closely collaborates with the IEC because the later is responsible for standardization in electronics beyond the ISO scope. Their common forum is ISO/IEC *Joint Committee on Information Technology* (JTC 1, formerly TC97 ISO). Its subcommittee 21 (*SC21*) is responsible for information processing systems and **OSI**.

The ISO may be contacted as follows:

- http://www.iso.ch

IEC

The **International Electrotechnical Commission** (IEC) is the international standards and conformity assessment body for all fields of electrotechnology collaborating with the ISO. The IEC was founded in 1906 as the world organization that prepares and publishes international standards for all electrical, electronic, and related technologies. There are about 50 member countries.

The IEC charter embraces all electrotechnologies (beyond the ISO scope) including **electronics, magnetics and electromagnetics, electroacoustics, telecommunication**, and energy production and distribution, as well as associated general disciplines such as terminology and symbols, measurement and performance, dependability, design and development, safety and the environment.

The IEC is one of the bodies recognized by the World Trade Organization (WTO) and entrusted by it to monitor the national and regional organizations which have agreed to use the IEC's international standards as the basis for national or regional standards as part of the WTO's Technical Barriers to Trade Agreement. The adoption of IEC standards by any country, whether it is a member of the Commission or not, is entirely voluntary.

The IEC may be contacted as follows:

- http://www.iec.ch

ANSI

The **American National Standards Institute** (ANSI) was founded in 1918 as a private, non-profit membership organization with nearly 1000 members (private and public sector organizations, government agencies, institutional and international members). ANSI is the sole US representative and dues-paying member of the ISO (its founding member) and the IEC.

The work of international technical committees is carried out by volunteers from industry and government, not ANSI staff, therefore the success of these efforts is often dependent upon the willingness of US industry and the US government to commit the resources required to ensure strong US technical participation in the international standards process. ANSI has produced standards in networking, such as the FDDI or Fibre Channel, ISDN and Frame Relay. **Conformity Assessment** (steps taken by both manufacturers and independent third parties to assess conformance to standards) also remains a high priority for the Institute. ANSI's program for accrediting third-party product certification has experienced significant growth in recent years, and the Institute continues its efforts to obtain worldwide acceptance of product certifications performed in the US and the promotion of reciprocal agreements between US accreditors and certifiers.

ANSI may be contacted as follows:

■ **http://www.ansi.org**

IEEE

The **Institute of Electrical and Electronics Engineers** (IEEE), although based in the US and having origins in US engineers' activities (founded in 1894), nowadays works as an international organization of professionals volunteering in standardization work. The IEEE has many committees of which only the 802 committee (founded in 1980) is dedicated to networking standardization (LAN/MAN). Its first approved standard was IEEE 802.3 in 1983.

The IEEE may be contacted as follows:

■ **http://www.ieee.org** (info on standards **http://standards.ieee.org**)

ETSI

The **European Telecommunications Standards Institute** (ETSI) is a non-profit making organization whose mission is to produce telecommunications standards. Based in France it has 789 members (from 52 countries, not only from Europe), representing administrations, network operators, manufacturers, service providers, research bodies, and users. Any European organization proving an interest in promoting European telecommunications standards has the right to represent that interest in ETSI and thus to directly influence the standards-making process.

ETSI's approach to standards-making is innovative and dynamic. It is ETSI members that fix the standards work program as a function of market needs. Accordingly, ETSI produces **voluntary standards** – some of which may go on to be adopted by the European Commission as the technical base for EU Directives or Regulations – but the fact that the voluntary standards are requested by those who subsequently implement them means that the standards remain practical rather than abstract. ETSI promotes the worldwide standardization process whenever possible. Its Work Programme is based on, and coordinated with, the activities of international standardization bodies, mainly the ITU-T and the ITU-R.

ETSI may be contacted as follows:

■ http://www.etsi.fr

CEN/CENELEC

The **Comité Européen de Normalisation** (CEN) has the mission to promote voluntary technical harmonization in Europe in conjunction with worldwide bodies and its partners in Europe. CEN works in partnership with CENELEC (The European Committee for Electrotechnical Standardization) and ETSI.

CEN works through procedures which guarantee respect for the following principles:

■ openness and transparency (all interested concerns take part in the work while representation is secured first through the national standards bodies which have the duty of sending balanced delegations to the policy-making bodies and technical committees);

■ consensus (European Standards are developed on the basis of voluntary agreement between all the interested parties);

■ national commitment (the formal adoption of European Standards is decided by a weighted majority vote of all CEN National Members and is binding on all of them);

■ technical coherence at the national and European level (standards form a collection which ensures its own continuity for the benefit of users, both at the European and national level through the compulsory national implementation of European Standards and the withdrawal of conflicting national standards);

■ integration with other international work (ISO).

The **Comité Européen de Normalisation Electrotechnique** (CENELEC) was founded in 1973 as a non-governmental body and was approved by the European Commission as a European standardization body in 1983.

CEN/CENELEC may be contacted as follows:

■ http://www.cenorm.be
■ http://www.cenelec.org

Consortia and interest groups

Although networking vendors are more and more active in the standards bodies, new specification development work is still carried on outside of these officially recognized bodies, in industry consortia or interest groups. These organizations also take care of the promotion of and education in the technologies of their particular scope. Among the major drivers (or recently established consortia having an influence in the areas covered here) belong the following (Internet related organizations are discussed next).

ATM Forum

The **ATM Forum** (founded in 1991) is an international non-profit organization formed with the objective of accelerating the use of ATM (Asynchronous Transfer Mode) products and services through a rapid convergence of interoperability specifications. In addition, the Forum promotes industry cooperation and awareness. The ATM Forum consists of a worldwide Technical Committee, three Marketing Committees for North America, Europe, and Asia-Pacific, as well as the User Committee through which ATM end users participate. It collaborates with the ITU-T, ANSI, ETSI, IETF, and other fora.

The ATM may be contacted as follows:

■ http://www.atmforum.com

Broadband Wireless Internet Forum

The **Broadband Wireless Internet Forum** (BWIF) has developed a specification for vector OFDM (VOFDM). The BWIF voted to approve version 1.0 VOFDM specifications. However, critics point out that the BWIF's lack of participation in the IEEE 802.16 working groups is a sign of isolation. One of the major criticisms of the BWIF is that it does not consider OFDM implementations other than Cisco's.

The BWIF may be contacted as follows:

■ http://www.bwif.org

EIA

Accredited by the ANSI and founded in 1924 (as the *Radio Manufacturers Association*), the **Electronics Industry Association** (EIA) provides a forum for the industry to develop standards and publications in the following technical areas: electronic components, consumer electronics, electronic information, and telecommunications. The EIA also collaborates with the ITU-T.

The EIA may be contacted as follows:

■ http://www.eia.org

FCIA

The **Fibre Channel Industry Association** (FCIA) is an international organization (founded in 1993) of manufacturers, systems integrators, developers, systems vendors, industry professionals, and end users. With more than 190 members and affiliates in the United States, Europe, and Japan, the FCIA is committed to delivering a broad base of Fibre Channel infrastructure to support a wide array of industry applications within the mass storage and IT-based arenas. FCIA Working Groups focus on specific aspects of the technology that target both vertical and horizontal markets, including storage, video, networking, and SAN Management.

The FCIA may be contacted as follows:

- http://www.fibrechannel.com

Frame Relay Forum

The **Frame Relay Forum** (FRF), founded in 1991, is an association of vendors, carriers, users, and consultants committed to the education, promotion, and implementation of Frame Relay in accordance with international standards. FRF specifications are publicly available as **Implementation Agreements** (IA).

The FRF may be contacted as follows:

- http://www.frforum.com

GEA

The **Gigabit Ethernet Alliance** (GEA) founded in 1996, was recently renamed as 10 Gigabit Ethernet Alliance. It is an open forum whose purpose is to promote industry cooperation in the development of (10) Gigabit Ethernet.

- http://www.10gea.org

HSTRA

The **High-Speed Token Ring Alliance** (HSTRA) was founded in 1997 by leading Token Ring vendors. Its mission was to rapidly develop the technologies, standards, and products necessary to deliver 100 Mbps Token Ring to the still very sizeable Token Ring customer base. The alliance was highly successful in meeting its original goals, with standard work completed in record time and products delivered in the second half of 1998. After successfully delivering on its original goals, the alliance turned its focus to its current mission which is to provide educational information on High-Speed and general Token Ring technologies.

The HSTRA may be contacted as follows:

- http://www.hstra.com

IrDA

The **Infrared Data Association** (IrDA) was founded in 1993 as a non-profit organization. The IrDA is an international organization that creates and promotes interoperable, low-cost infrared data interconnection standards that support a walk-up, point-to-point user model. The standards support a broad range of computing and communications devices.

The IrDA may be contacted as follows:

- http://www.irda.org

MPLS Forum

The MPLS Forum is closely monitoring progress in all MPLS related areas, with a current goal of overall market education and a focus on areas that are inadequately addressed by other standards bodies. The ITU is also becoming active in MPLS. With the efforts of all these organizations, the opportunity exists to produce a cohesive set of standards. While standards for traditional MPLS are expected in 2001 before those for MPλS, this will not stop deployment of MPLS.

The MPLS Forum may be contacted as follows:

■ http://www.mplsrc.com

Mal– Switching Forum (MSF)

Founded in 1998, the MSF represents service providers and system suppliers developing open and multiservice, multiservice and switching systems.

The MSF may be contacted as follows:

■ http://www.msforum.org

OFDM Forum

The **OFDM** (orthogonal frequency division multiplexing) Forum consists of several companies that were key in developing the 802.11 wireless LAN standard. The OFDM Forum's goal is to harmonize on a specific proposal for OFDM that it can present to the IEEE. During the IEEE's 802.16 Wireless MAN meeting in November, the OFDM Forum submitted a PHY layer proposal to the 802.16.3 subcommittee. This working group is currently considering standards for both single channel QAM, QPSK, multichannel OFDM solutions, and hybrid systems that are agnostic to any modulation technology for sub-11-GHz wireless bands. During that meeting at least nine OFDM proposals were made along with proposals for CDMA and single channel. Out of those proposals a few multichannel OFDM proposals were retained; one single channel and the CDMA proposals were thrown out.

The ODFM Forum may be contacted as follows:

■ http://www.ofdm-forum.com

Optical Domain Services Interconnect Forum

The **Optical Domain Services Interconnect** (ODSI) Forum has used the concepts of MPLS, including the structural approach of the LDP/CR-LDP (Label Distribution Protocol/Constraint Based-Label Distribution Protocol), to produce a new specification, the **Optical Gateway Protocol** (OGP). The challenge for the ODSI Forum is to gain acceptance for its alternative solution in the face of the combined efforts of the IETF and the OIF.

The ODSI Forum may be contacted as follows:

■ http://www.odsi-coalition.com

Optical Interworking Forum

The **Optical Interworking Forum** (OIF) for the optical market has the expertise to identify those aspects that are significant to establishing LSPs through optical networks. The OIF is working closely with the IETF (see below). Although the specific focus of each organization is different, the MPLS protocol standards themselves are in broad alignment, and the expertise of these two organizations can be leveraged to streamline the standardization process.

The OIF may be contacted as follows:

■ http://www.oiforum.com

Quality of Service Forum

The **QoS Forum** (QOSF) is an international, industry forum accelerating the adoption of standards-based QoS technologies. Utilizing a comprehensive set of education, marketing, and testing services, the goal of the QoS Forum is to educate the market and facilitate deployment of QoS-enabled IP products and services. The QOSF is *not* a standards-setting group. Where appropriate, it works with standards bodies such as the IETF.

The major objectives of the forum are to align understanding and create a common terminology to advance the deployment of QoS products and services and to increase awareness of the benefits and opportunities of QoS solutions including the technical aspects of QoS.

The QoS Forum may be contacted as follows:

■ http://www.qosforum.com

TIA

The **Telecommunications Industries Association** (TIA), formed in 1988, is the leading trade association in the communications and information technology industry with more than 1100 member companies that manufacture or supply the products and services used in global communications. The TIA represents providers of communications and information technology products and services for the global marketplace through its core competencies in standards development, domestic and international advocacy, as well as market development and trade promotion programs. The TIA concentrates on user premises equipment, network equipment, wireless communications, fiber optics, and satellite communications. EIA/TIA standards are mostly known in the areas of interfaces and cabling (examples are EIA/TIA 232 and 449, formerly recommended standards, RS).

The TIA may be contacted as follows:

■ http://www.tiaonline.org

WLANA

The **Wireless LAN Association** (WLANA) is a non-profit educational trade association, comprised of the leading thinkers and technology innovators in the local area wireless technology industry.

The WLANA may be contacted as follows:

■ http://www.wlana.com

Internet community

The Internet community is currently organized into the following four groups:

- the **Internet Society** (ISOC) and its Board of Trustees;
- the **Internet Architecture Board** (IAB);
- the **Internet Engineering Steering Group** (IESG);
- the **Internet Engineering Task Force** (IETF).

The first IETF meeting was held in January 1986 at Linkabit in San Diego with 15 attendees. The 14th IETF meeting held in 1989 marked a major change in the structure of the IETF universe. The **IAB** (then the Internet Activities Board, now the Internet Architecture Board), which until that time oversaw many 'task forces,' changed its structure to leave only two: the **IETF** and the **IRTF**. The IRTF is tasked to consider the long-term research problems in the Internet. After the **Internet Society** (ISOC) was formed in January 1992, the IAB proposed to ISOC that the IAB's activities should take place under the auspices of the Internet Society. During INET92 in Kobe, Japan, the ISOC Trustees approved a new charter for the IAB to reflect the proposed relationship.

Internet Society

The **Internet Society** (ISOC) is a professional membership organization that is concerned with the growth and evolution of the worldwide Internet, with the policies and practices of Internet use, and with the social, political, and technical issues which arise as a result. The ISOC Trustees are responsible for approving appointments to the IAB from among the nominees submitted by the IETF nominating committee.

The ISOC may be contacted as follows:

- **http://www.isoc.org**

Internet Architecture Board

The **Internet Architecture Board (IAB)** is a technical advisory group of the ISOC. It is chartered to provide oversight of the architecture of the Internet and its protocols, and to serve, in the context of the Internet standards process, as a body to which the decisions of the IESG may be appealed. The IAB is responsible for the following:

- *IESG selection*. The IAB appoints a new IETF chair and all other IESG candidates from a list provided by the IETF nominating committee.
- *Architectural oversight*. The IAB provides oversight of the architecture for the protocols and procedures used by the Internet.
- *Standards process oversight and appeal*. The IAB provides oversight of the process used to create Internet standards. The IAB serves as an appeal board for complaints over the improper execution of the standards process.

- *RFC series and IANA.* The IAB is responsible for the editorial management and publication of the Request for Comments (RFC) document series, and for administration of the various Internet assigned numbers.
- *External liaison.* The IAB acts as the representative of the interests of the Internet Society in liaison relationships with other organizations concerned with standards and other technical and organizational issues relevant to the worldwide Internet.
- *Advice to ISOC.* The IAB acts as a source of advice and guidance to the Board of Trustees and Officers of the Internet Society concerning technical, architectural, procedural, and (where appropriate) policy matters pertaining to the Internet and its enabling technologies.

The IAB may be contacted as follows:

- **http://www.iab.org**

Internet Engineering Steering Group

The **Internet Engineering Steering Group** (IESG) is responsible for the technical management of IETF activities and the Internet standards process. As part of the ISOC, it administers the process according to the rules and procedures which have been ratified by the ISOC Trustees. The IESG is directly responsible for the actions associated with entry into and movement along the Internet 'standards track,' including final approval of specifications as Internet Standards. The IESG members are selected according to the procedures specified in RFC 2727: IAB and IESG Selection (2000, Best Current Practice).

The IESG may be contacted as follows:

- **http://www.ietf.org/iesg.html**

Internet Engineering Task Force

The **Internet Engineering Task Force** (IETF) is the protocol engineering and development arm of the Internet. It is an open international community of network designers, operators, vendors, and researchers concerned with the evolution of the Internet architecture and the smooth operation of the Internet. It is the principal body engaged in the development of new Internet standard specifications. Though it existed informally for some time, the group was formally established by the IAB in 1986.

The IETF is open to any interested individual: membership in a mailing-list of any IETF working group (see below) means effectively membership in the IETF.

The IETF's mission includes:

- identifying, and proposing solutions to, pressing operational and technical problems in the Internet;
- specifying the development or usage of protocols and the near-term architecture to solve such technical problems for the Internet;
- making recommendations to the IESG regarding the standardization of protocols and protocol usage in the Internet;
- facilitating technology transfer from the IRTF to the wider Internet community;
- providing a forum for the exchange of information within the Internet community between vendors, users, researchers, agency contractors, and network managers.

TABLE B-3   Standard IETF protocols (as per RFC 2900)

Protocol	Title	RFC number	STD number
--------	Internet Official Protocol Standards	3000	1
--------	Assigned Numbers	1700	2
--------	Requirements for Internet Hosts – Communication Layers	1122	3
--------	Requirements for Internet Hosts – Application and Support	1123	3
--------	[Reserved for Router Requirements. See RFC 1812.]		4
IP	Internet Protocol	791	5
ICMP	Internet Control Message Protocol	792	5
---------	Broadcasting Internet Datagrams	919	5
---------	Broadcasting Internet datagrams in the presence of subnets	922	5
--------	Internet Standard Subnetting Procedure	950	5
IGMP	Host extensions for IP multicasting	1112	5
UDP	User Datagram Protocol	768	6
TCP	Transmission Control Protocol	793	7
TELNET	Telnet Protocol Specification	854	8
TELNET	Telnet Option Specifications	855	8
FTP	File Transfer Protocol	959	9
SMTP	Simple Mail Transfer Protocol	821	10
SMTP-SIZE	SMTP Service Extension for Message Size Declaration	1870	10
MAIL	Standard for the format of ARPA Internet text messages	822	11
NTP	[Reserved for Network Time Protocol (NTP). 305.]	See RFC	12
DOMAIN	Domain names – concepts and facilities	1034	13

TABLE B-3   Continued

Protocol	Title	RFC number	STD number
DOMAIN	Domain names – implementation and specification	1035	13
--------	[Was Mail Routing and the Domain System. Historic.]	Now	14
SNMP	Simple Network Management Protocol (SNMP)	1157	15
SMI	Structure and identification of management information for TCP/IP-based internets	1155	16
Concise-MI	Concise MIB definitions	1212	16
MIB-II	Management Information Base for Network Management of TCP/IP-based internets:MIB-II	1213	17
EGP	[Was Exterior Gateway Protocol (RFC 904). Historic.]	Now	18
NETBIOS	Protocol standard for a NetBIOS service on a TCP/UDP transport: Concepts and methods	1001	19
NETBIOS	Protocol standard for a NetBIOS service on a TCP/UDP transport: Detailed specifications	1002	19
ECHO	Echo Protocol	862	20
DISCARD	Discard Protocol	863	21
CHARGEN	Character Generator Protocol	864	22
QUOTE	Quote of the Day Protocol	865	23
USERS	Active users	866	24
DAYTIME	Daytime Protocol	867	25
TIME	Time Protocol	868	26
TOPT-BIN	Telnet Binary Transmission	856	27
TOPT-ECHO	Telnet Echo Option	857	28
TOPT-SUPP	Telnet Suppress Go Ahead Option	858	29
TOPT-STAT	Telnet Status Option	859	30

▶

TABLE B-3   Continued

Protocol	Title	RFC number	STD number
TOPT-TIM	Telnet Timing Mark Option	860	31
TOPT-EXTOP	Telnet Extended Options: List Option	861	32
TFTP	The TFTP Protocol (Revision 2)	1350	33
RIP1	[Was Routing Information Protocol (RIP).by STD 56.]	Replaced	34
TP-TCP	ISO transport services on top of the TCP: Version 3	1006	35
IP-FDDI	Transmission of IP and ARP over FDDI Networks	1390	36
ARP	Ethernet Address Resolution Protocol: Or converting network protocol addresses to 48.bit Ethernet address for transmission on Ethernet hardware	826	37
RARP	Reverse Address Resolution Protocol	903	38
IP-ARPA	[Was BBN Report 1822 (IMP/Host Interface). Historic.]	Now	39
IP-WB	Host Access Protocol specification	907	40
IP-E	Standard for the transmission of IP datagrams over Ethernet networks	894	41
IP-EE	Standard for the transmission of IP datagrams over experimental Ethernet networks	895	42
IP-IEEE	Standard for the transmission of IP datagrams over IEEE 802 networks	1042	43
IP-DC	DCN local-network protocols	891	44
IP-HC	Internet Protocol on Network System's HYPERchannel: Protocol specification	1044	45
IP-ARC	Transmitting IP traffic over ARCNET networks	1201	46
IP-SLIP	Nonstandard for transmission of IP datagrams over serial lines: SLIP	1055	47
IP-NETBIOS	Standard for the transmission of IP datagrams over NetBIOS networks	1088	48
IP-IPX	Standard for the transmission of 802.2 packets over IPX networks	1132	49

TABLE B-3   Continued

Protocol	Title	RFC number	STD number
ETHER-MIB	Definitions of Managed Objects for the Ethernet-like Interface Types	1643	50
PPP	The Point-to-Point Protocol (PPP)	1661	51
PPP-HDLC	PPP in HDLC-like Framing	1662	51
IP-SMDS	Transmission of IP datagrams over the SMDS Service	1209	52
POP3	Post Office Protocol – Version 3	1939	53
OSPF2	OSPF Version 2	2328	54
IP-FR	Multiprotocol Interconnect over Frame Relay	2427	55
RIP2	RIP Version 2	2453	56
RIP2-APP	RIP Version 2 Protocol Applicability Statement	1722	57
SMIv2	Structure of Management Information Version 2 (SMIv2)	2578	58
CONV-MIB	Textual Conventions for SMIv2	2579	58
CONF-MIB	Conformance Statements for SMIv2	2580	58
RMON-MIB	Remote Network Monitoring Management Information Base	2819	59
SMTP-Pipe	SMTP Service Extension for Command Pipelining	2920	60
ONE-PASS	A One-Time Password System	2289	61

The **IETF** is divided into eight functional **areas**: *Applications, Internet, IP: Next Generation, Network Management, Operational Requirements, Routing, Security, Transport and User Services*. Each area has one or two area directors. The area directors, along with the IETF/IESG chair, form the IESG. Each area has several working groups where the actual technical work of the IETF is done. Much of the work is handled via mailing lists. The IETF holds meetings three times per year. The IETF meeting is not a conference, although there are technical presentations.

A **working group** is a group of people who work under a charter to achieve a certain goal (see Working Groups directory at **http://www.ietf.org/html.charters/wg-dir.html**). That goal may be the creation of an informational document, the creation of a protocol specification, or the resolution of problems in the Internet. Most working groups have a finite lifetime. That is, once a working group has achieved its goal, it disbands. As in the IETF, there is no official membership for a working group.

Unofficially, a working group member is somebody who is on that working group's mailing list; however, anyone may attend a working group meeting. Areas may also have **Birds of a Feather** (BOF) sessions. These generally have the same goals as working groups, except that they have no charter and usually only meet once or twice. BOFs are often held to determine if there is enough interest to form a working group.

The IETF may be contacted as follows:

■ **www.ietf.org**

IETF deliverables: RFCs and Internet Drafts

The IETF documents are entitled Request for Comments (RFC) which reflects their true meaning. There are now two special sub-series within the **RFCs**: FYIs and STDs. The **For Your Information** (FYI) RFC sub-series was created to document overviews and topics which are introductory. Frequently, FYIs are created by groups within the IETF User Services Area. The **Standard** (STD) RFC sub-series was created to identify those RFCs which do in fact specify Internet standards. Every RFC, including FYIs and STDs, has an RFC number by which they are indexed and by which they can be retrieved. FYIs and STDs have FYI numbers and STD numbers, respectively, in addition to RFC numbers.

Internet Drafts are working documents of the IETF. Any group or individual may submit a document for distribution as an Internet Draft. These documents are valid for six months, and may be updated, replaced, or made obsolete at any time. Drafts are publicly available and retrievable in the same way that RFCs are. An Internet draft, if it is commented on and attracts enough attention, becomes an RFC. Its status will depend on whether the RFC is part of the **standards track**: first it is a **draft standard** RFC, then it might be promoted to a **proposed standard** RFC, and if approved it may eventually become a **standard** RFC; however, there are not more than 60 standard RFCs (see Table B.3). (The standard track RFCs may eventually become **historic** if they are no longer in use; in cases of very old RFCs the status is sometimes shown as 'unknown.')

It is important to recognize the difference between technical and applicability statement RFCs where the former specify the technology while the latter give guidelines to its deployment and are not standards per se. Additionally, there are specific RFCs denominated as **best current practices**.

There are still other types of RFCs such as **informational** or **experimental** (these are mostly vendor specifications which are not intended or likely to be widely adopted). The RFC index is updated continuously and always shows the latest status of every RFC. As the RFCs are sequentially numbered, the index also shows which RFCs have become obsolete and which newer RFCs supersede them.

Key links to bookmark and watch in relation to IETF work and its deliverables (it is possible to subscribe to the IETF and receive notification of new RFCs and Internet Drafts) are as follows:

■ to the current list of RFCs and their status – **http://ftp.rfc-editor.org/in-notes/rfc-index.txt** (the list changes any time there is a new RFC approved or when an old RFC changes status);

■ to the RFCs – **http://www.ietf.org/rfc.html** or **http://www.rfc-editor.org/rfcsearch.html** (there are several new RFCs usually endorsed and made public every month; the only RFCs which might not be taken too seriously are those published on April 1!);

■ to the Internet drafts – **http://www.ietf.org/ID.html** (every day there appear new Internet Drafts).

Internet Research Task Force

The **Internet Research Task Force** (IRTF) has a mission to promote research of importance to the evolution of the Internet by creating focused, long-term, small research groups working on topics related to Internet protocols, applications, architecture, and technology. The IRTF is composed of a number of small research groups, which are usually focused and long term, though short-lived 'task force' like groups are possible.

The research groups work on topics related to Internet protocols, applications, architecture, and technology, and are expected to have the stable long-term (with respect to the lifetime of the research group) membership needed to promote the development of research collaboration and teamwork in exploring research issues. Participation is by individual contributors rather than by representatives of organizations.

The IRTF is managed by the IRTF chair in consultation with the Internet Research Steering Group (IRSG). The IRSG membership includes the IRTF chair, the chairs of the various research groups and possibly other individuals ('members at large') from the research community. The IRTF chair is appointed by the Internet Architecture Board (IAB), while the research group chairs are appointed as part of the formation of each group and the IRSG members at large are chosen by the IRTF chair in consultation with the rest of the IRSG and on the approval of the IAB.

In addition to managing the research groups, the IRSG may from time to time hold topical workshops focusing on research areas of importance to the evolution of the Internet, or more general workshops to, for example, discuss research priorities from an Internet perspective. The work of the IRTF follows the principles laid down in RFC 2014 (1996, Best Current Practice).

The IRTF may be contacted as follows:

■ http://www.irtf.org

Internet Assigned Numbers Authority

The **Internet Assigned Numbers Authority** (IANA) is the central coordinator for the assignment of unique parameter values for Internet protocols. The IANA is chartered by the Internet Society (ISOC) to act as the clearing house to assign and coordinate the use of numerous Internet protocol parameters. Regionally IANA assigns IP addresses and autonomous numbers through its regional registries. The IANA maybe contacted as follows:

■ http://www.iana.org

The **Regional Internet Registries** (IR) are as follows:

■ *ARIN* (*American Registry for Internet Numbers*) – for the Americas and sub-Saharan Africa, contact:
  – **http://www.arin.net**

■ *RIPE NCC* (*Réseaux IP Européens Network Coordination Center*) – for Europe, the Middle East, and part of Africa, contact:
  – **http://www.ripe.net**

■ *APNIC* (*Asia Pacific Network Information Center*) – Asia-Pacific region, contact:
  – **http://www.apnic.net**

APPENDIX C

Quick guide to internetworking troubleshooting

Networks are about connectivity, hence connectivity is the main target of any network administrator. Communication, data, and services accessibility and availability is what is visibly important to the network users. Connectivity is, in fact, invisible to them in many cases (is data locally or remotely stored, is application on local computer or not – users do not care much, unless they do not get from the networking system what they ask for). Users are not always happy even if they can use the application they want. Why? Well, if they have to wait for response from the system more than several seconds they get angry and if the application during peak time hangs, they can easily get mad. Therefore network availability and its performance is based on response time, throughput, and reliability.

Basic troubleshooting therefore deals with the following issues:

- **connectivity** – none, partial, intermittent;
- **performance** – response time, resource management.

Troubleshooting routing problems

Symptom	Possible cause	Action
No connection	■ Router down ■ Routes aging ■ Routes removed from routing table ■ (Mis)configured filter(s)	■ Verify router's functionality ■ Verify configuration – support for particular protocol ■ Verify configuration – static routes and routing protocols consistency ■ Verify filters
Sudden loss of connection	■ Invalid router configuration due to recent reboot or remote reconfiguration	■ Verify router's configuration, restore previous one if necessary

Symptom	Possible cause	Action
	■ Invalid end system/other routers configuration ■ Physical connectivity down	■ Verify configuration of other routers under the same administration (routing processes and filters) ■ Validate IP addresses across network ■ Verify end-system configuration (IP address or DHCP enabled; default gateway) ■ Check physical connections
Poor network and router performance problems	■ Misconfiguration ■ Excessive changes resulting in frequent routing tables recomputing ■ Routing loops/rerouting	■ Monitor routing updates and tables, debug routing protocol information ■ Verify routes in routing table against physical topology ■ Verify loop-free routing ■ Check timers' setting across collaborating routers ■ Monitor routing errors

Note. For all **internetworking devices' benchmarking** see: Informational **RFC 2544:** *Benchmarking Methodology for Network Interconnect Devices* (1999). The RFC discusses and defines a number of tests that may be used to describe the performance characteristics of a network interconnecting device. In addition to defining the tests this document also describes specific formats for reporting the results of the tests. Appendix A lists the tests and conditions that are believed should be included for specific cases and gives additional information about testing practices. Appendix B is a reference listing of maximum frame rates to be used with specific frame sizes on various media and Appendix C gives some examples of frame formats to be used in testing.

Troubleshooting LAN switching

Symptom	Possible cause	Action
No connection	■ Switch down ■ Port disabled ■ (Mis)configured VLAN ■ (Mis)configured filter	■ Reboot switch ■ Enable port ■ Clear address/VLAN tables or use management tools to find out VLAN membership ■ Verify filters
Loss of connection	■ Port disabled ■ Bad connector at switch ■ Learning mode turned off	■ Enable port ■ Verify link status ■ Turn on learning mode
Persistent connection and network performance problems	■ Excessive broadcast/multicast traffic ■ Broadcast storm ■ Loop ■ Address table full ■ Switch excessively cascaded leading to timouts ■ Excessive dropped frames	■ Monitor amount of broadcast/multicast traffic, set thresholds ■ Monitor network for broadcast storm ■ Detect and isolate loop, verify spanning tree operation is turned on across all switches ■ Verify that switch does not prematurely age out entries in address table due to full occupancy ■ Analyze rate of frame dropping

Note. For **switch benchmarking** see: Informational **RFC 2889:** *Benchmarking Methodology for LAN Switching Devices* (2000). The RFC provides a methodology for benchmarking local area network (LAN) switching devices. It extends the methodology already defined for benchmarking network interconnecting devices in Informational RFC 2544 (*Benchmarking Methodology for Network Interconnect Devices*, 1999) to switching devices. RFC 2889 primarily deals with devices which switch frames at the Medium Access Control (MAC) layer. It provides a methodology for benchmarking switching devices, forwarding performance, congestion control, latency, address handling, and filtering. In addition to defining the tests, this document also describes specific formats for reporting the results of the tests.

APPENDIX D

Overview of transmission speeds

A condensed list of references to the commonly used abbreviations relating to speeds, bandwidth, and/or signaling is provided in the table below which it is hoped the reader will find useful. Notes on more technical details related to the table are also provided below.

DS	
DS0	64 kbps
DS1 = T1	1.544 Mbps (24 DS0)
DS2 = T2	6.312 Mbps (4 DS1, 96 DS0)
DS3 = T3	44.736 Mbps (28 DS1, 672 DS0)
DS4	274.176 Mbps (4032 DS0)

SONET/SDH	
STS-1 = OC-1	51.84 Mbps
STS-3 = OC-3 = STM-1	155.52 Mbps (3 STS-1)
STS-9 = OC-9 = STM-3	466.560 Mbps (9 STS-1)
STS-12 = OC-12 = STM-4	622.08 Mbps (12 STS-1)
STS-18 = OC-18 = STM-6	933.120 Mbps (18 STS-1)
STS-24 = OC-24 = STM-8	1244.16 Mbps (24 STS-1)
STS-48 = OC-48 = STM-16	2488.32 Mbps (48 STS-1)
STS-192 = OC-192 = STM-64	9953.28 Mbps
OC-768	39.813 Gbps

ANSI	
STS-1	51.84 Mbps
STS-3c	155.52 Mbps (concatenated)
STS-12c	622.08 Mbps (concatenated)
DS3	44.736 Mbps

CCITT/ITU-T	
DS1	1.544 Mbps
E1	2.048 Mbps
DS2	6.312 Mbps
E2	8.448 Mbps
E3	34.368 Mbps
DS3	44.736 Mbps
E4	139.264 Mbps
STM-1	155.52 Mbps (= STS-3)
STM-4	622.08 Mbps (= STS-12)

ATM Forum	
DS1	1.544 Mbps
E1	2.048 Mbps
J2	6 Mbps
E3	34.368 Mbps
DS3	44.736 Mbps
STS-1	51.84 Mbps
STM1/STS-3c	155.52 Mbps
STM4/STS-12	622.08 Mbps
STM-8/STS-24	1244.16 Mbps
STM-16/STS-48	2488.32 Mbps
STM-64/STS-192	9953.28 Mbps

Notes

1 STS is used in the US, STM in Europe.

2 Although often used interchangably, and rightly so, technically DS3 or Digital Signal-3 is different to T-3 or T-Carrier-3. A DS3 channel is comprised of seven DS2 channels, which is comprised of four DS1s, which is 24 DS0s:

DS0 = 64K × 24 = DS1
DS1 = 1.536M (1.544M w/T-carrier overhead) × 2 = DS2
DS2 = 3.072M (3.152M w/T-carrier overhead) × 7 = DS3
DS3 = 43.008M (44.736M w/T-carrier overhead)

There is also a DS-1C (concatenated), which is two DS-1s, but this is rarely seen. (More is given overleaf in the layering note.)

3 T1 is a high-speed digital carrier facility developed by AT&T in the 1950s to support long-haul pulse-code modulation (PCM) voice transmission. T1 provides digital voice circuits or channels. There are 24 channels per each T1 line or 'trunk.' AT&T describes their Digital Carrier System as a 'two-point, dedicated, high capacity, digital service provided on terrestrial digital facilities capable of transmitting 1.544 Mbps. The interface to the customer can be either a T1 carrier or a higher order multiplexed facility.' T1 refers to the transport of a DS-1 formatted signal onto a copper, fiber, or wireless medium for deploying voice, data, or video-conferencing services. The T1 is part of an extensive digital hierarchy that starts with 24 DS0s at 64 kbps. These individual DS0s are used to provide voice or digital data to support point-to-point or network applications. By combining multiple DS0s, a high-speed interface can be provided to support a synchronous interface to an LAN router or voice PBX. For distances longer than one mile, a repeater is placed every mile to regenerate the signal. T1 is also sold in parts as **fractional T1**.

4 **E1** is the European equivalent to the American T1. Although both E1 and T1 use 64 kbps channels, they differ in many aspects. E1 is a point-to-point, dedicated, 2.048 Mbps communications circuit that carries 32 channels in contrast to T1's 24 channels. Of these 32 channels, 30 channels transmit voice and data. Unlike T1, E1 always provides clear channel 64 kbps channels. Of the two remaining channels, one uses time slot 16 and is used for signaling and carrying line supervision (such as whether the telephones are on-hook or off-hook). The other remaining channel uses time slot 0, and is used for synchronization, channel control, and framing control. There are two options for the physical media:

   – 120 ohm twisted pair cabling, typically foil shielded – this is called a balanced interface and uses a DB-15 or eight-pin modular connector;

   – 75 ohm coaxial cable – this is called an unbalanced interface because the two conductors do not have an equal impedance to ground and use a BNC connector.

5 **T3** is a physical transmission medium, which varies from DS3, which is the actual data, video, and voice that is transmitted over the medium. DS3 can be transmitted over microwave radio, fiber optics, and 75 ohm coaxial cable (in-house wiring with distance limitations of 450 feet). The line coding for a T3 line is Bipolar Three Zero Substitution (B3ZS). The framing formats available are M12/M23, M13, or C-Bit Parity. DS3 can be delivered channelized or non-channelized. Channelized DS3 is delivered as 28 individual DS1s and 672 individual DS0s. Each DS1 may come from a remote location. The telephone company's central office will do the subdivision of the DS3 to each site. Non-channelized DS3 involves no DS2 or DS1 multiplexing. This service is delivered as a T3 pipe with a bandwidth of 44.2 Mbps. It is generally used in point-to-point applications (one customer sending data to one remote site). Any subdivision of bandwidth is performed at each customer site rather than the central office. M13 and C-Bit parity formats support both of the applications above. T3 is also sold in parts as **fractional T3**.

6 **TAXI 4B/5B** (Transmitter/receiver Interface 4-byte/5-byte) is an encoding scheme used for FDDI LANs, as well as for ATM. It supports speeds of up to

100 Mbps over multimode fiber. TAXI is the chipset that generates 4B/5B encoding on multimode fiber. Five bit encoding provides 16 data symbols (0–F), eight control symbols (Q, H, I, J, K, T, R, S), and eight violation symbols (V). The coding of these symbols is done such that in normal situations there will never be four consecutive zeros in a row.

Layering note

At the lowest level are the signal (i.e. electrical or optical) standards that define single bits. These may be associated with a particular connector, but they also have particular timing characteristics. DS1 and E1 describe bit streams that run at certain data rates:

- 1.544 Mbps for DS1;
- 2.032 Mbps for E1.

T1 is a DS1 signal specifically running over copper pairs. It is possible to have radio or optical DS1 that is not on wire. DS-x is also a level in a digital multiplexing hierarchy. DS-x or E-x streams are isochronous: bits have to fall into time slots in the stream, but there are no in-stream timing bits (as with asynchronous signals) or external timing (as with synchronous signals).

For the next layer up, there are constraints on the bit stream. These constraints are used to maintain signal quality, for limited control (e.g. triggering loopbacks), etc. Bit level framing includes algorithms such as AMI and B8ZS. The next level up synchronizes multiple streams into frames so the frames can be associated with multiplexed subchannels. SF and ESF are common methods, along with CAS and CCS as means of sending control information.

On top of the subchannels goes the basic data link framing from protocols such as frame or ATM with AAL. Both of these families go up yet another layer, with a protocol type field starting the data field, a field based on 802.2.

There is a technical difference when referring to DS1 vs. T1 (or DS3 vs. T-3). When the reference is to signaling and framing, technically it is to a DS<n> (DS<n> stands for digital signal level <n>). However, if the reference is to the entire physical layer, including the cabling, interfaces, connectors, etc., then it is technically about a T<n>. This technical difference is an important one if a distinction is needed as to what carries what. It is absolutely incorrect to say that a T1 is carried by a DS1. If anything, it is the other way around, though it would really be incorrect to say that one carries the other since there is some overlap in what the two terms define. 'T1' and 'DS1' tend to be used interchangeably, but it is a misconception that the two terms are equivalent. When referring to the whole multiplexing hierarchy, it is usually simply the 'T-carrier,' or alternatively the PDH (plesiochronous digital hierarchy).

Second, a T1 does not add framing and overhead to the DS1. The DS1 defines the framing bits, and anything other signaling that forms the 0s and 1s that are eventually sent over a physical medium. The only thing that the T1 does that the DS1 does not is provide a physical medium for the DS1 to travel over.

Since every level in the hierarchy employs different framing and multiplexing schemes, it is not wise to assume that what is true for a DS1 is also true for a

DS3. For example, DS1 defines byte-interleaving, whereas DS3 uses bit-interleaving, which is a big difference. Other differences are discussed below.

DS1 interleaves 24 DS0s in a byte-wise fashion. Every level above the DS1 interleaves signals from the next lower level in a bit-wise fashion. The process to get from a DS1 to a DS3 in an M13 (pronounced M-one-three) multiplexor is as follows. First, four DS1s are interleaved bit-wise to form a DS2. Next, seven DS2s are multiplexed bit-wise to form a DS3. Note that each level in the hierarchy adds its own framing bits before being multiplexed to the next level, which is why a DS3 has many more bits in its frame than 28×193 (there are 193 bits in a DS1 frame). Also note that many levels exist entirely in a digital state within the multiplexor, and that typically the signal will not be seen on a physical cable (e.g. T2 which includes a physical medium in addition to the DS2 signal, although a DS2 exists at some point every time DS1s are multiplexed together to form a DS3). Also DS3 signals frequently are placed in a Sonet STS-1 frame for transport over fiber (OC-n), in which case there is also no T3. This is the reason that DS<n> terminology is used instead of T<n>.

Also note that when considering DS<n> 'frames,' these frames are not analogous to the more familiar data-link frames. Transmission frames reside more at the physical layer than at any other layer, if you were to try to map them to the OSI model. The problem with T-carrier is that each level uses different framing formats. Also the use of bit-interleaving (at higher levels) combined with the T-carrier's plesiochronous (meaning 'nearly synchronous') nature creates problems that are only solved by adding bits to the frame known as 'stuff bits.' So, as the multiplexor is pulling individual bits from buffers that contain bits from lower level signals there may be situations where, due to timing differences, the next bit to be multiplexed has not yet arrived in the buffer. (Note that individual bits are switched and/or multiplexed as soon as they arrive which is why these devices have latencies that are measured in numbers of microseconds.) In this situation, a stuff bit is used instead and the real bit will be grabbed the next time around.

Stuff bits from the DS2 frame are rolled up and multiplexed in with new stuff bits at the DS3 level. In order to expose individual lower level signals, the whole DS3 needs to be demultiplexed in order to remove the stuff bits (etc.) and get back the original signals. This is one reason why Sonet is superior – because the multiplexing is identical at every level, and all of it uses byte-wise multiplexing. Therefore individual DS0s can be pulled out of the frame without having to demultiplex the whole thing.

APPENDIX E

Useful numbers

For quick reference this appendix provides at a glance the **most common IP numbers**:

- **protocol numbers**;
- **port numbers**;
- **multicast addresses**.

In addition, the appendix includes a small but handy **conversion table between decimal, binary, and hexadecimal numbers.**

Protocol numbers

The following section provides commonly used numbers specified by the IETF in RFC 1700 (ftp://ftp.isc.org/pub/rfc/rfc1700.txt), protocol and port numbers respectively. The RFC should be consulted for up-to-date number status and for less frequent numbers not contained herein. In the IPv4 (RFC 791) the *Protocol* field identifies the next level protocol. This is an eight-bit field. In IPv6 (RFC 1883) this field is called the *Next Header* field.

Assigned Internet Protocol Numbers

Decimal	Keyword	Protocol	References
0	HOPOPT	IPv6 Hop-by-Hop Option	[RFC1883]
1	ICMP	Internet Control Message	[RFC792]
2	IGMP	Internet Group Management	[RFC1112]
3	GGP	Gateway-to-Gateway	[RFC823]
4	IP	IP in IP (encapsulation)	[RFC2003]
5	ST	Stream	[RFC1190,IEN119]
6	TCP	Transmission Control	[RFC793]
7	CBT	CBT	[Ballardie]
8	EGP	Exterior Gateway Protocol	[RFC888,DLM1]
9	IGP	any private interior gateway (used by Cisco for their IGRP)	[IANA]

Decimal	Keyword	Protocol	References
10	BBN-RCC-MON	BBN RCC Monitoring	[SGC]
11	NVP-II	Network Voice Protocol	[RFC741,SC3]
12	PUP	PUP	[PUP,XEROX]
13	ARGUS	ARGUS	[RWS4]
14	EMCON	EMCON	[BN7]
15	XNET	Cross Net Debugger	[IEN158,JFH2]
16	CHAOS	Chaos	[NC3]
17	UDP	User Datagram	[RFC768,JBP]
18	MUX	Multiplexing	[IEN90,JBP]
19	DCN-MEAS	DCN Measurement Subsystems	[DLM1]
20	HMP	Host Monitoring	[RFC869,RH6]
21	PRM	Packet Radio Measurement	[ZSU]
22	XNS-IDP	XEROX NS IDP	[ETHERNET,XEROX]
23	TRUNK-1	Trunk-1	[BWB6]
24	TRUNK-2	Trunk-2	[BWB6]
25	LEAF-1	Leaf-1	[BWB6]
26	LEAF-2	Leaf-2	[BWB6]
27	RDP	Reliable Data Protocol	[RFC908,RH6]
28	IRTP	Internet Reliable Transaction	[RFC938,TXM]
29	ISO-TP4	ISO Transport Protocol Class 4	[RFC905,RC77]
30	NETBLT	Bulk Data Transfer Protocol	[RFC969,DDC1]
31	MFE-NSP	MFE Network Services Protocol	[MFENET,BCH2]
32	MERIT-INP	MERIT Internodal Protocol	[HWB]
33	SEP	Sequential Exchange Protocol	[JC120]
34	3PC	Third Party Connect Protocol	[SAF3]
35	IDPR	Inter-Domain Policy Routing Protocol	[MXS1]
36	XTP	XTP	[GXC]
37	DDP	Datagram Delivery Protocol	[WXC]
38	IDPR-CMTP	IDPR Control Message Transport Protocol	[MXS1]
39	TP++	TP++ Transport Protocol	[DXF]
40	IL	IL Transport Protocol	[Presotto]
41	IPv6	Ipv6	[Deering]
42	SDRP	Source Demand Routing Protocol	[DXE1]
43	IPv6-Route	Routing Header for IPv6	[Deering]
44	IPv6-Frag	Fragment Header for IPv6	[Deering]
45	IDRP	Inter-Domain Routing Protocol	[Sue Hares]
46	RSVP	Reservation Protocol	[Bob Braden]

Decimal	Keyword	Protocol	References
47	GRE	General Routing Encapsulation	[Tony Li]
48	MHRP	Mobile Host Routing Protocol	[David Johnson]
49	BNA	BNA	[Gary Salamon]
50	ESP	Encap Security Payload for IPv6	[RFC 1827]
51	AH	Authentication Header for IPv6	[RFC 1826]
52	I-NLSP	Integrated Net Layer Security	TUBA [GLENN]
53	SWIPE	IP with Encryption	[JI6]
54	NARP	NBMA Address Resolution Protocol	[RFC 1735]
55	MOBILE	IP Mobility	[Perkins]
56	TLSP	Transport Layer Security Protocol using Kryptonet key management	[Oberg]
57	SKIP	SKIP	[Markson]
58	IPv6-ICMP	ICMP for IPv6	[RFC 1883]
59	IPv6-NoNxt	No Next Header for IPv6	[RFC 1883]
60	IPv6-Opts	Destination Options for IPv6	[RFC 1883]
61		any host internal protocol	[IANA]
62	CFTP	CFTP	[CFTP,HCF2]
63		any local network	[IANA]
64	SAT-EXPAK	SATNET and Backroom EXPAK	[SHB]
65	KRYPTOLAN	Kryptolan	[PXL1]
66	RVD	MIT Remote Virtual Disk Protocol	[MBG]
67	IPPC	Internet Pluribus Packet Core	[SHB]
68		any distributed file system	[IANA]
69	SAT-MON	SATNET Monitoring	[SHB]
70	VISA	VISA Protocol	[GXT1]
71	IPCV	Internet Packet Core Utility	[SHB]
72	CPNX	Computer Protocol Network Executive	[DXM2]
73	CPHB	Computer Protocol Heart Beat	[DXM2]
74	WSN	Wang Span Network	[VXD]
75	PVP	Packet Video Protocol	[SC3]
76	BR-SAT-MON	Backroom SATNET Monitoring	[SHB]
77	SUN-ND	SUN ND PROTOCOL-Temporary	[WM3]
78	WB-MON	WIDEBAND Monitoring	[SHB]
79	WB-EXPAK	WIDEBAND EXPAK	[SHB]
80	ISO-IP	ISO Internet Protocol	[MTR]
81	VMTP	VMTP	[DRC3]
82	SECURE-VMTP	SECURE-VMTP	[DRC3]

Decimal	Keyword	Protocol	References
83	VINES	VINES	[BXH]
84	TTP	TTP	[JXS]
85	NSFNET-IGP	NSFNET-IGP	[HWB]
86	DGP	Dissimilar Gateway Protocol	[DGP,ML109]
87	TCF	TCF	[GAL5]
88	EIGRP	EIGRP	[CISCO,GXS]
89	OSPFIGP	OSPFIGP	[RFC1583,JTM4]
90	Sprite-RPC	Sprite RPC Protocol	[SPRITE,BXW]
91	LARP	Locus Address Resolution Protocol	[BXH]
92	MTP	Multicast Transport Protocol	[SXA]
93	AX.25	AX.25 Frames	[BK29]
94	IPIP	IP-within-IP Encapsulation Protocol	[JI6]
95	MICP	Mobile Internetworking Control Pro	[JI6]
96	SCC-SP	Semaphore Communications Sec. Pro.	[HXH]
97	ETHERIP	Ethernet-within-IP Encapsulation	[RXH1]
98	ENCAP	Encapsulation Header	[RFC1241,RXB3]
99		any private encryption scheme	[IANA]
100	GMTP	GMTP	[RXB5]
101	IFMP	Ipsilon Flow Management Protocol	[Hinden]
102	PNNI	PNNI over IP	[Callon]
103	PIM	Protocol Independent Multicast	[Farinacci]
104	ARIS	ARIS	[Feldman]
105	SCPS	SCPS	[Durst]
106	QNX	QNX	[Hunter]
107	A/N	Active Networks	[Braden]
108	IPPCP	IP Payload Compression Protocol	[Doraswamy]
109	SNP	Sitara Networks Protocol	[Sridhar]
110	Compaq-Peer	Compaq Peer Protocol	[Volpe]
111	IPX-in-IP	IPX in IP	[Lee]
112	VRRP	Virtual Router Redundancy Protocol	[Hinden]
113	PGM	PGM Reliable Transport Protocol	[Speakman]
114		any 0-hop protocol	[IANA]
115	L2TP	Layer Two Tunneling Protocol	[Aboba]
116	DDX	D-II Data Exchange (DDX)	[Worley]
117–254		Unassigned	[IANA]
255		Reserved	[IANA]

Port numbers

The port numbers are divided into three ranges:

- **well known ports** are those from 0 through 1023;
- **registered ports** are those from 1024 through 49 151 – the registered ports are listed by the IANA and on most systems can be used by ordinary user processes or programs executed by ordinary users;
- **dynamic and/or private ports** are those from 49 152 through 65 535.

Well known port numbers

The well known ports are assigned by the IANA (contact: **http://www.isi.edu/in-notes/iana/assignments/port-numbers**) and on most systems can only be used by system (or root) processes or by programs executed by privileged users.

Ports are used in the TCP (RFC 793) to name the ends of logical connections which carry long-term conversations. For the purpose of providing services to unknown callers, a service contact port is defined. This list specifies the port used by the server process as its contact port. The contact port is sometimes called the 'well known port.' To the extent possible, these same port assignments are used with the UDP (RFC 768).

The assigned ports use a small portion of the possible port numbers. For many years the assigned ports were in the range 0–255. Recently, the range for assigned ports managed by the IANA has been expanded to the range 0–1023.

Port assignments

Keyword	Decimal	Description
	0/tcp	Reserved
	0/udp	Reserved
#		Jon Postel <postel@isi.edu>
tcpmux	1/tcp	TCP Port Service Multiplexer
tcpmux	1/udp	TCP Port Service Multiplexer
#		Mark Lottor <MKL@nisc.sri.com>
compressnet	2/tcp	Management Utility
compressnet	2/udp	Management Utility
compressnet	3/tcp	Compression Process
compressnet	3/udp	Compression Process
#		Bernie Volz <VOLZ@PROCESS.COM>
#	4/tcp	Unassigned
#	4/udp	Unassigned
rje	5/tcp	Remote Job Entry
rje	5/udp	Remote Job Entry

Keyword	Decimal	Description
#		Jon Postel <postel@isi.edu>
#	6/tcp	Unassigned
#	6/udp	Unassigned
echo	7/tcp	Echo
echo	7/udp	Echo
#		Jon Postel <postel@isi.edu>
#	8/tcp	Unassigned
#	8/udp	Unassigned
discard	9/tcp	Discard
discard	9/udp	Discard
#		Jon Postel <postel@isi.edu>
#	10/tcp	Unassigned
#	10/udp	Unassigned
systat	11/tcp	Active Users
systat	11/udp	Active Users
#		Jon Postel <postel@isi.edu>
#	12/tcp	Unassigned
#	12/udp	Unassigned
daytime	13/tcp	Daytime (RFC 867)
daytime	13/udp	Daytime (RFC 867)
#		Jon Postel <postel@isi.edu>
#	14/tcp	Unassigned
#	14/udp	Unassigned
#	15/tcp	Unassigned [was netstat]
#	15/udp	Unassigned
#	16/tcp	Unassigned
#	16/udp	Unassigned
qotd	17/tcp	Quote of the Day
qotd	17/udp	Quote of the Day
#		Jon Postel <postel@isi.edu>
msp	18/tcp	Message Send Protocol
msp	18/udp	Message Send Protocol
#		Rina Nethaniel <---none--->
chargen	19/tcp	Character Generator
chargen	19/udp	Character Generator
ftp-data	20/tcp	File Transfer [Default Data]
ftp-data	20/udp	File Transfer [Default Data]

Keyword	Decimal	Description
ftp	21/tcp	File Transfer [Control]
ftp	21/udp	File Transfer [Control]
#		Jon Postel <postel@isi.edu>
ssh	22/tcp	SSH Remote Login Protocol
ssh	22/udp	SSH Remote Login Protocol
#		Tatu Ylonen <ylo@cs.hut.fi>
telnet	23/tcp	Telnet
telnet	23/udp	Telnet
#		Jon Postel <postel@isi.edu>
	24/tcp	any private mail system
	24/udp	any private mail system
#		Rick Adams <rick@UUNET.UU.NET>
smtp	25/tcp	Simple Mail Transfer
smtp	25/udp	Simple Mail Transfer
#		Jon Postel <postel@isi.edu>
#	26/tcp	Unassigned
#	26/udp	Unassigned
nsw-fe	27/tcp	NSW User System FE
nsw-fe	27/udp	NSW User System FE
#		Robert Thomas <BThomas@F.BBN.COM>
#	28/tcp	Unassigned
#	28/udp	Unassigned
msg-icp	29/tcp	MSG ICP
msg-icp	29/udp	MSG ICP
#		Robert Thomas <BThomas@F.BBN.COM>
#	30/tcp	Unassigned
#	30/udp	Unassigned
msg-auth	31/tcp	MSG Authentication
msg-auth	31/udp	MSG Authentication
#		Robert Thomas <BThomas@F.BBN.COM>
#	32/tcp	Unassigned
#	32/udp	Unassigned
dsp	33/tcp	Display Support Protocol
dsp	33/udp	Display Support Protocol
#		Ed Cain <cain@edn-unix.dca.mil>
#	34/tcp	Unassigned
#	34/udp	Unassigned

Keyword	Decimal	Description
	35/tcp	any private printer server
	35/udp	any private printer server
#		Jon Postel <postel@isi.edu>
#	36/tcp	Unassigned
#	36/udp	Unassigned
time	37/tcp	Time
time	37/udp	Time
#		Jon Postel <postel@isi.edu>
rap	38/tcp	Route Access Protocol
rap	38/udp	Route Access Protocol
#		Robert Ullmann <ariel@world.std.com>
rlp	39/tcp	Resource Location Protocol
rlp	39/udp	Resource Location Protocol
#		Mike Accetta <MIKE.ACCETTA@CMU-CS-A.EDU>
#	40/tcp	Unassigned
#	40/udp	Unassigned
graphics	41/tcp	Graphics
graphics	41/udp	Graphics
name	42/tcp	Host Name Server
name	42/udp	Host Name Server
nameserver	42/tcp	Host Name Server
nameserver	42/udp	Host Name Server
nicname	43/tcp	Who Is
nicname	43/udp	Who Is
mpm-flags	44/tcp	MPM FLAGS Protocol
mpm-flags	44/udp	MPM FLAGS Protocol
mpm	45/tcp	Message Processing Module [recv]
mpm	45/udp	Message Processing Module [recv]
mpm-snd	46/tcp	MPM [default send]
mpm-snd	46/udp	MPM [default send]
#		Jon Postel <postel@isi.edu>
ni-ftp	47/tcp	NI FTP
ni-ftp	47/udp	NI FTP
#		Steve Kille <S.Kille@isode.com>
auditd	48/tcp	Digital Audit Daemon
auditd	48/udp	Digital Audit Daemon

Keyword	Decimal	Description
#		Larry Scott <scott@zk3.dec.com>
tacacs	49/tcp	Login Host Protocol (TACACS)
tacacs	49/udp	Login Host Protocol (TACACS)
#		Pieter Ditmars <pditmars@BBN.COM>
re-mail-ck	50/tcp	Remote Mail Checking Protocol
re-mail-ck	50/udp	Remote Mail Checking Protocol
#		Steve Dorner <s-dorner@UIUC.EDU>
la-maint	51/tcp	IMP Logical Address Maintenance
la-maint	51/udp	IMP Logical Address Maintenance
#		Andy Malis <malis_a@timeplex.com>
xns-time	52/tcp	XNS Time Protocol
xns-time	52/udp	XNS Time Protocol
#		Susie Armstrong <Armstrong.wbst128@XEROX>
domain	53/tcp	Domain Name Server
domain	53/udp	Domain Name Server
#		Paul Mockapetris <PVM@ISI.EDU>
xns-ch	54/tcp	XNS Clearinghouse
xns-ch	54/udp	XNS Clearinghouse
#		Susie Armstrong <Armstrong.wbst128@XEROX>
isi-gl	55/tcp	ISI Graphics Language
isi-gl	55/udp	ISI Graphics Language
xns-auth	56/tcp	XNS Authentication
xns-auth	56/udp	XNS Authentication
#		Susie Armstrong <Armstrong.wbst128@XEROX>
	57/tcp	any private terminal access
	57/udp	any private terminal access
#		Jon Postel <postel@isi.edu>
xns-mail	58/tcp	XNS Mail
xns-mail	58/udp	XNS Mail
#		Susie Armstrong <Armstrong.wbst128@XEROX>
	59/tcp	any private file service
	59/udp	any private file service
#		Jon Postel <postel@isi.edu>
	60/tcp	Unassigned

Keyword	Decimal	Description
	60/udp	Unassigned
ni-mail	61/tcp	NI MAIL
ni-mail	61/udp	NI MAIL
#		Steve Kille <S.Kille@isode.com>
acas	62/tcp	ACA Services
acas	62/udp	ACA Services
#		E. Wald <ewald@via.enet.dec.com>
whois++	63/tcp	whois++
whois++	63/udp	whois++
#		Rickard Schoultz <schoultz@sunet.se>
covia	64/tcp	Communications Integrator (CI)
covia	64/udp	Communications Integrator (CI)
#		'Tundra' Tim Daneliuk
#		<tundraix!tundra@clout.chi.il.us>
tacacs-ds	65/tcp	TACACS-Database Service
tacacs-ds	65/udp	TACACS-Database Service
#		Kathy Huber <khuber@bbn.com>
sql*net	66/tcp	Oracle SQL*NET
sql*net	66/udp	Oracle SQL*NET
#		Jack Haverty <jhaverty@ORACLE.COM>
bootps	67/tcp	Bootstrap Protocol Server
bootps	67/udp	Bootstrap Protocol Server
bootpc	68/tcp	Bootstrap Protocol Client
bootpc	68/udp	Bootstrap Protocol Client
#		Bill Croft <Croft@SUMEX-AIM.STANFORD.EDU>
tftp	69/tcp	Trivial File Transfer
tftp	69/udp	Trivial File Transfer
#		David Clark <ddc@LCS.MIT.EDU>
gopher	70/tcp	Gopher
gopher	70/udp	Gopher
#		Mark McCahill <mpm@boombox.micro.umn.edu>
netrjs-1	71/tcp	Remote Job Service
netrjs-1	71/udp	Remote Job Service
netrjs-2	72/tcp	Remote Job Service
netrjs-2	72/udp	Remote Job Service

Keyword	Decimal	Description
netrjs-3	73/tcp	Remote Job Service
netrjs-3	73/udp	Remote Job Service
netrjs-4	74/tcp	Remote Job Service
netrjs-4	74/udp	Remote Job Service
#		Bob Braden <Braden@ISI.EDU>
	75/tcp	any private dial out service
	75/udp	any private dial out service
#		Jon Postel <postel@isi.edu>
deos	76/tcp	Distributed External Object Store
deos	76/udp	Distributed External Object Store
#		Robert Ullmann <ariel@world.std.com>
	77/tcp	any private RJE service
	77/udp	any private RJE service
#		Jon Postel <postel@isi.edu>
vettcp	78/tcp	vettcp
vettcp	78/udp	vettcp
#		Christopher Leong <leong@kolmod.mlo.dec.com>
finger	79/tcp	Finger
finger	79/udp	Finger
#		David Zimmerman <dpz@RUTGERS.EDU>
http	80/tcp	World Wide Web HTTP
http	80/udp	World Wide Web HTTP
www	80/tcp	World Wide Web HTTP
www	80/udp	World Wide Web HTTP
www-http	80/tcp	World Wide Web HTTP
www-http	80/udp	World Wide Web HTTP
#		Tim Berners-Lee <timbl@W3.org>
hosts2-ns	81/tcp	HOSTS2 Name Server
hosts2-ns	81/udp	HOSTS2 Name Server
#		Earl Killian <EAK@MORDOR.S1.GOV>
xfer	82/tcp	XFER Utility
xfer	82/udp	XFER Utility
#		Thomas M. Smith <Thomas.M.Smith@lmco.com>
mit-ml-dev	83/tcp	MIT ML Device
mit-ml-dev	83/udp	MIT ML Device

Keyword	Decimal	Description
#		David Reed <--none--->
ctf	84/tcp	Common Trace Facility
ctf	84/udp	Common Trace Facility
#		Hugh Thomas <thomas@oils.enet.dec.com>
mit-ml-dev	85/tcp	MIT ML Device
mit-ml-dev	85/udp	MIT ML Device
#		David Reed <--none--->
mfcobol	86/tcp	Micro Focus Cobol
mfcobol	86/udp	Micro Focus Cobol
#		Simon Edwards <--none--->
	87/tcp	any private terminal link
	87/udp	any private terminal link
#		Jon Postel <postel@isi.edu>
kerberos	88/tcp	Kerberos
kerberos	88/udp	Kerberos
#		B. Clifford Neuman <bcn@isi.edu>
su-mit-tg	89/tcp	SU/MIT Telnet Gateway
su-mit-tg	89/udp	SU/MIT Telnet Gateway
#		Mark Crispin <MRC@PANDA.COM>
########### PORT 90 also being used unofficially by Pointcast #########
dnsix	90/tcp	DNSIX Securit Attribute Token Map
dnsix	90/udp	DNSIX Securit Attribute Token Map
#		Charles Watt <watt@sware.com>
mit-dov	91/tcp	MIT Dover Spooler
mit-dov	91/udp	MIT Dover Spooler
#		Eliot Moss <EBM@XX.LCS.MIT.EDU>
npp	92/tcp	Network Printing Protocol
npp	92/udp	Network Printing Protocol
#		Louis Mamakos <louie@sayshell.umd.edu>
dcp	93/tcp	Device Control Protocol
dcp	93/udp	Device Control Protocol
#		Daniel Tappan <Tappan@BBN.COM>
objcall	94/tcp	Tivoli Object Dispatcher
objcall	94/udp	Tivoli Object Dispatcher
#		Tom Bereiter <--none--->
supdup	95/tcp	SUPDUP
supdup	95/udp	SUPDUP

Keyword	Decimal	Description
#		Mark Crispin <MRC@PANDA.COM>
dixie	96/tcp	DIXIE Protocol Specification
dixie	96/udp	DIXIE Protocol Specification
#		Tim Howes <Tim.Howes@terminator.cc.umich.edu>
swift-rvf	97/tcp	Swift Remote Virtural File Protocol
swift-rvf	97/udp	Swift Remote Virtural File Protocol
#		Maurice R. Turcotte
#		<mailrus!uflorida!rm1!dnmrt%rmatl@uunet.UU.NET>
tacnews	98/tcp	TAC News
tacnews	98/udp	TAC News
#		Jon Postel <postel@isi.edu>
metagram	99/tcp	Metagram Relay
metagram	99/udp	Metagram Relay
#		Geoff Goodfellow <Geoff@FERNWOOD.MPK.CA.US>
newacct	100/tcp	[unauthorized use]
hostname	101/tcp	NIC Host Name Server
hostname	101/udp	NIC Host Name Server
#		Jon Postel <postel@isi.edu>
iso-tsap	102/tcp	ISO-TSAP Class 0
iso-tsap	102/udp	ISO-TSAP Class 0
#		Marshall Rose <mrose@dbc.mtview.ca.us>
gppitnp	103/tcp	Genesis Point-to-Point Trans Net
gppitnp	103/udp	Genesis Point-to-Point Trans Net
acr-nema	104/tcp	ACR-NEMA Digital Imag. & Comm. 300
acr-nema	104/udp	ACR-NEMA Digital Imag. & Comm. 300
#		Patrick McNamee <--none--->
cso	105/tcp	CCSO name server protocol
cso	105/udp	CCSO name server protocol
#		Martin Hamilton <martin@mrrl.lut.as.uk>
csnet-ns	105/tcp	Mailbox Name Nameserver
csnet-ns	105/udp	Mailbox Name Nameserver
#		Marvin Solomon <solomon@CS.WISC.EDU>
3com-tsmux	106/tcp	3COM-TSMUX
3com-tsmux	106/udp	3COM-TSMUX
#		Jeremy Siegel <jzs@NSD.3Com.COM>

Keyword	Decimal	Description
rtelnet	107/tcp	Remote Telnet Service
rtelnet	107/udp	Remote Telnet Service
#		Jon Postel <postel@isi.edu>
snagas	108/tcp	SNA Gateway Access Server
snagas	108/udp	SNA Gateway Access Server
#		Kevin Murphy <murphy@sevens.lkg.dec.com>
pop2	109/tcp	Post Office Protocol - Version 2
pop2	109/udp	Post Office Protocol - Version 2
#		Joyce K. Reynolds <jkrey@isi.edu>
pop3	110/tcp	Post Office Protocol - Version 3
pop3	110/udp	Post Office Protocol - Version 3
#		Marshall Rose <mrose@dbc.mtview.ca.us>
sunrpc	111/tcp	SUN Remote Procedure Call
sunrpc	111/udp	SUN Remote Procedure Call
#		Chuck McManis <cmcmanis@freegate.net>
mcidas	112/tcp	McIDAS Data Transmission Protocol
mcidas	112/udp	McIDAS Data Transmission Protocol
#		Glenn Davis <davis@unidata.ucar.edu>
ident	113/tcp	
auth	113/tcp	Authentication Service
auth	113/udp	Authentication Service
#		Mike St. Johns <stjohns@arpa.mil>
audionews	114/tcp	Audio News Multicast
audionews	114/udp	Audio News Multicast
#		Martin Forssen <maf@dtek.chalmers.se>
sftp	115/tcp	Simple File Transfer Protocol
sftp	115/udp	Simple File Transfer Protocol
#		Mark Lottor <MKL@nisc.sri.com>
ansanotify	116/tcp	ANSA REX Notify
ansanotify	116/udp	ANSA REX Notify
#		Nicola J. Howarth <njh@ansa.co.uk>
uucp-path	117/tcp	UUCP Path Service
uucp-path	117/udp	UUCP Path Service
sqlserv	118/tcp	SQL Services
sqlserv	118/udp	SQL Services
#		Larry Barnes <barnes@broke.enet.dec.com>

Keyword	Decimal	Description
nntp	119/tcp	Network News Transfer Protocol
nntp	119/udp	Network News Transfer Protocol
#		Phil Lapsley <phil@UCBARPA.BERKELEY.EDU>
cfdptkt	120/tcp	CFDPTKT
cfdptkt	120/udp	CFDPTKT
#		John Ioannidis <ji@close.cs.columbia.ed>
erpc	121/tcp	Encore Expedited Remote Pro.Call
erpc	121/udp	Encore Expedited Remote Pro.Call
#		Jack O'Neil <---none--->
smakynet	122/tcp	SMAKYNET
smakynet	122/udp	SMAKYNET
#		Mike O'Dowd <odowd@ltisun8.epfl.ch>
ntp	123/tcp	Network Time Protocol
ntp	123/udp	Network Time Protocol
#		Dave Mills <Mills@HUEY.UDEL.EDU>
ansatrader	124/tcp	ANSA REX Trader
ansatrader	124/udp	ANSA REX Trader
#		Nicola J. Howarth <njh@ansa.co.uk>
locus-map	125/tcp	Locus PC-Interface Net Map Ser
locus-map	125/udp	Locus PC-Interface Net Map Ser
#		Eric Peterson <lcc.eric@SEAS.UCLA.EDU>
unitary	126/tcp	Unisys Unitary Login
unitary	126/udp	Unisys Unitary Login
#		<feil@kronos.nisd.cam.unisys.com>
locus-con	127/tcp	Locus PC-Interface Conn Server
locus-con	127/udp	Locus PC-Interface Conn Server
#		Eric Peterson <lcc.eric@SEAS.UCLA.EDU>
gss-xlicen	128/tcp	GSS X License Verification
gss-xlicen	128/udp	GSS X License Verification
#		John Light <johnl@gssc.gss.com>
pwdgen	129/tcp	Password Generator Protocol
pwdgen	129/udp	Password Generator Protocol
#		Frank J. Wacho <WANCHO@WSMR-SIMTEL20.ARMY.MIL>
cisco-fna	130/tcp	cisco FNATIVE
cisco-fna	130/udp	cisco FNATIVE
cisco-tna	131/tcp	cisco TNATIVE

Keyword	Decimal	Description
cisco-tna	131/udp	cisco TNATIVE
cisco-sys	132/tcp	cisco SYSMAINT
cisco-sys	132/udp	cisco SYSMAINT
statsrv	133/tcp	Statistics Service
statsrv	133/udp	Statistics Service
#		Dave Mills <Mills@HUEY.UDEL.EDU>
ingres-net	134/tcp	INGRES-NET Service
ingres-net	134/udp	INGRES-NET Service
#		Mike Berrow <---none--->
epmap	135/tcp	DCE endpoint resolution
epmap	135/udp	DCE endpoint resolution
#		Joe Pato <pato@apollo.hp.com>
profile	136/tcp	PROFILE Naming System
profile	136/udp	PROFILE Naming System
#		Larry Peterson <llp@ARIZONA.EDU>
netbios-ns	137/tcp	NETBIOS Name Service
netbios-ns	137/udp	NETBIOS Name Service
netbios-dgm	138/tcp	NETBIOS Datagram Service
netbios-dgm	138/udp	NETBIOS Datagram Service
netbios-ssn	139/tcp	NETBIOS Session Service
netbios-ssn	139/udp	NETBIOS Session Service
#		Jon Postel <postel@isi.edu>
emfis-data	140/tcp	EMFIS Data Service
emfis-data	140/udp	EMFIS Data Service
emfis-cntl	141/tcp	EMFIS Control Service
emfis-cntl	141/udp	EMFIS Control Service
#		Gerd Beling <GBELING@ISI.EDU>
bl-idm	142/tcp	Britton-Lee IDM
bl-idm	142/udp	Britton-Lee IDM
#		Susie Snitzer <---none--->
imap	143/tcp	Internet Message Access Protocol
imap	143/udp	Internet Message Access Protocol
#		Mark Crispin <MRC@CAC.Washington.EDU>
uma	144/tcp	Universal Management Architecture
uma	144/udp	Universal Management Architecture
#		Jay Whitney <jw@powercenter.com>
uaac	145/tcp	UAAC Protocol

Keyword	Decimal	Description
uaac	145/udp	UAAC Protocol
#		David A. Gomberg <gomberg@GATEWAY.MITRE.ORG>
iso-tp0	146/tcp	ISO-IP0
iso-tp0	146/udp	ISO-IP0
iso-ip	147/tcp	ISO-IP
iso-ip	147/udp	ISO-IP
#		Marshall Rose <mrose@dbc.mtview.ca.us>
jargon	148/tcp	Jargon
jargon	148/udp	Jargon
#		Bill Weinman <wew@bearnet.com>
aed-512	149/tcp	AED 512 Emulation Service
aed-512	149/udp	AED 512 Emulation Service
#		Albert G. Broscius <broscius@DSL.CIS.UPENN.EDU>
sql-net	150/tcp	SQL-NET
sql-net	150/udp	SQL-NET
#		Martin Picard <<---none--->
hems	151/tcp	HEMS
hems	151/udp	HEMS
bftp	152/tcp	Background File Transfer Program
bftp	152/udp	Background File Transfer Program
#		Annette DeSchon <DESCHON@ISI.EDU>
sgmp	153/tcp	SGMP
sgmp	153/udp	SGMP
#		Marty Schoffstahl <schoff@NISC.NYSER.NET>
netsc-prod	154/tcp	NETSC
netsc-prod	154/udp	NETSC
netsc-dev	155/tcp	NETSC
netsc-dev	155/udp	NETSC
#		Sergio Heker <heker@JVNCC.CSC.ORG>
sqlsrv	156/tcp	SQL Service
sqlsrv	156/udp	SQL Service
#		Craig Rogers <Rogers@ISI.EDU>
knet-cmp	157/tcp	KNET/VM Command/Message Protocol
knet-cmp	157/udp	KNET/VM Command/Message Protocol
#		Gary S. Malkin <GMALKIN@XYLOGICS.COM>

Keyword	Decimal	Description
pcmail-srv	158/tcp	PCMail Server
pcmail-srv	158/udp	PCMail Server
#		Mark L. Lambert <markl@PTT.LCS.MIT.EDU>
nss-routing	159/tcp	NSS-Routing
nss-routing	159/udp	NSS-Routing
#		Yakov Rekhter <Yakov@IBM.COM>
sgmp-traps	160/tcp	SGMP-TRAPS
sgmp-traps	160/udp	SGMP-TRAPS
#		Marty Schoffstahl <schoff@NISC.NYSER.NET>
snmp	161/tcp	SNMP
snmp	161/udp	SNMP
snmptrap	162/tcp	SNMPTRAP
snmptrap	162/udp	SNMPTRAP
#		Marshall Rose <mrose@dbc.mtview.ca.us>
cmip-man	163/tcp	CMIP/TCP Manager
cmip-man	163/udp	CMIP/TCP Manager
cmip-agent	164/tcp	CMIP/TCP Agent
smip-agent	164/udp	CMIP/TCP Agent
#		Amatzia Ben-Artzi <---none--->
xns-courier	165/tcp	Xerox
xns-courier	165/udp	Xerox
#		Susie Armstrong <Armstrong.wbst128@XEROX.COM>
s-net	166/tcp	Sirius Systems
s-net	166/udp	Sirius Systems
#		Brian Lloyd <brian@lloyd.com>
namp	167/tcp	NAMP
namp	167/udp	NAMP
#		Marty Schoffstahl <schoff@NISC.NYSER.NET>
rsvd	168/tcp	RSVD
rsvd	168/udp	RSVD
#		Neil Todd <mcvax!ist.co.uk!neil@UUNET.UU.NET>
send	169/tcp	SEND
send	169/udp	SEND
#		William D. Wisner <wisner@HAYES.FAI.ALASKA.EDU>

Keyword	Decimal	Description
print-srv	170/tcp	Network PostScript
print-srv	170/udp	Network PostScript
#		Brian Reid <reid@DECWRL.DEC.COM>
multiplex	171/tcp	Network Innovations Multiplex
multiplex	171/udp	Network Innovations Multiplex
cl/1	172/tcp	Network Innovations CL/1
cl/1	172/udp	Network Innovations CL/1
#		Kevin DeVault <<---none--->
xyplex-mux	173/tcp	Xyplex
xyplex-mux	173/udp	Xyplex
#		Bob Stewart <STEWART@XYPLEX.COM>
mailq	174/tcp	MAILQ
mailq	174/udp	MAILQ
#		Rayan Zachariassen <rayan@AI.TORONTO.EDU>
vmnet	175/tcp	VMNET
vmnet	175/udp	VMNET
#		Christopher Tengi <tengi@Princeton.EDU>
genrad-mux	176/tcp	GENRAD-MUX
genrad-mux	176/udp	GENRAD-MUX
#		Ron Thornton <thornton@qm7501.genrad.com>
xdmcp	177/tcp	X Display Manager Control Protocol
xdmcp	177/udp	X Display Manager Control Protocol
#		Robert W. Scheifler <RWS@XX.LCS.MIT.EDU>
nextstep	178/tcp	NextStep Window Server
nextstep	178/udp	NextStep Window Server
#		Leo Hourvitz <leo@NEXT.COM>
bgp	179/tcp	Border Gateway Protocol
bgp	179/udp	Border Gateway Protocol
#		Kirk Lougheed <LOUGHEED@MATHOM.CISCO.COM>
ris	180/tcp	Intergraph
ris	180/udp	Intergraph
#		Dave Buehmann <ingr!daveb@UUNET.UU.NET>

Keyword	Decimal	Description
unify	181/tcp	Unify
unify	181/udp	Unify
#		Vinod Singh <--none--->
audit	182/tcp	Unisys Audit SITP
audit	182/udp	Unisys Audit SITP
#		Gil Greenbaum <gcole@nisd.cam.unisys.com>
ocbinder	183/tcp	OCBinder
ocbinder	183/udp	OCBinder
ocserver	184/tcp	OCServer
ocserver	184/udp	OCServer
#		Jerrilynn Okamura <--none--->
remote-kis	185/tcp	Remote-KIS
remote-kis	185/udp	Remote-KIS
kis	186/tcp	KIS Protocol
kis	186/udp	KIS Protocol
#		Ralph Droms <rdroms@NRI.RESTON.VA.US>
aci	187/tcp	Application Communication Interface
aci	187/udp	Application Communication Interface
#		Rick Carlos <rick.ticipa.csc.ti.com>
mumps	188/tcp	Plus Five's MUMPS
mumps	188/udp	Plus Five's MUMPS
#		Hokey Stenn <hokey@PLUS5.COM>
qft	189/tcp	Queued File Transport
qft	189/udp	Queued File Transport
#		Wayne Schroeder <schroeder@SDS.SDSC.EDU>
gacp	190/tcp	Gateway Access Control Protocol
gacp	190/udp	Gateway Access Control Protocol
#		C. Philip Wood <cpw@LANL.GOV>
prospero	191/tcp	Prospero Directory Service
prospero	191/udp	Prospero Directory Service
#		B. Clifford Neuman <bcn@isi.edu>
osu-nms	192/tcp	OSU Network Monitoring System
osu-nms	192/udp	OSU Network Monitoring System
#		Doug Karl <KARL-D@OSU-20.IRCC.OHIO-STATE.EDU>
srmp	193/tcp	Spider Remote Monitoring Protocol

Keyword	Decimal	Description
srmp	193/udp	Spider Remote Monitoring Protocol
#		Ted J. Socolofsky <Teds@SPIDER.CO.UK>
irc	194/tcp	Internet Relay Chat Protocol
irc	194/udp	Internet Relay Chat Protocol
#		Jarkko Oikarinen <jto@TOLSUN.OULU.FI>
dn6-nlm-aud	195/tcp	DNSIX Network Level Module Audit
dn6-nlm-aud	195/udp	DNSIX Network Level Module Audit
dn6-smm-red	196/tcp	DNSIX Session Mgt Module Audit Redir
dn6-smm-red	196/udp	DNSIX Session Mgt Module Audit Redir
#		Lawrence Lebahn
		<DIA3@PAXRV-NES.NAVY.MIL>
dls	197/tcp	Directory Location Service
dls	197/udp	Directory Location Service
dls-mon	198/tcp	Directory Location Service Monitor
dls-mon	198/udp	Directory Location Service Monitor
#		Scott Bellew <smb@cs.purdue.edu>
smux	199/tcp	SMUX
smux	199/udp	SMUX
#		Marshall Rose <mrose@dbc.mtview.ca.us>
src	200/tcp	IBM System Resource Controller
src	200/udp	IBM System Resource Controller
#		Gerald McBrearty <---none--->
at-rtmp	201/tcp	AppleTalk Routing Maintenance
at-rtmp	201/udp	AppleTalk Routing Maintenance
at-nbp	202/tcp	AppleTalk Name Binding
at-nbp	202/udp	AppleTalk Name Binding
at-3	203/tcp	AppleTalk Unused
at-3	203/udp	AppleTalk Unused
at-echo	204/tcp	AppleTalk Echo
at-echo	204/udp	AppleTalk Echo
at-5	205/tcp	AppleTalk Unused
at-5	205/udp	AppleTalk Unused
at-zis	206/tcp	AppleTalk Zone Information
at-zis	206/udp	AppleTalk Zone Information
at-7	207/tcp	AppleTalk Unused
at-7	207/udp	AppleTalk Unused
at-8	208/tcp	AppleTalk Unused

Keyword	Decimal	Description
at-8	208/udp	AppleTalk Unused
#		Rob Chandhok <chandhok@gnome.cs.cmu.edu>
qmtp	209/tcp	The Quick Mail Transfer Protocol
qmtp	209/udp	The Quick Mail Transfer Protocol
#		Dan Bernstein
		<djb@silverton.berkeley.edu>
z39.50	210/tcp	ANSI Z39.50
z39.50	210/udp	ANSI Z39.50
#		Mark Needleman
#		<mhnur%uccmvsa.bitnet@cornell.cit. cornell.edu>
914c/g	211/tcp	Texas Instruments 914C/G Terminal
914c/g	211/udp	Texas Instruments 914C/G Terminal
#		Bill Harrell <---none--->
anet	212/tcp	ATEXSSTR
anet	212/udp	ATEXSSTR
#		Jim Taylor <taylor@heart.epps.kodak.com>
ipx	213/tcp	IPX
ipx	213/udp	IPX
#		Don Provan <donp@xlnvax.novell.com>
vmpwscs	214/tcp	VM PWSCS
vmpwscs	214/udp	VM PWSCS
#		Dan Shia <dset!shia@uunet.UU.NET>
softpc	215/tcp	Insignia Solutions
softpc	215/udp	Insignia Solutions
#		Martyn Thomas <---none--->
CAllic	216/tcp	Computer Associates Int'l License Server
CAllic	216/udp	Computer Associates Int'l License Server
#		Chuck Spitz <spich04@cai.com>
dbase	217/tcp	dBASE Unix
dbase	217/udp	dBASE Unix
#		Don Gibson
#		<sequent!aero!twinsun!ashtate.A-T.COM!dong@uunet.UU.NET>
mpp	218/tcp	Netix Message Posting Protocol
mpp	218/udp	Netix Message Posting Protocol
#		Shannon Yeh <yeh@netix.com>
uarps	219/tcp	Unisys ARPs
uarps	219/udp	Unisys ARPs

Keyword	Decimal	Description
#		Ashok Marwaha <---none--->
imap3	220/tcp	Interactive Mail Access Protocol v3
imap3	220/udp	Interactive Mail Access Protocol v3
#		James Rice
		<RICE@SUMEX-AIM.STANFORD.EDU>
fln-spx	221/tcp	Berkeley rlogind with SPX auth
fln-spx	221/udp	Berkeley rlogind with SPX auth
rsh-spx	222/tcp	Berkeley rshd with SPX auth
rsh-spx	222/udp	Berkeley rshd with SPX auth
cdc	223/tcp	Certificate Distribution Center
cdc	223/udp	Certificate Distribution Center
#		Kannan Alagappan
		<kannan@sejour.enet.dec.com>
#	224-241	Reserved
#		Jon Postel <postel@isi.edu>
direct	242/tcp	Direct
direct	242/udp	Direct
#		Herb Sutter <HerbS@cntc.com>
sur-meas	243/tcp	Survey Measurement
sur-meas	243/udp	Survey Measurement
#		Dave Clark <ddc@LCS.MIT.EDU>
dayna	244/tcp	Dayna
dayna	244/udp	Dayna
#		Steve Bateman <SBATEMAN@dayna.com>
link	245/tcp	LINK
link	245/udp	LINK
dsp3270	246/tcp	Display Systems Protocol
dsp3270	246/udp	Display Systems Protocol
#		Weldon J. Showalter
		<Gamma@MINTAKA.DCA.MIL>
subntbcst_tftp	247/tcp	SUBNTBCST_TFTP
subntbcst_tftp	247/udp	SUBNTBCST_TFTP
#		John Fake <fake@us.ibm.com>
bhfhs	248/tcp	bhfhs
bhfhs	248/udp	bhfhs
#		John Kelly <johnk@bellhow.com>
#	249–255	Reserved
#		Jon Postel <postel@isi.edu>

Internet multicast addresses

Host Extensions for **IP Multicasting** (RFC 1112) specifies the extensions required of a host implementation of the Internet Protocol (IP) to support multicasting. The multicast addresses are in the range 224.0.0.0 through 239.255.255.255. Current addresses are listed below.

The range of **multicast addresses** between **224.0.0.0 and 224.0.0.255** inclusive, is **reserved** for the use of routing protocols and other low-level topology discovery or maintenance protocols, such as gateway discovery and group membership reporting. Multicast routers should not forward any multicast datagram with destination addresses in this range, regardless of its TTL.

224.0.0.0	Base Address (Reserved)	[RFC1112,JBP]
224.0.0.1	All Systems on this Subnet	[RFC1112,JBP]
224.0.0.2	All Routers on this Subnet	[JBP]
224.0.0.3	Unassigned	[JBP]
224.0.0.4	DVMRP Routers	[RFC1075,JBP]
224.0.0.5	OSPFIGP OSPFIGP All Routers	[RFC2328,JXM1]
224.0.0.6	OSPFIGP OSPFIGP Designated Routers	[RFC2328,JXM1]
224.0.0.7	ST Routers	[RFC1190,KS14]
224.0.0.8	ST Hosts	[RFC1190,KS14]
224.0.0.9	RIP2 Routers	[RFC1723,GSM11]
224.0.0.10	IGRP Routers	[Farinacci]
224.0.0.11	Mobile-Agents	[Bill Simpson]
224.0.0.12	DHCP Server / Relay Agent	[RFC1884]
224.0.0.13	All PIM Routers	[Farinacci]
224.0.0.14	RSVP-ENCAPSULATION	[Braden]
224.0.0.15	all-cbt-routers	[Ballardie]
224.0.0.16	designated-sbm	[Baker]
224.0.0.17	all-sbms	[Baker]
224.0.0.18	VRRP	[Hinden]
224.0.0.19	IPAllL1ISs	[Przygienda]
224.0.0.20	IPAllL2ISs	[Przygienda]
224.0.0.21	IPAllIntermediate Systems	[Przygienda]
224.0.0.22	IGMP	[Deering]
224.0.0.23	GLOBECAST-ID	[Scannell]
224.0.0.24	Unassigned	[JBP]
224.0.0.25	router-to-switch	[Wu]
224.0.0.26	Unassigned	[JBP]
224.0.0.27	Al MPP Hello	[Martinicky]

224.0.0.28	ETC Control	[Polishinski]
224.0.0.29	GE-FANUC	[Wacey]
224.0.0.30	indigo-vhdp	[Caughie]
224.0.0.31	shinbroadband	[Kittivatcharapong]
224.0.0.32	digistar	[Kerkan]
224.0.0.33	ff-system-management	[Glanzer]
224.0.0.34	pt2-discover	[Kammerlander]
224.0.0.35	DXCLUSTER	[Koopman]
224.0.0.36	UDLR-DTCP	[Cipiere]
224.0.0.37–224.0.0.250	Unassigned	[JBP]
224.0.0.251	mDNS	[Cheshire]
224.0.0.252–224.0.0.255	Unassigned	[JBP]
224.0.1.0	VMTP Managers Group	[RFC1045,DRC3]
224.0.1.1	NTP Network Time Protocol	[RFC1119,DLM1]
224.0.1.2	SGI-Dogfight	[AXC]
224.0.1.3	Rwhod	[SXD]
224.0.1.4	VNP	[DRC3]
224.0.1.5	Artificial Horizons – Aviator	[BXF]
224.0.1.6	NSS – Name Service Server	[BXS2]
224.0.1.7	AUDIONEWS – Audio News Multicast	[MXF2]
224.0.1.8	SUN NIS+ Information Service	[CXM3]
224.0.1.9	MTP Multicast Transport Protocol	[SXA]
224.0.1.10	IETF-1-LOW-AUDIO	[SC3]
224.0.1.11	IETF-1-AUDIO	[SC3]
224.0.1.12	IETF-1-VIDEO	[SC3]
224.0.1.13	IETF-2-LOW-AUDIO	[SC3]
224.0.1.14	IETF-2-AUDIO	[SC3]
224.0.1.15	IETF-2-VIDEO	[SC3]
224.0.1.16	MUSIC-SERVICE	[Guido van Rossum]
224.0.1.17	SEANET-TELEMETRY	[Andrew Maffei]
224.0.1.18	SEANET-IMAGE	[Andrew Maffei]
224.0.1.19	MLOADD	[Braden]
224.0.1.20	any private experiment	[JBP]
224.0.1.21	DVMRP on MOSPF	[John Moy]
224.0.1.22	SVRLOC	[Veizades]
224.0.1.23	XINGTV	[Gordon]
224.0.1.24	microsoft-ds	<arnoldm@microsoft.com>
224.0.1.25	nbc-pro	<bloomer@birch.crd.ge.com>

224.0.1.26	nbc-pfn	<bloomer@birch.crd.ge.com>
224.0.1.27	lmsc-calren-1	[Uang]
224.0.1.28	lmsc-calren-2	[Uang]
224.0.1.29	lmsc-calren-3	[Uang]
224.0.1.30	lmsc-calren-4	[Uang]
224.0.1.31	ampr-info	[Janssen]
224.0.1.32	mtrace	[Casner]
224.0.1.33	RSVP-encap-1	[Braden]
224.0.1.34	RSVP-encap-2	[Braden]
224.0.1.35	SVRLOC-DA	[Veizades]
224.0.1.36	rln-server	[Kean]
224.0.1.37	proshare-mc	[Lewis]
224.0.1.38	dantz	[Zulch]
224.0.1.39	cisco-rp-announce	[Farinacci]
224.0.1.40	cisco-rp-discovery	[Farinacci]
224.0.1.41	gatekeeper	[Toga]
224.0.1.42	iberiagames	[Marocho]
224.0.1.43	nwn-discovery	[Zwemmer]
224.0.1.44	nwn-adaptor	[Zwemmer]
224.0.1.45	isma-1	[Dunne]
224.0.1.46	isma-2	[Dunne]
224.0.1.47	telerate	[Peng]
224.0.1.48	ciena	[Rodbell]
224.0.1.49	dcap-servers	[RFC2114]
224.0.1.50	dcap-clients	[RFC2114]
224.0.1.51	mcntp-directory	[Rupp]
224.0.1.52	mbone-vcr-directory	[Holfelder]
224.0.1.53	heartbeat	[Mamakos]
224.0.1.54	sun-mc-grp	[DeMoney]
224.0.1.55	extended-sys	[Poole]
224.0.1.56	pdrncs	[Wissenbach]
224.0.1.57	tns-adv-multi	[Albin]
224.0.1.58	vcals-dmu	[Shindoh]
224.0.1.59	zuba	[Jackson]
224.0.1.60	hp-device-disc	[Albright]
224.0.1.61	tms-production	[Gilani]
224.0.1.62	sunscalar	[Gibson]
224.0.1.63	mmtp-poll	[Costales]
224.0.1.64	compaq-peer	[Volpe]

224.0.1.65	iapp	[Meier]
224.0.1.66	multihasc-com	[Brockbank]
224.0.1.67	serv-discovery	[Honton]
224.0.1.68	mdhcpdisover	[RFC2730]
224.0.1.69	MMP-bundle-discovery1	[Malkin]
224.0.1.70	MMP-bundle-discovery2	[Malkin]
224.0.1.71	XYPOINT DGPS Data Feed	[Green]
224.0.1.72	GilatSkySurfer	[Gal]
224.0.1.73	SharesLive	[Rowatt]
224.0.1.74	NorthernData	[Sheers]
224.0.1.75	SIP	[Schulzrinne]
224.0.1.76	IAPP	[Moelard]
224.0.1.77	AGENTVIEW	[Iyer]
224.0.1.78	Tibco Multicast1	[Shum]
224.0.1.79	Tibco Multicast2	[Shum]
224.0.1.80	MSP	[Caves]
224.0.1.81	OTT (One-way Trip Time)	[Schwartz]
224.0.1.82	TRACKTICKER	[Novick]
224.0.1.83	dtn-mc	[Gaddie]
224.0.1.84	jini-announcement	[Scheifler]
224.0.1.85	jini-request	[Scheifler]
224.0.1.86	sde-discovery	[Aronson]
224.0.1.87	DirecPC-SI	[Dillon]
224.0.1.88	B1RMonitor	[Purkiss]
224.0.1.89	3Com-AMP3 dRMON	[Banthia]
224.0.1.90	imFtmSvc	[Bhatti]
224.0.1.91	NQDS4	[Flynn]
224.0.1.92	NQDS5	[Flynn]
224.0.1.93	NQDS6	[Flynn]
224.0.1.94	NLVL12	[Flynn]
224.0.1.95	NTDS1	[Flynn]
224.0.1.96	NTDS2	[Flynn]
224.0.1.97	NODSA	[Flynn]
224.0.1.98	NODSB	[Flynn]
224.0.1.99	NODSC	[Flynn]
224.0.1.100	NODSD	[Flynn]
224.0.1.101	NQDS4R	[Flynn]
224.0.1.102	NQDS5R	[Flynn]
224.0.1.103	NQDS6R	[Flynn]

224.0.1.104	NLVL12R	[Flynn]
224.0.1.105	NTDS1R	[Flynn]
224.0.1.106	NTDS2R	[Flynn]
224.0.1.107	NODSAR	[Flynn]
224.0.1.108	NODSBR	[Flynn]
224.0.1.109	NODSCR	[Flynn]
224.0.1.110	NODSDR	[Flynn]
224.0.1.111	MRM	[Wei]
224.0.1.112	TVE-FILE	[Blackketter]
224.0.1.113	TVE-ANNOUNCE	[Blackketter]
224.0.1.114	Mac Srv Loc	[Woodcock]
224.0.1.115	Simple Multicast	[Crowcroft]
224.0.1.116	SpectraLinkGW	[Hamilton]
224.0.1.117	dieboldmcast	[Marsh]
224.0.1.118	Tivoli Systems	[Gabriel]
224.0.1.119	pq-lic-mcast	[Sledge]
224.0.1.120	HYPERFEED	[Kreutzjans]
224.0.1.121	Pipesplatform	[Dissett]
224.0.1.122	LiebDevMgmg-DM	[Velten]
224.0.1.123	TRIBALVOICE	[Thompson]
224.0.1.124	Unassigned (Retracted 1/29/01)	
224.0.1.125	PolyCom Relay1	[Coutiere]
224.0.1.126	Infront Multi1	[Lindeman]
224.0.1.127	XRX DEVICE DISC	[Wang]
224.0.1.128	CNN	[Lynch]
224.0.1.129	PTP-primary	[Eidson]
224.0.1.130	PTP-alternate1	[Eidson]
224.0.1.131	PTP-alternate2	[Eidson]
224.0.1.132	PTP-alternate3	[Eidson]
224.0.1.133	ProCast	[Revzen]
224.0.1.134	3Com Discp	[White]
224.0.1.135	CS-Multicasting	[Stanev]
224.0.1.136	TS-MC-1	[Sveistrup]
224.0.1.137	Make Source	[Daga]
224.0.1.138	Teleborsa	[Strazzera]
224.0.1.139	SUMAConfig	[Wallach]
224.0.1.140	Unassigned	
224.0.1.141	DHCP-SERVERS	[Hall]
224.0.1.142	CN Router-LL	[Armitage]

224.0.1.143	EMWIN	[Querubin]
224.0.1.144	Alchemy Cluster	[O'Rourke]
224.0.1.145	Satcast One	[Nevell]
224.0.1.146	Satcast Two	[Nevell]
224.0.1.147	Satcast Three	[Nevell]
224.0.1.148	Intline	[Sliwinski]
224.0.1.149	8x8 Multicast	[Roper]
224.0.1.150	Unassigned	[JBP]
224.0.1.151	Intline-1	[Sliwinski]
224.0.1.152	Intline-2	[Sliwinski]
224.0.1.153	Intline-3	[Sliwinski]
224.0.1.154	Intline-4	[Sliwinski]
224.0.1.155	Intline-5	[Sliwinski]
224.0.1.156	Intline-6	[Sliwinski]
224.0.1.157	Intline-7	[Sliwinski]
224.0.1.158	Intline-8	[Sliwinski]
224.0.1.159	Intline-9	[Sliwinski]
224.0.1.160	Intline-10	[Sliwinski]
224.0.1.161	Intline-11	[Sliwinski]
224.0.1.162	Intline-12	[Sliwinski]
224.0.1.163	Intline-13	[Sliwinski]
224.0.1.164	Intline-14	[Sliwinski]
224.0.1.165	Intline-15	[Sliwinski]
224.0.1.166	marratech-cc	[Parnes]
224.0.1.167	EMS-InterDev	[Lyda]
224.0.1.168	itb301	[Rueskamp]
224.0.1.169	rtv-audio	[Adams]
224.0.1.170	rtv-video	[Adams]
224.0.1.171	HAVI-Sim	[Wasserroth]
224.0.1.172	Nokia Cluster	[O'Rourke]
224.0.1.173–224.0.1.255	Unassigned	[JBP]
224.0.2.1	'rwho' Group (BSD) (unofficial)	[JBP]
224.0.2.2	SUN RPC PMAPPROC_CALLIT	[BXE1]
224.0.2.064–224.0.2.095	SIAC MDD Service	[Tse]
224.0.2.096–224.0.2.127	CoolCast	[Ballister]
224.0.2.128–224.0.2.191	WOZ-Garage	[Marquardt]
224.0.2.192–224.0.2.255	SIAC MDD Market Service	[Lamberg]
224.0.3.000–224.0.3.255	RFE Generic Service	[DXS3]

224.0.4.000–224.0.4.255	RFE Individual Conferences	[DXS3]
224.0.5.000–224.0.5.127	CDPD Groups	[Bob Brenner]
224.0.5.128–224.0.5.191	SIAC Market Service	[Cho]
224.0.5.192–224.0.5.255	Unassigned	[IANA]
224.0.6.000–224.0.6.127	Cornell ISIS Project	[Tim Clark]
224.0.6.128–224.0.6.255	Unassigned	[IANA]
224.0.7.000–224.0.7.255	Where-Are-You	[Simpson]
224.0.8.000–224.0.8.255	INTV	[Tynan]
224.0.9.000–224.0.9.255	Invisible Worlds	[Malamud]
224.0.10.000–224.0.10.255	DLSw Groups	[Lee]
224.0.11.000–224.0.11.255	NCC.NET Audio	[Rubin]
224.0.12.000–224.0.12.063	Microsoft and MSNBC	[Blank]
224.0.13.000–224.0.13.255	UUNET PIPEX Net News	[Barber]
224.0.14.000–224.0.14.255	NLANR	[Wessels]
224.0.15.000–224.0.15.255	Hewlett Packard	[van der Meulen]
224.0.16.000–224.0.16.255	XingNet	[Uusitalo]
224.0.17.000–224.0.17.031	Mercantile & Commodity Exchange	[Gilani]
224.0.17.032–224.0.17.063	NDQMD1	[Nelson]
224.0.17.064–224.0.17.127	ODN-DTV	[Hodges]
224.0.18.000–224.0.18.255	Dow Jones	[Peng]
224.0.19.000–224.0.19.063	Walt Disney Company	[Watson]
224.0.19.064–224.0.19.095	Cal Multicast	[Moran]
224.0.19.096–224.0.19.127	SIAC Market Service	[Roy]
224.0.19.128–224.0.19.191	IIG Multicast	[Carr]
224.0.19.192–224.0.19.207	Metropol	[Crawford]
224.0.19.208–224.0.19.239	Xenoscience, Inc.	[Timm]
224.0.19.240–224.0.19.255	HYPERFEED	[Felix]
224.0.20.000–224.0.20.063	MS-IP/TV	[Wong]
224.0.20.064–224.0.20.127	Reliable Network Solutions	[Vogels]
224.0.20.128–224.0.20.143	TRACKTICKER Group	[Novick]
224.0.20.144–224.0.20.207	CNR Rebroadcast MCA	[Sautter]
224.0.21.000–224.0.21.127	Talarian MCAST	[Mendal]
224.0.22.000–224.0.22.255	WORLD MCAST	[Stewart]
224.0.252.000–224.0.252.255	Domain Scoped Group	[Fenner]
224.0.253.000–224.0.253.255	Report Group	[Fenner]
224.0.254.000–224.0.254.255	Query Group	[Fenner]
224.0.255.000–224.0.255.255	Border Routers	[Fenner]
224.1.0.0–224.1.255.255	ST Multicast Groups	[RFC1190,KS14]

224.2.0.0-224.2.127.253	Multimedia Conference Calls	[SC3]
224.2.127.254	SAPv1 Announcements	[SC3]
224.2.127.255	SAPv0 Announcements (deprecated)	[SC3]
224.2.128.0–224.2.255.255	SAP Dynamic Assignments	[SC3]
224.252.0.0–224.255.255.255	DIS transient groups	[Joel Snyder]
225.0.0.0–225.255.255.255	MALLOC (temp - renew 1/01)	[Handley]
232.0.0.0–232.255.255.255	VMTP transient groups see single-source-multicast file	[DRC3]
233.0.0.0–233.255.255.255	Static Allocations (temp – renew 03/02) [Meyer2]	
239.000.000.000–239.255.255.255	Administratively Scoped	[IANA,RFC2365]
239.000.000.000–239.063.255.255	Reserved	[IANA]
239.064.000.000–239.127.255.255	Reserved	[IANA]
239.128.000.000–239.191.255.255	Reserved	[IANA]
239.192.000.000–239.251.255.255	Organization-Local Scope	[Meyer,RFC2365]
239.252.000.000–239.252.255.255	Site-Local Scope (reserved)	[Meyer,RFC2365]
239.253.000.000–239.253.255.255	Site-Local Scope (reserved)	[Meyer,RFC2365]
239.254.000.000–239.254.255.255	Site-Local Scope (reserved)	[Meyer,RFC2365]
239.255.000.000–239.255.255.255	Site-Local Scope	[Meyer,RFC2365]
239.255.002.002 rasadv		[Thaler]

There is also the concept of **relative addresses** to be used with the **scoped multicast addresses** (for more details on multicasting in IP see Section 11.6 in Part IV). These relative addresses are listed below:

Relative	Description	Reference
0	SAP Session Announcement Protocol	[Handley]
1	MADCAP Protocol	[RFC2730]
2	SLPv2 Discovery	[Guttman]
3	MZAP	[Thaler]
4	Multicast Discovery of DNS Services	[Manning]
5	SSDP	[Goland]
6	DHCP v4	[Hall]
7	AAP	[Hanna]
8–252	Reserved – To be assigned by the IANA	
253	Reserved	
254–255	Reserved – To be assigned by the IANA	

These addresses are listed in the Domain Name Service under MCAST.NET and 224.IN-ADDR.ARPA.

Note that when used on an Ethernet or IEEE 802 network, the 23 low-order bits of the IP multicast address are placed in the low-order 23 bits of the Ethernet or IEEE 802 net multicast address 1.0.94.0.0.0. For MAC multicast addresses refer to Chapter 2 in Part I; for mapping IP to MAC multicast addresses see Chapter 11 in Part IV.

Decimal, hex, binary conversion

The following table presents the conversion of decimal numbers 1–50 to hexadecimal and binary.

Dec	Hex	Bin	Dec	Hex	Bin
0	0	0000 0000	27	1B	0001 1011
1	1	0000 0001	28	1C	0001 1100
2	2	0000 0010	29	1D	0001 1101
3	3	0000 0011	30	1E	0001 1110
4	4	0000 0100	31	1F	0001 1111
5	5	0000 0101	32	20	0010 0000
6	6	0000 0110	33	21	0010 0001
7	7	0000 0111	34	22	0010 0010
8	8	0000 1000	35	23	0010 0011
9	9	0000 1001	36	24	0010 0100
10	A	0000 1010	37	25	0010 0101
11	B	0000 1011	38	26	0010 0110
12	C	0000 1100	39	27	0010 0111
13	D	0000 1101	40	28	0010 1000
14	E	0000 1110	41	29	0010 1001
15	F	0000 1111	42	2A	0010 1010
16	10	0001 0000	43	2B	0010 1011
17	11	0001 0001	44	2C	0010 1100
18	12	0001 0010	45	2D	0010 1101
19	13	0001 0011	46	2E	0010 1110
20	14	0001 0100	47	2F	0010 1111
21	15	0001 0101	48	30	0011 0000
22	16	0001 0110	49	31	0011 0001
23	17	0001 0111	50	32	0011 0010
24	18	0001 1000	…	…	…
25	19	0001 1001	255	FF	1111 1111
26	1A	0001 1010			

APPENDIX F

Recommended reading

Books

There are a great many networking books on the market but only a few may truly be recommended either as information sources dedicated to an individual topic among those covered here, or as additional sources of information on related topics:

Berkowitz, Howard C., *Designing Addressing Architectures for Routing and Switching*, New Riders Publishing, 1998.

Berkowitz, Howard C., *WAN Survival Guide: Strategies for VPNs and Multiservice Networks*, John Wiley & Sons, 2000.

Davie, Bruce, Doolan, Paul, and Rekhter, Yakov, *Switching in IP Networks: IP Switching, Tag Switching, & Related Technologies*, Morgan Kaufmann Publishers, 1998.

Gray, Eric W., *MPLS: Implementing the Technology*, Addison-Wesley, 2001.

Halabi, Sam and McPherson, Danny, *Internet Routing Architectures*, 2nd edn, Cisco Press, 2000.

Jones, Vincent C., *High Availability Networking with Cisco*, Addison-Wesley, 2001.

Malkin, Garry Scott, *RIP: An Intra-Domain Routing Protocol*, Addison-Wesley, 2000.

Moy, John T., *OSPF: Anatomy of the Internet Routing Protocol*, Addison-Wesley, 1998.

Oppenheimer, Priscilla, *Top-Down Network Design*, Cisco Press, 1999.

Pužman, Josef and Pořízek, Radek, *Communication Control in Computer Networks*, John Wiley & Sons, 1980.

Pužman, Josef and Kubín, Boris, *Public Data Networks*, Springer-Verlag, 1992.

Retana, Alvaro, Slice, Don, and White, Russ, *EIGRP for IP: Basic Operation and Configuration*, Addison-Wesley, 2000.

Perlman, Radia, *Interconnections: Bridges, Routers, Switches and Internetworking Protocols*, 2nd edn, Addison-Wesley, 2000.

Stewart, John W. III, *BGP4: Inter-Domain Routing in the Internet*, Addison-Wesley, 1999.

Articles, surveys and research notes

There are many networking journals and magazines which bring news on and insights to the technology. Most of them are more aimed at regular network users or network managers. However, for more substantial reading the interested network professional should look for peer-reviewed magazines publishing on topics under development and showing the technology directions, research results, and tutorials. Among these the primary recommendation is the journal of the **IEEE Communications Society**. Any member of the Society is eligible for this monthly journal available in printed and electronic versions (*IEEE Communications Interactive* at **http://www.comsoc.org/ci/**). Any member of other IEEE societies may also subscribe to this invaluable source of information.

The following is a list of the latest recommended articles on hot topics worth reading:

Andersen, Niels Engell (Tellabs Denmark), Arturo Azeorra (University of Carlos III of Madrid), Erik Bertelsen (Aarhus University), Jorge Carapinha (PT Inovacao), Lars Dittmann (Technical University of Denmark), David Fernandez (Technical University of Madrid), Jens Kristian Kjaergaard (Ericsson Telebit), Iain McKay (University of Edinburgh), Janusz Maliszewski (Telekomunikacja Polska SA), and Zdzislaw Papir (University of Mining and Metallurgy), 'Applying QoS Control through Integration of IP and ATM,' *IEEE Communications*, July 2000.

Armitage, Grenville (Bell Labs Research Silicon Valley, Lucent Technologies), 'MPLS: The Magic Behind the Myths,' *IEEE Communications*, January 2000.

Awduche, Daniel O. (MCI Worldcom), 'MPLS and Traffic Engineering in IP Networks,' *IEEE Communications*, December 1999.

Awduche, Daniel (Movaz Networks) and Yakov Rekhter (Juniper Networks), 'Multiprotocol Lambda Switching: Combining MPLS Traffic Engineering Control with Optical Crossconnects,' *IEEE Communications*, March 2001.

Banerjee, Ayan, John Drake, Jonathan P. Lang, and Brad Turner (Calient Networks), Kireeti Kompella (Juniper Networks), and Yakov Rekhter (Cisco Systems), 'Generalized Multiprotocol Label Switching: An Overview of Routing and Management Enhancements,' *IEEE Communications*, July 2001.

Barakat, Chadi, Eitan Altman, and Walid Dabbous (INRIA), 'On TCP Performance in a Heterogeneous Network: A Survey,' *IEEE Communications*, January 2000.

Bernet, Yoram (Microsoft), 'The Complementary Roles of RSVP and Differentiated Services in the Full-Service QoS Network,' *IEEE Communications*, February 2000.

Bonenfant, Paul and Antonio Rodriguez-Moral (Lucent Technologies), 'Optical Data Networking,' *IEEE Communications*, March 2000.

Bux, Werner, Wolfgang E. Denzel, Ton Engbersen, Andreas Herkersdorf, and Ronald P. Luijten (IBM Research), 'Technologies and Building Blocks for Fast Packet Forwarding,' *IEEE Communications*, January 2001.

Callegati, Franco (University of Bologna), and Hakki C. Cankaya, Yijun Xiong, and Marc Vandenhoute (Alcatel), 'Design Issues of Optical IP Routers for Internet Backbone Applications,' *IEEE Communications*, December 1999.

Chakrabarti, Satyabrata (Lucent Technologies), and Amitabh Mishra (Virginia Tech), 'QoS Issues in Ad Hoc Wireless Networks,' *IEEE Communications*, February 2001.

Chao, Jonathan (Polytechnic University), 'Saturn: A Terabit Packet Switch Using Dual Round-Robin,' *IEEE Communications*, December 2000.

Chase, Jeffrey S., Andrew J. Gallatin, and Kenneth G. Yocum (Duke University), 'End System Optimizations for High-Speed TCP,' *IEEE Communications*, April 2001.

Chen, Thomas M. and Tae H. Oh (Southern Methodist University), 'Reliable Services in MPLS,' *IEEE Communications*, December 1999.

Cocca, Roberto and Stefano Salsano (CoRiTeL), and Marco Listanti (University of Rome 'La Sapienza'), 'Internet Integrated Service over ATM: A Solution for Shortcut QoS Virtual Channels,' *IEEE Communications*, December 1999.

Copley, Amy (Sycamore Networks), 'Optical Domain Service Interconnect (ODSI): Defining Mechanisms for Enabling On-Demand High-Speed Capacity from the Optical Domain,' *IEEE Communications*, October 2000.

Doverspike, Robert and Jennifer Yates (AT&T Labs), 'Challenges for MPLS in Optical Network Restoration,' *IEEE Communications*, February 2001.

Eichler, Gerald (Deutsche Telekom Technologiezentrum), Heinrich Hussmann (Dresden University of Technology), George Mamais and Iakovos Venieris (National Technical University of Athens), Christian Prehofer (Siemens AG), and Stefano Salsano (CoR), 'Implementing Integrated and Differentiated Services for the Internet with ATM Networks: A Practical Approach,' *IEEE Communications*, January 2000.

Elmirghani, Jaafar M. H. (University of Wales Swansea) and Hussein T. Mouftah (Queen's University), 'All-Optical Wavelength Conversion: Technologies and Applications in DWDM Networks,' *IEEE Communications*, March 2000.

Elmirghani, Jaafar M. H. (University of Wales Swansea) and Hussein T. Mouftah (Queen's University), 'Technologies and Architectures for Scalable Dynamic Dense WDM Networks,' *IEEE Communications*, February 2000.

Gao, Jun, Peter Steenkiste, Eduardo Takahashi, and Allan Fisher (Carnegie Mellon University), 'A Programmable Router Architecture Supporting Control Plane Extensibility,' *IEEE Communications*, March 2000.

Gerstel, Ori (Nortel Networks), 'Optical Layer Signaling: How Much Is Really Needed,' *IEEE Communications*, October 2000.

Gerstel, Ornan and Rajiv Ramaswami (Xros), 'Optical Layer Survivability: A Services Perspective,' *IEEE Communications*, March 2000.

Ghani, Nasir, Sudhir Dixit, and Ti-Shiang Wang (Nokia Research Center), 'On IP-over-WDM Integration,' *IEEE Communications*, March 2000.

Ghanwani, Anoop, Bilel Jamoussi, and Don Fedyk (Nortel Networks USA), Peter Ashwood-Smith (Nortel Networks Canada), Li Li (8 Networks), and Nancy Feldman (M. T. J. Watson Research Center), 'Traffic Engineering Standards in IP Networks Using MPLS,' *IEEE Communications*, December 1999.

Golmie, Nada, Thomas D. Ndousse, and David H. Su (NIST), 'A Differentiated Optical Services Model for WDM Networks,' *IEEE Communications*, February 2000.

Green, Paul, 'Progress in Optical Networking,' *IEEE Communications*, January 2001.

Hunter, David K. and Ivan Andonovic (University of Strathclyde, UK), 'Approaches to Optical Internet Packet Switching,' *IEEE Communications*, September 2000.

Iida, Katsuyoshi and Kenji Kawahara (Kyushu Institute of Technology), Tetsuya Takine, (Kyoto University), and Yuji Oie (Kyushu Institute of Technology), 'Performance Evaluation of the Architecture for End-to-End Quality-of-Service Provisioning,' *IEEE Communications*, April 2000.

Jia, Weijia (City University of Hong Kong), Dong Xuan and Wei Zhao (Texas A&M University), 'Integrated Routing Algorithms for Anycast Messages,' *IEEE Communications*, January 2000.

Jourdan, Amaury, Dominique Chiaroni, and Emmanuel Dotaro (Alcatel CIT), Gert J. Eilenberger (Alcatel SEL), Francesco Masetti (Alcatel US), and Monique

Renaud (Opto+), 'The Perspective of Optical Packet Switching in IP-Dominant Backbone and Metropolitan Networks,' *IEEE Communications*, March 2001.

Keshav, S. and Rosen Sharma (Cornell University), 'Issues and Trends in Router Design,' *IEEE Communications*, May 1998.

Kou, Kuei Y. (NEC America, Inc.), 'Realization of Large-Capacity ATM Switches,' *IEEE Communications*, December 1999.

Kumar, Vijay P., T. V. Lakshman, and Dimitrios Stiliadis (Bell Laboratories, Lucent Technologies), 'Beyond Best Effort: Router Architectures for the Differentiated Services of Tomorrow's Internet,' *IEEE Communications*, May 1998.

Li, Bo, Mounir Harndi, Dongyi Jiang, and Xi-Ren Cao (Hong Kong University of Science and Technology), and Y. Thomas Hou (Fujitsu Laboratories of America), 'QoS-Enabled Voice Support in the Next-Generation Internet: Issues, Existing Approaches and Challenges,' *IEEE Communications*, April 2000.

Li, Tony (Procket Networks, Inc.), 'MPLS and the Evolving Internet Architecture,' *IEEE Communications*, December 1999.

Listanti, Marco and Vincenzo Eramo (University of Rome 'La Sapienza'), and Roberto Sabella (Ericsson Lab Italy), 'Architectural and Technological Issues for Future Optical Internet Networks,' *IEEE Communications*, September 2000.

Manchester, James, Jon Anderson, Bharat Doshi, and Subra Dravida (Bell Laboratories), 'IP over SONET,' *IEEE Communications*, May 1998.

Minkenberg, Cyriel and Ton Engbersen (IBM Research), 'A Combined Input and Output Queued Packet-Switched System Based on PRIZMA Switch-on-a-Chip Technology,' *IEEE Communications*, December 2000.

Neukermans, Armand and Rajiv Ramaswami (Nortel Networks), 'MEMS Technology for Optical Networking Applications,' *IEEE Communications*, January 2001.

Nong, Ge and Mounir Harndi, 'On the Provision of Quality-of-Service Guarantees for Input Queued Switches,' *IEEE Communications*, December 2000.

Ohba, Yoshihiro (Toshiba R&D Center), 'Issues on Loop Prevention in MPLS Networks,' *IEEE Communications*, December 1999.

Okamoto, Satoru, Masafumi Koga, Hiro Suzuki, and Kenji Kawai (NTT Network Innovation Laboratories), 'Robust Photonic Transport Network Implementation with Optical Cross-Connect Systems,' *IEEE Communications*, March 2000.

O'Mahony, Mike J., Dimitra Simeonidou, David K. Hunter, and Anna Tzanakaki, 'The Application of Optical Packet Switching in Future Communication Networks,' *IEEE Communications*, March 2001.

Qiao, Chunming (SUNY at Buffalo), 'Labeled Optical Burst Switching for IP-over-WDM Integration,' *IEEE Communications*, September 2000.

Rajagopalan, Bala, Dimitrios Pendarakis, Debanjan Saha, Ramu S. Ramamoorthy, and Krishna Bala (Tellium, Inc.), 'IP over Optical Networks: Architectural Aspects,' *IEEE Communications*, September 2000.

Roberts, Jim W. (France Telecom R&D), 'Traffic Theory and the Internet,' *IEEE Communications*, January 2001.

Shiomoto, Kohei, Masanori Uga, Masaaki Omotani, Shigeki Shimizu, and Takeshi Chimaru (NTT Network Service Systems Laboratories), 'Scalable Multi-QoS IP+ATM Switch Router Architecture,' *IEEE Communications*, December 2000.

Strand, John (AT&T Laboratories), and Angela L. Chiu and Robert Tkach (Celion Networks), 'Issues for Routing in the Optical Layer,' *IEEE Communications*, February 2001.

Swallow, George (Cisco Systems), 'MPLS Advantages for Traffic Engineering,' *IEEE Communications*, December 1999.

Tschudin, Christian and Henrik Lundgren (Uppsala University), and Henrik Gulbrandsen (Ericsson Research), 'Active Routing for Ad Hoc Networks,' *IEEE Communications*, April 2000.

Van de Voorde, I. and C. M. Martin (Alcatel Corporate Research Center), and J. Vandewege and X. Z. Qiu (IMEC – INTEC), 'The SuperPON Demonstrator: An Exploration of Possible Evolution Paths for Optical Access Networks,' *IEEE Communications*, February 2000.

Veeraraghavan, Malathi (Polytechnic University) and Mark Karol (Lucent Technologies), 'Internetworking Connectionless and Connection-Oriented Networks,' *IEEE Communications*, December 1999.

Veeraraghavan, Malathi (Polytechnic University), Mark Karol (Avaya Inc.), Ramesh Karri (Polytechnic University), Reinette Grobler (University of Pretoria), and Tim Moors (Polytechnic University), 'Architectures and Protocols that Enable New Applications on Optical Networks,' *IEEE Communications*, March 2001.

Xu, Lisong, Harry G. Perros, and George Rouskas (North Carolina State University), 'Techniques for Optical Packet Switching and Optical Burst Switching,' *IEEE Communications*, January 2001.

Yao, Shun and Biswanath Mukherjee (University of California), and Sudhir Dixit (Nokia Research Center), 'Advances in Photonic Packet Switching: An Overview,' *IEEE Communications*, February 2000.

Yao, Shun, S. J. Ben Yoo, and Biswanath Mukherjee (University of California), and Davis Sudhir Dixit (Nokia Research Center), 'All-Optical Packet Switching for Metropolitan Area Networks: Opportunities and Challenges,' *IEEE Communications*, March 2001.

Yoo, Myungsik (Soongsil University), Chunming Qiao (State University of New York at Buffalo), and Sudhir Dixit (Nokia Research Center), 'Optical Burst Switching for Service Differentiation in the Next-Generation Optical Internet,' *IEEE Communications*, February 2001.

The IEEE also publishes on-line, since October 1998, the journal *Communications Survey and Tutorials* (**http://www.comsoc.org/pubs/surveys/**), the quarterly issues of which are currently free of charge. The latest issue, however, only appeared in the third quarter of 2000. Some of the surveys recommended for interested readers are as follows:

Andrikopoulos, I., A. Liakopoulos, G. Pavlou, and Z. Sun, 'Providing Rate Guarantees for Internet Application Traffic Across ATM Networks,' *IEEE Communications Survey and Tutorials*, Vol. 2, No. 3, Third Quarter 1999.

Arpaci, Mutlu and John A. Copeland (Georgia Institute of Technology), 'Buffer Management for Shared-Memory ATM Switches,' *IEEE Communications Survey and Tutorials*, Vol. 3, No. 1, First Quarter 2000.

Labrador, Miguel A. and Sujata Banerjee (University of Pittsburgh), 'Packet Dropping Policies for ATM and IP Networks,' *IEEE Communications Survey and Tutorials*, Vol. 2, No. 3, Third Quarter 1999.

Mangues-Bafalluy, Josep and Jordi Domingo-Pascual (Technical University of Catalonia), 'Multicast Forwarding over ATM: Native Approaches,' *IEEE Communications Survey and Tutorials*, Vol. 3, No. 1, First Quarter 2000.

Ramalho, Maria (Alcatel Corporate Research Centre), 'Intra- and Inter-Domain Multicast Routing Protocols: A Survey and Taxonomy,' *IEEE Communications Survey and Tutorials*, Vol. 3, No. 1, First Quarter 2000.

Additional recommended articles from the journal *Computer Communications* are as follows:

Cheng, Sheng-Tzong (National Cheng Kung University, Taiwan), 'Backtrack Routing and Priority-Based Wavelength Assignment in WDM Networks,' *Computer Communications*, 22 (1999), pp. 1–10.

Fan, Z. (University of Cambridge), 'New Trends in ATM Networks: A Research View,' *Computer Communications*, 22 (1999), pp. 499–515.

On-line sources – vendors vs. standardization bodies

The Internet represents indisputably a vast source of publicly available information – of different scope, quality, and targeted readers. With relation to the topics covered or referred to throughout this book, the **networking vendors' sites** are offering nowadays not only vendor- and product-specific information, but increasingly more technical information in the form of white papers, technical and application notes, tutorials, guides, glossaries, etc. Anyone interested should be aware, however, that the prime source of technical information on the standardized technologies, mechanisms, and tools is always the standards and specifications themselves, available from their respective issuing bodies.

Among the networking vendors the most extensive on-line library available to the public at large and (even more topics for) registered users that of Cisco Systems (Cisco Connection On-line at **http://www.cisco.com**). There readers can find not only Cisco-specific but also background information such as:

■ *Internetworking Technology Overview*:
   http://www.cisco.com/univercd/cc/td/doc/cisintwk/ito_doc/index.htm

■ *Internetwork Design Guide*:
   http://www.cisco.com/univercd/cc/td/doc/cisintwk/idg4/index.htm

As noted in Appendix B, most internationally recognized **standardization organizations** do not make their standards freely publicly available, but are for sale only (and costly). Nevertheless, searching through the IEEE, ISO, or ITU-T sites, just to name a few among the standards bodies, can bring information about the evolution of technologies and their specifications, plus tutorials and presentations on emerging topics. The Internet community work is open to the public and all RFCs and Internet Drafts are available on the Internet for free. Fortunately, the format and language used in the IETF documents is very easy to absorb (as opposed to some of the international standards). For those interested in a particular area it is recommended to search for the **IETF working group** (**http://www.ietf.org/html.charters/wg-dir.html**) under whose wing the topic is being developed, and follow (or even contribute to) its work. Key links to bookmark and watch for (you may subscribe to the IETF to receive notification on new RFCs and Internet Drafts) are as follows:

- to the current list of RFCs and their status – **http://www.isi.edu/in-notes/rfc-index.txt** (the list changes any time there is a new RFC approved or when an old RFC changes status);

- to the RFCs – **http://www.ietf.org/rfc.html** (there are several new RFCs usually endorsed and made public every month; note that the only RFCs which might not be taken too seriously are those bearing the date of April 1!);

- to the Internet Drafts – **http://www.ietf.org/ID.html** (every day there appear new Internet Drafts).

Index